The Jossey-Bass/AHA Press Series translates the latest ideas on health care management into practical and actionable terms. Together, Jossey-Bass and the American Hospital Association offer these essential resources for the health care leaders of today and tomorrow.

Risk Management Handbook

American Society for Healthcare Risk Management

Roberta Carroll, Editor

Risk Management Handbook

FOR HEALTH CARE ORGANIZATIONS

Third Edition

JOSSEY-BASS
A Wiley Company
San Francisco

Health Forum, Inc.
An American Hospital Association Company
CHICAGO press

Jossey-Bass books and products are available through most bookstores. To contact Jossey-Bass directly, call (888) 378-2537, fax to (800) 605-2665, or visit our website at www.josseybass.com.

Substantial discounts on bulk quantities of Jossey-Bass books are available to corporations, professional associations, and other organizations. For details and discount information, contact the special sales department at Jossey-Bass.

Library of Congress Cataloging-in-Publication Data
Risk management handbook for health care organizations /
  American Society for Healthcare Risk Management:
  Roberta Carroll, editor. —3rd ed.
     p. cm.
  Includes bibliographical references and index.
  ISBN 0–7879–5553–1
    1. Health facilities—Risk management. I. Carroll, Roberta.
  II. American Society for Healthcare Risk Management.
  [DNLM: 1. Health Facilities—economics. 2. Health Facilities—
organization & administration. 3. Risk Management.
  WX 157 R59533 2000]

RA971.38.R58   2000
362.1'1'068—dc21

          00–055479

THIRD EDITION
HB Printing   10 9 8 7 6 5 4 3 2 1

Contents

List of Exhibits, Figures, Tables, and Appendixes

EXHIBITS

FIGURES

TABLES

APPENDIXES

About the Contributors

Kathryn T. Allen is a senior consultant with AIG Consultants, Inc., Healthcare Management Division in Houston, Texas. With more than twenty years of health care quality assurance and risk management experience, she has extensive expertise in ambulatory, long-term care, and acute health care settings. She has designed, implemented, and directed integrated facility-wide risk management and performance improvement programs. Prior to joining AIG, Allen consulted in the areas of quality management, health information management, risk management, and operations improvement in the health care management practice of Coopers and Lybrand. She has spoken nationally on outcome measurement, quality improvement, and JCAHO survey preparation. Allen is a registered health information administrator with a bachelor of science degree in health information management from Stephens College, Columbia, Missouri, and is a Certified Professional of Healthcare Quality. She is a member of the National Association of Healthcare Quality and the American Health Information Management Association. Allen has met the requirements of the State of Texas Insurance Code and is designated by the Texas Department of Insurance as a Texas Field Safety Representative with specialties in the areas of hospitals and workers' compensation.

Ellen L. Barton, JD, CPCU, DFASHRM, is vice president, risk management for Med-Star Health, Inc., Columbia, Maryland. She served as president of Neumann Insurance Company, and director of risk management for the Franciscan Health System in Aston, Pennsylvania, from May 1987 to December 1996. She also served as general counsel for Franciscan Health System from July 1993 to July 1996 and as senior vice president legal services from July 1994 to July 1996. In addition to those responsibilities, Barton sat on the boards of several insurance companies and as a captive insurance company management firm. Other past positions include: vice president and health care practice leader, Aon Risk Services, Inc. of Maryland; vice president, legal services, American Radiology Services, Inc., Baltimore, Maryland; chief operating officer and general counsel of New American Health, LLC, Glen Burnie, Maryland; director of risk management at the University of Pennsylvania; associate director and director of risk management at the University of Cincinnati; assistant editor of the FC&S Bulletins at the National Underwriter Company, Cincinnati, Ohio; independent claims adjuster for Lloyd R. Deist Insurance Adjusters, Inc., Cincinnati, Ohio. Barton received her judicial degree from the University of Cincinnati in 1978. She has written numerous articles and book chapters on risk management issues, and conducted seminars on a national as well as regional level. Barton is admitted to the Bars of Ohio, Maryland, and Pennsylvania and holds membership in the Maryland and American Bar Associations, the Society of Chartered Property and Casualty Underwriters, the American Health Lawyers Association, the Risk and Insurance Management Society, and the American Society for Healthcare Risk Management, of which she was president for 1990–1991. Barton was the recipient of ASHRM's Distinguished Service Award in 1993.

Dorothy Bazan, RN, BS, FASHRM, is the director, risk management, Presbyterian Intercommunity Hospital in Whittier, California. She has held a variety of positions, including president, Bazan & Associates, Burbank, California; risk management coordinator, Citrus Valley Health System in Covina, California; consultant director risk and quality management services, Professional Risk Management Group, Long Beach, California, serving international clients; vice president risk management services, Alexander & Alexander Health Care Division, Pasadena, California; and manager education and professional liability representative, Farmers Insurance Group of Companies, Los Angeles. Bazan's responsibilities have varied throughout all aspects of risk management components. She has served on the ASHRM Board of Directors. She has also served on the SCAHRM Board of Directors for eight years and is past president. Bazan enjoys numerous speaking and teaching engagements, as well as committee activities.

Karen E. Bedford, BSN, MSW, is senior vice president of Aon Healthcare Specialists. She is responsible for the management of a specialized division dedicated to providing medical professional liability coverage and consulting services to physician group practices and integrated heath care systems located throughout the United States. Prior to joining Aon in 1993, Bedford worked for an insurance brokerage firm and was responsible for the development and management of insurance programs for physician group practices, including IPAs, PHOs, and MSOs on a national basis. Bedford began her insurance career in 1983 at CNA Insurance Companies in Chicago, following positions in clinical nursing and medical social work. Bedford received her master of science degree in social work with a specialization in medical and health care from Indiana University. She is a licensed registered nurse and received her bachelor of science degree in nursing from the University of North Carolina. She is an affiliate member of the Medical Group Management Association and is a frequent guest speaker on medical professional liability and medical risk management.

Sylvia M. Brown, RN, JD is vice president, risk management, of the Insurance Management Services program associated with Premier, Inc. She has eight years of experience as a nurse in a variety of clinical settings, and is an attorney with bar membership in the state of Virginia. In addition, Brown has developed clinical risk management service programs for Willis Corroon, PLCM Group (an Aon Company), The Virginia Reciprocal, and The Medical Protective Company (a General Electric Company). She served on the ASHRM Communications and Resources Committee from 1992 to 1995, and chaired the committee from 1993 to 1994.

Jane M. Bryant, MHSA, DFASHRM, is director of risk management at Oconee Memorial Hospital, Seneca, South Carolina. A former ASHRM board member, Bryant has participated in the development of basic risk management education programs for ASHRM. She was ASHRM's president in 1985 and received the Distinguished Service Award in 1994.

Berni H. Bussell is senior vice president, Aon Health Risk Specialists, Aon Risk Services, Inc. He has led Aon Risk Services' provider risk practice in the northeast for the last six years. Through aggressive reengineering of traditional insurance products, use of nontraditional funding mechanisms, and attention to provider risk management and loss control needs, he has built the northeast practice into the east coast's leading intermediary for provider risk solutions. His clients include leading provider organizations ranging from local medical groups and managed self-insured health plans to regional health care delivery systems and national, provider-sponsored health plans. Nationally, Bussell serves as a shared managed care resource through the Aon Healthcare Alliance and is a member of the Alliance's Managed Care Steering Committee. Prior to joining Aon, Bussell spent ten years as a hospital CEO and COO specializing in hospital turnarounds. He holds a bachelor's degree from Boston University and a master's degree in business administration from Northeastern University.

Roberta Carroll, RN, ARM, MBA, CPCU, CPHQ, DFASHRM, is senior vice president and manager of the health care unit, Aon Risk Services of Northern California, Inc., in San Francisco. Previously, she held a variety of positions, including vice president of risk and insurance management at UniHealth in Burbank, California; manager of the Healthcare Division of Corroon & Black of Illinois in Chicago; vice president and trust administrator at Premier Healthcare Alliance/PAIC; and director of risk management at Mount Sinai Medical Center, Miami Beach, Florida. Carroll served on the ASHRM board for six years and is a past president. She is the editor of the *Risk Management Handbook for Healthcare Organizations* (2nd ed.) (1997) and has received the following awards: 1997 Distinguished Service Award from ASHRM, 1998 Distinguished Alumni Achievement Award from Nova Southeastern University in 1998, most contributing member to risk management in 1996 from Southern California Association of Healthcare Risk Management (SCAHRM), and most valuable contribution to the field of risk management in 1993 from SCAHRM. She is a member of HFMA, Society of CPCU, ASHRM, and CSHRM. As an expert and educator in the health care risk management areas of risk financing, claims administration, loss control strategic planning and reengineering, her speaking engagements and committees activities are numerous.

Christopher Cassirer, ScD, MPH, is an internationally known teacher, researcher, and consultant with special expertise is the fields of strategy, risk management, and patient safety. He currently serves as the Vernon E. Weckwerth Professor of Healthcare Executive Studies with the University of Minnesota's Carlson School of Management. In that position, he is responsible for continuing expansion of the Carlson School's international graduate health care executive education programs including the ISP/Executive Studies Program, a distance-learning program currently operating in thirty-three countries. In addition, Cassirer continues to lecture on medical malpractice and best practices in risk management for The Johns Hopkins University School of Public Health. As a member of the Harvard research team responsible for producing information on rates of patient injury in Colorado and Utah hospitals, Cassirer led the assessment of hospital risk and safety management activities among organizations participating in that study. Recent publications include a chapter on risk management program evaluation for an upcoming book from the American Hospital Association, and, as co-author, a chapter on medical malpractice and clinical risk management for the book *Managing Quality in a Cost-Focused Environment.* Formerly, Cassirer held the position of assistant vice president for knowledge services with MMI Companies, Inc., a multinational liability insurance and health care risk management services company.

Ward R. H. Ching is senior vice president and director, strategic solutions group, at Aon Risk Services in San Francisco. He developed a number of innovative management consulting approaches designed to assist clients to better handle their strategic and financial management of both insurance and business risk. These approaches range from comprehensive risk management audits to integrated risk mapping techniques to alternative risk financing including the use of captive insurance facilities. Ching conducts numerous consulting assignments for a variety of international and domestic clients across a broad spectrum of industries. Typical assignments include: planning and change integration, reengineering, process mapping, workers' compensation cost management and managed care analysis and integration, organizational effectiveness review, and program benchmarking. Ching teaches and has published articles relating to risk management, finance, and international relations. He is a frequent speaker on numerous topics at industry events. Ching currently is working on his PhD in International Relations from the University of Southern California. He earned a master's of science degree in international relations and economics from the University of Southern California and a bachelor of arts degree in international relations and political science from the University of Southern California.

Mark Cohen, ARM, RPLU, CPHQ, serves as a risk management consultant to Sutter Health, an "integrating" system of twenty-six acute care hospitals, as well as home health and hospice agencies, occupational health services, medical foundations, and medical research institutes. Cohen provides a broad range of consulting services to Sutter Health's affiliate organizations relating to risk management program review and development, risk assessment, and loss prevention and loss control education. He is a past president of both the Southern California Association for Healthcare Risk Management and the California Society for Healthcare Risk Management, and the currently serves as editor of CSHRM's quarterly journal. Cohen is the current chair of ASHRM's Information Technology Task Force, a member of ASHRM's Modules faculty, and he is a board member and treasurer of the Sacramento Risk Management Forum.

Dominic A. Colaizzo is regional vice president serving the Aon Risk Services offices of Philadelphia, Baltimore, Pittsburgh, Washington, D.C., and Hershey, Pennsylvania. He has sixteen years of experience in health care administration and thirteen years of insurance broking and consulting experience. He has a particular focus on the development and use of captive insurance programs and serves as a national resource in this regard. Colaizzo has earned a master of business administration from the Leonard Davis Institute for Health Economics at The Wharton School of the University of Pennsylvania and a bachelor of arts degree in economics and mathematics from Washington and Jefferson College. He is a diplomat of the American College of Health Care Executives and a member of ASHRM, The American Hospital Association, and the Health Care Financial Management Association.

Kirk S. Davis, JD, is a Florida Bar board-certified health care attorney. He was appointed as an inaugural member of the Health Law Certification Committee and was its chair in 1998–1999. He served as chair of the Florida Bar Health Law Section in 1992–1993. He also serves as a Supreme Court of Florida certified court mediator. Davis joined the health care group of the Tampa office of firm Akerman Senterfitt & Eidson, P.A. in September 1997 where his health law practice includes representation of hospitals and other health care providers in general health care matters, primarily of a civil and administrative trial nature. He has extensive experience in the medicolegal aspects of the health care practice, and in all aspects of medical staff matters from both the physician and hospital perspectives, including hospital-based physician contracting. Davis has been practicing law in the area of civil litigation and health care since 1983. He received his bachelor of science in biology from Stetson University and his judicial degree from Stetson University College of Law.

Corbette S. Doyle, CPCU, ARM, is CEO of Aon Healthcare Alliance. She is responsible for coordinating Aon's broking, consulting, claims, and risk management services for the health care industry. Her areas of expertise include the design, marketing, and implementation of alternative loss financing programs for national and multinational firms. Doyle has published articles in numerous journals including *Risk Management, Best's Review, Nursing Homes, National Underwriter, American Economist,* and ASHRM's *Journal of Healthcare Risk Management.* Doyle won the latter publication's 1995 Award for Writing Excellence. She is a frequent speaker at industry seminars, particularly on topics related to medical professional, D&O, and workers' compensation. She has served on both the ASHRM Board of Directors and the Governing Board of the CPCU Risk Management Section. Doyle received her master's of business administration degree from Vanderbilt University and her bachelor of the arts degree from the State University of New York at Oswego.

Jeffrey F. Driver, JD, MBA, FASHRM, is corporate risk manager and compliance officer of Children's Hospital and Health Center of San Diego, California. He is also the president of Children's Hospital Insurance Ltd. Driver is the current chair of the Advocacy Committee of ASHRM, past chair of the Legislative and Regulatory Committee, as well as past president of the San Diego Association for Healthcare Risk Management. He is an author and frequent speaker on various topics of interest on risk and compliance management issues.

Sheila Hagg-Rickert, MHA, MBA, DFASHRM, JD, is senior vice president, strategic consulting services, for Marsh, Inc. in Atlanta, Georgia. She is a past member of ASHRM's board of directors, and its special projects, bylaws, and communication and resources committees. Hagg-Rickert has served as faculty at numerous ASHRM educational programs, including the annual conference and modules.

Judy M. Hart is vice president, chief marketing officer, for GE Risk Solutions. She is responsible for the coordination of marketing for GE Risk Solutions Healthcare Segment, including Employer's Reinsurance Corporation (ERC), The Medical Protective Company, Industrial Risk Insurers, and Westport Insurance Company. In addition, she is a team consultant on major accounts assisting in the identification and analysis of risk and the development of innovative solutions to address the financial impact of the risk. Prior to joining ERC in 1997, Hart was deputy national director for the Healthcare Practice of Alexander & Alexander. In that capacity, she served as a national resource to A&A health care personnel and their clients. She has been developing risk financing programs for health care organizations for more than twenty years. Hart is a frequent speaker and author on risk management issues associated with all aspects of alternative risk financing, managed care issues, and the evolving risks associated with health care integration. She attended Southeast Missouri State University and Washington University in St. Louis.

Rebecca Havlisch, RN, JD, is vice president of risk services for Catholic Health West in San Francisco. She is responsible for all aspects of the corporate risk management program including loss prevention, occupational health and safety, risk financing, claims management, and licensing and accreditation. She has been in the field of risk management for twelve years, beginning her career as a staff nurse in newborn intensive care. Since 1987, after obtaining a judicial degree from William Mitchell College of Law, she has been employed in the field of health care risk management and health law. Havlisch was one of the founding members of the Minnesota ASHRM chapter. She is currently a member of ASHRM, CSHRM, and American Health Lawyers Association.

Michael G. Hercz, JD, is an associate in the health industry practice of Akin, Gump, Strauss, Hauer & Feld, L.L.P. based in Los Angeles, where he focuses on health care litigation, government regulatory investigations, compliance, and Medicare certification. He also advises clients on a wide range of medical staff issues, including peer review, bylaws, hearings, and credentialing. Hercz received his bachelor's degree in psychology from the University of Pennsylvania and his doctor of law from the University of Southern California.

Thomas M. Hermes is a consulting actuary with Tillinghast-Towers Perrin in its Hartford office. He is a principal of Towers Perrin. He holds a bachelor's degree in mathematics from State University of New York at Plattsburgh. Hermes is a fellow of the Casualty Actuarial Society, member of the American Academy of Actuaries, fellow of the Conference of Consulting Actuaries, member of the Casualty Actuaries of New England (past secretary/treasurer), and member of the Hartford Actuaries Club. Prior to his firm's merger with Tillinghast in 1985, Hermes served as president and chairman of the board (1981–1985) of Independent Actuarial Services of Connecticut, Inc., president and chairman of the board (1979–1981) of Independent Actuarial Services of Bermuda, Ltd., and CEO of Integrated Risk Information Systems, Inc. For twelve years Hermes managed the Hartford office of Tillinghast. Hermes's experience as a casualty actuarial consultant has included a broad range of assignments for captive and domestic insurance companies, self-insureds, and joint underwriting associations. In particular, Hermes's consulting experience includes extensive work in the medical professional liability industry. He has provided ratemaking, reserving, and strategic and financial planning services to more than forty captive insurers, as well as numerous JUAs, PCFs, and self-insured programs formed since 1975. Projects have also included development of sophisticated retrospective rating and allocation models, determining the financial accrual impact of self-funded programs and liability and portfolio duration and cash flow analysis to maximize investment yield while minimizing risk. Hermes has served on several committees of the Casualty Actuarial Society and the Conference of Consulting Actuaries, and has been a panelist for numerous conferences, including several of the Casualty Actuarial Society loss reserve seminars.

Sandra K. Johnson, RN, ARM, FASHRM, is regional manager of corporate compliance and risk management for Imperial Point Medical Center in Fort Lauderdale, Florida. She began her career in risk management twenty-two years ago, working for PHICO Insurance Group, Inc., in Mechanicsburg, Pennsylvania. Past positions include director, risk and insurance, for Keystone Health System, in Drexell Hill, Pennsylvania; director, risk and insurance, at Holy Cross Hospital in Fort Lauderdale, Florida; and system director of risk management at Intracoastal Health System, West Palm Beach, Florida. She has served on many ASHRM committees, as faculty at the 1988 Annual Conference, as past board member, and on the nominations committee. Currently, she is serving another term on the ASHRM board. While in Philadelphia, she held various officer and committee positions with the Philadelphia Area Society for Health Care Risk Management and the Pennsylvania Society for Health Care Risk Management. She is serving on the Florida Society for Health Care Risk Management Board of Directors and is secretary for the Broward County Risk and Insurance and Management Society. Additionally, she is a member of the Advisory Board for the publication *Healthcare Risk Management,* published by American Health Consultants. She was awarded the ARM designation in 1990 and the FASHRM designation in 1991.

Thomas M. Jones is a partner in the Chicago office of McDermott, Will & Emery, an 800-plus attorney international law firm. Jones's practice has specialized over the past eighteen years in legal matters concerning the establishment and operation of self-insurance and risk transference mechanisms, with particular emphasis on related insurance regulatory, tax, security law and similar issues. Jones regularly advises on formation and restructuring of trusts, risk retention and risk purchasing groups, and offshore or onshore liability captives, fronted and unfronted. He has substantial experience in stock, both in mutual and reciprocal formats. In this context, he has worked with the businesses and trade associations in a variety of industries. One of his special interests is advising on formation of trusts and offshore and onshore captives for tax exempt and taxable health care providers. Jones received his doctor of law and his master's of business administration degrees from Cornell University and has been an adjunct faculty member at Loyola University Law School in Chicago, where he taught international tax planning. He is a frequent speaker at insurance seminars and conferences, including Barbados, Bermuda, Cayman Islands, Hawaii, and Vermont seminars on offshore and onshore captive insurance companies and numerous presentations to trade groups on self-funding, workers' compensation, professional and product liability, and similar topics.

Mark A. Kadzielski, JD, is the partner in charge of the West Coast Health Law practice at Akin, Gump, Strauss, Hauer, & Feld, L.L.P., based in Los Angeles. His practice focuses on individual and institutional health care providers throughout the United States. Kadzielski speaks and publishes frequently on matters of health law. He has been selected, on the basis of peer evaluations, to be included in the Healthcare Law Section of *The Best Lawyers in America* for the past several years. He currently serves on the board of directors of the American Academy of Healthcare Attorneys, and has served on many advisory bodies in the health care industry. Kadzielski is a graduate of the University of Pennsylvania Law School.

Lillian P. Karson, DFASHRM, has enjoyed a twenty-year career as a registered nurse specializing in critical care and a subsequent twenty-two-year career as a risk management consultant and Property Casualty Broker. Karson is principal of QA/RM Consultants and L & J Insurance Services in Santa Ana, California. While president of Southern California Association of Healthcare Risk Management, the ASHRM Chapter was awarded the National Achievement Award. Karson has served on many SCAHRM and AHSRM committees as well as various other health care organization boards and committees. Karson contributed to the ASHRM publication *Pearls* and has co-authored "Risk Management in a Private OB/GYN Practice," a national publication for 501-C3 outpatient clinics. Karson is guest faculty at the University of Arizona, Vanderbilt University, and The Institute of Medical Law.

Leilani Kicklighter, RN, ARM, MBA, DFASHRM, is assistant administrator, risk management services, at the North Broward Hospital District, in Fort Lauderdale, Florida.

Kicklighter began her career as a registered nurse. Her career in health care risk management of more than twenty-three years has afforded her experience in the large teaching hospital environment, in a university medical school setting, and in a variety of other health care provider settings, including the large multispecialty medical clinic, the for-profit community hospital, and the not-for-profit integrated health care multifacility system, and a large HMO. Before joining the North Broward Hospital District, the fourth largest public hospital system, she was a health care risk management consultant with a large international insurance broker. She has been active in state and local health care risk management organizations and a member of ASHRM for twenty years, serving on committees, the board of directors, and as president in 1997–1998. In addition to earning the ARM and a master's of business administration, she has been awarded the DFASHRM designation from ASHRM and is currently working toward the CPCU designation.

Frances Kurdwanowski, FASHRM, is a risk management consultant based in Cornwall, New York. She has eighteen years' experience as risk manager at St. Joseph's Hospital and Medical Center, Paterson, New Jersey, in all aspects of that role. Kurdwanowski has been a member of ASHRM since 1984, serving on the Communication and Resources Committee, the Editorial Review Board of the *Journal of Healthcare Risk Management,* and the ASHRM Board of Directors for two terms (1993–1994 and 1996–1997). She also worked on the first and second edition task forces of the handbook along with co-authoring in both editions. Kurdwanowski currently serves on the ASHRM historical and journal writing excellence task forces.

Maria D. Lain, MBA, has twenty years of health care organization experience working with organizations to implement business solutions that achieve profitability and growth by integrating customer value and operations effectiveness. She has implemented credible performance management systems that ensure accountability, vision and strategy achievement, and effective organization performance and advancement.

Robert J. Marder, MD, is vice president for medical affairs at Holy Cross Hospital, a 350-bed community hospital in Chicago with eighteen hospital-owned clinical practice sites. His responsibilities include quality and resource management, risk management, medical records, and medical staff program development. Marder has been professionally involved with quality management for more than ten years. From 1988–1991, he served as project director for clinical indicator development at the Joint Commission on Accreditation of Healthcare Organizations (JCAHO) and conducted extensive training workshops in the use of performance measures in quality improvement. From 1991–1998, Marder was at Rush Presbyterian-St. Luke's Medical Center in Chicago as the medical director for quality management and assistant vice president, quality management. He has served on local and national quality-related committees, including the Institute of Medicine, the American Cancer Society, the Illinois Hospital and Healthcare Association, and the Lincoln Foundation for Business Excellence. Marder received his doctor of medicine at Rush Medical College and completed his residency training in pathology at Rush Presbyterian-St. Luke's Medical Center.

Peggy Berry Martin, MS, MEd, ARM, DFASHRM, is director of education for the Risk Management Foundation (RMF) of the Harvard Medical Institutions. In this role she serves as consultant to RMF staff and their clients for the development, production, and presentation of educational programs and products. Her background includes experience in loss prevention, institutional risk management, and risk management education.

Martin was a founding member and first president of the Massachusetts Society for Healthcare Risk Management; has served as faculty for local, state, and national conferences; and teaches an undergraduate course in health care risk management at a local college. She is a former ASHRM board member and committee chair, and currently serves as chair of the ASHRM Education Committee.

Jane C. McConnell, RN, MBA, JD, is executive director of the Maryland Medicine Comprehensive Insurance Program, a joint venture between the University of Maryland Medical System Corporation and University Physicians, Inc., that pools the liability risk of physician group practices and health care entities into a self-insurance and reinsurance program. In reporting directly to the board of directors, McConnell is responsible for the integration of all system-wide risk and insurance management functions, as well as the Terrapin Insurance Company domiciled in the Cayman Islands. Before that, she was vice president, insurance and risk management, for the Franciscan Sisters of Allegany Health System, Inc. (AHS), in Tampa, Florida, and president of S.A. Insurance, Ltd., the AHS captive company. Other past positions include vice president, risk management for FOJP Service Corporation in New York City, deputy executive director of the New York County Health Service Review Organization, director of nursing at the Brooklyn Cumberland Medical Center, and director of quality assurance with the New York City Health Department. McConnell received her law degree from Fordham University School of Law, two master's degrees from New York University, a nursing degree from St. Vincent's Hospital in New York, and has earned the associate in risk management designation from the Insurance Institute of America. She is a past president of ASHRM and a member of the AAHA and the ABA.

William J. McDonough, MPAH, ARM, FASHRM, is a senior vice president with HealthSpectrum, the global health care practice at MARSH, Inc. He is located in Boston and is the practice leader for risk management consulting and oversees efforts by MARSH to serve the home health care industry. McDonough has a bachelor of science degree from the University of Miami; a master's in public health administration from Suffolk University; and a doctorate in health, law and policy from Northeastern. McDonough is also a fellow of the American Society of Risk Management and a certified mediator for health care. He speaks frequently both regionally and internationally on the topics of compliance, risk management, and sentinel event investigation. He had more that fifteen years' experience in health care administration in New England before joining MARSH in 1992.

Peggy L. B. Nakamura, RN, MBA, JD, DFASHRM, is executive director of risk management/associate counsel of Adventist Health, a multistate/multihospital health care system in the western United States. Nakamura is a past president of ASHRM and the California Chapter (CSHRM) and served on the boards of ASHRM and CSHRM. She has more than twenty-five years of experience in the health care field, including critical care nursing, nursing administration, serving as a medical malpractice defense attorney, and developing multihospital system risk management programs. In her current position, she oversees a comprehensive risk management department, including self-administered and self-insured programs in workers' compensation, professional, general, and managed care liability. In 1997, Nakamura received the Outstanding Advocate Award from The American Association of Nurse Attorneys (TAANA) and has lectured frequently on risk management topics.

Brad R. Norrick, CPCU, is a senior vice president at Marsh USA Inc., Cleveland, Ohio. Norrick joined a predecessor firm to Marsh in 1981, after graduation from Amherst

College and employment with a major insurance company. He has worked in the Seattle, Portland, and Detroit offices, and opened an Indianapolis office in January 1995. He went to Cleveland in the fall of 1997. Norrick has specialized in consulting for health care providers for more than twenty years. He has been a frequent contributor to ASHRM and RIMS as well as to the previous editions of this handbook.

James E. Orlikoff is president of Orlikoff and Associates, Inc., a Chicago-based consulting firm, specializing in health care leadership, organizational development, quality, and strategy. Orlikoff was director of AHA's Division of Hospital Governance and director of the Institute on Quality of Care and Patterns of Practice. He has served on many health care and related boards, and has been a mentor of the Governing Council of South Suburban Hospital in Hazel Crest, Illinois.

Pamela J. Para, BSN, RN, MPH, is the director of professional and technical services at ASHRM. In this role, she is responsible for coordinating educational programs, products, and other resources that are available to ASHRM members. Prior to joining ASHRM in November 1999, Para was a health care consultant with AIG Consultants, Inc., Healthcare Management Division, in Chicago. Para received a bachelor of science degree in nursing from DePaul University and a master's degree in public health from the University of Illinois at Chicago.

Grena G. Porto, RN, ARM, DFASHRM, is currently the director of clinical risk management in the insurance services division at VHA, Inc., an alliance of more than 1,800 leading community-owned health care organizations around the country. She has twenty years' experience in all aspects of health care risk management, including loss control, claims administration, and risk financing. Her past positions include regional claims manager for a national surplus lines insurer and director of risk management at a large academic medical center. Porto is active in the American Society for Healthcare Risk Management (ASHRM) and served as its president in 1999. She serves as a member of the board of directors of the National Patient Safety Foundation, and is a past president of the Philadelphia Area Society for Healthcare Risk Management. She is a registered nurse and holds a master's degree in health administration. She has been awarded the designations of Distinguished Fellow (DFASHRM) by ASHRM and Associate in Risk Management (ARM) by the Insurance Institute of America. She has published and lectured extensively in her field.

Benjamin A. Post, Esq., has handled a wide variety of medical malpractice lawsuits, representing hospitals and physicians throughout Pennsylvania. He has spoken at several hospitals on topics including the Federal Anti-Dumping Law, and reimbursement restraints on hospitals and physicians, and has addressed hospital personnel on their preparation for depositions and trial. Post graduated from Franklin and Marshall College in 1981, and from Villanova University Law School in 1984, where he was a published member of the Law Review. He has been a partner at Post & Schell, P.C., since 1990.

William B. Reisbick, Esq., is system director of risk management, Providence Health System, Seattle, Washington. His responsibilities include oversight of self-insured, general, and professional liability claims for thirty-four facilities in four states. Reisbick handles placement of commercial insurance coverages and risk management education programs. From 1994–1999, Reisbick was director of risk management at Virginia Mason Medical Center in Seattle. For seventeen years, he was in private practice in Portland, Oregon, focusing on medical liability and product liability cases. Reisbick received his bachelor's degree from Portland State University and his juris doctor from Willamette University. His service to ASHRM includes a 1998–1999 term on the board of directors and a year on the Annual Conference Committee.

Kathleen M. Roman, MS, is assistant vice president, risk management education services, for The Medical Protective Company, headquartered in Fort Wayne, Indiana. She has more than twenty years of experience as a health care writer, having served in the past as a community health liaison, community health needs assessment leader, and as a health issues writer for several newspapers. Roman writes extensively on the topics of risk management and quality improvement for medical and dental journals. She is a popular speaker on these same issues and is in demand throughout the country for presentations to physicians, dentists, practice managers, and staff. Roman serves on an ad hoc advisory council to the American Dental Association related to professional liability insurance. She is a member of the American Medical Writers Association as well as ASHRM and the Indiana Society of Healthcare Risk Managers, where she most recently has served on the education committee. She is also a member of the Alliance for Continuing Medical Education.

John F. Roskopf is Senior Managing Director, AON University. He is responsible for Management Training and Development Programs. Roskopf has twenty-five years' experience in risk management and corporate treasury functions. A frequent lecturer on the risk management discipline, he has published numerous articles on such topics as benchmarking in risk management, M&A due diligence, and effective risk management practices. Prior to joining AON, Roskopf was a consultant with Tillinghast. Before that, he held several positions in risk management and treasury operations. His Academic background includes a master's of business administration from Loyola University as well as the associate in risk management designation from the Insurance Institute of America. Roskopf has published numerous articles and is a nationally recognized speaker on management and the risk management discipline.

Fay A. Rozovsky, JD, MPH, DFASHRM, is senior vice president for Marsh Health Spectrum. Rozovsky has more than twenty years' experience as a health care risk management consultant and attorney. Rozovsky has lectured extensively and authored or co-authored more than 500 articles and several books including *Consent to Treatment: A Practical Guide; Liability and Risk Management in Home Health Care Law; Medical Staff Credentialing: A Practical Guide;* and *Liability and Risk Management in Managed Care.* Her most recent book is *Corporate Compliance in Home Health: Establishing a Plan, Managing the Risks*. Rozovsky's expertise in consent law has been recognized by several courts, including the U.S. Supreme Court and the highest courts in Hawaii, Kentucky, West Virginia, and several other states. A graduate of Providence College, Rozovsky received a juris doctor from Boston College Law School and a master's degree in public health from the Harvard School of Public Health. She is an affiliate associate professor in the legal medicine and health administration departments at the Medical College of Virginia. Rozovsky is admitted to the practice of law in Florida and Massachusetts. Rozovsky is a Distinguished Fellow of the American Society for Healthcare Risk Management and president of the society. In 1998, she was awarded the Distinguished Service Award, the highest honor bestowed on a member of ASHRM.

Jeannie Sedwick, ARM, is regional marketing manager for health care organizations for The Medical Protective Company in Fort Wayne, Indiana, owned by Employers Reinsurance Company, Overland Park, Kansas. She is formerly the corporate director of risk management at Wake County Hospital System, Inc., in North Carolina where she was responsible for the risk management program, including risk identification, loss prevention, loss control, claims administration, educational programs, risk financing, and management of the hospital insurance portfolio. Sedwick received her associate in risk management designation from the Insurance Institute of America, and completed the ASHRM Health Care Risk Management Certificate Program, as well as the Hospital Administrators Management Improvement Program from Duke University Medical Center. Sedwick was named to the 1997 Business Insurance "Risk Manager of the Year Honor Roll" for her contributions to risk management and innovations in the development of the risk management program at Wake County Hospital System. She is a past president of both ASHRM and the North Carolina chapter of ASHRM.

Ronni P. Solomon, JD, is vice president, legal affairs, and director, risk management services, at ECRI, a nonprofit health services research agency located in suburban Philadelphia that specializes in health care risk management and technology assessment. Solomon has approximately eighteen years' experience in health care risk management, law, and regulation. She has published numerous articles, and lectured frequently in the United States and abroad. She has received ASHRM's Award for Writing Excellence.

Kathleen Stillwell, RN, MPA, HSA, is president of SQM Consulting Group, and is a nationally recognized expert in health care risk management and quality management, including program assessment, claims management and administration, health care strategic planning, and organizational development. Stillwell has more than sixteen years of direct health care quality and risk management experience and has held senior positions with major health care providers and managed care organizations throughout the United States. For the past nine years, Stillwell has provided professional consulting services to health care clients nationwide and to select international clients. Her expertise includes risk management and insurance program assessment, redesign, professional liability claims management, auditing, development of allocation models, and due diligence reporting for mergers and acquisitions of health care corporations. Her consulting practice includes the evaluation and development of alternative health care delivery systems, home health, long-term care, subacute health care services, school health services, and the development of community-based clinics. In addition to her risk management, insurance, and quality management activities, Stillwell has held faculty appointments at the University of San Francisco in the departments of organizational behavior and public management, and at Woodbury University in the department of business and management. She is a frequent presenter at state and national health care conferences. She is past chair, Healthcare Division for the American Society for Quality, and trained as an international lead auditor for the ISO 9000 series. She chaired the Long-Term Care Think Tank for ASHRM and serves as faculty for the national risk management certification program sponsored by ASHRM. She is actively involved in numerous volunteer business and community advocacy projects and serves on the board of several organizations.

Sally T. Trombly, RN, MPH, JD, DFASHRM, is director of regulatory services for Risk Management Foundation (RMF) of the Harvard Medical Institutions, Cambridge, Massachusetts, and senior consultant to RMF Strategies, a division of RMF. She serves as a resource to Harvard-affiliates and outside clients for loss prevention concerns, legislative and regulatory issues, and relevant legal trends. Her background includes extensive risk management experience in sites ranging from multihospital academic systems to community care settings. She has served on ASHRM's board of directors, its legislative committee, and the board of the Massachusetts Society for Healthcare Risk Management. Currently, she is a member of ASHRM 2000's advocacy committee and serves on the boards of the Professional Liability Foundation, the Anesthesia Patient Safety Foundation, and as a member of the Executive Committee of the National Practitioner Data Bank. She has written and lectured on a variety of risk management and health law topics.

Glenn T. Troyer is a senior partner for the law firm of Locke Reynolds LLP located in Indianapolis, Indiana. He holds a bachelor of arts degree from Wittenberg University, Springfield, Ohio; a master's in health administration from Indiana University; and a doctor of jurisprudence from Capital University Law School, Columbus, Ohio. With more than twenty years of experience in health care law, he concentrates his practice on the representation of hospitals, physicians, mental health centers, nursing facilities, and other health care providers in business transactions, health law matters, and compliance-related issues. Troyer has written several articles and given numerous presentations on a variety of health law risk management topics and in 1986, co-authored and co-edited *Handbook of Health Care Risk Management.* He is a founding director and past president of the American Society of Health Care Risk Management, is a member of the American Health Lawyers Association, and chaired its physician recruitment task force, which authored *Physician Recruitment and Retention Guidebook* in 1997. Prior to joining Locke Reynolds in 1982, he served in various hospital administrative capacities in Columbus, Ohio; Chicago, Illinois; and Indianapolis, Indiana, including five years as general counsel and director of risk management for Methodist Hospital of Indiana, Inc.

Michael P. Warnick was admitted to the Illinois Bar in 1993. He received his bachelor's degree in history and economics from Northwestern University in 1990, and his doctor of law, *cum laude,* from Loyola University of Chicago in 1993. He has a diverse insurance practice representing general liability, professional liability, employment practices liability, health care professional liability, and life, health, and disability, domestic and international insurers and reinsurers. Warnick has represented insurers and reinsurers in cases involving a variety of general liability exposures, including environmental bodily injury and property damage and mass product losses.

In the environmental coverage area, Warnick was counsel for certain insurers in *Fruit of the Loom v. Travelers and Transportation Ins. Co.,* 284 Ill. App.3d 485, 672 N.E.2d 278 (1st Dist. 1986), which was the first decision after the Illinois Supreme Court's adverse decision in *Outboard Marine Co.,* interpreting the sudden and accidental pollution exclusion to uphold summary judgment for an insurer on the pollution exclusion. Warnick also has written articles on environmental coverage issues, including the article, "The Illinois Insurer Estoppel Doctrine: The Consequences of Wrongful Denial of the Duty to Defend," 7 *Environmental Claims Journal 5* (Summer 1995), which was expressly relied upon by the Illinois Appellate Court in *Employers Ins. Co v. Ehlco Liquidating Trust,* Ill. App. 3d, 687 N.E.2d 82 (1st Dist. 1997) in holding that estoppel does not preclude on insurers from asserting a late notice defense.

John C. West, MHA, JD, DFASHRM is a principal in West Consulting Services, LLC in Cincinnati, Ohio, which specializes in risk management consulting services for health care organizations. He has twenty years' experience in assisting health care organizations to develop occupational safety and health programs and was board certifed in the comprehensive practice of industrial hygiene in 1983. He has published numerous articles on various aspects of risk management and is a frequent speaker at national and regional educational programs.

Rando W. H. Wick, JD, is a partner in the Seattle law firm of Johnson, Graffe, Keay & Moniz. He specializes in the defense of health care law, including the defense of medical negligence claims. He is a board member of the Washington Health Care Risk Management Society and a member of the American Society of Health Care Risk Management. He is a former board member of the Washington State Society of Health Care Attorneys. Wick has assisted health care providers with the implementation of new health care legislation and regulations. Wick received his judicial degree from the University of Washington School of Law and a certificate in health care ethics from the University of Washington School of Medicine.

Kimberly Willis, MBA, CPCU, ARM, is vice president of Aon Healthcare Alliance. She has spent more than fourteen years developing risk management programs for the health care industry. Her responsibilities include marketing, policy analysis, statistical loss analysis, product development, and financial evaluation of risk vehicles. She also provides sales, resource support, and senior account management to Aon staff and clients worldwide. Willis is currently a speaker for ASHRM Module IV: Cents and Sense of Risk Management. In addition, she teaches the economics and accounting modules for the CPCU designation. She is a member of the Society of Chartered Property and Casualty Underwriters, ASHRM, and Missouri Society for Healthcare Risk Managers.

Sheila Cohen Zimmet, BSN, JD, is senior counsel for Georgetown University Medical Center. Zimmet started her professional career as a neonatal intensive care nurse after earning her undergraduate nursing degree from Georgetown in 1971. After she received her judical degree from Georgetown in 1975, Zimmet pursued a legal career with the federal government in the fields of occupational and mine safety and health. She returned to Georgetown University in 1984, where her legal practice has focused on her primary areas of interest in clinical, bioethical, and biomedical research issues, in addition to educational law issues involving students, faculty, and staff that are common to academic medical centers.

M. Michael Zuckerman, JD, is a regional vice president of Healthcare Services, Eastern Region, for AON Risk Services in Philadelphia, Pennsylvania. In this role he coordinates risk management services to clients. Previously Zuckerman served as associate vice president for risk management and insurance for a large university medical system including four hospitals.

He has more than nine years of experience with international insurance brokerage firms, during which he designed self-insurance programs for workers' compensation and medical professional liability including captives, among other consulting activities. Most recently, Zuckerman served Temple University Fox School of Business and Management as a full-time insurance and risk management faculty while he also pursued a private consulting practice.

Zuckerman earned a bachelor of business administration in accounting from Temple University's Fox School of Business and Management. He also earned his juris doctor from the John Marshall Law School in Chicago and received a master of business administration from Temple University's Fox School. Zuckerman maintains memberships in the Philadelphia Area Society of Healthcare Risk Management, the American Risk and Insurance Association, and the American Society of Healthcare Risk Management.

Preface

It is predicted that the changes in health care over the next ten to fifteen years will far outweigh the changes made in the last 150 years. When one ponders that statement, it makes one realize how fast the industry is moving forward and just how far it has come. Health care is not an isolated industry experiencing this rapid advancement. All one has to do is look at the communications and information technology field to see the accelerated pace of change over the past decade or two. Computers and the Internet are changing the way we communicate, internally and externally, professionally and personally, and how health care is delivered, managed, and paid. Advancements made through research in diagnostic and treatment methodologies are also rapidly changing the picture of health care.

Another significant area of growth that will forever transform the health care landscape is the aging of the population. Increases in life expectancy, the ability to maintain good health, and the escalation in population growth will necessitate a different approach to health care delivery methods and payment structures. It requires that we take a second look at how resources are deployed and how we are all stakeholders in the success of the "system." Consumers will aggressively manage their own health and will take an unprecedented role in these changes, particularly those affecting choice and service. Those changing dynamics clearly indicate that we *all* have a role to play.

Consolidation through mergers and acquisitions continues to affect the health care industry as well. To illustrate this point, look at the consolidation and expansion of markets among pharmaceutical companies, clinical laboratories, hospitals, medical groups, insurance companies, accounting and actuarial firms, and insurance brokers and consultants.

What we have not successfully advanced is greater satisfaction with how our care is delivered, managed, and paid. Every year the cost of health care takes a bigger bite out of our income while our access to care and our general feeling of satisfaction diminishes.

How does this all affect health care risk management and the risk manager? What does it mean to us and how do we manage within this changing environment? On one front, it clearly indicates that the risk management profession continues to offer challenges and opportunities. Viewing health care risk management as purely a hazard mitigation process will leave behind many who are engaged in the practice of risk management in the future. Enterprise risk management in which the total organization's exposure to loss over a continuum of operating units is managed will be the norm. Risk management will be a key component of an organization's strategic planning process, instrumental in the organization's success, and a method to increase value to its shareholders. This will require enhancements and a change in the current skill set of most health care risk managers. How we manage change and accept challenge will dictate how we respond.

We hope that this third edition of the *Risk Management Handbook for Health Care Organizations* will assist the risk manager in the advancement of those skills necessary for the future. The logistics of publishing a book of this nature as a volunteer project are complex. The ASHRM Handbook Revision Work Group was composed of the following individuals: Michael Zuckerman, Sheila Hagg-Rickert, Peggy Martin, Ellen Barton, and Leilani Kicklighter. We owe them a heartfelt *thank you* for their energy, spirit, hard work, and dedication to detail. This truly was a collaborative effort and one not achievable without their assistance. We also want to thank the many contributing authors whose efforts made this book possible. There are too many to personally name, but as you read through the contents and identify them by name please say "thanks" for a job well done the next time you see them. Lynne Mangan, manager of communications for ASHRM, was our staff liaison. She was instrumental in coordinating our efforts and is very much appreciated for her time and availability.

Our goal was for this edition of the handbook to be used as a guide for anyone interested in health care risk management—from the CFO to the human resource executive, to the director of managed care, to, of course, the health care risk manager. We have attempted to offer the audience what the risk management implications are in the subject material and advise on possible solutions. We have also taken this opportunity to write on a variety of new risk management subjects for the first time, bringing the value of this book to a wider range of professionals and broadening the reader's education. We have included a new section on managed care, as well as new chapters on advertising liability, enterprise risk management, risk mapping, corporate compliance, emerging risk associated with joint ventures, partnerships, legal review of the exposures in different organizational settings, and risk management program evaluation.

We hope you learn as much from using the *Risk Management Handbook for Health Care Organizations* (3rd ed.) as we all did in collaborating on its publication.

December, 2000

Roberta Carroll
Editor

About This Book

The *Risk Management Handbook for Health Care Organizations* (3rd ed.) was written as a reference test for the health care industry on the topic of risk management. This edition was particularly challenging, as the contributing authors researched and wrote twelve new chapters on material not previously covered. Scan through the chapters, and you will quickly see that it is a compilation of many subjects (thirty-eight chapters) by numerous authors (fifty)—truly a collaborative effort. Each chapter stands on its own, taking on the writing style of its author(s). The chapters can be read one at a time, in any sequence or order of preference, and the book can be used daily or on an as needed basis. If one looks at health care risk management on a continuum, this text is meant take the reader from the basics of program development through the more sophisticated concepts of enterprise risk management.

While we acknowledge that the largest audience for this book will be health care risk managers, it was written with multiple audiences in mind. The authors were asked to emphasize the risk management implications inherent in their subject material and identify possible techniques and treatments to manage the risk they addressed. To this end, the authors have included 120 various tools in the form of exhibits, figures, tables, and appendixes to assist the reader with the daily operations of risk management.

This book is divided into six parts with each part having multiple chapters (except for Part Three, which is a stand-alone section). The parts on managed care and risk financing are both new to this edition. Starting with the Framework for Health Care Risk Management in Part One, we continue with Part Two on Health Care Exposures, the largest part with fourteen chapters. Providers and Managed Care (Part Three) is offered as a primer on managed care issues. This part educates a variety of audiences and starts with the basics of managed care following through to the more advanced issues. For this edition, we have separated Risk Management Treatments and Techniques (Part Four) from Risk Financing (Part Five), as we felt risk financing issues were of particular importance in today's atmosphere of cost containment and the advancements in alternate risk financing arrangements. Monitoring and Evaluating (Part Six) ends the book. A comprehensive index for locating topics easily and quickly is included, and each author has attempted to offer an extensive references list as well as topical suggested readings.

Framework for Health Care Risk Management

art I offers basics tools for risk management program development. It offers, as its title so aptly suggests, the framework from which a risk management program can be implemented. It identifies all the elements and necessary functions of a risk management program, as well as key supporting relationships. The American Society for Healthcare Risk Management (ASHRM) role delineation study (as described in Chapter 1) identified for the first time an inventory of related job functions for a health care risk manager. That survey tool and responding answers are included in this section as they highlight the *who, what, where, when*, and *how* of health care risk management. This survey is also the basis for ASHRM's educational initiatives and certification program.

Organizational support for risk management programs must come from the governing body. How to gain that support and sustain it are highlighted as well as the issue of using the services of outside providers to supplement risk management staff. How to manage data, a topic much in debate, is discussed in great detail, and issues of confidentiality and privilege are explored. The chapter on enterprise risk management closes this part and offers the strategic risk manager a glimpse of what might quite possibly be their future role in health care risk.

1

The Health Care Risk Management Professional

Jeannie Sedwick
Grena G. Porto

Health care has changed dramatically over the past thirty years, and this has led to an expansion in the role and responsibilities of health care risk management professionals. In the early years of the profession, health care risk managers focused primarily on exposures relating to general and professional liability. Today, health care risk management professionals must manage not only those exposures but also exposures related to managed care and capitation risks, mergers and acquisition, employment and workers' compensation risks, and even risks related to corporate compliance and organizational ethics. Despite the significant changes of the past three decades, the risk management process itself has remained virtually unchanged and continues to serve the same purpose: to maintain a safe and effective health care environment for patients, visitors, and employees, thereby preventing or reducing loss to the organization.

This chapter provides an overview of the role of the health care risk management professional and the skills necessary for performing this function in an ever-changing health care environment. Information is provided about the educational and experiential backgrounds of risk management professionals as well as commonly held designations. Information about the availability of educational programs for those who wish to enter the field or for those in the field who wish to further their education is also discussed.

THE RISK MANAGER'S JOB—FUNCTIONAL AREAS OF RESPONSIBILITY

The roles and responsibilities of health care risk managers vary widely (see Table 1.1). Risk management program components—and therefore the role of the risk manager—are greatly influenced by the size and structure of the organization as well as the risk

TABLE 1.1.   Current Job Functions

Title	Percentage of importance
Risk Identification and Evaluation	90.0
Loss Prevention	79.0
Regulatory Compliance	74.0
Claims Handling	65.9
Education	58.0
Management and Administration	57.0
Medical Staff Issues	50.4
Legal Affairs	48.8
Contract Review	42.3
Quality	39.6
Ethics	37.3
Safety Administration	37.0
Insurance Program	35.7
Insurance Purchasing Decisions	35.7
Loss Financing	31.2
Workers' Compensation	26.8
Patient Representative Program	21.5
Security	17.6
Utilization Review	11.8
Case Management	9.4
Employee Benefits	4.5
Other	15.7

Base: 381 respondents—multiple responses

Source: Reprinted, with permission, from the American Society of Healthcare Risk Management, Healthcare Risk Manager National Role Delineation Study, 1999.

financing strategies it employs. The profession itself has evolved along functional needs and growing regulatory mandates, without benefit of extensive scientific study or a well-defined body of knowledge. Until recently, no attempt had been made to quantify the many activities that have come to comprise the health care risk manager's functional job responsibilities. Thus, it is not possible to describe the "typical" health care risk manager's job.

In 1999, the American Society for Healthcare Risk Management (ASHRM) conducted the first role delineation study in health care risk management. The purpose of this study was to identify those activities that comprise a health care risk manager's job and thereby define health care risk management's body of knowledge. A list of approximately 160 task statements describing various risk management functions and activities was sent to 2,500 health care risk management professionals, who were asked to rate the importance of each task (see Exhibit 1.1 on page 20). The findings suggest that the health care risk manager's job responsibilities can be divided into six major functional areas: loss prevention and reduction, claims management, risk financing, regulatory and accreditation compliance, risk management operations, and bioethics. Each of these areas is described here.

Loss Prevention and Reduction

This category encompasses all aspects of risk identification, loss prevention, and loss reduction and represents the largest functional area. Activities included in this category are:

- Developing formal and informal mechanisms for risk identification, such as incident reporting, staff referrals, medical record reviews, review of patient complaints, and review of pertinent quality-improvement information.

- Developing and maintaining collaborative relationships with key departments, such as quality management, nursing, medical staff, and infection control, in order to enhance program effectiveness.

- Developing statistical and qualitative reports on risk management trends and patterns, and communicating this information effectively to appropriate audiences.

- Developing policies and procedures in key areas of risk management interest, such as informed consent, product recalls, confidentiality, and handling of sentinel events.

- Developing educational programs for all levels of staff on a variety of risk management topics.

- Developing a program for management of exposures resulting from contracts, such as affiliation agreements, construction agreements, leases, management contracts, and purchase agreements.

- Serving as a resource to organizational staff on issues related to professional liability and other risks.

Claims Management

This category includes all activities associated with managing actual or potential claims, from reporting and investigation to resolution. Key activities included in this category are:

- Notifying carriers of actual or potential claims.
- Establishing claim files and coordinating investigation.
- Supervising investigators, third-party administrators (TPAs), and defense counsel.
- Coordinating the organization's response to discovery requests and interrogatories.
- Developing standards for the selection and evaluation of service providers.
- Setting expense and indemnity reserves.
- Approving and authorizing settlements.
- Ensuring that the organization's administrators are kept informed of high exposure cases and aggregate claims experience, including their impact on the risk financing program.

Risk Financing

This category includes all those activities associated with financing losses, whether the organization transfers or retains the risk. Activities included in this category are:

- Maintaining and coordinating exposure data for the organization.
- Coordinating insurance applications and renewals.
- Collaborating with brokers, underwriters, actuaries, and other service providers to determine the risk financing needs of the organization.
- Evaluating coverage limits, deductibles, attachment points, and lines of coverage to ensure that all exposures are adequately covered.

- Evaluating risk financing options such as commercial insurance, retention, captives, and risk retention groups, and selecting the best option based on the organization's needs.
- Monitoring and evaluating the organization's risk financing program.

Regulatory and Accreditation Compliance

This category includes all activities associated with compliance with accreditation standards as well as with major health care regulations. Activities included in this category are:

- Promoting compliance with requirements to report specific incidents to state and federal agencies.
- Promoting compliance with regulations such as Americans with Disabilities Act (ADA), Occupational Safety and Health Administration (OSHA), Patient Self-Determination Act (PSDA), Safe Medical Devices Act (SMDA), Emergency Medical Treatment and Active Labor Act (EMTALA), Health Care Quality Improvement Act (HCQIA), and Health Insurance Portability and Accountability Act (HIPAA).
- Promoting compliance with Joint Commission on Accreditation of Healthcare Organizations (JCAHO) requirements, including those pertaining to sentinel events.
- Promoting compliance with requirements to report deaths to the medical examiner or coroner.
- Collaborating with key department to ensure compliance with life safety codes.
- Promoting compliance with specific regulatory initiatives such as Project Lookback programs.

Risk Management Operations

This category covers those activities associated with managing a risk management department. Activities included in this category are:

- Developing an organizational risk management policy statement and plan.
- Training and supervising risk management staff.
- Coordinating and administering risk management committees.
- Developing annual goals for the risk management department.
- Evaluating the effectiveness of risk management activities.

Bioethics

This category includes all activities related to issues such as do not resuscitate (DNR) orders, brain death criteria, advance directives, withdrawal of life support, and human subjects research. Activities included in this category are:

- Reviewing policies and procedures related to end-of-life issues for conformance with ethical principles and adherence to applicable regulation.
- Reviewing policies and procedures relating to human subjects research for adherence to applicable regulation and organizational policy.

- Providing risk management consultation for specific ethical dilemmas.
- Providing education for staff, patients, families, and communities on patients' rights.

············

HEALTH CARE RISK MANAGEMENT ACROSS A SPECTRUM OF SETTINGS

As mentioned earlier in the chapter, the roles and job responsibilities of health care risk managers are determined by the characteristics of the organizations in which they work. The size and structure of the organization determine the needs of the organization, and this in turn influences the size, structure, and function of the risk management program. The risk financing strategies of the organization are also important determinants of risk management program structure and function.

The following sections examine the role of the risk manager in several health care settings—the acute care hospital or medical center, the academic medical center, the integrated delivery system (IDS), multihospital systems, and ambulatory care settings. For each setting, the relative importance of each of the six major functional areas of responsibility are examined, as are other unique characteristics of risk management programs in these settings.

The Acute Care Hospital or Medical Center

According to ASHRM's 1995 membership survey, 50 percent of respondents are employed in an acute care hospital or medical center, by far the largest category. Acute care hospitals or medical centers can range in size from less than one hundred licensed beds to more than five hundred licensed beds. They can be classified as community hospitals, which tend to be smaller and typically do not have their own residency programs, and teaching hospitals, which tend to be larger and often have multiple residency programs.

Acute care hospitals or medical centers offer a range of services, although not all hospitals offer every type of service. Patient care services typically offered in acute care hospitals or medical centers include general medicine and surgery, medical and surgical subspecialties such as cardiology and orthopedic surgery, and primary care services such as family medicine, pediatrics, and obstetrics. Most have intensive care units of some type and also have emergency departments. More complex services, such as transplant surgery and advanced trauma care, are typically found in academic medical centers, which are discussed later in this section. The types of services a hospital offers are typically controlled through the state's certificate of need program.

Even within this category, risk management program structure and function varies widely. At a *small-to-medium-sized community hospital*, it is common practice for the risk manager to assume responsibilities for several related areas, such as quality improvement, safety, or infection control. The limitations of the hospital's resources, together with a smaller workload, make this arrangement an attractive one for these organizations. More recently, risk managers in such settings have also been called upon to assume the role of the corporate compliance officer.

Small-to-medium-sized hospitals are usually commercially insured, thereby decreasing the administrative burden for the risk financing and claims management functions on the risk management department itself. Responsibilities for workers' compensation programs often rest with the human resources department. Thus, the risk manager's role in such settings often focuses on the activities associated with loss prevention and reduction: risk identification and analysis, management of serious adverse events, staff education, and policy and procedure review and development. Risk managers in these hospitals also often have responsibility for ensuring compliance with major health care regulations and requirements and for accreditation activities. Smaller hospitals often face risks associated with access to care, specifically access to specialized or intensive care, not faced by larger hospitals. The risk manager may be quite involved in clinical ethics consultations as well, because smaller organizations typically do not have the resources to employ an ethicist.

The risk manager's role in risk financing at smaller hospitals is often limited to collecting and coordinating exposure data and managing the insurance renewal process. The chief financing officer typically assumes the burden for evaluation of carriers and insurance options, selection of new carriers, and decisions regarding risk financing options. The risk manager's interaction with brokers and underwriters may be limited.

When risk is transferred, responsibilities for claims management also decreases. In a smaller commercially insured hospital, the risk manager's role in claims management is limited to coordinating the investigation and defense activities of the investigators, adjustors, and attorney employed or retained by the insurance carrier. The risk manager is not responsible for setting reserves or authorizing settlements, as this is usually the exclusive right and responsibility of the carrier.

Risk managers in small-to-medium-sized community hospitals often enjoy high visibility. They are often viewed as the primary resource on a wide range of topics because the organization cannot afford to employ a number of experts in a variety of disciplines. They very often function as the hospital's liaison to outside counsel and as such become involved in a variety of interesting legal issues. Risk managers in such settings have the opportunity to work and interact with nearly every health care discipline. Thus, these positions offer excellent opportunities for learning and collaboration, and also opportunities for advancement by assuming responsibility for related areas.

In *medium-to-large community hospitals or medical centers,* risk managers typically have somewhat greater and better defined responsibilities than they do in smaller hospitals. They generally retain responsibility for all loss prevention and control functions, but may be assisted by one or more staff persons. Such staff assistants often have clinical experience or expertise that enables them to interact very effectively with patient care providers. The nature of loss prevention and reduction activities at such hospitals is essentially the same, though the volume tends to be greater than at smaller facilities. Credentialing and informed consent issues assume greater significance in these settings because of the greater number of specialists on staff and the riskier nature of treatments and procedures offered.

Medium-to-large hospitals and medical centers usually employ a greater number of professionals specializing in a variety of disciplines, so that risk managers in such hospitals are less likely to assume multiple job responsibilities. Usually, safety and infection control professionals are employed, and often the quality improvement function is separate from risk management. Thus, the risk manager in such settings focuses almost exclusively on risk management functions, and there is little confusion among the staff as to who the risk manager is or what the function comprises.

While many are commercially insured, medium-to-large hospitals and medical centers are often in the position to use alternative risk financing strategies. It is common for such organizations to have in place self-insured trusts, large deductibles, or captive insurance companies to finance primary liability risks. If that is the case, the risk manager has a greater role in risk financing and claims management. The risk manager typically works collaboratively with the chief financial officer and other executives in the development of loss exposure data, setting reserves, monitoring of program results, and evaluating existing and alternative arrangements. Claims management also becomes a higher risk management priority in such circumstances, and the risk manager is often responsible for directing the activities of an in-house claims staff or of third-party claims administrators, investigators, and attorneys. Risk managers in such settings typically have a great deal of interaction with brokers, underwriters, and actuaries. They may also have responsibility for self-funded workers' compensation programs.

Risk managers in medium-to-large hospitals and medical centers are often quite involved in regulatory compliance, but in many cases there is a designated compliance officer with responsibility for the corporate integrity program. Thus, the risk manager's role becomes more advisory in nature in this area, serving as a content expert in those areas that relate to risk management. Most often risk managers in these settings continue to play a significant role in accreditation, but this is usually a collaborative role with other administrators. They are involved in ethics consultations, as are their counterparts in smaller hospitals, but their role may be more advisory in nature because larger hospitals typically have more developed ethics programs and may even employ an ethicist. As the risk management department in larger hospitals also tend to be larger, the risk manager in such a setting typically devotes more time to department administration.

Risk managers in medium-to-large hospitals and medical centers require the same skill set as risk managers in smaller hospitals. Effective communication skills and the ability to work collaboratively in other disciplines are critical success factors for risk managers in either setting. In addition, risk managers who work in larger and more complex settings need to develop a better understanding of those more complex risks as well as of risk financing and claims management.

The job descriptions found in Exhibit 1.2 on page 30 and Exhibit 1.3 on page 33 are most consistent with the functions of the risk manager in the acute care hospital or medical center.

Academic Medical Centers

Academic medical centers pose unique risk management challenges. They tend to be large and complex organizations, and the care they provide is equally complicated. Risk managers in these settings must deal with risks ranging from simple clinical misadventures to complicated issues involving clinical research, affiliation agreements, and academic freedom.

Academic medical centers tend to have risk management departments with several professional staff members. Most often, at least one staff member has clinical training. This is a great advantage given the complex nature of the clinical risks encountered in these settings.

Risk prevention and reduction activities in academic medical centers are made more difficult because of the many individuals involved in patient care. Unlike other hospitals, patients in academic medical centers are often cared for by students, residents, fellows, and a variety of specialists not commonly found in other settings. Because of the involvement of so many individuals in patients' care, there is a greater potential for error; thus, risk is increased. In addition, staff rotations and turnover tends to be higher in academic medical centers, and there is a constant need for education and reinforcement of risk management policies and procedures, including reporting requirements.

Risk managers in academic medical centers often spend a great deal of time in educating staff about risk management principles and practices. They also devote a great deal of time to the investigation of incidents, because facts and circumstances tend to be more complicated and harder to discern. Credentialing and human subjects research pose special risks in academic medical centers.

Because of the larger size of the academic medical center, the risk management department does not typically assume responsibility for related functions. Instead, there is a greater need for the risk management department to work collaboratively with related disciplines.

Academic medical centers often face unique risks that make commercial insurance vehicles unattractive options for them. As a result, academic medical centers are often involved in alternative risk financing arrangements such as captives. The risk manager in an academic medical center is likely to have some involvement in these risk financing arrangements and must therefore have expertise and knowledge in this area. The level of the risk manager's involvement will depend on many factors, including whether or not the organization is involved in a group arrangement and on the culture of the organization. Very often, academic medical centers' risk financing functions are administered at high administrative levels, and the risk manager's role in these functions may be limited.

Claims management in an academic medical center is usually handled within the organization rather than outsourced. This requires that the risk manager have the ability to effectively investigate claims, manage the activities of defense counsel, and establish appropriate reserves. The volume of claims in an academic medical center is such that several dedicated claims professionals may be required. This is especially true if the department is also expected to manage other types of claims, such as general liability, directors' and officers' liability, and property claims.

Regulatory and corporate compliance and accreditation activities in academic medical centers are complicated and time-consuming activities usually handled by professional staff dedicated to those functions. However, the risk manager typically serves as an advisor in those functions.

Bioethics consultation in an academic medical center is usually a collaborative effort in which the risk manger plays an important role. Because of the strong research orientation of academic medical centers, they often have strong clinical ethics programs with dedicated staff. Risk managers may be members of the ethics committee and institutional review board (IRB).

Risk management department operations consume much of the risk manager's time because the department tends to be larger in an academic medical center. Also, the risk manager in an academic medical center may be expected to support the organization's teaching and research mission by accepting interns, teaching in the medical school, and assisting in risk management related research. All of these activities increase the administrative burden of the risk management department.

The job description found in Exhibit 1.4 on page 36 is most representative of the scope of responsibilities in an academic medical center.

Integrated Delivery Systems

An integrated delivery system (IDS) is an organization that encompasses many different types of providers under one corporate structure. An IDS often includes acute care facilities, physician group practices and multi-specialty clinics, and post-acute care facilities and homecare services. Providers may be employees, independent contractors, or they may be loosely affiliated with the organization in some other way. IDSs often cover broad geographical areas and can be very large and complex organizations in terms of corporate structure. In many cases, an IDS comprises facilities across several states. For all of these reasons, IDSs pose particular challenges for risk managers who seek to develop coordinated and consistent risk management plans and strategies.

In an IDS, there is usually a corporate risk manager who assumes overall responsibility for the IDS's overall risk management program. The corporate risk manager is responsible for risk financing activities and has oversight responsibilities for claims management. This position is typically responsible for risk management activities only and does not assume other related responsibilities. Risk prevention and reduction activities are carried out by risk management staff at the facility level who may report to the corporate risk manager or to the facility administrator. In many instances, the risk management function is assumed by a clinician or other facility staff member with no formal risk management training. This requires that the corporate risk manager be an effective teacher and mentor.

The degree of integration and standardization of risk management practices, and of clinical practice, across the IDS is often quite variable and produces significant risk that must be managed. The corporate risk manager establishes broad goals and objectives for the risk management program, thus providing the framework for the individual facilities to follow. These general guidelines allow individual facilities to adopt policies and practices that address issues unique to their setting. It may take some period of time before all elements of the IDS can be successfully incorporated into a coordinated risk management program within the IDS. Very often, individual facilities are permitted to remain in existing risk financing arrangements because standardization and change across the IDS is too difficult to manage. Thus, the corporate risk manager may be required to manage and oversee a complex program with many different and varied components.

In addition to the risks noted above, IDSs are particularly vulnerable to the risks associated with merger and acquisition activity. Thus, the corporate risk manager's role in pre-merger due diligence takes on added significance in an IDS. Establishing strong relationships and being perceived as a valuable resource is essential in order for the corporate risk manager to influence decisions, and eliminate or mitigate risk, prior to these organizational changes (see Chapter 12 for more information on mergers and acquisitions).

Risk identification can be accomplished in a variety of ways in the IDS. Health plan utilization decisions that limit or deny services require a consistent approach based on currently accepted medical practices and on insuring agreements. Close study of contracts, credentialing practices, marketing and sales initiatives, capitation agreements, health benefit claims and denials, and member and patient satisfaction data are other mechanisms for identifying potential risks.

The risk manager may oversee or be directly responsible for claims administration, including investigating, analyzing, reporting, and establishing reserves.

The corporate risk manager in an IDS must be well-versed in all aspects of risk financing and must have excellent skills in contract management. The risk manager must also be able to work well with a variety of other people to achieve corporate objectives, even though the risk manager may exercise no control over these individuals. The job description in Exhibit 1.4 most closely corresponds with the role of the corporate risk manager in an IDS.

Multifacility Health Care Systems

Health care systems are composed of multiple facilities providing similar services owned by a single corporation or parent organization. In many ways, health care system risk management programs are similar to IDS programs. They both manage risks across discrete organizations that may have entirely different cultures and identities. However, systems do not face the same challenges that IDSs face in that their practices and procedures tend to be standardized across the system. Thus the corporate risk manager in a system is unlikely to be faced with a broad array of risk financing arrangements or facility-based practices within the system. The risk management program in a system is usually well coordinated and fairly standardized across the system.

The risk manager in a health care system most often functions as a senior executive in the organization. Risk prevention and reduction activities are usually carried out at the facility level under the direction of the system risk manager. The system risk manager is unlikely to have other duties in addition to risk management.

As in the IDS, the corporate risk manager in a system will likely be responsible for risk financing activities. Systems often employ alternative risk financing strategies to control costs, and the corporate risk manager usually directs this program. Claims management activities are often centralized and may be handled internally by dedicated claims staff.

System risk managers usually work collaboratively with others in the organization in the areas of regulatory and accreditation compliance and bioethics. They are likely to serve in a consultative capacity, or this responsibility may be delegated within the department. System risk managers often direct large departments and thus have significant operations responsibilities.

The job description in Exhibit 1.4 most closely approximates the duties of the health care system risk manager. The position requires significant risk management knowledge and experience, and the ability to stay ahead of the complexities involved in a changing health care environment.

Ambulatory Care Organizations

Ambulatory care organizations (ACOs) include physicians' offices, multispecialty clinics, freestanding surgical centers, urgent care or walk-in medical clinics, and community health or public health facilities. The organizational structure of outpatient care can be as varied as the facilities, with the owner of a practice, often a physician, functioning as the administrator to whom the risk manager reports. Larger facilities more often have a governing body to guide the organization. As in a small hospital setting, the individual responsible for the risk management function may serve in several capacities.

ACOs pose unique risks because of the large number of patient encounters, which increases the risk of exposure to loss. In addition, because patients themselves control the progress of their health care, there is a greater chance that care may be fragmented or prolonged, and a provider may not recognize changes or deterioration in a patient's condition. Finally, ACOs often do not have access to other departments that support critical risk management functions, such as safety, infection control, and biomedical engineering, as hospitals do.

Risks in ACOs vary with the type of setting. In most ambulatory settings, loss of patients to follow up is a major risk management concern. The use and maintenance of equipment often pose risk management concerns. Adherence to safety standards, universal precautions, and other requirements are often challenging in ACOs and can be a source of risk to both patients and staff.

Day surgery centers are concerned with appropriate discharge criteria and procedures. Emerging risks include the performance of a growing number of procedures, including surgery, in outpatient and office settings. Credentialing is of particular concern because ambulatory settings lack the procedural rigors of hospitals in this area.

Incident reports and occurrence screening often provide the mechanisms for risk identification. Patient complaints are also good sources of information about potential risks.

Risk financing strategies used by ACOs may vary, but rarely will an ACO be involved in a self-managed alternative risk financing arrangement. Most ACOs are commercially insured or are part of the risk financing program of a larger organization, often a hospital. In that case, the parent organization assumes most of the responsibility, and the ACO risk manager plays only a minor role in risk financing. This is usually limited to coordinating exposure data and renewals.

Most ACOs do not manage their own liability claims internally. Instead, this function is handled by the insurance carrier or a Third Party Administrator (TPA) employed by the parent organization. The ACO risk manager may be called upon to assist in the coordination of investigation and defense of claims, but will usually not have any direct responsibility beyond that.

Risk managers in ACOs typically do not have significant responsibilities for regulatory or accreditation issues. Bioethics issues also are less commonly seen in these settings.

The job description in Exhibit 1.2 most closely corresponds to the scope of responsibility of an ACO risk manager.

············
REQUIRED SKILLS FOR THE SUCCESSFUL HEALTH CARE RISK MANAGER

In order to be successful, health care risk managers must develop a variety of skills necessary for performing an often difficult job in a complex environment. Health care risk managers are called upon to interact with all levels of authority within the organization as well as with patients and other customers. They often act as the organization's "official" representative in very sensitive circumstances. This means that they must have the skills necessary to interact effectively with all types of people and to make themselves clearly understood, and they must be able to do this under often trying circumstances. Of primary importance is *communication,* which includes writing, listening, and speaking. Health care risk managers are often called upon to conduct educational sessions for other health care workers, both professional and nonprofessional providers and employees. They must also frequently deliver formal presentations to administrators or to board members or trustees. For this reason, excellent oral communication skills and a thorough understanding and application of effective presentation styles are of critical importance to a successful health care risk manager.

In addition to communicating well orally, successful health care risk managers must also be able to communicate well in writing. Health care risk managers must often prepare detailed reports of individual cases as well as reports of trends and patterns. Also, risk managers are often called upon to develop policies, procedures, and other guidance documents that will be used by others at all levels of the organization. For this reason, the health care risk manager must have the ability to communicate clearly, accurately, and succinctly in writing.

Finally, the ability to listen well is another essential component of excellent communication skills needed by the successful health care risk manager. An essential function of the health care risk manager is fact-gathering following a serious event. This involves interviewing those involved, carefully listening to their stories, and reconstructing the events that occurred. The health care risk manager must also be able to glean information about risks and exposures from a variety of other sources, including committee reports and informal discussions. The successful health care risk manager must be able to carefully listen to all information without passing judgment and to carefully and objectively process that information as well as pass it on to others who may need it. Thus, the ability to listen well is a complex and critical skill for the health care risk manager.

Another important skill for the successful health care risk manager is *the ability to negotiate*. The health care risk management professional often serves as negotiator in a variety of situations, such as the resolution of claims or patient complaints, securing broker services or insurance coverage, or in developing indemnification agreements or contract language. For this reason, the successful health care risk manager must have or develop the skills used by expert negotiators.

Another critical skill for a health care risk manager is *the ability to remain objective*. Health care risk managers are often involved in emotionally charged situations, and they are often called upon to provide support and direction to those most closely associated with these events. They must also take charge of discovering the facts and determining the best course of action. In order to do this effectively, the health care risk management professional must have the ability to maintain objectivity and professional detachment, even in emotionally difficult situations, and to pursue the best course of action for the organization regardless of personal feelings.

Finally, another critically important skill for the health care risk manager is *the ability to maintain confidentiality*. Because of the nature of their work, health care risk managers often come into contact with situations and fact patterns that have the ability to seriously damage or destroy the organization and the individuals who work there. The health care risk manager must be able to perform those activities necessary to protect the organizations and individuals while also being able to refrain from sharing information needlessly, regardless of how tempting or trying the situation might be. Maintaining confidentiality is critical not only to protect those involved in an adverse event or potentially damaging circumstance, it is also necessary to win and maintain the trust of those who might provide important information to the health care risk manager in the future.

············

RISK MANAGEMENT ETHICS

One hallmark of a true profession is a code of ethical conduct to which its practitioners must adhere. This is a familiar concept in health care, as medicine's own code of ethics dates back to the Hippocratic Oath. Nursing, law, and other disciplines related to health care risk management likewise have codes of ethical behaviors that guide practitioners in those fields.

ASHRM's own Code of Professional Responsibility spells out the standards of conduct to which its members must adhere. This code is included in Exhibit 1.5 on page 39, and provides a useful roadmap for health care risk managers who wish to maintain the highest level of professional conduct.

....

A PROFILE OF THE HEALTH CARE RISK MANAGER

Because of the way in which the health care risk management profession has evolved, health care risk management professionals come from a variety of professional and educational backgrounds, including nursing, law, administration, quality assurance, and insurance. According to the results of ASHRM's 1999 role delineation study, approximately 88 percent of respondents held at least a bachelor's degree, and 52 percent held a graduate degree.

Health care risk management professionals hold a variety of professional designations. Table 1.2 illustrates the results of the survey's findings regarding professional designations held by health care risk managers.

Respondents in this study had been in their current position an average of six years and 25 percent of respondents indicated they had been in their current job more than ten years. The average tenure in risk management was nine years, which is consistent with the 1995 ASHRM membership survey.

....

EDUCATION AND PROFESSIONAL RECOGNITION PROGRAMS

An important characteristic that distinguishes a true professional is the desire to further develop and refine his or her mastery of the chosen profession. One of the ways professionals pursue growth and development is by continuing their education through both formal and informal means. In turn, the profession recognizes the efforts of these professionals by bestowing designations extolling their achievements. Thus, continuing education and professional recognition of achievement are important components of a continuously evolving profession and important milestones for the health care risk management professional.

Academic Training

A growing number of colleges and universities either currently offer or are developing programs leading to a baccalaureate or master's degree in health care risk management. (Information about such programs is available on the ASHRM Web site at

TABLE 1.2.   Professional Designation

Designation	*Percentage*
RN	53.5
ARM	15.0
CPHQ	11.5
HRM	10.2
CHSP	2.6
CSP, CHEM, CPA, ALCM (.3 each)	1.2
ABHRM	1.0
RPLU	1.0
AIC	0.8
Other	29.1

Multiple responses: Average of 3.2 designations per respondent

Base: 381 respondents

Source: Reprinted, with permission, from the American Society of Healthcare Risk Management, Healthcare Risk Manager National Role Delineation Study, 1999.

www.ashrm.org.) This trend signifies the increasing recognition of health care risk management as a discipline worthy of academic attention. As the profession continues to evolve, more entrants into the field will come equipped with formal academic training rather than experiential training, as has been the case in the past. See Table 1.3 for the breakdown of academic backgrounds of ASHRM members responding to the recent Role Delineation Study. If the trend continues, it is possible that one day formal academic training in health care risk management will be a requirement for entry into the field. This requirement would also help to provide a steady stream of new and qualified candidates for health care risk management positions. However, that day is still far away, as such programs are not yet widely available.

Continuing Professional Education

While academic programs fulfill an important role for the profession, they may not meet the needs of those that already hold academic degrees but seek further professional education in the field of health care risk management. Thus, it is important that other means exist for health care professionals to obtain continuing education in the field of health care risk management. Fortunately, that is the case. In addition to academic programs, several other avenues exist for health care risk management professionals to further their education and professional development.

The major source of professional education programs for health care risk managers is ASHRM. ASHRM has developed a number of educational programs for health care risk managers that are available to both members and nonmembers. The Health Care Risk Management Certificate Program, which covers key aspects of risk management, is designed for the beginning risk management professional. The program consists of five modules covering such topics as the fundamentals of risk management, claims management and legal issues, clinical risk management, risk financing, workers' compensation, safety and security, contract review, and other critical topics for beginning risk managers. Upon completion of all five modules, attendees are issued a certificate of completion by ASHRM and they also earn continuing education credits.

ASHRM also presents programs on more advanced topics, such as risk financing, regulatory developments, and other critical issues for health care risk managers throughout the year. At its annual conference, ASHRM presents programs on a wide variety of topics both within the field of health care risk management and more broadly within health care as well. As with other offerings, attendees earn continuing education credits.

In addition to ASHRM, major health care liability insurance carriers and brokers also offer educational programs specifically designed for health care risk managers. While

TABLE 1.3.   Academic Achievement

Education	*Percentage*
Associate's degree	12.1
Bachelor's degree	35.9
Master's degree	38.3
Doctoral degree	13.7
	100.0
Base: 365 respondents	

Source: Reprinted, with permission, from the American Society of Healthcare Risk Management, Healthcare Risk Manager National Role Delineation Study, 1999.

these programs are often limited to clients or insureds, they often cover timely topics and feature nationally known speakers.

Certification

Certification provides evidence of mastery of a defined body of knowledge by requiring certificants to successfully complete an objective test, such as a written examination. It helps to set professional standards by identifying a minimum level of knowledge, which all certificants must possess. It also helps to ensure continued growth and development of the profession and of individuals practicing the profession by requiring recertification at predetermined intervals.

Currently, there is only one certification program specifically for health care risk managers in the United States. This program, administered by the American Hospital Association Certification Center (AHACC), in cooperation with ASHRM, offers the designation of Certified Professional in Healthcare Risk Management (CPHRM). An individual who meets eligibility criteria and successfully completes a qualifying examination becomes certified. Eligibility standards include prior work experience as well as certain educational requirements. The CPHRM examination tests the applicant's knowledge in each of the six domain areas identified by ASHRM's role delineation study: loss prevention and reduction, claims management, risk financing, regulatory and accreditation compliance, operations, and bioethics. Certificants are required to become recertified every three years.

The Insurance Institute of America (IIA) also offers risk management education in the form of its Associate in Risk Management (ARM) program. This is a designation program consisting of three courses and accompanying examinations that focus on the risk management process (designated as ARM 54), loss control (ARM 55), and risk financing (ARM 56). Upon successful completion of the examinations, the student earns the designation Associate in Risk Management, or ARM, which is recognized throughout the insurance industry. Although the ARM program does not focus specifically on health care risk management, it offers significant educational benefits to the health care risk manager who is interested in furthering his or her education beyond the borders of health care.

Other designation programs are also offered through the Insurance Institute of America and the American Institute for Chartered Property and Casualty Underwriters, including the Associate in Claims (AIC) and the Chartered Property and Casualty Underwriter (CPCU). Many equate a CPCU designation to a master's in insurance. Further information is available at the institutes' Web site at www.aicpcu.org.

Professional Recognition Programs

Professional recognition programs serve a valuable function for a profession and the individuals practicing the profession by encouraging continued growth and development of individuals, in turn elevating standards in the profession. Such programs are typically administered by professional societies and membership organizations.

ASHRM offers the designations of distinguished fellow (DFASHRM), which is awarded for outstanding achievement in the profession, and the designation of fellow (FASHRM), which is awarded for superior achievement. Criteria for both designations include a combination of educational, leadership, and publication experience and achievement, and designations are awarded to all members who meet the criteria.

ASHRM's highest award, the Distinguished Service Award (DSA), recognizes a health care risk management professional whose efforts have advanced the profession and practice of risk management and who has made an outstanding contribution to ASHRM. The award is given only to those whom the board of directors feels is deserving of the award.

Other organizations sometimes also offer awards in recognition of superior achievement. *Business Insurance,* a nationally recognized insurance publication, offers recognition to the Risk Manager of the Year as well as to the members of the Risk Management Honor Roll. These awards are given to winners from all industries, and health care risk managers have been honored on several occasions.

. . . .

CONCLUSION

The growth and evolution of the health care risk management profession has mirrored that of the health care industry as a whole, although its basic components and processes have not changed. The goal of an effective health care risk management program continues to be to maintain a safe and effective health care environment for patients, visitors, and employees, thereby preventing or reducing loss to the organization. Risk management continues to compose an important part of the delivery of health care, and it has become even more important because of the greater emphasis on patient safety brought about by legislative activity in early 2000.

The role of the health care risk manager has become more clear as a result of the role delineation study conducted by ASHRM in early 1999. For the first time, there is an accurate assessment of the various tasks that are comprised in the health care risk management function as well as their relative importance. Loss prevention and reduction, claims management, risk financing, regulatory and accreditation compliance, risk management operations, and bioethics are the major functional areas that together make up the health care risk manager's job. The depth and breadth of these functions, as well as their vital importance to an organization's survival, have been amply demonstrated by this study.

Health care risk managers are a diverse group of professionals from a variety of backgrounds. Most are highly educated and many have clinical experience. They value continuing education and professional achievement as demonstrated by the demographic data obtained in the ASHRM study.

Successful health care risk managers must possess certain critical skills. The ability to communicate well, to negotiate effectively, to remain objective and to maintain confidentiality are key to the ability of the health care risk manager to function effectively.

Opportunities for health care risk managers to enhance their professional growth and development abound. Academic training programs in health care risk management are increasingly common, and continuing education opportunities have always been plentiful. A new opportunity for health care risk managers to enhance their professional development and recognition comes with the health care risk management certification program developed by ASHRM in conjunction with the American Hospital Association.

The continuing challenge for health care risk managers will be to stay abreast of developments in health care that lead to new exposures, and to develop new techniques to manage those exposures. There is also the ever-present need to help other health care colleagues understand the purpose and function of health care risk management, as well as their role in it.

Suggested Readings

American Society for Healthcare Risk Management. "Healthcare Risk Management National Role Delineation Study." Analysis by Applied Measurement Professionals, Lenexa, Kansas, 1999.

Carroll, R. (ed.). *Risk Management Handbook for Health Care Organizations* (2nd ed.). Chicago: AHA American Hospital Publishing, 1997.

Business Insurance, Apr. 22, 1996, p. 135.

American Hospital Association. "Mapping Your Risk Management Course in Integrated Delivery Networks." Chicago: American Hospital Publishing, Inc., 1995.

American Hospital Association. "Mapping Your Risk Management Course in Stand-Alone Hospitals." Chicago: American Hospital Publishing, Inc., 1995.

American Hospital Association. "Mapping Your Risk Management Course in Ambulatory Care." Chicago: American Hospital Publishing, Inc., 1995.

Youngberg, B. J. *The Risk Manager's Desk Reference.* Rockville, Md.: Aspen, 1994.

EXHIBIT 1.1.   ASHRM Risk Manager Task Inventory

     American Society For
Healthcare Risk Management

Task Inventory

For purposes of this inventory, a general job definition has been included. Please thoroughly read this definition before you proceed any further.

Practitioner Definition

The ASHRM Certified Healthcare Risk Manager's primary objectives include the prevention, reduction, and control of loss to the healthcare organization, its patients, visitors, volunteers, physicians, other healthcare professionals and employees. Regardless of the healthcare delivery system in which the individual works, the Certified Healthcare Risk Manager interfaces with a number of healthcare professionals in the accomplishment of these objectives. These include but are not limited to: finance, regulatory/compliance, consumer advocacy, quality assurance, human resources, legal counsel, utilization review, and infection control. The Certified Healthcare Risk Manager possesses knowledge of the various types of insurance coverage and risk financing strategies; incident investigation, tracking, trending and evaluation; and claims management.

  < On pages 3-9, read and consider each task with respect to their content areas (e.g., I,. Loss Prevention/Reduction)
  < Read each task and consider its **importance** with regard to the effective performance of a Certified Healthcare Risk Manager as defined in the Practitioner Definition
  < Rate each task for importance by circling the appropriate number (0 - 5) using the importance scale given below.

<u>Importance</u> How important are the tasks on the following pages to the effective performance of a Certified Healthcare Risk Manager as defined in the Practitioner Definition?

0 = No importance	3 = Average or medium importance
1 = Minimal importance	4 = Above average or high importance
2 = Below average or low importance	5 = Extreme importance

These example ratings are for illustrative purposes only, and do not reflect actual ratings.

	Importance
I. Loss Prevention/Reduction	
1. Develop statistical and qualitative risk management reports.................................1.	0 1 2 3 4 5
2. Develop and maintain communications and relationships with key departments and functions, including but not limited to:	
a) human resources...2.	0 1 2 3 4 5

Before you begin however, please respond to the Background Information questions on pages 1-2.

If you have any questions about completing this inventory, please call:
Andrew J. Falcone, PhD, Program Director
Applied Measurement Professionals, Inc.
Lenexa, Kansas 66214-1579

(Continued)

EXHIBIT 1.1.   ASHRM Risk Manager Task Inventory (*Continued*)

ASHRM Risk Manager Task Inventory

Section I:
Background Information

Please answer the following questions about your background by filling in the appropriate circle, or by writing in the requested information. This information is confidential and will only be used to analyze the data across different groups of task inventory respondents (e.g., respondents from different states).

A. Location of facility or organization in which you work:
   (select only one response)

1. ☐	AK	14. ☐	ID	27. ☐	MT	40. ☐	RI			
2. ☐	AL	15. ☐	IL	28. ☐	NC	41. ☐	SC			
3. ☐	AR	16. ☐	IN	29. ☐	ND	42. ☐	SD			
4. ☐	AZ	17. ☐	KS	30. ☐	NE	43. ☐	TN			
5. ☐	CA	18. ☐	KY	31. ☐	NH	44. ☐	TX			
6. ☐	CO	19. ☐	LA	32. ☐	NJ	45. ☐	UT			
7. ☐	CT	20. ☐	MA	33. ☐	NM	46. ☐	VA			
8. ☐	DC	21. ☐	MD	34. ☐	NV	47. ☐	VT			
9. ☐	DE	22. ☐	ME	35. ☐	NY	48. ☐	WA			
10. ☐	FL	23. ☐	MI	36. ☐	OH	49. ☐	WI			
11. ☐	GA	24. ☐	MN	37. ☐	OK	50. ☐	WV			
12. ☐	HI	25. ☐	MO	38. ☐	OR	51. ☐	WY			
13. ☐	IA	26. ☐	MS	39. ☐	PA					

52. ☐ Multi-state
53. ☐ National Practice
54. ☐ Other: _____

B. Location (setting) of the facility/organization in which you work: **(select only one response)**

   1. ☐ Urban
   2. ☐ Suburban
   3. ☐ Rural

C. Highest level of academic education: **(select only one response)**

   1. ☐ Associate Degree
   2. ☐ Bachelor's Degree
   3. ☐ Master's Degree
   4. ☐ Doctoral Degree (PhD, EdD, JD)

D. Professional designations earned: **(select all that apply)**

   1. ☐ RN
   2. ☐ CPA
   3. ☐ CPCU
   4. ☐ CPHQ
   5. ☐ ARM
   6. ☐ ABHRM
   7. ☐ CHEM
   8. ☐ AIC
   9. ☐ ALCM
   10. ☐ CSP
   11. ☐ CHSP
   12. ☐ AU
   13. ☐ HRM
   14. ☐ RPLU
   15. ☐ Other: _____

E. Number of years of experience in your current position:

   _____ years

F. Number of years of experience in Healthcare Risk Management:

   _____ years

G. The majority of formal training you received in Risk Management: **(select only one response)**

   1. ☐ College Courses
   2. ☐ Professional Development Courses (e.g., ARM, CPCU)
   3. ☐ ASHRM Seminars/Certificate Programs

H. Type of setting which most accurately represents your *primary* risk management activities: **(select only one response)**

   1. ☐ Acute Care Medical Center
   2. ☐ Academic Medical Center
   3. ☐ Pediatric Hospital
   4. ☐ Psychology/Behavioral Healthcare
   5. ☐ Military/Federal/VA
   6. ☐ IDS Corporate Office
   7. ☐ Managed Care Provider
   8. ☐ Ambulatory Care

(*Continued*)

EXHIBIT 1.1.   ASHRM Risk Manager Task Inventory (*Continued*)

ASHRM Risk Manager Task Inventory

H. Type of setting which most accurately represents your primary risk management activities: **(continued)**

   9. ☐ Rehabilitation Facility
  10. ☐ Assisted Living
  11. ☐ Home Healthcare Agency
  12. ☐ Long Term Care Facility
  13. ☐ Risk Management Consultant
  14. ☐ Risk Mgt. Consultant/Self-employed
  15. ☐ Insurance Broker
  16. ☐ Insurance Company/Captive/Trust
  17. ☐ Physician Practice Management
  18. ☐ Law Firm
  19. ☐ Multi-system Hospital
  20. ☐ Other: _____

I. Current job title:
  (select only one response)

   1. ☐ President
   2. ☐ Senior Vice President
   3. ☐ Vice President
   4. ☐ Assistant Vice President
   5. ☐ Medical Director
   6. ☐ Director
   7. ☐ Assistant Director
   8. ☐ Administrator
   9. ☐ Assistant Administrator
  10. ☐ Manager
  11. ☐ Assistant Manager
  12. ☐ Claims Manager
  13. ☐ Risk Manager
  14. ☐ Corporate Risk Manager
  15. ☐ Coordinator
  16. ☐ Consultant
  17. ☐ Attorney
  18. ☐ In-House Legal Counsel
  19. ☐ Director of Risk Management
  20. ☐ Director of Risk Mgt./Quality Assurance
  21. ☐ Nursing Administrator/Director
  22. ☐ Quality Assurance Coordinator/Director
  23. ☐ Regulatory Compliance Officer
  24. ☐ Other: _____

J. Current job function(s).
  (select all that apply)

   1. ☐ Management/Administration
   2. ☐ Risk Identification and Evaluation
   3. ☐ Claims Handling
   4. ☐ Regulatory Compliance
   5. ☐ Quality
   6. ☐ Insurance Purchasing Decisions
   7. ☐ Utilization Review
   8. ☐ Case Management
   9. ☐ Employee Benefits
  10. ☐ Education
  11. ☐ Ethics
  12. ☐ Loss Prevention
  13. ☐ Loss Financing
  14. ☐ Legal Affairs
  15. ☐ Contract Review
  16. ☐ Safety Administration
  17. ☐ Patient Representative Program
  18. ☐ Insurance Program
  19. ☐ Security
  20. ☐ Worker's Compensation
  21. ☐ Medical Staff Issues
  22. ☐ Other: _____

(Continued)

EXHIBIT 1.1.   ASHRM Risk Manager Task Inventory (*Continued*)

Importance: 0 = No importance   3 = Average or medium importance
1 = Minimal importance   4 = Above average or high importance
2 = Below average or low importance   5 = Extreme importance

Healthcare Risk Manager
Role Delineation

Section II:
Task Statements

Importance

I.   *Loss Prevention/Reduction*

1. Develop statistical and qualitative risk management reports	1.	0	1	2	3	4	5

2. Develop and maintain communications and relationships with key departments
and functions, including but not limited to:

a) human resources	2.	0	1	2	3	4	5
b) infection control	3.	0	1	2	3	4	5
c) nursing	4.	0	1	2	3	4	5
d) medical records	5.	0	1	2	3	4	5
e) quality management	6.	0	1	2	3	4	5
f) medical staff	7.	0	1	2	3	4	5
g) patient relations	8.	0	1	2	3	4	5
h) high risk clinical departments	9.	0	1	2	3	4	5
i) utilization management	10.	0	1	2	3	4	5
j) plant operations	11.	0	1	2	3	4	5
k) biomedical ethics	12.	0	1	2	3	4	5
l) pharmacy	13.	0	1	2	3	4	5
m) safety	14.	0	1	2	3	4	5
n) security	15.	0	1	2	3	4	5
o) credentialing	16.	0	1	2	3	4	5
p) employee health	17.	0	1	2	3	4	5
q) marketing/public relations	18.	0	1	2	3	4	5
r) regulatory compliance	19.	0	1	2	3	4	5
s) finance	20.	0	1	2	3	4	5
3. Collaborate/participate in Sentinel Event Reporting Policy	21.	0	1	2	3	4	5
4. Communicate results of analysis regarding trends/risks	22.	0	1	2	3	4	5

5. Design, implement, and maintain risk management data collection system:

a) written incident reports	23.	0	1	2	3	4	5
b) referrals by staff, committees, or other departments	24.	0	1	2	3	4	5
c) patient complaints	25.	0	1	2	3	4	5
d) quality management referrals	26.	0	1	2	3	4	5
e) medical record requests	27.	0	1	2	3	4	5
f) billing disputes	28.	0	1	2	3	4	5
g) consults/queries	29.	0	1	2	3	4	5
h) policy queries	30.	0	1	2	3	4	5
i) reports of Potential Compensatory Events (PCEs)	31.	0	1	2	3	4	5
j) device reporting and tracking logs	32.	0	1	2	3	4	5
k) clinical indicators	33.	0	1	2	3	4	5
l) employee accident reports	34.	0	1	2	3	4	5
m) security reports	35.	0	1	2	3	4	5
n) loss runs	36.	0	1	2	3	4	5

EXHIBIT 1.1.   ASHRM Risk Manager Task Inventory (*Continued*)

Importance:	0 = No importance	3 = Average or medium importance
	1 = Minimal importance	4 = Above average or high importance
	2 = Below average or low importance	5 = Extreme importance

6. Ensure that a product recall program exists...37. 0 1 2 3 4 5

7. Ensure that appropriate policies, procedures, and mechanisms exist for
obtaining an informed consent..38. 0 1 2 3 4 5

8. Design, implement, and maintain educational programs on risk management
related topics for:
   - a) board...39. 0 1 2 3 4 5
   - b) medical staff..40. 0 1 2 3 4 5
   - c) nursing staff and other clinical staff..41. 0 1 2 3 4 5
   - d) non-clinical employees...42. 0 1 2 3 4 5
   - e) administrative staff...43. 0 1 2 3 4 5
   - f) pre-hospital care providers...44. 0 1 2 3 4 5
   - g) agency personnel..45. 0 1 2 3 4 5
   - h) house staff/students...46. 0 1 2 3 4 5
   - i) community...47. 0 1 2 3 4 5
   - j) law enforcement..48. 0 1 2 3 4 5
   - k) vendors...49. 0 1 2 3 4 5
   - l) volunteers..50. 0 1 2 3 4 5

9. Implement a program for control of contractual risk:
   - a) review contract for -
     1. risk exposures..51. 0 1 2 3 4 5
     2. risk assumptions..52. 0 1 2 3 4 5
     3. insurance provisions/requirements...53. 0 1 2 3 4 5
     4. hold harmless clause...54. 0 1 2 3 4 5
     5. indemnification...55. 0 1 2 3 4 5
     6. regulatory compliance...56. 0 1 2 3 4 5
   - b) recommend/implement modifications to address identifed risks.............57. 0 1 2 3 4 5
   - c) ensure that a program exists for tracking maintenance and retention
     of contracts..58. 0 1 2 3 4 5

10. Design, implement, and maintain a system for analyzing and trending risk
management data from all pertinent sources including:
   - a) written incident reports...59. 0 1 2 3 4 5
   - b) referrals...60. 0 1 2 3 4 5
   - c) patient, family, and guest reports..61. 0 1 2 3 4 5
   - d) medical record requests...62. 0 1 2 3 4 5
   - e) billing inquiries...63. 0 1 2 3 4 5
   - f) consults..64. 0 1 2 3 4 5
   - g) clinical indicators..65. 0 1 2 3 4 5
   - h) employee accident reports...66. 0 1 2 3 4 5
   - i) regulatory inquiries..67. 0 1 2 3 4 5
   - j) security reports..68. 0 1 2 3 4 5
   - k) police queries...69. 0 1 2 3 4 5
   - l) reports of Potential Compensatory Events (PCEs)................................70. 0 1 2 3 4 5
   - m) referrals and reports from committees and departments.......................71. 0 1 2 3 4 5
   - n) chaplain logs..72. 0 1 2 3 4 5
   - o) credentialing..73. 0 1 2 3 4 5
   - p) satisfaction surveys..74. 0 1 2 3 4 5
   - q) accreditation reports...75. 0 1 2 3 4 5
   - r) legal complaints..76. 0 1 2 3 4 5
   - s) utilization reports..77. 0 1 2 3 4 5

(*Continued*)

EXHIBIT 1.1.　　ASHRM Risk Manager Task Inventory (*Continued*)

Importance:	0 = No importance 1 = Minimal importance 2 = Below average or low importance	3 = Average or medium importance 4 = Above average or high importance 5 = Extreme importance

t) denial of benefits..78. 0 1 2 3 4 5

u) grievances..79. 0 1 2 3 4 5

v) recall notices..80. 0 1 2 3 4 5

w) third party and external reports and inquiries (e.g., media, insurance
carriers, fiscal intermediaries)...81. 0 1 2 3 4 5

11. Report the results of risk management activities to various committees..................82. 0 1 2 3 4 5

12. Respond to risk management concerns about professional liability and
physical liability from organization personnel and staff members...........................83. 0 1 2 3 4 5

13. Ensure that a program in the organization exists to require non-employed
staff members, vendors or contractors to maintain adequate insurance to
cover the organization's exposures..84. 0 1 2 3 4 5

14. Collaborate in the preparation of public relations responses to the
media/external inquiries regarding incident/occurrences...85. 0 1 2 3 4 5

15. Promote appropriate procedures for retention, access, and destruction of
medical records and other key business records...86. 0 1 2 3 4 5

II. Claims Management

1. Approve/authorize settlements..87. 0 1 2 3 4 5

2. Set expense and indemnity reserves...88. 0 1 2 3 4 5

3. Notify carriers of potential or actual claims...89. 0 1 2 3 4 5

4. Direct claims specific management strategy and activities including:

a) assignment of counsel..90. 0 1 2 3 4 5

b) assignment of Third Party Administrators (TPA)...91. 0 1 2 3 4 5

c) attendance at depositions..92. 0 1 2 3 4 5

d) attendance at settlement conference..93. 0 1 2 3 4 5

e) attendance at trials..94. 0 1 2 3 4 5

f) attendance at mediation and arbitration hearings...95. 0 1 2 3 4 5

g) discovery requests/interrogatories..96. 0 1 2 3 4 5

h) investigations..97. 0 1 2 3 4 5

i) selection of experts..98. 0 1 2 3 4 5

j) settlement authority..99. 0 1 2 3 4 5

k) ongoing monitoring of defense activities...100. 0 1 2 3 4 5

5. Set-up claim file...101. 0 1 2 3 4 5

6. Ensure that accurate and timely loss runs are maintained......................................102. 0 1 2 3 4 5

7. Develop and implement criteria for defense counsel reporting - including
reporting and billing...103. 0 1 2 3 4 5

8. Develop and implement criteria for Third Party Administrators (TPAs)
activities..104. 0 1 2 3 4 5

9. Develop standards for the selection and evaluation of defense counsel..................105. 0 1 2 3 4 5

10. Develop standards for the selection and evaluation of Third Party
Administrators (TPAs)...106. 0 1 2 3 4 5

11. Develop standards and procedures for the management and resolution of
claims in compliance with federal and state fair claims legislation.........................107. 0 1 2 3 4 5

12. Ensure that administration is kept informed of high exposure cases and aggregate
claims experience including its impact on the risk financing program....................108. 0 1 2 3 4 5

(*Continued*)

EXHIBIT 1.1.   ASHRM Risk Manager Task Inventory (*Continued*)

Importance: 0 = No importance   3 = Average or medium importance
1 = Minimal importance   4 = Above average or high importance
2 = Below average or low importance   5 = Extreme importance

III. Risk Financing

1. Maintain and coordinate exposure data for organization.....................................109. 0 1 2 3 4 5
2. Collaborate with actuaries to develop exposure data...110. 0 1 2 3 4 5
3. Complete insurance applications and renewals..111. 0 1 2 3 4 5
4. Ensure that a mechanism exists for retention, access and destruction of all
   insurance contracts, certificates of insurance, insurance schedules, and other
   key documents relating to the risk financing function...112. 0 1 2 3 4 5
5. Collaborate with brokers/underwriters to determine risk financing/coverage
   needs of organization...113. 0 1 2 3 4 5
6. Collaborate with brokers/actuaries to complete insurance coverage/risk
   financing program renewals..114. 0 1 2 3 4 5
7. Evaluate adequacy of coverage limits, deductibles, and attachment points........115. 0 1 2 3 4 5
8. Evaluate lines of coverage to determine that all exposures are covered..............116. 0 1 2 3 4 5
9. Evaluate risk financing options for organization including commercial insurance,
   retention, captives, and risk retention groups...117. 0 1 2 3 4 5
10. Evaluate alternative carriers/markets and select best option for organization......118. 0 1 2 3 4 5
11. Engage consultants to determine feasibility of alternative risk financing
    techniques for the organization..119. 0 1 2 3 4 5
12. Develop comprehensive risk financing strategies to address organizations'
    areas of exposure, including:
    a) automobile...120. 0 1 2 3 4 5
    b) directors and officers (D&O)..121. 0 1 2 3 4 5
    c) general liability (GL)..122. 0 1 2 3 4 5
    d) professional liability (PL)..123. 0 1 2 3 4 5
    e) environmental impairment liability (EIL)...124. 0 1 2 3 4 5
    f) property...125. 0 1 2 3 4 5
    g) Worker's Compensation (WC)...126. 0 1 2 3 4 5
    h) employment practices liability (EPL)..127. 0 1 2 3 4 5
    i) managed care errors and omissions (E&O)..128. 0 1 2 3 4 5
    j) crime and fiduciary..129. 0 1 2 3 4 5
    k) other...130. 0 1 2 3 4 5
13. Conduct ongoing monitoring/evaluation of risk financing program.....................131. 0 1 2 3 4 5

IV. Regulatory/Accreditation Compliance

1. Promote compliance with state agencies governing the reporting of specific
   events 132..132. 0 1 2 3 4 5
2. Promote compliance with the requirements of the following federal
   acts/regulations:
   a) Americans with Disabilities Act (ADA)...133. 0 1 2 3 4 5
   b) Nuclear Regulatory Commission (NRC)...134. 0 1 2 3 4 5
   c) Organ Procurement Organizations (OPO)...135. 0 1 2 3 4 5
   d) Occupational Safety and Health Administration (OSHA)..............................136. 0 1 2 3 4 5
   e) Patient Self-Determination Act (PSDA)...137. 0 1 2 3 4 5
   f) Health Insurance Portability and Accountability Act (HIPAA)........................138. 0 1 2 3 4 5
   g) National Practitioner Data Bank (NPDB)...139. 0 1 2 3 4 5
   h) Emergency Medical Treatment and Active Labor Act (EMTALA/COBRA).....140. 0 1 2 3 4 5
   i) Safe Medical Devices Act (SMDA)..141. 0 1 2 3 4 5
   j) Rehabilitation Act Section 504 (RAS 504)..142. 0 1 2 3 4 5
   k) Balanced Budget Act of 1997 (BBA 1997)...143. 0 1 2 3 4 5

(*Continued*)

EXHIBIT 1.1.　　ASHRM Risk Manager Task Inventory (*Continued*)

Importance:	0 = No importance	3 = Average or medium importance
	1 = Minimal importance	4 = Above average or high importance
	2 = Below average or low importance	5 = Extreme importance

　　l) Healthcare Quality Improvement Act (HCQIA).......................144. 0 1 2 3 4 5
　　m) Taxpayers Bill of Rights II (TBOR II)...................................145. 0 1 2 3 4 5
　　n) Food and Drug Administration (FDA)...................................146. 0 1 2 3 4 5
3. Promote compliance with state specific legislation....................147. 0 1 2 3 4 5
4. Promote compliance with federal and state laws and regulations governing
　　patient confidentiality including:
　　a) voluntary termination of pregnancy or induced abortion.......148. 0 1 2 3 4 5
　　b) alcohol and drug abuse records.......................................149. 0 1 2 3 4 5
　　c) family planning services..150. 0 1 2 3 4 5
　　d) Human Immunodeficiency Virus (HIV) records....................151. 0 1 2 3 4 5
　　e) mental health treatment..152. 0 1 2 3 4 5
　　f) sexually transmitted diseases...153. 0 1 2 3 4 5
5. Promote compliance with state reporting requirements concerning:
　　a) abuse of developmentally disabled patients.......................154. 0 1 2 3 4 5
　　b) child abuse...155. 0 1 2 3 4 5
　　c) domestic violence..156. 0 1 2 3 4 5
　　d) elder abuse...157. 0 1 2 3 4 5
　　e) employee sexual misconduct...158. 0 1 2 3 4 5
6. Promote compliance with requirements governing violence in the workplace..............159. 0 1 2 3 4 5
7. Collaborate with maintenance and operations staff to promote compliance with:
　　a) Highly Protected Risk (HPR) standards..............................160. 0 1 2 3 4 5
　　b) life safety codes..161. 0 1 2 3 4 5
　　c) National Fire and Protection Association (NFPA)..................162. 0 1 2 3 4 5
　　d) Occupational Safety and Health Administration (OSHA)........163. 0 1 2 3 4 5
　　e) state and local facility code...164. 0 1 2 3 4 5
　　f) waste management...165. 0 1 2 3 4 5
8. Investigate and resolve human rights complaints......................166. 0 1 2 3 4 5
9. Promote compliance with local requirements of reporting deaths to
　　coroner/medical examiner..167. 0 1 2 3 4 5
10. Educate organizational staff on regulatory issues related to risk management..............168. 0 1 2 3 4 5
11. Promote compliance with state regulations regarding the investigation and
　　resolution of patient complaints..169. 0 1 2 3 4 5
12. Collaborate with other departments in the preparation of accreditation surveys..........170. 0 1 2 3 4 5
13. Promote compliance with regulations governing involuntary detention patients..........171. 0 1 2 3 4 5
14. Provide ongoing consultation to other departments to promote compliance with
　　accreditation standards..172. 0 1 2 3 4 5
15. Promote compliance with Food and Drug Administration (FDA) Project Look
　　Back requirements...173. 0 1 2 3 4 5
16. Consult with departments/organizations regarding planning for business
　　continuity, emergencies, and disaster preparedness.................174. 0 1 2 3 4 5
17. Coordinate on-site surveys and inspections by local, state, and federal
　　agencies..175. 0 1 2 3 4 5
18. Collaborate in the development of the organization's regulatory compliance plan........176. 0 1 2 3 4 5
19. Promote compliance with the Joint Commission on Accreditation of Healthcare
　　Organizations (JCAHO) Sentinel Event reporting requirements...................177. 0 1 2 3 4 5
20. Promote compliance with private accrediting/certification organizations including:
　　a) American Osteopathic Association (AOA)............................178. 0 1 2 3 4 5
　　b) American College of Surgeons (ACS).................................179. 0 1 2 3 4 5
　　c) College of American Pathologists (CAP).............................180. 0 1 2 3 4 5

(*Continued*)

28   *Framework for Health Care Risk Management*

EXHIBIT 1.1.   ASHRM Risk Manager Task Inventory (*Continued*)

Importance: 0 = No importance   3 = Average or medium importance
               1 = Minimal importance   4 = Above average or high importance
               2 = Below average or low importance   5 = Extreme importance

d) Council on Accreditation of Rehabilitation Facilities (CARF)................................181. 0 1 2 3 4 5
e) Clinical Laboratory Improvement Act (CLIA)...182. 0 1 2 3 4 5
f) International Standards Organization (ISO 9000)..183. 0 1 2 3 4 5
g) Joint Commission on Accreditation of Healthcare
   Organizations (JCAHO)..184. 0 1 2 3 4 5
h) National Committee on Quality Assurance (NCQA)...185. 0 1 2 3 4 5
i) Utilization Review Accreditation Commission/The Commission (URAC).............186. 0 1 2 3 4 5
21. Promote compliance with federal and state laws regarding all insurance programs.. 187. 0 1 2 3 4 5

V. Operations
1. Perform administrator on-call duties...188. 0 1 2 3 4 5
2. Provide input in the preparation of organizational budgets.....................................189. 0 1 2 3 4 5
3. Supervise risk management staff..190. 0 1 2 3 4 5
4. Develop/maintain department policies and procedures and modify as required........191. 0 1 2 3 4 5
5. Prepare risk management department budgets...192. 0 1 2 3 4 5
6. Develop organizational risk management statement...193. 0 1 2 3 4 5
7. Coordinate/administer risk management committees..194. 0 1 2 3 4 5
8. Dovolop annual goals for risk management department...195. 0 1 2 3 4 5
9. Develop annual goals for service providers...196. 0 1 2 3 4 5
10. Train risk management staff..197. 0 1 2 3 4 5
11. Develop risk management plan...198. 0 1 2 3 4 5
12. Evaluate the effectiveness of risk management activities (e.g, expense/indemnity
    ratios, percent of cases identified prior to claim, number of cases closed without
    payment, comparison of reserves to payouts, interval between identification
    and resolution of claim)..199. 0 1 2 3 4 5
13. Serve as liaison to law enforcement agencies...200. 0 1 2 3 4 5
14. Develop policies and procedures for acceptance of legal documents
    (e.g., summons, complaints, subpoenas, court orders)...................................201. 0 1 2 3 4 5
15. Develop confidentiality provisions regarding the release of incident and/or
    claims information...202. 0 1 2 3 4 5

VI. Bioethics
1. Coordinate/provide administrative direction for Bioethics committee.......................203. 0 1 2 3 4 5
2. Review policies, procedures, forms, and practices pertaining to:
   a) advance directives for conformance with ethics principles and
      applicable regulations..204. 0 1 2 3 4 5
   b) brain death criteria..205. 0 1 2 3 4 5
   c) withdrawal of life support...206. 0 1 2 3 4 5
   d) Do Not Resuscitate Orders (DNR)...207. 0 1 2 3 4 5
   c) organ donation...208. 0 1 2 3 4 5
   f) human subjects research for compliance with applicable regulations...................209. 0 1 2 3 4 5
3. Provide risk management consultation for specific ethical dilemmas (cases)............210. 0 1 2 3 4 5
4. Provide education/in-service for staff, patients, families, communities on
   patients rights (e.g., end of life decisions)..211. 0 1 2 3 4 5

(*Continued*)

EXHIBIT 1.1.   ASHRM Risk Manager Task Inventory (*Continued*)

Importance: 0 = No importance   3 = Average or medium importance
                    1 = Minimal importance   4 = Above average or high importance
                    2 = Below average or low importance   5 = Extreme importance

Additional Healthcare Risk Manager Tasks

_____............... 212. 0 1 2 3 4 5

_____............... 213. 0 1 2 3 4 5

_____............... 214. 0 1 2 3 4 5

_____............... 215. 0 1 2 3 4 5

_____............... 216. 0 1 2 3 4 5

_____............... 217. 0 1 2 3 4 5

_____............... 218. 0 1 2 3 4 5

_____............... 219. 0 1 2 3 4 5

_____............... 220. 0 1 2 3 4 5

Considering the importance of each of the major sections of the task list to the Healthcare Risk Managers' job, what percentage of a certification examination would you allocate to each of the following areas?

      _____%   I.   Loss Prevention/Reduction

      _____%   II. Claims Management

      _____%   III. Risk Financing

      _____%   IV. Regulatory/Accreditation Compliance

      _____%   V.   Operations

      _____%   VI. Bioethics

  100%

How well did this inventory cover the important tasks of the Healthcare Risk Manager?

1_____completely   2_____adequately   3_____inadequately

If inadequately, please specify:

_____

_____

_____

_____

Thank you for completing this inventory.

EXHIBIT 1.2.   Risk Manager Position Description, Level One

Position Summary

The risk manager is responsible for the facility's risk management activities, which include coordinating insurance coverage and risk financing, managing claims against the facility, interfacing with defense legal counsel, administering the risk management program on a day-to-day basis, managing and analyzing risk management data, and conducting risk management educational programs, and complying with risk management related standards by JCAHO, all with the objective of controlling and minimizing loss to protect the assets of the facility. The level one risk manager performs these functions at the direction of first-level management. This individual participates in formulating policy or organizational changes, but must seek advice and approval from higher authority.

Insurance and Risk Financing

Overview:

The level 1 risk manager has general knowledge of, and is familiar with, the facility's insurance coverage against liability and casualty loss, including self-insurance funding and budgeting for payment of deductibles, risk retention, and coinsurance. Participates in management reviews of insurance coverage and related issues. May prepare summaries of the facility's insurance program for information of management and staff.

Specific Activities:

- Notifies the liability insurance carrier of all actual and potential claims, including primary and excess carriers as necessary.
- May verify that each voluntary physician provides proof of adequate professional liability insurance.
- Acts as liaison with the insurance carrier; completes insurance applications and responds to surveys; prepares materials necessary for renewal of primary and excess insurance policies.
- Provides insurance information to outside agencies; assists in compliance with state insurance reporting requirements.

Claims Management and Incident Reporting

Overview:

The level 1 risk manager receives complaints claims related to professional liability and transmits that information to the insurance carrier or legal counsel. At the request of management, legal counsel, or the adjuster, participates in responding to the complaint or claim to obtain information and facilitate settlement at an early stage. Works in coordination with patient ombudsman or acts as same to resolve complaints before they develop into professional liability claims. Receives incident reports and other information regarding untoward occurrences in the facility, such as quality assurance outliers or variations, and collates such information systematically to permit analysis pursuant to risk management policy and procedure. Reviews collated data to identify trends regarding accidents or occurrences, and recommends corrective action to management, if appropriate. Prepares reports to management regarding data systems and findings. Recommends electronic data programming initiation and improvement, working with data-processing professionals.

Specific Activities:

- Designs, implements, and maintains a direct referral system for staff to report potential claims against the facility through such input sources as medical records, business office, patient advocate, nursing, medical staff, quality assurance, etc.
- Designs, implements, and maintains a facility-wide incident reporting system.
- Investigates and analyzes actual and potential risks in the institution; assesses liability and probability of legal action for potential notification of insurance carriers.
- Receives and investigates reports of product problems to determine appropriate response (in-house recalls, independent evaluations, etc.).
- Participates on select committees related to assessment of patient care.
- Directly refers to administration those incidents with claims potential; reports to higher authority any serious event involving actual or potential injury to patients, visitors, or employees

(Continued)

EXHIBIT 1.2. Risk Manager Position Description, Level One (*Continued*)

- Takes steps to ascertain that risks are minimized through follow-up and actions on all regulatory insurance survey report recommendations deficiencies.
- Assists in processing summons and complaints served on present and previous employees; assists defendants in completing necessary documents.
- With director of patient representatives, reviews patient complaints that may be the source of potential legal action; discusses and offers solutions when possible to resolve with patient and/or family any grievances perceived as potential liability claims.
- Participates in evaluation of claims for settlement; negotiates settlement of small claims within administrative authority; advises collection department of appropriate action for unpaid accounts involved in litigation; approves payment for or replacement of lost property after evaluating claim.
- Reviews national and local claims data; analyzes prior claims, lawsuits, and complaints against the facility.
- May have on-call responsibility.

Program Administration

Overview

The level one risk manager has specific responsibilities regarding gathering and analyzing data and preparing reports to management and outside agencies as required (the latter subject to final approval by facility management). Responsible for keeping management advised of developments in professional liability, entailing ongoing review of applicable literature. May recommend budget items to management.

Specific Activities:

- Develops, coordinates, and administers facility-wide systems for risk identification, investigation, and reduction; maintains a network of informational sources and experts; performs risk surveys and inspects patient care areas; reviews facility and equipment to assess loss potential.
- Maintains risk management statistics and files in compliance with JCAHO and state and federal agencies; ensures maximum confidentiality and access of such information. Also ensures that the following information is accurate, available, and secure: medical records, patient billing records, policies and procedures, incident reports, medical examiner's reports (if available), as well as any other data pertinent to a particular claim.
- Collects, evaluates, and distributes relevant data concerning patient injuries: aggregate data summaries, monthly trend analyses of incidents, claims profiles, and workers' compensation trends; provides aggregate analysis of risk data; maintains statistical trending of losses and other risk management data.
- Informs directors of service and department heads regarding occurrences, issues, findings, and risk management suggestions; provides feedback to directors at all levels in the effort to eliminate risks; assists clinical chairs and department heads in designing risk management programs within their departments.
- Advises security on procedures to prevent or minimize loss of property or assets.
- Provides assistance to departments in complying with Joint Commission risk management related standards.
- Recommends appropriate revisions to new or existing policies and procedures to prevent future occurrences; recommends ways to eliminate risks through organization, equipment, or other changes; reviews and revises facility policies as appropriate to maintain adherence to current standards and requirements.

Legal Interface

Overview

On request of legal counsel, the level one risk manager may provide assistance in gathering information regarding individual claims or claims history. Seeks approval from management before requesting legal opinions or advice.

Specific Activities:

- Works with legal counsel to coordinate the investigation, processing, and defense of claims against the facility; records, collects, documents, maintains, and provides to attorneys any requested information and documents necessary to prepare testimony in pending litigation.
- Responds to professional liability and facility liability questions posed by physicians, nurses, and other personnel.
- Maintains awareness of legislative and regulatory activities related to health care risk management.

(Continued)

EXHIBIT 1.2.   **Risk Manager Position Description, Level One** (*Continued*)

Educational Services

Overview

The level one risk manager presents periodic in-services and routine orientation for facility employees, medical staff regarding health care risk management and related subjects. This position may be authorized to obtain outside speakers and faculty for such programs, subject to the approval of management, and may coordinate such efforts with the facility's education department.

Specific Activities:

- Provides in-service training to medical center personnel to enhance their awareness of their role in reducing liability exposures.
- Disseminates information on claim patterns and risk control, as well as legislative and regulatory changes.
- Maintains a risk management education calendar.

Source: Reprinted, with permission, from the American Society for Healthcare Risk Management.

EXHIBIT 1.3.   Risk Manager Job Description, Level Two

Position Summary

The risk manager is responsible for the facility's risk management activities, which include coordinating insurance coverage and risk financing, managing claims against the facility, interfacing with defense legal counsel, administering the risk management program on a day-to-day basis, managing and analyzing risk management data, and conducting risk management educational programs, complying with risk management related standards by JCAHO, all with the objective of controlling and minimizing loss to protect the assets of the facility. The level two risk manager performs these functions reporting to management at the vice-president level. This individual is responsible for reviewing and formulating policy or organizational changes and making recommendations for final approval by the vice-president, CEO, and governing body.

Insurance/Risk Financing

Overview

The level two risk manager performs or coordinates the functions outlined under level one and, in addition, participates in negotiating coverage issues with carriers or trust administrators, including levels of coverage, scope of coverage, and premiums. Participates in formulating recommendations for purchase of coverage or funding of self-insurance for submission to management for final approval. Participates in preparing other financial analyses of facility's insurance program for the information of management and the governing body.

Specific Activities:

- Reviews and maintains insurance policies; analyzes existing policies for coverage and exclusions; anticipates and deals with policy expirations.
- Participates in managing the facility's insurance programs and financing by preparing statistical data to support the continuation or reduction of premiums paid or reserves.
- Participates in negotiating policy provisions.
- May assess appropriate reserve funding levels, both insured and self-insured, in conjunction with an actuary.

Claims Management and Incident Reporting

Overview

The level two risk manager performs the functions outlined under level one and, in addition, works actively with legal counsel or the adjuster in investigating claims, developing defense strategy, and evaluating the monetary value of the claim. Participates as a team member in negotiating settlements for management approval. In litigated claims, assists legal counsel in accessing facility records and personnel and may act as a corporate representative during pretrial and trial. Recommends defense strategies for approval by CEO, governing board, and legal counsel. Provides advice to senior management or the chief financial officer regarding reasonableness of expenses for claims defense.

Specific Activities:

- Oversees investigation of all incidents/accidents/events that could lead to financial loss, including professional liability, general liability, and workers' compensation.
- Ensures investigation of all risks involving actual or potential injury to patients, visitors, and employees; ensures collection of all information necessary to prepare for the defense of claims.
- Serves as liaison to brokers and insurance company representatives in negotiating and settling specific general liability claims; directs conferences with claimants, attorneys, and insurance carriers, when applicable.
- Interacts with legal counsel, insurance carrier, and patients/families to effect quick settlement.
- Provides direction and advice to medical staff, as necessary, in connection with malpractice litigation and medicolegal matters.
- Reports patient care-related incidents to the Department of Health as required by law; directs investigation and development of corrective plans; submits required reports to state and federal agencies.

(Continued)

EXHIBIT 1.3.   Risk Manager Job Description, Level Two (*Continued*)

Program Administration

Overview

The level two risk manager performs the functions outlined under level one and, in addition, manages a facility department or office of risk management. Is responsible for data management, claims management, and the education components of the facility's risk management program. Develops department budget for management approval.

Specific Activities:

- Has full responsibility for all operations of the risk management program.
- Directs loss control/loss prevention activities.
- Supervises the statistical trending of losses and analyzes patterns.
- Designs and implements risk management surveys and studies; conducts surveys, studies, and special projects to assist in long-term planning and changes to facility policies and systems that reduce risk and losses.
- Designs and/or administers safety systems and procedures to prevent or minimize loss from employee casualties, and ensures compliance with OSHA regulations.
- Analyzes the risk of loss versus cost of reducing risk.
- Supervises accumulation of risk management cost data for budgetary and historical purposes: prepares budgets for departmental operations.
- Develops and maintains risk management profiles on individual physicians and ensures integration of that information into the credentialing process in compliance with state and federal agencies, Joint Commission, and institutional requirements.
- Submits recommendations for changes in the existing risk control and risk-financing procedures based on changes in properties, operations, or activities.

Legal Interface

Overview

The level two risk manager performs the functions outlined under level one and, in addition, works directly with legal counsel as a team member in the defense of claims. Has ongoing access to facility liability defense counsel to consult regarding both preventive and corrective measures to be taken in situations having legal connotation. On request, may provide information to facility management concerning reasonableness of cost and quality of legal services

Specific Activities:

- Evaluates correspondence from attorneys, patients, and other outside sources, and formulates responses, as necessary.
- Records, collects, documents, maintains, and communicates to insurance carrier and/or attorney any information necessary to prepare testimony in pending litigation.
- Directs and coordinates release of records and information in response to subpoenas, court orders, attorney requests, state and federal agency investigations, and other inquiries from outside sources.
- Maintains all legal case files and ensures maximum protection from discoverability of all such files.
- Approves defense postures or settlement values at lower levels routinely.
- Answers medical/legal inquiries of physicians, nurses, and administrators regarding emergent patient care issues and loss control.
- Is available to resolve treatment issues, including patient decisions made against medical advice (AMA), refusals of treatment, and consent issues; initiates court orders as appropriate via in-house and outside legal counsel.
- Reviews relevant contracts for risk exposure and insurance purposes before approval, including affiliation agreements, leases, construction agreements, and purchase orders, as appropriate.
- Maintains awareness of legislative activities that may affect risk management programs and participates in the legislative process.

(*Continued*)

EXHIBIT 1.3.   Risk Manager Job Description, Level Two (*Continued*)

Educational Services

Overview

The level two risk manager performs the functions as outlined under level one and, in addition, organizes and manages facility-wide educational programs on health care risk management and related subjects for health care practitioners. Presents such programs in conjunction with the facility's education department or other organization. Develops a budget for health care risk management educational activities, or recommends risk management educational items in facility education budget for management's final approval.

Specific Activities:

- Plans, develops, and presents educational material to administration, the medical staff, nursing personnel, and other department personnel on topics related to risk management as they affect personnel.
- Develops and implements educational programs to reduce or eliminate potential safety hazards throughout the facility.

Source: Reprinted, with permission, from the American Society for Healthcare Risk Management.

EXHIBIT 1.4.   Risk Manager Position Description, Level Three

Position Summary

The risk manager is responsible for the facility's risk management activities, which include coordinating insurance coverage and risk financing, managing claims against the facility, interfacing with defense legal counsel, administering the risk management program on a day-to-day basis, managing and analyzing risk management data, and conducting risk management educational programs, complying with risk management related standards by JCAHO all with the objective of controlling and minimizing loss to protect the assets of the facility. The level three risk manager performs the functions described in levels one and two reporting directly to the CEO, chief financial officer, or governing body. This position reviews, formulates, and implements policy and organizational changes, working within general programmatic authority delegated by the CEO, chief financial officer, or governing body.

Insurance/Risk Financing

Overview

The level three risk manager performs or coordinates the functions outlined under levels one and two and, in addition, manages the facility's or system's insurance or self-insurance program within broad guidelines established by the CEO, chief financial officer, or governing body. This position has authority to finalize selection and retention of carriers or self-funding mechanisms in conjunction with the chief financial officer. Sees to the preparation of loss experience reports and summaries for the information of the CEO, chief financial officer, and governing body.

Specific Activities:

- Evaluates property exposures, including new construction and renovation programs, to ensure coverage and minimize risk.
- Develops familiarity with insurance markets through frequent market contact and attendance at meetings and market symposiums.
- Plans, coordinates, and administers a broad, comprehensive insurance program involving such activities as insurance purchasing, insurance consulting, administering self-insured coverage, and coordinating claims handling for all insurance lines.
- Directs and coordinates all aspects of insurance management for the institution, including developing alternatives such as self-insurance, excess insurance, and other risk-financing mechanisms.
- Develops and manages the overall risk management program, involving risks of all types, which may include using deductibles, self-insurance, captive insurance companies, financial plans, commercial insurance, and insurance/reinsurance programs.
- For property insurance, boiler and machinery insurance, crime insurance, student health insurance, automobile insurance, and all other purchased insurance coverage, analyzes values and ensures that exposures are adequately insured; in the event of a loss, prepares data required by brokers and carriers and manages process through to settlement of claim.
- Develops familiarity with insurance markets through frequent market contact.
- Prepares specifications for competitive bidding; negotiates with brokers, agents, or companies on insurance coverage, premiums, and services.
- Establishes and administers self-insurance trust funds for various types of insurance needs.

Claims Management and Incident Reporting

Overview

The level three risk manager performs the functions outlined in levels one and two and, in addition has authority within broad guidelines established by the CEO, chief financial officer, or governing body to approve settlement of all claims against the facility or system. Has authority to direct legal counsel and other personnel involved in claims management and to give final approval to defense strategies. Approves payment of fees of defense counsel and payment of other expenses of claims defense.

- Manages the claims program, which contains the following components:

    Reporting procedures

    System maintenance

    Detailed claim investigations

(Continued)

EXHIBIT 1.4.   Risk Manager Position Description, Level Three (*Continued*)

Establishment of reserves

Selection and monitoring of legal counsel, as indicated

Conferring directly with claimants, attorneys, physicians, employees, brokers, carriers, and consultants

Settlement of claims

Selection and utilization of actuarial firms, as needed and/or required

Compliance with Medicare/Medicaid regulations

Recommendations to senior management for funding requirements and necessary limits of coverage

Reporting claims information to senior management

- Directs activities of investigators
- Directs all claims handling and defense preparation activities of the insurance company and defense counsel
- Is responsible for administering claims initiated in the boiler/machinery, fire, and other loss areas
- Procures outside loss prevention services
- Projects future costs of losses, services, insurance, and other risk management devices

Program Administration

Overview

The level three risk manager performs the functions outlined under levels one and two and, in addition, oversees all aspects of data management and analysis for the organization's loss control program. Establishes budget for data management and analysis aspects of loss control. Works within broad guidelines established by the CEO, chief financial officer, or governing body regarding the use and integration of loss control data with other types of organizational data systems for audit and accountability purposes on a facility- or system-wide basis.

Specific Activities:

- Conducts systems analyses to uncover and identify patterns that could result in compensable events.
- Assists clinical chairs and department heads in designing risk management programs within their departments.
- Develops and implements departmental and facility policies and procedures that affect liability exposures.
- Minimizes risk by responding to all regulatory/insurance survey report recommendations/deficiencies.
- Selects and utilizes services of consulting services, brokers, carriers, etc.
- Provides board summary reports on incidents, claims, reserves, claim payments, etc.
- Develops and maintains risk management profiles on individual physicians and ensures integration of that information into the credentialing process in compliance with state and federal agencies, the JCAHO, and institutional requirements.

Legal Interface

Overview

The level three risk manager performs functions outlined in levels one and two and, in addition, has authority to retain, direct, and approve compensation of defense counsel.

Specific Activities:

- Ensures compliance with various codes, laws, rules, and regulations concerning patient care, including those mandated by state and federal agencies, incident reporting, and also includes the investigation activities of federal, state, and local enforcement authorities.
- Implements relevant statutes and regulations, including mandated mechanisms of physician monitoring with feedback to medical staff office, reappointment process, etc.
- Assumes responsibility for contract compliance within appropriate guidelines and legal concepts; in preparing contracts for board approval, provides advice on contract language necessary to fulfill insurance and risk management requirements; evaluates each contract negotiated by the organization to ensure that insurance and liability issues are adequately addressed and that risk is transferred to the other party, if feasible; establishes insurance requirements for all projects and contracts; where appropriate, negotiates changes in contracts with other parties; ensures that affiliated institutions have adequate insurance coverage.
- Reviews and approves all plans and specifications for new construction, alterations, and installation of equipment.

(*Continued*)

EXHIBIT 1.4.   Risk Manager Position Description, Level Three (*Continued*)

Educational Services

Overview

The level three risk manager performs the functions outlined under levels one and two and, in addition, develops loss control educational programs for the organization's use. This position establishes education budget, subject to approval of the CEO, chief financial officer, or governing body. May develop educational programs relative to health care risk management utilizing well known experts in the field for national or regional representation. May develop risk management educational programs with broad appeal for marketing to other organizations.

Specific Activities:

Plans and implements a facility-system wide program for both loss prevention and loss control, and a comprehensive orientation program; those programs will be directed to all current and future employees of the board, physicians, and employees to advise them of their responsibilities, obligations, and part in the facility's risk management program.

• Directs and conducts educational sessions on risk management for medical staff and employees.

Source: Reprinted, with permission, from the American Society for Healthcare Risk Management.

EXHIBIT 1.5.　　**American Society for Healthcare Risk Management Code of Professional Responsibility**

• **Preamble**

Healthcare risk management professionals must acknowledge and address multiple and potentially conflicting responsibilities on a daily basis. This involves balancing the needs of employers or clients; patients and visitors; employees, independent contractors and volunteers serving their employers or clients, vendors; fellow healthcare risk management professionals; local, regional, national, and international communities; with their own needs. The healthcare risk management professional must maintain standards of professional conduct which will withstand the scrutiny of all constituencies served.

The American Society for Healthcare Risk Management (ASHRM) issues this Code of Professional Responsibility to assist its members in determining ethically appropriate professional conduct and avoiding conduct which does not meet this standard.

• **Confidentiality**

The healthcare risk management professional continually encounters information of a highly confidential nature relating to the business of the employer or client as well as to patients and others served. The healthcare risk management professional must maintain the confidentiality of that information by:

• Disclosing confidential information only when such disclosure is appropriately authorized or when such disclosure is required by law; and,

• Verifying that appropriate protocols exist or supporting the development of protocols to protect the confidentiality and privacy of patients, employers, clients, and others served, within the scope of the healthcare risk management professional's authority.

• **Conflict of Interest**

A conflict of interest exists when the healthcare risk management professional is called upon to serve competing interests. Some conflicts of interest, such as transactions with a former employer or dealings with past business associates, may be acceptable as long disclosure of the conflict is made to all involved parties. Other conflicts, such as business transactions which inure to the benefit of the healthcare risk management professional or his/her family members at the expense of others, are unacceptable even if disclosure to all involved parties is made. In order to avoid conflict of interest, the healthcare risk management professional must:

• Exercise good faith in all transactions;

• Act always for the benefit of the employer or client and avoid any interests, investments or activities which conflict or appear to conflict with the interests of the employer or client;

• Make full disclosure of all facts of any transaction which involves possible conflict of interest to all parties involved; and,

• Avoid accepting gifts or other considerations which might unduly influence the healthcare risk management professional's judgment.

• **Professional Integrity**

The healthcare risk management professional must maintain professional integrity at all times by:

• Practicing the profession with honesty, fairness, integrity, respect and good faith, and avoiding conduct which would result in unjust harm to others;

• Discharging all professional duties competently and consistently;

• Maintaining loyalty to the employer or client and the profession;

• Obeying all laws and regulations relating to professional activities, and supporting the development and enforcement of all laws and regulations which enhance the competent and ethical practice of the healthcare risk management profession

• Maintaining and improving professional skills, knowledge and competence through a program of ongoing self-assessment and continuing professional education;

• Enhancing the public understanding of the healthcare risk management profession;

• Assisting in maintaining and raising professional standards in the healthcare risk management profession by supporting research, fostering the professional development of other healthcare risk management professionals, and refraining from participating in any activity that demeans the credibility and dignity of the healthcare risk management profession;

• Upholding the mission of the American Society for Healthcare Risk Management; and,

• Upholding the integrity of this Code of Professional Responsibility by agreeing to abide by all rules of conduct prescribed by this Code and by ASHRM's Bylaws.

Source: Reprinted, with permission, from the American Society of Healthcare Risk Management, Healthcare Risk Manager National Role Delineation Study, 1999.

2

Development of a Risk Management Program

Jane M. Bryant
Sheila Hagg-Rickert

Organizations, as well as individuals, have no doubt always sought ways to identify and reduce the risks that threatened their existence. In primitive agrarian societies, where families and villages produced barely enough to meet their most basic needs, the loss of a year's harvest, whether to forces of nature or to the plunder of warring tribes, surely spelled disaster. As societies developed into industrialized economies, individuals and organizations continued to seek ways to understand and anticipate the risks associated with natural disaster, theft, fire, and other perils, to protect valuable property from such threats, and ultimately to establish mechanisms for transferring the financial consequences of such losses.

Despite this age-old concern with protecting valuable assets from the risks associated with accidental losses, risk management as a recognized management discipline has only existed for about fifty years.[1] Health care risk management in its present form did not really begin to emerge until the malpractice crisis of the mid-1970s, when hospitals and other health care entities saw rapid rises in claims costs, and subsequently insurance premiums, and witnessed the exit of several major professional liability insurers from the market.[2] This crisis formed the basis for health care organizations to develop risk management programs as a loss prevention technique with innovative alternative risk financing options.

In response to this heightened interest in risk management among health care organizations, the American Society for Hospital Risk Management (ASHRM) was born. ASHRM had its beginnings in 1978 when the American Hospital Association (AHA) received a request to develop an affiliated society for health care risk managers.[3] The AHA had previously established a number of other personal membership groups to provide networking and educational opportunities for various groups of health care operations professionals and to provide the AHA with technical expertise to support its goals of advocacy, education, and representation.[4] The AHA Board of Trustees approved the request to establish the new society in May 1979 and a Risk Management Advisory panel was convened to draft qualifications for membership, develop bylaws, prepare a state of officers, and plan an initial organizational meeting.[5] The first Board of Directors meeting took place in January 1980 with the organizational and initial educational meeting held in New Orleans in March of that year.[6] A second meeting was held in November 1980 with more than three hundred risk management professionals attending.[7] Membership in the new society exceeded six hundred by the end of the year.[8]

Today ASHRM, renamed the American Society for Healthcare Risk Management to reflect the growing diversity of its membership, provides a number of educational offerings, including not only an annual educational meeting and trade exhibition, but also a comprehensive five-part educational module series and a variety of seminars and telephone conferences on current risk management topics. A quarterly scholarly journal, the *Journal of Healthcare Risk Management,* the *ASHRM Forum,* a timely membership newsletter, a series of *Pearls* on specific risk control issues, and the new third edition of the *Risk Management Handbook for Healthcare Facilities* continue to provide society members with up-to-date resources to assist them in meeting the ever-changing demands facing today's health care risk manager in the twenty-first century.

Over the years, health care risk management has moved from a discipline focused almost exclusively on professional liability issues to a profession concerned with all of the risks associated with accidental losses facing a health care organization.[9] In addition to hospitals, managed care organization, physicians' practices, long-term care, and ambulatory care, providers have realized the value of effective risk management and developed programs.[10] Increasingly, risk management is moving beyond traditionally insurable risks to consideration of the myriad of complex legal, regulatory, political, business, and financial risks facing health care organizations. As risk management moves toward this more strategic orientation and risk managers prepare themselves for new roles as chief risk officers, the value of diverse work experience, higher education, and new and broad-based business, financial and technical skills will be needed by health care risk management professionals more than ever before.[11]

· · · · · · · · · · ·

RISK MANAGEMENT PROGRAM DEVELOPMENT

Whatever the health care setting or the sophistication of the risk management professional, an effective risk management program requires certain elementary building blocks: key structural elements, sufficient scope to cover all applicable categories of risk, appropriate risk strategies, and written policies and procedures. This chapter focuses on those building blocks, giving the novice risk manager guidance to develop a program and the mature risk manager a program overview that can be used as an assessment guide.

The structural elements are those program components that enable the risk manager to develop and enforce the risk management plan and enact needed changes in policy. The scope of risk to be covered includes an examination of risks associated with patients, medical staff, employees, government bodies, property, automobiles, and other things that subject the health care organization to potential liability or the threat of loss. Risk management strategies represent the mix of techniques employed to prevent or reduce losses and preserve the organization's assets. The final building block is a set of written policies and procedures to ensure program uniformity and consistency, and to communicate the program to impacted parties. This chapter describes how each of these four important elements contributes to an effective risk management program.

KEY STRUCTURAL ELEMENTS OF THE RISK MANAGEMENT PROGRAM

The exact structure of a given health care organization's risk management program depends on the size and complexity of its facilities as well as the scope of patient care and other services it offers. Nevertheless, several key structural components are necessary for any health care risk management program to succeed. Whether an entity is just beginning to organize its risk management program or is seeking to revamp or expand an existing program, attention to these structural factors will help ensure that the program has a solid foundation.

Authority

The risk manager in a health care organization must maintain sufficient authority and respect to enact the changes in clinical practice, policy, and procedure and in employee and medical staff behavior necessary to fulfill the essential functions of the risk management program. He or she must deal on a daily basis with highly sensitive and confidential information that directly affects the organization's public image and financial status. Moreover, the risk manager is responsible for coordinating risk management activities with members of the medical staff and outside parties as well as managers and employees at all levels. For these reasons, the risk manager's position must be relatively high in the organizational hierarchy.

Ideally, the risk manager should report directly to the CEO, or at least to another member of the senior administrative management team. Risk managers whose positions rank below the department manager level on the organizational chart will almost certainly face difficulty in dealing authoritatively with medical staff, nursing administration, and with department managers. They also may have difficulty gaining the attention of senior management and representing the organization in its relations with insurers, attorneys, and other outside parties involved in the risk management process.

Visibility

The position of risk manager should be highly visible in a health care institution. No one can perform every function of a comprehensive risk management program single-handedly, even in the smallest health care facility. Therefore, it is necessary for the organization's risk manager, through consciousness-raising, education, and communication, to foster an awareness of risk management practices and techniques among medical staff members and hospital employees at all organizational levels. His or her position must be structured so as to enhance opportunities for interaction through serving on appropriate committees, participating in educational activities such as employee orientation and staff in-service offerings, and having access to organization-wide communications mechanisms.

Communication

As health care facilities merge into alliances and networks and acquire physician practices, clinics, and managed care organizations to form integrated delivery systems (IDSs), many issues relating to potential liability, insurance coverage, claims management, and loss control emerge. To anticipate risk management pitfalls and opportunities in this quickly changing environment, the risk manager must be an insider who is provided with information on proposed mergers, acquisitions, and joint ventures early in the due diligence process. (For further information on this subject, please refer to the chapters in this book on mergers, acquisitions, and divestitures, as well as partnerships, joint ventures, and other collaborations.) Equipped with such information, the risk manager is in a position to advise senior management on the risk management implications of various new business arrangements, many of which can be substantial, but frequently are overlooked by executives not attuned to risk management requirements.

Coordination

Because of the wide range of risk management functions and the diversity of activities necessary for a successful risk management program, the health care organization should establish both formal and informal mechanisms for the coordination of the risk management program with other departments and functions. To adequately integrate and coordinate risk management with other functions, the risk manager should establish reporting and communication relationships with key individuals, including:

- The CEO, who provides a vital link to the entity's governing board and medical staff. He or she also sets the tone and provides necessity support for the risk management program. The CEO serves as the key decision maker for many activities crucial to the risk management program, such as authorizing the settlement of larger claims and establishing insurance limits. Additionally, the CEO often heads the team of senior managers responsible for the development of new business opportunities, mergers, and acquisitions.

- The chief financial officer (CFO), who may, depending on the entity and the financial sophistication of the risk manager, establish limits on self-insured retentions or trusts, monitor the financial operations of captives, and oversee the performance of actuarial analyses. In some organizations, the CFO is the primary purchaser of insurance coverage and must therefore rely on information provided by the risk manager to make effective decisions on behalf of the institution.

- The quality improvement director, who serves as an important source of information on adverse clinical events occurring within the facility that may have serious risk management implications. The risk management standards promulgated by the Joint Commission on Accreditation of Healthcare Organizations (JCAHO) emphasizes the interdependence of risk management and quality improvement activities.[12] The quality improvement director may also be able to assist a risk manager who lacks clinical training in interpreting and analyzing information contained in the medical record and in providing clinical loss prevention services.

- The infection control nurse (or staff epidemiologist), who provides information on patient infections that may give rise to liability claims. He or she can assist the risk manager in understanding infection control protocols aimed at reducing the frequency and severity of nosocomial infections and in establishing guidelines for coping with AIDS, tuberculosis, and other communicable diseases.

- The safety officer, who may assist the risk manager in performing fire safety, hazardous materials management, disaster planning, and employee safety activities in compliance with JCAHO standards[13] or may have primary responsibility for those activities. He or she usually chairs safety committees, which serve as a vital source of risk management information and problem solving.

- The patient representative (or ombudsman), who relays information to the risk manager on patient complaints and dissatisfaction. Patient representatives, whether employees or volunteers, must be trained to recognize and appropriately handle potential risk management concerns that may arise in the course of their dealings with patients and their families.

- The employee health nurse (or workers' compensation coordinator or personnel director), who may manage the daily operational activities related to the hospital's workers' compensation program and provide claims and injury information to the risk manager. Often this individual also is instrumental in managing transitional duty return-to-work and other injury management programs. In many health care organizations, the risk manager may be personally responsible for the operation of workers' compensation programs.

- The medical records director, who notifies the risk manager of requests from attorneys for medical records, which may signal initiation of a professional liability action. The risk manager must work with the medical records director to develop policies and procedures relating to the documentation of patient care activities and patient confidentiality, and the release of information.

- The medical director (or vice president of medical affairs or chief of staff), who serves as a liaison between the risk management program and the medical staff, and assists the risk manager in "selling" risk management to physicians. In addition, the risk manager must work with the medical director to ensure that the organization's medical staff appointment, credentialing, privileging, and disciplinary procedures are conducted in accordance with sound risk management practices.

- The patient accounts representative, who works with the risk manager to identify patient complaints and concerns that surface during the billing and collections process. Such concerns may be based on perceived patient care problems and hold the potential for liability claims.

- Nursing and departmental managers, who offer the risk manager the technical and clinical expertise necessary to identify and analyze potential risks, and assist with the investigation of liability claims and incidents. Middle management personnel play a crucial role in building and maintaining support for the risk management program and in educating and raising the risk management consciousness of employees within their areas.

- The education director (or in-service program coordinator), who can assist the risk manager in identifying staff education needs. He or she also can be of assistance in planning, organizing, and presenting in-service education programs pertaining to risk management.

Accountability

Just as the risk manager needs sufficient authority to perform assigned functions, he or she should be held accountable for that performance. Every health care organization's risk manager, including those in small institutions that have job duties in addition to risk management, should have a written job description that outlines key risk management responsibilities. Annual performance appraisals assessing the risk manager's achievement of specific, measurable risk management goals and objectives should be conducted to gauge and document the individual's effectiveness. The risk manager should prepare and distribute to senior management and the governing board an annual report that summarizes claims, insurance, and risk management program activities.

....

SCOPE OF THE RISK MANAGEMENT PROGRAM

The primary purpose of a health care risk management program is to protect the health care organization against loss. Therefore, one of the building blocks of an effective program is sufficient scope to cover all potential sources of risk. Although many risk managers tend to focus on the professional liability aspects of health care risk management, the discipline extends into many other areas that are equally important to the survival of the modern health care organization. Defined broadly, health care risk management is concerned with a tremendous variety of issues and situations that hold the potential for liability or casualty losses for an institution. To be truly comprehensive, a risk management program must address the full scope of the following categories of risk:

- Patient care-related risks
- Medical staff-related risks
- Employee-related risks
- Property-related risks
- Financial risks
- Other risks

(For a more comprehensive overview of other risks, please refer to the chapter on enterprise risk management.)

Patient Care-Related Risks

Throughout much of the late 1970s and early 1980s, U.S. health care institutions and practitioners experienced a "malpractice crisis" evidenced by escalating numbers of professional liability claims, as well as by rising settlement amounts, jury verdicts, and insurance premium.[14,15] As many state legislatures debated tort reform proposals aimed at slowing the trend,[16] and some states enacted statutes mandating specific health care risk management programs,[17] increasing national attention was focused on the patient care aspects of health care risk management. In the 1990s, much of that focus moved to managed care and the gatekeeper functions of HMOs and their contracted primary care physicians in limiting patient access to care[18] and to the liabilities associated with alleged fraud and abuse committed by health care providers.

Therefore, it is not surprising that many health care risk management efforts begin with patient care-related issues. Patient care or clinical risk management, including information gathering, loss control efforts, professional liability risk financing, and claims management activities, forms the core of most health care risk management programs. Although most patient-related risk management activity focuses on direct clinical patient-care activities and the consequences of inappropriate or incorrectly performed medical treatments, other important patient-related issues also confront the risk manager, including:

- Confidentiality and appropriate release of patient medical information.

- Protection of patients from abuse and neglect and from assault by other patients, visitors, or staff.

- The securing of appropriate informed patient consent to medical treatment.

- Nondiscriminatory treatment of patients, regardless of race, religion, national origin, or payment status.

- Protection of patient valuables from loss or damage.

- Appropriate triage, stabilization, and transfer of patients presenting to emergency departments (EDs).

- Patient participation in research studies and the use of experimental drugs or medical procedures.

- Utilization review decisions related to the timing of patient discharges and the provision of medically necessary services under various third-party payer arrangements.

Medical Staff-Related Risks

Closely aligned with patient care-related management issues are those experienced by a medical staff and other clinically privileged practitioners. Many, if not most, of the potentially serious occurrences related to the delivery of clinical patient care also involve the facility's medical staff. It is therefore imperative that the health care risk manager includes physicians in clinical loss prevention and claims management programs and elicits their support of overall risk management activities.

Risk management concerns stemming from the unique relationship between a health care organization and its medical staff merit the risk manager's particular attention. Of special importance are:

- Medical staff peer review and quality improvement activities.

- The confidentiality and protection of the data generated through such processes.

- The medical staff credentialing, appointment, and privileging processes.

- Medical staff disciplinary proceedings and related issues of due process, antitrust, and restraint of trade.

- Various business arrangements and incentives to physicians that may have fraud and abuse implications under federal Medicare regulations.[19,20]

- Physician gatekeeper obligations under various managed care plans.

In this area of expanding legal theories of corporate liability and broadened notions of vicarious liability, the activities of the medical staff often are deemed the activities of the health care organization. It has become increasingly difficult for defense attorneys to persuade judges and juries to distinguish between the institution and its physicians. As physicians increasingly become business partners with health care entities and assume ownership interests in new ventures, and as hospitals and other organizations purchase or assume management of physician practices, the distinctions become even more blurred.

Employee-Related Risks

Several issues relating to the employment of personnel deserve the health care risk manager's attention. Of obvious importance are maintaining a safe work environment for employees, reducing the risk of occupational illness and injury, and providing for the treatment and compensation of workers who suffer on-the-job injuries and work-related illnesses. In this regard, it is important that the risk manager maintain a working knowledge of relevant state workers' compensation law as well as federal regulations promulgated by the Occupational Safety and Health Administration (OSHA). This will allow the risk manager to work effectively with the human resources department, employee health nurse, and designated safety officer.

Posing particularly serious problems for today's health care organization are those issues involving allegations of discrimination in recruitment, hiring, and promotion based on age, race, sex, national origin, or disability; wrongful termination; and other claims filed with the Equal Employment Opportunity Commission (EEOC). Claims involving alleged sexual harassment are also increasingly common.[21–23] The risk manager must work with the facility's human resources director to help minimize such claims exposures, manage the claims, which do occur, and finance the costs associated with these losses.

Property-Related Risks

Many complex health care entities have significant property assets, including large hospital and clinic structures, medical office buildings, and valuable medical and data processing equipment. It is therefore incumbent upon the risk manager to protect these assets from risk of loss due to fires, floods, windstorms, earthquakes, and other perils that may damage or destroy such property. In addition, health care institutions typically maintain a large volume of paper and/or electronic records—patient medical, business, and financial—that are essential to the ongoing operations of the entity and that must be protected from damage or destruction.

Finally, many health care employees routinely handle cash, checks, and credit cards in the course of their job duties. In addition, hospital and nursing homes often are called on to safeguard cash and other valuables belonging to patients and residents. Home health workers, who may function independently and without direct supervision in a client's home, are particularly vulnerable to allegations of theft. Thus, it is important for the risk manager to evaluate hiring and screening protocols for such workers, to review policies and procedures for handling cash and safeguarding valuables, and to consider various bonding and insurance alternatives to adequately protect the facility from such losses. Obviously, the costs associated with repairing and replacing damaged assets can be significant and the revenues lost during the period of business interruption can have disastrous effects on the organization.

Financial Risks

Although the ordinary business risks associated with new ventures or services and the continued financial viability of the organization's existing operations traditionally are considered to be outside the sphere of risk management concerns, there are at least two areas of financial risk with which the risk manager should be concerned.

First, the directors and officers of health care organizations, like those of other corporate entities, may face liability imposed by suits from shareholders or others alleging inappropriate conduct in the fulfillment of their respective duties. Corporate charter or bylaws frequently require the entity to defend and indemnify its directors and officers for such claims. Likewise, the entity itself may face similar actions. It is therefore important for the risk manager to understand the corporate structure of the organization; any requirements imposed by charter, bylaws, or other documents; and the opportunities to transfer such risks through policies of insurance in order to adequately protect the organization's assets.

Second, risk managers who represent the interests of health care providers who contract with managed care organizations (MCOs) on an "at-risk" basis (typically through capitated payment arrangements) need to consider available options for limiting the financial risks inherent in such agreements. These risks may be characterized as either specific, in which the costs associated with providing care to an individual plan subscriber greatly exceed expectations, or aggregate, in which the total costs of providing required health care services under the plan agreement are higher than anticipated. Various options for contractual transfer of risks above a certain level back to the MCO or for the purchase of "stop-loss" insurance coverage may be explored to manage such risks effectively.

Other Risks

There are, of course, other areas of potential interest for the health care risk manager. Among these are property and liability losses relating to the operation of automobiles, trucks, vans, and ambulances owned or leased by the organization. Additionally, many facilities own or operate helicopters or fixed-wing air transport services, or maintain heliports or helipads that pose additional liability and property risks.

Because hospitals and most other health care entities are open to the public, they are vulnerable to a wide variety of general liability claims stemming from visitor injuries caused by slips, falls, and other mishaps. The risk manager must therefore be concerned with the overall maintenance of buildings, parking lots, and sidewalks, as well as visitor control. (Please refer to the chapter on safety and security.)

Hazardous materials management is yet another area of risk management that has gained much recent attention. Ensuring that appropriate protocols are in place for the safe storage, use, and disposal of myriad toxic chemicals and radioactive materials is a highly regulated[24] and increasingly important risk management activity. The implications for patients and employees as well as for the community at large, should such materials find their way into the environment, are chief considerations in managing hazardous materials. Infections biological waste generated by hospitals came under increased public scrutiny after contaminated syringes and other medical waste products washed up on eastern U.S. beaches in 1988,[25] making the assurance of proper disposal procedures all the more important.

Special issues involving auxilians and other volunteers who may provide services at hospitals, and students involved in clinical training experiences who may sustain injury in the course of their duties or may inflict harm on others, also merit the risk manager's attention.

Requirements for training and supervision of volunteers and students as well as clearly delineated duties appropriate for such non-employees must be clearly defined.

············
RISK MANAGEMENT STRATEGIES

Viewing risk management as a process helps the risk manager set priorities. In conjunction with a vigorous claims management and risk-financing program, the risk management process assists in ensuring a comprehensive risk management effort.

The risk management process consists of five steps:

1. Identify and analyze loss exposures.
2. Consider alternative risk management techniques.
3. Select what appears to be the best risk management technique or combination of techniques.
4. Implement the selected technique(s).
5. Monitor and improve the risk management program.

The sections that follow describe how each step of the risk management process must be considered in developing a comprehensive risk management program.

Risk Identification and Analysis

Risk identification is the process through which the risk manager becomes aware of risks in the health care environment that constitute potential loss exposures for the institution. Such exposures can include loss of the facility's financial assets through liability judgments and out-of-court settlements as well as casualty losses to its physical plant and property, human losses through death or injury, and less tangible losses to its public image and reputation.

The risk manager can use many information sources to identify potential risks. Incident reporting, in which employees report accidents and occurrences not consistent with normal operating routine, is the cornerstone of most risk identification systems. In addition, the following resources provide valuable information to assist the risk manager in identifying risks:

- Generic occurrence screening, often performed as part of the organization's quality improvement programs.
- Patient complaints and satisfaction survey results tallied by patient representatives (or community relations or marketing departments).
- Prior professional liability, property and casualty, and workers' compensation claims data.
- Surveys by the JCAHO,[26] the National Committee on Quality Assurance (NCQA),[27] liability or other insurers, or risk management consultants.
- State licensure surveys.

Contracts, leases, and other agreements entered into by the health care facility often reveal additional risk exposures, as does information generated through the facility's infection control and quality improvement functions, which the risk manager should routinely review to the extent permitted by law. (Some concerns have been expressed that free access to medical staff peer review information by a risk manager for use in preparing a defense for professional liability claims may waive statutory protections provided under state peer review protection statutes. The reader is advised to seek the counsel of an attorney when developing a mechanism for reviewing such information.) Finally, informal discussions with line managers and other staff members are excellent sources of information about potential risks.

Risk analysis is the process of determining the potential severity of the loss associated with an identified risk and the probability that such a loss will occur. Together, those factors establish the seriousness of a risk and guide the risk manager's selection of an appropriate risk treatment strategy. Risk managers need to give priority to areas that hold the greatest potential risk of financial loss, such as anesthesia or obstetrical mishap, even though claims in these areas may occur infrequently. Ordinarily, less emphasis should be given to small claims that may occur more frequently, unless the total costs associated with a certain type of incident are especially significant.

Although risk analysis is, in part, an "art"—a judgment call based on the training, experience, and instincts of the risk manager—it also is a "science," in that certain data and other sources of information are taken into consideration. In particular, closed claims data, which reveal the frequency of occurrence and financial consequences of prior losses, should be reviewed to gain insight into the analysis of current risks. The hospital's legal counsel, insurance brokers, and insurance carriers also may be consulted for additional information.

....

EXAMINATION, SELECTION, AND IMPLEMENTATION OF ALTERNATIVE RISK TREATMENTS

Risk treatment refers to the range of choices available to the risk manager in handling a given risk. Risk treatment strategies include two general categories—risk control and risk financing. Under the risk control category are the treatments or techniques of:

- Risk avoidance or prevention
- Risk reduction or minimization

Under risk financing are:

- Risk acceptance or risk retention
- Risk transfer

In addition to exploring these risk treatments individually, the risk manager can fashion the combination of treatments or techniques that is best suited to managing a given risk exposure.

Risk Acceptance or Retention

One strategy for managing an identified risk is risk acceptance or risk retention. This treatment involves assuming the potential losses associated with a given risk and making plans to cover any financial consequences of such losses, either through access to the general assets of the institution, by creating a special set-aside fund or self-insurance mechanism, or by establishing a line of credit with a financial institution so that it may borrow funds should losses occur. Risk acceptance is most appropriate for managing (1) those risks that cannot be otherwise reduced, transferred, or avoided; (2) those risks for which the probability of loss is not great and for which the potential consequences are within the institution's ability to self-fund; (3) those losses that are quantifiable and predictable; and (4) those small risks (such as missing dentures and eyeglasses) for which cost-effective insurance may be difficult to purchase.

For the purposes of illustration, assume that a hospital risk manager has identified a risk of birth trauma injury associated with the facility's obstetrical services. Because the hospital's governing board and administration may have identified obstetrical services as central to both its mission and market-positioning strategy, the hospital may be unwilling to forgo providing such services as a means of eliminating the risk. The hospital may then choose to self-insure for losses associated with birth trauma injury, or perhaps to purchase an insurance policy to cover such losses (a risk transfer strategy), but with a self-funded deductible or retention as a means of risk acceptance.

Likewise, a physician's office practice in California may elect (absent any loan covenants, mortgage restrictions, or FEMA requirements to the contrary) not to purchase earthquake insurance coverage on its office building. The risk manager may determine that the chances of the buildings being seriously damaged or destroyed in an earthquake are sufficiently remote and the costs of securing such coverage sufficiently high to merit "going bare" for the exposure. If such a risk acceptance strategy is employed, it may be appropriate for the risk manager to increase risk reduction or minimization efforts, such as the installation of sway bracing near sprinkler heads to reduce potential water damage in the event of an earthquake. Thus risk acceptance, like other available risk treatment strategies, should not be viewed in isolation, but as part of a combined strategy for managing an identified risk.

Risk Avoidance

Risk avoidance represents another risk treatment strategy. When a given risk poses a particularly serious threat that cannot be effectively reduced or transferred, the conduct or service giving rise to the risk may be avoided. Avoidance is the only risk treatment that reduces the probability of a loss to zero. In the obstetrical example, for instance, the hospital might elect not to provide obstetrical services, thus avoiding the risk of a birth trauma claim. Although that strategy may be very effective in terms of controlling risk exposure, it may come at the high cost of a loss of hospital mission effectiveness, market share and revenues, patient satisfaction, and medical staff relations, which could well outweigh its benefits.

For the physician's office, a risk prevention strategy would be to relocate the practice to a geographic area not subject to earthquakes. Because, theoretically, an earthquake can occur virtually anywhere, there is no fail-safe way to avoid this risk, although the risk might be significantly reduced if the practice were moved to a less earthquake-prone locale. Business necessity in the health care environment often precludes absolute avoidance of risks. Although there are some instances in which an identified risk may be totally avoided, such as substitution of a non-hazardous cleaning product used by an organization's housekeeping department for one posing known environmental or health risks, the risk manager is more often called on to identify strategies for coping with a risk that cannot be completely avoided. Risk prevention as a loss control technique reduces the likelihood of an event or the frequency (numbers of times the event occurs) of the event. Risk prevention efforts are at the heart of most health care risk management programs and are proactive in nature. Some of these activities include staff education, policy and procedure review and revision, and other interventions aimed at controlling adverse occurrences without completely eschewing potentially risky activities.

Risk Reduction or Minimization

Risk reduction or minimization involves various loss control strategies aimed at limiting the potential consequences of a given risk without totally accepting or avoiding it. Risk reduction or minimization efforts focus on reducing the severity of an event that has already occurred. This generally equates into the reduction or minimization of total dollars spent. Other risk reduction treatments are: prompt incident investigation, disaster and business continuity drills and written plans, fire drills, and building with noncombustible or fire retardant materials.

A risk reduction strategy in an obstetrical case may be to save the placenta for pathological review. This review will allow for and encourage an early settlement if the review is unfavorable and does not support quality care. If the review does support the care rendered, the pathological findings becomes an excellent defense tool.

In the physician's office example, the risk manager, although unable to control the frequency of earthquakes, may reduce the adverse effects or severity of such occurrences that do occur by electing to install sway bracing for water pipes and sprinkler heads, secure shelving units to walls, keep duplicates and electronic "backups" of records (also called duplication, another loss control treatment), and make other physical modifications to the property. These are all clear examples of risk reduction or mitigation techniques.

Risk Transfer

Risk transfer techniques involve shifting the risks of financial loss to another entity, either through contract or by purchasing insurance. Through risk transfer, an institution can continue to engage in a risk-reducing activity while, for a price, transferring the financial risk of loss. In the obstetrical example, the hospital may purchase a professional liability policy to pay for any losses associated with an adverse obstetrical occurrence, thereby transferring the financial obligation for the loss to another party. Or the hospital may contract with another facility to provide such services as methods of risk avoidance. In either scenario, the hospital has transferred the financial obligation for the loss to someone else. Likewise, the physician's practice may elect to lease office space and thus transfer the risk of loss to the building to the landlord, although losses to the contents of the building and business interruption losses experienced by the practice while the repairs of the earthquake damage were being made would not ordinarily be so transferred. However, such risks could be transferred along with the risks of actual structural damage to the building via a policy of insurance.

It should be clear from the preceding discussion that, for most identified risks, the health care facility may employ a combination of risk treatments and techniques to best manage a given risk. In the obstetrical example, a hospital would likely accept a certain amount of risk through an insurance deductible or self-insured retention, avoid potential risk by not offering high-risk obstetrical services, reduce the severity of risk already incurred by the implementation of transfer arrangements with a high-risk neonatal nursery, and prevent risk through in-service education and appropriate staffing and credentialing, and transfer the financial risk by purchasing insurance. For the physician's office, a policy of insurance featuring some level of deductible and a program of building retrofitting to reduce the severity of potential earthquake losses might be employed.

EVALUATE AND MONITOR THE RISK MANAGEMENT PROGRAM

The final risk management strategy is to evaluate and monitor the risk management program, whereby the effectiveness of the techniques employed to identify, analyze, and treat risks is gauged and assessed. Risk management evaluation involves not only the risk manager, but also senior management, the medical staff and governing board, insurers, claims managers, and legal counsel. This multidisciplinary approach to evaluating the effectiveness of a risk management program ensures that the impact of various risk management activities is measured accurately and appropriately and that additional risk management opportunities are fully explored. To facilitate the risk management evaluation process, the risk manager needs to prepare a comprehensive annual report of risk management activities highlighting significant claims activity, new program developments, changes in insurance coverage, and contractual modifications. These results should be compared against some clearly defined benchmarks that have been identified in advance of the review. These benchmarks can be internal or external to the organization and can be as simple as comparing the current program results against previous year's results. The risk manager could also use data from an independent but like organization against which to benchmark. One area that seems to lend itself to benchmarking in risk management is in the claims or litigation management area. This area deals with frequency and severity of risk, which translates into numbers of events and dollars impacted by their occurrence. (For more on benchmarking and program evaluation, refer to other chapters in this book.)

············

PILLARS OF AN OPERATIONAL RISK MANAGEMENT PROGRAM

Another way to look at the elements of a risk management program is to consider the three essential pillars of risk management operations: loss control, claims management, and risk financing. For each of the risks identified as facing the health care organization, the risk manager must develop and implement strategies that: (1) seek to prevent or minimize the occurrences giving rise to losses; (2) investigate, evaluate, defend, and settle claims resulting from such occurrences; and (3) establish risk financing mechanisms to pay for the losses. Virtually all of the day-to-day operational functions of an effective risk management program fall under one of these pillars. In order to ensure that an organization's risk management program is truly comprehensive, it is imperative that the risk manager address the loss control, claims management, and risk financing dimensions of each risk identified as having significant potential to adversely impact the health care organization's ability to meet its objectives.

Loss Control Activities

Loss control activities form the heart of most risk management programs and include the strategies employed to prevent the frequency of occurrences that give rise to losses and to reduce the severity of such occurrences. Loss control strategies related to professional liability may include employee orientation and in-service education programs, policy and procedure development, and preventive maintenance programs for patient care equipment. For a property loss control program, the risk manager may evaluate the adequacy of sprinkler and other fire-suppression systems within buildings and the resistance of various roofing materials to windstorm damage.

Obviously, one of the great challenges for the health care risk manager is the tremendous diversity of loss control strategies that must be employed to successfully address all of the risks facing today's complex health care organizations. While a thorough understanding of clinical issues and practices is generally considered a prerequisite for a successful health care risk management career, familiarity with safety, engineering, legal, and financial issues, to name a few, is also important.

Claims Management Activities

Despite the implementation of a myriad of loss control strategies by health care organizations, losses and claims continue to occur. Lapses in human judgment, equipment malfunctions, inadequate staffing, and a variety of systems issues can lead to injuries to patients and visitors, which can result in liability claims. Additionally, such parties may bring meritless claims against the health care organization in an effort to gain unwarranted financial compensation. While the institution may ultimately prevail in successfully defending such claims, mechanisms to investigate, evaluate, and manage them must be established including the impact they may have on market share and reputation of the organization.

So-called first-party losses occur when the institution itself sustains a direct loss such as a property loss due to flood, fire, windstorm, or earthquake, collision damage to an automobile owned by the facility, or the theft of computer equipment from hospital offices. The risk manager must make certain that such losses are promptly reported to the appropriate insurance carriers and that all information required to substantiate the nature and scope of the loss is provided. For complex casualty losses, especially when a significant business interruption loss has been sustained, the investigation and adjustment process may continue for months or even years. Such claims present a real challenge to even an experienced risk manager.

For health care organizations that elect to self-insure, a successful claims management program may contribute greatly to the overall effectiveness of the risk management effort.

Risk Financing Activities

Risk financing activities encompass all of the mechanisms utilized by health care organizations to pay for claims and losses or those techniques aimed at transferring the financial obligation to someone else. Today's sophisticated organizations frequently employ combinations of traditional insurance coverage, self-insurance, captive insurance companies, and other risk financing vehicles to fund losses. The novice risk manager will no doubt find forecasting future losses for each identified category of risk, selecting the appropriate types and limits of insurance coverage, utilizing the best and most cost-effective insurance carriers, and identifying the most advantageous self-insured retentions and deductibles daunting tasks. Even experienced risk management professionals may rely heavily on the organization's chief financial officer and other members of the senior management team, as well as the advice of outside brokers and insurance consultants, in making the major risk financing decisions for their organizations.

DEVELOPMENT OF THE RISK MANAGEMENT PROGRAM

As the delivery of health care continues to change, so must the structure of risk management programs. The existing and emerging principles that apply to risk management will need to adapt in order to continue to ensure safe, cost-effective, and clinically effective care. The health care organization as it is known today will be different in the future, with multiple levels and both horizontal and vertical integration. Interdependency on organizational strategic and financial goals must be integrated into risk management program development and must meet the needs of the changing customer base and payer mix. It is possible that within one organization there will be a need to create different risk management program structures and take different steps in assessing risk management needs in the health organization's different areas.

············

SELECTING AN APPROPRIATE RISK MANAGEMENT PROGRAM STRUCTURE

A variety of risk management program structures can be considered based on organizational size, scope of services and activities, available resources, and locations. Generally, acute care hospitals have preexisting systems for the introduction and enhancement of risk management program components, whereas integrated delivery systems (IDSs), long-term care settings, physician's office practices, home health care, and ambulatory care centers are less likely to have formalized risk management efforts.

The overall level of risk management responsibility can vary greatly. It can be any one of the following (or a combination, depending on organizational structure and expectations):

- *All related risk management functions:* This structure requires a vast array of resources and expertise able to address each type of service provided within the organization. Knowledge of and experience in clinical care delivery, plant engineering, safety, claims, and finance are particularly helpful in large, multi-institutional organizations. In many situations, on-site risk management coordinators work to coordinate activities with the corporate or home office. In many smaller organizations, all related risk management activities may be managed out of one department or by one person. A physician's office practice is a good example where one employee may have responsibility for risk management, quality improvement, safety, medical records, disaster planning, infection control, and so on.

- *Responsibility for a set of defined risk management activities and services:* This structure seems to still be the model of choice at acute care hospitals and hospitals in a system. Responsibility in this structure is spread among multiple departments. The coordination and facilitation of activities that impact risk management activities should still be managed and controlled out of a single office, preferably the risk management department. In this structure there are generally separate departments for safety, security, quality improvement, corporate compliance, education and in-service, risk financing, contract review and negotiating, claims administration, and so on. The CFO could have responsibility for the risk financing program, the in-house legal administration responsibility for the claims administration and contract review, or the director of the emergency department responsibility for disaster planning, just to give few examples. The hospital or other health care setting that is part of a system also has a limit to the breadth and depth of risk management responsibility. In many cases, the corporate office mandates the risk financing program and may also manage all claims. These positions at the single site generally revolve around loss control activities. This kind of coordination is far more common these days than is control of all functions. The intent of these programs is to create a general operational structure that encourages consistency and cost control but also allows for flexibility and timeliness and places accountability at the lowest possible levels.

- *Consultative and outsourcing only:* At specific times, an organization may chose to outsource its risk management responsibility. Even with the consulting and outsourcing structure model, there needs to be a structure in place to internally manage the flow of information and to facilitate communication. Consultative and outsourcing structures generally are used during times of merger, acquisition, and divestiture, when the organization faces severe financial constraints, has a loss of key risk management personnel, or is undergoing reengineering efforts or management change. It is not unusual that in this structure there is still the need for a risk manager. As a matter of fact, this would be the ideal. This person then becomes the point person between the outsourced organization or consultant and senior management, and the outsourced organization becomes the risk management "backroom."

Regardless of the health care organization's choice of formal structure, its risk management program should incorporate the basic elements, components, and functions described throughout this chapter. All risk management activities require alignment with the organization's mission and strategic plan.

············
ASSESSING AREAS OF THE ORGANIZATION THAT NEED RISK MANAGEMENT

There are various ways to approach any assessment, but most risk managers find that having written guides helps prevent them from overlooking key points. There are many such tools from which to choose, one of which is the *Risk Management Self-Assessment Manual*.[28] Other sources can be found through literature searches and in outside organizations such as insurance companies, regulatory agencies, and consulting firms.

Identify the Various Areas for Assessment

In general, profiling the organization's current services and relationships is important in identifying the various areas for assessment. This process could be seen as "taking inventory" of activities that may have potential risk, as well as finding a starting point for developing or renewing the risk management program's focus. This inventory includes a systematic review of the organization's functions, data, budget, and workforce, as well as a survey of perceptions about the effectiveness of systems and processes already in place. The assessment may reveal findings and needs that differ according to the organization's various areas. An example could be if organization decides to institute a research department, but lacks a defined and operational institutional review board (IRB), which could result in regulatory noncompliance and direct-patient risk.

Analyze Systems Already in Place

The second phase of the assessment would be to analyze those systems that are already in place for minimizing risk and then to determine their current effectiveness. Profiles should include identification of key contacts and responsibilities, level and types of risk financing, contractual relationships, and risk management activities (including policies, orientation, job and credentialing requirements, and integration into current organizational structure). Areas or topics to be inventoried (some of which are discussed in other chapters of this book) may include:

- Educational relationships—levels and types of agreements, formal or informal.
- Staff relationships—employed, contracted, independent, network (where staff float from one entity of a large organization to another), or consulting (may involve the assessment of staff issues).
- Scope of services—not only types, but also where and to what degree.
- Subsidiaries owned, partnered, or otherwise associated with the organization.
- Accreditations, licenses, certifications, or other designations in which any or all parts of the organization participate.
- Human resources issues, with focus on pre-employment screening and competency.
- Information management methodologies, computerized information and access, as well as other information issues such as retention and release.
- Clinical technology issues—selection, maintenance, and user training.
- Loss assessment data, loss runs, as well as results of inspection by regulatory agencies.
- Credentialing and orientation processes for non-employee staff, both initially and at reappointment.
- Contract management protocols.
- The safety management program structure and its integration and effectiveness.

Each of these areas should have systems in place that have risk management-related processes. Identifying similarities and shortfalls will assist in developing a cohesive program.

Determine External Needs and Demands

Risk management programs must not only meet organizational needs but also provide support for meeting the requirements of outside entities that, by either choice or mandate, make demands on the health care organization's operation. The demands in the managed care market may not only come with a list of activities and reporting provisions, but also require that certain accreditations be maintained. Rules set forth by regulatory agencies must also be factored into the activities and processes as the risk management program develops and expands. One should first review and analyze the most recent findings of all external reviews, inspections, and surveys, as well as any reports from consultants. These reports (and the status of the action taken in response), along with appropriate standards issued by various bodies, can be used to compile assessment tools that can assist in evaluating the risk management program and in planning for improvement.

Review the Assessments

Assessments are performed to identify risk management program strengths as well as opportunities for improvement. Analysis should include categorizing findings according to severity, frequency, impact of the organization's strategic plan, areas identified for improvement, as well as best practices identified. Good practice without supporting documentation should be assessed as both a practice strength and an information weakness. For example, even if it is identified that the patient care process may need no immediate attention, the recording or tracking of patient care information may well require integration into a better-defined information process in order to substantiate practice patterns.

Set Priorities for Program Implementation

Established risk management programs should undergo continuous reassessment, particularly in new areas or those previously identified as weak. Regulations and other external mandates, along with areas of severe loss, should command the most immediate attention. Organizational emphasis (what the strategic plan and mission support) will also need to be factored into the list of areas to be addressed first. The key is to map out a strategy to take advantage of the many activities that are interdependent. Some risk management activities that may seem less important may need to be initiated in order to lay the groundwork for success in high-impact areas. An example might be the development of a variety of reporting or early identification tools that are adapted for the organization's various departments and services for ease of use (and are therefore more likely to be used). However, the weak area may turn out to be the timely reporting of potential litigious situations. Such a project could be multidisciplinary and supported by various areas within the organization, which can lead to an enhanced quality-improvement database. In setting priorities for program implementation, risk managers need to clearly define the desired outcome. Having done an analysis, the risk manager should be aware of the organization's strengths and weaknesses, as well as improvements or expansions that need to be accomplished. Preliminary work may consist of collecting data and drafting early versions of future measurement tools. Identifying levels of understanding not only during the assessment but also once an analysis is formulated is another key item. The result of action or inaction must be clearly defined in relation to the direct impact on the organization.

············

KEY COMPONENTS FOR GETTING STARTED

For any risk management program to meet its goals, several key components must be in place. Organizational commitment—that is, acceptance of roles as well as support for program aspects by the various levels of leadership, starting with the board—is a necessity. Commitment is often demonstrated through assignments of responsibility, approval of the program, and participation in aspects requiring support and action. The ultimate goal is to achieve integration of risk management components, systems, and strategies into the overall organizational culture. Access to all levels of the organization, with defined accountabilities and identification of resources, also is part of the initial structure formation. No risk management program can function in isolation; its integration with other initiatives is critical to its success. By relying on already established relationships, risk managers can enhance programs with limited resources by strengthening operational linkages and avoiding duplication of efforts. Negative perceptions about the risk management program might damage its credibility before it even gets under way. Physicians often perceive that risk management's involvement after an event has occurred only makes matters worse or that their only interest is to keep the cost down. Frequently, risk management programs are viewed as reactive to crisis rather than proactive. First, risk management activities should focus on support and service, using facilitative techniques in guiding the clinicians' understanding of the nonnegotiable forces (regulatory fines, accreditations, citations, and agency requirements) and the alternatives available. Clinical staff should have input into not only the risk management process but also the analysis and monitoring stages. Most program elements that affect clinical functions require that the clinical staff members become committed to risk management concepts and understand the desired outcome. Ensuring that duplication of effort is minimized can be a key selling point to staff in accepting their roles in the risk management effort. Simplification of any process is always welcome. A method for seeking continual staff feedback also should be developed to ensure ownership of the program by all staff.

WRITING A RISK MANAGEMENT PROGRAM

The written risk management program includes an overview of the purpose, structure, and process of risk management activities within the organization. Within this framework, organizational performance objectives can be developed. Built into this framework will be policies and guidelines that support the identified processes that maximize achievement of the program's objectives. It is critical to maintain an integrated approach at this point of development in order to achieve a consistency of purpose within the organization and to avoid duplication of effort. Rather than create new systems for the risk management process, the risk manager should evaluate how best to enhance existing systems.

As with all programs that have a data collection and monitoring function, reports, memos, and minutes will be generated as communication tools. To be most effective, these tools must meet the needs of those responsible for the implementation and change of risk management practices. Therefore, it is important that those to be served by such information have input into its ultimate design and format as a means of maximizing its usefulness.

ACHIEVING PROGRAM ACCEPTANCE

Often the quickest way to gain support for a program is to provide visibility and education on its related topics. A well-formed risk management program will go nowhere unless staff at all levels understand its purpose and methods. In some cases, the risk manager may even provide unrelated service simply as a means to gain the acceptance and trust vital to the program's success. Often it is the support of an interested medical staff member serving as an advocate that paves the way for others to become familiar with the merits of the risk management program.

Ways for risk management programs to gain visibility include participation in employee orientation and continuing education activities. Maintaining a subject file on risk management topics such as consent, information release, falls, and credentialing allows the risk manager to have supplemental resources when participating in in-services and continuous quality improvement projects.

CONCLUSION

Establishing a risk management program is no simple task, particularly in today's complex health care environment. Assessment of the health care organization's internal and external relationships and forces will provide an overview of the issues the risk management program must address. Obtaining commitment to the program from all levels of the organization, top to bottom, can be a slow process in some instances, but must be achieved for full integration to occur. Translating a written plan into functional risk management processes requires collaboration and facilitation skills now more than ever. No matter how defined the risk management plan, the program will always be "getting started" as it adapts to the changes in health care.

Endnotes

1. Kuhn, A. M. "Introduction to Risk Management." In B. Youngberg, *The Risk Manager's Desk Reference.* Gaithersburg, Md.: Aspen Publishers, 1988.

2. *Ibid.,* p. 1.

3. Archives of the American Society for Healthcare Risk Management.

4. Ryan, W. "The Growth and Development of Hospital Risk Management." *Perspectives in Hospital Risk Management, 3*(2), Spring 1983, pp. 31–32.

5. Archives of the American Society for Healthcare Risk Management.

6. *Ibid.*

7. *Ibid.*

8. *Ibid.*

9. Taravella, S. "The Rise of Risk Management." *Modern Healthcare,* Oct. 8, 1990.

10. *Ibid.*

11. *Ibid.*

12. Joint Commission on Accreditation of Healthcare Organizations. *1996 Comprehensive Accreditation Manual for Hospitals.* Oakbrook Terrace, Ill.: JCAHO, 1995.

13. *Ibid.,* p. 326

14. DiPaulo, S. "Spiraling Premiums Predicted." *Modern Healthcare, 9*(2) Dec. 1979, p. 56.

15. Missouri Hospital Association. *Crisis in Missouri: Case Study on Medical Malpractice Insurance.* Jefferson City, Mo.: MHA, 1985, p. 6.

16. "Professional Liability Legislation: Looking to '86." *Medical Staff, 14*(2), Oct. 1985.

17. Nelson, S. "States Adopt Risk Management Regulations." *Hospitals, 62*(6), Jan. 20, 1988, p. 56.

18. Mulholland, D. M. "Managed Care Liability for Medical Malpractice and Utilization Review." *The Medical Staff Counselor, 7*(2), Spring 1993, p. 35.

19. 42 USC 1320.

20. 2 CFR Part 1003.

21. *Laughinhouse v. Risser,* 786 F. Supp. 920 (Kan. 1992).

22. *Trotta v. Mobil Oil Corp.,* 798 F. Supp. 1336 (DC NY 1992).

23. *Jewell v. Palmer Broadcasting Ltd.,* Iowa District Ct. No. CL94-56040, Dec. 30, 1993.

24. Hazard Communication Standard. Final Rule. Occupational Safety and Health Administration. 29 CFR.1910.1200.

25. Holthaus, D. "States Seek Tighter Rules on Infectious Waste." *Hospitals, 62*(17), Sept. 5, 1988, p. 70.

26. JCAHO, p. 3D16.

27. National Committee on Quality Assurance. NCQA Standards for Accreditation (CR 8.0, CR 13.0) Washington, D.C.: NCQA, 1995.

28. *Risk Management Self-Assessment Manual.* Chicago: American Hospital Association, 1991.

Suggested Readings

Brown, B. L. *Risk Management for Hospitals: A Practical Approach*. Rockville, Md.: Aspen, 1979.

Harpster, L. M., and Veach, M. S. *Risk Management Handbook for Health Care Facilities*. Chicago: American Hospital Publishing, 1990.

Healthcare Risk Control (published monthly by the Emergency Care Research Institute [ECRI], 5200 Butler Pike, Plymouth Meeting, Penn. 19462).

Hospital Peer Review (published monthly by American Health Consultants, Inc., 3525 Piedmont Rd. N.E., Bldg. 6, Ste. 400, Atlanta, Ga. 30305).

Hospital Risk Management (published monthly by American Health Consultants, Inc., 3525 Piedmont Rd N.E., Bldg. 6, Ste. 400, Atlanta, Ga. 30305).

Jessee, W. F. *Quality of Care Issues for the Hospital Trustee: A Practical Guide to Fulfilling Trustee Responsibilities*. Chicago: Hospital Research and Educational Trust, 1984.

Journal of Healthcare Risk Management (published quarterly by the American Society for Healthcare Risk Management of the American Hospital Association, One North Franklin, Chicago, Ill. 60606).

Kraus, G. P. *Health Care Risk Management: Organization and Claims Administration*. Owings Mills, Md.: National Health Publishing Co., 1986.

Monagle, J. F. *Risk Management: A Guide for Health Care Professionals*. Rockville, Md.: Aspen, 1985.

Orlikoff, J. E., and Vanagunas, A. M. *Malpractice Prevention and Liability Control for Hospitals* (2nd ed.). Chicago: American Hospital Publishing, 1988.

Richard, E. P., and Rathburn, K. C. *Medical Risk Management: Prevention Legal Strategies for Health Care Providers*. Rockville, Md.: Aspen, 1983.

Risk Management Pearls Series (published by the American Society for Healthcare Risk Management of the American Hospital Association, One North Franklin, Chicago, Ill. 60606).

Rowland, H., and Rowland, B. *Hospital Risk Management: Forms, Checklists, and Guidelines*. Gaithersburg, Md.: Aspen, 1993.

Troyer, G., and Salman, S. L. *Handbook of Health Care Risk Management*. Rockville, Md.: Aspen, 1986.

Wade, R. D. *Risk Management Hospital Professional Liability Primer*. Columbus: Ohio Hospital Insurance Co., 1983.

3

The Health Care Organization Governing Board

James E. Orlikoff

The governing board of any health care organization, whether hospital, multihospital system, or integrated delivery system (IDS), is ultimately responsible and accountable for the operation of the organization.* This includes, among other things, the quality of care provided, the performance of the physicians, and the effectiveness of the organization's risk management and quality improvement programs. Though these responsibilities are constants, other aspects of governance have been undergoing change as a result of the revolutionary changes in U.S. health care.

This chapter presents an overview of these changes and their effects on health care organization governing boards. It then examines the relationship between governance and risk management, and offers guidelines on effective ways to educate the board on risk management concerns. It also discusses directors' and officers' liability and the part that risk management can play in minimizing organization and trustee exposure to liability.

HEALTH CARE—AND GOVERNANCE—IN TRANSITION

Governance, like health care, is in transition. To understand the nature of this change, it is first necessary to understand the unprecedented, revolutionary changes the U.S. health care system is experiencing. The emergence of better-informed and more aggressive payers and employers, the growth of managed care and at-risk capitation, the increasing

*The introductory section has been adapted from Orlikoff, J. E., and Totten, M. K. *The Future of Health Care Governance: Redesigning Boards for a New Era.* Chicago: American Hospital Publishing, Inc., 1996, pp. 1–13.

availability of high-quality data to purchasers and consumers, reductions in Medicare payments, the linking of health care financing and delivery systems, the movement away from inpatient acute care, the increasing emphasis on wellness and illness prevention, the growth and acceptance of alternative medicine—all these changes are creating new forms of health care delivery organizations and forcing existing ones to choose between an unprecedented type and pace of change and extinction.

Accelerating the health care revolution is the decline of fee-for-service health care and the rise of managed care. Aggressive payers realize that the best way to control the growth in health care costs is to make the providers of care assume the financial risk. Thus, the trend of at-risk capitation is quickly growing. These reversed financial incentives are transforming hospitals from freestanding, revenue-generating centers into cost centers that are part of integrated health care delivery systems.

At the same time, the focus of health care delivery is shifting from one that predominately provides services to ill or injured people to one that provides services designed to prevent or minimize illness or injury to people in a given community. Because of this shift in focus and the changing financial incentives, many health care providers are beginning to offer a variety of services that, today, fall into the category of "alternative medicine." Like all medical services, these services come with their own unique risks, which must be recognized, minimized, and overseen by the governing board.

As health resources become scarcer and more tightly controlled, hospitals will have to integrate their services with those of other health care providers to use those resources more efficiently. This includes integration of physicians, clinical services, information systems, inpatient and outpatient access points, governance, quality improvement, risk management, and all parts of the health care continuum. The forces of the market, in its demand for efficiency, push health care providers to create, evolve into, or affiliate with IDSs.

Integration is defined as "the extent to which functions and activities are appropriately coordinated across operating units . . . so as to maximize the value of services delivered."[1] The promises of integration are clear: better service to the community, greater continuity of care, greater control over quality and costs, and increased efficiency, to name a few.

Briefly, an IDS has the following characteristics:

- Integration of the delivery of care with the financing of care—that is, not only providing health care, but also performing functions associated with insurance companies (accepting premiums, processing claims, and calculating claims-cost-per-life and medical loss ratios).

- Integration of the physicians with the organization, resulting in the sharing of risk and the alignment of economic incentives with physicians.

- Provision of a highly accessible continuum of care based on decentralized primary care provider locations, and on smooth and efficient access to specialty care, hospital care, and ancillary services.

- Accountability for the health status of specific populations in defined geographic areas.

- Provision of high-quality, cost-effective care as a result of the integration of different individuals and entities that provide similar levels of care.

- Utilization of an effective, unified cost and quality information system, which is essential to the integration of patient care and the ability to monitor and control quality and cost efficiency.

- Integration of physicians at all levels of leadership structures and planning activities—key to IDS success.
- Creation of a new form of integrated, systems-oriented governance.[2]

Whether the IDS emerges as the dominant form of health care organization or as a transitional form, massive changes are ahead for hospitals, multihospital systems, and all health care providers. As new forms of health care organizations emerge, new forms of governance are emerging to lead them. Governance will have to oversee and manage interdependent relationships involving multiple institutions and boards, physicians and senior managers, the community, and the purchasers, to name a few. These complex and sometimes transitory relationships must be forged and nurtured effectively for the system to be successful.

The transitions that health care governance is undergoing affect not only the structure and function of the board, but also the extent and nature of its responsibility for and oversight of risk management. Among the more significant governance transitions are:

- *The transition from an emphasis on the local community and focused constituencies to a more regional focus with more disparate constituencies:* An IDS board finds itself with a broader constituency than that of a hospital board due to the expanded geographical coverage and to a new emphasis on the health of the entire community, not simply a segment of it that avails itself of the services of the health care organization.
- *The transition from market share defined as admissions and inpatient census to market share defined as covered lives and physicians:* With the rapid rise of managed care and capitation, standard measures of capacity (such as number of hospital beds) and demand (such as admissions and census) are yielding to new measures. The new measures of health care organization or IDS capacity include the number of aligned physicians and the proper balance between primary care and specialists among the physicians. New measures of demand include the number of covered lives of the organization or system, as well as the size of the communities for which the system accepts accountability for health. Boards in this environment must transition to, and become adept at, maneuvering new levers of control to balance capacity and demand. This is a critical transition for governance. Managed care reduces costs by not only reducing inpatient days and eliminating unnecessary treatment, but also forcing the reduction of health care capacity. In some markets, this means a reduction in the number of hospitals or hospital beds, or specialist physicians.
- *The transition from cost-based pricing to price-based costing:* In inefficient markets, the provider of a product or service develops price based on its cost. Under this method, the price is determined simply by adding a margin on top of the cost. As markets become more efficient, cost-based pricing loses currency because the market demands lower prices. When the market is efficient, it does not care what the cost of a product or service is, only what the lowest price is. At this point, cost-based pricing yields to price-based costing. Under this method, the provider of a product or service determines what the market is willing to pay for the commodity, then reengineers the process to produce the product or service at a cost below the market price. A classic example of this dynamic is the transition of fee-for-service health care to capitation. Boards must change their focus to cope with, and preferably lead, this transition by ensuring that the costs of the services provided by their system are known, that they are appropriate relative to the capitated rate, and that constant organizational efforts to lower costs are under way.

The risk management challenge is to do this while maintaining acceptable and even superior levels of quality and service to minimize loss through malpractice and other legal claims, such as restraint-of-trade claims filed by physicians who have been "deselected" from the systems contracts.

• *The transition from managing stability to leading change:* In past, stable times, the role of the board was to be reactive—that is, to monitor the past. In times of turmoil and massive change, the fundamental role of the board changes to become one of creating the future through forward-thinking, proactive planning and action. This shift requires boards to move away from a cumbersome, slow decision-making process to a streamlined, rapid one. It also requires that boards develop an increased tolerance for risk.

• *The transition from institutional (local) board authority to system (central) board authority:* As IDSs form through mergers and affiliations of hospitals and other health care providers, many boards that previously had ultimate authority for their organizations now find that they are subordinate to a system board. The reconciliation of this diminution of authority, along with the specific clarification of relative roles and authorities between the subordinate and system boards, is crucial to effective system governance and risk management. This transition has particular significance for risk management because in many systems, the institution-specific authority for quality and risk management is delegated to a subordinate, institutional board, such as a hospital board. In a system with multiple hospitals and organizations, the system board also must have responsibility for risk management, not only within the hospitals of the system, but for all the many and varied functions of the system.

• *The transition from representational governance to systems-thinking, mission-driven governance:* Many hospital and health care organization boards are composed of members who were chosen, or believe it is their role, to represent specific constituencies or organizations. This perception gives rise to representational governance, in which the members of the system board focus on the best interests of component parts of the system rather than on the best interests of the system as a whole. Representational governance is the antithesis of integration.

One does not overcome representational governance by emphasizing structural matters, such as how board members are chosen or whether there are few or many boards. Rather, one overcomes representational governance through an emphasis on mission and systems thinking. *Systems thinking* means, in part, that the board members of local institutions recognize that the interests of their institutions, communities, or constituents will be best served in the long run if the system as a whole pursues and achieves its mission. It also means that every member of a system board places the best interests of the system above those of the constituency or institution from whence he or she came.

• *The transition from the governance of facilities to the governance of services:* As IDSs and hospitals push patient care outside the boundaries of the acute care environment, and as they increasingly focus on providing preventive and wellness services to a broader community, the context of health care delivery transcends the building or institution. Thus, IDS governance moves away from governance based on institutions toward governance based on services. This shift presents a challenge because it is easier to govern (and oversee risk management) in a building such as a hospital than in a disparate collection of services provided in a widely dispersed manner and area.

• *The transition from an acute care and illness care approach to a continuum of care and prevention approach:* A law of economics known as the "fallacy of composition" states that what is good for the individual is not good for the group and, conversely, what is good for the group is not good for the individual. Until recently, health care has focused on the sick individual, resulting in a diversion of resources away from community health. This, in turn, has resulted in a decline in the health status of the population.

With the growth of managed care and capitation, financial incentives for health care providers are shifting away from sickness care and toward prevention, wellness, and health maintenance. Under managed care and capitation, a health care organization has a clear incentive to provide services that keep its enrolled population or covered lives healthy. The downside of this is that boards will have to balance the needs of the group against those of the individual. Managed care involves population-based health care, which means that more emphasis is placed on community health (the group) than on sickness care (the individual). To make this goal a reality, boards will need to recognize that the more resources that are devoted to the community, the fewer resources are available to provide services to sick individuals. In the near future, all IDS and hospital boards will need to address the issue of rationing care to individuals. This has significant implications for risk management because malpractice law still emphasizes damages to the individual and corresponding compensation.

• *The transition from simply delivering care to delivering and financing care:* As mentioned earlier, one characteristic of an IDS is that it performs functions relating to the financing of care. These include the acceptance and processing of premium dollars, actuarial assessment and management of risk, and the calculation and monitoring of medical loss ratios (how much of the premium dollar is actually devoted to health care). As a result, IDS boards will need to merge a focus on health care delivery (such as that of a hospital board) with a focus on health care financing (such as that of an insurance company board). This dual focus will entail new skills, new structures, and new challenges for governance. For example, boards will have to oversee not only the traditional medical risk management functions, but also insurance and financial risk management functions.

• *The transition from governance oversight of physicians to physician involvement in governance and leadership of the system:* For an IDS to be successful, physicians must be integrated into all aspects of the system, including the board(s) and other leadership structures. Boards will need to reconceptualize their relationships with physicians, which, at a minimum, will necessitate a greater involvement of physicians in governance.[3]

Research confirms that the governance of health care organizations is changing in response to an industry in transition. Two studies conducted by the Governance Institute, one on the boards of fifty not-for-profit hospitals, and one on sixty-five not-for-profit health systems, reveal emerging differences between hospital boards and health system boards. According to the studies, governance differences are evident in that system boards are smaller, meet less frequently, compensate their members more often, and spend more time on formal education than do hospital boards.[4,5] Specific differences can be seen in Table 3.1, which was drawn from the two Governance Institute studies.

············

RISK MANAGEMENT AND THE BOARD

Board accountability for risk management and quality is a relatively recent development. Consequently, few boards, especially system boards, effectively oversee and set the direction for their organizations' risk management programs. Risk management preserves and protects the health care organization's assets and maintains and improves the quality of care provided by the system or hospital. As a critical health care function, risk management should be an ongoing board priority. However, the board is not responsible for

TABLE 3.1.   Hospital and System Boards

Characteristics of Sample	Hospital Boards	System Boards
Average size	18 members	13 members
Range in board size	5 to 45 members	6 to 51 members
Percent that offer cash compensation to their board members	4 percent	14 percent
Percent that impose term limits for board members	78 percent	70 percent
CEO is a member of the board	77 percent	76 percent
Average amount of time devoted to formal board education per year	16 hours	23 hours
Percent that meet:		
Monthly	74 percent	44 percent
Bimonthly	18 percent	29 percent
Quarterly	8 percent	27 percent
Average number of standing committees of the board	6	5
Percent with the following committee:		
Finance	93 percent	78 percent
Executive	79 percent	75 percent
Planning/Strategy	79 percent	56 percent
Nominating	46 percent	53 percent
Compensation	31 percent	48 percent
Quality Improvement	65 percent	28 percent
Percent that have a line item in budget for		
governance (education, development, and so on)	28 percent	26 percent
Average number of non-board members who attend board meetings	8	6

Compiled from two Governance Institute studies published in 1995 and 1996.

"doing" risk management; instead, its role is to provide direction for the hospital's or system's risk management program and to ensure that the various risk management activities are functioning effectively.

The board's oversight role includes verifying that the organization's definition of risk management and the structure and function of the risk management program are consistent with and support the organization's mission. The board also must integrate risk management into the strategic planning process to ensure that the system undertakes new activities in a manner that will minimize liability exposure and maximize high-quality care and asset preservation. Consistent with its oversight role, the board should review and approve the system's or hospital's risk management plan annually and hold the CEO responsible for ensuring that all components of the program are functioning effectively and consistently with the plan.

To help the board discharge its role effectively, the risk manager must report to the board regularly on the activities of the risk management program and on new developments or major exposures to liability. The risk management reports should be comprehensible, establish the necessary, two-way communication between board and risk manager, and enable the board to understand what is required to provide organizational support and effective resource allocation to the risk management program. Board oversight and support are critical to the program's ongoing effectiveness.

Risk Management's Role in Educating the Board

A board cannot effectively discharge its oversight role in risk management until it knows what that role is and what the purposes, functions, and activities of risk management are.[6] Consequently, the risk manager and the hospital or system CEO must educate the board about risk management.

One of the basic risk management concepts about which the board must be educated is the difference between custodially related patient injury and iatrogenic (medically related) patient injury. A custodially related patient injury is not caused by medical intervention, but rather by custodial or administrative action, inaction, or circumstance. Typical examples of custodially related patient injury include slips and falls in wet hallways, from bed, on the way to the bathroom, and in the bathroom. In contrast, an iatrogenic patient injury is directly related to or caused by medical or professional health care. Examples of iatrogenic patient injury include a bowel perforated during a colonoscopy, an operation performed on the wrong patient, removal of the wrong body part during surgery, an anaphylactic reaction to a prescribed drug or chemical agent, and post-operative infections.

The board must be familiar with the distinction between custodial and iatrogenic injuries in order to ensure that the resources of the risk management program are appropriately apportioned. Although iatrogenic injuries occur much less frequently than custodially related ones, they generally are much more severe and result in much greater liability dollar losses. Consequently, the board may wish to direct the risk management program to devote more of its resources to preventing iatrogenic injury occurrence and liability.

The board also must be familiar with the operating risk that is associated with managed care. When the provider of care assumes the financial risk for the provision of that care via capitation or other payment mechanisms, the concern of risk management with the preservation of the system's resources takes on striking new dimensions. The minor complications, nosocomial infections, and other inefficiencies that in the past rarely, if ever, generated traditional malpractice liability now inexorably chip away at the organization's resources and revenues. As such, they may pose a more insidious threat than the specter of a multimillion-dollar malpractice judgment.

Consider the case of nosocomial infection. In a fee-for-service environment, the costs of treating the infection were borne by the insurer or the patient. In a managed care environment, the costs of treating the infection, or any other iatrogenic complication, are borne directly by the health care organization. This new reality forces the board to integrate the traditional risk management functions with those of quality improvement and operational efficiency improvement to oversee the organization's risk exposures and control mechanisms.

In addition, the board should be familiar with:

- The organization's definition of risk management and the scope of the organization's risk management program.
- The role and the job of the risk manager.
- The relationship between the insurance and claims functions and the risk management program.
- The relationship between the system's or hospital's quality improvement program and medical staff credentialing function, and the risk management program.
- The risk management program's data-gathering and risk identification techniques— incident reporting, occurrence reporting, generic screening, patient complaints, or other methods.
- The highest-risk areas of patient injury and malpractice claims within the hospital and throughout the system and how they compare with national data.
- Insurance coverage and costs.
- The organization's claims history.

- The part the board plays in preventing patient injury and malpractice liability and reducing overall liability exposure by effectively discharging its risk management oversight role.
- The role of ineffective governance in generating liability losses.

These concepts can be communicated to the board through a risk management orientation program conducted by the risk manager, the hospital CEO, the hospital attorney, the medical staff director, or by regular risk management reports. The risk manager must recognize that failing to educate the board may mean that the board will be unable to oversee the risk management program effectively, may be unreceptive and unresponsive to the risk management reports, and may be unwilling to provide support to the risk manager.

Content and Format of Reports to the Board

There are three general types of information in a system or health care organization: management and financial information, clinical information, and governance information. Boards respond to the information they are provided. If a board is given management information, it will manage. If a board is given clinical information, it will attempt to practice medicine. Therefore, it is critical that boards be provided with governance information. Unfortunately, many boards do not receive governance information in their agenda materials. Instead, they get operational detail, warmed-over management reports, and detailed clinical information. Figure 3.1 lists information that risk management reports to the board should, at various times, present.

Following are some common flaws and weaknesses in providing information and reports to boards:

- Reports and information do not flow from or support the explicitly defined role of the board regarding the issue.
- There are no guidelines on what information should be reported to the board or how it should be reported.
- Reports provide data, such as cross-sectional indicators, but not information, such as longitudinal trends or projections. *Data* convey individual facts or statistics; *information* conveys knowledge.

FIGURE 3.1.   Contents of Reports to the Board

- Analyses of trends identified through incident reports and occurrence screens.
- Summary and status of open malpractice claims.
- Analyses of trends identified through patient complaints.
- An example of the risk management incident investigation and problem resolution process.
- Open- and closed-claims trends and costs of claims.
- Actual losses.
- Losses by area, by physician distribution, and by organization within a system.
- Results of insurance audits and costs.
- Incident reports compared with claims compared with losses.
- Staff turnover trends and patterns of staff complaints.
- Reports outlining operational efficiency improvements that are instrumental in minimizing an organization's exposure to operating risk.

- Meeting minutes are used as a vehicle for providing information to the board.
- Too much material is presented in the reports.
- Governance reports are simply retitled management or medical staff information.
- Ineffective report formats blunt the board's understanding of important information.
- Thick agenda packets are distributed to board members so close to the scheduled board meeting that there is insufficient time to read all the material.
- Significant amounts of informational materials are routinely distributed to board members for review at, rather than before, the board meeting.

To be meaningful to the board, the risk management reports should be brief and understandable and should either enhance the board's understanding of an issue or facilitate its taking action. They should present summary information in a graphic format that compares data over time. For example, a graph of incident report trends by area for the past quarter compared to those trends over the past several years would enable the board to determine whether progress was being made in increasing incident reporting in areas likely to generate medically related patient injury. For a system board, reports graphically comparing risk management trends and indicators across the different hospitals and institutions in the system is a necessity.

To be most effective, the risk management reports should not present too much information and should vary the content presented. For example, one report could present claims information; another, incident report graphs; another, insurance information; and yet another, patient complaint trends. Brief, graphic, and varied reports will best educate the board about the purposes of risk management. The risk manager may wish to refer to the following guidelines in preparing reports:

1. Informational reports to the board should be brief and in graphic format, whenever possible.
2. Any narrative reports provided to a board should be prefaced by a brief executive summary.
3. All risk management information provided to a board should relate directly to the system or organizational risk management strategy and goals.
4. Meeting minutes should never be used as the primary vehicle for providing information to a board. (Meeting minutes are valuable only to the group whose meeting is reflected in them. Thus, the only minutes a board should review are those of its own meetings.)
5. The board, with input and guidance from the risk manager, should annually develop and select a series of risk management indicators that will be routinely presented to the board. These indicators will allow the board to perform its monitoring functions in a condensed and efficient manner.
6. Once the indicators are selected, threshold or target levels for each should be developed. (For example, upper and lower limits can be established for most indicators. If the indicator is within established limits, the board will not spend any time reviewing it. However, if an indicator trendline has approached or exceeded an upper or lower limit, the board will devote attention to it.)
7. Indicators, along with upper and lower limits or thresholds, should be presented to the board in graphic format. This facilitates quick board review of the indicators, as well as provides the board with a big-picture view of the issues.

8. An annual calendar for the reporting of routine or required information to the board should be developed and used. Many risk management issues the board must address can be anticipated. These routine reports can then be scheduled for presentation to the board in sequenced and manageable detail through the use of an annual board reporting calendar.

....

DIRECTORS' AND OFFICERS' LIABILITY PREVENTION

As a result of the rapid changes in the health care system, as well as the increasingly difficult decisions faced by boards, IDS and hospital boards increasingly are exposed to directors' and officers' (D & O) liability. Risk managers can assist their boards in developing a board risk management program to minimize both the organization's and the individual trustee's exposure to liability. In so doing, the board will recognize the importance of risk management and come to regard the risk manager as a valuable resource. This will facilitate effective two-way communication between board and risk manager as well as effective board oversight of the organization's risk management program.

A board risk management program starts with the following three-step risk analysis and reduction process:

1. Determination of potential areas of board liability exposure.

2. Assessment of the degree of liability exposure in such areas.

3. Implementation of corrective action to minimize liability exposure in high-risk areas or activities.[7]

Determination of Potential Areas of Board Liability Exposure

To determine potential areas of board liability exposure, the risk manager should first list all D & O insurance policy coverage limitations and exclusions. Next, he or she should research the most common types of D & O lawsuits brought against hospitals, systems, or other health care organizations. Finally, the risk manager should list all current and planned activities that have significant implications for the organization, its medical staff and physician groups, its employees, the community, or other area health care organizations.

In IDSs or other multi-institution organizations, great care must be taken to clarify the different roles and authority among the different boards. For example, in a system with several hospitals where each has a board, and all the boards are subordinate and report to a system board, which board bears ultimate accountability and liability for medical staff credentialing? Unless this and similar issues are made extremely clear, boards may be exposed to significant, and surprising, liability. Thus, assessment of the clarity of role and responsibility distinction among different boards within a system is a crucial component of potential governance liability exposure.

Most insurers have identified the areas of greatest risk of loss and either exclude them from coverage or restrict coverage. Common D & O policy coverage limitations and exclusions include:

- Discrimination in employment.
- Medical staff appointment and reappointment, including restriction or revocation of staff medical privileges.

- Failure to maintain adequate general and professional liability insurance for the hospital.
- Hospital pollution, hazardous waste, nuclear perils, and any illegal board activities.
- Antitrust, or restraint of trade.

Most institutions indemnify their directors and officers through an indemnification provision in the organization bylaws. An indemnification provision ensures that board members will be compensated by the organization for losses that trustees are legally obligated to pay and that are related to their being trustees or directors. Indemnification may be used to reimburse a trustee for losses not covered by insurance, or it may be used instead of D & O liability coverage. Governing boards that rely solely on indemnification provisions may be placing their organizations and themselves at financial risk if the organization does not have the available funds to cover a large settlement or award. If the organization cannot pay, the governing board members may be personally liable for the balance. Moreover, most indemnification provisions contain limitations or exclusions of indemnity that may be significant. Those items also should be added to the list of potential areas of board liability exposure.

Another way to determine potential areas of board liability exposure is to list all recent and planned board decisions, noting their implications for any significant groups related to the system or hospital. As hospitals and systems increasingly pursue nontraditional business and marketing strategies, D & O liability allegations against governing boards are likely to increase. Such allegations also are likely to follow from governing board decisions involving the closing of facilities, mergers, sales to other organizations, financial failures, elimination of medical staffs, exclusive alignment with specific physician groups, and corporate restructuring.

Assessment of the Degree of Liability Exposure

Once the greatest potential areas of board liability exposure have been identified, the next step is to assess as accurately as possible the degree of board liability exposure in each area. This assessment is the most critical step of the risk analysis and reduction process. By honestly assessing each area of potential liability exposure, the board will clarify the most effective means of eliminating or reducing that exposure. This step may be lengthy because it involves a critical review of past and pending board actions for each potential risk area. For example, a board and a risk manager would review the process the board employs for credentialing and privileging of medical staff applicants and members to confirm that it is based on objective, reasonable, nonarbitrary, and noncapricious criteria and that it is applied equally to all medical staff applicants and members.

Many boards include local businesspeople among their members. Conflicts of interest can arise when the board approves contracts or arrangements with local businesses that are represented on the board. Frequently, local attorneys, insurance agents, or construction contractors who serve as board members may have an interest that conflicts with the hospital's interest. The board should have an approved conflict-of-interest policy that distinguishes between duality of interest and conflict of interest. At a minimum, board members must be required to disclose potential conflicts of interest and abstain from voting on any issue where there may be a perception that the board member is putting personal interest ahead of the best interest of the hospital. The policy should be reviewed annually, and board members should be given the opportunity to disclose any personal interest that has the potential to conflict with the hospital's best interest. Board members' statements of potential conflicts of interest should be kept on file.

Implementation of Corrective Action

The last step in the risk analysis and reduction process is taking corrective action based on the results of the liability assessment. The board may be advised to revise board policies, procedures, and certain decision-making processes to minimize future liability.

••••••••••••

CONCLUSION

Ensuring the quality of care that the health care organization provides, being accountable for the performance of its physicians, and preventing liability are major responsibilities of a health care governing board, which also require an effective governing board risk management program. Governing board risk management helps to improve the functioning of a board and enables it to protect itself and its organization. It also heightens board awareness of and interest in the organization's risk management program, which facilitates improved communication between risk manager and board and improves board oversight of the organization's risk management program. The risk manager's role in helping the board discharge its responsibilities includes educating the board members in basic risk management concepts and providing appropriate governance information by means of brief, understandable reports.

Endnotes

1. Gillies, R. R., Shortell, S. M., Anderson, D. A., and others. "Conceptualizing and Measuring Integration: Findings from the Health Systems Integration Study." *Hospital and Health Services Administration, 38*(4), June 1993, pp. 467–489.

2. Orlikoff, J. E., and Totten, M. K. *The Future of Health Care Governance: Redesigning Boards for a New Era.* Chicago: American Hospital Publishing, 1996.

3. *Ibid.*

4. The Governance Institute. *Governance Trends and Practices in Hospitals: 1996 Bi-Annual Survey of Hospital Boards.* La Jolla, Calif.: The Governance Institute, 1996.

5. The Governance Institute. *Governance Trends and Practices in Hospitals: 1995 Panel Survey of System Boards.* La Jolla, Calif.: The Governance Institute, 1995.

6. Veach, M. "Minimizing the Hospital's Risk of Liability Exposure: The Trustee's Role." *Trustee, 40*(6), June 1987, pp. 16–18.

7. Orlikoff, J. E., and Vanagunas, A. M. *Malpractice Prevention and Liability Control for Hospitals* (2nd ed.). Chicago: American Hospital Publishing, 1988.

4

Statutes, Standards, and Regulations

Mark Cohen

"It will be of little avail to the people . . . if the laws be so voluminous that they cannot be read, or so incoherent that they cannot be understood; if they be repealed or revised before they are promulgated, or undergo such incessant changes that no [one] who knows what the law is today can guess what it will be tomorrow." *The Federalist Papers,* no. 62.*

This should not come as much of a surprise, but health care is one of the most regulated of all sectors of commerce. Much of this regulation, such as federal and state law, are mandates; others, such as the requirements of the Joint Commission on Accreditation of Healthcare Organizations (JCAHO), are voluntary. In either case, the number and variety of laws and regulations that govern our profession is staggering. Risk managers should become familiar with key legislation and regulations and actively work to establish their organization's compliance. An understanding of key laws and regulations is an important element of the risk manager's risk control efforts. Risk managers are strongly advised to use all available resources (corporate counsel, federal and state agency representatives, professional journals, newsletters, and so on) to help them understand the intent of a law or regulatory requirement.

---

*The Federalist Papers are a collection of 85 essays written over a two-year period (1787–1788) by James Madison, Alexander Hamilton, and John Jay. The intent of these essays, originally submitted to New York newspapers by all three authors under the collective pseudonym of "Publius," was to persuade the citizens of New York, and, specifically, the New York delegation to the Constitutional Convention, to support ratification of the newly drafted Constitution.

Space permits a review of just a fraction of the total number of laws, regulations, and guidelines that affect health care. The discussions are meant to provide the reader with a brief introductory overview of the laws and should not be considered a comprehensive review of each of their elements, or the final word on compliance. As laws, regulations, and other pieces of legislation are subject to revision, court interpretation, suspension, or repeal at any time, the reader is cautioned to always refer to the most current version of the law.[†] Citations have been provided to identify the source or authority of the law.

Note: To avoid redundancy, laws, regulations, interpretive guidelines, conditions of participation, and so on will be referred to collectively as "laws" even though the issue being addressed may not actually be a "law." Also, references to a "patient" includes surrogate decision makers appointed by the patient, a court, and/or anyone acting lawfully on the patient's behalf. Finally, as English is not a gender-neutral language, when third-party personal pronouns "he," "she," "his," and "her" are used, the reader is asked to regard it as embracing the complementary gender as well.

············

PATIENT CARE

Following are several examples of laws that affect patient health care.

Emergency Medical Treatment and Active Labor Act

The Emergency Medical Treatment and Active Labor Act (Social Security Act 1867 codified as 42 USC 1395dd; 42 CFR 489 et al.) is also known as EMTALA or COBRA. One of many measures found in the Consolidated Omnibus Budget Reconciliation Act of 1986 (the source of the COBRA acronym), this law is essentially a nondiscrimination statute that was enacted in response to the then common practice among hospital emergency departments to either refuse service, or refer to increasingly crowded public hospitals, patients who lacked the ability to pay. This practice, known as "patient dumping," occasionally resulted in patient injury or death. In response to this alarming trend, California congressman Pete Stark drafted this law. EMTALA imposes an unfunded mandate on hospitals. Specifically, anyone who comes to a hospital seeking aid in diagnosing or treating an "emergency medical condition" must be offered and provided diagnostic and/or therapeutic services necessary to (a) determine if an "emergency medical condition" exits, (b) clinically stabilize, to the degree possible given the facility's available resources, any medical condition that poses an immediate threat to the health of the patient, and (c) in the absence of sufficient resources to treat the patient's condition, transfer him to someplace that does. Everything else within this law serves to support these objectives. However, years after the law was written and the final regulations published, many facilities continue to struggle with compliance. The United States Supreme Court has ventured into this arena only once, but the issue at hand (the so-called "improper motive" required within some jurisdictions for a plaintiff or patient to proceed with an EMTALA action) was dismissed. As the case involved a patient who had been hospitalized for six weeks prior to the transfer in question, the question arises whether EMTALA extends into inpatient areas. The Court would not say, but a recent Special Advisory Bulletin issued jointly by the Health Care Financing Administration (HCFA) (the division of the federal Department of

---

[†]CAUTION: When in doubt as to the meaning of a law or regulation, always consult legal counsel. No exceptions.

Health and Human Services that oversees the Medicare and Medicaid programs) and the Office of the Inspector General (OIG) suggests that this may now be the case.[1]

This law applies to Medicare-certified hospitals and their satellite clinical operations that operate under the facility's Medicare provider number. Everyone who presents herself at a hospital (or clinic operating under the hospitals' Medicare provider number) seeking care or assessment for what she believes may be an emergency medical condition (EMC) is entitled to a screening assessment and any needed stabilizing treatment. Signs must be posted "conspicuously . . . in a place or places likely to be noticed by all individuals entering the emergency department" that explain the patient's right to such evaluation and treatment.

As patients are entitled to such care irrespective of their ability to pay for it, financial screening is permitted as long as there is *no delay whatsoever* in providing all of the services noted above. A growing number of hospitals now postpone their financial screening until the medical screening examination has been completed to avoid accidentally violating this requirement. In response to the requirement of many managed care organizations for enrollees to obtain prior authorization for out-of-network services, HCFA has made it clear in their Special Advisory Bulletin[2] that a hospital should not attempt to obtain the authorization of the patient's primary care giver or health plan to provide a medical screening examination (MSE), "stabilizing" treatment, or to arrange for a transfer to another hospital if necessary.

Every facility must maintain a central log of individuals who come to the facility seeking emergency assessment and care. This requirement also extends to those units or clinics that provide labor checks for expectant mothers, walk-in "urgent/primary care" clinics, and so on, whether they are on or off the hospital's premises, provided they are aligned with the hospital and use its Medicare certification number.

Emergency departments must maintain a roster of physicians (representing each of the clinical services offered by the hospital) who are on-call to the emergency department to provide consultation or care. Although twenty-four hour, seven-day per week on-call coverage for every service would be ideal, HCFA recognizes that this just is not possible for many facilities. As such, if full-time on-call coverage cannot be provided, the hospital must make and document its efforts to arrange for such coverage to the best of its ability—for example, through transfer agreements, contracts with specialty medical groups, and so on. The issue of "dual staffing," a system of on-site E.D. physician coverage initiated by managed care plans as a cost control effort, merited comment by HCFA and the OIG in their 1999 Special Advisory Bulletin.[3] Although not prohibiting this practice outright, HCFA counsels hospitals to be aware of the potential for violation inherent in a system that is based upon drawing a distinction made among patients based upon their insurance status.

Medical staff bylaws and/or rules and regulations must reflect the obligations of medical staff to participate in the on-call rotation as well as provide time frames within which on-call physicians must respond to consultation requests. Although many physicians remain skeptical of the "on-call" mandate, civil monetary penalties of up to $50,000 per violation[4] may be imposed against a physician for noncompliance, as well as loss or suspension of Medicare or Medicaid provider status.

Patients with unresolved emergency conditions may be transferred to another facility if the transferring hospital lacks the resources to adequately care for them. However, under no circumstances may such transfers result from financial considerations alone. Specific requirements of the transfer process are defined within the regulations and interpretive guidelines.

The law requires hospitals to make every reasonable effort to advise patients of the medical risks of leaving before completion of their screening assessment or treatment. These efforts must be documented and, whenever possible, the patient should be asked to sign confirmation that it occurred.

Risk Management Implications   Failure to comply with any element of this law may result in investigation by the state licensing authority, state professional review organization (PRO), HCFA, OIG, and, under certain circumstances, the Justice Department. A schedule of fines and penalties is noted within the law [5] and the prospect of losing its Medicare or Medicaid provider agreement should make a believer out of every risk manager and hospital administrator. Hospitals that receive an inappropriately transferred patient have a duty to report the circumstances to their state licensing authority or HCFA. Failure to do so can result in a violation by itself. Severe penalties have been set for any individual or organization that retaliates against either a physician or other "qualified" individual who refuses to authorize the transfer of an unstable patient, or anyone who reports a suspected EMTALA violation to the state regulatory agency or to HCFA.

Health Care Quality Improvement Act of 1986

The Health Care Quality Improvement Act (USC 42 11101; 45 CFR Part 60, Public law 99–660), also known as HCQIA, went into effect on November 14, 1986. In its statement of findings, Congress noted that the law was enacted to address the nationwide increase in medical malpractice claims, a corresponding need to improve quality of care, and a method of accomplishing this objective, for example, by encouraging meaningful professional peer review. For peer review to be effective, Congress established a broad immunity from civil liability for physicians and others who participate in good faith in the process. The establishment of such protection at the federal level was felt by Congress to be more effective than the piecemeal, state-by-state approach then in effect.

This law applies to peer (professional) review committees in hospitals, their members, and contributors, as well as medical staff members and certain allied health care professionals. Qualified immunity from liability in civil actions was established for physicians and other specified providers engaged in legitimate peer review if the review action is taken:

- To further high-quality health care.
- After a reasonable effort has been made to ascertain the facts of the matter.
- After notice and fair hearing opportunities are provided by the involved provider.
- In the reasonable belief that the action is supported by the facts.

The notice of a proposed professional review action submitted to a physician under review must include the reasons for such review, the time frame within which the physician may request a hearing, and a summary of his fair hearing rights.

HCQIA established the National Practitioner Data Bank for Adverse Actions Against Physicians and Other Health Care Practitioners—commonly known as the NPDB or "Data Bank." The Data Bank acquires information from a variety of sources in connection with claims of professional negligence that were resolved with either a judgment found against the practitioner or a settlement made on her behalf, regardless of the amount.

Health care entities must report to their state board of medical examiners (BOME) any action taken that adversely affects a practitioner's medical staff membership or clinical privileges for a period exceeding thirty days, or a physician's voluntary relinquishment of membership privileges submitted to avoid disciplinary action. Health care entities may, but are not required to, report actions taken against other health care practitioners (such as nurse midwives) as well. A BOME must, in turn, report to the Data Bank any actions taken against the licenses of physicians or dentists. *Note:* Time frames within which reports must be made to the Data Bank are specifically defined within the law. Pay close attention to them.

Hospitals must request information from the Data Bank on applicants for medical staff membership or in connection with the periodic renewal of their clinical privileges. In any case, the Data Bank must be queried about individual practitioners no less frequently than every two years. Although there is no provision for imposing civil money penalties against facilities that fail to query the Data Bank as required, they remain accountable nonetheless. In addition, a plaintiff's attorney will be given access to otherwise confidential Data Bank information about a defendant physician if he can establish that the hospital did *not* query the Data Bank as required under this law. Provisions are also made for state licensing board, as well as the practitioners themselves, to request information from the Data Bank under specific circumstances.

Risk Management Implications Complying with the reporting and querying elements of this law is essential. As noted, a hospital that fails to do so may provide a plaintiff's attorney with access to what would ordinarily be unobtainable, confidential information about a physician. This would not sit well with the medical staff. The important "immunity" provisions of this law support peer review by providing an incentive for physicians to actively participate in the process. Peer review, when performed as intended, is a vital element of a risk management program.

The Bureau of Health Professions of the Health Resources Service Administration (HRSA) has noted that they believe facilities significantly underreport. Unfortunately, they probably have good cause for arriving at this conclusion. Consequently, the HRSA has advocated for increasing penalties for violators of this law. Make every effort to ensure that your organization remains compliant with all HCQIA requirements.

Patient Self Determination Act of 1990

Final regulations implementing the Patient Self Determination Act of 1990 (42 USC 1395cc) went into effect on July 27, 1995. The tragic case of accident victim Nancy Cruzan and the exhaustive efforts of her parents to gain the right to make end-of-life decisions on her behalf[6] spurred Congress to address these issues in this landmark statute that defines the right of patients to make legally enforceable decisions now about the course their health care will take, even if they should become unable to express them later on. The law imposes an obligation on a broad range of providers to provide written information to their patients, clients, or enrollees at the time of admission or initial contact about these rights, as well as to ask whether the individual has completed an "advance directive" as provided for under the law.

This law applies to hospitals, hospices, skilled nursing facilities (SNFs), providers of home health care or personal care services, hospice programs, and health maintenance organizations (HMOs). The notification requirements do not apply to providers of outpatient services or physicians. The law defines an "advance directive" as a written instruction, such as a living will or durable power of attorney for health care, recognized under state law, that relates to the provision of health care when adult individuals are unable to express their own wishes regarding medical treatment (see the sample directive in Exhibit 4.1 on page 103). By requiring health care providers to furnish information regarding an individual's rights, patients are encouraged to actively participate in this process by establishing guidance for others to follow when they are no longer able to express their wishes themselves.

Risk Management Implications   Develop policies and procedures that address each element of the law. Retain patient advisory materials that are distributed to patients. Familiarize yourself with the specifics of your state's law relating to this advance directives (if such law exists) in order to ensure uniform compliance at all levels. See the chapter on ethics and patient care for an expanded discussion on this topic.

Patient's Rights Conditions of Participation

Also known as the Patient's Rights COP, this law (HCFA-3018-IFC, Medicare and Medicaid Hospital Conditions of Participation, 64 *Federal Register* 36070 [July 2, 1999] 42 CFR 482.13) was first published in December 1997 as a proposed rule. It was later finalized and enacted in 1999. This Medicare/Medicaid condition of participation (COP) established six standards relating to a variety of patient's rights issues that Medicare/ Medicaid-participating hospitals must adopt. It applies to acute care hospitals and psychiatric treatment units within them, psychiatric hospitals, and skilled nursing facilities.

The six standard key points are:

1. *Notice of Rights:* Hospitals must inform each patient or, when appropriate, the patient's representative, of their rights "in advance of furnishing or discontinuing patient care whenever possible." HCFA has not yet defined how to accomplish this; however, your policy should reflect, at a minimum, how, when, and where to provide patients with this information. Facilities are also directed to establish a formal process for investigating and resolving patient grievances and must advise each patient whom to contact if they wish to file one. The law delegates to the hospital's governing body the responsibility to oversee this process. They, in turn, may redelegate this responsibility to a committee. After the committee reviews the grievance, it must provide the patient with a written notice of its findings, including, (1) the name of the hospital contact person, (2) the steps taken to investigate the complaint, (3) the actual results or findings, and (4) the date of completion. HCFA also expects that issues of note that arise during the investigation are referred to appropriate quality improvement, utilization, or peer review groups. HCFA has not defined the term "grievance" nor has it made a distinction between a "grievance" and a "complaint" (if, in fact, one exists). As such, it is up to each facility to develop a reasonable means of compliance on its own.

2. *Exercise of Rights:* Patients must be advised of their rights to:

- File a grievance and to know whom to contact to do so.
- Participate in the development and implementation of their plan of care.
- Make informed decisions regarding their course of treatment.
- Be continually informed of the status of their health by their providers.
- Formulate advance directives and to have these directives followed.
- Obtain privacy.

- Receive care in a safe and non-abusive setting.
- Access their hospital records as well as access to them.
- Be free from restraints and seclusion used for coercive or punitive reasons or the convenience of the staff.
- Notify a family member and their private doctor at the time of their admission.

Note: Ensure that all patient's federal and state-mandated patient's rights are posted, as may be required. As there are many such rights, so be sure to address them all. For the sake of convenience, consider developing a consolidated list of the various patient's rights directives—each with its corresponding citation—within a single posting. Check with counsel, as well as the state licensing authority, to see if this is feasible. Develop a policy that addresses posting and other means of notifying patients of their rights.

3. *Privacy and Safety:* Patients are entitled to personal privacy and to receive care in a safe environment without the threat of harm, abuse, or harassment. Although the requirements are self-evident, specific guidance as to compliance may be referred to in the yet-unpublished interpretive guidelines.

4. *Confidentiality of Patient Records:* This standard reiterates each patient's long-held right, as reflected under most state's laws, to confidentiality of their health care records. This standard was developed in response to concern that patient confidentiality was steadily eroding as a result of the increasing flow of personal health care information to regulatory agencies, insurers, accreditation agencies, researchers, and others. In addition, this standard entitles patients to access their medical records without undue delay. There are, however, some restrictions imposed on such access and they should be reviewed in detail with the hospital's medical records or information management department.

5. *Restraints in Acute Medical and Surgical Care:* This is the first of two standards relating to the use of restraints. In effect, this standard defines what constitutes a restraint and the conditions under which its use is permitted. This standard generally, but not exclusively, applies to the acute care and surgical settings. Hospitals are mandated to provide ongoing staff education relating to the use of restraints. Developing and implementing a formal training protocol is essential to establish compliance.

6. *Seclusion and Restraint for Behavior Management:* This second "restraint" standard was enacted in response to a series of articles published in the *Hartford (Massachusetts) Courant* newspaper that reported a series of patient injuries and deaths within psychiatric care settings resulting from both the apparent abuse and misuse of restraints and/or seclusion. Specific requirements regarding issuing and monitoring restraint orders are detailed, including requiring a "licensed independent practitioner" to personally see the patient and evaluate the need for restraint or seclusion within one hour after initiating its use. This particular requirement drew a quick response from the health care community. Risk managers are advised to see the "one hour" issue as only one element of the overall standard and not to lose sight of the need to comply with the rest. Finally, patient deaths resulting from the use of restraints, or while the patient was in seclusion, are to be reported to HCFA.

Risk Management Implications   Nothing can substitute for a complete review of each element of each of these standards. As HCFA and the OIG have left the development of much of the means of compliance to the hospitals, leeway is given to facilities to develop measures that will work best for themselves. Compliance must be a facility-wide initiative. Due to the ambiguous nature of some of these standards, advice from counsel is suggested (although they are often just as much in the dark as anyone else). In any event, compliance with these COPs, very much as with the case of the EMTALA statute noted previously, will likely take some time to fully mature, although they went into effect on August 2, 1999. As is the case with all conditions of participation in the Medicare program, failure to comply with all or part of the law may result in HCFA's terminating the facility's Medicare/Medicaid provider agreement.

Safe Medical Devices Act of 1990

The purpose of the federal Food and Drug Administration (FDA) is to protect the public health by regulating commerce involving foods, drugs, medical devices, and related commodities. As part of the Safe Medical Devices Act of 1990 (SMDA, Medical Device Amendments of 1992: 21 USC 360i[a]; 21 CFR 803), the FDA gathers information regarding the safety of medical devices, including adverse incidents attributed to their use. In 1984, under authority granted by the federal Food, Drug and Cosmetic Act of 1938 and the 1976 Medical Device Amendments, the FDA issued reporting regulations for medical device manufacturers. Subsequently, the agency discovered that the number of device-related incidents that resulted in injury or death was underreported, especially those incidents that occurred in hospitals. In response, the FDA sought congressional support for a more stringent set of reporting requirements. As a result of the enactment of the SMDA, final *device-tracking* regulations went into effect on August 16, 1993, and final *reporting* regulations were published on December 11, 1995, and went into effect on July 31, 1996. An excellent overview of the reporting requirements ("Reporting Problems with Medical Devices") was prepared by the Office of Surveillance and Biometrics of the FDA's Center for Devices and Radiological Health.

This law applies to hospitals, ambulatory surgical facilities, nursing homes, home health care agencies, ambulance providers, rescue squads, rehabilitation facilities, psychiatric facilities, and all outpatient diagnostic and treatment facilities that are not physicians' offices. When a death or serious injury occurs that may be related to the use of a medical device, facilities must file "MedWatch" medical device reports (MDRs) (see Exhibit 4.2 on page 108) with manufacturers or directly with the FDA if the name of the manufacturer is unknown. All deaths are also reportable to the FDA. When advised of adverse incidents attributed to, or associated with, the use of their product or device, manufacturers are obligated to submit MDRs to the FDA as well.[7] *Note:* Exempt from reporting are physicians' offices, chiropractors, optometrists, nurse practitioners, employee health clinics, dental offices, and freestanding care units.

A reportable event is defined as ". . . information [from any source] that reasonably suggests that a device has or may have caused or contributed to a death or serious injury. . . ." "Serious injury" refers to an injury that (1) is life threatening, (2) results in permanent impairment of a body function or permanent damage to a body structure, or (3) requires medical or surgical intervention to preclude such permanent impairment or damage.

Note: To preserve any confidentiality protections that may be afforded by state law, investigations involving potential SMDA reportable events should occur under the auspices of a protected peer review or administrative structure, if such exists. The investigation team may be brought together on an ad hoc basis to conduct the investigation, prepare (or direct the preparation of) a report to the FDA—if one is warranted—and submit their findings to the board or other responsible body through their primary committee. As committee findings and the MDR reports may reflect sensitive liability and/or peer review information, efforts at establishing whatever protections may exist are highly recommended.

Reporting   Using the MedWatch program, device users must report to manufacturers (or to the FDA if the manufacturer's identity is not known) within ten days of becoming aware of an event involving a serious patient injury or death using the MedWatch form (Exhibit 4.2). The FDA must be notified as well within the same time frame in cases where a death is involved. A facility "becomes aware" when any medical personnel employed by or affiliated with a user facility learns that a potentially reportable event has occurred. In addition, facilities are required to report to the FDA semiannually (January 1 and July 1) a summary of MDR reports made during the previous six months.

Upon learning of a "reportable" incident involving the use of their product or device, manufacturers are also required to submit an MDR to the FDA. At the FDA's request, a "Five-Day" report must be submitted by a manufacturer when the FDA believes that immediate intervention is called for to prevent risk of harm to the public health.

Submitting Reports   Report forms, instructions, and event code books are available from the FDA. On-line submissions also are acceptable with prior approval from the agency. Although facilities are obligated to maintain copies of these reports for a minimum of two years, risk managers are advised to keep them for at least five years (or longer) in recognition of any liability issues that may be present. Ask counsel, your insurer, and your state hospital association for guidance in this regard.

Medical Device Tracking Rules   The SMDA also requires the tracking of certain medical devices, such as implantable items, from the point of manufacture to the end user. The goal is to protect public health and safety by facilitating the transmission of newly acquired device safety information, such as product recall data.

Although primary responsibility for tracking rests with manufacturers, others in the distribution chain (physicians, retail pharmacies, hospitals, and so on) have responsibilities as well. Hospitals, for example, are asked to submit to the FDA patient-identifying information of patients who receive implants. The FDA does not make such information available to the public.

Risk Management Implications   Identifying factors that directly or indirectly contribute to patient endangerment is a fundamental component of the risk management process. Complying with the reporting requirements of this law compels the health care sector to actively participate in an important oversight process that directly impacts risk management efforts. The Manufacturers and User Facility Device Experience (MAUDE) database[8] is an excellent source of information relating to the FDA's adverse event tracking efforts.

Mammography Quality Standards Act of 1992

The Mammography Quality Standards Act of 1992 (42 USC 263b, 21 CFR parts 16, 900, 1308 and 1312, 42 CFR part 498) was reauthorized by Congress in 1998 and final regulations went into effect on April 22, 1999. This law was enacted in response to the public's increasing awareness and concern about breast cancer screening and treatment. Although the law focuses primarily on issues related to improving the diagnostic and technical standards of mammography, the importance of communicating results to referring practitioners and their patients is addressed as well. As of this writing, there are more than 10,000 facilities in the United States and its territories that are certified under this law to provide mammography services. If your organization is one of them, or intends to become one, a close review of this complex law is necessary.

This law applies to facilities, practitioners, and specified personnel involved in the provision of breast cancer screening, diagnosis, and treatment, and covers a variety of areas. Specific requirements imposed on facilities and identified professionals by this law include:

- Ensuring the competency and qualifications of interpreting physicians, medical physicists, and radiological technicians.

- Maintaining facility accreditation in connection with annual facility compliance inspections performed by the FDA or any one of five FDA-approved accrediting bodies.[9]

- Adhering to specified equipment testing and maintenance protocols.

- Developing and implementing quality assurance and quality control programs.

- Reporting mammogram results to the referring health care provider as well as to the patient in a prescribed manner.

Risk Management Implications   The FDA has published an MQSA guidance document[10] that is an excellent resource for facilities and practitioners to help in understanding the many facets of this complex law. As is the case with virtually every law, the risk manager is not expected to be an expert on each of its constituent elements, but rather to understand its basic tenets including the penalties or other risks of not complying. If your facility falls within the application of this law, an in-depth review of all required elements of compliance should be carried out, including ongoing review to identify additions or other changes.

The Newborns' and Mothers' Health Protection Act of 1996

In the face of the increasing incidence of "drive-through" short-stay deliveries, Congress enacted the Newborns' and Mothers' Health Protection Act of 1996 (42 USC 300gg–300gg-63, 300gg-91, 92; 42 CFR 144.101, 146.130). The law provides protections for mothers and their newborns from restrictions that may be imposed by managed care organizations (MCOs) and health plans on hospital lengths-of-stay permitted following childbirth.

It applies to group health plans, health insurance issuers in the group and individual markets, obstetricians, and facilities providing obstetrical services. Health plans and health insurance issuers may not restrict covered benefits for a mother and her newborn to less than forty-eight hours following a vaginal delivery and ninety-six hours following a cesarean section. Discharging a patient within a period of time *less* than provided for by this law is permitted only with the mutual agreement of the attending provider and mother.

Health plans and other insurers are prohibited from pressuring or coercing the mother or her provider to agree to an early discharge. In addition, providers are not required to obtain an MCO's or insurer's prior authorization for these prescribed lengths-of-stay. State laws that address this issue may supercede this federal statute as long as they meet one or more of the following requirements:

- Minimum allowable lengths-of-stay meet or exceed the forty-eight- or ninety-six hour requirements.

- Coverage provided by health plans and insurers comply with guidelines established by the American College of Obstetricians and Gynecologists, the American Academy of Pediatrics, or any other established professional medical association.

- Decisions regarding the post-partum length-of-stay are left exclusively up to the provider in consultation with the mother.

Risk Management Implications   Violation of these requirements may result in the suspension or termination of a health plan or health insurer's license. Physicians, nurse midwives, or other licensed providers who fail to comply with this law run the risk of being accused of unprofessional conduct, fraud, or professional negligence. As a final note, hospitals are *not* considered "providers" under this act.

National Organ Transplant Act of 1984

Prior to the enactment of the National Organ Transplant Act of 1984 (42 USC 273 NOTA. HCFA Conditions of Participation for Organ, Tissue and Eye Donation [June 22, 1998, 63 *Federal Register* 33856] Amendments to Final Rule, Oct. 1999), the system within the United States for allocating and distributing organs for transplant was quite fragmented. By enacting NOTA, Congress established a set of unified standards to be followed by organ procurement organizations (OPOs) throughout the country. To implement the act, the Organ Procurement Transplant Network (OPTN) was established and is currently operated under contract with the Department of Health and Human Services (DHHS) by the United Network for Organ Sharing (UNOS). In 1997, the National Organ and Tissue Donation Initiative was also launched in support of this general program. HCFA enacted a new regulation[11] that required hospitals to work collaboratively with local organ procurement organizations to enhance access to potential donors. Amendments to the Final Rule relating to the management and oversight of the OPTN were released by HCFA on October 18, 1999.[12] These amendments were the result of a study performed at the behest of Congress by the National Academy of Science's Institute of Medicine. The amendments established greater accountability of the OPTN to develop and implement improved criteria for organ allocation, mandated the establishment of an Advisory Committee on Organ Transplantation, revised and clarified oversight responsibility for program enforcement, developed specific performance criteria, and made changes with respect to the composition of the OPTN Board of Directors.

This law applies to hospitals, transplant centers, and organ procurement organizations. Member hospitals of the OPTN working in collaboration with their regional OPO, tissue, and eye bank must:

- Implement a working agreement with the OPO by which it will notify them of individuals either whose deaths are imminent or who have died. The responsibility for determining whether a patient is a suitable donor rests with the OPO, not the hospital.

- Develop a similar agreement with at least one tissue bank and one eye bank.

- Collaborate with the OPO to inform the families of potential donors of their options with respect to organ donation. Although this activity is mandated to hospitals by law, it should always be carried out in a manner that is sensitive to the circumstances and to the cultural or religious beliefs of the family.

- Work with the OPO to educate hospital staff on identifying and reporting potential donors, tissue testing, and so on.

Risk Management Implications   As noted, these regulations are Conditions of Participation in Medicare and Medicaid programs. Non-compliance may not only result in loss of the facility's Medicare/Medicaid provider agreement, but loss of participation within the OPTN.

Protection of Human Research Subjects

Protection of Human Research Subjects Act:

- (45 CFR part 46) These regulations relate to human subject research conducted or supported by federal departments or agencies (for example, the Food and Drug Administration). Specific categories of research that are exempted from regulation under this section are also identified. The section further defines the applicability of state laws and regulations, as well as those of foreign countries and international treaties, to human subject research. This section also establishes the standards for Institutional Review Boards (IRBs) including composition, operations, research review, records, and so on.

- (21 CFR parts 50, 56, 312 and 812) These regulations address various additional issues primarily relating to research performed under the guidance of the FDA. Among the many issues addressed within these regulations are the various requirements relating to obtaining a research subject's informed consent, mandatory reporting, the investigational use of new drugs and devices, and a delineation of penalties that may be imposed for failure to comply with these requirements including, but not limited to, disqualification of an IRB from further FDA-approved research activities, as well as exposure of both the research investigator and his or her institution to claims of civil liability.

Risk Management Implications   Risk managers in facilities that carry out research protocols must become familiar with these regulations as they may be asked to serve on committees that function as institutional review boards (IRBs). Members of IRBs need to develop an in-depth understanding of requirements relating to patient informed consent and research-related record keeping. Non-compliance may result in the loss of federal (and private) funding of the research activities, as well as investigation and possible sanctions imposed by the state licensing agency.

············

FRAUD AND ABUSE

Following are several examples of laws that deal with the issues of fraud and abuse within the health care industry.

Health Insurance Portability and Accountability Act of 1996 (HIPAA)

Also known as the Kassebaum-Kennedy bill, this intricate and far-reaching legislation (Public Law 104-191, 104th Congress, 26 USC Subchapter A) amends elements of the Employee Retirement Income Security Act (ERISA), the Public Health Service Act

(PHSA), and the Internal Revenue Code of 1986. The act establishes a variety of health insurance coverage protections including access to insurance markets for small businesses and the self-employed, access and transferability of coverage for individuals who change jobs, and access by individuals who have pre-existing medical conditions. The establishment of individual Medical Savings Accounts (MSAs) is another feature of this law. However, the focus of this review is Title II of the act, "Preventing Health Care Fraud and Abuse."

In short, HIPAA makes the commission of health care fraud a federal criminal offense. The act establishes and funds a new health care fraud and abuse control program overseen by the OIG of DHHS. The operating capital for the department's enforcement efforts (for example, investigations, audits, inspections, provider and consumer education, and prosecutions) comes from the Health Care Fraud and Abuse Control Account, which was established specifically for this purpose. The account is funded from civil monetary penalties (CMPs), criminal fines, and proceeds from the disposition of forfeited property and assets obtained in connection with enforcement actions taken by the OIG.

The Health Care Integrity and Protection Data Bank   Section 221(a) of the act establishes a data collection program involving "adverse" actions taken against individual providers, manufacturers, and suppliers. Such actions include (1) civil judgements (*not* including professional liability actions, which fall within the purview of the National Practitioner Data Bank) obtained against suppliers and providers in either state or federal court, (2) criminal convictions, (3) actions taken by federal or state agencies responsible for licensing or certifying practitioners, providers, or suppliers, (4) exclusion from federal or state health care programs, and (5) any other actions that DHHS determines are reportable. Settlements in which no findings or admissions of liability have been made are excluded from reporting. Mandatory reporting is required only of health plans and, as indicated, involved federal and state agencies. Providers, practitioners, suppliers, and manufacturers are not required to self-report, but may query the data bank. (See the chapter on data management for more information.)

Medicare Integrity Program   This program permits DHHS to contract with outside entities, known as "intermediaries," to carry out various program oversight functions, such as (1) reviewing utilization, fraud prevention, and general program compliance activities related to individuals or entities who furnish items or services subject to Medicare reimbursement; (2) auditing cost reports relating to payments made for services provided to program beneficiaries; (3) determining whether payments made to Medicare secondary payers (for example, Medicare managed care plans) were appropriate; (4) providing broad-based education to providers and beneficiaries regarding payment integrity and benefit quality assurance issues; and (5) developing and periodically updating a list of safe harbors (or, permitted activities) and durable medical equipment items that are subject to prior authorization requirements.

Risk Management Implications   Suffice it to say that the federal government is serious about its efforts to control fraud in the health care setting. In summary, Section 242 of the act provides jail time and/or fines for anyone convicted of (1) defrauding, attempting, or conspiring to defraud *any* health care benefit program (not just Medicare or Medicaid); (2) theft or embezzlement of money, securities, or other assets of a health care plan; (3) making false or fraudulent statements or representations relating to the

delivery or payment of health care benefits or services; (4) obstructing in any way a criminal investigation into alleged health care offenses; or (5) laundering money in connection with any federal health care offense.

False Claims Act

This statute (31 USC Section 3729) is the oldest one represented in this chapter. First enacted in 1863 to combat fraud committed by suppliers to the Union army during the Civil War, the act, also called the Lincoln Law due to the president's strong support, has had a checkered history. After remaining dormant for years, the act resurfaced briefly during World War II and then, most notably, at the height of the Pentagon procurement scandals of the 1980s. The law was amended in 1986 and has played a key role in the government's fraud and abuse control activities ever since.

In a brief summary, the act prohibits anyone from submitting a false or fraudulent claim for payment to the federal government. Although the act defines other illegal activities as well, its use by HCFA in responding to fraudulent Medicare/Medicaid claims has put it in the forefront of health care fraud abuse and control activities. One of the better known elements of the act provides for recognition of the right of citizens—called "relators" or more commonly, "whistleblowers"—to bring private civil actions (on behalf of the government) against suspected violators. These lawsuits are known as *qui tam* actions, from the Latin *"qui tam pro domino rege quam pro se ipso in hac parte sequitir,"* which means, "he who brings an action for the king as well as for himself." The government has broad leeway in how it investigates and prosecutes *qui tam* actions. In the event of monetary recovery by the government, the relator is entitled to at least 15 percent, but no more than 25 percent, of the proceeds of recovery. Even if no prosecution occurs, the court may still award the relator a percentage of proceeds recovered by way of settlement.

Risk Management Implications   A *qui tam* action brought by a former employee of a well-known provider of health care services helped spark the government's current fraud and abuse control efforts. Risk managers must be keenly aware of the penalties for submitting fraudulent claims to the government. Even if the claim is submitted with no intent to defraud, if it is subsequently determined that it was submitted "in deliberate ignorance of the truth or falsity of the information," or "in reckless disregard of the truth or falsity of the information," a violation may be found which may, in turn, result in the severe penalties provided for under the law.

Civil Monetary Penalties, Assessments, and Exclusions

This federal regulation (42 CFR Section 1003) defines the penalties associated with filing inappropriate claims under the Medicare, Medicaid, Maternal and Child Health Services, or Social Services Block Grant programs. Penalties may involve the payment of CMPs, forfeiture of assets, or exclusion of a practitioner or provider from participating in the Medicare and Medicaid programs Additionally, guidance from HCFA has reaffirmed that such penalties may be applied to providers who hire or do business with individuals or entities that have been excluded by HCFA from the Medicare/Medicaid programs. Risk managers should be particularly sensitive to the fact that such fines and penalties are invariably excluded from coverage under almost every form of insurance contract. In addition, a number of prominent organizations have gone out of business or divested themselves of considerable holdings in response to penalties assessed by federal regulators.

············

EMPLOYMENT AND NON-DISCRIMINATION

Although there are more than twenty-five federal statutes that relate to employment matters, this chapter provides a review of just a few. The enforcement of several of these laws falls within the purview of the Equal Employment Opportunity Commission (EEOC). The EEOC's implementing regulations may be found at 29 CFR parts 1600–1691.

As each law represents a distinct employment practices liability (EPL) exposure, the risk manager should become familiar with them as the frequency of employment-related litigation is escalating rapidly. Please bear in mind that the following brief summaries of these laws do not, in any way, represent a comprehensive overview. A discussion of the Family and Medical Leave Act of 1993 is also included although its enforcement does not fall within the jurisdiction of the EEOC. An in-depth discussion of employment-related issues may be found later in the book.

Title VII of the Civil Rights Act of 1964

Commonly known simply as "Title VII"(42 USC 2000e et seq.), this act is one of the most important of a long line of employment laws enacted in the last century. Essentially, Title VII prohibits discrimination in employment based upon an individual's race, color, religion, sex, or national origin. Federal law requires employers to post notices detailing employee rights under these laws. Such notices must be accessible to employees with visual impairments as well.

Sexual Harassment   Among the most common allegations brought under the act are those that relate to sexual harassment. One type of harassment singled out under the act is called *quid pro quo* (something for something), and occurs when an employee's supervisor or other person in a position of authority, either implies or explicitly demands the employee's acquiescence in response to a sexual overture of any kind as a condition of continued employment, advancement, and so on. A claim characterized as reflecting a "hostile work environment" may arise if an employee is subjected to offensive, sexually related comments, writings, or pictures, for example. Multi-million-dollar judgements have been awarded in a number of high-profile cases arising from such conduct, including one for more than seven million dollars against the largest law firm in the world[13] and an eighty-one-million-dollar verdict against an international package delivery service.[14] One of the common denominators in most of these cases is management's persistent failure to establish and/or enforce a zero-tolerance environment for such behavior.

Employers are mandated to establish and strictly enforce anti-harassment policies and complaint procedures. Every employee should be provided with a copy of these documents. An anti-harassment policy should reflect (1) a clear and comprehensive explanation of prohibited conduct, (2) assurances that an employee who either reports an act of suspected harassment, or who participates in the investigation of such an allegation, will not be retaliated against, (3) how to file a complaint, (4) an assurance of confidentiality to the extent possible, and (5) an assurance that the employer will take any indicated corrective action if a finding that harassment is made.

Race and Color Discrimination   To put it simply, it is against the law to discriminate against an employee or a job applicant based upon her race or color. This prohibition is a cornerstone of Title VII as well as its predecessor, the Civil Rights Act of 1957. Discrimination may be alleged whenever someone believes that his race or color was unlawfully considered in the context of an application for employment, assignment, promotion, or other job-advancement opportunity. Allegations of ethnic or racial slurs, and sexist and other derogatory language are common elements found in hostile work environment claims. Employers and supervisors must be sensitive to the perceptions of job applicants and employees in this regard and, as is the case with any discriminatory behavior, establish a zero-tolerance climate at all levels of the organization.

National Origin Discrimination   Title VII also prohibits discrimination based upon an individual's birthplace, ancestry, culture, or "linguistic characteristics common to a specific ethnic group." Although employers are required by the Immigration Reform and Control Act (IRCA) of 1986 (Public Law 99-603) to ensure that employees are legally authorized to work in this country, requesting such verification only of applicants based upon their ancestry, accent, or place of birth may result in a violation of both Title VII and the IRCA. If your organization customarily asks applicants for evidence of such authorization, be certain that the request is made of *everyone*. By extension, requiring United States citizenship as a *condition* of application or promotion may also violate the IRCA. Seek input from an experienced human resources manager and/or labor attorney before implementing any "English only" language restrictions.

Religious Accommodation   Accommodating an employee's religious beliefs is required under Title VII unless the employer can establish that doing so will impose an "undue hardship." Claims relating to a "hostile work environment" can be made when employees feel that they are subjected to offensive proselytizing in the workplace, or that participation in certain religious activities are condoned, encouraged, or required by management unless, of course, such activities are part of the job description.

Fair Credit Reporting Act

This law (15 USC 1681 et seq. FCRA) addresses a couple of issues of particular significance to risk managers. The first provides rules for performing background checks on prospective employees. The second relates to investigating sexual harassment claims and is the focus of this discussion. In April 1999, an attorney for the Federal Trade Commission issued the opinion[15] that outside consultants (including attorneys) retained to perform or investigate allegations of sexual harassment meet the definition of a consumer reporting agency (CRA) as defined within the act and as such must comply with all rules applicable to CRAs.

If an employer elects to initiate a sexual harassment investigation of an employee using the services of a CRA, the employer must notify the target employee of the intent as well as obtain his written authorization to proceed. The disclosure must also inform the employee of his right to request the employer to disclose the nature and scope of the investigation. Once the report is completed, the CRA must provide a summary of the employee's rights under the law to the employer who, in turn, must certify that it recognizes the employee's rights, including the right to have a copy of the investigative report given to him should the employer elect to take an adverse employment action.

Risk Management Implications   The Federal Trade Commission's (FTC) opinion letter is just what it says it is—an opinion. However, such letters are generally given deference. Risk managers are cautioned to review the letter's implications with their organization's counsel and human resources manager. Due to the implications of this opinion, consultation with an attorney specializing in labor issues is advised. If an organization intends to use outside consultants or agencies to participate in sexual harassment investigations, it may consider having new employees authorize such investigations in writing at the time of hire. Another option simply remains to perform such investigations using only employees of the organization, thereby precluding the application of the FCRA. Unfortunately, depending upon the nature of the investigation, or *whom* you are investigating, this option may not always be possible or even desirable. As of this writing, legislative efforts are underway to address this important issue.

Civil Rights Act of 1991

In response to a series of United States Supreme Court rulings that were felt to have weakened the Civil Rights Act of 1964, Congress enacted amendments to the act that served to reverse elements of some of the Court's decisions. Among the changes enacted was shifting some of the burden of proof of the complaining party (plaintiff) to the respondent (defendant) when attempting to establish that one or more unfair employment practices had a "disparate impact" on a protected group of employees. The 1991 act also permits the complaining party to request a jury trial, and the opportunity to recover compensatory and punitive damages (as opposed to simply equitable relief) in cases where the respondent acted "with callous indifference to the federally protected rights of others." The act also establishes that an act of discrimination need not be the sole contributing factor to the violation under review, but merely that it was a contributing factor.

Americans with Disabilities Act

In 1990, Congress passed this landmark legislation. The intent of the Americans with Disabilities Act (ADA) (42 USC 12101) was to provide disabled citizens with equal opportunity rights. The act makes it unlawful to discriminate in employment against a qualified individual with a disability (QIWD). The ADA also prohibits discrimination against disabled individuals relating to access to state and local government services, public accommodations, transportation, and telecommunications. Following is a brief overview of the Title I employment highlights.

Who Is Subject to the ADA?   All employers with fifteen or more employees are subject to the nondiscrimination in employment provisions of the ADA. State and local government employers have no employee minimum to trigger these requirements.

Who Is Protected under the ADA?   QIWDs are protected from employment discrimination. A disabled person is regarded as someone who has (or has a record of, or is regarded as having) a physical or mental impairment that substantially limits a major life activity. He must have a substantial impairment, defined as a significant restriction on a major life activity. The disabled person also must be qualified to perform the essential functions of the job with or without reasonable accommodation.

How Is the ADA Enforced?   Complaints falling within Title I are referred to the Equal Employment Opportunity Commission (EEOC). Absent a state or local law with specific filing deadlines, a charge of discrimination must be filed within 180 days. The available remedies mirror those available under Title VII of the Civil Rights Act of 1964.

Risk managers involved in human resources issues should review all state and local antidiscrimination laws that may also apply.

The ADA requires that places of public accommodation (such as hospitals, physicians' offices, long-term care facilities, and so on) be accessible to disabled persons. As such, it would be prudent for risk managers to suggest that an ADA analysis be made at the time plans for new construction are reviewed, renovations are contemplated, and when realty is leased or purchased.

Title III of the ADA also includes requirements for places of public accommodation to ensure that the disabled are not treated differently due to the absence of "auxiliary aids and services," which include interpreters, readers, specialized equipment, and so on. An entity may be exempted from developing accommodation measures if it can demonstrate that doing so would alter the nature of the business or be unduly burdensome.

Risk Management Implications   Risk managers should bear in mind that there may be complementary state laws on this issue. In addition, the U.S. Supreme Court and a number of lower courts have made numerous rulings on ADA cases over the past several years. Risk managers are advised to keep abreast of these decisions and to work closely with the human resources department, environmental services, planning department, and labor counsel, if available, to ensure compliance.

Age Discrimination in Employment Act

The ADEA—not to be confused with the ADA—was enacted in 1967 and amended in 1974. In 1996, the ADEA cautioned employers, employment agencies, and labor organizations not to use an individual's age alone as a factor in hiring, advancement, recruiting, or other work-related activities. The act does acknowledge the existence of bona fide occupational qualifications, seniority systems, and similar age-based criteria that may be taken into account under defined circumstances. However, restrictive hiring notices, conditions of employment, pension benefit plan rules, and so on are among the areas that are specifically addressed by this law.

The Family and Medical Leave Act of 1993

In response to the changing dynamics of family life and the perception that employers often fail to take into account employees' responsibilities to their families, this law ([FMLA] 29 USC 2601 et seq., 25 CFR 825.100 et seq) was enacted to extend a measure of recognition and accommodation of these issues. FMLA specifically recognizes that a disproportionate share of the responsibility for family care-taking falls on women. Accordingly, the act serves to "even the playing field" in a manner consistent with the Equal Protection Clause of the Fourteenth Amendment.

The act applies to employees who have been employed for at least twelve months and for at least 1,250 hours of service during the previous twelve-month period. The act encompasses employers who have employed fifty or more employees during each of the twenty or more work weeks in the current or preceding calendar year.

The FMLA entitles an eligible employee to up to twelve weeks of leave during any twelve-month period for any one or more of the following reasons:

1. Childbirth and the care of the newborn.
2. Adoption.

3. To care for a seriously ill spouse, child, or parent.

4. To accommodate any health condition of the employee that precludes her from performing the functions of her job.

A sign or poster displaying information relating to employees' FMLA rights must be posted conspicuously at the worksite.

During leave periods, an employee's position remains protected and the benefits that the employee is otherwise entitled to must continue to be provided. Although the twelve weeks allowed is cumulative, time taken for childbirth or adoption-related reasons may not be taken intermittently, or on a reduced leave schedule, unless the employee and employer mutually agree to it. However, intermittent leave or a reduced schedule must be accommodated by the employer for requests of leave taken for purposes of caring for seriously ill family members, or the employee herself.

If, however, an employee requests intermittent leave, or a reduced leave schedule, for these purposes, the employer may require her to transfer temporarily to an available alternative position for which she is qualified. This position must have equivalent pay and benefits of the position the she has temporarily vacated, and must better accommodate her needs for the modified work schedule. If an employer provides paid leave for fewer than the twelve weeks provided for under the act, it is not required to pay for time off taken under the act that is not otherwise covered under the established employee benefit plan.

The employee is obligated to give his employer at least thirty days' notice when taking such leave is foreseeable. In addition, an employer may require that the employee's request for leave be supported by certification by a health care provider. If the employer doubts the validity of this certification, it may require, at its own expense, that the employee obtain a second opinion from a provider designated or approved by the employer. Recertification by a health care provider may be requested by the employer "on a reasonable basis." Upon completion of the FMLA leave, an employee may be required to provide evidence from his health care provider that he is able to go back to work.

Risk Management Implications   Violations of the act are common due to an inadequate understanding among many employers, supervisors, and human resources professionals of its often complex procedural requirements. Management and supervisory staff must commit to learning, and complying with, the act's mandates, or run the risk of lawsuits filed by employees, and fines imposed by the Department of Labor. As there are notable areas of overlap between FMLA and the ADA, risk managers and human resource professionals are advised to develop a sound understanding of the elements of both laws, or run the considerable risk attendant to noncompliance.

....

MISCELLANEOUS

Following are several examples of laws that affect the health care industry in various areas.

Medicare Regulations for Long-Term Care Facilities

Since the original legislation and regulations (42 CFR 483; 42 CFR 488; 42 USC 1395i-3) were enacted, long-term care has been the recipient of increasing attention by federal and state authorities. In 1998, HCFA's Office of the Inspector General (OIG) published "Quality of Care in Nursing Homes: An Overview"[16] which reflected that although the overall number of deficiencies found during nursing facility surveys was decreasing, the number of "quality of care" and other serious deficiencies was increasing. Long-term care facilities, along with the rest of the health care industry, came under increasing surveillance by the OIG with respect to allegations of Medicare billing irregularities. In the October 29, 1999, edition of the *Federal Register* (vol. 64, no. 209), the OIG published its "Draft OIG Compliance Program Guidance for Nursing Facilities," which delineates their expectations with respect to efforts by facilities to curb fraud and abuse. HCFA has notified states to crack down on facilities that are found to have repeatedly violated health and safety requirements. HCFA's Web site (www.medicare.gov/Nhcompare/Home.asp) provides consumers with information regarding residents' health status (including the prevalence of bedsores, incontinence, and other conditions) at every Medicare/Medicaid-certified nursing facility.

In brief, nursing facilities have been ordered, as a condition of maintaining their Medicare/Medicaid provider agreements, to (1) develop initiatives to improve the overall level of care provided (including special focus on reducing the use of restraints whenever possible), (2) reduce the incidence of bedsores and malnutrition, and (3) ensure that all rights entitled to by patients are recognized and supported in practice and not just relegated to a sign posted in the front office. Patients have the right to:

- Information about their physical condition, medical benefits, and associated costs.
- Access to a physician.
- Copies of their medical records.
- Active participation in making treatment decisions, including refusal of recommended treatment.
- Freedom from physical restraints and psychoactive drugs that are not required as part of the medical plan of care.
- The ability to file formal complaints about infractions of any rights.

The rules also impose certain staffing requirements on facilities, such as nursing coverage, physician examinations, and follow-up visits. In addition, the regulations require facilities to provide formal training and certification of nursing assistants, as well as to establish a quality assurance (QA) committee that meets at least quarterly.

Implementing a comprehensive compliance program that addresses identification and prevention of fraud should be a key priority. In support of this objective, the OIG published its "Compliance Program Guidance for Nursing Facilities" in the March 16, 2000 issue of the *Federal Register* (vol. 65, no. 52). This article may be accessed on the Internet at the OIG's "Compliance Program Guidance" page: www.dhhs.gov/progorg/oig/modcomp/index.htm.[17]

Risk Management Implications   Recent enforcement actions have made headlines across the country. Enforcement regulations enacted in 1995 empower survey agencies (either the state agency and/or HCFA) to impose a wide range of sanctions (including civil money penalties or fines of up to $10,000 per day), denial of payment for new admissions, and termination from the Medicare and Medicaid programs on noncompliant providers. Sanctions imposed by the regulators will depend on the agency's characterization of the level and pervasiveness of harm. The flexibility and speed with which the new sanctions may be imposed is a change from the old rules. As not all survey actions are subject to appeal, it is important for providers of long-term care services and their risk managers to understand the regulations, participate actively in the survey process, and maintain an ongoing dialogue with reviewers. Above all, providers must be prepared. State inspectors, employing new inspection protocols, have been told by the HCFA that they must stagger surveys and conduct visits on weekends, early mornings, and evenings, the times when quality, safety, and staffing problems are most likely to be apparent.

Risk managers should become familiar with the JCAHO's current standards as reflected in the Comprehensive Accreditation Manual for Long Term Care (CAMLTC). Although all elements of the standards are important, of particular focus by risk managers are the sections reflecting the "dimensions of performance"—that is, the nature and extent of services provided residents as well as the effectiveness of service delivery. Credentialing practices associated with all licensed "independent practitioners" also should be reviewed to ensure that they are carried out thoroughly and consistently.

Health Maintenance Organizations Act

Two pieces of federal legislation are of particular significance to managed care organizations (MCOs). The first is the Federal HMO Act, (42 USC 300e, 42 CFR 417.1 et seq.), passed in 1973, that promoted the growth of prepaid health care organizations by requiring most employers to offer an HMO option to employees if a federally qualified HMO was available. This act describes the characteristics of a federally qualified HMO, the basis for providing services to Medicare recipients, and the scope of offerings made to senior citizen HMO subscribers.

Employee Retirement and Income Security Act

The second piece of legislation relating to MCOs is the Employee Retirement and Income Security Act, or ERISA (29 USC 1001). Risk managers with responsibility for managed care operations should be intimately familiar with this 1974 federal statute. Although the purpose of ERISA was to standardize the administrative functions of employee welfare benefit plans throughout the country, ERISA also established a federal preemption of state laws that cover plan benefits. The practical effect of the ERISA preemption was the removal of lawsuits filed in connection with the provision of plan benefits from state courts to federal courts, thereby limiting the few remedies available to plaintiffs to those provided under this law. Although there have been a number of high-profile, high-dollar lawsuits involving managed care plans, they have usually involved health plan enrollees who were employees of governmental agencies, whose health care plans are not covered under ERISA. However, a number of important court decisions throughout the United States have eroded some of the MCO's protections afforded by ERISA. Texas and California are among a growing number of states that have enacted legislation that now permits health plan enrollees to sue their MCOs, in defiance of the ERISA preemption. Although court challenges have been filed to overturn some of these new laws, it appears that MCOs may find themselves more accountable for treatment decisions than ever before as the plaintiffs' attorneys try out new theories of liability to penetrate the shield of the ERISA preemption.

Risk Management Implications Remember, health plans may deny payment for services, but they may not deny a patient access to the service itself. To help lessen your organization's liability exposure within this area of law, ensure that staff understand their independent duty of care to their patients as health care providers and patient advocates. Staff should document all of their efforts in contesting what they reasonably believe to be inappropriate treatment denials. Such documentation should, at a minimum, include a description of the information provided to support the appeal and the subsequent response by the MCO or plan representative. Staff must advise their patients of treatment denials made by their health plans and review with them reasonable alternative courses of treatment that may be available, irrespective of whether the health plan may cover it or not. Again, these discussions should be thoroughly within the patient record.

Nuclear Regulatory Commission

Established under the auspices of the Atomic Energy Act of 1954, the federal Nuclear Regulatory Commission (NRC) (42 USC 2011 et seq.; 10 CFR 35) established rules for the handling, storage, and use of radioactive substances (by-product material) within the health care environment. Part 35 of Title 10 of the CFR (Medical Use of By-Product Material)[18] provides a detailed set of instructions for the management of by-product material in the health care setting.

Among the many issues covered by the regulations are:

- Human subject safety (including informed consent requirements).
- Reporting misadministrations of nuclear by-product material to the local NRC Regional Office within fifteen days of discovery.
- Extensive staff training requirements.
- The establishment of a quality management program.
- Provision of penalties for violations.

The role of the facility's radiation safety officer is defined as well as facility's detailed record-keeping responsibilities. Due to the enormous risk attendant to these services, continual monitoring of these services is essential.

Risk Management Implications   Risk managers of facilities that provide diagnostic or therapeutic services using radioactive substances are advised to familiarize themselves with the applicable regulations. The rigorous monitoring and reporting requirements found within the regulations must be adhered to or the facility faces loss of its NRC license, the implications of which are considerable.

Violations of the regulations generally invite swift response by the NRC. In 1999, a facility in Michigan was the focus of an NRC investigation arising from the misadministration of iodine-131 used in the treatment of a patient with thyroid carcinoma. Instead of receiving 150 millicuries as ordered, the patient was administered 100 millicuries. After realizing his mistake, the technician deliberately altered the prescribing physician's written order to cover up the error. Subsequently, the physician discovered the alteration and notified hospital administration who, in turn, notified the NRC's Regional Office as required by regulation. The NRC's Office of Investigations responded within two weeks, found that deliberate misconduct had been made by the technician, and issued (through the Office of Enforcement) a Confirmatory Order requiring that individual to notify any current or prospective NRC-licensed employer of the findings of the results of the investigation.

Risk Management Regulation

Risk managers in a few states have their professional practice regulated under specific risk management laws. In 1987, the American Society for Healthcare Risk Management (ASHRM) developed and published a model risk management program. Although ASHRM does not endorse a state legislative scheme for health care risk management, its model prescribes the elements of an acceptable health care risk management program. Those elements include a system for identifying, evaluating, and handling risk exposures; employment of a qualified risk manager; data sharing and continuing education; and, most important, commitment from the governing body to the risk management effort (see Appendix 4.1 on page 111). In addition, ASHRM developed sample statutory language for confidentiality of all risk management-related documents and immunity for participants in risk management activities. As the states overhaul their medical malpractice statutory schemes, these concepts are gradually working their way into state code books.

·············

CHILD AND ELDER ABUSE REPORTING

The following breaks down a few of the laws related to the responsibilities of those in the health care industry to report suspected abuse.

Children

It has been estimated that 3.195 million cases of suspected child abuse or neglect were reported to state Child Protective Service (CPS) agencies in 1997.[19] These cases fell under several categories: neglect (57 percent), physical abuse (26 percent), sexual abuse (7 percent), emotional maltreatment (4 percent), and other miscellaneous causes (11 percent).[20] Every state has enacted, to one degree or another, mandatory reporting requirements relating to suspected child abuse and neglect. Among the notable federal initiatives in this area are the Child Abuse Accountability Act; the Child Abuse, Domestic Violence, Adoption and Family Services Act of 1992; the Child Abuse Prevention, Treatment and Adoption Reform Act of 1978; and the Child Abuse Victims' Rights Act of 1986. Although state statutes often differ in their definition of terms, most define abuse as representing harm or threatened harm to a child's health or welfare.[21] Abuse can be characterized in many ways: physical injury, sexual contact, sexual exploitation, and so on. Neglect is generally defined in terms of the deprivation of adequate food, clothing, shelter, or medical care. Exceptions to such reporting do exist and generally relate to children who are under treatment by spiritual means.

Elder Adults

The National Elder Abuse Incidence Study,[22] conducted in 1996 by the National Center on Elder Abuse and funded by the Department of Health and Human Service's Administration for Children and Families and the Administration on Aging, attempted to determine the scope of domestic elder abuse and neglect in this country. Because the legislative mandate limited the study to the assessment and preservation of violence in domestic settings, elders living in nursing homes, assisted-living facilities, and other institutional or group facilities were not included in the study. Information on substantiated cases of abuse or neglect was gathered from Adult Protective Service (APS) agencies and other sources from twenty counties in fifteen states. The study confirmed that reported cases of abuse and neglect (including self-neglect) represent only "the tip of the iceberg." An estimated 551,000 elderly persons, aged sixty years and over, were the victims of abuse and/or neglect in domestic settings in 1996. The study further estimated that only approximately 115,000 (21 percent) of these cases were ever reported and substantiated by state APS agencies.

Risk Management Implications   Risk managers must become familiar with all mandatory reporting requirements, including permitted statutory exceptions, relating to child, elder, and dependent adult abuse and neglect. Hospital staff, including medical staff, must be advised (and reminded periodically) of their individual reporting obligations under your state's laws. To encourage reporting, many states have enacted immunity provisions protecting the reporters from civil liability. Even the laws that regulate the disclosure of patient's records related to federally funded substance abuse treatment programs,[23] expressly permit reporting suspected child abuse to state agencies. Significant penalties up to and including the loss of licensure, allegations of unprofessional conduct, and exposure to civil litigation are possible for individuals or facilities that fail to comply with these important reporting obligations.

INSURANCE LAWS AND REGULATIONS

Although federal regulations (such as the Health Insurance Portability and Accountability Act [HIPAA] and the Employee Retirement Income Security Act [ERISA] described earlier) have a significant impact on insurance practices within the country, state insurance codes define operationally how the business of insurance is carried out. Commercial insurance, captives (and other self-insurance programs), managed care plans, and other insurance mechanisms are generally tightly regulated. Risk managers are strongly encouraged to familiarize themselves with the regulatory controls over the insurance programs in place within their organization. When considering establishing alternative risk financing strategies for the organization, risk managers, in consultation with their corporate counsel and broker(s), must explore the many complex financial and legal implications. Contact your state department of insurance for information on the current regulatory initiatives that may affect your programs.

TORT REFORM

Since the appearance of the professional liability insurance crisis of the 1970s, the frequency of malpractice litigation has proliferated. In fact, the genesis of today's health care risk management profession can be traced directly to industry efforts to address the alarming rise in the number (and cost) of negligence lawsuits. From the beginning, efforts have been made by risk managers, insurers, and health care industry leaders to control the growth of this litigation. These efforts have generally taken the form of statutory controls. California's landmark Medical Injury Compensation Reform Act (MICRA) has served as a benchmark for other states' tort reform efforts. Enacted in 1975 as emergency legislation, MICRA established several basic tenets that influenced similar efforts throughout the country: (1) a cap (limit) of $250,000 was set for non-economic ("pain and suffering") damages, (2) allowing periodic payments of future damages in excess of

$50,000 were set to insure that a steady source of money remained in place to cover costs over time, (3) juries were allowed to have information on collateral sources of payment made to the patient/plaintiff to ensure that the plaintiff did not benefit from excessive financial remuneration from multiple sources, and (4) the rates of attorney's contingency fees were fixed by statute to ensure that plaintiffs were not taken advantage of by unscrupulous lawyers. Many states have established their own successful tort reforms efforts based upon this model.

Risk Management Implications The road to meaningful tort reform has been a rocky one. A number of state courts have overturned or curtailed all or part of many tort reform efforts. At the same time, 1999 saw a number of successful efforts throughout the country to control frivolous or excessive civil litigation. Risk managers should become very familiar the issues associated with tort reform initiatives in their states and, to the degree possible, managers should support efforts to establish reasonable and balanced means of resolving disputes and negligence claims. Examples include employing alternative dispute resolution techniques (such as arbitration or private judges) and working closely with injured patients and their families early on to reach an equitable and mutually satisfactory resolution to the dispute. Although a defense of nonmeritorious lawsuits should be provided whenever necessary, the many claims that reflect "gray" areas of liability should be addressed proactively and creatively. By so doing, the risk manager contributes to the successful loss control efforts of her program.

Professional Practice Acts

Risk managers are often called upon during the course of an investigation to consider "scope of practice" issues. For example, a question may arise as to whether a nurse, therapist, or other licensed health care professional performed an act that, under state statute, was outside the scope of professional practice as defined by her licensing board or agency. The state's pertinent professional practice act should be reviewed under such circumstances to help make such an assessment. From an insurance standpoint, coverage determinations are often dependent on such findings. For each group of health care professionals licensed by the state, laws and regulations define the scope of practice and outline the oversight authority vested in their professional regulatory boards. Professional practice regulatory boards are established by statute. Specific requirements regarding professional practice are generally found within both law and state regulation. They detail the process of licensure, including the state's requirements, if any, for mandatory continuing education, the definition of "unprofessional conduct" (such as unlawful use of controlled substances), and mandatory reporting requirements. For example, many states require a medical professional to report a colleague to the licensing board if there is a reasonable belief that the public welfare may be compromised as a result of the colleague's substance abuse.

Risk Management Implications A risk manager cannot always clearly assess the professional liability exposure present in a given situation unless she understands the standards of professional practice that are applied to the individual involved. A classic example is the scope of practice of nonphysician "qualified medical personnel" involved in performing medical screening examinations pursuant to the Emergency Treatment and Active Labor Act (EMTALA). In addition, familiarity with such standards is critical in controlling risk during the development and implementation of new and alternative treatment regimens. From an employment liability standpoint, state-imposed disciplinary and licensure mandates should be clearly understood by risk managers and human resources personnel alike.

PEER REVIEW

A hospital's responsibility to establish physician peer review stems from a series of well-publicized cases that arose in the 1970s and 1980s. Typical of these findings was that of the 3rd District Court of Appeals in *Elam v. College Park Hospital*[24] in which the court found that "a hospital is accountable, under the doctrine of corporate negligence, for negligently screening the competency of its medical staff to insure the adequacy of care rendered to its patients. . . . Furthermore, the hospital itself had a direct and independent responsibility to its patients of insuring . . . the quality of care provided." With the enactment of the Health Care Quality Improvement Act (HCQIA) in 1986 (covered earlier in this chapter) and the publicity associated with the United States Supreme Court's findings relating to an Oregon hospital's medical staff peer review committee's alleged anticompetitive activities (*Patrick v. Burget*),[25] the need for hospitals to establish a thorough and above-board peer review protocol was driven home.

The objective of peer review is to promote patient safety and well-being through the ongoing monitoring of physician performance. This obligation is generally vested in an organization's board of directors, who in turn delegates its operational elements to the medical staff. To encourage physician involvement in this process, a number of states have enacted laws that provide protection from civil liability for individuals who participate in peer review activities. At the federal level, the HCQIA provides similar protections.

Risk Management Implications   Confidentiality of peer review deliberations and records is provided for under the laws of many states as well as the HCQIA. Sometimes the confidentiality is provided through the application of a legal privilege to committee records. In others, the protection is afforded by establishing an immunity from subpoenas or other "discovery" arising out of civil litigation. Consequently, both hospital and medical staff should be reminded periodically that such protections are important in preserving the integrity of the peer review process, and that these often fragile, narrowly defined safeguards may be relinquished if the protected information is released inappropriately or otherwise used for purposes for which it was not intended. Depending upon the nature of your state's laws, consider having participants sign a "confidentiality" statement when joining or otherwise taking a part in peer review activities. Doing so will help reinforce the confidentiality provisions of the peer review process, as well as provide some measure of liability control.

POLICY AND PROCEDURE MANUALS

Policy and procedures establish an organization's internal "regulatory" practices. They are viewed by regulatory and accreditation agencies as evidence of the organization's acknowledgement of and compliance with required standards. Plaintiff's attorney routinely demand access to them to assess whether professional or operational standards were breached. Unfortunately, for many organizations, policies, procedures, medical staff bylaws, best-practice guidelines, and so on are often neglected. Out-of-date policies, or those that no longer comply with changes in the law, serve little practical purpose from an operational standpoint, and they pose a significant risk exposure to the organization. Policies must be reviewed periodically to ensure that they reflect key regulatory and practice requirements. Remember, policies do not have to address everything. Individual departments should be given the flexibility to establish, and modify, guidelines and procedures on an ongoing basis to ensure that they represent current practices. As the function of such manuals is to provide a resource to optimize the quality of care and operations of the facility, attention should be paid to their development and ongoing review and maintenance.

Risk Management Implications Policies, procedures, and guidelines must remain subject to change as circumstances dictate. Input from risk managers and legal counsel during the creation and review of such manuals is encouraged so that reasonable and achievable standards are developed.

Risk managers should recognize the value of maintaining out-of-date and modified policies, manuals, and similar materials. This effort has significant risk management implications as it allows the organization to establishment what its "standard of care" was at a given point in time, should it become an issue during litigation. Modified policies and protocols should be afforded the same consideration as any noncurrent business records. Store them in such a manner that they can be accessed when the need arises.

CASE LAW

Statutes and regulations enacted by Congress and the states certainly do not cover every possible situation in which they may apply. Under certain circumstances, litigants may ask appellate courts at both the state and federal level to review unfavorable decisions. When that court renders a decision in the form of a written opinion, the opinion becomes part of the body of the law and should be recognized and given the same consideration as enacted legislation. Decisions by these courts should be routinely monitored by risk management professionals. A variety of resources are available to help the risk manager achieve this objective—for example, regulatory updates published by state health care organizations, law firm advisories, and the Web page of the American Society for Healthcare Risk Management (ASHRM).

CONCLUSION

Risk managers must be prepared to help their organization understand and comply with the entire spectrum of regulation. As failure to comply exposes the organization and, in many cases, individual staff, to a wide range of penalties, persistent efforts by the risk manager in providing guidance in this regard is essential (see Exhibit 4.3 on page 110 for an example). Remember that complying with laws and regulations is somewhat like playing a game whose rules are constantly changing. You cannot afford to ignore this area of risk control. Ideally, subscribe to newsletters or other resources that will help identify changes in the ever-changing legal and regulatory landscape. Make an effort to ensure that everyone within your organization with a "need to know" is apprised of additions or significant modifications of the law. With the flood of new regulations flowing from the federal government, as well as increasing focus on health care issues at the state level, especially with regard to managed care and patient privacy, today's health care risk managers most certainly have their hands full.

Endnotes

The author would like to acknowledge and thank Patricia Scully, JD, for her previous work which contributed greatly to this chapter.

1. EMTALA Special Advisory Bulletin. *Fed. Reg., 64*(217), Nov. 10, 1999, www.dhhs.gov/progorg/oig/oigreg/frdump.pdf

2. *Ibid.*

3. *Ibid.*

4. 42 USC 1395dd (d)(1).

5. *Ibid.*

6. *Cruzan v. Director, Missouri Department of Health,* 497 US 261 (1990).

7. www.fda.gov/cdrh/mdr.html

8. www.fda.gov/cdrh/maude.html

9. The American College of Radiology and designated state agencies under contract with the FDA in California, Arkansas, Iowa, and Texas.

10. Available from the FDA or at www.fda.gov/cdrh/mammography/guidance.html

11. Hospital Conditions of Participation for Organ, Tissue and Eye Donation., 63 *Fed. Reg., 64*(33856), Jan. 22, 1998.

12. An excellent review is available at www.hhs.gov/news/press/1999press/99101a.html

13. *Weeks v. Baker & McKenzie,* 98 *Daily Journal,* DAR 4634 (May 6, 1998).

14. *Channon v. United Parcel Service, Inc.,* U.S. District Court, Polk County, Ia., 1998.

15. Available from the Federal Trade Commission or at www.ftc.gov/os/statutes/fcra/vail.htm

16. DHHS Office of the Inspector General Report OEI-02-98-0031.

17. Draft OIG Compliance Guidance for Nursing Facilities, *Fed. Reg., 64*(209), Oct. 29, 1999, or at www.dhhs/gov/progorg/oig/modcomp/draftc.pdf

18. www.access.gpo.gov/nara/cfr/waisdx_99/10cfr35_99.html

19. *Current Trends in Child Abuse Reporting and Fatalities: The Results of the 1997 Annual Fifty State Survey.* The Center of Child Abuse Prevention Research, www.childabuse.com/50ddata97.htm

20. *Ibid.*

21. National Clearinghouse on Child Abuse and Neglect Information.

22. www.aoa.dhhs.gov/abuse/report/Cexecsum.htm

23. 42 USC 290dd-2; 42 CFR Part 2.

24. *Elam v. College Park Hospital,* 132 Cal. App. 3d 332 (1982).

25. *Patrick v. Burget,* 486 US 94 (1988).

EXHIBIT 4.1.   Advance Health Care Directive

(California Probate Code Section 4701)

Explanation

You have the right to give instructions about your own health care. You also have the right to name someone else to make health care decisions for you. This form lets you do either or both of these things. It also lets you express your wishes regarding donation of organs and the designation of your primary physician. If you use this form, you may complete or modify all or any part of it. You are free to use a different form.

Part 1 of this form is a power of attorney for health care. Part 1 lets you name another individual as agent to make health care decisions for you if you become incapable of making your own decisions or if you want someone else to make those decisions for you now even though you are still capable. You may also name an alternate agent to act for you if your first choice is not willing, able, or reasonably available to make decisions for you. (Your agent may not be an operator or employee of a community care facility or a residential care facility where you are receiving care, or your supervising health care provider or employee of the health care institution where you are receiving care, unless your agent is related to you or is a coworker.)

Unless the form you sign limits the authority of your agent, your agent may make all health care decisions for you. This form has a place for you to limit the authority of your agent. You need not limit the authority of your agent if you wish to rely on your agent for all health care decisions that may have to be made. If you choose not to limit the authority of your agent, your agent will have the right to:

(a) Consent or refuse consent to any care, treatment, service, or procedure to maintain, diagnose, or otherwise affect a physical or mental condition.
(b) Select or discharge health care providers and institutions.
(c) Approve or disapprove diagnostic tests, surgical procedures, and programs of medication.
(d) Direct the provision, withholding, or withdrawal of artificial nutrition and hydration and all other forms of health care, including cardiopulmonary resuscitation.
(e) Make anatomical gifts, authorize an autopsy, and direct disposition of remains.

Part 2 of this form lets you give specific instructions about any aspect of your health care, whether or not you appoint an agent. Choices are provided for you to express your wishes regarding the provision, withholding, or withdrawal of treatment to keep you alive, as well as the provision of pain relief. Space is also provided for you to add to the choices you have made or for you to write out any additional wishes. If you are satisfied to allow your agent to determine what is best for you in making end-of-life decisions, you need not fill out Part 2 of this form.

Part 3 of this form lets you express an intention to donate your bodily organs and tissues following your death.

Part 4 of this form lets you designate a physician to have primary responsibility for your health care.

After completing this form, sign and date the form at the end. The form must be signed by two qualified witnesses or acknowledged before a notary public. Give a copy of the signed and completed form to your physician, to any other health care providers you may have, to any health care institution at which you are receiving care, and to any health care agents you have named. You should talk to the person you have named as agent to make sure that he or she understands your wishes and is willing to take the responsibility.

You have the right to revoke this advance health care directive or replace this form at any time.

* * * * * * * * * * * * * * * * * *

(Continued)

EXHIBIT 4.1.   **Advance Health Care Directive** (*Continued*)

PART 1
POWER OF ATTORNEY FOR HEALTH CARE

(1.1) DESIGNATION OF AGENT: I designate the following individual as my agent to make health care decisions for me:

_____
(name of individual you choose as agent)

_____
(address)   (city)   (state)   (ZIP code)

_____
(home phone)   (work phone)

OPTIONAL: If I revoke my agent's authority or if my agent is not willing, able, or reasonably available to make a health care decision for me, I designate as my first alternate agent:

_____
(name of individual you choose as first alternate agent)

_____
(address)   (city)   (state)   (ZIP code)

_____
(home phone)   (work phone)

OPTIONAL: If I revoke the authority of my agent and first alternate agent or if neither is willing, able, or reasonably available to make a health care decision for me, I designate as my second alternate agent:

_____
(name of individual you choose as second alternate agent)

_____
(address)   (city)   (state)   (ZIP code)

_____
(home phone)   (work phone)

(1.2) AGENT'S AUTHORITY: My agent is authorized to make all health care decisions for me, including decisions to provide, withhold, or withdraw artificial nutrition and hydration and all other forms of health care to keep me alive, except as I state here:

_____

_____

_____
(Add additional sheets if needed.)

(1.3) WHEN AGENT'S AUTHORITY BECOMES EFFECTIVE: My agent's authority becomes effective when my primary physician determines that I am unable to make my own health care decisions unless I mark the following box. If I mark this box ☐, my agent's authority to make health care decisions for me takes effect immediately.

(1.4) AGENT'S OBLIGATION: My agent shall make health care decisions for me in accordance with this power of attorney for health care, any instructions I give in Part 2 of this form, and my other wishes to the extent known to my agent. To the extent my wishes are unknown, my agent shall make health care decisions for me in accordance with what my agent determines to be in my best interest. In determining my best interest, my agent shall consider my personal values to the extent known to my agent.

(1.5) AGENT'S POSTDEATH AUTHORITY: My agent is authorized to make anatomical gifts, authorize an autopsy, and direct disposition of my remains, except as I state here or in Part 3 of this form:

_____

_____

_____
(Add additional sheets if needed.)   (*Continued*)

EXHIBIT 4.1.   **Advance Health Care Directive** (*Continued*)

(1.6) NOMINATION OF CONSERVATOR: If a conservator of my person needs to be appointed for me by a court, I nominate the agent designated in this form. If that agent is not willing, able, or reasonably available to act as conservator, I nominate the alternate agents whom I have named, in the order designated.

PART 2
INSTRUCTIONS FOR HEALTH CARE

If you fill out this part of the form, you may strike any wording you do not want.

(2.1) END-OF-LIFE DECISIONS: I direct that my health care providers and others involved in my care provide, withhold, or withdraw treatment in accordance with the choice I have marked below:

☐ (a) Choice Not To Prolong Life

I do not want my life to be prolonged if I have an incurable and irreversible condition that will result in my death within a relatively short time, I become unconscious, and, to a reasonable degree of medical certainty, I will not regain consciousness, or the likely risks and burdens of treatment would outweigh the expected benefits, OR

☐ (b) Choice To Prolong Life

I want my life to be prolonged as long as possible within the limits of generally accepted health care standards.

(2.2) RELIEF FROM PAIN: Except as I state in the following space, I direct that treatment for alleviation of pain or discomfort be provided at all times, even if it hastens my death:

_____

_____

_____

(Add additional sheets if needed.)

(2.3) OTHER WISHES: (If you do not agree with any of the optional choices above and wish to write your own, or if you wish to add to the instructions you have given above, you may do so here.) I direct that:

_____

_____

_____

(Add additional sheets if needed.)

PART 3
DONATION OF ORGANS AT DEATH (OPTIONAL)

(3.1) Upon my death (mark applicable box):
☐   (a) I give any needed organs, tissues, or parts, OR
☐   (b) I give the following organs, tissues, or parts only.

_____

☐   (c) My gift is for the following purposes (strike any of the following you do not want):
     ☐ (1) Transplant
     ☐ (2) Therapy
     ☐ (3) Research
     ☐ (4) Education

(*Continued*)

EXHIBIT 4.1.   Advance Health Care Directive (*Continued*)

PART 4
PRIMARY PHYSICIAN (OPTIONAL)

(4.1) I designate the following physician as my primary physician:

_____
(name of physician)

_____
(address)   (city)   (state)   (ZIP code)

_____
(phone)

OPTIONAL: If the physician I have designated above is not willing, able, or reasonably available to act as my primary physician, I designate the following physician as my primary physician:

_____
(name of physician)

_____
(address)   (city)   (state)   (ZIP code)

_____
(phone)

* * * * * * * * * * * * * * * * * *

PART 5

(5.1) EFFECT OF COPY: A copy of this form has the same effect as the original.
(5.2) SIGNATURE: Sign and date the form here:

_____   _____
(date)   (sign your name)

_____   _____
(address)   (print your name)

_____
(city)   (state)

(5.3) STATEMENT OF WITNESSES: I declare under penalty of perjury under the laws of California (1) that the individual who signed or acknowledged this advance health care directive is personally known to me, or that the individual's identity was proven to me by convincing evidence, (2) that the individual signed or acknowledged this advance directive in my presence, (3) that the individual appears to be of sound mind and under no duress, fraud, or undue influence, (4) that I am not a person appointed as agent by this advance directive, and (5) that I am not the individual's health care provider, an employee of the individual's health care provider, the operator of a community care facility, an employee of an operator of a community care facility, the operator of a residential care facility for the elderly, nor an employee of an operator of a residential care facility for the elderly.

_____   _____
First witness   Second witness

_____   _____
(print name)   (print name)

_____   _____
(address)   (address)

_____   _____
(city)   (state)   (city)   (state)

_____   _____
(signature of witness)   (signature of witness)

_____   _____
(date)   (date)

(*Continued*)

EXHIBIT 4.1.   **Advance Health Care Directive** (*Continued*)

(5.4) ADDITIONAL STATEMENT OF WITNESSES: At least one of the above witnesses must also sign the following declaration:

I further declare under penalty of perjury under the laws of California that I am not related to the individual executing this advance health care directive by blood, marriage, or adoption, and to the best of my knowledge, I am not entitled to any part of the individual's estate upon his or her death under a will now existing or by operation of law.

_____   _____
(signature of witness)   (signature of witness)

PART 6

SPECIAL WITNESS REQUIREMENT

(6.1) The following statement is required only if you are a patient in a skilled nursing facility—a health care facility that provides the following basic services: skilled nursing care and supportive care to patients whose primary need is for availability of skilled nursing care on an extended basis. The patient advocate or ombudsman must sign the following statement:

STATEMENT OF PATIENT ADVOCATE OR OMBUDSMAN

I declare under penalty of perjury under the laws of California that I am a patient advocate or ombudsman as designated by the State Department of Aging and that I am serving as a witness as required by Section 4675 of the Probate Code.

_____   _____
(date)   (sign your name)

_____   _____
(address)   (print your name)

_____
(city)   (state)

Source: California Legislative Information www.leginfo.ca.gov/pub/bill/asm/ab_0851-0900/ab_891bill_19991010_chaptered.html

EXHIBIT 4.2. **Medication and Device Experience Report**

MEDWATCH
THE FDA MEDICAL PRODUCTS REPORTING PROGRAM

For use by user-facilities, distributors and manufacturers for MANDATORY reporting

Page _____ of _____

Form Approved: OMB No. 0910-0291 Expires: 11/30/99
See OMB statement on reverse

Mfr report #

UF/Dist report #

FDA Use Only

PLEASE TYPE OR USE BLACK INK

A. Patient information

1. Patient identifier	2. Age at time of event: or ———— Date of birth:	3. Sex ☐ female ☐ male	4. Weight _____ lbs or _____ kgs

In confidence

B. Adverse event or product problem

1. ☐ Adverse event and/or ☐ Product problem (e.g., defects/malfunctions)

2. Outcomes attributed to adverse event (check all that apply)
- ☐ death _____ (mo/day/yr)
- ☐ life-threatening
- ☐ hospitalization – initial or prolonged
- ☐ disability
- ☐ congenital anomaly
- ☐ required intervention to prevent permanent impairment/damage
- ☐ other: _____

3. Date of event (mo/day/yr)	4. Date of this report (mo/day/yr)

5. Describe event or problem

6. Relevant tests/laboratory data, including dates

7. Other relevant history, including preexisting medical conditions (e.g., allergies, race, pregnancy, smoking and alcohol use, hepatic/renal dysfunction, etc.)

C. Suspect medication(s)

1. Name (give labeled strength & mfr/labeler, if known)
#1
#2

2. Dose, frequency & route used	3. Therapy dates (if unknown, give duration) from/to (or best estimate)
#1	#1
#2	#2

4. Diagnosis for use (indication) #1 #2	5. Event abated after use stopped or dose reduced #1 ☐ yes ☐ no ☐ doesn't apply #2 ☐ yes ☐ no ☐ doesn't apply

6. Lot # (if known) #1 #2	7. Exp. date (if known) #1 #2	8. Event reappeared after reintroduction #1 ☐ yes ☐ no ☐ doesn't apply #2 ☐ yes ☐ no ☐ doesn't apply

9. NDC # – for product problems only (if known)
____ – ____ – ____

10. Concomitant medical products and therapy dates (exclude treatment of event)

D. Suspect medical device

1. Brand name

2. Type of device

3. Manufacturer name & address	4. Operator of device ☐ health professional ☐ lay user/patient ☐ other: _____

6. model # _____ catalog # _____ serial # _____ lot # _____ other # _____	5. Expiration date (mo/day/yr)
	7. If implanted, give date (mo/day/yr)
	8. If explanted, give date (mo/day/yr)

9. Device available for evaluation? (Do not send to FDA)
☐ yes ☐ no ☐ returned to manufacturer on _____ (mo/day/yr)

10. Concomitant medical products and therapy dates (exclude treatment of event)

E. Initial reporter

1. Name & address	phone #

2. Health professional? ☐ yes ☐ no	3. Occupation	4. Initial reporter also sent report to FDA ☐ yes ☐ no ☐ unk

FDA
FDA Form 3500A

Submission of a report does not constitute an admission that medical personnel, user facility, distributor, manufacturer or product caused or contributed to the event.

(Continued)

EXHIBIT 4.2. **Medication and Device Experience Report** (*Continued*)

Medication and Device Experience Report
(continued)
Refer to guidelines for specific instructions

Submission of a report does not constitute an admission that medical personnel, user facility, distributor, manufacturer or product caused or contributed to the event.

Page _____ of _____

U.S. DEPARTMENT OF HEALTH AND HUMAN SERVICES
Public Health Service • Food and Drug Administration

FDA Use Only

F. For use by user facility/distributor–devices only

1. **Check one**
   ☐ user facility ☐ distributor

2. **UF/Dist report number**

3. **User facility or distributor name/address**

4. **Contact person**

5. **Phone Number**

6. **Date user facility or distributor became aware of event** (mo/day/yr)

7. **Type of report**
   ☐ initial
   ☐ follow-up # _____

8. **Date of this report** (mo/day/yr)

9. **Approximate age of device**

10. **Event problem codes** (refer to coding manual)
    patient code _____ – _____ – _____
    device code _____ – _____ – _____

11. **Report sent to FDA?**
    ☐ yes _____ (mo/day/yr)
    ☐ no

12. **Location where event occurred**
    ☐ hospital   ☐ outpatient diagnostic facility
    ☐ home
    ☐ nursing home
    ☐ outpatient treatment facility   ☐ ambulatory surgical facility
    ☐ other: _____ specify

13. **Report sent to manufacturer?**
    ☐ yes _____ (mo/day/yr)
    ☐ no

14. **Manufacturer name/address**

G. All manufacturers

1. **Contact office – name/address** (& mfring site for devices)

2. **Phone number**

3. **Report source** (check all that apply)
   ☐ foreign
   ☐ study
   ☐ literature
   ☐ consumer
   ☐ health professional
   ☐ user facility
   ☐ company representative
   ☐ distributor
   ☐ other:

4. **Date received by manufacturer** (mo/day/yr)

5.
   (A)NDA # _____
   IND # _____
   PLA # _____
   pre-1938 ☐ yes
   OTC product ☐ yes

6. **If IND, protocol #**

7. **Type of report** (check all that apply)
   ☐ 5-day   ☐ 15-day
   ☐ 10-day   ☐ periodic
   ☐ Initial ☐ follow-up # _____

8. **Adverse event term(s)**

9. **Mfr. report number**

H. Device manufacturers only

1. **Type of reportable event**
   ☐ death
   ☐ serious injury
   ☐ malfunction (see guidelines)
   ☐ other: _____

2. **If follow-up, what type?**
   ☐ correction
   ☐ additional information
   ☐ response to FDA request
   ☐ device evaluation

3. **Device evaluated by mfr?**
   ☐ not returned to mfr.
   ☐ yes ☐ evaluation summary attached
   ☐ no (attach page to explain why not) or provide code: _____

4. **Device manufacture date** (mo/yr)

5. **Labeled for single use?**
   ☐ yes   ☐ no

6. **Evaluation codes** (refer to coding manual)
   method [____]–[____]–[____]–[____]
   results [____]–[____]–[____]–[____]
   conclusions [____]–[____]–[____]–[____]

7. **If remedial action initiated, check type**
   ☐ recall   ☐ notification
   ☐ repair   ☐ inspection
   ☐ replace   ☐ patient monitoring
   ☐ relabeling ☐ modification/adjustment
   ☐ other: _____

8. **Usage of device**
   ☐ initial use of device
   ☐ reuse
   ☐ unknown

9. **If action reported to FDA under 21 USC 360i(f), list correction/removal reporting number:**

10. ☐ **Additional manufacturer narrative** and/or 11. ☐ **Corrected data**

The public reporting burden for this collection of information has been estimated to average one-hour per response, including the time for reviewing instructions, searching existing data sources, gathering and maintaining the data needed, and completing and reviewing the collection of information. Send comments regarding this burden estimate or any other aspect of this collection of information, including suggestions for reducing this burden to:
FDA Form 3500A - back

DHHS Reports Clearance Office
Paperwork Reduction Project (0910-0291)
Hubert H. Humphrey Building, Room 531-H
200 Independence Avenue, S.W.
Washington, D.C. 20201

"An agency may not conduct or sponsor, and a person is not required to respond to, a collection of information unless it displays a currently valid OMB control number."

Please DO NOT RETURN this form to this address.

EXHIBIT 4.3.   **An Example of a Risk Manager's Report to Staff**

LEGISLATIVE UPDATE

SUTTER HEALTH RISK MANAGEMENT DEPARTMENT

Prepared by Mark Cohen, ARM, RPLU, CPHQ   ***Risk Management Consultant***

November 1998

SB 2056: HIV TESTING RELATED TO EMPLOYEE EXPOSURE

DESCRIPTION: Under current California law, an employee who is exposed to a patient's blood, other body fluids, or tissues may initiate a process to have the source patient's blood tested for HIV. This "clean-up" legislation closes a couple of the loopholes in this law; specifically, those involving testing blood of incapacitated or deceased patients. This new legislation addresses this oversight by permitting HIV testing on available blood or other "patient samples" obtained in the course of providing health care services at the time of the exposure to such patients. With respect to incapacitated patients, testing of available blood may be performed only if no authorized representative has been identified and the patient is not expected to regain his/her capacity within the following seventy-two hours. Testing of available blood of deceased patients is also now permitted without need for notifying, or obtaining the consent of, the decedent's next-of-kin or other representative.

WHO NEEDS TO KNOW: Administrators, Patient Care Executives, Clinical Department Managers, Infection Control, Human Resources.

WHAT NEEDS TO BE DONE: Modify existing protocols covering this issue to provide for the testing of the blood or tissues of incapacitated or deceased patients. Sample protocols relating to permissible HIV testing of source patient blood may be obtained from your Risk Manager or Sutter Health Risk Management.

Appendix 4.1.

MODEL LANGUAGE FOR A HEALTH CARE RISK MANAGEMENT PROGRAM

....

AMERICAN SOCIETY FOR HEALTH CARE RISK MANAGEMENT LEGISLATIVE TASK FORCE

Rev. November 1987

I. A risk management program shall include but not be limited to the following components:

A. There must be a person designated as the facilities risk manager. A risk manager is defined as that person charged with the responsibility for the implementation, coordination, and effectuation of the risk management program. The risk manager shall be empowered with the authority and responsibility from the governing body, medical staff, and administration that is necessary to carry out the functions and activities of the internal risk management program.

The incumbent shall be qualified by education, training, and/or experience to coordinate the functions and activities of the internal risk management program.

B. The risk manager must evidence at least eight (8) hours of continuing education per calendar year in areas that are relevant to the risk management functions and activities described in these regulations. Risk management programs acceptable for continuing education credits shall include, but not be limited to programs sponsored by the American Society for Healthcare Risk Management (ASHRM), affiliated state and local risk management societies, American Hospital Association (AHA), American Medical Association (AMA), state hospital and medical associations, and Joint Commission on Accreditation of Hospitals (JCAH).[*]

C. The risk manager, in order to carry out these functions, activities, and the position's responsibility, shall have access to all necessary, relevant hospital and medical staff data including but not limited to committee minutes, medical records, and medical staff files.

---

[*]The American Society for Healthcare Risk Management's (ASHRM) Board and the Legislative Task Force are not suggesting nor do we mean to support the concept or advocate statutorily required risk management programs. However, ASHRM is cognizant of the need and their responsibility to give guidance where needed and requested in the area of health care risk management. The Legislative Task Force has therefore drafted language for a model risk management program that can be utilized by any interested party.

D. A commitment from the governing body to the risk management program including resources (manpower and financial) necessary for implementation and the daily functions of the program that is evidenced in writing by a policy statement formally adopted by the governing body, medical staff, and administration.

E. A system for the identification of:

   i. Unexpected or unanticipated outcomes which may have caused injury or may have the potential to cause injury.

   ii. Identification of risks which have or could potentially have caused an injury or the impairment of patient safety.

   This system for identification can utilize and include, but not necessarily be limited to the following:

   1. Criteria-based outcome studies.
   2. Monitoring systems based on objective criteria.
   3. Incident reports.
   4. Patient grievances (for example, written complaint letters relating to the quality of care issues).
   5. Committee reports and minutes including quality assurance, credentialing, peer review, morbidity, and mortality.
   6. Legal complaints and suits.
   7. Third-party reports (that is, JCAH, state licensure, departments of professional regulations).
   8. Cases referred to the medical examiner or coroner.
   9. Outside request for medical records, x-rays, laboratory reports.
   10. Security or police reports.
   11. Nursing, administrative, and/or administrator-on-call reports.

F. An internal procedure for the expeditious review and investigation of all serious unanticipated or unexpected outcomes where a patient injury has occurred or patient safety has been impaired.

G. A system for the analysis of all identified risk exposures to include the following components:

   1. Centralization of all identified risk data.
   2. A means to share and integrate risk management data collection and analysis activities with other appropriate clinical and administrative departments. (For example, this could include sharing clinical risk data of a given specialty with a chief of service, quality assurance committee, or other administrative departments such as safety or infection control.)
   3. The results of the analytical review are to be forwarded by the risk manager to the person charged with the responsibility for the clinical areas involved to review, evaluate, and respond back to the risk manager. Any corrective action taken in response to the review and evaluation should be forwarded to the risk manager.

H. The risk manager shall provide reports to the governing body at designated times, but at least annually, for the purpose of reviewing and evaluating the activities of the risk management program. These reports can be written or given verbally through a formalized committee structure.

I. The risk manager should coordinate, plan, and implement educational programs to minimize the risk of harm to patients. These educational programs should address but not be limited to:

1. The medical staff on initial appointment and during the reappointment process.
2. General orientation for all new employees.
3. Specific programs tailored to the individual institution to address the high risk clinical areas, in particular: operating suite, labor and delivery, emergency department, and anesthesia.

The risk manager shall be empowered to effectuate the implementation of other programs to reduce the possibility of patient injuries and financial loss.

J. The risk manager shall forward to those committees empowered to evaluate the competency of the medical staff, any and all pertinent data, such as claim and litigation histories, quantitative data from incident reporting or occurrence screening systems, and knowledge of adverse outcomes or questionable medical practice. These committees may include medical executive committee, credentials committee, and governing body committees.

K. The risk manager should perform, coordinate, and/or assist with the risk financing and claims administration functions for the institution.

II. Immunity

No individual or institution reporting, providing information, opinion, counsel, or services to a medical or incident review committee, or any other medical staff, administrative, or governing body committee that evaluates quality of care issues or as part of the internal risk management program shall be liable in a suit for damages based on such reporting, providing information, opinion, counsel, or services provided that such individual or institution acted in good faith and with a reasonable belief that said actions were warranted in connection with or in furtherance of the functions of the internal risk management program.

III. Confidentiality

Any and all documents and records that are part of the internal risk management program as well as the proceedings, reports, and records from any of the above committees shall be confidential and not subject to subpoena or discovery or introduced into evidence in any judicial or administrative proceeding except for proceedings by the department responsible for disciplinary and/or review action of any professional.

Reprinted, with permission, from the American Society for Healthcare Risk Management. Credited to Roberta Carroll, chairperson; Lawrence Herron; James Holzer; and Stephen Trosty.

5

Data Management

Kirk S. Davis
Jane C. McConnell

The management of patient-specific data and information is an important risk management responsibility. Within a system that provides a continuum of care comprising many types of data, including inpatient and outpatient health care records, incident reports, quality assurance reports, committee meeting minutes, and medical staff performance reviews, information whether in electronic or written form must be handled appropriately and protected under the confidentiality provisions and privileges of state and federal law. The protection of such data is necessary because it ensures patient privacy and encourages active peer review and quality improvement.

Over time the ability to keep information confidential has become a more significant challenge and public concern. This is due to the advances of electronic technology in the health care industry and the linking of many types of patient care facilities, providers, health plans, payers, employers, and vendors through centralized databases such as e-mail and computer-based medical record systems. Technological advances affecting data management also have required additional security safeguards to protect the integrity of patient and health care business data and the inadvertent release of confidential information. Until recently there were only a few federal laws protecting confidentiality with state regulations predominating. Since state protections were uneven and there were large gaps in these protections in certain states, Congress recognized the need for minimum national health care privacy *and security* standards through the passage of the Health Insurance Portability and Accountability Act of 1996 (HIPAA).[1]

In accordance with HIPAA, the Secretary of the Department of Health and Human Services (DHHS) set forth for Congress a framework for federal privacy legislation for individually identifiable health information as follows:

- Allow for the smooth flow of individually identified health information for treatment, payment, and related operations, and for specific additional purposes related to health care that are in the public interest.

- Prohibit the flow of individually identified health information for any additional purposes unless specified and voluntary authorization is given by the subject of the information.

- Put into place fair information protections that allow individuals to know who is using their health information and how it is to be used.

- Establish fair information practices that allow individuals to obtain access to their records and obtain amendments or corrections to them where there is inaccurate or incorrect information.

- Require persons who hold individual identifiable health information to safeguard that information from inappropriate use or disclosure.

- Hold those who use the individual identifiable health information accountable for their handling of this information and to provide legal recourse to persons harmed by misuse.

- Allow health information to be disclosed without an individual's authorization for certain national priorities and purposes (such as research, public health, and oversight) but only under defined circumstances.

On August 21, 1999, or three years since the passage of HIPAA when Congress failed to pass a privacy statute by that date, the authority to promulgate privacy regulations passed to DHHS. Under these circumstances and in accordance with HIPAA's more limited legislative direction, on November 3, 1999, DHHS did issue proposed regulations in a Notice of Proposed Rule Making (NPRM) on National Medical Records Privacy Rules pertaining to individual identifiable health information privacy and security. These proposed regulations are more limited than their 1997 recommendations with regard to the entities covered (health plans, health care clearinghouses, and health care providers) and pertain only to individual identifiable health information maintained or transmitted by these entities in electronic form.[2] According to DHHS in their introductory statements in the regulations, they are also more limited with regard to strong enforcement provisions and the private right of action for individuals. However, despite these limitations and varied opinions about what the final regulations should contain and whether or not Congress should intervene and pass additional legislation, federal regulations in some form will most likely predominate in the future. They also will preempt state laws that are in conflict with their regulatory requirements and that have less stringent privacy protections.

While there are many potential changes under way with regard to privacy and security concerns, this chapter focuses on some of the basic principles concerning the confidentiality and privacy management of health care information. This is done through the examination of existing state and federal statutes, some aspects of the proposed federal regulations, and practical advice. While in the past, the term *medical record* was used almost exclusively in reference to data management, according to the newly proposed federal regulations and some new state regulations, the terms *health information, health care information,* or *individual identifiable health information* are also used in describing types and forms of information associated with confidentiality and privacy protections. This health information referred to in the proposed federal regulations relates to a person's physical or mental health, the provision of health care, or the payment of health care. It is information that could identify or be used to identify a person, created by or received from a covered entity, and has been electronically maintained or transmitted by a covered entity. Because the medical record is usually the key document risk managers are concerned about, this chapter will continue to use this term as well as health information in discussing confidentiality and security concerns. Because the law of health care data management continues to evolve as this chapter is being written, risk managers must be alert to the release of the final federal regulations and possible congressional intervention. They should also be aware of its impact on specific state laws to have more precise information to develop the required policies and procedures to comply with the confidentiality and security requirements for the protection of health information.

CONTENT AND PURPOSE OF THE MEDICAL RECORD

The medical record is the primary document in which health care information about a patient is recorded. It should include results of physical examinations, a medical history, treatment reports, x-ray reports, physician orders, clinical laboratory reports, consultation reports, anesthesia records, operative reports, signed consent forms, nurses' notes, and any other reports, including computer reports and graphs that may be generated during the patient's treatment. Emergency department (ED) records may require additional information to be in compliance with some state regulations and the federal Emergency Medical Treatment and Active Labor Act (EMTALA).[3]

Whether handwritten, typed, or computerized, the medical record should be complete, legible, and accurate. The computerized record can aid the information network in knowing a patient, enhancing completeness and accuracy of information, and achieving the record's immediate availability to authorized personnel. Accuracy is enhanced in computerized records because they often automatically record the date and time of each entry and identify the person entering the data.

The medical record serves a number of purposes. As a repository of information, it is a means of communicating among physicians and other providers involved in the patient's care throughout the health care delivery system. The Joint Commission on Accreditation of Healthcare Organizations (JCAHO) requires that all facilities treating patients maintain adequate medical records "which contain sufficient information to identify the patient, support the diagnoses, justify the treatment, document the course and results, and promote continuity of care among health care providers."[4] Additionally, the medical record is an important business record that may be accessed by many departments and personnel not involved in direct patient care, such as physicians engaged in peer review, the billing departments, health plans, HMOs, or health care clearinghouses. Outside the health care system, it is used by various government agencies, government-funded organizations, and accreditation bodies to monitor the health care entity and individual provider performance. Medical records also are reviewed by third-party payers for reimbursement and under certain circumstances used for research purposes. From time to time, the medical record, as well as other documents peripherally related to patient care, such as operative logs and physician peer review records, may be requested by legal counsel, the patient, or the patient's spouse or family. Often, it is the most important document available to a health care facility and a practitioner in defending a negligence action and ordinarily is admissible as evidence of what transpired in the care of the patient.

Thus, with medical records as accessible as they are to so many users and for so many purposes, it is essential that users recognize the obligation to keep information confidential. The health care entity and/or network must have clear policies that comply with federal and state laws, regulations, and credentialing bodies regarding who may make entries on the medical record and how those entries may be corrected and completed to ensure record authenticity. Also necessary are policies on privacy and security measures to prevent tampering or loss, actions to undertake when unauthorized access or use occurs, and stipulations as to how long data is to be retained.[5] Additional privacy protections to be required under the newly proposed federal regulations are discussed later in this chapter.

Record Authentication

Most state regulations require a signature or other authentication by a health care practitioner to ensure the reliability of the information in the medical record. The JCAHO requires that all entries in the record be dated and authenticated and that a method be established to identify their authors. Entries can be authenticated by written signature, identifiable initials, electronic signature, or computer key.[6] The Medicare Conditions of Participation require that the person responsible for ordering, providing, or evaluating the service performed personally authenticate the record.[7]

Because errors in medical record entries are inevitable, in addition to authentication of the record, formal procedures must be adhered to for making corrections to the record.[8] As a general rule, the person who made the incorrect record entry should correct it. If the correction is significant, a senior person designated by facility policy should review it to ensure that it complies with facility guidelines for record amendments. Health care personnel should make changes that are within their scope of practice, as defined by state licensing and certification laws. To ensure compliance with the procedures developed, a quality control procedure must be in place.

Record Retention

The length of time that a medical record is retained will be determined by federal or state laws and regulations or, in their absence, by sound administrative policy and medical practice. Record retention also will be influenced by the nature of the health care entity and resources available—for example, whether the entity has access to off-site storage facilities, microfilming arrangements, or optical disks.

A few states have acts and regulations that establish general medical record retention requirements. Some states also have specific retention requirements for particular parts of medical records, such as x-rays, or specific classifications of patients, such as minors, the mentally ill, and the deceased.[9] For example, the Florida Hospital Association has promulgated a compliance standards manual. It goes further into record retention by review of a variety of sources. The Office of the Inspector General's *Model Compliance Guide for Hospitals* indicates a hospital compliance program should provide for the implementation of a records system. This system should establish policies and procedures regarding the creation, distribution, retention, storage, retrieval, and destruction of documents. The types of documents developed under this system should include all records and documentation, such as clinical and medical records and claims documentation, required by either federal or state law for participation in federal health programs, and all records necessary to protect the integrity of the hospital's compliance process and confirm the effectiveness of the program.[10]

In looking at the development of a record retention policy, it is also important to consider the Statute of Limitations under the False Claims Act.[11] This act states that an action for a false claims violation "may not be brought (1) more than six years after the date on which the violation . . . is committed, or (2) more than three years after the date when facts material to the right of action are known or reasonably should have been known by the official of the United States charged with responsibility to act in the circumstances, but in no event more than ten years after the date on which the violation is committed, whichever occurs last."[12]

Each health care entity should, with input from its risk management department, establish its own policy governing medical record retention. Clearly, medical records should be retained for as long as there is a medical or administrative need for them—for example, for subsequent patient care, medical research, review and evaluation of professional and hospital services, and defense of professional or other liability actions. Additionally, health care entities should consult state laws that may require a longer retention period for the medical records of minors.

However, it may be impractical to retain certain types of medical information in the medical record. Thus, within the record retention policy, special attention should be given to radiology films, EKG and EEG tracings, slides, videotapes, and fetal monitor strips, because these are types of medical information that pose unique record retention problems. For example, a heart patient might have a number of EKG tracings, or a maternity patient might have hours of fetal monitoring strips containing important documentation of the events of the birth. X-rays, as well as scanning technologies such as computed tomography, mammograms, and ultrasound, produce medical information in a pictorial rather than written form that also may be difficult or impossible to include in the record. Although the physician's reports and interpretations of the tests will certainly be part of the record, they may not be sufficient information in defense of a medical malpractice case. Paper records should ideally be stored together; however, other methods to retain these original films, strips, slides, videotapes, and scans must be developed.[13]

Record Destruction

Some states have enacted statutes and regulations specifying the method by which a record may be destroyed after the retention period has concluded or after the record has been copied onto microfilm, entered into a computer, or converted to some other machine-readable form. Other states require health care entities to prepare a permanent abstract of the record before destroying it. After the record destruction policy is created, it should be applied uniformly. Otherwise, the court may allow a jury to infer from the unavailability of the records that the health care entity acted improperly in treating the patient.[14]

....

ACCESS TO MEDICAL RECORDS

Although the health care entity or the physician is viewed as the owner of the medical record, the record is maintained for the benefit of the patient, who generally is viewed as having some proprietary rights to the information it contains. Many states have adopted laws regarding patients' access to their own records. These laws set forth specific guidelines delineating the circumstances under which a patient has access to his or her record and whether that access may ever be denied. Even in states that do not have a specific statute, from both a patients' rights and a public relations perspective, it is advisable for a facility to develop a policy that allows patients reasonable access to their medical records.[15] Under the NPRM, individuals will be able to obtain access to protected health information about them. This would include a right to inspect and obtain a copy of their medical record and request amendments or corrections if there is inaccurate or incorrect information. In addition, the right of access includes an accounting of the disclosures made.

Confidentiality and the Physician-Patient Privilege

The legitimate needs of individuals not involved in a patient's care to have access to the patient's information conflict with the principle that patient information is confidential. There is both an ethical and a legal basis for confidentiality of medical information. The ethical principle originates from the idea that an assurance of confidentiality encourages patients to seek needed medical care and to be candid with their physicians about their condition. Confidentiality also is necessary to protect the patient's inherent privacy interest. People receiving medical care are entitled to privacy with regard to their bodily condition. A recent Ohio Supreme Court decision concluded that there is a common law right to privacy and established an independent tort of unauthorized disclosure of medical information based on the physician-patient relationship.[16]

The legal basis for confidentiality derives from the physician-patient privilege, set forth by statute in almost all states. This is one of several relationships recognized as special by law. The others are attorney-client, husband-wife, and priest-penitent; in all these, preservation of confidentiality is viewed as essential to the maintenance of the relationship. The patient has a privilege to refuse to disclose (and to prevent any other person from disclosing) confidential communication made for the purpose of obtaining medical services and eliciting medical advice. The physician-patient privilege provides that, absent patient authorization or waiver or an overriding law or public policy, medical information on a patient is insulated from the process known as discovery, through which parties to a lawsuit normally can compel disclosure of relevant evidence.[17]

Professionals Covered by the Physician-Patient Privilege

In most states, the physician-patient privilege extends beyond physicians to protect the patient's relationship with other health care professionals, such as psychologists and social workers. For example, the U.S. Supreme Court ruled that psychotherapists and social workers who offer counseling generally cannot be forced to provide evidence about their patients. Courts also have interpreted the physician-patient privilege to protect information provided by a patient to employed nurses, physician assistants, and other professionals working for a physician. However, in the absence of a statute, there generally is no privilege on the information provided by a patient to a nurse who has acted independently.[18] Risk managers should check the law of their jurisdiction to ascertain which health care professionals are specifically covered by the privilege.

Information Covered by the Physician-Patient Privilege

To be privileged, patient information must satisfy certain criteria. For example:

- It must have been communicated in the context of the physician-patient relationship.
- It must have been given with the expectation that it remain confidential.
- It must be necessary for the diagnosis and treatment of the patient.

Once the privilege is determined to exist, it is found consistently to extend beyond oral communications between physician and patient to cover written entries in the patient's record. Also covered are x-rays, cardiograph strips, lab results, and other past or future health information on a patient's physical or mental condition that is kept by the individual provider or health care entity.[19] However, other information, such as the patient's name and address and the fact that he or she is receiving medical treatment, is not privileged because that information is not necessary for the patient's diagnosis and treatment.[20]

Assertion of the Physician-Patient Privilege

The physician-patient privilege belongs to the patient because it is for his or her benefit that it exists. Frequently, however, the patient is not available and does not even have knowledge that records concerning his or her treatment have been requested. In such a case, the privilege must be asserted on the patient's behalf by the physician or the entity where the patient received treatment.[21] A patient claiming negligence in the performance of a particular procedure might seek a judicial order allowing discovery of the records of other patients who underwent similar surgeries. In those situations, the administrator should raise the issue of privilege for these patients' records.[22] If records are released, the court may order names and other identifying details to be removed from copies of the records. Even though this may change under the proposed federal regulations, in those states where a legal responsibility to maintain confidentiality ends with the death of the patient, it is still advisable to obtain authorization from the patient's legal representative.[23]

Waiver of the Physician-Patient Privilege

Unlike assertion of the physician-patient privilege, a waiver of the privilege may be made only by the patient or, in cases of incompetency, infancy, or death, by his or her legal representative. Waiver may be either express or implicit. Obviously, a patient may expressly waive the privilege by authorizing the provider to release information to a third party, such as an insurance carrier or an attorney. Under the proposed federal regulations in order to ensure voluntary authorization to release the minimum amount of protected health care information necessary, the form must state what is to be disclosed and its purpose. When a health care provider receives a letter from an attorney requesting copies of a patient's medical record, the records custodian should confirm that the letter is accompanied by an authorization from the patient allowing release of the records to the requesting attorney or that the request otherwise complies with state law on release of records.

Implicit waiver of the privilege occurs when a patient brings a personal injury action concerning a medical condition for which he or she was treated, or when he or she otherwise discloses or consents to disclosure of a significant part of the communications previously made to a treating physician. Here, because the patient has placed information about his or her medical condition in issue, he or she may no longer claim the privilege.[24]

Risk managers sometimes must decide whether a patient who has not yet commenced a lawsuit but has performed some affirmative act, such as sending an "attorney request letter," has waived the privilege and thereby entitled the physician or the hospital to turn over the patient's medical records to its liability insurance carrier. Courts have held that, where a physician has a reasonable basis for believing that a claim of malpractice will be made, the physician and his or her insurer are entitled to investigate and prepare for an anticipated lawsuit, justifying his or her disclosure of the medical records to the attorney and/or insurer.[25]

In some instances, defense counsel in a malpractice action may seek information on a litigant's medical condition that is not the subject of the suit. For example, to impeach the credibility of the plaintiff's claim about a lasting physical injury, the defense may wish to show that the plaintiff has received psychiatric treatment.[26] In birth injury cases, the defense frequently seeks discovery about the medical condition of the infant's siblings and about other prenatal and labor and delivery records of the mother in an effort to prove a genetic cause for the infant's condition.[27] Court decisions vary from jurisdiction to jurisdiction on whether waiver of the privilege extends to other conditions, and, if it does, how information about them can be obtained from treating physicians who are not parties in the suit.

Courts generally permit liberal discovery of records of subsequent treatment by physicians who have treated the plaintiff for the condition that is the subject of the litigation or is demonstrably related to it. However, even if the defendant is permitted to obtain access to information from the plaintiff's nonparty treating physicians, courts are divided as to whether the plaintiff's condition can be discussed with those physicians in the absence of plaintiff's attorney (*ex parte*), or whether they must go through formal discovery proceedings.[28] Most courts have held that, even though there has been a waiver of the physician-patient privilege, the defendant must use formal discovery methods.[29]

RELEASE OF CONFIDENTIAL INFORMATION WITHOUT PATIENT CONSENT

The right of confidentiality and the physician-patient privilege are never absolute. Certain interests of society outweigh the physician's duty to maintain confidentiality of patient records even when there has been no waiver or authorization. Most states have laws mandating physicians and/or hospitals to report communicable diseases, incidence of cancer, cases of suspected child abuse or neglect, gunshot or knife wounds, physician misconduct, and incidents of adverse patient care.[30] The statute or regulation mandating disclosure usually will contain a confidentiality provision restricting the ability of the public to gain access to that information.[31] In the proposed federal regulations covered entities could use or disclose individual identifiable health information without authorization for treatment, payment, health care operations, and national priority activities.[32] With regard to business partners, in the federal regulations covered entities can release protected health care information only if satisfactory assurance is obtained that will safeguard this information. For a breach by the business partner is deemed a breach by the covered entity.[33]

Physician Duty to Third Persons in Psychiatric Cases

One of the most difficult areas concerning unauthorized disclosure of privileged patient information arises in psychiatric cases. The guarantee of confidentiality is especially important in the patient-psychiatrist relationship. Statutes in many states require institutions to implement special procedures to prevent any disclosure of mental health records. The new proposed federal regulations also contain protections.[34] At the same time, situations may arise in which psychiatrists and other mental health professionals treating a potentially violent patient may find a conflict between their fiduciary obligation to maintain confidentiality and their countervailing duty to disclose that a third party may be a potential victim of their patient's violent acts.

First set forth in the landmark case of *Tarasoff v. Regents of the University of California*,[35] a judicial doctrine was developed that has been codified in most states:

when a patient is determined to be a danger to others, the treating psychiatrist or therapist has a responsibility to disclose the danger to the extent necessary to protect potential victims.[36] Some state courts have held that the endangered third party must be specifically identified, whereas others have held that a general threat is a sufficient basis for breach of confidentiality. Before developing a policy for the institution or advising affiliated mental health professionals about disclosure to endangered third parties, the risk manager should review any applicable state statutes and consult with counsel.

Records of Alcohol and Drug Abuse Patients

Special federal rules exist regarding confidentiality of information on patients treated or referred for treatment for alcohol and drug abuse.[37] In general, the regulations prohibit any disclosure or release of patient information, whether recorded or not, that would identify the patient as a substance abuser. The regulations were amended in 1987 in an attempt to make them clearer and to narrow their application with respect to general care hospitals. Under the amendments, a general medical facility is not subject to the regulations unless it has either a distinct substance abuse program or specialized personnel whose primary function is treatment, diagnosis, or referral for treatment of substance abuse patients. Even then, the rules apply only to that special program or unit unless the hospital elects to place the entire facility under the regulations. Therefore, in a situation where a patient who is a substance abuser is being treated for a medical problem other than substance abuse in the general part of the hospital, information on that patient will not be covered by the regulations. On the other hand, the records of a patient who is in a substance abuse program are protected, and his or her records may not be released or transferred, even to another department of the hospital, without a special consent. The regulations require that patients be given a written summary of the confidentiality regulations.

Under the regulations, information may be released with the patient's consent if the consent is in writing and contains all of the following elements:

- Name of the program.
- Name of the proposed recipient of the information.
- Name of the patient.
- Purpose or need for the disclosure.
- Extent and nature of the information to be disclosed.
- Signature of the patient or of the person authorized to give consent if the patient is a minor, incompetent, or deceased.
- Date on which the consent is signed.
- A statement that the consent is subject to revocation at any time.
- Date, event, or condition on which the consent will expire if not revoked before that time.

The regulations contain a sample consent form. Each disclosure made with the patient's written consent must be accompanied by a specific written statement, set forth in the regulations, prohibiting redisclosure.

The regulations permit disclosure without patient consent if the disclosure is to medical personnel to meet any individual's bona fide medical emergency, or to qualified personnel for research, audit, or program evaluation. They also permit disclosure for certain specified purposes, pursuant to a court order, after the court has made a finding that (1) "good cause" exists, (2) the information is not otherwise available to the requesting party, and (3) the public interest in disclosure outweighs the potential harm to the patient. The person requesting court-ordered disclosure has the burden of demonstrating its necessity. A subpoena or similar legal document then must be issued in order to compel disclosure.

If a hospital receives a request for disclosure of patient information that does not comply with the regulations, it must respond with a noncommittal answer that will not reveal that a specific patient has been diagnosed or is being treated for substance abuse. If the request is for treatment information on a patient known to be a substance abuser, the hospital should respond either with the noncommittal answer or by sending a copy of the regulations and an attached statement that they restrict disclosure of substance abuse records. It is permissible, however, for a hospital to state that a specific person is not, and never has been, a patient of the program if such is the case.[38]

Medical Records Containing HIV- or AIDS-Related Information

Because of discrimination against an individual that may result from dissemination of information on his or her HIV status, such information is highly confidential. States have enacted a variety of laws addressing the confidentiality of HIV test results and treatment records. Most states make available anonymous HIV testing but also establish non-anonymous, but confidential, testing programs under which public health officials have access, under specific conditions, to the names of those testing positive.[39]

Risk managers must review the law in their state and develop written policies that conform to their hospital procedures regarding disclosure to the applicable statute. In the absence of such a statute, it may be advisable to model the hospital's policy after the federal drug and alcohol rules so that no HIV or AIDS information is released without patient authorization or a court order.[40]

Release of Patient Information to Law Enforcement Agencies

Risk managers frequently ask how they should respond to subpoenas and other, less formal requests for patient information received from law enforcement officers, including police officers, district attorneys, and grand juries. In general, without a specific statute compelling disclosure, law enforcement officers have no authority to examine a patient's medical records. This means that the results (for example, blood alcohol levels on a patient brought into the ED) should not be disclosed to the police unless required by statute.[41] Subpoenas and other legal processes issued by law enforcement agencies also should be carefully scrutinized, in consultation with the health care facility's attorney, prior to releasing privileged information. Within the proposed regulation is a specific provision for use and disclosure of protected health information for law enforcement purposes without the authorization of the individual. These purposes relate to a legitimate law enforcement inquiry, for identifying a suspect or victim as well as for national security activities and health care fraud.[42]

············

RELEASE OF PATIENT INFORMATION IN CIVIL LITIGATION

After a lawsuit is commenced, both sides engage in "discovery," whereby they gain access to factual information about the dispute in the control of either their adversary or persons who are not parties to the suit. Whether this information will later be "admissible" in a trial is a separate inquiry.

With respect to parties to the lawsuit, discovery of documents is initiated by serving a notice specifying, with reasonable particularity, the documents sought to be reviewed, as well as the time, place, and manner of inspection. Document discovery from nonparties (for example, the hospital where a patient was treated when only the patient's private physician has been sued) also is authorized but is more cumbersome. Usually, it involves a two-step process: serving a discovery notice on all other parties to the lawsuit, and then serving a subpoena or court order on the nonparty in possession of the documents.

It is important to understand that, despite its official-looking appearance, a subpoena is rarely issued by the court itself. A subpoena may be issued by a clerk or a judge where there is no clerk, administrative agencies, an arbitrator or referee, any member of a board or commission, and, in criminal cases, a prosecutor. In civil litigation, subpoenas are issued frequently by the attorney of record of any party to an action. Under the procedural law of most jurisdictions, an attorney, as an officer of the court, has the power to issue such a directive without the court's specific authorization. Therefore, risk managers should carefully scrutinize all subpoenas, including those signed by a judge, and challenge them in appropriate circumstances when the subpoenas request privileged material. In most jurisdictions, it is the health care entity's responsibility to assert the physician-patient privilege on behalf of a patient who is not a party to the lawsuit. In addition, many other records maintained by the hospital may be privileged and not subject to discovery by way of a subpoena or otherwise.

As custodians of their patients' medical records, health care entities frequently receive subpoenas for records in the context of litigation not involving allegations of medical malpractice. For example, when an accident victim sues the other party to the accident, hospital medical records contain information necessary to prosecute the suit. Those records may be subpoenaed by one or both of the parties to the lawsuit.

As a practical matter, a risk manager who believes that a subpoena is requesting privileged materials should contact the attorney issuing the subpoena and request that it be modified or withdrawn. If that is not successful, an application to the court, called a "motion to quash" or a "motion for a protective order," is the appropriate and proper method to test the subpoena.[43]

DISSEMINATION OF INFORMATION TO INTERNAL OR EXTERNAL REVIEW ORGANIZATIONS

Patient authorization is not a prerequisite to dissemination of information to either internal or external review organizations. The generally accepted rule is that consent is not required for:

- Use of a medical record for automated data processing of designated information.
- Use in activities concerned with the monitoring and evaluation of the quality and appropriateness of patient care.
- Departmental review of work performance.
- Official surveys for compliance with accreditation, regulatory, licensing standards.
- Educational purposes and research programs.

Increasingly, official agencies such as state health departments and professional review organizations (PROs) are accessing patient records for purposes of quality-of-care outcomes. Those agencies, themselves bound to maintain confidentiality of the information they review, must be permitted access to the patient's medical records, although no privilege has been waived. Educational use is generally understood to be for the benefit of the providers associated with the organization, not for a for-profit educational company.

Usually, those agencies make confidential all information reviewed or generated by them (other than general summaries or aggregate statistical data) that explicitly or implicitly identifies an individual patient, practitioner, or reviewer. However, increasingly, the laws and regulations are amended to contain exceptions to total nondisclosure, and the risk manager should consult with counsel about how to proceed when dealing with a special situation or quasi-governmental agency such as a PRO. It is suggested that health care entities have specific confidentiality policies and educate their staff accordingly. In fact, some may require certain members of their staff to sign an agreement that they will maintain confidentiality of this information and records. There is at least one case where an employee was terminated for violation of a hospital's confidentiality policy.[44] Additionally, some states have statutes that impose criminal or civil penalties on persons for unlawful disclosure of medical information.[45]

CONFIDENTIALITY OF BUSINESS AND OTHER RECORDS

A health care facility's business records may contain a number of different kinds of documents, including incident reports and reports of hospital and medical staff committees. Incident reports usually are generated following any event that is inconsistent with routine operation of a facility or an adverse event. They provide the facility with the information necessary to determine what happened and how it could be possibly avoided in the future.

Most states have adopted legislation protecting clinical information generated as part of a hospital's quality assurance (QA) activities from discovery or admission into evidence. This includes the incident report as well as peer review documents generated to review a physician's performance.[46]

Incident Occurrence Reports

Incident reports can be a source of incriminating evidence if they are discoverable. Consequently, the discoverability of incident reports has been litigated in many states. If they are protected, protection usually depends on state QA and peer review statutes, or statutes creating an attorney-client or insurer-insured privilege.

In many states, incident reports describing occurrences where the hospital has an expectation that it will be sued may be protected under the attorney-client privilege, the attorney work product doctrine, or a similar qualified immunity accorded to reports made to an insurer by an insured in anticipation of, or preparation for, litigation.[47] However, with respect to minor occurrences that happen very frequently in the hospital, such as patient falls or medication errors, routinely prepared incident reports are more in the nature of accident reports maintained in the ordinary course of business. In most states, such reports are discoverable even if they ultimately are used in connection with litigation of a claim. Discoverability generally will turn on whether the accident report has a "mixed purpose"; it will be protected only if it was prepared exclusively in anticipation of litigation, not if it was prepared also for hospital administrative purposes.[48] In a state with a more comprehensive QA statute, incident reports involving serious occurrences that were prepared both in anticipation of litigation and as part of the hospital's effort to evaluate and improve the quality of health care should be protected.[49]

Incident reports should be labeled and treated as confidential, and their distribution limited. The risk manager should conduct in-service programs on how to write such a report. Incident reports should contain only a summary of objective facts and should avoid subjective analysis, conclusion, *mea culpas,* or finger-pointing. They should be addressed to the hospital's lawyer or insurance carrier. Depending on the breadth of state law, the risk manager may consider forwarding a copy of the report to the QA committee.[50]

Even in a state with broad protection, a court may find that the privilege is not absolute and, upon a showing of "exceptional necessity" or "extraordinary circumstances," a plaintiff will be permitted to obtain incident reports generated by the hospital's internal risk management program, as well as related peer review committee documents.[51]

Credentials Files

The JCAHO requires a process for delineating clinical privileges, as well as for reappointment to the medical staff and reappraising of such clinical privileges. Collection and review of information regarding credentials also are required by most state statutes and by the federal Health Care Quality Improvement Act (HCQIA).

Regardless of the extent of protection from discovery accorded to credentials files, they should by maintained with an awareness that, in the future, they might be accessed by a wide variety of third parties, including physicians who have been denied privileges, the JCAHO, and state and federal regulatory organizations. In addition, there are cases in which malpractice plaintiffs who were treated by private attending physicians have asserted a separate cause of action for negligent credentialing against the hospital. As part of the claim of corporate liability, they have sought discovery of credentialing files. It is unclear at this time how many states will recognize that cause of action, but even in those states that currently grant protection from discovery to credentials files, it cannot be guaranteed that such existing qualified protections will be maintained.[52]

Ironically, regardless of any statutory protection that might exist, if a hospital is sued for negligent credentialing, it may find itself in a catch-22 situation in which the only way it can defend itself is with the very documents it is seeking to protect. In those states where the statute granting protection does not specifically allow the hospital to use those documents in its defense, some lawyers advise the hospital never to voluntarily disclose peer review or credentialing documents even if, in a particular case where the process was carried out well, they may be helpful to the hospital defense. Selective disclosure may end up being detrimental in a subsequent case because of the legal precedent that is set.

Some hospitals choose to place only relatively mundane information in individual credentials files and "reference" by code the more sensitive information that located elsewhere in the hospital, such as the risk management case files, the QA files, or the offices of individual department chairpersons. Only at the time of credentials review is all the information brought together for the credentials committee's consideration.

Other hospitals maintain a bifurcated system in which sensitive qualitative information is kept in the credentials files, including information obtained from other institutions, information regarding the physicians history of medical malpractice and professional misconduct, and information on the physician's delivery of medical care obtained through the hospital's QA process. In contrast, the physician's separately maintained personnel file contains objective factual information, such as educational qualifications, date of licensure, salary, and title, but does not include any evaluation comments. The majority of discovery requests can then be satisfied by producing only the personnel file, and the hospital can reserve its confidential arguments for the more sensitive credentials files.

Release of Information to the National Practitioner Data Bank

The federal HCQIA, passed in 1986, established the National Practitioner Data Bank (NPDB), which contains a centralized source of information on physicians, dentists, and other licensed health care professionals. The act requires that each person or entity, including an insurance company, which makes a medical malpractice payment under an insurance policy, self-insurance, or otherwise for the benefit of a physician, dentist, or other health practitioner in settlement of, or in satisfaction in whole or in part of, a written claim or judgment against such physician, dentist, or other health care practitioner must report this information to the NPDB and the appropriate state licensing board(s). It also requires (following due process procedures) (1) state medical and dental boards to report disciplinary actions taken against the license of a physician or dentist, (2) hospitals and other health care entities to report their professional review actions that adversely affect a physician's or dentist's appointment or clinical privileges, and (3) medical and dental societies to report adverse membership actions based on professional competence or conduct.[53] In addition, hospitals must request information directly from the NPDB on each physician, dentist, or health care practitioner they are considering for appointment, and at least every two years, on those on their medical staff to whom they have granted clinical privileges previously.

Although there is great political pressure to make this information more available to the public, in general, the information reported will be considered confidential and may not be disclosed. However, it will be disclosed to the physician or practitioner involved and to a hospital or health care entity that needs information concerning a physician, dentist, or other health care practitioner who either is on its medical staff or has clinical privileges, or is entering an employment or affiliation relationship with it. With respect to malpractice cases, a plaintiff's attorney may obtain confidential information on a specific physician, dentist, or health care practitioner named in the action or claim upon a showing that the hospital did not, as part of its credentialing and appointment process, obtain information on the individual involved from the NPDB. The plaintiff's attorney also must agree that the information will be used solely for that specific litigation. Failure to adhere to the confidentiality provision and its use solely for the purpose requested could result in a $10,000 penalty.

....

HEALTHCARE INTEGRITY AND PROTECTION DATA BANK

Included in the Health Insurance Portability and Accountability Act (HIPAA) was the creation of another national data bank to contain information on certain final adverse actions taken against health care providers, suppliers, and practitioners. This bank is called the Healthcare Integrity and Protection Data Bank (HIPDB) and its purpose is to foster quality health care and help stem health care fraud and abuse. The information to the data bank will be reported by state and federal law enforcement organizations, state and federal agencies responsible for licensing or certifying any type of health care practitioner, provider, or supplier; federal agencies that administer or provide payment for health care; and private health plans. The information that they are to report includes:

- Civil judgments, with the exception of malpractice judgments, against health care providers, suppliers, and practitioners in federal or state courts related to the delivery of a health care item or service.

- Federal or state criminal convictions against health care providers, suppliers, and practitioners related to the delivery of health care items or service.

- Actions by federal or state agencies responsible for the licensing and certification of health care providers, suppliers, and practitioners.

- Exclusion of health care providers, suppliers, and practitioners from participation in federal or state health care programs.

The HIPDB is currently requiring reports and will be fully operational in early 2000 to receive requests for reports. All reporting agencies must provide information on all reportable final adverse actions taken since August 21, 1996. Settlements in which no finding or admissions of liability have been made will be excluded.

Information reported to this data bank is confidential. Access to HIPDB is also strictly limited by statute; the general public, as well as health care entities, other than private health plans, do not have access. Where managed care organizations once asked the hospital to provide credentialing information on a physician, it now may be necessary for the hospital to ask the managed care organization for such information. To avoid overlap and confusion, a single NPDB-HIPDB Integrated Querying and Reporting Service will be used to report and query both data banks on the World Wide Web.

The statute provides that only the government agencies and private health plans required to report to the data bank will be authorized to obtain data bank information. However, subjects of reports may obtain access to their reports. Information may be requested for privileging and employment information, professional review, licensing, certification or registration, fraud and abuse investigation, certification to participate in a government program, and civil and administrative actions. It is the prevailing belief that other health care entities such as hospitals, should have access to this information and legislation has been recently introduced to expand HIPDB access.[54]

Peer Review Privilege

In some states, the so-called peer review privilege is quite narrow, protecting only those proceedings in which physicians review the quality of medical care delivered. More recently, as part of comprehensive tort reform legislation in a large number of states, the privilege has been extended to include all the professional committees, such as credentials, utilization review, and QA, as well as to cover other documents maintained in connection with programs to monitor and improve the quality of care, regardless of whether they are related to a specific committee performing a medical review function.[55]

Courts generally have recognized, even in the absence of statute, that a guarantee of confidentiality and protection from discovery is necessary to promote an important state interest in effective peer review proceedings. Only a few courts have given greater deference to a plaintiffs need for all relevant information to prove a case.[56] Some malpractice plaintiffs' attorneys have argued that the proceedings and records of peer review committees, physician credentials files, and other QA documents contain relevant evidence about a physician's general qualifications as well as information about the particular case in suit.

Sometimes attorneys try to circumvent the privilege related to those documents by arguing that the applicable statute should be construed to cover only a very narrow category of documents and information. The issue most often arises in lawsuits alleging malpractice by physicians for whom the hospital may have vicarious liability, such as ED physicians. With greater frequency, however, it is being raised as part of a claim of corporate negligence on the part of the hospital for negligently credentialing the treating physician.[57]

It is important to emphasize that even in states with a relatively broad privilege, the applicable statute frequently protects only the review process itself. The statute may cover discussions at committee meetings, as well as records and documents specifically created for a committee, but may not protect documents otherwise available from nonprotected sources, such as accident reports made in the ordinary course of business, some patient record information, personnel records, and other administrative records of the hospital, even if they are necessary to the committee's deliberations. In addition, actions taken as a result of the committee's deliberations, such as curtailment of a physician's privileges or other disciplinary action, may not be privileged.[58]

A very significant exception, incorporated into almost every statute, is that the prohibition against discovery does not apply to any statements made by a person at the meeting who subsequently is a party to an action concerning the subject matter reviewed at that meeting.[59] Therefore, if a physician whose practice is being reviewed participates in the meeting, any statements he or she makes may be discoverable in a subsequent malpractice action against the physician and the hospital.

Because of questionable protection for certain types of information and documents, the policy concerning peer review materials prepared outside a committee must indicate that they were created to further the work of a committee whose records are privileged under the statute.[60] Some risk managers stamp each such document with a statement that the document has been prepared at the request of a peer review or QA committee and is confidential under the relevant statute.

Other practical suggestions to maximize protection include controlling distribution of and access to peer review committee records; distributing and collecting minutes at the meeting rather than mailing them; destroying all copies except the original; prohibiting names of patients and physicians from being recorded in minutes; and inserting provisions in medical staff bylaws that recognize the confidentiality of peer review activities and prohibit unauthorized or voluntary disclosure of peer review information.[61]

The scope of activities, the types of committees, and the specific information and documents that are protected vary widely from state to state. Prior to establishing the hospital's procedures for generating and maintaining records in this area, it is important to become familiar with case law, statutes, and regulations of the state. The entity's bylaws and its QA and risk management plans and practices should be developed to maximize the protection from discovery available in the jurisdiction. In addition, the risk manager, in coordination with legal counsel, should develop systems for reviewing all discovery requests for each type of information to avoid inadvertently releasing a document that may be privileged.

Attorney-Client Privilege

If the state has a very narrow peer review privilege, as mentioned previously, another privilege that may be available to protect committee minutes and other sensitive documents is the attorney-client privilege. The precise limits of the attorney-client privilege and the extent of protection from discovery afforded to an attorney's work product vary by jurisdiction. In general, however, where legal advice is sought from a lawyer, the confidential communications between client and attorney relating to that advice are protected from disclosure, unless the client waives the privilege.[62] Therefore, when a committee discusses a patient care incident and a strong possibility exists that the hospital will be sued, it may be advisable to have outside legal counsel in attendance. The drawback to relying solely on in-house counsel in those circumstances is that some courts have found that in-house counsels function in a dual capacity as administrator and attorney, rendering communication with them not privileged.[63] With outside counsel present, it may be possible to argue that the issues were discussed in anticipation of litigation and are protected from discovery under the attorney-client privilege. If the lawyer keeps the minutes of the meeting and also writes an advisory memo about the committee's deliberations to hospital administration, which contains the lawyer's advice and opinions on the matter, those records probably will be protected by the privilege.

....

ELECTRONIC RECORDS

Computerization is increasing the volume and sophistication of patient information and the complexities of the records containing that information. New technology makes it possible to collect, store, and analyze worldwide bases of information at a relatively low cost. However, although the principles of medical record keeping have remained the same in the electronic format, computerization has brought with it additional problems.

The advantages of computerized medical records include enhanced patient care brought about by instant access to records by a variety of health care professionals and the creation of legible and complete records that are difficult to lose or destroy. However, the disadvantages include potential review of confidential records by unauthorized users, authentication and accuracy issues, lack of durability of the storage media, and a lack of clear, uniform legislation protecting the records.

The Health Privacy Project working group has outlined its eleven best principles for health privacy. The 1999 report discusses nonidentifiable information; privacy protections follow the data; right of access; notice; safeguards; authorization; organizational policies; research; law enforcement; discrimination; and remedies.[64]

The DHHS-proposed national standard is designed to protect the privacy of the information, whether oral or written, not just the specific record. In the proposal, while DHHS may not have the authority to protect all medical records, including paper records, it attempts to broaden its scope of application. If the information has been maintained or transmitted electronically, then DHHS intends to apply the privacy standard to the source record and to subsequent electronically generated records.[65]

Other criticisms and disadvantages of electronic records include that HIPAA does not allow DHHS to issue standards for records that are maintained by other insurers or by employers for workers' compensation purposes. The proposed rule does not establish appropriate restrictions on the use of redisclosure of such information by likely recipients such as researchers; life insurance issuers; marketing firms; or administrative, legal, and accounting services. DHHS also lacks the authority to provide Americans the right to take action in court when their medical information is used inappropriately, a critical consumer protection that only Congress can provide. The president has called upon Congress to close these gaps and enact comprehensive national legislation to insure that all medical records are protected.[66]

Legal Requirements

Many states permit hospitals and health care facilities to have fully computerized patient records; however, these states carefully regulate how those electronic records are kept. For example, a California statute requires that licensed health care providers utilizing electronic record-keeping systems for patient records comply with additional requirements, unless hardcopy versions of patient records also are retained.[67] Some of those requirements include use of an off-site backup storage system, an image mechanism able to copy signature documents, and a mechanism to ensure that once a record is input it is unalterable.[68] Additional requirements include development and implementation of policies and procedures to outline safeguards against unauthorized access to electronically stored patient health records, including authentication by electronic signature keys.[69] The 1998 *Accreditation Manual for Hospital Standards* has an entire section dedicated to management of information. The standards focus on organization-wide information planning and management processes. The standards attempt to provide guidance as to:

- Insuring timely and easy access to complete information throughout the hospital.

- Improving data accuracy.

- Balancing requirements of security (the protection of data from intentional or unintentional destruction, modification, or disclosure, and ease of access).

- Using the aggregate (combination of standardized data and information) and comparative data to pursue opportunities for improvement.

- Redesigning information-related processes to improve efficiency.

- Increasing collaboration and information sharing to enhance patient care.

Electronic medical records necessarily include electronic signature standards and DHHS issued a proposed rule regarding these.[70] In electronic signatures, there should be an attribute affixed to an electronic document to bind it to a particular entity. An electronic signature secures the user authentication—that is, supplying proof of the claimed entity at the time the signature is generated. It creates the logical manifestation of a signature that will include the possibility for multiple parties to sign a document and have the order of application recognized and proven. It further supplies additional information such as a time stamp and signature purpose specific to that user. The electronic signature also insures the integrity of the signed document to enable the transportability of data, interoperability, independent verifiability, and continuity of signature capability. Verifying a signature on the document substantiates the integrity of the document and its associated attributes and verifies the identity of the signer. The standard for an electronic signature is based on cryptographic methods that use a set of rules and parameters so that the identity of the signer and the integrity of the data can be verified.

In addition to the JCAHO standards, individual states are promulgating requirements for hospitals and other facilities that must be met for electronic authentication of medical record entries to be permitted. For example, some states require that medical records be dated and authenticated and their authors identified. Entries may be confirmed by written signature or initials, rubber stamp, or computer "signatures" (or sequence of keys). Any practitioner who uses a rubber stamp or computer signature to authenticate entries signs a statement that he or she alone will use it. A stamp or computer signature authorized for one person is not used by anyone else.[71] Each state law should be reviewed particularly with the continuing changes being promulgated within the JCAHO standards, as well as the new proposed federal regulations.

System and Data Security

With electronic collection, storage, and analysis of data comes increased access. A variety of problems including those of confidentiality and security arise as a result. Unfortunately, no security system in general use today can withstand the efforts of a skilled computer expert who is determined to break into a system.

The standard of computer security legally required for computerized patient records is not always clear. What is clear, however, is that computer and data security for computerized patient records must be, at a minimum, reasonable.[72] Whether security is reasonable depends on a number of factors. The American Health Information Management Association (AHIMA) has created the following criteria to be considered in determining the reasonableness of security:

- The state of commercially available computer technology.
- The affordability of security technology, procedures, and techniques.
- The likelihood of failure of security and the risk that such a failure could be caused intentionally.
- The magnitude of harm that could result if security fails, is inadequate, or is breached.
- Known and reasonably anticipated threats to security.
- Standards promulgated by nationally recognized standard-setting organizations and professional associations in the fields of health information, health care informatics, and computer security.[73]

Security Threat Technologies

Even insurance companies, managed care companies, pharmaceutical firms, physicians, and outside ancillary health care providers dialing in from their computers pose a threat to data security because they may inadvertently access unauthorized information. Finally, the addition and integration of new medical record technology into an existing medical record-keeping system can threaten the security of data because such integration often requires exposure of data so that systems specialists can make sure that the integrated system is working properly. Fortunately, the computer security technology that we thought was available only in the movies is with us today.

Passwords often are used as a security measure to ensure data confidentiality because they are based on something a user knows. However, problems can occur, including cracking, sharing passwords, and simply forgetting the appropriate password, particularly if it is changed on a routine basis. Because of the problems with passwords, some institutions have begun to protect their documents by using biometrics technology. Biometrics permit entry based on some characteristic of a user, for example, fingerprints, voice patterns, hand geometry, retinal patterns, and facial recognition.[74] The advantages of this type of technology include the fact that this information is difficult to crack and not easily shared. The disadvantages include false acceptance and an individual's hesitancy to have this technology utilized on him or her.

Tokens provide another form of data security. These may include credit cards or calculator-sized devices that generate passwords.[75] There are some problems with tokens; one major disadvantage is cost, particularly for large organizations where employee turnover is constant and where tokens are easily lost.

Less costly ways of improving data security include the use of software that renders computer terminals inactive after a certain time frame and logs out certain users or otherwise prohibits their access. In addition, certain systems make their users go through multiple levels of authentication, and others have one set of computers as a boundary between the end product and the outside world. Finally, data can be *encrypted,* that is, scrambled in such a way as to be unintelligible to anyone without the appropriate information to unscramble them.

Medical information should be made available only to those with the need to know. Therefore, it is essential that the accountability of the people who have access to sensitive information be ensured. Risk management issues that need to be addressed to ensure data accountability include:

- Establishing written policies for employees to maintain security and confidentiality and discipline violaters.
- Tracking of user activities as to the time and nature of modifications made to the data.
- Auditing to reflect the logging-in on the system.
- Intrusion detection, which flags undesired behavior.
- Provision of a mechanism for users to validate that information they receive electronically came from the person who claims to have sent it.
- Digital signatures that may use encryption technology.

Protection of Confidentiality with Vendors and Data Clearinghouses

Health information system contracts are complex.[76] In a typical vendor form contract, such as medical record copy services, medical record transcription services, and claims adjudication services, the only restriction on the vendor's use or disclosure of patient and provider data is that no patient will be identified by name. Such a restriction is inadequate to protect patient confidentiality in an environment where combining and cross-matching data are possible and inferences are available for determining the identity of record subjects. In fact, in the current environment, there is no certain protection of patient confidentiality in data disclosed by the vendor, unless the data are aggregated into cells of sufficient minimum size that the probability of anyone identifying a patient whose data are included in the cell approaches zero.

It is interesting to note that the new contracts between the United Auto Workers and the Big Three automakers and their largest parts suppliers include new provisions to ensure the privacy of employee medical records. The contract provision states that the company will use medical information only for the purposes for which it is initially given.[77]

A provider should agree to permit vendor use of its data only if the agreement includes detailed confidentiality obligations applicable to the vendor, its agents, employees, and subcontractors. In addition, the agreement should protect patient identifiable data, any information identified as proprietary information of the provider and its affiliates, and practitioner- or provider-identified data. The agreement also should include detailed procedures and protocols the vendor must follow in handling the provider's data.[78]

Contracts with clearinghouses and other third parties handling unencrypted data also should include protections such as clear delineation of ownership rights in the data and detailed provisions stating the extent to which the clearinghouse or third party may disclose or distribute data to others. The contract should contain a clear statement of the purpose(s) for which the third party is being granted access to the data. Such provisions may be important in preventing third-party access to data, even pursuant to subpoena. For example, if the third party has access to data for purposes of performing peer review or utilization review, a privilege may apply in some states.

Detailed data quality standards, delineation of procedures for maintaining data quality, and provisions for auditing data quality also should be included in a contract with a vendor or other third party. As a part of maintaining quality standards, it is important to require the third party to comply with the provider's security requirements if the third party will be granted remote access to the provider's patient information system.

Because a third party presumably will have several employees reviewing confidential data, it is necessary that all employees, agents, and subcontractors of the third party sign confidentiality agreements before being given access to those data. These confidentiality agreements should contain clear definitions of the information to be held in confidence. It is particularly important that the agreements be signed by anyone who will have access to patient-identifiable information in unencrypted form. However, the provider also may wish to protect as confidential any proprietary information of the provider and its affiliates and any information that identifies the provider or an affiliate or a practitioner.

In addition, the contract should provide for remedies for breach of confidentiality obligations, including injunctive relief. Provisions limiting the third party's liability for breach should be avoided, if possible. The contract should anticipate protections on data security after termination of the relationship with the third party. A provision stating that confidentiality obligations survive termination of the agreement and requiring the third party to return all copies of the provider's data upon termination should be included. Finally, the contract should include provisions requiring that the third party indemnify the health care provider for any actions brought against the provider as a result of the third party's breach of confidentiality obligations.[79]

There also must be a real concern for patient rights regarding record disclosure between entities. This issue becomes even more troublesome when confidential information, such as HIV status, mental health treatment, and alcohol or drug abuse treatment, is discussed.

· · · · · · · · · · · ·

MOTIVATIONS FOR ADDRESSING SECURITY IN HEALTH CARE SYSTEMS

Legislative requirements, regulations by accrediting organizations, conformance with which the system may be required to operate, and litigation by individuals who are harmed due to the revelation of private medical information because of inadequate safeguards provided by a health care worker or the organization are all motivations for addressing security in health care systems.

The legal requirements for maintaining the security of health care records (whether in electronic or paper form) are based on a complex mix of federal and state regulations.[80] A portion of the HIPAA's provisions directs the development and implementation of uniform national standards for the secure electronic transmission of health information.

A series of definitions demonstrates the expansiveness of the act. *Health information,* that is, information created or received by a health care provider, health plan, public health authority, employer, life insurer, school, university, or health care clearinghouse, relates to an individual's past, future, or present physical or mental health or condition, receipt of health care, or payment for such health care. DHHS has been directed to adopt standard "data elements" and "code sets" for the electronic encoding of health information. These standard data elements and code sets must work for all financial and administrative transactions involving health claims, enrollment and eligibility, referrals, and authorizations, as well as first reports of injury and coordination of benefits. These data cannot permit the disclosure of trade secrets or confidential information and must reduce the administrative costs of providing and paying for health care. Each of the organizations that are covered will be assigned a unique health identifier.

DHHS issued a NPRM proposing the security standard called for in HIPAA on August 12, 1998. Presently there is no date set for the issuance of the proposed security standards in final form. Succinctly, the security standard consists of requirements that a health care entity must address to safeguard the integrity, confidentiality, and availability of electronic data. Additionally, the standard describes the features that must be implemented to satisfy the rule. There are four security standard categories:

- Administrative procedures.
- Physical safeguards.
- Technical security services.
- Technical security mechanisms.

Failure to use these standards results in penalties unless the organization has reasonable cause.

The act also stipulates specific health data privacy requirements in order to maintain "reasonable and appropriate" safeguards for the integrity and confidentiality of health information. Any "reasonably anticipated" threats to the security or integrity of individually identifiable health information and unauthorized use or disclosure of that material must be prevented.

Specific security provisions must consider (1) the technical capabilities of health information record systems, (2) security measure costs, (3) personnel training, (4) audit trails for computerized record systems, and (5) the needs and capabilities of small and rural health care providers. Penalties for breach of privacy where there is knowing procurement or disclosure of individually identifiable health information include a $50,000 fine and a one-year prison sentence. If this information is utilized through false pretenses, the fine increases to $100,000 and the prison term to five years. If there is an intent, transfer, or use of the information for commercial advantage, personal gain, or malicious harm, the fine increases to $250,000, and the prison term extends to ten years. Until DHHS issues final regulations, state laws protecting the privacy of individual patient data are not preempted. Ultimately, the most stringent requirements, whether state or federal, to protect privacy rights are mandated to be followed.

The proposed DHHS regulations outline many compliance requirements, which health plans, for example, will be required to follow.

- Develop a notice of information practice for distribution to customers.
- Designate a company privacy official.
- Develop accounting procedures for tracking disclosures.
- Train employees on privacy requirements.
- Develop safeguards for the protection of information.
- Develop information sharing policies and procedures.
- Draft contracts for arrangements of business partners to share protected information.

············

CONCLUSION

Advances in computer technology, combined with advances in health care, have created complex legal and ethical considerations for all health care providers and entities. With the increase in the electronic storage and transmission of health care information, the legal framework within which confidentiality, security, patient care, and other critical issues are addressed will change. Furthermore, as the health care marketplace continues to evolve, greater demands will be placed on hospitals, health systems, health plans, and other providers for access to confidential patient and peer review information. To be effective, mechanisms to protect confidentiality and security of health care information must be a part of a complete security package. This includes well thought-out security policies and procedures, security training, and security management and maintenance. A comprehensive security management program is a significant undertaking but is well worth the investment of required resources and under future federal regulations may be required.

Endnotes

1. P.L. 104-91, 110 Stat. 1936 [hereinafter HIPAA], § 264 (a).
2. NPRM Preamble § I.E. 1.b.
3. Conner, C., LL.L. "Medical Records." *Hospital Law Manual (vol. III)*. Gaithersburg, Md.: Aspen, 1999.
4. Joint Commission on Accreditation of Healthcare Organizations (JCAHO). Management of Information. *Comprehensive Accreditation Manual*. Oakbrook Terrace, Ill.: JCAHO, 1998.
5. Conner, pp. 4–5.
6. JCAHO, 1998.
7. 42 CFR §482.24. See Security and Electronic Signature Standards, 63 *Fed. Reg.* 43241 (1998) (to be codified at 45 CFR pt. 142) (Proposed Aug. 12, 1998).
8. 42 USC §1395.
9. In states that have adopted the Uniform Preservation of Private Business Records Act, a three-year preservation requirement applies to the medical records maintained by private hospitals, even though the act does not specifically address medical records.
10. For example, documentation that employees were adequately trained; reports from the hospital's hotline including the nature and results of any investigation that was conducted; modifications to the compliance program; self-disclosure; and the result of the hospital's auditing and monitoring efforts. Further, Medicare's Conditions of Participation Requirement states that hospital records regarding Medicare claims be retained for a minimum of five years. (42 CFR § 482.24 [b][1] and HCFA Hospital Manual §413 [C][12-91]).
11. 31 USCA 3731 (b).
12. The suggested retention schedule was compiled from information in the Code of Federal Regulations, basic IRS regulations, corporate records retention manuals, Healthcare Financial Management Association reference materials, the Medicare Hospital Manual (Publication 10), the College of American Pathologists, Joint Commission of Accreditation of Healthcare Organizations, Florida's General Records Schedule (GS-4) for Public Hospitals, Health Care Facilities, and Medical Providers, and state laws.
13. Connor, pp. 4–5.

14. Connor, pp. 4–5.

15. The Uniform Health Care Information Act of 1985 has been adopted in Montana and Washington, but many states have passed legislation that accomplishes the same objective. See, for example, Colo Rev. Stat. Tit. 25-1-801; 735 Ill. Comp. Stat. Ann.5/8-2001. In states without a statute, courts sometimes will find a common-law right of access.

16. *Biddle v. Warren General Hospital,* 715 N.E. 2d 518 (Ohio 1999). In the case of *Weld v. CVS Pharmacy, Inc.,* (1999 WL 494114 [Mass. Super. Ct.], Massachusetts's Superior Court regarding the marketing of pharmacy information held that there was a common-law right of privacy. *Cossette v. Minnesota Power & Light,* 188 F.3d 964 (8th Cir. 1999). Here the Eighth Circuit of Appeals determined that the Americans with Disabilities Act (ADA) created its own set of privacy restrictions for medical information, and that these protections were not limited to "disabled" persons but would apply to any employee or other person potentially covered by the ADA. States differ as to whether there is a legal, as opposed to a moral or ethical, "right to privacy." Under a variety of legal theories, most states protect some type of privacy interest. Some state courts have held that breach of the duty of confidentiality is a tort and that a cause of action for breach of confidentiality may exist in circumstances where there has been extrajudicial disclosure of confidential information, or in cases such as custody disputes where the plaintiff's physical condition is not in issue. See generally, Annotation, Physician's tort liability for unauthorized disclosure of confidential information about patients (48 *ALR* 4th 668, 1985). A medical provider that reveals privileged information by mailing patient's medical records in lieu of attending a deposition as required by a subpoena may be sued in tort for breach of the fiduciary duty of confidentiality. State ex rel. *Crowden v Dandurand,* 970 S.W. 2d 340 (Mo. 1998). Expert affidavit submitted by patient in malpractice action against psychologist was adequate despite contention that expert's opinion was premised on violation of professional ethical standard, which could not alone serve as basis for malpractice action; expert did not merely opine that psychologist's alleged disclosure of confidential information violated ethical standard, and expert specifically stated that disclosure was deviation from "standard of care" of psychologist, although such statement was followed by reference to ethical rule. OCGA § 9-11-9.1 *Bala v. Powers Ferry Psychological Associates,* 225 Ga. App. 843, 491 S.E. 2d 380 (1997), cert. denied (Sept. 4, 1997). A medical malpractice claim may be based on the unauthorized disclosure of confidential information. G.S. § 8-53. *Jones v. Asheville Radiological Group,* P.A., 129 N.C. App. 449, 500 S.E. 2d 740 (1998), related reference, 506 S.E.2d 254 (N.C. 1998). *Horne v. Patton,* 287 So.2d 824, 1973 (physician disclosed confidential information to plaintiff's employer); *MacDonald v. Clinger,* 84 AD 2d 482, 446 NYS 2d 801, 1982 (psychiatrist revealed confidential information to patient's wife). Probably a more logical basis for finding liability is that, as part of an implied contract between physician and patient, the physician agrees not to release information about the patient without his or her consent. *Hammonds v. Aetna Casualty and Surety Co.,*243 F. Supp. 793, ND OH, 1965. Suits against practitioners for invasion of privacy typically allege an unwarranted exploitation of the patient's personality or a publication about his or her private affairs that would cause outrage, mental suffering, shame, or humiliation. See, for example, *Barber v. Time, Inc.,* 348 Mo. 1199, 159 SW 2d 291. That type of action might be brought when a photograph or description of the patient is published without permission. As to whether there is a constitutional right of privacy, although not explicitly stated anywhere in the Constitution, the Supreme Court has held that there is a fundamental right of privacy emanating from various provisions in the Constitution that limit the extent to which the government may interfere with an individual's privacy. See, for example, *Griswold v. Connecticut,* 381 US 479, 1965; *In re Search Warrant,* 810 F.2d 57, 3d Cir. cert. denied, 107 S.Ct. 3233, 1987 (patients have a privacy interest under the Constitution in their medical records in the possession of their physicians; however, the protection afforded by the right to

privacy is not absolute and must be balanced against the legitimate interests of the state in securing the information contained therein).

17. The four traditional criteria for a privileged communication are: (1) It originates in confidence that it will not be disclosed, (2) the element of confidentiality is essential to the full maintenance of the relationship between the parties, (3) the relationship is one that the community thinks ought to be fostered, and (4) the injury to the relationship that would occur from the disclosure would be greater than the benefit gained by the aid-giver to the litigation. 8 Wigmore, *Evidence* §2285 at 527, McNaughton rev., 1961.

18. 8 Wigmore, *Evidence §2380. Hinzman v. State,* 53 Ark. App. 256; 922 S.W.2d 725 (1996). Because psychologist notified patient that findings from their session would be reported to the prosecuting attorney's office, communications were not confidential and therefore not subject to psychologist-patient privilege. *Halacy v. Steen,* 670 A.2d 1371 (Me. 1996). When assailant agreed that his pre-sentence investigation report from a related criminal proceeding could be released to a particular third party, he did not waive his psychologist-patient privilege over those reports as to other third parties. *Me. R. Evid.* 503 (physician- and psychotherapist-patient privilege).

19. Annotation, physician-patient privilege as extending to patients' medical or hospital records, *10 ALR* 4th 552, 1981. Hospital records are included within physician-patient privilege. VAMS §491.060(5). State ex rel. *C.J.V. v. Jamison,* 973 S.W.2d 183 (Mo. Ct. App. E.D. 1998). Personal injury plaintiff waived physician-patient privilege in her medical records insofar as they concerned medical condition at issue under pleadings. State ex re. *Jones v. Syler,* 936 S.W.2d 805 (MO. 1997). Patient was entitled to obtain dates on which his physician had obtained medical treatment in six months prior to and sixty days following patient's surgery, where patient alleged that physician was suffering from disability or illness that limited his ability to perform surgery, patient sufficiently showed through physician's admissions to patient regarding his own medical condition that physician's physical condition was in controversy and physician-patient privilege did not protect dates on which physician received treatment. *Klein v. Levin* 242 A.D.2d 682,662 NYS 2d 792 (2d Dep't 1997). Probationer could not have reasonably expected that his communications with psychologist would be privileged and could not claim psychologist-patient privilege, and thus trial court abused its discretion in denying motion in negligence supervision suit against city on behalf of child raped by probationer to compel discovery, where municipal court had ordered probationer to participate in treatment as conditions of continued probation and probationer signed consent form for release of information to probation officer. West's RCWA 18.83.110 *Hertog v. City of Seattle,* 943 P 2d 1153 (Div. 1 1997). Patient records and files were indispensable to insurer's defense in action by insured, a physician, under disability insurance policy; insurer was entitled to records from insured's medical practice to determine whether he was unable to perform substantial and material duties of his job, and insured could not hide behind Ohio's statutory physician-patient privilege to impair insurer's ability to defend itself. Ohio R.C. §2317.02 *Varghese v. Royal Maccabees Life Ins. Co.* 181FRD 359 (S.D. Ohio 1998) Defendant was not entitled to production of witness's confidential drug treatment records, to show extent of witness's addiction and payments made to clinic by witness, who defendant claimed was perpetrator of charged robbery; because information was available through other means, defendant's need for information did not outweigh statutory emphasis on keeping treatment records confidential. Public Health Service Act, §543, as amended, 42 USCA §290dd-2. *U.S. v. Obele,* 136 F3d 1414, (10th Cir. 1998), cert. denied, 119 S. Ct. 197 (U.S. 1998).

20. See, for example, *Payne v. Howard,* 75 FRD 465, DDC, 1977 (court permitted plaintiff to discover the names and addresses of patients of plaintiff's physician who had received similar treatment so that plaintiff could contact them and determine whether they would be willing to waive the statutory privilege attaching to their records); *Hirsh v. Catholic Medical Center,* 91 AD 2d 1033, 458 NYS 2d 625, 2nd Dept., 1983 (disclosure of the

name of a nonparty patient who may have witnessed an occurrence would not violate the privilege). *Contra, Schecket v. Kesten,* 126 NW 2d 718, MI, 1964 (names of nonparty patients are protected by physician-patient privilege and are not subject to discovery); *N.O. v. Callahan, 110* FRD 637, D. MA, 1986 (plaintiffs complaining of inadequate state psychiatric facilities could tour facilities but could not videotape other patients without their consent).

21. See, for example, *Tucson Medical Center Inc. v. Rowles,* 21 AZ App. 424, 520 P.2d 518, 523, 1974. ("Our decision . . . that hospital records are covered by the physician-patient privilege where neither the patient nor his physician are parties to the proceedings. To hold otherwise would deprive a patient of the confidentiality granted him by [the statute] simply because neither the patient nor his physician are parties to the proceeding." The court then reviewed the record in camera to ascertain if there was any relevant nonprivileged information and denied access.)

22. See, for example, *Ziegler v. Superior Court of the County of Pima,* 134 AZ 390, 656 P.2d 1251, AZ Ct. App., 1982. Other courts have rejected this approach because of the perceived danger that the nonlitigant patient's identity would not remain confidential. *Parkson v. Central Du Page Hospital,* 105 IL App.3d 850, 435 NE 2d 140, 1982.

23. If there is an executor of the deceased patient's estate, authorization of the executor usually should be sought before releasing information. If there is no executor, authorization should be obtained from the next of kin. *Claim of Gurkin,* 434 NYS 2d 607 NY Sup. Ct., 1980 (wife authorized release); *Emmentt v. Eastern Dispensary and Casualty Hospital,* 396 F.2d 931, 935 DC App., 1967 (son authorized release; the court stated, "In our view, a son and only child has so vital an identification with any cause of action potentially arising upon his father's negligently caused demise as would enable him to waive the privilege when there is no personal representative to act in his behalf"). If there is known conflict among next of kin, authorization of all the nearest kin available should be obtained.

24. *In re Lifschutz,* 85 CA Rptr. 829, 467 P.2d 557, 1970, quoting *San Francisco v. Superior Court,* 37 CA 2d 227, 232, 231 P.2d 26, 1951; *Hoenig v. Wesohal,* 52 NY 2d 605, 439 NYS 2d 831, 1981 (by commencing personal injury action, plaintiff waived any privilege she previously had and was required to produce reports of treating physicians).

25. *Hammonds v. Aetna Casualty and Surety Co.,* supra note 16; *Rea v. Pardo,* 132 AD 2d 442, 552 NYS 2d 393, 4th Dept., 1987.

26. See, for example, *Friedlander v. Morales,* 70 AD 2d 501, 415 NYS 2d 831, 1st Dept., 1979 (court permitted defendant to discover records of plaintiffs treating psychiatrist in case where plaintiff alleged defendant's malpractice caused serious physical and emotional injury). However, courts will not allow so-called blunderbuss notices for discovery. Although waiver of the physician-patient privilege has occurred, its scope is limited and does not permit discovery information involving unrelated illnesses and treatments.

27. See, for example, *Williams v. Roosevelt Hospital,* 66 NY 2d 391, 497 NYS 2d 348, 1985. (Infant plaintiff alleged Erb's palsy and brain damage caused by cephalopelvic disproportion and defendant's failure to perform cesarean. Court ruled mother could not refuse to answer questions during her deposition concerning condition of plaintiff's siblings and mother's obstetrical history, although court did not decide, in this case, whether defendant also could gain access to actual medical records of plaintiffs siblings and mother.)

28. Most jurisdictions disapprove of *ex parte* interviews. See generally, Annotation, Discovery: right to *ex parte* interview with injured party's treating physician. 50 *ALR* 4th 714, 1986; see also, *Petrillo v. Syntex Laboratories Inc.,* 148 IL App.3d 581, 102 IL Dec. 172, 499 NE 2d 952, 1986 (court held patient's implied consent, in filing suit, was

only to release medical information relevant to suit; *Anker v. Brodnitz, 98* Misc.2d 148, 413 NYS 2d 582, 1979, aff'd, 73 AD 2d 589, 422 NYS 2d 887, 2nd Dept., 1979 (court prohibited private interviews with treating physicians during the pretrial discovery phase absent patient's express consent or a court order). But see *Nielson v. John G. Appison, MD, PC,* 138 Misc.2d 74, 524 NYS 2d 161, trial term, 1988 (limiting this prohibition to the pretrial discovery stage of litigation and permitting defendants to privately interview plaintiffs treating physicians in anticipation of presenting them for testimony at trial). No court, however, has permitted recovery against a physician for breach of confidentiality under facts such as these.

29. Cases permitting *ex parte* interviews include: *Doe v. Eli Lilly & Co.,* 99 FRD 126, DDC, *1983; Langdon v. Champion,* 745 P.2d 1371 AK, 1987; *Coqdell v. Brown,* 531 A.2d 1379, NJ Super. L., 1987; *Moses v. McWilliams,* 549 A.2d 950, 959. PA Super., 1988 (interpreted a statutory exception to the privilege for "civil matters brought by the patient" to apply to *ex parte* disclosures by physicians, court noted "*ex parte* interviews are less costly and easier to schedule than depositions, are conducive to candor and spontaneity, are a cost-efficient method of eliminating nonessential witnesses . . . and allow both parties to confer with the treating physicians").

30. For examples of mandatory reporting statutes, see, for example, CA Penal Code §11160 (1999) (injury caused by deadly weapon); 325 Ill. Comp. Stat. Ann.5/4, 1999 (child abuse); *Conn. Gen. Stat.* §19a-215, 1994 (communicable diseases); *Minn. Stat. Ann.* §144.34, 1998 (occupational diseases, including poisoning from lead, phosphorus, carbon monoxide, and so on).

31. The federal Freedom of Information Act (FOIA), 5 USC §552-a, sets forth a general rule of disclosure for records in the possession of the executive branch. The statute contains an exception for "personnel and medical files and similar files the disclosure of which would constitute a clearly unwarranted invasion of personal privacy," 5 USC 552(b)(6). State freedom of information laws contain similar exclusions.

32. 45 CFR Part 164.910 Uses and Disclosures Permitted without Individual Authorization.

33. 45 CFR Part 164.506(e) Application to Business Partners.

34. 45 CFR Part 164.506 (c) Exception for Psychotherapy Notes.

35. In *Tarasoff,* the victim of the therapist's patient was clearly identified. Subsequently, in *Thompson v. County of Alameda,* 167 CA Rptr. 70, 27 CA 3d 741, 614 R2d 728, 1980, the California Supreme Court held that the duty to warn depends on and arises from the existence of a prior threat to a specific identifiable victim. A few courts have gone beyond *Tarasoff* to hold that psychotherapists also will be liable for their patients' violent acts against persons who are not identifiable in advance but are "foreseeable victims." In those cases, liability arises where the therapist or psychiatric facility negligently releases a potentially dangerous patient who subsequently harms a third party. See, for example, *Leverett v. State,* 61 OH App.2d 35, 399 NE 2d 106, 1978 ("A hospital may be held liable for the negligent release of a mental patient only when the hospital, in exercising medical judgment, knew or should have known that the patient, upon his release, would be very likely to cause harm to himself or others.").

36. See, for example, 740 Ill. Comp. Stat. Ann.110/1, et seq., 1999, which requires that confidential records and communications be disclosed "when, and to the extent, a therapist, in his sole discretion, determines that such disclosure is necessary to initiate or continue civil commitment proceedings or to otherwise protect against a clear imminent risk of serious physical or mental injury or death to the patient or another. Like most statutes, this one allows, but does not require, a psychiatrist to warn.

37. 42 CFR Subchapter A, Part 2.

38. For an excellent article on the amendments to the alcohol and drug abuse regulations, see: Kramer, D. V. "Confidentiality of Patient Alcohol and Drug Abuse Information." *Kentucky Hospitals,* Spring 1988.

39. George Washington University, Intergovernmental Health Policy Project, State AIDS Policy Center, *State AIDS Reports,* #7, Feb.–Mar. 1989, p. l.

40. Discovery was allowed in *Belle Bonfils Memorial Blood Center v. Denver District Court,* 763 P.2d 1003, solo. 1988; *Tarrant County Hospital District v. Hughes,* 734 SW 2d 675, TX App. 1987, cert. denied, 484 U.S. 1065, 108 S.Ct. 1027, 1988. Discovery was denied in *Rasmussen v. South Florida Blood Service, Inc.,* 500 So.2d 533, 1987; *Krygier v. Airweld,* 137 Misc.2d 306, 520 NYS 2d 475, 1987.

41. *State v. Copeland,* 680 SW 2d 327, MO App., 1984. A few medical record confidentiality statutes authorize disclosure of medical records information without patient authorization or a subpoena when necessary to cooperate with law enforcement agencies.

42. 45 CFR Part 164.510 (f) Disclosure for Law Enforcement.

43. See also proposed Federal Regulations 45 CFR Part 164.510(d) Uses and Disclosure for Judicial and Administrative Proceedings. Interestingly, a physician-patient privilege may not be asserted to quash a *subpoena ad testificandum* on the theory that a witness cannot assert the privilege in advance of the questions being asked. However, the witness can refuse to answer a question seeking privileged material, in which case the questioner could ask a court to determine if the privilege has been raised appropriately and, if not, to order an answer.

44. *Tehven v. Job Service North Dakota and St. Luke's Hospital,* 488 NW 2d 48, ND, 1992.

45. See also proposed Federal Regulations 45 CFR Part 154.510(g) Uses and Disclosure for Governmental Health Data Systems and 164.51(c) Use and Disclosure for Health Oversight Activities. *Tenn. Code Ann. §68-11-311.*

46. For examples of peer review statutes, see: *Arizona Rev. Stat. Ann.* §36.445.01A, West, 1999; *Cal Evid Code* §1157, 1999; §§ 395.0193, 395.0197 and §766.101, *Fla. Stat.,* 1999. 735 Ill. Comp. Stat. Ann.5/8-2101, 1999; NY CLS Public Health §2805-m, 1996; *Bayfront Medical Center, Inc. v. State Agency for Healthcare Administration,* 741 So. 2d 1226 (Fla. 2d DCA 1999), where the appellate court ruled that the Medical Center's report of the results of a peer review investigation, as contrasted to the actual records of the investigative procedures of the peer review panel, was not privileged from disclosure to the state agency reviewing the Medical Center's risk management procedures. Without a statute, courts have refused to create a privilege. *Davison v. St. Paul Fire and Marine Ins. Co.,* 75 WI.2d 190, 248 NW 2d 433, 1977 (declining to apply retroactively a subsequently enacted statute granting protection from discovery in malpractice cases and rejecting argument in favor of a common-law peer review privilege).

47. For a discussion of the attorney-client privilege, the insured-insurer privilege, and the work product doctrine, see generally, Jones, *Evidence* §19: 18–19: 19, 1972. *Hickman v. Taylor,* 329 US 495, 1957, remains the seminal case on the question of protection afforded to attorney work product. Some states, such as Florida, specifically provide that incident reports required under a hospital's risk management program "shall be considered to be part of the work papers of the attorney defending the establishment in litigation relating thereto . . ." making them subject to discovery only upon a showing of undue hardship. §395.0197, *Fla. Stat., 1999, Fla. R. Civ. P* 1.280(b)(2). Without a privilege, an incident report would represent a contemporaneous statement of fact generated in response to a specific event and would not be protected.

48. *Sims v. Knollwood Park Hospital,* 511 So.2d 154, AL, 1987 (patient who fractured hip when she fell in hospital may discover incident report about the fall because it is not work product protected by the attorney-client privilege; the mere possibility of eventual litigation is not enough to protect the report); but see *Enke v. Anderson,* 733 SW 2d

462, MO App., 1987 (incident report was still entitled to the more limited protection available to materials prepared for litigation under the attorney work product doctrine). See also *Shaffer v. Rogers,* 362 NW 2d 552, IA, 1985 (routine internal investigation report was protected even though it might serve a variety of possible future uses; its primary purpose was in anticipation of litigation).

49. See, for example, *Mass. Ann. Laws, Ch.* 111 §205(b), 1999, which provides protection for incident reports as records necessary to comply with risk management and QA programs; *Gallagher v. Detroit Macomb Hospital Association,* No. 95084, MI Ct. App. Oct. 3, 1988 (discovery of an incident report about a patient's fall from bed not permitted; report came within statutory protection afforded to records prepared for hospital quality-of-care data collection purposes; hospital administrator for legal affairs had testified that incident reports on unusual occurrences were routinely forwarded to internal safety and QA committees).

50. Conner, C., LL.L. "Medical Records." *Hospital Law Manual (vol. III).* Gaithersburg, Md.: Aspen, 1999.

51. For example, Florida allows discovery of materials protected as work product "upon a showing that the party seeking discovery has need of the material in preparation of his case and that he is unable without undue hardship to obtain the substantial equivalent of the materials by other means." Rule 1.280, Florida Rules of Civil Procedure. But, in application, this is a difficult standard for a plaintiff to meet. *Bay Medical Center v. Sapp,* 535 So.2d 308, FL App. 1st DCA, 1988 (where plaintiff was not entitled to production of incident reports in absence of required showing of undue hardship and inability to obtain substantially equivalent materials by other means).

52. Many statutes specifically state that the privilege does not apply to proceedings in which a health care provider contests denial or status of staff privileges or authorization to practice. See, for example, *Cal. Evid Code* §1157 (c); *Kan. Stat Ann. §65-4915; La. Rev. Stat. Ann.* §§13:3715-3; 735 Ill. Comp. Stat. Ann.5/8-2101. Case law is divided on this question. See, for example, *Roseville Community Hospital v. Superior Court,* 70 CA App. 3d 809, 139 CA Rptr. 170, 1977 (statements made by individuals at a committee meeting of hospital's medical staff were discoverable by persons whose requests for staff privileges were denied); *contra, Parkview Memorial Hospital v. Pepple,* 483 NE 2d 469, IN App., 1985 (Indiana's peer review confidentiality law applies to civil actions brought by physicians challenging private hospitals' decisions concerning staff privileges as well as malpractice cases).

53. 42 USCA §11111.

54. 45 CFR Part 61 Governing the Healthcare Integrity and Protection Data Bank.

55. See Conner, C., LL.L. "Medical Records." *Hospital Law Manual, (vol III).* Gaithersburg, Md.: Aspen, 1999. For example, in 1986, New York law was amended to provide confidentiality protection for all information required to be collected and maintained as part of a hospital's coordinated program of quality assurance and risk management, including records, documentation, committee actions, and incident reports required to be made to the state health department. *NY CLS Pub. Health* §2805-m, 1999. The former peer review statute (which remains in effect) protected a more narrow category of records and proceedings relating to performance of a medical review function. *NY CLS Educ.* §6527, 1999. The Massachusetts law was similarly amended in 1987 to provide protection for records necessary to comply with risk management and QA programs, *Mass. Ann. Laws, Ch.* 111, §205(b), 1999.

56. See, for example, *Humana Hospital Desert Valley v. Superior Court County of Maricopa,* 154 AZ 396, 742 P.2d 1382, 1386, AZ App., 1987 ("If this court were to eliminate the peer review privilege, it would negate an important state interest. . . . The confidentiality of peer review committee proceedings is essential to achieve

complete investigation and review of medical care. These deliberations would terminate if they were subject to the discovery process."). See also *Willing v. St. Joseph Hospital,* *176* Ill. App-3d 737, 531 NE 2d 824, IL App. lst Dist., 1988; *Caroll v. Nunez,* 137 AD 2d 911, 524 NYS 2d 578, NY AD 3d Dept., 1988. See generally, Annotation, Discovery of hospitals' internal records or communications as to qualifications or evaluations of physicians. 81 *ALR* 3d 944, 1977; Cunco, M. K. "Disclosure versus Confidentiality of Hospital Peer Review Records." *Medical Trial Technique Quarterly,* Fall 1984, pp. 172–83; Goldberg, B. A. "The Peer Review Privilege: A Law in Search of a Valid Policy." *American Journal of Law and Medicine, 10*(151), 1984. Under Florida law, no public policy reasons barred disability insurer from obtaining discovery of insured physicians' peer review materials in suit to recover disability benefits; insurer made a sufficient showing of exceptional necessity or extraordinary circumstances to justify production of the small portions of the hospital applications possibly stating that the physician suffered from no physical or mental limitations impairing ability to practice medicine. *Toyos v. Northwestern Mut. Life Ins. Co.* 1 F. Supp. 2d 1462 (S.D. Fla. 1998). Provision of Nurse Practice Act allowing claims for retaliatory acts relating to peer review committees did not include within its definition of "peer review" the evaluation of a licensed vocational nurse; such a nurse was not a proper subject for "peer review." Vernos' Ann. Texas Civ. St. art 4525b, §6 *Clark v. Texas Home Health, Inc.* 971 SW2d 435 (Tex.1998) State statutes prohibiting disclosure of physician peer review procedure were inapplicable to a malpractice action brought under the Federal Tort Claims Act. 28 USCA §2671 et seq.: NY McKinney's CPLR 4504; *Syposs v. US* 179 FRD 406 (WDNY 1998) Letter from doctor, allegedly a letter of reference to third-party confidential assessment of physicians' professional competence, generated at request of hospital's credentialing committee for use in determining whether permanent privileges should be extended to physician, could be privileged from discovery under Medical Studies Act in medical malpractice litigation between patient and physician and hospital, as granting or limiting staff privileges could constitute internal quality control. SHA 737 ILCS 5/8-2101, 8-2102. *Stricklin v. Becan,* 689 NE 2d 328 (4th dist. 1997) Statutory peer review privilege did not apply to physicians' action against hospital seeking damages for actions of its peer review committee that restricted his staff privileges, such that privilege did not preclude discovery of hospital's peer review committee records, even those documents regarding matters unrelated to the physician. *VAMS* §537.035 State ex rel. *Health Midwest Development Group, Inc. v. Daugherty,* 965 S.W. 2d 841 (Mo. 1998), reh'g denied (Apr. 21, 1998).

57. In cases alleging corporate negligence of hospitals, most decisions appear to protect against disclosure of peer review records. See, for example, *Terre Haute Regional Hospital, Inc. v. Basden,* 524 NE 2d 1306, IN App., 1988; *Humana Hospital Desert Valley v. Superior Court, supra; Shelton v. Morehead Memorial Hospital,* 318 NC 76, 347 SE 2d 824, 1986; *Snell v. Superior Court,* 158 CA App.3d 44, 204 CA Rptr. 200, 1984; *Somer v. Johnson,* 704 F.2d 1473, 11th Cir., 1983; *contra, Byork v. Carmer,* 109 App. Div.2d 1087, 487 NYS 2d 226, 1985; *Greenwood v. Wierdsma,* 741 P.2d 1079, WY, 1987.

58. See, for example, *Willing v. St. Joseph Hospital,* 176 IL App.3d 737, 531 NE 2d 824, IL App. 1st Dist., 1988 (Interpreting the Illinois Medical Studies Act, the court stated, "Records and documents are protected under the Act if they are utilized as part of the peer review process and not as a result or consequence thereof. . . . the privilege will be accorded only after each document is scrutinized in light of the Act's purpose."); *Byork v. Carmer* (upholding but limiting state's peer review statute to the records of the proceedings of peer review committees and not protecting knowledge gained from other sources); *Harris Hospital v. Schattman,* 734 SW 2d 759, TX App., 1987 (holding that nondiscoverable records include only those documents generated by committee, but not communications between hospital and physician); *Humana Hospital v. Superior*

Court, supra, note 46 (evidence possessed by credentials committee that was not otherwise privileged could be discovered, although credentials committee files themselves were protected); *Richter v. Diamond,* 108 IL 2d 265, 483 NE 2d 1256, 1985 (statutory privilege applies to the peer review process but is not accorded to the imposition of restrictions that may result from the process).

59. See, for example, *Cal. Evid. Code* §1157 (c), 1999: The prohibition relating to discovery of testimony does not apply to the statements made by any person in attendance at . . . a meeting of any of those committees who is a party to an action or proceeding the subject matter of which was reviewed at that meeting; *Carroll v. Nunez,* 137 AD 2d 911, 524 NYS 2d 578, 1988 (in motion for protective order, court held plaintiff was not entitled to physician's personnel folder or copies of complaints made against him for performing unnecessary surgery, but was to be furnished with any statement made by physician at the hospital's peer review committee proceedings regarding the subject matter of the suit).

60. *Jordon v. Court of Appeals,* 701 SW 2d 644, TX 1985 (privilege protects documents prepared by, or at direction of, hospital committee for committee purposes; does not apply to documents that have been created without committee impetus and purpose).

61. For suggestions on how to protect peer review records, see Fishman, L. W. "Confidentiality of Medical and Peer Review Records." Paper presented at National Health Lawyers Association, 1988.

62. 8 Wigmore, *Evidence,* §2292, McNaughton rev., 1961.

63. The attorney-client privilege, especially in the corporate context, only protects disclosure of communications; it does not protect disclosure of the underlying facts by those who communicated with the attorney. The application of the privilege is determined on a case-by-case basis. An analysis of this concept can be found in *Upjohn Co. v. United States,* 449 U.S. 383, 1981. Additionally, the Florida Supreme Court has established set criteria to judge whether a corporation's communications are protected by the attorney-client privilege: (1) the communication would not have been made but for the contemplation of legal services; (2) the employee making the communication did so at the direction of his or her corporate superior; (3) the superior made the request of the employee as part of the corporation's effort to secure legal advice or services; (4) the content of the communication relates to the legal services being rendered, and the subject matter of the communication is within the scope of the employee's duty; (5) the communication is not disseminated beyond those persons who, because of the corporate structure, need to know its contents. *Southern Bell Telephone and Telegraph Co. v. Deason,* 632 So.2d 1377, FL 1994. These and similar cases should be consulted for in-depth discussions of these issues.

64. Lo, B., Chair, *Best Principles for Health Privacy,* The Health Privacy Project Working Group, Georgetown University, July 1999.

65. 45 CFR 164.505.

66. United States Department of Health and Human Services, *DHHS Fact Sheet,* Oct. 29, 1999.

67. *Cal. Health & Safety Code,* §123149, 1996.

68. *Ibid.*

69. *Ibid.*

70. See endnote 7.

71. JCAHO, 1998.

72. *Estate of Behringer v. Medical Center at Princeton,* 249 NJ Super. 597, 592 A.2d 1250, 1991 (finding defendant hospital negligent for failure to take reasonable steps to maintain confidentiality of a patient's medical records).

73. American Health Information Management Association. "Model Language for Health Information Legislation on Creation, Authentication, and Retention of Computer-Based Patient Records." Unpublished, 1995.

74. "One system that uses the iris of the eye for identification because it has more unique physical characteristics than fingerprints claims annual fate of 1 in 131,158." Taken from "ATMs May Make Eye Contact." *St. Petersburg Times,* May 28, 1996, p. 8A.

75. Although tokens traditionally have been implemented as hardware devices, software-only versions of tokens have recently been developed.

76. For a checklist of contractual items to address, see *Health Information Systems and Electronic Medical Records Practice Guide*, American Health Lawyers Association, Washington, D.C., 1997.

77. *BNA's Health Law Reporter, 8*(44), Nov. 11, 1999, p. 1804.

78. For example, an electronic medical records contract uses language indicating that the vendor will abide by all laws and regulations on confidentiality that are now, or may become, applicable to the records. Ensure that the vendor warrants and represents that it will not use any data it obtains in any form.

79. All system usage, including e-mail, must have stated employee regulations. These regulations include a warning that no employee who communicates through the system should expect that his or her communication will be private. Further, it should be stated that the system is to be used only for business purposes and that its misuse will result in termination. Moreover, it should be stated that information access is limited without proper authorization; no personal disks can be used, no files can be copied, and violation of the policies will result in discipline.

80. See the Electronic Privacy Information Center (www.epic.org) and the Privacy Page (www.privacy.org).

Suggested Readings

American Bar Association, *Health Care Facility Records: Confidentiality, Computerization and Security*. Chicago, Ill.: Forum on Health Law of the American Bar Association, 1995.

Blair, J. S. *Overview of Standards Related to the Emerging Health Care Information Infrastructure*. Schaumburg, Ill.: The Computer-Based Patient Record Institute, Inc., 1995.

Daniels, A. R. "Confidentiality of Medical Records." Presentation for the National Health Lawyers Association, Chicago, Ill., June 1994.

Guidelines for Establishing Information Security Policies at Organizations Using Computer-Based Patient Record Systems. Schaumburg, Ill.: The Computer-Based Patient Record Institute, Inc., 1995.

Guidelines for Information Security Education Programs at Organizations Using Computer-Based Patient Record Systems. Schaumburg, Ill.: The Computer-Based Patient Record Institute, Inc., 1995.

Jones, R. T. "Computerized Medical Records: A 'Practical Guide' for Avoiding the Legal Hazards of the Computerized Hospital Record." *LegaLetter.* Florida Hospital Association, June 19, 1995.

Waller, A. A., Broccolo, B. M., and Fulton, D. K. "The Electronic Medical Record." Paper presented at the 16th Annual Meeting and Education Conference, American Society for Healthcare Risk Management of the American Hospital Association, Nov. 3, 1994.

Electronic Medical Records: Effective Risk Management after HIPAA. Annual Conference and Exhibition of American Society for Healthcare Risk Management, Chicago, Ill., Oct. 3–6, 1999, presented by Adele A. Waller.

6

Creative Staffing

Dorothy Bazan
Lillian P. Karson

As health care institutions respond to changes brought about by managed care, they are faced with the need to broaden their scope of services. From a risk management point of view, the institution may be assuming more risk from additional activities such as managed care contracting and health care mergers and acquisitions. At the same time, many institutions are downsizing, and the resulting process changes caused by the elimination of positions also may create greater exposure to risk.

Risk management departments are not immune to cutbacks in staff. Thus, the risk manager must be prepared to face the reality of accomplishing normal department functions with potentially fewer resources. To prepare for the future, he or she must develop a creative staffing plan that will enable the department to survive the inevitable disruptions caused by reductions in staff. The plan's primary purpose is to *create* new resources for the department. This can be accomplished in three separate, but related, ways:

1. *Internal transfer:* Shifting selected department functions to other departments.
2. *Internal resource utilization:* Utilizing "spare" or underutilized personnel in other departments to perform some functions.
3. *External resources:* Covering some functions through outsourcing.

The degree to which the staffing plan succeeds will depend on the risk manager's creativity in developing additional resources and on the plan's soundness and practicality. A simple plan that is well executed and managed should enable the risk manager to build and maintain a successful risk management team.

This chapter describes a five-step process for identifying and prioritizing various staffing options. After following this process, the risk manager will have created a flexible and responsive plan of action that can be implemented if resources are reduced. To help facilitate this process, the chapter includes a model and other tools that risk managers can use as "road maps" to plot their course.

....

DEVELOPING A CREATIVE STAFFING PLAN

Putting together a creative staffing plan entails careful consideration of department functions. The risk manager must assess the full range of department operations to decide which ones must be accomplished by the department and which ones can be reassigned. To meet the challenges of this complex task, he or she should follow a process that both identifies potential staffing options and assists in prioritizing them to best meet the organization's circumstances and objectives.

Five major steps are involved in developing a creative staffing plan. These are:

1. Assessing the full range of current functions.
2. Evaluating options for internal and external transfer of functions.
3. Determining a new staffing plan after functions are transferred.
4. Establishing processes to manage the external resources effectively.
5. Developing monitors to assess the plan's effectiveness and make changes as necessary.

The sections that follow examine each of these steps in detail.

Step 1. Assessing the Full Range of Current Functions

The first step in designing and planning a creative staffing plan is to thoroughly assess the full range of functions currently performed by the risk management department. To ensure that the listing is complete, the risk manager should make every effort to separate the functions that are accomplished from the job positions to which they are assigned. A good technique for this process is to conduct a department-wide brainstorming session. Such a session can enable the manager to capture undocumented functions that otherwise might be overlooked. Moreover, by involving staff in the planning process, the risk manager increases the likelihood that they will support the plan should it become necessary to implement it in the future.

The risk manager also should thoroughly document, or "spell out," each function's specific elements. Defining all the elements will help ensure that a vital responsibility is not inadvertently overlooked if, in the future, it is shifted to someone outside the department.

After all the functions are listed, the manager must pare them down to a workable set. This can be done by consolidating overlapping or parallel functions into clearly understandable categories. The creative staffing prioritization model in Exhibit 6.1 provides an example of the types of categories that might be included. The left-hand side of the model includes the three major categories of loss control and management, risk finance, and claims administration. These categories can, of course, be tailored to meet the needs of the institution. However, the model works best when the categories are limited to three or four major areas.

Additionally, the risk manager should review the list to identify strengths and weaknesses in the current staffing plan. (This task is not illustrated in the prioritization model because strengths and weaknesses vary widely from institution to institution.) To accomplish this, the risk manager might consider elements such as staff expertise, cost of managing the exposure, and amount of time allocated to particular projects or risk

EXHIBIT 6.1. Sample Creative Staffing Prioritization Model

Range of Alternatives for Moving the Function or Position

This is a sample model of a tool for use in developing and displaying the organization's priorities for moving functions outside the risk management department. To use it, the risk manager would follow four basic steps.

1. List all functions or positions to be evaluated and prioritized.
2. Determine and list the appropriate alternatives for the organization.
3. List the top three priorities for each function being evaluated.
4. Review the process with the management team to get other input.

Function or Position	Internal Sources				External Sources			
	Permanent assignment	Project assignment	Short-term assignment	Limited-function employee	Permanent contractual	Contractual by project	Outside consultant	Vendors as prepaid service
Loss Control and Management								
Department manager	1				2		3	
Legal counsel		3			2	1		
OSHA training	2		3					1
Fire and safety surveys	1		2					
Regulatory compliance		1	2				3	
SMDA		1		2				3
Medical staff credentialing		1	2		3			
Staff education						2		3
Policy and procedure review			2	1			3	
ADA compliance			2	1	3			
Disaster control training		1				2		3
Risk Finance								
Contract review and negotiations	1		3			2		
Premium audit		1		2		3		
Broker selection	1	2			3			
Insurance purchasing	1	2			3			
Insurance application processing			1	2		3		
Risk analysis	2			1	3			
Claims Administration								
Medical records liaison				1			2	3
Variance report tracking		2		1			3	
Claims analysis		2		1	3			
MSC attendance	1	3					2	
Legal file maintenance	1				3		2	
Staff education (reporting)		1				3	2	
Loss ratio						2	1	3

functions. Particular attention should be paid to the amount of department involvement in the management of risk-financing, claims, and loss control activities. Involvement in each of these activities is paramount to the risk management program's success and thus should not be minimized without due consideration.

Step 2. Evaluating Options for Internal and External Transfers of Functions

This second step in the planning process requires the most creativity. During this step, the risk manager must think beyond today's operations to identify all potential resources, both internal and external, that could be part of the final plan. Two resources should be considered:

1. Other people or departments that could serve a function for the risk management department, typically on a part-time basis.
2. Potential outsourcing of complete or partial functions.

Developing the possible alternatives to performing the full range of risk management functions within the department can be very difficult without the use of a management tool. The model in Exhibit 6.1 can serve as a tool the risk manager can use in both preparing and presenting alternatives in a clear and easily understood manner.

The risk manager also must understand and be able to communicate which functions are best accomplished by the risk management department, which ones may be transferred to other staff within the institution, and which ones could be outsourced. Once again, by using the creative staffing prioritization model as a tool, the risk manager can assign a priority to each of the identified functions. A priority of 1 means that a function is best accomplished by that alternative. A priority of 2 would be assigned to the next best alternative, and so on. The purpose of the model is to provide a tool to help the risk manager consider prioritizing and treating a variety of risks.

Internal Staffing Opportunities   Through imagination and creativity, the risk manager can develop internal sources for assigning one or more risk management functions. Identifying other internal resources may reap the additional benefit of allowing the institution to more fully utilize the services of an individual who cannot be fully utilized in his or her primary assignment. Thus, both the risk management department and the institution as a whole benefit. The health care organization encompasses a wide range of expertise that could be used effectively for risk management functions. Many risk management projects may require short-term staffing, which an internal personnel pool could supply. Staff may be put on limited duty for a number of reasons, such as pregnancy, health situations, or workers' compensation rehabilitation periods. (Back-to-work assignments are discussed in Chapter 25.) The number of risk management tasks that can be assigned to "newly created staff" is limited only by the risk manager's imagination and ability to create new staffing opportunities. The following examples illustrate just a few of these opportunities:

- *Home office workers:* Data collection, off-site auditing, and preparation of meeting materials.
- *Workers' compensation or limited-work persons:* Updating policy and procedures, trending of data, assignment to various committee meetings, and research.
- *Americans with Disabilities Act:* Policy and procedure review, development of loss and trending information, auditing, credentialing functions, and committee assignment.

- *Physical therapist:* Ergonomics, staff education, safety committee assignments, and health and exercise programs.
- *Safety and security staff:* Staff education, assignment to various committees that contribute to the risk data collection process.

Outsourcing To utilize all resources fully, the risk manager must not only analyze functions that can be outsourced but also identify resources to accomplish the outsourcing. The cost-effective availability of an outside resource could lead to a decision to outsource a particular function that otherwise would have been kept within the department. Areas to be evaluated include:

- Pre-accreditation survey for a specific department.
- OSHA education for a high-risk employee group.
- Preconstruction survey and building compliance.
- Staff development and education.
- Third-party administration of claims.
- Contract review and negotiations.

Risk managers new to outsourcing may need guidance in locating reputable, well-qualified persons to become part of the risk management team. Following are some of the outsourcing options that are available to supplement the risk management team:

- Risk consultants.
- Insurance brokers.
- Insurance companies.
- Contractors.
- Waste disposal consultants and vendors.
- Security and alarm consultants and vendors.
- Community disaster organizations.
- Disaster planning personnel.
- Legal resources.
- Third-party administrators (TPAs).

Examples of how these resources may be utilized include:

- *Risk consultants:* Providing focus or full-facility surveys, addressing targeted risk concerns, presenting educational programs, or helping to develop and implement a risk management program.
- *Insurance brokers:* Providing assistance in the proper and accurate completion of insurance applications, promoting the updating of the organization's insurable interests and maintaining a current inventory of those insurables, and introducing new insurance products that may be of significant benefit to the organization.
- *Insurance companies:* Providing on-site risk management surveys or educational consultations via telephone to address immediate risk concerns or guidance. (The various professionals available include industrial hygienists, safety engineers, workers' compensation case managers, and ergonomic technicians.)
- *Contractors:* Depending on the identified need, consultants provide a gamut of support for an internal risk program. Expertise can range from support for the waste

disposal program to OSHA by waste disposal consultants and vendors to security risk management issues managed by security and alarm consultants and vendors.

- *Disaster planning personnel:* Involving local community disaster planning staff (fire department, emergency medical technicians, rescue units) can expand and improve the disaster planning process. Benefits to the risk program will include on-site education for staff, updating of current fire and evacuation safety issues, and enhanced communication with the disaster planning personnel.

- *Legal resources:* Communicating updated legal information, staff education programs (including medical staff and the board) as well as attendance at any meetings requiring legal attendance (Mandatory Settlement Conference, special hearings, and so on) will be of benefit to the overall wellness of the risk management program.

- *TPAs:* Assisting the organization in the management of deductibles, maintenance of the legal claim files, and Mandatory Settlement Conference (MSC) attendance. Of course, management of the allegations through legal completion is an expertise that should be considered for outsourcing.

Cost must be carefully considered before outsourcing a function. With the exception of the risk consultant, who usually works on a fee-for-service basis, external resources usually are prepaid as part of an existing contract or an insuring agreement.

Step 3. Determining a New Staffing Plan After Functions Are Transferred

During this step, the risk manager will need to make the difficult decisions on which functions or positions to reduce or eliminate in the event of a cutback. Because such decisions are specific to a department and an institution and involve personnel issues, there are no set guidelines to follow. However, the practical basis for making such decisions and for communicating the rationale behind them can be found in the creative staffing model.

After identifying the functions to be transferred, the model should be revised with the newly planned resources included. This will help the manager quickly identify areas where the greatest economies can be obtained in reducing staffing and transferring additional functions. For example, if a function is outsourced, the person currently performing that function will be available to take on other responsibilities or will be transferred to another assignment within the organization. The visible listing of the required functions will assist in recognizing opportunities and "holes" because the various staffing alternatives are included in the model.

Step 4. Establishing Processes to Manage External Resources

To develop a creative staffing plan that is both effective and manageable, the risk manager must design a flexible program that will integrate the newly assigned resources into the existing department structure. He or she will need to utilize different management techniques and processes because the personnel accomplishing the functions will not be reporting within the traditional department structure. However, by adapting a few basic processes to the new situation, the risk manager can ensure a manageable situation. For example, he or she should have the following in place:

- A policy for assignment within the risk department.
- A credentialing process for all candidates (internal and external) (Exhibit 6.2).
- An orientation for all staff members (Exhibit 6.3).

EXHIBIT 6.2. **Risk Management Department Credentialing Checklist**

Name: _____ Area of expertise: _____

Position: _____

Project: _____

Qualifications required:

Degree requirements:

Years of experience:

Experience level:

Certification:

Confidentiality statement:

Curriculum vitae:

License(s):

OSHA training:

The applicant/consultant _____ received OSHA training

on _____ at _____. A certificate of completion is attached.

The applicant/consultant will require OSHA training prior to any assignment at _____

_____. Upon completion, the certificate of completion must be included in

the credentialing file.

References:

1.

2.

3.

References submitted by candidate: Yes _____ No _____ Date _____

Permission to contact references: Yes _____ No _____ Date _____

References returned:

1._____ Date _____ Reviewed _____

2. _____ Date _____ Reviewed _____

3. _____ Date _____ Reviewed _____

- A mandated confidentiality statement.
- A project-tracking mechanism to effectively evaluate the progress, needs, and expectations of the various assignments (Exhibit 6.4).

The creative staffing plan must include a mechanism to ensure that properly qualified personnel are assigned to manage specific risk functions. Monitoring of the various internal and outsourced staff projects is critical to the risk management program's success. Therefore, it is strongly suggested that some of these tools and processes be utilized for all risk management projects, whether the person involved is internal or external, temporary

EXHIBIT 6.3.   Risk Management Department Orientation

Name: _____   Date: _____

Project: _____   Site: _____

Consultant   Yes _____   No _____

Employee   Yes _____   No _____

Date	Department	Initials (department head)

Identification badge   Physical plant tour
Keys   Key personnel (introductions)
Computer and security clearance   Job description
General safety   Project summary
Computer introduction   Human relations
OSHA education   Confidentiality
Policy and procedures   Organizational chart

RM dept
Committee assignment

Date _____ Committee _____ Location _____

or permanent. For example, the risk management department project summary example shown in Exhibit 6.4 could be used as the one common tracking and management tool for most of the department's projects. The format should be tailored to the institutional circumstances, but the concept of using consistent tools for documenting projects in a common format is essential when working with diverse and changing personnel.

To manage the risk management program effectively, the risk manager must promote and maintain communication with every person on the risk management team as well as the affected managers in other departments of the organization. Key to this communication is the current status information on the various projects. Identified changes in the status of each must be clearly communicated, and the reasons for those changes understood.

Step 5. Developing Monitors to Assess Staffing Plan Effectiveness

The final step in the process is to create a separate mechanism for monitoring and displaying the results of the overall department after the new structure is in place. By determining in advance what results should be expected, the risk manager can work with the assigned individuals to assess the level of contribution they are making and whether the expectations for the new structure are reasonable.

A good deal of time and effort will be required to jointly develop a reasonable and easily measured performance status (metric) for each individual component. However, the investment will pay off handsomely in ease of monitoring and reporting the current status.

Exhibit 6.5 is an example of a monitoring tool that can be used for this purpose. Its organization and format are drawn from the creative staffing model (Exhibit 6.1) developed previously so that the two correlate. This same summary sheet can be used for reporting outside the department so that the organization's management is informed of

EXHIBIT 6.4. **Risk Management Department Project Summary**

Project: _____ Site location: _____

Goal: _____ Estimated start date: _____

Estimated completion date: _____

Reports to: _____ _____
Telephone: _____
Fax: _____
Pager: _____

Personnel assigned to: _____ Project: _____

1. Name _____ Dept._____ Tel. _____ Fax _____

2. Name _____ Dept._____ Tel. _____ Fax _____

Committee attendance required: Yes _____ No _____

1. Committee _____ Scheduled date/time _____ Location _____

2. Committee _____ Scheduled date/time _____ Location _____

Project progress report requirements

Forward all progress reports to: _____

     Due by _____ day of each week/month

Progress reports to include:

1.   Summary of activity

2.   Goals attained in previous week/month

3.   Projected new goals for upcoming week/month

4.   Detailed expense/budget report to date

5.   Explanation of overbudget items

6.   Expected completion date

the effect of the restructuring and the department's progress in maintaining or improving on the previous level of service provided.

This summary presentation will permit the risk manager to continually monitor and display the status of the individual assignments, and will quickly highlight any need to reallocate resources.

· · · · · · · · · · · ·

RISK MANAGEMENT IMPLICATIONS OF CREATIVE STAFFING

There are many individual and corporate loss control specialists in the risk management consulting field. Consultants usually market their ability to perform loss control functions within a particular scope of expertise, such as risk financing, general and/or professional liability, ethics, workers' compensation, or litigation management. Some

EXHIBIT 6.5. Sample Monitor Tool for Risk Management Function

This is a sample model of a tool for use in monitoring the organization's performance after moving some functions outside the risk management department. To use it, the risk manager would follow three basic steps.

1. List all functions or positions to be monitored.
2. Determine an appropriate progress measure (metric) for each item to be tracked and display the plan status (ahead, on plan, behind plan).
3. Review the progress and the process with the individuals on a regular basis.

Departmental Summary

See individual project-tracking sheets for detailed data

Function	Individual assigned and source			Measurement and plan progress			
Loss Control and Management	Individual/ organization	Internal resource	External resource	Measurement (metric)	Ahead of plan	On plan	Behind plan
Legal counsel	Marques, Shawn & Little		X	% of responses deemed timely		X	
OSHA training	M. Robinson		X	% of training completed		X	
Fire and safety surveys	Vacant			Not available			XXX
Regulatory compliance	J. Jones	X		% of required audits completed		X	
SMDA	Vacant			Not available			XXX
Medical staff credentialing	S. Glover	X		% of staff with complete records			X
Staff education	N. McNew	X		% of required training completed	X		
ADA compliance	J. Scherz	X		# of outstanding issues		X	
Disaster control training	ADC Inc.	X		% of required training completed		X	

Risk Finance

Contract review and negotiations							
Premium audit							
Insurance application processing							

Claims Administration

Variance report tracking							
Claims analysis							
MSC attendance							
Legal file maintenance							

consultants may also market loss control services in areas where they may not have an expertise. To meet clients' needs and fulfill outsourcing contracts, consultants may sub-contract to another risk consultant those areas where they feel their expertise is lacking. Keep in mind that any subcontractor who engaged to work on a contract needs to be approved by the client as well. Both consultants and subcontractors will work in unison to complete the contract.

As stated earlier, risk management departments are not immune to cutbacks in staff. A frequent assumption is made that the risk management department staff includes a minimum of three people: risk manager, loss control specialist, and an administrative assistant. In reality, many risk management departments' staff includes only a risk manager (this could be a part-time position), a shared clerical support, and possibly limited use of a data analyst. In addition, the risk manager may have responsibilities for other department functions outside of risk management. Utilization of the resource plan and supporting model tools will enable the risk manager to maintain and retrieve information as well as afford a hands-on approach to monitoring compliance of outsourced activities. However, outsourcing any risk management functions has potential risk management implications.

············
RISK MANAGEMENT OUTSOURCING IMPLICATIONS

Using the model or grid shown in Exhibit 6.5, the risk manager is able to measure and weigh the importance of selected risk management outsourced responsibilities. The risk manager needs to be aware of potential risk management concerns that may arise not only within the specific outsourced risk function but also those concerns that arise from the engagement of a specific consultant. Risk management outsourcing implications for the consultant that should be reviewed prior to his or her engagement are the following:

- Credentials and references.
- Timeline to complete services and ability to perform.
- Health care risk management expertise needed.
- Extraneous services that may not be of value to your entity.
- End-work product, written and/or data management.
- Literacy in risk management information system (RMIS) and computer applications.
- Ability to communicate with a wide range of professionals.

············
DUE DILIGENCE

It is usually wise to engage the human resource and legal departments before signing a contract for outsourcing services. They offer invaluable insight and will assist in eliminating risk associated with a poorly drafted contract.

Due to the sensitivity and confidentiality of the information to which the consultant will be privy, in addition to the above information requested, it is suggested as part of the background check that a detailed work history be obtained to determine if the following may be of concern:

- Fraudulent financial practices.
- Failed prior fiduciary relationships.

- Criminal record.
- Failure to timely complete contract.
- Lack of knowledge concerning insurance products, coverages, or exclusions.
- Inability to understand various computer programs and related software platform functions for creating a data management system.
- Fraudulent disclosure of completion of particular education or certification programs.
- Political sensitivity to the culture, style, and needs of the organization.

....

THE CONSULTANT AGREEMENT

After a consultant has proposed to offer outsourcing services and has been interviewed by key staff, the next step is to draft a service agreement to memorialize the specifics of the engagement. The service agreement should be reviewed by in-house counsel if available, as well as by human resources. The agreement is the document by which the consultant's results will be evaluated. Compensation to the consultant will usually be based on services identified in the service agreement. Basic contact requirements are listed in Chapter 11, and at a minimum should include:

- Scope of the project.
- Timeline for completion.
- Account team and biographical sketches of team members.
- Compensation.
- Service standards.
- Cancellation clauses.
- Confidentiality statements.
- Evaluation criteria.

....

CONCLUSION

The day may come when a risk manager must cut department staff. The manager with an organized creative staffing plan will be equipped to cope with the changes and contribute to the cost-saving goals of the institution while still maintaining a level of control over the department's vital risk management functions.

By utilizing the creative staffing model, the risk manager can develop and communicate a plan that will accommodate various levels of staffing cutbacks depending on the circumstances of the institution. Once functions are transferred outside the department, the risk manager needs to put processes in place to manage them despite the absence of direct control. The need to thoroughly document qualifications, project status, personnel training, and other aspects of the creative staffing program will increase with the reduction in staffing. To best manage the processes, the risk manager should develop and use tools that make the management and documentation consistent and easy. Regardless of whether cutbacks occur, creation of a creative staffing plan helps the manager assess the risk management program's current strengths and weaknesses, and is thus a worthwhile endeavor.

7

Enterprise Risk Management: Emerging Concepts and Applications in Health Care

Ward R. H. Ching

Within the past three years, enterprise risk management (ERM) has emerged as a powerful, new financial, operational, and strategic management tool. At the heart of the ERM process is the recognition that traditional definitions of risk are inefficient and can lead to suboptimal allocations of resources, unintended misrepresentations of material risks within the organization, or the misapplication of financial and operational solutions. ERM commenced in for-profit business but is taking hold in the not-for-profit arena as well.

Risk has been traditionally defined as either "speculative or pure" or "fortuitous" risks. Speculative or pure risks are those for which the probability of financial gain exists along with the probability of loss. For example, stock market speculation carries with it the opportunity to make money on a stock trade or options transaction at the same time that a calculable probability of a financial position loss also exists. The speculator, or risk taker, understands the probability of gain or loss at the onset of the transaction by analyzing historical patterns of gains or losses by watching the performance of the stock or options market. Fortuitous risks differ because they do not offer the risk taker the opportunity for financial or operational gain. Fortuitous risks, normally associated with insurance risks (property, casualty, directors and officers, workers' compensation) are risks where the probability of loss can usually be calculated and an associated transfer cost to a disinterested third party can be established.

Financial managers have discovered that within a corporation, risk has been identified and managed in "functional silos." Hazard risks are usually handled by the corporate risk manager; treasury risks, such as foreign exchange or hedging risks, are handled by the treasurer; capital acquisition and market risks are usually handled by the chief financial officer; risks associated with the day-to-day management of the business enterprise are handled by line mangers and the chief operating officer; human resources risks, ranging from benefits, health care, and retirement program management to quality of the workforce and succession planning, are normally handled by the director of human resources; and finally, the reputation risks of a business, those acts that could materially effect stock price or "brand quality," are handled by the board of directors. Under these conditions, the number of potential risks can be large, as can the number of potentially unrelated sources of risk management and mitigation. For corporations that must operate in a market environment where financial precision, operational speed, or management decision nimbleness is essential, the traditional forms of risk management have become dangerously ineffective. Mismanagement of risk could put the corporation in jeopardy of extinction.

This chapter explores the market forces that have rendered traditional risk management obsolete and outlines the ERM framework and applications associated with the ERM approach. The ERM framework will be generally described and, where possible, direct linkage with health care risk management will be made. The two central questions being answered here are (1) based on observed market conditions, why the move to ERM? and (2) what is ERM, and how does it work?

WHY THE SHIFT TO ERM?

A number of market conditions have converged to render the traditional method for handling risk obsolete. If we confine our observations first to the general risk market (which includes both hazard and nonhazard risks) we find that:

- Companies are now intensely focused on maximizing shareholder value. Particularly those companies that have large institutional shareholders, management have realigned their financial and organizational priorities to drive as much profit into shareholder equity as possible. Recent observations of the North American stock market has shown that for those companies that have not refocused their business priorities appropriately, the market has responded by penalizing their stock price.

- Right or not, companies will continue to use price as the key risk financing purchasing criteria, due in part to a continued soft insurance and capital market. Danger lurks for those who buy by price alone. In some areas, such as provider stop loss, HMO reinsurance, managed care errors and omissions (E&O), and workers' compensation, we see the cycle turning.

- Enlightened companies will seek to redefine "value" in their purchasing decisions. Many are now openly talking about and employing the concept of "solution partner" to characterize what they want and need from their service providers. The fundamental question going forward will be: Assuming that insurance or other risk mitigation methods are nothing more than alternative sources of capital, and that the real risk management problem is finding ways to eliminate or neutralize measurable financial volatility of the firm's risk, which capital method should be used? ERM represents a method to understand, identify, and measure the volatility of risk from wherever it originates and helps define which capital solutions should be used.

- Significant and continued insurance industry and financial services mergers and acquisitions will open business opportunities for enhanced risk management techniques due to current client frustrations with a perceived overconcentration of brokerage and financial services resources. A new player in the risk-financing arena (particularly for traditional hazard risks) will be the capital markets. Currently, there is more than $15 trillion of new capital being focused on the enterprise risk solutions market space. As capital finds new employment, market shifts will occur in response to price and risk transfer approaches. A new financial equilibrium will emerge only after significant shakeouts in the financial service markets occur.

• New risk-financing approaches are emerging that transcend traditional hazard risk. Enterprise risk solutions that started as multiline/multiyear insurance contracts are now starting to incorporate market, operational, and reputational risks. Some of these programs, also referred to as "integrated risk programs," have been written for the larger health care risk environments, such as health care systems or integrated delivery networks. *Market risks* are those that exist exogenous to a corporation, which can have a negative effect on stock or capital value. Market risks can include the entry of a new competitor, changes in tax rates, political risk, or unexpected regulation (both domestic and foreign). *Operational risks,* some of which can originate as hazard risks, are those risks that exist within the corporation's production function or value chain, which, if left untreated, can diminish a corporation's stock or capital value. Such risks include poor technology, bad internal communications systems, disruptive senior management decision-making processes, or unclear strategic vision. *Reputational risks,* while at times related to market or operational risks, focuses on those risks that effect a corporations "brand." Product tampering or poor product design that leads to the erosion of public or market confidence are examples of this highly volatile risk. The public perception of health care has eroded over the past few decades and continues to deteriorate, particularly in the area of managed care and financial incentives.

• New information technologies that take advantage of e-commerce methods will become a major part of the risk financing landscape. The broker, carrier, or capital market that gets to the customer first with the most product or service flexibility will have a significant advantage.

Some of the key market drivers include:

• The almost slavish focus on maximizing shareholder value will drive markets to develop new ways to use risk as part of the competitive differentiation of a corporation. Risk is no longer just a defensive issue (risk is bad, therefore it should be avoided) but is becoming a component of the new management's vision of the competitive landscape (Exhibit 7.1). What this exhibit shows is a situation where a corporation is looking at risk in terms of how well it understands it and manages it relative to its competition. For an organization to succeed there must be a more strategic understanding of risk and ways found to use its ability to manage risk as part of its competitive arsenal.

• The penalties for mismanagement of resources have intensified. Consistent with the last point made above, risk managers, treasurers, and CFOs are looking for ways to mitigate and manage risks that:

1. Are focused on promoting the core business strategy of the business.

2. Are quickly implemented.

3. Are measurable both financially and within a specified time frame.

4. Are simple.

5. Are leverageable to the extent that a risk mitigation solution may treat a number of risks together to achieve a consolidated outcome.

EXHIBIT 7.1.　Risk Can Be Used to Develop a Competitive Advantage

Two strategic questions:

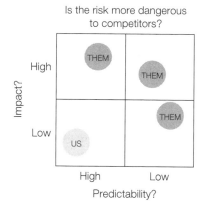

THE CONCEPT OF RISK IS CHANGING

As suggested earlier, the concept of risk is changing. Risk has taken on a new and more complex definition. At the ERM level, risk is being defined in terms of large risk domains. These include hazard risks, operational risks, market risks, reputational risks, and human capital risk management risks. Within these risk domains is the notion that risks do not exist in isolation. Risks exist within a corporation in a connected web-like fashion. For example, hazard risks, with the exception of property risk, are either direct or indirect results of market or operational risks. A poor-product recall will give rise to a reputation risk, which could lead to the loss of key people—a human resources risk management risk. Traditional risk management identification and account methods have structured artificial "functional" definitions of risk and risk mitigation. With risks now recognized as being more fundamentally interdependent and the probability of conjoint negative outcomes statistically measurable, more sophisticated frameworks for identifying and measuring risks are needed.

Additionally, more analytically robust and dynamic definitions of risk are increasingly showing up as part of the strategic goal-setting process. As corporations gain confidence in connecting risks and risk profiles together into manageable portfolios, managers will shift the concept of risk forward to take advantage of it as a product or service differentiator.

WHAT ABOUT HEALTH CARE?

One would have to have been entirely sheltered from the academic and popular literature for the past five years not to notice that extraordinary changes are taking place within the health care delivery system. For health care, the concept of risk and risk management takes on a heightened perspective. Some simple observations:

- Someone is turning fifty every eight seconds in the United States.
- In 1930, the percent of the U.S. population over the age of sixty-five was around 6 percent; in 1990 it hovered around 13 percent; in the year 2030 it will reach 20 percent.

As the U.S. population ages, the health care delivery system will be substantially unable to deliver necessary health care services.

Another way of looking at it, as quoted in *Atlantic Monthly,* May 1996: "By 2025, the proportion of all Americans who are elderly will be the same as the proportions in Florida today. . . . America, in effect, will become a nation of Florida." Imagine how far we have come since 1996?

- Globally, the picture appears about the same or worse. China's elderly population will hit 20 percent; Japan's 32 percent; UK's 28 percent; and Italy's 35 percent by 2005.
- More change will occur in the health care technology in the next ten years than in the last one hundred years, where the public expectation, at least in the United States, is for health care to be of high quality, anytime, anywhere, and from any one location. Will the financial infrastructure associated with the current health care delivery model allow this?
- There will be a downward change in the public's attitude and their increased negative perception of health care and the providers within it.
- Financially, without significant support, the Medicare system will continue to be financially insecure with the trust fund potentially going broke in three to five years.
- Health care premiums paid by employers are going to dramatically shift upward due to the aging demographics.
- Not surprising, as the cost of health care increases, the financial burden will be shifted from the employer to the employee; in effect, more expensive care, possibly less effective care, in a system that cannot handle it now. As cost increase and cost shifting occurs, there will be a lessening of provider access, which will lead to employee dissatisfaction and distrust of both employer and health care system, which ultimately leads to employee performance erosion (human capital risk management risk).

Health care is not the only industry that is experiencing these issues. Evidence suggests that almost every industrial and service sector is experiencing the same enterprise-level issues. Strategic vision, ability to anticipate market changes, proactive husbandry of capital, and nimble decision-making processes appear to be at the forefront of management's mind at the moment. So enters enterprise risk management.

············
THE ERM FRAMEWORK AND APPLICATIONS

Enterprise risk management represents a more robust and dynamic extension of various forms of risk management.

Exhibit 7.2 identifies many different, yet related, risk management methodologies that have been used to assist corporations define, identify, and manage risks.

As you move up the level of sophistication dimension, the first real tool was classical hazard risk identification. Focused mainly on insurable issues, risks were identified by insurance classification as a function of their experience (how many losses over a period of time) and exposure (the number of staffed and available acute care beds; the number of visits or encounters; the insurance unit of account, such as the number of full-time employees, general receipts, rolling stock, numbers of shifts, and so on.) A second-order tool introduced statistical modeling and forecasting to determine future loss levels across preidentified risk categories. Loss forecasting is the mainstay of the actuarial profession and has contributed mightily to the new ERM methods. Risk mapping, prioritization, and

EXHIBIT 7.2.   ERM as an Analytical Framework

Represents an evolving and integrated analytical framework within which to evaluate risk on a dynamic financial and operational basis

portfolio analysis techniques represent the analytical backbone of the ERM approach. Risk mapping is a method by which various risk domains can be evaluated simultaneously and rigorously against financial materiality thresholds to graphically illustrate the importance of risks and risk families. Prioritization uses the mapping method to explore and construct risk remediation or countermeasure solutions and put them into financial and organizational context. Maps and prioritization leads to the development of risk portfolios that are designed to take advantage of noncorrelative risk effects to provide the corporation with either a more stable risk financing package or a competitive advantage tool (forward pricing contracts, warranties, service programs, and so on).

For purposes of this discussion, ERM is defined as a series of conceptual frameworks and tools that contribute to solutions that focus on maximizing corporations' competitive advantage. This definition is illustrated in Exhibit 7.3.

The ERM process takes advantage of frameworks and tools from every part of the corporation. As shown in Exhibit 7.4, tools can be highly quantitative and/or qualitative in design. The key is knowing how to use these tools within a framework that ultimately provides decision makers with useful strategic information.

Exhibit 7.5 illustrates one of the common macro-overviews of the ERM process. As can be seen, this process encounters a significant number of data sources, process methods, and outputs.

A more common project level ERM process diagram appears in Exhibit 7.6. In this four-phased work plan, the ERM process starts with a problem definition exercise. This leads to Phase I, which deals with identifying and modeling the various sources of risk. Phase II deals with linking identified risks to meaningful financial measures including materiality thresholds. Phase III seeks to match current risk remediation methods against identified risks and financial measures to determine whether the current portfolio of risks is being properly handled. Phase IV takes the output from the first three phases and formulates both a quantitative assessment of the risk portfolio as well as suggested management next steps.

Exhibits 7.7 and 7.8 illustrate risk maps and portfolio perspectives. Risk maps represent one of the first methods to identify and evaluate risks across predefined risk

EXHIBIT 7.3. ERM Definitions

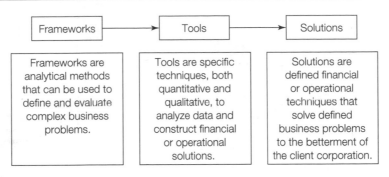

EXHIBIT 7.4. Solution Support

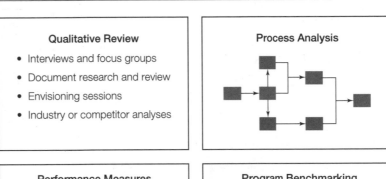

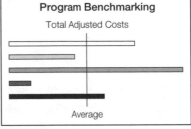

Each solution is supported by well-developed frameworks and tools

domains. Maps provide management with a prioritization scheme that they can then use to do further data collection, analysis, and capital management on a portfolio basis. (See Chapter 21 for more about the origins and applications of risk mapping.)

Exhibit 7.9 illustrates an overview of a corporation's attempt to utilize the results of an ERM process. In this case, the corporation sought to tie a number of key organizational risk areas together to create a more fluid risk identification and remediation tool. The corporation used the frameworks shown in Exhibits 7.5 and 7.6 to construct a virtual risk management process that acted like an information pump into management's decision processes. The idea was that as risks were identified and measured, they needed to account for their portfolio impacts. Immaterial risks were left untreated, where material risks (those that financially exceed a prespecified and auditable threshold) had to be aggressively managed. As risks were managed, feedback

EXHIBIT 7.5.   The Enterprise Risk Management Framework

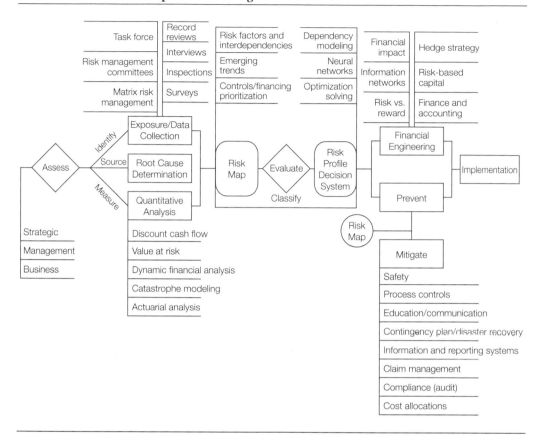

regarding the effectiveness of the management process was recorded and used as future inputs into the risk mapping, prioritization, and portfolio management process.

············

CONCLUSION

Enterprise risk management is an emerging framework accompanied by a series of analytically robust and dynamic tools focusing on helping a company achieve competitive advantage. This new approach is gaining wider and wider acceptance because it seeks to redefine the nature and boundaries of business risk, is more analytically complete, can deal with real-world data deficiencies, and focuses on what counts most—driving shareholder value. While the entire ERM process appears daunting from a project management perspective, bits and pieces of the ERM method can be used to treat specific management questions without compromising the integrity of the overall effort.

For the most part, ERM has been applied in the technology and financial sectors, but is potentially one of the more important analytical weapons that the health care industry can use.

EXHIBIT 7.6.   Process Proposed Utilizing Rigorous Methodology

Process Phase	Phase I: Model the Various Sources of Risk	Phase II: Link Risk Sources to Financial Measures	Phase III: Identify Portfolio of Risk Remediation Strategies	Phase IV: Optimize Risk Financing/ Mitigation Strategies
Key Worksteps	• Envisioning meeting • Set project mechanics • Establish project office • Scope of work validation • Initiate data retrieval • Interview document development and scheduling	• Quantitative assessment (simulation and financial modeling) • Conduct interviews • Link qualitative and quantitative assessments • Develop map metrics • Map identified risks against metrics	• Map risks against remediation methods • Determine value of remediation • Hazard risk	• Develop map-enhanced risk remediation strategy • Develop implementation method
Deliverables	• Clear scope of work • Identify key participants • Develop interview guide • Project office initiated • Data book developed • Peer review standards established • Materiality thresholds determined	• Risk map/score and Strategic risk management report	• Risk map/score portfolio	• Strategic risk management report

The process we propose focuses on answering specific client questions utilizing a rigorous methodology

---

EXHIBIT 7.7.   Sample Map Layout

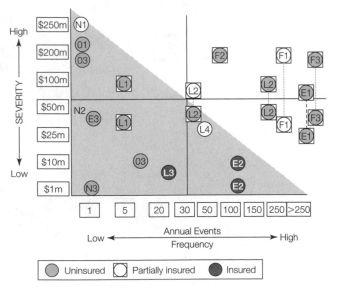

EXHIBIT 7.8.   Connecting the Map

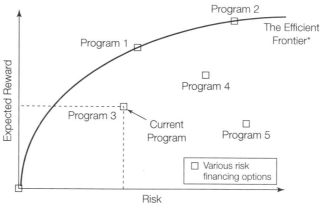

Connecting the map elements to a workable financial solution is the final goal

*The efficient frontier is the point at which there is no greater expected reward for a given level of risk, and vice versa.

EXHIBIT 7.9.   Virtual RM^{2000}

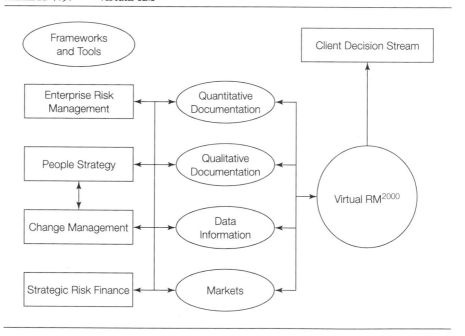

PART *II*

Health Care Exposures

A wide variety of chapters compose this section of the book. The single thread that weaves throughout all fourteen chapters is that each identifies unique and specific health care exposures to loss. Those exposures are as varied as the health care settings in which they occur. Several new chapters in this edition identify exposures and the potential liability associated with: advertising, partnerships, joint ventures, collaborative relationships, documentation, risk in cyberspace and telemedicine, the legal liabilities in different organizational settings, corporate compliance programs, and a new strategic risk management identification tool called "risk mapping." Chapters on health care provider credentialing, occupational and environmental risk exposures, mergers, acquisitions, and divestitures, as well as the risk associated with high-risk clinical areas and information technologies are also discussed in detail.

As health care changes, new exposures to loss are identified and analyzed. The process to identify new exposures never stops; it is a continuous process and one that the risk manager tackles daily. This section will offer the health care risk manager many suggestions, and it will share many tools on how to discover those new exposures and determine just what they mean to their organization.

8

Systems for Risk Identification

William J. McDonough

At the heart of every effective risk management program are systems for identifying (incident reporting mechanisms) near misses, actual loss-producing events, and risks leading to future losses. The purpose of risk identification systems is to identify potential losses, opportunities for improvement, or potential claims. Early identification is important so that a prompt investigation can be initiated while information is still fresh and available; early intervention can be considered, with the potential of eliminating or reducing the cost of the claim; and appropriate risk transfer or financing can be planned with earlier and more accurate reserve setting, claims adjudication, and litigation management.

The systems for identifying potential risks and loss-producing events are quite varied, ranging from the informal to formal, many of which are computerized and others that are driven from voice-activated software or telephonic exchange. This chapter briefly discusses all these systems as well as their use in acute care settings, long-term care, home health care, as well as in the private office setting of physicians.

FORMAL RISK IDENTIFICATION SYSTEMS

Formal risk identification systems are those that follow established policies and procedures. Typically these systems are implemented in order to compliment self-insurance mechanisms (such as captives or trusts), comply with regulatory requirements (state statutes), and/or meet standard requirements such as those promulgated by the Joint Commission on Accreditation of Healthcare Organizations (JCAHO). Four formal means of identifying potential risks and loss-producing events are incident reporting, sentinel event tracking, occurrence reporting, and occurrence screening.

Incident Reporting

Traditionally, incident reporting has been the cornerstone of health care risk management. Generally, an *incident* is defined as any happening that is not consistent with the routine care of a particular patient or an event that is not consistent with the normal operations of a particular organization, such as a strike threat, homicide, or major physical disaster. The occurrence of an incident should trigger completion of a report form for transmittal to risk management and other necessary parties dependent on organization policy and, a general rule of thumb, referred to as a "need to know." Incident report data should be collected, studied for trends, and analyzed to determine whether there are any trends that represent real or potential problems in the delivery of care or service. The results of this analysis should be distributed and discussed with the individuals and departments involved and who possess the authority to promote changes in protocol, policy, and procedure. The analysis may reveal positive findings, which may be disseminated to employees, as well as problem issues that should be addressed in a timely manner utilizing the committee structures, problem resolution processes, and peer review mechanisms (if applicable) at the organization.

The incident report was originally developed in the early 1970s by commercial insurance companies as a means of loss notification. This type of report was not solely a health care report of loss; all industries used incident reports to make notice to their carriers of a loss. In health care specifically, these reports were forms on which to record basic information on the patient (or other potential claimant) or third party (in the case of general liability claims) and the incident(s)—that is, patient name, patient identifying information, and a brief description of the incident. In addition many forms required "follow up" information confirming that the incident has been adequately addressed with appropriate care and intervention. Forms such as these were adopted for use in the majority of U.S. hospitals and health care organizations. In fact, many insurance companies still provide the incident report forms to be used by the facility.

More recently, long-term care, managed care organizations, home health care, and assisted living facilities have designed and implemented reporting mechanisms to capture necessary data for risk management efforts. Historically these organizations have afforded less emphasis on true risk identification systems typically given their minimal medical malpractice experience.

Content of the Incident Report

Today's incident report forms vary in content and structure and vary from organization to organization throughout the continuum of care. Recent emphasis has been placed on making forms "user friendly," less cumbersome, and a tool that employees are more likely to utilize. Some forms have only preprinted data elements for check-off, which simplifies computer entry, whereas others have extensive narrative portions. Regardless of format, some basic information that is contained in most incident reports includes:

● Demographic information including name, home address, and telephone number of the patient, visitor, or employee involved in the incident. (For patients, medical record numbers also may be recorded as part of the identifying information.) This information is used to identify the potential claimant and witnesses in case of litigation. Typically most forms, particularly those in acute care settings, will have a section on the form in which a patient's identifier "plate" can be imprinted directly on the form.

● Facility-related information, such as admission or visit date, patient identification number, patient room number, and admitting diagnosis or presenting complaint. This is used as aggregate data to determine whether certain units of the system are more incident-prone. Trending this information promotes risk management intervention and actions plan to react to frequency or severity in incidents reported.

● Socioeconomic data on the individual involved in the occurrence, such as age, gender, marital status, employment, and insurance status. This information aids in assessing potential loss. For example, collecting employment status assists the risk manager and counsel in determining the potential for wage loss or economic (loss of salary) damage. Other questions that can be answered with this data include: Is there a possible consortium claim? Are there co-payments from other sources?

● Description of the incident, as well as facts surrounding the event, such as location of the incident; type of incident (such as medication error, treatment error, diagnostic error, slip or fall, lost property, elopement); extent of injury incurred at the time of the incident; pertinent environmental findings (such as position of bed rails, condition of floor surfaces, physical defects in equipment); and results of any physical examination of the patient, visitor, or employee by clinical staff, often provided by staff of the emergency department.

Staff Participation in Incident Reporting

Incident reporting should be the responsibility of all staff including employed and voluntary members of the medical personnel, not just the nursing department. To enhance the effectiveness of the incident report as a tool for risk management, the risk manager should encourage physicians, pharmacists, and laboratory and other ancillary service personnel to report incidents.

For the health care risk manager in the integrated delivery system (IDS), this presents a significant challenge. The various facilities that make up the IDS are usually geographically distant from each other; as a result, promoting the consistent and timely reporting of incidents demands effective staff education. Simplicity of the reporting system, as well as easy accessibility to training in how to use it, is especially important in encouraging staff in widely dispersed locations to report incidents.[1] For these systems, risk managers must include training and development for home health care providers, private physician offices, ambulatory care centers, and mobile mammogram units, for instance.

One of the greatest challenges risk managers face today is dealing with the negative perceptions of incident reports. One example is that staff view reporting as a routine task or low-priority paperwork. These misconceptions result in slow reporting and delayed follow-up on incidents. By providing feedback on the results of investigation and problem resolution, the risk manager can demonstrate the value of incident reporting. Once staff see the value of systematically identifying and addressing problems in patient care, they often are more motivated to participate in reporting incidents on a timely basis. Further examples that should be used in improving this perception are trending and analysis reports that lead to changes in protocol, procedures, or equipment based on these findings. This increases the effectiveness of the reporting process overall.

Sometimes, staff are reluctant to report incidents because they fear the report is an admission of negligence that exposes them to liability and could be used against them in court or as a punitive personnel tool.[2] To alleviate such fears, the risk manager should ensure that the incident report is not used as either a punitive measure in disciplining employees or a vehicle for airing interpersonal disagreements. This is not to say that the incident itself, such as repeated medication errors that lead to patient injury, may not involve some form of discipline. This should not be construed as the incident report leading to discipline but rather the event itself. Incident report training must stress that the report should be a factual account of what happened; no finger-pointing or accusatory language should be included. Incident reports are meant to collect "just the facts," avoiding subjective hearsay or third-party opinions of what did or did not happen. If a grievous error was made resulting in a severe outcome for the patient, an employee may require counseling regarding the incident and measures to prevent recurrence, but the incident report should not be used as evidence against the employee in a disciplinary procedure.

Numerous studies suggest that passive surveillance systems (such as incident reporting) identify far fewer adverse events that active surveillance systems (such as computerized detection system for medical administration). Following are reasons why incident reports may not be filed when policy directs staff to do so:

- Observer is too busy to complete the report when a narrative section is required.
- Staff believe that reporting is of little value due to lack of feedback.
- Staff fear disciplinary action based on the report.
- Nonphysicians are reluctant to report incident involving physicians.
- Staff are concerned that the report may lead to a lawsuit leading to personal responsibility.
- Staff failed to recognize that an incident occurred.
- Staff do not understand the definition of an incident.[3]

Supporting the theory that current incident reporting systems capture very little in organizations, Donald Berwick, MD, cites a 0.2 percent adverse drug event rate in hospitals based on self-reporting mechanisms such as incident reports or adverse drug event reports. When record review is performed, those rates of drug events increase threefold to 0.7 percent. When computerized screening is performed, the rate increases dramatically to 3.8 percent. Finally, when a chart review is combined with computerized screening, the incident rate increases to 10 percent.[4]

Effectiveness of the reporting process also can be maximized by written policies and procedures that clearly define a reportable incident. Traditionally, incident reports have been used to report major categories of events including patient slips and falls, medication errors, intravenous infusion problems, and lost valuables, among others. This limited use of the report is due, in part, to the mistaken belief that it is a document prepared for the facility's safety committee. Although events such as patient falls may occur frequently, claims studies clearly show that they are not the areas of greatest pay-out in health care-related claims. By indicating through in-service training, the design of the form, and written definitions of what constitutes a reportable incident, the risk manager can broaden the types of incidents reported to include clinically related events. Many organizations have used national claims data to dictate which events must reported and have included them in the redesign of their internal form. For instance, diagnostic errors account for a high proportion of malpractice claims and payments. Autopsy studies have indicated rates as high as 35–40 percent of missed diagnoses causing death.[5] One large professional liability carrier, St. Paul Fire and Marine, reports that diagnostic errors account for five of the top ten allegations in terms of frequency during claims year 1995.

More recent results from this carrier suggest similar findings with diagnostic error as a loss leader in malpractice.[6]

Finally, the risk manager should encourage staff to complete the incident report promptly, accurately, and completely. Ideally, the form should be completed at either the time of occurrence or immediately afterward. Many organizations utilize a "twenty-four-hour rule" for reporting, within twenty-four hours of the event or knowledge of the event. For accuracy's sake, the incident should be reported by the individual who has the most knowledge about the event—that is, the staff member involved in the occurrence, who witnessed it, or to whom it was reported. Second-hand knowledge often includes subjective information related to the event. If the incident report form requires follow-up information to be entered directly on it, policies should ensure that this information is transmitted rapidly, perhaps by telephone to the risk manager and that the completed incident report be forwarded to the risk manager as soon as possible. Any delay in transmitting information may prevent the risk manager from reacting immediately to the event and doing the appropriate follow-up within a day or two of the incident. Immediacy of information and action based on the report information is critical in any incident reporting system.

It is useful to think of the incident report and the process within the framework of recording information relating to who, what, when, where, how, and why.[7] This format also works well as the foundation in incident reporting development and training. Included in this training, risk managers should highlight key do's and don'ts for participants such as members of the medical staff, office managers, and home health aides:

- DO notify risk management within twenty-four hours of an incident.
- DO NOT route incident reports through any other department for any reason.
- DO NOT delay incident reports for follow-up or extra review and signatures.
- DO record in the patient's medical record a factual account of any unanticipated events involving patient injury.
- DO NOT indicate in the patient's medical record that an incident report was completed.
- DO NOT allow the incident report to become a part of the medical record.
- DO NOT assign blame or admit liability on the incident report or the medical record.[8]
- DO NOT make photocopies of the incident report for any reason.

Guidelines for Preserving Report Confidentiality

Although completed incident reports are a statement of fact and, therefore, contain readily available information from other sources, risk managers and staff should strive to maintain the confidentiality of these reports and related information. The preservation of confidentiality:

- Encourages accurate and frequent reporting.
- Ensures the factual information and promotes honesty of reports.
- Prevents the perception (usually introduced by plaintiff's counsel) that something "wrong" has occurred.
- Supports a defense attorney's ability to provide appropriate defense.

In order to protect the confidentiality of the document, one of two common approaches can be taken: to provide protection under state statutes regarding quality assurance studies and/or peer review activities or to provide protection under the attorney-client privilege, also referred to as work product protection.

To maintain confidentiality, the original report should be sent to the risk manager immediately upon completion. As mentioned previously, copies should never be made, and the report must *never* be made part of the medical record.

Frequently, a follow-up sheet is attached to the incident report form. This usually is completed by a departmental manager, the nursing supervisor, or nursing home administrator (or other responsible administrator) who has investigated the occurrence and, when possible, ascertained the fact pattern of events (cause) leading to the incident. It is important to protect the confidentiality of this addendum and other related information such as photographs, staffing records, and so on, as well as the actual incident report.

If managers use incident reports to support quality assurance (QA) studies or insist on having the reports for any reason, risk managers should suggest that managers review the originals in the risk manager's office. Once again, it is important to ensure that copies are not made and the originals are not removed from the file.

If the incident report is best protected through assertion of attorney-client privilege, the incident report should be reviewed by legal counsel in a timely fashion (depending on the nature of the incident) and maintained in specifically identified and appropriately designated files. If report confidentiality is best achieved through statutory protection afforded to QA data and peer review activities, the reports must be reviewed through the established QA program. This review can be accomplished when there is a distinct operational linkage between risk management and quality assurance (performance improvement) departments. It is best to discuss these options with legal counsel to determine the most appropriate method for preserving confidentiality, keeping in mind local and state case law. Likewise, the risk manager should consult with legal counsel regarding procedures for reviewing and maintaining the reports.

Risk management professionals and defense counsel have worked tirelessly to ensure protection of this type of information. However recently, health care organizations have found increasing numbers of challenges to this protection by plaintiff attorneys and the courts. Thus, it is important to remember that while organizations work diligently to protect this information, it must be assumed that all health care information is "discoverable." Given that belief, the recording of facts only on incident reports is of utmost importance given that this information could be found in other documents including the medical record.

Occurrence Reporting and Screening

As previously mentioned, a potential problem with incident reporting is that staff view it as a vehicle for reporting nonclinical incidents only. To ensure that clinically related adverse patient occurrences are properly reported and tracked, many health care organizations have modified their data collection and reporting systems. Three approaches often used are focused occurrence reporting, occurrence screening, and generic screening.

The fact that occurrence reporting is a mandatory function in most JCAHO accredited organizations is one of the features that distinguishes it from incident reporting, which is voluntary or considered a passive surveillance system. Also, the events to be identified through occurrence reporting are clearly specified.[9]

Focused-Occurrence Reporting

With focused-occurrence reporting, staff are given clear guidelines and specific examples of reportable incidents. For example, these incidents may include:

- Occurrences of missed diagnosis or misdiagnosis that result in patient injury, such as failure to diagnose acute myocardial infarction, fractures, serious head trauma, or appendicitis.

- Surgically related occurrences, such as the wrong patient being operated on, the wrong procedure being performed, an incorrect instrument or sponge count, or an unplanned return to the operating room.

- Treatment- or procedure-related occurrences, such as reactions to contrast material used in a diagnostic procedure, inappropriate exposure to x-rays, or burns resulting from improper use of hot packs.

- Blood-related occurrences, such as the wrong type of blood given to the patient, transmission of disease via infected blood, or inappropriate use of blood.

- Intravenous-related occurrences, such as the wrong solution being administered, infiltration of solution, or an inappropriate infusion rate.

- Medication-related occurrences, such as administration of the wrong medication or dosage, or administration to the wrong patient.

- Lack of appropriate follow-up, such as failure to notify a patient of abnormal laboratory findings or failure to schedule required screening tests such as annual PAP smears or mammograms.

- Falls.

- Other occurrences that result or may result in injuries to patients or visitors.[10]

The majority of these examples apply to acute care setting but many are applicable to other parts of the continuum. Medication-related occurrences should be reported and tracked in all health care settings including the private office setting. Falls, which are a prevalent cause of injury in long-term care facilities, can occur in any setting, as can the development of decubitus ulcers, patient elopement, failure to refer, and Emergency Medical Treatment and Active Labor Act (EMTALA) violations. With the elderly, the resulting injury can be severe. Finally, as we witness more and more care being provided in alternate settings such as in the home, these providers must design incident reporting system that track treatment variances and errors and equipment malfunctions leading to patient or client injury.

To further focus the reporting process, many health care organizations define reportable occurrences by designated clinical areas, such as the emergency department (ED), surgical suite, labor and delivery room, high-risk nursery, and so on. For larger integrated delivery systems (IDSs) and stand-alone alternate care settings, reportable occurrences are designed specific to that type of service offered. By developing lists of specific adverse outcomes or events in these high-risk areas, the clinical focus of occurrence reporting is addressed, as well as the definition of incidents that need to be reported. In this process, the incident report form or a similar form is used to report those occurrences and the policies and procedures define what is to be reported. (Exhibits 8.1 and 8.2 illustrate focused-occurrence reports.) The risk manager receives these reports directly. Because of their highly clinical nature, in most facilities the data collected through this process also are reported to the performance improvement (or QA)

EXHIBIT 8.1.   Ambulatory Care Surgical Occurrences Criteria

1. Perioperative death.
2. Perioperative cardiac or respiratory arrest.
3. Perioperative acute myocardial infarction.
4. Wrong procedure performed (for example, wrong side for breast removal, wrong space for laminectomy).
5. Wrong patient operated on.
6. Unplanned return to the operating room during the same admission or within ten days of discharge (excluding staged procedures).
7. Postoperative neurological deficit not present on admission.
8. No written consent (except in medical emergencies) or improper consent for procedures or incomplete consent (such as untimed, undated, unsigned).
9. Patient injury resulting from chemical, physical, laser, or electrical hazards (for example, burns or abrasions).
10. Incorrect needle, sponge, or instrument count that is unspecified.
11. Instrument breakage or malfunction.
12. Foreign object or material found during surgery (except for bullets, knife plates, or other objects related to trauma requiring surgery).
13. Adverse reactions to anesthesia (except those with no residual effect beyond four hours postoperatively).
14. Intubation or extubation resulting in injury (including injury to teeth).
15. Patient operated on for repair of a laceration, perforation, tear, or puncture of an organ subsequent to the performance of an invasive procedure.
16. Reintubation in operating room or Post Anesthesia Care Unit (PACU) (for example, inadequate reversal or over narcotization).
17. Lost specimen.
18. Any other untoward event such as falls, accidents, or medication errors resulting in patient injury.
19. Transfusion error.
20. Unplanned admission to hospital related to ambulatory surgical procedure (except for observation patients).
21. Recovery discharge criteria not met—patient leaves AMA unaccompanied by a responsible adult, or elopes.
22. Patient callback reveals medical concerns relating to the procedure requiring physician contact by a hospital employee.

Reprinted with permission, from Chicago Hospital Risk Pooling Program.

committee for peer review to perform a root cause analysis and prepare action plans and incident follow-up. At the very least, aggregate reports of this information should be reported to quality assurance, as well as to stand-alone risk management committees.

There are many ways to enhance the effectiveness of the reporting process. These include:

- Ensuring that departmental and medical staff are involved in development of the list of reportable occurrences so that there is agreement as to the need for reporting.

- Streamlining the reporting process so that the paperwork is not burdensome and reporting is easy. Because many of the items on the list of reportable incidents occur frequently (for example, patients leaving the ED against medical advice), checklists may be more useful than lengthy narrative reports. Again the intent and best practice at this time in health care is to improve reporting. Increasing the number of reports may not be the ultimate goal but rather receiving reports on events that require risk management review and afford an opportunity to reduce the likelihood of legal liability.

EXHIBIT 8.2.   Ambulatory Care Non-Surgical Occurrences Criteria

1. Death.

2. Cardiac or respiratory arrest.

3. Serious patient complications as a result of diagnostic and/or therapeutic services (for example, bowel perforation, patient burn or scarring, or amniocentesis complications).

4. Unexpected return to center or unplanned hospital admission for complications or incomplete management of problems on previous outpatient visit(s). (specify)

5. Patient discharged with altered state of consciousness, neurological deficit, or unstable vital signs with no follow-up plans documented.

6. Initial diagnosis of fracture made subsequent to previous patient visit(s). (specify)

7. Patient injured resulting from chemical, medication, or equipment adverse event (for example, equipment failure or malfunction, extravasation of cytoxic drug). (specify)

8. Patient refuses treatment or exam or leaves AMA. (specify)

9. Other-patient or visitor fall, medication error, or patient accident. (specify)

10. Results not on chart forty-eight hours after test done, except when test takes longer than forty-eight hours to obtain results (for example, cultures or state lab results).

11. Diagnostic test omitted when ordered.

12. Lost specimens.

13. Failure to perform pregnancy test on female patients of childbearing age who present with abdominal complaints or symptoms requiring abdominal x-ray.

14. Pregnancy undelivered at forty-two weeks of gestation, or in which there is no documentation that the well-being of the fetus has been carefully evaluated clinically and through use of testing (for example, nonstress test, biophysical profile).

Reprinted, with permission, from Chicago Hospital Risk Pooling Program.

- Ensuring that the results of the reporting are given to the departments involved as quickly as possible for their review and consideration, thus emphasizing the utility of identifying problems in the quality of patient care rather than the punitive aspect of claims involvement.

Occurrence Screening   Another method that attempts to identify adverse patient occurrences in clinical areas is the occurrence screening process, as originally developed by Joyce Craddick of Medical Management Analysis International. This system, and many others like it that followed, utilizes a clearly defined list of patient occurrences with which patient medical records are screened. The screeners are looking for deviations from practice, policy, and procedures. Criteria for the screens are established in areas that are considered to be either high risk, have a high number of incidents that have been reported as quality of care "red flags" to be further evaluated, or areas where the effects of an untoward event occurring can have disastrous results from an injury standpoint. In the past, most screens were centered around clinical events and related administrative events but they can just as well be used for regulatory and financial issues. Criteria are developed and exceptions are listed if appropriate. As an example, in the operating room or surgery, one specific criterion that may be screened for is appropriate informed consent documentation. An exception to this criterion may be for a case of emergency surgery, where either the patient is unable to give consent or there is not time to obtain consent. Another criterion to screen for and evaluate regardless of location in the health care setting is an unexpected death. There are no exceptions to this criterion. In the emergency department, criteria may include misread x-rays or readmissions within twenty-four hours.

In an inpatient setting, all patient records are reviewed against the criteria within forty-eight to seventy-two hours of admission and every three or four days thereafter until the patient is discharged. The patient chart also is reviewed approximately two weeks after discharge to ensure that compliance with all criteria has been assessed.

Results of this screening process are prepared for each admission by trained data-retrieval personnel (screeners). The abstract is then forwarded to the QA office for follow-up and data collection. When identified, serious occurrences are reported immediately by the patient care reviewers to the appropriate person for action. All occurrences are aggregated to aid in identifying any trends that reflect patient care problems requiring remedial action.

Occurrence screening can be effective in other settings as well; ambulatory care organizations (ACOs), group practices, and clinics, in particular, have found this method useful in identifying sources of risk. Using a checklist, ACO staff review their outpatient records for items such as documentation of patient allergies, prescription refills, patient notification of test results, and telephone communication. The records are also reviewed to see whether they are sufficient for another practitioner to continue the patient's care.[11]

Although occurrence screening is an effective method for identifying adverse occurrences, its implementation in most institutions is done entirely under the QA program. The major challenge of this system is how to ensure appropriate involvement of the risk manager. In some institutions, the risk manager is notified by having the patient care reviewer complete a separate risk management notification form for serious adverse patient occurrences. In other instances, the risk manager is part of the quality management team and is apprised of the results of the occurrence screening through departmental or QA committee meetings.

Regardless of the method chosen, the risk manager should have ready access to these data in order for this process to be useful to the risk management program. In addition, the risk manager should play a key role in identifying and implementing action plans relating to abnormal and increasing negative data trends.

············

INFORMAL RISK IDENTIFICATION SYSTEMS

In addition to the more structured systems of risk identification, such as incident reporting, occurrence reporting, and occurrence screening, there are many other sources of information available to the risk manager for identifying actual loss-producing events and potential risks. Some of these include:

- *Committee meeting minutes,* such as from those dealing with performance improvement, quality assurance, safety, infection control, and bioethics; and those from departmental committees such as morbidity and mortality, tissue review, pharmacy and therapeutics, and other quality-related committees.

- *Claims data,* including a review of both the facility's loss experience over a period of time and any national or regional trends as reported in various publications. For instance, risk managers will serve their organizations well tracking regional or national loss trends even if those types of incidents have not occurred (or been reported) in their organization. Planning and being proactive to avoid known risks is reflective of a mature risk management program.

- *Survey reports,* including those from the JCAHO, the National Committee on Quality Assurance (NCQA), the Commission on Accreditation of Rehabilitation Facilities (CARF), Occupational Safety and Health Administration (OSHA), the state fire marshal, state licensure surveys, broker or underwriter site assessments, consultant findings, and private review organization study results.

- *Floor rounds,* in which the risk manager is visible and available to staff members and encourages the sharing of information that may be viewed by certain individuals as too sensitive for a written report. Having a routine presence on the floor and availability in the office or by pager are important factors in the continuous effort to enhance the early reporting of incidents.

As before, availing themselves of these data sources, risk managers should contact legal counsel to determine how best to protect the confidentiality of any data collected.

INTEGRATION OF RISK-IDENTIFYING SYSTEMS WITH CLAIMS MANAGEMENT

While all systems discussed support claims management, some of the previously mentioned systems are better than others at identifying potential claims immediately. The incident reporting system is the one originally designed for this purpose. However, for this system to be most effective, the staff must be educated as to what a reportable incident is and why it is necessary to quickly report serious incidents directly to the risk manager. In home health care, for instance, given the geographic barrier between staff and a risk manager, there must be user-friendly processes for staff to report incidents. Requiring staff to return to the central office to complete a report after an incident may not be the most effective protocol and would likely lead to less reporting or reporting not done in a timely manner.

Occurrence reporting has the advantage of providing a better definition of reportable incidents but may be too clinically specific, thus limiting reports of nonclinical events. When designing occurrence reporting programs in a long-term care setting, it is important to keep in mind that a large percentage of losses are directly related to nonclinical intervention (treatment), such as falls, abrasions, resident-to-resident violence, molestation, and elopement.

The occurrence screening system that utilizes periodic record review is perhaps the least immediate and effective for claims management purposes. However, the benefits of its comprehensiveness and consistency of review can be enhanced by adding a mechanism to ensure immediate reporting of potential or known claims (defined well in advance) to risk management. A screening tool that highlights direct reports to risk management can serve the organization well in this instance.

COMPUTERIZED OCCURRENCE TRACKING

With the ready availability and use of personal computers, bedside monitors, and recently, the palm pilot in the health care field, there has been concomitant computerization of risk management data. There are many commercially available prepackaged software programs designed to track risk management data including front-end reporting, statistical analysis, and claims management. There also are many database management software programs that can be used to customize an individual's risk management information needs.

The kinds of data that can be tracked by computer include but are not limited to:

- Incident report data.
- Occurrence screening information.
- Claims data, including professional liability claims, general liability claims, workers' compensation claims, and others, as needed.
- Litigation management data including defense costs, defense counsel hours, standard answers to interrogatories, depositions and motions filed on behalf of the insured organization, and limited access to legal counsel's database for the limited review of motions filed, research, and discovery information.
- Insurance-related data, such as schedules of insurance, premium costs, premium allocation methodologies, excess-carrier information, claims and incident reporting requirements, and brokerage service agreement.

More recently, many risk management information systems (RMIS) are beginning to promote statistical analysis and offer benchmarking capabilities all allowing the risk manager to compare their organization with similar organizations or by significant national trends. (For more information on benchmarking and program evaluation, please refer to Chapters 34 and 35, respectively.)

The important elements of a computerized system, regardless of the system used or the data input, are:

- Data collection.
- Data screening, review, and coding.
- Data processing.
- Report generation in an easily comprehensible format.
- Information analysis and feedback.[12]

An effective RMIS must have a data collection form that collects information accurately, quickly, and in a manner that facilitates coding and entry. For example, incident report forms should be either precoded or designed for easy coding to ensure fast and accurate entry and easy retrieval of information. These forms usually contain many check-off boxes and limited narrative description. New technology such as scanning software promotes an easy way to convert a paper document to soft data, which then can be manipulated using the computer software program.

The most important element of a successful computerized system is its ability to generate useful and readable reports. Without the capacity to produce aggregate reports and data trends, the utility of a computerized system is minimal. The whole purpose of automating the data is to permit easy tracking and trending in order to identify patterns and problems and compare current data with those of last month, last year, and perhaps the past five years.

The kinds of variables related to occurrences that could be analyzed include:

- *Date of the occurrence.* This information is valuable for providing trending information to determine whether the number of occurrences is increasing, decreasing, or remaining stable over time.
- *Type of occurrence.* Looking at types of occurrences (for example, falls, medication errors, diagnosis-related occurrences, treatment-related occurrences, and so forth) and their frequency is important when trying to identify priorities in loss prevention activities.

- *Location of the occurrence.* By analyzing where adverse occurrences are most likely to happen, loss prevention activities can be more readily targeted. Also, this allows for providing profiles to various departments, as requested.

- *Severity of injury.* By focusing on occurrences with the highest likelihood of severe injury (for example, Apgar scores below five at five minutes or anesthesia accidents), one can identify and respond to possible claims with the potential for the greatest severity.[13]

In addition to those variables, other elements of the occurrence that can be examined for trends include:

- Patient characteristics, such as age, gender, marital status, occupation, method of payment, and diagnosis.

- Staff characteristics, such as name, title, employment status (for example, agency versus staff nurse) of all employees involved in the occurrence; or name, department, and specialty of all involved physicians.

- Other occurrence-related data, such as time and shift of the occurrence, physical environment at the time of the occurrence (such as wet floor, inoperative call light, inappropriate bed-rail position), location of occurrence within the system, or the status of family training in home-care situations.

Choosing a computerized system to support the risk management function is not an easy task. Expense, ease of use, and utility are important factors in selecting a system to manage reporting and data manipulation. Compatibility with the clinical and financial data systems currently in place at the organization is a key decision element as well.

Recent Developments regarding Incident Reporting

There have been three major developments relating to medical error and reporting within health care organizations: the JCAHO Sentinel Event Policy, the release of the Institute of Medicine's report "To Err is Human: Building a Safer Health System," and the severe increase in malpractice claims in both the managed care industry and the long-term care environment. These developments have led to increased public scrutiny, more oversight by regulatory and voluntary accrediting bodies, and an increased emphasis on accountability as defined by consumers of health care. Accountability in any health care organization demands the development of valid and reliable measures of quality and outcomes, avoiding (of course) poor or negative outcomes.

JCAHO Sentinel Events[14]

The Joint Commission's Sentinel Event Policy is designed to encourage the self-reporting of medical errors to learn about the relative frequencies and underlying causes of sentinel events, share "lessons learned" with other health care organizations, and reduce the risk of future sentinel event occurrences. Accredited organizations must update their internal reporting systems to minimally identify these types of events, which are fully defined below.

According to the JCAHO, a sentinel event is any unexpected occurrence involving death or serious physical or psychological injury, or the risk thereof. Serious injuries specifically include a loss of limb or function. The phrase "or the risk thereof" includes any process variation for which a recurrence would carry a significant chance of a serious adverse outcome.

Any time a sentinel event occurs, the accredited organization is expected to complete a root cause analysis, implement improvements to reduce risk, and monitor the effectiveness of those improvements. While the immediate cause of most sentinel events is due to human fallibility, the root cause analysis is expected to dig down to underlying organization systems and processes that can be altered to reduce the likelihood of human error in the future and to protect patients from harm when human error does occur.

A standard that creates explicit expectations regarding the internal identification and management of sentinel events was added to the leadership chapter of all accreditation manuals and became effective January 1, 1999.

Voluntary Self-Reporting of Sentinel Events   Under the Sentinel Event Policy, a defined subset of sentinel events are subject to review by the Joint Commission and may be reported to the Joint Commission on a *voluntary* basis. Only those sentinel events that affect recipients of care (patients, clients, and residents) and that meet one of the following criteria fall into this category.

- The event has resulted in an unanticipated death or major permanent loss of function, not related to the natural course of the patient's illness or underlying condition.[15]
- The event is one of the following (even if the outcome was not death or major permanent loss of function):[16]
    a. Suicide of a patient in a setting where the patient receives around the clock care (such as in a hospital, residential treatment center, or crisis stabilization center).
    b. Infant abduction or discharge to the wrong family.
    c. Rape.[17]
    d. Hemolytic transfusion reaction involving administration of blood or blood products having major blood group incompatibilities.
    e. Surgery on the wrong patient or wrong body part.[18]

An organization that experiences a sentinel event that does *not* meet the criteria for review under the Sentinel Event Policy is still required to complete a root cause analysis. However, according to JCAHO policy, the root cause analysis does not need to be made available to the Joint Commission.

Sentinel Events That Are Not Self-Reported   Each accredited health care organization is encouraged, but *not* required, to report to the Joint Commission any sentinel event meeting the aforementioned criteria for reviewable sentinel events. Alternatively, the Joint Commission may become aware of a sentinel event by some other means such as from a patient, family member, or employee of the organization, or through the media.

Whether the organization voluntarily reports the event or the Joint Commission becomes aware of the event by some other means, there is no difference in the expected response, time frames, or review procedures.

Joint Commission Response   If the Joint Commission becomes aware (either through voluntary self-reporting or otherwise) of a sentinel event that meets the definition of a reviewable sentinel event, the organization is required to

- Prepare a thorough and credible root cause analysis and action plan within forty-five calendar days of the event, or of its becoming aware of the event.

- Submit to the Joint Commission its root cause analysis and action plan or otherwise provide for Joint Commission evaluation of its response to the sentinel event under an approved protocol, within forty-five calendar days of the known occurrence of the event.

The Joint Commission will then determine whether the root cause analysis and action plan are acceptable.

Advantages to Reporting a Sentinel Event   There are several advantages to the organization that reports a sentinel event.

- Reporting the event enables the addition of the "lessons learned" from the event to be added to the Joint Commission's sentinel event database, thereby contributing to the general knowledge about sentinel events and the reduction of risk for such events in many other organizations.

- Early reporting provides an opportunity for consultation with Joint Commission staff during the development of the root cause analysis and action plan.

- The organization's message to the public that it is doing everything possible to ensure that such an event will not happen again is strengthened by its acknowledged collaboration with the Joint Commission to understand how the event happened and what can be done to reduce the risk of such an event occurring in the future.

Submission of Root Cause Analysis and Resulting Action Plan   The Joint Commission has initiated a number of procedures to protect the confidentiality of sentinel event information shared by accredited organizations and in the Joint Commission's possession.

The Joint Commission advises health care organizations not to provide patient or caregiver identifiers when reporting sentinel events to the Joint Commission.

An organization that experiences a sentinel event should submit two separate documents to the Joint Commission: (1) the root cause analysis and (2) the resulting action plan. The root cause analysis will be returned to the organization once abstracted and information is entered into the Joint Commission database. If copies have been made for internal review, they will be destroyed after the review. Also, once the action plan has been implemented to the satisfaction of the Joint Commission, it will be returned to the organization.

In addition, if the organization has concerns about increased risk of legal exposure as a result of sending the root cause analysis documents to the Joint Commission, the following alternative approaches to review of the organization's response to the sentinel event are acceptable.

- An organization brings root cause analysis documents to the Joint Commission headquarters for review and then takes the documents back on the same day.

- A specially trained surveyor conducts an on-site visit to review the root cause analysis and action plan. The organization will be assessed a charge sufficient to cover the average direct costs of the visit.

- A specially trained surveyor conducts an on-site visit to review the root cause analysis and findings, without directly viewing the root cause analysis documents, through a series of interviews and review of relevant documentation. For purposes of this review activity, "relevant documentation" includes, at a minimum, any documentation relevant to the organization's *process* for responding to sentinel events and the action plan resulting from the analysis of the subject sentinel event. The latter serves as the basis for appropriate follow-up activity. The organization will be assessed a charge sufficient to cover the average direct costs of the visit.

- Where the organization affirms that it meets specified criteria respecting the risk of waiving legal protection for root cause analysis information shared with the Joint Commission, a specially trained surveyor conducts an on-site visit to interview staff and review relevant documentation to obtain information about:

   a. The *process* the organization uses in responding to sentinel events.

   b. The relevant policies and procedures preceding and following the organization's review of the specific event and the implementation thereof, sufficient to permit inferences about the adequacy of the organization's response to the sentinel event.

Institute of Medicine's "To Err is Human: Building a Safer Health System"

This report is just but one in a series of reports produced by the Committee on Quality Health Care in America project. This project was initiated by the Institute of Medicine in June 1998 with the charge of developing a strategy that will result in a threshold improvement in quality over the next ten years.[19]

This first report focusing on patient safety was released in November 1998 and has evoked tremendous scrutiny and comment. Although the report is still being analyzed by many in health care, it does highlight the need for change. The report, extrapolating data from previous hospital-based studies, estimated that between 44,000 and 98,000 Americans die yearly due to preventable medical error. The report goes on to say that if one were to look at the smaller number (44,000) and make some comparisons that it would show that it is greater than the eighth leading cause of death.

The report also estimates that the occurrence of preventable adverse events is understated because the studies reviewed only included those errors that are mentioned in the medical record, only considered those events that resulted in a specified level of harm, and imposed a high threshold to determine whether the adverse event was preventable or negligent.

The results of this report will support those risk management activities that emphasize risk prevention. It puts the risk manger in the position of having tremendous impact on the organizations' response to this report. It encourages the risk manager in all health care delivery settings to review policy and procedures related to patient safety and the reporting of adverse events. It also supports a close working relationship with quality on process improvement activities. Risk managers have an opportunity now more than ever before to assist the board of directors, senior management, and the medical staff with proactive risk control activities.

Future reports of the Committee on Quality Health Care project will address other quality-related issues such as redesigning the health care system, aligning financial incentives, and developing information technology.

Managed Care Organizations

Over the past decade managed care organizations have met with increasing frequency and severity of malpractice claims (for example, see *Fox v. HealthNet*, Calif., 1996). Relying on the protections afforded Managed Care Organizations (MCOs) by Employment Retirement Income Security Act (ERISA) preemption and arguments that HMOs do not provide care, MCOs had not experienced the large losses historically as other parts of the health care delivery system have. The court recently began allowing patients and their representatives access to courts for quality of care issues resulting in harm (particularly denial of care and failure to refer) and breach of fiduciary responsibility. Reacting to a severity trend, MCOs have formalized risk management efforts including steps such as:

- Recruitment of risk management professionals.
- Development of a risk management plan and program.
- Design of incident reporting systems both for the corporation and the network.
- Development of patient grievance systems that not only afford members (patients) due process but assist in identifying "incidents" for risk management oversight.
- Formal educational programming for MCO staff and the network addressing risk management and incident reporting.

Examples of reportable events for an MCO are included in Exhibit 8.3. Of importance to note is that MCOs must focus their reportable events on clinical, operational, and financial "events" such as "denial of benefits."

············

CONCLUSION

A meaningful, organization-wide reporting system that identifies and promotes response to adverse patient occurrences is the backbone of an effective risk management program. It is essential that the risk manager work on the design and implementation of an effective data-gathering system—whether it be incident reporting, occurrence reporting, or

---

EXHIBIT 8.3.   MCO Suggested Reportable Events and PCEs

1. Written executive inquiry demanding damages or services.
2. Reversal of benefit determination after two earlier denials.
3. Final benefit determination rendered more than forty-five days after initial grievance filed.
4. Experimental treatment benefit determination reversal after earlier denial.
5. More than three calls to provider relations or member services regarding a single incident or event.
6. Provider complaints that accounts receivable is more than sixty days old.
7. Global capitation contracts with providers are executed without financial guaranteed required.
8. Member's readmission to a hospital within seven days of discharge.
9. Member admitted to hospital within twenty-four hours of visit to emergency room.
10. Surprise lawsuit (no previous event reported to legal or risk management).
11. Appropriate board-level minutes do not reflect at least quarterly report of audit results for delegated functions (such as credentialing, utilization review, claim payment, and so on).
12. Early and vocal alignment of PCP with member's cause.
13. Loss of accreditation based on quality of care or service.
14. Bankruptcy or financial difficulties involving bond issues or licensing bodies.
15. Network disruption, percentage of network physicians nonrenewal of contract.

Reprinted with the permission of the Center for Excellence in Healthcare Risk Management, MARSH USA, Inc.

occurrence screening, or a combination of systems—and that the purposes and value of that system be clearly identified for all members of the health care team.

It is also important to always keep in mind that any reporting system relies heavily on the human element to make it successful.

Endnotes

The author would like to gratefully acknowledge and thank Audrone M. Vanagunas for her earlier work, which contributed greatly to the development of this chapter.

1. Maley, R. A. "Building Risk Management into Integrated Healthcare Delivery Systems." *Journal of Healthcare Risk Management, 16*(4), Fall 1996, pp. 31–40.

2. Orlikoff, J. E., and Vanagunas, A. M. *Malpractice Prevention and Liability Control for Hospitals* (2nd ed.). Chicago: American Hospital Publishing, 1988.

3. Cullen, D., and Associates. "The Incident Reporting System Does Not Detect Adverse Drug Events: A Problem for Quality Improvement." *Journal of Quality Improvement, 21*(10), 1995, pp. 541–548.

4. Berwick, D. M., and others. "Reducing Adverse Drug Events and Medical Errors." Presented at the National Forum on Quality Improvement in Health Care Conference, New Orleans, La.: Dec. 4–6, 1996.

5. Kern, K. A. "Diagnostic Errors: The Utility of Statistical Process Control in Preventing Misdiagnosed Breast Cancer." Presented at Examining Errors in Health Care Conference, Rancho Mirage, Calif.: Oct. 13–15, 1996.

6. St. Paul Fire and Marine Insurance Company: Year-End Report, 1995.

7. ECRI, Healthcare Risk Control, Incident Reporting and Management, p. 1, July 1996.

8. *Ibid.*, p. 2.

9. Quinlan, W. C. "How Do Risk Managers Really Learn about Potential Claims?" *Journal of Healthcare Risk Management, 15*(2), Spring 1995, p. 3–6.

10. Orlikoff and Vanagunas, pp. 57–58.

11. American Society for Healthcare Risk Management. *Mapping Your Risk Management Course in Ambulatory Care.* Chicago: ASHRM, 1995, pp. 12–13.

12. Kraus, G. P. *Health Care Risk Management, Organization and Claims Administration.* Owings Mills, Md.: Rynd Communications, 1986.

13. Orlikoff and Vanagunas, p. 68.

14. *Sentinel Events: Evaluating Cause and Planning Improvement* (2nd ed.). Joint Commission, 1998.

15. "Major permanent loss of function" means sensory, motor, physiologic, or intellectual impairment not present on admission requiring continued treatment or lifestyle change. When major permanent loss of function cannot be immediately determined, applicability of the policy is not established until either the patient is discharged with continued major loss of function, or two weeks have elapsed with persistent major loss of function, whichever occurs first.

16. A distinction is made between an adverse outcome that is related to the natural course of the patient's illness or underlying condition (not reviewed under the Sentinel Event Policy) and a death or major permanent loss of function that is associated with the treatment, or lack of treatment, of that condition (reviewable).

17. The determination of "rape" is to be based on the health care organization's definition, consistent with applicable law and regulation. An allegation of rape is not reviewable

under the policy. Applicability of the policy is established when a determination is made that a rape has occurred.

18. All events of surgery on the wrong patient or wrong body part are reviewable under the policy, regardless of the magnitude of the procedure.

19. Corrigan, J., and others. *To Err is Human: Building a Safer Health System.* Committee on Quality of Health Care in America Project and the Institute of Medicine, Washington, D.C.: National Academies Press, 1999.

9

Occupational and Environmental Risk Exposures for Health Care Facilities

John C. West

ealth care professionals have long been concerned about the safety of the delivery of health care services. But until relatively recently, this concern was focused exclusively on the safety of patients. In the distant past, the delivery of health care services was generally an unsafe occupation, and many health care providers became ill or were injured in the course of their employment. During that less-litigious time, occupational hazards were an accepted part of health care service delivery. Health care professionals and analysts of the field only recently have begun to raise concerns about the safety and health of health care workers and potential damage to the environment as a result of health care operations. To some degree, this trend reflects the change in the perception of health care from an altruistic field to a business.

This chapter focuses on the myriad regulations promulgated by the Occupational Safety and Health Administration (OSHA) and the Environmental Protection Agency (EPA), as well as the standards of the Joint Commission on Accreditation of Healthcare Organizations (JCAHO), that affect how health care services can be delivered. As a general rule, these regulations and standards are essential components of successful loss prevention programs. The direct losses the facility should seek to avoid in this regard include:

- Workers' compensation payments.
- Employment-related litigation.
- Environmental impairment claims.
- Property damage claims.
- Civil penalties.
- Loss of accreditation.
- Potential criminal actions.

There also are indirect benefits to be obtained from implementation of good programs to manage these risks, including increased productivity, improved employee morale, improved community relations, and a general improvement in the global environment, which benefits all of us.

This chapter will also provide advice on ways to create programs that are effective, efficient, and in keeping with regulatory requirements. A key component to the success of these programs is the facility's commitment to effective implementation. If policies and procedures are developed but never followed, or programs are implemented but never evaluated or enforced, the effort is simply a waste of time.

Unfortunately, the voluminous amount of information on occupational health and environmental risk exposures cannot be covered in a few pages. Consequently, this chapter focuses on issue spotting, which will help the health care risk manager recognize relevant issues when they arise and guide him or her to more definitive sources of information.

··········

OCCUPATIONAL SAFETY AND HEALTH CONCERNS

The primary regulatory agency in the field of occupational safety and health is OSHA, a federal agency within the U.S. Department of Labor. A number of states also have implemented programs equivalent to the federal OSHA program. As of this writing, twenty-four states and territories have received certification for their programs (meaning that developmental steps have been completed).[1] Fourteen of these twenty-four states have received final approval for their programs.[2] It should be pointed out that federal enforcement ceases for issues covered by a state plan.[3] To qualify as a state plan, the state agency must promulgate regulations at least as stringent as the federal regulations. States are free to promulgate more stringent regulations if they so desire. Due to the large number of state programs, this chapter addresses federal regulations only. Health care risk managers in states with their own OSHA programs are encouraged to consult their state regulations for further guidance. The following subsections address the principal health concerns for which OSHA has developed safety standards.

Asbestos

Asbestos is a naturally occurring magnesium silicate mineral fiber that was used extensively in the construction of commercial buildings, including hospitals and long-term care facilities, from shortly after World War II until the late 1970s. In 1989, the EPA attempted to ban the use of asbestos under the Toxic Substances Control Act, but much of the ban was struck down by the U.S. Court of Appeals for the Fifth Circuit.[4] In reality, asbestos-containing material (ACM) was seldom used in the construction or renovation of any buildings or portions of buildings after 1980.

Asbestos, as regulated by the various federal agencies, includes chrysotile, amosite, crocidolite, tremolite (asbestiform only), anthophyllite (asbestiform only), and actinolite (asbestiform only) fibers. Nonasbestiform fibers from these latter three materials may be regulated under OSHA's total particulate (inert or nuisance dust) standard.[5] Unless ACMs have been removed from a building constructed or renovated between World War II and the late 1970s, either by an abatement program or through more recent renovation, it is generally to be expected that there may be some ACM still present. Although asbestos has been the subject of a great deal of hysteria on the federal, state, and local levels, it probably is not as dangerous as many people believe. Having asbestos in a building is somewhat akin to having a rattlesnake: it may not be the best idea to have it there, but it will not hurt anyone unless it is disturbed. Asbestos fibers are only hazardous if they are inhaled by people. Consequently, only ACM that is capable of releasing airborne fibers (friable ACM) is of pressing concern. Any ACM that is damaged, or that is otherwise subject to disturbance, may need to be removed. Other ACM may very well be capable of management in place.[6,7]

ACM is an extremely effective fire and heat retardant. It is usually encountered in one of three categories: sprayed-on fire retardant (usually on structural supports); thermal system insulation (wrapping on pipes, boilers, or water heaters); or construction materials (for example, acoustic plaster, floor and ceiling tiles, siding, and roofing materials). As a general rule, exposure to asbestos in health care facilities occurs during building renovation or demolition; the risk of exposure during application or use is remote because asbestos is not used for anything in health care facilities at this time.

Asbestos has been regulated by OSHA since 1971 and currently is regulated under both the General Industry Standards[8] and the Construction Standards.[9] The General Industry Standards apply to any activities unrelated to demolition or renovation, such as housekeeping in areas where ACM is present. These standards set 0.1 fibers per cubic centimeter (f/cc) of air (one fiber in ten cc's of air) as an eight-hour, time-weighted average as the permissible exposure limit, although they allow for a thirty-minute excursion limit up to a level of one f/cc. The General Industry Standards usually are a problem only for workers who actually handle ACMs. It is extremely uncommon for undisturbed ACM to generate airborne fibers at levels high enough to be of concern. As a result, they are a consideration only when housekeepers accidentally disturb ACM or when plant operations personnel need to remove it to repair piping or equipment.

The Construction Standards apply in any circumstances surrounding demolition or renovation, including cleaning up afterward. The exposure limits imposed by OSHA in the Construction Standards are the same as those imposed in the General Industry Standards, but in renovations the potential for exposure is infinitely greater. The potential for spreading the contamination throughout the facility also exists unless proper containment measures are implemented. In addition, the Construction Standards contain stringent personal protection, handling, clearance, and disposal requirements. As a general rule, unless the renovations are essentially minor, the best policy is to turn the abatement project over to a licensed contractor.

The EPA also has regulatory authority in controlling exposure to asbestos. The EPA regulations are discussed in greater detail later in this chapter in the section entitled Environmental Impairment.

Bloodborne Pathogens

Bloodborne pathogens[10] include any microorganisms that may be transmitted by contact with the blood or body fluids of an infected person. The pathogens of major concern are the human immunodeficiency virus (HIV) and the hepatitis B virus (HBV). Briefly, the Bloodborne Pathogens Standard requires that health care workers practice universal precautions when working with blood and body fluids, that they be offered hepatitis B immunizations, that infectious waste be handled appropriately, and that certain housekeeping and work practice controls be implemented.

Universal Precautions Universal precautions require exactly what the term implies: that adequate precautions be taken whenever a health care worker is dealing with, or has the potential for exposure to, the blood or body fluids of any patient. For purposes of this discussion, potentially infectious body fluids include blood, semen, vaginal secretions, cerebrospinal fluid, synovial fluid, pericardial fluid, pleural fluid, amniotic fluid, and saliva (seldom a concern except if visibly contaminated with blood, such as during a dental procedure). Infectious body fluids do not normally include urine, feces, tears, or saliva, unless these materials are visibly contaminated with blood. However, any body fluid must be treated as infectious if its origin is questionable or unknown.

As the name implies, bloodborne pathogens are carried in the infected person's bloodstream and certain other body fluids, and may be transmitted to another person only by contact between the infected person's body fluids and the other person's body fluids. Consequently, transmission may be by various routes, including parenteral (for example, needle sticks); splashing (if the infected body fluids contact mucous membranes, open sores, or lesions); or sexual contact. Universal precautions are intended to minimize the potential for this transmission by placing barriers to contact whenever possible.

Health care providers sometimes argue that they should be allowed to test all patients prior to certain procedures, such as surgery, or upon admission to the hospital. However, this assertion generally flies in the face of the most basic element of universal precautions—that they be universally applied. One must assume that the health care provider who wishes to know the HIV status of a patient wants this knowledge in order to act on it in some way. The provider will either treat the patient with a higher degree of caution than normally employed or refuse to treat the patient at all. Refusal of treatment constitutes a violation of the Americans with Disabilities Act (ADA),[11] and is beyond the scope of this chapter. The former alternative (treating an HIV-infected patient with a higher degree of caution) implies that patients who are believed to be HIV-negative may be safely treated with a lower degree of caution. This position is unacceptable because there is a window of at least ninety days from infection to conversion to the positive status, meaning that a number of infected, but not yet diagnosable, patients would be treated with an unacceptably low degree of caution. Health care workers should treat all patients, regardless of HIV status, as if they were infected.

Protective Devices   A number of products that rely on engineering controls have been developed recently to assist in isolating the worker from the hazard. Specific devices include needleless systems, blunt needles, self-sheathing sharps systems, and magnetic trays. There are four general categories of safety systems or devices: passive safety systems that are always in effect and need not be activated by the user; active devices that require activation by the user; integral safety devices that are built in to the device and cannot be removed; and accessory devices that are external to the device and must be carried to or affixed at the point of use.[12] The passive and integral safety systems are clearly the best choices because they are least dependent upon the user for proper use. Any health care facility seeking to employ safer devices should be careful to review the entire range of devices available, and to select those that will serve its needs most closely.

Even in the presence of engineering controls, personal protective devices are required to isolate the health care worker from contact with the blood or body fluids of patients. Although personal protective devices generally are not considered the first choice for the protection of employees, they are appropriate in this context because there often is no other way to control the hazard. Examination gloves, probably the most commonly encountered protective devices, are required for phlebotomy, surgical procedures, examinations of body cavities, or any procedure that might involve exposure to potentially infectious materials. Although it generally is conceded that gloves will not deter a determined scalpel or needle, they do protect the hands (the skin of which is frequently not intact) from contact with gross blood. Other protective devices, such as face shields, masks, goggles, aprons, or impervious clothing, may be required, depending on the likelihood of contact with potentially infectious materials through splashing.

Hepatitis B Immunization   The OSHA standard requires that all employees who are potentially exposed to blood or body fluids be offered the hepatitis B immunization within ten days of starting work and after the required training program.[13] The employer cannot require the employee to take the immunization. The employer need not offer the immunization if the employee has previously been immunized, and may not make participation in a prescreening program (analysis of antibody titers) a prerequisite for immunization. If the employee declines to be immunized, he or she must sign a declination form that contains the wording prescribed by OSHA.[14] The immunization of registry or pool personnel is not the responsibility of the hospital but, rather, the agency that employs them. Neither the school that they attend, nor the hospital where they receive clinical training, appears to be required to immunize students. It appears to be the students' responsibility, and the school appears to be able to require it as a condition of admission.

Infectious Waste Handling and Sharps Disposal   OSHA has incorporated numerous requirements in the standard for the handling of infectious waste and the disposal of sharps.[15] Although the standard originally prohibited the bending, removal, or recapping of sharps, it presently allows these practices if they can be accomplished by a mechanical device or a one-handed technique and there is no feasible alternative to the practice. Containers used for the disposal of infectious waste, or those used to store blood specimens or reusable sharps, must be closable, leak-proof, puncture resistant, and properly labeled or color coded. Broken glassware that may be contaminated must be picked up using mechanical means, such as gloves or a broom and dustpan. Contaminated laundry must be properly bagged so that the contents of the bag are readily identifiable. Additionally, the bag must be constructed so as to prevent leakage of blood or body fluids.

As mentioned earlier, states may implement their own regulations governing disposal of infectious waste and these regulations may be more stringent than OSHA's. The health care risk manager would be well advised to be aware of, and adhere to, all regulations on this subject. If the regulations appear to conflict, the facility should adhere to the more stringent regulations.

Capillary Tubes   Capillary tubes are widely used in health care to collect and process blood for a variety of laboratory tests. They are often used in the centrifugation of blood to analyze its formed elements, as in a hematocrit. Glass capillary tubes are generally very thin and relatively fragile, which commonly leads to breakage. A consortium of federal agencies (Food and Drug Administration [FDA], Centers for Disease Control and Prevention [CDC], National Institute for Occupational Safety and Health [NIOSH] and OSHA) have issued a joint advisory to health care entities regarding this problem.[16] The use of glass capillary tubes should be avoided whenever possible. They can break during routine use, when their ends are plugged with clay for centrifugation, or during centrifugation. Breakage at any point during use presents the possibility of inoculation to the user with, or dermal or airborne contact with, human blood. One death has been attributed to the use of these tubes and OSHA estimated that approximately 2,800 such injuries occur each year due to the use of glass capillary tubes.[17]

There are alternatives available to the use of glass capillary tubes. These include capillary tubes made of materials other than glass (such as plastic), capillary tubes wrapped in puncture resistant film, products that use a sealing method other than plugging one end, and the measurement of hematocrits by methods that do not involve centrifugation.

Sharps Injury Prevention Programs   Health care entities should approach the problem of injuries due to sharps in an integrated manner, rather than attempting to solve it piecemeal. In this, as in all things, health care facilities exist in a world of ever dwindling and scarce resources, and do not have the luxury of fixing all of their problems in one fell swoop. They should develop a management plan to study, implement, monitor, maintain, and improve upon necessary corrective action.

The first step in the process is to assemble an interdisciplinary team to review the issues associated with the problem and to investigate it. The team should include, at a minimum, representatives from the following functions: nursing, laboratory, medical staff, infection control, risk management, safety, purchasing and materials management, and other clinical users of devices. This team should set goals and priorities for itself, and should set a firm time line for its activities. The team will probably never disappear, but its function will evolve out of a problem-solving mode into a maintenance and performance improvement mode over time.

The next step is to determine where and how injuries are occurring in the facility. Can a specific device, or type of device, be implicated as a prime offender in causing incidents? Do the incidents have the potential for serious injury? Are there incidents that may happen relatively infrequently, but which bear an extremely high risk of infection? Studies of this sort can be done retrospectively, assuming that the facility has been collecting and tracking the necessary data. A retrospective look at the injuries will give the answers that the facility seeks in the most expeditious manner. If the necessary data has not been collected or tracked by the facility, a prospective review of injuries may be necessary. Although this may consume valuable time, it is extremely important to approach this problem with a good idea of the actual parameters of the problem.

Once problem areas and devices have been recognized, the team should carefully evaluate the needs of the users in the context of the needs of the patient population. There will always be a tension between the needs of production and the needs of protection. If one attempts to neglect the needs of production in favor of protection, the users will inevitably find a way to circumvent the protective measures in order to get the job done. It cannot be emphasized enough that any solution that is implemented without input from the users will invariably fail to meet its objective.

Once the team has identified problem areas and devices, and has solicited and considered input from the user population, it should develop design and performance criteria for the protective devices that it will evaluate. It is always helpful to know, in advance, what one is looking for. If the needs of the facility have been carefully evaluated, each product can be held up to the light of the facility's needs and evaluated on an objective basis. This helps to avoid the "whiz-bang" phenomenon, which occurs when one encounters a really nifty device, but one that does not really meet one's needs or solve one's problem(s). Once all of the relevant products have been demonstrated and investigated, the facility should undertake clinical trials of the devices to see how well they function under real world clinical conditions. Test users should be asked to evaluate the device and give careful and unbiased feedback.[18]

If the device performs as it was hoped it would, the facility should adopt it. This, of course, does not end the process. The team should begin investigating the next most troublesome sharps problem, and apply the same procedure to it. Eventually, all of the troublesome problems will have been solved, and the team can begin evaluating new products on the market to determine whether they are more effective than the devices previously adopted by the facility. The team can also monitor the effectiveness of the devices adopted to ensure that they are as effective as hoped.

This dissertation on sharps injury prevention programs is not meant to fully explain all facets of the issue. The reader is advised to consult with specialized treatises on the subject for further information.[19]

Although the facility's goal must be to eliminate sharps injuries, it must also be prepared to treat the injured employee appropriately if such an injury occurs. Such post-injury treatment and prophylaxis has improved considerably in recent years, especially with respect to possible infection with the human immunodeficiency virus. Again, a complete discussion of this topic is beyond the scope of this chapter, and the reader is referred to more specialized treatises.[20]

Cadmium

Cadmium is a bluish-white metal often used in radiation oncology departments in molds used in radiation therapy. It is commonly encountered in alloys, in which it is mixed with lead, and also may be encountered in the plant operations department in soldering material used to join metallic surfaces. Exposure to cadmium may occur through the inhalation of cadmium fume during any operation in which cadmium is heated to high temperatures. As a result, operations involving the heating of cadmium to high levels should be done only in areas where the general ventilation is adequate or, preferably, in an area where there is local exhaust ventilation to remove the fume.

The OSHA permissible exposure limit for cadmium is 0.1 milligram per cubic meter of air (mg/m^3) as an eight-hour, time-weighted average and 0.3 mg/m^3 as a ceiling value.[21]

Confined-Space Entries

The OSHA Permit-Required Confined Spaces Standard[22] regulates any spaces within the facility or on its grounds that are large enough for a person to enter and perform work, have limited methods of entrance or exit, and are not designed for continuous employee occupancy. Health care facility examples include pipe tunnels, valve pits, transformer pits, sewers, and grease traps. These areas present hazards because they may contain hazardous gases, vapors, or dusts, or may have an insufficient concentration of oxygen.

The employer must take a number of steps to comply with this standard. The first step is to identify all confined spaces on the premises. The confined spaces should then be separated into two classes: those that employees may enter without any special precautions and those that require precautions. The latter include any confined spaces in which a *hazardous atmosphere* exists, defined as an atmosphere that contains either flammable gases or vapors in excess of 10 percent of their lower flammable limit, combustible dusts at or above their lower flammable limit, less than 19.5 percent oxygen, more than 23.5 percent oxygen, or any OSHA-regulated compound in any concentration at or above its dose or permissible exposure limit. These spaces should be designated as permit-required spaces. If the employer allows employees to go into permit-required spaces, it must evaluate the space to determine the nature of the hazard present and any precautions necessary for an employee to enter the space. If the employer does not allow employees to enter such spaces, it must take all steps necessary to prevent entry.

Ergonomics Programs

Ergonomics, when reduced to its fundamental components, is the study of adapting the environment to the person (worker) in order to avoid musculoskeletal or cumulative traumatic disorders (MSDs). The adaptation of the environment can take many forms, including alteration of the physical environment, alteration of work practices, or the addition of engineering controls. Unfortunately, the typical health care workplace does not always present many viable alternatives to the facility's current environment or work practices. Some aspects of health care (such as food service, materials management, plant operations, central processing/sterile, business office, and so on) are amenable to an ergonomic approach to injury reduction. In these areas one has some latitude to redesign the work place layout, to implement engineering controls (such as through assistive mechanical devices, and so on), or to implement different work practices (such as reducing the size and weight of objects to be moved, minimizing tasks that require twisting, or performance in awkward positions). However, in the clinical setting, the options are far more limited.

The world of the clinical setting is far less regular, routine, or capable of standardization. The musculoskeletal injuries often seen among clinical health care providers very often include strains or other injuries caused by overexertion. The provider often tries to lift more weight than she is capable of lifting safely, finds a patient unduly cumbersome, or experiences an unforeseen strain on her musculature. This is often the case because patients are seldom of a uniform size or shape, they have no convenient handles for grasping to assist with the lifting process, and they tend to fall or stop cooperating at inopportune moments. All of this makes the application of ergonomic interventions more challenging, but it does not preclude the use of such mechanisms.

OSHA has, as of this writing, proposed a standard that would require certain employers to implement ergonomics programs.[23] The proposed standard has not yet been promulgated. The standard applies to manufacturing jobs, manual handling jobs, and jobs that may cause musculoskeletal disorders (however, the job activities must be the type that can cause musculoskeletal disorders and the activities must be a core part of the employee's job).[24] The proposed standard will not apply to the entire workplace. Rather, it will only apply to relevant jobs.[25] The proposed standard has six program elements:

1. Management leadership and employee participation.[26]
2. Hazard information and reporting.[27]
3. Job hazard analysis and control.[28]
4. Training.[29]
5. MSD management.[30]
6. Program evaluation.[31]

Management leadership requires top-level support for the program. It is recognized that virtually all project plans in health care begin with "Get top level support," but it is especially true in this case. Because the provision of health care is so seldom routine or regular, the best ergonomic intervention is frequently the availability of more staff to assist with transferring the patient or other tasks involving heavy exertion. In an era of ever-dwindling resources, only top-level support will make the resources available to assist with the necessary interventions. Alterations in the work environment and changes in work practices can be expensive and can disrupt, if only temporarily, productivity. Since there is little point in studying a problem for which there is no hope of a solution, top-level support is crucial in these endeavors.

Employee participation requires that employees have a way to report the signs and symptoms of MSDs and that the employer will be required to respond promptly to their reports. Employees will be allowed access to the standard and to information regarding the program. Finally, the employer must provide a mechanism for employees to be involved in developing, implementing, and evaluating each element of the program.

The *hazard information and reporting* element will require the employer to furnish new and existing employees with information about common MSD hazards, MSD signs and symptoms, and the need to report the ways in which reports can be made, and a summary of the standard. It will also require that the employer designate a person to receive and evaluate reports.

The *job hazard analysis and control* element will require the employer to analyze jobs that may cause MSDs for ergonomic risk factors. The hazards must then be either eliminated, reduced to the extent feasible, or materially reduced using an incremental abatement process (described in the standard). If the employee with the MSD is the only employee at risk, the job hazard analysis may be confined to that employee.

The employer will be required to provide *training* for employees in problem jobs and for their supervisors. This training involves many of the aspects of the program already discussed, but also must include protection from acquiring MSDs and job-specific controls to prevent MSDs from occurring. The employer must also provide appropriate training for persons who will be responsible for designing, implementing, and maintaining the ergonomics program.

The employer is also required to provide *MSD management* when employees are found to have developed an MSD. The management of an MSD entails a prompt response to the report of the signs or symptoms of an MSD, a prompt determination of the need for light or restricted duty, the provision of appropriate medical care (evaluation, treatment, management, and follow-up), and obtaining a written opinion from the health care provider, which must be shared with the employee. The employer is responsible for providing the health care provider with the information necessary for the provider to evaluate and treat the employee.

The employer must periodically *evaluate* the program to ensure that it is effective. This must be done not less frequently than every three years. The evaluation must include consultations with employees in problem jobs to assess their perceptions of its effectiveness. The evaluation must also determine whether the program is actually eliminating or materially reducing MSDs.

This discussion of ergonomic interventions is but a glancing blow to the subject. If the reader wishes to pursue the subject in more detail, reference should be made to the actual language of the OSHA standard and to the literature of the subject.[32]

Back Belts

Back belts include any device that is worn around the user's lower abdomen and lower back, and are also known as weight lifting devices, supports or aids, abdominal belts, spinal braces, supports, corsets, and orthoses. The term loosely includes devices intended for use by the general public and also devices used by injured persons as part of a therapeutic regimen. Because back injuries constitute approximately 20 percent of all occupational injuries, and cost an estimated 20 to 50 billion dollars per year,[33] it is clear that American industry is acutely aware of the problem and the need for a solution. This has created a great deal of interest in and use of back belts to prevent injury.

To date, however, there has been little scientific evidence that conclusively proves any beneficial effect from wearing back belts, at least among persons who have not experienced a back injury previously.[34] The use of back belts as part of a therapeutic regimen for the treatment of back injuries is a recognized therapy.

Back injuries are a highly complex constellation of injuries that can be brought on by a number of occupational, environmental, and lifestyle conditions. They are not susceptible to an easy solution of any sort. Back belts have been touted, and perceived, as a relatively quick and easy solution to the problem. In all likelihood, the only way to minimize back injuries (there is probably *no* way to eliminate them) is through a comprehensive ergonomics program, coupled with training on the contribution of the performance of tasks beyond the worker's capacity, as well as the benefits of losing weight and getting regular exercise. Any facility that believes that it can solve its back injury problem by handing the employee a back belt will invariably be disappointed with the results of the intervention.

Ethylene Oxide

Ethylene oxide (EtO) is a colorless gas that has a sweetish odor. It is commonly encountered in the central or sterile processing department, where reusable items and surgical packs are sterilized. It is often used to sterilize items that may be heat-sensitive and that cannot be sterilized using steam (EtO sterilizers usually operate at 140°F [60°C], as opposed to steam sterilization, which often requires temperatures as high as 270°F [132°C]). Generally, EtO sterilizers are one of two types: larger models that typically use a mixture of 12 percent EtO and 88 percent Freon,[35] or smaller models that use 100 percent EtO. The former variety usually has external supply cylinders that can sterilize a number of loads, whereas the latter usually employs small cylinders that are placed inside the sterilizer chamber and punctured.

EtO is regulated by OSHA as a carcinogen. The OSHA standard for EtO allows for a permissible exposure limit of one part per million of air (ppm) as an eight-hour, time-weighted average and an excursion limit of five ppm over a fifteen-minute period. The action level under this standard is 0.5 ppm as an eight-hour, time-weighted average.[36]

The control of exposure to EtO generally is accomplished by modifications to the sterilizer and local exhaust ventilation. The sterilizer should be connected to a duct system that conveys the exhaust from the sterilizer to the exterior of the building (additionally, the exhaust port should be located at least twenty-five feet from a ventilation system intake). Also required is a mechanism for controlling any exhaust that may be present at the location where the water (condensate) from the sterilizer is discharged to a floor drain or the sewer system. Local exhaust ventilation should be provided through a hood located immediately above the door to the sterilizer. The air movement into this hood should be strong enough to capture any vapors that escape when the sterilizer door is opened (the amount of vapor escaping should be rather small due to the purge cycles of the sterilizer prior to completion of the cycle, and the capture of these vapors is facilitated by the generally upward movement of the heated vapors). This hood also should be connected to a dedicated duct system that exhausts the air from the sterilizer directly to the exterior of the building. The entire system of controls must be inspected on a regular basis to ensure that all of its components are functioning properly.

Personal protective equipment is available to protect employees from exposure to EtO. This equipment includes face shields and heavy gloves. Although effective equipment is bulky and cumbersome, it can be useful for certain tasks, such as changing the external EtO cylinders. Surgical masks provide no protection whatsoever.

The hospital also must have an emergency procedure policy that can be followed in the event of a spill or release of EtO. The procedure should allow for complete segregation of any area in which a release could occur, including mechanical rooms, tank storage areas, and the sterile-processing work area. In addition, the ventilation system for the affected area should be segregated from the ventilation system for the rest of the hospital. There should be an emergency alarm system that will alert employees to increased levels of EtO or to the failure of required ventilation systems, so that the emergency procedure plan can be implemented.

The employer is required to monitor the levels of EtO in the air of the workplace, the frequency of which is dependent on the levels measured. All sampling for exposure to EtO should be done at the employee's breathing zone (within inches of the mouth or nose). If the initial monitoring, or periodic monitoring (at least two samples taken at least seven days apart), reveals levels below the action level (0.5 ppm), monitoring for that employee should be repeated only if his or her work practices change. However, if it reveals levels at or above the action level but at or below the permissible exposure limit, monitoring for that employee needs to be done every six months. If the levels are above the permissible exposure limit, monitoring for that employee must be performed every three months. In all cases, the employee must be advised of the results of the monitoring.

Formaldehyde

Formaldehyde has a characteristic pungent odor. It is regulated by OSHA as a potential carcinogen. The OSHA permissible exposure limit is 0.75 ppm as an eight-hour, time-weighted average, with a short-term excursion limit of two ppm for no more than fifteen minutes.[37] Formaldehyde is commonly used as a tissue preservative and also may be used as a disinfectant. It may be present in the laboratory (especially pathology and the morgue), surgery, and dialysis. It is commonly encountered as Formalin, which is a solution of formaldehyde (10 percent), methyl alcohol, and water. The 10-percent concentration is sufficient for virtually all applications in the hospital. If a product is labeled as formaldehyde, it typically contains 37-percent formaldehyde. As a cost-saving measure, hospitals frequently purchase it in the 37-percent concentration and dilute it to the 10-percent strength.

Control of exposure to formaldehyde is best accomplished by local exhaust ventilation at the area where it is used, or where specimens preserved in it are handled. Personal protective equipment, such as goggles, gowns, aprons, and gloves, should be used whenever there is a possibility that the employee might be splashed with the material or otherwise come in direct contact with it.

Control of exposure also can be accomplished by changes in work practices. For example, purchasing the product already diluted to 10-percent strength, rather than purchasing the 37-percent concentration and diluting it on site, removes a potential source of exposure. Additionally, the spigots of jugs of Formalin should be positioned over a sink (rather than a counter or floor) so that spillage can be quickly and readily discarded without requiring a health care worker to come into contact with the material.

It must be noted that many health care workers, especially physicians, have worked with formaldehyde for years (since gross anatomy class, if not before), and may have a very cavalier attitude toward the hazards it presents. Vigilant monitoring and rigorous training may be necessary to impress upon such people the importance of controlling exposure to this potentially dangerous substance.

Glutaraldehyde

Glutaraldehyde, used as a cold sterilant for sensitive equipment, is frequently encountered in endoscopy or respiratory therapy departments, where it often is used to sterilize scopes and other equipment. Glutaraldehyde was formerly regulated by OSHA with a permissible exposure limit of 0.2 ppm of air as an eight-hour, time-weighted average, but a defect in the promulgation process caused OSHA to withdraw its standard. Because glutaraldehyde is highly toxic, highly irritating, and has been shown to be fetotoxic and mutagenic in animal studies,[38] it should be carefully handled, and employee exposure should be carefully controlled.

There are a number of relatively simple ways by which exposure to glutaraldehyde may be controlled. The room in which a tub of glutaraldehyde is used (instruments are normally soaked in a calm vessel of the solution) should be adequately ventilated. Whenever instruments are not being placed into or removed from the tub, it should be covered with a tight-fitting lid. Personnel placing instruments into or removing them from the tub should wear utility gloves and protective goggles or a face shield to prevent accidental contact. If employees complain of irritation, or exposure monitoring indicates high levels of the material in the air, the hospital should consider installing a local exhaust hood over the work area in which the tub is located, bearing in mind that the vapors should be pulled away from the employee's breathing zone.

Hazard Communication Standard

The Hazard Communication Standard, also referred to as the employee's right-to-know rule, requires employers to inform employees of all hazards associated with the materials with which they must work.[39] If a product poses a health or physical hazard for employees, it is covered. A product poses a health hazard if studies have shown that it may produce acute or chronic health effects in humans. All compounds regulated by OSHA, or for which the American Conference of Governmental Industrial Hygienists[40] have set a threshold limit value, are automatically included in this category. A product presents a physical hazard if it is flammable, combustible, reactive, water-reactive, explosive, or pyrophoric, or if it occurs in the form of a compressed gas, an oxidizer, or an organic peroxide. If a product is subject to other regulations, such as pesticides, foods and food additives, or distilled spirits, or if it is a consumer product used in the workplace in the same way that consumers use it, it may not be subject to this standard.

This standard requires that containers of hazardous products be properly labeled and that the employer not deface or remove these labels. The labels must identify the hazardous chemicals contained in the product, give appropriate warnings, and give the name of the manufacturer. Stationary vessels can have temporary placards attached, and temporary vessels, such as buckets and small containers, do not need to be labeled if they are for the immediate use (that is, use within that shift) of the employee making the transfer. Hazardous drugs or medications dispensed to a health care provider for administration to a patient do not need to be labeled under this standard.

The manufacturer or distributor of the product is required to supply the customer with a material safety data sheet (MSDS) on the product. Most manufacturers routinely supply MSDSs with each shipment of a product. These sheets must be in English, although the employer may also provide them in other languages. The MSDSs must be available to employees for their use. This requirement has many implications. For example, employees must know where the MSDSs are stored, how to find the one they need, and how to read it once they find it. To ensure that these requirements are met, employees should be trained in the hazards associated with the products with which they work. They must be given information on this standard, operations in the work area that involve exposure to hazardous products, the location and availability of the written hazard communication program, and the location and availability of the MSDSs. Employees also need to be trained in the detection of hazardous chemicals in the workplace (in the event of a spill or a release), the physical and health hazards associated with the products with which they work, measures they can take to protect themselves, an explanation of the labels, and an explanation of the relevant MSDS. Care must be taken in explaining the MSDSs because, to the average person, an MSDS is virtually indecipherable. To audit the effectiveness of the program, employees should periodically be asked to retrieve the MSDS for a given product and to explain the hazards of working with it. It also is advisable to maintain a complete set of all MSDSs in the emergency department (ED) or other area in which emergency care is rendered, so that personnel have immediate access to required emergency information in the event of a splash or other accidental contact.

Health care risk managers should note that the Hazard Communication Standard covers all employees in the hospital except for laboratory employees, who are covered by the Laboratory Standard, discussed later in this section. The only requirements in the Hazard Communication Standard with respect to laboratories are that the employer must maintain all labels on incoming containers, must maintain all MSDSs received, and must train the laboratory's personnel regarding the location, availability, and use of MSDSs.

Hazardous Waste Operations and Emergency Response

The Hazardous Waste Operations and Emergency Response Standard (HAZWOPER) is designed to protect workers who are involved in cleaning up hazardous waste disposal sites, but it also may have implications for health care facilities.[41] Any worker who is required or expected to respond to a spill or a release of hazardous material needs to be equipped and trained according to the requirements of HAZWOPER.

The standard differentiates between types of spills or releases. An *incidental release* does not pose an imminent health or safety hazard and may be cleaned up by personnel without specialized training. Spills of cleaning materials normally fall into this category. However, any release that is not incidental may require cleanup by personnel who have had specialized training. Releases or spills of EtO, mercury, formaldehyde, glutaraldehyde, ammonia (often used as a refrigerant in food service), or flammable liquids fall into this category.

The standard also requires different levels of training for personnel, depending on the role they are to play in the response to the release. When attempting to determine the level of training an individual may require, the facility should imagine the worst case to which the employee might be expected to respond, then train the person accordingly. The most basic level of training is the First Responder Awareness Level. This level of training must be given to persons who may discover a release and are expected to notify the proper authorities. The next level of training is First Responder Operations Level. This must be given to those persons who will respond to the release and attempt to contain or confine it until more qualified people can arrive at the scene. These individuals should not attempt to stop the release. The next level, Hazardous Materials Technician Level training, is intended for those persons who will perform this function, generally by sealing the container that is leaking. There are higher levels of training mandated by HAZWOPER, but they are designed for hazardous waste cleanup sites and generally have little applicability for health care facilities. It is clear that many hospital personnel will require some level of training under this standard.

The facility is required to have an emergency response plan that lays out, in some detail, the anticipated responses to every potential spill or release. The plan should specify not only the internal responses that are expected, but also those expected from external sources (for example, the fire department and hazardous waste spill response team). It should specify when to contact external sources and the method by which they are to be contacted, including the name and telephone number of the agency or contact person. If external responders are to be used, they should be familiar with the facility, the types of materials that could be spilled or released, and the types of activities that could be expected of them. The plan also must specify the persons who will be in charge of the spill or release response.

Hospitals also may find themselves subject to the requirements of HAZWOPER when they respond to a disaster in the community. In the event of a disaster, the hospital will need to designate an area as a decontamination area. For all intents and purposes, this decontamination area will be very similar to the scene of a spill or release. Certain persons, such as physicians, may require no more training than a quick briefing on the nature of the contamination at the time of the emergency. However, those employees who will be expected to actually perform decontamination procedures must have at least First Responder Operations Level training.

Hydrogen Peroxide

Hydrogen peroxide is a colorless liquid with a bitter taste that is completely miscible in water. With the burgeoning reuse of medical devices that are labeled for single use only, and the move away from ethylene oxide as a sterilant for health reasons, hydrogen peroxide is becoming more widely used as a cold sterilant in health care. It can be encountered in vapor phase and gas plasma sterilizers. Although it is far more reactive than ethylene oxide, which makes it inappropriate for sterilizing some materials (including porous cellulose wrapping materials, rubber, nylon, and certain metals), and it lacks the penetrating qualities of ethylene oxide, its use is becoming more widespread.[42]

The primary health concerns surrounding the use of hydrogen peroxide involve local irritation of the skin, eyes and mucous membranes, and, at a systemic level, pulmonary irritation ranging from mild bronchitis to pulmonary edema. It may cause irritation and a bleaching effect at low concentrations. It may cause severe eye injuries at high concentrations.[43] The permissible exposure limit set by OSHA for hydrogen peroxide is one part per million (1 ppm) or 1.4 milligrams per cubic meter (1.4 mg/m^3).[44]

Laboratory Standard

As previously noted, the Hazard Communication Standard is not fully applicable to the employees of the laboratory. OSHA promulgated a separate standard the Occupational Exposure to Hazardous Chemicals in Laboratories Standard to deal with the specific requirements of laboratories.[45] In exempting laboratory employees from some of the requirements of the Hazard Communication Standard, OSHA recognized that laboratories often deal with large numbers of chemicals, but with a relatively small quantity of any given chemical. For the purposes of this standard, the term *laboratory* refers to an area in which multiple chemicals are used, in relatively small quantities, in processes that are not meant to produce chemicals or chemical compounds. Thus, it is not applicable to areas of the facility that perform very minor laboratory procedures, such as dipstick urine analyses or blood sugars using test strips.

The cornerstone of the Laboratory Standard is the chemical hygiene plan. This plan needs to prescribe the procedures, equipment, personal protective equipment, and work practices required to ensure that employees are not exposed to any hazardous chemicals at or above any of OSHA's permissible exposure limits. It needs to contain standard operating procedures and criteria for the implementation of control measures to ensure the safety of employees when they are working with hazardous chemicals. And it needs to address the proper use and maintenance of engineering controls (for example, hoods and ventilation systems), personal protective equipment, and hygiene practices. The chemical hygiene plan must be carefully drafted because it will be the first thing an OSHA compliance officer will ask to see when coming into the laboratory.

Employees need to be properly trained concerning the Laboratory Standard and the chemical hygiene plan. More specifically, they must be informed that a plan exists and what its purposes are, how they are to use it, where it is kept, what hazards are associated with exposure to the chemicals with which they work, how to recognize the signs of overexposure, and what means they can use to protect themselves.

Lead

Lead is a gray, highly malleable metal that is occasionally used in radiation oncology and plant operations. Radiation oncology uses lead to form molds, which requires that it be melted and reformed in the proper shape. Lead also is present in solder used by plant operations, although it should not be used to join pipes in water supply lines in the plumbing system. The OSHA standard for lead is 0.2 milligrams per cubic meter (mg/m^3) of air.[46] Lead should be melted or heated to high temperatures only in well-ventilated areas or in areas where local exhaust ventilation is present.

Lockout or Tagout Standard

OSHA regulates exposure to high levels of energy under the Control of Exposure to Hazardous Energy Standard, more familiarly known as the lockout or tagout rule.[47] This standard applies to any situation in which the unexpected energization of a piece of equipment, or the release of stored energy, could cause an employee injury. It applies to any piece of equipment during maintenance or repair procedures. If the equipment can be locked out (rendered unusable unless a lock is removed), the employer must provide for a means to lock it out. If it cannot be locked out, the employer must provide a tag system that will warn other employees not to turn the equipment on. Either system must identify the employee who has locked or tagged out the equipment.

Mercury

Mercury is a silver-white metal that is liquid at room temperature. It is used in health care institutions primarily in medical devices such as sphygmomanometers, thermometers, and gauges. Exposure to employees usually occurs either during the servicing of such devices or when a device breaks or leaks. Consequently, the extent of potential exposure to employees is relatively self-limited. Exposure to mercury can cause significant damage to the central nervous system. The OSHA standard for mercury is 2 mg/m^3, but that is predicated upon chronic and routine exposure, rather than episodic acute exposures.[48]

There are numerous devices available today that are effective substitutes for devices that contain mercury. These mercury-free devices should be used whenever possible. If health care facilities do use devices that contain mercury, they need to be prepared to deal with spills or other accidental releases. There are a number of commercially available spill kits that appear to work well if used in conformity with the manufacturer's specifications. It must be remembered, however, that exposure can occur by both inhalation and contact with the skin. Employees must be carefully trained and equipped to protect themselves from either avenue of exposure.

Methyl Methacrylate

Methyl methacrylate is used primarily in hospitals as a cement to attach prosthetic devices to bone. To apply methyl methacrylate, it is necessary to mix a powder and a liquid together immediately before use. The OSHA permissible exposure limit for this material is 100 ppm of air as an eight-hour, time-weighted average.[49] Reported data indicate that levels of up to 280 ppm can be detected immediately after mixing, but that these levels fall off quickly thereafter.[50]

Methyl methacrylate should be mixed under a hood or in an area that offers other local exhaust ventilation. Although it is difficult to install local exhaust ventilation near enough to the operative site to obtain good capture of contaminants, it should be possible to use an apparatus such as a smoke evacuator to draw off the methyl methacrylate vapors that may evolve during the application of the cement. If a smoke evacuator is used, it must be equipped with an activated carbon filter or a scrubbing device because simple particulate filtration will not remove the contaminant.

Miscellaneous Solvents

Any number of solvents may be present at various locations throughout the health care facility. Many of them are subject to standards promulgated by OSHA.[51]

Acetone   Acetone is a relatively benign solvent that sometimes is sold as nail polish remover. However, because acetone is highly flammable, it should be stored in a flammable liquid storage location if significant volumes (i.e., more than one gallon) are kept. Frequently, acetone can be found in the laboratory, sometimes in relatively high volumes, but also may be found almost anywhere else in the hospital. The OSHA permissible exposure limit is 1,000 ppm.

Alcohol, Ethyl   Ethyl alcohol, also known as ethanol or grain alcohol, is used in relatively large quantities in hospitals and may be present in virtually any department. Because ethyl alcohol also is highly flammable, it should be kept in a flammable liquid storage location if it is stored in great quantity. The OSHA permissible exposure limit for ethyl alcohol is 1,000 ppm, and the effects of exposure by inhalation are not greatly different from the effects of exposure by ingestion. This latter remark is subject to the caveat that ethyl alcohol, as it is used in hospitals, sometimes is adulterated to discourage ingestion.

Alcohol, Isopropyl   Isopropyl alcohol, also known as rubbing alcohol, may be encountered virtually anywhere in the hospital. As with ethyl alcohol, isopropyl alcohol is highly flammable and should be stored in a flammable liquid storage location. The OSHA permissible exposure limit is 400 ppm.

Alcohol, Methyl   Methyl alcohol is also known as methanol or wood alcohol. It sometimes is encountered in laboratories as a relatively pure compound, and it also is encountered in Formalin. Because methyl alcohol is a flammable liquid, it should be stored in a flammable liquid storage location. The OSHA permissible exposure limit is 200 ppm. Exposure to high concentrations of methyl alcohol can cause damage to the optic nerve and, possibly, blindness.

Benzene   Benzene is regulated by OSHA as a carcinogen because it has been shown to cause aplastic anemia and leukemia in humans. Although benzene was once commonly encountered in hospitals, its use has been greatly diminished as it has been replaced by safer compounds. The OSHA standard for benzene is 1 ppm as an eight-hour, time-weighted average, with a short-term exposure limit (not more than fifteen minutes) of five ppm.[52]

Toluene   Toluene is also known as methyl benzene, although it does not share the more harmful effects seen in benzene exposure. Toluene may be found in the laboratory and occasionally in plant operations. The OSHA standards for toluene are 200 ppm as an eight-hour, time-weighted average, with a ceiling concentration (a level that is not to be exceeded) of 300 ppm, with the exception of short-term exposures of ten minutes or less, which are permissible up to 500 ppm.[53]

Xylene   Xylene is also known as dimethyl benzene, although it, too, does not share the high degree of hazard that benzene poses. Xylene is commonly used in laboratories and, occasionally, plant operations. The OSHA standard for xylene is 100 ppm.

Noise

The OSHA Noise Standard requires that employers protect their employees from exposure to excessive noise.[54] Employees may be exposed to constant noise according to a sliding scale found in the OSHA standard. As noise levels increase, the employee may be exposed to it for shorter and shorter periods of time, unless adequate hearing protection is provided.

Noise levels high enough to require compliance with the OSHA standard can be measured in a number of locations in the hospital. These include plant operations areas (especially near boilers and generators, in carpentry shops, or during grinding operations), and in food service areas. The noise level should be measured in any area where it is difficult to have a conversation in a normal speaking voice or where employees complain about the noise.

The employer is required to implement a hearing conservation program for all employees who are exposed to noise levels consistently above 85 dBA over an eight-hour period. As part of this program, affected employees must have an annual audiometric examination and should be provided with hearing protection. The employer should make every effort to reduce the noise level by engineering modifications of the workplace. Additionally, high noise areas should have warning signs posted that indicate that hearing protection is required in that area.

Personal Protective Equipment

A hierarchy of safety and health hazard control measures ranks available control measures according to their effectiveness and efficiency. Engineering controls (for example, increased ventilation, sound-dampening materials) are the most effective and desirable control measures because they remove the hazard from the workplace. Administrative controls (for example, changes in work practices or limits on the duration of exposure) are acceptable, but are less desirable because they do not remove the hazard and may not protect sensitive individuals. Personal protective equipment is the least desirable method for protecting employees because they either do not like to wear the devices, forget to wear them, or may not be adequately protected by them. It is against this backdrop that OSHA has promulgated its generic standard regarding personal protective equipment.[55]

The employer is required to obtain and provide to the employee, at the employer's cost, all personal protective devices that the employee may require to perform his or her job safely. The employer is required to maintain the devices in a sanitary manner and in a way that ensures their reliability. Moreover, the employer is required to assure the adequacy of the devices as a whole, as well as the adequacy of each device as it relates to each employee who is required to wear it. Any personal protective device must be selected, obtained, and maintained in a manner that will give the affected employee maximal protection.

Respiratory Protection

The employer may use respiratory protection to reduce hazards if employees are exposed to airborne contaminants at levels at or exceeding OSHA permissible exposure limits, or to other contaminants that could cause illness or injury, and it is not feasible to implement engineering controls to abate the hazard. If respiratory protection is chosen as a course of action, the employer also must implement a respirator selection program that complies with the OSHA standard.[56] There also are certain other requirements that may be imposed by OSHA under other standards or enforcement policies, such as the asbestos standard and the enforcement guidelines for exposure to tuberculosis.

The respiratory protection program must address a number of issues. It must have written specifications for the selection of respirators for protection against different hazards. In addition, it must specify the ways by which the employer will ensure that employees use the respirators, as well as the ways in which the program will be monitored and evaluated. Further, the program must ensure that the employee is capable of wearing the respirator safely and of performing necessary tasks while wearing it. This latter requirement may require a physical examination, including a pulmonary function study (spirometry). The program must also specify the manner in which respirators will be maintained, cleaned and/or sterilized, used, and stored.

Tuberculosis Exposure Control

At one time in this country, tuberculosis (TB) was considered to be a disease on the decline. However, in the early 1990s, the Centers for Disease Control and Prevention (CDC) noted a marked increase in the number of new cases of TB in the United States, and OSHA took notice. The enforcement guidelines that OSHA promulgated are based on the CDC's *Guidelines for Preventing the Transmission of Tuberculosis in Health-Care Settings,* which was published in 1990.[57]

The CDC guidelines follow a logical sequence in identifying and addressing the potential hazard. They require that each facility conduct risk assessments, identify infected persons or high-risk areas, rapidly isolate infected persons, and take steps to control the spread of the disease. To prevent the TB organism from escaping into the rest of the facility, infected persons should be placed in respiratory isolation rooms that are under negative air pressure relative to the corridor or the rest of the ventilation system. The organisms that cause TB (most commonly *Mycobacterium tuberculosis*) are found in droplet nuclei (particles in the one- to five-micron size range) that are expelled by infected persons, and these droplet nuclei can, under certain conditions, travel long distances before settling out. The exhaust from the isolation room can be vented to the exterior of the building or may be passed through high-efficiency particulate air (HEPA) filters and recirculated. However, if filtration is used, the dirty filters should be considered infectious waste and handled accordingly.

The CDC guidelines require that each facility develop and implement a written exposure control plan. As part of the plan, each facility must perform a risk assessment to determine the level of risk of exposure to which its employees are subject. The risk assessment dictates the level of monitoring the facility will need to undertake, including the frequency with which employees need to undergo skin testing. The exposure control plan must include procedures for rapidly identifying TB patients, treating known and suspected TB patients, and effectively isolating them until they are no longer infectious.

Employees must use personal protective equipment, even if engineering controls are in place, when entering a room housing a known or suspected TB patient, when administering cough-inducing procedures on such patients, or in other situations where engineering controls may not reduce the risk of transmission of TB (such as when transporting TB patients). Although the CDC originally recommended powered, self-purifying respirators (which are expensive, complicated, and cumbersome) for use with TB patients, it now recommends HEPA masks, which are relatively simple to use and may be disposable. However, facilities should be careful when selecting HEPA masks. Some of the commercially available masks have an exhalation port that delivers the wearer's breath directly to the outside of the mask without filtering it. Obviously, such masks should not be used in surgery (unless a second mask also is worn) or recommended for a TB patient to wear.

··············

OCCUPATIONAL HEALTH ISSUES NOT DIRECTLY ADDRESSED BY OSHA

A number of occupational health issues are not addressed by existing OSHA regulations. However, because such issues are not addressed by OSHA regulations does not necessarily mean that OSHA cannot require compliance with the recommendations of other agencies or groups. The general duty clause, a provision in the Occupational Safety and Health Act, requires that each employer shall furnish to each of his employees employment and a place of employment that are free from recognized hazards that are causing or are likely to cause death or serious physical harm to his employees.[58] A hazard is a *recognized* hazard to the extent that it is recognized as such in the industry, by authoritative bodies or in the trade literature, or in the workplace in question. Accordingly, OSHA has jurisdiction under the general duty clause to require an employer to abate any recognized hazard, even if there is no standard to cover it. Some occupational health issues that may present recognized hazards are discussed below.

Electric and Magnetic Fields (EMF)

There has been a great deal of debate, often fired by private interests and the media, on the health effects of electromagnetic, or electric and magnetic, fields (EMF). The alleged hazard can be created by everything from video display terminals and televisions to fluorescent lighting, electric toothbrushes, and household wiring.[59] It is true that virtually all electrical appliances and devices, even when they are plugged in but not turned on, generate EMF, but this does not necessarily mean that they are dangerous.

To put this in perspective, electromagnetic fields are generated by electrical current and usually generate extremely low frequencies (1 to 300 hertz [cycles per second]), although power lines can generate waves of up to approximately 10^5 hertz. By contrast, radio and television waves are in the range of 10^5 to 10^7 hertz, while microwaves are in the range of approximately 10^8 to 10^{11} hertz. The range of visible light is approximately 10^{15} hertz, and x-rays are in the range of 10^{17} to 10^{20} hertz. While there is ample evidence of injury or other biological effects caused by energy in the range of microwaves and higher frequency energies, these are far removed from the ranges of electromagnetic fields.

To date, the neutral and objective scientific evidence on the health effects of EMF has been inconclusive.[60] While there does not appear to be cause for undue alarm at this point in time, this is a subject that both the government and industry are continuing to scrutinize, and it is one that health care should continue to monitor.

Hazardous Drugs

A number of drugs may constitute a health hazard for health care workers who are exposed to them. These drugs include the antineoplastic/chemotherapy drugs, as well as Pentamidine and Ribavirin. Many of these drugs are known mutagens, teratogens, or carcinogens, and any exposure to health care workers should be prevented. Although OSHA does not have a standard on this subject, it has issued guidelines in its *Technical Manual*.[61]

Potential exposure to these drugs can occur at any time during their handling. Many hazardous drugs must be reconstituted shortly before use. This procedure should be undertaken in a Class II Biological Safety Cabinet (BSC), preferably one vented to the exterior of the building. Cabinets equipped with HEPA filters may be used but are less desirable than those vented to the outside. Cabinets of this sort employ an airflow that descends vertically from the top of the interior of the cabinet and is exhausted out the bottom of the interior. This forms a virtual air curtain that neither pulls air in nor blows air out. The former aspect of the cabinet's operation is important in maintaining sterility of the product. The latter is important because aerosolized particulate is not blown into the breathing zone of the employee performing the reconstitution. In addition to the BSC, the employee also should wear personal protective equipment, such as goggles or safety glasses, gloves, and a disposable impervious gown. The gown and the gloves should not be worn out of the preparation area and should be discarded after use. Employees administering hazardous drugs also should wear personal protective equipment.

All waste materials, including contaminated sharps, empty vials, gloves, and gowns used in reconstituting or administering the drugs, as well as the materials used to clean up spills or decontaminate the cabinet, must be properly discarded. The most desirable method of disposal is by incineration. The problem with these materials is not that they may contain potentially infectious material but, rather, that the drugs are toxic. Consequently, other methods of disposal of infectious materials, such as autoclaving or disinfection with shredding, are inappropriate. Most infectious waste disposal contractors (at least those that incinerate the wastes) are willing to handle hazardous drug waste, although they may require that containers of hazardous drug waste be specifically labeled as such.

Indoor Air Quality

Indoor air quality is a term used by occupational health professionals to describe a situation in which they know or believe there is a problem with a given work area, but may be unable to determine its cause. It must be remembered that it is relatively easy to determine the concentration of a known contaminant in air, but exceedingly difficult to determine what contaminants are in the air if their identities are unknown. Indoor air quality problems can be classified into two groups: sick building syndrome, which normally involves irritation of the throat, eyes, or mucus membranes; headaches; nausea; or other relatively nonspecific complaints; and building-related illness, which includes Legionnaire's disease, asbestosis, asthma, or other disorders involving hypersensitivity.

Any number of potential culprits can cause indoor air quality problems, including cements used to lay carpeting, fabric treatments, building materials, exhaust from copiers, cigarette smoke, improperly positioned air intake vents, paint, wall coverings, malfunctioning heating devices, and multipart forms. Potential pollutants include formaldehyde, carbon monoxide, ozone, truck or car exhaust, radon, ammonia, cleaning agents, molds, fungi, bacteria, smoke, and asbestos.

As a general rule, inadequate ventilation causes most sick building syndrome problems. (To some extent, the truth of this statement is substantiated by the fact that the problem was not apparent prior to the invention of the tight or energy-efficient building.) If an increase in the ventilation rate does not cure the problem, or if the rate cannot be increased, more attention may need to be paid to the cause of the problem. Indoor air quality problems may arise if air intake grilles are located near areas where cars or trucks idle, or where a large number of cars drive by, allowing exhaust to be pulled into the ventilation system. A problem with the heating system may allow the products of incomplete combustion to enter the ventilation system. Or, furnishings or building materials may cause air quality problems that can be remedied only by replacement or renovation.

Sick building syndrome may be a chronic condition, it may have a gradual onset, or it may appear suddenly. If it is a chronic condition, or it has evolved gradually, it may be necessary to perform a wholesale review of all of the building's systems and furnishings. If it has appeared suddenly, however, the most important question to be answered may be, "Why now?" When one discovers what has changed in the environment, the solution to the problem may be evident.

Building-related illnesses, on the other hand, may require more careful analysis of the heating or cooling system. Molds, fungi, and bacteria can grow in the heating and cooling system and spread throughout the building. Dusts and allergens can accumulate in duct work and cause hypersensitivity reactions among sensitized individuals. Asbestos can become airborne if disturbed and cause asbestosis or lung cancer. Radon, an isotope that occurs naturally in many areas of the country, can cause lung cancer. Although renovation or modification of the heating and cooling system may be necessary to solve some sick-building problems, others can be solved by the less drastic measure of increasing ventilation in affected areas.

Infectious Waste Handling and Disposal

Infectious waste handling, with the exception of requirements in OSHA's Bloodborne Pathogen standard discussed previously, is largely regulated by state or local law. Different jurisdictions may prescribe certain treatment or disposal methods and may not allow other methods, even though they may be widely used in the industry. Different jurisdictions may have different classification systems for identifying wastes as infectious wastes. It is important to be thoroughly familiar with the regulations of the authority having jurisdiction over the facility prior to implementation of a program to handle infectious waste.

Each facility should have an infectious waste program that conforms with relevant OSHA standards, as well as all state or local laws. The program should have specific directions for identifying infectious waste. It should mandate a system for segregating infectious waste from ordinary solid waste, and this segregation should occur as close to the point of generation as possible. It should specify the proper packaging of infectious waste, ensuring that containers are immediately recognizable as infectious waste containers (red bags emblazoned with the universal biohazard symbol are recommended). The plan also should provide for storage of the material, preferably in a location that can be locked, is relatively free of traffic, and can be kept in a sanitary condition (free of vermin). Further, it should specify the appropriate treatment method for each type of infectious waste, or for all infectious waste if only one method is employed. The program also should address proper disposal of the waste and include emergency procedures for use in the event of a spill or release of infectious waste. Finally, the program must address the training that will be provided to employees regarding the routine handling of infectious waste, as well as any emergency procedures that may be applicable.

Although different jurisdictions may use different definitions for *infectious waste*, the term generally includes isolation wastes, cultures of infectious agents, blood and body fluids (including dressings), pathological wastes, contaminated (and sometimes uncontaminated) sharps, contaminated animal bodies or body parts (from research labs), and contaminated animal bedding. It must be remembered that, regardless of state or local regulations, often the ultimate arbiter of the identification of material as infectious waste is the landfill operator or solid waste disposal contractor. If either of these parties decides that something is infectious waste, the facility undoubtedly will need to treat it as such. In short, despite the added cost, it usually is advisable to err in favor of treating a material as an infectious waste rather than ordinary solid waste.

There are various types of treatment methods for rendering infectious waste noninfectious. However, despite the variety of methods, incineration and steam sterilization (autoclaving) are perhaps the most popular and can, with few exceptions, be used to treat any form of infectious waste. Incineration can be used to dispose of any type of infectious waste and has the distinct advantage of rendering the waste unrecognizable as infectious waste after treatment (a very distinct advantage in the case of sharps). Steam sterilization can be used to treat all of the above types of waste, with the exception of large matter (for example, body parts, animal bodies, or animal bedding), although the fact that the waste is still recognizable is a disadvantage. Cultures of infectious agents can be treated by the above methods, or may be treated by either thermal inactivation or chemical disinfection. Bulk blood or blood products often can be discharged to the sanitary sewer system if this is acceptable to the local sewage treatment system. Once infectious wastes have been properly treated, they may be sent to an ordinary landfill.

Laser and Electrocautery Devices

The word *laser* is an acronym for light amplification by stimulated emission of radiation. Lasers are usually named after their lasing medium. The most commonly encountered lasers in health care are carbon dioxide, neodymium:YAG, dye, argon, and krypton. Additionally, lasers are classified according to the degree of hazard they present. Class I and II lasers are relatively benign and need not be of great concern (though it is not never advisable to shine any laser into someone's eyes). Class III and IV lasers, the types used in surgical procedures, are of the most concern.

Laser Optical Hazards   The optical hazard presented by lasers is a combination of various characteristics of the laser beam. In assessing the hazard, a number of factors must be considered: the laser's power or energy output (the higher the energy, the greater the hazard), the wavelength of the beam (different wavelengths react differently with different target materials), the beam diameter, the beam divergence (as one moves away from the laser itself, the beam decreases in coherence and hence in the degree of hazard), the pulse repetition frequency, and the potential for reflection. Different lasers may present completely different health hazards based on the combination of the above factors presented by the laser and the environment in which it is used.

Any facility that uses Class III or Class IV lasers should have a laser safety officer (LSO) to administer a laser safety program. Depending on the number of lasers and the safety requirements of the program, this position may be full- or part-time. The LSO should evaluate the laser program for the degree and nature of hazards, evaluate the environment to remove potential hazards (such as reflective surfaces and use of flammable preparation materials), and implement necessary programs to ensure that the lasers can be used safely.

Lasers present a tremendous hazard for operating room (OR) employees because of the potential for injury to the eyes. The beams of many lasers will pass through the lens and chambers of the eye without significant attenuation, and the lens of the eye also may help to focus the beam on the retina. High-energy lasers produce a great deal of heat when focused on human tissue (see the discussion of laser plume below); hence, shining a laser into an eye may actually cause a burn on the retina. Employees should wear protective eyewear whenever lasers are in use, and all areas in which lasers are in use should have appropriate signs in place to warn personnel to wear protective eyewear. In addition, reflective surfaces should be kept to a minimum in the OR when a laser is in use, and care should be taken to avoid allowing the laser beam to escape the room through windows.

Laser and Electrocautery Plume   Laser and electrocautery plume is caused when tissue is heated to high temperatures during laser surgery or the use of an electrocautery knife, such as a Bovie. The increase in temperature causes the water in tissue to boil and vaporize, resulting in the virtual explosion of cells. This process releases steam, smoke, and particulate matter (ejecta), all of which may be collectively termed *plume*. Recent studies have shown that plume may contain intact viral DNA (including human papillomavirus, which causes warts and HIV),[62,63] bacteria,[64,65] chemical vapors and gases,[66] and mutagenic materials,[67] as well as smoke particles. The mutagenic potential of plume appears to be comparable to that of cigarette smoke,[68] which exposes all OR personnel to second-hand smoke. Additionally, studies have documented the presence of coal tar pitch volatiles (carcinogens),[69] cyanides (toxic materials),[70] and formaldehyde[71] in plume. Studies with animals have shown that direct exposure to plume can cause severe pulmonary inflammation.[72,73]

There are many models of smoke evacuators on the market that employ a number of different filtration methods. The most common type employs a HEPA filter. This type is excellent for removing particles that are 0.3 microns or larger, but it does not filter out chemical vapors or gases. Other evacuators use a HEPA filter and an activated carbon filter. In addition to particulates, this system removes odors and some organic vapors. Another type of evacuator uses an ultra-low penetration air filter, which filters out particles down to 0.1 micron but, again, does not filter out chemical vapors or gases. A final type of evacuator uses a scrubber and a chlorine solution, which filters out particulate and most chemical vapors and gases. The facility should carefully consider the type of evacuator that will deliver the most protection to the OR staff.

Latex Sensitivity

The process by which someone may become allergic to a substance is well known and understood in the abstract, but is usually poorly understood on the level of the individual or as a measurable process. It is well understood that a person must be exposed to a substance before he or she can become allergic to it. No one is born with an allergy to something. Additionally, the substance must be an allergen of some sort, and not all substances are allergens. Once a person has been exposed to an allergen, there is a certain level of probability that she may become allergic to it. The process by which the person becomes allergic to the substance is known as sensitization. The amount of exposure to the allergen necessary to cause sensitization is generally unknown, and will vary greatly from one individual to another. It is known that higher levels of exposure will cause higher rates of sensitization in potentially sensitive individuals. The number of exposures to the material necessary to cause sensitization is also largely unknown, and some persons do not develop a sensitivity to a material until they have been exposed to it on numerous occasions. The degree of reaction by sensitive individuals when they contact the allergen to which they are sensitive will vary according to the individual, the allergen in question, and the level and route of exposure.[74]

The National Institute for Occupational Safety and Health (NIOSH) estimates that between 8 and 12 percent of health care workers who are exposed to latex have become sensitized to it,[75] but OSHA estimates the number of sensitized workers at between 6 percent and 17 percent of health care personnel exposed to latex.[76] It is generally recognized that rates and levels of sensitization have increased among health care workers in recent years due to OSHA's requirement that health care workers wear gloves whenever they are potentially exposed to blood or body fluids as part of the Bloodborne Pathogen Standard.[77] Latex sensitivity can range from dermatitis (rash and inflammation) to respiratory irritation and asthma. It may cause shock in rare cases.[78]

Although one normally thinks of gloves when one thinks of devices or products containing latex, there are any number of devices and products present in the health care environment that may contain latex. These include blood pressure cuffs, stethoscopes, airway tubing, endotracheal tubes, tourniquets, IV tubing, syringes, electrode pads, surgical masks, goggles, catheters, wound drains, injection ports, tops on multidose vials, and dental dams. Persons at high risk of sensitization include health care workers with high levels of exposure, as well as persons with multiple allergic conditions and persons with spina bifida. Latex allergy may also be associated with allergies to adhesive bandages, avocados, potatoes, bananas, tomatoes, chestnuts, kiwi fruit, and papayas.[79]

There are a number of possible solutions to the problem of latex sensitivity. Of primary concern should be the prevention of sensitization in the first place through a reduction in exposure to all health care workers. It is much more easily managed if one is not sensitized. There are numerous ways to avoid exposure. Nonlatex gloves should be used whenever possible, consistent with sound infection control processes. If latex gloves must be used, they should not be powdered and should have reduced protein levels (the allergens are certain proteins in latex). These proteins can be absorbed by powder and then more easily transmitted to the skin, or the powder can become airborne and inhaled by the wearer. Hypoallergenic gloves do not reduce the risk of latex allergy, but they may reduce the risk of contact dermatitis due to a reduction in the chemical additives often found in other types of gloves. Oil-based hand creams or lotions should not be used if latex gloves are to be worn. The wearer should wash his or her hands with soap and water after wearing latex gloves. Work areas should be cleaned regularly to remove dust that could contain latex from contaminated areas and equipment.[80]

If a health care worker has become sensitized to latex, the task of preventing reactions can be much more complicated. The sensitized person must avoid all contact with products or devices containing latex. The person should avoid areas where he or she might inhale dust particles containing latex. The person's employer and all health care providers who provide care for the person must be aware of the sensitivity. The person should wear a medical alert bracelet, or a similar device, to warn of the sensitivity.[81]

Video Display Terminals

Video display terminals (VDTs) have been investigated for radiation exposure, eye strain, ergonomic and repetitive motion disorders, and complications in pregnancy. With the exception of eyestrain, fatigue, and repetitive motion disorders, most of the complaints lodged against VDTs remain unproven. VDTs do generate electric and magnetic fields (discussed previously), but the amount generated is minimal. If one wishes to minimize the risk in an excess of caution, one should not sit closer than twenty-nine inches (seventy-six centimeters) from the screen, or within four feet (122 centimeters) from the sides and back of the VDT.[82]

The complaints regarding repetitive motion disorders are really aimed at keyboard use rather than at the VDTs themselves. VDT use has been implicated in the development of tendonitis, tenosynovitis, trigger finger, gamekeeper's thumb, Guyon's canal syndrome, epicondylitis, cubital tunnel syndrome, low back pain, and carpal tunnel syndrome.[83] Many of these problems are caused by awkward positions, localized pressure, holding static positions, excessive use of force, and repetition. Many of the complaints can be avoided if the workstation is fully adjustable, so that it can be tailored to the employee's needs and physical characteristics, which will minimize operations performed in awkward positions. Many of the problems can also be avoided by regular rest breaks.[84] Complaints of eyestrain often are due to lighting issues or inappropriate placement of the screen. The screen should be placed in a position that will minimize glare from overhead lighting or sunlight. Lighting in the office should be analyzed because the overhead lights may be significantly brighter than the screen. This may lead to adaptation problems with the user's eyes. Additionally, the screen refresh rate should be at least 60 hertz (cycles per second) to avoid screen flicker, which may be associated with eye strain.[85]

Many, if not all, of the ills associated with work at VDTs can be alleviated by careful attention to the environment and the allowance of regular rest periods.[86] Because many of the problems lie within the province of the employee for correction, employees need to be trained in the use of VDTs just as they are trained in the use of any other equipment. They should be informed of the benefits of safe work practices and the risks of unsafe work practices. They should be encouraged to adopt safe work practices, even if this means lower production on an hourly basis.[87]

Waste Anesthetic Gases

The primary anesthetic gases presently in use include nitrous oxide and various halogenated agents, such as halothane, enflurane, and isoflurane. Exposure to these agents normally occurs among OR staff, post-anesthesia care unit staff, dentists, and dental assistants. Nevertheless, exposure to nitrous oxide also can occur in the ED, where small tanks of nitrous oxide are sometimes used for analgesia in trauma cases. Exposure to waste anesthetic gases has been linked to decreased reproductive ability (increased rates of spontaneous abortion, even among the mates of exposed males); embryotoxicity; liver and kidney disease; and various nonspecific complaints such as headache, drowsiness, depression, nausea, and fatigue.[88]

OSHA has not promulgated specific standards for any of these materials but has issued guidelines for the evaluation of anesthetizing locations.[89] In 1977, NIOSH recommended a standard for anesthetic gases that was never adopted by OSHA.[90] NIOSH recommends that levels of nitrous oxide be monitored and maintained below twenty-five ppm. If this level is achieved, exposure to the halogenated agents will normally be maintained below two ppm. This is a sensible plan because it allows a facility to monitor for only one contaminant, rather than several. Monitoring should occur at the breathing zones of affected employees. The individual most affected in the OR (other than the patient) is typically the anesthesiologist or anesthetist.

Exposure generally occurs due to leakage at a coupling or a valve, deficiencies in the scavenging system, use of a mask that fits poorly on the patient, or the exhalations of patients after extubation. Even if the levels of nitrous oxide are consistently below twenty-five ppm, each anesthesia machine should be checked on a regular basis, including wall or column supply connections and the scavenging system, using a real-time (instantaneous readout) monitoring device to detect any leakage. If leakage is detected, it should be corrected as soon as possible by appropriate service personnel. The operating and recovery room ventilation rates also should be monitored on a regular basis. If the air in the room is exchanged at a high rate, it will mute the adverse effects of a leak, should one occur. The ventilation rate should be in the neighborhood of fifteen room air changes per hour.

· · · · · · · · · · · ·

GENERAL SAFETY ISSUES NOT ADDRESSED BY SPECIFIC OSHA STANDARDS

The foregoing section dealt with occupational health issues that are either not covered, or covered only cursorily, by specific OSHA regulations. Those issues concern agents or conditions that could cause *illness* or another morbid condition. This section deals with safety issues not strictly regulated by OSHA, but these issues involve agents or conditions that may cause or threaten *injury* to employees, patients, or visitors, or that may result in property damage. Again, the lack of specific regulations does not mean that OSHA cannot regulate an employer's conduct with regard to these issues. OSHA has the authority, under the general duty clause to require the employer to provide a safe and healthful workplace free of recognized hazards.[91] The following issues concern some of those recognized hazards.

Compressed Gases

Most health care facilities utilize a number of compressed gases in their day-to-day operations, including nitrous oxide, oxygen, carbon dioxide, carbon monoxide, propane, and acetylene. The storage and delivery vessels for these gases range in size from very large stationary tanks to relatively small, portable cylinders. The primary hazard associated with compressed gases is the unanticipated and sudden release of their contents. If the head is knocked off of a cylinder, the cylinder can become a virtual torpedo. This hazard is compounded if the contents are flammable or combustible.

All employees who deal with compressed gas cylinders need to be carefully trained and monitored regarding their handling and storage. Cylinders, even empty ones, should always be secured when in storage or while in use. Only reasonable numbers of cylinders and amounts of compressed gases should be stored on site. They should be stored away from all sources of ignition or flame. Flammable or combustible gases should never be stored near oxidizers, such as oxygen. Proper ventilation should be provided to avoid the creation of a hazardous environment in areas where toxic (for example, carbon monoxide) or flammable (such as acetylene) gases are stored. Cylinders should only be transported in appropriate conveyances, such as hand trucks or carriers. If stored outdoors, they should be kept out of direct sunlight. These precautions should be followed carefully because an accident involving a compressed gas cylinder is potentially disastrous.

Flammable Liquids and Solvent Storage

Bulk quantities of flammable liquids (for example, acetone, alcohols, benzene, ether, toluene, and xylene) should be stored only in approved locations. Flammable liquid storage cabinets are acceptable for interior storage of moderate amounts of flammable liquid. Many such cabinets can be vented to the exterior of the building, which prevents some degree of employee exposure to fugitive vapors. However, the facility must be careful to use piping that has the same fire resistance as the cabinet (for example, cast iron), or the integrity of the cabinet may be compromised.

If kept in large quantities, flammable liquids should be stored in a designated flammable liquid storage room. Ideally, such a room has blowout panels that will allow an explosion to be directed away from occupied areas of the building. The door to the room should have a dike, or the floor may be recessed, to prevent spilled liquid from exiting the room. The lighting in the room, including the light switch (if inside the room), must be explosion-proof. It may be easier to position the light switch outside the door. The room should be as free of combustible material as possible: deliveries should be broken down as soon as they are received, cardboard boxes should be removed as soon as possible, and shelving material should be made of metal. Large drums of liquid should have grounding wires to avoid static sparks. Acids, alkalis, oxidizers, and reactive materials should not be stored with flammable liquids. All locations in which flammable liquids are stored must be conspicuously labeled with warning signs. Appropriate fire extinguishers should be located nearby (not inside a flammable liquid storage room).

Radiation Safety

Ionizing radiation may be a natural phenomenon that occurs when a radioactive isotope undergoes decay, or it may be artificially created, as in the case of x-rays. Disintegration of an isotope causes the release of a particle that is thrown off and can travel for some distance in air. Different particles present different levels and types of hazards. Alpha particles, for example, are relatively large particles that do not travel very far in air and have limited ability to penetrate human tissue. However, they can be hazardous if inhaled or ingested. An example of an alpha emitter used in hospitals is radium (radium 226 and radium 222), which is used in implanted material. Beta particles are smaller than alpha particles and have greater ability to travel in air or in tissue. Internal exposure to beta particles is more hazardous than external exposure, but external exposure also presents risk.

Beta emitters used in hospitals include iodine 131, radium 226, and cobalt 60. Gamma rays are capable of traveling great distances and are able to penetrate tissue readily. Gamma rays are produced by materials such as cobalt 60, cesium 137, iridium 192, and radium 226. X-rays are electromagnetic radiation and are similar to gamma rays, except that x-rays have longer wavelengths, lower frequencies, and less energy than gamma rays. X-rays are produced when high-energy electrons strike the nuclei of a target material, such as tungsten.

Exposure to radiation, even in small amounts, can cause adverse health effects, including cancer (myelogenous leukemia, bone, skin, and thyroid), lung fibrosis, kidney fibrosis, cataracts, aplastic anemia, sterility, radiodermatitis, and a shortening of the life span generally.[92] Radiation exposure can occur in a health care facility during procedures involving diagnostic x-rays, fluoroscopy, angiography, computerized tomography, therapeutic radiology, nuclear medicine, and the implantation of radioactive materials.

Each facility that uses devices or materials that produce ionizing radiation should employ a radiation protection officer who will direct an integrated program to protect employees. All employees who are potentially exposed should wear dosimeters to measure exposure levels as well as appropriate personal protective equipment. Areas where radioactive materials are used or stored should have appropriate barrier material in place to prevent the escape of radiation. These areas should be monitored regularly to detect any loss or escape of radioactive materials. Ideally, waste radioactive material should be returned to the radiopharmacy for storage or disposal, although many facilities store waste material with short half-lives on-site. This latter practice is acceptable if the volume is not excessive, the material can be stored safely in a secured area, it does not present a hazard for employees in the general area, it is monitored regularly to detect any release, and it is carefully evaluated to ensure that it has decayed to background levels prior to disposal.

Workplace Violence

Violence in the health care workplace has been a problem for a considerable period of time and has become a topic of concern for regulators in the relatively recent past. Between 1980 and 1990, approximately 106 health care providers were killed at work, including pharmacists (twenty-seven), physicians (twenty-six), registered nurses (eighteen), nurses' aides (seventeen), and others (eighteen). Another report in 1989 indicated that a psychiatric hospital experienced sixteen assaults on its employees per 100 employees per year. This compares to a rate of 8.2 assaults per 100 employees per year for all industries.[93] While violence may be a fact of life in health care, that does not mean that there is nothing to be done about it. Like most aspects of the health care business, it must be managed if it is to be reduced.

Worksite Analysis   The first step in the process is to analyze the facility's current problems with violence and to look for weaknesses in its defenses. It is important to ensure that employees are reporting violent acts, since it is entirely possible that they are not being reported unless someone has gotten hurt. *All* violent acts need to be reported if the facility is to understand its problems.

The facility should also undergo a worksite analysis to determine where its potential problems may lie. It is important to remember that there are numerous classes of assailants, or types of assaults, as follows:

- Patient assaults on staff.
- Staff assaults on patients.

- Visitor assaults on staff.
- Visitor assaults on patients.
- Visitor assaults on visitors.
- Third-party (nonvisitor) assaults on staff.
- Third-party (nonvisitor) assaults on patients.
- Third-party (nonvisitor) assaults on visitors.
- Family member assaults on patients.
- Family (or estranged family) member assaults on staff.

Assaults may be motivated by criminal tendencies (robbery, rape, and so on), by rage or revenge, by persons who are unable to control their actions, or by a myriad of other factors. With particular regard to assaults by criminals or would-be criminals, there are some common elements in all of this that the facility should keep in mind while performing its worksite analysis.

The first element is opportunity. As a general rule, assailants will generally limit their assaults to situations that they think they can control, where the assault will proceed as they have planned, and where they may be able to accomplish it without detection by anyone other than the assaulted party. Hospitals present unique opportunities because they are accessible, to some extent, twenty-four hours per day. The presence of more than one person, security officers, adequate lighting, limitations on access, alarm systems, and the like tend to be deterrents to assaults. The facility should evaluate its premises for opportunities for assaults, and it should not restrict this to the middle of the day. Such evaluations may need to be made at 2:00 a.m.

The second element is attraction. Assailants are often attracted by something that serves as the motivation for the assault. Unfortunately, hospitals and health care facilities are ripe with attractants. They have drugs on the premises that may attract substance abusers with criminal tendencies (although the motivation was not described in the previous section, it is probably not mere coincidence that pharmacists had the highest number of occupational fatalities in the study). They often have money on the premises. They also have a predominantly female workforce, which may attract sex offenders. Knowing the potential reasons for an assault can give the facility the advantage. If a facility can minimize the opportunity for assaults, and minimize the attractiveness of its facility to those bent upon assaulting someone, the facility will definitely be a safer place.

Hazard Prevention and Control   There are a number of engineering controls that can be applied to reduce the possibility of workplace violence. Engineering controls usually involve a change in the environment in which the employees work in order to build in protections. The level of controls necessary will depend to a large extent on the facility's need for protection, which can be determined by the facility's geographic location, history, experience, and patient population. A rural facility may not feel the need for as high levels of security as an inner city facility may feel. The facility's culture may also be a factor in determining the level of security: it may be important to the facility to avoid the appearance of a fortress.

Engineering controls are largely of three types: environmental controls, barriers, and alarms. Environmental controls can include increased lighting in a dark area, doors that are locked and cannot be entered from the outside, metal detectors, providing two exits from meeting rooms, providing secured areas for staff (such as staff restrooms or locker rooms), or other controls that may make the environment less attractive to would-be assailants or amenable to assaults. Barriers can include locked doors or units, waiting rooms with controlled access to the department or unit, plexiglass shields in front of cashiers, and so on. Alarms can be installed at doors that are not to be used in the ordinary course of the facility's business and panic buttons can be installed wherever someone might have an immediate need for assistance. In addition, cellular telephones or noise devices can be tremendously beneficial in an emergency.

Administrative controls can also be helpful to reduce the threat of violence. They generally do not alter the environment, nor do they depend upon an individual using them. Examples of administrative controls that might be helpful in these situations might include increased staffing to avoid having people work alone late at night, strict enforcement of visiting hours, monitoring visitor access to sensitive areas (such as the newborn nursery, ED examination rooms), having a trained emergency response team available, or having multiple employees work with an agitated patient or distraught family member.

In spite of all of the preparations, a facility may experience an act of violence on its premises. The facility needs to be prepared to deal with the immediate medical and emotional needs of the injured party, the emotional needs of his or her coworkers, the police, and the media. The time to decide on the proper way to handle all of the demands of a situation like this is well in advance of the need to do so.

Training and Education   All personnel need to be trained regarding personal safety and the security features of the facility. They need to understand that they must always be aware of their surroundings, that they should avoid unsafe areas or areas that they may perceive to be unsafe, and how they may be able to prevent an assault. They must be told to report all acts of actual or threatened violence.

Clinical personnel need to be trained in recognizing, managing, deescalating and controlling assaultive behavior, in addition to the general training given to all employees. They need to be aware of the risk factors that can lead to assaultive behavior and how to avoid them. This training should include discussions of their interactions with all persons, including patients, family members, and visitors.

Recordkeeping and Program Evaluation   The facility needs to keep careful records of all acts of actual or threatened violence, including the nature of the act, the parties involved, the location (including any relevant aspects of the location, such as obstructed visibility, poor lighting, and so on), and the date and time of the event. The facility must continually monitor the effectiveness of its program through incident analysis, but also through monitoring of employee comfort levels and anxiety.

∙∙∙∙∙∙∙∙∙∙∙∙

JOINT COMMISSION ON ACCREDITATION OF HEALTHCARE ORGANIZATIONS (JCAHO) ISSUES

The JCAHO is a private organization that accredits, among other entities, hospitals. Recently, it has undertaken a transformation that is intended to move its accreditation process away from an emphasis on structures and toward one on performance improvement. As part of this transformation, the chapter formerly titled "Plant, Technology and Safety Management" in the *Accreditation Manual for Hospitals* now is entitled "Management of the Environment of Care" in the *Comprehensive Accreditation Manual for Hospitals*.[94] The standards found in this chapter can be divided into eight groups: safety management, security, hazardous materials management, life safety management, emergency preparedness, equipment management, utilities management, and management of the social environment. Each of the standards requires certain activities in common, such as employee training and education, performance standards, program monitoring and evaluation, and designation of individuals responsible for the programs required by the standards. The following subsections look at the standards for each of these areas.

Safety Management

The JCAHO standards on safety management provide a structure on which the facility should base its safety program. These standards require that each facility provide an environment that is free of hazards to life and health. The facility needs to have a designated safety officer, appointed by the CEO, who is responsible for the development, implementation, and evaluation of the safety program. The safety officer needs to have authority to intervene whenever there is an imminent hazard to life or health. The facility also needs to have a safety committee composed of representatives from administration, clinical services, and support services. This committee is responsible for identifying and analyzing safety trends and issues, and developing recommendations for abating any hazards. The safety management program also needs to have a reporting system that reports all incidents involving injury, illness, or property damage. The facility needs to have safety policies and procedures, both departmental and facility-wide, that are both practiced and enforced, and that are revised as necessary and reviewed at least once every three years. Finally, it needs to have a risk assessment program in place that identifies all factors that may have an impact on patient, employee, and public safety.

Security

Under the new JCAHO standards, facilities are required to develop and implement a security management plan that will address security concerns; identification procedures for staff, patients, and visitors; control of access to sensitive areas; and control of traffic in emergency service areas. The program must have a person or persons designated to be responsible for management of the program, and there must be a mechanism for reporting all security incidents. Of particular concern in the security management program should be sensitive areas such as the ED (assaults against personnel or patients), the pharmacy (control of dangerous drugs), and the nursery (infant abductions).

Hazardous Materials Management

Each facility must have a hazardous materials and waste management program. For the purposes of these standards, hazardous materials would include hazardous chemicals, sharps, and other infectious wastes, hazardous gases, radioactive wastes, waste antineoplastic agents, and any other material that would be classified as a hazardous waste under federal, state, or local regulations. The program should provide for the selection of hazardous materials, including techniques to minimize their quantity and number. It also must address the proper storage, handling, and disposal of hazardous wastes, and must provide a system for reporting all incidents involving hazardous materials. The hazardous materials management program should specify all facets of a material's journey through the facility, from receipt to use to final disposal. Each employee who comes into contact with a hazardous material must be carefully trained regarding his or her role in the material's use in the facility, including the proper response to an emergency situation.

Life Safety Management

Life safety management involves protecting patients, employees, visitors, and buildings from the threat of fire. Each facility is required to be in compliance with the *Life Safety Code* with regard to the structure and fire protection features of the building.[95] Different standards in the code are applicable to different occupancies (for example, buildings that house patients overnight, business occupancies, and so on). If the facility is not in compliance with the code, it must have either a documented equivalency from the JCAHO or a plan of correction. It also must have a written life safety management program that addresses the protection of patients, visitors, and employees from fire and the products of combustion; maintenance of all structural features necessary for compliance with the code; maintenance and testing of all fire detection, alarm, and suppression systems; evaluation of acquisitions of bedding, wall coverings, and furnishings for fire hazards; and proper responses to fire emergencies. The program must be understood by all employees and must be monitored and evaluated to ensure its effectiveness.

Emergency Preparedness

Each health care facility must be prepared to respond to and handle foreseeable natural or other disasters, whether within or outside the facility. To accomplish this, each should have a written emergency preparedness program that is tested periodically and evaluated after every drill or actual emergency. Such a plan needs to address mechanisms for notifying personnel of the emergency, including a callback system for employees not on duty, and must specify employees roles and responsibilities in emergency situations. Further, it should specify the logistics of providing triage and care for the victims of a mass casualty, including situations in which the victims may be the facility's own employees or patients. And finally, it must address mechanisms for notifying local authorities and for obtaining supplies.

Equipment Management

Health care facilities need to have a program in place for managing medical equipment to minimize risks to patients and employees. Such a program should identify equipment that will be subject to its requirements. It must address methods for equipment selection, inspection (both prior to first use and periodically thereafter), evaluation, maintenance, and repair. The plan also should address product recalls or alerts issued by manufacturers. It should have mechanisms for identifying equipment subject to a recall or alert (such as a current and comprehensive inventory) and for providing whatever service is required to resolve any potential problem. The facility must have a system for reporting all incidents involving equipment malfunction, as well as all those involving actual or potential injury to patients due to equipment use, misuse, or malfunction. Finally, the equipment management program must address all training and orientation necessary for employees to use equipment safely.

Utilities Management

Health care facilities are highly dependent upon their essential utility systems (electricity, water, heat, sewage, ventilation, and so on). This dependence often is taken for granted until the systems are inoperable. The primary goal of the facility's utilities management program is to ensure the operational reliability and reduce the risk of failure of the various utility systems through inspection, testing, maintenance, repair, and training of employees responsible for their maintenance. The program must identify the distribution system for each utility system, including the valves or controls necessary for shutting down all or a portion of the system. It also should address any backup or contingency plans the facility could implement to minimize the effect of a system failure.

Social Environment

Health care facilities need to address the various aspects of the social environment in which care is rendered. This includes provisions for appropriate and adequate space, privacy protection, and activities geared toward the patient's needs. The environment must foster a positive self-image for the patient and preserve his or her human dignity. This standard also now addresses the facility's smoking policy as part of the social environment. The facility needs to have a policy that prohibits smoking throughout the building, unless authorized for an individual patient in writing by a licensed practitioner, which must be made in conformity with criteria developed by the medical staff.

············

ENVIRONMENTAL IMPAIRMENT

The laws governing impairment of the environment are a complex mixture of federal, state, and local regulations that sometimes overlap and contradict one another. As a general rule, the federal laws constitute a framework on which the state or local authorities may build. State and local regulations may be stricter than the federal laws, but federal laws take precedence if state or local laws are less strict. Among the most important federal laws governing this subject are the Resource Conservation and Recovery Act (RCRA),[96] the Comprehensive Environmental Response, Compensation and Liability Act (CERCLA),[97] the Clean Water Act,[98] the Clean Air Act,[99] and the Toxic Substances Control Act.[100] Because it is virtually impossible in a treatise of this sort to address all state and local regulations, the following subsections address only general concerns related to the federal laws and regulations.

Underground Storage Tanks

Most hospitals, as well as some long-term care facilities, have underground storage tanks (USTs) on their premises. These tanks most commonly contain diesel fuel, which is used to power the emergency generator(s) and to provide a backup fuel source for the boilers. Such tanks may range in size from a few hundred gallons to 20,000 or 30,000 gallons. Hospital USTs also may contain gasoline or various grades of fuel oil. The risk of impairment to the environment posed by the leakage of a large UST is considerable. The risk of leakage for any particular tank is subject to a complex set of factors. For example, the construction of some tanks (for example, bare steel) will make them more prone to corrosion and leakage. The type of soil around a tank may promote corrosion. The existence of groundwater in the vicinity of the tank also may cause it to corrode quickly. Finally, improper original installation of the tank is often a major cause of leakage.

A regulated UST is one that, including piping, has at least 10 percent of its volume underground and contains a regulated substance. Regulated USTs do not include tanks that contain substances regulated as hazardous wastes under RCRA, equipment or machinery tanks that contain regulated substances for operational purposes, tanks that contain only a *de minimis* amount of regulated substance, tanks that contain only regulated substances related to an emergency spill or overflow, septic tanks, tanks located in an underground area (such as a basement) if the tank is above the floor, or tanks that store heating oil for consumption on the premises where stored. *Regulated substances* include petroleum products and any substances that are considered to be hazardous substances under CERCLA.

Certain tanks have been granted a deferral from portions of the regulations. These include wastewater treatment tanks that are not part of a wastewater treatment facility and tanks that contain fuel solely for use in emergency power generators, which are exempt from release detection requirements.

Some performance standards are applicable to both existing (installed prior to December 22, 1988) and new USTs (installed after December 22, 1988). All USTs must be, and should have been, installed by certified installers. All UST operators must ensure that releases due to spilling or overfilling will not occur. This can be accomplished by ensuring that fittings are tight and that there is more volume available in the tank than the amount of product to be transferred.

Each UST should be monitored to detect any releases as quickly as possible. Release detection can be accomplished by tightness testing, installation of a tank gauging system, inventory control methods, groundwater monitoring, vapor monitoring, or interstitial monitoring. *Tightness testing* involves pressurizing the tank to determine if it is leaking. This method should be capable of detecting a leak as small as 0.1 gallons per hour. *Installation of a tank gauging system* involves monitoring the volume of liquid in the tank (as a fuel gauge monitors the amount of gasoline in an automobile's tank). The employees of the facility should periodically monitor and record the level of the liquid, since unexplained reductions may indicate that the tank is leaking. However, this method provides only rough approximations of the volume of liquid in the tank; hence, it should only be used in conjunction with a more accurate leak detection method. *Inventory control methods* require that the volume of the tank be measured manually on a regular basis and records of usage, withdrawal, and input are kept to balance with the measured volume. This method should normally be used in conjunction with another method because it is often not capable of detecting a small leak. *Groundwater monitoring* is a viable method of monitoring for leak detection, as long as there is groundwater that can be reached with a probe (less than twenty feet below the surface), the product in the tank is not immiscible in water, and the method is sensitive enough to detect very small amounts of product. *Vapor monitoring* is conducted in the excavation zone—that is, that area around the tank that is filled with backfill after installation of the tank. *Interstitial monitoring* is conducted by monitoring the space between the tank and a secondary containment or barrier. Any tightness testing or modification of the tank should be performed by a certified installer because personnel with less training often do not realize they may have caused a leak while trying to detect or prevent one.

Serious consideration should be given to upgrading older tanks to make them more leak resistant. This can be accomplished by adding either an interior lining or cathodic protection, or by a combination of the two. However, even if a tank is upgraded, the facility must continue to monitor for releases and should plan on replacing all old tanks in the foreseeable future. Any tank not presently in service should be promptly emptied and removed from the ground, or filled with an inert material. The state agency having jurisdiction over USTs must be informed of their closure prior to removal or final closure.

Facilities must report significant releases or spills within twenty-four hours of discovery. If the spill causes a sheen on surface water or more than twenty-five gallons were released, the facility should commence cleanup operations immediately.

The federal regulations also have mandatory financial responsibility standards, although their applicability to most hospital-owned USTs may be questionable. Many states have responded to the federal requirements by instituting financial responsibility pools. UST owners often can participate in these funds for rather nominal amounts (usually only $100 to $200 per tank per year). However, UST owners should be careful to ensure that their tanks qualify as regulated tanks prior to paying the fees.

Aboveground Storage Tanks

Aboveground storage tanks include day tanks on generators and other vessels that do not have at least 10 percent of their volume below ground. They generally contain the same types of materials as do USTs but are invariably smaller than USTs. They also generally present less of a threat to the environment because they are more accessible for visual inspection and repair. However, they do present a threat of which the facility should be aware.

Aboveground tanks often are placed in equipment areas and may be located near a floor drain. In the event of a leak or release, the contents of the tank would be discharged to the sewer system. A barrier or secondary containment mechanism should be implemented to prevent this release. In order to be fail-safe, the secondary containment mechanism should be capable of holding more liquid than the volume of the tank ideally, 150 percent of the tank's volume. Moreover, if the aboveground tank contains hazardous or flammable liquids, adequate signs should be posted in the vicinity warning employees of the potential danger.

Asbestos Removal

The EPA has extensive requirements for the control of asbestos exposure under the National Emission Standard for Hazardous Air Pollutants (NESHAP),[101] the Asbestos Hazard Emergency Response Act (AHERA),[102] Resource Conservation and Recovery Act (RCRA),[103] and the Toxic Substances Control Act.[104] For the purposes of this discussion, the NESHAP regulations are of the greatest concern.

The NESHAP regulations apply to any demolition or extensive renovation of any facility that contains potential ACM, as well as to the transportation and disposal of the resulting debris. All potential ACM must be identified and its condition assessed. Basically, the standard for demolition, renovation, and disposal is that there can be no visible emission of fibers during the operation. This generally means that friable asbestos (materials that may release fibers if crushed or disturbed) must be removed prior to demolition, especially if it is in a deteriorated condition. Other nonfriable ACM (such as floor tiles) may be left in the building, as long as the potential for emissions is low. Once the material is removed from the building, it must be kept wet, in sealed containers, and may not be crushed during transportation or disposal. However, ACM is not regulated as a hazardous waste under RCRA; hence, in the absence of more stringent state or local regulations, it may be disposed of in public or private landfills so long as there are no visible emissions during the process.

It should be noted that asbestos is considered a hazardous material under the reporting requirements of CERCLA.[105] Under these regulations, the release of more than one pound of asbestos into the atmosphere must be reported to the National Response Center.[106]

As a practical matter, ACM is a material that needs to be managed, rather than the subject of hysterical overreaction. Except in situations where it has become deteriorated, or where it may be friable, if it can be left undisturbed it can usually be managed in place. The first step is to identify it as ACM and to catalog its condition. Identification should be accomplished by an AHERA-accredited inspector, although, in reality, there is nothing to stop a building manager from treating suspected ACM as real ACM and managing it accordingly.

Once all the potential ACM has been identified, an operations and maintenance (O&M) program for managing the material should be developed. This program will address all the material present in the building and prescribe all future courses of action with regard to it. The O&M program should be integrated into the master plan for the building, if one exists. As soon as the O&M program has been implemented, all the employees in the building must be notified of the presence of ACM and the ways in which they will be able to continue to work around it.

The next step in the O&M program is to remove all severely deteriorated or readily disturbed friable material. In this instance, abatement may be by encapsulation, containment, enclosure, repair, or removal. However, it is important to be aware that quick fixes in managing ACM are not always the best practices. If the ACM is friable and severely deteriorated, it will have to come out of the building eventually, whether during demolition or renovation. Consequently, it may be wisest to simply remove severely damaged ACM as it is encountered. The rest of the ACM (reasonably undamaged) may be left in place, or may be repaired, enclosed, or encapsulated. It should be kept in mind that ACM continues to be some of the best insulating material ever developed and, if undamaged, will continue to provide a great deal of energy efficiency for thermal systems or fireproofing for structural members. The EPA has published two documents that provide far more detail on this subject than it is possible to provide here.[107]

Disposal of Hazardous Waste

Disposal of hazardous waste is regulated under RCRA, although liability for improper practices in the past would be imposed under CERCLA. This act provides a mechanism for making all persons or entities (known as potentially responsible parties) who may have disposed of hazardous waste at a contaminated site (a Superfund site) liable for all or a portion of the costs of cleaning up the site. This liability may be enormous and potentially disproportionate to the amount of waste actually dumped at the site. It cannot be foisted upon the contractor who removed, transported, treated, or disposed of the waste. Consequently, facilities need to pay careful attention to the disposal of hazardous waste.

The facility should develop a waste management program that identifies all types of waste and mandates minimization techniques, employee training, segregation, proper storage, treatment, and disposal that are appropriate for the status of the generator, and that meet the requirements of the JCAHO standards relating to hazardous materials.

Hazardous wastes must be solid wastes to be governed by the definition of hazardous wastes under RCRA. However, the term *solid waste* includes semisolids, liquids, and compressed gases. Thus, hazardous wastes are any solid wastes that possess certain characteristics, including ignitability (any waste that could start a fire during storage or disposal, wastes having a flash point below 140°F, or oxidizers), corrosivity (pH less than two or greater than 12.5), reactivity (readily undergoes violent change, reacts violently with water, or produces toxic gases when mixed with water), or toxicity (contains certain toxic materials or otherwise shows evidence of toxicity).

Conditionally exempt small-quantity generators (SQGs) are those generators of hazardous wastes that produce less than 1,000 kilograms (kg) of hazardous waste per month, or that do not violate the storage requirements established for SQGs.[108,109] SQGs can be further classified as those that produce less than 100 kg per month, and those that produce between 100 and 1,000 kg per month. This latter category is exempt from some, but not all, of the EPA's requirements for hazardous waste generators.[110] SQGs (less than 100 kg per month) are exempt from the requirement to use a manifest with shipments of hazardous waste to disposal sites, and facilities in the intermediate category (more than 100 but less than 1,000 kg per month) also are exempt if the waste is recycled, although most transporters require manifests (despite this exemption) and facilities are well advised to use them to document proper disposal. Additionally, SQGs are not required to have an EPA identification number, although facilities in the intermediate category are required to obtain one. Neither of these types of generators is required to file biennial reports with the EPA. However, both types are required to have a permit to store hazardous wastes if they store the material for longer than 180 days.

Any facility that stores hazardous waste must be careful to store it appropriately. For example, the waste must not react with the container in which it is stored. To prevent a fire or explosion in the event of a spill or leak, incompatible substances should not be stored near one another. Wastes should be stored in a secure area and only authorized personnel should have access to the area. Additionally, they should not be stored near compressed gas cylinders. If the wastes are flammable, adequate precautions must be taken, as described above.

Any facility that disposes of hazardous waste also must ensure that the disposal is performed appropriately. The facility should ensure that all manifests are returned after disposal and must report those not returned within forty-five days to the EPA. The facility also should monitor and periodically audit the process, including a trip to the treatment or disposal facility.

On-Site Medical Waste Incinerators

Many hospitals still have on-site medical waste incinerators, although they are used much less frequently than in the past, when most, if not all, hospitals had an incinerator of some sort. These were frequently pathological waste incinerators, designed to burn body parts. (It was aesthetically unappealing to send these to a garbage dump or landfill, and burial in a cemetery was often more expensive than maintaining an incinerator.) As the states and the federal government began to implement clean air and infectious waste regulations, hospitals began to shut down many of these pathological incinerators, and installed more complex incinerators to handle higher volumes of waste (a pathological incinerator is often little more than a set of gas jets, a small combustion chamber, and a chimney). Unfortunately, the onslaught of regulations has continued, and most hospitals find it difficult to maintain an on-site incinerator. The EPA has issued performance standards for medical waste incinerator installations. A complete dissertation of the regulation of medical waste incinerators is beyond the scope of this discussion, and the interested reader is urged to consult with the EPA's publications on the subject.[111]

Clean Air Act

The Clean Air Act contains numerous provisions that could affect health care facilities.[112] The medical waste incinerator standards and guidelines noted previously were issued pursuant to the mandates of this act. The act also mandates a phaseout of ozone-depleting chemicals, such as the chlorofluorocarbons typically used in air-conditioning systems. The Clean Air Act also requires that the National Emission Standard for Hazardous Air Pollutants (NESHAP) impose limits for EtO, formaldehyde, and xylene. However, these limits are very high and it is unlikely that a health care facility would exceed them. Additionally, hospitals, physician offices, and other health care facilities are, for now, exempted from the EtO emissions standard. Individual states, however, may have emissions standards for EtO that do not exempt health care facilities. The Clean Air Act sets emissions standards for steam-generating units, such as hospital boilers, but the EPA has noted that natural gas-fired boilers have such low emissions of particulate and sulfur dioxide that control technologies presently available are not reasonable. The EPA suggests that oil-fired boilers be run on low-sulfur oil, and has set its limits for coal-fired boilers based on available control technologies. The act also requires permits for major sources of air pollution.

· · · · · · · · · · · ·

ENVIRONMENTAL ISSUES IN ACQUISITIONS

As noted previously, CERCLA can impose liability on landowners or other potentially responsible parties for past activities on a particular piece of property. Thus, the EPA can assess all or a portion of the costs of cleanup against persons or entities that may have contributed to the problem. This should be of particular importance to hospitals, or to any other entity that has ever disposed of hazardous waste, because the potential for liability does not depend on illegal activity (the activities may have been perfectly legal at the time), connection with the property (the entity may not have even known where its waste was going), culpability (the entity may have done everything necessary to attempt to stay within the law or good practice), or even any activity involving hazardous waste (the owner of contaminated property may be required to pay for all or a portion of the cleanup, even if it never dumped waste on the property). It is this latter aspect of CERCLA liability that is implicated in the performance of environmental risk assessments prior to the acquisition of real property.

There is a defense to liability under CERCLA that is available to the innocent landowner. To avail itself of the defense, the landowner needs to show, by a preponderance of the evidence, that he or she had no knowledge, at the time of purchase (which must be after all dumping has occurred), that hazardous substances had ever been dumped at the site. The defense is further available only if, at the time of purchase, the buyer exercised due diligence and made all appropriate inquiry into previous ownership and past uses of the property as would be consistent with good commercial practice. The defense is not available for previous landowners. The question, of course, then revolves around the amount of inquiry necessary to assure a buyer that the property has not been contaminated by past use. This is the purpose of the environmental risk assessment.

Environmental Risk Assessments

An environmental assessment should be performed by a knowledgeable individual or individuals, though there is little consensus at present about an assessor's training or even the breadth and scope of the assessment. There is little in the way of certification or credentialing available for consultants who perform environmental risk assessments. Professional engineers, industrial hygienists, or specially trained environmental specialists are good choices for this type of engagement, as long as they have expertise in environmental risk assessment. Prior to hiring a consultant, a facility would be well advised to request résumés and references and then should be careful to investigate them. However, it also is advisable to bear in mind that this is one area of endeavor in which the clients are seldom completely satisfied with the consultant's work, regardless of his or her skill or expertise.

Three levels of environmental risk assessment may be undertaken in assessing a proposed acquisition. The Phase I assessment is the most basic. It exists only to identify potential risks, without any development of the severity of the risk. If the Phase I assessment gives a reasonable basis to believe that a significant environmental risk exists on the property, a Phase II assessment is necessary. The Phase II assessment seeks to confirm or deny the presence of contamination, using valid scientific sampling methods. The Phase III assessment is performed only if the Phase II assessment yields evidence of environmental contamination. The Phase III assessment seeks to document the extent of the risk and to assess the feasibility of engineering controls or other cleanup measures.[113] Only the Phase I assessment is required in the vast majority of acquisitions; hence, the discussion that follows will center on this type of analysis. In general, a Phase I assessment involves a thorough inspection of the subject parcel of property and a review of public records on both the property and surrounding properties.

Inspection of the Property A physical inspection of the property may be the most valuable part of the Phase I assessment. This should involve a thorough inspection of the structure of the building, including its contents and fixtures. One of the more valuable aspects of the physical inspection is an interview with the director of plant operations, or with maintenance personnel who have worked in the facility for a long time. Each of the following topics should be discussed with plant operations personnel and then verified by inspection:

- *Presence of ACM:* Although there probably is no potential CERCLA liability associated with ACM, as noted previously, virtually all friable ACM and some nonfriable ACM must come out of a building sooner or later, and it must be dealt with whenever renovations are undertaken or the building is razed. ACM may be present as thermal system insulation (pipe wrap, or jackets on water heaters or boilers), which may require access to pipe chases and other concealed areas. Sprayed-on fireproofing for structural members commonly contains asbestos. ACM also may be present in acoustic plaster, which was used in the ceilings and walls of auditoriums, chapels, and corridors. Asbestos in any of these materials may be friable; hence, care should be taken during the inspection not to disturb them. ACM may be present as floor tile (old nine-by-nine-inch floor tiles often contain asbestos), and asbestos also may be found in the mastic that holds floor tiles down. Ceiling tiles, as well as roofing materials, can contain asbestos. These latter types of ACM usually are not friable, which generally means that they are less dangerous during day-to-day operations but still may present problems in renovations. The quantity and condition of all materials suspected to be ACM should be carefully recorded during the assessment.

- *Presence of USTs:* There may be filling ports, air vents, or lines coming through the wall of the boiler or generator rooms if USTs are present on the property. If the USTs are still in service, plant operations personnel should be asked about leak detection methods, and these records should be reviewed. It is possible that there may be USTs on the property that are no longer in service. These may or may not have been closed properly, and state law may require that such tanks be removed.

● *Presence and condition of any electrical transformers:* Although such uses are now prohibited, in the past, transformers were filled with fluid that was often adulterated with polychlorinated biphenyls (PCBs). These chemicals served to reduce the fire hazard presented by the transformer. In the event of a spill or a fire, however, the building could be, or could have been, contaminated with PCBs, which are relatively expensive to dispose of. The EPA regulates PCB waste, which it defines as waste containing 50 ppm of PCB in the fluid.[114] The local utility company may be able to determine whether a transformer contains PCBs, or may have previously labeled the transformer as being free of PCBs.

● *Areas for bulk storage of waste materials:* It is entirely appropriate to have some waste on hand that has not yet accumulated to a large enough quantity to warrant removal. However, more than one drum of any particular type of waste should be cause for concern. Similarly, rusted or leaking drums, or any drums that appear to have been stored for long periods, also are cause for concern.

● *Signs of hazardous waste dumping on property outside the building:* Lawn areas in which grass does not grow, or areas that have bare spots in peculiar patterns, should be noted, as should distressed vegetation, such as an inordinate number of dead trees or shrubs. A sheen on puddles, creeks, or ponds may indicate past dumping or leaks from USTs. Sidewalks and driveways also should be inspected for stains, which could indicate the presence of hazardous materials.

Records Review   The review of public records should include a title search for the property going back to when it was virgin land. The title search should elicit information on ownership that can then be crosschecked with other materials (such as a federal or state census of manufacturers) to determine the type of industry present at the site. If the previous use was in an industry known to have used large quantities of hazardous materials, further scrutiny is advisable.

Other public records also are available for review. Aerial photographs may be available in the county engineer's office that would show buildings and potential waste dumps, such as barrels, drums, or lagoons. In addition, historical photographs that depict activities at the site may be available. Court records can be reviewed to determine whether previous owners were sued for nuisance complaints.

The federal EPA and several state agencies maintain a priority list of known hazardous waste sites, showing their relative priority for cleanup. Obviously, the list should be checked to see if the subject property is on it, but it also should be checked to see if any listings are close to the subject property. Many of the state agencies also have lists of UST locations, including listings of sites on which leaking USTs have been discovered. This list should be checked to see if there have been any leaks near the subject property. If any such entries are discovered, further investigation of possible site contamination due to migration or transport of hazardous materials should be undertaken.

Records do not necessarily need to be public in order to qualify for review. If the property contains a going concern, its records also should be reviewed. Of particular importance are records of hazardous waste disposal. The facility should have received a completed manifest from every shipment of hazardous waste that indicates the date and manner of final disposal. An inquiry can be made to the state EPA regarding any problems that the disposal contractor may have had in the past. Purchasing records may give an indication of the quantities of solvents or other chemicals previously obtained by and used at the facility.

....
CONCLUSION

Occupational safety and health and environmental impairment are issues of ever-increasing importance for health care facilities. Gone are the days when a health care facility could blithely assume that whatever it did was correct and that it was not subject to regulation by external agencies. The penalties for disregarding these issues may come in the form of civil monetary penalties, criminal indictments, class action lawsuits, lawsuits brought as a result of nuisances, increased community dissatisfaction with its uncaring neighbor, and increased illness and injury rates, with a concomitant increase in workers' compensation costs and decrease in productivity.

Fortunately, none of this is insurmountable. Each health care facility needs a program by which it can manage these exposures. The first step in any such program is to identify each potential exposure. The facility must then be certain that it understands all the federal, state, and local regulations that might apply to the problem. Next, the facility should implement a workable plan that will adequately and effectively resolve the situation, and that can be monitored for effectiveness. All employees need to understand the plan as well as their roles therein. They must appreciate the potential for exposure or damage that exists in these matters so that they will perform their jobs carefully and diligently. Unfortunately, if the facility neglects to implement a program or manage these exposures, there are any number of agencies and entities out there that will not only penalize them for their neglect but also mandate management of the exposures on their terms.

Endnotes

1. These states and territories include Alaska, Arizona, California, Connecticut, Hawaii, Indiana, Iowa, Kentucky, Maryland, Michigan, Minnesota, Nevada, New Mexico, North Carolina, Oregon, Puerto Rico, South Carolina, Tennessee, Utah, Vermont, Virgin Islands, Virginia, Washington, and Wyoming.

2. These states and territories include Alaska, Arizona, Hawaii, Indiana, Iowa, Kentucky, Maryland, Minnesota, South Carolina, Tennessee, Utah, Virgin Islands, Virginia, and Wyoming.

3. Bureau of National Affairs. *BNA's Health Care Facilities Guide (Suppl.)*. Washington, D.C.: BNA, 1994, §2100, pp. 4001–4003.

4. *Corrosion Pipe Fittings v. EPA*, F.2d., No. 89-4596 (5th Cir. Oct. 18, 1991).

5. 29 CFR §1910.1000, Table Z-3.

6. U.S. Environmental Protection Agency. *Managing Asbestos in Place: A Building Owner's Guide to Operations and Maintenance Programs for Asbestos-Containing Materials*. Washington, D.C.: U.S. EPA, 1990.

7. Fumento, M. "The Asbestos Rip-Off," *American Spectator*, Oct. 1989, pp. 21–26.

8. 29 CFR §1910.1001.

9. 29 CFR §1926.1101.

10. 29 CFR §1910.1030.

11. *Bragdon v. Abbott*, 524 U.S. 624, 118 S. Ct. 2196 (1998).

12. Occupational Safety and Health Administration. *How to Prevent Needlestick Injuries: Answers to Some Important Questions* (OSHA Pub. No. 3161).

13. 29 CFR §1910.1030(f)(2).

14. The wording of the declination is found at 29 CFR §1910.1030, Appendix A. It reads: "I understand that due to my occupational exposure to blood or other potentially infectious materials I may be at risk of acquiring hepatitis B virus (HBV) infection. I have been given the opportunity to be vaccinated with hepatitis B vaccine, at no charge to myself. However, I decline hepatitis B vaccination at this time. I understand that by declining this vaccine, I continue to be at risk of acquiring hepatitis B, a serious disease. If in the future I continue to have occupational exposure to blood or other potentially infectious materials and I want to be vaccinated with hepatitis B vaccine, I can receive the vaccine series at no charge to me."

15. 29 CFR §1910.1030(d)(2),(4).

16. Occupational Safety and Health Administration. "Glass Capillary Tubes: Joint Advisory About Potential Risks," Feb. 22, 1999.

17. *Ibid.*

18. An excellent evaluation tool can be found in OSHA's *How to Prevent Needlestick Injuries: Answers to Some Important Questions* (OSHA Pub. No. 3161).

19. Pugliese, G., and Salahuddin, M. *Sharps Injury Prevention Program: A Step-by-Step Guide.* Chicago, Ill.: American Hospital Association, 1999; Occupational Safety and Health Administration. *How to Prevent Needlestick Injuries: Answers to Some Important Questions* (OSHA Pub. No. 3161); Occupational Safety and Health Administration. "Record Summary of the Request for Information on Occupational Exposure to Bloodborne Pathogens Due to Percutaneous Injury," May 20, 1999.

20. 29 CFR §1910.1000, Table Z-2. Centers for Disease Control and Prevention. "Public Health Service Guidelines for the Management of Health-Care Worker Exposures to HIV and Recommendations for Post-Exposure Prophylaxis." *Morbidity and Mortality Weekly Report, 47*(RR-7), May 15, 1998. pp. 1–28.

21. 29 CFR §1027.

22. 29 CFR §1910.146.

23. Proposed 29 CFR §1910.900, as published at 64 *Fed. Reg.* 65768, Nov. 22, 1999.

24. Proposed 29 CFR §1910.901, as published at 64 *Fed. Reg.* 66068.

25. Proposed 29 CFR §1910.903, as published at 64 *Fed. Reg.* 66069.

26. Proposed 29 CFR §§1910.911-.913, as published at 64 *Fed. Reg.* 66069-66070.

27. Proposed 29 CFR §§1910.914-.916, as published at 64 *Fed. Reg.* 66069.

28. Proposed 29 CFR §§1910.917-.922, as published at 64 *Fed. Reg.* 66070-66072.

29. Proposed 29 CFR §§1910.923-.928, as published at 64 *Fed. Reg.* 66072.

30. Proposed 29 CFR §§1910.929-.935, as published at 64 *Fed. Reg.* 66072-66073.

31. Proposed 29 CFR §§1910.937-.938, as published at 64 *Fed. Reg.* 66073.

32. National Institute of Occupational Safety and Health. *Elements of Ergonomic Programs.* Washington, D.C.: USGPO (NIOSH Pub. No. 97-117, 1997); National Institute of Occupational Safety and Health. *Musculoskeletal Disorders and Workplace Factors: A Critical Review of Epidemiological Evidence for Work-Related Musculoskeletal Disorders of the Neck, Upper Extremity, and Low Back.* Washington, D.C.: USGPO (NIOSH Pub. No. 97-141, 1997); Fragala, G. *Ergonomics: How to Contain on-the-Job Injuries in Health Care.* Chicago, Ill.: Joint Commission on Accreditation of Healthcare Organizations, 1996; Bureau of National Affairs. *Cumulative Trauma Disorders in the Workplace: Costs, Prevention and Progress.* Washington, D.C.: Bureau of National Affairs, 1991; Occupational Safety and Health Administration. *Preventing Work-Related Musculoskeletal Disorders,* Feb. 1999; Occupational Safety and Health Administration. *OSHA Technical Manual.* Washington, D.C.: USGPO (OSHA Instruction No. TED 1.15, 1999).

33. National Institute for Occupational Safety and Health. *Back Belts: Do They Prevent Injury?* June 1997.

34. National Institute for Occupational Safety and Health. *Back Belts: Do They Prevent Injury?* June 1997; National Institute for Occupational Safety and Health. *Workplace Use of Back Belts: Review and Recommendations* (NIOSH Pub. No. 94-122). Washington, D.C.: USGPO, July 1994; National Institute for Occupational Safety and Health. "NIOSH Facts: Back Belts," July 1997.

35. EtO sterilizers often use dichlorodifluoromethane (CFC-12) as the diluent, although its production is banned by the Clean Air Act (42 USC §7401, et seq.) after January 1, 1996. It may be possible to substitute HCFC-124 for CFC-12 without modifying the equipment. (HCFC-124 will not be banned by the Clean Air Act until 2030.)

36. 29 CFR §1910.1047(b)(c).

37. 29 CFR §1910.1048(c).

38. National Institute for Occupational Safety and Health. *Registry of Toxic Effects of Chemical Substances.* Washington, D.C.: NIOSH, 1985, p. 1351; as noted in NIOSH, *Guidelines for Protecting the Safety and Health of Health Care Workers* (Pub. No. 88-110). Washington, D.C.: US GPO, 1988, p. 5–13.

39. 29 CFR §1910.1200.

40. American Conference of Governmental Industrial Hygienists, 1330 Kemper Meadow Drive, Cincinnati, OH 45240.

41. 29 CFR §1910.120.

42. Canadian Healthcare Association. *The Reuse of Single-Use Medical Devices: Guidelines for Healthcare Facilities.* Arlington, Va.: Association for the Advancement of Medical Instrumentation, 1996.

43. National Institute for Occupational Safety and Health. *Occupational Diseases: A Guide to Their Recognition* (Pub. No. 77-181). Washington, D.C.: USGPO, 1977.

44. 29 CFR §1910.1000, Table Z-1.

45. 29 CFR §1910.1450.

46. 29 CFR §1910.1025.

47. 29 CFR §1910.147.

48. 29 CFR §1910.1000, Table Z-1.

49. 29 CFR §1910.1000, Table Z-1.

50. NIOSH, *Guidelines for Protecting the Safety and Health of Health Care Workers*, pp. 5-30, 5-31.

51. Unless otherwise noted, all of the permissible exposure limits for the following miscellaneous solvents are found in 29 CFR §1910.1000, Table Z-1.

52. 29 CFR §1910.1028.

53. 29 CFR §1910.1000, Table Z-2.

54. 29 CFR §1910.95.

55. 29 CFR §1910.132.

56. 29 CFR §1910.134.

57. Centers for Disease Control and Prevention. "Guidelines for Preventing the Transmission of Tuberculosis in Health-Care Settings." *Morbidity and Mortality Weekly Report,* RR-17, Dec. 1990.

58. 29 USC §654(a)(1).

59. Lechter, G. S. "A Survey of Present Knowledge Concerning Low-Frequency Electromagnetic Radiation from Power Lines, Home Wiring, Appliances, Televisions and Computer Displays," *Medical Electronics,* available on Safe Technologies Corporation's Web site at www.milligauss.com. Safe Technologies Corporation sells ultra-low frequency computer monitors and Gauss meters (used to measure EMF).

60. See, for example, National Institute for Occupational Safety and Health. *NIOSH Fact Sheet: EMFs in the Workplace* (Pub. No. 96-129). Washington, D.C.: USGPO, 1996; Occupational Safety and Health Administration. "OSHA Technical Links: ELF Radiation," Sept. 27, 1999; New York State Health Department. "Info for Consumers: Power Lines Project—Questions and Answers," Oct. 1999, available at www.health.state.ny.us; Occupational Safety and Health Administration. *Working Safely with Video Display Terminals* (Pub. No. 3092), 1997.

61. Occupational Safety and Health Administration. "Controlling Occupational Exposure to Hazardous Drugs." *OSHA Instruction TED 1.15.* Washington, D.C.: OSHA, 1995, as referenced in *BNA's Health Care Facilities Guide.* Washington, D.C.: BNA, 1995, §500, pp. 4505–4602.

62. Gloster, H. M., and Roenigk, R. K. "Risk of Acquiring Human Papillomavirus from the Plume Produced by the Carbon Dioxide Laser in the Treatment of Warts." *Journal of the American Academy of Dermatology, 32*(3), Mar. 1995, pp. 436–441.

63. Johnson, G. K., and Robinson, W. S. "Human Immunodeficiency Virus-1 (HIV-1) in the Vapors of Surgical Power Instruments." *Journal of Medical Virology, 33*(1), Jan. 1991, pp. 47–50.

64. Ediger, M. N., and Matchette, L. S. "In Vitro Production of Viable Bacteriophage in a Laser Plume." *Lasers in Surgery and Medicine, 9*(3), Mar. 1989, pp. 296–299.

65. Matchette, L. S., Faaland, R. W., Royston, D. D., and Ediger, M. N. "In Vitro Production of Viable Bacteriophage in Carbon Dioxide and Argon Laser Plume." *Lasers in Surgery and Medicine, 11*(4), Apr. 1991, pp. 380–384.

66. Bryant, C., Gorman, R., Steward, J., and Whong, W. *NIOSH Health Hazard Evaluation Report: Bryn Mawr Hospital, Bryn Mawr, Pennsylvania* (Pub. No. 85-126-1932). Washington, D.C.: NIOSH, Sept. 1988.

67. Tomita, Y., and others. "Mutagenicity of Smoke Condensates Induced by CO2-Laser Irradiation and Electrocauterization." *Mutation Research, 89,* 1981, pp. 145–149.

68. *Ibid.*

69. Bryant, C., Gorman, R., Steward, J., and Whong, W. *NIOSH Health Hazard Evaluation Report: Bryn Mawr Hospital, Bryn Mawr, Pennsylvania* (Pub. No. 85-126-1932). Washington, D.C.: NIOSH, Sept. 1988.

70. Moss, C. E., and others. *NIOSH Health Hazard Evaluation Report. University of Utah Health Sciences Center, Salt Lake City, Utah* (Pub. no. 88-101-2008). Washington, D.C.: NIOSH, Feb. 1990.

71. *Ibid.*

72. Baggish, M. S., Baltoyannis, P., and Sze, E. "Protection of the Rat Lung from the Harmful Effects of Laser Smoke." *Lasers in Surgery and Medicine, 8*(3), Mar. 1988, pp. 248–253.

73. Wenish, B. L., Stenson, K. M., Wenig, B. M., and Tracey, D. "Effects of the Plume Produced by the ND:YAG Laser and Electrocautery on the Respiratory System." *Lasers in Surgery and Medicine, 13*(2), Feb. 1993, pp. 242–245.

74. See, for example, Fischer, A. *Contact Dermatitis* (2nd ed.). Philadelphia, Pa: Lea & Febiger, 1973.

75. National Institute for Occupational Safety and Health. *NIOSH Alert: Preventing Allergic Reactions to Natural Rubber Latex in the Workplace* (NIOSH Pub. No. 97-135). Washington, D.C.: USGPO, 1997.

76. Occupational Safety and Health Administration. "Technical Information Bulletin— Potential for Allergy to Natural Rubber Latex Gloves and Other Rubber Products," Apr. 12, 1999.

77. National Institute for Occupational Safety and Health. *NIOSH Alert: Preventing Allergic Reactions to Natural Rubber Latex in the Workplace* (NIOSH Pub. No. 97-135). Washington, D.C.: USGPO, 1997.

78. National Institute for Occupational Safety and Health. "NIOSH Facts: Latex Allergy," June 1997.

79. *Ibid.*

80. National Institute for Occupational Safety and Health. *Latex Allergy: A Prevention Guide* (NIOSH Pub. No. 98-113). Washington, D.C.: USGPO, 1998.

81. *Ibid.*

82. National Institutes of Health, Cognitive Sciences Branch. "Guidelines for Designing Effective and Healthy Learning Environments for Interactive Technologies," 1996.

83. *Ibid.*

84. *Ibid.*

85. *Ibid.*

86. The Human Factors Society. *American National Standard for Human Factors Engineering of Visual Display Terminal Workstations*, Santa Monica, Calif.: The Human Factors Society, Inc., 1988.

87. Occupational Safety and Health Administration. *Working Safely with Video Display Terminals* (Pub. No. 3092), 1997.

88. National Institute for Occupational Safety and Health. *Criteria for a Recommended Standard . . . Occupational Exposure to Waste Anesthetic Gases and Vapors* (Pub. No. 77-140). Washington, D.C.: USGPO, 1977.

89. Occupational Safety and Health Administration. *Technical Manual* (Instruction CPL 2-2.20B), Ch. 7, 1990, as referenced in *BNA's Health Care Facilities Guide*, §500, 1994, pp. 3005–3008.

90. National Institute for Occupational Safety and Health. *Criteria for a Recommended Standard . . . Occupational Exposure to Waste Anesthetic Gases and Vapors* (Pub. No. 77-140). Washington, D.C.: USGPO, 1977.

91. P.L. 91-596, §5(a)(1); 29 USC §654(a)(1).

92. National Institute for Occupational Safety and Health. *Occupational Diseases: A Guide to Their Recognition* (Pub. No. 77-181). Washington, D.C.: USGPO, 1977; National Institute for Occupational Safety and Health. *Guidelines for Protecting the Safety and Health of Health Care Workers*.

93. Occupational Safety and Health Administration. *Guidelines for Preventing Workplace Violence for Health Care and Social Service Workers* (OSHA Pub. No. 3148), 1998.

94. Joint Commission on Accreditation of Healthcare Organizations. *Comprehensive Accreditation Manual for Hospitals*. Oakbrook, Ill: JCAHO, 1996.

95. National Fire Protection Association. *Life Safety Code* (NFPA 101), Quincy, Mass.: NFPA, 1991.

96. 42 USC §6901, et seq.

97. 42 USC §9601, et seq.

98. 33 USC §1251, et seq.

99. 42 USC §7401, et seq.

100. 15 USC §2601, et seq.

101. 40 CFR §61, subpart M.

102. 40 CFR §763, subpart E, as extended by the Asbestos School Hazard Abatement Reauthorization Act (ASHARA), 40 CFR §763, subpart E, Appendix C, to all types of institutional and commercial buildings.

103. 42 USC §6901, et seq.

104. 40 CFR §§763.160–179.

105. 42 USC §9601, et seq., as required by 40 CFR part 302, Table 302A.

106. The National Response Center may be reached by calling (800) 424-8802. Reports must also be made to the appropriate regional administrator of the EPA.

107. U.S. Environmental Protection Agency. *Managing Asbestos in Place: A Building Owner's Guide to Operations and Maintenance Programs for Asbestos-Containing Materials* (Pub No. 20T-2003). Washington, D.C.: EPA, 1990; *Guidance for Controlling Asbestos-Containing Materials in Buildings* (Pub. No. 560/5-85-024). Washington, D.C.: EPA, 1985.

108. Conditionally exempt SQGs of hazardous waste are permitted to store up to 1 Kg of acutely hazardous waste, 100 Kg of residue or materials cleaned up after a spill of acutely hazardous waste, or 1,000 Kg of hazardous waste. Acutely hazardous wastes are listed in 40 CFR §§261.31, 261.32 and 261.33(e). None of these materials are commonly encountered in health care facilities.

109. 40 CFR §261.5.

110. See 40 CFR parts 262 266, 268, 270, 124; and RCRA Section 3010.

111. U.S. Environmental Protection Agency. *Operation and Maintenance of Hospital Medical Waste Incinerators*, Order No. EPA625689024 (available from the National Service Center for Environmental Publications, P.O. Box 42419, Cincinnati, OH 45242-2419).

112. 42 USC §7401, et seq.

113. See, for example, Wilson, A. R. *Environmental Risk: Identification and Management*. Chelsea, Mich.: Lewis Publishers, 1991.

114. 40 CFR part 761.

10

Physician and Allied Health Professional Credentialing

Mark A. Kadzielski
Michael G. Hercz

Credentialing is an area in which risk managers can significantly minimize the liabilities inherent in the health care industry. To do so, the risk manager documents credentialing policies and procedures, periodically reviews a facility's policies on credentialing, and keeps abreast of current developments in health care. Risk managers also should be prepared to function proactively by continually discovering new methods to prevent or minimize the potential liabilities associated with the provision of health care.

Historically, increased regulation has proven to be costly and has tended to increase regulatory scrutiny. Notwithstanding the fact that credentialing increases costs and scrutiny (as do malpractice awards), the institution and maintenance of written credentialing policies and procedures by a health care facility are among the most effective preemptive risk management tools available. Although facilities have little, if any, control over the practice of medicine, they can exercise substantial control over the qualifications and competence of physicians and allied health professionals (AHPs). Credentialing is a necessary and vital tool with which facilities can make strides in utilization patterns and quality outcomes. The concomitant costs and inconveniences are clearly outweighed by the benefits.

This chapter discusses aspects of credentialing for both physicians and AHPs, including sources of potential liability, state and federal credentialing provisions, and accreditation standards. It also describes AHP qualifications and scope of authority, as well as laws and regulations regarding AHP scope of practice.

CREDENTIALING OF PHYSICIANS

Credentialing is the process by which health care organizations review an applicant physician's licensure, certification, references, and other professional information pertaining to his or her qualifications and ability to provide health care services. It entails a decision by a health care organization that determines whether the applicant is qualified to provide health care services for that organization.

Credentialing involves granting medical staff membership to physicians and/or granting them clinical privileges, two diverse concepts that require the analysis of different criteria. Accordingly, health care organizations should clearly differentiate between them. Membership provides practitioners with a voice in the governance of the health care organization, while clinical privileges provide physicians with the opportunity to practice their clinical skills without being embroiled in the organization's affairs.

From a risk management perspective, granting privileges is more critical than granting membership alone, since significant potential liability accompanies the ability to perform surgical or nonsurgical procedures. But, as set forth in this chapter, such liability may be minimized by competent risk management.

The Joint Commission on Accreditation of Healthcare Organizations (JCAHO) defines *credentialing* as "[t]he process of obtaining, verifying, and assessing the qualifications of a health care practitioner to provide patient care services in or for a health care organization."[1] JCAHO further defines the process as a "series of activities designed to collect relevant data that will serve as the basis for decisions regarding appointments and reappointments to the medical staff, as well as delineation of clinical privileges for individual members of the medical staff."[2] The National Committee for Quality Assurance (NCQA), a private, not-for-profit organization that assesses and reports on the quality of managed care plans broadly defines *credentialing* as "the process [by which managed care organizations] select and evaluate the practitioners who practice within its delivery system."[3]

Credentialing is a multistep process that must be tailored to fit the specific needs of each health care organization, whether a hospital, a managed care organization (MCO), an integrated delivery system (IDS), an independent practice association (IPA), or some other type of delivery system. Tailoring can be accomplished by documenting credentialing processes in bylaws, rules and regulations, and policies and procedures, as applicable. However, facilities should not attempt to cut costs by applying another organization's bylaws, rules and regulations, or policies and procedures to their own operations. This practice can result in the application of inappropriate and inconsistent policies that can negatively affect accreditation status and the quality of care provided in the facility.

Credentialing standards ensure the uniform treatment of all staff members being considered for appointment and reappointment and provide the individual staff member with a fair, known, and systematic information collection process. Further, strict adherence to a documented credentialing system can protect a facility in credentialing disputes. Health care institutions should not fall prey to the mistaken belief that only large organizations with plentiful resources can afford to scrutinize applicants' credentials carefully and discipline errant physicians in a uniform and systematic manner. No organization, large or small, should underestimate the importance of the credentialing function.

Federal Law on Credentialing

An integral part of risk management is a working familiarity with federal and state laws concerning credentialing and accreditation standards specific to the health care delivery system in which they will be applied. Various credentialing laws and accreditation standards are set forth here.

The Medicare Conditions of Participation for Hospitals provide that "[t]he medical staff must examine credentials of candidates for medical staff membership. . . ."[4] They also require the collection of credentialing information for purposes of reappointment to the medical staff.[5] The Medicare Conditions of Participation for Long Term Care Facilities provide that "[p]rofessional program staff must be licensed, certified, or registered, as applicable, to provide professional services by the State in which he or she practices."[6] The Conditions of Participation for Home Health Agencies provide that "[p]ersonnel practices . . . are supported by appropriate, written personnel policies. Personnel records include qualifications and licensure that are kept current."[7] The Medicare Conditions of Participation for Comprehensive Outpatient Rehabilitation Facilities provide that "[p]ersonnel that provide service must be licensed, certified, or registered in accordance with applicable State and local laws."[8] Medicare also prescribes similar Conditions of Participation for Critical Access Hospitals,[9] and for Clinics, Rehabilitation Agencies, and Public Health Agencies as Providers of Outpatient Physical Therapy and Speech-Language Pathology Services.[10]

State Law on Credentialing

To varying degrees, most states supplement federal statutory credentialing provisions with their own legislative pronouncements on credentialing. Through the enactment of regulations, many states require a health care facility to credential its physicians before granting clinical privileges. For example, in California, "all members of the medical staff [are] required to demonstrate their ability to perform surgical and/or other procedures competently and to the satisfaction of an appropriate committee . . . at the time of application for appointment to the staff and at least every two years thereafter."[11] Further, the doctrine of corporate liability for negligent credentialing, a state law tort theory, necessitates implementing and maintaining written credentialing policies and procedures.

Accreditation Standards

Accreditation standards require that physicians be credentialed prior to being granted privileges to practice medicine at a facility. Apart from state law and the Medicare Conditions of Participation for Hospitals, a governing body's responsibility for credentialing physicians who practice within its hospital is established by accrediting bodies such as the JCAHO. The JCAHO standards require that the mechanisms for appointment or reappointment to the medical staff and the initial granting and renewal or revision of clinical privileges be fully documented in the medical staff bylaws, rules and regulations, and policies.[12]

Outside the hospital context, similar standards exist for MCOs and ambulatory surgery centers (ASCs) through accrediting bodies such as the NCQA and the Accreditation Association for Ambulatory Health Care (AAAHC), as well as a number of others. For example, the NCQA requires that "[t]he managed care organization document the mechanism for the credentialing and recredentialing of MDs, DOs, DDSs, DPMs, DCs, and other licensed independent practitioners with whom it contracts or employs who treat members outside the inpatient setting and who fall within its scope of authority and action."[13]

Internet Credentialing

With the advent of the Internet, new opportunities are available for facilities in their ongoing efforts to credential practitioners. Online databases, such as the Office of Inspector General's (OIG) List of Excluded Individuals/Entities (LEIE) and Web sites maintained by state licensing authorities, provide additional information regarding practitioners to the public, including consumers and individuals not otherwise entitled to similar information maintained by the National Practitioner Data Bank (NPDB) or the Healthcare Integrity and Protection Data Bank. The existence of these databases may also establish a new standard of care regarding the frequency of checking whether practitioners have been disciplined. The OIG may impose a Civil Monetary Penalty of up to $10,000 for each item or services furnished by an individual excluded from participation in a federal health care program (such as Medicare, Medicaid, and so on) *on any individual or entity which contracts with the excluded individual.* For liability to be imposed, the provider submitting the claims for health care items or services furnished by an excluded individual must either "know or *should* know" that the person was excluded.[14] Thus, the OIG "urges health care providers and entities to check the OIG List of Excluded Individuals/Entities on the OIG Web site (www.hhs.gov/oig) prior to hiring or contracting with individuals or entities."[15] Providers should also "periodically check the OIG Web site for determining the participation/exclusion status of current employees and contractors." Although the OIG does not expressly state how often providers should check the Web site, one may infer the appropriate frequency from the fact that the OIG updates the LEIE monthly.

············

DOCUMENTATION OF CREDENTIALING CRITERIA

Key to the uniform application of credentialing criteria is documentation of the criteria in a facility's governance documents, such as the bylaws, rules and regulations, and policies, procedures, and protocols. Each of these documents serves a different function. Generally, the *bylaws* provide an organization's basic framework. In the hospital context, medical staff bylaws delineate the staff's responsibilities, the basic framework for committees and members, the process by which staff members are disciplined, and the delegation of functions. The *rules and regulations* provide additional details on operational aspects of performing the responsibilities assigned by the bylaws. At a minimum, documentation of, and adherence to, written credentialing criteria delineated in governance documents invalidates the argument that a facility randomly and discriminatorily applies its credentialing criteria. A health care organization's *policies, procedures, and protocols* contain the detailed rules and regulations that govern day-to-day operations. These documents can contain as much detailed information as is deemed necessary. In fact, it is advisable in many circumstances that they contain the most detailed information available in order to guide the medical staff and ensure consistency in the day-to-day decision making of the organization's physicians.

Written credentialing criteria should be directly related to patient care and based on objective factors such as education, experience, and current competence rather than on arbitrary distinctions based on title. If distinctions are to be made between the types of services that can be provided by two groups of practitioners (for example, radiologists and emergency department physicians, orthopedists and podiatrists, or psychiatrists and psychologists), they should derive from *objective criteria* and the *standard of care in the community* to avoid the appearance of discrimination based solely on profession. Properly developed and documented credentialing criteria that are applied appropriately should withstand the strictest scrutiny.

In addition, written credentialing criteria should be facility-specific and based upon such factors as a facility's license capacity and availability of equipment, personnel, and services. Physicians should not be granted privileges to perform procedures that exceed the facility's financial and personnel resources. Drafters and reviewers of credentialing criteria should be cognizant of the health facility's assets and limitations when reviewing the credentialing criteria.

Documentation of credentialing criteria should not be done haphazardly, at the last minute, or after the fact. Credentialing criteria must be reviewed by committees and/or bodies that are responsible for establishing those criteria, such as a credentialing committee, an executive committee, and the hospital governing body. To minimize legal liabilities, it is vital for leadership such as the executive committee and the governing body to provide oversight and input, as well as final approval.

············

POTENTIAL LIABILITIES RELATED TO CREDENTIALING

Risk managers play an important role in minimizing potential liabilities. Specifically, they must be vigilant in advocating the establishment and maintenance of written policies and procedures. Health care facilities that credential physicians may be liable to those very same physicians for discrimination; restraint of trade; economic credentialing; violation of the facility's bylaws, rules and regulations, and policies and procedures; and a plethora of other actions or inactions. Risk managers must be wary of not only the acts or omissions for which a facility may be liable to physicians who exercise privileges there, but also the potential liabilities a facility may have to patients, their families, estates, and/or legal representatives.

Early implementation of written policies and procedures or protocols can be accomplished only when risk managers keep abreast of the rapidly evolving health care sector and are able to identify potential liabilities before they occur. Failure to perceive potential liability issues early will result in a lack of written policies and procedures and the absence of a uniform and sound approach to risk issues, thus increasing the risk of litigation.

Almost all risk managers and health care providers are familiar with the liability associated with less than optimal outcomes and the importance of maintaining guidelines intended to minimize such liability. Sometimes overlooked, however, is the need to advocate the implementation of policies to minimize the legal risk associated with negligent credentialing, economic credentialing, breach of privacy, violation of the Americans with Disabilities Act (ADA), and a physician's breach of a "duty to warn."

Negligent Credentialing

Traditionally, there was no institutional liability for the negligence of individual providers. However, beginning in 1965 with *Darling v. Charleston Community Memorial Hospital*, various state courts began recognizing a new doctrine called "hospital corporate liability."[16] In *Darling*, the Supreme Court of Illinois held that the hospital had an independent duty to ensure that high-quality care was rendered at its facility, and held the hospital accountable for negligently screening the competency of its medical staff. Numerous states have adopted some form of the hospital corporate liability theory thereby providing some legal relief for the tort of negligent credentialing, including Arizona, California, Colorado, Georgia, Michigan, Nebraska, Nevada, New Jersey, New York, North Carolina, North Dakota, Pennsylvania, Rhode Island, Texas, Washington, West Virginia, and Wisconsin.[17]

Health care facilities and providers should not be surprised to see the doctrine of corporate liability extended to MCOs, IPAs, and IDSs in the near future.[18] Like hospitals, courts will likely conclude that such entities have a duty to credential and recredential affiliated physicians and monitor the quality of care provided by affiliated physicians. And if health care delivery systems credential physicians, such systems have a duty to credential them thoroughly and properly. If an MCO, IPA, or IDS breaches its duty to provide high-quality care to a patient by failing to screen out incompetent physicians or take appropriate measures against physicians who are providing substandard medical care, the entity may be negligent based on a theory of corporate liability.

The nexus between the health care delivery system and the medical care provided may be based on a health care system's advertising claims. Advertising campaigns used by health care entities to attract new consumers generally contain representations regarding the qualifications of affiliated physicians and the high quality of care that patients can expect from a particular plan's physicians. Representations regarding the quality of care to be provided by physicians affiliated with MCOs, IPAs, and IDSs are much more direct than the implied representations attributed by courts to hospitals upon which corporate liability was based in the 1960s. Thus, based on the same theoretical underpinnings, liability may be easily extended to MCOs, IPAs, and IDSs.[19]

Moreover, we may see corporate liability further extended to management services organizations (MSOs) and other independent contractors that credential physicians on behalf of a hospital, MCO, IPA, or IDS. Risk managers in MSOs must be aware of such potential liability and should advocate the institution and maintenance of uniform written credentialing procedures if the facility has contracted for, or is entrusted with, credentialing functions.

Economic Credentialing

Currently, economic credentialing is a bone of contention between some physicians and health care institutions. The term *economic credentialing* has been used to denote a credentialing, selection, or termination action based, at least in part, on economic considerations. The current absence of a definitive determination by state legislatures, courts, and professional associations on the parameters of using economic criteria in credentialing decisions and the legal and medical communities' failure to provide an acceptable definition of the term may render the use of economic criteria a double-edged sword with costly consequences.

In simple terms, economic credentialing is the use, in the credentialing of a physician, of data that indicate his or her effect on the financial success of a facility. This term also refers to the use of data that reflect the proportion of indigent patients admitted or treated by a particular physician at a facility. The economic factors generally relate to a physician's utilization of health care resources and a provider's profits for the facility resulting from his or her payer mix, market share, charges, and collections.

Apart from the position (or lack thereof) of professional associations, the legislatures, and the courts on economic credentialing, the economic pressures on health care systems make it probable that economic factors will continue to be used in credentialing decisions. To minimize potential liability, risk managers who are employed by facilities that use economic credentialing should advocate and assist in the development of a written protocol addressing the use of economic credentialing.

Hospital-based risk managers must be familiar with Medicare's position on the use of economic credentialing by hospitals. The Medicare Conditions of Participation for Hospitals provide that "[t]he governing body must . . . [e]nsure that under no circumstances is the accordance of staff membership or professional privileges in the hospital dependent solely upon certification, fellowship, or membership in a specialty body or society."[20] Accordingly, if economic criteria are to be used in hospital credentialing decisions, they should not be the *sole* basis for terminating or granting medical staff privileges. If this does occur, the risk manager should be alert to the possibility of not merely civil liability but also potential administrative penalties that the Health Care Financing Administration can impose, such as exclusion from the Medicare program.

Using economic criteria in a uniform, reasonable manner to educate practitioners and to identify the links between economic factors and quality of care may minimize potential liability. For example, disclosure of reasons for refusal to grant privileges or for termination of privileges may diminish the legal liability associated with economic credentialing. Risk managers also may advocate educating physicians about the efficient use of health care resources. One such approach is to use physician profiling of cost, quality, and utilization data. Sharing profiled information with physicians allows them to change their approach to a more cost-effective one while preserving the quality of care. Furthermore, challenges to economic credentialing may hinge on inclusion of these procedures in written governance documents such as the bylaws, especially in states such as Florida, where bylaws are deemed to be a contract between facility and physician.

Breach of Patient Privacy

A breach of a patient's privacy rights may occur in a variety of ways, ranging from intrusion on a patient's privacy in his or her room to the unauthorized disclosure of patient-identifiable medical information. Although it may be relatively easy to prevent intrusion into a patient's room, other breaches of privacy, such as improper disclosure of either patient information or individual providers' quality outcome information, can be much more difficult to control. As a result, it is essential that a facility implement and maintain written policies and procedures pertaining to disclosure. Accordingly, the risk manager should be familiar with state law regarding privacy rights.

In addition, Medicare's recently added "Patients' Rights" Condition of Participation for Hospitals expressly states that the "patient has the right to personal privacy" and "the right to confidentiality of his or her clinical records."[21] Although Medicare has yet to explain how it will interpret this Condition of Participation, it is certain that patient privacy has become a top concern among government investigators, due in part to the advent of the Internet and the increased accessibility of information via such developments as the electronic medical record.

Disclosure of Patient-Identifiable Information

In this era of managed care, compliance with state law regarding disclosure of patient-identifiable information is becoming increasingly difficult because of the proliferation of contracts between individuals and entities pertaining to medical or administrative support functions. Further, the proliferation of complicated delivery systems that affiliate with different types of providers has made it more difficult to determine to whom medical records may be released. And in most states, state law has failed to keep pace with the rapid changes in the health care sector, thus increasing the risks associated with the provision of health care.

Although the disclosure of patient-identifiable information may be an unavoidable reality in the race for managed care contracts, facilities should not risk the liability associated with the wrongful disclosure of patient-identifiable information in contravention of applicable state law. Any disclosure of patient-identifiable information should be reviewed, in detail, by legal counsel prior to the execution of agreements containing promises regarding disclosure of such information. Risk managers should notify and assist in educating the medical records department—and all other appropriate departments—about the liability associated with wrongful disclosure and identify the release of medical information as an area of risk. Further, facilities should maintain written guidelines on disclosure of such information.

Disclosure of Individual Providers' Quality Outcome Information

Driven by the need to compete in a changing health care market, many different entities, such as managed care plans, payers, and employers, may seek quality outcome information from a health care delivery system. The quantifiable nature of such information renders it an effective marketing tool that can be easily disseminated to the public, which can then compare individual providers and make informed choices about the quality of the providers associated with a managed care plan. Quality outcome information also allows employers to easily ascertain which managed care plan will be the best one for its employees.

However, legal and regulatory constraints are often imposed on health care delivery systems that can result in the nondisclosure of information or the limitation of the types of information that can be disclosed. The entities to whom quality outcome information can be disclosed should be independently determined by each health care facility with the assistance of its legal counsel, which will play a crucial role in maneuvering the facility through the quagmire of legal and regulatory provisions. By creating written protocols and guidelines for disclosure, the risk manager can assist the organization in handling such highly sensitive and confidential information.

First, such protocols should be based on applicable state law—if it exists. Second, facilities should determine whether quality outcome information is protected from discovery. Statutory privileges accorded to peer review information may protect quality outcome information if such information is discussed and analyzed in the peer review process for peer review purposes. Whether a facility is willing to disclose such information should be dependent, in part, on whether the information is protected by state law. Third, if a facility's written policy permits the release of such information, the facility should obtain written authorization from physicians allowing its release. Preferably, such release should be obtained upon the physician's membership in the organization rather than at the time that such information is requested.

Depending on the scope of payers' requests, facilities may want to consider disclosing quality outcome information—provided that patient and physician anonymity are maintained. Disclosure of provider-specific quality outcome information, however, is plagued with peril. The provider whose quality outcome information is released may have some legal rights. The wrongful disclosure of provider-specific quality outcome information may embroil a facility in costly litigation. Accordingly, quality outcome information should be released only in accordance with a written policy based on applicable state law and reviewed by the appropriate facility departments and individuals.

Violation of the Americans with Disabilities Act and/ or the Rehabilitation Act

As of 1999, the impact of the Americans with Disabilities Act (ADA) and Section 504 of the Rehabilitation Act on the credentialing of health care practitioners remains unclear. The ADA prohibits discrimination based on the physical or mental status of an individual.[22]

Section 504 of the Rehabilitation Act similarly prevents discrimination based on the physical or mental status of an individual in any program or activity receiving federal financial assistance, and thus Section 504 presumably applies to any health care facility "participating" in either Medicare or Medicaid.[23]

Courts have begun to address the applicability of the ADA to credentialing decisions at private hospitals and/or other nonpublic health care facilities. In *Menkowitz v. Pottstown Memorial Medical Center*, the Third Circuit held that both the ADA and Section 504 of the Rehabilitation Act prohibits disability discrimination against a medical doctor with staff privileges at a hospital.[24] In *Menkowitz*, a physician claimed he had been discharged in violation of the ADA and Section 504 of the Rehabilitation Act when his clinical privileges were summarily suspended after he disclosed to the medical staff that he had been diagnosed with attention-deficit disorder. However, despite *Menkowitz*, it unclear whether and how the ADA applies to practitioner credentialing.

Facilities are granted broad discretion to collect and verify different types of information in the credentialing process. According to the JCAHO, each facility must independently determine the applicability of the ADA to its medical staff.[25] Thus, a facility has the discretion to determine whether it will require information pertaining to the physical or mental condition of the medical staff applicant.

The NCQA similarly gives MCOs the following guidance on questioning applicants regarding their physical and mental health status: "[t]he applicant completes an application for membership. The application includes a statement by the applicant regarding reasons for any inability to perform the essential functions of the position, with or without accommodation; [and] the lack of present illegal drug use. . . ."[26] The NCQA further provides that "[t]he exact statement or inquiry may vary depending on applicable legal requirements such as the Americans with Disabilities Act."[27]

Clearly, the JCAHO explanation of intent behind the standard—"the act does not appear to prohibit inquiry as to the ability of the applicant . . . to perform the specific privileges requested"[28]—is ambiguous. The NCQA similarly provides little guidance on the issue of the applicability of the ADA to private hospitals. Whether the ADA is applicable to health care facilities, and exactly when a facility can inquire about applicants' mental and physical health status, will remain unclear until the ADA's applicability to the credentialing process is further clarified by legislative or judicial intervention.

For guidance, facilities may want to review the Equal Employment Opportunity Commission (EEOC) enforcement guidelines on ADA applicability. Although these guidelines do not provide guidance on ADA applicability to health care facilities, they may be useful in determining what types of health status questions can be posed to applicants and when.

Based on accreditation standards and the EEOC enforcement guidelines, it appears reasonable to request information from practitioners regarding their physical and mental ability to perform the clinical privileges requested in connection with their application to the facility. However, ideally the information should be considered *only after* the applicant has otherwise been approved for medical staff membership and/or clinical privileges in order to avoid the inference that an adverse decision was based solely on the disclosed disability. If the practitioner discloses a disability covered under the ADA (or Section 504 of the Rehabilitation Act), the facility should assess whether reasonable accommodation would allow the practitioner to exercise clinical privileges and/or perform medical staff duties consistent with the standards imposed upon nondisabled practitioners. The facility should also carefully consider the manner in which questions regarding physical and mental ability are phrased. As a result, all policy documents and applications addressing health status inquiries should be reviewed by legal counsel. Risk managers may, however, minimize liability by warning appropriate departments and individuals of such perils and advocating a review of existing bylaws, rules and regulations, and applications.

Breach of Duty to Warn

At the first take, the doctrine of a physician's duty to warn appears rather simple: physicians must discuss their patients' medical condition and course of treatment with them or their legal representatives. Often, however, facilities fail to implement written protocols pertaining to a physician's duty to warn. At times, physicians also neglect to carry out that duty.

In 1995, the health care industry eagerly awaited adjudication of *Reisner v. Regents of the University of California.*[29] In *Reisner*, a physician and a hospital were sued by the sexual partner of a teenager who had died of AIDS—contracted after receiving a transfusion. Although the hospital and the physician knew of the patient's exposure to HIV within days of its occurrence, the physician apparently failed to warn her. Three years later, the patient, unaware that she had contracted the virus, engaged in sexual relations with the plaintiff and exposed him to the virus. A California court held the hospital liable for the physician's failure to warn his patient that she had contracted HIV. (*Reisner* should not be confused with *Tarasoff v. Regents of the University of California*, in which a psychiatrist was sued because he failed to warn a third party of potential harm from his patient.[30])

Such liability might have been avoided by implementation of, and adherence to, a carefully drafted protocol pertaining to effective communication between a physician and his or her patient or the patient's legal representative. Although the *Reisner* decision is not applicable outside California, risk managers should: (1) be familiar with a physician's duty to warn his or her patients; (2) advocate and assist their facilities in developing and implementing written policies and procedures aimed at minimizing such risks through notification and counseling of patients, including exposed or infected patients, in accordance with state law; and (3) advocate educating physicians regarding their duty to warn and the liability associated with the failure to do so.

INFORMATION SHARING AND THE CONTRACTUAL ALLOCATION OF RISK

The proliferation of IDSs and the continuing consolidation of health care facilities raise issues of information sharing between affiliated health care facilities. The development of credentialing policies and procedures for physicians and AHPs, as well as the actual credentialing of health care providers, is costly and time-consuming. Health care facilities can decrease the time spent on such activities and the associated costs, as well as eliminate duplication, by engaging in information sharing. Nevertheless, although information sharing is efficient and cost-effective if executed correctly, there are some accreditation limitations and legal concerns that must be considered when determining the extent of information sharing and the protection and use of the shared information.

Initially, analyzing and implementing an information-sharing system will require a commitment of significant time and resources. If such a system is to be implemented, it should be documented in a written agreement. Also, bylaws, rules and regulations, and appointment and reappointment applications of all participating facilities should be reviewed and amended to reflect the information-sharing system and to ensure a certain degree of consistency between facilities. Confidentiality agreements also should be executed and enforced between facilities and their peer review members, and issues pertaining to the release of patient-identifiable medical information, fraud and abuse, the National Practitioner Data Bank, and the Healthcare Integrity and Protection Data Bank should be analyzed. Proper implementation of an information system can be efficiently accomplished with the assistance of risk management personnel who can identify and analyze facility-specific risk issues that may arise before, during, and after implementation of an information-sharing system.

Contractual Provisions for the Confidentiality of Information

Sharing confidential peer review information poses questions regarding the discoverability of this sensitive information. Some states, including California, protect peer review documents of licensed health facilities such as hospitals and federally certified ASCs. Based on a state's definition of a health care facility and the concomitant protections that may be available, myriad health care entities, ranging from hospitals to MCOs and ASCs, can share information.

Notwithstanding the statutory protections afforded peer review documents, facilities should be wary of sharing confidential peer review information because any subsequent disclosure of peer review committee records could result in a loss of this protection. Clearly, providing an entity with confidential information makes it harder to control its dissemination. The risk of such disclosure and the possible loss of statutory protection, if it is available, can be reduced if health care facilities enter into written agreements limiting the sharing of such information for the purpose of peer review. Moreover, contract provisions should prohibit the further release of such information, identify the parties entitled to review it, identify the method in which it should be maintained, and delineate a facility's liability for failing to comply.

Facilities engaged in information sharing can mitigate the risk of voluntary disclosure of peer review information by executing confidentiality agreements between not only the health care facilities, but also each health care facility and each of its peer review committee members. To avoid dissemination of additional information, facilities also should consider removing identifying information on practitioners (other than the practitioner under consideration) and patients' names from shared peer review documents.

Obtaining Appropriate Releases

Practitioners who are damaged professionally by an unauthorized release of confidential peer review information may have some legal rights. To avoid any such risk, facilities should require providers to sign a release specifically authorizing the sharing of credentialing information between facilities. Execution of such a release is particularly important because it serves as documentation of authorization, notifies the physician of the conditions for release of information, and provides a facility with a certain degree of immunity from liability. In addition, the facility's bylaws should contain a provision that infers consent to release such information from an application for clinical privileges or medical staff membership.

Release of Patient-Identifiable Medical Information

Another concern with information-sharing is the release of patient-identifiable medical information, which is governed by state law. Unless state law provides that a health care facility may release patient-identifiable information without the patient's written consent, a facility should remove patient-identifiable information from medical records and peer review documents before releasing them to another health care facility.

Fraud and Abuse Concerns

Risk managers also must be aware that fraud and abuse concerns may arise because the responsibilities undertaken by one facility for the benefit of another could be viewed as a benefit. To comply with applicable state and federal laws, any information-sharing arrangement should be undertaken in an arm's-length transaction and pursuant to a written agreement. (An arm's-length transaction pertains to a relationship between two or more contracting parties unblemished by any other connections or relations that may bias the judgment of the contracting parties.) Such an agreement should specify the responsibilities of the parties, the term of the agreement, and the fair market value cost(s) associated with performing such services.

National Practitioner Data Bank (NPDB)

Federal law prohibits the release of National Practitioner Data Bank (NPDB) reports except to hospitals.[31] The NPDB contains adverse *licensure* action reports on physician and dentists (including revocations, suspensions, reprimands, censures, probations and surrenders for quality purposes); adverse *clinical privilege* actions against physicians and dentists; adverse *professional society membership* actions against physicians and dentists; and *medical malpractice payments* made on all health care practitioners. Groups that have access to this data system include: (1) hospitals, (2) other health care entities that conduct peer review and provide or arrange for care, (3) state boards of medical or dental examiners, (4) other health care practitioner state boards, and (5) practitioners conducting a self-inquiry. Unauthorized release of information contained in the NPDB may result in a $10,000 fine for each individual and entity involved in the release. However, a hospital can be appointed as an agent of another health care facility and then obtain such information on its behalf without violating federal law. Any such principal-agent relationship should be formally documented to avoid any disputes between facilities and claims by physicians about the unauthorized release of information. Under such circumstances, an agent must submit a separate request for information for each entity on whose behalf it is acting.

Healthcare Integrity and Protection Data Bank (HIPDB)

Federal law also prohibits the release of information contained in the Healthcare Integrity and Protection Data Bank (HIPDB), opened in 1999, to anyone except federal and state government agencies, health plans, and self-queries from health care suppliers, providers, and practitioners.[32] As of 1999, hospitals do not have direct access to the HIPDB. The HIPDB contains information regarding certain final adverse actions against health care providers, suppliers, or practitioners. Final adverse actions include: (1) civil judgments against a health care provider, supplier, or practitioner in federal or state court related to the delivery of a health care item or service, (2) federal or state criminal convictions against a health care provider, supplier, or practitioner related to the delivery of a health care item or service, (3) actions by federal or state agencies responsible for the licensing and certification of health care providers, suppliers, or practitioners, (4) exclusion of a health care provider, supplier, or practitioner from participation in federal or state health care programs; and (5) any other adjudicated actions or decisions that the secretary establishes by regulations. Settlements in which no findings or admissions of liability have been made are excluded from reporting. However, any final adverse action emanating from such settlements and consent judgments otherwise reportable under the statute will be reported in the data bank. All final adverse actions are required to be reported *regardless of whether such actions are being appealed by the subject of the report.*

In order to ensure that the NPDB and HIPDB contain all relevant information, federal law imposes specific reporting requirements on entities which collect information on practitioners.[33] Failure to report such information can lead either to the imposition of severe monetary sanctions or to the withdrawal of immunity under federal law for peer review activities.[34] It is therefore crucial that any facility required to report information to either the NPDB or HIPDB maintain policies and procedures that ensure that timely reporting is made.

....

CREDENTIALING OF ALLIED HEALTH PROFESSIONALS

In today's rapidly evolving health care market, facilities may be motivated to extend the role of AHPs such as nurse midwives, physician assistants (PAs), nurse anesthetists, and nurse practitioners. The rapid push of AHPs to the forefront of medicine has been motivated by not only the advent of managed care, social reform, economic pressures, and financial concerns, but also by AHPs eager to assume the tasks and responsibilities for which they have been trained. However, such forces must be tempered by progression based on qualifications, training, experience, and current competence.

Licensure, certification, and registration are three forms of credentialing mechanisms that assist facilities in defining AHP qualifications and competence. Risk managers must be familiar with these mechanisms and the role they play in credentialing AHPs.

Registration is mutually exclusive of licensure, whereas certification is interdependent with licensure. Unlike licensure and certification, registration is devoid of any nexus to the provision of high-quality services or an attempt to standardize the profession to allow for the production of benchmarks linking education, training, and experience to high-quality services. In contrast, certification is a method of not only distinguishing members within a profession but also of providing facilities, employers, patients, and the public with a valid mechanism by which to identify the level of training a particular AHP has received.

Decisions to delegate responsibilities to AHPs that are not within the scope of their licensure or are outside the facility's protocol can have serious civil, criminal, and financial ramifications. For example, if a service or treatment that can be performed only by a physician is delegated to an AHP, a violation of the state's medical practice act may have occurred. Depending on the facility's marketing and advertising strategies and oral representations—made to patients—such conduct also may result in claims of misrepresentation.

Sources of Potential Liability

Risk managers must be familiar with the circumstances under which liability may be imputed to health care facilities, supervising physicians, and AHPs resulting from the provision of services by AHPs. For example, a facility may expose itself to liability if it fails to ensure adequate physician supervision or if it permits an AHP to perform procedures outside the scope of his or her license or outside the facility's approved protocols. Supervising physicians likewise face exposure should they fail to adequately supervise. AHPs face exposure if they fail to exercise appropriate clinical judgment, and facilities can be exposed to liability if they do not rigorously enforce the standards established in their protocols.

Another source of potential liability is a facility's failure to educate AHPs about risk management issues. According to a study conducted by the American Academy of Physician Assistants Risk Management Task Force in 1992, 40 percent of survey respondents indicated that they did not receive orientation in risk management issues.[35] Accordingly, investing resources in orienting AHPs, including PAs, about risk management issues specific to the setting in which they practice may reduce liability.

Dependent versus Independent AHPs

There are two categories of AHP—dependent and independent. *Dependent AHPs,* or practitioners, cannot provide patient care services without direction or supervision by a physician. For example, PAs are dependent AHPs. In the hospital context, dependent AHPs may not be members of the medical staff and are not required to have prerogatives.

On the other hand, *independent AHPs* may provide patient care services without direction or supervision by a physician. Nurse midwives are an example of independent AHPs. In the hospital context, although independent AHPs must have delineated clinical privileges, certain classes of them may be members of the medical staff. For example, clinical psychologists are often medical staff members.

The credentialing of independent AHPs differs markedly from the credentialing of dependent AHPs. Most facilities recognize that federal law, state law, and accrediting bodies do not require that dependent AHPs be credentialed. Thus, facilities generally do not expend scarce resources on credentialing this class of practitioner. However, they should maintain a written dependent AHP credentialing policy because these individuals provide patient care services. In addition, the OIG can impose severe civil monetary penalties for submitting claims for services provided by AHPs whom the facility "knows or should have known" have been excluded from participation in Medicare. The JCAHO, among others, requires periodic verification of competence using clinically valid, objective criteria.

Laws Regarding Scope of Practice

Scope-of-practice issues are almost exclusively within a state's domain, codified in state law and regulations; federal law does not address scope of practice. Guidelines promulgated by licensing boards and associations are additional sources of information that can be used in determining a class of AHPs' scope of practice. However, distinctions must be clearly drawn between legal authority that is enforceable by the state and that may result in criminal and/or civil sanctions if violated, and guidelines that are merely recommended by professional associations. AHPs' scope of practice within a facility should be based on the interrelation of various factors such as state law, regulations, accreditation standards, and association guidelines.

Accreditation Standards Regarding Scope of Practice

Whether an AHP functions in an acute care hospital, a psychiatric hospital, an ASC, or some other health care facility will dictate which accreditation standards are applicable to the exercise of his or her practice privileges. Generally, scope-of-practice issues either will not be addressed in accreditation standards or will be deferred to state law and regulations governing the practice. For example, the 1999 JCAHO *Accreditation Manual for Hospitals* provides that "[i]ndividuals are granted the privilege to admit patients to inpatient services in accordance with state law. . . ."[36]

Although accrediting bodies generally do not limit the independent AHPs' scope of practice, the accreditation guidelines may expressly reference the type of patient care that may be appropriately provided by independent AHPs. The 1999 JCAHO manual provides that ". . . licensed independent practitioners who are permitted to provide patient care services independently may perform all or part of the medical history and physical examination, if granted such privileges."[37]

In contrast, dependent practitioners generally are not addressed by accrediting bodies such as the JCAHO, NCQA, AAAHC, and others. Thus, each facility must determine the scope of dependent practitioners' practice in its protocols based on state laws, regulations, and the licensing board's guidelines, if any; AHPs' functions within the clinical setting; the degree of supervision required; and the facility's needs.

Identification of Clinical Services to Be Provided

All individuals who are permitted by law and by a hospital to provide patient care services independently must have delineated clinical privileges, whether or not they are medical staff members.[38] Thus, whenever a request is received from an AHP for medical staff membership or practice privileges, the health care facility should have a documented procedure that it follows as early as forwarding the application.

If a class of AHP that currently is not employed at a hospital applies for practice privileges, a hospital should investigate whether there is a need for the services of this class of AHP, document its findings, and make recommendations based on objective findings. Similarly, other types of health care organizations should investigate and document their need for AHPs.

The following issues are paramount in determining whether to allow a particular class of AHP to practice at a facility:

- The education, training, and skills that such a class of AHP must possess to perform patient care services.
- The legal scope of practice for the applicable class of AHP.
- A determination of the necessity of supervision of the AHP and the extent of such supervision.
- The number and types of facilities in the area that provide the services offered by such AHPs.
- The extent of demand for such services at this facility.
- The criteria that will be used to credential this class of AHP.

Additionally, all facilities, including hospitals, should identify the qualifications that a supervising physician must possess to oversee the AHP, if applicable. Some states even require specific licensure for supervisors. Apart from identifying whether a sufficient number of physicians are available and willing to supervise dependent AHPs, input from physicians regarding the credentialing of AHPs should be limited to information pertaining to matters that affect the quality of care and the operation of the facility to avoid any semblance of protectionism of existing economic interests, conspiracy, claims of antitrust, and defamation.

············

QUALIFICATIONS AND SCOPE OF ALLIED HEALTH PROFESSIONAL AUTHORITY

Nurse midwives, PAs, clinical psychologists, physical therapists, nurse anesthetists, and nurse practitioners are representative of different classes of AHPs. Educational requirements vary for each class of AHP, as do the clinical practice and degree of autonomy each class of AHP can exercise based on state law and the setting in which the AHP practices. Although each enumerated class of AHP (and several other classes of AHPs that have not been mentioned) are worthy of evaluation, the scope of this chapter does not permit a complete listing. Only nurse midwives, PAs, and nurse anesthetists are discussed herein.

Nurse Midwives

The practice of midwifery comprises two distinct components. Some states recognize both lay midwives and nurse midwives. *Lay midwives* are those individuals who perform midwifery services but do not possess a nursing degree. Whether they can practice midwifery and the types of services they can provide depend on state law. *Nurse midwives,* on the other hand, are registered nurses who have completed a state-mandated course of formal education after basic nursing education. They possess the advanced formal training, knowledge, and ability to provide gynecological care, prenatal care, and low-risk obstetrical care such as delivery and postpartum care.

To minimize risks, facilities should maintain written policies addressing the credentialing of nurse midwives, with particular emphasis on scope of practice issues. Liability also can be minimized by implementing written protocols, based on state law, regarding the prescription and administration of medication by midwives. Further, to reduce risks, midwives should be required to document thoroughly all patient care and comply with a facility's consultation and referral policies.

Scope of Practice   Nurse midwifery practice is legal in all fifty states and the District of Columbia. However, the scope of nurse midwifery practice is dependent on state law and the clinical setting in which midwives practice. For example, in California nurse midwives may provide care and advice in a variety of settings during the antepartal, intrapartal, postpartal, interconceptional, and family planning stages. More specifically, they can conduct deliveries on their own responsibility and care for newborns, including preventive measures and the detection of abnormal conditions in the mother and child.[39]

Prescriptive Authority   Nurse midwives have prescription-writing authority in forty-one states.[40] Risk managers should be familiar with the statutory limitations that apply to nurse midwives' prescriptive authority. For example, nurse midwives cannot prescribe controlled substances in California, Idaho, Nevada, New Mexico, Tennessee, and Virginia. Other states maintain different restrictions on nurse midwives' prescriptive authority. Failure to be familiar with the limitations of midwifery can result in the imposition of significant liability on a facility.

Physician Assistants

Physician assistants (PAs) are health professionals licensed to practice medicine with physician supervision. Except for Mississippi (the only state that does not recognize PAs), each state requires PAs to be licensed, certified, or registered before they can engage in the practice of medicine. Approximately twenty-one states require PAs to pass a national certifying examination administered by the National Commission on Certification of Physician Assistants before commencing practice. Passing the examination entitles the PA to use the title of physician assistant-certified.

Based on state law, PAs may be able to perform clinical services such as patient evaluation, patient monitoring, and diagnosis; to provide therapeutic treatment such as administering injections; to provide immunizations and suture; to provide wound care; to manage certain conditions produced by infection or trauma; and to counsel patients on complying with therapeutic regimens and injection of medications. The physician-PA relationship, however, is a dependent one that requires supervision by a physician. A PA is an agent of the supervising physician. Accordingly, physicians may be liable for the negligent acts of PAs because they select and/or supervise PAs and exercise control over them.

Sources of Liability Specific to PAs   Facilities may be liable for less than optimal care rendered by PAs and for negligently credentialing PAs. Such potential liability underscores the importance of professional liability insurance for PAs as well as physicians. Facilities may be held responsible for paying a judgment against a physician and/or the PA if either of the individuals is uninsured or underinsured. Accordingly, the scope of coverage and policy limitations also must be reviewed and understood prior to granting practice privileges to PAs.

Some states, including California, also require that a physician obtain licensure as a PA supervisor prior to supervising PAs. As part of the credentialing process, prior to allowing a physician and his or her assistant to provide direct patient care, a facility should establish mechanisms to ensure that a supervising physician maintains appropriate current licensure as a PA supervisor.

Prescriptive Authority   Currently, approximately thirty-eight states grant prescriptive writing authority to PAs. Prescriptive authority can encompass prescribing, dispensing, and/or merely transmitting prescriptive orders. Familiarity with the degree of prescriptive authority PAs are legally permitted to exercise is essential. For example, in the District of Columbia, PAs are limited to prescribing noncontrolled substances. In California, hospital regulations provide that PAs are limited to transmitting, orally or in writing, a prescription from the supervising physician, and that such transmission, if written in the patient's medical record, must be reviewed, dated, and countersigned by the supervising physician within seven days of transmission.[41] To minimize liability, it is necessary to be familiar with the degree of prescriptive authority PAs may exercise.

Accordingly, facilities should implement and maintain written protocols regarding PAs' prescriptive authority, transmittal authority (oral or written), and dispensing authority, if any. Pharmacy personnel and PAs should also be provided with such written protocols.

Nurse Anesthetists

Nurse anesthesia is an advanced clinical nursing specialty. Nurses can become certified registered nurse anesthetists (CRNAs) after attending an accredited nurse anesthesia education program and passing a national certification exam. CRNAs practice in a variety of settings, ranging from hospitals, ASCs, and pain clinics to physicians' offices.

CRNAs can manage patients' operative anesthesia needs as well as pre- and post-operative needs. Depending on state law and the clinical setting, they may be legally authorized to perform physical assessments, prepare patients for anesthetic management, administer anesthesia, maintain anesthesia intraoperatively, oversee recovery from anesthesia, and manage the patients' postoperative course. Proper utilization of CRNAs subject to strict controls through proper credentialing can result in high-quality and cost-effective care, thus benefiting facilities, employers, physicians, and patients alike.

The issue of CRNA supervision continues to be hotly debated in the health care sector. Statutory requirements regarding the degree of supervision and supervisors' qualifications vary among states. Many states, such as California, recognize the independent practice of CRNAs. In California, absent any restrictions that may be imposed by a facility, CRNAs may lawfully perform all anesthesia service without physician supervision after the physician has ordered the administration of anesthesia. However, the area of supervising physicians' qualifications is less clear. Some states require CRNAs to be supervised by a physician, although such supervision does not necessarily need to be provided by an anesthesiologist. Accordingly, risk managers should be familiar with whether limited-license practitioners, such as dentists and podiatrists, can supervise CRNAs, and the degree of independence CRNAs are legally authorized to exercise.

Although the battle lines have been drawn for years and many can predict which side each camp will take, it is likely that the issue of CRNA supervision will remain hotly debated. Based on financial pressures that are continually being exerted on health care systems nationwide, however, it also is likely that CRNAs who provide high-quality care will gain a stronger foothold in today's health care market.

Verification of Credentials

It also is important to reverify AHPs' credentials vigilantly, including PAs', after the initial grant of practice rights. According to the American Academy of Physician Assistants Risk Management Task Force study mentioned earlier, 96 percent of the respondents indicated that hospitals required initial verification of PAs' credentials, but only 81 percent reverified them.[42]

There should be *no* discrepancy between verification rates during credentialing and recredentialing. Reverification of pertinent information such as current licensure; current competency; maintenance of malpractice insurance; initiation of legal actions and/or judgments against AHPs, including PAs; verification of current participation and exclusion status regarding federal health care programs; and other such malpractice information is an important risk management tool. A facility's failure to diligently maintain current credentialing information on all those who practice in its midst can affect its accreditation rating, quality outcomes, and reputation in the community.

....

MINIMIZING POTENTIAL LIABILITY IN THE COURSE OF CREDENTIALING

Several steps can be taken to reduce the risk of liability associated with credentialing. First and foremost, developing a risk management plan that addresses qualifications, credentials, and practice guidelines should eliminate a substantial degree of inconsistency and minimize liability. A risk management plan should be based on a state's licensure laws, state and federal regulations, and the facility's needs. In addition to risk management plans for different liability issues and different classes of practitioners, facilities must institute and maintain written protocols. Written protocols provide systematic guidance to administrators, surveyors, physicians, and other entities and individuals who are entrusted with credentialing functions.

After implementing credentialing protocols, compliance with such protocols should be sought. For example, credentialing decisions should be clearly delineated in an applicant's file. The denial and grant of practice privileges should be based on objective factors that are documented in an applicant's file. Justification of credentialing decisions, as opposed to conclusory statements such as "practice privileges granted" or "practice privileges denied," will support a facility's claim that a practitioner's privileges were denied based on objective factors used to evaluate members of such class of AHP.

As a rule, facilities should not communicate credentialing decisions orally. Statements made by facility employees may be admissible in a hearing challenging the facility's credentialing decision. All employees involved in the credentialing process should be aware that any and all information regarding credentialing should be communicated only in writing by individuals with the authority to do so.

Too often, in today's extremely competitive health care market, decision makers fail to take necessary actions in accordance with their facility's written protocols or make exceptions for practitioners who are well respected in the community or who have been on the hospital staff for many years. However, such a practice is hazardous, to not only patients but also the facility's licensure, Medicare and Medicaid certification, accreditation status, and financial condition. Uneven application of rules and policies is likely to result in legal liability.

Implementing effective communication strategies is also an important risk management tool. Effective communication strategies should be implemented to provide prompt reporting and resolution of problems. Facilities should be careful not to implement policies, procedures, and protocols with which the staff cannot or will not comply. Implementation of written standards that are not strictly followed may expose facilities to liability for failure to comply with their own standards.

....

CONCLUSION

Credentialing poses several potential sources of liability for the health care organization. Discrimination, restraint of trade, inadequate supervision of allied health professionals, negligent credentialing, failure to check whether the practitioner has been excluded from participation in federal health care programs, and wrongful disclosure of peer review and quality outcome information are among the most serious.

Risk management plays a significant role in minimizing those sources of potential liability. By documenting, and ensuring adherence to, the health care organization's credentialing policies and procedures, and periodically reviewing them, the risk manager can minimize potential liabilities associated with this process. Also, the ongoing and rapid changes in health care are bringing changes in potential sources of liability. By staying familiar with current developments in health care, the risk manager will be better able to foresee new areas of potential liability and address them early.

Endnotes

The authors would like to acknowledge and thank Elona J. Kogan, JD, for her previous work which contributed to this chapter.

1. Joint Commission on Accreditation of Healthcare Organizations. *1999 JCAHO Accreditation Manual for Hospitals*. Oakbrook Terrace, Ill.: JCAHO, 1999.

2. *Ibid.*

3. National Committee for Quality Assurance. *Draft 1999 Managed Care Organization (MCO) Accreditation Standards.* Washington, D.C.: NCQA, 1999.

4. 42 CFR § 482.22(a)(2).

5. 42 CFR § 482.22.

6. 42 CFR § 483.430(b)(5).

7. 42 CFR § 484.16.

8. 42 CFR § 485.54(b).

9. 42 CFR § 485.604.

10. 42 CFR § 485.705.

11. 22 CCR § 70701 (a)(7).

12. Joint Commission on Accreditation of Healthcare Organizations. *1999 JCAHO Accreditation Manual for Hospitals* (MS 5.3.2). Oakbrook Terrace, Ill.: JCAHO, 1999.

13. National Committee for Quality Assurance. *NCQA Standards for Accreditation.*

14. 42 CFR § 1003.102(a)(2).

15. 64 *Fed. Reg.* 52791, 52793 (Sept. 30, 1999) (OIG Special Advisory Bulletin).

16. 211 N.E.2d 253 (Ill. 1965).

17. In California, the theory of corporate liability for negligent credentialing was established in *Elam v. College Park Hospital,* 132 Cal. App.3d 332 (1982).

18. In *McClellan v. Health Maintenance Organization,* 604 A.2d 1053, *allocatur denied,* 616 A.2d 985 (Pa. 1992), the court held that an HMO may be held liable under the theory of ostensible corporate liability for failing to "select and retain only competent individuals."

19. In *Petrovich v. Share Health Plan,* 1999 WL 773524 (Ill. 1999), the Illinois Supreme Court recently considered portions of the health plan's member handbook that referred to the "comprehensive high quality services" purportedly provided by plan physicians to hold that an HMO could be held vicariously liable under an apparent authority theory for the malpractice of its independent contractor physicians.

20. 42 CFR § 482.12(a)(7).

21. 42 CFR § 482.13, as reported in 64 *Fed. Reg.* 36070 (July 2, 1999).

22. 42 U.S.C. §§ 12101-12213.

23. 29 U.S.C. § 794; see also *Menkowitz v. Pottstown Mem'l Med. Ctr.,* 154 F.3d 113, 123-24 (3d Cir. 1998).

24. *Menkowitz,* 154 F.3d 113.

25. Joint Commission on Accreditation of Healthcare Organizations. *1999 JCAHO Accreditation Manual for Hospitals* (MS. 5.4–5.4.3 & accompanying "Intent").

26. National Committee for Quality Assurance. *NCQA Standards for Accreditation* (CR 4).

27. National Committee for Quality Assurance. *NCQA Standards for Accreditation* (CR 4 and footnote).

28. Joint Commission on Accreditation of Healthcare Organizations. *1999 JCAHO Accreditation Manual for Hospitals* (MS. 5.4–5.4.3 & accompanying "Intent").

29. 37 Cal. Rptr.2d 518 (1995).

30. *Tarasoff v. Regents of the University of California,* 551 P.2d 334 (1976).

31. 45 CFR § 60.13.

32. 45 CFR § 61.14.

33. 45 CFR § 60.4–9; 45 CFR § 61.4–11.

34. 45 CFR §§ 60.7, 60.9; 45 CFR §§ 61.9, 61.11.

35. American Academy of Physician Assistants Risk Management Task Force. *Hospital Practice Survey*. Alexandria, Va.: AAPA, Apr. 1992.

36. Joint Commission on Accreditation of Healthcare Organizations. *1999 JCAHO Accreditation Manual for Hospitals,* p. 267 (MS.6.1).

37. Joint Commission on Accreditation of Healthcare Organizations. *1999 JCAHO Accreditation Manual for Hospitals,* p. 268 (MS.6.2.2).

38. Joint Commission on Accreditation of Healthcare Organizations. *1999 JCAHO Accreditation Manual for Hospitals,* p. 263 (MS.5.14).

39. 16 CCR § 1463.

40. American College of Nurse Midwives. *A Handbook of State Legislation*. Washington, D.C.: ACNM, 1995.

41. 16 CCR § 1399.541(h).

42. American Academy of Physician Assistants Risk Management Task Force. *Hospital Practice Survey*. Alexandria, Va.: AAPA, Apr. 1992.

11

A Contract Review Primer
for Risk Managers

Peggy L. B. Nakamura

In the ever-changing world of a health care organization, knowledgeable risk managers involved in the contract review process are a valuable resource to the senior management team. The risk manager can assist in protecting the assets of the organization through involvement in the contracting process, wherever that process might begin. Contract review is similar to many other management techniques in that a systematic approach can minimize problems due to inadequate knowledge of the subject matter or lack of time to devote to the project. The risk manager is best suited by training and experience to focus on areas of liability, insurance, hold-harmless and indemnification, and other risk elements common to many health care contracts such as qualifications of service providers or reporting claims and lawsuits. The systematic review does not eliminate the need for competent counsel's involvement in major contracts; rather, the risk manager's involvement augments the organization's thoughtful consideration of all contractual relationships.

To accomplish an efficient review of any health care contract, the risk manager must understand the type of contract being considered, the contractual responsibilities (performance) of the various parties, and the importance of identifying the negative consequences in the event a poorly drafted contract is executed.

This chapter provides the health care risk manager with basic tools to develop a contract review process that includes the major areas of liability assumption and transfer through idemnification and hold-harmless provisions, insurance requirements, and standard contract terminology.

CONTRACT STRUCTURE

A contract, according to *Black's Law Dictionary,* is defined in part as "an agreement between two or more persons that creates an obligation to do or not to do a particular thing."[1] A contract can also be known as an agreement, letter contract, letter of intent, memorandum of understanding, lease, purchase agreement or order, or oral contract.

A contract contains legally binding obligations between two or more parties, and provides one or more of the parties with a legal remedy if another party fails to perform as specified in the document. For a contract to exist, all the legal essentials must be included. The essentials are:

- The parties to the contract are competent.

- The contract represents a "meeting of the minds" between the parties.

- There is consideration; a bargained-for exchange of legal value exists between the parties.

- The purpose or object of the contract is legal.

- The contract is documented in writing if required for legal enforcement in that state.

A well-written contract serves to confirm the understanding between the parties and avoids future disagreements about terms, conditions, and definitions critical to the relationship. Essential contract terms should *always* be clear and contain adequate detail so as to avoid subsequent misunderstanding.

Parties to the Contract

The correct and legal names of all parties to the contract should be listed in the opening paragraph. If a shortened name (for example, "facility," "entity," "contractor," and so on) is used, it should be identified clearly and used consistently throughout the document. Changing terms (for example, "contractor" to "vendor") within the body of the contract should be avoided. Also, it is advisable to determine the proper contracting entity on behalf of the organization (PHO, MCO, MSO, corporate, or parent) *before* drafting the contract so that the legal names accurately reflect the parties involved in the contract relationship.

To identify the appropriate legal names, it is beneficial for the risk manager to have easy access to a current listing of all subsidiary entities, affiliates, joint ventures, and other legal partnerships, with the correct names as taken from the incorporation documents. As *dbas* ("doing business as") become more plentiful within health care, it will be necessary to have knowledge of their existence and basic structure. In its definition of *dba*, *Black's Law Dictionary* remarks:

> The doing of business is the exercise in the state of the ordinary functions for which the corporation was organized. What constitutes "doing business" depends on the facts in each particular case. . . . The determination as to what constitutes "doing business" may differ as to whether the term is being used with reference to amenability to service of process or taxation, and also may vary in definition from state to state.[2]

When, and if, a *dba* becomes incorporated, the risk manager should request notice because of the new liability created with this legally distinct entity upon incorporation.

Performance Expectations

Written performance expectations for one or both parties, including definitions and time frames for completion, are key to a successful business relationship and should be memorialized in the contract. The description should be easily understood by both parties and cover standards for performance, as well as specific remedies for nonperformance. It is important to quantify and qualify, to the extent possible, standards the receiver of the services will use to determine whether the anticipated service quality has been met. In certain situations, failure to meet the "quality standard" should result in automatic termination of the contract without financial penalty to the receiver of such services.

The performance area is one appropriate section for requiring the contractor to meet the Joint Commission on Accreditation of Healthcare Organizations (JCAHO) standards if considered a contract service (for example, security, dietary, biomedical engineering, reference laboratory, temporary staffing agency) affecting patient care delivery in the hospital.

For example, JCAHO standards specify that when patient care services are provided by another source, a patient should receive the same level of performance from that source as from the organization. Leaders must also participate in the selection of sources for needed services not provided by the department or organization.[3] Additional standards apply to the quality control processes required in clinical laboratory services, radiology, dietetic services, nuclear medicine, and radiation oncology.

Any health care organization anticipating a JCAHO accreditation survey should consider contract services as a potential—and probable—area of scrutiny. The risk manager can provide invaluable assistance in this area through the development of comprehensive performance requirements when contracting for patient care services.

Contract provisions might include a description in the performance standards area that the contractor must meet or exceed JCAHO standards (or other standards of accrediting or licensing bodies that apply to the service) and that the contract may be terminated for failure to meet those standards. In addition, the contractor's qualifications and competency should be considered as applicable to the type of service provided and any ongoing education or training necessary to maintain the requisite skills (for example, licensure, basic life support, or continuing education). The risk manager might also consider the addition of appropriate quality control or performance improvement activities, after consultation with knowledgeable professionals in that particular field. These may include specific *measurable* standards in the performance expectations area, as well as a requirement that the contractor meet employee health requirements for the organization.

············

TERMINOLOGY

Most contracts encountered in the health care setting contain section headings (or provisions) that organize the document and make it easier to review. It is important for any risk manager to have a basic understanding of "contract vocabulary" prior to beginning a meaningful review.

Typical section headings include:

TERM and TERMINATION

The *effective date* of the contract is the date on which it takes effect. The *termination date* is the date the contract has been fully performed or completed. The period of time between the *effective date* and the *termination date* equals the contract *term*. The beginning, end, and date of signing the contract (*execution date*) should be readily apparent in the document.

Within this section, the risk manager should carefully consider *automatic extensions* or *renewals* to the contract term. For instance, the following typical provision should warrant further scrutiny:

This contract shall have an initial term of three years commencing on the date first written above, and shall automatically renew for successive three year terms.

The risk manager, when confronted with this provision, should ask the following questions:

1. Is there a provision permitting the termination of the contract prior to the end of the term?

2. Is the termination "without cause" so that the contract relationship can be cancelled in the event the quality of services has deteriorated or the business climate has changed?

3. If a termination "for cause" provision exists, does it clearly specify what constitutes "for cause?"

The termination provision should allow as much flexibility as possible, enabling the organization to terminate the contract for reasons of changing need or poor performance.

However, there may be contractual relationships that necessitate financial penalties if a party cancels the contract prior to expiration of the term. A common example is one in which a party incurs significant costs at the beginning of the term with the anticipation of a long-term commitment, warranting the outlay of "up-front" services such as major equipment installations or relocation costs for individuals recruited to assume a critical role.

Amendments

Contracting parties can amend contracts, but the new requirements or contract language should *always* be in writing and signed by both parties. The original contract provisions that now are deleted or changed should be noted in the amendment as well as a statement in the original contract that all amendments must be in writing and signed by both parties.

From a practical standpoint, many contractual relationships do not always proceed as specified in the contract and yet the parties are satisfied with the arrangement. For instance, the services provided may change in focus or scope during the contract term and without benefit of a written amendment to the original contract and as signed by both parties. If the receiving party continues to compensate the other party according to the contract terms, a strong argument can be made that the receiving party implied consent to the changes in performance and cannot later plead breach of contract. Contract litigation is expensive and rarely rewarding. Therefore, any changes in the contractual relationship during the term should be mutually acknowledged in writing to avoid subsequent problems.

Additional section headings include:

- *Indemnification*—written to protect one party to the contract against the liability and costs associated with claims arising from the acts or omissions of the other party to the contract.

- *Relationship of the parties*—the parties classification of the relationship, such as not-for-profit entity or independent contractor.

- *Insurance requirements*—should include each type of insurance necessary to cover the risks and liabilities of all parties to the contract.

- *Alternative dispute resolution*—permits other resolution methods, such as arbitration or mediation as a substitute for litigating disputes between the parties. (See Chapter 26 for further detail.)

- *Changes or compliance with laws and regulations*—specifies the effect changes in statutes or regulations affecting the health care industry will have on the contract terms and also that the parties are required to comply with applicable laws and regulations.

- *Inspection of books and records*—42 USC section 1395x (b)(1)(I) requires contractors providing services for $10,000 or more for a hospital during any twelve month period to allow the government access to all pertinent books and records.

- *Force majeure*—protects the parties from being in breach of the contract due to unavoidable causes.

- *Choice of law*—specifies which jurisdiction will be used to govern the construction and interpretation of the contract.

- *Assignment*—governs the ability of one party to transfer its rights under the contract to another party.

- *Confidentiality*—essential to any contract involving health care providers or organizations; requires the parties to maintain the confidentiality of certain information.

- *Exhibits*—specifies that each exhibit is a part of the contract; all exhibits should be attached to the contract and reviewed concurrently.

············
CONTRACT REVIEW IN INTEGRATED DELIVERY SYSTEMS (IDSs)

The major challenge in reviewing IDS contracts is identifying the proper individuals to be involved in the review, negotiation, and signing of applicable contracts. One suggestion is for the risk manager to review existing contract review policies and recommend revisions based on the change in corporate structure.

Significant problems have been encountered when the insurance or self-insurance programs have not been properly addressed in the contract language. Also, the new legal names or structures sometimes do not receive appropriate acknowledgment in existing insurance documents or other legal contracts. Often the "legal" name has changed for many affiliated entities, much to their chagrin, at the time of subsequent negotiations. The risk manager is encouraged to request, or develop, a legal name organizational chart, with backup files on historical names. Tracking entities and insurance coverages is an area of significant value to any developing IDS.

Key questions for the risk manager to ask include:

- Who has administrative responsibility and control of the various entities and employees?

- Are the entities properly reflected on the respective contracts, leases, policies, and so on?

- Are all the proper parties "on notice" of the new legal entities or names, including *dbas*?

- Are the coverage limits adequate for the expanded organization and the new types of exposure that may result from operations?

- Who has responsibility for filing legal documents relating to legal structure?

- Where are the documents maintained?

. . . .

IMPLICATIONS AND ISSUES FOR TAX-EXEMPT ORGANIZATIONS

Internal Revenue Service Revenue Procedure 93-19 (IRS Rev. Proc. 93-19) has particular significance in contract review involving a tax-exempt-bonds-financed facility and a nongovernmental service provider. IRS guidelines set forth its view on the compensation of a *service provider* providing services under a *service contract* to a 501(c)(3) organization. Service contracts may involve all, a portion, or any function of a facility, such as a contract for the provision of management services for an entire hospital or specific department, janitorial services at a facility, or physician services to patients of a hospital.

According to the procedure, the service provider must receive *reasonable* compensation for services rendered, which may not be based on a share of net profits. In addition, at least 50 percent of the compensation must be based on a periodic fixed fee. In the term and termination areas, the term of the contract, including renewal options, must not exceed five years. After three years into the term, the facility owner must be able to cancel the contract for any reason without penalty. And, lastly, the facility owner and the service provider cannot be members of the same controlled group or related parties as defined in the regulations.

As the risk manager assumes greater responsibility in the area of contract review and file maintenance, it is essential to recognize if the facility is covered by this IRS procedure and establish close communication with knowledgeable counsel. It is conceivable that a seemingly innocuous service contract may result in the IRS imposing sanctions on the errant facility.

. . . .

HEALTH CARE CONTRACTS AND CORPORATE COMPLIANCE

The contract review process in a health care organization should be integrated with the corporate compliance program. (Chapter 20 on corporate compliance should be referenced for more detail on this topic.) In general terms, federal and state laws prohibit health care providers from paying for the referral of patients or other business, thus requiring careful legal scrutiny of all contractual arrangements between health care organizations, physician providers, medical groups, or other potential referral sources.

While legal compliance experts are essential to the process of drafting appropriate contracts as respects compliance with these complex federal and state laws, risk managers should become involved in reviewing the contracts for risk management-related issues such as insurance requirements, indemnification provisions, and performance expectations.

. . . .

CONTRACTUAL RISK TRANSFER

One of the most important concepts to master for a risk manager is that of transferring (or assuming) financial risk through contractual provisions. In essence, the contract becomes the governing law as respects the risks assumed by the parties to the contract. Therefore, understanding the contractual methods of transferring risk is the crucial first step in the process of risk management's review.

Contractual risk transfer may occur in the following provisions of a contract:

- Indemnification or hold-harmless.

- Liability limitations.
- Subrogation waivers.
- Insurance requirements.

Each of these provisions serves to restrict, transfer, or require financial risk assumption in a manner specific to the particular relationship embodied in the contract. Careful attention to detail is required as each provision is considered.

Indemnification Provisions

As a general rule, hold-harmless or indemnification provisions should be included in a contract. Such provisions require one party to the contract (the indemnitor) to assume the financial liability that may arise from the contract performance. The party lacking such responsibility (the indemnitee), or held harmless from the liability, is entitled to a defense and satisfaction of any resulting judgment from the indemnitor.

Indemnification provisions may range from the basic and easy to understand to the legally complex, with confusing terms and responsibilities. However, most provisions can be dissected as to the indemnitor's scope of responsibility and the reasonableness of the risk assumption in the particular contract.

A few considerations for the risk manager in reviewing the contract include:

- Can the assumption of risk fit into the insurance or self-insurance coverages available?
- What risks can the health care organization afford to assume if coverage is unavailable?
- Will the insurance policy or self-insurance document allow coverage for liability assumed by contract?
- Will the risk assumed through the indemnification requirements impact the limits of coverage for the organization?

In most situations, it is appropriate for each party to the contract to retain responsibility and liability for those contract activities and operations under its control. This includes acts of omission or commission by employees or agents. An ideal contract provision would specify that each party is responsible for its own actions, and the indemnifying party will reimburse the second party for any costs the second party incurs as a result of the indemnifying party's negligence.

One example of basic mutual indemnification language follows:

Each party, Health Care Entity and Contractor, agree that with respect to any claim or lawsuit arising out of the activities described in this contract, each party shall only be responsible for that portion of any liability resulting from the actions or omissions of its own directors, officers, employees, and agents.

Each party, Health Care Entity and Contractor and their respective directors, officers, employees, and agents, shall defend, indemnify, and hold harmless the other party from and against any and all liability, loss, expense, reasonable attorneys' fees, or claims for injury or damages arising out of the performance of this contract, but only in proportion to, and to the extent that, such liability, loss expense, attorneys' fees, or claims for injury or damages are caused by or result from the acts or omissions or the indemnifying party.

The risk manager is well advised to work with corporate counsel to develop basic indemnification language, as appropriate, that might serve as a template for contract review. Many contractors or companies are amenable to alternate contract language, if provided in a timely and professional manner.

....

LIABILITY LIMITATIONS

A liability limitation provision (most often found in architects', construction, supplier, or manufacturing contracts) transfers risk by limiting the liability of one party in favor of another party. This provision limits the party's liability to a predetermined level or amount of damages, thereby transferring the liability exposure beyond that level to the other party.

Assuming that the health care entity provider is the recipient of this provision in a contract, it is prudent to consider the reasonableness of the liability limitation and the risk being assumed by the entity. Particular attention should be given to liability limitation provisions regarding errors and omissions, professional acts, breach of contract, personal injury, and property damage.

Waiver of Subrogation Rights

Another consideration in listing insurance requirements is the use of a "waiver-of-subrogation" clause. A waiver of subrogation rights is the voluntary relinquishment by the insurer or self-insurer of the right to recover from a third party. One common subrogation example occurs when a contractor's employee is injured on the health care organization's premises while performing services under the contract. When the contractor's workers' compensation carrier receives the claim, it will often pursue a premises liability or negligence cause of action against the organization. A waiver of subrogation would "relinquish" the workers' compensation carrier's right to pursue subrogation against the organization.

As is obvious in the noted example, the insurer's "rights" are affected. Therefore, parties to the contract should notify their insurer anytime a waiver of subrogation is included in the contract and receive authority or approval from the insurer before proceeding.

Insurance Requirements

Requiring the party (or parties) to a contract to procure and maintain insurance is one way to ensure that the indemnifying party (indemnitor) can satisfy the financial obligations arising from the indemnification or hold-harmless provisions. In large part, the type of contract dictates the specific types of insurance that should be required by the contracting parties. For instance, any contract covering professional services should require the service provider to have adequate minimum amounts of professional liability and general liability insurance. Property, business automobile, fidelity, workers' compensation, and major medical health coverage also are reasonable insurance requirements for many service and maintenance contracts. It is important to consider the possible losses or claims that may arise from the contract performance and then anticipate the various insurance coverages necessary to cover them.

The key elements to review whenever insurance requirements are contemplated include: limits of coverage, cancellation provisions, evidence of coverage for the other party, financial security of the insuring company,[4] whether parties are named as additional insureds or certificate holders, and whether self-insurance will be accepted in lieu of a commercial insurance policy.

Insurer Solvency

Within the insurance requirement section, a few phrases may be added to ensure, to the greatest extent possible, that the insurer used by the contracting party will remain financially solvent and able to pay any claims on behalf of its insureds.

Language for insurance requirements might be:

Acceptability of Insurers

Prior to commencement of services, CONTRACTOR shall furnish ENTITY with evidence of insurance coverage as required in this CONTRACT and agree that all insurance has been placed with insurers with an A. M. Best rating of no less that A-VII and are also licensed and/or authorized to do business in the state in which services will be rendered.

....

MANAGED CARE CONTRACTS

Many health care organizations now have administrative staff assigned to the task of drafting, negotiating, and reviewing managed care contracts. However, this area requires a coordinated team approach to best consider the multitude of requirements and provisions that affect the financial viability and operational units of the organization.

What role does the risk manager play in the managed care-contracting environment? First and foremost, he or she must be conversant about the expansive risks an organization assumes as it enters into managed care contracting relationships. Of particular concern are the requirements related to:

- Utilization management and quality assurance (QA) protocols.
- Provision for medical screening examination in an emergency department (ED).
- Credentialing and privileging of physicians and midlevel practitioners by the managed care organization (MCO).
- Reporting of medical malpractice claims and lawsuits.
- Reporting of actions related to licensure of privileges of facility, staff, and physicians.
- Release of historical claims data.
- Insurance and indemnification requirements.
- Access to peer review and QA committee proceedings.
- Financial responsibility in the event of health plan insolvency.
- Ability of health plan to remove providers from provider panel.
- Appeal processes.
- Stop-loss provider excess or risk-limiting protection arrangements.

Many health care organizations, particularly those encompassing acute care facilities, fail to consider managed care liability as a significant exposure, because of commonly held definitions of an MCO. However, as health care providers form integrated delivery systems or networks (IDSs or IDNs) or establish business partnerships, ventures, or networks for contracting purposes, the potential for managed care liability expands significantly. For instance, a health care organization that develops an exclusive provider organization (EPO) for its own employees has in essence created its own MCO. The health plan coverage document, preauthorization requirements, establishment of "exclusive providers" from which the employees must choose, and other administrative processes related to traditional health plans now are a part of the organization's administrative responsibility.

Another example of significant managed care liability exposure is when the health care organization assumes *by contract* delegated functions from a health plan, such as utilization management or provider credentialing. The organization's staff assuming this delegated role must meet the accrediting agency's requirements (for example, the National Committee for Quality Assurance [NCQA]), as well as any managed care provider manual or policies/procedures detailing the delegated function. Does the contract limit the liability assumed by the organization to that delegated function only? How will this professional service be covered under existing insurance or self-insurance programs? Are the staff performing this service properly trained, credentialed, and qualified?

Unfortunately, many managed care business liability exposures are not properly identified in the organization's risk-financing program. Once again, the risk manager can be a valuable resource, identifying new and expanding areas of risk exposure for the organization and integrating risk management concepts, strategies, and techniques into the managed care contracting arena.

When conducting a risk management review of a managed care contract, unique aspects of the business relationship should be addressed.

Identification and Relationship of the Parties   The contract should clearly identify in the opening paragraphs each legal corporate entity involved in the relationship, including affiliate corporations. The status of the parties (such as payor, provider, provider organization) should also be clear without ambiguity, and state that the relationship of the parties is one of independent contractors.

Terminology   Managed care contracts should contain an extensive list of defined terms so as to avoid subsequent disputes regarding interpretation of key words. A review should also remove from any definition terminology such as "highest quality," "least expensive," or "immediate."

EMTALA Issues   Many managed care contracting staff are unaware of a hospital's obligations under the Emergency Medical Treatment and Active Labor Act (EMTALA). The risk management review of the contract should include particular attention to any provision requiring prior authorization before screening or stabilization of the patient, definitions of covered emergency services which differ from EMTALA, and any references to reviewing financial obligations with the patient. For example, any language requiring the hospital to seek (from the managed care plan) authorization prior to administering stabilizing medical care is a potential EMTALA violation.

Notification and Release of Information   Managed care contracts often contain provisions regarding the obligations of the provider or provider organizations to notify the payor when litigation, claims, or adverse events occur. However, care should be taken to protect any confidential or sensitive information and to limit the information to only that which is necessary and/or legally permissible. Risk managers should work with legal counsel to develop preferred contract provisions to incorporate applicable federal and state law, and review the provisions with the enactment of new confidentiality laws or statutes.

Insurance and Indemnification   The risk manager should carefully review the types of insurance required and the limits of liability as it impacts the various legal entities involved. For instance, if a self-insurance program is in place, do the insurance requirements permit this coverage? Are individual providers required to have multiple coverages such as managed care errors and omissions or comprehensive general liability, which the provider might not have in place?

Additionally, contractual risk transfer in managed care contracts contained in the indemnification provisions must be carefully reviewed to limit the risk assumed to only those services or activities under the control of the provider or provider organization.

A comprehensive discussion of managed care-contracting issues for the risk manager is beyond the scope of this chapter. However, involvement of risk managers in the process and inclusion of affected staff beyond the managed care department (for example, utilization management and discharge planning) benefit the organization. Because they are particularly complex and often time-sensitive, managed care contracts may be potentially devastating to an organization. A managed care contract review presents a perfect opportunity for the risk manager to showcase his or her risk management expertise in risk identification, treatment, and analysis.

············
CONFIDENTIALITY PROVISIONS

Many contractual relationships in health care organizations have confidentiality (or privacy) issues contained within the document. As contracts are reviewed, serious thought should be given to including a confidentiality provision specific to the proprietary nature of business records of the organization, in addition to other protected and sensitive information such as patient information, medical staff records, committee proceedings, personnel files, payroll, and compensation.

Negligent disclosure of protected information exposes the custodian of the information to legal liability. Therefore, access to the organization's protected or sensitive information must be limited to that which the contracting party has a valid "need to know." Any unauthorized disclosure by the contractor and its employees should subject the contractor to the resulting financial liability from the negligent act.

The risk manager is well advised to work with legal counsel in developing sample confidentiality provisions, which can be inserted into the health care contract as necessary.

············
CONTRACT FILE MANAGEMENT

The key to success in contract review is to establish a workable system for managing the renewal process and categorizing the type of contract being reviewed or filed. One suggestion is to develop contract files under the following names: management services, home health, maintenance and repair, temporary staffing, consulting services, professional services, leases, purchase agreements, construction, clinical affiliation agreements, physician-related, managed care, and pending mergers or acquisitions. Within each file, all contracts should be listed by contracting party name, time period, and anniversary date. All requested documentation regarding insurance coverages (such as certificates and additional insured endorsements) should be maintained with each contract in an easily retrievable manner.

A tickler system should assist the risk manager in reviewing pending contracts for required certificates of insurance (or coverage) or additional-insured endorsements *prior* to the contract effective date, as well as a process for reviewing renewing contracts well in advance of any anniversary or termination date with applicable notice requirements. The tickler system should list the anniversary date and notice requirement prior to renegotiation or termination, and allow for adequate time to involve the necessary parties in reviewing the terms and suggesting improvements in performance expectations.

At the time of renewal or renegotiation, the risk manager should impart to the negotiating parties any newly enacted or contemplated legislation, statutes, or regulations affecting the contract. For instance, Safe Medical Device Act (SMDA) reporting obligation, affect many health care organizations, providers, and vendors yet rarely are included within the contract specifications.

It is advisable to include a statement in the contract that each party agrees to comply with all applicable federal and state laws, and local ordinances or regulations. However, certain federal or state mandates (for example, SMDA, Patient Self Determination Act [PSDA], Occupational Health and Safety Act [OSHA]) have such a major impact that it is best to delineate each party's actions in order to comply with the law and alleviate any misunderstandings as to the appropriate party's responsibility for compliance.

Developing a policy or procedure for the organization related to who may sign contracts on its behalf, maintenance of the contract document, appropriate parties who must review the contract before signing, and the contracts that warrant risk management and legal review is particularly beneficial. Involved managers should participate in the process to some degree because they are key organizational contacts for the contracting party. Further, the person responsible for insurance programs or self-insurance coverages must be included in the process of contract review, preferably before signing the document, to ensure that appropriate insurance or coverage language is used.

....

SPECIFIC RISK ISSUES IN CONTRACTUAL RELATIONSHIPS

Additional areas of a health care organization's contractual relationships require the risk manager's particular attention. These include clinical affiliations, arrangements with temporary or independent contractors, supplemental staffing agencies, consulting services, equipment purchases, construction contracts, and building leases.

Clinical Affiliations

Student affiliations encompass many clinical experiences and departments in the health care organization. For instance, occupational therapy, physical therapy, advanced professional training for licensed providers, and other dependent or independent practitioner "on-site" programs occur in many locations every day. A few key ideas to consider are:

- The sponsoring educational institution should specify responsibility for health plan, workers' compensation, and professional liability coverage. Although the student may be required to obtain his or her own professional liability coverage, the limits of coverage and liability responsibility for professional acts should be clearly defined.
- The health care organization cannot transfer responsibility or accountability for the care of its patients to an educational institution despite the presence of students in a

clinical area. Therefore, although a student might be assigned patient care duties, the organization's staff must supervise and monitor all care delivered to the patient and not use students as "replacement staff."

This should be reflected in the contract, as in the following wording: "The health care organization retains full administrative and clinical responsibility for the care of its patients. Students and faculty, as participants in this education program, will not replace organization staff and will follow organization policies and procedures in the rendering of patient care."

• The health care organization should be allowed to remove any student from the patient care area for infractions of policy or procedure. Protecting patients from potential injury is of paramount importance.

• The ratio of instructor to student and supervisory responsibility should be clearly noted. For instance, does the facility provide a dedicated individual to fulfill this obligation? Will the school provide faculty on site to supervise the students?

• Both students and faculty should abide by the facility's policies and procedures including dress code, employee health requirements, confidentiality, and behavior.

• Responsibility for lost or damaged property should be listed in the agreement, with the school reimbursing the facility for lost or damaged equipment or property as a result of student or faculty actions.

Temporary or Independent Contractors

Under certain circumstances and applicable federal or state law, an organization may become liable for injuries sustained by a temporary or independent contractor while performing the contract services, particularly in the area of hazardous materials or medical waste handling. The contract should clearly delineate responsibilities for the handling and disposal of hazardous materials and, if possible, require the employer of the temporary or independent contractor to train its employees accordingly. Responsibility for the safe handling and disposal of hazardous materials or other medical waste will rest with the producer of such materials, unless noted in the contract. The organization must decide whether health plan coverage and workers' compensation insurance are to be required for temporary and contract workers, given the scope of services provided.

The contract should also specify that the organization is not liable for any employee benefits, workers' compensation, payroll taxes, and so on for the independent contractor. However, it might be wise to require the "solo" contractor to have health plan coverage in the event an accident occurs during contract performance or to require a company of multiple employees to maintain workers' compensation insurance limits as required by state law.

Temporary Staffing Agencies

Critical to this type of contract is the responsibility of the staffing agency to ensure the competency and qualifications of the staff it sends to the organization. For instance, a temporary staffing employee previously convicted of a felony assault may create a significant problem for the organization if the agency has failed to "uncover" his or her history. The unsuspecting health care organization may now expose its patients to a convicted felon and ultimately an unsafe situation. If the temporary staffing agency has minimal or inadequate coverage for the negligent acts of its employees, or the contract fails to specify which party has responsibility for claims arising from the services provided by the agency, the organization may become the "deep pocket" or inadvertent responsible party in any subsequent civil action involving the patients.

The staffing agency should perform the initial licensure and competency evaluation of all employees it sends to facilities under the terms of the contract. However, the receiving facility has a duty to supervise, monitor, and intervene in the temporary staff's patient care activities once they arrive for duty.

Consulting Services

Many contracts for specific consulting services fail to properly reflect the performance expectations as originally intended by the health care organization. Consultants should provide evidence of professional liability, or errors and omission coverage, for their consulting services. Of greater importance, however, is the need for the organization to clarify or articulate its expectations of the consultant's performance. Undoubtedly, many organizations have incurred great expense for consulting services, yet when the consultant's report arrives and the recommendations simply gather dust on a manager's shelf, any benefit to the organization is lost. At the root of this problem lies the inadequate preparation on the part of the health care organization to arrive at a clear understanding of needed services *before* the contract was drafted or negotiations completed. In addition, the organization should have a clear understanding of how the consultant's recommendations will be used when received. Expectations and performance standards must be clearly articulated and documented prior to signing any consulting service contract to avoid this frustration and unnecessary expense.

Equipment Purchases

The risk manager should become familiar with the process followed in ordering, receiving, and installing new equipment within the organization. Because the Uniform Commercial Code generally governs these transactions, risk managers should acquaint themselves with this body of law. Common issues in equipment purchase include:

- What warranties does the vendor supply?
- Who, how, and where will the service and maintenance be provided on this equipment?
- If a new upgrade is developed, who pays?
- Who is responsible for patient injury from equipment failure?
- Can the organization pay, at least in part, *after* the equipment is installed and operating as intended?
- Who pays if the equipment malfunctions and no facility services can be provided?
- Will the vendor provide emergency service? At what cost?
- What type of notice is required before a service repair technician will respond? What is the time frame?
- Will the vendor train facility staff in the proper use of equipment?
- Can the contract be terminated (the equipment returned) if it fails to produce as advertised? Are there any penalties involved?
- What is the responsibility of biomedical engineering vendors in the area of preventive maintenance and documentation?

Construction Contracts

Because of financial ramifications and local and state building code requirements, among other considerations, the majority of construction contracts will be negotiated and implemented apart from the risk manager. For purposes of this discussion, the risk manager is encouraged to request the services of the property insurer, facility operations manager, and local counsel to evaluate the adequacy of the commercial insurance requirements to obtain bonds and secure necessary permits, dispute resolution requirements, and indemnification and hold-harmless provisions. Many property insurers will provide valuable review of construction plans upon request.

Building Leases

A simplistic approach to reviewing a building lease is to ask the following questions and consider whether the "responsible" party in the lease is appropriate.

- Which party is responsible for damage to the building, contents, surrounding property, and so on?
- Who is responsible for preexisting conditions, such as toxic waste?
- Does each party grant a waiver of subrogation rights?
- Who is responsible for sprinkler damage, fire, earth movement, or flooding?
- If the organization is leasing space to physicians, does the lease meet all necessary requirements?

Once again, building leases most often will involve legal counsel in drafting and negotiating terms. If presented with a lease, the risk manager is best served by contacting legal counsel for assistance.

············

HOME CARE CONTRACTS

As IDSs and IDNs develop, the home care area is one that frequently evolves into another cost center or revenue producer for the parent organization. Stand-alone or multilocation home care agencies often are integrated into the organization, as well as new agencies developed. Private duty (nonlicensed services), hospice, and durable medical equipment (DME) providers often are included under the home care "umbrella."

The risk manager must first look to the insurance coverages for this type of operation. Does the organization separately insure or cover this operation? Who is the legal "employer" for home care staff? How are workers' compensation and automobile liability exposures covered? If DME is included in the operation, is product liability coverage considered? How will third-party crime impact the coverages available?

Next, any licensing or accrediting body requirements should be reviewed. If an accrediting body has specific requirements, the various required elements should be considered *before* reviewing any contracts in order to save time and effort. In the home care area, two accrediting agencies are often used: Community Health Accreditation Program (CHAP) and JCAHO. Also, it should be determined whether any state or federal laws are applicable to this endeavor. For instance, should the DME or home care staff report patient injury under the Safe Medical Device Act (SMDA)? Are the Patient Self Determination Act (PSDA) responsibilities addressed?

A common practice is for the home care agency to subcontract for certain services, particularly when the service volume does not reasonably afford the hiring of such staff (for example, occupational or physical therapy). Therefore, the use of an independent contractor in home care is common, and the provider must be qualified by licensure, education, and training to provide such services. He or she should produce evidence of current professional liability coverage by a certificate representing the amount of coverage and the insured's name. An additional area to consider is the IRS's scrutiny of independent contractor arrangements as it relates to the "control" of the provider's services.

It is important that the home care agency not be misled as to the qualifications or liability coverage for the contractor, subcontractors, and employees. For instance, an occupational or physical therapist must be knowledgeable and agree to meet the accreditation requirements of the home care agency. After all, the contractor is holding itself out to the agency as being in a provider business and should be held to the provider's standard. Also, it is best to specify the amount of coverage required and to maintain a certificate of coverage with the contract file. In certain instances, the organization may request that the provider's professional liability insurer include the organization as an additional insured as respects the provider's activities under the contract. This is particularly helpful if the provider is performing direct patient care activity.

Additional areas of concern in home care are the agency's requirements for client education in relation to medical equipment usage, a medical director's review of practices and policies within the agency, and the safety of employees in the client's home and community. Additional requirements for home care agency contracting may be found in the CHAP or JCAHO standards, which list contract requirements for the many areas mentioned above, such as applicable standards, licensure required, and evaluation of the independent contractor's services.

· · · · · · · · · · · ·

CONCLUSION

Contracts should not intimidate risk managers. By carefully reviewing contracts, considering the language and reasonableness of the provisions, and developing a system for filing and analyzing key contract provisions, the risk manager will contribute significantly to the avoidance or mitigation of liability for the health care organization. The contract review described in this chapter is limited in scope and in no way purports to replace legal counsel's involvement in contract drafting or negotiating. However, the risk manager is trained to identify risk exposures for the organization, which should include exposures contained in contracts. The greater the risk manager's expertise and skill in contract review, the greater the savings to the organization due to decreased use of legal services and decreased liability exposure for the organization.

Endnotes

1. Black, H. C. *Black's Law Dictionary*. St. Paul, Minn.: West Publishing Co., 1991.

2. *Ibid.*

3. Joint Commission on Accreditation of Healthcare Organizations. *1999 Comprehensive Accreditation Manual for Hospitals*. Oakbrook Terrace, Ill.: JCAHO, 1999.

4. A.M. Best Company, an independent analyst of the insurance industry, uses financial criteria to rate insurance companies. Factors such as profitability leverages, liquidity, assets, spread of risk, and so on are used to determine the rating.

Every state has a guarantee or insolvency fund to protect insureds and claimants if an insurer becomes insolvent or otherwise unable to fulfill its financial obligations. The funds generally cover only the failure of insurers licensed to do business in that state and offer limits lower than the defunct policy provided. However, such insurer insolvency protection is the best available at this time.

Suggested Readings

Benda, C. G., and Rozovsky, F. A. *Managed Care and the Law, Liability and Risk Management: A Practical Guide.* Boston: Little, Brown and Company, 1996.

Clifford, R. C., and Sleeth, B. *Insurance Law Handbook.* Carlsbad, Calif.: Parker and Son, 1992.

Hall, J. L., and Williams, T. A. "Important Provisions and Features of Any Contract Involving Health Care Providers." *Health Law Handbook,* 1998, pp. 309–341.

Hillman, D. C. "A Primer on PHO Capitation Contracts." *Journal of Health and Hospital Law, 29*(5), April. American Academy of Healthcare Attorneys.

Ino, A. W. *Managed Care and Capitation Contracting for Home Health Agencies.* Gaithersburg, Md.: Aspen, 1996.

Keckeissen, F. G., and Grube, K. S. "Independent Contractor or Employee? The Rules and Ramifications of Worker Classification in the Health Care Industry." *Health Law Handbook,* 1998, pp. 413–441.

Miller, T. R., and Belt, J. E. "Conducting a Managed Care Contract Review." *Healthcare Financial Management,* Jan. 1998, pp. 40–41.

Pozzar, G. D. *Legal Aspects of Health Care Administration* (6th ed.). Gaithersburg, Md.: Aspen, 1996.

Wiehl, J. G. *The Direct Contracting Manual: A Strategic Guide to Hospital-Employer Health Care Agreements.* Alexandria, Va.: Capitol Publications, 1992.

Wielinski, P. J., Woodward, J. W., and Gibson, J. P. *Contractual Risk Transfer: Strategies for Contract Indemnity and Insurance Provisions.* Dallas: International Risk Management Institute, Inc., 1995.

12

Mergers, Acquisitions, and Divestitures

Karen E. Bedford
Corbette S. Doyle
John F. Roskopf

Before an acquisition closes, the risk manager must work to ensure that critical risk-related issues are brought to light. This process is known as due diligence. The risk manager has a unique position from which to view an acquisition. Involvement with both staff and operating departments provides a broad perspective, insight into exposures, and an appreciation of the working relationships between various departments throughout the organization. However, the risk manager has to maintain a delicate balance between technical concerns and the strategic issues inherent in any acquisition. Consequently, his or her objectives in the due diligence process, though grounded in technical analysis, should simultaneously focus on tactics that will:

- Reduce the acquisition purchase price.
- Improve postacquisition earnings and/or cash flow.
- Improve risk management effectiveness throughout the organization.
- Insulate the organization from unanticipated costs.

It is only through achievement of these strategic objectives that the true contributions of the risk management function are manifest. This chapter outlines some of the major concerns risk managers must address to perform their due diligence responsibilities from both the technical and strategic perspectives.

CONCEPT OF SUCCESSOR LIABILITY

A number of legal issues are associated with an acquisition; two of the more important ones are the distinction between a stock acquisition and an asset purchase, and the concept of successor liability. In a *stock acquisition,* the acquiring company acquires, and is legally liable for all the liabilities, known and unknown, of the target company. In an *asset purchase,* only specific assets are acquired and, historically, there is no transfer of liability. In recent years, however, state courts and legislatures have developed the concept of *successor liability,* under which the acquiring company can be held liable for the torts of the target company's previous owners. This is particularly true when there is an asset acquisition of an entire company and the acquirer continues to operate the company under the same name, with little or no outward indication of the change in ownership. If the public does not perceive a difference in ownership or the previous owners are subsequently bankrupt, the current owner can, in certain instances, be held liable. Generally, the successor corporation may be held liable in the following situations:

- If it expressly or implicitly assumes liability for the defective product or service.
- If the transaction amounts to a consolidation or merger of the two corporations.
- If the transfer amounts to a continuation or reincarnation of the predecessor corporation.
- If the transaction is fraudulent or lacking in good faith.

The acquisition document in an asset acquisition often includes a list of the specific assets to be acquired. Risk management should be careful about acquiring the insurance policies of the target company, particularly if it is a division or subsidiary of another company. Acquiring the insurance policies may limit the purchaser's ability to pass certain claims back to the seller. Worse yet, some courts view acquisition of the insurance policies as an indication of the company's intent to accept responsibility for all claims, including those that occurred prior to acquisition.

It should be noted that the concept of successor liability is not limited to the United States, but is coming into use in Europe as well. The risk manager, along with legal counsel, should examine both the acquisition and proposed operations of the target company after the acquisition. Examination is particularly important when existing facilities and staff, either employed or contract, will continue to be used.

....

ELEMENTS FOR RISK MANAGEMENT REVIEW

In addition to the due diligence process (discussed in detail in a later section of this chapter), a review of several other important elements should be performed. Those elements include the indemnity and insurance provisions of the company being acquired, its historic claims data, and senior management's concerns about hidden issues.

Indemnity and Insurance Provisions

The entire acquisition contract should be reviewed thoroughly, with particular attention to any indemnification language. Concurrent with the contract review, the risk manager should review all applicable liability policies, going back at least five years or further, depending on the exact nature of the exposures. In addition, a matrix should be constructed that identifies at least the following information for each policy period:

- Coverage and form.
- Limits and self-insured retentions (SIRs), deductibles.

- Carriers.
- Insolvent carriers.
- Paid claims.
- Open reserves.
- Aggregate limits erosion.
- Aggregate retention erosion.
- Key coverage exclusions.
- Excluded operations and businesses.
- Policy form retro dates.
- Retro dates.
- Named insureds and critical endorsements.
- Premiums and funding.
- Allocation methodologies.

Depth of the analysis depends on factors such as the tail, or lag, in reporting claims, claim frequency, and potential severity. The importance of this analysis cannot be overstated. Inadequate insurance, for whatever reason, has a direct impact on the cash flow and profitability of the venture.

Traditionally, insurance has been used to support or collateralize the indemnification provisions of the contract. However, as lawyers and negotiators become more creative, this distinction has become blurred. Particularly in the case of the sale of a division or subsidiary, the selling parent might warrant that it will be responsible for all claims of the division or subsidiary for events prior to the close, but only to the extent that it has insurance. If there is no insurance, the limits are exhausted, or the carriers insolvent, the acquiring company must pay the claim. If a claim results in increased costs to the seller, such as, for example, retro charges, the acquiring company also must reimburse the seller. The numerous implications of such onerous clauses should be reviewed in detail.

Historic Claims Data

Historic claims data should be reviewed to determine whether claim trends are within acceptable bounds. As with the insurance review, adverse claim trends can have a material impact on both cash flow and profitability. Whenever possible, an actuarial analysis and loss forecast should be performed. Some of the more important questions to ask in a claim review are:

- *Valuations:* Are individual claims properly valued and reserved by the claims administrator?
- *Reserves:* Has the target company properly accrued for all open claims and an appropriate estimate of incurred but not reported (IBNR) claims?
- *Projections:* How do projections of ultimate cost compare with the applicable limits of insurance?
- *Litigation:* Has the target company initiated any litigation against its insurers over claim practices or coverage disputes?

- *Trends:* In addition to general claim trends, are there any precedent-setting cases that may have a material impact on future negotiations?
- *Philosophy:* What is the target company's philosophy with regard to the claim management process?

An absence of claims is not necessarily an indication of a good operation; it may be just good luck or timing. Conversely, the way a company approaches claims—both professional liability loss prevention and management of specific cases—can provide subtle indications of the general quality of the management team.

Senior Management Concerns

Senior management's overriding concern is its ability to make the deal work. This concern is manifest in two ways. First, specific issues such as directors' and officers' (D&O) liability, professional liability, or pollution problems are raised. They are the big, obvious exposures. Although the solutions can be quite complex, their identification is often relatively simple.

The second concern is more subtle. Senior management has a certain, sometimes unquantifiable concern about hidden issues that may not surface until well after the deal is consummated. Exhibit 12.3 on page 293 contains a sample of documents to review and questions to ask. The risk manager's job is to ferret out as much of the operating and exposure information as possible, assimilate the data, and present a highly focused report. The report should include all the answers to two basic questions: What does management *want* to know, and what *should* management know? Of course, what management should know is anything that can have a material impact on the four areas cited in the introduction to this chapter—price of acquisition, postacquisition earnings or cash flow, effectiveness of risk management, and insulation against unanticipated costs.

Determination of materiality is a function of the size of the acquiring company, the size of the target company, loss potential, and similar factors peculiar to each transaction. For example, any problems associated with a hospital that is being acquired by a one-hospital entity may well be material. On the other hand, those same problems may be deemed immaterial if the acquirer is a multibillion-dollar corporation. In general, the due diligence process and issues of concern are the same regardless of the size of the acquirer or the entity being acquired. The key differences are that: (1) larger organizations tend to move more quickly in acquisitions and divestitures (thus allowing less time for the due diligence process) and (2) fewer issues will be deemed material (that is, significant enough to derail a merger).

DIVESTITURES

To a certain extent, the information discussed in the mergers and acquisitions due diligence process also can be used for divestitures. It simply necessitates a shift in perspective. However, certain administrative issues need to be addressed by the divesting company. Typically, the divesting company will be interested in:

- Analysis of the key variable costs—for example, claim reserves or IBNR calculations and potential cost fluctuations.
- Analysis of the impact of the divestiture on the remaining insurance program.

- Assistance with data collection for the new owners, including loss and exposure history, loss control reports, operating contracts, procedures, and so on.

Although divestitures are not viewed as the attention getters that mergers and acquisitions are, they frequently generate more work for risk managers. This is particularly true if the divesting organization has sophisticated loss-financing arrangements and sells the liabilities of an entity. The risk manager may need to establish elaborate cost accounting and billing mechanisms with the acquiring organization.

Exhibit 12.1 on page 289 contains a synopsis of some of the major administrative issues. The risk manager will want to revise this outline to meet the specific requirements of each divestiture, particularly if the transaction involves physician groups.

....

DUE DILIGENCE PROCESS

From a risk management perspective, the purpose of the due diligence process is to ensure that critical risk-related issues are brought to light before an acquisition closes. *Critical issues* are those issues that could impact the price or terms of the acquisition or conceivably alter the decision to proceed with a planned acquisition. This section addresses the specific exposure, risk-financing, and administrative issues that risk managers need to evaluate for the due diligence process.

The key steps in the due diligence process are to:

1. Collect the necessary information.
2. Analyze the subject organization's exposures to loss.
3. Assess its risk-financing programs.
4. Evaluate its risk management policies and procedures.

Results of the analysis should then be reported to management in a format that will assist in the decision-making process. Once a decision is made to proceed with a transaction, several steps must be taken to merge the risk management programs of the new and existing entities. (See Exhibit 12.2 on page 291.)

Exposure Issues

The first step is to identify the past, current, and planned future operations of the target entity. Each of these exposures should then be evaluated for known and hidden liabilities and/or costs in excess of those currently planned for or funded. The following sections identify the broad categories of issues that risk managers need to evaluate. The specific concerns for each category are delineated in the checklist in Exhibit 12.1 on page 289.

Contractual Liability

Risk management should obtain a list of key operating contracts, including managed care contracts, that will continue after the acquisition is completed. The risk manager should then review the hold-harmless, indemnification, and insurance provisions of these contracts to determine whether the company has assumed the liability of others (for example, nonemployed physicians or contract services) and whether risk management will be able to provide the appropriate insurance to comply in the future. This may be problematic if, for example, managed care contracts have been signed with broadly worded hold-harmless provisions.

The risk manager also should review incidental contracts (building leases, equipment leases, maintenance agreements, and so on) to be sure that all the insurance terms are appropriate and have been met. Capital leases and long-term financing agreements, as well as some loan documents, frequently contain insurance and indemnity provisions. If a captive is involved, the risk manager should evaluate any contractual provisions such as a mandate for admitted and/or Best's rated insurance coverage.

In addition, the risk manager should review any prior acquisitions and divestitures to determine what liabilities may be lingering from prior transactions. In larger transactions and any transactions involving publicly traded companies, the law firms typically assemble a list of all documents, which are then made available to interested parties. Typically referred to as the "bank book," this is an excellent source of information. Certificate of insurance records also can be helpful. Once the transaction is completed, the risk manager should amend any existing contracts that will be maintained to reflect the merger and acquisition or divestiture.

Loans and financing agreements may also contain requirements for the maintenance of specific insurance, both property and liability. These documents should be reviewed to ensure continued compliance.

Professional Liability

The long-term nature of the exposures, the significance of retained losses (versus losses transferred to others), and the frequency of claims-made coverages render professional liability one of the most complicated and critical steps in the due diligence process. If the liabilities of a heavily self-insured organization will be assumed, an actuarial evaluation should be obtained to establish the adequacy of reserve levels.

The adequacy of protection afforded by the professional liability policies should be evaluated in conjunction with loss reserves. Narrow coverage may, for example, require increased reserve levels for uninsured losses. Key considerations include:

- Policy limits.
- Definition of named insured (including committee coverage).
- Definition of claim and notice.
- Incident-reporting trigger (versus coverage only for claims actually asserted).
- Vicarious medical professional coverage for managed care activities.
- Errors and omissions (E&O) protection for the administrative exposures of managed care activities. (The risk manager should check for a comprehensive definition of covered exposures that includes all existing activities.)
- Existence of a captive insurance company, which may require a separate due diligence analysis.

Physician acquisitions have become commonplace in the past few years, and divestitures of group practices have already begun as a result of strategic realignments. Many of the issues discussed above apply equally to physician professional liability issues. There are additional points for consideration, however, such as billing procedures, scope of managed care contracts, and adequacy of the internal credentialing procedures. The checklist in Exhibit 12.3 covers the pertinent issues in detail.

Directors' and Officers' Liability

Directors' and officers' (D&O) liability coverage review is one of the most critical steps in the due diligence process because (1) it is often the first line of defense if problems arise and (2) the cooperation and satisfaction of the insured individuals may be critical to ongoing operations. As such, the merger and acquisition agreement generally mandates runoff protection for the outgoing directors and officers if they are subsequently sued as a result of the transaction. Sources of D&O claims can include conflict of interest, antitrust, personal profit, refusal to consider competing offers, and so on. The scope of runoff coverage required should be compared with the existing D&O policy in case the former is broader than the latter.

Separate runoff coverage for the acquired entity can be purchased (from either the acquiree's insurer, the organization's insurer, or even a third insurer), or risk management can ask the organization's insurer to roll the coverage into the organization's own policy. For organizations that make a large number of acquisitions, "rolling runoff" coverage can be negotiated so that risk management can automatically roll the runoff into the parent's policy.

Consider the following example. Two large, nonprofit systems agreed to merge. The merger agreement included significant financial penalties if either firm pulled out of the merger. The chairman of one board felt the proposed management structure for the combined company was inappropriate and encouraged his board to pull out, with the result that the board of the second company sued him and his board for breaching the contract and invoked the financial penalties. The first board and its chairman are counter-suing and also attempting to invoke the financial penalties.

Provider Excess and Capitation Coverage

Provider excess coverage, also commonly known as *stop loss,* is usually structured to insure claims that are incurred during a twelve-month period and reported no later than three to six months after expiration of the policy. Because many administrative details can fall by the wayside during merger and acquisition negotiations, it is critical to ensure that payable claims are reported to the carrier in time to invoke recovery.

Risk management should determine whether the underlying managed care contracts are transferable and, if so, whether the provider excess coverage is transferable to a new owner. If liabilities will be assumed, it may be necessary to have an actuarial review of the managed care contract rates and loss experience to identify any potential material losses. Because these losses pay out quickly, the "pain or gain" will be recognized quickly. For example, one West Coast health care system used its captive to reinsure its provider excess exposure. Unfortunately, the underlying rates were inadequate and the captive suffered a $4 million loss in one year. With no time lag in the loss payout, there was not even an opportunity to earn investment income to offset the size of the loss.

Workers' Compensation

Risk management should examine all insurance policies, state filings, loss runs, Occupational Safety and Health Administration (OSHA) reports, and so on. In addition, historical actuarial analyses should be obtained, if available. If not available, loss runs should be examined for trends in frequency and severity. Risk management should look for signs of deteriorating loss profiles and areas for potential loss reduction efforts, such as opportunities to improve the profitability of the organization postacquisition.

The risk manager also should obtain details on the nature of the current loss-financing programs if his or her organization will be assuming liabilities. For loss-sensitive programs, it is important to obtain copies of *all* side indemnification agreements. In states where the company qualifies as self-insured, risk management should evaluate the process for maintaining self-insured status.

In addition, risk management should determine how the seller plans to handle current disability claims. Because of their open-ended nature, it is preferable that the buyer not assume any responsibility for employees on disability at the date of close.

Safety and loss prevention programs also should be reviewed to help ensure that they are well structured and effective and to gain insight into management's approach to workers' compensation. For example, risk management should find out whether there have been any significant OSHA fines or citations.

Property Exposures

In addition to examining the typical direct-damage exposures, risk management should perform an analysis of business interruption and contingent business interruption exposures. Cash flow may be extremely important in the transaction, and the new owners may not have a complete grasp of the business interruption exposure or potential adverse financial impact. Analysis may be particularly important if there are properties with significant wind or earthquake exposures.

It is common to have a formal property appraisal in the acquisitions. The client also should instruct the appraisal company to provide actual cash value and replacement cost values, using the insurance definitions of those terms.

If possible, complete loss runs, loss prevention reports, and any engineering data available (including probable maximum loss and maximum foreseeable loss projections) should be obtained. Although the reporting lag on property claims typically is short, those who suffered losses from the Northridge earthquake learned just how long this process can take—and how often necessary data are lacking.

Bonds

Generally, bonds other than fidelity, self-insured, and patient compensation fund bonds are not a major issue for health care organizations. However, they do merit attention because the issues are a bit different.

Risk management should obtain a schedule of all outstanding bonds and determine the collateral requirements. Frequently, loan covenants restrict the ability to issue letters of credit or other acceptable collateral to bond underwriters. The risk manager should examine the superseded suretyship provisions in the acquiring company's fidelity coverage and determine the impact on the limits available if the target company's coverage is subsequently dropped.

Pollution

Pollution issues are complex, involving legal and operating issues that are beyond the scope of this chapter. The client should retain appropriate legal and environmental consulting services. At a minimum, most buyers will want to perform a Phase I audit of the property, which includes a review of plant or property records, interviews with local regulatory officials, review of appropriate regulatory databases, a historical ownership and usage search, and an on-site risk assessment. Phase I audits usually do not include testing, soil or water sampling, and so on.

Many businesses are engaged in litigation over past disposal practices. Regulation of hazardous waste at the federal level mushroomed in 1976 with passage of the Resource Conservation and Recovery Act (discussed in Chapter 9). Many companies that currently are environmentally sound can have problems from past practices, particularly those involving waste storage and disposal.

Specific pollution liability policies (for example, underground storage tank coverages) and pollution coverage provisions and exclusions in other liability policies (both current and prior) should be reviewed in detail.

Among the numerous pollution liability cases that illustrate the dangers of potential liability, one that stands out involves a charitable organization that we will refer to as Gamma Association. In 1984, Gamma Association received a donation of an eight-acre lot in an industrial area. The donor was Alpha Corporation, which apparently had been unaware that previous Alpha operations had dumped chemicals at the site. The state EPA is now holding Gamma liable for the cleanup costs, which will be measured in multiples of Gamma's annual revenue. Alpha has apologized but declined to take back the property or contribute to the cleanup costs.

Occupational Disease Exposures

Occupational disease claims that surface after the close of the transaction can come as a surprise and be quite expensive. To avoid this problem, risk management should examine all occupational disease exposures thoroughly and review the target company's compliance with OSHA requirements and right-to-know regulations.

Telemedicine and E-Medicine Exposures

Technology is rapidly changing the face of health care and the relationship between providers and patients. Critical new exposures include confidentiality clinical advice across state lines, redefining the criteria for a physician-patient relationship, e-mail documentation and record keeping, and copyright infringements. The due diligence process should include a review of existing Web sites and procedures for reviewing information posted on them, and the use of e-mail, including confidentiality and documentation issues.

Risk-Financing and Administrative Issues

Risk-financing issues are most critical if the liabilities will be included in the acquisition. The key issues are the nature and extent of retained losses (whether self-insured or included in a loss-sensitive financing program), and the scope of historic and current coverage (discussed at the beginning of this chapter). The detailed information needed for these analyses is spelled out in the checklist in Exhibit 12.3.

Quantification of Reserves and IBN

In examining adequacy of the reserves, risk management should review the reserving philosophy for methodology, adequacy, and consistency. Reserves on the insurance company loss runs should be reviewed, as should accruals on the target company's books.

Individual case reserves may have to be examined prior to determining whether the aggregate reserves are adequate. It is only after the aggregate reserves have been reviewed that a projection of the IBNR can be properly developed. Depending on the type of claims, frequency, and severity, an independent actuarial analysis may be required.

When explaining the potential for adverse development in claim and reserve patterns, the risk manager should ensure that management understands the impact on both the purchase price and the ongoing profitability of the company. For self-insurance, captives, and other loss-sensitive plans (such as retros), a schedule should be developed of maximum cost by year, amounts paid to date, open reserves, and potential additional costs up to any maximums or loss limits.

The importance of this process is illustrated in the following example. A large hospital system was self-insured for professional liability, and all the claims were managed by the in-house legal department. The legal department also established the reserves. It was discovered that the department was only reserving for indemnity and was paying outside legal expenses on a current basis. The inclusion of outside defense costs increased the claim reserves by several million dollars.

Administrative Issues

Risk managers should examine every aspect of combining the target company or facility with their organization's current insurance program. In some instances, it may be advantageous to keep the two programs separate (for example, in the case of a hospital acquiring a group practice for the first time, even if it means more administration).

Administrative costs, though not always significant, can be troublesome. If risk management does not have (and cannot obtain) adequate staff support to handle the paper trail of the merger and/or the increased activity levels post-merger, support should be solicited from external service providers, such as brokers and insurers.

Consider the example of a large health care system that sold its West Coast facilities. As a precaution, the system wanted to recall or void all outstanding certificates of insurance for the division, estimated to be in the hundreds. (The new owners also were curious about the number of outstanding certificates.) It was then that employees of the system discovered that they had neither tracked requests for certificates nor retained copies of certificates. The certificates that the system had were issued in the name of the parent "including all divisions and subsidiaries." The system is hoping that its customers read about the sale and contact the new owners for replacement certificates.

Loss-Adjusting Cooperation

Cooperation is easiest if the entire organization, all its staff, and all its employees are acquired. When the target company is a subsidiary of a larger organization, the new owner and the old owner should agree to cooperate in the handling of all liability claims, whether or not known at the time of close. Health care professionals, risk managers, medical directors, lawyers, and other appropriate parties at the old owner should be available for deposition or testimony if required for the defense of a future claim. The same cooperation is necessary when the old owner has retained the liabilities of a spin-off facility and needs the testimony of transferred employees. Similarly, it would be inappropriate for the prior owner to quickly settle old claims just for the sake of disposing of them, thereby developing a pattern that may affect the new owner's ability to settle future claims more judiciously.

The acquisition document should contain a clause providing the acquiring company access to data and personnel from the old company (or vice versa if liabilities are retained) as required for the investigation and defense of claims of all types.

··········

TIPS FOR THE DUE DILIGENCE PROCESS

The due diligence process is different for every transaction, even though the overall objectives remain unchanged. The following tips will help ensure uniformity in approach and documentation.

Use of Source Documents

Whenever possible, original documents, particularly policies and loss runs, should be used. The source of the information and valuation date of data should always be stated. If specific documents are unavailable, or if copies appear to be incomplete, the risk manager's due diligence report should note the deficiencies.

Obtainment of Written Confirmation

Documentation of critical issues should include written confirmation from the target company or its representatives. At a minimum, risk management should obtain confirmation that all policies are currently in effect, all premiums have been paid, and all loss runs are accurate and complete. If written confirmations are not possible, the sources of all verbal confirmations and responses to questions should be cited.

Development of an Action Plan

Risk management should formulate a list of issues to examine, documents to review, and people to interview—and time frames for each. Although it is best to concentrate on the critical issues, seemingly minor areas, such as lease reviews, should not be ignored. Often these secondary issues can provide useful insight into a company's diligence and attention to risk management issues. The sample checklist in Exhibit 12.3 provides a useful starting point for developing an action plan.

Adoption of a Flexible Work System

Deadlines and priorities can change in an instant. Therefore, risk management should consider developing a short list of the most important questions that, if necessary, someone else could ask on the risk manager's behalf. Conversely, the risk manager should see what information can be obtained from fellow employees participating in other areas of the due diligence review.

Focus on Risk Management

Due diligence is not just an insurance policy and loss history analysis. Risk management should review internal policies and procedures, information systems, and related records. The level of risk management awareness throughout the company also should be determined.

Respect for the "Other Guy"

It is important to maintain respect for the people, procedures, and culture at the target company. Just because the other organization does things differently does not mean its processes are wrong or inappropriate. The risk manager and the rest of the team should keep an open mind at all times.

Likewise, it is easy to find fault with an acquisition target. The risk manager should consider whether his or her organization would fare any better under the scrutiny of the due diligence process. He or she should be honest and look for ways to make the deal work for the benefit of everyone.

Awareness of Audience

The risk management due diligence report should be written with the needs of the audience clearly in mind. Focus should be on the main issues, and issues should be ranked by category of importance. If detail and support documents must be included, the report should include an appendix. Risk managers should remember that reports reflect their authors, and should therefore project themselves as attuned to the big picture, not as technical insurance specialists.

Quantification of Major Issues

Risk management should attempt to quantify the financial impact of major issues, even if the best available information is a range of costs. It is not adequate, for example, simply to state that one of the excess carriers is insolvent or that claims are not managed properly. Information on potential costs is material in negotiating the acquisition price.

•••••••••••

CONCLUSION

Risk management is essential in identifying the known and unknown liabilities of a potential acquisition or merger candidate, or an entity being considered for divestiture. Proper and timely analysis provides three vital benefits. The first is a contribution toward determining the appropriate value of the acquisition, merger, or divestiture target. Second, risk management analysis can identify issues that will have a direct impact on future profitability. Finally, thorough analysis helps to identify and anticipate the administrative issues involved in these processes. Although mergers and acquisitions are extremely challenging, they provide the risk manager with an outstanding opportunity to demonstrate the scope and impact of risk management throughout the entire organization.

EXHIBIT 12.1. Divestiture Checklist

Review Terms of Divestiture Agreement

- Transfers of liabilities, assets, employees.
- Retained liabilities.

Property Insurance

- Notify carriers of impending change.
- Prepare insurance specifications for new owner.

  Location schedule

  Insurance coverage

  Loss history

  PLC and engineering reports

  Appraisals
- Calculate return premium estimates.

Liability Insurance

- Notify carriers (primary and excess) of impending change.
- Prepare insurance specifications for new owner.

  Current coverage

  Exposure base (beds, visits, vehicles, and so on)

  Loss history

  Specific liability issues, such as trust agreements, service agreements, key contracts (especially managed care contracts)
- Calculate impact on premium and self-insured reserves.
- Calculate ultimate loss levels, including IBNR if necessary, for liability transfer.
- Requirements for tail coverage.
- Handling of IBNR claims.

Workers' Compensation

- Notify carriers.
- Prepare insurance specifications for new owner.

  Payroll

  Locations

  Loss history

  Safety surveys

  OSHA logs
- Summary of current funding.

  Retro or loss sensitive

  Self-insured
- Calculate impact on current program and loss reserves.
- Calculate ultimate loss levels, including IBNR if necessary, for liability transfer.
- Impact on self-insurance bonds.
- Collateral requirements.

(Continued)

EXHIBIT 12.1.   Divestiture Checklist (*Continued*)

D&O Liability

- Notify carriers.
- Indemnification agreements with key employees.
- Examine the need for tail coverage.

Bonds

- Bond schedule.
- Supporting collateral.

Fidelity and Fiduciary Liability

- Notify carriers.
- Calculate return premiums.
- Comply with ERISA on timing of pension or benefit plan transfers.

Other Property or Casualty Coverages

- Notify carriers.
- Prepare insurance specifications for new owner.

    Coverage

    Exposure base

    Loss information

- Calculate impact on current program.

General Cooperation

- Provide new owners with whatever assistance is necessary, including the placement of coverage during the transition.

    Certificates of insurance (recall old certificates)

    Bonds

    Loss-adjusting cooperation

EXHIBIT 12.2.   Steps in the Due Diligence Process

Action Steps	Responsibility/ Assignments	Completion Date	Notes

1. Compile data on existing insurance programs. See separate insurance program summary. Consider the following exposures:
  1. Property (including earthquake and windstorm)
  2. Crime
  3. Professional liability
  4. Excess liability
  5. Workers' compensation (or alternative, if opted out)
  6. Motor vehicle
  7. Heliport
  8. Aircraft
  9. Environmental (storage tanks)
  10. D&O (and general partners' liability)
  11. Employee-related practices
			Information submitted and reviewed. Interviews completed. X report completed and submitted. Y report being completed this week and will be submitted by 2/28.

2. Review existing risk management policies and procedures.			Have reviewed policies. X updating claims procedures. Request sent to get copies of Y and Z items.
3. Evaluate existing financial exposures and recorded financial reserves.			Completed with Item 1 above.

4. Prepare recommended insurance program parameters to include:
  1. Desired coverages
  2. Per claim SIR or deductible
  3. Aggregate SIR or deductible
			Unable to complete due to ongoing negotiations with Z. Information prepared to submit to X for evaluation.

5. Develop global risk management policies and procedures.			Will convene task force as soon as policies and procedures submitted.
6. Review and approve insurance program parameters.			Outstanding pending completion of Item 4.
7. Prepare a timetable for the combination of all coverages and related cancellation of existing policies.			Outstanding pending completion of Item 6.

(Continued)

EXHIBIT 12.2.   Steps in the Due Diligence Process (*Continued*)

Action Steps	Responsibility/ Assignments	Completion Date	Notes
8. Review and approve risk management policies and procedures.			Outstanding pending completion of Item 5.
9. Issue risk management policies and procedures together with contact lists and other pertinent data to facility CEOs and risk managers.			Outstanding pending completion of Item 8.
10. Evaluate level of training required for facility risk managers.			Outstanding.
11. Determine methods of cost allocation to facilities.			Outstanding pending completion of Item 6.
12. Identify sources (TPAs, and so on) of claims data and compile historical claims information for use in future underwriting efforts. Compile data in a manner useful to actuarial reserve analysis.			Sources identified and claims data available for past policy periods per Item 1. Reserve analysis outstanding.
13. Design ongoing cost allocation methods.			Outstanding pending completion of Item 11.
14. Review and approve ongoing cost allocation methods.			Outstanding pending completion of Item 12.
15. Develop training programs for facility risk managers.			Outstanding pending completion of Item 12.
16. Design activity reporting system for professional liability and workers' compensation programs for use by corporate, regional, and facility senior management and by risk managers.			Outstanding.

Source: Sheila Hagg-Rickert.

EXHIBIT 12.3.   Sample Checklist for Mergers and Acquisitions

The following loss control, risk management, and insurance items are recommended for consideration when reviewing a health care entity for mergers or acquisitions:

Transaction

- Provide specific details on the transfer of liabilities, reserves, and ultimate costs
- Review copies of the following items:

    Transaction agreement

    Letters of intent

    Related documents

Demographic Information

- Provide the following descriptive and statistical information for the most recent fiscal year:

    Patients

    - Number of patient visits per month per physician and per allied health care professionals
    - Patient mix percentage (fee for service, managed care, Medicare, Medicaid, other)
    - Patient demographics by age, sex, and utilization of services

    Facilities and personnel

    - Number of locations
    - Geographic location and overall condition (for example, age and construction) of each facility
    - Length of time in operation for each facility
    - Number of physicians, allied health care professionals, and other personnel at each facility by specialty
    - Numbers of full-time, part-time, and contracted staff
    - What are the qualifications of employees and contracted staff?

        Current licensure

        Current certification

    What has the turnover been during the past five years for:

        Physician staff

        Allied health care professional staff

        Management

        Administrative staff

        Other

    Review of accreditation reports and surveys conducted by NCQA, JCAHO, AAAHC, other

    Investigations by government agencies such as Medicare, FDA, and so on

    Services provided

    - Range of medical and administrative services provided
    - Services provided by the following personnel:

        Physician

        Mental health

        Nursing

        Social services

        Pharmacy

        Risk management

        Laboratory

        Other

(*Continued*)

EXHIBIT 12.3.   Sample Checklist for Mergers and Acquisitions (*Continued*)

Existing professional service contracts

Provide copies of agreements and contracts for:

HMOs, PPOs, and others

Physical therapy, occupational therapy, home health, other

ED physicians, radiology, anesthesiology, other specialty physician contracts

Other

Organizational Structure

- Provide information on:

Ownership

Type of ownership

Organizational structure

Other businesses or companies health care entity owns or is involved in
Flowcharts of operations

Prior acquisition, merger, and divestiture transaction agreements

Annual report

Risk Management

- Provide policies and procedures for:

Quality assurance plan

Risk management manual and statement of risk management philosophy

Incident reporting

Violence in the workplace

Claims reporting

Complaint handling process

Outcome monitoring

Sexual harassment

Patient satisfaction program

Patient relations and communications

Staff training and continuing education

Employee communication process

Employee orientation program, including employment practices guidelines and
education

Peer review

Credentialing

Recredentialing

Informed consent

General information available to patient, including on-line information

Billing and collection

Research

Telemedicine and e-medicine including: disclaimers and consent forms for the
Web sites, procedures for incorporating e-mail into patient file, and the use of
audits to assess system security and compliance

Physician orientation and mentoring programs

Medical records

Record-keeping deficiencies

(*Continued*)

EXHIBIT 12.3.   Sample Checklist for Mergers and Acquisitions (*Continued*)

     Documentation requirements, including e-mail communications

     Catastrophe plans, including technology backup systems

     Impaired physicians or other employees

     Nursing and other services

     Chain of command

- Provide copies of the following information:

     Structure of risk management and employee benefit departments

     Cost allocations

     Handling and recording of certificates of insurance

     If a captive is used, procedures and records for filing self-procurement taxes

     Workers' compensation filings for self-insured states

     Personnel policies

     Contact information: Brokers—and direct writers—names, titles, and telephone numbers; listing of service providers for engineering, loss control, claims management, claim audit, risk management consulting, and other insurance and risk management services

     Contract review procedures: who drafts and reviews contract wording? to what degree are contracts standardized? who has authority to bond the company into such contracts?

     Web site and e-mail policies and procedures

     Compliance policies and procedures

Insurance Information

- For the most recent five years, a matrix should be constructed that identifies at least the following information for each policy period:

     Coverage

     Limits

     Carriers

     Insolvent carriers

     Paid claims

     Open reserves

     Aggregate limits erosion

     Aggregate retention erosion

     Key coverage exclusions

     Excluded operations and businesses

     Policy form retro dates

     Retro dates

- This matrix should be used to review policies and contracts for the following insurance coverages and programs:

     Professional liability insurance

     General liability

     Workers' compensation and employer's liability

     Automobile liability

     Property liability

     Earthquake fund

     Difference in conditions

     Excess or umbrella liability

     Environmental impairment liability (pollution)

(*Continued*)

EXHIBIT 12.3.   Sample Checklist for Mergers and Acquisitions (*Continued*)

D&O liability

Liquor liability (if separate from general liability policy)

Employee benefit liability (if separate from general liability policy)

Employment practices liability

Employed lawyers

Volunteer liability

Products liability (if separate from general liability policy)

Advertising liability (if separate from general liability policy)

Aircraft liability

Fidelity and employee theft

Business interruption

Fiduciary liability

Errors and omissions liability

Any other insurance policy that addresses liability to third parties

- Obtain copies of the most recent renewal applications for the above coverages
- Provide a description of the primary casualty insurance program for the past five years, including:

Type (for example, retro, dividend, SIR, purchasing group, and so on)

Retentions by line of coverage

Per occurrence and aggregate limits

Claims made versus occurrence form policies

Collateral used, such as letters of credit, bonds, and so on

Premiums

Financial stability of insurance carriers utilized

Provide a schedule of all bonds

Has the entity ever been cited by OSHA, EPA, OIG, FDA, EEOC?

Non-Insurance Risk-Financing Programs

- Provide descriptions of:

Unfunded self-insurance plans

Funded self-insurance plans

Captive operations, including:

- Coverages written
- Reinsurance
- Net retentions
- Management company
- Financial underwriting reports

Claims Review

- Evaluate open and closed claims for all insurance coverages for the past five- to ten-year period and summarize:

Frequency

Severity

Trends with allegations, procedures, staff involvement (medical professional liability)

- Some of the more important questions to ask in a claims review are:

Valuations: Are individual claims properly valued and reserved by the claims administrator?

(Continued)

EXHIBIT 12.3.   Sample Checklist for Mergers and Acquisitions (*Continued*)

Reserves: Has the target company properly accrued for all open claims and an appropriate estimate of IBNR?

Projections: How do projections of ultimate cost compare to the applicable limits of insurance?

Litigation: Has the target company initiated any litigation against its insurers over claim practices or coverage disputes?

Trends: In addition to general claims trends, are there any precedent-setting cases that may have a material impact on future negotiations?

Philosophy: What is the target company's philosophy on the claims management process?

- Obtain copies of:

    Actuarial analysis of self-insured reserves and loss projections to ultimate, and any other actuarial studies performed for the property and casualty programs

    Ledger pages that document accruals for self-insured programs

    Descriptions of pending litigation cases (pollution, products liability, D&O, and so on)

    Are outside actuarial resources used to calculate reserves and develop loss projections to ultimate?

    Who performs claims handling, claim audits, loss control, and any other risk management and employee benefit services?

    Who produces the various loss runs, and how are the data analyzed?

    Is there an in-house facility to develop reports and analyses?

Other

If you can afford the luxury of time, there are additional items for review:

- Clinical review

    Review of medical procedure, policies and protocols, practice guidelines, and so on, by medical specialty or department, such as:

    - Anesthesiology
    - ED
    - Obstetrics/gynecology
    - Pediatrics
    - OR/surgical services
    - NICU
    - Radiology
    - Critical care units
    - Cardiac catheterization lab

- Medical record review

    Random audit of medical records at all locations

- Review of physician background

    Education

    If a foreign medical school graduate, confirm if certified by the Educational Council for Medical School Graduates

    Specialty

    Board certifications

    All places of licensure (active and inactive) and license numbers

    Present and previous hospital affiliations and staff memberships

    Type of staff privilege

    Any facilities where privileges were suspended, reduced, revoked, or not renewed for disciplinary reasons

(Continued)

EXHIBIT 12.3.   **Sample Checklist for Mergers and Acquisitions** (*Continued*)

Appearance before a state regulatory or review committee for alleged misconduct or malpractice

Any current or past challenges to medical or drug licenses

Proof of professional liability insurance, including the following information for the past five years:

- Limits of liability
- Current and past insurance carriers and coverage dates with each carrier
- Indicate type of coverage (occurrence or claims made) with each carrier
- Indicate if professional liability insurance has ever been denied, cancelled, or nonrenewed
- Expiration date
- Prior acts date
- Any criminal convictions
- Any present or history of substance abuse
- Investigations by government agencies, such as Medicare, FDA
- Revocation of membership or contracts with managed care organizations
- Fee complaints or professional relations complaints registered with medical association, hospital, or licensing authority
- Review of claims history for past ten years
- All malpractice suits in which applicant was or is a named defendant (including open, closed, and pending claims)
- Most recent report from National Practitioner Data Bank
- Most recent loss run from current and previous insurance carriers

13

Emerging Liabilities in Partnerships, Joint Ventures, and Collaborative Relationships

Rebecca A. Havlisch

In the last twenty years, health care has evolved from freestanding entities to conglomerations of hospitals, health plans, physician practices, and other services designed to address the needs of patients throughout the continuum of care. In the last five years, we have found the formation of integrated systems and the purchase of physician practices has not always resulted in the efficiencies and profits expected at the outset. Organizations have found that "bigger is not always better" and acquisition and merger does not always result in the control and cost effectiveness predicted.

Other models, such as partnerships, joint ventures, and other collaborative relationships, are being used increasingly to respond to the demands of the marketplace that were not successfully addressed with integrated systems and other acquisition and merger business structures. The management of the risks associated with the evaluation of partners, development of the business structure(s), implementation of the business plan, and day-to-day management of such business structures are the subject of this chapter.

CHARACTERIZATION OF THE BUSINESS RELATIONSHIP

The three business relationships exist on a continuum with partnerships on one end and collaborative relationships at the other extreme. Risk managers are familiar with many of the strategies necessary to manage the risks of these types of business structures no matter where they fall on the continuum. However, inherent in these structures are unique legal liabilities and exposures that require special consideration and attention. The following sections provide an overview of each business structure as a starting point for assessing the unique liabilities and exposures of each.

Partnership

A partnership is a voluntary contract between two or more competent persons to place their money, effects, labor, and skill, or some or all of them, in lawful commerce or business, with the understanding that there will be a proportional sharing of the profits and losses between them.[1] This contract is bilateral or reciprocal, in which the parties expressly enter into mutual engagements, each binding himself to the other. There is mutual participation in the profits that may accrue from property, credit, skill, or industry, furnished in determined proportions by the parties. An example of a partnership is two small physician groups that consolidate their practices in one location to decrease overhead and improve their ability to contract effectively with payers.

State law governs the formation and operation of partnerships. Nearly all states have adopted the Uniform Partnership Code into their state statutes. The Uniform Partnership Code defines a partnership as "an association of two or more persons (who) come together to carry on, as co-owners, in a business for profit."[2]

In many states, the existence of a partnership is not wholly dependent on the intent of the partners to form a partnership, but can be inferred from their actions.[3] For example, in California, an association must be evaluated as a whole. The parties' actions and any written agreement will be scrutinized in determining whether a partnership exists.[4]

The terms of a partnership relationship are created by the partners in their partnership agreement.[5] These terms can affect partners' ability to accept and delegate risk. State statutes frequently limit the provisions of partnership agreements. For example, partnership agreements may not:

- Unreasonably restrict partners' right of access to books and records.
- Eliminate partners' duty of loyalty or duty of care.
- Eliminate partners' obligations of good faith; however, the partnership agreement may prescribe reasonable standards by which that obligation is measured.
- Vary the power to dissociate a partner.
- Restrict the rights of third parties with respect to the partnership.[6]

Partners are jointly and severally liable "for all obligations of the partnership unless otherwise agreed by the claimant or provided by law."[7] However, a partner who is admitted to an existing partnership is not liable for any obligation that incurred before his addition.[8] Limited partnerships are subject to different rules, with liability dependent on the partner's role as either a general or limited partner.[9]

Joint Venture

A joint venture is a legal entity in the nature of a partnership engaged in the joint pursuit of a particular transaction for mutual profit.[10] It requires a community of interest in the performance of a subject matter, a right to direct and govern the policy in connection therewith, and a duty, which may be altered by agreement, to share in both profit and losses.[11] An example of joint venture may be a hospital and a radiologist who come together to make advanced technology available twice a week at the hospital.

Joint ventures are similar to partnerships with respect to parties' rights and responsibilities. The important difference between partnerships and joint ventures is the more limited business scope in joint ventures. The distinction is well-described as follows: "A partnership, ordinarily, is formed for the transaction of general business of a particular kind, while a joint venture relates to a single transaction of a particular kind."[12] Joint ventures have additionally been defined as "a partnership limited to one or several transactions."[13]

While there is some law to the contrary, the majority of cases and secondary authority hold that each of several joint venturers has the power to bind the others and to subject them to liability in matters that are within the scope of the association.[14] Hence, the shared liability of joint venturers is likely to the same as that of partners in a partnership.[15] In matters within the scope of the venture, joint venturers are likely to be held jointly and severally liable.

Unlike a partnership, a joint venture does not entail a continuing relationship among the parties. It is a one-time grouping of two or more persons in a business undertaking.

Collaborative Relationship

Collaborative business relationships can be characterized as those in which parties cooperate in an endeavor related to the needs of one or the other or both. There is no statutory or case law that governs liability of the business relationship in and of itself. Obligations may be outlined in a contract, memorandum of understanding, or letter of intent. Hence, the traditional tenets of contract law govern the rights and responsibilities of the parties.

The scope of a collaborative relationship is usually more limited than a joint venture. It may not involve the exchange of financial resources. Rather, it is more likely to focus on information, skill, services, or expertise that is valuable for two or more parties to reach a goal or accomplish a project that will benefit each of the parties individually. An example of a collaborative relationship is Catholic health systems collaborating on physician education initiatives or sharing testing data related to Y2K compliance.

The potential risks of a collaborative relationship vary depending on the subject and nature of the collaboration. The method chosen to memorialize the collaboration will also be determinative of potential liabilities and exposures.

············
EVALUATING POTENTIAL BUSINESS PARTNERS

The success of any new business relationship is contingent upon the completion of a thorough due diligence review of the proposed new entity.

Due Diligence

Key executives are frequently very enthusiastic about new business relationships. When a business relationship is being considered and designed, the risk manager should become involved as early as possible in evaluating the pros and cons of the proposed partner(s) and the business structure. The risk manager must maintain the delicate balance between the strategic importance of a business relationship and alerting key decision makers to downside risks. This evaluation, commonly referred to as *due diligence,* has become a competency of many risk managers due to the number of mergers and acquisitions in the last twenty years.

Site Visits   Many organizations utilize due diligence procedures for purposes beyond a pure paper evaluation of the potential business partner(s). When due diligence includes site visits and interviews with key people in the proposed partner's organization, the evaluation process is not only augmented, but the opportunity to design effective procedures and practices to mitigate identified risks is enhanced. For example, if there is documentation of several Health Care Financing Administration (HCFA) investigations for Emergency Medical Treatment and Active Labor Act (EMTALA) violations, the risk manager's plans to mitigate the risk is very different if there is an interview with the "new" emergency department (ED) manager who has already begun education programs versus visiting with an ED manager who states the investigator is "after him."

Site visits create a foundation for the integration process, which occurs following the finalization of the business relationship. They allow those who will be working together when the business relationship is consummated to get acquainted on a personal and professional level. It allows representatives of the partners to gain an overview of the strategic, programmatic, and operational plans and programs in place for the major functional areas within the scope of the planned relationship. Best practices and processes that support the success of the proposed business relationship can be identified. Finally, site visits and interviews create an opportunity to answer questions raised by the document review.

Due diligence, which includes both document review and site visits, facilitates the identification of concerns or opportunities that need to be addressed or improved prior to consummating the business relationship and/or during the integration process. It also identifies, with a greater degree of certainty, significant patterns, trends, concerns, or issues that need to be incorporated into the memorandum of understanding, contract, or other documentation that describes the terms of the business relationship. Finally, both processes facilitate identification of significant issues that suggest the one partner should reevaluate plans to choose another partner.

Exhibit 13.1 on page 315 is a draft of a site visit agenda that utilizes two individuals in a broad scope evaluation of an acute care facility. One individual has risk financing expertise. A second individual evaluates the facility with a focus on clinical risk and loss prevention. Exhibits 13.2 and 13.3 on pages 316 and 318, respectively, are examples of interview questions focused on an organization with documented quality issues. Exhibits 13.4 and 13.5 on pages 320 and 321 are tools that could be used to evaluate services commonly undertaken as joint ventures, laboratory, and radiology.

Due diligence procedures must be designed to accommodate the breadth of the proposed transaction and business structure. In some cases, such as the physician practice partnership mentioned above, due diligence with a scope that would be used for an acquisition for both parties would be appropriate. The site visit would include interviews with the office manager, the quality and risk manager, a coder, the referral specialist, the lead physician, the physician in charge of quality and risk management, the compliance officer, a representative of an allied health professionals employed by the clinic (such as the lead nurse practitioner), the individual responsible for risk financing (if different from the individual with quality and risk management responsibilities), a human resources manager, and someone from medical records or information management. A review of a sample of medical records is also suggested. More frequently than not, records are made available provided you sign a confidentiality agreement.

In the case of joint venture for radiology services, the interviews would likely be limited to the physician, the business manager, an individual responsible for equipment maintenance, and one of the radiologist's employees. Depending on the documentation of repairs and the age of key equipment, a technical inspection of the equipment may be warranted.

In case of a collaborative relationship, due diligence is most often an informal process with a very narrow focus. Individuals will become aware of a service or competency had by another organization or group, such as education programs or a list of Y2K medical equipment testing results. Their organization or group is in need of that service or information. After interviewing key personnel from the group with the desired product and, perhaps, a reference provided by the group, a decision is made about the credibility and usefulness of the product. There may be payments, which generally cover the cost (with no or minimal profit) of the education program or other product. In the case of a group of Catholic health systems that jointly plan physician education programs, the cost to those who attend cover only the overhead of hosting the conference. Hence, continued participation is based on the value attributable to each health system as delivered by the physician education program.

Environmental Assessment   Whenever the proposed business structure includes incorporation of a physical location (for example, the building, office, campus, or property), the risk manager plays the role of evaluating hazards and insurable exposures. A facility or campus walk-through is very important when the contemplated relationship is a partnership or a joint venture. Exhibits 13.6, 13.7, and 13.8 beginning on page 322 identify documents required for environmental due diligence and an agenda for a site visit. As indicated above, depending on the scope of the proposed business relationship, it will be necessary to customize the breadth, depth, and type of documents and interviews requested.

Document Review   Risk managers are but one member of the due diligence team. There are likely multiple disciplines, including legal, finance, managed care, information management, quality, and reimbursement involved in the process. Some of the documents those disciplines scrutinize closely are very helpful to the risk analysis. In particular, the minutes of the board and board committees, executive committees, finance committees, and other governing bodies going back three to five years are very useful in identifying potential significant issues and exposures that may lead to expenditures after the partnership or joint venture is consummated.

The annual audit letter from the accounting firm can help identify the funding status of self-insurance and pension programs that may be difficult to ascertain from actuarial reports only. The new business relationship may be responsible for making up inadequate funding by the other partner(s) of the partnership or joint venture.

Finally, the annual legal audit letter or assessments assist in determining the status of current litigation, insured and uninsured, that may affect the bottom line of the proposed business relationship. This is particularly important when the proposed business relationship is a partnership and there is no continuing organization to bear the costs of litigation.

Chapter 12 on mergers, acquisitions, and divestitures outlines an extensive list of documents. As indicated previously, the scope of the proposed business transaction will dictate the type and level of detail of the documents requested.

Report Out   In addition to a written report, a meeting where all the disciplines involved in the due diligence process share their findings can be critical to the success of the future business relationship. It allows the risk manager to contrast his or her perceptions with those of all the other disciplines. This gathering, like the site visits and interviews, allows the risk manager to further evaluate opportunities and strategies to effectively mitigate identified risks and exposures.

Compliance   The high level of activity out of the Office of the Inspector General, (OIG) HCFA, and the Department of Justice (DOJ) require most if not all potential partnerships and joint ventures due diligence processes to incorporate a compliance assessment. This may be accomplished by legal, financial, compliance, or risk disciplines, depending on the expertise of the involved individuals. The risk manager should ensure that this assessment is conducted and tailored to the proposed business transaction. Business arrangements that include significant billing functions should be highly scrutinized.

Coverage   The standard insurance coverages will require at least the same level of scrutiny in the due diligence process as for a proposed acquisition or merger. Because of compliance and other risks inherent in the formation process of partnerships and joint ventures, a careful evaluation of existing risk financing vehicles is important to be sure these risks are covered. If not, it may often be advisable to obtain new or additional coverage during the business development time period.

A second reason to carefully scrutinize existing risk financing strategies is to ensure coverage for known liabilities is adequate. In a partnership, one or more of the partners' original organizations may cease to exist. If insurance limits or reserves are not adequate or extending reporting (tail coverage) is not specifically addressed, the new relationship may become responsible for preexisting claims. These additional liabilities could significantly impact the business success of the new relationship.

In a joint venture, one of parties may not have had insurance as they were not "in the business" previously. The other partner may also not carried insurance for exposures within the scope of the joint venture as this is a new line of business for them. A comprehensive analysis of available insurance is imperative to protect both parties during the time the business is being developed.

In addition, it is important to understand nonscope liabilities of partners who are new to the business. While business deals can be structured to prohibit one partner's preexisting liabilities from impinging on the bottom line of the new relationship, the constraint on the partner's personal finances may be such that he cannot contribute as required by contract.

Chapter 12 outlines due diligence procedures by coverage line. This chapter will only identify the nuances related to partnerships, joint ventures, and collaborative relationships.

Directors' and Officers' Coverage   In both partnerships and joint ventures, it is imperative that all partners have coverage for their officers and board members during the negotiation and business development process. It is important to evaluate the adequacy of limits given existing liabilities. It may be necessary to increase limits during the business development phase. Carriers should be put on notice of business development strategies to acquire, merge, or form a partnership or joint venture.

In addition, the coverage terms and deductibles should be evaluated. Consider an example: an organization with a thirty-member board, fifteen officers, and a $250,000 deductible per claim enters into discussion with a large physician practice management company to form a reference laboratory joint venture. Multiple issues arise when compliance issues become a concern for the organization that backs out. The physician practices bring multiple suits with individualized causes of actions. The organization must assess its ability to put up reserves to cover the deductibles of claims. In the absence of adequate capacity, the organization should consider altering the terms of the coverage during the formation of the new relationship.

Particularly in joint venture situations, one or more of the parties may not have been involved in an independent business and/or may not have carried directors' and officers' coverage. The partner(s) with insurance should insist on coverage with terms similar, if not identical to their own coverage.

It is important to begin to assess the cost of coverage for the new entity during the due diligence process. For new exposures and/or previously uninsured parties, directors' and officers' coverage may be difficult or expensive to obtain. It may be necessary to pursue alternatives to a separate freestanding policy for the partnership or new joint venture after the deal closes. An alternative may be to endorse coverage for activities within the scope of the business relationship, particularly joint ventures, onto the directors' and officers' policies of the parent corporations, if coverage existed and the parent corporations are continuing.

The cost of tail or runoff must be included in a due diligence evaluation. The scope of runoff coverage required should be compared with the current coverage in case the former is broader than the latter. Ultimately, questions about who will bear the cost of the run-off insurance, the length of the tail, and deductibles for all partners should be addressed in the final agreement.

Property Coverage   Frequently, the development of a new business relationship includes a new location for delivering services or products within the scope of the new business structure. In addition to gathering information on the additional values of buildings, property, and contents, a new, off-premises business operation has business interruption exposures. The risk manager must assess the likely extent of revenue and income loss if damage is caused by fire or extended perils. It is also important to assess the new location for the potential of catastrophic loss, such as flood or earthquake, which may not be an exposure at either partners' current business location. Evaluation of the alternatives and cost of business recovery, for example, at a temporary location with leased equipment, and the expense of coverage for these new exposures should be included in the due diligence process.

Chapter 12 discusses the advisability of formal property appraisals. In a broad scope partnership, such an evaluation may be warranted. However, many partnerships and joint ventures may not warrant the expense in light of their scope. For example, a hospital and group of hand surgeons joint venture a hand therapy clinic in an empty suite next door to the surgeons' office. Limited due diligence would be required in this scenario.

The pricing for a freestanding policy for the new organization should be explored during the due diligence process. If one of the partners already has a large, consolidated program, it may be very inexpensive to add the joint venture to that coverage, if the terms of the policy allow. Frequently, if the joint venture is "controlled by" the parent, it may covered under the organization's policy. Partnerships, because they are reciprocal relationships by definition, frequently are not "controlled by" the parent and will require a stand-alone policy.

Product Liability   Some partnerships, joint ventures, and collaborative relationships involve the sale of products. The relationship to the product may be manufacturer, wholesaler, supplier, advisor, or some combination. Under all these circumstances, the product liability provisions of the comprehensive general liability policy should be analyzed in light of the proposed scope of the business relationship. The due diligence process should be used by the risk manager to gain an understanding of the nature of the product to be provided, proposed product flow, loss history, and the liability implications. In this way, the risk manager develops a knowledge base to propose endorsements to outline proper coverage.

Comprehensive General Liability   For new exposures and/or previously uninsured parties, particularly those structured as joint ventures, it is important to determine a source of coverage during the negotiation and development process. For business relationships the organization will "control," the carrier for the organization should be advised of the formation, emphasizing the interrelatedness of the corporate structure. For those partners who will not "control,"such as those who possess ownership of less than 51 percent, separate policies should be explored for the negotiation and development phase. Frequently, these policies become the partnership or joint venture's policy after the deal is closed.

Assessing the cost of tail or runoff is also important to evaluate during due diligence. The scope of runoff coverage required should be compared with the current coverage in case the former is broader than the latter. Ultimately, questions about who will bear the cost of the runoff insurance, the duration of the runoff, and deductibles for all partners should be addressed in the final agreement. Discussion should begin early in the process about the policy terms on the partnership or joint venture's separate policy, who will bear the cost of tail coverage and the length and scope of tail coverage. For example, if clinical trials on human subjects are within the scope of the joint venture or partnership, the extended reporting time must be much longer than if the joint venture was established to provide billing services.

With the occasional exception of general liability coverage, collaborative relationships do not usually require a coverage evaluation. In these relationships, each partner looks to their own policies and self-insurance programs for coverage. In the sharing of data, issues regarding intellectual property may arise. Letters of intent and contracts outlining the information to be shared, the purpose, how it will be used, and the responsibilities can be utilized to minimize exposures in this area.

If education sessions are being orchestrated, it is important that copyright permission is obtained. If a claim were to arise, it is likely the risk financing mechanisms of all partners would be invoked. Given the narrow scope of collaborative relationships and the relative low risk of an exposure occurring, time and energy spent on due diligence is probably better spent on accomplishing the goal of the collaborative relationship.

Errors and Omissions or Fraud and Abuse   Given the increasing number of OIG and Department of Justice (DOJ) investigations of billing practices, any business relationship that includes the billing function must be closely scrutinized. When the billing function is large or the focus of the new relationship (for example, multiple physician practices joint venturing a billing company), current coverage provisions, or lack thereof, for fraud and abuse and billing irregularities and alternatives for future insurance coverage should be explored as part of the due diligence process.

It is likely that the compliance and/or legal functions will conduct an audit of existing billing practices. Monitoring the process of the audit is an important function. Should irregularities begin to appear, it is very important to reevaluate the potential partner in the business relationship. The DOJ will presume successor liability if, upon finding irregularities in a billing audit that is part of due diligence, the nature of the deal is changed to eliminate liability for prior acts and the audit is discontinued. (See Chapter 12 for a discussion of successor liability.)

While the DOJ has taken this position in cases related to mergers and asset acquisitions, it is conceivable that certain analogous fact situations in the formation of partnerships and joint ventures will arise where the DOJ might take the same position. In this situation, the business relationship would be liable for reimbursing the government monies owed due to inappropriate billing practices predating the formation of the business and penalties. While it has not yet imposed such fines, the Department of Justice could impose a $10,000 civil money penalty for each and every false billing in addition to being repaid amounts overbilled or not eligible for reimbursement. Particularly in a partnership, such financial fines and penalties could significantly impact the parent organization.

Workers' Compensation   Assessing the loss experience of the potential partners is important as alternatives for managing prior liabilities are explored. As mentioned previously, it is important to identify if reserves are adequate for past liabilities if the potential partners are self-funded. Particularly in a partnership, the business or parent corporations of the other partners may result in making up funding deficiency. Documentation of excess insurance and third-claims administration agreements from the inception of the self-insured program should be obtained and reviewed. It is not unusual for old claims, such as asbestos, to come to light or resurface after long periods of time. These documents are important to prevent the new relationship from taking past liabilities and claims management expenses.

It is important to evaluate the runoff provisions of the insurance contract or self-insurance mechanism. If your potential partner is self-insured, it is necessary to assess the adequacy of his letter of credit or bond posted securing his liabilities. In both cases, the claims servicing charges (meaning, the third-party administrator) need to be evaluated. In other cases, the cost of a third-party administrator will need to be added during the runoff period. In case of self-administration, resources may or may not be available. It will be important to assess whether it is desirable to have multiple groups managing prior claims. This situation is more likely to occur in a partnership than in a joint venture.

Professional Liability   Like workers' compensation, it is imperative that the loss experience of the potential partners be explored to assess alternatives for managing prior liabilities. This is particularly important if the scope of the new business relationship encompasses some of the same risks.

Also, as with workers' compensation, it is important to identify if reserves are adequate for past liabilities if the potential partners are self-funded.

∙∙∙∙∙∙∙∙∙∙∙∙

DEVELOPING THE BUSINESS STRUCTURE

Legal and business development disciplines frequently take the lead roles in developing the business structure. However, the risk manager needs to be well-informed on the business structure, operations, and anticipated financial transactions in order to most effectively mitigate exposures identified during due diligence and the coverage analysis. The risk manager also plays a role in ensuring that additional risks and exposures are not created unnecessarily in the design of the business structure.

Proposed Antitrust Guidelines for Collaborations among Competitors

As indicated previously, legal will generally take the lead in designing a proposed business structure that avoids compliance issues such as antitrust and inurement. The risk manager must have a basic understanding of this area of the law and the effect it has on business structures. Current reporters on the topic are very valuable since this area is always subject to changes and new interpretations.

The Federal Trade Commission (FTC) and DOJ (collectively "the Agencies") have released several guidelines addressing several special circumstances in which antitrust issues related to competitor collaborations may arise, including one focused on health-care.[16] The Agencies recently released "Antitrust Guidelines for Collaborations Among Competitors." The guidelines apply to a wide range of joint ventures, strategic alliances, and other collaborative relationships among competitors. They are intended to assist businesses in assessing the likelihood of an antitrust challenge to a collaboration with one or more competitors.

The guidelines begin with definitions of important terms. *Competitor collaboration* is defined as "a set of one or more agreements, other than merger agreements, between or among competitors to engage in economic activity, and the economic activity resulting therefrom." Competitor collaborations involve one or more business activities, including research and development, production, marketing, distribution, sales, and purchasing. *Competitors* include groups that are actual or potential competitors in a relevant market.

Competitor collaborations are distinguishable from mergers. Mergers completely end competition between the merging parties and are permanent. In contrast, most competitor collaborations preserve some competition among the participants and are usually of limited duration. Partnership, joint venture, and collaborative relationships fall into this category.

Collaborative agreements among competitors are subject to one of two types of analysis: *per se* and *rule of reason. Per se* analysis is applied to those agreements that are so likely to harm competition and to have no significant procompetitive benefit that they do not warrant the time and expense of a particularized inquiry into their effects. Agreements that always or almost always tend to raise prices or reduce output fall into this category. Agreements subject to *per se* analysis include price-fixing agreements and agreements to share and divide markets. A joint venture between competing hospitals to provide a service not available from another source in the relevant market must be carefully scrutinized.

A rule of reason analysis seeks to determine the overall competitive effect of the agreement. The central question is whether the relevant agreement likely harms competition by increasing the ability or incentive profitably to raise prices above or reduce output, quality, service, or innovation below what would likely prevail in the absence of the relevant agreement. Competitive effects are evaluated at the time of possible harm to competition, whether at the time of collaboration or later. Hence, avoiding the Agencies' scrutiny at the outset does not preclude the possibility of evaluation of the partnership or joint venture at some future point.

The first step in the rule of reasons analysis is an examination of the nature of the relevant agreement. This entails characterizing the business purposes of the agreement and evaluating evidence of the parties' subjective intent regarding competitive effects. If, after this evaluation, anticompetitive harm seems unlikely, the Agencies' analysis ends. If competitive harm appears possible, the Agencies continue with Step Two.

Step Two requires a more in depth analysis of the collaborative agreement. The Agencies identify, assess, and evaluate the following: the competitive effects of the agreement in the relevant markets, the market share and market concentration at issue, factors affecting the participants' and the collaboration's ability and incentive to compete independently, the likelihood of anticompetitive information sharing, and the duration of the collaboration. If, after examination of these factors, the Agencies are satisfied there is no potential anticompetitive harm, the analysis ends. If potential anticompetitive harm is identified, then the Agencies proceed to Step Three.

Step Three is a straightforward balancing test to determine whether procompetitive benefits offset anticompetitive harms. To identify procompetitive benefits, the agencies evaluate whether the collaborative agreement is reasonably necessary to achieve cognizable efficiencies. Cognizable efficiencies are efficiencies verified by the Agencies that do not arise from anticompetitve reductions in output or service, and that cannot be achieved through practical, significantly less restrictive means. If the collaborative agreement is reasonably necessary to achieve cognizable efficiencies, the Agencies compare the anticompetitive harms to determine the agreement's overall effect. As the level of anticipated harm rises, so too does the required level of cognizable efficiencies necessary to have an offsetting effect.

In establishing a business plan for a partnership and joint venture, attention must be given to identifying cognizable efficiencies. In the case of a service joint venture (such as a lab or radiology), these efficiencies may include less administration, ability to obtain most sophisticated technology by combining resources, and/or elimination of redundant rent. The business plan should also identify consideration of other less restrictive means and why they did not produce the same efficiencies. Because of the Agencies' ability to evaluate at any time, it is important to maintain this documentation.

Finally, the proposed guidelines describe *antitrust safety zones* designed to encourage procomeptitive collaborative agreements. Two types of safety zones are described. A general safety zone *provides* that competitor collaborations that collectively account for 20 percent or less of the relevant market will not be challenged by the Agencies. The *research and development safety zone* encourages competitors' collaboration in innovation markets as long as there are a sufficient number of similar and independent research and development programs. The general safety zone may protect many of the more limited scope joint ventures, depending how the relevant market is defined.

Compliance issues will likely be the largest risk to mitigate in the development of a partnership or joint venture. In most situations, compliance issues are unlikely to occur in collaborative relationships, unless there is sharing of sensitive information, such as payer rate schedules, contract prices on goods and services, and so on. Collaborative relationships frequently develop to share information to use for benchmarking purposes. Compliance issues are more likely to arise if the data is used for other purposes and more formal business agreements are developed based on the information.

Insurance Coverage

Several issues must be addressed in the decision to incorporate the new business operation into one of the existing partner's corporate insurance program or establish a separate, stand-alone program. The first (and potentially controlling) consideration is the preservation of the tax-exempt status of the self-insurance funding for not-for-profit operations. If nonprofit trusts are used to fund risk financing mechanisms and the business relationship is for-profit, extreme caution must be used in considering those trusts as a risk financing vehicle for the new business relationship. Infusing for-profit operations into such a trust could jeopardize its nonprofit status. If a nonprofit trust is involved, strong consideration should be given to a stand-alone program to avoid the tax implications of incorporating a for-profit business.

A second consideration is whether the operations are closely controlled by the parent. Previously, it was mentioned that self-insurance vehicles may require "control." Typically, this is defined as 51-percent ownership or management control over the operations. If there are no tax issues, a joint venture could be covered by corporate insurance programs providing the new business met the control requirements of the insurer or self-insurance vehicle. Partnerships are less likely to be able to be incorporated into existing programs because the reciprocal nature of the business relationship results in no controlling partner (meaning, the partners all share equally in profits and losses.)

A third consideration is whether the new operations are closely linked or interconnected to those of the parent. If the new business adds more of similar risks with limited scope, it may be prudent to access the parent's insurance. Separate programs may be prudent if the addition of the new business will negatively impact the parent's program by adding new risks not previously covered (such as a joint venture for reproductive assist technology) or a significant volume of high risks (such as a reference laboratory joint venture anticipating 500,000 tests annually).

In situations where past liabilities are uninsured and/or may not be completely covered by insurance limits, it may be prudent to consider a litigation buyout for certain claims or a loss portfolio transfer on group claims. Either of these alternatives minimizes, if not eliminates, future liabilities for the partners based on liabilities incurred prior to the new business relationship.

These techniques are being used increasingly to unencumber the balance sheets of for-profit entities to make them more attractive to partners in new business relationships and/or to increase their value. Hence, as part of due diligence, potential partners should be queried about their use of these vehicles and the purpose.

Finally, the breadth of available coverage from insurance or self-insurance must be evaluated. Frequently, the vehicles will permit coverage for controlled entities. However, coverage may be limited to the interest of the partner, not the entire new business. Hence, the other partner's insurance or another vehicle will be necessary to cover exposures not controlled by one partner. In this situation, a stand-alone program is advisable. Multiple insurers on the same risk is a heavy administrative burden and frequently leads to finger-pointing if claims should arise and conflicts with "other insurance" clauses on the partners' policies.

The need for new coverages should be evaluated during the due diligence process. If the new business includes billing services, serious consideration should be given to coverages for billing irregularities. Certain other lines of business (such as home care) would also warrant serious evaluation of this line of coverage given OIG and DOJ statements and activities.

Because of the nature of the risks or the relationship, it may be difficult and/or expensive to secure a stand-alone program. If that is the case, the risk manager must determine what the partner's insurers require to include the new entity. In some cases, only notice is required. In other instances, the underwriter or trust committee may want a full submission in order to endorse coverage.

Contracting

The risk manager must develop strong, interactive relationships with those who will be developing and finalizing the documents for the new business. Participation in the process provides risk managers with the opportunity to identify potential risks being assumed. Inclusion in the contracting process also affords the risk manager the opportunity to draft contract language and develop guidelines or protocols to minimize risks inherent to the scope of the new business and/or the chosen business structure (such as a partnership or joint venture). An exhaustive evaluation of contract review is contained in Chapter 11.

The following terms are considerations when drafting a partnership agreement:

- Insurer of the partnership must be reasonably acceptable to both parties to the contract.
- Type of coverage (occurrence versus claims made), variety of required coverages, and required limits are specified by contract.
- Insurer of the partnership must be reasonably acceptable to both parties to the contract.
- Management of prior liabilities specified (such as requirement of tail coverage, the length of tail, and limits of tail coverage) should be outlined by contract.
- Waiver of subrogation is included.
- Purchase of tail for all lines of coverage and, most important, directors' and officers' tail coverage for business development and negotiation phase is required.
- Liability for obligations of the partnership is delineated clearly.
- Duties and responsibilities of each party bound by the contract must be outlined.
- Indemnification clause is included.
- Statement is made that partnership is in full compliance with licensure and regulatory agencies.
- Reporting relationships and required communication with parent corporation(s) are outlined.

Given the more limited scope of joint ventures, the following terms are considerations when drafting a joint venture:

- Indication of whether stand-alone policies will be required or if new business will be incorporated into parent corporation's insurance program and terms.
- Insurer of the partnership must be reasonably acceptable to both parties to the contract.
- Type of coverage (occurrence versus claims made), variety of required coverages, and required limits are specified by contract.
- Management of prior liabilities specified (such as requirement of tail coverage, the length of tail, and limits of tail coverage) should be outlined by contract.
- Waiver of subrogation is included.
- Purchase of tail for all lines of coverage and, most important, directors' and officers' policy includes retro date preceding pre-work.
- Liability for obligations of the joint venture are delineated clearly.
- Method by which the profits will be distributed clearly articulated.
- Interest of partners relative to whole described (such as, who is the controlling party).
- Duties and responsibilities of each party bound by the contract must be outlined.
- Indemnification clause is included.

- Statement that joint venture is in full compliance with applicable licensure and requirements.
- Reporting relationships and required communication with parent corporation(s) outlined.

Agreements defining collaborative relationships, like the relationship themselves, are generally informal and simple. Contracts are generally used in limited situations. These situations include relationships where services, information, or products are provided in exchange for payments. The contracts outline the deliverables, time frames, format, and payment terms. These contracts generally contain clauses exculping all parties from liability.

In certain cases where information is shared by the collaborating organizations, the contract includes the intent of the agreement, the type of information to be provided, the format, deadlines, confidentiality requirements, prohibitions against subsequent release of information, limitations on the use of information, and restrictions on liability. These contracts were particularly important when integrated systems shared the results of their Y2K biomedical testing results. Contracts that were drafted prior to the federal legislation minimizing liability contained terms clearly indicating the information should not be relied on exclusively, prohibited rerelease of information, and the organization providing the information would be indemnified should someone sue them when a piece of compliant equipment failed.

The majority of collaborative relationships operate from mission and vision statements for the collaborative. Liabilities are not assumed by the group but rather by individual organizations for their own acts and omissions.

············
IMPLEMENTING THE BUSINESS RELATIONSHIP

In all cases, the risk manager must have a plan for all coverages for the new business prior to closing. Separate, stand-alone policies should be effective on the date of close. Evidence of tail coverage for directors' and officers', professional liability, general liability, and workers' compensation should be required before the signing of the documents. If a joint venture, the directors' and officers' policy should be scrutinized to be sure there is coverage during the evaluation and design phases of the new business. The retro date should not be the closing date; rather, the retro date should predate the business development phase.

The due diligence process laid the foundation for integration of activities. Education regarding risk management services is imperative in the time frame around closing. The type, focus, and audience for education will be driven by the source of risk management resources for the new business, such as new, internal resources, or support from the parent.

············
MANAGING DAY-TO-DAY OPERATIONS

The new relationship will require risk management support. In some situations, it may be prudent to manage the risks from the corporate function. This decision may be appropriate if the joint venture is limited in scope with risks not dissimilar from the parent, located somewhat near the parent, and of a size that additional staff is not warranted. In these cases, risk management guidelines should be expanded to include the additional business operations. At a minimum, notification procedures and clear lines of communication must be established for matters that have liability potential.

Safety protocols for the parent corporation should be expanded to include the new business relationship. Depending on the scope of the new business relationship, ongoing audit processes (billing, OSHA compliance, EMTALA, and so on) should be established.

In situations where the new business relationship is a completely new business with all new employees, managers should be alerted to and educated about the management of exposures in the following areas:

- Environmental impairment, including underground storage tanks and asbestos.

- Obligations for leased property or equipment.

- Business interruption due to faulty processes because health care procedures are interdependent; if one particular activity is interrupted, such as the lab or radiology, significant disruption of other operations is likely, including that of the parent organization who is dependent on the results of the joint venture or partnership.

- Business interruption caused by factors outside the new relationship—telephone service and electricity are two examples. Disaster plans and alternative sources must be incorporated and managers educated on how to access alternatives to minimize amount and length of disruption.

It may be that access to the entire premise had been limited prior to closing the deal.

After the deal is consummated, it is useful to conduct a thorough walk-through to evaluate the new business for unusual items maintained on the off-site premises to see if any special liability policies are required. Aircraft (owned or leased), helicopters (owned or leased), and boats and/or docks are examples.

In some new business relationships, it may be necessary to establish on-site risk management resources. Reasons to establish site-based risk management include the type of risks (those that are substantially different from the parent company's risks), the volume of risks, the physical size of the new operation, the location of the new operation (far from the parent or difficult to reach expeditiously), and/or the desires of management (independence from parent). If this model is chosen, the risk manager of the parent should become familiar with the administrative organization chart and lines of communication for the new relationship. It will be important for the parent's risk manager to know how to obtain urgently needed information about the new business operation during and after the hours of operation.

In some situations, the parent may provide administrative support, including insurance certificates and the site-based resources employed to manage day-to-day clinical, operational, and/or safety exposures. It is important to outline roles and responsibilities to pertinent individuals at the parent level and within the new business. As above, defined lines of communication are imperative to seamless operations if the responsibilities are divided between multiple parties or the parent and the new business.

············

CONCLUSION

Risk managers are uniquely situated to identify potential exposures in the development of new business relationships. They are an integral part of the due diligence, negotiating, and integration team when new business relationships are explored, designed, and eventually consummated.

Endnotes

1. *Burr v. Greenland,* Tex. Civ. App. 356 S.W.2d 370, 376; *Preston v. State Industrial Accident Commission,* 174 Or. 553, 139, P2d 957, 961, 962.

2. Uniform Partnership Act, § 6(1).

3. See, for example, California Corporations Code § 16202(a), which states that a partnership is "the association of two or more persons to carry on as co-owners of a business . . . whether or not the persons intend to form a partnership."

4. To determine whether an association is a partnership, the California Corporations Code § 16202(c)(1999) provides:

   (1) (J)oint tenancy, . . . joint property, . . . or part ownership does not by itself establish partnership, even if the co-owners share profits made by the use of the property.

   (2) The sharing of gross returns does not by itself establish a partnership, even if the persons sharing them have a joint or common right of interest in property from which the returns are divided.

   (3) A person who receives a share of the profits of a business is presumed to be a partner in the business, unless the profits were received for any of the following reasons:

   (a) In payment of a debt by installments or otherwise.

   (b) In payment for services as an independent contractor or of wages or other compensation to an employee.

   (c) In payment of rent.

   (d) In payment of an annuity or other retirement benefit to a beneficiary, representative or designee of a deceased or retired partner.

   (e) In payment of interest or other charge on a loan, even if the amount varies with the profits of the business, including a direct or indirect present or future ownership of the collateral, or rights to income, proceeds, or increase in value derived from the collateral.

   (f) In payment for the sale of the goodwill of a business or other property by installments or otherwise.

5. See, for example, California Corporations Code § 16103(a)(1999).

6. California Corporations Code § 16103(b)(1999).

7. California Corporations Code § 16306(a)(1999).

8. California Corporations Code § 16306(b)(1999).

9. See generally, California Corporations Code § 15501-15533 (1999).

10. *Tex-Co Grain Co. v. Happy Wheat Growers, Inc.,* Tex. Civ. App., 542 S.W.2d 934, 936.

11. *Russell v. Kelin,* 33 Ill. App.3d 1005, 339, N.E.2d 510, 512.

12. *Tufts v. Mann,* 116 Cal. App. 170, 177 (1931).

13. In re Gotfried, 45 F. Supp. 939, 941 (1942).

14. 12 AmJur Prof 2d 295 § 5.

15. See *Orlopp v. Willardson Company,* 232 Cal. App.2d 75, 754-55 (stating that "the relations of joint venturers as between themselves and as to third parties are generally the same as those of partners and to the extent they are the same, the law of partnerships applies to both" and holding that "a creditor is entitled to recover from all the partners when discovered, though the debt was not originally charged to all").

16. The *Statements of Antitrust Enforcement Policy in Health Care* outline the Agencies' approach to certain health care collaborations, among other things. The *Antitrust Guidelines for the Licensing of Intellectual Property* outline the Agencies' enforcement policy with respect to intellectual property licensing agreements among competitors, among other things.

EXHIBIT 13.1.   Site Visit Draft

DUE DILIGENCE CLINICAL		Site Visit
Total Hours	*Risk Financing Review*	*Clinical Risk Review*
Day One:		
4 to 6 hours	Document Review	Document Review
Day Two:		
1 hour	Administrator	Administrator
1 hour	Risk Manager	Chief Nurse Executive
1 hour	Manager, Medical Staff Services	Manager, Medical Staff Services
45 minutes	Human Resources Manager	Quality Management/Performance Improvement
45 minutes	Lead, Managed Care Contracting	Chief of Staff/Chief Medical Officer
30 minutes	Facilities or Construction Manager	Director, Maternal Child Health
30 minutes	Manager, Outpatient Services	Director, Emergency Department
30 minutes	Workers' Compensation Coordinator	Director, Surgery Department
1 hour	Claims Manager/Third-Party Administrator Representative	Claims Manager/Third-Party Administrator Representative
1 hour	Insurance Broker	Directors, Other High Risk Departments

EXHIBIT 13.2.   **Performance Improvement (PI) Review and Assessment Tool**

	Name of Facility:
Date: _____	Reviewers:

#	*Indicators*	*Findings*		
1.	Medical staff has a leadership role in establishing a planned, systematic, organization-wide PI plan with measurements?	Yes ☐	No ☐	Comments
2.	The PI activities are interdisciplinary and are part of a team effort?	Yes ☐	No ☐	Comments
3.	The PI process for the hospital and new or added process are well designed?	Yes ☐	No ☐	Comments
4.	Performance indicators are written for old and new processes along with expectations	Yes ☐	No ☐	Comments
5.	All performance indicators require a means for measuring results?	Yes ☐	No ☐	Comments
6.	Data is collected for the following purposes:			
	• To establish and define a baseline for outcomes.	Yes ☐	No ☐	Comments
	• To identify opportunities for improvement.	Yes ☐	No ☐	Comments
	• To identify changes that will lead to improvement.	Yes ☐	No ☐	Comments
	• To monitor practice and changes implemented to ensure improvement?	Yes ☐	No ☐	Comments
7.	The organization collects data to monitor its performance. In which way does this occur in your facility?	Yes ☐	No ☐	Comments
8.	Is data collected used for profiling members of the medical staff with regard to outcomes?	Yes ☐	No ☐	Comments
9.	Does the organization have a mechanism for reporting performance improvement issues to the PI committee when problems occur?	Yes ☐	No ☐	Comments
10.	The data collected and aggregated ongoing for PI is used to monitor and provide information on:			
	• Medical staff performance (physician profiles)?	Yes ☐	No ☐	Comments
	• Risk management issues and sentinel events?	Yes ☐	No ☐	Comments
	• Targeted areas where problems were identified?	Yes ☐	No ☐	Comments
	• Monitor areas where corrective actions have been implemented?	Yes ☐	No ☐	Comments
11.	Data analyzed is communicated to the organization using appropriate PI tool? How is physician-related data displayed?	Yes ☐	No ☐	Comments
12.	The hospital uses reliable organizations and agencies to compare, and it benchmarks its results and outcomes?	Yes ☐	No ☐	Comments
13.	The hospital or medical staff conducts more intensive review and evaluation on problem areas identified and unacceptable trends?	Yes ☐	No ☐	Comments
14.	Medical staff PI includes peer leadership and process measurement in the following areas:			
	• Treatment and assessment of patients?	Yes ☐	No ☐	Comments
	• Medication usage and IRB activities?	Yes ☐	No ☐	Comments
	• Blood and blood product usage?	Yes ☐	No ☐	Comments
	• Operative and invasive procedures?	Yes ☐	No ☐	Comments
	• Departures from practice norms and appropriateness of patient management?	Yes ☐	No ☐	Comments

(Continued)

EXHIBIT 13.2. **Performance Improvement (PI) Review and Assessment Tool** (*Continued*)

	Name of Facility:
Date: _____	Reviewers:

#	Indicators	Findings
15. Does the medical staff provide the education chairman with important topics (for example, referred by the PI committee, as a result of PI findings, topics for improvement, and so on) for continuing education programs?		Yes ☐ No ☐ Comments
16. When relevant PI findings occur that merit further actions does the medical staff ensure that appropriate measures (peer review, summary suspension, proctoring, and so on) are implemented?		Yes ☐ No ☐ Comments
17. Does the PI review or medical record review process include a system for monitoring the medical records for timeliness, legibility, and accuracy of entries?		Yes ☐ No ☐ Comments
18. Does the PI review or medical record review monitor the three guidelines for autopsy identifying criteria when an autopsy should be required? Process for documenting permission for an autopsy completed? System for notifying the attending physician?		Yes ☐ No ☐ Comments
19. All results, conclusions, recommendations, and other actions are communicated to the appropriate medical staff committee and forwarded to the MEC and governing board for final approval and recommendations?		Yes ☐ No ☐ Comments

EXHIBIT 13.3.   **Medical Staff Review and Assessment Tool**

Date: _____

Name of Facility:
Reviewers:

#	*Indicators*	*Findings*		
1.	The medical staff bylaws, rules, and regulations reflect current practices in the medical center?	Yes ☐	No ☐	Comments
2.	The medical staff bylaws, rules, and regulations provide reasonable language to allow the physicians to practice with some degree of freedom and confidence utilizing their medical judgment?	Yes ☐	No ☐	Comments
3.	The medical staff bylaws, rules, and regulations provide for a formal peer review process to maintain quality medical care in the hospital?	Yes ☐	No ☐	Comments
4.	The medical staff peer review process includes mechanisms to:			
	• Identify peer review issues?	Yes ☐	No ☐	Comments
	• Work through the process?	Yes ☐	No ☐	Comments
	• Document and report the review findings and outcomes?	Yes ☐	No ☐	Comments
5.	The medical staff has developed quality indicators for monitoring physicians performance and opportunities or improvement?	Yes ☐	No ☐	Comments
6.	The medical staff has approved clinical indicators to identify opportunities to improve care delivered to patients:			
	• Complications?	Yes ☐	No ☐	Comments
	• Undesirable outcomes?	Yes ☐	No ☐	Comments
	• Mortalities?	Yes ☐	No ☐	Comments
7.	The medical staff has operational indicators in place to monitor patient-focused functions and identify opportunities for improvement?	Yes ☐	No ☐	Comments
8.	The medical staff has a physician well-being committee to ensure that the health (physical and mental) and well-being of physicians are addressed? (DHS Standard)	Yes ☐	No ☐	Comments
9.	The medical staff has in place outcome indicators to determine if desired results were achieved and physician performances were adequate?	Yes ☐	No ☐	Comments
10.	Indicators used are meaningful, facility specific, and have a measurement component?	Yes ☐	No ☐	Comments
11.	Corrective actions are monitored to ensure process improvement?	Yes ☐	No ☐	Comments
12.	Identify medical staff-related PI projects that have a positive outcome and desired result?	Yes ☐	No ☐	Comments
13.	Is quality improvement data-aggregated, benchmarked, and utilized to create meaningful physician profiles for reappointment?	Yes ☐	No ☐	Comments
14.	The medical staff has a leadership role in performance improvement? (JCAHO requirement)	Yes ☐	No ☐	Comments
15.	The medical staff is actively involved in the following performance improvement processes:			
	• Treatment and medical assessment of patients?	Yes ☐	No ☐	Comments
	• Use of blood and blood products?	Yes ☐	No ☐	Commentsl
	• Use of medications?	Yes ☐	No ☐	Comments
	• Use of operative and other invasive procedures?	Yes ☐	No ☐	Comments

(Continued)

EXHIBIT 13.3.   **Medical Staff Review and Assessment Tool** (*Continued*)

Date: _____

Name of Facility:
Reviewers:

#	*Indicators*	*Findings*		
16.	The medical staff initiates peer review for medical staff members who violate medical staff bylaws, rules, or regulations?	Yes ☐	No ☐	Comments
17.	The medical staff has developed a point system and action plan based on the severity of a violation (such as failure to pay due; bylaws, rules, or regulations violation; practice issues; behavior issues)?	Yes ☐	No ☐	Comments
18.	Who is responsible and accountable for the peer review process? Does this individual maintain or review all documents, making sure procedural steps in the process are followed in accordance with the bylaws, rules, and regulations?	Yes ☐	No ☐	Comments
19.	The medical staff bylaws, rules, and regulations address physicians who fail to appear as requested for peer review meetings, hearings, and/or other medical staff requests?	Yes ☐	No ☐	Comments
20.	Each medical staff department has an effective physician leader who:			
	• Upholds the bylaws, rules, and regulations?	Yes ☐	No ☐	Comments
	• Assures MEC that peer review is conducted in a timely manner, and that a fair hearing process is completed?	Yes ☐	No ☐	Comments
	• Follows up to ensure that corrective action has been implemented and opportunities for improvement determined?	Yes ☐	No ☐	Comments
	• Keeps MEC informed on key issues regarding the hearing process and works with the medical staff department to maintain confidentiality of information?	Yes ☐	No ☐	Comments
21.	How many medical staff peer review actions have occurred during the past three years?	Yes ☐	No ☐	Comments
22.	How many physician peer review-related problems and issues were not acted upon?	Yes ☐	No ☐	Comments
23.	How are medical staff peer review issues identified in minutes of meeting—performance improvement, department, MEC, and so on—which:			
	• Are pending without final action?	Yes ☐	No ☐	Comments
	• Were noted in minutes but were never acted upon by the medical staff?	Yes ☐	No ☐	Comments
	• Were acted upon and the process can be followed by documentation?	Yes ☐	No ☐	Comments
24.	If the peer review process is not working, what is the root cause of the problem?			
	• Need for reestablishing an appropriate peer review process?	Yes ☐	No ☐	Comments
	• Education and training of the medical staff on various peer review topics including the importance of internal peer review and/or why peer review is essential in your facility?	Yes ☐	No ☐	Comments
25.	How many physicians were reported to the State Board of Medical Examiners and Board of Osteopathic Examiners in Medicine and Surgery (BOMEX) over the past two years?	Comments		
26.	How many physicians were reported to the National Practitioner's Data Bank over the past two years? (Include reasons.)	Comments		
27.	Additional questions and findings:	Comments		

EXHIBIT 13.4.   Due Diligence Assessment Form: Pathology and Laboratory Services

Focus Areas	*Yes*	*No*	*OFI**
1. Laboratory is licensed by appropriate authorities and the licensing documents are retained.			
2. All individuals involved in specimen collection are trained, supervised, and evaluated for hospital competence.			
3. There were written laboratory instructions for all procedures that are reviewed and revised at least every three years.			
4. The accuracy of all procedures is documented by tracking reports that are regularly reviewed by the direction laboratory supervisor and director as appropriate.			
5. All employees are instructed in the legal requirements for HIV testing and confidentiality.			
6. Laboratory results are recorded on forms specific to the procedure or a test.			
7. There are written listings of critical panic values that are distributed to all staff and physicians.			
8. There is an effective communication system for critical panic value results. This information needs to be communicated to the physician and recorded in the medical record noting the date, time, to whom the information was reported, the communication method, and the person communicating.			
9. All laboratory testing done while the patient is under the care of the hospital is done in the hospital's laboratory or In an approved referenced laboratory.			
10. Evidence indicates that there is a mechanism designed for determining the reference laboratory's performance, acceptability, and compliance with federal standards.			
11. There are laboratory policies and procedures that address at least the following: • Specimen collection. • Specimen preservation. • Instrument calibration. • Quality control and remedial action. • Equipment performance evaluation. • Test performance.			
12. Quality control checks are conducted on each procedure as defined by the organization (at a minimum, manufacturer's instruction are followed).			
13. The laboratory meets all CLIA regulations.			
14. There is a list of laboratory procedures done in the laboratory.			
15. There is a description of the process used to send lab work to a reference laboratory from specimen collection to receipt of report.			

*Opportunities for Improvement (OFI).

<u>**EXHIBIT 13.5.**</u>   **Due Diligence Assessment Form: Radiology**

Focus Areas	*Yes*	*No*	*OFI**

1. The organization defines its scope of service as it relates to radiology. Regardless of whether or not services are provided on-site or through a contractual arrangement, services need to be provided in a timely manner and must not delay patient's diagnosis and/or treatment.

2. Radiology services include at least the following:
   - Providing radiographic or fluoroscopic diagnostic and treatment services appropriate to the scope of services provided.
   - Interpreting x-ray films and other radiographs.
   - Supplying reports in a timely manner.
   - Providing summaries of performed radio therapy in a timely manner.
   - Maintaining duplicate reports of services and retaining film in the radiology department for a period of time in accordance with the policies of the hospital.

3. A radiologist authenticates reports of all examinations except those reports of specific procedures that may be authenticated by other physicians given privileges to do so.

4. There are signed and dated reports of all radiology examinations performed included in the patient's record.

5. There are a significant number of competent, appropriately trained, and educated and supervised personnel available to conduct radiology services.

6. Policies and procedures require a written order prior to the performance of a nonemergency radiology exam. (Screening mammography may be performed on the request of the patient.)

7. Radiology orders are accompanied by a concise statement of the reason for the examination. This is documented in the medical record.

8. There are written policies and procedures addressing the handling of hazardous materials and wastes from the point of entry into the health care organization to the point of disposal. Staff are educated and trained in the appropriate handling of these materials.

9. There is adequate space, equipment, and supplies for performing radiology services with optimal accuracy, precision, efficiency, and safety.

10. Specific safety factors in radiology include at least the following:
    - Precautions against electrical, mechanical, and radiation hazards.
    - Proper shielding where radiation sources are used.
    - Acceptable monitoring devices to be worn by all personnel in the area with a potential radiation hazard.
    - Maintenance of records on personnel exposed to radiation.
    - Instructions to personnel concerning safety precautions and the handling of emergency radiation hazards and periodic evaluation by qualified personnel of radiation sources and of all safety measures followed, including calibration of equipment.
    - Radiology tests are interpreted and results documented by qualified physicians.

*Opportunities for Improvement (OFI)

EXHIBIT 13.6.   Environmental Due Diligence Overview

Completion of an environmental site assessment (ESA) is a key component of the due diligence process. An ESA is performed to identify recognized environmental conditions (RECs) that potentially could effect the decision to purchase a particular property. Recognizable environmental conditions means the presence of or likely presence of any hazardous substances or petroleum products on the property under conditions that indicate an existing release, a past release, or a material threat of a release into structures on the property, into the ground, groundwater, or surface water of the property. Completion of a environmental site assessment (ESA) that meets the standards of the American Society for Testing and Materials (ASTM) protocols is intended to assist the user to satisfy one of the requirements to qualify for the *innocent landowner defense* to the Comprehensive Environmental Response, Compensations, and Liability Act (CERCLA) liability. Without such due diligence, the purchaser of the said property may incur all future and past liabilities related to poor environmental stewardship by prior owners.

In addition to the requirements set out by ASTM E 1528, one should also review the prior property owner's diligence in meeting their obligations under OSHA and other associated laws and regulations pertaining to occupational health and safety. This will provide the future owner with a fuller understanding of past operations and potential liabilities in this area.

A comprehensive ESA (Phase 1) includes (1) a review of all documents available, (2) interviews with staff familiar with past operations at the site, (3) a walking tour of the facility to include the exterior grounds and all locations on the site where hazardous substance may have been handled, used, stored, or disposed, and (4) a search of numerous governmental data, historical aerial photos, topographic maps, and geological data of the surrounding area.

EXHIBIT 13.7.   Environmental Due Diligence Document Request

Please have all of the following documents available for the document review session. If the facilities do not have any of those listed below, please indicate so.

- Safety committee minutes.
- Safety policies and procedures (such as bloodborne pathogens, tuberculosis, injury and illness prevention, and so on).
- Emergency preparedness program and/or plans.
- OSHA 200 Logs—past three years.
- Regulatory Agency inspection reports and/or citations—past three years.
    CalOSHA
    Fire departments
    Local department of health (as they pertain to environmental, health, and safety)
- Accrediting agency reports (such as JCAHO, NCQA).
- Full set of site plans.
- Hazardous materials business plan (California only).
- Hazardous materials inventory and MSDS files.
- Hazardous waste disposal documents.
    Waste determinations
    Manifests
    Disposal contracts
- Biohazardous waste documents.
    Tracking documents
    Disposal contract
    Medical waste management plan (California only)
- Asbestos reports and surveys.
- Prior environmental assessments (such as Phase I's, internal audits).
- Permits (air, water, biohazardous waste, ethylene oxide use, wastewater discharge, EPA).
- If laboratory services are provided:
    Chemical hygiene plan
    Exposure monitoring reports
- If radiological services are provided:
    Radiation safety committee minutes and documents
    Quarterly reports from radiation physicist
    State inspection reports
    Silver recovery documents and a summary of silver recovery process
- Disposal records of any radioactive materials.
- If underground storage tanks (UST) are maintained (emergency generators)
    All documents relating to UST
    Permits and certifications
- If above ground storage tanks (AST) are maintained
    All documents relating to AST

EXHIBIT 13.8. **Agenda for a Site Visit**

DUE DILIGENCE **Site Visit**
Environment of Care

Occupational Health/Facilities/Environment of Care	*Total Hours*	*CHW Team Member*
Day One:		
Document Review	8 hours	*Insert Name*
Day Two:		
Tour (can be combined with Clinical Team Tour)	1–3 hours	*Insert Name*
Safety Officer/Chair of Safety Committee	1 hour	*Insert Name*
Biomedical Engineering Lead	1 hour	*Insert Name*
Facilities Manager	1 hour	*Insert Name*
Individual responsible for employee health and workers' compensation coordination	1 hour	*Insert Name*
Security	30 minutes	*Insert Name*

14

Health Care Legal Liability Exposures in Different Organizational Settings

William B. Reisbick
Rando W. H. Wick

Liability can result in many health care settings, for a multitude of legal reasons. This chapter will focus principally on medical professional and general liability exposures. Key differences involving these two types of legal concepts and insurance coverages follow.

General Liability

This type is often referred to as premises liability, since many of these claims involve slips and falls and other premise-related injuries. Nevertheless, this category also includes many other injuries or legal theories such as: libel, slander, defamation, malicious prosecution, false arrest, wrongful eviction, assault and battery, advertising activities, environmental pollution, and so on. This category generally includes claims that allege negligence for nonpatient care activities. Claimants may include patients, physicians and other providers, family members, visitors, or even trespassers. Failure to provide a safe environment for the delivery of care under the new Joint Commission standards may result in either or both general and professional liability.

Professional Liability

Also referred to as malpractice liability, this liability involves allegations of negligent acts or omissions of health care providers or employees that result in patient injury. Patients, or their legal representatives, may allege separate theories of negligence against treating physicians, health care entities, nurses, and other employees.

To avoid confusion and insurance carrier "finger-pointing," it is recommended that these two coverages be written in a single policy with the same insurer. This is particularly true for hospitals.

History of Negligence

Under common law, negligence has been recognized as a separate "tort" or civil wrong. Early cases recognized that those individuals that held themselves out as having special competence (for example, a surgeon or nurse) assumed an obligation to give proper service. The breach of that duty by negligent conduct was found to result in legal liability. A cause of action (or legal theory) for negligence requires more than negligent conduct. The legal formula requires proof by the plaintiff of the following elements:

1. *A duty to exercise reasonable care.* The law implies a duty to exercise reasonable care whenever a patient or provider relationship has been formed. In some jurisdictions this may arise with the exchange of any communication with the patient. Consult your state's laws.

2. *Breach of the duty.* This is a failure to conform to the required standard. In malpractice cases this often involves the determination of the applicable *standard of care,* and whether it was not met.

3. *Causation in fact, and legal or "proximate" causation.* This requires proof by the plaintiff of a reasonably close causal connection between the alleged conduct and the resulting injury.

4. *Actual loss or damage.* The plaintiff must prove actual, rather than nominal, damages resulted.[1]

Standard of Care

For the application of negligence principles in health care, evidence as to the customary practice is usually admissible. The plaintiff must prove that the defendant's conduct did not meet recognized medical practices. "It is not enough that the expert witness to testify that he would not personally follow the defendant's practice, he/she must also testify that the practice was not recognized as valid."[2] Proof that the care did not meet the standard must be established by expert testimony unless:

1. The negligence is so obvious that is within the common knowledge of jurors, or

2. *Res ipsa loquitor,* which is Latin for "the thing speaks for itself." The cause of injury is under the exclusive control of the defendant, and this type of accident does not happen without negligence (for example, a foreign body left in at surgery).[3]

The expert witness traditionally stated the standard of care in terms of a practitioner in good standing in that community. This was called the "strict locality rule." Many jurisdictions evolved to the "similar community under similar circumstances" test to avoid the difficulty of obtaining experts in the same community to testify against each other. Many jurisdictions have now adopted the "national standard" to reflect the readily available information on computers, Medline, and through national certification for specialists.[4] Check your state laws to determine the applicable standard in your jurisdiction. Physicians who are specialists are usually required to meet a higher standard of care. In many states they are required to use that degree of care, skill, and diligence that is used by ordinarily careful specialists practicing in the same medical field.

The "Medical Malpractice Crisis" and Tort Reform

In the late 1970s and mid-1980s, an increase in the frequency and severity of malpractice claims produced a huge increase in malpractice premiums and decrease in coverage availability. State legislatures responded with changes in the law known as *tort reform.*

These changes affected standard of care, informed consent, maximum limits on noneconomic damages (pain and suffering, loss of consortium or services), punitive damages, and statutes of limitation (time limits for filing lawsuits).[5] Economic damages have survived in most states, and the cost of future care (life care plans) have kept settlement and verdicts high in many cases.

············

HOSPITALS AND MEDICAL CENTERS

Many early common law cases viewed hospitals in legal terms much the same as innkeepers. The role of hospitals was evolutionary, with many physicians treating patients at home. Early hospitals housed and fed patients, where they were treated by their doctor. By the early 1900s the development of aseptic technique and therapeutic and diagnostic capability resulted in liability for hospitals for maintaining facilities, providing equipment and supplies, and hiring and supervising nurses. In most jurisdictions, hospitals remained protected by the concepts of charitable or governmental immunity. However, by the 1950s, many courts began to impose liability on hospitals for providing direct health care to patients, and supervising staff.[6] The erosion of charitable and governmental immunity followed, when courts recognized that hospital liability insurance was available and affordable. Prior cases recognized hospital liability for "administrative acts," but not for "medical acts."[7] The rule allowing hospitals immunity for medical acts was abandoned in one jurisdiction after another.[8]

Respondeat Superior

The legal theory of Respondeat Superior applies where the acts of a hospital employee is within the course and scope of their employment (or, let the master answer for the acts of the servant). If the employee acted negligently, then courts have found hospitals liable even though they were not directly negligent in any way. For example, an eighteen-year-old male patient broke his leg in a college football game, and he was seen by a physician on emergency call at the hospital that day. The physician and other hospital personnel applied traction and a plaster cast. After the cast dried, the patient's toes became dark and swollen. The patient and family complained of increasing symptoms of poor circulation. Despite alerting staff about an increase in symptoms, no remedial steps were taken. In three days the cast was removed, at which time the leg had to be amputated. The plaintiff alleged negligence by both the physician and nursing staff. The court held that the concept that the hospital does not undertake to treat the patient, but merely procures doctors and nurses to do so on their own responsibility, was no longer valid. Patients expect that the hospital will attempt to cure them, not merely that its nurses or other employees will act on their own responsibility.[9] This case (*Darling v. Charleston Community Hospital*) is a landmark in the beginning of the concept of the corporate negligence liability of hospitals.

Thus, there have been two approaches to liability of hospitals for their employees. First, is the *respondeat superior (or control) theory* that finds liability when the employee's action was within the actual or implied scope of employment at the hospital. The second is the *enterprise theory*, which requires the hospital entity to pay damages on the theory that it is better situated to bear the loss.[10]

Negligent Credentialing Liability

In a landmark case imposing liability on the hospital for negligent credentialing, a patient underwent surgery to remove a pin fragment from his right hip. The surgeon was a member of the independent medical staff. During the course of the surgery the patient's femoral artery and nerve were injured causing atrophy and paralysis. The patient settled with the physician, and continued to sue the hospital for negligence in appointing the physician to its medical staff. The evidence demonstrated that reasonable inquiry by the hospital would have revealed suspension of privileqes at other facilities, as well as the existence of then other cases involving medical malpractice against the physician. The court held that the jury may find the hospital liable for negligent credentialing, or recredentialing, saying that a hospital owes a duty to its patients to exercise reasonable care in the selection of its medical staff, and in granting specialized privileges. This includes verifying the applicant's statements regarding medical education, training, experience, history regarding adverse privileging, and prior malpractice actions.[11] More recently, courts have charged hospitals with knowledge of what they knew, or could have known, regarding the physician applicant upon diligent inquiry. This includes inquiry with the state licensing body(s) and National Practitioner Data Bank (NPDA). A hospital that does not request information from the NPDA as required is presumed to have knowledge of any information reported.

Ostensible Agency or Apparent Authority

This legal concept is based on two factors that must be proven to hold a health care facility legally responsible for the actions of independent contractors or physicians: (1) that the patient looked to the institution rather than the individual physician for care; and, (2) that the hospital "held out" the independent contractor or physician as it's employee. The *Restatement of Torts* initially set this concept forth as follows:

> One who employs an independent contractor to perform services for another which are accepted in the reasonable belief that the services are being rendered by the employer or by his servants, is subject to liability for physical harm caused by the negligence of the contractor in supplying such services, to the same extent as though the employer were supplying them himself or by his servants.[12]

Since this form of legal liability is triggered by the patient's mistaken belief that the independent contractor or physician is an employee of the hospital, many facilities are careful to minimize the possibility of this misconception, such as through signage, name badges, letterhead, advertisements, and billing statements clearly identifying these individuals as independent from the hospital. See *Shepard v. Sisters of Providence* for a case holding the hospital liable for the apparent authority of a surgical resident from a nearby university medical school.[13]

Inherent or Essential Function Test

The courts have allowed juries to impose liability on hospitals for the acts of independent contractors or physicians where the nature of the service determines liability. In these cases the courts have held that the hospital has certain inherent functions for which it cannot delegate legal liability to others, such as the emergency department, radiology, pathology/lab, neurology, and so on. The theory is that public expectations have been created by hospitals through advertising that the institution has control over the safe performance of these functions. Also, most often the patient has little or no role in selecting or even knowing who these providers are. For interesting cases, see *Beeck v. Tucson General Hospital* (radiologist)[14] and *Adamski v. Tacoma General Hospital* (emergency physician).[15]

Nondelegable duty

This doctrine has been applied to impose legal responsibility on hospitals to retain responsibility for essential functions (like emergency departments) that are legally required. The lead case is the Alaska case of *Jackson v. Power*.[16] This case involved a seventeen-year-old male patient who was injured when he fell from a cliff in 1981. He was airlifted to Fairbanks Memorial Hospital where he was seen by the independent emergency physician on duty. His injuries included facial and scalp lacerations, multiple contusions and lacerations of the lumbar area, several fractured vertebra, and gastric distention suggesting the possibility of internal injuries. Dr. Power ordered several tests, but none that were focused on possible kidney damage. The patient had, in fact, sustained injury to his renal arteries and kidneys. This went undetected for nine to ten hours, causing the patient to lose both of his kidneys. The court held that patients receiving treatment at a hospital emergency room are deserving of safe and adequate treatment, and the hospital should not be able to transfer that duty to another. This duty is nondelegable. Other courts have found hospital-based services (radiology, pathology, and so on) to be "nondelegable." But other jurisdictions have rejected *Jackson v. Power*, where the patient knew who the physician (or radiologist) was prior to the procedure.[17]

Negligence *Per Se*

The standard of conduct of a reasonable hospital or health care provider may be established by a statute or regulation. Your state's hospital regulations may have this type of legal binding effect.

....

CLINICS AND PHYSICIANS

The legal principles of negligence, including duty, breach, causal connection, and damage, apply (with equal force) to clinics, physicians, and other independent providers. The provider's action (commission) or failure to act (omission) must be shown to be a departure from the acceptable standard of care, and the damage or injury must be causally related. Clinics, ambulatory surgery centers, dialysis centers, for example, and their physician owners or partners, have been the subject of many cases that have successfully alleged and proven liability for respondeat superior, ostensible agency, or apparent authority (much the same as the hospital cases cited previously).

It is important to remember that despite many technological advances, much of medicine, as it is still practiced, is an art rather than a science. There is no certainty that treatment will succeed. Many states have standard jury instructions stating that the physician is not a guarantor of cure. Most physician decisions are judgmental in nature, and even when they do not prove (with hindsight) to have been the best course, such decisions should not justify the filing of a malpractice action. While plaintiff lawyers have long been admonished to always seek the aid of medical experts with equivalent training to review the medical records prior to filing suit, we all know this practice is not always followed. The only legitimate exception to this practice is where the statute of limitations (time limit for filing a lawsuit) is about to expire.[18] Independent medical chart reviewers should make a bona fide effort to apply foresight (what the treating physician knew, or should have known, at the time of treatment), and not hindsight adding what is known retrospectively. For example, In a lawsuit alleging misdiagnosis of an ankle fracture, it was alleged that the physician misinterpreted the x-ray and incorrectly diagnosed an ankle sprain. The court held that the patient's experts were employing hindsight in reviewing the x-rays, because they knew before the review that a fracture existed.[19] In this case, the fracture was "extremely discreet."

Medical History

The physician has a duty to obtain a complete medical history from the patient before commencing treatment. This is true in all but extreme emergent situations when there is absolutely no time to do so.[20,21] A military physician prescribed a fifty-day supply of Valium to a soldier without taking any significant history of prior psychiatric illnesses, nor reviewing prior (local) Army psychiatric records. The patient overdosed and injured two other persons while driving erratically. The court held that the physician was liable to the third parties.[22] It is the standard of care to take an anesthesia history of the patient prior to surgery. The failure of the physician to ascertain that the patient had a prior history of adverse reaction to Halothane, resulted in liability for both the anesthesiologist and orthopedic physician. Conversely, the physicians were not found liable for a morphine allergic reaction leading to the patient's death where the patient had denied any drug allergies during a thorough medical history. Lack of an accurate history by the patient can result in the application of contributory negligence barring recovery, or comparative negligence reducing recovery by the prorated percentage of negligence by the patient (depending on the jurisdiction).[23] Taking a thorough medical history entails asking appropriate questions, active listening, pursuing responses in greater detail when answers are not clear and complete, and following up on any "lingering doubts." Failure to document and investigate ambiguities or changes in the history can result in liability.

Physical Examination

Upon completion of the medical history the physician should complete a physical examination[24] of the patient that meets the following standards:

- Taking care not to injure the patient (do no harm).
- Ordering appropriate diagnostic tests and imagery.
- Making appropriate referrals. Often performing the test and interpretation require an appropriately trained specialist.
- Proper utilization and use of the tests.

Key elements of a physical exam include checking the vital signs and an exam of the following systems: skin, head, eyes, ears, nose and sinus, mouth and throat, neck, breasts, respiratory, cardiac, gastrointestinal, urinary, genito/reproductive, peripheral/vascular, musculoskeletal, neurologic, endocrine, hematologic, psychiatric, and so on.

Ordering Appropriate Tests and Imagery

When an emergency physician failed to order an electrocardiogram for a middle-aged, female patient admitted to the emergency room with complaints of chest pain, the physician was found negligent as a matter of law.[25] When the physician failed to take additional steps to determine the cause of the patient's back pain, liability resulted. The physician should have known by a thorough history and record review that her symptoms signaled the risk of metastasis from her breast cancer.[26] As a general rule, the physician may rely upon customary diagnostic tests and procedures to confirm the diagnostic impression that was developed from the history and physical, as long as this diagnosis is not in conflict with the clinical presentation.[27]

When the physician knows, or should know, that a pregnant patient is of Eastern European Jewish background and he does not order a screen for potential Tay-Sachs disease, liability for the child's medical, hospital, nursing, and funeral expenses may result, as in *Howard v. Lecher*.[28] When the parents allege they would have terminated the pregnancy by legal abortion if advised, they were not allowed recovery for mental distress in this case. Misinterpretation or incomplete laboratory tests by the physician that result in harm can also result in liability.[29]

When a patient's symptoms suggested a common ailment, rather than a rare malignancy, the physician was not liable for the failure to order a biopsy to check for the rare condition, as in *Daigle v. St. Paul Insurance*.[30]

Differential Diagnosis or Clinical Impression

When the patient's clinical presentation is atypical, or lacks some or all of the usual symptoms or signs (rebound tenderness, fever, and so on), the physician may be able to avoid liability for failure to diagnose, treat, or refer. For example, refer to atypical presentation of appendicitis, as in *Hawkins v. Ozborn*.[31] There are many court decisions stating that the exercise of medical judgment still has elements of art, as well as science. These cases often hold that the physician will not be liable for an honest error in medical judgment if he or she complies with recognized medical standards and administers the treatment in a nonnegligent fashion.[32] With the advent of clinical practice guidelines (CPGs), the physician must carefully document why he or she varied from the guidelines to minimize legal exposure for doing so. For example, the State of Maine Clinical Guidelines create a disputable presumption that the standard of care is met if the guideline was followed. When a pediatrician ordered penicillin and streptomycin at 75 percent of the adult dose and ignored the label "Not for pediatric use," the physician was held liable for the child's permanent deafness.[33] There is also a line of cases that hold that where a treatment or procedure is one of choice among competent providers, a physician is not negligent if he or she selects the one that, according to best judgement, is most appropriate for the patient's needs.[34] This case, and others that reflect on the choice of contrast medium, will need careful interpretation in view of the clinical appropriateness versus managed care and cost issues in the use of ionic and nonionic contrast media. In a another case the court held that where alternative procedures are available, any of which are medically acceptable, a physician will not be held liable for electing to use one of the acceptable procedures instead of the other, such as an election to perform gallbladder tests, which did not reveal lymphoma in the epigastrium in the case of *Bellomy v. United States*.[35] In other words, when competent medical authority is divided, a physician may follow a course of treatment advocated by a considerable number of competent professional colleagues (the minority), if it is in accord with the exercise of reasonable clinical judgment.

Failure to diagnose and report potential child or dependent adult abuse may result in physician liability.[36] Most states grant immunity, or qualified immunity, for good faith reporting of suspected abuse. There have been recent long-term care and adult abuse developments in California.

As stated previously, no health care provider is an absolute insurer of a successful course of medical treatment, correct diagnosis, or cure. Atypical presentation or abnormal location of nerves, arteries, or organs can offer a viable theory of defense.[37] The physician must be very careful to avoid guaranteeing results. Example: "I will guarantee to make the hand 100 percent perfect." Liability can result on a theory of contract or breach of warranty.[38] This is particularly true in advertisements or before and after pictures shown to plastic or elective surgery patients.

Failure to Make Appropriate Referral

A physician's failure to seek appropriate consultation when not trained for the particular clinical situation or procedure is actionable negligence. A physician must know and act to seek help when he is in over his head. For example, in the case of *Buck v. United States*, failure to consult with an expert physician with knowledge of snakebites resulted in liability when the patient sued for foot-drop.[39] Referral to an inadequately qualified specialist can also result in liability. The physician retains legal responsibility to be aware of the training and experience of other health care providers to whom referrals are made.

Failure to Follow Patient or Give Appropriate Discharge Instructions

A lack of continuity of care frequently plays a large role in clinic and physician liability exposures. Oftentimes it is necessary to construct a timeline chronology of the care given to discern gaps, delays in care, or sequential relationships. Often, these gaps result in a patient condition deteriorating or a complication arising. Carefully elicited expert opinion on causation of injuries may be necessary to sort out delay (or lack of continuity) caused injuries from the underlying disease or injury process. There can be recovery for the extent of aggravation of preexisting or underlying disease or injury. A physician has the duty to follow the patient's progress, monitor the effectiveness of the treatment, and address possible adverse effects. Many patients will follow the physician's instructions literally. Thus, the legal duty is to give clear discharge and medication instructions that take into account reasonably foreseeable risks. A failure to advise or warn patients of adverse symptoms that could occur (and what to do in their event) could create legal exposure. For example, physician liability can result from ordering a patient to ambulate following a possible vertebral fracture from a diving accident, as in *Huff v. Condell Memorial Hospital*.[40] Whenever possible, it is prudent to instruct patients in writing: "If your condition WORSENS, return or call IMMEDIATELY, return to the office or ER, or call 911." A physician may also be liable for causing a patient to become foreseeably addicted to drugs.[41]

Abandonment

The establishment of any significant communication between the patient or their legal representative and the physician or clinic staff can result in the formation of a physician and patient relationship. This can, and often does, result in the duty to appropriately attend and treat the patient. If ongoing care is needed, the physician cannot withdraw without reasonable notice. The physician must either provide reasonable care or provide a competent physician in their place. A physician who leaves a patient, at a critical stage of the disease, without reason, or sufficient notice to procure another medical attendant, is guilty of a culpable dereliction of duty.[42] The American Medical Association (AMA) has concise guidelines for termination of care (and a suggested form letter). This includes offering to provide emergent care for up to thirty days, referral to another provider or medical association, and making photocopies of clinic records immediately available to the new provider upon receipt of proper authorization.

Lost Chance of Survival

For many years the courts have held that proof of a decreased chance of survival is not enough to take a proximate cause question to the jury.[43] These courts concluded that there should be no recovery where the patient would have died anyway. In a line of cases beginning in the late 1960s and early 1970s, other courts began to recognize legal liability where the health care provider's negligence deprived the patient of a significant chance to survive or recover. For a summary of these cases see *Herskovits v. Group Health*.[44] Some of these cases required the plaintiff to prove that the patient had a 51 percent or greater chance of survival, but for the negligence of the provider. *Herskovits* held that a reduction in chance of survival (cancer) from 39 percent to 25 percent was sufficient to go to the jury.

Other Legal Theories

Clinics and physicians have potential legal liability exposure on a host of other possible legal theories, including *negligence per se* for violation of legal statutes or regulations that result in patient injury. These include Emergency Medical Treatment and Active Labor Act (EMTALA) and COBRA violations. Others include consumer protection violations, unfair trade practice, assault and battery (inappropriate touching or sexual contact), and managed care liability. Clinics and owners also have potential liability for premises related general liability (slip and falls, lost property, and so on).

············

INTEGRATED DELIVERY SYSTEMS

For the risk manager, the recent rise in integrated delivery systems (IDSs) has created uncertainty as to who will bear the legal responsibility for the care of a patient by various health care providers. As primary care providers, specialists, pharmacists, and hospitals seek such systems as a means of sharing inherent financial risks, not surprisingly, the distinctions of professional liability have also become less clear. Primary care providers will be considered principally responsible for determining which patients are referred to specialists and which patients are to be hospitalized. Specialists will bear responsibility for determining which tests and to what extent testing is to be performed, as well as the length of hospital stays of a particular patient.

The evolving nature of IDSs also broadens the "gray area" in the context of principal and agent. Previously, a physician with hospital privileges was clearly considered an independent contractor for whom the hospital could usually not be held vicariously liable for any negligence. Additionally, specialists would not be held responsible for the negligence of the referring primary care provider, nor would the primary care provider be responsible for any negligence of the specialist. However, with the development of IDSs, arguments are surfacing that the various health care entities share some responsibility for other providers within that system to assure that appropriate care is being provided to their respective patients. Although there are no reported appellate court decisions against an IDS as yet, that in itself, does not mean they will be spared in the future. With the prevalence of IDSs and the overlapping lines of professional responsibility, medical malpractice cases in which a greater number of defendants are involved will certainly come.

As an example, consider liability exposure in the following scenario:

> Mr. Smith goes in for his annual visit to an optometrist who belongs to an IDS. Upon examination, the optometrist finds something that is a possible old retinal detachment. The optometrist arranges for an appointment for Mr. Smith to be seen by an ophthalmologist who is a member of an IDS. Before visiting the ophthalmologist, that optometrist, in consultation with Mr. Smith's family practitioner, also has Mr. Smith go in for blood work at a local hospital, which is also a member of the IDS. A request is made that the laboratory results from the hospital be sent to the ophthalmologist for further follow-up.
>
> The ophthalmologist receives the laboratory data from the hospital; however, Mr. Smith never shows up for his appointment. The ophthalmologist, not having seen Mr. Smith before, simply files away the laboratory data, awaiting Mr. Smith's appointment. A phone call is made by the ophthalmologist's clinic to Mr. Smith's home, leaving a message on the answering machine that he needs to reschedule his appointment. Nevertheless, Mr. Smith fails to reschedule an appointment.
>
> One year later, Mr. Smith returns to his optometrist, not having sought out any additional eye care during the previous year. At that point, the abnormality seen at the original examination has worsened. An immediate referral is made, once again, to an ophthalmologist. Diagnosis of an ocular melanoma is made. Unfortunately, as a result of the delay in treatment, metastasis had occurred to the liver, ultimately causing Mr. Smith's untimely death.
>
> Arguably, Mr. Smith shares some of the responsibility for failing to show up for his ophthalmology appointment; however, liability will likely be pursued against a number of entities. The optometrist is sued for allegedly failing to ensure that Mr. Smith has followed-up with the ophthalmologist, given the optometrist's concerns over the suspicious clinical findings. The ophthalmologist is sued for both failing to contact the optometrist to inform him that Mr. Smith never showed up and for failing to make a greater effort to ensure that Mr. Smith rescheduled his appointment, since the ophthalmologist was aware of the no-show at the initial appointment and had received the laboratory data. Finally, the hospital is brought into the litigation simply because they were involved in analyzing the laboratory data, had granted staff privileges to both the optometrist and the ophthalmologist, attesting to their professionalism and qualifications as health care providers, and due to the fact that they were all part of the same IDS.

Although juries may differ as to who they believe is primarily responsible for the failure to diagnosis Mr. Smith's condition and untimely death, the fact that the optometrist, ophthalmologist and hospital were all a part of the same system increases the likelihood that all three entities will be made parties to the litigation. Most defense trial lawyers will agree that defending a "system failure" is more challenging than defending an individual provider's medical judgment. When a plaintiff's lawyer pursues an action against several entities, claiming system failure, it depersonalizes the individual health care providers, thereby reducing the likelihood that a jury will empathize with the health care provider's position.

············

MANAGED CARE ORGANIZATIONS (MCO/HMO)

There is no single area under more scrutiny in today's legal environment than managed health care. At the forefront of federal legislation is a movement towards expanding the liability exposure beyond the individual health care provider and on to organizations, or insurers, who play a role in actually determining what health care is provided to patients.

Lately, the numbers of MCOs have mushroomed due to the inability of the fee-for-service system to prevent substantial health care inflation. Under the fee-for-service arrangement, when health care providers were compensated by a third party, there was often little or no deductible to be paid by the patient. Therefore, neither the health care provider nor the patient had a financial incentive to limit the amount of health care provided. When diagnostic tests were considered, the physicians knew that they would make more money if the tests were ordered. Likewise, patients would often desire to proceed with the recommended tests to ensure that all avenues of care were provided, especially given the fact that there was little or no financial incentive not to have such tests done since they would not be paying for it. Additionally, if the diagnostic procedures were not ordered, and the patients had negative outcomes, which could have been prevented had the procedures been performed, the physicians faced the risk of professional liability. With little or no incentive upon the physicians and patients to limit services, much more testing was done, even if it marginally useful. As a result, third-party payors expended a large amount of capital for such services, ultimately necessitating a change in the system to control costs.

Hence, MCOs were developed to decrease total costs of health care expenditures, reduce marginally useful procedures, and decrease the length of hospital stays. Financial incentives were available for underutilization, as opposed to overutilization, of such care.

Given the increasing role of third-party payors in determining what care is actually provided to patients, many are advocating for legislation to ensure that these same third-party payors are held responsible for adverse patient outcomes due to their utilization review or benefit decisions.

> Given the competition between the HMO's need for cost containment and the injured patient's need for compensation for harm received, an adjustment in our tort system is necessary to bring liability in line with managed care's increasing control over the delivery of health services. As our legal system struggles on its voyage between uncontrolled health costs and the tort liability arising out of cost containment activities, malpractice liability associated with cost-cutting initiatives should be jointly allocated among all culpable actors.[45]

As a result of pressures on physicians to place cost-cutting measures ahead of professional judgment, beneficial medical services may actually be omitted to achieve the MCO's bottom line. Nonetheless, physicians' fiduciary duty to patients and their exposure to liability for decisions that deviate from the applicable standard of care remain unchanged.[46] Where the standard of care has not been met, liability should properly attach, regardless of whether the conduct at issue was brought about by cost-cutting, economic imperatives. Clearly, as underutilization and cost containment strategies become more dominant, MCOs must shoulder their portion of the liability when patients are harmed by these negligent cost-cutting initiatives and the resulting substandard health care.[47]

The (Soon to Be) Former Defense of Employee Retirement Income Security Act (ERISA) Preemption

Some legal scholars have also argued that there should be a cause of action for denial of a physician-recommended therapy, when such conduct creates an unreasonable risk to the patient. An MCO will be held liable if its failure to permit such care increases the risk of harm or the harm is suffered.[48] In today's health care environment, some maintain that health maintenance organizations substitute their own expertise for that of the treating physicians and deny the physician-requested treatment due to financially-based considerations.[49]

One such highly publicized case, *Self v. CAMG,* which had begun as a garden-variety employment and contractual dispute case between a physician and a medical group, inevitably turned on this managed health care issue. Dr. Self, a gastroenterologist, sued his employer, Children's Associated Medical Group (CAMG), for wrongful termination and defamation. Although some reported that there was ample evidence to justify his termination (poor interactions with colleagues and staff, clinical incompetence, overtesting, and untruthfulness) and there was no written record of his advocacy, he was able to convince a jury that his dismissal had occurred solely because he protested a managed care utilization review (UR) decision. This isolated UR decision involving whether or not to perform a certain test prior to an endoscopy procedure on a child became the "smoking gun" in this case. The jury found in favor of Dr. Self, although the claims were settled for $2.5 million just days before the punitive damages phase of the trial. Dr. Self became the first physician to prevail in a case based on the California antiretaliation statute prohibiting retaliation against a physician who protests or appeals a payor's decision on grounds that it interferes with appropriate medical care. Indeed, this decision is instructive to risk managers and may reflect the prevailing attitude and frustration with managed care.

The mounting exposure of MCOs and insurers and payors for such health care services may be explained by the change from a retrospective utilization review in a fee-for-service system to a prospective utilization review under a managed care system. As in the *Houston Law Review:* "Whereas a mistaken retrospective review in a fee-for-service system would result only in the wrongful withholding of payment, an erroneous prospective utilization review process under our present managed care system will result in the wrongful withholding of necessary health care and immediate patient morbidity or mortality. In determining the propriety of a medical treatment decision for a particular patient, utilization reviewers have a fiduciary duty to use reasonable care when reviewing physician-recommended services."[50] Recent trends expanding the liability of health maintenance organizations are evidenced by the following cases and legislation.

Wickline v. Blue Cross. The *Wickline* case is one of the landmark cases in which MCOs have relied upon in the past to escape liability in medical negligence matters. The plaintiff in *Wickline* alleged that her insurer's decision to deny certification for additional hospitalization, as had been requested by her physician, resulted in amputation of her leg. Her original physician sought and obtained approval for surgery from the insurers, Medi-Cal. However, the plaintiff suffered circulatory problems and additional clotting in her legs, leaving her physicians to label her recovery "stormy." Her physicians requested eight additional hospital days' coverage in the hope of saving her legs. Medi-Cal denied the extended stay, allowing only four additional days. Nine days after her discharge from the hospital, the plaintiff was readmitted to have her right leg amputated, a result she claims stemmed directly from Medi-Cal's negligence in approving payment for a lesser amount of hospital time than her physician had ordered.

Though the court in *Wickline* denied liability because the patient's physician failed to adequately protest the utilization review findings by filing an appeal with Medi-Cal, the court opened the door to liability against the health care payor, stating that "[t]he patient who requires treatment and who is harmed when care which should have been provided is not provided should [be compensated] for the injury suffered from those responsible for deprivation of such care, including, when appropriate, health care payors."[51]

Shortly after the *Wickline* case was decided, the California courts ruled on *Wilson v. Blue Cross,* which shattered the MCO's false sense of security as to the liability preemption portions of ERISA. In the *Wilson* case, treating physicians recommended that Mr. Wilson should have been hospitalized for three to four weeks to stabilize his severe depression. Blue Cross denied payment for such services, alleging Mr. Wilson could be followed on an out-patient basis. Three weeks later, he committed suicide.

On the basis of the payor's utilization review and denial of coverage, the Wilson family sued both the insurer and its adjuster for tortious breach of the insurance contract, wrongful death, and tortious inducement to breach a contract. The court narrowed the *Wickline* decision. In such cases where a decision was made through utilization review and that decision complied with the medical standard of care, no action would be allowed against the insurer. The court held, however, that if the insurer's decision was a "substantial factor" in causing the plaintiff's injury and the denial of treatment was not within the standard of care, liability against the insurer could be found. The court did require that the patient's physicians make a good faith effort to advocate for the patient with the MCO or insurer before liability would be allowed against the MCO or insurer.[52]

Insurers' and health maintenance organizations' uneasiness with the decisions pertaining to utilization review, notwithstanding the liability of attending physicians, is understandable. In fact, one of the largest and most publicized medical negligence verdicts in the country was a case against a health maintenance organization, *Fox v. HealthNet.* In *Fox,* the plaintiff was denied a bone marrow treatment under utilization review when it was requested after Mrs. Fox was diagnosed with breast cancer. Mrs. Fox went through traditional forms of treatment, including two radical mastectomies and chemotherapy. Mrs. Fox's last chance for survival was having a bone marrow transplant, which her HMO denied as being experimental. Mrs. Fox and her husband sued the HMO for breach of contract, breach of the covenant of good and faith, and fair dealing and intentional infliction of emotional distress. The jury awarded Mrs. Fox $89 million, including $77 million in punitive damages. Rather than risk an adverse award standing as precedent, the HMO settled for an undisclosed amount prior to the entry of the final judgment.

Several states are following the example of Texas in advocating legislation that allows a patient to sue his HMO and other managed care entities for malpractice if an adverse medical necessity determination causes harm, injury, or death. Such legislation is pending in Arizona, California, Georgia, Virginia, and several other states.[53]

Many state courts are inclined to allow such lawsuits against HMOs. In Pennsylvania, the Supreme Court handed down a decision that tort claims against HMOs under state law are not barred by the ERISA preemption.[54] In one particular case, the Haverford Community Hospital was actually a third-party plaintiff against U.S. Health Care on claims that the HMO was at fault for not approving an immediate transfer of the plaintiff from Haverford's emergency room to a tertiary care hospital. The attending physician consulted with a neurologist and a neurosurgeon, all of whom concurred that the plaintiff's condition was a neurologic emergency. However, U.S. Health Care denied authorization for treatment at the university hospital selected by the attending physicians at Haverford, and delayed the patient's transfer for several hours in attempts to route him to one of three alternative facilities. As a result of compression to his spine, the plaintiff became a permanent quadriplegic. Though U.S. Health Care argued that such a lawsuit was pre-empted by ERISA, the Pennsylvania Supreme Court disagreed.[55]

Liability Theories Against Managed Care Organizations

The managed care organization (MCO) can be held liable under several different theories of liability whether in tort or contract. Those are vicarious liability, respondent superior, and ostensible agency.

Vicarious Liability   Vicarious liability is indirect liability. While not the direct or specific provider of medical services, the managed care organization may still be held liable for the negligence of those with whom it contracts based on an agency theory. In *Sloan v. Metropolitan Health Council,*[56] the court held that the staff model HMO may be responsible and hence liable for the negligent acts of its physician/employees. Also, in *Schleier v. Kaiser Foundation Health Plan,*[57] an appellate court upheld an $825,000 jury verdict against the Kaiser Plan for malpractice of an unaffiliated cardiologist. The basis of this holding was the finding that it was the plan's physician who had referred the patient to the consulting cardiologist and he, in turn, failed to diagnose coronary heart disease.

Respondeat Superior   In the staff model MCO, the physician and providers are employees. In this instance, liability is found under the doctrine of *respondeat superior.* This doctrine holds the employer liable for the negligence of their employees.

Ostensible Agency   Liability may also be found against an HMO under the doctrine of ostensible agency. This is an exception to the general rule that an employer is not liable for acts committed by an independent contractor employ. The factors in determining whether ostensible agency creates liability for the MCO are (1) whether the patient looks to the MCO rather than the individual physician for care, and (2) whether the institution holds itself out as offering medical services through its controlled, contracting physician and providers.[58]

For the most part, courts have ruled that physicians are independent contractors with respect to the hospitals and the HMOs that employ them. The courts have been more inclined to hold hospitals liable than HMOs. However, ostensible agency claims against HMOs are becoming more successful, especially where staff-model HMOs and group-model HMOs are involved, as well as when an HMO provides medical equipment and facilities.

Capan v. Divine Providence Hospital[59] was one of the first decisions to recognize this eroding façade of health care. The *Capan* court held the hospital liable for the conduct of a physician who treated a patient in an emergent situation by injecting the patient with a fatal dose of sedatives based on the theory of ostensible agency. The court recognized that patients often go to hospitals to receive medical services rather than to see a personal physician. The court noted the absurdity of requiring patients to inquire about the details of a physician's employment contract before deciding whether to accept emergency treatment. Similarly, the court refused to allow "secret limitations" in the employment contract, which effectively prevents a plaintiff's recovery where a hospital's representation that its physicians are competent, skilled professionals, is wrongful.[60]

Corporate Negligence

The corporate negligence of health care providers was first noted in the landmark case of *Darling v. Charlston Community Memorial Hospital.*[61] In *Darling,* the Illinois Supreme Court recognized that hospitals had an affirmative, nondelegable duty to supervise the competence of its staffmembers. This duty has since been expanded to include liability for the negligent selection of physicians for staff privileges at hospitals and HMOs and is the foundation for our present credentialing systems. The theory behind hospital, HMO, and payor liability rests upon the following: (1) the entities hold out the physicians as competent, and (2) their failure to investigate the physician's skills and qualifications, or their failure to supervise staffmembers, creates an unreasonable yet foreseeable risk of harm to patients. The court held the HMO has a duty to check on a physician's competency by making sure there is: (1) a thorough and complete application process, (2) verification of the provider or applicant's representations during the application process, (3) some form of peer review, and (4) evaluation of the applicant's current practice status. Some courts have held that expert testimony is required to establish a hospital's corporate negligence unless the hospital's negligence is obvious.[62]

Breach of Contract

Although direct liability quality of care claims against MCOs have been brought on the basis of negligent credentialing, breach of contract claims alleging failure to provide qualified health care services and providers, and misrepresentation of the availability of quality care, still face significant barriers to legal accountability to enrollees.[63]

Warranties regarding quality often result because of competitive pressures in the marketplace. These exposures are seldom insured because underwriters view the warranties as business risk. In the case of *Gladden v. Michael Reese Health Plan, Inc.,*[64] a subscriber died due to a physician's failure to examine and treat chest pain. The plaintiff's widow alleged that the HMO's advertisements and marketing constituted deceptive business practices because it did not inform others that the HMO's physicians received bonuses if their utilization costs were lower than budget.

Bad Faith Claims

Managed care organizations also potentially face liability for insurer's duty of good faith and fair dealing. Most states have a requirement that insurers act in good faith when paying claims of their insured. Patient advocates argue that MCOs should be permitted to deny valid claims for medical services only if requested health care is not within acceptable community standards.[65]

At least one court held that an HMO was liable on a bad faith theory. In *Williams v. HealthAmerica,*[66] the plaintiff went to her primary HMO physician complaining of a gynecological problem, including severe cramping and bleeding. Her primary care physician refused to allow the plaintiff to see a gynecologist, a decision that the HMO told her was left entirely up to her primary care physician. When the plaintiff finally saw a gynecologist, she was diagnosed with endometriosis. The court found that reasonable minds could conclude that HealthAmerica's failure to approve payment for an initial referral evidences a bad faith course of conduct on the part of the HMO. Importantly, such a cause of action only exists where courts imply a duty of good faith and fair dealing in contractual relationships, as in the state of Ohio, as well as Texas and California.

Breach of Fiduciary Duty

For the first time, one state court has held that a physician has a fiduciary duty to inform a patient of a managed care financial incentive arrangement that provides a benefit to that physician for underutilization. *Neade v. Portes*[67] held that the plaintiff was able to bring a separate cause of action against the physician for breach of fiduciary duty, distinct from the action of medical malpractice, when the facts revealed that the physician had a contractual relationship with the insurer, a health maintenance organization, that had a medical incentive fund that was used to pay for testing and referral to specialists, and that any monies not spent from this fund would be split between the HMO and member physicians. The plaintiffs in the *Neade* case alleged that if they had known of Dr. Porter's financial interest when he refused to authorize additional tests, they would have obtained a second opinion. The trial court originally struck all references to the fund from the plaintiffs' negligence claim and entirely dismissed the breach of fiduciary duty claim. However, the Illinois appellate court reversed the trial court ruling. This case has been reviewed and ruled on by the Illinois Supreme Court in an unpublished opinion.

At least two states, Texas and California, have enacted legislation that may substantially change the delivery of health care in the future. Among the California legislation is a law creating a new government agency, the Department of Managed Care (DMC). The purpose of this agency will be to oversee HMOs and to address many of the aforementioned issues, including health plan liability for failure to exercise ordinary care, independent review of health plan denials, mental health parity, and provider solvency. It will be the responsibility of the Financial Solvency Standards Board, created under the DMC, to develop and monitor financial solvency requirements for providers who enter into risk sharing contracts with health plans.

Long-Term Care Liability

General principles pertaining to medical negligence cases apply equally to long-term care facilities. For example, as in most medical negligence cases, expert support is still required in order for a plaintiff to establish a *prima facie* case. Experts are usually required to be in the same specialty or field as the provider being sued. For example, in *McIntyre v. Transitional Health Services, Inc.,*[68] the court held that an administrator and nurse were qualified to provide expert testimony regarding the standard of care and causation of injuries, respectively, in a medical malpractice action against a nursing home. This court also ruled that although North Carolina state law did not permit recovery under a theory of implied contract in medical malpractice actions, the claim alleging that the nursing home breached an express contract with the resident survived the defendant's motion for summary judgment.

An Alabama Court provides a good example of how not just any health care provider can provide the required expert testimony in a nursing home negligence case. In *Husby v. South Alabama Nursing Home,*[69] an action was brought against a nursing home and its employees on behalf of a patient who had fallen out of bed. The court found that to prove a breach of the standard of care, the plaintiff must present expert testimony from a nurse who was qualified to provide such testimony about the nursing care provided to the plaintiff. In this case, summary judgment was granted for the defendants because the plaintiff offered expert testimony through a nursing home administrator and an anesthesiologist. The court found that these two individuals could not provide testimony regarding the standard of care of "hands on" health care providers such as a nurse in a long-term care facility. Therefore, the case was dismissed.

Nursing homes can also be held liable to a patient's family when injury has occurred to the patient. Several cases nationwide have explored nursing home liability for patients who disappear from a facility. In *Nelson v. Four Seasons Nursing Center,*[70] the Oklahoma Court of Appeals ruled that a nursing home could be liable to an adult child of a resident for loss of parental consortium after the resident's disappearance from the facility. From a risk management perspective, greater precautions need to be made to make sure that patients who are prone to mental confusion are carefully monitored to ensure that they do not escape the facility. Juries appear to be inclined to expect nursing homes to have such protections in place.

When a number of nursing home residents are injured due to a poorly run facility, there may be an attempt to bring a class action lawsuit. However, one case has held that such residents do not form a properly formed "class" for such an action. In *Kohn v. American Housing Foundation*,[71] former residents of a nursing home brought an action against the owner and manager of the nursing home alleging inappropriate care, and they moved for class action certification. The court held that certification as a class was not warranted because of the circumstances of each plaintiff or patient's alleged injury were highly individualized and could not be separated from a causation inquiry.

Like all medical negligence actions, the statute of limitations applies, limiting the time frame for bringing an action against the nursing home. Some courts have ruled that this time period (which varies among the states, but is commonly two to three years) can be extended when the patient has been treated by the same provider over a long number of years. This is called the continuing course of treatment rule. However, the court in *Dunagan v. Shalom Geriatric Center*,[72] held that a nursing home resident who brought an action against the nursing home could not use the "continuing course of treatment" exception to the statute of limitations since there was more than one physician providing care during the resident's stay.

Another potential source of liability is for abuse of nursing home residents. Most states have statutes protecting the "vulnerable adult" similar to those statutes preventing child abuse. Violations of such statutes can result in an individual action by the patient, or on behalf of the patient. Liability for what is often intentional misconduct can limited by risk managers at long-term care facilities by assuring that (1) appropriate background checks are made into employees, (2) there is a well-established policy on reporting possible abuse, (3) all such reports of possible abuse are thoroughly investigated and the findings well documented, and (4) any employee found to have been abusive to a patient is terminated and reported to proper authorities.

Finally, long-term care facilities can potentially be found liable to spouses of their employees if appropriate infection control measures are not followed. The case of *Bolieu v. Sisters of Providence in Washington*[73] represents an aberrant ruling on a unique set of facts. In this case, the spouses of nursing assistants employed by the Sisters of Providence complained of a skin rash with itchy bumps. They were ultimately diagnosed with a staph infection. The employees filed workers' compensation claims. However, the spouses filed individual lawsuits the following year against the nursing home facility run by the Sisters of Providence, claiming that they had been infected as a result of their wives' staph infections. The court initially granted the defendant's motion for summary judgment, ruling that the Sisters of Providence had no duty to protect nonpatients or nonemployees from infectious agents. However, the Supreme Court of Alaska reversed, finding that the nursing facility had a duty of care to the spouses because the injury was foreseeable. The proximity between the conduct of the nursing facility and the injuries suffered, the moral blame attached to the conduct of the nursing facility, the policy of preventing future harm, the extent of burden to the nursing facility, the consequences to the community imposing a duty on the nursing facility, the availability of costs and the prevalence of insurance for the risk involved, all weighed heavily in favor of binding liability on behalf of Sisters of Providence for these plaintiffs' injuries.

Liability issues for health care providers have expanded in recent years. Many principles of risk management for hospitals are equally applicable to long-term care facilities. However, additional precautions should be made based upon the patient population, as is outlined in this chapter. The increasing parallels of health care liability, whether for hospitals or for long-term care facilities, have almost uniformly increased risk exposure for any provider. However, long-term care facilities are often heavily regulated by state agencies. Familiarity with these state regulations, and their reporting requirements, in critical for any risk manager of such a facility.

Endnotes

1. Wade, J., Schwartz, V., Kelly, K., and Partlett, D. *Cases and Materials on Torts* (9th ed.). Mineola, N.Y.: The Foundation Press, Inc., 1994, p. 130–131.

2. *Ibid.*, p. 180.

3. *Ibid.*, pp. 180, 233.

4. *Ibid.*, pp. 184–185.

5. *Ibid.*, p. 195.

6. Furrow, and others. *Health Law.* West Publishing, 1995, pp. 448–449.

7. *Bing v. Thunig,* 163 NYS2d 3, 143 NE2d 3 (NY, 1957).

8. *Schloendorf v. Society of N.Y. Hospitals,* 211 NY 125, 105 NE2d 92 (1914).

9. *Darling v. Charleston Community Hospital,* 33 Ill. 2d 326, 211 NE2d 253 (1965).

10. Wade, J., Schwartz, V., Kelly, K., and Partlett, D. *Cases and Materials on Torts,* pp. 642–643.

11. *Johnson v. Misericordia Community Hospital,* 99 Wis. 2d., 708, 301 NW 2d 156 (1981).

12. *Restatement of Torts,* Sec. 429 (1965).

13. *Shepard v. Sisters of Providence,* 750 P2d 500 (Or. App., 1988).

14. *Beeck v. Tucson General Hospital,* 18 Ariz. App. 165, 500 P2d 1153 (1972) (radiologist).

15. *Adamski v. Tacoma General Hospital,* 20 Wash. App. 98, 579 P2d 970 (1978) (emergency physician).

16. *Jackson v. Power,* 743 P2d 1376 (Alaska, 1987).

17. *Estate of Milliron v. Francke,* 793 P2d 824 (Mont., 1990).

18. Louisell, D., and Williams, H. *Medical Malpractice.* Matthew Bender, Inc., 1999.

19. *Jones v. Finley,* 170 Ga. App. 182, 316 SE2d 533 (1984).

20. *Kearns v. Hartford Fire Insurance Company,* 450 SO2d 1024 (La., 1984).

21. Bates, B. *A Guide to Physical Examination and History Taking* (3rd ed.). Rochester, N.Y.: Lippincott, Williams, & Williams.

22. *Watkins v. United States,* 589 F2d 214, (5th Cir., 1979).

23. *Howell v. Outer Drive Hospital,* 66 Mich. App. 142, 238 NW2d 553 (1975).

24. Bates, B. *A Guide to Physical Examination and History Taking* (3rd ed.). Rochester, N.Y.: Lippincott, Williams, & Williams.

25. *Keogan v. Holy Family Hospital,* 95 Wash. 2d 306, 622 P2d 1246 (1980).

26. *Schneider v. Memorial Hospital,* 473 NYS2d 524, 100 AD2d 583 (1984).

27. Fiscina, S. *Medical Law For The Attending Physician.* Carbondale: Southern Illinois University Press, 1982, p. 68.

28. *Howard v. Lecher,* 386 NYS2d 460 (1976).

29. *Marchese v. Monaco,* 52 NJ Super. 474, 145 A2d 809 (1958).

30. *Daigle v. St. Paul Insurance,* 323 SO2d 312 (1963).

31. *Hawkins v. Ozborn,* 383 F. Supp. 1389 (1974).

32. *Hoglin v. Brown,* 481 P2d 458 (1971).

33. *Koury v. Follo,* 158 SE2d 548 (NC, 1968).

34. *Ball v. Mallinkrodt Chemical Works,* 381 SW2d 563 (1964).

35. *Bellomy v. U.S.,* 888 F. Supp. 760, 765, (S.D., W. Va., 1995).

36. *First Commercial Trust v. Rank,* 915 SW2d 262, (Ark., 1996).

37. *Lightsey v. Bessemer Clinic,* 495 SO2d 35 (Ala., 1986).

38. *Hawkins v. McGee,* 146 A 641 (NH., 1929).

39. *Buck v. U.S.,* 433 F. Supp. 896 (MD, Fla., 1977).

40. *Huff v. Condell Memorial Hospital,* 280 NE2d 495 (Ill., 1972).

41. 16 ALR 4th 999 (1982).

42. *Norton v. Hamilton,* 92 Ga. App. 727, 731, 89 SE2d 809 (1955).

43. *Cooper v. Sisters of Charity of Cincinnati,* 27 Ohio 2d 242, 272 NE2d 97 (1971).

44. *Herskovits v. Group Health,* 99 Wash. 2d 609, 644 P2d 474 (1983).

45. Gonzales, Jose L., 35 Houston L. Rev. 715, 742 (1988).

46. 35 Houston L. Rev. at 736–37.

47. 35 Houston L. Rev. at 739.

48. 35 Houston L. Rev. at 753.

49. 35 Houston L. Rev. at 753.

50. 35 Houston L. Rev. at 754.

51. *Wickline v. Medi-Cal,* 192 Cal. App. 3d 1630, 239 Cal. Rptr. 810, 819 (1983).

52. *Wilson v. Blue Cross of Southern California,* 222 Cal. App. 3rd 660, 271 Cal. Rptr. 876, 883 (1990).

53. *Managed Health Care, 9*(7), July 1999, p. 24.

54. *Pappas v. Asbel.*

55. *Managed Health Care, 9*(7), July 1999, pp. 24–25.

56. 516 NE2d 1104 (Ind. App., 1987).

57. 876 F2d 174 (D.C. Cir., 1989).

58. 35 Houston L. Rev. at 743, citing *McClellan v. Health Maintenance Organization.*

59. 40 A.2d 647 (Pa. Super. Ct., 1980).

60. *Ibid.,* 649.

61. 211 NE2d 253 (Ill., 1965), *cert. denied,* 383 U.S. 946 (1966).

62. See, for example, *Welsh v. Bulger,* 698 A.2d 581 (Pa. 1987), in which the plaintiff sued for the hospital's failure to oversee staff and physicians properly, and for the hospital's negligently granting hospital privileges to the plaintiff's obstetrician in a case where prompt cesarean section by a qualified physician would have saved the plaintiff's child's life.

63. 35 Houston L. Rev. at 747.

64. Cause No. 89L-18551 (Cir. Ct. Cook County, Chicago, filed Dec. 22, 1989).

65. 35 Houston L. Rev. at 750.

66. 535 NE2d 717 (Ohio App., 1987).

67. 303 Ill. App. 3d 799 (1999).

68. 198 LEXIS 13965 (MD, N.C., May 20, 1998).

69. 712 So.2d 750 (Ala., Apr. 10, 1998).

70. 934 P.2d 1104 (Okla. Ct. App., July 30, 1996).

71. 178 F.R.D. 536 (D., Colo.. Mar. 26, 1998).

72. 967 S.W.2d 285 (Mo., App., Apr. 28, 1998).

73. 953 P.2d 1233 (Alaska, Feb. 13, 1998).

15

High-Risk Clinical Areas

Sylvia M. Brown

This chapter defines the bases for clinical risk exposure and presents strategies for addressing it in "classic" high-risk areas—that is, areas that are regularly distinguished by frequent or severe professional liability claims. Professional liability exposure trends reflect the forces driving change in the health care industry overall. Cost containment, for example, is increasingly shifting professional liability exposure from the inpatient to the outpatient setting. It is also broadening the scope of practice for some professions, and this has led to the increased naming of allied health professionals (AHPs) in professional liability actions. At the same time, technological advances continually impact the focus of professional liability exposure. As a result, clinical risk management issues are topical, and it is impossible to predict how today's "top ten" claim sources will rank next year. Given the rapid evolution of professional liability issues, this chapter does not attempt to describe every clinical risk management matter in high-risk areas but, rather, focuses on key issues and strategies likely to be applicable to more than one situation.

Professional liability theory is based on the theory of negligence. Negligence is proven when the provider has breached his or her duty to render reasonable care to a patient, resulting in substandard practice that, in turn, caused damage. For risk management, the primary challenge of minimizing liability exposure is the task of helping providers establish and document adherence to the standard of care that other reasonable providers would give under the same or similar circumstances. To help readers meet the challenge, this chapter lists key organization(s) that prescribe standards for each high-risk clinical area, then describes how to reduce risk exposure through the fulfillment of pertinent training, organizational, environmental, and technological needs. It also provides a risk management self-assessment tool for each area discussed.

....

OBSTETRICS AS A HIGH-RISK AREA

For more than twenty years, obstetrics has led, or been close to the top of, severity statistics for professional liability claims. The primary organizations guiding obstetrics are the American College of Obstetricians and Gynecologists (ACOG),[1] the Association of Women's Health, Obstetric, and Neonatal Nurses,[2] and the American Academy of Pediatrics.[3] Although standards of care for this specialty area are clearly prescribed, several issues continue to be problematic. Among them is the failure to identify fetal distress in a timely manner, to complete a cesarean section in a timely manner, and to comply with manufacturers' instructions on the administration of oxytocin. The self-assessment tool in Exhibit 15.1 provides an inventory of specific risk management concerns related to each of these problems.

Failure to Identify Fetal Distress

Much has been written about the worth of fetal monitoring.[4] The consensus is that it is a valuable diagnostic tool as long as the provider communicates with the parents to foster realistic expectations and discourages overreliance on technology, and as long as the equipment is used properly.

Training Needs   Respected professional guidelines[5] require that both physician obstetric practitioners and nurses[6] be properly skilled in the interpretation of the fetal heart monitor. It also must be noted that it is arguably adverse to the standard for strips to be

---

EXHIBIT 15.1.   Self-Assessment Tool—Obstetrics Area

I. Obstetrics Providers
   A. What number or percentage of physician providers are obstetricians? Family practice?
   B. What number or percentage of nursing staff are RNs with obstetric training, including documented specific education on fetal monitoring? If other staff interpret strips, what is their background and how are they trained for equivalency with the RN provider?

II. Emergency Cesarean Procedures
   A. If cesareans are performed in the OR, do procedures, including emergency cesarean, facilitate smooth transition of the patient, with continuity of care for mother and fetus?
   B. Are cesarean count procedures equivalent to other surgical procedures in approach?
   C. Does the cesarean team come together effectively within the thirty minutes necessary per ACOG guidelines?
   D. Is a pediatrician or neonatologist in attendance at c-sections? If not, who cares for the baby?

III. Fetal Monitoring
   A. Are policies specifying documentation on fetal monitor strips in place?
   B. Are fetal monitor strips retained so that they can be cross-referenced with the medical record?
   C. Is fetal monitoring and other support equipment, such as pulse oximetry, state of the art and maintained under a current comprehensive biomedical agreement?

IV. Administration of Oxytocin
   A. Do procedures support adequate medical evaluation for possible emergent care?
   B. Does the physician evaluate the patient immediately before induction and document same?
   C. If a physician cannot be present and turns the patient over to another physician while an induction is running, is there a specific discussion regarding the patient to support the second practitioner in her care, if necessary?

---

interpreted by nonobstetric practitioners or providers other than physicians and registered nurses (RNs). However, with cost containment pressures broadening the scope of practice in many clinical areas, the risk manager may well face a situation in which, for example, an RN is not available to fulfill these duties. In cases such as these, an alternative (though less desirable) risk management approach is to implement and document proper fetal monitor training and continual competence checks for a less-credentialed individual. In obstetrics, as in all areas of the health care operation, a finely tuned outcome screening process is critical to picking up quickly on risk management issues. Such a process is obviously beneficial in a high-risk area if an approach that is arguably below the standard of care is utilized (see Exhibit 15-1).

Another obstetric issue the risk manager faces due to cost containment is reengineering, which results in staff downsizing. In these circumstances some obstetric units crosstrain their staff to provide labor and delivery, post-partum, and nursery care. It is essential that crosstrained staff receive specifically documented training for each clinical area and each facet of clinical care in which they will be expected to participate. Examples of obstetric care in which training is particularly important from a risk management perspective are crash cesarean sections, charge nurse responsibility, and fetal monitor interpretation.[7]

Formal courses offered by manufacturers of fetal monitors can assist providers in achieving and maintaining skills in strip interpretation. As a supplement, in remote areas or because of financial constraints, providers can conduct their own training courses, including fetal strip "rounds" during which they interpret a particular strip and critique each other's interpretations. Formal education should be documented in the nurses' credentialing files. Informal education, such as weekly monitor strip rounds, should also be documented in this way.

Organizational and Environmental Needs   Protocols should specify what is to be documented on the fetal monitor strip by physicians and nurses, respectively, as well as when documentation is to occur. Variances from protocols should be documented through continuous quality improvement (CQI) efforts. This approach helps ensure consistency in the documentation of critical interventions, such as the initiation of Pitocin. Another issue related to obstetric medical records is the retention of fetal monitor strips. Because the entire consecutive strip must be kept, finding places to store strips can be challenging. Ideally, they should be placed on the mother's chart. At a minimum, strips should be cross-referenced and kept in a safe place that preserves confidentiality. Microfiche can provide a solution to strip retention problems if obstetric providers agree that the quality of reproduction is adequate and if an agreement can be reached with the microfiche organization. This agreement should contain confidentiality provisions and address the issue of liability for lost strips. Because in some states a cause of action by an infant may be viable until the age of majority, the fetal monitor strip may be a critical piece of evidence when no clinicians recall the case.

The importance of properly documenting and maintaining all obstetric medical records cannot be overemphasized. All clinically pertinent data, including provider interventions to counter fetal distress, must be documented objectively. In addition, medical records should be confidentially maintained, yet readily accessible for reference during care or when needed to prepare for the defense of any actions filed.

Technological Needs   Clearly, the proper maintenance of fetal monitoring equipment should be a top priority. A preventive maintenance program should be in place to provide for routine checks within manufacturer-recommended time frames. Equipment should not be kept after it becomes functionally obsolete, such as when parts are no longer available or monitoring capabilities are outmoded. When outdated equipment is disposed of, proper disposal should be documented.

Failure to Complete a Cesarean Section

ACOG standards require that an emergent cesarean section be performed within thirty minutes of the delivering physician's determination that it is necessary—or "from decision to incision," as it is commonly stated.[8] Myriad logistical issues must be addressed to facilitate timely and competent cesarean delivery under emergent conditions.

Training Needs   In many facilities, the obstetrics unit handles its own cesarean sections. A few organizations still have operating room (OR) staff perform surgery when a cesarean is necessary. Regardless of who is involved, proper training is necessary to ensure that staff achieve and maintain competence. For consistency's sake, it is preferable that all OR or all obstetric providers be trained and that completion of training be documented. However, certain tasks should not be delegated to nonobstetrics staff, regardless of training. For example, if the OR staff performs the procedure, the labor and delivery nurse should accompany the mother and continue fetal heart monitoring as long as possible. (It is understood that fetal monitoring, whether by machine or Doppler, cannot be continued after a sterile prep.) The continuation of monitoring and of the relationship with the labor and delivery nurse enhances continuity of care, provides ongoing documentation of fetal heart tones, and helps to reassure the mother.

Organizational Needs   Again, regardless of where the cesarean is performed, a consistent standard of care must be maintained. For example, obstetrical area count procedures for needles, sponges, instruments, and so on should be equivalent to those used in the OR.

It also is crucial to remember that the "thirty-minute rule" applies to all facilities, including those in rural areas. A chief consideration in meeting this standard is the real-time availability of obstetric practitioners and anesthesia support staff. In settings in which staff may be off-site, it can be challenging to assemble the team in a timely manner, especially during inclement weather. A useful approach for rural facilities that perform deliveries is to have key personnel stay overnight when weather threatens to block roads.

Technological and Environmental Needs   All facilities should develop efficient approaches for setting up the cesarean room. Proper equipment, including fetal monitors and pulse oximetry, must be readily available for use in the procedure.

The geographic layout of the obstetric area may present additional risk. For example, the distance between the labor and delivery room and the OR should be evaluated to ensure that it does not hinder the timely transfer of patients. Any other potential obstacles to efficient transfers also should be identified. For instance, an elevator transport might result in an unintentional, but clinically devastating, delay.

Administration of Oxytocin (Pitocin)

Oxytocin's drug circular requires that there be "adequate medical supervision in a hospital" during administration of the drug. Additionally, in the event of fetal distress, "the mother and the fetus must be examined by the responsible physician."[9] There has been much discussion of what constitutes adequate medical supervision in various settings. The simple truth is that if an emergent bad outcome is related to the induction, the case will be difficult to defend if the physician was not present. Many risk management issues are therefore related to this concern.

Training and Organizational Needs   An obvious risk management strategy for administration of oxytocin is to train appropriate staff and to enhance training periodically. In addition, policies and procedures should, at the least, require that physicians provide adequate medical supervision. Real-time expectations of physicians' physical availability must be considered. In many settings, practitioners prefer to continue seeing patients in their offices while oxytocin is running on a labor patient. Many organizations support this practice as long as practitioners can be physically available in five to ten minutes, and this argues that it is standard of care. Adherence to the five- to ten-minute time frame may be monitored through the CQI process.

In academic settings, the resident physician's role in the induction of patients should be clearly delineated. The resident physician's on-call duties should not include primary management of emergency medical care or the precipitous delivery of an induction patient. To participate in the care of induction patients, the resident physician must be able to provide documentation of relevant training, and there must be clearly specified and ongoing supervision by the attending physician of the resident.

Similarly, in private settings where attending physicians cover for one another, it is essential that an attending who will not be available communicate with the attending covering about the status of a laboring induction patient. For example, as attendings who perform elective surgery will be unavailable during the course of that surgery, they should share the patient's history with a qualified physician who can take over for them in an emergency. Steps to facilitate communication in situations like this should be discussed in a multidisciplinary forum.

Multidisciplinary committees can, in fact, be an invaluable aid in all high-risk areas. In the obstetrics area, for example, a perinatal committee might team physician and nurse practitioners with anesthesia and pediatrics staff. Through discussion, multidisciplinary groups can effectively identify, implement, and monitor solutions to many of the issues that arise as a result of the complexity of health care organization processes.

Technological and Environmental Needs   Fetal monitoring should be implemented for any induction patient. In planning the building of medical staff offices and similar projects, the proximity of obstetric providers to the facility should be an important consideration.

In closing the discussion of obstetric risk, it is important to mention that placental evaluations performed by pathologists according to specific criteria (about 50 percent of births have such indicators) can yield extraordinary information about the entire gestational life of the fetus.[10] This information can be helpful in understanding the causes of bad outcomes in obstetric cases, and, potentially, in increasing the defensibility of a related claim.

....

EMERGENCY SERVICES AS A HIGH-RISK AREA

The emergency department (ED) is a brief and volatile contact for both patients and providers. ED providers face many challenges, including a lack of familiarity with their patients' medical history and the sheer number of patients who may converge on the ED at the same time, all of them presenting with clinical crises. In many EDs, these challenges are compounded by barriers to effective provider-patient communication, such as language and cultural differences. Considering the nature of emergency setting patient provider contacts, it is not surprising that patient assessment is at the root of many risk management issues related to the ED. Specific standards that are critical to emergency services include those of the American College of Emergency Physicians (ACEP.)[11] (See the self-assessment tool in Exhibit 15.2 for an inventory of specific risk management concerns related to the ED.)

Medical Evaluation

It is a sign of our cost-conscious times that concerns about medical evaluation involve economic issues as well as clinical issues. More specifically, "antidumping" legislation has given rise to new concerns regarding medical evaluation. The Emergency Medical Treatment and Active Labor Act (EMTALA)[12] was put into place to prevent transfer of indigent emergent patients from one health care organization to another before their emergent condition could be assessed or stabilized. EMTALA represents a significant exposure for EDs and their practitioners.

The clinical adequacy of medical evaluation also is of concern to risk management. Among the many issues to which risk management should be alert are emergency service claims involving missed diagnoses of conditions such as myocardial infarction, fractures, and meningitis.

EXHIBIT 15.2.   Self-Assessment Tool—Emergency Services

I. Providers
  A. Are physicians covering the ED specialists in ED, internal medicine, or family practice? If not, what specialties are represented?
  B. Are specialties on call adequate to provide backup?
  C. Is RN staff trained in ED care? If other than RN staff is used, is training in place to facilitate equivalent competence?

II. Medical Assessment
  A. Are admitting and transfer procedures consistent with EMTALA requirements?
  B. Are clerical staff trained not to ask for financial information before clinical assessment has taken place, consistent with EMTALA?
  C. Are callback procedures in place for abnormal results and/or discrepancies?
  D. Are overreading procedures in place for radiology films and EKGs?
  E. Are medical records clinically sufficient and available in a timely manner, if dictated?
  F. Does a physician assess all patients?
  G. If telephone triage of any kind is used, are physician-approved specific protocols in place, supplemented by core assessment criteria, to identify high-risk callers?

III. Technological and Environmental Issues
  A. Are signs in place to inform patients of EMTALA rights?
  B. Do clothing and nametags of contracted emergency providers omit name of facility, to avoid ostensible agency considerations?
  C. Is the emergency area designed to facilitate patient flow with maximum security regarding the outside area, and to facilitate observation of high risk patients?

IV. Communication Issues
  A. Are all staff trained in communications skills, including clerical?
  B. Are discharge instructions specific to treatment and a copy given to the patient?

Training Needs   To comply with EMTALA, a thorough inservice on the many implications of the act is appropriate. Of particular note, emergency clerical staff must be trained not to ask new admissions about their source of payment for services before clinical evaluation or triage is performed. To meet the challenge of ED assessment, physicians, nurses, and AHPs must be kept informed about lab test reporting procedures and other clinical measures supporting medical evaluation. Physicians also must receive ongoing education on ED diagnoses. Emergency service medical practitioners must be prepared to address a variety of issues, including emergent delivery. Therefore, board certification in emergency medicine is a highly desirable qualification for ED physicians. Emergency services also should be supported by appropriately trained on-call physicians.

Organizational Needs   The importance of pertinent clinical documentation in the ED cannot be overstated. Although dictation systems enable physicians to document more clearly, dictation also can present a problem if information cannot be quickly and easily accessed by consulting physicians and subsequent caregivers. This problem can be solved through mechanisms such as voice-activated, confidential access by phone to the content of dictation.

Transfers of patients require especially careful documentation. To comply with EMTALA, there must be proper documentation of decisions regarding transfer, including communication with the receiving hospital and the signatures of patients who refuse transfer.

Triage policies and procedures must be in place. These should reflect an objective system of evaluation to be carried out by properly trained emergency nurse providers and physicians. In addition, follow-up approaches, such as overreading of radiology films and cardiograms, are essential, as is a procedure to recall patients if results are abnormal.

It is important that, whenever possible, emergency service evaluations of patients take place in person, rather than over the telephone. Phone assessments may trigger allegations of economically motivated treatment or substandard care, and thus should be discouraged. Telephone assessment of an ED patient by an attending physician, followed by nursing treatment without emergency physician involvement, is also to be avoided. At the same time, it is recognized that in some high-volume environments, including EDs and physician office practices, use of the telephone to triage patients is an increasingly accepted approach. Telephone triage is also increasingly utilized by managed care plans. If telephone triage is utilized, it should be implemented by registered nurses using diagnosis-specific protocols that have been reviewed and approved by physicians. Also, generic criteria should be developed to cover factors that may indicate that an otherwise routine caller is at risk, such as advanced age or a flat affect.[13]

Another risk management issue pertinent to the ED is *ostensible agency,* a major legal theory shifting responsibility for an independently contracted provider's medical evaluation and intervention to the health care organization. In brief, courts in many jurisdictions will imply an employment relationship if the patient perceives that one exists and relies on this perception. The ED, where patients have no reason to know that providers are not employees, is a particularly vulnerable area. To avoid allegations based on misperception, independently contracted physicians or agency nurses in the ED or other departments should be instructed to abstain from wearing scrubs with the health care organization's name on them. Nametags bearing the name of the employing organization are highly appropriate. It is also critical that contracts with independent contractors contain provisions addressing the independent contractor status of the provider, mutual indemnification, hold harmless and promise-to-defend clauses, and the responsibility of the provider for maintenance of adequate professional liability insurance.

Technological and Environmental Needs   Proper diagnostic equipment support is essential. In addition, thought must be given to the risk management implications of the department's physical layout. For example, the radio with which the ED communicates with ambulances in the field should be easily heard by providers.

Likewise, logistical issues such as distance between the ED and radiology should be evaluated. If the distance is great, ED staff might accompany elderly or unsteady patients to radiology to reduce the risk of falls in the hallway. Another logistical risk management intervention is to have RNs accompany patients who are potentially clinically unstable.

Communication Issues

The amount of time an ED provider has to talk with a patient is often limited by the demands of other patients, and the pressing need to perform a comprehensive medical evaluation. As a result, the potential for emergency services liability is intensified by communication issues.

Training Needs   All providers should receive training in communication skills, such as how to listen effectively, how to ask open-ended questions, how to interpret non-verbal communication, and how to give clear instructions. The importance of these skills is heightened for the emergency provider. Providers also should be made aware of cultural differences that can hinder effective communication and be trained in ways to overcome these barriers. For example, women of Middle Eastern origin or descent are traditionally brought up to avoid eye contact. This behavior might lead a practitioner to believe that such a patient is extraordinarily shy, less than forthright, or evasive. Strategies to conquer such barriers include additional patience on the practitioner's part, as well as sensitivity to cultural and individual differences.

Organizational Needs   Patient-provider communication can be enhanced through use of written materials such as discharge instructions. It is very important to ensure not only that the patient receives a copy of these instructions but also that he or she understands them. Instructions, like informed consent forms, should be written to a fifth to sixth grade audience. In addition, to accommodate the needs of patients who do not speak English, discharge instructions should be conveyed with the assistance of an interpreter from the health care organization's "language bank." If the ED sees a high percentage of non-English speaking patients, discharge instructions and informed consent forms should be available in the predominant foreign languages involved.

Technological and Environmental Needs   To facilitate communication between patients and providers, the physical layout of the ED should provide as much privacy as possible. In addition, it should accommodate the clinical needs of the routine population. For example, the ED should be equipped with rooms that permit observation of potential suicide patients awaiting transfer to a psychiatric environment.

As with obstetrics, a multidisciplinary forum in which providers can discuss issues can be of great benefit. Although trauma service and ambulance personnel sometimes are overlooked when ED multidisciplinary committees are formed, representatives from these areas should be included, as they can provide valuable input.

....

SURGICAL SERVICES AS A HIGH-RISK AREA

Understandably, surgical services have been at the risk management juncture between technological growth and cost containment pressures. Liability issues include those generated by the push into the outpatient area fostered by cost containment. (For an inventory of specific risk management issues related to surgical services, see the self-assessment tool in Exhibit 15.3.) The standard of care for surgical services is guided by organizations such as the American College of Surgeons[14] and the Association of Operating Room Nurses (AORN).[15]

Retained Procedural Item

It is critical to ensure that counts of all sponges, needles, and instruments take place per AORN standards. Traditionally, retained items have been one of the most indefensible liability issues among medical negligence cases. The legal theory *res ipsa loquitor* ("the thing speaks for itself") is often used in retained-object cases. Once circumstances supporting *res ipsa* are established, the theory shifts responsibility for proving the case from the plaintiff to the defendant, who must then establish a lack of culpability. Despite the fact that some of the most dramatic legal actions involve retained instruments, these implements still are sometimes not counted. The only instances in which some flexibility, judiciously considered, may be permitted in the counting of implements involves operative fields that are not large enough to encompass the instrument, for example, in the case of clamps used during eye surgery.

Training and Organizational Needs   A policy and procedure should be in place to support the proper approach to counts, including the ordering of a film if the count remains incorrect. Some caregivers have voiced concern about the time it takes to

---

EXHIBIT 15.3.   **Self-Assessment Tool—Surgical Services**

I. Providers
   A. Are surgical privileges specific, competence based, and documented, with a copy maintained in the OR?
   B. Are nurses in the OR specifically trained in OR nursing? If other providers are used, how is training performed to facilitate equivalent competence?

II. Count Procedures
   A. Are these performed on all instruments, needles, and sponges?
   B. Is nursing allowed, by policy, to call for a film if a count is incorrect?

III. Preoperative Evaluation
   A. Is this on the medical record preoperatively?
   B. If not, does the OR supervisor or anesthesiologist have authority to stop the case from going forward?

IV. Equipment
   A. Does a current biomedical agreement cover appropriate operative equipment, such as lasers?
   B. If lasers are utilized, are safety procedures in place?
   C. Is an SMDA reporting system in place?

V. Outpatient Surgery
   A. Is patient disposition (for example, caregiver to drive home) planned ahead of time?
   B. Are discharge criteria postanesthesia assessed by an anesthesia professional?
   C. Are discharge instructions clear and documented for the patient and caregiver, including what to do in an emergent circumstance?
   D. Is the environment appropriate for the procedures performed, for example, laser surgery?
   E. Are emergency support procedures and equipment in the outpatient surgical setting adequate?

---

perform additional counts while the patient is still on the table. This understandable concern should be addressed in the context of a multidisciplinary or perioperative committee, as appropriate.

Technological and Environmental Needs   Whatever mechanisms can be put in place to facilitate a complete count should be implemented. For example, count forms should be kept in an accessible and convenient location. A mechanism for tracking implants per the requirements of the Safe Medical Devices Act (SMDA) also is important.

Misidentification of the Patient or the Side on Which a Procedure Is to Be Performed

Just as inexcusable and potentially indefensible as retained instrument claims are claims involving misidentification. Unfortunately, such claims usually involve procedures that are routinely done in large numbers by surgeons at a given facility, suggesting that routinization desensitizes personnel to the need for identification.

Training and Organizational Needs   By policy, the final validating identification of the patient and the procedure should take place at the last possible moment in the operating room. The policy should also detail several preceding checks at logical points in the preoperative process, all of which are documented. The final check should also include a cross check of the physician's progress notes and the informed consent form in the medical record, and not rely solely on the acquiescence of a patient who has been premedicated. A policy that can be especially helpful in avoiding "wrong side" procedures will require that the surgeon mark the operative site during preoperative discussion with the patient with a standardized mark that is recognized by all operating room personnel.

Technological and Environmental Needs   The logistics of the preoperative process should facilitate the identification process. Obviously, the chart and all relevant information need to be easily accessible by those performing the checks. Operating room personnel should perform all final identification checks before the patient is draped, and should validate the procedure, location of the procedure, and identity of the patient with the surgeon before he or she makes the initial incision.

Of particular interest is the statement of the American Association of Orthopaedic Surgeons on "Wrong-Site Surgery," published in 1997. This position statement advocates that the surgeon place his or her initials on the operative site before the surgery.

Inadequate Preoperative Evaluation

Another traditional concern in the area of surgical services is inadequate preoperative evaluation. At the time of surgery, the medical record must include a completed history and physical. Inadequate preoperative evaluation is, perhaps, of even greater concern today because of the relatively short time patients are in the health care organization.

Training Needs   Practitioners should be made aware of the policy and procedure supporting the timely placement of essential clinical information in the medical record. These include the history, the physical, and all relevant test results.

Organizational Needs When proper documentation is missing from the record, the case may be delayed until essential records are in place. Authority for delaying the case should rest with anesthesia and/or the OR nursing supervisor.

Technological and Environmental Needs To ensure that histories and physicals are done preoperatively, it can be helpful to discuss ways to facilitate provider access to patients before surgery.

Outpatient Surgery

The increasing volume and acuity of cases in these areas present a continuing challenge regarding standard of care. It is essential that the standard of care in the outpatient setting be equivalent to that in the inpatient setting. Additional organizational standards concerning outpatient surgery and other clinical environments include those of the Accreditation Association for Ambulatory Health Care, Inc.[16]

Training Needs Surgeons and the OR nursing staff must be able to provide documentation of competence equivalent to that of their counterparts in the inpatient health care organization setting. Training and continuing education should be provided where indicated.

Organizational Needs Policies and procedures must be comprehensive. If the surgical setting is part of a hospital, inpatient procedures already in place arguably set the standard of care and should be evaluated for their appropriateness for the outpatient setting. Preoperative assessment should include a determination about what type of support the patient will need postoperatively. For example, a patient might need someone to take him or her home and/or to assist with postoperative care. Special attention must be paid to patient discharge criteria. This should be the province only of the anesthesiologist. Discharge instructions must be comprehensive, clear, and in writing so that the patient or home caregiver can take them to the home setting.

Technological and Environmental Needs Only those procedures that the environment can support should be performed in the outpatient or physician's office setting. Medical emergency capability should be evaluated, including proximity to the nearest hospital. To facilitate cooperation and a coordinated effort, the outpatient operation should communicate with the hospital before the setting is needed in an emergency. (The section of this chapter on conscious sedation on page 357 provides more information on this topic.)

....
ANESTHESIA AS A HIGH-RISK AREA

From a risk management perspective, anesthesia losses traditionally have been very severe, with the dollar value on cases corresponding to the severity of the alleged harm. Primary risk management issues include the technical proficiency and availability of providers. (For an inventory of specific risk management concerns, see the self-assessment tool in Exhibit 15.4.) The standard of care is prescribed by the American Society of Anesthesiologists[17] and the American Association of Nurse Anesthetists.[18]

EXHIBIT 15.4.   Self-Assessment Tool—Anesthesia

I. Providers
  A. Are anesthesiologists on staff? CRNAs?
  B. If CRNAs are utilized with anesthesiologists, is care coordinated so that anesthesiologists care for high-risk patients?

II. Training
  A. Do surgeons have privileges specific to the procedures they are performing, such as pediatric anesthesia?
  B. Do anesthesiologists participate in training other staff and/or assume responsibility for intubating the patient in a code outside the OR?
  C. Are anesthesia staff trained specifically on any new equipment?

III. Equipment
  A. Is the anesthesia area supported by pulse oximetry, end tidal CO_2?
  B. Does a current biomedical agreement cover anesthesia equipment and related monitoring devices?
  C. Does the medical record document an equipment check?
  D. Does anesthesia maintain the original or a copy of the preventive maintenance agreement?

IV. Conscious Sedation
  A. If conscious sedation is used, are staff trained and supplied with appropriate monitoring equipment, such as pulse oximetry?
  B. Is there a facility-wide protocol in place incorporating the outpatient and physician office area which has been developed with anesthesiology input?

Failure to Properly Intubate the Patient

Some of the most severe cases in the anesthesia area occur because of the failure to provide the general anesthesia patient with a patent airway.

Training Needs   Providers should demonstrate ongoing proficiency in this critical area. Those who are particularly proficient might be called on to train other providers, as appropriate. Pediatric cases, which are particularly challenging, should be handled only by practitioners who have specific expertise and maintain competence through hands-on experience.

Organizational Needs   Both in and out of the OR, code procedures should give responsibility for intubation to individuals with both expertise and experience. Credentialing should reflect these points.

Technological and Environmental Needs   Proper equipment should be available whenever and wherever intubation is to be undertaken. Pulse oximetry and capnography should be used to monitor progress of intubation on the patient.

Failure to Monitor Due to Equipment Performance Issues   Another serious problem in this area is the improper administration of anesthesia agents resulting from malfunctioning of the anesthesia machine.

Training Needs   All anesthesia personnel should be proficient in operating the equipment with which they work. The same applies to biomedical preventive maintenance personnel, who should have special additional training in the care of anesthesia equipment.

Organizational Needs   Anesthesia providers should maintain the biomedical preventive maintenance agreement pertaining to anesthesia equipment, and a copy also should be kept by biomedical preventive maintenance representatives and/or administration for the purpose of monitoring service issues. The medical record should contain a documented equipment checklist for every anesthesia case. This checklist is most often incorporated in the anesthesia record.

Technological and Environmental Needs   Anesthesia equipment must not be functionally obsolete. On occasion, but certainly too often for comfort, outdated equipment is shunted to a "less acute" surgical area. Instead, outdated equipment should be properly disposed of and its disposal documented. State-of-the-art monitoring, such as pulse oximetry and end tidal CO_2 monitoring, are essential to the process of anesthesia administration. Pulse oximetry also should be available in the post-anesthesia setting. As is true of all aspects of care, the same technological support must be available to both inpatients and outpatients.

Conscious Sedation

When Versed (generic name midazolam) was introduced several years ago, it was heralded as the "stingless Valium." Its benefits were twofold. First, it enabled patients to communicate with their providers during painful procedures such as endoscopy, yet have no recollection of pain afterwards. Second, with the administration of Versed, the aftereffects of anesthesia were avoided. However, concerns about the drug arose when it was discovered that a major complication of intravenous Versed administration was respiratory arrest. The primary risk management concern pertaining to conscious sedation is avoidance of this serious complication.

There has been much controversy about the proper credentials for practitioners who want to administer Versed. Because it often is used in outpatient practice (as well as by pulmonologists for bronchoscopies and gastroenterologists for endoscopy), it may not be possible to provide anesthesia support to administer the drug. There are at least two alternatives, both of which should be considered by a multidisciplinary group that includes anesthesia professionals. First, Valium is still available as a treatment choice. Second, if the determination is made to proceed with conscious sedation utilizing Versed, all practitioners who administer the drug should participate in a program of education designed by anesthesia professionals. This program should address development of patient selection criteria, dissemination of critical pharmaceutical information regarding dosage, and formalization of criteria for proper monitoring of conscious sedation patients.[19,20] Specific privileges for conscious sedation based on such training should be developed.

Organizational Needs   A facility-wide conscious sedation protocol should be designed and implemented to promote consistency of approach. Like the educational program previously described, the protocol should be developed with input from anesthesia. It is important to ensure that the approach developed addresses the needs of the entire organization.

Technological and Environmental Needs   All conscious sedation patients must receive pulse oximetry monitoring. If conscious sedation is performed in the outpatient setting, particular attention must be paid to the availability of proper emergency support. Crash carts in these clinical areas should contain an appropriate reversal agent.

Patient Care Responsibilities

Ideally, anesthesiologists should provide supervision of certified registered nurse anesthetists (CRNAs) and manage all critical patients. For smaller institutions in rural areas, however, this approach may be impractical.

Training and Organizational Needs   Anesthesia providers must demonstrate competence and ongoing proficiency. If anesthesiologists are available to supervise CRNAs, they should clearly have input into evaluation, regardless of whether the CRNA is independently contracted or employed by the anesthesiologist or the organization. Anesthesiologists also should participate in the development of appropriate policies and procedures and peer review. If they are unavailable, the responsibility falls to another physician, usually a surgeon. Because a practitioner of this specialty can fulfill the supervisory role only from the perspective of his or her own practice, it is prudent for the health care organization to form a relationship with anesthesiology support at an external facility. In this way, the organization can provide for telephone consultation with anesthesiologists and, possibly, chart review to augment other CQI measures.

Technological and Environmental Needs   Anesthesia coverage must address all emergent surgical needs. Practitioners should be immediately accessible and physically available within a reasonable amount of time.

∙∙∙∙∙∙∙∙∙∙∙∙

PSYCHIATRIC SERVICES AS A HIGH-RISK AREA

The risks inherent in this high-risk area are compounded by an increasingly acute psychiatric population and the pressures of cost containment. (For an inventory of specific issues, see the self-assessment tool in Exhibit 15.5.) Standards of care for psychiatric services are prescribed primarily by the American Psychiatric Association.[21]

Failure to Prevent Suicide

Some of the most severe claims in the psychiatric area are those alleging that clinical staff failed to properly monitor or protect a patient who later attempted or actually committed suicide.

Training Needs   The complexity associated with assessment of psychiatric patients necessitates ongoing education of staff. Potentially suicidal cases are one of the most important areas in which staff need information. Orientation to policies and procedures on management of these cases also is a critical risk management intervention.

Organizational Needs   Policies and procedures should clearly outline staff's responsibilities toward the patient. Specific behaviors should be correlated with intensity of supervision. For example, overt suicidal ideation arguably calls for one-on-one supervision. All providers who work with suicide-risk patients should receive appropriate training.

It also is essential that assessment and intervention be carefully documented in the medical record. It should be noted that psychiatric medical records are usually protected under state confidentiality laws. Chemical dependency medical records are protected by federal laws.[22]

EXHIBIT 15.5.   Self-Assessment Tool—Psychiatric Services

I. Providers
  A. Are physician and allied health professional privileges specific regarding diagnosis and procedure and supported by documentation of training?
  B. If allied health professionals other than RNs monitor patients, how is training arranged to provide for equivalent competence?
  C. Is staffing commensurate with acuity level of patients?

II. Suicide Prevention
  A. Are precautions defined clearly so that staff know when to implement and what levels of observation are necessary, as well as when to discontinue?
  B. Is there consistency between the approach taken with these precautions on other units, such as the ICU and the ED?

III. Medical Records
  A. Are mechanisms in place to facilitate confidentiality?
  B. Is documentation objective and thorough, including recording of suicide precaution checks of the patient?

IV. Restraints
  A. Does a physician order support restraints?
  B. Are all staff trained regarding purposes and safe implementation of restraints?

V. Medications
  A. Are patients routinely monitored for signs of any adverse reaction or side effects, including hypotension, heart rate changes, and signs of tardive dyskinesia?
  B. Is informed consent obtained for patients receiving psychotropic medications and medications with similar effects?

VI. AMAs
  A. Is the physician involved in a possible AMA to explain consequences of same to the patient?
  B. Do staff implement and clearly and objectively document any interventions taken on behalf of patients who have eloped or left AMA who may be a danger to themselves or others (for example, calling the police)?

VII. Outpatient
  A. Are outpatient and partial program admission and discharge criteria specific?
  B. If inpatient and outpatient traffic flows together, is patient identification and control over inpatients adequate to keep them from leaving with outpatients?

VIII. ECT
  A. Are dual-diagnosis patients assessed for chronic internal medicine issues as well as psychiatric diagnoses?
  B. Are the emergency care procedures that are in place adequate?
  C. Does an anesthesia professional administer anesthesia?

Finally, it is important to evaluate the need for consistency of approach between a psychiatric unit environment and other clinical settings, such as the intensive care unit and the ED.

Technological and Environmental Needs   The health care organization must provide psychiatric patients with a safe and secure environment. Specific safety precautions include placing the patient in an environment free of sharp objects, hooks on doors, or unsecured windows. If the patient is placed in a locked room, caregivers must be able to quickly open the lock in the event of fire. In addition, special precautions should be taken to prevent patient access to anything from which they could hang, such as clothing (which might be knotted), showerheads, shower curtain rods, and so on.

Outpatient Psychiatric Environment

Partial hospitalization programs and psychiatric outpatient settings have become increasingly popular because of reimbursement pressures. However, these programs bring with them special risk management concerns, including potential difficulty in managing clinical emergencies. Likewise, the subtle challenges inherent in evaluating psychiatric patients may result in an inaccurate determination of their readiness for a less supervised environment, increasing the risk of behavior-related exposures like suicidal ideation or violence toward others. Staff in the outpatient psychiatric environment should have training and access to education equivalent to that of inpatient staff.

Organizational Needs   Admitting and discharge criteria should be specific and reasonable, that is, reflective of what the setting can handle. Access to emergency care support, such as "911" emergency services and a hospital environment, should be proactively assessed and any necessary interventions implemented. As in the inpatient psychiatric environment, confidentiality of medical records must be respected. As previously noted, psychiatric patient medical record confidentiality is based on specific state legislation in many instances. In the case of chemical dependency patients, the obligation flows from federal law.

Technological and Environmental Needs   Security issues should be addressed as appropriate. If inpatient and outpatient environments flow together at all, traffic patterns and, in particular, exit locations should not jeopardize the inpatient population by allowing them to leave.

Restraints

This is a particularly challenging area because regulatory and accrediting organizations continue to promulgate requirements that health care organizations avoid use of restraints. This is true even for the use of restraints to prevent falls.

Training Needs   Staff should be trained regarding the purposes of restraints—for example, pharmaceutical restraints versus support for an elderly patient or prevention of patients' causing harm to themselves or others. Training also should include instruction in the effective and safe use of restraint devices. Ongoing competence in the purposes and proper uses of restraints should be documented.

Organizational Needs   By policy, a physician order should support all restraints. Staff should regularly evaluate the patient's safety and clinical well-being, including observation of skin integrity. Range-of-motion exercises should be carried out every hour if the patient is restrained, and circulation of extremities also should be assessed.

Falls of patients who are not candidates for restraints should be monitored through the CQI process. Staff should explore creative solutions to this problem, such as placing the patient's mattress on the floor (provided that infection control approves of this solution). Again, a multidisciplinary committee is an excellent forum for brainstorming solutions to problems.

Technological and Environmental Needs   If locked leather restraints are used, a qualified individual must be in charge of the psychiatric unit and physically present at all times, with a key readily available to enable the quick release of patients in the event of fire.

Psychopharmacology

Risk management issues arise from bad outcomes such as tardive dyskinesia, which is involuntary movement of facial and other muscles resulting from ineffective monitoring of psychotropic medication dosages.

Training   Providers should be trained regarding medications and their possible clinical implications, such as tardive dyskinesia.[23]

Organizational Needs   In both the inpatient and outpatient setting, physician ordering and prescribing patterns should be evaluated through quality monitoring. Informed consent should be obtained by the physician for administration of psychotropic medications. Staff should monitor patients for clinical side effects, such as orthostatic hypotension with administration of certain psychotropic drugs, including Mellaril, and also any signs of tardive dyskinesia.

Technological and Environmental Needs   Many psychiatric settings ban scheduled substances like narcotics in the medicine room because of the increased risk they bring to suicide-risk cases and patients with chemical dependency problems.

Electroconvulsive Therapy

Electroconvulsive therapy (ECT) has regained popularity in recent years, primarily as a treatment for depression. The primary risk management issues related to this procedure revolve around anesthetic support.

Training Needs   Staff should be trained in implications of the therapy and, in addition, should be certified in basic cardiac life support.

Organizational Needs   If ECT is performed on the psychiatric unit in the hospital setting, anesthesia support and emergency response resources should be evaluated for equivalence with the rest of the operation's approach. Anesthesia support should be provided by an anesthesia professional. Care of these patients, many of whom are elderly, depressed individuals who have other physical diagnoses such as heart disease or diabetes, should be evaluated through quality monitoring. It may be appropriate for an internist to work with the psychiatrist in assessing the appropriateness of the therapy for the patient and in monitoring specific physical problems.

Technological and Environmental Needs   The effectiveness of emergency response equipment and procedures should be evaluated.

RADIOLOGY SERVICES AS A HIGH-RISK AREA

Although radiology traditionally is not a high-risk area, the importance of claims arising from failure to diagnose, as well as other clinical risk management issues, now raises recent concerns in this clinical area. (The self-assessment tool outlined in Exhibit 15.6 provides an inventory of risk management issues related to this area.) Many standards in this area have been promulgated by the American College of Radiology.[24]

EXHIBIT 15.6.   Self-Assessment Tool—Radiology Services

I. Providers
  A. Are physician providers board-certified radiologists? If practitioners have specialties other than radiology, what are they and how are equivalent competencies maintained?
  B. Do allied health professionals other than radiology take radiology films or participate in other procedures? What is their role, and how are equivalent competencies maintained?

II. Equipment
  A. Is a current biomedical preventive maintenance agreement in place for equipment?
  B. Are staff trained specifically on all new equipment?

III. Avoidance of Failure to Diagnose
  A. Are physicians and other practitioners specifically trained regarding mammogram testing, interpretation, and so on, as appropriate?
  B. Does the CQI program call for an overread of mammogram results and peer review pertaining to same?

IV. Use of Contrast Media and Support in Emergency Circumstances
  A. Are all staff certified in basic cardiac life support?
  B. Is emergency equipment available and adequate?
  C. Do staff perform mock codes routinely?
  D. Is a reasonably developed approach for selecting patients to receive low-osmolar-weight contrast media in place, if it is not in place for all patients?

Management and Avoidance of Contrast Media Reactions

In the 1980s, much debate occurred concerning the possible effectiveness of low-osmolar-weight contrast media in reducing the chance of adverse reactions, including cardiac arrest. The difficulty with switching all media administered to the low-osmolar-weight product has been the expense, which can be many times that of high-osmolar-weight media.

Training Needs   Regardless of the type of contrast media used in a radiology department, staff must be trained in basic cardiac life support and should participate periodically in "mock codes."

Organizational Needs   Economic considerations are a poor defense to a professional liability action. Therefore, the concept of getting a patient's "informed consent" that he or she is willing to have administered a less expensive, but higher-risk dye is probably ineffective from a risk management standpoint. Group purchase arrangements for low-osmolar-weight contrast media can facilitate the lowering of this item's cost.

The patient population at risk for reactions—for example, those with allergies to seafood—should be identified and considered candidates for administration of low-osmolar-weight media. From an opposite perspective, procedures with lower risk for reactions, such as cardiac catheterization, should be identified. These procedures may be appropriate for administration of high-osmolar-weight media. In addition, case histories of patients who have had reactions should be assessed and the literature reviewed. All these factors can help the operation to develop a reasonable, clinically based approach to administration of contrast media.

Technological and Environmental Needs   If high-osmolar-weight contract media are in use, or if the radiology department sees unstable clinical patients on a routine basis, which is likely in today's acute environment, a crash cart should be kept in close proximity to the department.

Failure to Diagnose

As failure to diagnose breast cancer and other similar claims come to the fore in professional liability actions, the radiology area is assuming its share of loss exposure.

Training Needs Physicians should be up to date on mammogram interpretation techniques and related procedures. Similarly, staff should be trained in management of equipment and positioning of patients for mammogram.

Organizational Needs For quality improvement purposes, procedures in the radiology area should provide for callback for abnormal results and overreading.

Technological and Environmental Needs Investment in state-of-the-art equipment and maintenance of same under an appropriate contract or other arrangement are critical.

HOME HEALTH SERVICES AS A HIGH-RISK AREA

It has been said that the hospital will no longer exist in years to come, and all care will be provided in the home. If this prediction becomes reality, all the issues previously discussed in this chapter may someday be applicable to this section. Primary risk management concerns grow out of the lack of support resources available to caregivers in this area. (The self-assessment tool in Exhibit 15.7 provides an inventory of specific risk management concerns.) In this rapidly evolving field, many organizations are promulgating pertinent standards, including the American Medical Association,[25] the American Association for Respiratory Care,[26] and the American Hospital Association.[27]

Training Needs Home health personnel qualifications must be equivalent to those of other health care organization-based staff. Credentialing must take into consideration that the home health professional functions with a degree of autonomy unknown in any other part of health care. Skills must be commensurate, and procedures performed in the home must be appropriate to the setting.

EXHIBIT 15.7. **Self-Assessment Tool—Home Health Services**

I. Providers
   A. Are RN qualifications the same as those for providers in an inpatient setting?
   B. If providers other than nurses are used in the field, how are their qualifications made equivalent to those of RNs?
   C. Are physician providers involved in individual patient care routinely as necessary, and with regard to development of policies and procedures?

II. Equipment
   A. Does a proper biomedical preventive maintenance agreement cover same?
   B. Is staff specifically credentialed to care for any high-risk equipment, such as ventilators?

III. Medical Records
   A. Are medical records clinically sufficient?
   B. Do they document interaction with the physician provider as appropriate?

IV. Safety and Security
   A. Do staff work in the evening? If so, are they accompanied?
   B. Are they trained to avoid or manage potentially violent situations?
   C. Do they carry cellular phones?

Use of equipment such as ventilators and apnea monitors for infants is frequently seen in the home health setting, and providers must be appropriately trained and credentialed to manage such equipment when it is used.

Organizational Needs   Medical record documentation must be as thorough, and policies and procedures must be set up as specifically and comprehensively, as any developed elsewhere in the organization. Policies and procedures should include a format for assessing the family's or caregiver's strengths and weaknesses. Based on this, the staff can determine reasonable goals regarding the family's or caregiver's potential role in assisting the patient, and help to achieve them. Physician involvement in care also should be specifically addressed in policies and procedures, because physicians are physically removed from this care arena. Additionally, emergency care response (for example, "911") must be established, and staff must be certified in basic cardiac life support.

Technological and Environmental Needs   Biomedical preventive maintenance agreements for equipment used in the field must be evaluated with an eye toward ascertaining that proper insurance coverage is maintained by the providers of this service and that the contract describes a comprehensive arrangement. Staff security is an issue aside from, but as important as, the clinical risk management implications of this area. Interventions such as provision of cellular phones to providers should be considered.

Physician's Office Setting

Although not a traditional high risk setting, the physician's office does represent a unique set of risks. Of particular note, the standard of care in the traditional doctor's office has usually been less rigorous than that of the more highly regulated environment in the hospital. For example, non-nurses have given medications for many years in doctors' offices, but this approach is unacceptable in the hospital. A physician's practice that has been purchased by a hospital is therefore potentially vulnerable to allegations that their medication administration is below the standard of care.

Another aspect of physician's office risk is the same as that discussed in home care and outpatient surgery. Just like these settings, the acuity of the patient population in the physician's office, and of the procedures performed there, is on the rise.

Training and Organizational Needs   Many physicians' offices lack any elements of a formal risk management program, such as incident reporting, or training for the staff on documentation issues. They may also be in need of basic policy and procedure manuals and job descriptions to support day-to-day practice. One example of a policy that is essential to a physician's office setting is a formalized approach to transferring the patient in a medical emergency.

Technological and Environmental Needs   Physicians' offices sometimes also need assistance with basic safety and security programs. For example, physicians' laboratories are as vulnerable as those of hospitals to violations of the Clinical Laboratory Improvement Amendments (CLIA), the aspect of HCFA that governs laboratories. It is also important that physicians' office radiology facilities will be held to the standard of care equivalent to those in the hospital, even though they may not have implemented risk management strategies like overreading films.

Long-Term Care and Assisted Care

For many years, professional liability claim managers have thought of long-term care as a "low risk" area because of the perception that older people are inherently limited in capability to amass economic damages. With the implementation of elder abuse laws in many jurisdictions, supported by aging baby boomers, and a rise in the acuity of patients in the long-term care setting, which mirrors the intensity in the hospital, this view has changed drastically.

Assisted living, evolving as a boon to the aged, promises increased freedom and a more responsive set of care options. Yet it is, at this point, ill-defined and relatively unregulated. A product of the union between nursing homes and the hotel business, the professional liability risk associated with this setting is difficult to gauge, other than to say that it is potentially volatile at this point.

Training and Organizational Needs   Long-term care and assisted living facilities that are part of health care organizations may suffer as "step children" who inherit safety programs and other administrative approaches of the acute care setting with little modification. Apart from this, long-term care settings, which are intensely regulated by state law and Medicare, do have detailed medical record documentation systems in place, as well as systems with which to report resident harm and address complaints. Assisted living, in contrast, is not subject to these requirements in most places, and so may have little infrastructure with which to promote resident care and contain risk.

Technological and Environmental Needs   Long-term care and assisted living facilities must have technologic and environmental support that is commensurate to the needs of their populations. An example of a challenge for the long-term care environment is the need to provide for an increasingly diverse array of specialized long term care conditions like Alzheimer's disease and HIV. For assisted living, however, the challenge may more be to identify the process through which its residents may pass and address the evolution of their condition. A marble floor may be attractive to a would-be resident of sixty in good health, but constitute a high risk to the same individual ten years later. (See the self-assessment tools in Exhibit 15.8 and Exhibit 15.9 on page 366.)

·············
CONCLUSION

An increasingly diverse number of clinical services place the health care facility and its staff at high risk for liability claims. Certain areas such as obstetrics, emergency services, surgical services, anesthesia, psychiatric services, radiology services, and home health services particularly increase clinical risk exposure. Each of these areas faces specific risk management issues that should be addressed through examination of the service's training, organizational, environmental, and technological needs. Each service must attempt to develop clinical indicators with which to identify such issues, implement solutions based on a variety of resources, and monitor the success of resolution. Finally, perhaps the most important thing that health care facilities can do is to establish multidisciplinary forums to address risk management in today's increasingly complex health care organizational systems.

EXHIBIT 15.8.	Self-Assessment Tool—Assisted Living

I. Provider Training

    A. Are those who assist with self-medication in the assisted living setting specifically credentialed for this role?

    B. Are those who provide any form of clinical care licensed or otherwise specifically credentialed providers?

II. Criteria for Admission

    A. Are criteria for admission to the setting specific and clinically relevant, and are they developed with physician input?

III. Fall Risk

    A. Are clients assessed for fall risk on application? And, on identifying fall risk, is admission denied or, as an alternative, are appropriate preventive interventions initiated?

IV. Safety Program

    A. Is there a smoking policy in place?

    B. Is there a comprehensive fire plan and disaster plan with routine drills performed?

EXHIBIT 15.9.	Self-Assessment Tool—Long-Term Care

I. Fall Risk

    A. Are clients specifically assessed for fall risk and interventions documented?

II. Decubitus

    A. Is a specifically developed protocol in place addressing decubiti care, and including the use of photographs to document the assessment and progress of this care?

III. Wanderers

    A. Is a specific protocol in place to address concerns about wanderers, including the use of photographs of patients to familiarize staff with their identity, safety bracelet-alarm systems, frequency with which they are to be monitored, and plan to address any elopements?

IV. Restraints

    A. Is a restraint policy in place that supports care of the patient in the least restrictive environment, and provides for physician orders to be obtained routinely?

    B. Does the policy provide for staff to check circulation on a routine basis?

V. Acute Care Patients

    A. Is any acute care rendered, such as IVs, ventilators, and so on, supported by credentialed personnel and appropriate policies and procedures?

VI. Safety

    A. Is there a comprehensive fire safety, evacuation, and disaster plan?

Endnotes

1. American College of Obstetricians and Gynecologists, ACOG Resource Center, 409 12th St. SW, Washington, D.C. 20024 (telephone: 202-863-2518).

2. Association of Women's Health, Obstetric, and Neonatal Nurses, 700 14th St. NW, Suite 600, Washington, D.C. 20005-2019 (telephone: 202-662-1600).

3. American Academy of Pediatrics, 141 NW Pt. Bd., P.O. Box 927, Elk Grove Village, Ill. 60009 (telephone: 847-228-5005).

4. Bartlett, E. E. "Risk Management and Medical Technology: The Case of Obstetrical Malpractice." *Journal of Healthcare Risk Management, 13*(1), Winter 1993, pp. 9–13.

5. American College of Obstetricians and Gynecologists. "Fetal Heart Rate Patterns: Monitoring, Interpretation, and Management." ACOG Committee on Practices, *Technical Bulletins*, 1995, pp. 18–207.

6. Association of Women's Health, Obstetric, and Neonatal Nurses. "Issue: The Role of Unlicensed Assistive Personnel in the Nursing Care for Women and Newborns." AWHONN Position Statement no. 24. Approved by the AWHONN Executive Board, February 1997.

7. Mahlmeister, L. "The Perinatal Nurse's Role in Obstetric Emergencies: Legal Issues and Practice Issues in the Era of Health Care Redesign." *Journal of Perinatal and Neonatal Nursing, 10*(3), Dec. 1996, p. 32.

8. American College of Obstetricians and Gynecologists. "Fetal Distress and Birth Asphyxia." Unpublished committee opinions. Committee on Obstetric Practice, 1994.

9. *Physician's Desk Reference.* Montvale, N.J.: Medical Economics Data Production Co., 1995, pp. 2,708–2,709.

10. "Should You Conduct Placental Evaluations?" *American Journal of Healthcare Risk Management, 16*(2) Mar. 1996.

11. American College of Emergency Physicians, P.O. Box 619911, Dallas, Tex. 75261-9911 (telephone: 214-550-0911).

12. 42 USC §1395.

13. Wheeler, S. Q., with Windt, J. H. *Telephone Traige: Theory, Practice, and Protocol Development*. Albany, N.Y.: Delmar, 1993.

14. American College of Surgeons, 55 E. Erie St., Chicago, Ill. 60611 (telephone: 312-664-4050).

15. Association of Operating Room Nurses, 2170 S. Parker Rd., Suite 300, Denver, Colo. 80231-5711 (telephone: 303-755-6300).

16. Accreditation Association for Ambulatory Health Care, Inc., 9933 Lawler Ave., Skokie, Ill. 60077 (telephone: 708-676-9610).

17. American Society of Anesthesiologists, 520 N. Northwest Hwy., Park Ridge, Ill. 60068-2573 (telephone: 847-825-5586).

18. American Association of Nurse Anesthetists, 222 S. Prospect Ave., Park Ridge, Ill. 60068-4001 (telephone: 847-692-7050).

19. American Association of Nurse Anesthetists. "Role of the Registered Nurse in the Management of Patients Receiving IV Conscious Sedation for Short-Term Therapeutic, Diagnostic, or Surgical Procedures," (with American Association of Critical Care Nurses, American Association of Spinal Cord Injury Nurses, American Nurses Association, American Society of Post Anesthesia Nurses, Association of Operating Room Nurses, and Association of Women's Health, Obstetric, and Neonatal Nurses). *Position Statements,* 1991.

20. Association of Operating Room Nurses. "Monitoring the Patient Receiving Local Anesthesia." *Recommended Practices,* 1984 (rev. 1993).

21. American Psychiatric Association, 1400 K St. NW, Suite 1101, Washington, D.C. 20005 (telephone: 202-682-6000).

22. Confidentiality of Alcohol and Drug Abuse Patient Records. 42 CFR Part II, 1992.

23. American Psychiatric Association. *Tardive Dyskinesia: A Task Force Report of the American Psychiatric Association.* Washington, D.C.: APA, 1992.

24. American College of Radiology, 1891 Preston White Dr., Reston, Va. 22091 (telephone: 703-648-8900).

25. American Medical Association, 515 N. State St., Chicago, Ill. 60610 (telephone: 312-464-5000).

26. American Association for Respiratory Care, 11030 Ables Ln. Dallas, Tex. 75229 (telephone: 214-243-2272).

27. American Hospital Association, One North Franklin, Chicago, Ill. 60606 (telephone: 312-422-3000).

16

Information Technologies
and Risk Management

Ronni P. Solomon

ntil the early 1980s, risk management departments used typewriters. Incident reporting data were always tracked manually, and claims data were logged by hand into a giant ledger pad. A field was a place to play baseball, a screen was something to watch at a movie theater, and a printer was someone who made wedding invitations. Today, these words have taken on new meaning. Risk managers have access to new information technologies that will forever alter the way they work. Today's tools—personal computers, the Internet, telecommunications networks, fax machines, and palm devices—will fundamentally change the way that risk management knowledge is gathered, from sources close to home as well as around the world. Cyberspace has no geographical boundaries.

Likewise, rapid changes in the health care system are forcing many risk managers to face new challenges and responsibilities. Increasingly, risk management programs require more data, from more sources, more frequently. They require creating new loss prevention and control programs for new settings and new liability exposures. The challenges are many and varied, but a common theme is the need to turn data into meaningful information that underpins effective risk management action in a variety of health care settings.

Although the workload will inevitably shift and grow in ways yet unknown, the number of staff is likely to remain the same or decrease. As a result, risk managers will have to develop new approaches and broaden their base of knowledge. Information technologies, which foster collaboration and reduce turnaround time, will play a key role. Risk managers must learn to embrace these technologies—from establishing a risk management information system, to using Web-based resources, to encouraging the use of clinical information technologies.

Equally important, risk managers must identify the concerns posed by new information technologies. Electronic patient records, telemedicine, e-mail, fax transmissions, and the Internet introduce new variations of old concerns, such as patient privacy, authentication, and security. Thus, reasonable precautions must be established. The stakes are much higher because, unlike paper-based records, one electronic break-in can access hundreds of thousands of data. Artful risk managers will embrace and benefit from the new information technologies while helping to set and maintain the standards that govern their use.

This chapter identifies and describes the benefits of various technologies available to risk management for the gathering and communication of information. It also discusses the legal concerns that risk management information systems raise, particularly with regard to patient confidentiality and medical record security.

....

RISK MANAGEMENT INFORMATION NEEDS

Health care risk managers have myriad information technology needs to support effective judgement and decision making. The core need is to review the right information at the right time in order to make the best decisions. Specifically, risk managers need:

- Tools to automate various risk management processes, such identifying and analyzing incident and loss information.

- Answers to requests for information within minutes or hours, not days or weeks.

- Supporting information that spurs action to reduce and control losses in order to "sell" risk management to other managers.

- Ways of gathering the intelligence that will enable a shift from general risk management assessments and evaluations to more in-depth, focused analyses of specific areas that have high payback potential.

Information technologies, many with Web-based modules, can support all these risk management needs. These technologies help spot problems that were previously unidentifiable and, in minutes, access information that previously took weeks or months to gather.

Computers are a key to effectiveness. They not only aid in tracking and trending incidents but can also assist the risk manager in a variety of other ways, such as filing and retrieving incident information, performing statistical analysis of data, tapping into electronic libraries, and communicating with peers through list servers and discussion forums. Computers also assist the risk management function carried out by others, such as nurses, physicians, and pharmacists. Computers not only decrease the time it takes to perform a task but also can improve the quality of the information gathered and produced. This improvement in quality helps risk managers to focus loss prevention efforts at the right target and to be proactive about losses.

However, learning to use new computer technologies takes patience. Although, initially, the risk manager who is new to computers and on-line information services might feel frustrated, the time, effort, and energy invested will have a high payoff.

....

RISK MANAGEMENT INFORMATION SYSTEMS

To coordinate the diverse information needs of effective risk management, many health care facilities are using some form of risk management information system (RMIS) that automates many aspects of record keeping. Mergers, acquisitions, and joint ventures also have increased the need for RMISs, particularly those with network capabilities that serve multiple sites and locations. These software systems are critical for corporate risk managers who have responsibilities for multiple institutions. There is software that automates the variety of risk management functions, from incident reporting to risk assessment surveys to claims management.

RMISs consist of computerized databases, which, simply put, are comprehensive collections of information. (For definitions of other computer-related terms, see Appendix 16.1 on page 381.) Viewed from a manual record-keeping perspective, a departmental database may consist of all the written records in file cabinets, notebooks, and desk drawers. For risk managers, this collection of information might include incident or occurrence reports, claims tracking and administration data (including workers' compensation, professional liability, general liability, directors' and officers' liability, and other claims information), insurance policy information, reserves, regulatory compliance information, patient complaints, litigation management information, and so on.

RMISs are available from software vendors or can be developed by in-house staff. Internally provided systems can use a mainframe approach or a PC-based approach. Some insurance carriers, brokers, third-party administrators, and management service organizations also offer specialized systems that are easy to implement and use. Regardless of the source, risk managers should work closely with information systems (IS) staff in developing and reviewing the software specifications, ongoing support services, data entry and maintenance requirements, Web interfaces, and other key characteristics. Special needs and expectations are best discussed at the outset of a development project.

When record keeping is automated into a computerized database, new benefits arise. A key advantage is the ability to integrate and sort information located in different parts of the overall data collection. This helps to transform risk management data into risk management information. The database system has the capability to retrieve records and display them on the screen, to extract subsets of data, and to produce formatted reports. These computerized systems can be used for all the previously listed risk management functions. Each use, however, must be carefully planned to ensure that it will generate accurate, useful, and effective reports.

....

USING INFORMATION SYSTEMS TO GENERATE REPORTS

When envisioning reports, the risk manager should consider who will receive them, how they will be used, and how often they will be produced. With these facts in mind, he or she can decide what sources of data should be used and how best to present data—in graphics or in narrative form.

Risk managers will need to consider what factors they need to track and analyze. These will vary depending on whether it is an incident reporting, workers' compensation, or other system. The following examples illustrate the types of information that reports typically generate:

- Insurance policies and coverage limits.
- Newly reported losses or incidents.
- Losses or incidents by department or service.
- Losses or incidents by date reported.
- Losses or incidents by date of occurrence.
- Loss costs by accident type or part of body.

- Current status of open claims.
- Accident frequency by job and location.
- Number of employee injuries or patient incidents.
- Types of employee injuries or patient incidents.
- Lost work time.
- Actual medical costs versus average costs.
- Most frequent and most expensive causes of losses.
- Reserves.
- Allegations.
- Staff involved in incident or claim.
- Patient characteristics.
- Names of attorneys.
- Witnesses.
- Insurance carriers.
- Status of the claim.
- Actions taken.

INTEGRATING RISK MANAGEMENT AND QUALITY ASSURANCE

Through the use of computers, information from the facility's quality assurance (QA) information system can be referred to the risk management system, and vice versa. Information referral between risk management and QA helps to foster effective follow-up on patient safety issues. Certain indicators that are tracked for QA purposes should be referred to the RMIS (for example, dental injuries or ocular injuries in the operating room). This information could indicate the need for a risk management investigation or for setting up a potential claims file. Conversely, risk management incident trending reports can be incorporated into the QA information system. These reports could be coded numerically with the date, location, and individual who assessed the patient, as well as follow-up information.

INTERNET

The Internet, the World Wide Web, e-mail, and on-line discussion forums are all information technologies that contribute to the effectiveness of risk management. There is a vast and growing amount of health care information resources on the Web. Many are available free of charge; others are available through membership programs or fee-based searches. These information resources are invaluable for health care risk managers who need to stay on top of newly emerging risks in an era of change. Indeed, the need to access electronic information is becoming so compelling that failure to do so might be dubbed the equivalent of risk management malpractice.

The Internet was first developed in the 1960s by the U.S. Department of Defense as a strategy to prevent the risk that a nuclear attack would wipe out critical information on a single-wire government communication link. The system allowed information to survive through numerous linkages. For the next twenty years, the Net was primarily used by scientists and academic researchers operating in a profit-free mode. Today, over half of the adults in the United States have Internet access, and net culture—and dot.com companies—are pervasive. Commercial domains (the ".com" domain) are the largest and fastest growing segment; educational domains (".edu") are the second largest. The Internet is capable of supporting many different types of files—text, graphic, audio, video, 3-D, and interactive. There is an ever-expanding volume and variety of information available, such as:

- U.S. government information. Most branches and agencies have their own address (for example, "president@whitehouse.gov").
- U.S. legislative history, including the Congressional Record.
- Official government sites for a majority of countries throughout the world.
- Health and medical information.
- The U.S. Code and Code of Federal Regulations.
- News wire services, such as the Associated Press and Reuters.
- Scientific and research information.

This is just a small sampling. No one entity or government owns or controls the Internet; there is no president or CEO. The owners of each server or computer are responsible for their part of the worldwide network of networks.

············
WORLD WIDE WEB

The World Wide Web is a network of Web servers (computers that host one or more Web sites) that helps users navigate with ease through the Internet. An organization's or individual's uniform resource locator (URL) address on the Web constitutes a Web site, which contains one or more Web pages. The first page of a Web site is called a home page. Home pages contain highlighted links that, when clicked with a mouse, automatically take the user to another Web page, which may be on the same or another Web site. With its point-and-click approach, the World Wide Web is the fastest growing segment on the Internet.

On-line services, whether the Internet or a proprietary system, share a number of features.

············
ELECTRONIC MAIL

As the name implies, e-mail is a letter sent electronically. Pen and paper are replaced by typing a message onto a computer screen with a computer keyboard. The post office box or address is replaced by a "virtual" mailbox, called an e-mail address. The postal worker is replaced by the "send" command. To send or receive mail, users need only register their addresses. When they connect to the system, any messages sent to them will be waiting in their mailbox.

An Internet mailbox address consists of the identifying name or number of the mailbox, plus the name of the computing system where the mailbox is located—for example, rsolomon@ecri.org. The @ symbol separates the person's mailbox identifier (rsolomon) from the name of the computing system or server (ecri). In this example, *ecri* is the name of the organization; *org* stands for a nonprofit organization.

E-mail certainly has a number of advantages. It is easier than writing, printing, proofing, addressing, stamping, and sending a letter. It has revolutionized the exchange of contracts and other documents. It can reduce the costs that would otherwise be incurred through long distance telephone calls. And delivery time is almost instantaneous anywhere in the world. Messages can be sent at any time across the world as easily as across the office, to a group of people or a single recipient, without the sender leaving their desk. The recipient can collect their mail when they want, from wherever they are.

Over time, e-mail and other distance technologies will transform the way that medicine and health care are provided. Clinicians are beginning to use e-mail to communicate patient information to colleagues and to correspond directly with patients; and this and other uses can present a number of concerns for the risk management function. For example, e-mail has been used as evidence in civil trials. As evidence, e-mail may be more troublesome than hard copy communication for a number of reasons. By its nature, e-mail encourages informality with little, if any, proofreading or editing. As a result, messages may be speedily dashed off with little regard for tone or even content. E-mail messages can be altered with little trouble and forwarded on to new recipients. And the "delete" command deletes the message only from the screen, not from the system until the trash bin is emptied. And even then, they may reside in the network for a time.

Additionally, confidentiality and privacy might be jeopardized without appropriate transmission safeguards. As with paper-based correspondence, it is impossible to guarantee that the intended recipient is the only actual recipient. But unlike interceptions of paper transmissions, e-mail interceptions may go unidentified because the named recipient will still get the message. Also, e-mail systems may be down, and messages delayed by hours or even days. Thus, it is not reliable for transmitting urgent, time-sensitive information. An additional complication of using e-mail is that sound documentation and record-keeping practices may be infringed. If a clinician fails to print out e-mail messages and file them in the patient's medical record, problems in diagnosis and treatment could result. Although the facsimile (fax) transmission of patient information raises similar concerns, most fax transmissions have cover sheets that contain confidentiality statements; e-mail does not have this safeguard.

The usual authorization procedures for the release of medical information should be maintained. Thus, when information is e-mailed or faxed within the institution to those who have a need to know, patient consent to disclosure should not be needed. If, however, transmission is intended to go beyond that scope, the patient should be asked to sign a release. In any event, it is advisable to notify the intended recipient that patient information has been faxed or e-mailed and to ask for a response if the information is not received.

For these reasons, risk managers should participate in their institution's e-mail policy and procedure, and the organization's orientation and in-service education programs.

············

DISCUSSION FORUMS

A discussion forum (or newsgroup or listservers) is a public Internet conferencing area in which individuals exchange information on areas of common interest. For example, a risk manager who needs help on a specific issue can leave an open message to everyone who visits the forum, and someone with experience or knowledge on the topic is likely to reply. Many systems also allow subscribers to receive discussion entries via e-mail.

At their best, on-line forums generate a genuine spirit of enthusiasm and sharing among the participants, much like a roundtable discussion at a professional meeting.

Participants, who may be aware of each other's identities, may form a professional relationship that leads to an off-line relationship as well. An additional benefit of the electronic forum is that the information remains posted in the conference area so that future participants can access it at a later date. Thus, this type of forum can build overall risk management know-how.

CONSUMERS AND THE INTERNET

No doubt, the increasing availability of health information on the Internet will influence consumers. In the not-too-distant future, patients will have access to the same information on a condition, treatment, or new technology as their doctor. Consumers and physicians may use the same search engine, such as MEDLINE, to find the latest peer-reviewed medical journal article. They may read the same newsgroup discussions, review a health plan's on-line coverage criteria, or watch the same medical video clip. Before the Internet, consumers received information primarily by word of mouth from their physicians. Now, with the proliferation of health information on the Web, the problem is no longer finding information but assessing the credibility, relevance, and accuracy of Web information. Physicians will play a greater role in analyzing the mixed quality of medical information for patients.

CLINICAL SETTING

RMISs and access to the Internet are two important information technologies for the risk manager's own office. However, other computer programs may have a positive impact on medical malpractice, quality of care, and patient safely initiatives. Although risk managers might not be the primary users of these applications, they should nevertheless be aware of them and encourage physicians and other appropriate parties to use them.

Computer systems are transforming the way clinicians communicate, document, treat, and diagnose. Physicians can get on-line access from their homes or offices to laboratory and x-ray results, pharmaceutical profiles, clinical pathways, and medical references. For patient histories and physicals, voice-recognition technologies are being used in place of traditional dictation and transcription.

Laboratory information systems are widely used to improve the flow of information within as well as outside of clinical laboratories. These systems are designed to order tests, create bench worklists, verify specimens, report results, collate patient demographics with results for reports, and process or transfer billing information.[1] The systems may also help to simplify some information gathering required by the Clinical Lab Improvement Act (CLIA) or requested during a CLIA or College of American Pathologist (CAP) inspection.

Automated anesthesia record-keeping systems not only interface with anesthesia gas machines and patient monitoring equipment but also document drug administration, timing, and patient response more accurately and completely than manual record keeping. Indeed, the automated record might help to defend against charges of anesthesia malpractice.

Some emergency departments (EDs) no longer rely solely on physician judgment for a decision on whether to admit a patient for a cardiac workup. Artificial intelligence technology estimates the probability of an acute myocardial infarction based on the patient history and physical and ECG findings. This technology might help to reduce the frequency and severity of malpractice claims that allege failures in treating and diagnosing acute myocardial infarctions.

A number of pharmacy applications help to reduce the risk of errors. Examples include automated drug dispensing systems, drug interaction programs, drug allergy warnings, dosage cross-checking, side-effect data, drug and food interaction warnings, and others.

There also are computer-assisted protocols for antibiotic therapy that use real-time patient data to calculate antibiotic dose, duration of therapy, and cost-effective choices. These systems are able to pull patient information directly from bedside monitors in the intensive care unit (ICU).

Radiology systems are linked to remote viewing units, such as the ICU and off-site physician practices, thereby reducing film retrieval time from twelve hours to less than one minute. All these applications have the potential to reduce malpractice liability.

Other examples of computerized clinical applications include:

- Medical diagnostic programs.
- Drug interaction programs.
- Patient instruction and discharge sheets.
- Tickler systems for physician office visits and periodic screening examinations.
- Patient tracking systems.
- Medical device tracking systems.
- Medical equipment control programs.
- Health hazard appraisal systems.
- Medical device adverse-event reporting systems.
- Clinical pathways software.
- Automated record-keeping systems.

The list of available computer programs grows daily. Risk managers should view these as risk management tools that may help to reduce loss exposures in certain practice settings. At the same time, risk managers must continue to help develop and maintain policies and procedures that protect the security and confidentiality of electronic data.

ELECTRONIC PATIENT RECORDS

Many of today's systems still depend on paper-based records: Paper records are scanned into a document-imaging system, which then permits automated retrieval from various locations. Others, with computerized user entry, are further along the electronic evolutionary scale. Although they are just beginning to evolve, electronic patient records are already being hailed as an end to the paper chase. Fully electronic patient records are expected within the next decade.

Protecting the security of computerized medical records is further complicated as electronic links are established between geographically separate facilities in a health care system (for example, a hospital and a physician's office) or between hospitals and managed care organizations (MCOs). (For a detailed discussion of confidentiality and security issues related to electronic records, see the chapter on data management.)

An analysis of the legal aspects of computer-based patient records and record systems in *Medical Records and the Law* (1996) identifies various other issues that risk managers should address.[2] Among them are accessibility, durability, accuracy, and evidentiary concerns.

ACCESSIBILITY

Computer-based patient records can be altered, destroyed, or rendered inaccessible by computer viruses, or sabotaged by a disgruntled employee or disreputable software vendor. Excessive system downtime, whether related to sabotage or some less insidious cause, can jeopardize patient safety and expose a health care facility to negligence liability, regulatory violations, or Joint Commission on Accreditation of Healthcare Organizations (JCAHO) accreditation deficiencies. (JCAHO standards, Medicare conditions of participation, and many state licensure regulations require that patient records be accessible and permit prompt retrieval of information.)

DURABILITY

Some states require that medical records be retained for twenty-five years; research institutions may need to preserve them for as long as seventy-five years. But changes in technology can render a record storage system obsolete long before the requirements for record retention expire. Hospitals may have to maintain a computerized storage system even after they have switched to an updated system; thus, long-term equipment support and service may be important elements of computer purchase contracts or leases. If hospitals opt to copy records from old equipment onto new equipment, they will have to ensure that copied records comply with licensure laws. If records are copied, the hospital also will have to be able to prove the chain of copying to ensure that the copied records are admissible as evidence in court.

ACCURACY

Errors in computerized medical records can result from hardware or software defects. Regular maintenance and performance checks reduce the risk of such errors; the results of performance checks should be documented.

Errors also may occur because of inaccurate input by humans or machines. Mechanisms to minimize human error include periodic review of input data. (JCAHO standards require review of medical record entries for completeness, accuracy, and timeliness at least quarterly.)

EVIDENTIARY CONCERNS

In a court case, all medical records, regardless of form, are considered hearsay if offered as evidence to prove the truth of any matter asserted in the record. Therefore, they must fit within an exception to the hearsay rule to be admissible. Medical records made in the normal manner at or near the time care was delivered generally meet this exception. To ensure that computerized medical records are admissible, automated record systems should record the date and time of each entry and update to a medical record. The record also must have been made by or from information transmitted by someone with knowledge of the recorded events. Thus, the system should identify each person who makes an entry or changes a record.

Because the integrity of the computerized record is at stake, a secure access system is essential. Also, the health care facility should have an employee or computer consultant who can testify as to the reliability of the system's identification and entry dating process and the trustworthiness of the system as a whole, including its security features and procedures.

Regardless of the medium used for the patient medical record, the risk management mandate remains the same. The record must be accurate and patient privacy must be protected. Computers did not create confidentiality concerns for medical records; the technology only makes the issue more compelling.

TELEMEDICINE

Telemedicine is the use of telecommunications technology for medical diagnosis and patient care to sites that are at a distance from the provider. Thus, telemedicine permits providers to provide care without moving the patient.

There is a wide range of applications for this technology. Telepathology involves rendering diagnostic opinions on specimens at remote locations. Teleradiology is the electronic transmission of radiologic images from one location to another for the purpose of interpretation or consultation. Other uses exist and undoubtedly will evolve.

Telemedicine is not new. It got off the ground more than thirty years ago, briefly flourished, and then fell out of favor in the 1980s. Its current resurgence has been linked to changes in clinical needs, the growth of managed care, a reduction in the cost of telemedicine systems, and improvements in quality. Its viability will be shaped by the insurance reimbursement policies adopted by public- and private-sector payers.

Telemedicine carries a host of unresolved risk management issues and few legal or regulatory guidelines. One of the first hurdles is the state-based physician licensure system, which runs counter to telemedicine's "virtual" boundaries. The rules for licensure by endorsement and out-of-state consultations vary among the states and pose barriers to development of interstate systems. Risk managers will need to keep abreast of telemedicine initiatives at the state and federal level. Credentialing is a related problem, and poses the issue of whether practitioners would need to be granted telemedicine privileges at remote facilities. Refer to the chapter on telemedicine for more information on this subject.

SECURITY

Hackers have ably illustrated that computer and telecommunications technologies pose security risks. Although the risks are not entirely new, the ante has been raised because large amounts of data now can be accessed, stolen, or altered from a remote location. Computer hackers, disgruntled personnel, fires, floods, and disasters all threaten the safety and security of information technologies. The need to prevent the inappropriate disclosure of patient information is just as important to the electronic world as to the paper world. Various security technologies, such as data encryption, digital signatures, and virus protection software are being developed to minimize these problems. Numerous legislative and regulatory approaches have been initiated.

EXHIBIT 16.1.   **Security Checklist for Information Technologies**

- Develop and strictly enforce policies against disclosing or sharing passwords, access codes, key cards, and other means of access to the system.
- Develop policies and procedures for the assignment of passwords, as well as for their deactivation should an employee leave.
- Institute a "time-out" on computer terminals—that is, program terminals' screens should go blank after a certain period (for example, three minutes) of inactivity following the display of a patient record.
- Establish audit trails so that access to each record is tracked by the system.
- Sharply limit access to sensitive records or portions of records (for example, HIV-antibody test results).
- Protect against mass access and extraction of information.
- Educate staff about the importance of privacy and the problems that arise from sharing passwords.
- Ask medical staff members to sign confidentiality statements.
- Hold physicians liable for any entries to a record made by nurses or assistants using the physicians' password.
- Provide twenty-four-hour assistance to authorized users who forget their access codes or to persons who legitimately need one-time access.
- Provide mechanisms for minimizing human error, such as review of input data for accuracy. If bar codes or other programmed codes are used to record clinical observations, there should be a mechanism for visual confirmation or other verification of entries. Document accuracy reviews.
- To the extent possible, limit connections to, and electronic data sharing with, outside computer systems.
- Use disks from reputable software vendors only.
- Obtain antivirus software to protect against computer viruses.
- Require software vendors to indemnify against all damages and costs arising from viruses, bombs, and similar sabotage inserted into the software by the vendor or its agents.
- Explore the feasibility of using optical disk "write once, read many" (WORM) technology; although it is considered antiquated for other industries, it may be ideal for hospitals because records cannot be altered after they are initially recorded in this form.
- Properly maintain hardware, and thoroughly debug and maintain software.
- Include performance standards in any lease or contract with a vendor, as well as guarantees of reliability and ongoing maintenance support.
- Have adequate backup and emergency capability. (For example, frequent backup of databases; off-site as well as on-site computer tape storage; and emergency data processing capability are essential, as is electrical power during power outages.)
- Routinely monitor available security systems and ensure that existing measures are reasonable by current standards.

Risk managers must ensure that appropriate risk control measures are implemented and enforced. A security checklist for information technologies is provided in Exhibit 16.1; it summarizes major measures that organizations should take to help provide security for their information technologies. All employees should be educated on the hospital's confidentiality policy and given specific instructions on the release of patient information consistent with law and regulation. A confidentiality statement should be signed. Highly sensitive data, such as HIV tests and mental health records, should be specifically addressed; for example, the faxing of HIV-related information should be prohibited. Physical controls and policies on access to information must be designed in advance. Passwords should be used and changed frequently, and disclosure of passwords should be prohibited. There should be lockout triggers for users who go beyond their approved levels of access. The computer systems should be able to track access to records by each user.

Finally, physician bylaws should establish the requirements and prohibitions for access. Confidentiality agreements, signed by physicians and others, could spell out the duty to keep patient information confidential.

∙∙∙∙∙∙∙∙∙∙∙∙

CONCLUSION

The Internet and its associated technologies may well be the key development of our times. For health care risk managers, these technologies will promote more collaboration, faster response times, and an increased knowledge base—essential qualities for today's restructured health care industry. No one can underestimate the growth of on-line services and how they will alter the way business is conducted. At the same time, risk management information services will continue to yield new efficiencies and help to turn data into information that can be used to identify and analyze risks.

Endnotes

1. ECRI. "Healthcare Information Systems: Laboratory Information Systems." *Special Reports.* Plymouth Meeting, Pa.: ECRI, 1995.

2. Roach, W. H., Chernoff, S. N., and Esley, C. L. *Medical Records and the Law* (2nd ed.). Rockville, Md.: Aspen, 1996.

Appendix 16.1

Computer Glossary for Risk Managers

@—At. Separates the specific user ID and domain name of an Internet address.

Access—The ability to use a computer or program to store or retrieve information.

Address—A unique identification assigned to a specific computer. To send e-mail, the sender needs the Internet address, which usually consists of a user ID, the @ symbol, and a domain name, and can be in numbers rather than words.

Anonymous FTP—A public file transfer protocol (FTP) file archive that is made available for Internet users to access.

Application programs—These are designed to carry out specific tasks for the user. They may be purchased from commercial software companies or written by computer staff.

Archie—An Internet search tool used to locate files on anonymous FTP sites.

ASCII—American Standard Code for Information Interchange. A standard code used in computer telecommunications that allows computers to exchange text-based files between them.

Bandwidth—The volume of data that a particular transmission channel can carry at once. There are several media for transmission; two types are twisted-pair telephone wires and fiber optics.

BPS—Bits per second. The higher the rate, the more data that can be transmitted.

Browser—A type of software program that enables users to move around the World Wide Web to explore Web sites.

Bug—An error that occurs in a computer program.

BBS—Bulletin board system. Software that allows messages to be left on a computer from a remote computer.

Chat—A real-time typed conversation between two or more people over the Internet or a proprietary computer network such as America Online or CompuServe.

.com—A commercial organization's domain designation.

CPR—Computerized patient record.

Database—Entire collection of stored data.

Domain—The name of the computer that is connected to the Internet. Computers are uniquely identified by a series of numbers. The domain name system translates those numbers into a name to which users can relate.

Download—The transfer or capture of data files from a database to the user's computer storage area; to retrieve files from an external computer to one's own computer.

EDP—Electronic data processing. Represents the automation of routine manual clerical activity (for example, an association membership list).

.edu—An educational institution's domain designation.

Electronic signature—A feature that allows a physician to sign off on a report through the information system by using a special password, logging off, or other means that do not require signing a hard copy.

EPR—Electronic patient record.

FAQ—Frequently asked questions. A file that contains questions and answers about specific topics.

Field—Specific pieces of data that will be coded as a sequence of characters. Each field is given a name (incident type, incident location, date, shift).

File—A subset of the database that is stored and used as a unit.

FTP—File transfer protocol. A service that supports file transfers between local and remote computers.

Gateway—A hardware and software interface system that links two different types of computer systems, such as a mainframe and a LAN.

Gopher—A search tool that displays information through a system of menus and menu choices.

.gov—A government agency's domain designation.

Hardware—The pieces of equipment used by the system.

Home page—A location on the World Wide Web that identifies an individual or organization; generally used to refer to the first screen at a site. A home page welcomes visitors and points them to other information available at the Web site.

HTML—Hypertext markup language. The standard format for documents on the World Wide Web.

http—Hypertext transfer protocol. The protocol used by the World Wide Web for transmitting Web pages and other hypertext-linked files over the Internet.

Hypertext—Text that has contextual links to other related text. For example, if a document uses a term that is defined or explained in depth somewhere else, a hypertext document would include a link from that term to the related text.

In-Area Services—Health services rendered by providers located within the authorized service area.

Internet—Interconnected collection of computer networks.

IRC—Internet relay chat. Software that allows real-time typed conversations between two or more people over the Internet.

Listserve—A combination of e-mail software and mailing lists. It is commonly used for an electronic newsletter, where the writer of the newsletter sends it to the listserve, which then transmits it to all the subscribers. Another use for listserve is to facilitate a discussion of a special-interest group. All e-mail sent to the listserve is sent to everyone on the list.

Mailing list—A group discussion distributed through e-mail.

.mil—A military organization's domain designation.

MIS—Management information system. Generally for middle and operating management, an MIS integrates data from a variety of functional areas and produces much of its output on an on-demand basis.

Modem—An electronic device that translates computer signals into a form suitable for long-distance transmission, usually by telephone; *modulator/demodulator*, the hardware that translates between analog, and *digital,* so a digital computer can communicate through an analog telephone line.

.net—An Internet organization's domain designation.

Newsgroup—A discussion group on Usenet. Each newsgroup covers a specific topic. Within a newsgroup, there are initial postings listed by subject and subsequent response postings. Newsgroups are not real-time conversations; the postings are stored and forwarded, and often last for weeks or months.

Node—Any single computer connected to a network.

.org—A not-for-profit organization's domain designation.

Packet—A unit of data sent across a packet-switching network.

Prompt—On-screen instructions.

Protocol—A set of rules governing communication between computers on the Internet.

Record—A collection of related fields describing an entity.

Software—The programs required for the computer to perform desired operations.

Systems software—Software that makes the entire computer system operate efficiently. It is provided by the manufacturer.

TCP/IP—Transmission control protocol/Internet protocol. The standardized set of computer guidelines that allow different types of machines to talk with each other and exchange information over the Internet.

Telnet—Terminal emulation protocol that allows Internet users to log into a host computer from a remote location using a Telnet program.

Upload—Transfer of information or data files from a user's computer to another computer.

URL—Uniform (universal) resource locator. A unique identifier that points to a specific site on the World Wide Web.

Usenet—A collection of discussion areas (bulletin boards) known as newsgroups on the Internet.

Virus—Software designed to cause damage to computers or files. Viruses generally enter a computer system via files received on floppy disk or over networks.

Web site—An organization's or individual's Web pages, the first of which is called the home page.

17

Evolving Risk in Cyberspace and Telemedicine

Kathryn T. Allen
Pamela J. Para

Telemedicine has been defined as the use of telecommunications to provide medical information and services. It may be as simple as two health professionals discussing a case over the telephone, or as sophisticated as using satellite technology to broadcast a consultation between facilities in two countries using videoconferencing equipment.

Telemedicine is defined by the American Medical Association's Council on Medical Education and Medical Services as the "provision of health care consultation and education using telecommunications networks to communicate information," and also as "medical practice across distance via telecommunications and interactive video technology."[1]

The Institute of Medicine's Committee on Telemedicine defines telemedicine as "the use of electronic information and communications technologies to provide and support health care when distance separates the participants."[2] The term is now more commonly applied to computer-based, interactive communication and transmission of images such as x-ray films, pathology slides, scope images, and anatomical photographs. Other data that may be transmitted through telemedicine include patient records, EKGs, vital signs, pulse oximetry, and fetal monitoring.

In summary, telemedicine is a term used to describe the provision of medical services across distances utilizing the electronic transmittal of medical information.

While telemedicine is not a new phenomenon, increased interest and sophistication in technology in recent years has fostered a renewed awareness of the application of technological transmission of medical information. In addition, demands for accessible and cost-effective health care have encouraged a modified approach to health care delivery. Technology is moving swiftly to satisfy the demand for telecommunications and video that connect geographically separated health care organizations. Increased competitiveness in the medical marketplace has also resulted in a marked increase in the practice of telemedicine.

Although telemedicine's role is recognized as critical in the "new technological age in health care," it is merely one facet of a well-designed health care program. Advocates of this view stress a primary focus on the continued development of the health system, followed by the determination of the appropriate role and use of telemedicine.

This chapter will discuss the evolution of telemedicine, risk management issues and strategies, role of the risk manager, and "virtual" health care industry applications.

THE HISTORY OF TELEMEDICINE

The concept of telemedicine is recorded as far back as 1924, when radio news foretold "interactive video conferencing." Television was invented in 1927. The creation of teleradiology followed in the 1950s, and video two-way interactive television was utilized for neurological examinations. One of the first telehealth projects took place when the University of Nebraska College of Medicine, in Omaha, used microwaves to conduct group therapy at the Nebraska Psychiatric Institute and at Norfolk State Hospital, 122 miles away. In 1965, surgery to replace an aortic valve in Texas was transmitted via the Communications Satellite Corporation's "Early Bird" satellite to the Geneva University Medical School in Switzerland. The "experiment" was considered a successful international exchange of information. In 1967, voice radio channels transmitted EKG information from a fire department to a hospital for the first time. And in 1972, a hospital's television cable transmitted information to nurse practitioners providing primary care at a distant clinic. Throughout the 1970s and 1980s, a variety of telehealth research projects took place in the United States and Canada.

Before 1986, phone lines transmitted EEG information through scan speed television. In the late 1980s, although most research projects demonstrated that telehealth did indeed work and that its users were satisfied with its performance, programs ceased to exist because government grants were exhausted and the programs were no longer solvent.

Since 1990, however, there has been renewed interest in telehealth. Telemedicine applications have expanded at an accelerated rate. Current applications are unlimited, fostering international cooperation in health care endeavors. Early forms of telemedicine were confined by limitations in technology and subsequent high costs. Recent advances, such as fiber optics, satellite communications, data compression, and real-time video transmission, have minimized many of the technological and financial barriers that impeded the growth of telemedicine. With telemedicine's technical precursors, risk managers can build upon a health care organization's historical coping mechanisms to develop strategies for future technological growth opportunities.

TELEMEDICINE TODAY

The Healthcare Information Management and Systems Society (HIMSS) recently conducted their ninth annual survey of senior health care executives. Of the 1,754 respondents, 34 percent reported their organizations currently use telemedicine technologies, 10 percent plan to use telemedicine within the next twenty-one months, and 28 percent are investigating future uses.

Telemedicine is now generally classified into four types of applications: (1) interactive video, (2) store-and-forward teleconsultations, (3) IP (Internet protocol) video on the Internet, and (4) cable-based video. In the first three categories, data are transferred over telephone lines—via wide bandwidth such as ISDN, T1 lines, or ordinary telephone lines. Cable-based video connects the patient to the health care provider through television cable.

There are two types of technology that make up most of the telemedicine applications in use today. "Store and forward" is used for transferring digital images from one location to another. A digital image is taken using a digital camera ("stored") and then sent ("forwarded") to the receiving location. This is typically used for nonemergent situations, when a diagnosis or consultation may be made and returned in the next twenty-four to forty-eight hours.

The other widely used technology, two-way interactive television (IATV), is used when the patient, primary care provider, and specialist are involved in a consultation. Video-conferencing equipment at both locations, typically an urban and a rural location, allows a "real-time" consultation to take place. This means that the patient does not have to travel to an urban area to see a specialist and in many cases, IATV provides access to specialty care where none has previously been available. Most medical specialties have been found to be conducive to this kind of consultation. The primary users of the technology are psychiatry, internal medicine, rehabilitation, cardiology, pediatrics, and obstetrics and gynecology.

••••••••••••

TELEMEDICINE RISKS

In spite of the recognized value of telemedicine, there remain difficult policy issues that hamper wide-scale implementation. The risk manager should consider the following potential areas of concern involved in telemedicine practice:

- *Practice standards:* credentialing, licensure, clinical guidelines, and peer review.
- *Financial compliance:* anti-kickback or fraud and abuse, antitrust (monopoly, price fixing, restraint of trade), coding and reimbursement.
- *Regulatory implications:* state authority, Food and Drug Administration (FDA), Federal Communication Commission (FCC), Health Care Financing Administration (HCFA), Joint Commission on Accreditation of Healthcare Organizations (JCAHO), National Committee on Quality Assurance (NCQA), and so on.
- *Legal:* jurisdictional issues, potential penalties, and sanctions.
- *Medical malpractice (or "telemalpractice"):* including general agency, vicarious and physician liability, and liability of nonphysicians.
- *Data confidentiality and protection:* electronic access to patient records, electronic misappropriation of health information.
- *Technical shortfalls:* equipment and product liability exposures, contributory negligence of the patient, and ergonomics issues.

Practice Standards

Practice standards that are applicable to telemedicine include, but are not limited to: credentialing, licensure, clinical guidelines, and peer review.

Credentialing   Current accreditation requirements and credentialing standards for the medical staff and other independent practitioner members are inadequate to address the needs of "virtual" practice. In the absence of specific telemedicine standards, compliance with state law and private accrediting standards is more difficult. In an effort to clarify accreditation issues, the Interdisciplinary Telehealth Standards Working Group was organized by the American Nurses Association in 1997. Forty-one representatives from different professional associations and health care organizations participated. As part of that meeting, a smaller work group was charged with developing draft policy positions regarding professional standards in telehealth, to be used as a basis for advising related federal and state legislative, regulatory, and policy initiatives.

Because a remote telemedicine practitioner does not have the intimate relationship with a health care organization, as does a member of the on-site professional staff, experts recommend that organizations exercise careful scrutiny in the selection and retention of telemedicine physicians and other professional practitioners. In some way, every health care organization that offers telemedicine care to its patients must ensure that the remote physicians are qualified by education and demonstrate current clinical competence to practice medicine. Likewise, it is important to monitor the quality of services provided by any practitioner who is either employed or contracted to provide telemedicine services. This makes the granting of specific privileges and monitoring of practice activities through peer review a critical component of any telemedicine venture.

In several telemedicine trial programs, credentialing has not been required of the "distant" physician as long as the "host" physician requesting the consultation, who acts on the recommendations of the distant consultant, is properly credentialed. However, as telemedicine plays a more significant role in the delivery of health care services and telemedicine services become more invasive, credentialing requirements must be tightened.

Licensure   Currently each state requires separate medical licenses for physicians practicing inside state boundaries. While occasional consultations are now permitted between states, it is unclear whether regular consultations are accepted. However, the requirement for a practitioner to hold a full license in every state where practice occurs has proven burdensome and inconvenient. At least six states bar physicians without a state license from practicing distant telemedicine within their borders. Eighteen other states are currently considering similar restrictions. These licensure issues also apply to nurse practitioners, registered nurses, and other licensed professional providers, and physicians.

Proposal of Various Interstate Licensure Models   The Federation of State Medical Boards (FSMB) and the National Council of State Boards of Nursing (NCSBN) have proposed several interstate licensure models. The FSMB, an umbrella organization for sixty-eight state boards of medicine and osteopathy, has recommended a Model Telemedicine Act to establish a license specific for the practice of telemedicine. The act recommends a special license that would authorize the practice of telemedicine across state lines, emulating models set forth by the Defense Department, Department of Veterans Affairs, and the Indian Health Service.

The NCSBN has developed a model for mutual recognition of nurses to practice across state lines according to the licensing act in the state of practice. A state must voluntarily enter into an agreement with another state, have standardized language (similar to drivers' license agreements), and have the licensing act passed by the state legislature. Accountability for the licensing would be to the board of nursing in the state of residence.

In June of 1999, the House of Delegates of the American Nurses Association passed an action report that endorses the continuation of a strong state-based system and offered other approaches to regulating interstate and multistate practice. Negotiations are continuing with the NCSBN, state nurse licensing agencies, professional nursing organizations, federal agencies, and health care industry trade organizations to seek agreement on this issue.

In addition, an interstate telemedicine licensure bill called SB 600 is now before the Oregon State Legislature. SB 600 requires an out-of-state physician's license to be in good standing, meet basic educational and experiential requirements, and restricts the licensee to interstate telemedicine practice only. A mutual recognition model that holds practitioners responsible for their actions in each state in which he or she practices, in-person or "telemedically," is advocated by the Association of Telemedicine Service Providers.[3]

On September 24, 1996, California enacted a law which gives the state medical board the discretion to develop a proposed registration program that permits out-of-state physicians to practice telemedicine in California.

The American College of Radiology adopted a "Standard for Teleradiology" in 1994, which includes the recommendation that "physicians who provide the official, authenticated interpretation of images transmitted by teleradiology should maintain licensure appropriate to delivery of radiologic service at both the transmitting and receiving sites."[4]

The American Medical Association (AMA) House of Delegates voted in June 1996 to adopt a policy declaring that "states and their medical boards should require a full and unrestricted license for all physicians practicing telemedicine within a state."[5]

The College of American Pathologists has taken the position that "a physician rendering primary diagnosis and/or treatment should have a full and unrestricted license to practice medicine in the state in which the patient presents for diagnosis. In cases where specimens, slides or images are transported in interstate commerce, the patient is deemed to have presented for diagnosis in the state in which the specimen is taken or the image made."[6]

In summary, alternative models relating to licensure that could be applied to a health care professional providing telemedicine services include, but are not limited to, the following:

- *Consulting exceptions* allow a physician who is unlicensed in a particular state to practice medicine in that state at the behest of, and in consultation with, a licensed referring physician.

- *Endorsement* is currently used by most state boards to grant licenses to health professionals licensed in other states that have equivalent standards.

- Through *mutual recognition* systems, licensing authorities voluntarily enter into an agreement to legally accept the policies and processes (licensure) of a licensee's home state.

- *Reciprocity* denotes the relationship between two states when each state gives the residents of the other certain privileges, on the condition that its own residents shall enjoy similar privileges at the hands of the latter state.

- *Registration* of a health professional licensed in one state would inform the authorities of other states that he or she wished to practice part-time therein.

- *Limited licensure* requires health professionals to obtain a license from each state in which they practice, with the option of obtaining a limited license that allows the delivery of a specific scope of health services under particular circumstances.

- *National licensure* would involve the issuance of a license based on a standardized set of criteria for the practice of health care throughout the United States
- Through *federal licensure,* health professionals would be issued one license by the federal government based upon federally established standards related to qualifications and discipline.
- *Clinical guidelines* are set forth by a health care organization to define accepted practice. When established guidelines are not followed, negligence may be constituted on the part of a practitioner.

Courts often rely on existing professional standards to determine appropriate care. To date, only the American College of Radiology (ACR) has implemented standards for telemedicine, setting specifications for procedures, equipment, personnel, licensing and quality control in teleradiology. Similar protocols are being developed for telepathology.

The board of directors of the American Telemedicine Association (ATA) has adopted a set of clinical guidelines for the use of telemedicine for homecare. Members of the ATA's Homecare Task Force prepared the draft guidelines, which includes criteria for patient care, health providers, and technology used.

Financial Compliance

Issues of financial compliance that pertain to telemedicine include, but are not limited to: anti-kickback/fraud and abuse, antitrust, coding, and reimbursement.

Anti-Kickback/Fraud and Abuse   An incentive exists for telemedicine partners to refer to each other by virtue of their electronic proximity. The potential for violations of federal self-referral statutes such as STARK exist when physicians are investors in telemedicine projects, or where health care centers provide telecommunications equipment to smaller facilities. This may have the appearance of inducing referrals in violation of existing laws and regulations.

The question arises as to whether the host's subsidization of the system's capital or operating costs is intended to lock in a referral stream. To the extent that the host shoulders most of the costs and access to the host by distant physicians (and vice versa) results in referrals, thus an anti-kickback remuneration problem arises.

Antitrust   Regulators may view network physicians as engaging in price fixing despite the network facilitating consumer choice. A related risk involves regulators viewing network physicians as allocating the patient marketplace amongst them. Other antitrust allegations include monopoly and restraint of trade.

Coding and Reimbursement   Barriers to the expansion of telemedicine services and systems include the fact that no uniform federal payment policy for clinical and consultative services is provided for telemedicine. With the exception of laboratory services and radiologic imaging interpretation, Medicare reimburses for services only if the physician and patient are face to face, thus preventing payment for most telemedicine encounters. However, Medicaid gives individual states the flexibility to reimburse for services delivered via telemedicine. Several states' Medicaid programs reimburse for services delivered through telemedicine.

Although bills have been introduced at the federal level that would mandate Medicare reimbursement for telemedicine, the only federal law mandating any Medicare reimbursement for telemedicine thus far is the Balanced Budget Act of 1997. The act mandates that no later than January 1, 1999, Medicare shall reimburse under Part B for telemedicine consultations for beneficiaries residing in rural counties designated as health professional shortage areas. A bill was recently introduced into the 106th Congress to expand eligibility for Medicare reimbursement. The Health Care Financing Administration (HCFA) has expressed the following concerns about broad-scale coverage and payment for telemedicine services:

- Safety and clinical effectiveness of telemedicine applications.

- Absence of published standards.

- Extent to which current payment methods will accommodate telemedicine.

- Potential for overutilization.

- Increased financial liability on beneficiaries.

- Inevitable impact on the Medicare Trust Fund.

Medicare and Medicaid reimbursement billing codes for telemedicine encounters will need to be assigned to assist in monitoring the utilization of this mode of health care delivery, as well as to verify compliance.

Experts have been challenged with setting policy to define:

- What telemedicine services to reimburse and in what amount.

- How to reimburse physicians and other health care practitioners (for example, the referring versus the consulting practitioner).

- How to finance reimbursement for telemedicine services.

- What incentives would encourage reimbursement for telemedicine.

Regulatory Implications

Section 706 of the Telecommunications Act of 1996 directs the Federal Communications Commission (FCC) to examine whether advanced telecommunications capability, or broadband, is being made available to all Americans on a reasonable and timely basis. The commission concluded that the consumer broadband market is in the early stages of development, and that while it is too early to reach definitive conclusions, aggregate data suggests that broadband is being deployed in a reasonable and timely fashion.

The Department of Health and Human Services (DHHS) developed proposed standards for consideration by Congress designed, in the words of DHHS Secretary Donna Shalala, to "strike a balance between the privacy needs of our citizens and the critical needs of our health care system."[7]

It is anticipated that the Food and Drug Administration (FDA) may regulate the hardware and software that makes telemedicine possible. The FDA has defined the term "telemedicine" as the delivery and provision of health care and consultative services to individual patients and the transmission of information related to care, over distance, using telecommunications technologies, and incorporating (1) direct clinical, preventive, diagnostic, and therapeutic services and treatment; (2) consultative and follow-up services; (3) remote monitoring of patients; (4) rehabilitative services; or (5) patient education. A telemedicine system generally incorporates a mixture of equipment and software, some of which may have been designed specifically for medical use while other components of a system may be general purpose hardware or software put incidentally to a medical use. Future guidelines are expected to clarify regulations on classification and approval of these devices.

The JCAHO advises hospitals that physicians who provide telecommunications consultation need privileges if they are involved in direct patient care.

Legal

Legal theories that may have an impact on risk management strategies related to telemedicine include, but are not limited to, the following.

Lex Loci Delicti Commissi   The state where the injury occurred, or the one with the most ties to the issues involved, has jurisdiction (plaintiff's counsel will probably try to bring a claim in whatever state has what he or she believes to be the most sympathetic forum and the most favorable law from his or her client's perspective). This theory creates uncertainties as to how much insurance is sufficient to cover possible malpractice exposure.

The Doctor-Patient Relationship and the Quality of Care   The challenge of building good rapport with the patient in this era of high-tech diagnostic and therapeutic modalities, the increasing influence of third-party payers, and the adversarial atmosphere engendered by litigation or the threat thereof may be intensified by the distance (literal and figurative) inherent in "low-touch" telemedicine.

Duty   Litigation over whether a telemedicine consultant has a doctor-patient relationship with a plaintiff patient has not yet arisen, so predicting its outcome is speculative. If the patient's regular doctor regains control and responsibility for the management of the case, a defense to the telemedicine consultant may be provided.

Issues of choice of venue and law will need to be considered as states differ in statutory limits on malpractice awards.

Medical Malpractice

Traditional medical malpractice issues have become more complex with the advent of telemedicine. For example, there are now many more potential defendants (for example, the referring physician, the consulting physician, and the referring and consulting physicians' health care organizations). Telecommunications providers and their consultants could also be sued on the grounds that an equipment malfunction or software error contributed to the patient's injuries. Allegations may rest on acts of commission (such as inadequate telemedicine consultation) or omission (such as failure to obtain a telemedicine consult). Moreover, suits may be filed in numerous jurisdictions with varying requirements and standards of care.

A plaintiff must still generally satisfy four criteria to prove medical malpractice: (1) a physician-patient relationship existed in which the physician owed the patient a duty of care; (2) the physician breached that duty by failing to meet the standard of skill and knowledge required by the jurisdiction in which the suit is brought; (3) the physician's breach of that duty injured the plaintiff; and (4) damages occurred as a direct result of the physicians breach of duty. In the realm of telemedicine, the physician-patient relationship is unclear. The role of the remote physician is clarified either when the physician becomes more involved in the care of a patient or when the physician's role starts to resemble that of a specialist more than that of a second opinion.

General Agency and Physician Liability   The mere appearance of an agency relationship may, in a legal sense, create the relationship between a physician and a health care organization. Liability attaches to the hospital if the attending physician is the apparent or ostensible agent of the hospital. In telemedicine physicians will also provide consultations through agents, many of whom will not be physicians.

Vicarious Liability   Under the legal doctrine of *respondeat superior,* health care facilities may be held liable for the negligence of an employee committed while the employee is acting within the scope of his or her employment. Nurses, physician assistants, radiological technicians, and other health care facility employees are treated as agents of their employer, and so long as they are acting within the scope of their employment, their employer is liable for any damage caused by their negligent actions. Because some courts have expanded hospital liability for the acts of independent contractors based on theories of apparent and ostensible agency, it is possible for remotely located plaintiffs to sue the hospital for the negligence of a teleradiologist or other telemedicine consultant.

Liability of Nonphysicians in Telemedicine   Because telemedicine equipment is used to make life-or-death decisions, professional liability exposure for the acts of nonphysician consultants (such as, other health care providers, equipment technicians, computer programmers and operators) must be considered if a "wrong" system decision is made. With increasing dependence on informatics and telematics in health care, policies may shift away from the concept of liability evolving around the responsible health care professionals, to the idea of shared liability between the responsible health care professionals and those who have provided this technology.

Insurance Coverage   There is significant uncertainty at this time as to whether malpractice insurance policies adequately cover telemedicine services. Carriers and practitioners are either seeking to amend existing policies or create new ones to ensure proper coverage.

Additionally, since many medical centers have entered into international telemedicine agreements, insurance carriers are faced with coverage needs for suits brought outside the United States. Unless coverage is purchased by a carrier licensed abroad, health care providers may find themselves uninsured for suits brought outside of the United States.

Insurance territorial rating questions may need to be addressed as a greater number of claims arise from this new treatment modality.

Data Confidentiality

Telemedicine often demands that the medical record of the patient be shared across state lines. One can anticipate claims that confidential data were improperly revealed and/or that the patient was not adequately informed or warned about the potential for transmission of sensitive data.

The Health Insurance Portability and Accountability Act of 1996 (HIPAA) directed the U.S. Department of Health and Human Services to promulgate regulations mandating security standards for the electronic transmission of administrative and financial health care information and to report proposed legislation to Congress for protecting the privacy of individually identifiable health information. The former regulations are not relevant to the sorts of transmissions that will occur during telemedicine consultations, as those regulations only address information that, although electronically transmitted, does not allow one to learn specific health information about a particular individual. The latter report to Congress, which DHHS Secretary Donna Shalala submitted in September 1997, addressed concerns that will have an impact on telemedicine. JCAHO and the NCQA also have standards for maintaining the privacy of medical records.

Current federal or industry regulations governing the confidentiality and privacy of data specifically passing over an interstate telemedicine network is insufficient to protect the patient. Whether through legislation or professional organizations, the reliability and standardization of data and the protection of the electronic medical record needs to be established. Experts recommend that technical safeguards, such as, cryptography, token-based or biometric message authentication, personal identification, user verification, as well as administrative and procedural methodologies, be implemented.

Technical Shortfalls

The choice of equipment used in telemedicine is often determined by factors that are outside the control of the health care provider, such as equipment manufacturer, the telecommunication lines used to transmit the data, financial considerations, or even the patient.

To date, many telemedicine projects have been hampered by the lack of appropriate telecommunications technology. Regular telephone lines do not supply adequate bandwidth for most telemedical applications. Rural areas do not always have cable wiring or other kinds of telecommunications access required for more sophisticated uses. Therefore, Congress recently passed the Telecommunications Reform Act of 1996, which among other things will allow rural education and health care networks to get connectivity rates similar to those charged in urban areas.

Data compression, incomplete transmission of data, or poor quality image transmission can hinder and perhaps impair the quality of the consultation, leading to claims of medical malpractice. Such a claim may be complicated by, or combined with, a plaintiff's claim of product liability against a telecommunications company or equipment manufacturer. Related claims may be further complicated by contributory negligence on the part of the patient, who may be given certain responsibilities in a telemedicine setup, which are not followed through. The improper setup of equipment creates the potential for errors in interpretation of data.

Experts recommend the development and implementation of guidelines and standards for the manufacture, use, and training of all telemedicine equipment and the establishment of contingency plans in the event of equipment or human failure. Regulatory control of telemedicine equipment by the FDA is anticipated.

Since telemedicine is a means for health care professionals to provide services it is imperative that written contracts defining the responsibilities and potential liabilities for each party be obtained. Indemnification clauses are appropriate especially where equipment maintenance is concerned.

············

INVOLVEMENT OF THE RISK MANAGER IN TELEMEDICINE

Telemedicine represents the confluence of medicine, technology, and patient care. The record of advances in twentieth-century health care will include telemedicine as one of the factors having the most influence on the trajectory of care delivery in the twenty-first century. As with any great innovation, telemedicine is subject to the law of unintended consequences.

The previous section describes some of the identified risks. As technological advances extend the reach of telemedicine, others will emerge. It is the risk manager's role, duty, and responsibility to anticipate the unintended consequences and to interpose sound risk principles between the organization and loss. In the case of telemedicine, this means that the risk manager's presence shall be felt at every level of administration, from contracting to education to marketing. A risk management role, however, must begin with familiarity. The risk manager is responsible for learning about telemedicine, its current integration into the organization, and its place in the organization's strategic planning.

The health care risk manager should be involved at the start of all negotiations and decision-making junctures of telemedicine programs that an organization or individual practitioner undertakes. Doing so will enable appropriate decisions to be made with respect to insurance coverage, confidentiality, and integrity of data transmitted.

············

EDUCATION—BOARD OF DIRECTORS, MEDICAL STAFF, ADMINISTRATION, AND MANAGEMENT STAFF

A primary responsibility of risk management is to provide the organization with the knowledge of the risks involved in the practice of telemedicine from a legal liability perspective. The risk manager should provide sufficient information about the legal snags and responsibilities to all levels of the organization including the board of directors, administration, the medical staff, and department directors. It is important for each of the participants in the decision-making process to clearly understand the responsibilities and risks that are involved. One approach is to formally design a telemedicine risk management inservice that explains in general terms the liability issues created when telemedicine modalities are utilized in the provision of any of the hospital's medical services. The risk manager can present this to all of the above mentioned entities and field questions from the audience related to telemedicine risks.

Contracting for Telemedicine Services

For risk managers, contract review responsibilities still apply. Prior to signing any agreements for the provision of telemedicine services, the risk manager should be involved in the review process in conjunction with legal counsel.

Insurance Coverage

As with other insurance purchases, whether directly or indirectly involved in the purchase, the risk manager should provide input into the purchase of insurance coverage of telemedicine services. The risk manager's sixth sense for identifying potential issues should be exercised at the point of insurance coverage.

Incident Reporting and Monitoring

The incident reporting system should clearly identify reporting criteria and indicators for unusual occurrences that are potential compensible events in the telemedicine arena. One of the challenges of telemedicine is to identify and report incidents that occur at remote locations. Staff at these locations may be unfamiliar with reporting procedures and criteria.

Risk Management

In order to support loss control, there must be an effective interface with many systems, processes, and disciplines already in place. The risk manager serves as the facilitator for the interfaces.

Quality Management (Clinical and Operational Issues)

Include all telemedicine practitioners in the routine quality and peer review mechanisms.

Credentialing

The risk manager must ensure that all practitioners involved in cyber partnerships are credentialed through the same process as if they were practicing on-site.

Human Resources

Staff orientation should include telemedicine technologies. Initial telemedicine skills assessments and ongoing validation of competencies must demonstrate a clear understanding of telemedicine from an operational and record-keeping perspective.

Health Information Management

The medical staff, administration, and risk manager, working closely with the health information manager, should make decisions regarding what reports and records will be formally generated, how they will be stored, and in what format. The maintenance and security of all patient information are paramount responsibilities of all health providers. The risk manager should be familiar with policies and practices related to confidentiality, documentation, coding, release of information, and retention of records.

IS (Technical Issues)

The risk management challenge within this department is information access restriction.

Safety (Equipment Issues)

Procedures must be clearly defined and documented with respect to telemedicine equipment maintenance and back-up systems.

Marketing and Advertising

Telemedicine services marketing must not be overblown and should describe realistic and attainable benefits of the technology.

Managed Care Relationships

Unless the delivery sites are owned by the managed care organization (MCO), MCOs develop their networks through contractual agreements. The contracts generally call for accurate and timely claims reporting as well as compliance with two standards from the

NCQA: that the contracted organization provide the MCO access to treatment records and that the organization participate in the MCO's quality improvement activities. Both the organizations providing telemedicine services and the host should be aware of these contractual obligations. Reimbursement may be another issue. Unless the telemedicine provider is identified in the contract as an agent of the contracted organization, the MCO could justifiably declare that telemedicine services came from an out-of-network provider and refuse payment. By providing contract oversight, the vigilant risk manager can ensure that this interpretation docs not apply.

·············

"VIRTUAL" HEALTH CARE INDUSTRY APPLICATIONS

This particular section of the chapter could be called "the patient is the winner." However, there are many winners in an effective telemedicine program. The increased interaction among physicians helps keep physicians current and in communication with peers and specialists of all disciplines of medicine.

Hospitals

The hospital is the largest utilizer of telemedicine services in the areas of surgical evaluation, emergency, psychiatry, radiology, pathology, dermatology, and cardiology.

Organ, Tissue, and Blood Procurement

Telemedicine supports these programs in tracking of potential donors and recipients.

Home Health

Home health enables the patient and family to receive education and perform self-care through the use of videophone hook-ups. Nursing assessments can also be performed with the cooperation of the patient and family members.

Outerspace Utilization

Remote sensing and videoconferencing allows providers to monitor the health of U.S. astronauts during missions, while conducting scientific experiments and monitoring the results in real time.

Physician Office, Rural Health, and Dentistry

The solo practitioner becomes a virtual medical center with telemedicine capabilities (such as, two-way video monitoring).

Airports and Airlines

Illnesses and injuries in airports and on airplanes are no longer compounded with an absence of medical care and consultation. Telemedicine capabilities are able to provide the communication and guidance for interim treatment.

Leisure Telemedicine

With a boon to the ever-increasing leisure lifestyle, telemedicine brings the capability to provide state-of-the-art medical access through telemedicine technologies to remote and mobile vacation sites.

Web Sites

The question has recently arisen as to the liability of medical information provided over the Internet as well as the sale of medical supplies and pharmaceutical products.

Military and Veterans' Health

The advantages that telemedicine brings to military and veterans' health care include telecommunication linkages between base hospitals and remote military outposts; real-time battlefield imaging devices; radio transmission of ECG data; future ECG and skin sensors that allow battlefield tracking data, with communication of individual soldier location and physiologic information to base health care personnel; and future battlefield robotic surgery.

Medical Education and "Telementoring"

Educational programs delivered via telemedicine technology provide interaction among practitioners that has never been possible before. This practice virtually eliminates the old notion of community standards in the practice of medicine because of the widespread availability of medical knowledge.

Community and Public

Mobile health services use basic forms of telemedicine technology to transfer test results and medical information.

Telephone and Telemedicine Triage

The ability to diagnose and provide treatment guidance to formerly inaccessible locations, and during situations where patient transport is not possible, is an invaluable benefit.

International

The advances in telemedicine technology have virtually eliminated all manmade and natural boundaries. It has become an international, limitless practice of medicine. The use of telemedicine technologies is enabling the corporate practice of medicine within the United States and internationally.

Prison Health

Populations certainly benefit by having the access to sophisticated medical practices while at the same time maintaining the security of the prison population and reducing costs.

Research

This technology expands the availability of many practitioners, real-time study and data collection, and increased populations for study.

Remote Emergency and Trauma Support

More telemedicine connections provide more timely responses to emergency site locations and the ability to initiation intervention prior to arrival at trauma centers (or when trauma centers are not a reasonable alternative). Telemedicine applications are integral in improving the delivery of emergency care.

....

RISK ANALYSIS QUESTIONNAIRE

Ask yourself the following questions to determine if you are providing your organization with the safeguards necessary to ensure against the risks associated with the delivery of telemedicine.

1. Are you educating your facility on the risks associated with telemedicine (including the board of directors, department heads, administration, and medical staff)?

2. Are you involved in the contracting process when telemedicine services are under consideration?

3. Are all telemedicine partnerships clearly defined in the form of a written contract?

4. Are there back-up systems in place in case of technical failures in the telemedicine system?

5. Are the credentials and licenses of practitioners contracted to perform telemedicine being verified?

6. Have criteria or clinical standards for the telemedicine services been developed and are they being monitored?

7. Has the patient information and data been addressed in policies for protection of confidentiality in all aspects of the process?

8. Are mechanisms and policies in place to obtain informed consent of the patient involved in the telemedicine service?

9. Do you have established requirements for documentation of the telemedicine contact and patient information?

10. Has insurance coverage for related issues been investigated and discussed with your insurer?

11. Has a peer review mechanism been established for the telemedicine system, and is this system documented and integrated into your quality improvement program?

12. Does your incident reporting system include criteria and a mechanism for capturing occurrences involving telemedicine?

....

SUMMARY OF RISK MANAGEMENT STRATEGIES

The risk management strategies that are suggested for the telemedicine risks identified include, but are not limited to, the following:

● Federal procedures and state statutes must be monitored to maintain an awareness of venue and choice of legal theories in a telemedicine malpractice lawsuit.

● Telemedicine providers must monitor industry standards that may affect telemedicine technology and the delivery of care through telemedicine.

- Technical security safeguards must be ensured for computerized data, which include audit trails showing who accessed data. This will facilitate the identification of and thereby the prosecution or other appropriate action against anyone who may have used health records for illegal or improper purposes. The safeguards will limit access to those persons and entities with clearly defined and legitimate purposes for receiving it, will ensure mandatory education for all who gather or use individual health care information, and will ensure reasonable patient access to their own records. Technical safeguards (such as, cryptography, token-based or biometric message authentication, personal identification, user verification), as well as administrative and procedural methodologies, should also be established.

- The development and implementation of a system for quality oversight and peer review is imperative. The degree of accountability for individual practitioners, as well as jurisdictional issues are questions that need to be answered before the full potential of the liability exposures can be determined. With increasing reliance on informatics and telematics in health care there may come a shift away from the concept of liability evolving around the responsible health care professionals to the idea of shared liability between the responsible health care professionals and those who have provided this technology.

Experts recommend the implementation of a system for peer review of the telemedicine practice, such as a mechanism for "second reads" with results reported to the referring entity. In addition, it is recommended that contracts with telemedicine providers require peer review with results reported to the referring entity. This information should be incorporated into the quality improvement process of the organization with identified trends being shared on a timely basis with the risk management department.

- While no security system is immune from intrusion, health information managers need to implement systems that ensure high levels of clinical access and utility while maintaining secure and confidential patient information. Health care organizations are encouraged to design policies regarding information values, protection responsibilities, and organizational commitment to a set of laws, rules, and practices that regulate how an organization manages, protects and distributes sensitive information.

- Informed consent should address the risks of the care to be administered and any risks presented by virtue of the care being delivered via telemedicine. Health care organizations need to carefully assess their own telemedicine systems to identify specific risks about which they may need to inform patients.

- Before providing telemedicine services, providers and health care organizations need to ascertain whether or not their liability insurance extends to all referring and receiving jurisdictions, including other countries if telemedicine is practiced across international boundaries.

- Telemedicine providers must be cognizant of federal and state fraud and abuse laws and must examine their business relationships to ensure that prohibited practices do not occur.

- A means of identifying complications and adverse outcomes related to telemedicine must be incorporated into existing incident reporting systems, and these events must be reviewed to identify opportunities to improve patient care.

- Telemedicine providers must also ensure to the extent possible that telemedicine equipment is appropriate and that it is subject to routine inspection and preventive maintenance.

....

CONCLUSION

Significant hurdles remain, including legal and regulatory barriers and acceptance of the use of telemedicine by the traditional medical establishment. However, these barriers are coming down and a growing body of research data supports how telemedicine can improve patient outcomes and reduce health care costs. The future of telemedicine is left to our imaginations.

Endnotes

1. American Medical Association House of Delegates. Proceedings of the 145th Annual Meeting, June 23–27, 1996.

2. Institute of Medicine
   National Academy of Sciences
   2101 Constitution Avenue NW
   Washington, D.C. 20418
   (202) 334-2352

   "Telemedicine: A Guide to Assessing Telecommunications in Health Care," 1996.
   www.nap.edu/readingroom/records/0309055318.html

3. The Association of Telehealth Service Providers
   4702 SW Scholls Ferry Road #400
   Portland, OR 97225-2008

4. "The American College of Radiology Standard for Teleradiology," 1994, Resolution 21.

   American College of Radiology
   1891 Preston White Drive
   Reston, VA 20191

5. American Medical Association House of Delegates. Proceedings of the 145th Annual Meeting, June 23–27, 1996.

6. "Telemedicine Report to Congress: Legal Issues: Licensure and Telemedicine," p. 11. January 31, 1997.
   www.ntia.doc.gov/reports/telemed/legal.html

7. "Confidentiality of Medical Records: A Situation Analysis and AHIMA's Position," p. 4.
   www.ahima.org/professional.support/write.paper.html

Suggested Readings and Web Sites

"Advanced Technology Focus of 12 HPC Health Care Awards,"
www.nlm.nih.gov/research/telemedhpcc.html

Allen, B. "What Is Telemedicine and Who Uses It?" American International Group, Inc., Jan. 1998.

"American Medical Association Recommendations," July 31, 1996,
tie.telemed.org/scripts/getpage.pl?page=amadoc

American Nurses Association,
www.nursingworld.org

Antalis, J. "What Are the Implications of Telemedicine on Private Practice in Georgia?" *Journal of MAG 82*, May 1993, pp. 211–213.

Baur, H. J., and others. "How to Deal with Security Issues in Teleradiology." *Computer Methods and Programs in Biomedicine, 53* (1997), pp. 1–8.

Baquet, C. R. "An Overview of Telemedicine," www.som1.ab.umd.edu/~smadmin/TELEmed/BaquetCR-JAAMP.html

Belfiglio, G. "Bringing It All Back Home: Telemedicine Bridges the Distance Between Patient and Provide." *Healthplan,* Mar./Apr. 1998, pp. 31–37.

Berger, S. B., and Cepelewicz, B. B. "Medical-Legal Issues in Teleradiology." *American Journal of Roentgenology, 166,* Mar. 1996, pp. 505–510.

Brenner, R. J., and Westenberg, L. "Film Management and Custody: Current and Future Medicolegal Issues." *American Journal of Roentgenology, 167,* Dec. 1996, pp. 1371–1375.

Cepelwicz, B. B. "Telemedicine: A Virtual Reality, But Many Issues Need Resolving." *Medical Malpractice Law & Strategy, 13*(9), July 1996, pp. 1–3.

Chaffee, M. "A Telehealth Odyssey." *American Journal of Nursing, 99*(7), July 1999, pp. 27–32.

"Citations from Current Telemedicine Publications," Apr. 7, 1998, tie.telemed.org/scripts/getpage.pl?page=citations

"Compendium of Telemedicine Laws," 1998, www.legamed.com/compend.htm

Department of Defense, www.defenselink.mil/

"Fact Sheet: Telemedicine Related Programs," www.nlm.nih.gov/pubs/factsheets/telemedicine.html

Federal Telemedicine Gateway, www.tmgateway.org

"Funding for Telemedicine Projects," www.nlm.nih.gov/research/funding.html

Hartman, G. L. "The Telephone and the Practice of Medicine." *Physician Viewpoint, 3*(1), Winter 1998.

Health Care Financing Administration, www.hcfa.gov

Healthcare Open Systems and Trials (HOST), www.hostnet.org

"Health Information Systems and Telemedicine," www.arentfox.com/telemed/articles/licensenimplic.html

Herdman, R. C. "Protecting Privacy in Computerized Medical Information" (Office of Technology Assessment Digest), www.netreach.net/~wmanning/otadig.htm

Horton, M. C. "Licensure and Telehealth." *Nursing Management 28*(6), p. 10.

Horty, J. "Telemedicine: Liability of Physicians and Hospitals." *Medical Staff Monthly,* May 1997, pp. 1–4.

Horty, J. "Telemedicine: Licensure and Liability." *Medical Staff Monthly,* Apr. 1997, pp. 1–2.

Illinois Rural Health Association. Second Annual Telemedicine Conference, Mar. 23–24, 1998.

Japsen, B. "Kansas Hospital's Experiment in Home Health Telemedicine Cuts Costs, Visits." *Modern Healthcare,* Mar. 23, 1998, p. 47.

Johnson, D. P. "Telemedicine Breaks Distance Barrier," www.nlm.nih.gov/pubs/gyours/julaug97.html

Kamp, G. H. "Medical-Legal Issues in Teleradiology: A Commentary." *American Journal of Roentgenology, 166,* Mar. 1996, pp. 511–512.

Karp, D. "Malpractice in the New Millennium: Better Than Today?" *Alaska Medicine, 38*(3), July/Aug./Sept. 1996, pp. 106–108.

Kjervik, D. K. "Telenursing—Licensure and Communication Challenges." *Journal of Professional Nursing, 13*(2), Mar./Apr. 1997, p. 65.

Klein, S. R., and Manning, W. L. "Telemedicine and the Law." *Healthcare Information Management: The Journal of the Healthcare Information and Management Systems Society,* Summer 1995, www.netreach.net/~wmanning/telmedar.htm

Kovner, R., and Havens, D., and Hardy, M. "Telemedicine: Potential Applications and Barriers to Continued Expansion." *Journal of Pediatric Health Care, 10,* July/Aug. 1996, pp. 184–187.

Lally, J. F. "Teleradiology and a Specialty at Risk" *American Journal of Roentgenology, 169,* Aug. 1997, pp. 598–599.

LaMay, C. L. "Telemedicine and Competitive Change." *Spine 22*(1), 1997, pp. 88–97.

Laske, C. "Health Care Telematics: Who is Liable?" *Computer Methods and Programs in Biomedicine, 54,* 1997, pp. 1–6.

"Legal Issues—Licensure and Telemedicine." *Telemedicine Report to Congress,* Jan. 31, 1997, www.ntia.doc.gov/reports/telemed/legal.htm

Lott, C. M. "Legal Interfaces in Telemedicine Technology." *Military Medicine, 161,* May 1996, pp. 280–283.

McMenamin, J. P. "Telemedicine and the Law." *Virginia Medical Quarterly, 123*(3), July./Aug./Sept. 1996, pp. 184–189.

"National Library of Medicine's Telemedicine Projects," www.nlm.nih.gov/research/telfront.html

"NLM National Telemedicine Initiative," www.nlm.nih.gov/research/telemedinit.html

"NLM National Telemedicine Initiative Summaries of Awards," www.nlm.nih.gov/research/initprojsum.html

Norton, S. A., Lindborg, C., Delaplain, E., and Calvin, B. "Consent and Privacy in Telemedicine." *Hawaii Medical Journal, 52*(12), Dec. 1993, pp. 340–341.

Office for the Advancement of Telehealth, telehealth.hrsa.gov

Pedersen, S. "Telemedicine and New Technology." *British Journal of Hospital Medicine, 55*(6), 1996, pp. 372–373.

Pendrak, R. F., and Ericson, R. P. "Long Distance Lawsuits: Telemedicine Technologies are Outracing Liability Issues," www.phico.com/WN_Long_Distance_Lawsuits.htm

Perednia, D. A., and Allen, A. "Telemedicine Technology and Clinical Applications." *Journal of the American Medical Association, 273*(6), Feb. 8, 1995, pp. 483–488.

"Telemedicine: An Overview of Applications and Barriers," Rockville, Md.: Physician Insurers Association of America, 1996.

Rayman, R. B. "Telemedicine: Military Applications." *Aviation, Space, and Environmental Medicine,* Feb. 1997, pp. 135–137.

Reichertz, P. S. and Halpern, N.J.L., "FDA Regulation of Telemedicine Devices," www.arentfox.com/telemed/articles/fda_reg_telemed_dev.html

"Report of the Interdisciplinary Telehealth Standards Working Group," Jan. 6, 1998, www.arentfox.com/telemed/reports/telehlth.html

"Rockefeller Hosts Telemedicine Reception," www.nlm.nih.gov/pubs/nlmnews/maraug97.html

Scannell, K. M. "Telemedicine: Past, Present, Future," January 1966 through March 1995, www.nlm.nih.gov/pubs/cbm/telembib.html

"Secretary Shalala Announces National Telemedicine Initiative," Washington, D.C., Oct. 8, 1996, www.nlm.nih.gov/news/press_releases/telemed.html

Sharp, N. "Nurse Practitioners, Telemedicine, and the Federal Communications Commission." *Nurse Practitioner,* July 1996, pp. 99–103.

Shotwell, L. F. "Taming Liability of Telemedical Transactions: Technology Adoption Poses Catch-22 for Providers," www.arentfox.com/telemed/articles/tamingliab.html

Siebelt, B. "Telemedicine: What It Is and What It Isn't." Handouts from a presentation at AIG, May 22, 1997.

Skolnick, A. A., "Taking Telemedicine to the Top of the World." *Journal of the American Medical Association, 279*(11), Mar. 18, 1998, pp. 816–817.

Smith, S. Z. "Telemedicine." *KMA Journal, 96,* Mar. 1998, p. 108.

Sommer, T. J. "Telemedicine: A Useful and Necessary Tool to Improving Quality of Healthcare in the European Union." *Computer Methods and Programs in Biomedicine, 48,* 1995, pp. 73–77.

"State Legislation Relating to Telemedicine/Telehealth," www.ana.org/gova/telemedlg.htm

Swett, H. A., and others. "Telemedicine: Delivering Medical Expertise Across the State and Around the World." *Connecticut Medicine, 59*(10), Oct. 1995, pp. 593–602.

Tange-duPre, K. "Telemedicine—Opportunities and Issues." *White Paper, American Society for Healthcare Risk Management,* pp. 1–8.

Telehealth Magazine, www.telemedmag.com

"Telemedicine Presents New Malpractice Concerns According to Physician Insurers Association." *Journal of the Oklahoma State Medical Association, 90,* Mar. 1997, pp. 101–102.

"Telemedicine and Interstate Licensure: Findings and Recommendations of the Center for Telemedicine Law Licensure Task Force," www.ctl.org/ctlwhite.html

Telemedicine Research Center, tie.telemed.org

Telemedicine Today Magazine, www.telemedtoday.com

Telemedicine and the Law, www.arentfox.com/telemedicine.html

"The Western Governors' Association Telemedicine Action Report," www.netreach.net/~wmanning/wgovtel.htm

Trombly, S. "Transformation of Care by Telemedicine," Apr. 1996, www.rmf.org/b3404.html

"Types of Telemedical Services Performed, Studied and Evaluated Under the NLM Contract— A Brief Summary," www-abc.hsc.usc.edu/nlm/Telemedical_Services_Summary.html

Waters, R. J. "Licensure Laws Pose Interstate Tug-Of-War: Physicians Grapple with State Statutes, Liability Concerns," www.arentfox.com/telemed/articles/interslicense.html

Winn, J. R. "Draft Model Act to Regulate the Practice of Telemedicine Across State Lines: A Few Brief Comments," Aug. 21, 1995, www.netreach.net/~wmanning/fsmb.htm

Glossary

AHIMA—The American Health Information Management Association, a professional association representing 38,000 health information management professionals. Since its founding in 1928, the AHIMA has worked to protect the confidentiality of individually identifiable health information.

ATSP—The Association of Telemedicine Service Providers is a member-focused, international organization comprising health care service providers and technology vendors. The ATSP is dedicated to the business development of the telemedicine industry through advocacy, education, and information.

Bandwidth—The capacity of an electronic transmission medium to transmit data per unit of time. The higher the bandwidth, the more data can be transmitted.

CSU/DSU—Channel Service Unit/Data Service Unit is a hardware device that is needed to terminate a high-speed telecommunications connection.

DICOM—Digital Imaging and Communications in Medicine is an industry standard for connection of and communication among medical imaging devices.

Encryption—A mathematical transposition of a file or data stream so that it cannot be deciphered at the receiving end without the proper key; a security feature that assures that only the parties who are supposed to be participating in a video conference or data transfer are able to do so.

FDA 510K Approval—Product has met the Food and Drug Administration (FDA) approval criteria, or is similar to a product that has.

Federal Trade Commission (FTC)—Enforces a variety of federal antitrust and consumer protection laws. The commission seeks to ensure that the nation's markets function competitively and are vigorous, efficient, and free of undue restrictions. The commission also works to enhance the smooth operation of the marketplace by eliminating acts or practices that are unfair or deceptive. In general, the commission's efforts are directed toward stopping actions that threaten consumers' opportunities to exercise informed choice. Finally, the commission undertakes economic analysis to support its law enforcement efforts and to contribute to the policy deliberations of the Congress, the executive branch, other independent agencies, and state and local governments when requested. In addition to carrying out its statutory enforcement responsibilities, the commission advances the policies underlying Congressional mandates through cost-effective, non-enforcement activities, such as consumer education.

Firewall—A computer system that prevents the passing of Internet traffic to an organization's internal network; provides an added layer of protection against "hackers"; external type protects all internal systems from the outside world, and internal type protects only selected systems.

Frame rate—Frames per second displayed on a video monitor.

Freeze frame—Useful feature in medical consultation; allows the consultant to get a well-framed and focused still image for closer examination.

Frequency response—A relative measure of audio quality, measured in cycles per second; optimizes many electronic stethoscopes for either heart or lung sounds.

Ghosting—A motion artifact in monitor displays of compressed video image.

Graphic equalizer—Allows user to accentuate or deemphasize selected frequencies within an audio sample, such as when "tuning" heart and lung sounds in electronic stethoscopes.

HL7: Health Level 7—A standard interface between hospital information systems that defines the format for interchange of text files between health care databases.

Image management—The ability to sort, arrange, and manipulate stored images into functional groups.

INMARSAT—An international global telecommunications satellite network established by government treaty in 1979 with 79 member countries.

Integrator—A vendor that uses retail parts from other manufacturers to produce a product that other vendors might make and assemble within the company.

Interface—The manner in which the system enables information to be accessed and modified.

ISDN—Integrated Services Digital Network is a low-to-medium speed technology for digital telephony.

ISO—International Standardization Organization establishes and coordinates worldwide standards for electronic information exchange.

ITU-T Standards—International Telecommunications Union standards were founded in 1965 as a telegraphy standards body; now a United Nations agency.

ITV—Interactive televideo.

JPEG—Joint Photographic Experts Group is an international group that has developed standards for still image compression.

LAN—Local area network is a computer network linking computers, printer servers, and other equipment within an enterprise; can support audio, video, and data exchange.

LAN connectivity—The ability to connect the video system to a LAN within the health care facility; can allow access to and sharing of patient records, test reports, demographics, and so on during a videoconference.

Laser digitizer—Laser scanner; employs a laser to capture image information to digital form.

LEC—Local exchange company is the local telephone office that bridges between the long-distance carrier and the customer site.

Leveling—A software manipulation technique, using mathematical algorithm to compensate for a teleradiology monitor's inability to provide the same contrast and depth as the original hard copy x-ray.

Low-pass filter—A filter for leveling out the borders in the screen display of radiology image.

MCU—Multipoint control unit is a device that enables participants at more than two sites to participate in voice or video calls.

Modem—Enables transmission of digital data over standard analog phone lines and cable video systems.

Modem access for remote diagnostic support—Indicates that a technical support center can call into the system on a separate modem line to perform remote diagnostics.

MPEG—Moving Picture Experts Group is a group of standards for compression and storage of motion video.

Multiplexer—A hardware device that divides a digital transmission stream into two or more subchannels.

Network—An assortment of electronic devices (computers, printers, scanners, and so on) connected (by wires or wireless) for mutual exchange of digital information.

Network interface—Connectivity options for the system.

Ocular tube adapter—Allows a camera to be mounted to any microscope.

OEM—Original equipment manufacturer.

PACS—Picture archiving and communication system is an image system that embraces all modalities (x-ray, CT, MR, nuclear medicine, ultrasound) and links users with display workstations over a high-speed network to an image server, an archive, printers, and radiology information systems.

PC platform for data/applications access and storage—Indicates if a personal computer (PC) is integrated into the system and is available for use by PC applications.

PC applications as a video input source—Indicates whether a separate PC application can be run on the system during a video conference and sent as the video picture to the far end.

PC applications conferencing—Describes the ability to run a PC application on one end of a videoconference and to share that application with the PC at the other end of the videoconference.

Peripheral devices—Attachments to videoconferencing systems to augment their communications or medical capabilities (such as electronic stethoscopes, oto-/ophthalmoscopes, dermacopes, and scanners).

PIP—Picture in picture allows both ends of the videoconference to be viewed simultaneously on a single monitor.

Presets—Determines how many predefined camera positions can be set.

Primary user interface device—Indicates what type of device is used to control the video conferencing system.

Printer interface—Allows data and images sent or received via the PC to be sent to a printer; enables reports, images, and data shared in a videoconference to be rendered as hard copy for record keeping and teaching purposes.

Store and forward—This technology refers to capturing information such as a diagnostic image through use of medical equipment or by scanning and digitizing the image. The information is then stored and sent to the interpreting physician. This can happen immediately or it can be saved and transmitted later.

Real time—Sends and receives audio or video data simultaneously, without more than a fraction of a second delay; collaborative real-time video patient management allows a remote practitioner to observe and discuss symptoms with a patient or another practitioner. Two-way workstations produce quality digital motion pictures across long distances. Equipment needs include a communications network and peripheral equipment, such as an electronic stethoscope, otoscope, ophthalmoscope, and dermascope. Endoscopy equipment is used by some telemedicine centers. Future applications will allow higher-speed transmission of cinematographic data, such as angiography and echocardiography. Remote sensing involves the transmission of patient information from one site to another, including electrocardiographic (ECG) and digital x-ray data.

Resolution—The level of detail that can be captured or displayed (such as teleradiology or interactive video).

Telehealth—The use of telecommunications equipment and communications networks for transferring health care information between participants at different locations.

Telenursing—A subset of telehealth that allows a nurse to deliver care through a telecommunications system.

Telepathology—Now allows rapid analysis of frozen sections. Experts at the transmission site are responsible for forwarding the image in a way that can be analyzed accurately by the receiving consultant.

Telepresence—Combines robotics and virtual reality to allow a surgeon equipped with special gloves and proper video and audio equipment to manipulate surgical instruments at a remote site.

Teledermatology—Associated with telepathology and can either be accomplished with a store and forward or interactive mode of transmission. Digital images may be taken of skin diseases and sent to a dermatologist for diagnosis.

Telepsychiatry—Utilizes "real-time" observations.

Teleradiology—Involves the transmission of medical images (x-ray, MRI, and so on) to a radiologist for interpretation. This was one of the first uses of telemedicine to receive full reimbursement under U.S. Medicare and is the single-most widely employed use of telemedicine in the country.

Telehomecare—Uses personal computers and video equipment to transmit data over ordinary telephone lines so that home health providers can monitor patients and provide care at a much lower cost than technologies that use wider bandwidth telephone lines and more complex equipment.

Video teleconferencing—Transmits sound and images between two or more sites, permitting participants to interact.

18

Documentation

Sandra K. Johnson

The purpose of the medical record is to document the course of a patient's medical evaluation, treatment, and change in condition, regardless of the delivery setting. In other words, it is the day-to-day log of events, thought processes, actions, and results of actions, reflecting the care that is given to a particular patient. It is the primary means of communication among members of the health care delivery team. Documentation is the basis for reimbursement, establishes a medical history, and creates an accurate legal record in the event of a claim.

The medical record is the chief, single-most important means by which a provider plans and coordinates the patient's care during an episode of illness. Documentation is the essence of the medical record and risk managers have a vested interest in preserving the record and in enhancing the quality of documentation therein. A long-standing challenge for health care risk managers is to ensure complete, appropriate, and legible entries in the medical record.

Because documentation is a written form of communication, change of shift reports and physicians signing off to partners or other covering physicians can be particularly vulnerable areas. Documentation issues can even extend to reports of supervisory changes of shift. If there is a written report it should be prepared as directed by risk management, especially if adverse outcomes or incidents are included. This information may not be protected and, quite likely, may be discoverable.

Medicine is not an exact science and requires the experience, expertise, and judgement of the health care providers rendering care. They evaluate objective data and render opinions based on their experience, expertise, and judgement. This is an invaluable source of information and should be shared appropriately with other care providers. Errors do occur when providers chart value judgments and opinions (subjective) without supportive evidence rather than factual (objective) information. If you have ever read a malpractice case transcript, you would realize how much a jury relies on documentation. What the providers document or fail to document will certainly influence the outcome of any case.

Brevity is a desirable documentation attribute; however, the essence of effective documentation is to write enough to adequately cover the issue and convey all facts. Essential information should never be sacrificed for brevity. As far as a jury is concerned, an action that is not documented is not performed. This is obviously significant in cases of informed consent, medication, or treatment entries, and is also true of "routine" observations.

When there is no recorded continuity of the patient's status and deterioration occurs, an absence of documentation can support a claim of negligence. The best way for health care providers to look at their charting is to view it as an attorney would and ask themselves, if it were presented as evidence to a jury, would it be thorough and convincing?

The rules, which govern documentation, come from several sources:

- Federal Statutes—Medicare and Medicaid mandate medical records content.
- State Statutes and State Licenser Requirements—These vary from state to state and address such things as content, timeliness, retention procedures, maintenance, destruction, and signing of medical records.
- Professional Practice Standards—Organizations such as the American Nurses Association and the American Medical Association identify specific standards for documentation.
- Specific Healthcare Facility Protocols—These are not laws, but the law tends to support such policies.
- Insurance companies, managed care organizations, and other third-party organizations also have standards and may refuse to pay claims if the care rendered is not properly or thoroughly documented.
- Joint Commission for Accreditation of Healthcare Organizations (JCAHO)—This organization has very specific standards for medical record documentation.

At the very least, the sources referenced above require that the medical record contain certain minimum categories of information and must be accurate and complete.

How Records Are Used Adversely in the Event of a Claim:

- To determine the extent of injury.
- To show a series of events leading up to a patient's injury in the hospital, and to help determine where to place responsibility.
- To show failure of staff to use information available in the patient's record, and to prove that the patient suffered as a result.
- To show failure to transfer important information from one department to another.
- To show the failure to write clear medical orders.

How Records Can Be Used in the Affirmative Defense of a Claim:

- Documents all relevant medical information. ·
- Substantiates the rationale for care provided or not provided.
- Highlights the professional interaction between professionals.
- Creates a timeline for care rendered.
- Documents the psychosocial needs and concerns of the patients and relevant others.
- Preserves the medical history of patient care.

OWNERSHIP OF MEDICAL RECORDS

The medical record is an unusual type of property, since both the patient and the health care facility or provider have an ownership interest. The health care facility or provider owns the actual record but the patient owns the information contained therein. The record must remain in the facility; therefore, the facility has the responsibility to exercise control in the release of the documentation itself or the information contained therein. Patients and others who have a vested interest have a right to access the information contained in the record but there are limitations on this right, which vary by state.

In today's environment, many documentation issues arise relative to mergers, acquisitions, divestitures, and HMO provider contracts. One such issue is ownership of medical records. This is illustrated by a recent decision in the Florida Fourth District Court of Appeals in *Humana Medical Plan v. Fischman,* decided in December 1999. Humana terminated an agreement with a physician provider. This decision was based on a contract provision, which stipulated that the medical records relating to Humana members, during the term of their enrollment, would be the property of Humana.

Despite many requests, the physician provided only those records for which he had received prior written consent from his patients. The physician argued that, according to Florida Statute 455.667, governing the disclosure of patient medical records, Humana did not qualify as the "owner" of the records. Humana conceded that F.S. 455.667 did not authorize it to obtain these records and admitted it did not obtain written authorization from the insured in advance. The Florida Appeals Court upheld the lower court's decision in favor of the physician. Cases such as this demonstrate the importance of reviewing contract language, in advance, regarding the issue of ownership of the medical record.

RELEASE OF RECORDS

Communications between physician and patient during the patient's treatment are generally afforded the protection of confidentiality. Records should be released only as authorized by state and federal laws. Failure to follow proper release procedures can result in significant liability.

For example, a Virginia hospital involved in litigation was directed by its general counsel to send a copy of a medical record to the Neonatal Intensive Care Nurse in preparation for her deposition. The patient filed a claim for improper release of medical records. The court held the filing of a lawsuit did not waive any of the patient's rights with regard to unlawful disclosure. The award was $100,000.

TAMPERING WITH MEDICAL RECORDS

If the medical record is altered, unintentionally or purposefully, it can be misleading to others and documentation as to the care may be disputed. Falsification, including alteration of medical records, can be grounds for a criminal indictment or a civil claim for damages. Changing inaccurate information, filling in omissions, altering dates and times, rewrites, destroying records, adding to someone else's notes, and correcting or amending notes can be construed as "tampering with medical records." This can expose the health care facility and health care provider to many different types of claims, raise many other issues, and, quite possibly, could result in the loss of affirmative defenses in a negligence claim. Additionally, tampering may be reportable to external agencies and professional licensing boards and to the corporate compliance officer.

In the state of Florida, the Agency for Health Care Administration has provided: "The Board of Nursing shall impose disciplinary penalties upon a determination that a licensee . . . (d) Has falsely represented the patient's chart, patient flow sheets, narcotic records, or nursing progress records, or otherwise misrepresented the facts on records relating directly to the patient."[1]

While this illustrates a specific state's handling of this issue, risk managers should be thoroughly familiar with their respective state's disciplinary rules, promulgated by professional regulatory and licensing boards.

The risk manager should be notified and should assist in the investigation whenever it is determined that a record has been altered. The appropriate committees need to be notified to take disciplinary action, if warranted. Reports should also be filed with the external licensing board as appropriate. In addition, the risk manager can assist in the preservation of records and deter alterations. If a patient experiences a poor or unexpected outcome, the urge to alter the record to make the care appear more appropriate may be overwhelming. With this in mind, the risk manager should rely on established policy and procedures (developed in conjunction with legal counsel, medical records, and risk management) to preserve the current in-use record. One effective way to decrease alterations is to copy the current record that discuses the poor outcome and keep the copy in the risk manager's office. If this policy is consistently followed on potentially serious incidents and events, the likelihood of alterations decreases as news of this policy circulates; no one want to be caught altering a record when a copy of the original preserved record is available. For records that are stored in the medical record department it is prudent to have a policy and procedure on the release or availability of records to any requesting and appropriate party. Depending on the status of an identified event (incident, notice of intent to sue, claim being made, lawsuit, and so on), the record could be sequestered with the original not being made available unless under direct supervision. This policy will prevent the inadvertent alterations or misplacement of the record (see Exhibit 18.1).

············

FORENSIC DOCUMENT EXAMINATION

On occasion, additions or alterations are made in health care facility records that may not appear on originals, or are added as late entries without proper designation. For many years forensic documentation techniques have been utilized to analyze handwriting and signatures and chronology of entries. The techniques have not changed but the scope of the analysis has broadened. The following is a brief list of such forensic techniques. These techniques can be expensive, depending on the number of documents to be reviewed. For more information, contact your defense attorney. These forensic techniques can recreate missing information, which may be used in support or defense of a claim:

- Electrostatic Detection Apparatus—can detect latent impressions on the underlying pages of a document that have been amended. *Advantage:* provides a hard copy. *Disadvantage:* the equipment is not portable.

- Ink Analysis—can be used if there is a possibility the medical record was altered and is the only method to establish identifiers of the ink type used for entry. *Advantage:* may provide conclusive evidence of fabrication, if the ink contains certain markers.

EXHIBIT 18.1.   **Request for Records**

Risk Management Department

☐ IPMC Region   ☐ NBMC Region   ☐ CSMC Region   ☐ BGMC Region   ☐ Western Region

TO: ☐ Pathology
           ☐ Central Business Office
           ☐ Radiology
           ☐ QA/UR
           ☐ Medical Records
           ☐ Other _____

FROM: Risk Management: _____   _____   _____
                                    Name   Telephone #   Location

RE: Patient: _____   Medical Record # _____

           Admitted: _____   Discharged: _____   DOB: _____

In anticipation that the above patient may file a claim against his/her health care providers:

☐ Secure all specimens, slides, and blocks (itemize below)
☐ Secure all films, scans, and x-rays (itemize below)
☐ Prepare   ☐ One   ☐ Two itemized copy(ies) of bill
               ☐ One   ☐ Two copy(ies) of detailed billing notes; forward all to risk management
☐ Forward a copy of the QA/UR review on this patient to the person identified above.
☐ Forward _____ copy(ies) of the medical records to: ☐ District   ☐ Regional Risk Management

☐ Number the pages of the original medical record prior to copying

DATE DONE	NUMBER	TYPE

Secured originals are not to be released out of your department or viewed without authorization by risk management.

Please complete and return to risk management within five days of receipt

Disadvantage: because tiny ink samples are lifted from the original document, damage does occur. Many inks have not been tagged and there is no standardization.

- Infrared Exams—used to identify ink types but cannot be used to show inks are the same. *Advantage:* does not destroy the document. *Disadvantages:* the equipment is not transportable, so original documents need to go to a laboratory. Cannot distinguish among all ink types.

- Identification of Date Markers—date markers can identify most paper copy machines, printers, and typewriter ribbons. *Advantage:* objective and reliable. *Disadvantage:* very time consuming.

In the event an expert handwriting analysis is undertaken, risk management must ensure integrity of chain of custody of evidence. Often, this requires hand-carrying the original medical record or document to the analyst and remaining with it until it is returned to the original custodian. The custodian could be called upon to testify to the maintenance of this chain of custody of evidence.

CHARTING AND DOCUMENTATION MODELS

Risk managers are frequently queried as to the best tool for documentation. The response is that no one method is superior. Successful documentation models generally utilize a combination of narration and flow charts. Whichever tool is selected, compliance and consistency is paramount and education is the key.

DOCUMENTATION CHALLENGES

It is the responsibility of each health care professional to comply with the facility's policies and procedures for documentation. Documentation must be objective and free of speculation. Plaintiff's attorneys look for gaps and inappropriate language to discredit or cast doubt on the credibility of medical records. Verbiage such as "unintentionally," "inadvertently," and "unexpectedly" are not appropriate, because they reflect a judgment that something untoward happened. Words such as "appeared," "apparently," and "seems to be" are not specific, and can be used by plaintiff's attorneys to cast doubt. Additionally, many words can have different meanings to different people. Terms such as "ate well" and "feels better" are examples. Use of nonspecific language leaves the author open to criticism. If it is necessary to use these words, then supplemental information is needed to provide clarity.

Uncooperative or Noncompliant Patients

When dealing with noncompliant patients and families (those who fail to follow instructions on diet, medications, use of safety devices, or who tamper with medical equipment), the risk manager should advise staff to thoroughly document these issues objectively, including all education and reinforcement provided. In the event it becomes necessary to "administratively or permanently discharge" or refuse further care, the usual practice is to orally advise the patient and family of the intent to do so, followed immediately by written notice, sent certified mail, and return receipt. This written notice should give a time frame (usually thirty days) for continued care (sometimes limited to emergency care during the time frame). It should also include references for continued care, such as several names and phone numbers of physicians in the same specialty and the name and phone numbers of the local or regional Medical/Doctor of Osteopathy (DO) Societies. In some instances, a copy of the pages of some medical specialty listings from the phone directory may be included. Remember to keep a copy for your file and the patient's medical record. It is recommended that the risk manager check with legal counsel to verify such a process complies with specific state statutes and case law.

Correcting Errors in the Medical Record

The acceptable method for correcting an error is to draw one line through the entry, initial, or sign and date it. Then place the correct information above the drawn-through entry. If space is not available or if the corrected information is too lengthy to place adjacent to the incorrect entry, the corrected note should be place in the appropriate place on the record (progress notes, nursing notes, and so on) and it should be contemporaneous with that date's notes. It should be dated and signed and the reason for the correction noted. Never obliterate, erase, or use correction fluid, as these methods of correction may appear to be an attempt to conceal the entry. It is strongly recommended that nothing be added to the record after an adverse outcome, patient complaint, or request for records. In these instances, the risk manager may advise staff to do a memorandum or clarification on an incident report form directed to the risk management department or legal counsel.

Patient or Family Requests for a Correction to the Record

Patients have a direct interest their medical record and are concerned about the accuracy and reliability of what is documented. In those infrequent situations when a patient or the patient's family or legal representative requests an entry in the medical record be changed or added, it is recommended that the risk manager and medical record director collaborate. Depending on the issue, the attending physician may need to be consulted.

If the issue is a name change, the legal document verifying the patient's correct name should be copied and placed in the specific medical record. It is recommended that changing a progress note or nurse's note not be done for any reason. If the patient or family insists, it is suggested that they put their requested change in writing, so that it can be added to the medical record, or attached to an incident report and maintained by risk management.

A policy should be in place to govern such requests from patients or patient's family members, developed and approved by both the medical records and risk management departments. In addition, the risk manager should be aware of any state laws that govern such requests for correction.

Hearsay

The risk manager should advise staff that "hearsay," or statements made by persons other than the author of the entry, should not be documented as if they were fact. Instead, the method by which the author of the entry heard the statement and the fact that it was heard from another source should be documented, such as "the husband stated that his wife does not take her medications as prescribed." This should be done in quotation marks as illustrated.

Telephone Calls and Telephone Advice in Physician Office Practices

It is recommended that medical advice not be given over the phone unless it is known who is on the other end. However, if medical advice is provided then documentation is key and will prove invaluable in the event the quality of care is called into question. At a minimum, the date, time, and content of the discussion should be documented. All telephone messages must be filed in the medical record in chronological order. E-mails and faxes should also be preserved and maintained in the medical record.

Adverse and Incident Documentation

The occurrence of an adverse event or incident must be documented in the medical record to avoid possible allegations of "willful concealment." Documentation should not be an expression of opinion but a factual account. Document what was seen, record the patient's vital signs, note the physical condition and mental condition (if appropriate), and the patient's subjective complaints. The documentation should also include notification of the patient's physician if patient care was involved.

The completion of an incident report should never be documented anywhere in the medical record, because it may be considered confidential under state law and may unnecessarily raise a "red flag."

Pagination of Medical Record

It is recommended that defense counsel be consulted prior to pagination (numbering of pages) of a medical record for purposes of litigation. Number only those documents related to the actual medical record. Correspondence, such as requests to release medical records and other health care facility records, should not be paginated.

When Doctors Do Not Arrive

The staff member or nurse should carefully document the date and time of the notification of the physician, the content of the discussion, and the name of the individual taking the message. Responses from the physician need to be similarly documented. If the situation is serious and the physician has not responded in a timely manner, the nurse must follow the "chain of command" and contact the nursing supervisor or other appropriate person, in accordance with facility procedures. In addition, notice should also be provided to the chief of staff. Physician notification is of particular importance in intensive care units, the emergency department, obstetric unit, substance abuse units, mental health, and pediatrics.

Countersignatures

Countersignatures imply that the health care provider has done more than just read and signed an entry or order. The countersignature connotes that the health care provider agrees with the patient care described. Whenever a health care provider signs an entry in a medical record, he or she is responsible for whatever is contained in the entry.

Abbreviations

Abbreviations save time; however, they may be misinterpreted if they are ambiguous. Health care providers should be instructed to use universally accepted standard medical abbreviations and those specifically approved by the individual health care facility.

Authentication

JCAHO provides that entries in medical records may be made only by individuals given that right, as defined in facility policies and procedures and medical staff bylaws. All entries should be dated and signed by the author. In addition to the full name, the professional title should be reflected, such as MD, PA, ARNP, RN, RT, and so on. It is suggested that policies, procedures, and bylaws be reviewed to ensure there is no conflict among these documents. JCAHO will survey a facility's performance against its own guidelines and discrepancies can result in Type 1 recommendations, which is a recommendation or group of recommendations that addresses insufficient or unsatisfactory standards compliance in a specific performance area. Resolution of Type 1 recommendations must be achieved within stipulated time frames for an organization to maintain its accreditation.

The Health Care Financing Administration (HCFA) requires documentation of verbal orders or entries requiring countersignatures be signed as soon as possible. One physician cannot sign for another, unless both share joint responsibility. Facility policies and medical staff bylaws should define whether documentation by house staff and allied health professionals requires countersignatures.

Documentation Pitfalls

Some common documentation errors include:

- Failure to correct inaccurate dates or times.
- Failure to correct errors by other caregivers.
- Failure to note important laboratory results.
- Failure to record patient negative responses to medication treatment.
- Failure to be informed of negative findings.
- Failure to follow up on noted changes in conditions.
- Failure to record review of prior medical histories.
- Failure to note pertinent discussions with patients.

To avoid these pitfalls, staff should be instructed to:

- Be accurate, clear, and concise.
- Record patient response to medication and treatment.
- *Never* document in advance.
- Avoid general characterizations and nonspecific terms.
- Avoid corrections, erasures, and obliterations. Do not use correction fluid.
- Enter date, time, and legible signature with professional designation on all entries.
- Write legibly at all times—printing is necessary.
- Avoid accusatory or jousting language.
- Use preassigned employee numbers in addition to signatures, if appropriate (a good idea for rotating residents, interns, and others).
- Do not leave spaces between entries and do not squeeze entries into small spaces.
- Avoid time gaps and omissions.
- Avoid late entries.

- Use proper procedure to correct errors.
- Document patient and family education.
- *Never* document the completion of an incident report.

············
RISK MANAGER'S ROLE

For both new or "seasoned" risk managers, there are always opportunities to enhance the quality of medical record documentation, such as being proactive to avoid litigation woes. The risk manager should be ever vigilant in assessing medical record documentation. As stated before, thorough, appropriate documentation has many uses, but in the world of litigation, the quality of a medical record can sink or save a case.

The following are some suggestions to the risk manager addressing documentation issues:

1. *Interview Nurse Executive, Medical Records Professional, Quality Improvement Coordinator, and Medical Staff Coordinator*—Identify and assess past documentation issues and problems.

2. Collect all forms, policies, procedures, protocols, and standards relating to documentation in the medical record, and maintain them in a documentation binder.

3. Review the minutes of the medical records committee and closed records review proceedings for the past twelve months to assess issues being discussed.

4. Contact defense counsel for advice on documentation issues that have been identified in claims, and obtain a copy of pertinent documentation case law.

5. Review the medical staff bylaws and rules and regulations regarding documentation requirements.

6. Ask the medical staff coordinator for the protocol for handling inappropriate physician documentation and determine whether any physician has been reported to the state board of medicine for altered medical records.

7. Determine if there is a committee responsible for reviewing or approving all new and revised forms used in the medical record. This committee is a valuable asset to the facility, especially if it has been given the authority to develop and require a standardized format for medical record forms, to eliminate duplication, to ascertain the need for new forms, and to determine how they will be used and to control costs. If such a committee does not exist, the risk manager should work with administration and nursing for the opportunity to review forms intended for the medical record from a risk exposure viewpoint.

8. The risk manager should become familiar with all federal and state statutes, health care providers' licensure documentation requirements, Medicare conditions of participation, and other standards regarding documentation. Copies of these documents should be maintained in the documentation binder.

9. The risk manager should develop a collaborative relationship with the personnel responsible for coding medical records and for responding to subpoenas and requests for records from attorneys. In addition, the medical records department should be advised as to which attorney requests should be copied to the risk manager prior to the release of medical records.

10. The risk manager's annual report should include a discussion on documentation issues.

11. Risk management and documentation issues should be a part of the general orientation for all new employees. In addition, the risk manager should give at least a one-hour presentation to all newly hired professional staff as a part of the clinical orientation.

12. The risk manager should be familiar with federal and state reporting requirements relating to communicable diseases, domestic violence, child and elder abuse, births and deaths, organ donation, gunshot wounds, and other trauma potentially related to criminal activity.

13. The risk manager should consider conducting random audits of medical records to identify documentation issues. In 1993, the American Society for Healthcare Risk Management (ASHRM) published a self-assessment questionnaire in its publication *Risk Management Pearls for Physicians: Managing Risk Through Effective Communication* (see Exhibit 18.2). This may be useful when developing a documentation audit tool.

14. According to a recent conversation with the publication manager of ASHRM, approximately 60 percent of their members have access to the Internet. With the increased pressure to be cost efficient, the necessity for real-time access to information, the advent of telemedicine, the development of the electronic medical record, all coupled with an increasing array of delivery sites, the risk manager is required to develop the necessary computer and technological skills necessary to maintain and advance in his or her position.

15. After all of the above has been collected and assessed, the risk manager should do an executive summary, prioritize, and develop a plan of action to address documentation issues. The action plan should be shared with the key stakeholders, including

---

EXHIBIT 18.2.   Questions for Medical Record Review

- If the patient alleged some deficiency in patient care, could the record negate the patient's story?
- Is there a logical process presented in the record for coming to a decision about the course of treatment?
- Would any reasonable physician be likely to come to the same conclusion?
- Were the appropriate tests ordered in a timely manner?
- Do test results verify the course of treatment?
- Was appropriate consultation obtained?
- Do the consultants' reports agree with the course of treatment?
- If not, were the differences clearly explained and justified in the record?
- Did the physician comment on the interventions and results of treatments provided by other professionals (such as, nurses and therapists) that may have affected the condition of the patient or the treatment regimen?
- Do the progress notes indicate that the patient knew about the benefits and reasonably expected risks and alternatives before giving consent to high-risk or invasive procedures?
- Are the entries accurately timed, dated, signed, and above all, legible?
- Do they reflect professionalism (for example, no evidence of infighting with other members of the care team)?
- Is there any evidence of alteration of the record? (Even if this was done innocently, juries frown on even the appearance of fraud or cover-up.)
- Looked at in its entirety, does the medical record present a complete picture of the care provided, with no ambiguity, no unexplainable gaps in time for treatments or medications, no illegible entries, and so on?[2]

---

the chief of staff, nurse executive, medical records, and quality improvement professionals, to gain their support and input. Finally, the risk manager should meet with the management team to review the action plan.

....

CONCLUSION

As stated at the beginning, the purpose of this chapter is to emphasize and reinforce the role of risk management in properly documenting the medical record and preserving its integrity. The medical record is a communication link, which benefits both patients and health care providers. It is the basis for successful documentation of treatment of the patient and it provides a valuable tool in the defense of a negligence claim.

The medical record can be a risk manager's strongest ally, if it is accurate, complete, and timely. It can be the worst enemy if improperly prepared or maintained. Ensuring the appropriateness, thoroughness, and timeliness of medical record documentation is a significant loss prevention activity that should be undertaken by the risk manager.

Endnotes

1. Florida Administrative Code 59S-8.005.

2. American Society for Healthcare Risk Management. *Management Pearls for Physicians: Managing Risk Through Effective Communication.* Chicago, Ill.: American Hospital Association, 1993.

19

Advertising Liability—A Growing Risk Management Concern

Grena G. Porto
Benjamin A. Post

In an increasingly competitive environment, marketing and advertising have become the keys to survival for many health care organizations. Changes brought about by market reform initiatives aimed at controlling rising health care costs have left many providers aggressively competing for shrinking health care dollars. The recent trend among managed care organizations to provide patients with greater choices of providers has served to sharpen the competitive instincts of many providers. Indeed, in a recent study conducted by the Society for Healthcare Strategy and Market Development (SHSMD), health care marketing professionals identified achieving higher market share as their biggest challenge.[1]

Even with economic pressure to limit expenditures, hospital-specific marketing budgets have grown steadily since 1996 and accounted for approximately 2 percent of total operating budgets in 1998.[2] This translates to mean annual expenditures of $469,400 for a single hospital and $1.155 million for combined hospitals and systems.

By far the largest component of any health care organization's marketing budget is advertising. According to SHSMD's study, hospitals' commercial advertising budgets grew by 25 percent from 1996 to 1997, and posted another 13 percent increase in 1998. That year, the average hospital spent $206,180 in advertising alone, while hospital system expenditures for advertising averaged $529,590. This comprised 36.6 percent of all marketing expenditures.

Beyond helping health care organizations to survive and thrive by increasing market share, marketing and advertising in health care can also serve important functions for patients. Health care organizations' marketing efforts often include initiatives in community relations, consumer awareness programs, and wellness campaigns aimed at improving community health. Direct-to-consumer advertising plays an important role in educating consumers about their health needs and encouraging them to seek necessary treatment. Of course, these outreach efforts must be balanced to ensure that vulnerable patients are not manipulated or that unreasonable expectations are not created.

Like other core activities of health care organizations, marketing and advertising initiatives often lead to increased risk and liability. This chapter will explore the types of liability that can arise from a health care organization's advertising practices and will offer strategies to help reduce or eliminate these risks.

THE LINK BETWEEN ADVERTISING AND TORT LIABILITY

Liability for making unjustified claims about quality of care or results of treatment is a relatively rare phenomenon. For liability to attach to generalized statements about quality of services provided, the statements would have to include very specific representations about success rates or specific outcomes. Merely advertising that a provider's care is of high quality will generally not result in liability for the advertiser.

A good illustration of this can be found in *Pulvers v. Kaiser Foundation Health,*[3] in which a California court held that an HMO was not liable for advertising that its care met "high standards of medical service." The plaintiff in this case died as a result of an alleged delay in performing a biopsy, which would have resulted in an earlier diagnosis, possibly extending the plaintiff's life. The plaintiff's survivors sued the HMO for breach of warranty, claiming that the HMO's advertisement that it provided care that met "high standards" warranted nonnegligent care. The court held that the HMO was not liable because it did not "clearly and unequivocally" warrant that a course of treatment would produce a certain result.

By far the greatest exposures that health care organizations face as a result of their advertising campaigns occur when statements made in advertising create vicarious liability for the acts of nonemployed physicians. When these advertising claims have the effect of creating the public perception that physicians associated with the health care organization are in fact agents of the health care organization, the health care organization assumes liability for their actions. That has been the finding of several courts that have considered this issue.

In *Pamperin v. Trinity Memorial Hospital,*[4] the Supreme Court of Wisconsin held that when a hospital holds itself out to the public as providing complete medical care, the hospital can be held liable under the doctrine of apparent authority for the negligent acts of the physicians retained by the hospital, even if those physicians are independent contractors. In this case, the plaintiff was admitted to the emergency room after falling and injuring his leg. He was admitted under the care of the emergency room physician on duty rather than his own personal physician. The plaintiff's leg was x-rayed and a minor fracture of the ankle was diagnosed. A splint was applied and the plaintiff was discharged to his home. He was subsequently found to have a fracture of the proximal tibia at the knee, which had not been detected by either the emergency room physician or the hospital's radiologist. The court reasoned that because the hospital held itself out and advertised that it provided complete care, the hospital created the appearance that the hospital itself treated emergency room patients.

The case of *Boyd v. Albert Einstein Medical Center*[5] further illustrates the role that advertising can play in establishing vicarious liability for a health care organization. In this case, the plaintiff alleged that the HMO advertised that its physicians and medical care providers were competent, and that they had been evaluated for a period of six months prior to being selected to participate in the HMO program. The HMO advertised that it was "an entire health care system [and] provides the physicians, hospital and other health professionals needed to maintain good health. [It] assures complete security, when illness or injury arises."

The Pennsylvania Superior Court held that the HMO advertisement caused the consumer to reasonably conclude that the physicians were HMO employees and further, that it caused the consumer to select the HMO rather than an individual physician. Because the consumer looked to the HMO for care in response to an invitation from the HMO, the physician was found to be an ostensible agent of the HMO and the HMO was liable for the negligence of the physicians.

A similar finding was reached by an Indiana court in *Sword v. NCK Hospitals, Inc.*[6] The plaintiff alleged negligent placement of an epidural catheter during childbirth, which caused severe headaches and numbness. She sued the hospital based on its advertisements. Norton Children's Hospital advertised in brochures that its Women's Pavilion was ". . . the most technically sophisticated birthplace in the region." It also advertised that it offered ". . . instant access to the specialized equipment and facilities, as well as to physician specialists in every area of pediatric medicine and surgery. Every maternity patient has a private room and the full availability of a special anesthesiology team, experienced and dedicated exclusively to OB patients."

The Supreme Court of Indiana held that the hospital was liable for the errors of the anesthesiologist. It based its ruling on the hospital's advertisements that portrayed the anesthesiologist as a hospital agent.

In *Martell v. St. Charles Hospital,*[7] the New York Supreme Court held that as hospitals advertise themselves as full-service facilities, they will be held liable for the negligence of those physicians who treat patients in the emergency room and other physicians whom the patient does not choose, such as emergency room physicians, radiologists, and anesthesiologists.

Thus, there is ample legal precedent for finding a health care organization liable for the acts of its independent contractors based on statements it makes in its advertising literature. However, advertising can result in liability in other ways as well. The Pennsylvania Supreme Court established a new precedent in advertising liability in the case of *McClellan v. HMO of Pennsylvania.*[8] Following the ruling in *Boyd,* the court held this HMO liable under a theory of ostensible agency for the physician's negligence since the HMO advertised that it carefully screened its physicians. But it went one step further by holding that the HMO misrepresented the quality of its physicians.

The plaintiff's primary care physician failed to test and diagnose a malignant melanoma and the plaintiff subsequently died. Suit was brought against the physician as well as the HMO alleging that the physician was not qualified and failed to make referrals. The suit included allegations of fraud against the HMO for intentionally misrepresenting that the physician was qualified. The HMO advertised that each and every primary care physician satisfied criteria for participation as a qualified physician after passing rigorous screening criteria and that the primary care physician would promptly and properly refer patients to appropriate specialists.

The court held that the plaintiff not only had a cause of action against the HMO for the negligence of the physicians to whom it referred in its advertisements, the plaintiff also had a cause of action against the HMO for misrepresentation in its advertising that the physicians were competent, carefully screened, and made prompt referrals.

••••••••••••

REGULATORY IMPLICATIONS OF HEALTH CARE ADVERTISING PRACTICES

In addition to civil liability in the form of tort claims by patients, health care organizations also face potential regulatory liability for their advertising practices. The Federal Trade Commission (FTC) empowered by the federal government to regulate advertising practices can take action against any entity that it deems has engaged in "false advertising."

According to the FTC, a health care provider's advertising claims are false and misleading when there is no competent and reliable scientific evidence to substantiate the claims. *In the Matter of NME Hospitals*[9] is a case in which the FTC concluded that the health care provider engaged in false advertising because there was no scientific evidence to support the claims made.

NME Hospitals placed advertisements in periodicals of general circulation and mailed promotional materials to potential patients regarding services offered by the Continent Ostomy Center, which offered surgical treatment of bowel-related diseases, including ulcerative colitis. The advertisements made claims regarding the success of the surgical procedures performed by NME as well as the lack of certain known complications of the procedure. The advertisements alleged that NME's surgical procedure was ". . . recognized as the most successful alternative" to other comparable surgeries. Additionally, the advertisements claimed that there was more than a 50 percent chance that patients who had a particular procedure would not require additional surgery.

The FTC alleged that NME Hospitals misrepresented its success in treating ulcerative colitis and the comparative superiority of its procedure to other surgical procedures used to treat the disease. NME Hospitals did not have scientific evidence to support its claims, and the FTC therefore found its advertisement to be false and misleading.

The case involving Cancer Treatment Centers of America, Inc.,[10] is another illustration of the type of advertising that the FTC finds false and misleading. Cancer Treatment Centers of America was a group of three corporations, including a hospital, that offered cancer treatment and related health care services.

The hospital distributed a promotional brochure, which stated in part, ". . . Statistically our five-year survivorship is among the highest documented." The brochures also claimed that through a form of treatment known as whole body hyperthermia, the hospital treated certain forms of cancer that were unresponsive to conventional treatment. They further claimed that through a treatment called brachytherapy, the chances of survival for lung cancer patients were improved. The brochures included testamentary advertisements regarding the experience of patients.

The FTC found that this advertisement was a representation that statistical evidence demonstrated that the five-year survivorship rate for cancer patients in Cancer Treatment Centers of America's hospitals was among the highest recorded rates of survivorship for cancer patients. The FTC found this to be false and misleading because Cancer Treatment Centers of America did not have a reasonable basis, including scientific evidence, to support or substantiate these representations. The FTC also found the testamentary claims to be false and misleading because they did not represent the typical or ordinary experience of members of the public who use the program. All testamentary advertising must meet this criterion unless: (1) there is scientific evidence to show that this is a typical experience; (2) there is a disclosure of generally expected results; or, (3) there is a disclosure of limited applicability, indicating that one should not expect similar results.

The Cancer Treatment Centers of America case is also noteworthy because it involved false and misleading claims of endorsement by an independent medical organization. In connection with its whole body hyperthermia treatment, Cancer Treatment Centers of America advertised that it had ". . . received or was in the process of applying for accreditation, approval, or certification from the Joint Commission on Accreditation of Healthcare Organizations, the American College of Surgeons, the Association of Community Cancer Centers, and the College of American Pathology." In fact, Cancer Treatment Centers of America had not received any accreditation or approval from any of these organizations and no independent organization had approved the treatment. The FTC found these claims to be false and misleading as well.

The FTC can impose fines as well as other sanctions for violations of its regulations. Fines and penalties can vary but may not exceed $10,000 per violation.[11] Sanctions usually take the form of a consent and agreement order to cease and desist, a settlement that requires the advertiser to stop the objectionable advertising. Consent orders also frequently require the advertiser to maintain all documents that are relied upon in making a claim in advertising about the information covered in the agreement. A consent order is not a finding of fact and, unlike other types of settlements, is a matter of public record. They are published in the Federal Register before they become binding orders.

············

MANAGING ADVERTISING LIABILITY EXPOSURES— A RISK MANAGEMENT ROAD MAP

Marketing and advertising initiatives are critical to a health care organization's survival and, like other critical activities, they increase the risk of liability. However, as mentioned early in this chapter, marketing and advertising initiatives also provide an important service for patients. Thus, health care risk management professionals must approach advertising liability not as a "necessary evil," but as a risk associated with one of the organization's core functions that must be managed. As with other liability exposures, advertising liability can be managed with systematic approach for identification of risks and appropriate intervention to reduce or eliminate these risks.

Some key strategies for managing the risks associated with advertising are:

● Become familiar with professional standards relating to health care marketing and advertising practices. The American Hospital Association issued a management advisory on advertising for health care facilities in 1990.[12] The American Marketing Association has also developed standards that cover all aspects of marketing and advertising.[13] These documents provide standards and useful guidance that should be followed in designing advertising campaign strategies.

● Become familiar with the organization's marketing philosophy and planned advertising initiatives. This will provide the context for the decisions made and the priorities established in connection with the organization's marketing plan.

● Develop a partnership with the person responsible for the organization's marketing activities and become a resource for risk management implications of advertising campaigns and marketing activities.

● Develop a system for early review of proposed advertising initiatives to identify potential exposures.

● Avoid any statements about success rates or specific outcomes of treatments.

● Pay particular attention to advertising campaigns that may create the appearance of an agency relationship with independent contractors, particularly emergency room physicians, anesthesiologists, radiologists, pathologists, and other providers whom the patient does not specifically select. Ensure that appropriate notations in the advertising campaign spell out the nature of the relationship, and make sure that prominently posted signs and other notices to patients reinforce this message.

• If the appearance of an agency relationship is inevitable or necessary in the advertising campaign, develop indemnification language or other risk financing strategies to cover any resulting additional exposures.

• If the name of a specific physician or other provider is to be used in advertising, assume that the organization will be held vicariously liable for the acts of that provider. Plan risk financing strategies accordingly.

• Avoid any representations about the high quality of providers associated with the organization, and ensure that all providers are properly credentialed.

• Work with the organization's corporate compliance officer to ensure that all advertising campaigns meet the organization's standard for corporate integrity.

・・・・・・・・・・・

CONCLUSION

By far the greatest exposures that health care organizations face as a result of their advertising campaigns occur when statements made in advertising create vicarious liability for the acts of nonemployed physicians. When these advertising claims have the effect of creating the public perception that physicians associated with the health care organization are in fact agents of the health care organization, the health care organization assumes liability for their actions.

In addition to civil liability in the form of tort claims by patients, health care organizations also face potential regulatory liability for their advertising practices. The Federal Trade Commission (FTC) empowered by the federal government to regulate advertising practices can take action against any entity that it deems has engaged in "false advertising." The FTC can impose fines as well as other sanctions for violations of its regulations.

Risk managers can manage the increased liability risks associated with the organization's advertising activities by adopting a systematic approach for the identification of these risks and implementing appropriate interventions. This is best accomplished by developing and maintaining collaborative relationships with those responsible for the organization's marketing activities. By becoming a resource to those involved in developing marketing initiatives, the risk manager becomes a valuable partner in the process and helps the organization to avoid unnecessary risk.

Endnotes

1. *Marketing by the Numbers: Trends in Healthcare Marketing and Advertising Expenditures.* Chicago: Society for Healthcare Strategy and Market Development, 1998.

2. *Ibid.*

3. *Pulvers v. Kaiser Foundation Health,* 160 Cal. Rptr. 392 (Cal. Ct. App., 1979).

4. *Pamperin v. Trinity Memorial Hospital,* 423 N.W. 848 (Wisc., 1988).

5. *Boyd v. Albert Einstein Medical Center,* 547 A.2d 1229 (Pa. Super., 1988).

6. *Sword v. NCK Hospitals, Inc.,* 714 N.E.2d 142 (Ind., 1999).

7. *Martell v. St. Charles Hospital,* 523 N.Y.S2d 342 (N.Y., 1987).

8. *McClellan v. HMO of Pennsylvania,* 604 A2d. 1053 (Pa. Super., 1992).

9. *In the Matter of NME Hospitals,* 115 FTC 7998 (1992).

10. *In the Matter of Cancer Treatment Centers of America, Inc.,* 121 FTC 692 (1996).

11. 15 USC §45.

12. "Advertising by Health Care Facilities." Chicago: American Hospital Association *Management Advisory,* 1990.

13. *Code of Ethics,* Chicago: The Alliance for Healthcare Strategy and Marketing, 1999.

20

Corporate Compliance—
A Risk Management Framework

Jeffrey F. Driver
Glenn T. Troyer

To some health care risk managers, the term "corporate compliance" conjures visions of an incomprehensible matrix of laws and regulations that defy logic and control by even the most seasoned health care professional. Yet, corporate compliance is one of the most significant risk exposures facing a health care enterprise and therefore commands the risk manager's attention and comprehension. Many health care businesses have established "corporate compliance programs" and designated or hired "compliance officers" in order to proactively address fraud, abuse, and administrative error that has been reported to be widespread in the health care industry. Risk management professionals have various levels of involvement in compliance activities. In some health care settings, the risk management professional plays a central role in the compliance process or may even be designated the corporate compliance officer. In others, the role is more collaborative or supportive. In all settings, however, the contribution of the risk management professional and the skills that they bring to the compliance program are invaluable to protecting an organization and individuals from, among other things, financial loss, diminution of reputation, and criminal prosecution.

The purpose of this chapter is to eliminate some of the mystery surrounding compliance programs and activities. Afterall, fraud and abuse enforcement activities are just one of the several newer loss exposures facing health care organizations. This chapter first arms the risk management professional with a compliance fundamental primer on the fraud and abuse statutory and regulatory framework that is essential for the risk management professional working within a compliance program or collaborating on specific compliance situations. Included in this review are a listing and description of key federal and state agencies and their contractors. The second half of the chapter is devoted to applying what is learned in the first half of the chapter. Specifically, armed with compliance knowledge, the risk management professional can utilize familiar loss control and risk-financing strategies to approach compliance program development and solve specific compliance problems.

In summary, compliance management is *risk management* in the new millennium—with a few new twists. The "twists" include a new set of rules (laws and regulations), a host of government agencies to enforce the rules, and a prescribed yet flexible formula for implementing and managing a compliance program defined by the Office of the Inspector General (OIG) and the United States Sentencing Guidelines (USSG). Once the new twists are learned, application of tried-and-true risk management techniques empower compliance and risk management professionals to handle just about any problem facing the health care organization.

The terms "fraud" and "abuse" are often misused and overused to characterize many types of legal conduct. Consequently, an understanding of their use within specific statutes is essential to identify what conduct is legal and what is not.

·············
HEALTH CARE FRAUD AND ABUSE

Health care fraud, as defined by the Health Insurance Portability and Accountability Act of 1996 (HIPAA), is the knowing and willful execution or attempt to execute a scheme to defraud a health care benefit program to obtain, by means of false or fraudulent representations or promises, any money or other property owned by a health care benefit program.[1] Abuse generally encompasses incidents or practices that are inconsistent with sound fiscal, business, or medical practices that may result directly or indirectly in unnecessary program costs, improper payment, or payment for services that fail to meet professional standards of care or that are medically necessary.[2]

Taken together, some examples of the types of activities and conduct that are typically considered to be either fraudulent or abusive under the various applicable fraud and abuse statutes and regulations include:

- False claims and fraudulent billing.
- Bribes, kickbacks, excessive or unreasonable discounts and rebates, and profit-sharing agreements.
- Payment to induce referrals.
- Medical neglect of a patient.[3]

STATUTORY AND REGULATORY FRAMEWORK

The following discussion will focus on those criminal and civil statutes and their regulations that are used to prosecute fraud and abuse cases. Of these, the most commonly used enforcement laws are the following: (1) the 1977 Medicare-Medicaid Anti-Fraud and Abuse Amendment to the Social Security Act, including the anti-kickback provisions; (2) the Criminal False Claims Act; (3) the Civil False Claims Act; (4) the Civil Monetary Penalties Act; and (5) program exclusion provisions of the Social Security Act.

Anti-Kickback Statute   In general, the Anti-Kickback Statute, found at 42 U.S.C. § 1320a-7a, prohibits soliciting or receiving directly or indirectly communication in return for a referral for program reimbursable items or services as well as the giving of remuneration with intent to induce referrals for program reimbursable services to induce patient referrals. More specifically, the statute makes it unlawful for a provider to knowingly or willfully solicit, receive, offer, or pay remuneration for services paid for under any federal health care program.[4] Remuneration includes "a kickback, bribe or rebate."[5] The purpose of the statute is to prevent the misuse and overutilization of services paid for by federally funded health care programs.[6]

The Anti-Kickback Statute has both a criminal and civil component. The criminal component of the statute makes violation of the Anti-Kickback Statute a felony punishable by imprisonment and/or fine.[7] The civil component is associated with the Civil Monetary Penalty Law (CMPL), discussed in the next section.[8] Penalties for violating the Anti-Kickback Statute may also include mandatory or permissive exclusion from both federal and state programs.[9]

Regulations In 1991, OIG promulgated eleven Safe Harbor Regulations, which list certain types of transactions that are immune from federal prosecution under the Anti-Kickback Statute. In 1992, two additional safe harbors were added, and in 1996, those interim final rules were issued in final form.[10] On November 19, 1999, the OIG issued eight new Safe Harbor Regulations for a total of twenty-one as of this writing.[11] These Safe Harbor Regulations do not expand the scope of activities prohibited by the statute, but are designed to exclude transactions from prosecution that would, by their very nature, have no fraudulent or abuse impact on the health care program.[12] Each of the Safe Harbor proposals is based on the OIG's consideration of the effect that the proposal would have on important factors such as access, quality, competition, costs, and the potential for overutilization.[13]

As of November 19, 1999, the OIG had issued Safe Harbor Regulations for the following areas:

1. Investments in large publicly traded entities.*†
2. Investments in smaller ventures.*†
3. Lease of space and equipment rental.*†
4. Personal services and management contracts.*†
5. Sale of practitioner practice.†
6. Referral services.*†
7. Warranties.†
8. Discounts.*†
9. Employee compensation.†
10. Group purchasing organizations.†
11. Waiver of beneficiary coinsurance and deductible amounts.†
12. Managed care safe harbors.
13. Risk sharing arrangements.
14. Investments in underserved areas.
15. Practitioner recruitment in underserved areas.
16. Obstetrical malpractice insurance subsidies for underserved areas.
17. Sales of physician practices to hospitals in underserved areas.

---

*Clarified in 11/19/99 publication.[14]
†1991 Safe Harbors.

18. Investments in ambulatory surgical centers.

19. Investments in group practices.

20. Referral arrangements for specialty services.

21. Cooperative hospital service organizations.

A detailed list of the original Safe Harbor Regulations can be found at 42 CFR §1001.952.

OIG Advisory Opinions   HIPAA requires the Secretary of the Department of Health and Human Services (DHHS) to issue advisory opinions when a request is properly submitted.[15] The OIG, at the request of interested parties, will issue advisory opinions, which address specific questions arising out of the application of the Anti-Kickback statute.[16] These opinions are only binding on the Secretary and the party seeking the opinion.[17] The procedure for submitting a request for an opinion can be found at 63 Fed. Reg. 38,311 (July 16, 1998). Examples of questions which must be answered by advisory opinions include questions regarding what constitutes prohibited remuneration, satisfaction of criteria for exceptions to the statute, and satisfaction of criteria for safe harbor regulations. The OIG advisory opinions will not address factual questions like fair market value of goods or questions concerning certain employment relationships.

Fraud Alerts   Periodically, the OIG will issue fraud alerts interpreting the application of the Anti-Kickback Statute to certain practices observed throughout the industry. Fraud alerts identify questionable features of certain transactions.[18] While fraud alerts yield significant insight and understanding of the analysis used in enforcing the statute, they are not binding, and do not carry the weight of judicial precedent or advisory opinions.[19] Fraud alerts, however, still also serve as guidance for structuring payments and other financial relationships.[20] The fraud alerts are in place to encourage reporting of suspected violations to the government.[21] HIPAA also requires the OIG to publish a procedure for receiving public requests for additional fraud alerts.[22]

Stark I and II: The Ethics in Patient Referrals Act   Stark I, at 42 USC §1395nn, originally prohibited physicians from referring Medicare or Medicaid patients to clinical labs in which the physician has a financial interest. Under Stark I, labs were also prohibited from billing for services performed as a result of the prohibited referral.[23] In 1993, an amendment to section 1877 of the Social Security Act (Stark II) expanded the prohibited referrals to Medicare and Medicaid patients by creating ten additional "designated health services."[24] As a result, Stark II makes it unlawful for a physician, or any member of the physician's immediate family who has a financial relationship with an entity, to make referrals for use of the following designated health services:

- Clinical lab services.

- Physical therapy.

- Occupational therapy.

- Radiology services, including MRIs, computerized axial tomography scans, and ultrasound services.

- Radiation therapy services and supplies.

- DME and supplies.

- Parenteral and enteral nutrients, equipment, and supplies.

- Prosthetics, orthotics, and prosthetic devices.
- Home health services and supplies.
- Outpatient prescription drugs.
- Inpatient and outpatient hospital services.[25]

The intent of the Stark bills was to deter overutilization, referral to substandard providers, and unfair competition. Exceptions to Stark II apply to certain ownership or investment financial relationships and compensation arrangements.[26]

Violations of Stark II are civil in nature and carry the imposition of civil monetary penalties of between $5,000 and $10,000 per illegally referred claim.

HCFA Advisory Opinions   The Health Care Financing Administration (HCFA), at the request of interested parties, may issue advisory opinions about whether proposed transactions or relationships violate Stark I or II.[27] Opinions issued are only binding on the Secretary of Health and Human Services and the party requesting the opinion.[28] HCFA Advisory Opinions are case specific and intended to address the facts of a particular arrangement as described by the party requesting the information.[29] Opinions may include information on whether the party has an unexpected financial relationship with an entity, but will not issue opinions regarding a party's possible awareness that certain referrals violated Stark I or II regulations.[30]

False Claims Act   The False Claims Act, promulgated at 31 USC §3729, prohibits a person from knowingly submitting a false or fraudulent claim to the government for payment or approval. Specifically, seven types of activities are prohibited. These include:

- Presenting a false claim.
- Making or using a false statement to get a claim paid.
- Conspiracy involving federal claims.
- Embezzlement by government contractors.
- False certification of deliveries to the government.
- Purchase on the black market.
- Reverse false claims (for example, a provider withholds information or makes false statements to avoid or reduce an obligation to the government).[31]

The statute requires actual knowledge of information, deliberate ignorance of the truth of information, and reckless disregard of the truth of information.[32] Certain instances of gross negligence may also be considered a violation of the act.[33] Although the requisite intent is high and comparable to most criminal standards, this act is civil in nature. Under the act, violation is punishable by civil penalties of not less than $5,000 and not more than $10,000, plus three times the amount of damages sustained by the government.[34] For some examples, refer to: *U.S. v. Oncology Associates, P.C.*, 1999 WL 1215725 (4th Cir. 1999); *U.S. v. Columbia / HCA Healthcare Corp.*, 125 F.3d 899 (5th Cir. 1997); *U.S. v. Epic Healthcare Management Group*, 193 F.3d 304 (5th Cir. 1999); *Luckey v. Baxter Health Care Corp.*, 183 F.3d 730 (7th Cir. 1999).

However, criminal penalties may also be imposed under the Criminal False Claims Act. This promulgation is separate from the Medicare/Medicaid Antifraud and Abuse laws. While the Criminal False Claims Act is often used to prosecute fraudulent tax returns and Social Security fraud, there are several instances in which Medicare and Medicaid fraud have also been prosecuted.[35] Violation of the Criminal False Claims Act is a felony and penalties include a maximum prison sentence of five years per violation as well as a fine.[36] For some examples, refer to: *U.S. v. Bupack,* MM Cases 600 (D.C. Cir. 1997); *Pani v. Empire Blue Cross & Blue Shield,* MM Cases 6084 (2nd Cir. 1998); *U.S. v. Universal Rehabilitation Services,* 6158 (3rd Cir. 1999); *U.S. v. Guilliard,* MM Cases 6018 (11th Cir. 1998).

Qui Tam Lawsuits   Under the False Claims Act, the federal government or any person may bring a civil action for violation of the act.[37] *Qui Tam* lawsuits are actions brought by a person or entity other than the United States Attorney General.[38] *Qui Tam* lawsuits represent the United States government's efforts to control widespread fraud. *Qui Tam* provisions offer an incentive for whistleblowers to come forward to help the government discover and prosecute fraudulent claims by awarding them a percentage of the recovery.[39] A copy of the proposed complaint, together with substantial evidence and information about the allegations, is required to be filed with the United States Attorney's Office before an action may proceed.[40] Initially, all evidence will be considered, in private, by the United States Attorney who, within sixty days, must make a determination concerning whether or not the government will proceed against the violator on behalf of the whistleblower. If the government declines, the whistleblower may, nevertheless, move forward and file the complaint using private legal counsel.

Civil Monetary Penalties Act   Section 1128A of the Social Security Act found at 42 U.S.C. 1320a-7a is also known as the Civil Money Penalties Act (CMP Act), gives the Secretary of DHHS the authority to impose and assess civil money penalties for fraud and abuse against federal health care programs.[41] Penalties may apply to individuals, entities, agencies, or organizations that knowingly present prohibited, false, or improper claim for medical care, items, or services.[42] Penalties imposed under the CMP Act may be imposed in addition to other penalties that may be imposed by other laws.[43] Penalties vary depending on which section of the CMP Act is violated and range from $10,000 to $50,000.[44] In addition, for any offense, violators may not be assessed penalties more than three times the amount claimed for each item or service.[45]

In 1996, HIPAA incorporated certain changes into the CMP Act that allow civil monetary sanctions for fraudulent activity in the delivery of health care in *any* federal program.[46] HIPAA also clarifies the intent requirement of the CMP Act. It is now clear that the CMP Act can be violated if an action is completed with conscious disregard of the law.[47] In other words, the CMP Act now uses a "should have known" standard. The standard is satisfied when a person acts in deliberate ignorance with respect to the information, or acts in reckless disregard of the truth or falsity of the information.[48]

State Statutes   Additionally, many states have enacted legislation, which address health care fraud and abuse and antireferral provisions. Over thirty states have enacted antireferral laws, based on one of three models. Some state antireferral laws are modeled after federal Stark legislation. Other states have either disclosure statutes that do not prohibit physician ownership interests, but require disclosure of that interest; or statutes that allow self-referrals in special circumstances such as where the community needs dictate self-referral.[49] Additionally, some states have Medical Practice Acts that address referral practices by prohibiting "fee-splitting," with penalties such as revocation or suspension of physicians' licenses.[50]

Health care fraud charges may be brought under a variety of state statutes including theft, larceny, and forgery. However, many states (approximately twenty-six) have laws specifically directed at Medicaid fraud.[51] In addition, some states have included elements that specifically address false statements or claims, kickbacks and referrals, and civil and criminal penalties. Recently, some states (Alaska, Florida, and Rhode Island) have enacted statutes, that require access to records for fraud investigations. Finally, some states have employed the use of medical neglect statutes to support fraudulent billing cases.

Key Federal and State Agencies and Contractors

While a variety of governmental agencies, bureaus, and divisions may become involved in enforcement activities, the following is a list of those most commonly involved.

The Federal Bureau of Investigations   The Federal Bureau of Investigations (FBI) is a federal agency with broad authority to investigate crimes against the United States. As a result, the FBI may become involved in conducting investigations involving criminal aspects of health care fraud and abuse violations. The FBI has authority to execute warrants, make arrests, and pursue seizures, but typically has little or no involvement with civil health care fraud and abuse claims.

Office of Inspector General   The Office of the Inspector General (OIG) of the DHHS is responsible for conducting and supervising audits and investigations of entities that are under the control of DHHS. Organizations under the investigative authority of the OIG include those organizations that receive federal funding or payment from federal programs such as Social Security, Medicare, Medicaid, and Public Health Services. The OIG does not investigate private sector health care fraud. There are five divisions within the OIG, each responsible for duties affiliated with that office, including auditing, inspection, investigation, enforcement and compliance, and counsel. Additionally, the OIG oversees state Medicaid fraud control units. The OIG is also responsible for reporting all exclusions and monetary penalties to state licensing boards, as well as publishing quarterly lists of excluded providers. OIG agents cannot, however, execute search warrants or make arrests.

State Medicaid Fraud Units   State Medicaid fraud units are involved in both the criminal and civil aspects of health care fraud and abuse, and have the authority to prosecute violations of fraud and abuse statutes and regulations statewide. These agencies typically employ attorneys, investigators, and auditors, and operate as part of the state attorney general's office. Each state is required to have a Medicaid fraud control unit, which operates as a separate entity from the state Medicaid agency. The Medicaid fraud unit's primary duties include investigation of allegations of fraud, abuse, or neglect of patients.

Intermediary Fraud Units   Intermediary fraud units are responsible for assisting Medicare in diminishing the instances of fraud and abuse. Intermediary fraud units develop cases of suspected fraud and refer those cases to the OIG. The OIG, and not the fraud units, will make the determination of whether federal criminal or civil violations have occurred.

Adult Protective Service Agency   Adult protective services may be a division of state government with a primary duty to investigate instances of neglect and abuse involving the elderly or disabled. Since abuse may not be limited to physical abuse, but may logically include fraud or misrepresentations involving finances, such agencies may also investigate charges of Medicare or Medicaid fraud and abuse that result from health care services rendered to the elderly or disabled.

State Department of Health   Pursuant to authority granted by the DHHS, state departments or boards of health are entrusted with the authority to take all necessary steps to promote public health. This authority includes promulgation of and enforcement of health regulations (such as, conditions of participation in the Medicare programs, state licensure requirements, and so on), and may be delegated to local or county health agencies.[52] As such, state departments of health may take action to ensure that state and federal health care regulations and statutes are enforced.

Local Police Agencies   Local police agencies and/or sheriff's departments are entrusted with the primary duty of law enforcement, as a representative of the state's administrative department. Police officers' powers and duties include preserving peace and enforcing criminal law, by arresting and committing to jail all felons, traitors, and violators.[53] Under those sections of the Social Security Act, which impose criminal penalties for violations of health care laws, police officers may arrest offenders and commit them to prison.

United States Attorneys Office   United States attorneys are executive officials of the government under the direction of the U.S. attorney General. U.S. attorneys are appointed by judicial district and are charged with faithful execution of laws for the protection of the interest of the United States.[54] U.S. attorneys may act as the prosecuting attorney for the United States, and may therefore prosecute all criminal cases, and participate as a representative of the United States in civil matters that involve violations of federal health care laws.

County Prosecutors   County prosecutors are generally prosecuting attorneys whose duties are proscribed by state laws and constitutions and include prosecuting criminal charges on behalf of the state in a specific county or district. These attorneys act as representatives of the state to advocate public interests.[55] County prosecutors may participate in enforcing violations of health care laws in local or county courts on behalf of the state.

State Attorneys General   The attorney general in each state is the chief law officer of the state and has the duty of prosecuting all suits in which the state government is involved. State attorneys general also advise the governor and other administrative offices and officials in legal matters.[56] State attorneys general may, therefore, act as prosecutors or advocates on behalf of the state as well as issue advisory opinions in matters involving health care regulations.

....

A RISK MANAGEMENT FRAMEWORK FOR COMPLIANCE MANAGEMENT

Risk management professionals can be involved with compliance activities directly as a designated compliance officer, or as an internal resource to a compliance department or compliance officer. In either event, the risk management professional should be well versed in the general law previously outlined in this chapter, as well as the structure and goals of their organization's compliance program. Armed with this knowledge, the risk management professional can provide valuable input to the health care organization's compliance process, as well as tackle the inevitable compliance problems that intersect with traditional risk management problems.

Why Compliance Programs?

The primary purpose of a compliance program is to promote adherence to applicable federal and state law, and the program requirements of federal, state, and private health plans. Fundamentally, compliance program efforts should be designed to establish a culture that promotes the detection and resolution of conduct that does not conform to federal and state law—eventually, becoming the fabric of the organization's routine operations. The establishment of a compliance program in addition to an existing risk management program should, in theory, reduce the risk of unlawful or improper conduct. Most significantly, the OIG, following the Federal Sentencing Guidelines, will consider the existence of an effective compliance program that predates any governmental investigation when addressing the appropriateness of administrative penalties.[57]

Specifically, in 1991, the United States Sentencing Commission issued a series of guidelines[58] that judges must use when sentencing organizations that are convicted of federal crimes.[59] One provision of the Federal Sentencing Guidelines provides for more lenient punishment for organizations that adopt effective programs for detecting and preventing criminal conduct.[60] Also, the presence of an effective compliance program may influence the OIG when assessing whether to impose a permissive exclusion against a health care entity that engaged in impermissible activities.[61] Finally, the civil act provides that a person that has violated the act, but who voluntarily discloses the violation to the government, in certain circumstances, will be subject to not less than double (as opposed to treble) damages.[62]

United States Sentencing Guidelines Determine Minimum Compliance Program Elements

The Federal Sentencing Guidelines form the basis for the OIG-recommended compliance program elements.[63] The OIG believes that every hospital, whether small or large, urban or rural, for-profit or not-for-profit, multihospital or stand-alone, and integrated delivery systems should implement the recommended elements by tailoring them to fit the needs and financial realities of a particular hospital.[64] These essential elements include:

1. The development and distribution of written standards of conduct (often referred to as a "code of conduct").

2. The development of written policies and procedures that promote the hospital's commitment to compliance (including adherence to compliance as an element in evaluating managers and employees; developing medical and business record policies; and so on) and that address specific areas of potential fraud (such as claims development and submission processes, code gaming, and financial relationships with physicians and other health care professionals).

3. The designation of a chief compliance officer charged with the responsibility of operating and monitoring the compliance program, and who has access and directly reports to the CEO and the governing body.

4. The designation of a corporate compliance committee.

5. The development and implementation of regular, effective education, and training.

6. The maintenance of a process, such as a hotline, to receive complaints.

7. The adoption of procedures to protect the anonymity of complainants and to protect whistleblowers from retaliation.

8. The development of a system to respond to allegations of improper or illegal activities.

9. Enforcement of appropriate disciplinary action against employees who have violated internal compliance policies, applicable statutes, regulation, or federal health care program requirements.

10. The use of audits and monitoring as well as other evaluation techniques to audit and monitor compliance and assist in the resolution of identified problem areas.

11. The development of policies addressing the non-employment or retention of sanctioned individuals as identified in the OIG exclusion list.[65]

Defining and Understanding the Importance of Compliance Program Effectiveness

Under both the Federal Sentencing Guidelines and the OIG Compliance Program Guidance for Hospitals, only an "effective program to prevent and detect violations of law" will mitigate losses associated with violations of the law.[66] Therefore, it is absolutely essential that an organization be able to demonstrate effectiveness in program design and implementation on an ongoing basis. Swenson and Didier outline a particularly useful way of understanding effectiveness based upon four definitional components of the federal sentencing guidelines.[67] Beginning with an overarching principle from the sentencing guidelines, these authors maintain that these principles define how an effective program should be viewed and interpreted.

According to Swenson and Didier, there are four guiding principals regarding the demonstration of effectiveness.[68] The first, and perhaps most important, principle is identified as the "lens" or "overarching principle" for which the remaining principals should be viewed and interpreted.

1. The compliance program is reasonably designed, implemented, and enforced so that it will be generally effective in preventing and detecting criminal conduct. The hallmark of an effective program to prevent and detect violations of law is that the organization exercised due diligence in seeking to prevent and detect criminal conduct by its employees and other agents.

2. The organization must address the seven steps outlined by the United States Sentencing Guidelines.[69]

3. The compliance program must be designed and implemented so that it fits the unique characteristics of the particular organization involved. The design is dependant on a number of factors, including the size of the organization, the likelihood that certain offences may occur because of the nature of the business, and the prior history of the organization.

4. An organization's failure to incorporate and follow applicable industry practice or the standards called for by any applicable government regulation weighs against a finding of an effective program to prevent and detect violations of the law.

The remainder of this chapter focuses on the design, implementation, and enforcement of compliance programs from a risk management perspective.

Program Design—Identifying Loss Exposure—
Risk Identification and Analysis

Given the rapid pace of changes in health care and government fraud and abuse activities, it should be clear that compliance is a moving target. Every health care organization is unique with its own culture, institutional dynamics, and specific issues. While an effective compliance program will take into account these factors, it must also remain adaptable to endure the rigors of change within the health care industry and regulatory environment. Moreover, as explained previously, it is imperative, for establishing effectiveness, that the compliance program is established and implemented upon a carefully executed risk assessment.

Risk management in its most proactive form, in terms of fraud and abuse and compliance activities, is a process designed to prevent fraud, abuse, and administrative error. There are several steps an organization can take to ward off an investigation by law enforcement agencies. The first step is to conduct a comprehensive risk assessment. The purpose of this risk assessment is to discover inherent organizational weaknesses that could result in violations of laws or rules and regulations of health care funding programs, such as Medicare, Medicaid, and TriCare. By identifying these high-risk areas and modifying organizational practice to conform to the legal requirements, the organization will be better able to protect against investigation by outside agencies.

The risk assessment provides a baseline assessment—a "snapshot" of the organization. From this baseline, an organization should be able to demonstrate effectiveness by implementing corrective actions addressing high-risk areas discovered from the risk assessment. The risk assessment should consist of both an external and internal survey. These surveys and assessments should reveal organizational vulnerabilities, as well as areas where governmental investigative activities may be directed. Most important, risk assessment must be dynamic. In other words, the risk assessment should be both a formal established process (for example, annual, biannual, semiannual, and so on), as well as a daily operational process that responds to both external and internal information as it becomes available.

External Survey   As explained previously, the OIG has a variety of ways of notifying health care providers and the public of its concerns. At a minimum, this information should be reviewed at the inception of the compliance program. Additionally, a procedure for reviewing this information on an ongoing basis should be established as part of the day-to-day risk assessment process. Furthermore, an organization should develop a practice whereby a variety of external information is reviewed on a scheduled basis. With respect to billing issues, this review may include the documents listed below, most of which can be found at either the OIG Web site or the HCFA Web site.

OIG Compliance Guidance   Over the past several years, the OIG has drafted and/or issued compliance-related guidance for hospitals, clinical laboratories, home health agencies, hospices, third-party medical billing companies, durable medical equipment companies, and Medicare + Choice organizations.[70] Thus, as part of a baseline assessment, OIG compliance guidance documents that are pertinent to a particular health care entity's organizational operations should be reviewed as part of a baseline assessment. The guidelines should be tailored to fit the particular needs of an organization. While it may not be feasible to implement all guidelines fully, a good faith and meaningful commitment is essential.[71] For instance, the OIG in its compliance guidance for hospitals does not indicate that a "hotline" is the only process for receiving complaints.[72] However, if a hotline is not used, another method must be instituted and there must be measurable effectiveness.

OIG Work Plan   The OIG Work Plan[73] details the various projects of the DHHS, the Office of Audit Services (OAS), the Office of Evaluation and Inspections (OEI), the Office of Investigations (OI), and the Office of Counsel to the Inspector General (OCIG) that are to be addressed during a given fiscal year. The OIG does not provide information on the status of work projects contained in its work plan.

The 1998, 1999, and 2000 OIG Work Plans have addressed HCFA Projects, Public Health Service Agencies Projects, Administrations for Children and Families Projects (the 2000 Work Plan includes Aging), and DHHS-wide projects.[74]

Advisory Opinions   The OIG issues advisory opinions[75] to provide meaningful advice on the application of the Anti-Kickback Statute and other OIG sanction statutes in specific factual circumstances. These opinions are only legally binding on the requestor. Regardless, advisory opinions are helpful in understanding how the OIG applies the law in specific factual scenarios.

Additionally, HCFA issues certain written advisory opinions.[76] These advisory opinions discuss whether a physician's referrals relating to certain designated health services (other than clinical laboratory services) are prohibited under the Medicare program. Again, however, only the requestor may rely upon the advisory opinion.

OIG Exclusions   The OIG's List of Excluded Individuals/Entities (LEIE)[77] provides information to health care providers, patients, and others regarding individuals and entities that are excluded from participation in Medicare, Medicaid, and other federal health care programs. Information is readily available to users in two formats on more than 15,000 individuals and entities currently excluded from program participation through action taken by the OIG. Review of this information is important when considering hiring or contracting with an individual or entity. The public may obtain information about the Medicare or Medicaid participation status of an individual or entity as well.

OIG News Releases and HCFA Publications   The OIG releases special advisory bulletins, fact sheets, press releases, as well as other information that should be reviewed as part of assessment activities. For example, the OIG has historically addressed cutting-edge topics such as EMTALA (the patient anti-dumping statute), the Anti-Kickback Statute Safe Harbors, Healthcare Integrity and Protection Data Bank (HIRDB), and gain sharing arrangements. These documents can be found on the OIG's Web site.[78] Also, users can now subscribe to receive electronic notice of new OIG press releases.

Medicare, Medicaid, and Child Health Insurance Programs are administered by HCFA. HCFA maintains a "Plan and Provider" home page on its Web site,[79] which is touted as "the first stop" for physicians, health plans, health organizations, care providers, carriers, intermediaries, and other HCFA partners.

Additionally, HCFA publishes a quarterly list of all manual instructions, policy operations letters, interpretive regulations, and other *Federal Register* notices that have been published.[80] This information should be reviewed at program inception and regularly as part of ongoing risk assessment activities.

HCFA Provider Manuals, Fiscal Intermediary, and Carrier Directives   HCFA periodically issues manuals and letters for providers, fiscal intermediaries, and carriers (contractors for DHHS to administer "Part A" services located in various geographical areas across the country). These manuals provide instructions on how each fiscal intermediary is to administer the Federal Medicare Program. In addition, HCFA publishes program memoranda for fiscal intermediaries and carriers, including detailed discussions and interpretations of billing and reimbursement provisions. Individual fiscal intermediaries and carriers may subsequently issue newsletters, which outline relevant policy and procedure for their providers to follow.

National coverage policies for certain subjects may be issued by HCFA as well. Additionally, fiscal intermediaries and carriers may establish and issue Local Medical Review Policies (LMRP). LMRP are only relevant if HCFA has not issued a National Coverage Policy.

Agency Reports   Federal agencies are required to publish semiannual regulatory agendas that outline their policy goals for the coming six months. These agendas are a good source of information regarding enforcement initiatives. Therefore, as part of the baseline and ongoing risk assessment, the compliance professional should review on a regular basis the information available from federal and state agencies such as the Occupational Health and Safety Administration (OSHA),[81] Environmental Protection Agency (EPA),[82] and the Food and Drug Administration (FDA).[83]

Other Sources of External Information   An important element of the external risk assessment is to survey the experiences of other organizations that have been investigated or charged with violations of law or regulation. This information can be gleaned from professional organizations, local media reports, reports from hospital associations, various newsletters, and published compliance materials. Also, participation in compliance professional associations may provide timely and relevant information related to on-going risk assessment activities.

Internal Survey   It is important to recognize that while an external survey is an important part of any risk assessment, it is imperative that the external risk assessment be combined with an internal risk assessment that carefully analyzes and addresses the everyday, real issues facing a particular health care organization. An internal risk assessment should survey various aspects of the internal operations of a health care entity.

Policy and Procedure Review   The OIG, in its various compliance guidance publications, lists a number of policies and procedures that should be established as part of the compliance program.[84] For example, the OIG expects a hospital to establish and maintain policies and procedures that promote the hospital's commitment to compliance and that specifically address areas of potential fraud, such as claims development and submission processes, code gaming (such as improper code enhancement, upcoding, DRG creep, or unbundling laboratory panels into several codes), and financial relationships with physicians and other health care professionals.[85] In addition, policies and procedures to protect the anonymity of complainants and to protect whistleblowers from retaliation are required.[86] The OIG also requires policies addressing the nonemployment or retention of sanctioned individuals.[87]

Historical Internal and External Audit and Inspection Reports   Particularly useful in establishing a baseline risk assessment are previous audit or inspection reports. These reports may be from internal and external sources. The reports can identify particular compliance problems faced by an organization and steps the organization has taken to avoid future problems. It is important that historical findings and corrective actions taken are documented in an organizations ongoing compliance monitoring process.

Interviews, Surveys, Checklists, Contract Reviews, and Hotline Tips   One of the best sources of information for an internal risk assessment is to *ask* those that are closest to exposure-prone activities whether they are in compliance with law and regulation or know of any "red-flags." Internal communication may be facilitated by using surveys and checklists to prompt important probing questions to reveal potential fraud and abuse loss exposures. Contracts should be reviewed and analyzed also for compliance issues—especially physician contracts. Finally, the organization's "hotline" is an excellent source of information for the ongoing risk assessment.

Implementation of the Compliance Program—Examining and Applying Alternate Risk Management Techniques

From the comprehensive and ongoing risk assessment, potential loss exposures related to fraud and abuse enforcement activities should become apparent. The next step in the risk management process after the risk assessment is to apply sufficient risk management techniques to control identified fraud and abuse loss exposures, as well as pay for fines and expenses that may result from a government investigation or self-disclosure.

Loss Control Techniques   Loss control techniques include risk management techniques designed to minimize the frequency and/or severity of fraud and abuse loss. Typical loss control strategies include exposure avoidance, loss prevention, loss reduction, segregation of loss exposures, and contractual transfers designed to protect a health care organization from paying for fraud and abuse losses.

Exposure Avoidance   Avoiding or abandoning an activity that would generate a fraud and abuse type of loss eliminates, or at least mitigates, the possibility of loss entirely. The exposure avoidance technique is especially useful when certain loss-prone activities are discovered from the initial or ongoing risk assessment and avoidance of the activity has minimal consequences on the health care entity. Avoidance, however, is only feasible when eliminating the activity does not substantially alter the business of the health care enterprise. While avoidance should always be considered a first-line defense to potential fraud and abuse loss, in reality, many vital but inherently exposure-prone activities must continue for adequate health care business operations to continue. Therefore, other loss control activities must be considered and implemented.

Loss Prevention   The second loss control strategy, loss prevention, is designed to reduce the likelihood, and therefore frequency, of a fraud and abuse type loss. For example, the risk assessment may reveal particular loss-prone activities in relation to billing coding practices for health care services that are under scrutiny by the state or federal government. Instituting mandatory coding education or in-services and coding monitoring software are practical examples of effective loss prevention strategies designed to reduce the frequency of a fraud and abuse loss attributed to coding error.

Loss Reduction   The third loss control strategy, loss reduction (mitigation), aims to lower the *severity* of a particular loss. A health care organization's effective compliance program is the best loss mitigation strategy available when an organization faces a fraud and abuse type loss. As mentioned previously, the OIG, following the U.S. Sentencing Guidelines, will consider the existence of an effective compliance program that predates any governmental investigation when addressing the appropriateness of administrative penalties.[88] Also, the presence of an effective compliance program may influence the OIG when assessing whether to impose a permissive exclusion against a health care entity that engaged in fraudulent actions.[89]

Another practical example of loss reduction is self-disclosing to the government[90] billing discrepancies or apparent violations of law and/or regulation when they have occurred. This self-disclosure benefits the organization in several ways. First, it establishes cooperation and good faith with the OIG in addressing overpayment violations.[91] Second, self-disclosure may enhance the organization's ability to limit monetary loss in a settlement with the government.[92] Self-disclosure may also ward off permissive exclusion from participation in federal reimbursement programs.[93] Finally, voluntary disclosures under the False Claims Act in certain circumstances reduce treble damages to double.[94]

Self-disclosure should be considered carefully with the assistance of legal counsel. Overpayments that are the result of simple error may simply warrant repayment to the contractor. Participants in self-disclosure must be aware that other criminal, civil, or administrative sanctions may be taken as a result of the disclosure.[95] Additionally, a possibility exists that self-disclosure waives the attorney-client privilege and/or attorney-work product privileges regarding information collected and evaluated pursuant to the government's self-disclosure protocols.[96]

Loss Segregation   The fourth loss control strategy involves arranging the health care organization's activities so that no single event can cause simultaneous loss. For example, it may be prudent to distribute medical coding functions among several employees. Doing so increases the chances of discovering discrepancies and reducing the number of times the errors are repeated, and makes it more difficult for an employee to mislead or misinform others regarding coding of a particular diagnostic test.

Contractual Transfer   The final loss control strategy involves contractually transferring the activity to another individual or entity. This particular loss control strategy will effectively transfer *all* of the financial risk associated with a particular activity. An example, again within the coding context, would be for a hospital to subcontract medical coding functions to a qualified third-party vendor. The contract would be written to provide complete unilateral hold-harmless, defense, and indemnification provisions inuring to the benefit of the health care entity.

Risk Financing Techniques   While beyond the scope of this chapter, risk financing alternatives deserve brief mention. In addition to applying loss control strategies, the prudent health care organization will devise a strategy to pay for fraud and abuse type losses when they occur. Risk financing encompasses all of the ways that an organization generates funds to pay for financial losses, if and when they do actually occur. Risk financing is traditionally within the functional domain of the risk manager or similarly experienced individual within the health care organization. In the fraud and abuse context, financial losses principally include investigation and audit expenses, attorney fees, and financial damages associated with settlements or verdicts of lawsuits brought by the government and/or *Qui Tam* relators.[97] The health care organization can choose to pay financial losses using internally retained funds or by transferring the financial loss to a third party. Often an organization pays for financial losses through a combination of both methods.

Risk Retention   An organization may pay for financial losses drawing upon internal financial resources in one or more of the following ways:

- Expensing the fraud and abuse losses when they occur.

- Using an *unfunded reserve* whereby an accounting entry is entered in the organizations' financial records denoting a potential liability to pay for a fraud and abuse loss that is believed to have occurred.

- Using a *funded loss reserve* whereby funds are set aside and released specifically to pay for particular fraud and abuse losses.

- Borrowing funds to pay for fraud and abuse losses when they occur.

- Paying for fraud and abuse losses through a self-insurance vehicle, such as a captive insurance company.

Risk Transfer   Many health care entities choose to pay for financial losses (such as property and casualty) by purchasing commercially available insurance. In the context of fraud and abuse losses, several commercially available insurance products have become available recently both for physicians and for health care entities. However, these insurance products are generally limited in coverage.

For physicians, generally three types of insurance products are available: (1) *Med-Defense* endorsements to physician liability policies, (2) *Administrative Defense* insurance policies, and (3) stand-alone *Physician Billing Error* policies. However, for health care entities, stand-alone policies are primarily available.

Physician Med-Defense endorsements generally cover limited legal expenses subject to a retroactive date, nominal deductible and coinsurance percentage, and exclusion for criminal acts. Physician Administrative Defense and Physician Billing Error policies cover limited legal expenses for regulatory and administrative actions, including license actions, hospital staff issues, managed care panel actions, and/or limited reimbursement from public (Medicare) and private billing errors. These policies do not cover criminal acts or restitution for overbilling.

Institutional coverage for health care entities is available in much higher limits than that generally available for physicians, but are also subject to much higher deductibles or retentions. Some of the more popular commercial insurance products include coverage for both defense and settlement costs associated with billing errors, false claim allegations, whistleblower, Stark, anti-kickback, and program fraud civil remedies. However, many of these institutional insurance policies require an effective compliance program be in place and will provide retroactive coverage only to the date of the program's inception. As with the physician insurance products, there is no coverage for criminal acts or return and restitution of over billings.

············

PUTTING IT ALL TOGETHER

Health care compliance programs became important in the late 1990s in response to efforts by both state and federal governments to prosecute individuals and organizations involved in waste (fraud, abuse, and error) of financial resources in the public health care system. These enforcement activities spawned the new field of health care compliance, complete with an army of new health care professionals and compliance officers. Yet, corporate compliance is really risk management—with a few new twists.

The twists, as described previously, include the fact that compliance management has its own set of particular laws, regulations, and government agencies for which the risk management professional must develop a fundamental understanding. Second, formal compliance programs must be established, implemented, and enforced to demonstrate "effectiveness" based upon criteria fixed by the United States Sentencing Commission and elaborated upon by the OIG. Third, long-standing risk management techniques can be applied to solve risk management problems in the context of fraud, abuse, and billing error. The final risk management "twist" pertains to the high-stakes government overlay to compliance management with its resulting severe consequences if compliance programs are mismanaged or ineffective.

Compliance management requires due diligence in all its efforts, including program formation, risk assessment, loss control, and risk financing. Once problems are discovered they must be fully investigated and audited to determine the scope of the problem. Restitution should be made for funds received that a health care entity or individual is not entitled. Once problems are discovered, corrective actions must be instituted to prevent future violations of law or regulation and the health care entity must implement ongoing monitoring to ensure compliance. Thus, the function of compliance is no easy task and requires a conscientious commitment of resources, time, and organizational priority. Whether the risk management professional plays a central role or an advisory role in compliance management, the role is as critical as any role performed since the birth of the health care risk management profession in the early 1970s.

Endnotes

The authors wish to acknowledge Sybil M. Richard, a student at the Indiana University School of Law, and Brian K. Beeler, J. D., for their contributions in the drafting of this chapter.

1. Pub. L. No. 104-191.

2. Health Care Fraud and Abuse Compliance Manual, Section 2, *False Claims and Fraudulent Billing,* 2(1), 1999 (citing 3 Medicare & Medicaid Guide (CCH) ¶ 13, 913).

3. Health Care Fraud and Abuse Compliance Manual, Section 1, *Overview of Fraud and Abuse* 1:2 (1999).

4. 42 USC §1320a-7a.

5. 42 USC §1320a-7a.

6. Health Care Fraud: Enforcement and Compliance, Section 3.02[5][d].

7. Health Care Fraud: Enforcement and Compliance, Section 3.02 [5][a]-[d]; 42 USC § 1320a-7(b)(a)(1).

8. Section 1128A Social Security Act, 42 USC §1320a-7a.

9. Balanced Budget Act of 1997, Pub. L. No. 105-33 §4331(c).

10. "Inspector General Announces Eight New Anti-Kickback Statute Safe Harbors." *OIG News Release,* Nov. 18, 1999.

11. "Federal Anti-Kickback Law and Regulatory Safe Harbors." *OIG Fact Sheet,* Nov. 19, 1999; 64 *Fed. Reg.* 63518, Nov. 19, 1999.

12. Health Care Fraud: Enforcement and Compliance, Section 3.02[5][c].

13. *Ibid.*

14. 42 CFR 1001.952; 64 *Fed. Reg.* Nov. 19, 1999.

15. Pub. L. 104-191.

16. Health Care Fraud and Abuse Compliance Manual, Section 3, *Fraud and Abuse Prohibitions Under the Kickback Statute,* §2-7 (1999).

17. Health Care Fraud: Enforcement and Compliance, Section 3.02[5][d][d][iii][A].

18. Health Care Fraud: Criminal, Enforcement and Compliance, Section 3.02[5][d][ii].

19. *Ibid.*

20. *Ibid.*

21. *Ibid.*

22. Pub. L. 104-191.

23. 42 USC §1395 nn.

24. Omnibus Budget Reconciliation Act of 1993, Pub. L. No. 103-66.

25. *Ibid.*

26. Health Care Fraud and Abuse Compliance Manual, Section 4, *Federal Physician Self-Referral Prohibitions: The Stark Law*, §5-1 (1999).

27. Health Care Fraud and Abuse Compliance Manual, Section 4, *Federal Physician Self-Referral Prohibitions: The Stark Law,* §4-1 (1999).

28. Health Care Fraud: Enforcement and Compliance, Section 4.05[5].

29. *Ibid.*

30. *Ibid.*

31. Health Care Fraud: Enforcement and Compliance, Section 4.01[2][c].

32. 31 USC §3729.

33. *Ibid.*

34. *Ibid.*

35. Health Care Fraud and Abuse Compliance Manual, Section 2:5, *Fraudulent Claims and Fraudulent Billing,* (1999).

36. 18 USC 287.

37. 31 USC§3729.

38. Health Care Fraud and Abuse Compliance Manual, Section 2:27, *False Claims and Fraudulent Billing,* §3-3 (1999).

39. Health Care Fraud and Abuse Compliance Manual, Section 2:27, *False Claims and Fraudulent Billing,* §3-7 (1999).

40. Health Care Fraud and Abuse Compliance Manual, Section 2:27, *False Claims and Fraudulent Billing,* §3-6 (1999).

41. 42 USC 1230a-7a.

42. *Ibid.*

43. *Ibid.*

44. *Ibid.*

45. *Ibid.*

46. Pub. L. 104-191.

47. *Ibid.*

48. Health Care Fraud and Abuse Compliance Manual, *Overview of Health Care Fraud and Abuse* (1999).

49. Furrow, B. R., and others. *HEALTH LAW,* §5 at 618 (3rd ed. 1997).

50. Id. at 619 (citing Mass. Gen. L. ch. 112 §§ 12AA, 23P 1/2 [1991]).

51. 39 AM. JUR. 2D *Health,* §§1-4; 14-20 (1999).

52. 70 AM. JUR. 2d *Sheriffs, Police and Constables,* §46 (1987).

53. 63C AM. JUR. 2d *Prosecuting Attorneys,* §3 (1997).

54. 63C AM. JUR. 2d *Prosecuting Attorneys,* §21(1997).

55. 7 AM. JUR. 2d *Attorney General,* §§1-6; 27 (1997).

56. HHS/OIG Compliance Program Guidance for Hospitals at 4, n. 2 (1998).

57. U.S. Sentencing Commission, *Guidelines Manual,* Ch. 8, (1999).

58. *"Organization* means "a person other than an individual." 16 USC §18. The term includes corporations, partnerships, associations, joint stock companies, unions, trusts, pension funds, unincorporated organizations, governments and political subdivisions thereof, and nonprofit organizations. *See* USSG §8A1.1, comment, n. 1.

59. USSG, §8C2.5(f).

60. HHS/OIG Compliance Program Guidance for Hospitals at 3, n. 2 (1998).

61. *Ibid.*

62. HHS/OIG Compliance Program Guidance for Hospitals, at 7, n. 6 (1998).

63. HHS/OIG Compliance Program Guidance for Hospitals, at 4 (1998).

64. The seven steps elaborated by the OIG are further separated into eleven steps for purposes of this chapter.

65. *See* USSG §8C2.5(f) and HHS/OIG Compliance Program Guidance for Hospitals at 3, n. 2 (1998).

66. Swenson, W. M., and Didier, M. E. "The Health Care Compliance Professional's Manual." *The Federal Sentencing Guidelines: A Practical Overview of Their Background, Intent and Implications, 3-2:1, 3-2:5, 3-2:7 (1999).*

67. *Ibid.,* at 3-2:5 citing to the Sentencing Commission's definition for effective programs to prevent and detect violations of law set forth at USSG §8A-1.2, comment (n. 3(k)).

68. The seven steps, elaborated by the OIG, are further separated into eleven steps as presented in the preceding section of this chapter.

69. A complete list can be found on the OIG Web site at www.dhhs.gov/progorg/oig/modcomp/index.htm

70. Health Care Fraud and Abuse Compliance Manual, 5:20.1-5:20.7.

71. HHS/OIG Compliance Guidance for Hospital, at www.dhhs.gov/progorg/oig

72. *See* www.dhhs.gov/progorg/oig/wrkpln/index.htm

73. *Ibid.*

74. *See* www.dhhs.gov/progorg/oig/advopn/index.htm

75. *See* www.hcfa.gov/regs/aop/

76. *See* www.dhhs.gov/progorg/oig/cumsan/index.htm

77. *See* www.dhhs.gov/progorg/oig/medadv/index.htm

78. *See* www.hcfa.gov/audience/planprov.htm

79. *64 Fed Reg.* 90 (1999).

80. *See* www.osha.gov/

81. *See* www.epa.gov/

82. *See* www.fda.gov/default.htm

83. *See* for example, HHS/OIG Compliance Program Guidance for Hospitals, pg. 5 (1998). www.dhhs.gov/progorg/oig

84. *Ibid.*

85. *Ibid.*

86. *Ibid.*

87. HHS/OIG Compliance Program Guidance for Hospitals, n. 2 (1998).

88. *Ibid.*, p. 3.

89. *63 Fed. Reg.* 58, 399 (1998).

90. Snell, R., Saunders, B. L., Murphy, J. E., and Ryan, E. "The Health Care Compliance Professional's Manual." *Government Enforcement Trends,* § 1-4:3 (1999).

91. *Ibid.*

92. *Ibid.*

93. *Ibid.*

94. *Ibid.*

95. *Ibid.*

96. Collectively referred to as "fraud and abuse losses."

21

Risk Mapping—
A Visual Experience

M. Michael Zuckerman

R isk is generally defined as uncertainty about future outcomes. Risk management is the process by which an organization identifies, assesses, and manages risk or uncertainty. The goal of risk management, therefore, is to prevent or mitigate the potential adverse outcome so that it does not prevent the organization from achieving its goals. Or one can say that risk management is about maximizing an organization's value.

....
WHAT IS RISK MAPPING?

In mathematics, a map is the "correspondence of one or more elements in one set to one or more elements in the same set or another set."[1] In risk management, risk mapping[2] is a process that graphically depicts the significance of an organization's risks. The *risk map* graphically displays the relationship between frequency (how often the loss will occur) and severity (how much the loss will cost us) in such a way that it permits us to see how each risk may financially impact the organization. This chapter will explore the risk mapping process and how this graphical "snapshot" of an organization's risk may benefit its risk management program.

To construct a risk map, a firm must identify its loss exposures, which are its assets in which it has a legal and financial interest and that it uses to generate revenue.[3] Examples of loss exposures include a firm's employees and the activities, services, and products it sells. Both can cause a financial loss for an organization.[4] For example, if we own a building, it can burn down. We then need funds to replace the building so that we can continue our operations. Or a doctor can negligently perform a procedure causing bodily injury requiring a payment of damages to the injured patient. All will result in financial loss. Therefore, once loss exposures are identified, the organization must gain insight into the chance of a loss and then assess the potential financial impact if a loss should occur.

Assessing the potential financial impact of a loss requires a health care entity to estimate the dollar value of the losses that will occur. An estimate of expected losses for any risk is a function of average frequency and average severity. Therefore, when a firm quantifies risk and/or expected losses, these *elements*—frequency and severity—must be derived from empirical or subjective estimation. A firm can measure severity or financial impact as a specific dollar loss; and both frequency and severity on an aggregate (cumulative) basis over some period of time such as one year. A firm can then graph these elements per type of risk or loss. For example, frequency may be graphed on the *x*-axis referenced to a certain number of losses or events occurring within a specific period of time such as the number of losses that will occur in a month, quarter, year, and so on.

Severity can be graphed on the *y*-axis to represent the financial impact each loss or the aggregate of losses will have on the organization. Severity can be represented in terms of dollars, or as a percentage of some financial benchmark such as revenues, earnings per share, or margin. The method of graphing is left to the imagination of each individual risk manager. But you must take into consideration annual aggregates and how the risk is currently being treated. Aggregate exposure is the total amount of losses expected over a period of time. It can be distinguished, for example, from specific or per-loss events on the risk map by geometric coding. Exhibit 21.1 illustrates a common risk map plotting severity on the *y*-axis and frequency on the *x*-axis.

The risk map allows the risk manager to visualize the frequency and severity for the set of losses his or her organization will face over a defined period of time. Risk mapping, therefore, is a tool that can be used to strategically manage risk because it allows us to analyze our identified risks in terms of how they may financially impact the organization and how these risks are currently being managed. For example, the hurricane or windstorm peril may be insured, but the issue that remains is whether the policy limits are adequate in light of the maximum possible and/or maximum probable loss.

Medical malpractice is graphed in Exhibit 21.1 on a per loss (expected dollar range of an individual loss) and in the aggregate (potential high frequency and severity aggregate).

EXHIBIT 21.1.   Risk Map: Frequency and Severity Chart

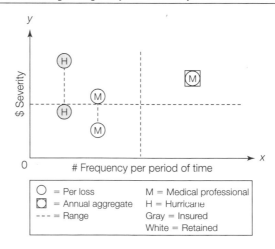

Again, if medical malpractice is graphed as partially retained up to a certain per dollar loss level, then one must ask whether this level of retention is appropriate. Are the excess liability insurance limits adequate, or should the program be structured on a multiyear, single-limit basis? (See Chapter 32 on Risk Financing Techniques.) Is there annual aggregate stop loss protection? If not, is it available in the commercial market, and at what cost?

The question is, what do we do with this information? Lewis Carroll wrote in *Alice in Wonderland*, "If you don't know where you are going, any road will get you there."[5] Risk mapping, clearly, is a key tool to aid the process of identifying what an organization's risk management goals should be—both short- and long-term. In other words, it is the risk map that can lead an organization down the right road in terms of identifying its risk management goals and establishing how risk management resources should be allocated to achieve these goals.

WHAT RISKS DO WE MAP?

It is impossible to map all risks that an organization faces. This project needs to have a focus and parameters. Any risk mapping project starts with *loss exposure and risk identification and assessment,* which will be discussed later. But the risk mapping process should focus on those risks believed to have the potential to financially impair the organization. Significance is defined by each organization depending upon the nature of its operation and financial condition.

The actual measuring of risk in terms of its financial impact depends upon the nature of the risk and the available data about that risk. To forecast an average medical professional liability loss and the total expected amount of professional liability losses for a specific period of time requires empirical data. Expected losses within a retained layer (the amount of losses being paid by your organization) for a specific period of time can be forecasted using your health care organization's own data, if it is credible. An actuary can help you define credibility. The alternative is to use industry data or a blending of both industry and organization data.

The actuary's role is critical to this process. An actuary will use statistical tools such as *Monte Carlo* simulations to estimate expected losses per risk that need to be analyzed.[6] This process will allow your organization to evaluate the risk of variation in actual from expected outcomes and develop acceptable expected loss estimation.

But, for example, if you operate a facility along the eastern coast of the United States, you know that you face the risk of a serious loss from a windstorm. But how can we predict the frequency and the financial impact of a potentially catastrophic event that will occur infrequently, thereby being very unpredictable by definition?

As we will discuss, any risk-mapping project must be based on the input of various disciplines from within your organization. The severity measures for some risks can be actuarially determined using empirical evidence. But severity measures for less predictable risks like hurricanes, earthquakes, or prosecution for fraud and abuse may be a subjective estimation derived from the input of many individuals with a specific perspective on that risk. Catastrophe modeling is another tool that may provide the appropriate risk management assessment for natural disasters such as hurricanes or earthquakes. Catastrophe modeling can "simulate the probability and outcome" of a natural catastrophe.[7] Reinsurers now use these models regularly.

How your organization defines risk is another determining factor used to decide which risks to map. The answer to this question will focus this risk-mapping project.

Traditionally, risk managers defined risk as "pure" risk (risks that present only a chance of a loss or no loss, but no chance of a gain), also known as "insurable risk" or "risk of accidental loss." In this context your organization will examine risk of loss from the perspective of:

1. Damage to property that an organization uses to generate revenue.

2. The disruption to an organization's revenue stream arising from a direct loss to its property or another's property upon which it is dependent, causing a net income loss and/or requiring an extraordinary expense to maintain the operation after the loss.

3. Third-party liability claims.

4. Personnel-workplace injuries.

In many organizations today, risk management is evolving to a more *holistic* approach by expanding the definition of risk to include speculative or operational risks— or, in other words, a movement towards Enterprise Risk Management as presented in Chapter 7 of this text. Financial risk is an example of speculative as opposed to pure risk.

Two forms of financial risk are price and credit risk.[8] Credit risk is the chance that your customers will not pay for services rendered.[9] For health care organizations, credit risk may include reimbursement risk, or the financial failure of an insurer (reimbursement source). Price risk can arise from the variation in interest rates, the cost of supplies used to operate your organization, and reimbursement for care provided that may impair your organization's margin, or earnings per share if you are a publicly traded "for-profit" organization.[10]

Another form of operational risk not traditionally insurable but that poses a significant risk of financial loss is regulatory risk. Regulatory risk is the failure to comply with regulations that may result in uninsurable financial penalties. Examples of such regulatory risk can arise from violations of regulation such as the Emergency Medical Treatment and Labor Act of 1986 (EMTALA) and the Occupational Safety and Health Act (OSHA), to name just two of many, which may result in significant uninsurable fines and penalties, not to mention damage to corporate reputation that may result in diminished market share.

An example of one approach to risk mapping appears in the Swiss Re publication *sigma*. The model risk map in this article presents a risk profile of a pharmaceutical firm that classifies risk into the following categories: third-party liability; workforce; terrorism; first-party damage and business interruption; financial; regulatory; and political risk.

Regardless of your organization's approach to defining and categorizing loss exposures and risk, parameters for the risk-mapping project must be adopted. The project must establish an understanding of just how representative or inclusive the risk map is of all organizational risk. In other words, the organization must define the scope of risk so that the risk mapping team knows what to look for.

WHAT IS THE RISK MAPPING PROCESS?

The risk mapping process can be defined as:

1. Identifying those significant risks that may materially impact an organization's earnings and financial strength.

2. Quantifying or measuring these risks in terms of frequency and severity on a specific or per loss basis, and in the aggregate for a defined period of time.

3. Identifying how risks are currently managed, analyzing which risks require a different risk management approach, further analysis, or are just in need of risk management attention.

The risk mapping process must begin with senior management support. Risk mapping requires a significant amount of resources including the input from various disciplines within the organization. The risk manager, therefore, must have jurisdiction to plan, organize, implement, and manage such an effort including eliciting the cooperation from the required disciplines.

The risk manager must now put a team together representing the various stakeholders in the risk management process. This team must represent all facets of the organization and bring together different perspectives on risk. A suggested list of participants, which is highlighted in Exhibit 21.2, include legal, financial, operations, public relations, facilities management, human resources, medical staff, nursing, security, environmental health, safety, and, of course, risk management. An insurance broker or consultant knowledgeable about risk mapping is a critical resource for the team. This list is not an exhaustive one and will vary according to the nature and make-up of the organization. But the risk manager must be the driver moving this process to conclusion.

The team must understand the definition of risk and, therefore, the scope of the project. In other words, just how holistic is your organization's approach to risk management? After that, the first order of business is to identify and assess the organization's loss exposures and risks.

The information sources for data on risk may include:

- Financial information such as financial reports and annual reports.

- Reports to the community, journal articles, and literature searches.

- Questionnaires designed to identify sources of risk that are to be completed by managers and supervisors within the organization.

- Internal documents such as budgets, business plans, board and committee meeting minutes, and procedure manuals.

EXHIBIT 21.2. Suggested List of Participants

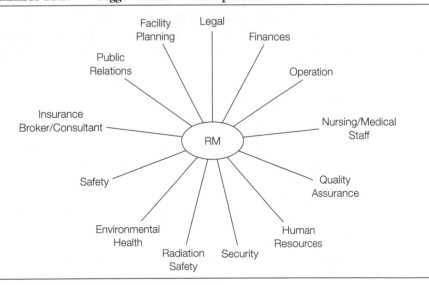

- Historical loss data.
- Physical inspections.
- Interviews of key personnel.
- Incident reports and occurrence screens.
- Insurance company loss prevention reports.
- Input from insurance brokers, consultants, and attorneys.
- Industry benchmarks.
- Insurance coverage checklists.

This is not an exhaustive list. Any tool or source of information that will uncover risk should be explored.

Other issues that the team should be considering as it identifies risk are:

1. What is the organization's environment, which can be defined in terms of its:
   - Regulators and regulations.
   - Competitors and trends in the industry.
   - Patients and their indigenous characteristics that may impact risk.
   - Geography and/or weather conditions such as exposure to earthquakes and hurricanes.
   - Political environment and expected changes in reimbursements and legal liability.

2. Does the organization have plans to expand, acquire new facilities, or merge with another organization, and what are the risks associated with this activity?

3. Will the organization begin to provide new services not previously offered?

4. What issues keep management up at night?

5. What is the nature of the patient population, and does that present any unusual or indigenous risks not faced typically by other health care organizations?

6. What could cause the organization to go out of business?

7. What is the organizational structure—publicly held for-profit or a nonprofit?

8. What is the organization's appetite for risk and ability to manage risk?

9. What is the threshold of materiality or significance, or at what dollar threshold does a potential loss become important or significant so that it must be managed? The choice of risk management tools, of course, includes risk control and risk financing. For purposes of this discussion, risk control is the process by which an organization attempts to prevent losses from occurring, and/or mitigate the financial impact of a loss after it does occur. And risk financing is the process by which an organization pays for loss prevention's failure through the use of risk transfer (insurance) or self-funding. Determining what is financially material will require input from financial management. The type and significance of the risk will trigger the types of risk treatment tools used to manage these risks.

All loss exposures and the risks an organization faces must be classified or organized in some form that makes sense for the organization. The traditional format[12] consists of classifying all loss exposures as:

1. *Property* in which the organization has a legal or financial interest and uses to generate income.

2. *Time element* loss exposures that consist of business interruption or net income, extra expense, or contingent business interruption or net income exposures. Time element losses are indirect or consequential losses arising from direct damage to the organization's property. But a contingent business interruption loss exposure arises from a dependency on someone else's property, damage to which can interrupt an organization's activities. Examples of the contingent business interruption exposure are dependency on a key supplier or a public utility.

3. *Third-party liability* loss exposures that arise from the activities of the medical staff, employees, trustees, and volunteers that can give rise to claims being made against the organization for damages resulting from negligence.

4. *Personnel* loss exposures, which arise from the injury or premature death to employees. This gives rise to a financial loss for the employee but also impacts the organization's productivity, and the organization's cost of workers' compensation and employee benefits.

If a more holistic approach is taken towards managing risk, then financial and regulatory risks, as previously discussed, may also be considered and added to this list.

Another method for classifying risks holistically, presented by Marsh, Inc.,[13] at the 1999 RIMS conference, is to classify your loss exposures according to:

1. *Natural* exposures such as earthquakes, fires, business interruption, and weather-related losses such as windstorm and flood.

2. *Liability* exposures such as services provided, products sold, construction projects, or other vendors used that could injure the public, the use and operation of ambulances and automobiles, managing hazardous waste, and professional liability.

3. *Employment* exposures such as work-related injuries, employment practices, and employee benefit issues.

4. *Operational* exposures such as tampering with medical devices, employee dishonesty, theft of inventory, and risks arising from mergers and acquisitions.

5. *Financial* exposures, which can arise from fluctuations in interest rates, credit risks, research and development losses, intellectual property, and other disruptions to earnings.

This is just another way of thinking about the risks that your organization faces as opposed to the risk classification system exemplified by the previously mentioned Swiss Re *sigma* article.[14]

The next step in the process is to map those risks according to frequency, severity, and the type of current risk management tool being used. To do this we must calculate an *empirical estimation* of frequency and severity according to our own historical data or industry data. An actuary can do this for your organization, or if the data is credible and available an experienced risk manager can also forecast expected losses.

If an empirical estimation is not possible then the risk mapping team must make a *subjective estimation* about frequency and severity of a particular risk. This subjective estimation may be based on industry data, topical literature, jury verdict reporters, input from outside consultants, and the instinct of team members.

After identification and assessment, the next step is to determine whether the risk is significant enough to warrant inclusion on the map. There are several issues that need to be considered when examining risk in terms of its financial impact as a single loss and/or in the aggregate for the appropriate time period.

First, are the expected losses and potential for capital impairment significant? In other words, will the loss have a material impact on the organization's financial strength, operations, earnings, or reputation? Again, this evaluation is dependent upon the organization's definition of what is significant and requires the input and insights of financial management.

Second, what is the potential for business interruption, such as a disruption of a revenue stream because of a direct loss to your organization's property or dependency on some other outside organization? This also includes the need to spend extraordinary amounts of money to mitigate the impact of a loss to get back into business as soon as possible to avoid loss of market share.

Finally, is there a potential for small losses to cumulatively impact the financial strength of the organization over a specific period of time such as one year? This is the aggregate accumulation of losses that exceed an acceptable amount of risk for your organization.

In summary, the actual mapping process can proceed by classifying risks to be mapped according to:

1. *The type of risk or loss potential* (see previous discussion about the loss exposure and risk identification classification scheme).

2. The *chance that a loss may occur.* What is a reasonable expectation versus the remote possibility that has no real meaning, such as the chance that space junk will fall to earth and hit your building as opposed to the chance that an ambulance will be involved in a high-speed collision?

3. The *expected frequency of loss.*

4. The *expected severity;* in other words, the range of possible dollar outcomes, or the average outcome, whether on a per loss or annual aggregate basis. Another way of thinking about severity is in terms of the financial impact that one loss or a number of losses will have on the financial well-being of the organization. Will margins shrink, resulting in the cancellation of capital projects? Or will future revenues be compromised because patients were forced to seek care elsewhere while the organization reacted to a loss that closed part of your facility, or some other internal crisis? The financial impact may also come from regulatory penalties.

5. *How the risk is currently being managed.* Are the risks:

   - Fully insured?

   - Insured using a significant deductible?

   - Retained (self-insured using some funding mechanism)?

   - Retained while transferring the catastrophic exposure?

   - Treated by a risk control program—loss prevention and loss reduction?

   - Passively retained (usually nonfunded)?

Each of the five aforementioned risk treatment techniques can be coded on the risk map. Color or geometric coding can be used in the risk map's legend to signify how the risk is currently being treated. The end result is a detailed risk map or maps that depict uninsured and insured risks (potential losses) by risk quadrant and relationship to frequency and severity. Exhibit 21.3[15] illustrates a hypothetical risk map prepared in this fashion.

EXHIBIT 21.3. **Hypothetical Risk Map**

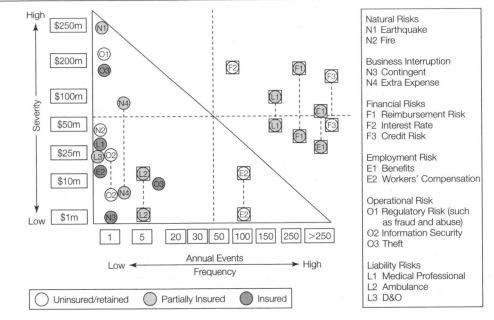

A sample risk coding legend is also included in Exhibit 21.3. Again the risk manager's own imagination will ultimately dictate how your organization codes its risks being mapped.

············

WHAT DO WE DO WITH THIS INFORMATION?

There are some general rules of risk management that an organization should consider at this point in the analysis of its risk map:

1. If the exposure to loss is characterized by low frequency and low per loss severity, then should it be retained and probably ignored? These are insignificant events with little or no financial consequence.

2. If the exposure to loss, such as workers' compensation, is characterized by high frequency and low per loss severity then retention of the risk should be considered if the aggregate expected loss forecast per specified time period such as one year is highly predictable.

3. If the exposure to loss is characterized by low frequency but high per loss severity, then there is a great deal of uncertainty and this risk should be transferred by way of insurance or contract.

4. If the exposure to loss is both high frequency and high per loss severity then unless the organization is going to avoid this activity all together the treatment decisions probably include risk control as well as risk transfer. Risk transfer, the purchase of insurance, will probably require that the insured assume some risk, in the form of a

deductible or self-insured retention, for these types of volatile risks. Examples of high frequency and high severity may be the operation of ambulances, or activity that generates high loss frequency with significant aggregate exposure. These general rules are illustrated on risk map model in Exhibit 21.4.

Some risks, such as workers' compensation, can be mapped in the lower right-hand quadrant because it is for the most part high frequency and low per loss severity. But it also poses a catastrophic risk from a single event that may be mapped in the upper left-hand quadrant, which is characterized by its low frequency but potential catastrophic or high per loss severity.

If a single event may present the possibility of a loss with a certain range of dollar outcome, it can also be mapped accordingly with the range represented by a dotted line between the two end points. For example, see N4 (extra expense) as graphed on Exhibit 21.3. The graphing displays a potential single loss ranging from $5 million to $95 million. Exhibit 21.3 is meant for discussion purposes only and does not represent any specific institution or set with data about these risks.

Again, the fact that risks are also mapped according to their current treatment presents an opportunity to analyze how the risk is currently treated, which begs the question whether or not the current strategy needs to be changed. See Exhibit 21.3 for examples about how risk treatment may be coded. The proper analysis of this information will require the services of a qualified insurance broker or consultant to bring an industry-wide perspective to this process.

To aid in this analysis, the risk manager should ask the following questions as he or she reviews how risks are currently being managed:

1. Is the risk control program adequately addressing the risk?

2. Are insurance policy limits adequate?

3. Are the deductibles appropriate—can the organization retain more risk?

4. If the risk is currently commercially insured, should risk retention be considered?

5. If the risk is untreated, why? Is it a conscious or unconscious decision to retain risk?

6. If the risk is retained, is the level of retention adequate and has the truly catastrophic exposure been transferred?

EXHIBIT 21.4.   Risk Map Model: General Rules

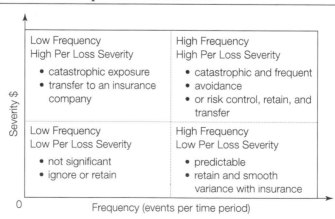

7. Are the commercial insurers used financially secure (will they be around to pay for claims) and providing the services requested?

This is not intended to be an all-inclusive list of possible action items but it does highlight the vast potential of the risk mapping process to enhance the strategic risk management process.

....

CONCLUSION

The benefits of risk mapping to an organization are that it:

1. Identifies in one place all *significant* risks facing the health care organization.
2. Permits a cross-discipline analysis of the organization's risks.
3. Quantifies the magnitude of the risk and the level of need for risk control and risk financing attention.
4. Focuses attention on risks that are material to the organization's financial viability.

With this information, an organization can then select the road it needs to travel to accomplish its risk management goals.

Endnotes

1. *The American Heritage Dictionary of the English Language* (3rd ed.). Boston: Houghton Mifflin Co. 1992. Anne H. Soukhanov, executive ed. for pp. 1096–1097.
2. The author acknowledges two 1999 Risk, and Insurance Management Society Annual Conference sessions on risk mapping: "Managing Balance Sheet Risk," presented by Kay K. Rahardjo of Liberty Mutual and Christopher M. Lewis of Ernst and Young, LLP; and "Risk Mapping: Discovering Hidden Treasures or Problems?" presented by Ken Zignorski of Marsh, Inc, Ron Loizzo of Colgate-Palmolive, and Russell Mulder of Zurich-American. These seminars were invaluable to the drafting of this chapter.
3. Head, G. L., and Horn II, S. *Essentials of Risk Management* (3rd ed.). vol. 1, Malvern, Pa.: Insurance Institutes of America, pp. 107–154.
4. *Ibid.*
5. I read this quote in Barbara J. Youngberg's *Risk Manager's Desk Reference* (2nd ed.) in which she defines strategic planning "as an organized process . . . used to define long-term goals and methods for achieving those goals." Youngberg, B. J., and Kuhn, A. M. "Risk Management Strategic Planning for a Changed Health Care Deliver System." *The Risk Manager's Desk Reference* (2nd ed.). Gaithersburg, Md.: Aspen Publishing, 1998, p. 61.
6. Vaughn, E. J. *Risk Management.* Wiley, 1997, p. 172.
7. Booth, G. "Surge in Losses Persuades Insurers to Use Software." *Financial Times (London),* Sept. 1, 1999, p. 12.
8. Harrington, S. E., and Niehaus, G. R. *Risk Management and Insurance.* Irwin/McGraw-Hill, 1999, pp. 3–6.
9. *Ibid.*
10. *Ibid.*
11. Swiss Re Insurance. *sigma* no. 2, 1999, p. 8.

12. Head, G. L., and Horn II, S. *Essentials of Risk Management* (3rd ed.). vol. 1, Malvern, Pa.: Insurance Institutes of America, pp. 107–154.

13. The author acknowledges two 1999 Risk and Insurance Management Society Annual Conference sessions on risk mapping: "Managing Balance Sheet Risk," presented by Kay K. Rahardjo of Liberty Mutual and Christopher M. Lewis of Ernst and Young, LLP; and "Risk Mapping: Discovering Hidden Treasures or Problems?" presented by Ken Zignorski of Marsh, Inc., Ron Loizzo of Colgate-Palmolive, and Russell Mulder of Zurich-American. These seminars were invaluable to the drafting of this chapter.

14. Swiss Re Insurance. *sigma* no. 2, 1999, p. 8.

15. Special thanks to Ward R. H. Ching of Aon Strategic Solutions Group in San Francisco, California, for developing this sample risk map. The author, with Mr. Ching's permission, made a few modifications.

III

Providers and Managed Care

C hapter 22 about providers and managed care is a new section to this third edition of the handbook. It was felt that managed care was of such importance to health care risk management that it deserved special attention; thus, a separate new section.

The goal of managed care, to deliver better health care at lower cost, has created much controversy and frustration within health care and in the mind and hearts of the public. One can't go a day without reading a newspaper or magazine article or hearing a news story about some new managed care dilemma. This section of the handbook was written as a primer on managed care and will be useful to a wide variety of audiences, from the health care risk manager to the health care CFO to the independent physician provider to the managed care contract professional to the health plan grievance coordinator. It will assist the reader in understanding the basic concepts of managed care from several different perspectives: that of the provider, the payor, the health plan, the provider organization, and the patient. To assist in that endeavor, a glossary of terms is provided, along with a number of exhibits.

The challenge of managed care offers risk managers unsurpassed opportunity for growth. It will teach risk managers new exposures, a new language, new coverage options, and new treatment techniques.

22

Providers and Managed Care

Berni H. Bussell

Controversial and frustrating, managed care has become a staple of most medical providers' business plans. Today, more than 100 million Americans participate in some type of managed care plan. Over 75 percent of all office-based physicians have at least one risk-based managed care contract.

Managed care has grown to prominence on the promise to deliver better care at lower cost. This promise is built on four basic premises: (1) financial incentives can be used to influence how care is delivered; (2) information systems can be developed that can provide timely and useful management tools; (3) the management information will be used to effectively manage the type and amount of services delivered; and (4) economies of scale and cost efficiencies will result from market competition. Controversy rages about whether managed care has succeeded. Nevertheless, the reality is this: aggressive and effective management of service cost and quality will remain the most significant challenge facing health care leaders over the next decade.

From the medical provider's perspective, managed care exposes them to more than just the financial risk that medical expense will exceed budget. It fundamentally changes the way clinicians and health care managers conduct their business. Managed care changes the way providers are paid for the treatments they provide and how they measure their performance. It requires learning the new skills and language to budget, account for, and manage prepaid health care. Effective care management demands providers access and integrate clinical and financial information in new ways. Managed care exposes them to a landscape of new regulatory and liability risks ancillary to managed care business activities. It plunges them headlong into a morass of conflicting interests and competing demands that result from multiple business interests and payment systems. Financial and risk managers must position themselves to manage these risks as well as adapt to constant change characteristic of the world of managed care.

In this chapter, we will survey the breadth of managed care's risk exposure. The chapter will provide perspective for understanding and organizing these issues, and offer a logical, common sense approach to managing them. We will focus on basics: understanding the many sources of loss, staying abreast of regulatory issues, and controlling medical expenses.

The reader will quickly discover that there is much more to be learned in any areas surveyed in the chapter. Some of these areas are detailed elsewhere in this textbook. Many more are available from the extensive publishing on the subject. The chapter's objectives are simple: provide financial and risk managers with a general overview of the information; help to identify, understand, and manage the breadth and depth of risks associated with managed care; and provide a platform for future personal learning plans.

We begin with some key concepts. Then, we will then look at general management issues. Finally, the chapter will offer some thoughts on managing contract performance and minimizing the impact of ancillary and third-party liabilities.

....

KEY CONCEPTS

The key concepts applicable to providers and managed care are addressed here. Some of these concepts are: managed care, contractual liability, prospective payment methods, capitation, and provider organizations.

Managed Care

Managed care is the process of delivering and financing better care at lower costs. Developed by payers in response to accelerating health care costs,[1] the primary goal of managed care was to find ways to reduce both the volume and price of services provided while improving patient care. See Table 22.1 for an overview of managed care history.

From the provider's perspective, managed care profoundly changes the way providers operate. It changes the way providers are paid for the treatments and how they

TABLE 22.1.   Health Care: The Last Fifty Years

Indicator	*1950–1970*	*1970–1990*	*1990–present*
Socioeconomic	Expansion	Rationalization	Consolidation and integration
Revenue source	Fee-for-service	Prospective payment	Capitation
Volume	Units	Episodes	Lives
Operating focus	Cost per unit	Cost per episode	Cost per member per year
Marketing	"Pull" doctors	"Push" doctors	"Pull" members
Quality assurance	Occurrence-driven	Process-driven	Utilization and outcome-driven
Monitoring technology	Nurses and doctors	Facility-based technology	Mobile technology
Treatment modalities	Limited hospital	Multiple facility-based	Multilocation
Government policy	Hill-Burton (1946) Medicare (1966)	SSA (1972) TEFRA (1983) SSA (1983)	HMO Act (1973) TEFRA (1983) HIPAA (1996) BBA (1997)

measure their performance. It requires learning new skills and the language associated with budgeting, accounting, and managing prepaid health care. It exposes them to a host of new regulatory and liability risks exposures. It forces them to manage multiple contracts, conflicting interests, and the competing demands of managed care's multiple constituencies.

Managed care is different from traditional indemnity health insurance. Under indemnity insurance, payers reimburse medical providers for services delivered. Medical providers remain relatively immune to the financial consequence of the treatment provided.

In managed care, payers reimburse or prepay the medical provider a fixed amount of money to provide the medical services needed to treat a patient's illness or injury. In theory, this preestablished or prospective payment creates the financial incentive for the provider to rationalize and better manage the medical services delivered. We will talk more about prospective payment shortly.

Prepayment of health care services forces medical providers to learn new budgeting, accounting, and management skills along with the language of prepaid health insurance. Prepaid health care also exposes providers to new business risks:

- *Insurance risk*—The risk that economic loss will result from failure of the prospective payment method to accommodate expect random variation of performance and/or unexpected cost variation due high severity or low frequency cases such as high-risk newborns and transplants.

- *Operating risk*—The risk that economic loss will result from the organization's failure to manage cost, cash, and quality within the prospective payment method and/or its inability to work with other providers to jointly coordinate care.

In addition, it exposes medical providers to risks that are ancillary to the management of care. These include:

- *Regulatory risk*—The risk that economic loss will result from the organization's failure to comply federal and state regulations.

- *Fiduciary risk*—The risk that economic loss will result from the organization's improper handling of the funds entrusted to it.

- *Third-party risk*—The risk that economic loss will result from the organization's liability for the harm it may have caused to patients, providers, employees, and others. This third-party exposure is heightened by several factors including the use of provider-owned entities as the nexus for manage care activities; a blurring distinction between who pays for and delivers medical care; the perception that financial incentives conflict with duty to patients; and need for medical providers to perform business activities that may not be directly related to the practice of medicine.

Managed care arrangements take on many forms and there are few standards. On the west coast, for example, providers receive capitated revenue. On the East Coast, providers are more likely to reimburse for service delivered and share risk on final performance. Nevertheless, all arrangements have four common characteristics:

1. Managed care contracts create a contractual liability for medical providers.

2. They use prospective payment as a financial incentive to manage care.

3. They require joint management of a broad range of health care services.

4. They involve defined provider organizations as the focal point for delivering health care services and sharing financial risk.

Contractual Liability

Let's begin with some basics. Managed care is a contractual liability. It results from a chain of contracts that link members to the health plan and downstream to the medical providers and the care they deliver. Depending on the type of contract, there may be up to five parties involved in any managed care arrangement:

1. *Patients*—Known in the health insurance world as "members" or "enrollees."
2. *Payers*—The third parties that pay the health insurance premium or direct medical cost (including government, employers, and individuals). Sometimes, the term payer extends to health plans as well.
3. *Health plans*—The health insurers or health insurance plans.
4. *Provider organizations*—Intermediary organizations made up of many providers.
5. *Providers*—The physicians, hospitals, health care facilities, and allied health providers that deliver patient care.

While there are no universal contracting standards, there are generally three contracting vehicles that together link the patient to the provider and create the contractual liability. They are:

- A *member or subscriber agreement* establishing the relationship between the patient (member), the payer, and the health plan. The subscriber agreement must include by law an easy-to-read summary plan description and list of coverage, benefits, eligibility, member rights, and appeal procedures.

- A *provider service agreement* creating the relationship between the health plan and the contracting provider organization.

- A *participating provider or contractor agreement* governing the relationship between the health plan or the provider organization and its contracting medical providers.

Sample risk contracts are illustrated in Figure 22.1.

FIGURE 22.1.   Sample Risk Contracts

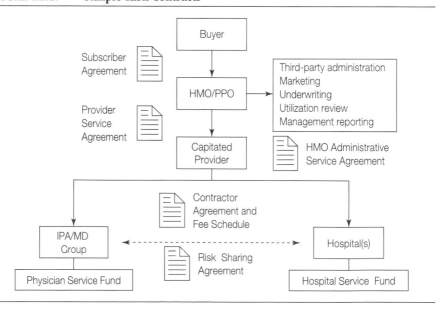

For our discussion, the provider service agreement performs three basic tasks. It transfers the financial risk for the delivery of a defined scope of medical services to the medical provider. It delegates the responsibility for administrative services among the contracting parties. It establishes who is responsible for collecting member premium and paying member medical costs. A basic provider service agreement includes the following components that are critical to the understanding of provider's financial responsibilities:

- A benefit plan articulating the services available to plan enrollees.
- A list of the medical services to be provided by the medical provider.
- A service matrix that assigns each medical service to a service fund for budgeting purposes.
- An administrative agreement between the provider and the health plan assigning responsibility for claims payment and utilization management.
- A compensation agreement.
- A risk sharing agreement.

The provider service agreement should clearly describe the medical services to be delivered. Generally, the contract does not require the medical provider deliver services in excess of the levels prescribed in the member's benefit plan.

Contractual arrangements with providers vary by payment type and contract length depending on the managed care plan and geographic region. Payments methods can be categorized into four types: negotiated discounts, fixed payment diagnostic related groups or (DRG-based fee schedules, per diems, case rates), fixed payments with risk sharing, and capitation or risk transfer. Contract forms and length vary from multiyear contracts with inflation adjustments to annual contracts that automatically renew unless terminated to single-year contracts that terminate unless renewed.

These contracts create legal obligations for providers. It is imperative that provider organizations thoroughly understand the contract expectations and assess their ability to meet them. While obvious, it bears repeating. The health plan generally creates the contracts to benefit the health plan, not the provider. The elements of these contracts and the critical analytic issues are discussed later in this chapter, but there is no substitute for careful legal review to ensure the provider's needs are adequately addressed.

Prospective Payment Methods

The building block of managed care is prospective payment. *Prospective payment* is a fixed payment intended to reimburse the expected future cost of the specified medical services. The prospective payment method determines how a provider generates revenue, the episode of care under management, and the breadth and depth of medical services to be managed. Most important, the prospective payment creates the financial incentive for providers to manage the cost of care.

Unlike fee-for-service medicine, prospective payment pays hospitals and physicians preestablished, fixed amounts to deliver a defined scope of health care services. The financial consequences of actual service costs exceeding these fixed amounts motivates the provider to control utilization and maximize the value of health care services they deliver. Payers prefer this payment method over fee-for-service because it fixes medical expense at predetermined amounts, thereby eliminating overutilization and unnecessary services.

There are many types of prospective payment methods. Some reimburse the provider a fixed amount for an episode of care (such as per diems for a day of service or DRGs for hospital admissions). Others, such as capitation, pay a fixed amount for the provision of a broad range of services to members over a defined period of time. Some methods include prepayment, others reimburse a fixed amount only after services are rendered.

The prospective payment method determines which units of service providers use to generate revenue. Medical providers grow their revenue (and medical expense budget) by increasing the unit of service or episode of care associated with each payment method. For example, providers paid a per diem would increase their revenue by increasing the days of service provided. Those paid a case rate would increase the volume of cases. Capitated providers would increase the number of members assigned to them.

Each prospective payment method also requires the provider risk-taker to successfully manage a different scope of medical services if they are to avoid economic loss. Using the prior examples, per diem payments require the management of the services delivered during a day of service. Case rates require management of the scope of services needed to complete the associated treatment. Table 22.2 highlights various prospective payment methods and their associated risk exposure.

There are four statistical concepts critical to understanding the inherent uncertainty of prospective payment:

- The prospective payment method is a projection or forecast of the average expected, not the maximum-probable, future cost of the underlying unit(s) of service. In other words, the payment amount is set at the point where there is an equal chance actual cost will be more or less than the projected payment.

- This projection is calculated using assumptions about a number of independent variables and *risk adjusters,*[1] and experience on *historical cost* and *utilization rates.*[2]

TABLE 22.2.   Risks by Prospective Payment Methods

	Unit Cost	*Units/Day*	*Units and Days*	*Acuity*	*Cost/year*
Discounted Charges Percentage of billed charges	X				
Fee Schedule Contracted fee schedule	X				
Per Diem Payment All inclusive payment per day	X	X			
DRG Payment Acuity-adjusted payment per discharge	X	X	X		
Case Rate All inclusive payment per procedure or discharge	X	X	X	X	
Capitation Fixed per capita payment	X	X	X	X	X
Percent-of-Premium Premium-driven per capita payment	X	X	X	X	X

- The projection has a relative frequency or probability of occurrence. The *"law of large numbers"* suggests that the likelihood this forecast will occur with the expected probability improve as the volume increases.

- Actual cost will always depart from this projected cost due to random and assignable cause variation. *Random variation* is the minor departure from the projected cost resulting from thousands of unknown factors. *Assignable cause variations* are major departures attributable to identifiable factors such as neonates, transplants, or other catastrophic cases.

These statistical concepts help illustrate the "insurance risk"[3] associated with prospective payment. In order to manage this insurance risk and ensure the reliable forecast of future cost, statistical theory tells us: (1) the assumptions used to develop the projection must be the same as those influencing future performance; (2) there must be sufficient volume to minimize variation from the average; and (3) the level of payment must be set, not at the average, but at the level needed to accommodate some degree of random variation. The organization's financial capacity and tolerance for risk determine the level of random variation for which the provider is willing to retain, or go "at-risk" for.

Capitation

The most complex and controversial prospective payment mechanism is *capitation*. Capitation is a fixed, monthly, per capita payment to medical providers for each of the health plan members assigned to them. In the language of managed care, these members are called *covered lives*. The capitation payment is based on an actuarially-determined rate or forecast of the member's future service cost. In exchange for the fixed capitation payment, the medical provider agrees to provide specified services to assigned members for a specified period of time regardless of the number of services the member actually uses.

Capitation has some advantages for providers. It captures a known patient population and provides a fixed revenue stream. On the other hand, capitation exposes medical providers to greater financial risk and requires them to rationalize and manage the financial aspects of medical care as part of their ongoing practice of medicine.

Capitation changes the performance metrics of health care. Revenue is no longer determined by the volume of procedures, but by the number of members assigned to the provider. The final outcome of the capitation arrangement depends on the accuracy of the rate assumptions and the provider's ability to manage the volume of services members use.

The capitation rate forecasts the average, not the maximum, expected future service cost of providing a specified level of benefits to the assigned members. This annual cost is allocated on a monthly basis or "per member month." The rate is developed using a number of factors including membership demographics, plan design, resources needed to treat the covered population, and historical cost and utilization experience.

Product and Plan Design Managed care contracts establish different expense budgets for different types of populations, such as: commercial populations (employed members and dependents under age sixty-five); Medicaid with and without aid for dependent children (AFDC); Medicare including primary and supplemental products; and individual members. The expense budgets for these populations vary because each exhibits a different utilization pattern. Utilization under the plans is also influenced by deductibles, coinsurance, and copayments imposed on members.

Enrollment Level and Growth Projections   The managed care contract covers a defined number of members. The number of members determines the provider's cash receipts, the aggregate revenue available under the contract, and the statistical reliability of the capitation rate. Growth projections are needed to compare revenue receipt against the timing of service demands.

Demographic and Other Risk Adjusters   The capitation rate is based on an assumed mix of members, the distribution of members by age and gender groupings, and risk adjusters including occupation, institutionalization, health status or illness acuity, recidivism, and chronicity. Like the major populations, the age and gender grouping with these populations also exhibit different utilization patterns. Attention to these demographic factors is critical, as a different member mix will yield different utilization projections and financial results.

Benefit Plan   The capitation rate is built to reflect the cost of the member's benefit plan. These benefit plans may vary by insurance product and reflect both mandated and voluntary levels of benefit. As the managed care contract typically requires the medical providers to deliver medical services consistent with the benefit plan, failure to quantify the cost impact of the plan may result in medical costs that exceed revenue.

Scope of Services   Many managed care arrangements put providers at risk for services they do not directly provide such as tertiary and specialty referrals, out-of-area services, and mental health and substance abuse services. Understanding the scope of services covered in the contract is important because financial results will depend on the utilization rates and price of these services.

Service Allocation   The contracted medical services are allocated to a medical expense fund or, in some cases, multiple expense funds called specialty service funds (such as an institutional service fund, a medical specialty fund, a primary care fund, a pharmacy fund, and so on). The service fund location of high-cost medical services such as chemotherapy significantly impact the capitation budgeted for the respective fund.

Historical Cost and Utilization Experience   More than any other prospective payment method, capitation exposes medical providers to a high degree of insurance risk. The capitation rate is a projection of the average, not the maximum, future cost needed to provide the specified benefit level to the assigned members. The rate consists of thousands of assumptions. It is expected the actual results will vary from this average due to random variation. This range of variation is minimized as membership increases.

There are two basic rate-making methodologies used to develop the capitation rate. *Experience-rating* develops the rate using historical experience on the actual subset of member population being served. It depends heavily on information of the defined member populations, their usage, and several years of continuous service to the defined population. *Community-rating* develops its rate based on the experiences of the overall member population rather than the particular subset of members being served. Community-rating is similar to pooling in that it spreads risk across a broader membership base. Table 22.3 illustrates a sample capitation budget.

The capitated provider must be prepared to deliver a broad range of services to its assigned members over the defined time period. This places them at greater financial risk than they would be under other prospective payment arrangements. Not only are they

TABLE 22.3. Capitation Budget with Utilization

Capitation Rate 5 (Enrollment By Age/Gender × Use Rate) × Average Unit Cost Member Months

Provider Organization Capitation Budget

Enrollment *149,033*

Category of Service	PMM	Units/1000	Unit Cost	Category of Service	PMM	Units/1000	Unit Cost
Physician and Ancillary Fund				*Hospital Fund*			
Physician Services				*Inpatient Services*			
Primary Care	$4.63	1,716	$32.38	Medical	$12.03	107	$1,345.00
Specialty Care	$5.20	1,882	$33.15	Surgical	$16.49	107	$1,838.00
Emergency Room	$1.12	272	$49.38	Maternity	$4.78	27	$2,102.00
Preventive Medicine	$2.79	889	$37.60	Psych and Substance Abuse	$0.99	19	$628.66
Allergy Services	$1.02	1,116	$10.95	*Outpatient Services*			
Hospital Visits	$1.19	276	$51.61	Test and Treatments	$6.64	1,088	$73.17
Surgery–Outpatient	$6.30	479	$157.61	Outpatient Facility	$8.21	181	$542.53
Surgery–Inpatient	$3.25	66	$585.75	Emergency Room	$2.27	242	$112.39
Maternity	$2.41	40	$717.72	Skilled Nursing	$0.0	8	$134.85
Anesthesia	$2.91	87	$399.35	Home Care	$2.44	268	$108.98
Asst Surgeon	$0.46	18	$297.76	Ambulance	$0.17	24	$83.72
Ancillary Services				DME	$0.40	142	$33.65
Laboratory	$8.59	4,012	$25.70	Therapy	$1.79	163	$131.31
Diagnostic Imaging	$12.26	1,383	$106.34				
Physician and Ancillary Fund Total	$52.13			*Hospital Fund Total*	$56.30		

responsible for delivering a broader array of services, but they also must manage jointly with other providers to coordinate services the capitated provider may not control.

There are many types of capitation contracts.

- *By payment type:* hard capitation or percent-of-premium capitation.[4]
- *By scope of contracted services:* full or carve-out services such as primary care, specialty care, physician or institutional service capitation.
- *By type of contracting provider organization:* network to physician panel capitation.
- *Based on who assumes premium handling and administrative responsibilities:* true capitation or shadow capitation.

True Capitation   In a "true" capitation, the at-risk provider organization receives the monthly capitation payment in advance. In exchange, it assumes the administrative cost and responsibility for paying medical providers for the services they deliver to its assigned members.

True capitation has many advantages for at-risk providers. They collect, manage, and control the premium, and benefit from any timing differences between their receipt of premium and service expenditure. True capitation provides an immediate financial incentive to manage care—avoid writing checks for unnecessary services and keep the cash received. Given that the at-risk providers pay their own claims, they theoretically have access to more timely and accurate management information.

True capitation also has disadvantages. The at-risk provider must have the liquidity and access-to-capital to meet the cash flow demands of the business. The provider assumes the cost of providing the administration and information management systems to pay the claims and manage the risk. As the result of accepting funds in advance, the provider assumes the fiduciary responsibility that the funds are available to pay any member's incurred medical costs. Due to this direct fiduciary responsibility, many states and health plans require providers accepting true capitation to post surety, demonstrate solvency and liquidity, and in some cases obtain an insurance license.

Budget or Shadow Capitation   Another common method of capitation is "budget" or "shadow" capitation. In this method, the managed care plan administers the capitation fund on behalf of the at-risk provider. The managed care plan collects the premium and pays member medical costs (including those to the at-risk provider) on behalf of the at-risk provider. These expenses are charged to the capitation budget. The health plan then reconciles actual expenses against the budgeted capitation and settles with the contracting provider. This settlement process results in the provider either receiving the budget surplus or paying the health plan for any deficit.

Shadow capitation would appear to be advantageous to the provider. The health plan handles all claims payment and administrative issues on behalf of the providers. Providers are paid fee-for-service, thereby eliminating the need to manage the cash flow of capitation. The fact that the health plan holds the premium may eliminate the need for the providers to meet licensing and regulatory requirements.

In fact, shadow capitation is a troublesome contracting method especially if the goal is managing care. It removes or defers the financial incentive to manage care. The providers are paid as they deliver services. The financial consequences of their managed care performance is delayed until the settlement process, six to eight months after the close of the contract year. As a result, providers generally look to maximize near-term cash receipts through higher volume and fees, forego management of care, and hope the accumulated cash will be sufficient to offset potential future fund deficits.

Under shadow capitation, the health plan functions as a third-party administrator collecting and holding member premium, paying member expenses, and reporting results periodically to the at-risk providers. As a result, the provider does not benefit from any timing difference between premium receipt and expense payment. Nor do they have access to timely information needed to monitor and correct performance.

Risk-Sharing   Many full-service, network capitation arrangements also carry internal risk-sharing arrangements. These arrangements are designed to share the financial risks and rewards between providers. These arrangements create separate capitation funds for related services (for example, a hospital services fund and a physicians services fund). Medical procedures are then allocated to a specific fund using a covered service matrix. The parties to the contract then create a risk-sharing agreement governing how the fund surpluses or deficits will be shared.

Determining settlements in these risk sharing arrangements is usually easier said than done. Timely settlements depend on the health plan or administrators ability to post and manipulate the necessary data. Lag times between service and payment dates and estimating incurred-but-not-reported (IBNR) claims add to the complexity of the settlement calculation.

Accounting Issues   All capitation contracts require providers to develop dedicated accounting skills and systems needed to monitor financial performance.

Whether providers receive capitation in advance of service delivery or are paid on an interim fee-for-service basis, the actual revenue earned under the contract will not be known until the year-end settlement is complete. This settlement generally occurs four to six months after the end of the contract year. In order to avoid the risk of over- or underrecording revenue during the contract year, providers must accurately capture enrollment, capitation revenue due, cash received, cash withheld, medical expenses paid, and medical expenses incurred by members but not yet recorded or reported. This information must be collected monthly and is critical to estimating amounts "due to" or "due from" the health plan at final settlement. Under accrual accounting principles, these estimated amounts should be recorded as either a receivable or payable each month.

Hospitals are much more familiar with these accounting practices than many physician practices. Hospitals already use accrual accounting techniques, whereas physicians more often account for their income and expenses on a cash basis.

Accurate financial reporting is further complicated by three factors. The health plan may provide insufficient data to allow for accurate reporting. There is an inherent lag between service and payment dates. Delays in reporting member enrollment and disenrollment information results in considerable retroactivity in revenue and medical expense estimates. Conservatism demands that proper accrual estimates be made to reserve for these unknowns.

The Continuance Table   Capitation is an effective tool for budgeting costs and aligning financial incentives. It is, however, a poor management tool. Capitation focuses on monitoring actual monthly expenses against an average annual expected cost allocated on a monthly basis. As such, it has three weaknesses: (1) actual expense is rarely in cycle with the monthly capitation budget, making it difficult to accurately monitor monthly performance; (2) the discovery of cost lags the management reporting system; and (3) it provides little information to medical providers about how to manage the care for individual patients.

The *continuance table,* also known as a frequency or claims distribution, is a management tool that translates capitation into individual, member-specific costs. It offers a more useful management perspective for clinical managers and physicians. The continuance table identifies the frequency of claims for single members by the amount of annual expense. It helps the provider understand that some number of high-cost members are assumed in the capitation budget. Providers can identify the type of patients or cases that result in specific levels of claim expense and develop appropriate, prospective patient management programs. Providers can compare expected and actual results on both a frequency and severity basis. Table 22.4 is an example of a continuance table.

Provider Organizations

Provider organizations are the focal point for most provider-based managed care efforts. These provider organizations allow providers to collectively negotiate contracts, and share administrative and risk expenses. The formation, governance, and management of these organizations create a host of additional risk exposures ancillary to the issues of managing care. Provider organizations are discussed here because the operation of the provider organization gives rise to the majority of third-party liability claims, and provider organizations may possess internal conflicts that impede the management of care.

Provider organizations have no single definition or structure. More commonly, these organizations are health care service entities, organized through ownership, contractual, or other relationships, to provide or arrange for the delivery of necessary medical services in a cost-effective manner. These provider organizations can contract with a health plan to deliver quality health care services to the plan's members for contracted prospective payment. The expectation is that the providers will control utilization within acceptable practice parameters to maximize profit.

The definition of a provider organization is not as important as understanding the objectives, structure, benefits, and drawbacks. Regardless of form or location, provider organizations have similar objectives:

- To link physicians and thereby increase and control patient flow.
- To market to and collectively bargain with health plans.
- To pool the financial risks of managed care among many providers.
- To share practice management, administration, and contract management costs.
- To integrate and coordinate needed medical services and service providers.

Provider organizations also add a level of complexity to the managed care effort.

- Joint ownership between physicians, hospitals, or both creates problems should the organization fail to meet expectations or be required to take corrective action against an owner.
- The provider organization may have business objectives that conflict with the job of managing care.
- Provider organizations are generally thinly capitalized and unable to invest in the infrastructure needed to operate the business.
- Provider organizations need to develop policies on internal reimbursement issues and the comparative level of risk assumed by each venture partners.

TABLE 22.4   Continuance Table and Claims Distributions

| | | | | | *Provider Organization Distribution* | | | | |
| | | | | | *Total Annual Member Claims* | | | | |
Total Annual Claims Cost	*Members*	*Distribution*	*Members Above Level*	*Percent Above*	*Paid Claims*	*Distribution*	*Paid Claims Above Level*	*Percent Above*	*Excess Claims Over Spec*
$0–$999	110,222	74.0 percent	149,033	100.0	$41,921,016	16.0 percent	$220,620,008	100.0	$220,620,008
$1,000–$4,999	30,848	20.7 percent	38,811	26.0	$67,083,294	30.4 percent	$178,698,992	81.0	$178,698,992
$5,000–$9,999	4,981	3.3 percent	7,963	5.3	$34,134,427	15.5 percent	$111,615,698	50.6	$111,615,698
$10,000–$19,999	1,825	1.2 percent	2,982	2.0	$25,134,245	11.4 percent	$77,481,271	35.1	$47,661,271
$20,000–$29,999	460	0.3 percent	1,157	0.8	$11,047,339	5.0 percent	$52,347,026	23.7	$29,207,026
$30,000–$39,999	266	0.2 percent	697	0.5	$9,242,742	4.2 percent	$41,299,687	18.7	$20,389,687
$40,000–$49,999	149	0.1 percent	431	0.3	$6,569,476	3.0 percent	$32,056,945	14.5	$14,816,945
$50,000–$99,999	214	0.1 percent	282	0.2	$14,213,752	6.4 percent	$25,487,469	11.6	$11,387,469
$100,000–$199,999	55	0.0 percent	68	0.0	$7,414,299	3.4 percent	$11,273,717	5.1	$4,473,717
$200,000–$299,999	8	0.0 percent	13	0.0	$1,960,061	0.9 percent	$3,859,418	1.7	$1,259,418
$300,000–$399,999	4	0.0 percent	5	0.0	$1,344,504	0.6 percent	$1,899,357	0.9	$399,357
$400,000 +	1	0.0 percent	1	0.0	$554,853	0.3 percent	$554,853	0.3	$154,853
Total	149,033				$220,620,008				

Example: Provider stop loss will reimburse 90 percent of the expense excess of $100,000 per members per policy period.

- From the patient's perspective, provider organizations further blur the distinction between who pays for and who delivers the care, as well as the clinical and financial decision making.
- They expose the providers to a host of new and evolving regulatory requirements and liability exposures.

Provider organizations are one type of a broad category of entities called managed care organizations. Ranging from utilization managers to health plans to provider organizations, each type of managed care organization approaches the management of care differently. They are differentiated by the level of risk they assume and transfer, whether they handle patient premium, and their responsibilities in selecting and integrating providers, controlling utilization or benefit administration, and delivering medical care.

Provider organizations take on various forms. These are illustrated in Exhibit 22.1. Provider organizations vary in their ability to integrate providers, coordinate care, provide autonomy, attract managed care contracts, and create economies of scale. Each also has different governance, operational, legal, financial, and political implications.

Providers should take care to understand how each organizational type impacts critical risk exposures such as:

- Medicare and Medicaid fraud and abuse.
- Private inurement and benefit.
- Restrictions on access to capital.
- Employment or contractor status.
- Corporate practice of medicine.
- Antitrust and noncompetitive practices.
- Pension plans.
- Self-referral and Stark II violations.
- Securities issues.
- Health planning and licensing laws.
- Fee splitting.
- Insurance laws.
- Business and professional liability.

············

SENIOR MANAGEMENT CONCERNS

For most provider organizations, managing care is not their only business objective. First, managed care remains only one of many lines of business operated by the organization's owners. Second, risk-based contracts represent a relatively small percentage of the provider's payer mix. Finally, the owners see the provider organization as an opportunity to attract physicians, stabilize patient flow to other business lines, capture the fixed revenue stream generated by covered lives, enhance the reimbursement for and thereby keep its key physicians, and generate additional revenue by providing management and contracting services to the physicians. These other benefits may be of higher priority and greater magnitude than any potential gains and losses under the managed care contract.

EXHIBIT 22.1.   Managed Care Organizations By Type

Utilization Management Companies

Utilization management companies are private companies, sometimes known as peer review organizations, that provide utilization management and cost and quality review to insurance carriers. They oversee and evaluate the medical services delivered by others.

A *third-party administrator (TPA)* is an independent organization that provides administrative services including claims processing and payment.

Health maintenance organizations (HMO) are licensed insurance companies. They finance and provide a comprehensive medical care at a fixed monthly premium per member. HMOs collect premiums from plan enrollees and provide or arrange for the provision of the medical care provided under their benefit plans. There are two basic types of HMOs:

- An employment or staff model where the HMO employs physicians who deliver the care.

- A contracted model where the HMO contracts with an independent practice association or group practices.

A *point of service (POS) plan* is a type of health plan allowing the member to choose providers. In exchange for this choice of provider, the member agrees to pay different amounts or experience different benefit levels based on the provider chosen.

Preferred provider organizations (PPO) are not truly insurers. They generally arrange to provide health care services through a network of providers at a discount rate. They do not usually assume risk in their agreements with members. In these arrangements, the health plan creates a benefit structure for its enrollees that includes financial incentives for the enrollees to use certain medical providers. Unlike HMOs, PPOs permit members to obtain care outside the network, but at a higher cost.

A *provider sponsored plan* is, as the name implies, a managed care plan or PPO developed by a single hospital, group of hospitals, or group of physicians. They are generally formed to contract directly with employers and other buyers.

Provider Organizations

A *management service organization (MSO)* is a wholly-owned subsidiary of a hospital created that purchases the hard assets of the physicians practices and manages the practices on behalf of the physicians.

An *independent practice association (IPA)* is an entity, often structured as a corporation, consisting of independent physicians or small groups of physicians for the purpose of contracting with a single managed care plan. The IPA in turn contracts with its member physicians.

An *independent practice organization (IPO)* is similar in structure to an IPA except that the IPO is formed to contract with multiple managed care plans.

A *group practice without walls* is a quasi-group practice sharing administrative and marketing expenses. Unlike a group practice, each physician maintains a separate office.

An *open-panel physician hospital organization (PHO)* is a legal entity formed by a joint venture between a hospital and its medical staff for the purpose of negotiating managed care contracts. In an open panel PHO, all members of the medical staff may join by virtue of their staff privileges.

A *closed-panel physician hospital organization* is a legal entity formed by a joint venture between a hospital and its medical staff for the purpose of negotiating and operating managed care contracts. Unlike an open panel PHO, membership is limited to medical staff meeting pre-established eligibility criteria.

An *integrated delivery system (IDS),* also known as a "super PHO," is a system consisting of multiple PHOs that form together to service a large geographic area with a vertically integrated range of medical care services.

These competing needs may shift the organization's focus away from managing care and cause them to ignore appropriate actions that would otherwise reduce the risk exposures related to care management. For example, many a provider organization has overlooked a target acquisition's managed care deficiencies in the interest of adding the physicians and their associated revenue stream to the corporate family.

This reference is made not in the context of judging the validity of any of these business decisions, but to suggest that the pure management of care is usually compromised by other factors. Risk management faces the challenge of navigating these competing demands, while still making good decisions about the assumption and management of risk.

············

ELEMENTS FOR RISK MANAGEMENT REVIEW

From a risk management perspective, managed care contracts and the provider organization create a host of new risk exposures. The manager must understand these exposures on a stand-alone basis and address their impact on the rest of the provider's business. Unfortunately, every contract and managed care relationship is different, so each arrangement requires analysis. Fortunately, the overall objectives remain similar. The following approach will help managers identify critical issues that impact rate, profitability, or the decision to proceed.

Financial and risk managers should focus their management activities in three areas:

1. Understanding and quantifying the many sources of economic loss.

2. Staying abreast of changing regulatory requirements.

3. Establishing basic loss control practices that avoids and control loss cost. These practices should include:

   - Thorough due diligence in advance of executing any managed care contract or provider acquisition.

   - Development of clear financial incentives.

   - Development of accurate and timely information and accounting systems.

   - Focus on referral and case management.

Managed care, however, remains a volatile, ever-changing business. To avoid potential errors and omissions, provider organizations should utilize external consultants, lawyers, brokers, and actuaries with a high level of managed care finance experience.

Understanding the Sources of Loss

Managed care loss originates from two sources: the performance of the capitation contract; and costs resulting from ancillary issues such as operation of the provider organization, regulatory compliance, and third-party liability.

Contract Performance   As with any business, managed care success depends on revenue exceeding costs. While medical providers attribute operating shortfalls to inadequate revenue, the shortfalls are due more to the high cost of medical care delivered. There are two major cost components: medical costs, and sales and administrative expense. Of the two, medical costs is the largest representing 85–90 percent of revenue. The business is also exposed to unexpected expense resulting from business interruption and contractual linkage costs.

Revenue   Medical providers perceive revenue shortfalls as a significant problem in managed care contracts. While the dominant issue is really the high cost of care and not revenue shortfalls, the potential for revenue shortfall does exist. These shortfalls may result from failure to capture revenue due or inadequate capitation.

The most immediate source of loss is failure to capture all the revenue due to the provider. The failure results from poor accounting and collection practices, and the difficulties encountered in reconciling member enrollment and eligibility. This reconciliation process is needed to ensure the organization has received the revenue it is due. Difficulties in revenue reconciliation result from retroactivity in posting member enrollment, disenrollment, provider assignment, and benefit plan eligibility.

The other source of loss is inadequate payment or capitation rates. To understand shortfalls resulting from inadequate capitation rate or revenue, we must distinguish these premium shortfalls from operating shortfalls. Premium shortfalls or inadequate rate occurs when the budget assumptions used to determine the capitation rates are inaccurate, the plan experiences adverse selection, the rate is insufficient to accommodate expected variation, or the enrollment is insufficient to minimize variation.

As we described earlier in the chapter, the capitation rate is based on many assumptions. These assumptions range from enrollment to demography to utilization rates. Should any of these assumptions prove inaccurate, both the premium rate and the total revenue may not meet expectations.

Premium shortfalls may also result from adverse selection. *Adverse selection* occurs when the provider group attracts patients who are in need of immediate medical care or require ongoing medical treatment. This is a typical scenario for provider organization anchored by tertiary and teaching hospitals. In this situation, the member does not contribute premium commensurate with their service requirements. Providers should work with the health plan to understand the screening processes used to identify and avoid employer groups likely to generate a high degree of adverse selection.

Rate shortfalls also result from unpredictable aberrations in utilization. These aberrations are called *random* or *assignable cause* variation. The capitation rate must be set to anticipate this variation.

The most common reason for capitation shortfall is market factors. Health plans set premiums at unrealistically low levels and ignore groups with poor experience in order to gain market share. Health plans transfer the risk to providers only if the transfer cost (capitated rate) is less than the plan's historical cost. The lower utilization and premium rates require the provider to make significant reduction from historical experience simply to break even. Meanwhile, they have paid medical providers more than the budgeted amounts to build loyal provider networks.

There are four common-sense steps to take in order to avoid inadequate capitation.

1. Ensure underwriting and actuarial assumptions used to determine the capitation rate are sound. Anticipate some level of random variation from the expected average plan results within the rate.

2. Know your direct cost of care. Do not pay yourself more than the budgeted rates without adjusting your performance expectations.

3. Increase your membership. Membership increases aggregate revenue while minimizing the range of variation around the capitation rate.

4. Be wary of health plans undergoing rapid membership growth.

The provider organization should perform a detailed financial analysis on every proposed contract and determine whether it is feasible to provide services within the rates proposed. The rate should also allow for some degree of random variation. This evaluation of a managed care contract requires providers to consider a set of issues with which they may not be familiar: actuarial expectations, the resources needed to treat the covered population, and cost and utilization patterns. It is important to understand the assumptions, develop a rate that is actuarially sound, and test it against historical experience. As referenced earlier in the chapter, the following are critical issues in determining the adequacy of the rate.

- Product design.
- Enrollment level and growth projections.
- Demographic and other risk adjusters.
- Benefit plan.
- Scope of services.
- Service allocation.
- Cost and utilization experience.

Management should involve an actuary to assist in establishing loss development and INBRs for any incomplete claims years, and in developing statistically credible forecasts in the event of small enrollments or minimal claims years. Absent historical experience, management should engage an actuary to develop the forecast.

Inadequate revenue may also be the result of several other issues. They include:

- Failure to account for medical inflation—the use of new more expensive treatment technologies.
- Changes in the benefits plans.
- Lower enrollments than expected.

Operating Expense   The other major source of loss is operating expense. Operating expense consists of two major cost components: medical costs, and sales and administrative expense.

Managing medical costs is the primary operating risk of the managed care contract. It is the risk that, assuming the assumptions on the capitation rate hold true, the provider will be able to produce the expected result. Potential sources of higher-than-expected medical expense include:

- Medical expense in excess of budget.
- Inadequate accounting and reporting systems.
- Unplanned business interruption and linkage expense.
- Inadequate stop-loss provisions.

Medical Expense   The most common cause of loss is the high cost of medical care. Medical costs consist of costs incurred by the contracted provider for services it directly provides to members, amounts the contracted provider pays to referral providers for service they provide, and consequential costs resulting from the need to add clinical resources or capacity in order to better meet members' needs. Measured as a *medical loss ratio*,[5] medical expense loss can be caused by any of several failures.

- Inadequate financial accounting and management reporting systems.
- Inability to audit medical expense for duplication of expense, inaccurate payment, inappropriate payment, and member eligibility at the date of service.

- Artificial pricing of services.
- Failed financial incentives.
- Ineffective management of referrals, length-of-stay, and high-risk cases.
- Failed stop-loss coverage.
- Extra expense for noncovered services or services or costs provided in excess of benefit plan limits. These issues include: providing services than are not authorized or covered by the health plan; Medicare/Medicaid eligibility and continuation of coverage requirements greater than those included in the health plan contract; and revenue reductions resulting from contractual discounts the provider offers to the health plan.

Information Systems Failures   Access to timely, accurate information is the key to managing care. Inadequate systems or system failures will inhibit the organization's ability to track and audit claims expense, monitor and correct its performance, forecast loss, develop reserves and IBNR, or provide the concurrent clinical and financial information that drives case management. More on information systems is included later in the chapter.

Artificial Pricing of Services   Some providers, particularly those under shadow capitation agreements, may pay themselves artificially high fees-for-service to maximize cash flow. Charging these artificially high rates against the capitation budget will increase the chance of operating deficits.

Failed Financial Incentives   The financial incentives created by the prospective payment method drive the management of care. In the case of capitation, the threat of a deficit (or promise of a surplus) focuses the provider on managing the cost of the members' care. Unfortunately, intermediate payment methods like those used in a shadow capitation may negate or reduce the effectiveness of capitation as an incentive.

Ineffective Management Systems   Capitated providers are required to work with other physicians to jointly manage care. Failures in this joint management, preauthorization of services, referral management, utilization management, and case management all would yield high medical costs.

Failed Stop-loss Coverage   Provider organizations can reduce the risk associated with unexpected claims frequency or severity by purchasing stop-loss insurance. stop-loss insurance will be discussed later in the chapter. It is important to note here that stop-loss coverage is expensive and may contain exclusions and limitations that result in less coverage than expected. Provider organizations should take great care in purchasing a stop-loss program and should only utilize insurance brokers with significant experience in managed care finance and placing provider stop-loss insurance.

Business Interruption and Linkage Expense   Providers need also to consider some of the potential hidden expenses of the contract. Business interruption either at the provider site or among referral providers may disrupt planned service delivery and result in the extra expense of paying noncontracted replacement providers. In addition, "most favored nation" clauses in any of the providers managed care or other contracts may result in unexpected revenue reductions to the provider. The contracts containing these clauses require the conversion of the contracted rates to the lowest available rate offered by the provider. Contracted providers may also be contractually obligated to provide service for other health plan products or offer the health plans insurance product to the provider's employees.

Ancillary Sources of Loss   Providers may also experience unexpected costs resulting from ancillary issues such as operation of the provider organization, regulatory compliance, and third-party liability.

Regulatory Compliance   As provider organizations assume more responsibility for handling premium dollars and managing service utilization and member benefits, they face heightened regulatory scrutiny. This regulatory environment changes rapidly. Failure to monitor regulatory compliance requirements may result in unexpected expense to the plan. Today, at-risk providers may face regulatory compliance expenses relating to:

- State licensing.
- Capital and solvency requirements.
- Standards for the security and transmission of patient data.
- Patient's rights, mandated health benefits, and quality assurance.
- Corporate compliance with federal fraud and abuse statutes.
- Fidelity requirements for handling patient and physician funds.

Third-Party Risk Exposures   Unanticipated operating expenses may also be the result of the defense and settlement costs relating to third-party liability. This third-party liability originates from four sources:

1. Operation of the managed care contract and the management of care.
2. Vicarious liability for the acts or negligence of business partners.
3. Handling of patient and provider funds.
4. Formation and operation of provider organizations.

The operation of a managed care contract requires providers to do more than practice medicine. They must provide a number of professional services relating to the management of care and administration of benefits. Medical management and referral activities common in the practice of medicine take on new meaning when financial incentives are involved. Some of the managed care business activities providers may be involved in include:

- Underwriting and enrollment of members and groups.
- Marketing and sales of health plans.
- Provider contracting, credentialling, and peer review.
- Provider network development.
- Utilization management and review.
- Interpretation and administration of health benefits.
- Coordination, continuation-of-care, and referral of medical providers.
- Claims handling and adjusting.

In addition, at-risk medical providers face vicarious medical malpractice exposure for the care delivered by referred physicians and hospitals. The directors and officers may be liable for failure to implement appropriate systems and controls to safeguard the entities and shareholder's assets, breach of contract, and noncompetitive practices. The provider organization may have general liability exposure relating to patient safety and nonmedical products.

There are three theories under which a provider organization may be held liable. They include: corporate negligence; *respondeat superior*—holding the employer responsible for the acts of its employees; and ostensible agency, based on the perception that an agency relationship exists between the parties to a managed care contract. A review of managed care cases reveals the following negligence theories being used to prosecute claims against HMOs and provider organizations:

- Direct negligence theories including negligent design of systems and benefits, failure to refer, negligent provider selection and credentialling, failure to monitor, and claims handling.
- Breach of contract, warranty, and fiduciary responsibility.
- Antitrust violations.
- Fraud and misrepresentation.
- Product liability.
- Denial of benefits.
- False claims made in government transactions.

Exhibit 22.2 outlines the major third-party loss exposures.

Three types of claimants account for the majority of the claims made: patients, physicians, and customers. The remainder of the claims made came from a variety of other plaintiffs, including government and federal agencies. The professional activities primarily responsible for the claims made include:

- *The processes of managing care.* The managed care contract places the financial and legal responsibility on the contracting providers for managing the medical care received by their members. This exposes the contracted provider to liability for its decision making, utilization review, and benefit determinations.
- *Provider credentialling and peer review.*

The remaining claims come from other sources such as:

- Vicarious liability for actions or malpractice by others.
- Breach of contract.
- Traditional operations and employment risks.
- Anticompetitive acts particularly in the case of exclusive contracts.
- Shareholder suits.
- Due diligence.
- Fraud.
- Government health care fraud enforcement.
- Failure to maintain confidentiality.
- Turning away patients.

The overwhelming majority of successful suits involve negligent utilization review.

The sources of liability continue to grow. The current legal battles center around agency liability, negligence, fiduciary duty, federal disability and corruption laws, mandated benefits, and the erosion of the protections afforded health insurance under the

EXHIBIT 22.2.   Sources of Third-Party Losses

Potential Defendants	*Potential Claimants*
• Provider entity	• Patients and families
• Directors	• Physicians
• Officers	• Contractors
• Employees	• Employees
• Contractors	• Health plans
• Affiliates	• Regulatory agencies
• Business partners	

Cause of Loss and Perils Include:

Managed care business activities
- Sales and marketing
- Cost containment and referrals
- Benefit determinations
- Underwriting and enrollment
- Claims processing
- Information processing
- Actuarial and risk financing
- Selection of providers
- Credentially
- Warranties of quality

Contracting issues
- Provider credentialing
- Antitrust violations and non competitive practices
- Good faith and fair dealing
- Peer review
- Vicarious exposure
- Apparent authority or ostensible agency

Direct and vicarious malpractice

Employment practices

Subcontractor compliance

Benefits determinations
- Failure to follow appeals processes
- UR/QA activities
- Good faith and fair dealing

Breach of fiduciary trust
- Turning away patients
- Acting for personal gain
- Fiduciary liability or misuse of funds

Regulatory compliance

Patient confidentiality, consent, and communications
- Disclosure and patient communication issues
- Failure to maintain confidentiality

Ancillary business activities
- Vicarious exposure for above issues
- Formation risks
- Network development and mergers and acquisitions due diligence
- Provider selection and enrollment
- Credentialing
- Network administration—command, control, and compliance systems
- Physician office administration

Employee Retirement Income Security Act (ERISA). Although there are considerable potential liabilities facing a managed care organization, the ERISA preemption has prevented ERISA-qualified employee benefit plans from being sued for punitive damages and limited damages to actual medical expenses. The Federal Employee Health Benefit Act (FEHBA) provides federal employee benefit plans with similar protections. Recently, legislative initiatives and new theories of liability have begun to erode these traditional protections.

Staying Abreast of Regulatory Requirements

As referenced earlier in this chapter, the regulatory environment surrounding managed care is extensive and changing rapidly. The current regulatory scrutiny is driven by a rising concern over increased health plan and provider insolvency, and an increasing number of member complaints about benefit denials and the quality of their health care. In addition to a basic understanding of the risks associated with managed care contracting, financial and risk managers need a solid understanding of this changing regulatory environment. Several areas warrant particular attention:

- State licensing.
- Capital and solvency requirements.
- Standards for the security and transmission of patient data.
- Patients' rights, mandated health benefits, and quality assurance.
- Corporate compliance with federal fraud and abuse statutes.
- Fidelity requirements for handling patient and physician funds.
- Accreditation issues.
- Regulations promulgated by the Securities and Exchange Commission (SEC) and the Internal Revenue Service (IRS) governing the formation and tax status of provider organizations.

The breadth and depth of this discussion requires more space than allotted here. Nevertheless, we will briefly discuss areas driving the majority of the regulatory issues.

State Licensing   Depending on the state, providers may need to be licensed in order to perform managed care tasks such as utilization review, or to provide health benefits for a prepaid periodic charge. The development of provider licensing parallels the concern regulators had about health plans. Regulators want provider organizations that accept prepayment to provide the same member protections required of HMOs. In most states, this would subject these provider organizations to state regulations governing solvency, quality assurance, marketing disclosure requirements, or appeal processes. In some states, however, these regulatory requirements trigger earlier. State regulations applying to the HMO are passed on to the provider when they join the HMO's delivery network.

The common practice of sharing risk between the health plan and providers or between providers themselves remains a gray area regarding regulation. The central issue appears to be whether the state believes that risk has been transferred to the provider organization to such a degree that the provider engages in the business of insurance. While the answers vary by state, generally regulators have limited their jurisdiction to only those arrangements where the provider has accepted a capitation payment. Budgeted capitation arrangements or narrow risk-sharing arrangements have fallen outside the insurance regulation. The environment continues to change. Providers should be aware that they are taking a calculated risk if they proceed with a risk-sharing arrangement without the specific approval of the state's regulatory agency.

Risk-Based Capital Requirements   Over the last several years, the National Association of Insurance Commissioners (NAIC) has become increasingly concerned about a rising number of HMO and provider insolvencies. In September 1998, the NAIC adopted a risk-based capital formula to monitor the financial solvency of managed care organizations and to articulate minimum capital requirements. The NAIC uses the methodology to monitor any organization capitating licensed medical providers in advance in anticipation they will deliver health benefits directly to individuals or employer groups. The NAIC's objective was to implement a uniform solvency standard and extend the standard to previously unregulated risk-takers such as provider organizations. Compliance with the standards ensures covered members will not experience a disruption in care, unpaid expenses, or lost premium.

The risk-based capital methodology calculates the organization's available liquid capital and compares this liquid capital to the amount needed to protect the members from any organization insolvency. The amount of capital and surplus needed is based on the organization's size, structure, and method and amount of retained risk. The calculation is complex and will not be detailed here. In simple terms, the output of the calculations is a ratio comparing of the organization's risk-adjusted capital (the numerator) and a minimum capital requirement (the denominator).

For our purposes, it is important to understand three things about risk-based capital:

1. It is fiscally prudent for every provider organization to try to meet risk-based capital requirements. Every managed care organization should prepare a compliance strategy for when this regulation is passed in its state. Understand and test the risk-based capital requirements in your state, review your managed care contracts, and estimate future capital and surplus requirements.

2. The provider reimbursement method directly impacts the risk-based capital requirement. As provider reimbursement methods move from fee-for-service through prospective payment to capitation, the required level of risk-based capital generally decreases.

3. Risk transfer vehicles such as surety bonds and reinsurance may reduce risk capital requirements.

While the types of organizations affected by the risk-based capital requirements will vary by state, any risk-taking organization may be required to seek state approval and meet the risk-based capital level prescribed by the state. Provider organizations seeking to go at-risk for Medicare programs are also required to meet state solvency requirements or apply for a federal waiver and meet federal requirements.

These federal requirements require provider organization preparing to go at-risk for Medicare + Choice programs to meet solvency standards. These standards include prefunding a level of potential loss, providing surety, and maintaining specified levels of net worth and cash.

Health Insurance Portability and Accountability Act of 1996   Financial and risk managers should be familiar with the details of the Health Insurance Portability and Accountability Act of 1996 (HIPAA) as it defines many of the regulatory objectives being advanced. Among the many issues covered in HIPAA, two have significant and immediate effect on providers—security for electronic patient data and medicare and Medicaid fraud and abuse protections.

The Department of Health and Human Services (DHHS) began rolling out the final HIPAA regulations on security of patient date in late 1999. All payers and providers will have two years from publication to implement systems to ensure these security changes. The regulations cover security of electronic patient data and electronic transactions while introducing standard data elements and interfaces.

HIPAA also establishes a comprehensive program to combat fraud committed against all health plans, both public and private. The program has several objectives.

- It coordinates federal, state, and local law enforcement efforts relating to health care fraud.

- It investigates and enforces civil, criminal, and administrative statutes on health care fraud.

- It provides industry guidance on avoiding fraudulent practices.
- It also incents people with knowledge of fraudulent practices to report them to the federal government.

The act requires health care providers to set up a corporate compliance to identify and correct fraudulent activity.

While initial enforcement efforts focused on fraudulent billing practices, more recent activity focuses on managed care activities. Specifically, investigators and auditors are focusing underutilization of services; self-referral; fraudulent payment data collection; member enrollment and disenrollment relating to Medicare, Medicaid, and TriCare members; and kickback violations that may result from the structure of the provider organization.

For further information, please refer to Chapter 20 on corporate compliance.

Other Regulatory Issues   Financial and risk managers should also be aware of other regulatory issues that might apply to them. For example, the Health Care Finance Administration (HCFA), Department of Justice (DOJ), and the Federal Trade Commission (FTC) have developed policies governing the enforcement of antitrust in health care. These policies articulate the type of collective activity among providers that would trigger scrutiny. The Health Care Quality Improvement Act of 1986 (HCQIA) provides standards for peer review processes and may offer some corporate immunity when standards are used. The ownership structure and income-sharing characteristic of many integrated provider organizations may require compliance with the IRS code and SEC code governing the sale of equity shares.

Accreditation   While not regulatory bodies, provider organizations generally seek to comply with accreditation standards established by the National Commission for Quality Assurance (NCQA), Joint Commission for Accreditation of Healthcare Organizations (JCAHO), and Utilization Review Accreditation Commission (URAC).

Other Compliance Issues   Many health plans are beginning to require provider organization to evidence their ability to perform the responsibilities under the contract. Specifically, the health plan is interested in verifying the provider organization will be able to reimburse the health plan for any cash deficits resulting form the risk sharing program. While letters of credit and surety products are available to meet this need, many physician practices have neither the assets nor creditworthiness to meet the underwriting requirements.

••••••••••••
LOSS CONTROL

Risk management strategies in loss control are addressed here.

Using Due Diligence

From a risk management perspective, the purpose of due diligence is to ensure that critical risk-related issues are identified before the managed care contract or relationship with a provider affiliate becomes a reality. These critical issues may have a significant impact on price, terms, or the decision to proceed.

Due diligence plays a critical role in the process of avoiding significant and unexpected managed care risk. It is used to conduct internal operational assessment as well as to evaluate potential health plans, provider organization affiliations, or managed care contracts. The due diligence and contractual analysis processes are discussed in greater depth elsewhere in this book. For our purposes, this section will highlight some of the due diligence objectives and criteria unique to managed care.

Internal Analysis and Analysis of Potential Partners   The basic objective in any internal assessment or due diligence process is to identify critical issues that may have a significant impact on price, terms, or the decision to proceed. Due diligence allows financial and risk managers to determine several things about the potential transaction:

- Will it provide the sustainable enrollment and revenue growth?
- Will it provide the expected operating income and positive cash flow?
- Does it provide access to needed clinical services?
- Does it maintain good business practices and reliable financial reporting systems?
- Does it maintain good systems for managing care?
- Does it have a compatible and appropriate governance and structure?
- Is it relatively free of troublesome prior liabilities arising from poor claims experience, understated IBNR and financial reserves, ineffective stop-loss and insurance programs, and liability for third-party claims?

Managers should collect and evaluate the following information:

- Enrollment and revenue projections.
- Operating and medical expense ratios.
- Cash flow and capital structure.
- Underwriting, rating assumptions, and rating methodology.
- Reinsurance, stop-loss, and insurance programs.
- Financial, accounting, and information systems.
- Loss control systems including underwriting, preauthorization, referral management, case management, disease management, and pharmacy benefit management systems.
- Governance, organizational, and legal issues.
- Managed care experience and past performance.
- Assignability of contracts.
- Assumed contractual liabilities.
- Funds flow and risk-sharing provisions.

Managers should pay special attention to potential unfavorable conditions such as:

- Small, managed care enrollments.
- Managed care arrangements for Medicare, Medicaid, and pharmacy benefits.
- Lack of claims history or financial reporting.
- Heavy dependence on stop-loss insurance.
- Weak financial and clinical loss control systems.
- Open-panel provider groups without provider deselection criteria.

Contract Analysis   As described earlier, contracts are a key component of managed care. They create the chain of liability between the patient and provider. They also describe the expectations of the business relationship between the health plans, the provider organization, and the participating providers. They affect payment, practice operation and operating procedures, and clinical decision making. Contract analysis is therefore a key step in due diligence.

The contract analysis should address two areas: (1) due diligence on the health plan offering the contract, and (2) analysis of the contract itself. For this purpose, two due diligence checklists are provided in Exhibits 22.3 and 22.4.

Provider organizations need to be aware that contractual agreements have serious implications regarding the transfer of risk. The agreements need to be reviewed relative to risk management strategies. It is important to understand two things: the managed care contract is generally written by the health plan for the plan's benefit, and there are no universal standards for managed care contract forms or wording. Legal counsel is a necessity in evaluating these contracts.

The primary objective in any contract analysis is to identify the contract expectations and determine the feasibility of meeting the expectations within the compensation offered. The underwriting factors for determining economic feasibility are discussed earlier in the chapter. They include:

- Capitation rate setting assumptions and methodology.
- Profitability analysis.
- Internal capabilities review (for example, information systems).

The secondary objective is to identify potential liabilities that may inure to the provider. Particular attention should be paid to financial, professional liability, and errors and omissions hazards such as:

- The medical and administrative services to be provided.
- The liability and indemnification of the parties.
- The contractually required utilization review, credentialling, quality assurance, and appeals policies and procedures.
- The payment terms and financial impact.
- Governing law.
- Risk pools and risk-sharing arrangements.
- Stop-loss.
- Settlement provisions.
- Contract period and service period.
- Dispute resolution.
- Coordination of benefits.
- Termination provisions and duties after termination.
- Disclosure and insurance requirements.

Please refer to Chapter 11 on contract review for more information.

Information Risk Management

The foundation of any good loss control program is good information systems. Data support and information management systems are critical in tracking performance and utilizing a data-driven medical management process. The task of building these systems is complex and costly, particularly when a provider organization has numerous managed

EXHIBIT 22.3.　　Managed Care Organization Analysis

Performance

Revenue growth
- Enrollment level by product
- Year-over-year growth by product
- Premium growth

Profitability
- Operating expense allocation and trend
- Medical loss ratio and trend
- Interest expense analysis
- Fixed cost analysis

Capital Structure and Credit Risk Analysis
- Cash on hand
- Current assets and current ratio
- Cash flow statements
- Past due provider payables (days on hand, percentage of total assets)
- Payment history
- Risk-based capital

Integrity of Financial Statements and Reporting Systems

Threat to Retained Earnings (ability to keep gross margin)

Ability to Withstand Upward Pressure Medical Prices
- Provider contracts by type and renewal
- Geographic market diversity
- Provider concentration

Ability to Withstand Downward Pressure on Premium
- Group contracts by type, renewal date, and size
- Geographic market diversity
- Employer concentration
- Regulatory sanctions, reviews, or investigations
- Civil or criminal litigation

Reputation

Accreditation

Managed Care Support Systems

- Underwriting criteria and procedures
- Underwriting screens
- Provider manual
- Availability of timely paid claims data and management reports
- Regular access to preapproval information on emergency visits, hospital referrals, and concurrent identification of high-risk cases.
- Preapproval criteria and process
- Referral management procedures
- Case management systems and managers
- Disease management systems and managers
- Pharmacy benefit management systems and managers
- Discharge planning

Qualitative

Type
- Group Model HMO
- Staff Model HMO
- Individual Practice Association
- Provider Sponsored Health Plan

Ownership
- Not-for-profit
- For-profit
- Provider group

Longevity—Years in Business

Licensure and Qualifications
- Appropriate licenses
- Compliance with federal requirements
- Meet solvency standards

Quantitative

Market Share and Service Area
- Enrollment
- Annual growth rate
- Employer groups

Benefit Plan Description
- Subscriber agreements and marketing materials

Performance Statistics
- Utilization statistics
- Days and procedures per thousand members
- Visit per member
- Cost per visit
- Allocation of premium

EXHIBIT 22.4.   Contract Analysis

Benefit Plan
- Services covered under the contract
- Allocation to service funds

Reimbursement
- Method payment
- Timely payment requirements
- Policies on co-payments and deductibles
- Remedies
- Most favored nation and other linkage clauses

Utilization review
- Payment linked to adverse utilization decisions
- Appeal procedures for benefit denials

Operational Issues
- Delegation of administrative services
- Referral and pre-authorization requirements
- Credentialling
- Subscriber eligibility
- Reconciliation of enrollment, eligibility, revenue, and expense
- Data delivery schedule

Subcontracting

Compensation and Risk-sharing
- Funding of deficits
- Cashflow

Fraud and Abuse Hazards
- Risk-sharing provisions
- Referral guidelines
- Representations
- Contractual inducements
- Measurement of quality outcomes

Terms and Conditions
- Effective and termination dates
- Termination provisions
- Duties after termination
- Representations and warranties
- Hold-harmless provisions
- Insurance provisions and requirements
- Dispute resolution
- Situs and jurisdiction

Historical Claims Information with Corresponding
- Member months
- Fee schedules
- Age-gender and risk adjusted population

Underwriting and Financial Analysis
- Risks assumed
- Quarterly or annual settlement of fund surplus or deficits
- Share the risk with others
- Limits to the risk or risk corridors

Enrollment or Disenrollment Penalties

Surety Requirements

Rate Making Assumptions
- Covered services, exclusions, and limit
- Fee schedules, copays, and deductibes
- Assumptions: enrollment, age, gender, units of service, unit price, and reimbursement method
- Historical utilization, cost, and claims
- Rating-making methodology: experience rated, community rated, or forward-thinking forecast

Financial Responsibility in the Event of
- Member ineligibility
- COBRA/COC
- Insolvency

care contracts are dependent on data that is incomplete, inconsistent, and poorly defined.

In the past, provider organizations have incorrectly assumed that claims processing systems alone will provide the information for all its management needs. In fact, the provider organization needs a more robust system to effectively manage its contracts. The key objectives for any managed care information system are:

- To support prospective reporting and case management.
- To support referral management systems.
- To track claims payment and expense.
- To drive appropriate financial accounting.

- To provide useful clinical-financial management reports.
- To forecast loss.
- To provide useful contracting information.

Prior to determining the appropriate information system, managers should carefully map the basic sources of data and how the data will be used.

Prospective Reporting   A fundamental requirement of managed care is the avoidance and prospective management of medical costs. For this to work, members with the potential to generate high costs need to be identified early. Internally, managers should ensure physicians, physician practice administrators, patient accounting staff, nurse case managers, and the hospital risk managers fully understand the need to flag prospective high-cost patients and immediately report those to the managed care financial and case management staff.

Expense Tracking   The information system should give the organization the ability to monitor significant expense items on both a member specific and per-member month basis and compare them with budget. The outputs of this system will be used to drive the concurrent management of patient needs. It also provides the information to separately track performance by risk group and product line.

Reconciliation   Due to timing differences in the accounting of expense and recognition of changes in member eligibility, the records between the health plan and the provider organization will vary. These variances should be researched and resolved to ensure proper recognition of capitated revenue and elimination of any claims expense for ineligible members.

Audit and Cost Recovery   Managed care contracts pay medical providers through a number of different payment mechanisms. The more differentiated the payment schedules, the more important it is for providers to carefully review the accuracy of all payments to (1) ensure no duplication, and (2) verify providers have been paid consistent with the payment schedule.

Cash Management and Accounting   Provider should interface the financial accounting and claims system to ensure proper cash management, develop accrual accounting statements that take into consideration account reserves and IBNRs, and support allocation of surplus or deficit.

Loss Development   Management should utilize a methodology to project future costs on known claims and estimate IBNR claims liability. These functions will ensure the provider organization maintains adequate financial reserves for claims payments and more accurately state the organization's financial position.

Many provider organizations have delegated claims payment and data collection responsibilities to the health plan. Managers should:

- Map the process and logic for installing the paid claims information and contract terms into the claims payment system.
- Understand the schedule and format for delivering the paid claims information to the provider organization.

- Evaluate the data delivery schedule for compatibility with stop-loss reporting requirements and the timing of final settlements.

- Request review and approval of authorized claims prior to payment.

- Establish processes to audit enrollment, capitation, and claims payments to ensure proper accounting.

A high-quality information system is also critical in securing the physician involvement and cooperation. Good information will help minimize the physicians' inevitable criticism of case management decisions. Poor or untimely information is useless.

Controlling Operating Losses   The challenge in controlling operating losses is establishing the priorities. The most immediate loss control priority is the diagnosis and management of the most volatile components of operating costs. As medical cost represents 85–90 percent of operating expenses, it becomes the most immediate priority.

Experience suggests that case and referral management activities yield a greater near-term benefit than efforts to reduce overall utilization. These management activities immediately focus physicians at two areas they are accustomed to managing. While utilization reduction is critical to long-term survival, the results take a long time to materialize. Without parallel efforts to reduce high-cost areas, the organization risks its short-term viability.

A basic loss control program should include the following steps:

1. Use due diligence and contract analysis to avoid unnecessary risk.

2. Establish an internal audit and cost recovery program.

   - Review all authorized claims prior to payment.

   - Review all authorized payments against provider fee schedules.

   - Review all stop-loss reimbursements against requested amounts and take corrective action.

3. Take steps to reduce referrals to providers other than provider organization affiliates.

   - Develop a preauthorization process and referral management program to avoid out-of-network referrals.

4. Identify prospective high-cost cases and begin a prospective and concurrent case management.

   - Managers may want to prospectively flag the following diagnoses: AIDS; cancer; bowel procedures; high-risk maternity and neonates; severe coronary conditions; spinal cord injury; stomach, esophageal, and duodenal procedures; and organ and blood marrow transplants.

   - Cancer (DRG 203,274-5,366-7,400-414,473)

   - Bowel procedures (DRG 148)

   - High-risk maternity (DRG 372,383)

   - Premature birth (DRG 385-390)

   - Severe coronary conditions (DRG 75,104-8,110,141,191,475)

   - OR procedure—infection (DRG 415)

   - Spinal cord injury (DRG 34)

   - Stomach, esophageal, duodenal procedure (DRG 154)

   - Transplants (DRG1-3,442,444,446,483-486)

5. Reduce expense in high-cost lines of service.

- Develop a replacement provider fee schedule for contracted providers and reprice claims.
- Review access to PPO contracts for out-of-network services and verify that out-of-network expenses have been repriced to the PPO rates.
- If hospitals are paid on a per diem basis, aggressively manage length of stay.
- Negotiate favorable pricing on outpatient services, particularly chemotherapy.
- Introduce a closed formulary for managing pharmacy benefits.

6. Understand regulatory requirements.

7. Utilize stop-loss programs to minimize the impact of unfavorable results.

Third-Party Loss Control

There are four major areas in which steps can be taken to control third-party loss: due diligence, patient communication, policies and procedures, and risk transfer. The seven steps listed below offer a starting-point.

1. Use the due diligence process and contract analysis to identify critical risk issues on inbound managed care contracts and provider groups.

2. Develop a written plan for provider selection, credentialling, and peer review. The selection, credentialling, and peer review of participating providers is a potential source of claims against the provider organization. A written plan should be established that includes participation requirements, performance metrics, corrective action, and appeals processes. The Health Care Quality Improvement Act of 1986 (HCQIA) provides standards for peer review processes and may offer some immunity when in compliance.

3. Prepare and monitor written utilization review and quality assurance plans. Given the severe liability exposures associated with this function, clearly defined policies and procedures should be established. The plan should include minimum qualifications and experience for individuals and entities performing this function. The utilization review program should also include standards for evaluating both the appropriateness and underutilization of services.

4. Develop a written plan guiding appropriate patient communication. Given that provider risk-taking and provider organizations blur the distinction between who pays for and who provides medical care, patient communication is a key loss control tool. Any patient communication plans should include guidelines for:

- Disclosing financial arrangements with payers.
- Differentiating treatment decisions from coverage decisions.
- Ensuring that managed care patients following the same treatment protocols and have the same access to service as nonmanaged care patients.
- Obtaining informed consent or refusal on recommended treatments.
- Outlining and discussing all possible treatment outcomes with patients.
- Describing and following grievance and appeals procedures.

5. Develop effective billing procedures to ensure the quality, timeliness, and consistency of all data used in the management of care.

6. Maintain an ongoing continuing education program for providers.

7. Utilize insurance and other risk transfer mechanisms.

- Use indemnification clauses to limit liabilities transferred between the health plan and provider organization.

- Require providers to sign hold harmless agreements and provide evidence of adequate insurance coverage including managed care errors and omissions coverage.

- Identify coverage available under the provider organization's current insurance programs and secure any additional coverage that is needed.

INSURANCE AND RISK FINANCING

The treatment of third-party liabilities by insurance and alternate risk financing techniques are discussed here.

Third-Party Liabilities

The concept of risk transfer is reviewed first.

Risk Transfer   There are four types of coverage that can provide liability protection:

1. *Directors' and officers' insurance*—Protects directors and officers from economic loss resulting from their liability for any wrongful acts in managing a corporate entity.

2. *Managed care directors' and officers' insurance*—Protects directors and officers from economic loss resulting from their liability for any wrongful acts in managing a managed care organization.

3. *Managed care errors and omissions insurance*—Protects the managed care entity from economic loss arising from the entity's negligence or wrongful acts in managed care business activities.

4. *Malpractice insurance*—Protects the managed care entity from economic loss due to its liability for direct bodily injury cause by the entity or its physicians.

Traditional directors and officers liability insurance may not meet the specific needs of managed care organizations. Particular attention should be paid to coverage for high-risk areas that may not be covered including:

- *Employment practices.*

- *Anticompetitive acts*—Network development activities including provider selection and deselection may be perceived as obstructing competition.

- *Due diligence and network development*—The organization may be liable for selecting inappropriate partners, neglect of assets, failure to manage or supervise, or improper delegation.

- *Shareholder liability*—Provider organizations, even when privately held, may face suits from its physician and hospital shareholders alleging misuse of funds or failure to disclose material information.

- *Fiduciary issues.*

Directors' and officers' coverage does not cover the biggest exposure facing a managed care organization—wrongful acts from the management of care. Managed care errors and omissions covers the economic injury arising from managed care business activities. Special attention should be paid to:

- The definition of managed care business activities.
- The definition of wrongful acts and the claim trigger.
- Damages covered under the policy. The majority of managed care claims are for economic damages or regulatory violations.
- Coverage for vicarious liability.
- Exclusions.
- How the policy treats "insured versus insured claims."
- Severability issues.

The coordination of insurance coverage is key. The organization's medical malpractice, institutional liability, general liability, directors' and officers', managed care errors and omissions, employment practices liability, and fiduciary liability insurance may afford some limited protection against managed care claims. While insurance carriers are improving policy forms to accommodate the changing needs of providers, it is best to assume insurance protection may not exist. These policies need to be reviewed carefully to ensure the broadest possible coverage is available.

For more information, see Chapters 30–32 on risk financing.

Operating Losses

Most provider organizations are marginally capitalized. So the overriding goal of any risk financing program is to develop a methodology for funding aggregate fund deficits that might occur; ensure appropriate funding, liquidity, and solvency; and address tax and accounting implications. The challenge is to accomplish this without eliminating the financial risk intended to motivate the management of care.

Management has three financing alternatives: (1) establish reserves and retain the loss, (2) share the loss, or (3) transfer the loss.

When retaining the loss, management must be concerned with two things: ensuring providers have access to funds to pay the loss, and negotiating favorable payback terms. Management can mix and match three tools to ensure the providers have available funds: a monthly reserve accrual, withholds on fees paid to at-risk providers or reinsurance recoveries, or letters of credit and other surety vehicles. A provider's access to letters of credit and surety vehicles is a function of their creditworthiness. As many providers, particularly physician practices, have minimal assets, the availability of letters of credit and surety availability may be a problem.

Management can also negotiate with the HMO to pay back any deficit through extended payment terms. Options include paying off the deficit over several years or off-setting the loss against future surpluses. Providers should avoid funding paybacks through future reductions in capitation rates or additional discounts on fee schedules. Reduction in capitation rates will increase the probability of future deficits. Reduction in fees may eventually leave the provider in the position of providing services to HMO members without cash reimbursement.

Another method of funding deficits is to transfer the risk for the deficit using aggregate stop-loss insurance. *Aggregate stop-loss insurance* indemnifies the provider for a percentage of any deficit excess of an aggregate retention or deductible per policy period. This aggregate deductible is defined as a percentage of the capitation. Aggregate stop-loss coverage is generally unavailable in today's market. Stop-loss carriers view this type of coverage unfavorably, believing it removes the provider's incentive to control losses.

Managers might look to the HMO or the independent stop-loss marketplace for this coverage. The underwriting process will be rigorous because the insurer will want to make sure the expected claims experience aligns well with the capitation. Price, control of coverage terms and claims data, and pooling are the key decision factors when deciding the best source for aggregate coverage.

Providers can also look to minimize the chance that deficits will occur. One method is to reduce the medical costs that accrue toward the fund by purchasing specific stop-loss insurance. *Specific stop-loss insurance* indemnifies the provider for a percentage of a single member's medical costs excess of a specific retention or deductible per member per policy period. It is the more common form of stop-loss coverage and functions whether the overall managed care contract is generating a surplus or deficit. Similar to aggregate stop-loss, specific stop-loss insurance is available through the HMO or from the independent stop-loss marketplace. As with agregate coverage, price, control of coverage terms and claims data, and pooling are the key decision factors when deciding the best source for specific stop-loss coverage.

Stop-Loss Insurance   Provider excess of loss insurance, also known as *stop-loss* or *reinsurance*, is an excess contractual liability insurance product used to limit the annual medical expenses incurred by individual health plan members, and/or to limit annual aggregate fund deficits. The policy indemnifies the provider (insured) for a portion of the loss excess of the attachment points (retention or deductible). Generally, the insurer is not involved in direct management of the claim.

There are two types of excess of loss policies: specific and aggregate. Both coverage structures require the insured to coinsure a portion of any recoveries. This coinsurance is intended to minimize the insured's incentive to push a claim past any stop-loss attachment points, or stop managing the claim once it exceeds the attachment point.

Stop-loss insurance has a claims-made and reported coverage trigger that requires all claims be incurred and reported within a defined period. Many policies carry an extended reporting period that allows claims to be reported up to six months after the expiration date. Some policies require that the covered loss (the underlying medical expense) also be paid within the same defined period. Some policies offer a thirty-first-day retroactive date or carry-over provision as a renewal incentive.

The insuring agreement typically states that the insurance company will indemnify the insured for any covered loss excess of the attachment and coinsurance. Covered loss is defined as the eligible expense for covered services provided to a covered member, and incurred, paid, and reported consistent with the notification provisions of the policy.

The stop-loss insurance policy may contain one or several limitations. Table 22.5 illustrates the financial impact of these limits.

- Per diem or case rate limits that cap the eligible expense.
- Specific limit that imposes a maximum benefit per member per year.
- Aggregate limit that imposes a maximum benefit per policy per year.

The policies may also have limitations on amount of medical costs that can accrue as loss and form the basis for recovery.

Administratively, prospective claims must be reported monthly. Consequently, the number of prospective and actual claims to be handled is large. In addition, proof-of-loss

TABLE 22.5. How Coverage Terms Affect Recovery

Cost Limitations

Many policies further restrict the costs that accrue toward the deductible and form the basis of the recovery by imposing per diem limits. These limits are usually averaged over the length of the admission. In these cases, the insured retains the risk for all costs excess of these limits.

Service Valuation

Insured services can be valued at "actual cost" (cost-to-charge ratio, and so on) or the payment rates in the underlying HMO contract. When using the contract payment rates, the insured retains the risk for actual costs excess of the payment. **Referral services** charged to the insured are valued at 100 percent of amounts paid.

XYZ Medical C...

Claims Summ...

Policy Number:	T0001B95	Member Name:	John Smith
Policy Period:	10/1/95 to 10/1/96	Date of Birth:	6/24/40
Paid Period:	10/1/95 to 12/31/96	Eligibility Date:	2/1/93
Population Type:	Commercial	Status:	Active

820415*01

Deductible: $50,000 pmpy

Provider #	Provider Name	Dates of Service From	To	LOS	Service Type	Per Diem Limitation	Maximum Allowable	Amounts Paid/Charged	Cost Adj	Net Cost	Covered Expense
10002	XYZ Medical Ctr	(Multiple Dates of Service)			Outpt			$5,957.00	64%	$3,812.48	$3,812.48
10002	XYZ Medical Ctr	5/5/96	5/7/96	2	Inpt	1500	3000	$3,303.90	64%	$2,114.50	$2,114.50
Total XYZ Medical Center											$5,926.98
10008	Religious Med Ctr	5/7/96	5/8/96	1	Inpt	2500	2500	$11,572.70	100%	$11,572.70	$2,500.00
10008	Religious Med Ctr	6/13/96	6/14/96	1	Inpt	2500	2500	$9,981.53	100%	$9,981.53	$2,500.00
10008	Religious Med Ctr	7/30/96	7/31/96	1	Inpt	2500	2500	$11,651.48	100%	$11,651.48	$2,500.00
10008	Religious Med Ctr	9/23/96	9/29/96	6	Inpt	2500	15000	$24,381.99	100%	$24,381.99	$15,000.00
Total Referred Inpatient Services											$22,500.00
10258	Ambulance	5/7/96			Transport			$715.00	100%	$715.00	$715.00
10003	ABC Hospital	5/17/96			Visit			$19.20	100%	$19.20	$19.20
10008	ABC Hospital	9/16/96			Visit			$168.57	100%	$168.57	$168.57
8247	Ambulance	9/16/96			Transport			$31.99	100%	$31.99	$31.99
Total Referred Services											$934.76
Total Physician Charges	Multiple (See Detail)							$49,131.11	RBRVS	$49,131.11	$49,131.11
										Total Eligible Expense	$76,378.35

Total Eligible Expense	$76,378.35
Less Deductible	($50,000.00)
Amounts Recoverable	$26,378.35
Coinsurance	90%
Net Recovery	$23,740.52

Deductibles and Retentions

The provider excess program or stop loss incemnifies the insured for member costs that exceed a specified deductible or self-insured retention per member per year. Choosing the appropriate deductible is a function of enrollment levels, risk capacity, and risk tolerance.

Coinsurance

Many underwriters request that the insured also retain a percentage of the costs excess of the deductible. Their objective is to ensure that the insured does not stop managing the claim after the deductible has been penetrated.

documentation usually consists of thousands of lines of expense and procedure data downloaded from electronic files, or submitted as paper UB-92 and HCFA 1500 standard billing forms.

Claims adjudication consists of comparing line-item procedure data, date of service, and expense data against the definition of eligible expenses and covered services contained in the insurance policy. There are situations where medical judgement determines the eligibility of expenses—so many claim settlements are the result of negotiation rather than technical adjudication.

Underwriters evaluate a number of key factors in determining the price of stop-loss coverage:

- The nature of the risk arrangement.
- The geographic location of the provider and the provider's delivery network.
- The enrollment and utilization projections.
- The provider payment schedules.
- The loss experience.
- Medical expense payment responsibilities.
- Availability of claims data.

Stop-loss premiums continue to rise at an incredible annual rate. There are three causes for these increases: high claims costs, artificially low premium rates, and the inappropriate use of low deductibles to cover controllable pricing and management failures. As premium rates increase, providers must reassess the amount of risk they are retaining and the most efficient ongoing use of stop-loss insurance. The checklist in Exhibit 22.5 may provide some useful guidance.

··············

TIPS FOR ADDRESSING MANAGED CARE RISK

In this chapter, we have covered many issues. Here are a few more tips for avoiding some of the potholes into which many an at-risk provider has fallen.

Carefully Review How the Managed Care Contract Delegates Administrative Services

Many risk-taking providers look to the HMO to perform several key administrative functions including preauthorization of services, utilization management, management reporting, and third-party administration and claims payment. As consideration for these services, the HMO receives, or holds back, a portion of the capitation payment. Despite the importance of these services and the overall, the parties rarely develop a separate service agreement that describes scope of work, performance metrics, and roles and responsibilities. To avoid misunderstandings and ensure accountability, providers should separately negotiate and prepare service agreements with the HMO.

Fully Develop Losses and IBNRs Prior to Analyzing Performance

As explained earlier in this chapter, the discovery of medical expense generally lags management reporting, sometimes by up to six months. In order to evaluate performance at

EXHIBIT 22.5.   **Stop-Loss Analysis**

Risk Financing Program Objective

To eliminate expense volatility at lowest cost of capital. Self-insure only the predictable and controllable expenses plus an additional level of risk tolerable to the organization.

Analysis

1. What is the current performance of my stop loss policy?
2. How sustainable is my current program in the stop loss marketplace?
   - Assumptions: Over time, the market will correct itself. Future price for stop loss coverage will equal projected losses plus insurer load. True cost of coverage is the net present value of the insurer's profit stream adjusted for the insured's gain or loss from cashflow.
   - What is the state of the current stop loss market?
3. How predictable are my losses?
   - What is the quality of my loss information? What is being done to correct deficiencies?
   - Are historical losses a reasonable predictor of future losses?
   - How credible is my loss history? Do I have sufficient enrollment and claims years to be statistically credible and at what confidence level?
4. How tolerable are my current loss expenses, and what corrective action is being taken?
   - By threshold, is my loss expense stable or volatile and over what time period?
   - If it is volatile, is the cause claims frequency or claim severity? What corrective action is being taken?
   - If it is stable, are expenses within or in excess of budget? What corrective action is being taken?
5. How confident am I that the corrective actions will yield the desired result, and on what do I base this?
6. What is my organization's capacity and tolerance for providing the ongoing risk capital to support this contract?
   - How much risk capital do I need to support this contract?
   - How much capital do I need to fund my self-insured retention?
   - Are there internal sources of funds available to meet these responsibilities?
   - Do I have access to external sources of funds? What is the cost of this capital?
   - Do I have the debt capacity to acquire this external capital?
   - Are there other, noncontract-related demands for funds (such as fund operating deficits, capital projects, and so on)?
7. How can I refine the coverage parameters to yield a better, more sustainable result?
   - Revise "covered services."
   - Revise "covered loss" definitions and loss limits.
   - Raise or lower thresholds and coinsurance.
   - Raise or lower maximum specific and aggregate benefits.
   - Review cashflow programs.

---

any given point in time, the organization must account for this lag in reporting. This is done by developing a financial reserve called a claims IBNR—claims incurred but not yet reported. The IBNR has two components: an estimate covering the further development of paid losses on known claimants, and an estimate for the discovery of unknown claimants.

While IBNR is not a cash expenditure, failure to account for IBNR may result in an inaccurate assessment of current performance and unplanned cash expenditures later in the contract year.

Manage Internal Pricing Issues

Perhaps the most common problem among provider risk-takers is the failure to effectively manage internal pricing issues—the costs the risk taker "pays" itself for the services it renders. This is a particular problem for providers with shadow capitation contracts who, for cash flow purposes, generally negotiate a prospective cash payment for services rendered that is then charged to the capitation budget. If the prospective payment amounts are higher than those allowed for in the capitation budget, the potential for a year-end deficit increases. This year-end deficit may result in additional cash expenditure and offset any marginal benefit derived from the high prospective payment.

The purpose of referencing this item is not to discourage maximization of cash flow. It is to caution managers to conduct a full analysis and develop and internal pricing strategy that considers all cash receipts and expenditures. Managers also need to take into account all aspects of this issue when evaluating the performance of the capitation contract.

Differentiate Between the Risk Financing Needs of the Physician Groups and the Needs of the Network

One of the benefits of a provider network is to pool all of its managed care lives to spread risk and make collective purchases. To maximize this leverage, the network may want to buy excess of loss coverage at higher levels that the provider might buy individually. The risk financing designs need to be fully explained to providers.

These benefits may directly conflict with the needs of the individual physician or hospital risk-takers who may not understanding pooling or want to pool risk with others. Remember, the concept of pooling is to average both the good and bad experiences of pool members. As such, future performance and costs will always be determined by the collective experience of the pool members. As members with more favorable experience always feel like they are "subsidizing" those with less favorable experience, proper expectations regarding pooling need be established.

Develop Covered Service Matrix

Many capitation, subcapitation contracts, and risk-sharing agreements create specific service funds. The description of what medical services are included in the fund is one of the factors determining the capitation rate. A majority of all disputes on claims payments result from disagreements on whether a particular medical procedure belongs in a specific service fund. Management must take care to understand and articulate which medical procedures are assigned to each specific fund and who makes these determinations.

Identify Cash flow Requirements

The cash flow associated with any risk-based contract will greatly determine how providers behave. Most providers are more loss adverse than risk adverse. They are more concerned about potentially paying out something they already have (cash), than the prospects of receiving a future profit or bonus.

Pay Attention to Unfavorable Conditions

Most provider contracts fail, not because of unknowns, but because managers refused to recognize obvious problems and take necessary action to avoid them. To prevent inadequate plan or contract performance, avoid making decisions based on limited information. Providers should exercise extreme caution if the business opportunity contains small enrollments; involves Medicare, Medicaid, and pharmacy benefits; provides no historical claims information; or contains forward-thinking assumptions.

Providers should take care to avoid accepting contracts if the provider organization has limited control over claims payment, inadequate management reporting systems, and lack of accounting systems.

Assess the capabilities of all business affiliates and avoid affiliating with other provider organizations who:

- Possess weak financial and clinical loss controls.
- Possess a lack of audit and recovery systems.
- Manage utilization rates instead of cases or episodes of care.
- Are heavily dependent on stop-loss programs.

· · · · · · · · · · · ·

CONCLUSION

Moving forward, health care leaders need to continually and aggressively improve the management of medical service cost and quality. Regardless of the form it takes, managed care will remain a dominant factor in the delivery and financing of better care at lower cost. All managed care initiatives will require financial and risk managers to effectively address the four success factors of managed care:

1. Effective use of financial incentives.
2. Access to timely and accurate information systems and management reports.
3. Integration of clinical and financial information into effective clinical management tools.
4. Development of economies of scale and cost efficiencies.

The responses and application of these basic premises will fundamentally change the practice and business of medicine.

As managers wrestle with these issue and their application in an ever-changing world, they must carefully assess how their actions affect a host of risk exposures, from insurance risk to operations risk to third-party risk. They must evaluate and quantify these risk exposures, not just in the context of the managed care contract, but from the organization's overall position as well.

The ability of financial and risk managers to provide timely, thoughtful, and cost-effective solutions to managing the risks of "providing better care at lower cost" will further enhance their organization's effectiveness at managing and allocating its risk capital.

Endnotes

1. Risk adjusters include age, gender, occupation, institutionalization, health status or illness acuity, recidivism, and chronicity. Each of these adjusters utilizes medical services at a different rate.
2. Utilization rates are expressed in units per thousand members. Utilization rates are segmented by risk adjuster and exist for admissions, discharges, inpatient days, procedures, and so on.

3. Insurance risk is the risk that economic loss will result from failure of the prospective payment method to accommodate random and assignable cause variation in actual results.

4. Hard capitation is a fixed per-capita amount regardless of the premium paid by members. Percent-of-premium capitation is a fixed percentage of the premium paid allowing the aggregate revenue to vary as premium increases or decreases.

5. Medical loss ratio is defined as medical expense divided by the premium allocated to cover the medical expense.

Appendix 22.1

Glossary

Activities of Daily Living—Activities performed as part of a person's daily routine of self-care such as bathing, dressing, toileting, transferring, continence, and eating.

Actuarial—Having to do with probabilities. Actuarial studies normally consist of projections of utilization and costs of specific benefits for a defined population.

Actuary—An accredited person trained in the mathematics of insurance who calculates rates, reserves, dividends, and other valuations, and who makes statistical studies.

Administrative Loading—The amount added to the projected actuarial cost of health services for expenses of administration, marketing, and profit.

Admissions/1000—The number of hospital admissions per 1,000 plan members per year.

Adverse Selection—A term used to describe a situation in which a carrier enrolls poorer risk that the average risk of the group.

Aftercare—Follow-up services after hospitalization or rehabilitation.

Age/Gender Factor—A measurement used in underwriting which represents the age and sex risk of medical costs of one population relative to another. An age/sex factor greater than 1.00 indicates a higher than average demographic risk of expected medical claims.

Aggregate Excess Coverage—A form of stop loss coverage that protects the insured against the abnormal accumulation of claims or an unusually high period of utilization. Aggregate excess applies to the experience of the group as a whole rather than an individual member. With aggregate, protection is triggered when per member month costs exceed a preestablished dollar limit. Aggregate excess is typically used by insureds who have minimal catastrophic risk.

Allowable Costs (or eligible costs)—The amounts paid or incurred for services rendered by a health provider that qualify as covered expenses.

Broker—A term generally used to describe a person licensed to place insurance business with more than one insurance carrier and who has no exclusive contract requiring that all business be offered to a single carrier. Unlike an agent who represents an insurance carrier, a broker has a legal duty to represent a buyer client.

Budgeted Capitation—A method of payment for health care services in which the provider receives a predetermined payment for services rendered and the total of payments received are compared to a budgeted fixed fee per member per month and the difference reconciled through a contractual risk sharing arrangement.

Capitation—A fixed dollar amount per member per month established to cover the projected cost of health services for an individual and covered population.

Carrier—The insurer who agrees to underwrite and assume a risk in exchange for a premium payment.

Case Management—The process by which all health-related matters of a patient's case are managed by a physician, nurse, or designated health professional. The process coordinates, evaluates, and manages the components of care delivered with respect to quality, cost, and service utilization.

Case Mix—The clinical composition of a hospital's inpatient population among various diagnoses. A measure of the relative frequency and intensity of care delivered by a hospital, it is factor used in determining cost and rate setting.

Claim—Information submitted by a provider to establish that medical services, covered as benefits in an insurance contract, were provided to a covered person.

Claim Lag—The time interval between the incurred date of a claim and its submission to an insurer for payment.

Claim Management—The process by which the information and documentation of services rendered are collected, compiled, evaluated, repriced, and submitted to an insurer for reimbursement.

Coinsurance—The portion of the risk borne by the insured as a cash payment. Usually a percentage of potential recoveries, coinsurance usually applies equally across the vertical range of costs.

Concurrent Review—Review of a procedure or hospital admission by a health professional other than the one providing the care.

Contract Size—The number of members covered under the managed care contract.

Conversion Privilege—The contractual provision allowing an individual member's costs incurred under one covered plan to apply toward a second covered plan when they switch managed care plans.

Contract Year—The period of time from the effective date of the contract to the expiration date of the contract.

Coordination of Benefits—A typical insurance provision whereby responsibility for primary payment of services is allocated among multiple responsible insurance carriers. A form of subrogation, this provision avoids the possibility of being reimbursed twice for the same service.

Covered Costs—See *Allowable Costs.*

Covered Lives—A term referring to the number of persons covered by a managed care or insurance contract.

Covered Person or Member—An individual who meets the eligibility requirements and for whom premium payments are paid for specific benefits of the contractual agreement.

Covered Plan—Managed care contract or benefits that meet eligibility requirements for coverage by an insurance contract.

Covered Service—The health services that meet the eligibility requirements for coverage by an insurance contract.

Date of Service—The date on which health services are provided to the covered person.

Deductible—Amounts required to be paid by the insured before the insurer will make payment for eligible benefits as stipulated by the insurance contract. A deductible is different from a specific retention in that a deductible typically erodes the maximum benefit provided in the contract whereas a specific retention does not.

Deductible Carry-Over—Costs applied to the deductible for services during the last month of a contract year simultaneously apply toward the deductible in the following year.

Demographics—The statistical characteristics of a defined population including age, gender, income level, race, education, occupation, employment status, and housing.

Diagnosis—The identification of disease or condition through analysis and examination.

Diagnostic Related Group (DRG)—A federally mandated program in which hospital procedures are classified and rated based on principal diagnosis and comorbidities and a payment rate applied.

Discharge Planning—The evalaution of a patient's medical needs in order to arrange for appropriate care after discharge from an inpatient facility.

Discounted Fee-for-Service—A reimbursement system whereby a provider agrees to provide services on a fee-for-service basis with the fees discounted by a certain percentage.

Effective Date—The date a contract becomes in force.

Eligibility—Status with respect to receiving coverage.

Eligibility Date—The date a covered person becomes eligible for benefits under an existing contract.

Eligible Expenses—Reasonable and customary charges or the agreed upon contract amount or fee for health care services and supplies to be covered by an insurance contract.

Eligible Person—An individual who meets the eligibility requirement specified in the contract.

Enrollee—An individual who is enrolled for coverage under a health plan contract and who is eligible to to receive health services under the contract.

Enrollment—(1) The total number of covered persons in a health plan. (2) The process by which a health plan signs up individuals for membership.

Exclusions—Specific conditions or circumstances listed in the contract for which the policy will not provide payment.

Expected Claims—The projected claim level of a covered group for a defined contract period.

Experience Rating—The process of setting rates based partially or in whole on evaluating claims experience and then projecting required revenues for a future policy year.

Experimental Procedures—Medical, surgical, psychiatric, substance abuse, or other health services, supplies, treatments, procedures, therapies, or devices that have not been approved by the Federal Trade Commission, are not generally accepted by informed health care professionals as effective in treating the specified condition, and have not been proven effective by scientific evidence.

Extended Care Facility—A nursing home or nursing center licensed to provide twenty-four-hour skilled nursing care.

Fee Schedule—A comprehensive listing of fee maximums used to reimburse medical providers.

First Dollar Coverage—A policy that has no deductibles and covers the first dollar of a member's expense.

Frequency—The number of times a service is provided.

Funding Level—The amount of revenue required to finance a medical care program. Under an insured program, this is the premium rate, which typically consists of expected claims costs, stop loss or reinsurance premium, and other administrative expenses.

Funding Method—The means by which a risk-taker funds a medical benefit plan. The most common methods are: self-funding from operating, debt, or equity funds; risk sharing; and risk transfer (insurance) on either a prospective or retrospective basis.

Gatekeeping—The process by which a primary care physician directly provides primary care and coordinates all diagnostic testing and patient referrals.

Grace Period—A set number of days past the due date of a premium payment during which medical coverage may not be cancelled.

HCFA—Health Care Financing Administration. The federal agency responsible for administering Medicare and the states' administration of Medicaid.

HCFA 1500—A universal billing form developed by HCFA for the billing of professional fees to health carriers.

HCFA Common Procedural Coding System (HCPCS)—A standard listing of medical services, procedures, and supplies provided by physicians and other medical providers. HCPCS include Common Procedural Terminology (CPT) codes, national alpha-numeric codes, and local alpha-numeric codes.

Health Maintenance Organization (HMO)—A risk-taking entity that provides, offers, or arranges for coverage of designated health services in exchange for a fixed, prepaid premium. There are four basic types of HMOs defined by the characteristics of their medical delivery system: group models, network models, staff models, and independent practice associations.

Health Service Agreement (or Subscriber Agreement)—The detailed procedure and benefit description given to each enrolled member.

Home Health Agency—A facility or program duly licensed to provide home health services.

Hold Harmless—A clause frequently found in contracts whereby both parties hold each other not liable for malpractice or corporate malfeasance if either party is found to be liable.

Hospice—A facility or program duly licensed to provide palliative and supportive care to the terminally ill.

In-Area Services—Health services rendered by providers located within the authorized service area.

Incurred But Not Reported (IBNR)—A term that refers to the costs associated with a medical service that has been provided, but for which a claim or bill has not yet been received. IBNR reserves are recorded to account for estimated liability based on studies of prior lags in claims submissions.

Incurred Claims—A term referring to the actual liability for a period that includes all claims with dates of service within the specified period.

Incurred Claims Loss Ratio—The result of incurred claims divided by premium.

Indemnity—An insurance program in which the insured person is reimbursed for covered expenses.

Injury—Physiological damage other than sickness including all related conditions and recurrent symptoms.

In-Network Services—A term describing the treatments provided to covered persons by providers participating in the insured's delivery system.

Inpatient—An individual who has been admitted to a hospital as a registered bed patient and is recieving services provided under the direction of a physician.

Intermediate Care Facility—A facility providing a level of care to individuals who do not require the level of care provided in a hospital or skilled nursing facility, but who require care above the level of room and board.

International Classification of Diseases, Ninth Edition (ICD-9)—A standard listing of diagnoses and identifying codes for reporting diagnoses.

Long-Term Care—Assistance and care for people with chronic disabilities who require help with the activities of daily living or who suffer from cognitive impairment.

Loss Ratio—The result of paid claims plus incurred claims plus expenses divided by premium.

Manual Rating—Rates developed based on the health plan's average claims data and then adjusted for group specific demographic, industry factor, or benefit variation.

Medicaid—A federal program administered by the states that provides medical benefits to eligible low income persons needing health care.

Medical Loss Ratio—The cost ratio of health services used compared to revenue received.

Medically Necessary—A service or treatment that is: appropriate and consistent with the diagnosis; is in accordance with generally accepted medical practice; and could not have been omitted without adversely affecting the individual's condition or the quality of medical care rendered.

Medicare—A federal program covering the costs of hospitalization, medical care, and some related services for eligible persons. Medicare has two parts: Part A covering inpatient costs reimbursed prospectively on a DRG basis; and Part B, which covers outpatient costs.

Member—A participant in a health plan.

Member Month—A unit of volume measurement that records one member for each month the member is eligible to receive benefits.

Morbidity—The incidence and severity of sicknesses and accidents in a well-defined class or classes of persons.

Mortality—The death rate at each age as determined by prior experience.

Out-of-Area—A term describing the treatment obtained by a covered person outside of the network service area.

Out-of-Network—A term describing the treatments provided to covered persons by providers who do not participate in the insured's delivery system.

Outlier—Patient case that have an extremely short or long length of stay of extraordinarily high or low costs when compared to similar cases.

Outpatient—A person who receives health care services without being admitted to the hospital.

Peer Review—The evaluation of quality of total health care by medical staff with equivalent training.

Per Diem Rates—A method of payment based on allowable costs per patient day.

Per Diem Costs—Actual costs incurred by the provider to provide a day of service.

Per Diem Limitation—The maximum costs per day covered under an insurance contract.

Per Member Per Month (PMPM)—The unit of measure related to each effective member for each month the member was eligible.

Physician's Current Procedural Terminology (CPT)—A standard five-digit listing of medical services and procedures performed by physicians and other providers.

Place of Service—The location where the health services were rendered.

Point-of-Service—A type of health plan providing different benefit or payment levels based on where the covered person chooses to receive services from providers.

Pooling—The process of combining risk for all groups or number of groups into a single risk pool.

Pre-Existing Condition—Any medical condition that was diagnosed or treated prior to a specified date.

Premium—The consideration paid to an insurance carriers for providing the coverage specified in the insurance contract.

Primary Care—Basic or general health care services traditionally provided by family practice, pediatrics, and internal medicine physicians.

Primary Coverage—Under coordination of benefits rules, the insurance plan that pays its eligible expenses first and without consideration of any other coverage.

Prior Authorization—The process of obtaining coverage approval for a service or medication.

Proof of Loss—The documentation providing the detail supporting a claim.

Prospective Claim Report—A requirement under a stop loss contract whereby the insured reports, on a monthly basis, all members whose costs have exceeded 50 percent of the specified deductible.

Provider—A physician, hospital, group practice, nursing home, pharmacy, or any other individuals, groups of individuals, or facilities providing a health care service.

Provider Excess of Loss Coverage—Insurance purchased by provider from an insurance company to protect itself against all or part of the losses it may incur in meeting its responsibilities under a risk-based contract.

Quality Assurance—A formal set of activities to review and affect the quality of the services provided.

Quality Improvement—A continuous process that identifies problems, tests solutions, monitors results, and acts on the results to correct or initiate further solutions.

Rate—The amount of money paid to a carrier for coverage. Rates are usually charged on a monthly basis.

Rating Process—The process of evaluating a group to determine a premium rate in regard to the type of risk it represents. Key components include: age, gender, location, occupation, industry, base capitation, plan design, average family size, demographics, and administrative costs.

Reasonable and Customary—A term referring to the commonly charged or prevailing fees for health services within a geographic area.

Recidivism—The frequency of the same patient returning to the hospital for the same presenting medical problem.

Referral—A recommendation by a physician and/or health plan for a member to receive care from a different provider.

Referral Provider—A provider that renders service to a member who has been sent to them by a provider participating in the health plan.

Reinsurance—Insurance purchased by a licensed risk-taker (insurance company or HMO) or self-funded employer from another insurance company to protect itself against all or part of the losses it may incur.

Reserves—Fiscal method of providing a fund for incurred but not reported claims or other financial liabilities.

Resource Based Relative Value Scale (RBRVS)—A classification system used as a financing mechanism to reimburse physicians and other providers for health care services. RBRVS values the skill and training required to perform a given health care service.

Retention—The portion of the medical costs that are kept and self-funded by the insured.

Retrospective Review—A method for determining medical necessity and appropriate billing practice for services already rendered.

Risk Pool—A defined account to which revenues and expenses are posted.

Secondary Care—Services provided by medical specialists who do generally not have first contact with the patient.

Secondary Coverage—Under coordination of benefits rules, the plan responsible for paying eligible charges not covered by the primary coverage.

Section 125 Plan—A flexible benefit plan paid for in pretax dollars as described in IRS Section 125.

Self-Funding—The funding of benefit plan obligations without purchasing insurance.

Service Area—The geographic area serviced by the health plan or provider as specified in the participation agreement.

Shared Risk—An arrangement in which financial liabilities are apportioned among two or more entities.

Skilled Nursing Facilities—A facility that accepts patients in need of rehabilitation and care qualifying for Medicare-eligible skilled coverage. SNFs must be certified by Medicare and meet specific requirements including twenty-four-hour nursing care, availability of physical, occupational and speech therapy, and others.

Solvency—The financial condition in which an organization is able to pay its debts as they come due.

Specific Excess Coverage—The form of stop loss coverage that protects the insured against the abnormal severity or frequency of claims by an individual member or specific service, case, or demographic risk.

Stop Loss Insurance (Excess Coverage)—Insurance coverage whereby absorption of prepaid patient expenses are limited by limiting lossess on an individual or aggregate basis.

Subrogation—A procedure under which and insurance company can recover from third parties the full or partial amounts paid by the insurer.

Subspecialist/Specialist—A physician who is recognized to have expertise in a specialty of medicine or surgery.

Tertiary Care—Health care services provided by highly specialized providers such as neurosurgeons, thoracic surgeons, and intensive care units usually requiring the use of university-affiliated or teaching hospitals with extensive diagnostic and treatment capabilities.

Third-Party Administrator (TPA)—An independent person or corporate entity who administers group benefits, claims, and utilization review.

Third-Party Payer—An organization that acts as a fiscal intermediary between the covered person and the provider.

Title XIX—Commonly refers to the Medicaid program.

Title XVIII—Commonly refers to the Medicare program.

Totally Disabled—A typical exclusion in a stop loss contract that denies coverage to any covered person who is hospitalized on the effective date of the coverage until they are discharged.

Total Disability—Disability due to an injury, illness, or pregnancy that: (1) requires regular care and attendance by a physician; and (2) renders the person, in the opinion of a physician, unable to perform the duties of their occupation.

Underwriting—The process of selecting, classifying, evaluating, and assuming risks according to their insurability.

Uniform Billing Code of 1992 (UB-92)—A federal directive requiring hospitals to follow specific billing procedures iteminzing all services included and billed on each invoice.

Usual, Reasonable, and Customary—See *Reasonable and Customary.*

Utilization Management—Systematic means for reviewing and controlling a members use of medical services and the providers use of medical resources.

Utilization Review—System of review conducted by professional personnel of the appropriateness, quality, and need for health care services rendered to members.

Utilization—The patterns of rates of use of a service or type of service within a specific contract period. Utilization is generally expressed in units per 1,000 persons.

Withhold—The portion of the capitation or payment to providers withheld by the HMO until year-end in order to create a financial incentive for efficient care.

PART IV

Risk Management Treatments and Techniques

T his section will highlight those techniques that can *prevent* or *reduce* the number of adverse events from occurring in a variety of health care delivery settings. Several "hot topics" in today's environment are discussed in detail. How to manage one of the most valuable resources of a health care organization, the employee, is discussed in detail in the chapters on human resources issues, workers' compensation, and safety and security. Patient-related concerns are identified in the chapters on ethics and informed consent. A risk manager's efforts to control losses are discussed in the chapters on claims and litigation management and biomedical technology.

While this section gives the reader a broad overview of a variety of different risk management techniques to treat loss exposure, it is by no means complete. As new exposures to loss are recognized, new treatments and techniques are identified and implemented every day to manage them.

23

Informed Consent as a Loss Control Process

Fay A. Rozovsky

Securing the informed consent of a patient marks the culmination of an important step in the care provider-patient relationship. "Consent," the act of agreeing to a specific diagnostic test or treatment, is not merely the completion of a form but, rather, a process[1] premised on effective communication and a meeting of the minds regarding what is and is not to be done to the patient. Characterized in this way, consent to treatment is like a contract for agreed-on services by the provider in exchange for valuable consideration (payment) by the patient or payer.[2]

In other ways, however, consent to treatment is different from other contracts. It is the cement that holds together the ongoing health care provider-patient relationship. It is platform for communication between patient and caregiver that starts at the outset of the care-giving relationship and ends with the completion of treatment. It is marked by extensive case law and guided by both federal and state laws that set forth not only the broad parameters for a valid treatment authorization,[3] but also specific diagnostic interventions and surgery. Included in this latter category are state laws governing consent to HIV testing, breast cancer surgery, and abortion.

Despite all the judicial interpretations, statutes, and regulations, consent—or lack of it—remains a persistent basis for claim in professional liability lawsuits. This is true whether the consent claim is adjunctive to other tort allegations or a stand-alone basis for action.

Consent litigation has moved beyond negligence claims and intentional torts, such as battery, to new levels of legal argument. These include "breach of contract" in situations in which patients argue that the caregiver "guaranteed" a specific outcome, and claims based on misrepresentation, deceit, or fraud. Utilizing state-based legislation governing unfair and deceptive trade practices, caregivers can find themselves on the receiving end of litigation that relies on such laws in lawsuits involving misrepresentation.

Unlike traditional negligence litigation, consent claims based on misrepresentation may involve punitive damages.

Some state legislation literally ties consent litigation to laws governing unprofessional conduct. This is an interesting risk management issue. Not only would a caregiver be exposed to a traditional negligent consent claim, the state professional licensing body may pursue an investigation or hearing for unprofessional conduct based on the same set of facts and circumstances. Defending on "two fronts," the caregiver has new risk exposure than in years past.

From a risk management perspective, it is disturbing that consent litigation persists. As a communication process and an integral part of the provider-patient relationship, a successful consent process can be used to pinpoint and address at-risk situations. To appreciate management of the consent process as a loss control or risk management technique requires an understanding of the elements of a valid treatment authorization, of the right to make an informed refusal-of-care decision, and of common problem areas involving minors or patients whose competence is in question. At the same time, the risk manager should be familiar with recurrent problems such as those emanating from the managed care arena, compulsory treatment situations, and the absence of appropriate documentation of the consent process.

Consent-to-treatment responsibilities belong to the care provider who is to conduct the proposed test or treatment. Educating providers about their respective roles and responsibilities is a function that is well disposed to health care risk managers. Treating consent as a tool to avoid liability exposure, the risk manager also can use it as a means of facilitating greater trust among patients and care providers in health care systems undergoing dynamic change.

This chapter identifies the contemporary legal drivers for the consent process. It describes the basic elements of the consent-to-treatment process from risk management's perspective. It also discusses the principal exceptions to the consent process and suggests measures that can be taken to avoid liability exposure with regard to consent to treatment.

··············

LEGAL DRIVERS FOR THE CONSENT PROCESS

The Consumer Bill of Rights and Responsibilities proposed by the President's Advisory Commission on Consumer Protection and Quality in the Health Care Industry and published in November 1997, not only reiterated the fundamental framework of consent to treatment, it set in place the cornerstone of future federal legal initiatives on the topic. The Commisssion said:

In order to ensure consumers' right and ability to participate in treatment decisions, health care professionals should:

- Provide patients with easily understood information and opportunity to decide among treatment options consistent with the informed consent process. Specifically,
    - Discuss all treatment options with a patient in a culturally competent manner, including the option of no treatment at all.
    - Ensure that persons with disabilities have effective communications with members of the health system in making such decisions.
    - Discuss all current treatments a consumer may be undergoing, including those alternative treatments that are self-administered.
    - Discuss all risks, benefits, and consequences to treatment or nontreatment.

- Give patients the opportunity to refuse treatment and to express preferences about future treatment decisions.

- Discuss the use of advance directives—both living wills and durable powers of attorney for health care—with patients and their designated family members.

- Abide by the decisions made by their patients and/or their designated representatives consistent with the informed consent process.

To facilitate greater communication between patients and providers, health care providers, facilities, and plans should:

- Disclose to consumers factors—such as methods of compensation, ownership of or interest in health care facilities, or matters of conscience—that could influence advice or treatment decisions.

- Ensure that provider contracts do not contain any so-called "gag clauses" or other contractual mechanisms that restrict health care providers' ability to communicate with and advise patients about medically necessary treatment options.

- Be prohibited from penalizing or seeking retribution against health care professionals or other health workers for advocating on behalf of their patients.[4]

The Rights and Responsibilities Statement serves as the basis for a recurrent theme in subsequent "federal drivers" on the topic of informed consent. It also encapsulates federal requirements on informed consent that date back to the 1970s in the area on human research as well as more contemporary legislation and regulations that address "patient dumping" under the Emergency Treatment and Active Labor Act (EMTALA-COBRA) and its accompanying rules.[5]

There are other "federal drivers" that promote consent as a process. Some of these provisions, however, are not part of laws or regulations directly related to patient care. Instead, these are regulations designed to protect and promote civil rights. For example, the regulations under the 1964 Civil Rights Act that bar discrimination on the basis of race, color, or national origin also impact consent practices. Hospitals and other health care organizations that provide services to recipients of federally assisted programs must take reasonable steps "to provide information in appropriate languages to such persons."[6] This means that patients enrolled in federally assistance programs who do not speak English enjoy some language service protection. Failure to meet such requirements could subject a health care organization to enforcement activities through the auspices of the U.S. Department of Justice, Office of Civil Rights.

The Civil Rights Act is part of a body of legislation and regulations that address compliance with standards set by the federal government. Some of these standards involve consent to treatment and advance directives. Examples include the Conditions of Participation (COPs) for health care facilities receiving Medicare and or Medicaid dollars. The provisions for hospitals state in part that:

> The patient or his or her representative (as allowed under State law) has the right to make informed decisions regarding his or her care. The patient's rights include being informed of his or her health status, being involved in care planning and treatment, and being able to request or refuse treatment.[7]

Health care organizations involved in corporate compliance activities purport to adhere to such requirements. Evidence of nonconformity with the Conditions of Participation, EMTALA, or the Civil Rights Act of 1964 may constitute noncompliance under the entity's corporate standards of conduct. The failure to take corrective action for non-conforming consent practices may cast doubt on the corporate compliance plan, and in some instances involving billing or coding issues, or patient complaints, it may trigger a regulatory investigation. Hence, corporate compliance, a voluntary program for health care organizations, may actually be a "federal driver" in the area of informed consent. (For further details on corporate compliance, see Chapter 20.)

The cadre of federal legislation, rules, and regulations shaping patients' rights and responsibilities creates legal concerns and risk exposures. The risks can be quite serious, including decertification from federal funding programs, civil monetary penalties, and in the case of corporate compliance, a corporate integrity program. Insurance coverages may be limited when dealing with the costs of defending a regulatory proceeding. Insurers will not reimburse health care organizations for criminal fines. Hence, there is a substantial financial loss exposure that stems from the "federal drivers" of consent. Coupled with the fallout from adverse media coverage, the reputational and financial loss exposure merits innovations in using the consent process as a loss control tool. Getting to this point requires the risk manager to have a firm knowledge of the basic elements of the consent process.

....

BASIC ELEMENTS OF CONSENT TO TREATMENT

Although the laws vary from jurisdiction to jurisdiction, a number of elements generally are recognized as integral to the consent process. These factors apply to so-called elective care situations in which there is sufficient time to obtain relevant history and to exchange pertinent information. These elements include:

- A disclosure of the nature and purpose of the proposed test or treatment.
- A description of the probable risks and benefits of the test or treatment.
- An explanation of alternate tests or treatment and the probable risks and benefits associated with these options.
- An explanation of the probable risks and benefits of foregoing proposed or alternate tests or treatment.
- An opportunity to ask questions and receive understandable answers.
- An opportunity to make a decision free of coercion and undue influence.

As a practical starting point, the consent conversation must be geared to the comprehension level of the patient. Medical jargon is unacceptable for most patients. However, talking down to a patient to the point that he or she is insulted and "turned off" is equally unacceptable.

The degree or extent of disclosure is a matter of sharp legal differences of opinion. The majority position, the "patient need" standard requires disclosure of "material" or significant information that a reasonable person in the same or a similar position as the patient would want to know in order to make a treatment choice. The minority perspective is based on what the "medical community" believes the patient should know.

Whether the risk manager works in a jurisdiction that follows the patient need or the medical community standard, the risk management stand is to furnish relevant, understandable information that will prevent or eliminate any misinformation or misunderstanding. In practical terms, this means conveying to patients information regarding:

- The risk of death, disability, disfigurement, or major change in lifestyle.
- The degree of pain, dysfunction, or discomfort associated with the test or treatment.
- The urgency to undergo the test or treatment.
- The consequences of deferring the test or treatment.

Generally speaking, remote risks need not be disclosed except in a few well-defined situations. If, however, a remote risk involves death, discussion should proceed on the topic. The risk of death from anesthesia, for example, is in this category. The anesthesiologist or nurse anesthetist is obliged to disclose to the patient that death is a possibility, albeit a remote one. In this instance, the risk management point to convey to care providers who are uneasy about such discussions is that their effectiveness rests on two important elements: what is said to the patient, and how the message is delivered. Remote risks can be put in an appropriate context to enable patients to make informed choices.

············

EXCEPTIONS FROM THE GENERAL RULES OF CONSENT

The requirements for a valid consent to treatment are not absolute. Indeed, the law recognizes a number of exceptions to the rule,[8] including exceptions for emergency treatment, therapeutic privilege, and compulsory treatment situations.

Emergency Treatment Exception

The emergency treatment exception is well recognized in case law[9] and in legislation.[10] Although the specifics vary from jurisdiction to jurisdiction, the basic criteria are the same:

- The patient presents with a life-threatening illness or injury that requires immediate attention.
- The patient is unable to either communicate or take part in a communication process.
- There is no time to secure a treatment authorization from someone else who might be empowered by law to act on the patient's behalf.

When these criteria are met, the law implies a treatment authorization on behalf of the patient for such diagnostic tests or treatments as are medically necessary to alleviate a life-threatening event. In doing so, the law assumes that if the patient were capable of participating in the consent process, he or she would readily agree to the course of treatment provided.

The emergency treatment exception authorizes only care that is medically necessary to rectify the urgent situation. Medically necessary care can be quite expansive, including removal of organs, amputation of limbs, and the causing of a miscarriage. However, it does not exonerate a care provider from doing tests or treatments that are not immediately required. Thus, a surgeon may be within the scope of the emergency exception in removing a patient's ruptured spleen, but not in removing a pigmented nevus on that patient's abdomen.

From a risk management perspective it is important to understand that the law will not sanction the application of the emergency exception when a patient is temporarily incapacitated by a preoperative medication and there is neither a life- nor health-threatening event that necessitates urgent surgical intervention. A *competent* patient in the midst of a health-threatening event still enjoys the right to refuse treatment.

The emergency exception does not preempt the competent patient's right to refuse treatment.

Caregivers often have difficulty accepting the fact that a competent person may decline life-saving care when confronted with the potential of death or serious harm from a heart attack, stroke, allergic reaction, or asthmatic attack. As health professionals trained to save life they feel that the better approach is to intervene to provide treatment. In doing so they minimize the power of the law and the significance of the principle of individual choice making. Judges and juries alike are apt to react quite negatively in cases in which the patient had made clear a choice not to undergo treatment when confronted with a life- or health-threatening event. In such instances, the risk is one of a battery claim in which there need not be proof of actual harm to the individual.

The right to refuse life-saving care is closely connected today with end-of-life decision making. (For more on this, see Chapter 28.) While there is a substantial amount of overlap of the two topics, it should be understood that the competent patient can decline treatments designed to save life or health without the situation involving a terminal illness. This is particularly true in EMTALA-style cases and emergency department treatment decisions.

Risk managers know that most emergency cases are not "black and white" episodes. Indeed, many cases are filled with shades of gray that necessitate teasing out factual information to substantiate that a true emergency does exist. To this end, the are several steps that can be taken to minimize inappropriate use of the exception including:

- Clinical pathways for declaring an emergency.
- Decision-trees for declaring an emergency.
- Education on the emergency treatment exception for new-hires and in-service for regular staff.
- Mandatory training and in-service for contracted employees of the emergency and urgent care departments.
- Documentation to substantiate the declaration of an emergency.
- Documentation to substantiate compliance with a patient directive declining treatment in an emergency.

Therapeutic Privilege Exception

In comparison to the emergency treatment provision, the therapeutic exception is a far more nebulous concept. This exception usually applies in narrowly drawn circumstances in which the disclosure of certain information is believed to cause the patient a risk of significant harm (likely to be psychogenic or psychobiologic in nature).

To invoke the therapeutic privilege exception, certain criteria must be met. These include a full assessment of the facts and circumstances of the patient's case and condition, and a medical opinion that a full disclosure of information will have a significant or seriously adverse effect on the patient.[11]

The therapeutic privilege exception does not exculpate the obligation to inform the patient. Rather, it grants the care provider leeway in the degree of disclosure surrounding those details that are apt to cause harm to the patient. From a risk management perspective, the exception requires careful application and detailed documentation to evidence the fact that it was used appropriately.

Compulsory Treatment Situation

The compulsory treatment situation is another type of exception from the general rules of consent. In essence, the law makes a value judgment that the rights and liberties of the individual must give way for the greater good and health of the community. As such, the compulsory treatment exception is largely rooted in public health legislation, empowering officials to quarantine, test, or treat individuals with infectious illnesses.[12] Even in the context of this exception, however, there are safeguards to obviate inappropriate use of public health legislation as a mechanism for circumventing the law of consent to treatment.

....

EFFECTIVE COMMUNICATION IN THE CONSENT PROCESS

Communicating in practical terms that the patient can understand may involve use of a number of communication channels. In addition to face-to-face verbal explanations, media may include video displays, interactive computer programs, and print items such as brochures, pamphlets, or information sheets. From a risk management perspective, the key point is that the message conveyed in all the media must be consistent because discrepancies create an opportunity to challenge the integrity of the consent process. It also is important to remember that multimedia resources, though useful tools, are ancillary to the care provider-patient communication that underpins the consent process.

In today's Internet society, communication is a serious issue in terms of informed consent. Patients access the Web and may find a host of sites that offer information pertinent to their needs. Some of the Web sites are legitimate locations that contain valid information. Other sites, however, although crafted by well-intentioned individuals, contain personal observations or "life experiences" that cannot be validated or replicated for others. Reliance on such information could lead to imprudent health choices by patients.

Why do patients "surf the Web" if their caregivers are furnishing them with salient information? The answer is that there is a level of distrust among today's health care consumers that they are not getting the "full story" and that they should do their own independent research lest they rely on inadequate information in making treatment decisions. Marketing by self-help and health information Web sites promotes such activity.

Confronted with a multitude of pamphlets, brochures, booklets, information sheets, and videotapes, there is a danger that patients can be confused rather than informed in making choices. Add to this abundant Internet material that contradicts or casts doubt on details provided by caregivers, and there is a shift from confusion to doubt or uncertainty. Patients are primed to confront caregivers with challenges demanding to know why they were not told about risks or treatment alternatives *they* found on the Internet. Indeed, enterprising plaintiffs' counsel will use such information to raise questions about the completeness of the "informed" consent process.

The role of the risk manager is to restore order to consent as a "communications process." This may involve preemptive practice assessments including:

- Inventory of media used for conveying information to patients.
- Consistency of information disseminated to patients.
- Providing "sanctioned" Web addresses to patients.
- Warnings that some Web addresses may contain information that is not scientifically proven or valid and to exercise caution in relying on treatment details at these sites.

Patients today are also hearing more and more about alternate and complimentary medicine. Some have embarked upon the use of herbal supplements or remedies to treatment mood swings, joint pain, and the symptoms of menopause. The failure to acknowledge this practice may lead to misdiagnosis or treatments with severe adverse results. Part of the contemporary risk management consent toolkit is to ask salient questions during the communication process that highlights such treatment practices. Once the information is in hand, appropriate treatment plans can be recommended to the patient.

Another communication-related consideration is the choice of messenger. Ideally, the person who is to perform the test or treatment should secure the patient's authorization. This step does not involve the administrative or clerical act of securing the patient's signature on a treatment authorization. Rather, the focal point of the consent process is on the communication exchange—the solicitation of critical information from the patient and the dissemination of relevant details in return. Another care provider is less likely to complete a successful consent process because he or she is less familiar with the patient's history, needs, and desires. Thus, relying on another to fulfill this task may create information gaps that culminate in consent claims.

What is sometimes missing in the communication aspect of informed consent is *confirmation* of the successful exchange of information. A consent form is evidence of the process; however, it typically provides little to substantiate that decisions were made with an understanding of benefits, risk, alternatives, opting for alternative and complimentary therapy, and the consequences of declining all care.

The confirmation aspect of communication can occur in a number of ways. Establishing a consistent protocol of questions that substantiates a confirmation of communication is one method. Making it a "usual and customary practice" may suffice in some states. However, a better approach is to use a checklist or some other forms of documentation. Posing confirmatory questions is a useful risk management tool. Rather than asking patients, "Do you understand what I have been saying?" the approach would be to ask open-ended questions such as, "Tell me in your own words what you understand to be involved in the operation?" That patients respond with appropriate answers is a confirmation of the communication process. Documenting that patients gave knowledgeable responses to such questions affirms that the communication was effective.

···········

IMPORTANCE OF AN INFORMED REFUSAL OF CARE

Although most health care professionals recognize the importance of informed choice in leading to a patient's agreeing to some type of diagnostic test or treatment, the same level of recognition is not always present in regard to informed refusals of care. Because the law has given particular recognition to the need for patients to decline tests or treatment on the basis of informed choice making,[13] informed refusal is an important concept.

The leading case on the topic involved a patient in California who repeatedly declined recommendations from her primary care physician to undergo a Pap smear.[14] Ultimately, she died of cervical cancer, leaving two minor children as survivors. The children sued the primary care physician for lack of informed refusal of care, successfully persuading the court that it was not sufficient for a care provider simply to recommend a diagnostic test. Instead, they argued, the duty to inform goes further, requiring the care provider to ensure that a patient's decision to refuse or decline tests or treatment is an informed decision.[15]

The California case has become a legal benchmark. To the extent that it is practical to do so, care providers are encouraged to discuss with their patients the consequences of declining tests or treatment and to document this phase of the consent process. In this way, patients are hard-pressed to claim later that a decision to forgo tests or treatment was based on inadequate disclosure of information. Informed refusal of care has even broader applications than routine care in the physician's office. It is equally applicable in emergency department (ED) settings where decisions to forego transfer to another facility or to decline admission for care have profound legal implications under so-called Emergency Medical Treatment and Active Labor Act (EMTALA) provisions under applicable federal and state law. (See Chapter 4 for additional information.)

For an informed refusal of care to be valid, the patient must be legally and mentally capable of making a choice. When he or she is unable to meet these criteria, a duly authorized surrogate decision maker may make the determination. Like the patient, the surrogate decision maker must be properly informed about the consequences of a determination to refuse care.

Once the patient has made an informed choice to refuse care, it is incumbent upon care providers to respect such a determination.[16] Care providers sometimes find this concept difficult to apply. Nonetheless, the law does not permit them—however well intentioned—to substitute their values and beliefs regarding what is "best" for those of their patients. Furthermore, the law expects that in providing patients with the requisite degree of information needed to make a treatment choice, care providers will deliver the details about the pros and cons of treatment even-handedly. Failure to do otherwise creates a needless risk of exposure for lawsuits based on lack of informed refusal of care.

• • • • • • • • • • • •

THE RIGHT OF THE PATIENT TO WITHDRAW CONSENT

Patients have the right to withdraw a valid treatment authorization. From a risk management standpoint, it is important to ask "when" can a patient make such a decision. A Wisconsin ruling offers an answer on the issue of "change of mind" in the informed consent process.[17]

A patient, pregnant for the third time, was informed by her doctor that although she had previously undergone cesarean deliveries, she should have a vaginal birth after cesarean (VBAC) this time. The doctor suggested that if medically necessary, a cesarean section would be performed. During admission the patient signed both a consent form for a vaginal delivery and a cesarean section. Several hours later when the doctor came in to see the patient she told him she wanted to have a cesarean section. The doctor responded by encouraging her to stick to the original delivery plan. When the patient's labor was not proceeding as had been anticipated, the doctor broke the amniotic sac to accelerate the process. The patient suffered such severe abdominal pain that the medication did not work. Once again, the patient informed the doctor that she had changed her mind and that she wanted a cesarean section. The doctor indicated that if he acceded to all such requests, all deliveries would be accomplished by cesarean section.

When the baby's heart rate dropped, an emergency cesarean section was performed. The outcome was poor. The mother's uterus had ruptured and the lack of oxygen left the child with spastic quadriplegia, unable to speak and unable to move below her neck.

In remanding the case for a determination of damages, the Supreme Court of Wisconsin reasoned that once a medical procedure has commenced the patient does not relinquish the right to withdraw consent to treatment. Much depends on the circumstances of each case and treatment alternatives in deciding when there is no turning back. In this case, cesarean section was an alternative form of delivery and therefore, the patient was able to withdraw her consent to vaginal childbirth. By changing her mind the patient set in motion a responsibility to complete a new informed consent discussion.

This "change of mind" case points out a critical component of risk management training on informed consent. It is imperative to sensitize caregivers to recognize consent "speed bumps" put in place by patients or substitute decision makers. As long as the point of no return has not been reached and there are treatment options, the patient has the right to opt out of an agreed-upon course of care.

· · · · · · · · · · · ·

NEEDS OF SPECIFIC PATIENTS IN THE INFORMED CONSENT PROCESS

Many states have singled out specific categories of patients for special consideration under the law of consent to treatment. These categories include minors, elderly patients, mentally disabled or challenged persons, and those undergoing tests or treatment for certain diseases such as HIV, blood transfusion therapy, or breast cancer.

Care should be exercised in generalizing about the requirements for consent with regard to specific patient groups or types of tests or treatment. Much of the law is quite state specific, necessitating specific legal advice and policy and procedure to address these matters.

Notwithstanding the fact that state law is so specific in this area, it is important to remember the basic requirements for a valid consent process. The law presumes that a patient possesses both legal competency and mental capability to make a treatment choice. Only in certain situations does the law require a different approach to the consent process. This requirement goes into effect when:

- Legislation varies the general rules of consent.
- Court orders require specific treatment or bar certain care.
- The facts of a given consent trigger the need for a determination of legal competency or mental capacity to make a treatment choice.

Aside from the law, there are very practical reasons for managing the consent process differently with certain categories of patients. These include:

- Auditory, speech, or visually impaired patients.
- Culturally sensitive consent situations.
- Linguistic barriers between patients and care providers.

Preliminary screening of patients can eliminate the risk that the process will unravel due to the patient's inability to hear, speak, or see sufficiently to engage in a valid consent process. Indeed, this risk can be obviated by telling patients at the outset that the care provider or facility is sensitive to such needs and encourages patients to disclose them. By the same token, care providers should be trained in methods that help detect those patients who need assistive devices, such as TDD (telephone devices for the deaf) or TTY (teletype).

As indicated earlier in the chapter under the Americans with Disabilities Act (discussed in Chapter 4), most health care entities are required to make reasonable accommodation to meet the needs of patients with a disability that could impair the consent process.[18] Some states have gone further, requiring the use of interpreters for those who confront a linguistic barrier to an effective consent process.[19] These are laws that have heightened awareness about regulatory compliance.

Cultural sensitivity also is important.[20] Although sometimes difficult to embrace in policy and procedure, cultural sensitivity reflects an awareness of what is disclosed to a patient and by whom. For example, discussion of urogenital anomalies or surgery by a male clinician with a female patient can be culturally charged and may cause the consent process to become derailed. In other situations, the cultural context of patients from other countries may inhibit reliance on "general understanding" of such things as the meaning of over-the-counter medications, home remedies, and so on. Good risk management in this regard demands identification of the cultural needs in the catchment area served by the health care organization. In addition, consent policy and procedure should be flexible enough to accommodate the needs of patients who object to such discussions.

Although the law views consent as a process between patient and care provider, it is not uncommon for family members to be involved in the discussion. This "family focused" consent process is also a practice sanctioned by the Joint Commission on Accreditation of Healthcare Organizations (JCAHO). Family involvement is not necessarily a sign that the patient distrusts the care provider. Indeed, family members may facilitate the process by furnishing additional details that the patient is unable to recall. Furthermore, from a loss control perspective, family involvement affords an opportunity to set expectations and establish a strong relationship. This rapport may be beneficial in short-circuiting potential litigation if untoward consequences result from tests or treatment.

From a risk management standpoint, it is critical that consent policy and procedure recognize state-specific exceptions and delineate an appropriate, practical process for securing a treatment decision in these matters. This approach can avert needless risk exposure and potential litigation.

....

CONSENT IN A MANAGED CARE ENVIRONMENT

The inroads exhibited by managed care in the health care delivery process have received much attention in legal and risk management circles.[21] Not the least of this attention has focused on consent to treatment in managed care.

Like other components of the health care delivery system, managed care requires consent for treatment. The standards of practice for consent are the same whether the patient is a recipient of services in a hospital, ambulatory care clinic, surgicenter, freestanding urgent care center, or home health care program. What do change, however, are the payment mechanisms and controls imposed on care providers under managed care arrangements. Some illustrations help to demonstrate this point.

- A primary care physician belongs to a fifty-physician independent practice association (IPA). The IPA has a risk-sharing contract with a managed care organization (MCO). The individual physicians in the group also have a financial bonus arrangement whereby they can receive as much as 12 percent per annum of the aggregate they save the IPA in terms of staying within the parameters of its risk-sharing contract with the MCO. Does this financial arrangement need to be disclosed to patients as part of the consent-to-treatment process?

- A radiologist determines that a subscriber referred to him by a primary care provider should undergo an intravenous pyleogram (IVP). Based on the specialist's determination, the gatekeeper at the subscriber's MCO approves an ionic contrast dye for the IVP. Even though the radiologist does not believe the subscriber is in a risk-prone category that would trigger the need for a nonionic contrast dye, do the principles of informed consent mitigate toward disclosing this as a diagnostic option?

The issue in both cases comes down to the financing of the proposed health care. In both instances, however, it also affects the consent process. Traditionally, physicians have not been required to disclose potential pecuniary conflict of interest as a risk factor in the consent process.[22] The reason is simple: it is unrelated to the proposed test or treatment. However, when the care provider's financial interests may impede his or her ability to secure a valid consent, a genuine issue of concern is raised about the legality of a patient's treatment authorization. Moreover, when a care provider permits pecuniary self-interest to dominate clinical judgment, a legitimate issue of professional misconduct is raised, an issue that could culminate in professional disciplinary proceedings.

The fact that physicians may be participants in an MCO's incentive bonus program came to have negative connotations after a well-publicized case, *Fox v. Health Net of California.*[23] Subsequently, much publicity has been focused on the fact that physicians may be so preoccupied with their personal financial interests that they are blind to instances in which there may be a lack of information or treatments offered to MCO patients.

As a result, the Health Care Financing Administration (HCFA) promulgated rules mandating disclosure of physician incentive plan arrangements in prepaid plans.[24] The disclosure provision applies with respect to Medicare beneficiaries in prepaid health care organizations. The duty to disclose, however, lies with the prepaid health care organization and not the physician. More can be anticipated in terms of disclosure laws on the state level.

The second illustration is more straightforward. Regardless of the source of payment, a patient who is a candidate for an elective, investigative procedure is entitled to information about treatment alternatives. Failure to disseminate information about treatment alternatives can vitiate the consent process.[25] Hence, the patient subscriber should be apprised that the nonionic contrast dye is a viable alternative, even if it is not approved by a gatekeeper and would require an out-of-pocket expenditure by the patient subscriber.

Many physicians have been reluctant to share such information for fear that they could provoke a confrontation between the patient subscriber and the MCO. Indeed, some have referenced the so-called gag rule in their provider agreements with MCOs as a deterrent to their disseminating such information.[26] The gag rule refers to contractual terms that bar a physician from communicating information to patients that might either undermine their relationship with the MCO or result in dissemination to subscribers of such propriety information as payment rates, utilization review procedures, and so on. Such practices have been condemned by legal scholars as barring physicians from being honest with their patients.[27] Moreover, at least one state has moved to eliminate use of the gag rule as a bar to effective physician-patient communication.[28]

Given the adverse publicity associated with managed care in the popular press, it is likely that further inroads can be expected to enhance effective, open, honest exchanges of information between care providers and subscribers. In addition, changes have been implemented with respect to managed care gatekeepers using individual patient financial responsibility as a deterrent to seeking care in a hospital ED. To the extent that financial pressures are used in this regard, risk exposure increases for undue influence or coercion vitiating the patient decision-making process.

In short, management of the consent process presents many challenges for MCO risk managers. The key is to identify risk-prone practices and to address the problems they present before claims emerge for invalid consents.

············

RESULTS OF A BREAKDOWN IN THE CONSENT PROCESS

Traditionally, consent litigation was premised on battery, an intentional tort that did not require proof of actual harm. In most states, patients can sue on several different legal theories for ineffective consents. These include:

- *Negligent consent:* An unintentional tort that requires actual injury emanating from failure to follow appropriate standards for completing the consent process resulting in causally linked and reasonably foreseeable harm.

- *Misrepresentation or deceit:* The failure to honestly disclose important information or the act of presenting details in a way that misstates such details, resulting in an authorization that otherwise would have been withheld by the patient. In many jurisdictions, this type of claim carries with it the prospect of punitive damages.

- *Breach of contract:* A claim premised on traditional notions of contract law in which the patient asserts that the care provider guaranteed or promised a certain result that was not achieved. This is most likely to happen in elective procedures involving plastic surgery, orthodontics, or other restorative fields of endeavor.

- *Battery:* The traditional basis for claims involving an unauthorized test or treatment. It also can be asserted in cases in which a patient has withdrawn consent and the care provider proceeds with the test or treatment.

- *Corporate liability:* The least likely basis for a consent claim, but nonetheless a source of consternation for health care risk managers. Traditionally, consent responsibilities have been reviewed as a duty of care of the attending care provider. However, to the extent that health care facilities intrude into, and impose conditions and requirements upon, the consent process, the risk of corporate liability for defective consents has increased. It also may follow from "constructive notice" of a flawed consent process known to an allied health professional who did not follow health care facility policy and procedure and warn a supervisor of the problem. Coupled with a health care facility mission statement, bylaws, and policies and procedures that speak to the institution's responsibility to safeguard patient care and well-being, the groundwork may be in place for such a claim.

By far, the most likely basis for claim is negligent consent. It may be asserted as an ancillary claim in a professional liability lawsuit or may proceed as a separate basis for claim. The point to remember is that consent is a viable basis for litigation. With the prospect of punitive damages for battery or misrepresentation,[29] consent is an issue ripe for risk management treatment.

············

RISK MANAGEMENT APPROACH TO CONSENT TO TREATMENT

From a risk management perspective, several measures can be taken to avoid liability exposure involving consent to treatment. These involve:

- Consent policies and procedures.
- Consent risk identifiers.
- Education.
- Documentation.

Each of these is discussed in the following sections as a component of a comprehensive approach to consent as a loss control mechanism. Taken together, these measures represent a practical, hands-on approach to lessening consent litigation.

Consent Policies and Procedures

Consent policies and procedures are central to a loss prevention program; they should be comprehensive, yet practical. The content should address frequently encountered problems, providing health care professionals and management with reasoned, legally appropriate responses. In addition, consent policies and procedures should address all aspects of the health care delivery system reflected in health care organizations. Thus, a hospital network that merges with a group of nursing homes or purchases a home infusion company needs to expand its consent policies and procedures to address these additional components of the system.

Certain basic components should be reflected in the consent policies and procedures. Some issues to address include:

- Requirements for a valid consent to treatment.
- Assessment for legal and mental capacity to give consent.
- Admission requirements.
- Patient self-determination requirements.
- Surrogate decision makers.
- Assessment for legal and mental capacity to give consent.
- Requirements for a valid consent to participate in human experimentation.
- EMTALA consent requirements.
- Managed care consent requirements.
- Documentation requirements.
- Handling specific situations:
  - Anesthesia consents
  - Advance directives
  - Do-not-resuscitate orders on requests
  - Organ procurement
  - Authorizations for autopsies
  - Handling refusals of care
  - HIV testing
- Requests not to use certain types of care, such as blood transfusion therapy.

As with other policies and procedures, the content should be field-tested to ensure that it is practical and understandable to end users. Further, it should be reviewed and updated periodically to make certain that any changes in federal or state law, including judicial decisions, are reflected in the documentation.

Consent Risk Identifiers

A comprehensive loss program should include monitoring for consent risk exposures. A broad sweep would include the use of quality outcome data, patient satisfaction information, and the results gleaned from incident reports and loss run and litigation files.

In addition, personnel should be encouraged to report concurrent consent risk situations, including disputes among family members regarding appropriate treatment for an incompetent relative, managed care-linked EMTALA problems in the ED, and refusals of care from questionably "capable" individuals. Ideally, effective patient history screening is a potent tool in identifying potential consent problems. For example, a patient and/or family member who presents with conflicting history information may be withholding important data that could affect the risk-benefit analysis of one form of care over another. This can happen with placement of an elderly person in an institutional care setting, when the relative selectively discloses information in the hope that the elderly patient will be situated in an assisted-living environment rather than a nursing facility or skilled nursing facility.

In other situations the information disclosed by the patient and/or relative may reveal inordinate expectations of care or treatment outcome. This, too, is risk-prone activity that should be addressed accordingly.

In some instances, a risk identifier may be found in the way in which the consent process is designed to work. For example, consent documentation includes provision for patients to participate in autologous blood storage programs. The notification is dated the same day or the day before an elected procedure. The operation is likely to require the use of blood products. That the patient was not notified or informed of the autologous blood program until it was too late to participate in this transfusion plan would be glaring evidence of an inadequate consent process. Here the inadequacy would be one based on time.

Traditionally, incomplete consent documentation has been viewed as a sentinel indicator of risk. Although this is a valid consent risk identifier, it does not relieve a health care entity of the need to ferret out exposures earlier in the process.

Education

Risk managers should never assume that health care professionals know how to properly secure a valid consent to treatment. Much is learned in clinical mentoring, including inappropriate methods for communicating information to patients and recording a treatment authorization. To lessen the likelihood of liability exposure, it is prudent to include orientation and regular in-service education on the proper way to secure a valid consent to treatment.

Education may become far more expansive than in previous times. With hospitals and other health care entities taking on increased roles in home health care, hospice, long-term care, subacute care, and ambulatory care, the horizon has broadened with respect to who must—and actually does—obtain consent to treatment. In view of these developments, it is important for risk managers to think broadly about who needs education on consent-to-treatment processes and practices.

Documentation

Consent documentation is important as a mechanism for memorializing in writing the scope of a treatment authorization. It is not a replacement for the consent process. Selecting the best method or methods for documenting consent is a collaborative activity involving care providers, legal counsel, and the risk manager.

Some health care entities prefer the *long-form consent,* which delineates risks, benefits, alternatives, and additional information. Others prefer the *short-form consent,* which basically indicates that a valid consent transaction occurred. A third approach calls for a *detailed note* in the patient record. The note should record the time and date of the transaction and should be signed by the provider who informed the individual and secured the authorization. This customized approach is considered to be more credible and genuine than a standard "boiler plate" consent form. A fourth method is the *checklist consent form,* which has categories that are checked off by the care provider securing the patient's consent. Once the consent process is completed, the form is signed by the provider and, in some locations, the patient. The form, designed to meet state law requirements, provides ample room for the care provider to detail the probable risks, probable benefits, and treatment alternatives for the patient, along with the risks of foregoing care. This approach is seen as a compromise between the traditional long-form consent and the detailed note in the record. Because it is streamlined and allows for the document to be customized to a specific patient, the checklist consent form is seen as a reasonable approach to memorializing the consent process.

Whatever method of consent documentation is selected, the key is to use it consistently. Failure to do so is a signal of potential risk. As such, it is important to engage health care professionals in the design and development of the documentation system to be certain that they will cooperate and use it effectively.

•••••••••••
CONCLUSION

Consent is a double-edged sword. When completed properly, the consent process is a potent tool for averting liability claims and the basis for a strong defense to assertions that a patient was not properly informed. However, when the consent process is inadequate or incomplete, it can be used as a weapon against a health care facility or professional.

Viewing consent as a loss control mechanism means designing a process that is practical and used consistently. It means drawing from legal requirements at the state and federal level, and from the experience of care providers regarding what will and will not work. Further, as with other aspects of loss control, vigilance is important in terms of monitoring for and managing risks that emerge on a concurrent basis. This latter point is critical in the contemporary vortex of change in the health care field, where further modifications can be anticipated that are central to the consent process.

Endnotes

1. See Rozovsky, F. A. *Consent to Treatment: A Practical Guide* (2nd ed.). Boston: Little, Brown and Co., 1990 (with annual supplements). Consent as a process is the same throughout most of the common-law world and in jurisdictions that follow the Napoleonic Code.

2. Note, however, that payment is not necessary for consent to be informed or valid.

3. The cases most often described as the benchmarks for the contemporary approach to consent to treatment include *Canterbury v. Spence,* 464 F.2d 772 (DC Cir. 1972); *Cobbs v. Grant,* 501 P.2dl (CA 1972); and *Wilkinson v. Vesey,* 295 A.2d 676 (1972). These cases marked a watershed in the field of health law, the repercussions of which have been noted in extensive case law and statutory law on the subject of consent to treatment.

4. *Consumer Bill of Rights and Responsibilities,* Chapter Four, "Participation in Treatment Decisions." President's Advisory Commission on Consumer Protection and Quality in the Health Care Industry, Nov., 1997.

5. 42 USC §1395dd. The regulations are at 42 CFR §498.24 (1998).

6. 28 CFR §42.405 (1998).

7. *Federal Register, 64*(127): 36088, (July 2, 1999).

8. For a detailed examination of the topic, see Rozovsky, Chapter 2, supra note 1.

9. Case law on the topic can be found as early as 1906. See, for example, *Pratt v. Davis,* 79 N.E. 562 (Ill., 1906).

10. See, for example, GA Code.

11. See Rozovsky, supra note l at ¤ 2.4.1.

12. Rozovsky, at ¤ 2.5

13. *Truman v. Thomas,* 611 P.2d. 902 (Cal., 1980).

14. *Truman v. Thomas.*

15. *Truman v. Thomas.*

16. See *Stamford Hospital v. Vegas,* P 236 Conn. 646 (1996).

17 *Schreiber v. Physicians Insurance Company of Wisconsin,* 588 NW2d 26 (Wis., 1999).

18. See 42 USC sec.12101, et seq. (1990). Title III provides the pertinent legislative requirements on the topic. Although exemptions are provided for certain religious facilities, many have chosen to follow the law.

19. See, for example, 210 ILCS 87/1, et seq. (Smith-Hurd 1994). (Language assistance is required if 5 percent of the population served by a health care facility on an annual basis do not speak English or are limited in their ability to speak English.)

20. For an interesting insight on the topic, see Gostin, L. "Informed Consent, Cultural Sensitivity, and Respect for Persons." *JAMA 274*(10), Sept. 13, 1995, pp. 844–845.

21. See, for example, Benda, C. B., and Rozovsky, F. A. *Liability and Risk Management in Managed Care.* Gaithersburg, Md. Aspen Publishers, Inc., 1998. (with annual supplementation).

22. Benda and Rozovsky.

23. No. 219692 (Cal., Superior Ct., 1993).

24. See 42 CFR sec.417.479 (Mar., 1996).

25. *Logan v. Greenwich Hosp. Ass'n,* 465 A.2d 294 (Conn., 1983).

26. See Woolhandler, S., and Himmelstein, D. U. "Extreme Risk: The New Corporate Proposition for Physicians." *New England Journal of Medicine 333,* Dec. 21, 1995, pp. 1706–1708.

27. See Mariner, W.S.K. "Managed-Care Gag Cheats the Patients." *National Law Journal,* Feb. 5, 1996, p. A19.

28. Massachusetts enacted such a law, which was signed into effect Jan. 19, 1996.

29. See, for example, *Lunsford v. Regents, University of California,* No. 837936 (Superior Ct., San Francisco County, Cal., Apr. 19, 1990).

Suggested Reading

Joint Commission, *Ethical Issues and Patients' Rights Across the Continuum of Care.* Oakbrook Terrace, Ill.: JCAHO, 1998.

Rozovsky, F. A. *Liability and Risk Management in Home Health Care.* Gaithersburg, Md.: Aspen Publishers, Inc., 1998 (with annual supplementation).

24

Safety and Security

Leilani Kicklighter

$\mathbf{I}$f health care organizations are to survive the demands of government, business, and other payers for lower-cost health care, they must reduce costs and yet still deliver high-quality patient care. Well-structured, well-administered safety and security programs help accomplish this goal. Such programs can prevent the loss of physical assets and reduce loss resulting from work-related injury or illness and visitor accidents.

Moreover, as the emphasis of health care delivery shifts from the traditional acute care setting to the outpatient setting, so do the risk exposures. Risk identification and treatment techniques must change to address not only the risk, but also the setting of the risk.

This chapter examines safety and security issues in the traditional acute care setting, and also includes new exposures and issues relevant to extended delivery settings such as home health care, long-term care, and ambulatory care. The principles involved in treating acute care risk exposures can be applied to, and implemented in, any of those alternative delivery settings.

SAFETY PROGRAM DEVELOPMENT AND IMPLEMENTATION

Every health care organization is mandated by federal and state law and private accrediting agencies to develop and implement a safety program whose goal is to provide safe working conditions and procedures for all employees. Although all the states had passed workers' compensation laws by 1948, it was not until 1970 that Congress passed Public Law 91-596, known as the Occupational Safety and Health Act. The agency charged with implementing that legislation is the Occupational Safety and Health Administration (OSHA).

Every employer whose business "affects commerce" is subject to OSHA regulations. A business affects commerce if any of the tools, equipment, materials, or devices used in it were manufactured in another state. Employers are subject to either civil or criminal sanctions for OSHA violations.

One benefit of good safety performance is the positive effect that control of employee incidents can have on staffing. When employees are unable to work because of occupational injury or illness, often they must be replaced to maintain adequate staffing levels. Orientation of new staff places an added burden on supervisors and employees alike. Safe working conditions and procedures contribute significantly to a reduction in employee absences resulting from workplace injury and illness.

From a business standpoint, a safety program also contributes toward conservation of financial resources. The frequency and severity of accidents, injuries, and occupational disease affect workers' compensation insurance premiums. By controlling the number of employee accidents and illnesses, a health care organization reduces its costs through improved experience modification rates, which lowers premiums (or funding requirements).

Many factors should be taken into account in setting up a safety program, including the type of organization (acute care, ambulatory care, long-term care, and so on) as well as its mission, size, range of services, number of employees, and organizational structure. In addition, the Joint Commission on Accreditation of Healthcare Organizations (JCAHO) has promulgated guidelines and standards for the environment of care, effective as of 1995. The Environment of Care program (EOC) and resultant committee structure, as required by the JCAHO standards, can be configured in any way the health care organization desires.

Laws or rules that exist in the state where the organization is located provide another source of guidance. JCAHO standards and guidelines, as well as state laws, are useful in designing a model for a safety program. Regardless of the program's structure, risk management should be an integral and integrated component of it. In addition, the program requires the commitment and involvement of management, supervisors, and employees.

It should be noted that depending on the size, location, and type of organization (rural, specialty, extended care, university, and so on), the responsibilities for risk management, safety, security, and workers' compensation may be assigned in different ways. For example, in some settings, those functions are assigned to individuals as single responsibilities; in others, they are assigned in combination with other types of responsibilities or with more than one of those listed here. For the purposes of this discussion, each of those responsibilities has been assigned to a specific individual. The following model program, which adheres to JCAHO guidelines, can be used as a framework for a safety program.

••••••••••••

POLICY STATEMENT

Following is a sample mission and policy statement for a safety program. This particular statement combines the safety and security programs, although this is not always the case. However, combined or not, safety and security programs should always be coordinated with the risk management program.

A highly visible program shall be established throughout the organization to emphasize and maintain safety and security practices as they relate to patients, medical staff, employees, visitors, equipment, and property on an ongoing basis. Additionally, this program will be concerned with loss control and the prevention of incidents that relate to safety and security. This program will be coordinated with, and an integral component of, the overall risk management program.

Methods of Implementation

Membership on the EOC safety and security subcommittees should be determined according to the guidelines outlined in the JCAHO standards for EOC and/or applicable state laws. The committees should meet at least monthly, and more often when the agenda shows that problems need to be addressed in a more timely fashion. The health care organization's board should review and approve annually a resolution granting the EOC committee authority to act in the event of an emergency. The following is a model program for the operation of the EOC committee and subcommittees.

- The chair of the EOC committee will be appointed by the executive director of the organization and is responsible for setting the agenda of the meetings and for monitoring to ensure implementation of the actions taken by the committee.
- The EOC safety and security subcommittees will determine the need, subject, and audience of safety- and security-focused in-service programs. That is, if a problem is recognized as relating to particular departments or groups of employees, programs to address it will be developed and presented for those employees. In addition, the subcommittees will ensure that the required annual educational programs are presented (such as the right to know, bloodborne pathogens, and others).
- As necessary, the chair of the EOC committee or of a subcommittee may assign individuals or ad hoc committees to investigate or more thoroughly analyze identified problems and charge them with reporting back to the parent committee or subcommittee. (This should be coordinated with risk management so that duplication of effort is minimized.)
- On an ongoing basis, the EOC committee and subcommittees shall be kept abreast of all new and modified standards, statutes, and regulations that affect the safety and security programs.
- As necessary, the EOC committee and subcommittees will use the expertise available in the community, state, and nation to supply references, ideas, or in-service programs when available and pertinent.
- The risk manager or a safety officer will serve as administrative staff to the EOC committee and subcommittees and work closely with the respective chairs, with input from the safety and security officer(s).
- Committee meeting minutes will be forwarded to the executive director, administrative management group, and executive medical staff committee (if applicable) for information and/or action on pertinent points, as necessary.

Role and Responsibilities of the Safety Officer

An organization should designate an individual as the safety officer. This person will provide a focal point for all safety-related activities and be accountable for the effectiveness of the safety program. Again, the size, type, and location of the facility will determine if the safety responsibilities should be full-time or in addition to other functions. The safety-related experience and education of the safety officer will, of course, impact the effectiveness of the overall program, but how extensive a background the organization will require from the designated individual will depend on the position's focus and the organization's needs. Following are some examples of the responsibilities of the safety officer.

- Monitoring employee injuries in a timely fashion by maintaining a log listing all injuries by individual, pay classification, and unit or department and including a summary of the incident; contributory negligence or other factors, or determination of cause; and time lost to date.

- Analyzing employee injuries and providing information to the divisions, units, and departments involved so that they can implement programs to resolve identified problems.

- Investigating all employee injuries, including viewing the site of the accident, interviewing the employee and witnesses involved, and devising prevention strategies or educational programs.

- Developing a method for tracking and trending an individual employee's accident record, and providing any necessary counseling and retraining through the appropriate department head.

- Maintaining a working relationship with the state workers' compensation offices. (In some institutions, the functions listed to this point may be the responsibility of the workers' compensation coordinator; however, because of the safety officer's expertise, it is always a good idea to collaborate with that individual to determine appropriate intervention for preventing recurrences of accidents.)

- Being knowledgeable in the field of safety as it relates to medical institutions and as required by JCAHO, the applicable state health care organization licensing agencies, OSHA, and other applicable federal, state, and local regulations.

- Making routine monthly environmental rounds of all nursing units and other departments to view each area for potential safety-related problems. Recommendations resulting from those surveillance rounds will be documented and referred to the appropriate director of the area for implementation within ten days (or for feedback to the safety officer as to why implementation is not feasible at the time). Continued noncompliance should be reported to the appropriate EOC subcommittee.

- Ensuring that fire drills are held as required in each unit and department, and that appropriate documentation is provided. The JCAHO and the National Fire Protection Association (NFPA) have detailed guidelines for the frequency and location of fire drills to which health care organizations should adhere; for instance, in acute care inpatient facilities the requirement is one monthly fire drill per shift per building.

- Developing and facilitating approval of the organization's disaster plan; recognizing the specific types of natural disasters, depending on the location of the facility, that pose a potential risk; providing educational programs on disaster preparedness; holding and evaluating disaster drills; and evaluating the response to real "disaster" events.

- Maintaining adequate documentation of safety education programs to comply with JCAHO standards, applicable state health care licensing standards, and OSHA, as well as other federal, state, and local regulations, as required. (See Chapter 9 on occupational and environmental risk exposures.)

- Maintaining a close working relationship with the workers' compensation department, if self-insured, or claims handling agency (third-party administrator [TPA] or carrier).

- Facilitating and coordinating identification of all substances governed by the right-to-know regulations, ensuring reporting to proper authorities, and maintaining all material safety data sheets, in-service programs, and other records. (See Chapter 9.)

- Identifying hazardous waste in the facility, monitoring and evaluating its disposal, and taking corrective action, as necessary. The safety officer also ensures appropriate maintenance of the waste disposal manifest forms for future reference, if necessary. (See Chapter 9.)

JOB OR POSITION DESCRIPTIONS WITH QUANTIFIABLE PHYSICAL-BASED CRITERIA

Specific job or position descriptions that reflect quantifiable physical-based requirements are necessary and form the basis for many of the other activities subsequently discussed. Without quantifiable physical-based job descriptions, there is no basis against which to evaluate a person's physical capabilities to safely perform tasks. Such specificity will assist in determining appropriate job placement against physical requirements and abilities, evaluating capabilities for returning to work, and assessing the work-hardening rehabilitation program. When developing the position-specific physical criteria, hearing and vision requirements should not be overlooked.

PREPLACEMENT AND POSTOFFER PHYSICAL EVALUATIONS

Each organization should develop a statement of the goal(s) of the preplacement physical evaluation and circulate it to all practitioners who will be conducting physical examinations. A copy of the individual's position description should be made available to the examining practitioner as a guide against which to evaluate the employee's capabilities to safely function in that role. The risk manager also should evaluate the purpose of all laboratory, radiology, and other tests against the statement of goals; tests not required by the individual state law, rules, or regulations or other federal laws or guidelines should be evaluated against cost and benefit. For instance, although preplacement chest x-rays should be taken in concert with the current Centers for Disease Control and Prevention tuberculosis guidelines, chest x-rays to identify tumors may not be cost-effective or in concert with established goals.

The preplacement physical evaluation should be conducted following an offer of employment or a transfer to a new position, but prior to the actual commencement of the job. In some organizations, there is such a need to fill certain positions that the preplacement physical evaluation is not done until weeks or even months after the employee begins work. Such a deviation from the intent of the preplacement process also results in failure to obtain baselines, such as audiology tests, vision examinations, and purified protein derivative (PPD) skin tests of those who are placed in positions either exposed to high noise or active tuberculosis or requiring 20/20 corrected vision to function safely. For consistency, practitioners specified by the organization should conduct preplacement evaluations. Allowing the employee's private practitioner to conduct the evaluation may not meet the goals set down by the organization.

Baseline Examinations

Baselines such as vision and hearing, obtained on initial preplacement evaluation and annually thereafter, are important as to whether claims of work-related vision or hearing-level deterioration can be shown to be preexisting. The types of positions and types and frequency of baseline examinations should be developed into a policy and procedure, and consistently applied to all employees who function in any of those positions. For instance, baseline vision exams should be administered to any employee whose job functions require a significant amount of work at a computer monitor, and audiology exams should be administered to helicopter ambulance crew and support staff.

Position-Specific Orientation and Annual Skill Assessment

Upon initial employment, as a part of departmental orientation, each employee's skills and abilities should be evaluated. Specifically, any employee whose job will require lifting should demonstrate proper lifting and body mechanics. Also, workstations should be evaluated ergonomically to ensure that six-foot-tall employees are not assigned to ones previously designed for five-foot-tall employees. Employees who will be using equipment such as saws or drills in the maintenance department or cleavers in the kitchen should be observed annually to verify that they are using proper safety techniques.

Employee Health Program

An employee health program is a strategic component of an effective employee safety program. The health care organization may be able to realize substantial savings and generate employee goodwill by having programs that enhance employee health. Health education, wellness promotion, preplacement medical evaluations, and initial treatment and follow-up of occupational injuries and illnesses are the basics of an employee health program.

An employee health office (EHO) staffed with an advanced registered nurse practitioner can provide routine immunizations; perform scheduled preplacement and other medical evaluations; screen and refer non-job-related injuries and illnesses; evaluate, treat, or refer job-related injuries, exposures, and illnesses; and monitor the care and rehabilitation of employees who have suffered job-related injuries or illnesses that resulted in time lost from work. In addition, many health care organizations are marketing their occupational health services to the community. A well-organized, cost-effective EHO that provides services to the parent health care organization is an effective component of marketing. Through such an EHO program, the institution can stay in contact with the employee and, when appropriate, bring him or her back to work in a capacity that is physically compatible with his or her job-related functions. Maintaining contact with the employee and the appropriate physician to monitor the employee's recuperation assists in planning for additional or substitute personnel or reassignment of duties. Case management is coming more into its own as a way to control costs and to facilitate appropriate and timely care for injured employees. Case management can be coordinated through, or done by, the EHO staff.

The employee health records kept in the EHO are valuable sources of information on the frequency and severity of injuries suffered by individual employees. Based on that information, the health organization's administrators may address the problem of repetitive "accidents" through counseling or retraining. Maintenance of EHO employee health records should be in compliance with the standard practices of the organization's medical records department and with OSHA guidelines. (See Chapter 9 on occupational and environmental risk exposures.)

Accident Prevention Program

An effective accident prevention program requires the commitment of all organization staff. Following are specific suggestions for supervisors and employees regarding accountability for accidents.

Supervisors   By policy, supervisors should be held accountable for the incidence of work-related accidents occurring in their respective areas of responsibility. Annual evaluations should include this accountability as one criterion of review. As part of their management responsibilities, supervisors should be responsible for the timely evaluation of each work-related accident, with and without injury or lost time, that occurs in their area of responsibility. Intervention and corrective action should be initiated immediately, based on the outcome of the evaluation. The supervisor's written evaluation should be forwarded to the safety officer to include in the database for analysis. In addition, the safety officer should evaluate the supervisor's investigation, conclusion(s), and intervention for thoroughness, completeness, timeliness, and appropriateness.

Employees By policy, employees should be held accountable for unsafe work practices. Annual evaluations are one way to address the accountability issue. One method of monitoring work-related accidents by employee is that the safety officer develops an index of divisions and the departments or units within. As each employee accident report is received, a search for prior accidents involving that employee is made. If none is found, a record is begun that lists the employee's name, date of birth, length of employment, assigned unit, position, date of the accident, type of accident (using the generic OSHA codes), known injury, and lost time days. The individual employee's record is filed by department. In the event of a third accident being entered on an employee's record in any twelve-month period, a notice would be sent to the employee's supervisor. This notice, in addition to listing the dates and types of accidents, would advise the supervisor that in keeping with the organization's safety committee mandate and personnel policy, he or she must counsel the employee and determine follow-up action, if necessary (that is, retraining, disciplinary action, workstation ergonomic design evaluation, or other). The supervisor's response is to be forwarded to the employee's personnel file and to the safety officer.

....

LIGHT- OR MODIFIED-DUTY OR EARLY RETURN-TO-DUTY PROGRAM

Consistently applied to all eligible employees, a formal light- or modified-duty or early return-to-duty program has the potential to return injured employees to work quickly while reducing overall costs. The personnel director, risk manager, safety officer, employee's department head, position ergonomic evaluator, and employee health nurse should be involved in determining the employee's suitability for light duty in relation to the prospective position assignment.

For examples of light- or modified-duty or early return-to-duty programs, please refer to Chapter 25 on workers' compensation.

....

RETURN-TO-WORK EVALUATIONS

In addition to the light- or modified-duty or early return-to-work program, a system should be in place to clear all employees to return to work after absence from any type of accident or surgery, whether or not work-related. The interests of the surgeon or physician who clears an employee who was injured in an auto accident (not related to work) or who has recovered from surgery to return to work are not the same as those of the employer. The returning employee should be evaluated with regard to the physical requirements of his or her job description. Failure to clear such employees could result in claims of aggravation or complications that could result in workers' compensation claims. On the other hand, the employer has a need to verify that employees have recovered to a point that they can perform their job activities safely.

Many states have implemented workers' compensation managed care arrangements or programs. Within those programs there may be rules governing clearance for return to work. It is suggested that the responsible party be thoroughly familiar with their respective state's rules in this regard.

Contact with Employees

Trust between employee and employer is one of the greatest aspects of loss control and prevention of workers' compensation claims. Genuine concern about an employee's progress and recuperation is one way to convey to the employee that the employer cares. Supervisors should initiate periodic, but frequent contact with injured employees. Sharing updates from the workplace makes the employee feel he or she is still a part of, and valuable to, the organization. In those instances when the employee requires assistance, the supervisor can notify the proper party (personnel or risk management) to contact the workers' compensation carrier or social services. Moreover, the supervisor should encourage coworkers to periodically contact injured employees who are absent to let them know they are missed. Often cards and notes are used to convey the same thought.

USE OF OWNED AND NONOWNED VEHICLES

Driving a company-owned vehicle or one's own vehicle for work-related activities is common practice. In home health care, most often it is the personal vehicle that is used to make the home visit. To deliver supplies, pharmaceuticals, and equipment to homebound patients or other providers, such as a long-term care facility, company-owned vehicles usually are used.

Employees whose jobs require them to drive company vehicles or their personal vehicles as a part of their responsibility can pose a risk exposure to the organization. Employees with less-than-acceptable driving records or with a history of driving under the influence (DUI) convictions may be unacceptable to the commercial automobile or fleet insurance carrier. Company or personal vehicles that are not properly maintained and are found to be in an unsafe condition (for example, poor tread on tires, windshield wipers that need replacing, lights that do not work) also are a risk exposure to the organization, especially if they become involved in a motor vehicle accident.

Exhibit 24.1 on pages 555–564 includes several examples of policies and procedures appropriate to a fleet risk management program; they can be adapted to meet the health care organization's needs, size of fleet, and type of organization.

SECURITY PROGRAM DEVELOPMENT AND IMPLEMENTATION

The goal of the health care organization's security program as described in the risk management policy statement is to maintain and foster an environment that is free of harm, enhancing the opportunity to deliver low-cost, high-quality health care. In addition to providing a safe environment for staff, patients, and visitors, security officers serve to protect their and the organization's valuables and other property.

Security Risk Assessment Plan

It is essential that a security risk assessment be conducted as the basis for the development of a security risk exposure plan. It is recommended that an on-site visit be made to each location throughout the organization. At each location security risk exposures should be identified and analyzed. The plan should discuss the security risk exposures identified and the action plan to address the exposures at each location and a prioritization of the most significant risks. It is suggested that this plan be the basis of the security program's annual goals and activities. Annually the plan should be reviewed and updated as necessary. The progress of addressing the exposures should be monitored on an ongoing basis and periodically reported to the security environment of care committee and to the risk management committee and/or to board of governors.

The presence of narcotics, other controlled substances, and syringes poses an additional burden of surveillance and protection on a health care facility's security personnel. The JCAHO requires a security plan to be developed and implemented. The monitoring of the plan's effectiveness is a component of JCAHO's EOC standard.

Security Program Staffing

The structure of the security program depends on the location of the facility, its management philosophy, and the organization's particular needs. The program's effectiveness depends on many variables, one of the most important of which is personnel.

Should an organization decide to maintain the security program in-house, staffing requirements will need to be analyzed. In addition to adequate staffing on all shifts, relief personnel must be available to cover for days off (such as sick days, holidays, and vacation time), for time off to attend in-service programs, and for personnel vacancies. In compliance with specific state laws, background investigations and character checks of all employed security personnel are necessary, in addition to the usual references obtained for all prospective employees. It is suggested that the director of the organization's in-house security program be experienced in personnel management as well as security.

Some health care organizations choose to contract with an independent agency to provide security. In that event, the risk manager must review the contract carefully for risk exposure, checking to ensure that it contains hold-harmless and indemnification clauses and adequate insurance requirements. The contract also should require that the security staff provided by the contractor meets any state statutory guidelines for security personnel and that they be required to participate in appropriate in-service programs at periodic intervals. Whether or not the security services are contracted, it is suggested that the director of the program be an employee of the health care organization. The employed director would have oversight of, and a vested interest in, the program's effectiveness.

Some organizations augment their security personnel with off-duty law enforcement officers. Even though such personnel are governed by their sworn duty to uphold the law, the health care organization employer might have risk exposure if those officers handle their duties differently from the organization's wishes. The risk manager should recognize and manage these exposures.

The assistance provided to the risk management and safety activities by security personnel is invaluable. Security officers patrol all parts of the facility's building and grounds and interact with staff, patients, and visitors. The extra eyes and ears can only enhance the overall effectiveness of the facility's risk management, safety, and security program goals.

Small, rural, and long-term care health care organizations may not have a formal security department because they either are unable to afford such a structured, formal program or do not perceive the need for one. Regardless, the JCAHO requires a security plan to be developed and implemented. It is suggested that the risk manager be involved in the development of such a plan. Home health care agencies and managed care organizations (MCOs) may not have a formal security program because their health care delivery is dispersed rather than in a centralized location; additionally, if the JCAHO or a similar agency does not accredit them, they are not required to have one. In such instances, the risk manager can develop relationships with the local law enforcement agency so as to enhance the visibility of its officers and vehicles on the organization's grounds. For emergencies, a "hotline" or "panic button" system connected directly to the law enforcement agency can be installed. Offering free coffee and pastries in the emergency department (ED), at the nurses' station, and in other strategic areas, particularly on the late evening and night shifts, can encourage visits by law enforcement officers. Their visibility both deters trouble and provides a sense of security for evening and night shift personnel. In institutions without a separate security staff or department, the staff of the entire organization will need to be conversant with its security plan and assume responsibility for being observant and protective of patients, visitors, and property. In fact, all institutions would do well to alert all staff to the purpose of the security department and the roles that all staff, security or otherwise, can play in fostering a secure environment.

Security Program Functions and Activities

Whether the security program is in-house or provided by a contract service, certain functions are to be performed by the person who is accountable for the institution's security. These are as follows (but are not all-inclusive):

- To establish a system for surveillance throughout the facility on all shifts and on all days of the week so that areas will be monitored to prevent bodily harm and loss or damage of property.

- To devise and implement a system for the prompt reporting of all losses of, or damage to, property and to implement corrective or preventive action.

- To monitor unauthorized ingress to and egress from the facility.

- To provide support personnel to subdue patients who may cause harm to themselves, others, or property, and to assist staff when requested and needed.

- To work with department heads to develop and implement a monitoring system to prevent loss of supplies and equipment.

- To develop and implement in-service programs to enhance employee sensitivity to security problems and teach employees how to act in specific situations.

- To maintain appropriate documentation to ensure compliance with JCAHO standards, applicable state health care licensing regulations, OSHA, and other federal, state, and local regulations, as required.

- To develop and maintain a working relationship with all applicable law enforcement agencies.

- To maintain current knowledge, theoretical and practical, so as to conduct a program and manage a staff with the ability to respond and interact appropriately in any situation that threatens people or property.

- To provide the EOC committee with monthly reports of security incidents and to recommend appropriate correction or prevention.

Use of Weapons

If security personnel are to carry guns, nightsticks, MAG lights (long, heavy black flashlights), batons, stun guns, sprays (pepper, chemical, and other), or handcuffs, they need additional training in their use. (Risk managers should be aware of applicable state and local laws regarding licensure and certification requirements for weaponry.) The security director and the risk manager, perhaps in conjunction with the CEO or other top-level manager, should establish guidelines specifying who may carry weapons, in what circumstances they are appropriate, and what training is required for each type of weapon. It also would be wise to include the health care organization's counsel in discussions on the benefits and risks involved in the arming of security staff. Training guidelines should conform to those used by local law enforcement personnel. When weapon use is permitted, background and character investigation of security personnel is imperative. Other issues to be decided are policies on how often weapons should be inspected, whether the employee owns the weapon, and whether weapons may be carried off the premises when personnel go off duty. Each security officer authorized to carry a weapon should be responsible and accountable for its care and upkeep.

The risk manager should discuss the health care organization's policy on weapons with its insurance agent, broker, or carrier to verify that coverage is available should a claim arise as a result of weapon use. Endorsements or additional coverage may be needed to provide coverage for such exposures. Some carriers consider weapon use to be an intentional tort and exclude such incidents from coverage. The risk manager should evaluate the risk benefit to the organization of weapon use and provide that analysis to senior management.

If weapons are to be used by security personnel provided through a contract, the risk manager must verify that it contains appropriate language to transfer the risk exposure for use of the weapons to the contractor, appropriate and adequate insurance, and background checks and mandatory annual education programs and firing range practice.

Use of Guard Dogs

Some health care organizations augment their security force with the use of guard dogs. When choosing this program, organizations must weigh the risks against the benefits. If possible, the same rules that apply to police dogs should apply to using guard dogs in health care facilities. Each dog should be assigned to an individual who is specially trained in the animal's care and control and who also is willing to take on the responsibility of caring for the dog once it is retired from service. The risk manager should be involved in the development of policies governing in which instances dogs should be used to contain or restrain an individual. In addition, he or she should verify that any claims that might arise from guard dog use are covered.

Use of Restraints

Because security personnel often are called on to assist in restraining patients, they should be trained in the application of both soft and leather restraints. Documentation of attendance at in-service programs on the proper use of restraints should be maintained for reference in the individual's personnel file. Policies on restraints should emphasize that restraints are applied only at the direction of nursing or medical personnel. The risk manager should ensure that all restraint policies and procedures comply with the Conditions of Participation, JCAHO, other accrediting and state licensing bodies, and applicable state and federal laws, rules, and regulations.

When security personnel are called on to subdue a patient or a visitor, risk management should be made aware of the incident either orally or through an incident report. Whether he or she is notified when restraints are applied depends on whether a claim may be brought because of the incident.

Handling of Combative or Disturbed Persons

Security personnel often are called on to assist in handling combative patients and visitors. When subduing a patient or a visitor, staff members have a responsibility to use care to prevent injury to other patients, staff members, and visitors who may be in the immediate area. Moreover, every effort should be made to protect property.

Security personnel, strategic nursing personnel, and others should be trained in how to subdue a combative individual using proper techniques and without being injured. Evidence of the successful completion of such training should be maintained in the individual's personnel file. Thus, should a claim be asserted against the institution and its personnel for injuries suffered as a result of such handling, evidence is available that the employee was trained to use techniques in keeping with the organization's established policies and procedures to protect the restrained individual and others from harm.

Handling of Patients Who Are Prisoners

Patients who are prisoners pose special problems for security and risk management especially if they are shackled (although it is suggested that if at all possible shackles not be used in any circumstances) or under police guard. The institution's policies on the care of prisoners must be developed in cooperation with area law enforcement agencies but should include the requirement that a key to the prisoner's shackles, if used, be accessible to nursing personnel in case of fire or other emergency. The key may be maintained in the narcotic cabinet and accounted for on each shift. When the patient is discharged, the shackle key should be returned to the appropriate law enforcement agency and a receipt obtained. It should be noted that JCAHO guidelines for restraints should be followed in developing guidelines for shackle use.

Other policies should address how to or whether to discharge patients who are not shackled but are subject to police holds under state or local law. Because ambulatory care clinics are the site of choice for nonemergent care in those locations where a prison clinic is not available, ambulatory care clinics in these locales may see an increase in their prisoner-patient population. Also, prisoners with urgent or emergent medical needs may be brought into a local ED for care. In these settings, the risk manager should contact local jail or prison authorities to develop policies on how to care for prisoners without creating a risk to the other patients waiting or being cared for. If possible, a system for scheduling a prisoner-patient should be established. Policy discussions should include all relevant institution staff (for example, risk management, security, and senior management).

Handling of Patients in Protective Custody

Inpatients who are in protective custody pose yet another challenge to security and risk management. They should be assigned to rooms that are easy to secure; for example, they should not be located near an exit stairwell or an elevator, or on an outside wall by a window if there is a building nearby. Additionally, these patients should not have roommates. Security or police guards, if used, should be posted inside the patient's room, not in the corridor. Consideration might be given to registering the patient under an alias, but after the patient is discharged, all the medical records should reflect his or her real name.

Dealing with the Media

Media issues may arise from the admission of or care provided to a patient who is a celebrity or in protective custody. A cooperative plan between risk management and public and media relations should be developed to respond promptly to inquiries. In the case of celebrities, protection of privacy may be a challenge; therefore, acknowledgment of admission of care should be made only with the patient's permission. Even then, employees may leak information. One way to protect a celebrity's privacy is by using an alias.

Those patients who are in protective custody pose a challenge of a different type. Acknowledgment of admission and information about conditions or treatments should be provided only in compliance with the guidelines for releasing patient-related information in general. That the patient is in protective custody should be weighed when considering what information to be released. Risk management should be involved, and the potential for risk to the safety of the staff should be evaluated.

Preservation of Evidence

When a crime suspect is treated in a hospital or outpatient facility, security personnel or other staff may need to assist local law enforcement agencies with preserving evidence for the prosecution of that crime. For example, auto accident victims may have their blood tested for levels of alcohol or controlled substances, or patients may be brought to the facility's ED or outpatient surgical center for the removal of bullets and other projectiles or for the removal from body cavities of condoms filled with cocaine or other controlled substances. Law enforcement officers may require that they be allowed to observe the removal and take immediate possession of the removed object. Having policies in place to deal with such issues is advisable, and they should be developed in cooperation with local law enforcement agencies.

Preserving the chain of custody of the evidence should be part of those policies and procedures. Procedures for maintaining the chain of custody should be developed with the assistance and input of the local law enforcement agencies and risk management personnel. In prosecuting crime, law enforcement officers must be able to identify evidence and demonstrate that it has been in continual custody since retrieval. Often hospital personnel are an essential link in the chain of custody, particularly when law enforcement officers are not in attendance or when evidence is obtained in places other than the operating room (OR) setting.

When the procedures are established, all patient care personnel, including physicians, especially in the ED, the outpatient surgery center, the OR, and pathology, should receive in-service education.

Searches of Private Belongings

Generally, searching the private belongings of the health care organization's patients and employees is an acceptable practice if done as advised by hospital legal counsel. Procedures for searches of employees for stolen hospital property may differ from those of patients for weapons or drugs. Therefore, policies specifying who is authorized to conduct searches, circumstances under which they may be conducted, involvement of the security force, and other issues related to searches that involve patients, visitors, and employees should be developed with the guidance of legal counsel and risk management personnel.

Authority to Make Arrests

Some jurisdictions provide that security personnel can be deputized to make arrests. The risk manager who is knowledgeable about those laws can develop policies and procedures regarding the circumstances in which officers may make arrests. The risk manager should be notified, orally or by incident report, of any arrests in the facility so that claims of injury from an arrest or allegations of false arrest can be investigated before a claim is brought.

Maintenance of Shift Reports

Some security supervisors require security officers to keep a log or shift report that notes all activities, observations, and circumstances that were out of the ordinary during a shift. In addition to the time and date, each entry includes a brief description of the situation, the location, the persons involved, and the manner in which the situation was handled. No reference should be made in the log as to whether an incident report was completed, because in some jurisdictions an incident report is a confidential document whereas a security report is not. Reference to an incident report in a security log produced as evidence may lead to requests for production of a risk management report that might otherwise not be requested.

Loss or Theft of Property

Patients who lose property may bring a claim against the hospital for their loss. Sometimes a patient who has a bad encounter during one aspect of his or her hospital experience may be more likely to bring a claim for malpractice if another incident or an unsatisfactory outcome occurs. Therefore, developing ways to manage claims for lost property, especially dentures, is an important security department function.

Responsibility for investigating lost patient, employee, hospital, and visitor property belongs to the security department. The risk manager is notified when trends are identified, when items of significant value are lost, and if there is criminal activity or negligence on the part of the hospital. Working together, security and risk management can develop and implement appropriate loss control measures. To assist the security department, the risk manager can offer education programs to teach the principles of investigation and interviewing. (Improper methods of investigation or a delay in reporting a loss may result in denial of coverage for a claim.)

To manage claims appropriately, risk management should develop, and recommend for board and CEO review, policies whereby the loss of property above a designated amount must be reported to the risk manager. The risk manager then determines how to handle the claim. In any case, if reimbursement is appropriate, the risk manager should authorize it. However, the patient should submit proof of value before any reimbursement is made. The risk manager may decide to replace the item, reimburse the patient for the cost of replacement, or reimburse for its depreciated value. In those instances where the loss or theft is a result of facility or staff negligence and payment is paid, the payment should be applied against the budget of the unit that is responsible for the loss or theft. It also might be advisable to obtain a release in such situations. In some instances, the patient can be advised to file a claim against a homeowner's policy. In the interest of continued patient relations, many organizations will agree to reimburse all or part of a "lost" item or to replace it even when there is no negligence on the organization's part; but even in those instances, the amount should be applied against the budget of the unit where the loss occurred.

The theft of patient property may be more likely to occur during visiting hours, especially in the obstetrics unit where patients and visitors frequently leave patient rooms to go to the nursery windows to look at the babies. During those hours, increased rounds by staff and security personnel may serve as a deterrent to theft.

The institution also should have policies and procedures for handling patients' valuables and belongings and the property of deceased patients. For example, patients should be encouraged to avoid bringing valuables to the facility. Their belongings should be itemized, and patients might be asked to sign a form stating that they are responsible for their personal belongings. In this way, the facility can be alleviated of liability. The hospital's attorney and the risk manager should assist in drafting or reviewing those policies.

Protection of Money

Security personnel protect those areas of the facility where money is handled, such as the cashier's office, the pharmacy, the cafeteria, and the gift shop. Consideration should be given to the installation at each cashier's location of silent alarms that connect to either the local police department or the facility's security department. When personnel take money to the bank or cashier's office, risk management principles dictate that the trips are made at staggered times, by different personnel, using different vehicles or hallways over different routes. The ideal way to transport money to and from the bank is by armored car; however, when a contract service is unavailable or undesirable, not establishing a routine is one of the best loss prevention methods.

Visitor Control

Visitor control can be another challenge to both risk management and security personnel. Many health care facilities have liberalized their policies on visiting hours. In obstetrical units, the practice of rooming-in with family members means that policies on visiting hours and who may visit may be even more liberal than on other units.

As a means of identifying visitors, some facilities use badges with the date and unit to be visited. The facility may choose not to monitor visitors during the day and early evening shifts. (This policy generally does not extend to children under twelve.)

Access to the facility by outsiders after visiting hours is another challenge and poses a significant exposure to employee and patient safety. One suggestion to control visitors after hours is as follows: After the end of visiting hours is announced, security personnel make rounds on each patient care unit. Visitors and family members who remain must have doctor's orders allowing them to do so, or in the case of the intensive care unit (ICU), be clearly identified to an ICU patient. Those visitors who may not remain will be escorted out by security. Those who are allowed to stay must abide by these rules:

- After-hours visitors will be logged in by security. This log will contain the date; the patient's name, unit, and room number; and the visitor's name.
- Visitors will be issued a dated stick-on badge with the name of the unit and the room number prominently displayed. Each visitor also will be given a list of after-hours visiting rules.

• Visitors must remain either on the patient's unit or in designated areas (such as the closest vending machine area or cafeteria). If such visitors are found in any other area, they may be challenged or ejected from the facility. Because all employees should be required to wear their name badges and all after-hours visitors should be required to wear stick-on badges, unidentified individuals will be readily recognized. Security then can intercede to determine whether the individual is on the property appropriately and handle the situation accordingly. This after-hours visiting procedure can be of great assistance to the late-evening and night nursing staff, and can convey a sense of security to night shift personnel.

• Many health care organizations require that vendors have an appointment, and a permit issued for that appointment only, before they can enter the facility. Stick-on badges that clearly identify the department with which the vendor has an appointment can be used. All vendors should be advised of the appointment-only policy and that its violation will result in termination of visiting privileges. Such a system will preclude the vendors from wandering the halls and attempting to have unscheduled meetings with department heads to sell their wares.

Security Surveillance

When facilities are assessed for potential security risks, two major considerations are the type of organization (acute care, ambulatory care, mental health, and so on) and the organization's location (for example, inner city, suburban, rural). These considerations usually dictate the potential threats from the community to the organization, visitors, patients, and staff. Fences, security cameras, lighting of outer grounds, control of ingress and egress, and patrols are among the methods that can be considered to provide security measures. Each method must be evaluated in conjunction with the organization's philosophy. If cameras are used, the same issues discussed further in this chapter regarding constant monitoring and timely response must be considered.

Routine surveillance of the grounds, including parking lots and facility entrances and exits, is important for the security of property and the safety of personnel. The institution should have clear policies on basic security procedures such as lockdown and key control. Incidents when doors that should be locked are found unlocked should be logged. A short-form notice regarding unlocked doors should be sent to the department head. If the same door is found unlocked more than once, increased surveillance may be justified. As they make their rounds, if security personnel notice that personal property of patients, employees, or visitors is unattended or left in an unsecured place, they may leave a warning on a brightly colored two- by three-inch card or sticker that says, for example, "If I were a thief, this would be gone! Your friendly security personnel."

Escort Services and Parking Surveillance

Many security departments offer staff and visitors an escort service to parking areas. If such a service is offered, notice of its availability should be posted and circulated. Forty-five minutes to one-half hour prior to and after each shift change or closing of the clinic or center, security should increase surveillance of all parking areas. This surveillance increases the safety, both actual and perceived, of employees who are going off or coming on duty, especially at night.

Key Control

Responsibility for key control should be delegated to the security department. The dispensing of keys, especially masters and submasters, should be strictly controlled. A policy that keys are turned in upon separation from employment should be enforced.

Human Resources Issues

If the institution plans a layoff of a large number of people, the security department should be notified to be alert to potentially violent situations. In instances of individual terminations, security personnel may be called on to give assistance should the individual become hostile.

Another service that security may perform for the human resources department is to do background checks on applicants for employment, especially for those positions where cash handling or access to the storeroom is included in the job responsibilities.

Fires, Disasters, and Traffic Control

Security personnel play a major role in traffic control in the event of fires, other disasters, and "code blues." Security personnel should participate in disaster planning, and all security officers should receive in-service training on their responsibilities during a disaster.

Use of Local Agencies

Local law enforcement and fire departments can help health care facilities to enhance their safety and security programs. For example, police officers can conduct in-service education programs for staff on self-defense, and firefighters can instruct on home and workplace fire prevention. Development of positive relationships with these public service agencies and their respective personnel also can enhance the health care facility's public and community image.

Special Risks

Each health care organization faces unique security-related risks determined by the type of organization it is (long-term care, home health, acute care, and so on). If the organization is accredited by the JCAHO there is a requirement to address "special" security risks.

In conjunction with risk management, a health care organization's security department should identify such special or high risks specific to the organization. The organization's overall security plan should address these special risks and plan to mitigate the exposure. A few such risks are discussed in this section.

Infant and Child Kidnapping   Infants and children are kidnapped with greater frequency than one would like to acknowledge, and many from health care clinics, hospital newborn nurseries, and health care on-site day-care centers. These risks pose a different type of challenge to the risk manager and are a security and safety issue as well. Risk and security management also should assess other units that house children, such as pediatrics or the ICU.

To deter the kidnapping of infants from the nursery, many hospitals have installed various types of security systems, such as sensors, swipe cards, and video cameras. Because no one system is perfect, many institutions combine various methods to strengthen security. This is especially important for institutions that permit rooming-in, which adds another variable to the security equation.

One type of system uses sensors placed in infants' clothing. The sensors set off alarms placed at strategic egress points in the maternity and nursery unit. However, a weakness of this system is that it can be bypassed if the clothing with sensors is replaced with regular clothing. Another method uses the same type of sensor but is embedded in the infant's identification band. A weakness of this method is, of course, that the band can be cut off. Yet another method is to match the baby with the mother by using photos of each. In addition, some nursery and maternity units strictly enforce traffic with swipe cards to allow access and egress. This system can be effective, as long as no one loses a card or fails to turn one in upon separation from the organization. In addition, it is difficult for security to control traffic from housekeeping and other ancillary staff, such as lab and x-ray. Still other organizations have installed security cameras to monitor the hallways and doors leading to the nursery and maternity unit. However, to be effective, the cameras must be monitored at all times, and ward staff cannot be asked to monitor the screens and perform their normal duties simultaneously. Even with constant monitoring, cameras do not provide complete security. For example, it can be very difficult to identify who does and does not belong from a video screen that may be monitored some distance from the security camera. If video monitoring is done, risk management, security, and legal counsel should develop policies on how long to maintain the films, where, and by whom. Specific state guidelines should be used in developing such a policy.

Clinics are vulnerable because a kidnapper, posing as staff, may succeed in taking the child from the unsuspecting parent's arms, claiming to need to take him or her for tests in preparation for seeing the physician. One way to prevent this scenario is to mandate that in the ambulatory setting no staff will carry a child. In this way, security can validate that the person with the child is, indeed, on legitimate business.

Day-care centers also can present security problems. For example, problems can occur when a parent with whom staff usually interact has someone else pick up a child at the end of the day. Another potential situation is the taking of a child from the playground when staff may be less than vigilant in their observation of all the children. One way to circumvent this is to use code words to identify unknown persons authorized to pick up children. Photos and code words are another way to better identify authorized pickups. Needless to say, background checks on all day-care center personnel are imperative (most states require such checks by law). The risk manager should conduct periodic inquiries and reviews of files to verify that such checks are conducted and actually reviewed by senior staff to ensure the timeliness and thoroughness of the process.

Threats of Violence   OSHA's *Guidelines for Preventing Workplace Violence for Health Care and Social Service Workers* became effective in 1996. These guidelines are not standards. The four elements of these guidelines are:

- Management commitment and employee involvement.
- Work-site analysis.
- Hazard prevention and control.
- Safety and health training.

Through these guidelines, *reasonable* parameters have been established. The risk manager and the safety director should collaborate to develop, implement, and provide in-services on these guidelines and policies and procedures. Should the health care organization have an incident, and it is determined that the organization did not have these *reasonable* guidelines in place, the organization might be held liable due to not having done enough to prevent violence.

Wanderers   Long-term care facilities are the settings with the most frequent challenges related to wanderers, although acute care facilities experience occasional incidents. The key to prevention is to identify patients who are likely to wander. Special steps then can be taken to decrease such incidents. One system used in these instances is an identification band with a sensor that activates an alarm when passed through certain points. When using these devices, the risk manager should evaluate where the point of turning off the alarm is placed. It is suggested that the only place the alarm can be deactivated is at the point where the alarm was tripped. Thus, to deactivate the alarm, staff must go to the point and, it is hoped, to the patient who tripped it. In addition, staff should have a system for periodically monitoring and charting that the patient still wears the sensor bracelet so that it can be replaced if it has been removed or fallen off.

Should a patient elope, with or without the sensor bracelet, established policy should be followed to notify police and family and to initiate a search. Risk management should be involved in developing such a policy and procedure. In addition, risk management should be notified immediately of any patient elopement from the facility.

Home Health Care

Home health care staff are required to go into all types of communities to provide services and deliver supplies and equipment. The safety and security of these personnel and contracted staff raise many risk management, safety, and security issues that should be kept in mind. Theft of supplies, equipment, or drugs is an exposure, and injury to the deliverer a potential exposure. Muggings and robbery of the staff as they go to or from the client's home, and accusations of theft of the client's personal property or monies, are other issues. Disposal of medical waste is another issue that should not be forgotten. (See Chapter 9 on occupational and environmental services.) Some risk managers have addressed aspects of these potential exposures and have issued cellular phones to all home health care staff; however, these phones are expensive and effective only if they can be used before the incident and if response is timely to deter the event. With more home health care being delivered in more inner city, high-risk areas, this may be one of the increasing challenges to risk managers.

Facilities for Psychiatric and Developmentally Disabled Patients

Many of the risk exposures inherent in this specialty area have been addressed in Chapter 15 on high risk clinical areas; however, attention should be given to the monitoring of knives (or sharps) in the kitchens of those facilities housed on more open campuses, especially adolescent psychiatric facilities. One way to monitor this exposure is to conduct a knife count before and after every meal, using the same system as used when counting controlled drugs. When not engaged in meal preparation, the knife storage area should be kept locked and the key maintained by the supervisor.

....

CONCLUSION

Safety and security are integral components of an overall effective program to manage the many and varied risk exposures of a health care organization. As such, the interrelationships, communication, and cooperation among those programs are strategic to each program's effectiveness and the overall risk management program as a whole. No one program functions independently of the other; all are interrelated and synergistic.

Suggested Readings

Occupational Health and Safety Administration. *Guidelines for Preventing Workplace Violence for Health Care and Social Service Workers.* Washington, D.C.: OSHA, 1996.

"ACEP Calls for Physician Role in Fighting Domestic Violence." *Emergency Department Law,* Oct. 18, 1994, pp. 3–4.

"The Everyday Face of Workplace Violence." *Risk Management, 47,* Feb. 2000, pp. 12–18.

Surveyer Mitiguy, J. "Facing Up to the Problem of Workplace Violence," RN, MS. *Nursing Spectrum,* Oct. 18, 1999, p. 29.

EXHIBIT 24.1.   Fleet Safety Policy

Authorizing Drivers

Policy

When any portion of an employee's job functions include the driving of a recognized motorized vehicle owned by, registered to, or leased to Anywhere Hospital (AH), the employee shall be required to secure and maintain a current, valid driver's license appropriate for the classification of the vehicle, issued by the State of _____. *Only* employees who meet the following stated guidelines are authorized to operate AH owned, leased, or rented vehicles.

Procedure

The Human Resources Department, on offer of employment of such an employee, shall secure the information as set forth in Section I above and forward this to the Risk Management Services Department.

Annually, in January of each year, the employees, as identified above, shall show their drivers' licenses to their respective Department Head or Nurse Manager who will transcribe the following information:

Name
Date of birth
Date of issuance
Date of expiration
License number

The above itemized information will be forwarded to the Risk Management Services Department and to the Human Resources Department by February 1 of each year.

The Risk Management Services Department shall submit to the State Division of Drivers' Licenses the list of information as submitted from the Department Heads, Nurse Managers, or Human Resources Department.

At any time that an employee whose job functions include driving an Anywhere Hospital vehicle is found to have within a twelve (12) month period, six (6) or more points against their driver's license, they shall be evaluated as to their driving habits and could be requested to take a defensive driver's course, be relieved from their driving functions, or otherwise disciplined.

If an employee's driver's license is suspended or revoked, it is grounds for immediate transfer, suspension, and/or dismissal.

Any employee who receives a moving traffic violation for any reason shall report such to their Department Head or Nurse Manager within five (5) days. This information shall then be forwarded to the Risk Management Services Department, points will be assigned, per violation as per the state Department of Highway Safety and Motor Vehicles.

DUI (.0? alcohol level)	Immediate Removal of Driving Duties
Speeding—15 MPH or less over posted speed	Points: 3
Speeding—16 MPH over posted speed	Points: 4
Reckless Driving	Points: 4
Moving Violation Causing an Accident	Points: 4

Any accident that occurs involving an AH vehicle, or a private vehicle used for official Anywhere Hospital business, shall be *immediately* reported to the Department Head or Nurse Manager *and* to the Risk Management Services Department.

Anywhere Hospital vehicles shall not be used for personal business unless assigned to specific individuals for their exclusive use, and shall always be garaged on AH grounds when not being used for Anywhere Hospital business.

Using Personal Vehicles for AH Business

Policy

Some AH employees have job descriptions that specify that they *must* have their own transportation to perform the required duties of their job function, such as home health care. These employees use their personal vehicles *at their own risk* and must maintain personal automobile insurance and have proof of same. Yearly, on the date of employment, the employee shall request a copy of insurance from their auto insurance carrier, to be sent to the Human Resources Department. The Human Resources Department will maintain the copy of insurance in the employee's personnel file. Employees using personal vehicles for AH business must ensure their vehicles meet a minimum auto safety standard at all times.

(Continued)

EXHIBIT 24.1.   Fleet Safety Policy (*Continued*)

Procedures

In the event an employee uses his or her personal vehicle for authorized, or required, company business, he or she will be entitled to reimbursement for mileage, in accordance to the personnel and finance policies of Anywhere Hospital.

In the event an employee receives a car allowance or is reimbursed for mileage, the car allowance and mileage reimbursement encompasses the following components:

Gas
Insurance
Wear and tear on the vehicle
Maintenance
Road toll charges

Upon hire date and then yearly on the date of employment, the employee shall request a copy of insurance from his or her auto insurance carrier to be sent to the Human Resources Department as proof of insurance.

In the event an employee is involved in an accident in his or her personal vehicle while on company business, his or her personal automobile insurance should immediately be notified of the accident. *The AH automobile insurance will not cover an accident that occurred while the employee was driving his or her personal vehicle on company business.*

Any accident that occurs involving a private vehicle used for official Anywhere Hospital business, shall be *immediately* reported to the Department Head or Nurse Manager *and* to the Risk Management Services Department.

A minimum safety standard of "Safe Driver" must be maintained at all times. The Risk Management Services Department shall submit to the State Division of Drivers' Licenses the list of information as submitted from the Department Heads, Nurse Managers, or Human Resources Department.

At any time that an employee whose job functions include driving an Anywhere Hospital vehicle is found to have within a twelve (12) month period, *six (6) or more points* against his or her driver's license, they shall be evaluated as to their driving habits and could be requested to take defensive driver's course, be relieved from their driving functions, or otherwise disciplined.

Adding or Deleting Vehicles to the Fleet

Policy

Each Department Head or Nurse Manager will immediately notify the Risk Management Department when adding or deleting any vehicle to or from the AH vehicle fleet.

Procedure

Use the vehicle acquistion/deletion form (Attachment A) to convey the information to the Risk Management Department.

The department's name, facility, and address will be entered on the form in the designated spaces. The type of vehicle will be indicated with a mark of "X" on Line 3. If the vehicle is not an automobile, a truck, or a van, the type of vehicle will be indicated in the space provided for "Other," such as *bus*. Enter in the space indicated "Make" the make (brand) of vehicle, such as Dodge, Buick, GMC. In the space indicated "Model" indicate such as Cutlass, 4-Door Sedan; Regency, 2-Door Sedan. Indicate in the area designated "Year" the year of the make of the vehicle. The "VIN" (vehicle identification number) is entered in the space provided. The VIN is obtained from the registration form. In the appropriate space, indicate the license tag number of the vehicle. If the vehicle currently carries a temporary tag, indicate such. Indicate the full purchase price in the space indicated. Attach a copy of the purchase papers to the form.

In the event a vehicle is leased, the leasing agency's name and address should be indicated in the space provided. In the space indicated "Use," indicate the use, *business* or *personal* (if it is to be assigned to an individual and the intended use of the vehicle, such as transport supplies, pick up and transport patients from their home and outpatient clinic). In the space indicated "Assigned To," enter the department to which the vehicle is assigned or the name of the person to whom the vehicle is to be assigned for either personal use or for use at work, such as Materials Management, Administration, Outpatient. In the space indicated "Garaged Where," indicate the name of the facility or the address of the department or individual to whom the vehicle may be assigned.

If the vehicle has been assigned to an individual for personal use, indicated the name of that individual, his or her current driver's license number, and the expiration date. Affix a copy of that individual's driver's license to the notification form.   (*Continued*)

EXHIBIT 24.1.   **Fleet Safety Policy** (*Continued*)

In the appropriate space indicated, enter the date that the vehicle was acquired, or the date that it was deleted from the fleet.

On the line indicated "Notice Date," indicate the date this form is completed, as well as the name and title of the person completing the notification form.

When the form is completed and all requested attachments are compiled, fax the form and attachments to the Risk Management Department, and send the original with attachments through the inter-office mail. The Risk Management Department will be responsible for notifying the agent/broker or insurance carrier to ensure appropriate addition or deletion from the policy. *NOTE:* If there are plans to purchase, lease, or rent long-term a vehicle, the Risk Management Department should be notified prior to finalizing the plans for such purchase or lease, so that appropriate certificates of insurance can be generated.

Attachment A

VEHICLE

ACQUISITION or DELETION

NOTIFICATION FORM

Dept. Name and Facility: _____

Address: _____

Automobile: _____   Truck: _____   Van: _____   Other: _____

Make: _____   Model: _____   Year: _____

VIN No.: _____   License Tag No.: _____

Purchase Price: _____

Leasing Agency: _____

Leasing Agency Address and Phone No.: _____

_____

_____

Intended Use of Vehicle: _____

_____

_____

Assigned To: _____

Garaged At: _____

If Assigned to an Individual, List the Driver's License Number and Expiration Date:

_____

Reason for Deletion (i.e., Lease Expired, Totaled): _____

_____

Acquisition Date: _____   Deletion Date: _____

Date of This Notice: _____   _____
                                                    Name

                                     _____
                                                    Title

(*Continued*)

EXHIBIT 24.1.   Fleet Safety Policy (*Continued*)

Automobile Insurance, Underwriting Information

Policy

The Risk Management Services Department will be responsible for maintaining a current list of all vehicles owned or leased by the facility. This information shall include the "make," "model," "year," "purchase price," "VIN," "use," "garage location," "person/department assigned," and "date of purchase."

Procedure

Four months prior to the renewal date of the Anywhere Hospital's automobile's insurance policy, the Risk Management Services Department will distribute a list reflecting the above itemized information to the department manager or individuals who have been assigned an AH-owned or leased vehicle. The department manager or individual will verify the vehicle information. This verified information shall be returned to the Risk Management Services Department within ten days of receipt.

The Risk Management Services Department will verify the returned information against the master list, making appropriate corrections where applicable.

On or prior to ninety days before renewal of the automobile's insurance coverage, the Risk Management Services Department will forward the updated, verified list of underwriting information to the agent/broker to include as part of the underwriting submission.

Insurance Information, Affixed in Each Vehicle

Policy

Upon renewal of the Anywhere Hospital automobile insurance, the Risk Management Services Department will forward to each department manager or individual to whom an Anywhere Hospital vehicle has been assigned, the new insurance card for each vehicle, instruction for reporting an accident, and instructions on reporting an accident (Attachment B) to the Risk Management Services Department. These documents will be affixed to the fire wall or the wall of the glove compartment of each vehicle.

Procedure

Upon receipt, the documents listed above will be placed in a baggie and affixed to the fire wall on the passenger side of the vehicle or to the wall of the glove compartment of the vehicle.

The baggie with the prior year's documentation will be removed and returned to the Risk Management Services Department for disposal.

In the event that the baggie is removed to utilize the information contained, for any reason, the Risk Management Services Department will be contacted immediately for replacement documents.

The documents should be consistently placed in the same location of the vehicle— either passenger side fire wall or on the inside wall of the glove compartment.

Monthly spot checks will be performed by the department manager to verify that the information is still affixed to the fire wall or glove compartment of the vehicle. This verification will be documented on the monthly vehicle check list.

Vehicles Not Assigned to an Individual for Their Personal Use— Signing Vehicles In and Out

Policy

All vehicles not assigned to an individual for personal use will be signed out either daily or at each reassignment of use. A sign-in/out log (Attachment C) will be at a central place (such as the key lock box) in each department for use when signing out vehicles assigned to that specific department.

Procedure

Departmentally Assigned Vehicles   Daily, the individuals assigned to specific vehicles in a particular department will sign out the vehicle at the beginning of the work shift and sign it in at the completion of the work shift or assigned task. Information for the log book will contain the make, model, and tag number of the vehicle, as well as the date, time out, mileage out, usage, time in, mileage in, and initials of the employee filling out the log. If there is a variety of uses of a particular departmental vehicle, the use for the shift will be so indicated.

(*Continued*)

EXHIBIT 24.1.   Fleet Safety Policy (*Continued*)

Carpool Vehicles   Employees having a need to use an Anywhere Hospital-owned or leased vehicle for hospital business assigned to another department shall sign out the vehicle by completing the information requested in the assigned department's log book. A current driver's license shall be shown to the individual responsible for the carpool vehicles before the vehicle is released. Upon the return of the carpool vehicle, the employee will indicate the time the vehicle has been returned, return the keys to the individual responsible for the carpool vehicles, and both will initial the log book entry. Annually, the log book for the carpool vehicles will be reviewed by the Risk Management Services Department, to ascertain any names of the employees who have used a vehicle, and have not been included in the semiannual driver's license review. Such individuals will be contacted by their department manager, and a copy of their driver's license will be made and forwarded to the Risk Management Services Department. The Risk Management Services Department will include that driver's license in the semiannual submission to the State Division of Motor Vehicles (DMV), to ascertain the status of that individual's diver's license and driving record.

Attachment B

ACCIDENT or INCIDENT REPORT FORM

This form has been designed to assist all parties involved in making an accident or incident report.

DRIVER 1—Name

Address

Business Phone

Home Phone

Driver License No. and State

Vehicle Owner

Owner's Address

Business Phone

Home Phone

Year and Make of Automobile

Tag No. and State

Insurance Company

Policy No.

DRIVER 2—Name

Address

Business Phone

Home Phone

Driver License No. and State

Vehicle Owner

Owner's Address

Business Phone

Home Phone

Year and Make of Automobile

Tag No. and State

Insurance Company

Policy No.

Location of Accident

(Continued)

EXHIBIT 24.1.   Fleet Safety Policy (*Continued*)

Time	

Time

Date

Witness

Investigating Officer

Badge No.

Department

Was a law enforcement Traffic Accident Report completed by the Investigating Officer? Attach a copy of the Police Case Number Card.

Was a traffic citation issued by the Investigating Officer?

Signature of Employee: _____   Date: _____

Investigating Accidents

Policy

The investigation of each accident will seek not only the specific cause, but go further into the conditions responsible, in order that the DDC program can be adjusted to correct the identified causes of accidents.

Procedures

Every driver who has an accident should be interviewed as soon as possible after the accident by his or her immediate supervisor.

Representatives from Risk Management Services Department, Human Resources Department, and the department director and/or manager of the individual involved in the vehicle accident or incident will review the pertinent circumstances.

If it is clear that the accident was nonpreventable and there were no contributory factors involving the employee, a letter to that effect will be entered in the employee's department driver record file.

If the accident is deemed preventable or there is contributory circumstances on part of the employee, a full investigative review will be conducted by the Risk Management Services Department. If the results deem that the accident or incident was in fact preventable, the Director of Human Resources will be notified for disciplinary action.

A *preventable accident* is defined as: Any accident involving a company vehicle that results in property damage and/or personal injury, regardless of who was injured, what property was damaged, to what extent, or where it occurred, in which the driver in question failed to exercise every *reasonable* precaution to prevent the accident.

The following actions are recommended guidelines for disciplinary action, but if there is proof of gross negligence by the employee, further action by the Director of Human Resource may occur.

Recommended Action for Employed Drivers

Number of Accidents	*Recommended Minimum Corrective Action*
First preventable or contributed to accident.	Written reprimand and remedial training.
Second preventable or contributed to accident within six (6) months of the first accident.	Suspension from duties not to exceed three (3) days and remedial training.
Third preventable or contributed to accident within six (6) months of the prior accident.	Loss of all company-owned, leased, or rented vehicle driving privileges, reassignment to a nondriving position if available, and suspension of three (3) days.

EXHIBIT 24.1.   **Fleet Safety Policy** (*Continued*)

Attachment C

VEHICLE

SIGNING IN or OUT LOG

Department Name/Facility _____

Vehicle Make/Model/Tag No. _____

Month/Year _____

Date	Time Out	Mileage Out	Usage	Time In	Mileage In	Initials

Sequential Page No. _____

Vehicle Maintenance Schedule

Policy

The department and individual to which or whom a vehicle is assigned (whether business or personal use) shall be responsible for ensuring that all vehicles in their care, control, and custody are maintained according to the owner's manual. A maintenance program based on mileage or operating hours will be the responsibility of the Department Manager responsible for the vehicle.

Procedure

A copy of the attached Vehicle Maintenance Schedule form (Attachment D), will be placed in the glove compartment of every vehicle owned or leased by Anywhere Hospital. The department manager or individual to whom the vehicle is assigned will be responsible for completing the form at the completion of each maintenance check.

This form will reflect all maintenance checks in sequential order for the life of the vehicle as long as it is owned or leased by Anywhere Hospital. (Use additional forms, stapled together, if necessary.)

After the completion of each sequential maintenance check, the department manager or the individual responsible for the vehicle will copy the Vehicle Maintenance Schedule form and forward the copy to the Risk Management Services Department.

The original of the Vehicle Maintenance Schedule form reflecting these sequential dates of the maintenance checks shall be maintained in the vehicle's glove compartment at all times.   (*Continued*)

EXHIBIT 24.1.   Fleet Safety Policy (*Continued*)

Attachment D

VEHICLE MAINTENANCE SCHEDULE

Page _____ of _____

Make: _____   Model: _____   Year: _____

VIN.: _____   Date Vehicle Acquired: _____

Department or Individual: _____

Date	Type of Maintenance	Odometer Reading	Where

Daily Vehicle Safety Maintenance Checklist

Policy

The department and individual to which or whom a vehicle is assigned (whether business or personal use) shall be responsible for ensuring that all vehicles in their care are maintained and operated safely.

Procedure

At the *beginning of each work day,* the individual who is assigned to a vehicle shall complete a safety maintenance checklist in accordance with the Vehicle Checklist (Attachment E). At the end of the shift, drivers will submit the Vehicle Checklist to their Department Manager. All vehicle reports and correspondence will be maintained in a vehicle jacket file within the department.

In the event a vehicle does not meet all the safety check items, the vehicle shall *not* be driven. The Department Director or Manager will schedule the vehicle for repairs through an approved Anywhere Hospital vendor.

At the end of each month, the driver will submit to the department manager a Vehicle Checklist, which will be reviewed and signed by the department manager. A copy of this report will be sent to the Risk Management Services Department.

Annually, in January of each year, the vehicle must pass the Vehicle Emission Inspection for tag renewal. Copies of this inspection will be forwarded to the Risk Management Services Department, no later than February 1 of each year.

(*Continued*)

EXHIBIT 24.1. **Fleet Safety Policy** (*Continued*)

Attachment E

DAILY VEHICLE SAFETY
MAINTENANCE CHECKLIST

Drivers should check their vehicles before each use. As necessary, at the end of each day drivers should submit a checklist of repairs or adjustments needed for their vehicle.

Items to be covered are:	*Acceptable*	*Needs Repair*	*Condition/Comments*	*Date Repaired*
Tire Condition	☐	☐	_____	
Tire Inflation	☐	☐	_____	
Lights (Headlights and Rear Lights)	☐	☐	_____	
Mirrors	☐	☐	_____	
Brakes	☐	☐	_____	
Exhaust System (Muffler)	☐	☐	_____	
Engine Belts	☐	☐	_____	
Windows (Wiper Blades)	☐	☐	_____	
Direction (Turn) Signals	☐	☐	_____	
Horn	☐	☐	_____	
Instrument Readings				
Oil	☐	☐	_____	
Water Temperature	☐	☐	_____	
Battery Charge	☐	☐	_____	
Fuel Indicator	☐	☐	_____	

Additional comments and concerns

_____
_____
_____
_____
_____
_____
_____

Signature of Driver: _____   Date: _____

By the last day of each month, each driver will submit to the department manager a completed Vehicle Checklist. This must be reviewed and signed by the department manager, and a copy of this report sent to the Risk Management Services Department. All vehicle reports and correspondences will be maintained in a vehicle jacket file within the Department.

Department Manager Signature: _____   Date: _____

Defensive Drivers Course (DDC)

Policy

Upon initial employment, and annually thereafter, all employees who will be operating an Anywhere Hospital-owned, leased, or rented vehicle as part of their job function will be required to attend a four (4) hour-long vehicle safety training course (Defensive Driving Course [DDC]) tailored to the needs of the job requirement and they must pass a written comprehensive test. Documentation of attendance will be maintained in each employee's personnel file. Copies of this documentation will be forwarded to the Risk Management Services Department.

(*Continued*)

EXHIBIT 24.1.   **Fleet Safety Policy** (*Continued*)

Procedures

Coordination of the DDC will be the responsibility of the Risk Management Department. This instruction is designed to teach the art of safe and accident-free driving. There will be a written comprehensive test at the conclusion of the presentation. Anyone failing the written test will have his or her driving privileges suspended until he or she repeats the course and passes the test.

Additional training will be required if there is a change in Anywhere Hospital-owned, leased, or rented vehicle being driven by the employee. This training will be the responsibility of the department manager as to orientation and familiarization of the new vehicle. Documentation of this training will be copied and forwarded to the Risk Management Department.

Reporting of Accidents

Policy

All employees involved in an automobile or vehicle accident while on company business, whether in a company-owned, leased, or rented vehicle or in their personal vehicle, will *immediately* report the accident to the local authorized police agency *and* to the Risk Management Department.

Procedures

The employee involved in an accident while on company business will complete the accident report form (Attachment B) found in the attached vehicle information package on the passenger side fire wall of the vehicle or attached inside the glove compartment. The accident report form may also be acquired through the Risk Management Department upon request.

Drivers involved in an accident or *incident* involving injuries to employee or others, or damage to property or vehicle must *immediately* notify their office and/or supervisor by radio or telephone of the incident. Should the event occur off company property, contact the local authorized police agency to investigate and document the accident. Should the vehicle be unable to be driven, the employee driving an Anywhere Hospital-owned or leased vehicle shall direct that the vehicle be towed to an Anywhere Hospital pre-designated authorized mechanical shop.

If the employee is injured or incapacitated, it shall become the responsibility of the department manager to obtain the required information, such as a police report, automobile accident report, and the accident investigation report. These reports must be submitted to the Risk Management Services Department for review within twenty-four (24) hours.

Employees who are driving their personal vehicles involved in accidents while on company business, in addition to notifying the Risk Management Services Department, shall also immediately notify their personal insurance carrier. Should the car require towing, this will be at the employee's expense and direction.

The Anywhere Hospital Risk Management Department may initiate its own accident investigation.

The Anywhere Hospital Risk Management Services Department must be notified immediately when events occur with a company owned, leased, or rented vehicle.

25

Workers' Compensation: A Risk or a Benefit?

Leilani Kicklighter

Cost containment is a challenge in today's business environment. If a health care organization is to survive and grow in today's climate, cost containment, while delivering quality patient care, is the "name of the game."

Historically, most health care organizations have placed more importance on medical professional liability exposures than on work-related injuries and illnesses, despite the fact that in some organizations, workers' compensation costs outpace professional liability costs. Typically, many key functions of the workers' compensation program are seated in safety, risk management, human resources, and employee benefits, while other still are managed through employee health. This lack of a single accountability for the workers' compensation program (ownership) commonly results in:

- A less than coordinated program to promote employee health.

- The lack of an opportunity to promote a safe work environment.

- The inability to minimize losses associated with work-related injuries.

Fortunately, health care organizations are realizing that work-related injuries are controllable and that there is a need to coordinate activities as well as control costs.

Workers' compensation is a growing concern for health care providers. As costs and premiums continue to rise, health care organizations are looking for mechanisms to control their workers' compensation loss experience. One cost containment technique to improve an organizations' bottom line is a well structured and administered workers' compensation program that can reduce the direct and indirect costs related to employee accidents and illnesses.

From a business standpoint, one of the most compelling reasons for an effective workers' compensation program is the need to conserve human and fiscal resources.

A health care organization benefits both directly and indirectly from controlling the costs of employee accidents and illnesses. As costs are removed from the system, insurance premiums are reduced through improved experience modification factor. Not only are costs reduced, but the corporate climate is enhanced and employee morale is improved.

In the author's experience, more than 75 percent of the efforts expended to control the workers' compensation costs at any given facility should be focused on *prevention*. Although it is acknowledged that good case management is an important component of a workers' compensation program, often little can be done to reduce the amount paid because of the state and federal rules and regulations that govern payment of lost wages and medical costs. Therefore, management of the workers' compensation risk should emphasize prevention of the accident in the first place.

In institutions lacking a full-time designated workers' compensation professional, the risk manager should work closely with the safety committee chairperson, the designated safety officer, and whoever else has responsibility for the workers' compensation program or program elements. The risk manager could also assume the responsibility for the workers' compensation program. This, of course, assumes the person not only has the initiative to do so but also has the requisite skills (management, insurance, human relation, communication, claims, regulatory, and financial).

All risk managers should have a working familiarity with the workers' compensation rules, regulations, claims management, and benefits as determined by their respective states, regardless of whether or not they have direct line responsibility for the program. State workers' compensation statues, rules, and regulations govern certain workers' compensation issues, policies, and procedures, whereas others, not as strictly regulated, should be cleared through personnel or human resources and legal counsel.

The risk manager should be familiar with the Americans with Disabilities Act (ADA) as it may relate to claims arising from discrimination during the hiring and placement practices of the organization. Such claims are usually brought in federal court and may or may not have coverage, depending on the coverages the specific organization has in place.

Each health care organization, as an employer, has the responsibility to develop and implement an employee safety program, the goal of which is to provide safe working conditions and procedures for all employees. This responsibility stems from regulatory, moral, and financial principles. Sec. (2) of Public Law 91-596 states, "The Congress finds that personal injuries and illnesses arising out of work situations impose a substantial burden upon, and are a hindrance to, interstate commerce in terms of lost production, wage loss, medical expenses, and disability compensation payments."[1] The purpose of the act is ". . . to assure so far as possible every working man and woman in the Nation safe and healthful working conditions and to preserve our human resources."[2]

PREVENTION

The prevention process begins with proper selection and placement of employees in positions in which they are physically and mentally capable of functioning, ongoing education on safe work practices, and provision of proper and adequate equipment and assistive devices. Ongoing analysis of empirical work-related accident data to identify where to focus energies and resources is also an important component of workers' compensation loss prevention activities. The following are discussions of the general components of a comprehensive workers' compensation program that can be tailored to fit different types of health care organizations. (See Exhibit 25.1 on pages 572–588 for a sample model workers' compensation program.)

Job or Position Descriptions with Quantifiable Physical-Based Criteria

Specific job or position descriptions that reflect quantifiable physical-based requirements are necessary and form the basis for many of the other activities subsequently discussed. Without quantifiable physical-based job descriptions, there is no basis against which to evaluate a person's physical capabilities to safely perform tasks. Such specificity will assist in determining appropriate job placement against physical requirements and abilities, evaluating capabilities for returning to work, and assessing the work-hardening rehabilitation program. When developing the job position, specific physical criteria, including hearing and vision requirements, should not be overlooked.

Interaction with Injured Employees

Trust between employee and employer is one of the greatest aspects of loss control and prevention of workers' compensation claims. Genuine concern about an employee's progress and recuperation is one way to convey to the employee that the employer cares. Supervisors should initiate periodic, but frequent contact with injured employees. Sharing updates from the workplace makes the employee feel he or she is still a part of, and valuable to, the organization. In those instances when the employee requires assistance, the supervisor can notify the proper party (human resources or risk management) to contact the workers' compensation carrier, employee assistance programs, or social or community services. Moreover, the supervisor should encourage coworkers to periodically contact injured employees who are absent to let them know they are missed. Often cards and notes are used to convey the same thought and are generally well received.

Light- or Modified-Duty or Early Return-to-Duty Program

A formal light or modified-duty or early return-to-duty program consistently applied to all eligible employees has the potential to return injured employees to work quickly and to reduce overall costs. The human resources (HR) director, risk manager, safety officer, department head to which the employee is to be assigned, position ergonomic evaluator, and employee health nurse should all be involved in evaluating the employee's suitability for light duty in relation to the prospective position to which he or she is to be assigned.

An example of a light- or modified-duty or early return-to-duty program is as follows:

● Identify light-duty positions or jobs and activities throughout the organization and develop specific job descriptions for these positions, including the physical criteria. When considering a candidate for the light-duty program, the position descriptions, the physical requirements, and the employee's regularly assigned job description should be made available to the treating physician(s).

● Assign eligible candidates to departments other than their regularly assigned unit, with salaries paid from a human resources or risk management fund allocated to support the light-duty program. In this manner, the injured employee's department budget will not account for an employee assigned through the light-duty program, either in salary or full-time equivalent overages. Additionally, if the employee is on an extended light-duty, the assignment to a light-duty-specific position could be limited to a defined period of time, not to exceed one to three months. Whether employees on light duty may accrue benefits is an individual organizational and state labor law determination.

• The light-duty program should ideally be an integrated program under the responsibility of the workers' compensation professional. The risk manager could assume this responsibility if necessary with assistance by the human resources and the director or safety officer. (For a description of a return-to-work benchmarking project, please refer to Chapter 34.)

In addition to the light- or modified-duty or early return-to-work program, a system should be in place to clear all employees to return to work after absence from any type of accident or surgery, whether or not work-related. Please refer to Chapter 24 on safety and security for examples.

Data Collection and Analysis

If the organization is self-insured, uses a third-party administrator (TPA) to handle claims, or is on a loss-sensitive program such as an incurred or paid loss retro, it is imperative that the risk manager monitor claims status, reserves, and payouts. The information on the loss runs provided by the TPA needs to be complete, in a readily understandable format and of use to the risk manager or safety department in identifying trends or patterns. Regardless of whether an organization is self-insured or commercially insured, consideration should be given to developing an in-house integrated information system that captures all work-related accidents and illnesses, medical-only costs, first-aid costs, and all other medical costs, with and without lost time. In addition, the system should capture information related to type of injury, type of accident, type of treatment or surgery, treating physician, lost days, and cost of medical treatment. Such information would allow the organization to analyze the data to determine types of treatment, costs of treatment, and lost time for comparable types of accidents and injuries, by physician. Also, should the organization develop a managed care program, preferred provider organization (PPO), or referral panel of physicians, this information may assist in selecting physician participants.

This system should be designed to capture all information related to accidents, with and without injury and/or lost time, and all costs, direct and indirect, in addition to information on the employee (position, age, length of employment, and so on) and the treating physician. This information should be analyzed monthly for trends and patterns. Data from work-related accident reports, with and without lost time, should be summarized, analyzed, and reported to the safety committee at each meeting. In addition, the workers' compensation professional should summarize the work-related incidents, with and without injury or lost time, by department, division, and floor or unit, monthly and quarterly, comparing the current period to the previous year's same time period. This report should be distributed monthly to the organization's senior management team.

The risk manager should maintain independent notes and questions regarding loss run prepared by the carrier or TPA on a monthly basis. These notes should be discussed and resolved. If the risk management information system will support the independent tracking of workers' compensation claims, that could be one method of ensuring that of all work-related accidents filed against the employer are accurate. Any discrepancies between the carrier or the TPA loss runs with risk management reports could be then clarified on a timely basis.

Reporting Employee Accidents

To promote complete reporting, an in-service program should be held for all employees to emphasize the requirement that all accidents, with and without injury, lost time, or any type of medical care, must be reported. In addition, it is recommended that a policy be developed to govern this reporting. Designing and implementing loss prevention based on accidents that result in injury without taking into account accidents (near misses) from which no injury occurred may not provide an accurate picture of the accident potential of a facility or department.

If an organization is self-insured and self-administered for workers' compensation, first notice may be when the supervisor or manager is made aware of the accident. The risk manager should be aware of the nuances of specific state rules related to reporting and should educate management staff frequently to those requirements. Failure to report promptly could result in fines for late reporting.

OSHA 200 Log

It is important that the OSHA 200 log be kept current and complete. Should OSHA come in to inspect the log and find it not current, a fine could be levied. One way to address this issue is to design a report on the workers' compensation information system that would translate the appropriate information from the accident reports entered in the OSHA 200 log which could be printed on request. Such software already may be available on the market.

Risk Financing

There are several methods to handle the risk financing of a workers' compensation programs. While this is a hybrid of a casualty line, the risk manager should work with the organization's broker or at least be involved in the process of placing the coverage for this line of insurance coverage. This is one reason the risk manager should have a working knowledge of the principles of workers' compensation in general and specifically in the risk manager's organization.

Workers' compensation costs are most frequently funded by guaranteed cost program, by self-insured programs, or through incurred- or paid-loss retro programs. It is customary that the primary limits of coverage are to the statutorily required level, which is a state-by-state set limit. Many organizations elect to carry excess coverage attaching over the primary limit. Many states require self-insureds to carry stop loss or excess coverage over the required statutory primary limit as well.

Guaranteed cost programs are often referred to as "fixed cost programs." There are two important considerations that are deserving of explanation:

1. The premium cost of this program (losses and expenses) is guaranteed (fixed) during the policy year subject only to a year-end audit to verify actual annual payroll and classification or rate codes. Annual premium cost is not affected by loss experience (either frequency or severity).
2. These programs are, with very few exceptions, written on a year-to-year basis.

Retrospectively rated programs are often referred to as "retro" or "loss sensitive" plans. There are three significant considerations that differentiate them from the guaranteed cost plan:

1. Unlike a guaranteed cost program, the final premium cost obligation in these programs is directly determined by the policy year loss experience (hence the reference to "loss sensitive").

   Unlike the "front-end" fixed premium cost of a guaranteed cost program, the actual and final premium cost obligation by the insured is determined "retrospectively" based on the actual loss experience.

2. While a guaranteed cost program is most often written on a year-to-year basis, retro plans are written with multiple year (three to five) loss or premium calculations at negotiated intervals usually yearly or at eighteen-month intervals. As a result, the ultimate premium cost obligation of the insured is not known for a period of time.

3. Unlike a guaranteed cost program, retro programs have a contractual obligation provision that is legally binding and enforceable as respects the payment by the insured or reimbursement to the insured of final premium cost.

Finally, there are two different types of retrospectively rated or "loss sensitive" programs:

1. *Incurred Loss Retro Plan*—This type of retro plan is written with a "fully funded" (estimated standard) premium calculation at the inception of the policy year. The insurer will collect the premium (the insurer generally gives the insured the option to pay the premium up front or in installments during the course of the year) and maintains control over loss costs and reserve funds until final loss adjustments and payments. As stated earlier, the final premium cost obligation will be determined by the actual loss experience.

2. *Paid Loss Retro Plan*—This is often referred to as a "cash flow" program. Unlike the incurred loss plan, which requires full premium funding, the paid loss plan allows the insured to "defer" a large premium cost component at policy inception in exchange for a financial security guarantee (such as a letter of credit or promissory note) to collateralize the balance of the premium obligation. In this program, the insured is typically required to fund only the estimated program expense and a claims escrow account or fund at policy inception. Instead of making scheduled premium payments during the year, the insured will only pay actual claim cost as billed by the insured. This discounting of annual premium cost obligation creates the cash flow advantage of this program. However, as stated earlier, and like the retro plan, the final premium cost obligation will be determined by the actual loss experience.

Experience Modification Factor

The experience modifier, often referred to as the "mod factor," affects workers' compensation costs by a factor that either credits or reduces *or* debits or increases the premium or assessments. Experience modification factors are computed every year. The standard premium is modified up or down by how much above or under 1.00 an organization's experience modifier is. Most states use an industry standard formula to calculate the experience modifier. It is recommended that each year the risk manager recompute the "mod factor" to verify accuracy.

The factors used in developing an experience modification are based on claims history, payrolls, each insured's claims experience, and other data for the previous three years (not including the current year).

It is suggested that the risk manager contact the local National Council of Compensation Insurance (NCCI) or other similar organization within their state for information regarding "mod factor" calculations in their respective state. In addition, the risk manager could purchase software to verify the annual calculation automatically; information for sources for such software may be available from the local NCCI.

Premium Rate Setting Basis

The premium for workers' compensation is based on classifications of employees grouped by job types and salaries. Certain senior management positions' salaries are capped so as not to skew the salary figure. It is important that the risk manager become familiar with the classifications and corresponding salaries to verify proper classification. Misclassifications have the potential to adversely impact the premium(s), which is why the risk manager should verify the classifications. When verifying the classifications, it is suggested the risk manager work with payroll to ensure that positions are correctly classified and that salaries are appropriately reported when requested for annual renewals and for the annual audits, if applicable.

....

CONCLUSION

Applying the principles of risk management—identification of the risk exposure(s), evaluation and analysis (through trends and patterns), determining the effectiveness of the treatment and intervention (loss prevention)—in most cases has shown that workers' compensation can be contained and possibly reduced. The financial ramifications of a workers' compensation program are easily assessed from the financial aspect. However, the risk manager must never lose sight that while money is an asset, the organization's employees are probably its largest asset, which must be protected from risk exposures like other identified assets. This chapter serves only to address the basics of the workers' compensation issue. Those risk managers who do not have a working knowledge of this line of coverage should be encouraged to learn more.

It must also be pointed out that effective programs to manage the risks related to work-related accidents and illnesses cannot be controlled through risk financing techniques alone. An effective, broad-based safety program, integrated with risk management and coupled with an appropriate risk financing method, have the most opportunity to result in reduction in direct and indirect costs.

Endnotes

1. Public Law 91-596, 91st Congress, S. 2193, *Occupational Safety and Health Act of 1970,* Dec. 29, 1970.
2. *Ibid.*

EXHIBIT 25.1.   Sample Model of Generic Workers' Compensation Program

Accountability		
Standard	*Rationale*	*Discussion*
Employee job descriptions and performance appraisals will reflect their responsibilities to adhere to safe work practices and comply with safety policies and procedures.	To show employees that preventing injuries is important to the organization; to ensure employee accountability regarding safety policies and procedures.	If employees do not adhere to safety policies, corrective and/or disciplinary action should be initiated. Accountability should be established in a positive manner; employees should understand that the organization values them so highly that preventing injuries is its number-one priority.
The job descriptions and the performance appraisals of supervisory and management personnel will reflect their responsibility to adhere to safe work practices and to ensure that their employees follow safety policies and procedures.	To ensure that supervisory and management personnel set the example for the rest of the staff; to ensure accountability for the work practices of their employees.	Establishing accountability for their employees provides supervisors with the necessary incentive to provide proper training, to intervene when unsafe practices are noted, and to institute corrective action and follow-up as needed.
Supervisor performance appraisals will reflect their accountability for the incidence (rate) of work-related accidents for their respective units.	To obtain the full cooperation of supervisors in the safety and loss prevention program.	Supervisory accountability via job descriptions and performance appraisals can provide additional incentive for supervisors to oversee their employees' work practices. Consideration also can be given to establishing goals for supervisors for the reduction of employee accidents.
Loss costs and premium allocations will be distributed to the facility CEO annually.	To provide motivation for managers to participate in the workers' compensation cost reduction process.	Some feel that this is a very effective tool to get the facility to "buy in" to efforts to reduce employee injuries and control workers' compensation costs. Some feel that without a financial incentive, loss prevention and loss reduction efforts may fail. This is a controversial issue as to effectiveness.
Individual facilities will distribute the loss costs and premium allocations to the cost centers; department managers will respond monthly and in writing to the budget variances.	To make the department heads or supervisors accountable for employee accidents.	Each department head or manager should be required, in writing, to summarize accidents, explain the reason for the increase or decrease, and provide an action plan on a monthly basis for preventing employee accidents. Similar reporting by the facility CEO to the corporate risk management department should also be required, if a multifacility organization.
Annual objectives for reduction of employee accidents will be established for all CEOs, and results will be measured against the objectives as part of the CEOs' evaluation.	To establish an incentive for CEOs to reduce the number of employee injuries.	Objectives and/or goals can encompass both the number of employee accidents and the elements of the loss prevention process, for example, safety training sessions. Objectives also can be set on an annual basis for the designated safety officer at each facility.

(Continued)

EXHIBIT 25.1. **Sample Model of Generic Workers' Compensation Program** (*Continued*)

Job Descriptions/Physical Capacities

Standard	*Rationale*	*Discussion*
Job descriptions will reflect specific physical-based criteria that provide an accurate profile of the positions; the bloodborne pathogens exposure level of the positions also will be reflected.	To provide an accurate profile of the physical requirements necessary for a position.	In addition to complying with the new federal Americans with Disabilities Act (ADA) and the Blood Borne Pathogens Act, the revised job descriptions should reflect the essential job functions for each position. Such specificity will assist in determining appropriate job placement against the physical requirements and abilities, in evaluation of capabilities for returning to work, and in the work-hardening rehabilitation program.
All employees will be evaluated by a medical practitioner as to their ability to perform the physical requirements of a position after an offer of employment has been made; an accurate physical-based job description will be provided to the practitioner.	To prevent new hires from entering into positions that may endanger patients or cause injuries to themselves or fellow employees.	The examining medical practitioner should be provided with a copy of the specific job description against which to evaluate a newly hired employee's ability to perform the essential functions of the position. *Note:* All physical examinations must be in compliance with the ADA.
Specific physical-based criteria will be sent to the examining practitioner and utilized in the evaluation of injured employee's ability to return to work.	To provide the examining practitioner with an accurate profile of the physical requirements of a position.	An accurate job description should be provided to the treating physician as soon as the employee begins treatment. One should also be provided to: all specialists; physical or occupational therapists; physicians who conduct independent medical examinations; the claims adjusters; or rehabilitation specialists, for example, medical management nurse or vocational counselor.
There will be an ergonomic evaluation of all workplaces and positions against the specific employee assigned to that place and job.	To determine that employees assigned to a particular job are capable of performing its physical requirements.	A workplace may have been modified or designed for an individual other than the incumbent; in addition, the physical attributes of the individuals assigned to a workplace on the three shifts may greatly differ. As a preventive measure, all workplaces should be evaluated ergonomically and appropriate accommodations made where necessary. Such evaluations and necessary physical accommodations can help to prevent work-related stress and injury; they also have the potential to increase productivity and enhance positive employee attitudes.
There will be a policy and procedure to give guidance on the handling of new-hire employees who do not meet the specific physical-based criteria of a position.	To ensure that all facilities handle this situation in a consistent manner and are in compliance with the organization's philosophy and with the Americans with Disabilities Act (ADA) and any other statutes.	This policy should be developed with input and advice from legal counsel to deal with newly hired employees who do not demonstrate the physical capabilities as described in the position-specific job description.
There will be a policy and procedure to handle those employees who are identified on an initial preplacement evaluation or periodic evaluation to have a condition or illness that may be a hazard to the employee or to the safe work practices of the facility.	To ensure the safety of the employee, other employees, and patients; to ensure that all facilities or units handle this situation in a consistent manner and in compliance with the ADA and any other statutes	Examples of such a condition are: brittle diabetes, labile hypertension, or cardiac arrhythmia. Should an employee with such a condition develop a complication (for example, a stroke), the condition could be considered compensable as an aggravation of a preexisting condition. Guidelines should describe how to refer the employee to a physician and what constitutes clearance to return to work.

(*Continued*)

EXHIBIT 25.1.   Sample Model of Generic Workers' Compensation Program   *(Continued)*

Job Descriptions/Physical Capacities

Standard	*Rationale*	*Discussion*
All policies, procedures, and systems that relate to pre-placement and return-to-work evaluations will comply with the ADA and state specific workers' compensation rules.	To limit potential liability as a result of noncompliance with the ADA.	The organization and the individual facilities, if a multifacility organization, may face risk exposure if actual practice, policies, and procedures are not consistent and in compliance with the ADA. In particular, employees who suffer impairment from a work-related injury may come under the protection of the ADA. Guidelines for ergonomic redesign of a workplace should be developed and consistently applied in compliance with the ADA; and legal guidance should be sought and incorporated.

Employee Orientation and Training

Standard	*Rationale*	*Discussion*
There will be evidence of ongoing in-services to address body mechanics, use of lifting equipment, and patient transfer techniques.	To provide periodic training in proper lifting and transferring techniques and to reinforce the emphasis on safe work practices.	Attendance should be documented to provide confirmation that facilities are meeting the minimal educational goal. Evidence should be in the form of sign-in sheets and documentation in the individual's personnel file.
There will be evidence of educational programs specific to areas identified from the analysis of accidents and correlated to patterns and trends of accidents.	To ensure that accident data are analyzed and used to prevent recurrence of accidents.	Loss prevention activities should be focused to address areas identified by accident reports, even those that reflect no apparent injury. The Environment of Care (EOC) Safety Committee should be responsible for identifying areas of concern. The committee meeting minutes should reflect discussion of the employee accident data, the identification of exposures, and the educational programs that are presented; the identification of the target audience should also be addressed.
Some educational programs, departmental or general, will be mandatory for all employees; evidence of attendance by all employees will be monitored.	To ensure that certain key educational programs are attended by all employees.	Attendance can be verified by sign-in sheets and periodic attendance checks. The mandatory topics should be identified so that all employees are aware of the requirement. Some examples of mandatory in-services are what to do in the event of an accident and proper lifting techniques.
Employee attendance at in-service programs will be a component of the individual employee performance appraisals.	To ensure that all employees fulfill their individual requirements as to education and training.	One facility required employees to attend all mandatory in-services before they could receive their annual performance appraisal and merit increase. This technique seemed effective in ensuring that all employees met their educational obligations.
A pre- and posttest will be administered at each formal safety and workers' compensation-related educational program.	To serve as a means to evaluate employee knowledge of the subject; to determine if the instruction was effective.	This system will allow facilities to document the employee's knowledge of a subject and to ensure that training sessions are informative and conducive to understanding of the subject. The results of these tests should be maintained in the employee's personnel files. The system should be implemented to accommodate those employees who have an inability to read, write, and/or comprehend English.

(Continued)

EXHIBIT 25.1. **Sample Model of Generic Workers' Compensation Program** (*Continued*)

Employee Orientation and Training

Standard	*Rationale*	*Discussion*
A program to enhance the employee's ability to read, write, and/or comprehend will be implemented.	To increase employee self-esteem, work habits, and loyalty to the organization.	A basic skills or literacy program (such as Project Step) can be developed and sponsored by the organization's staff. Increasing the literacy level of the nonprofessional staff can benefit both employees and organization. It is also recommended that an organization encourage those employees who lack high school diplomas to return to programs to obtain their GED.
There will be periodic educational programs for the respective facilities' senior and middle management to convey workers' compensation costs, corporate workers' compensation policies, and organizational philosophy.	To focus on the significant costs associated with employee injuries, in both dollar and human terms; to ensure that all managers understand what they can do to control costs and employee suffering.	These programs should be presented annually on a corporate level by the corporate risk management personnel. The organizational costs for premium and incurred losses, along with trends and patterns or other issues recognized across all regions should be addressed. Discussion should be encouraged among the attendees to enhance networking and sharing.
A series of educational programs will be developed for the individual supervisors, managers, department heads, and other administrative staff concerning workers' compensation-related issues.	To reinforce the importance of the organization's workers' compensation policies and procedures; to present changes in policies; to provide periodic updates on individual facilities' losses.	These programs can include: the respective state's workers' compensation laws, rules, and regulations; management's responsibilities, and why; employees' rights and obligations; and what management and supervisory personnel can do to control the costs of workers' compensation. The core program can be developed on a corporate level; changes can be made on a local level, if applicable. The internal claim department or the claims service provider, as applicable, and their defense counsel can assist in this program, especially when dealing with jurisdictional issues.
New employees will attend orientation in workers' compensation and safety policies and procedures prior to assuming their job duties.	To provide new employees with enough knowledge to perform their job duties in a safe manner; to demonstrate to employees the importance of safety policies and procedures; to instruct employees in the procedures to follow if they are injured on the job.	This should include, but not be limited to: general hospital safety policies and procedures; individual departmental safety policies and procedures; what to do in the event of a work-related accident; employees' and employer's rights and responsibilities in the event of a work-related accident; SARA, hazardous waste management and right to know, bloodborne pathogens, department-specific hazards, proper use of barrier equipment and other departmental equipment and procedures; and policies and procedures for disciplinary action for failure to comply with safe work practices and with safety policies and procedures. Consideration should be given to requiring yearly attendance at a refresher course in these subjects. Orientation also should be conducted for contract or pool personnel.

(*Continued*)

EXHIBIT 25.1.   Sample Model of Generic Workers' Compensation Program   (*Continued*)

Information Systems

Standard	Rationale	Discussion
OSHA 200 logs will be completed in full compliance with OSHA regulations.	To ensure accurate record keeping of employee accidents; to prevent fines for the violation of OSHA record-keeping violations.	The incorrect completion of OSHA logs and failure to keep the logs constitute a violation of OSHA regulations and can carry a fine of up to $7,000 per line. The complete instructions for completing the OSHA 200 logs are on the reverse of the log and, if read carefully, are self-explanatory. Because of potential OSHA violations, consideration should be given to appointing an individual who is responsible for checking the log's accuracy on a regular basis.
There will be a workers' compensation data and information management system developed and implemented on both the corporate and local levels to capture employee accident and injury data.	To track accident and injury data; to provide early warning of a developing problem; to evaluate the performance of managers.	Both a corporate and individual facility data system is needed so that trends can be identified company-wide and within the individual facility. The following data should be captured: all work-related incidents, with and without injury or lost time, "medical only," or first aid; costs of "medical only" or first aid; direct and indirect costs of incidents with and without injury or lost time; amount of all "write-offs"; type of injury, type of accident, type of treatment or surgery, treating physician; specific data related to employee, such as, age, length of employment, position, department, date, time, physician, lost time; the injuries of contract or pool personnel and volunteers should also be tracked.
There will be evidence that workers' compensation and employee accident data and information are analyzed no less than monthly for trends and patterns; these will be reported regularly to the Environment of Care Safety Committee and senior management.	To provide a system to identify trends and address the causes of accidents on a timely basis.	The safety officer can assume the responsibility of trending accidents. EOC Safety Committee notes should show evidence that any trends are thoroughly discussed and analyzed by the EOC Safety Committee. Senior management should also review and address these data.
Loss runs will be distributed to the individual facilities on a monthly basis.	To allow the facility to review the financial aspects of its losses on a timely basis.	Internal claims department or carrier loss runs should be distributed monthly to facilities so that they can be reviewed: to determine which claims are still open; to determine their accuracy; to examine the reserves and payments on each of their claims.

Loss Prevention

Standard	Rationale	Discussion
There will be a system to track all employee work-related accidents, with and without injury.	To establish trends and patterns of loss potential.	Trending and tracking incident data can identify areas where loss prevention or safety is needed. This should be the first step in establishing a loss prevention program that is proactive rather than reactive. A checklist-type of incident form can be developed to facilitate computer data entry. Injuries sustained by contract or pool personnel and volunteers should be included in these data.

(*Continued*)

EXHIBIT 25.1.   Sample Model of Generic Workers' Compensation Program   (*Continued*)

Loss Prevention

Standard	*Rationale*	*Discussion*
The incidence of work-related accidents will be monitored on a monthly basis to determine the need for supervisory intervention.	To provide for a permanent change in employee behavior that is monitored and maintained by the supervisor	Feedback to supervisors of accident review information on supervisory intervention is important. The EOC safety committee chairman, or other designated individual, should have responsibility for monitoring and analyzing employee accidents and for ensuring that recommendations for action and follow-up are transmitted to the individual supervisor.
Each facility will implement incentive programs to increase safety awareness and loss prevention activities.	To increase and maintain employee awareness and participation in safety and loss prevention program.	Incentive programs, using awards and rewards, can be set up so that a unit that goes without lost time accidents during a specified period of time, for example, quarterly, is given a desirable award such as an extra vacation day. Incentives also could include the choice of items from a specified catalog. A progressive point system can be used as well. Unit-wide incentive programs can put peer pressure to work in a given unit or shift to ensure the use of safe work practices. Bingo and small recognition awards to employees can also be effective, though controversial.
There will be an organized workers' compensation loss control suggestion program with corporate and facility support.	To encourage suggestions for loss prevention from all employees; to ensure that good ideas for on-the-job safety are not limited to a particular facility.	Discussions with the "front line" staff often result in simple, but effective ideas on preventing employee injuries. Awards for ideas could be monthly or quarterly and could include: time off (an extra vacation day), monetary awards, choices from a specified catalog of useful items, recognition in company newsletters, and/or performance reviews.
There will be a written safety policy statement that has been approved and signed by the corporate board, the president, and the local CEO, if applicable.	To develop employee awareness and communicate the company's commitment to provide a safe workplace.	This statement should address the corporate commitment to providing a safe work environment; identification of those responsible for managing the safety program; identification of those responsible for implementing the safety program; accountability of management for providing a safe work environment.
A safety program will be developed that will establish guidelines for the development of an Environment of Care Safety Committee.	To provide a framework for the reduction of employee injuries.	The safety program should: be supported by top management; have written policies and procedures; have a designated safety officer; provide for routine safety inspections; have involvement of employees; establish the function and responsibilities of the EOC Safety Committee; and provide for a periodic review of Committee activities.
There will be a separate incident report form for work-related accidents.	To provide for thorough reporting and analysis of employee accidents.	Often an incident report form is generic; used for both employee and patient injuries. Such a generic form may not protect risk management confidentiality. The design of the incident report form should be logical and should organize information into type and category of information needed.
Employees and/or supervisors will complete and forward employee incident reports for all accidents, with and without injury, within twenty-four hours to the designated workers' compensation coordinator.	To ensure that all employee accidents are reported promptly; to provide for a system of reporting all employee incidents.	The prompt completion of incident reports allows for a timely investigation of the incident and aids in prompt reporting to the carrier. All incidents, even those without injury, should be reported so that the information regarding the accident can be used in the analysis of accident data to prevent future accidents.

(*Continued*)

EXHIBIT 25.1.   Sample Model of Generic Workers' Compensation Program   (*Continued*)

Loss Prevention

Standard	*Rationale*	*Discussion*
The supervisor's investigation and causation analysis of each work-related accident, with and without injury, will be completed and forwarded to the designated safety officer within forty-eight hours of the accident.	To provide for prompt, accurate investigation and causation analysis of all employee accidents; to focus the supervisor's attention on causes and prevention of employee accidents.	Consideration should be given to creating a separate supervisor's accident investigation report form to include the following: What is the basic cause(s) of it? What other cause(s) contributed to the accident? What actions have been taken and by whom to reduce the chance of a recurrence of the injury or accident? What other actions and by whom should or can be taken to reduce the chance of recurrence?
There will be evidence of a thorough investigation and causation analysis of all accidents, appropriate supervisory intervention, and evaluation of the effectiveness of that intervention.	To ensure that appropriate action is being taken by all supervisors to prevent injuries and reduce the chance of recurrence of accidents.	The analysis of individual accident investigations and of intervention and corrective action should be completed by the hospital safety officer with further review by the EOC Safety Committee. Each analysis, intervention, and follow-up should be documented.
Individual and aggregate employee accident data will be routinely analyzed to determine causation factors, patterns, and trends. Based on this information, corrective actions, education, and development or modification of policies and procedures will be undertaken.	To determine critical factors causing employee injuries that are amenable to control and change.	Aggregate accident data analysis should look at such factors as injury type and accident type. Individual accident analysis should focus on causation factors, should be aggressive, and should proceed from the premise that the accident or injury could have been avoided. Analysis of accident data should include: conclusions, recommendations, actions, and follow-up.
There will be an individual designated as the facility safety officer who has responsibility and authority for all aspects of the safety program.	To give one individual the necessary responsibility and authority to achieve loss prevention objectives.	The title and responsibility of safety officer should only be given when it has been determined that the individual has the necessary background and time to perform the job effectively. Failure of the safety officer to perform effectively should be considered a failure of the management that appointed the individual.
A system will be developed to ensure that employees who feel they are at risk of a work-related injury or who have sustained an injury be given access to, and be encouraged to utilize, back-strengthening and work-hardening programs within the facility.	To encourage employees to use facility equipment to prevent or reduce the severity of on-the-job injuries.	The facilities have the necessary expertise and equipment to help employees strengthen muscle groups which may be weak, injured, or at risk for injury. Such a program would be a loss prevention effort and the benefits to the facility in preventing injuries should outweigh the costs of the program. Organizations that have implemented such a program appeared to have reduced the number and severity of lost workday injuries.
There will be an ergonomic evaluation of all positions with appropriate modification of the position, if indicated.	To reduce the number and severity of employee accidents related to ergonomic factors.	Often, investigation of various accidents or injuries and discussions with hospital personnel reveal that ergonomic factors were involved in many lost workday accidents, for example, in-room transfers. There are comparatively few different types of patient-focused positions within the facilities. An initial ergonomic evaluation of high injury-potential jobs in certain facilities or units could be followed by setting up ergonomic evaluation methods to follow in all facilities.

(*Continued*)

EXHIBIT 25.1. **Sample Model of Generic Workers' Compensation Program** (*Continued*)

Loss Prevention

Standard	Rationale	Discussion
There will be appropriate transfer and lifting equipment available in each patient care area and stockroom.	To provide a means for the transfer and/or lifting of heavy loads with minimum stress on employees' musculoskeletal systems.	Many facilities have the older types of lifting equipment available, for example, Hoyer lifts, but they are not always used by the staff. Certain newer types of lifting devices, for example, SARA lift by ARJO, are often greeted with much greater employee and patient acceptance. Also, properly designed and fitted quality lifting vests (commonly called back belts) can, when used properly, encourage proper employee lifting techniques and effectively reduce the chance of serious back strains.
There will be written policies and procedures on the proper use of the transfer and lifting equipment.	To provide proper direction in lifting and transferring patients; to prevent injuries to employees and patients.	Such policies and procedures should be derived from the manufacturers' suggested techniques where possible and should be very detailed. Lifting belt policies and procedures should also be very thorough.
There will be written, detailed policies and procedures for the in-room transfer of patients.	To reduce the number of employee injuries as a result of moving and lifting patients.	Often the most serious and frequent employee injuries occur during in-room transfer of patients; however, the techniques to be used in such transfers are seldom addressed in detail. The creation and review of policies and procedures should include substantial input from ergonomic job analyses. For example, a difference in height of five to six inches may make the difference between sliding and lifting a three hundred-pound patient; this will also make a substantial difference in the strain put on the employee.
In-service programs will be given to all new hires and annually thereafter to train employees in the proper use of the transfer and lifting equipment; these programs will be mandatory and attendance will be documented.	To reduce the number and severity of employee injuries due to failure to use transfer and lifting equipment properly.	It is important that such training be done before the employee assumes his or her job duties. Periodic refresher training helps to correct bad habits and to teach new techniques. Training should be of the "hands-on" type as much as possible in order to demonstrate errors in techniques and to give employees confidence in their ability to use the equipment.
There will be a system to verify the appropriate supervision and monitoring of the use of the lifting and transfer equipment.	To ensure that employees are using equipment properly and that necessary intervention is taken when equipment is used improperly.	The performance of personnel in the proper use of lifting and transfer equipment should be evaluated as part of their annual performance reviews. Supervisors should also be held accountable via their performance appraisals for monitoring and encouraging the proper use of the equipment.
There will be a mechanism for obtaining consultations from physical therapy personnel for the transfer and lifting of difficult patients.	To utilize existing facility resources to reduce employee injuries.	An example is to have physical therapy personnel provide a consultation on each patient to design a customized lifting procedure. The staff then can be trained in the procedure. The procedure can be indicated on a wipe-off board in the patient's room and updated as needed. This can prove to be a very effective means to ensure the proper lifting or transferring of patients.

(*Continued*)

EXHIBIT 25.1.   Sample Model of Generic Workers' Compensation Program   (*Continued*)

Loss Prevention

Standard	Rationale	Discussion
If applicable, each facility will designate an individual as the workers' compensation coordinator; this individual will have responsibility for coordinating all activities related to employee accidents.	To ensure use of effective claims management practices.	This individual should refer the injured employee to a gatekeeper physician, forward the employer's report to the internal claims department or insurance carrier claims service provider, explain the employee's rights and responsibilities, follow up with the treating physician on a regular basis, oversee the return-to-work program, contact the injured employee on a regular basis, contact and communicate regularly with the claims service provider, and hold in-person meetings with the claims service provider. If the organization is self-insured with in-house claims management, it may not be necessary that the workers' compensation coordinator perform all of these duties; certain responsibilities can be assumed by others. This should be implemented in concert with applicable state specific workers' compensation rules.
Each facility will have a formalized modified return-to-work program that is applied consistently to all employees.	To reduce the number of lost workdays as a result of employee accidents; to show employees they are needed on the job.	A modified return-to-work program is often the single-most effective claims management tool for reducing workers' compensation costs, other than prevention. Some states require a mandatory return-to-work program. It is suggested that the development and implementation of a modified return-to-work program be a mandatory requirement and applied equally to all employees. Each facility can develop its own formal return-to-work program. Every effort should be made to return injured employees to work within twenty-four to seventy-two hours to prevent "disability syndrome" from developing. Specific modified or light positions should be identified in each department. If an entire position cannot be identified, tasks should be identified to bring the employee back to work for a few hours each day. Consideration should be given to the impact on morale if an employee is returned to a modified-duty position in the area or on the unit to which he or she is regularly assigned.
There will be evidence of utilization of the return-to-work program, where appropriate, in all facilities.	To ensure that each facility utilizes a return-to-work program and applies it consistently to all injured employees.	Documentation as to the use of the return-to-work program should be evident in the employee's claim file. It should include contacts with the injured employee, the treating doctor, and the employee's department; job descriptions of any modified-duty positions; and physical capabilities forms completed by the physician.

(Continued)

EXHIBIT 25.1.   **Sample Model of Generic Workers' Compensation Program**   (*Continued*)

Loss Prevention

Standard	*Rationale*	*Discussion*
There will be an individual at each facility that is responsible for overseeing and coordinating the return-to-work program.	To ensure that the return-to-work program functions effectively.	The return-to-work coordinator can be the workers' compensation coordinator, the employee health nurse, or any other responsible party within the facility. This individual should be responsible and accountable for the effectiveness of the program and should coordinate activities with other individuals involved in the process, for example, supervisor or department manager. In any event, the return-to-work coordinator should be thoroughly knowledgeable about the philosophy and goals of the program and should enlist the assistance of the employee health nurse, the risk manager, and the safety officer in determining placement of a particular employee.
A specific training program will be developed detailing supervisors' responsibilities in the event of an employee accident; this program will be mandatory for all supervisory personnel.	To involve supervisors in the claims management process.	The relationship between supervisor and employee is critical. The supervisor can help to relieve employee uncertainties and ensure that all employees are treated fairly. Supervisory training should include: accident investigation and explaining why responding immediately is important, how to treat an injured employee, why all injuries should be treated as legitimate, what to do when fraud is suspected, and so on. A supervisory checklist can also be developed as part of the educational program.
There will be a corporate model claims management manual that is distributed to all facilities.	To provide the basic techniques of the organization's claims management program and to ensure continuity of the claims management program in the event of absences, turnover, and so on.	The manual will list the basics of what is expected by the organization and the workers' compensation insurance carrier, if applicable, in the area of claims management. It will cover: step-by-step instructions as to what should be done in the event of an accident; how to treat an injured employee; what to look for in a gatekeeper physician; what the organization will expect from the insurance carrier claims service provider; basic claims management techniques and how to use them, for example, surveillance, independent medical evaluations; warning signs of fraud; what to do when you suspect fraud; the basics of reserving; why follow-up with the provider is necessary, and how to follow up; medical cost containment techniques; and how to use the modified return-to-work programs.
There will be a facility-specific claims management manual at each facility that will be incorporated into the corporate manual.	To provide for different statutory rules and regulations that govern workers' compensation.	Certain "basics" to the jurisdiction should be included in the facility manual, for example, waiting period, maximum compensation rate, and so on. Most workers' compensation defense firms provide a monthly update on workers' compensation laws in their jurisdiction at no charge to the client. In addition, some have a fairly comprehensive synopsis of the workers' compensation act available. The workers' compensation insurance carrier claims service provider is an additional resource for jurisdiction-specific information.

(*Continued*)

EXHIBIT 25.1.   **Sample Model of Generic Workers' Compensation Program**   (*Continued*)

Loss Prevention

Standard	*Rationale*	*Discussion*
If an organization determines to pay the employee's wages during the specific state waiting period, it must be applied consistently to all employees.	Payment of the waiting period is considered a "goodwill" gesture on the part of the organization.	Some employers require employees to use sick or vacation pay or to go without pay during the statutory waiting period. This can present an undue hardship on employees if they do not or cannot use sick or vacation pay. In addition, under the waiting period system, employees who return to work quickly are penalized, whereas employees who stay out of work for extended periods are eligible for the waiting period and receive full pay. This should be addressed on a state-by-state and organization-specific basis, and should be applied in accordance with state statutes consistently to all employees.
All medical bills incurred as a result of work-related injuries will be submitted to the workers' compensation manager or carrier, as applicable.	To ensure that employees are not asked to submit medical bills incurred as a result of work-related injuries to their health insurance carrier.	State laws govern payment for work-related accidents and illnesses. Bills from work-related accidents and illnesses should not be submitted to employees' health insurance carrier. These bills are then subject to the employees' deductible and copayment. All bills from work-related injuries should be submitted to the workers' compensation carrier who then should determine whether they will be paid as part of a compensable injury. In the event that the workers' compensation carrier rejects the bills, they can then be submitted under the employees' health insurance.
An employee absence due to a work-related injury will not be considered an absence under the attendance policy.	To ensure that lost workdays as a result of a work-related injury are considered separate and distinct from the organization's attendance policy.	Some employers may "charge" an employee with an absence under the attendance policy when he or she sustained an accident on the job. Accordingly, the possibility exists that an employee could be put on corrective action for attendance or even terminated for missing time due to a work-related accident. Work-related injuries should be considered separate and distinct from the attendance policy.
An individual claim file will be created for the injured employee on all lost-time claims.	To provide for an organized method of gathering all information about an employee's workers' compensation claim.	The individual claim file should contain: a copy of the incident report, the employer's first report, copies of all applicable state forms, documentation of all contacts with the carrier, physician, and injured employee, all medical documentation, medical bills, and documentation of the use of the return-to-work program.
There will be evidence that the employers' first report of injury is forwarded to the carrier, if applicable, within seventy-two hours after receipt by the workers' compensation coordinator.	To ensure that the claims department or carrier has sufficient time to investigate the accident to make an informed decision as to compensability, and to make prompt payment to the injured employee.	Late reporting of workers' compensation claims can lead to confusion and anxiety for the employee, can lead to early attorney involvement, and result in state fines. The employer's report should be mailed or faxed to the appropriate claims office. To ensure the timely reporting of all facilities, a "lag" time report can be ordered from the claims service provider at regular intervals, for example, quarterly. This "lag" time report indicates the amount of time between the date of the accident and the date of receipt by the carrier's claims service provider.

(*Continued*)

EXHIBIT 25.1.   Sample Model of Generic Workers' Compensation Program   (*Continued*)

Loss Prevention

Standard	*Rationale*	*Discussion*
The claim file will show evidence that the workers' compensation coordinator has contacted the claims service provider, if applicable, within seventy-two hours, or as required by state guidelines, after the employer's report has been forwarded to them.	To develop good communication between the claims department or claims service provider and the workers' compensation coordinator.	The coordinator should obtain relevant information from the adjuster, for example, adjuster's name, claim number, and also furnish the adjuster with pertinent information, such as the case is questionable. It is important to develop a good working relationship with the claims adjuster in the initial stages of the case, because in most jurisdictions, once the case has been accepted as compensable, it is almost impossible to overturn this decision. The adjuster should also be aware that the employer is concerned about the outcome of the case and will be following the case to ensure proper handling.
The claim file will show evidence that the employee has been contacted within twenty-four hours after notification of a lost-time accident to furnish the employee with his or her rights and responsibilities and pertinent claim information, and to offer assistance to the employee.	To acknowledge that the organization is concerned about the employee and to eliminate any fears and doubts the employee has about his or her claim.	It is imperative that the employer let the employee know that it is concerned about the employee and will assist the employee during a difficult time. Many employees are anxious and afraid after they have been injured on the job; they have concerns about their health and income. Employees should be told of their rights and responsibilities so that there are no misunderstandings and the employee knows exactly what to expect. An employee pamphlet that covers this can be developed as a handout.
The claim file will show evidence that the potential for modified-duty work has been explored with the physician, the employee, and the claims service provider within twenty-four to forty-eight hours after notification of the accident.	To ensure that the possibility of return to work in some capacity is explored immediately.	A modified return-to-work program is most effective immediately following the accident. Studies have shown that the longer an employee is out of work, the more negative his or her attitude becomes toward returning to the workplace. The claim file should document that the possibility of return to work in some capacity is explored with all parties immediately after the accident.
The claim file will show evidence of ongoing communication with the injured employee.	To enhance positive relationships, minimize disputes, and keep the connection between employee and employer strong.	Ideally, regular contact should be made by the supervisor since the relationship between supervisor and employee is an important one. If contact by the supervisor is not appropriate, any designated individual can perform this function. The individual making the contact must be careful not to appear to be "checking up" on the employee; the individual should focus on how the employee is feeling and how the employee is missed by the department.
The claim file will show evidence of ongoing communication with the claims department or claims service provider, if applicable.	To show that employers who communicate regularly with their adjuster and stay involved in the claims management process receive better claims service.	The adjustment of the employee's claim should be a cooperative venture between employer and claims service provider. Many claims adjusters are overworked, and may only have time to work on a small percentage of their cases. Adjusters generally work on the cases of those employers who regularly monitor their cases. Regular communication should include discussion of claims management techniques, for example, independent medical evaluations, utilization review, and a strategy to move the case towards conclusion.

(*Continued*)

EXHIBIT 25.1.   Sample Model of Generic Workers' Compensation Program *(Continued)*

Loss Prevention

Standard	*Rationale*	*Discussion*
There will be an individual designated at each facility who will be responsible for initial and ongoing communication with the treating physician on all lost-time claims; the claim file will reflect evidence of this communication.	To ensure that there is adequate initial and ongoing communication with the treating physician.	The individual responsible can be the case manager, workers' compensation coordinator, employee health nurse, or any other involved party. This individual should contact the physician immediately after the first office visit to obtain the diagnosis, explain the modified return-to-work program, and obtain any limitations and restrictions the employee may have. This individual should also contact the treating physician on a regular basis to develop a rapport with the physician.
Personal meetings between facility personnel and members of the claims department will be held no less than semiannually.	To ensure effective communication between the facility and the claims department or claims service provider.	Personal meetings with the in-house claims department or the carrier's claims service provider help to develop a good working relationship with the adjusters and supervisors. This also provides a forum for discussing overall problems in the relationship. All pending claims should be discussed at these meetings and a mutually agreeable action plan for future handling should be developed. It can be effective to meet alternately at the facility and at the claims service provider's office. If the volume of claims warrants more frequent meetings, quarterly meetings should be held.
There will be an annual claim file audit of the claims service provider, if applicable.	To ensure that the organization is receiving effective claims service from the provider, if applicable.	The claim file audit should include an actual review of the claim service provider's physical claim file. The audit should include a review of the following claim file elements: investigation, documentation, timeliness, case management, litigation management, use of rehabilitation, medical cost containment, supervision, reserves, identification of subrogation, and/or second-injury fund reimbursement.
All facilities will designate a gatekeeper physician for referral of employees injured on the job, as provided by specific state workers' compensation rules.	To ensure that injured employees receive prompt, high-quality medical care from a physician who is familiar with the organization, shares its philosophy of early return to work, and will communicate effectively with the facility.	A gatekeeper physician should be chosen carefully. The facility can choose from staff or outside physicians. It is important to meet with and interview all potential gatekeeper physicians to find one that is right for the individual facility. A gatekeeper should provide prompt, high-quality care; be familiar with the organizational workers' compensation philosophy; be willing to communicate with the organization; share the organization's philosophy of early return to work. The implementation of a gatekeeper physician program should be introduced in a positive manner, for example, inviting the physician to give a seminar on a topic of concern to employees.
Meetings between the facility and the gatekeeper physician will be held no less than semiannually.	To provide a forum for discussion of concerns and problems; to ensure effective communication between facility and physician.	It is imperative that effective communication exists between the facility and the gatekeeper. During these meetings, overall concerns as well as individual cases can be discussed. Physicians should be invited to tour the facility during these meetings. If staff doctors are used as gatekeepers, regular meetings should still be held so that time is put aside to specifically address the treatment of injured employees and any problems associated with the program.

(Continued)

EXHIBIT 25.1.   **Sample Model of Generic Workers' Compensation Program**   (*Continued*)

Loss Prevention

Standard	Rationale	Discussion
All injured employees will be seen by a designated gatekeeper physician; referrals to the gatekeeper physician must be in compliance with individual jurisdictions.	To ensure that employees are evaluated, at least initially, in a consistent manner.	All employees should be referred to the gatekeeper except in actual emergencies. Certain jurisdictions allow the employee to choose the physician; even In these states, the employee should be encouraged to see the gatekeeper. Individual facilities should research their jurisdiction so that any referral to the gatekeeper is in compliance with state law; carrier or legal counsel advice should be sought and incorporated. Even in those jurisdictions that allow the employee to choose the treating physicians, many employees will stay with the gatekeeper if they feel they are receiving high-quality medical care.
Every facility will develop a panel of medical specialists if commercially insured, in conjunction with the carrier.	To provide for a panel of specialists who, like the gatekeeper, will provide prompt, high-quality medical care to employees, and who share the organization's philosophy on return to work.	Even facilities that have an effective gatekeeper should have a panel of approved specialists in the event the employee needs specialist care. A panel of specialists will ensure that the facility will not "lose" the employee to a physician who does not share the organization's philosophy. Again, any referral to a specialist must be in compliance with state law of the individual jurisdiction; carrier and/or legal advice should be sought and incorporated. Specialists should include, but not be limited to, orthopedics, neurology, ophthalmology, and internal medicine.
There will be a system in place to encourage the treating physician to use the organization's facilities for rehabilitation services.	To ensure that the employee receives the best possible medical care; to reduce insurance premiums or loss costs; to keep the connection between employee and workplace strong.	Treatment rendered by the facility can be very beneficial to employees. Often they are comfortable with the surroundings and have confidence in the staff. In addition, receiving treatment at the facility enables them to see their coworkers and this keeps the bond between employee and employer strong. The costs for medical treatment received at the facility should be "written off" to reduce insurance premiums.

Employee Health

Standard	Rationale	Discussion
There will be an established employee needle-stick policy in accordance with CDC and state guidelines.	To provide for prompt management and investigation of needle sticks; to protect and prolong employee life and health.	This should cover possible hepatitis B and C exposure, HIV exposure, and other diseases to which there may be bloodborne exposures. Testing of patients where possible and employees in compliance with state laws, baselines, and follow-up, for hepatitis and HIV is essential to protect not only the employee but also the facility. It must be emphasized that prompt reporting of such exposures is essential and delays will not be tolerated.

(*Continued*)

EXHIBIT 25.1.   Sample Model of Generic Workers' Compensation Program   *(Continued)*

Management

Standard	*Rationale*	*Discussion*
There will be a policy statement from the corporate office on employee rights and responsibilities relative to workers' compensation; the policy statement will be in writing and approved and signed by the board, the president, and the CEO of the local facility.	To provide an understanding of the organization's philosophy on workers' compensation; to demonstrate management's commitment to the philosophy.	This policy statement should include, but not be limited to, the overall philosophy of the organization towards employees injured on the job, how injured employees should be treated, what they can expect and what the organization expects, and the organization's position on providing modified work. The statement should be reviewed and signed by the board, president, and so on, to ensure that it accurately reflects the company's philosophy.
There will be evidence that patient acuity is developed and utilized in the setting of staffing levels.	To prevent employee injuries as a result of understaffing.	According to surveys, many employees feel that understaffing leads to careless work practices and unsafe acts, for example, trying to transfer a patient alone. Training is needed in how understaffing affects the potential for employee injuries. The EOC Safety Committee should address staffing at each individual facility to determine if it is having an effect on injuries. If a problem is noted, this should be brought before facility management and a plan devised to keep staffing levels appropriate and/or to deal with understaffing without posing a threat to employees.
It is the responsibility of each administrator to establish an atmosphere within the facility where employees feel that they are valued and feel that the facility will protect their interests.	To establish better employee relations that can help lower workers' compensation costs.	Often there is a correlation with the frequent and severe losses experienced in a facility or on a particular unit with poor overall morale. There is a direct correlation between employee morale and workers' compensation claims. When morale is poor, employees do not enjoy coming to work so they may stay out longer, even for a minor injury. Any effort to better employee relations can help to lower workers' compensation costs.
Each facility will develop a specific, formal program to show its concern for employees who have been injured on the job.	To express concern and establish a nonadversarial relationship with the injured employee.	It is important that all employees be treated with care and concern, especially when they are injured on the job. Employees must feel that they are missed and that they are needed on the job. Some of the ideas obtained from the surveys include get-well cards, flowers, personal visits, and invitations to departmental meetings.
There will be a survey conducted of employee attitudes after sustaining an accident on the job.	To determine how employees are being treated by both the facility and the claims service provider when they are injured on the job.	If employees are being treated in a negative fashion by the individual facility, it is likely that they will feel angry and resentful and the claim may escalate. In addition, it is important to know how the claims department or carrier is responding to the employee, for example, prompt contact, an explanation of benefits, prompt payment. Poor treatment from the claims service provider may cause the employee to seek an attorney. A questionnaire can help identify problems so that they can be addressed immediately. Also, it can let employees know that the organization cares enough to find out how they are treated when they were injured on the job. A corporate "get-well" card can also be sent.

(Continued)

EXHIBIT 25.1. **Sample Model of Generic Workers' Compensation Program** *(Continued)*

Management

Standard	Rationale	Discussion
The risk management report to the board will include information related to workers' compensation claims and costs.	To ensure that the board of directors is aware of the financial obligation and other issues as a result of the workers' compensation program.	The report should cover employee injury patterns and trends, direct and indirect costs, as well as loss prevention efforts and results.
The workers' compensation coordinator, the safety officer, and the employee health nurse will be given adequate time and incentive to fulfill their responsibilities relative to the workers' compensation program.	To ensure that individuals involved in the prevention and administration of employee injuries can function effectively.	A safety and claims management program will be effective only if the individuals involved in the administration of these programs have the necessary time and incentive to perform their duties effectively. Incentives can be built in through performance appraisals and/or bonus programs.
The workers' compensation coordinator, the safety officer, and the employee health nurse will be given adequate initial training in and ongoing education on the prevention and administration of employee injuries.	To ensure that individuals involved in the prevention and administration of employee injuries can function effectively.	Often the individuals involved in the workers' compensation program are lacking in the training and education needed to effectively perform their job duties. The educational needs of these individuals should be evaluated at each facility and any deficiencies addressed. Additional training can be provided at training sessions at the corporate headquarters, seminars, courses at local colleges, and so on. Some examples of areas where additional training may be warranted: infection control, workers' compensation rules and regulations, and claims management techniques.
There will be evidence that policies and procedures are in writing, and are reviewed and revised annually to comply with current federal or state requirements.	To ensure that all policies and procedures relative to the workers' compensation program comply with federal laws (such as ADA) and/or state law, and are updated and revised on a regular basis.	To prevent development of policies and procedures in conflict with state workers' compensation laws, ADA regulations and with the Family Leave Act, it is recommended that all current policies and procedures be reviewed on an annual basis by corporate counsel, labor attorneys, workers' compensation defense counsel, and the risk manager.
There will be evidence that all new human resource directors and personnel have, within six weeks of employment, attended an official, structured orientation on the workers' compensation program.	To ensure that all human resource managers fully understand the organization's workers' compensation philosophy and program; to ensure that they understand the duties associated with the position.	Often the workers' compensation program falls under the auspices of the human resource manager; it is imperative that all human resource managers understand their role in ensuring fair treatment of injured employees and in controlling workers' compensation costs. Many organizations throughout the country are recognizing that workers' compensation is a risk exposure to be managed, not a benefit, and are transferring the responsibility and accountability to risk management. Even in such instances, risk management and human resources must work in close coordination and collaboration.
Human resource policies and procedures will reflect that violations of safety policies will be grounds for disciplinary action.	To emphasize the importance the organization places on safe work practices and on preventing employee injuries.	This should be emphasized to all new employees and existing employees in a positive manner. The underlying reasons for this, that is, preventing employee injuries because employees are valuable to the organization and are needed on the job, should be stressed.

(Continued)

EXHIBIT 25.1.   **Sample Model of Generic Workers' Compensation Program**   *(Continued)*

Management		
Standard	*Rationale*	*Discussion*
Target rates for maximum employee turnover will be established for each facility; when a facility maximum turnover rate has been exceeded, there will be evidence that information relating to the turnover is analyzed to determine the causes and evidence of appropriate intervention.	To show that high turnover in an organization can adversely affect a program's ability to control workers' compensation costs.	High turnover rates can signify poor employee morale, which has an adverse effect on workers' compensation. Turnover also can increase injuries because new employees may not have enough experience to properly perform their job duties, and it can affect staffing; for example, a unit may be understaffed, leading to increased employee accidents.
Guidelines for contract language will be developed and promulgated regarding requirements for workers' compensation insurance from contractors and subcontractors; evidence of a current workers' compensation insurance policy also will be required.	To prevent potential liability for the injuries of contractors or subcontractors.	In many jurisdictions, if a contractor or subcontractor working on an organization's site does not have applicable workers' compensation insurance and one of its employees is injured on the job, the employee can be found to be a "statutory" employee of the organization and the organization's workers' compensation policy will apply. It should be noted that liability could still exist in certain jurisdictions even if the contract and insurance policy guidelines are met. Legal counsel should be sought and incorporated.
Guidelines for waiver of subrogation as it relates to the workers' compensation claims of a contractor's employees or subcontractors will be developed and promulgated.	To ensure a more favorable contract position with contractors and subcontractors for the organization.	If contractors or subcontractors agree to hold harmless and indemnify the organization, the organization could be exempted from liability for claims brought against them by contractors' or subcontractors' employees in certain jurisdictions. An employee of a contractor or subcontractor could be forced to go against the contractor or subcontractor for any tort recovery. The organization may be in a position, in some instances, to request and obtain such an agreement. Legal counsel should be sought and incorporated.

26

Claims and Litigation Management

Ellen L. Barton

Hospitals, health systems, integrated delivery systems (IDSs), physician-hospital organizations (PHOs), managed care organizations (MCOs), medical groups, clinics, home health companies, surgery centers, and health plans (hereafter collectively referred to as "health care organizations") have a major role to play in addressing medical professional liability, not only by ensuring high-quality care but also in managing claims. The health care organization and those individuals who represent it can directly affect the dollars paid in claims by the manner in which they administer those claims. Regardless of the nature of the health care organization, basic claims management principles apply, even though allegations may vary and different theories of liability may be relied on. All claims should be handled in a fair and equitable manner; that is, valid claims should be settled promptly and for a reasonable amount, and frivolous or nonmeritorious claims should be vigorously defended.

The risk manager's role in managing claims will vary, depending on the nature of the health care organization and its insurance program. If the organization is commercially insured, the risk manager's role is to monitor the activities of those with hands-on responsibility for claims management. However, if the organization is self-insured, the risk manager's role is to participate actively in claims management. This chapter sets forth principles of effective claims management applicable to all health care organizations and risk financing programs.

Sections of this chapter reprinted from *Nursing Economic$*, *3*(1), pp. 44–48, Jan.–Feb. 1985 and from *Nursing Economic$*, *3*(1), pp. 98–102, Mar.–Apr. 1985. Reprinted with permission of the publisher, Jannetti Publications, Inc., East Holly Avenue Box 56, Pitman, NJ 08071-0056; Phone (856) 256-2300; Fax (856) 589-7463. (For a sample issue of the journal, contact the publisher.)

·············

CLAIMS IDENTIFICATION AND INVESTIGATION

The organization's risk management plan will include a system for identifying and reporting actual and potential claims to the risk manager. This can be accomplished through both formal and informal information systems. (See Chapter 8 for a thorough discussion of risk identification systems.) The risk manager should review incident reports, minutes of selected committees (for example, quality management, medical executive, credentialing, and so on), and other similar documents, and follow up where necessary. In addition, the staff should report to the risk manager any complaints from patients, subscribers, or their families about either perceived injury or quality of care.

It is important that the risk manager have open lines of communication with the medical and nursing staffs, the patient representative, and all other ancillary personnel, as well as with administration. He or she should make the entire professional staff aware of the need to report dissatisfied patients or subscribers or *potentially compensable events* (PCEs). To further this goal, the risk manager should provide staff with ongoing education regarding trends in medical professional liability litigation and insurance coverage; reporting of events; release of medical records information; documentation of medical care; discussions with patients, subscribers, and their families; and other related topics.

If any health care provider or administrative personnel receive letters of representation, demands for damages, or formal legal papers, they should immediately send such notices to the risk manager, who, in turn, should forward them to the internal claims management department or appropriate primary and excess insurers, if applicable.

Reporting of Claims

It is the risk manager's responsibility to report actual or potential claims to the health care organization's insurance provider. It is impossible to list all events that should be reported; however, lawsuits, claims, and PCEs generally are considered reportable. Coverage documents should be carefully reviewed to determine the specific definitions of a "claim" or a PCE. Notice regarding claims or PCEs is particularly important when there has been a change in insurance carriers and a PCE was reported but no formal claim presented or suit filed. The current insurer may only cover incurred but not reported (IBNR) claims and the previous insurer may deny coverage because the event did not meet its definition of a claim.

Lawsuit   This category encompasses those cases where formal legal action for damages has been initiated. When a summons or complaint is served at the health care organization's offices, the individual receiving it should notify the risk manager immediately by telephone. The risk manager then should forward the suit papers to legal counsel or the insurance company (or broker) as soon as possible, noting the date the papers were received and by whom. The time periods for the filing of responsive (defense) documents will be measured from the date the papers were received. The risk manager should provide any other available information in a cover letter accompanying the suit papers.

Claim   A *claim* is defined as a formal notification, either orally or in writing, that monetary damages are being sought from the health care organization by a third party for an alleged injury. It may be made by a patient or subscriber or by the patient or subscriber's family, guardian, or attorney. Any organization personnel receiving such a demand should send copies of all such correspondence and summaries of any other available information to the risk manager as soon as possible.

Potentially Compensable Event   This category encompasses any incident in which there is neither an active claim nor institution of formal legal action. It includes those cases in which an unexpected event causing injury or potential injury has occurred in the course of a patient's or subscriber's treatment, including denial of treatment. It also includes those cases where, although there may be no injury, there has been some expression of dissatisfaction or perceived injury, short of an actual claim, by the patient's or subscriber's family.

The risk manager should investigate all incidents and potential claims to the extent necessary to determine whether a claim file should be opened. It is this decision that dictates the level of investigation needed and the responsibilities of the involved parties. He or she then can evaluate the situation and develop a plan of action to control effectively the loss or potential loss. A claim management checklist is one method for monitoring key steps in proactively handling a claim (Exhibit 26.1).

Initial Investigation

The most important aspect of claims handling is the initial investigation. All claims should be investigated as expeditiously as possible so that valid claims can be settled and non-meritorious claims can be defended. It is impossible to do either without a thorough investigation of the facts. Once facts are known, the appropriate standard of care may be determined and the potential liability assessed in light of the applicable law. The decision to settle or defend a case should be made only after a complete investigation.

Regardless of the risk financing mechanism chosen to address the professional or general liability exposure, the risk manager plays an important role in the investigative process. In those instances where he or she has the major responsibility for claims investigation, the risk manager should utilize all available resources, including in-house legal counsel, outside claims adjusters, and the insurance broker, as well as clinical personnel such as nursing and medical staff. However, in all cases, even where the health care organization is commercially insured, the risk manager should direct and maintain control of the investigation. He or she should provide an orientation to the investigative process for involved personnel to be interviewed and should remain present during all interviews by outside adjusters. To a large extent, the circumstances of each case will determine what information should be developed by the person assigned to the investigation. The following investigation checklist sets forth the minimum information required for the investigation of any lawsuit or claim:

- *Insured parties:* Name, address, phone number, employment or medical staff status, and role in the case. Generally, the insured parties include the health care organization and its employees who may have been individually named, as well as physicians for whom the organization has agreed to provide coverage. Health care organization employees also may have their own insurance coverage. In addition, the organization's insurer will want to know the coverages provided to named defendants.

- *Noninsured parties:* Actual or potential codefendants will need to provide name, address, phone number, employment or medical staff status, and role in the case. Parties not covered by the organization's insurance program usually are physicians and other health care entities who may have provided care and who will have their own coverage. Insurance coverage available on these parties should also be determined.

- *Dates:* Date of the incident (loss); date the risk manager was notified; date the insurer (commercial, captive, self-insurance trust fund) was notified; date the file was opened; and date the file was closed.

EXHIBIT 26.1.   Claim Management Checklist

MedStar Health, Inc.
Claim Management Checklist

Date of receipt of notice claim: _____

1. MedStar Coverage Confirmation Letter to Individual Insureds
   ☐ YES   Date: _____
   ☐ NO   Reason: _____
              _____
              _____ Date: _____

2. Investigator Assignment
   ☐ YES   Date of Assignment: _____
              Date of Receipt: _____
   ☐ NO   Reason: _____
              _____
              _____ Date: _____

3. MedStar Medical/Nursing Review
   ☐ YES   Date of Assignment: _____
              Date of Receipt: _____
   ☐ NO   Reason: _____
              _____
              _____ Date: _____

4. Indemnity Reserve
   Initial Indemnity Reserve _____ Date: _____
   Reserve Change _____ Date: _____

5. Expense Reserve
   Initial Expense Reserve_____ Date: _____
   Reserve Change _____ Date: _____

6. MedStar Liability Assessment
   ☐ Clear   ☐ Probable
   ☐ Remote   ☐ Questionable
   ☐ No Liability
   Remarks: _____
   _____
   Revisions: _____
   _____
   _____ Date: _____

7. Plan of Action: _____
   _____
   _____ Date:_____

8. Identification of Ethical Issues
   ☐ YES   ☐ NO
   Issue:_____
   _____
   _____ Date:_____

- *Insurance information:* Limits of liability, primary and excess insurance coverage of all parties, policy numbers, policy periods, potential for third-party actions, other coverage issues.
- *Claimant information:* Name, date of birth, age, gender, address, phone number, marital status, occupation, annual earnings, dependents.
- *Review of medical records:* Dates of treatment and, if applicable, dates of admission and discharge, medical record number, admitting and discharge diagnoses, treatment provided, summary of nursing notes.
- *Claimant's injuries:* Nature and extent of injuries alleged to have occurred, special damages, additional treatment required, subsequent treating physicians.
- *Current status of case:* PCE, claim, or suit; investigation or discovery pending.
- *Summary of claimant's allegations*: A summary of allegations of improper medical treatment.
- *Summaries of interviews:* Summaries of interviews with health care professionals or other parties involved in the incident.
- *Summary of facts*: A summary of the facts of the incident as developed by the investigator.
- *Copies of policies, procedures, and protocols:* Copies of any policies, procedures, and protocols in effect at the time of the incident that may have a bearing on the issues.
- *Copies of equipment maintenance reports:* If medical equipment is involved, copies of equipment maintenance reports are needed as well as findings of the clinical engineering department subsequent to the incident. Also needed are copies of any protocols for the maintenance and repair of the equipment in question. It is always helpful to maintain manufacturer information such as model number, make, serial number, date of purchase, and user literature and product information.
- *Summaries of results of peer review or expert review:* Summaries of any peer review or expert reviews conducted on the file.
- *Evaluation of legitimacy of damages:* Documents or other material that examines the legitimacy of damages claimed.
- *Investigator's evaluation of liability:* Recommendations for reserves and future handling of the claim file.
- *Known abilities and propensities of plaintiff's counsel.*

Guidelines for Investigating a Potentially Compensable Event

In those cases involving PCEs, it is equally important to conduct an investigation, although the process is slightly different. The following guidelines may be modified to address specific situations:

1. Ascertain the facts.

- Determine whether investigation must occur immediately or can wait for a more appropriate time. (*Note:* Prompt provision of necessary care should always take precedence over investigation of an event.)
- Identify all involved staff members and any witnesses to the event, including, as appropriate, nurses, physicians, and other ancillary personnel.
- Advise all involved staff that written and signed statements are not to be generated unless so directed by the risk manager, insurance carrier, and defense counsel.

- Advise all involved staff that no verbal statements to outside parties are to be made without prior knowledge and consent of the risk manager, insurance carrier, and defense counsel.
- Assist the insurance carrier and/or defense counsel, as appropriate, in assessing:

  Whether there is deviation from the applicable standard of care.

  Whether reasonable steps were taken to avoid the event.

  What the nature of the injury and prognosis were.

  Whether policies, procedures, and protocols were observed.

  Whether diagnostic tests and procedures, consultations, and any other surgical procedures and medical treatments were timely and appropriate.

  Whether there are contradictions, inconsistencies, or unnecessary time delays in care management.

  Whether the medical record contains obliterations, alterations, inconsistencies, omissions, or disparaging entries directed to patient, subscriber, staff, or physicians.

  Whether there is staff or physician impairment.

  Whether the acts or omissions of relatives or friends of the patient or subscriber led to the injury.

  Whether the acts or omissions of the patient or subscriber led to the injury.

2. Secure any and all evidence that may be pertinent to the effective defense of a future claim and define a chain of custody that sets forth those individuals who have access to the sequestered evidence.

   - Medical devices

     Remove from service and sequester under lock and key any and all medical devices involved in the event. Label all such devices for future identification.

     Do not clean, test, or alter any medical devices except as advised by the insurance carrier and/or defense counsel following consultation with an independent biomedical expert.

     Take photographs, as appropriate, after consultation with the insurance carrier and/or defense counsel.

     Determine responsibility for service and maintenance of all involved medical devices.

     Obtain and sequester under lock and key copies of all medical device maintenance and rental contracts, and any pertinent reports from the clinical engineering department generated before and after the event.

     Determine whether any medical device alerts were issued by the manufacturer, the distributor, or the Food and Drug Administration; and if so, whether the alerts were known and observed.

     Determine, in cooperation with the insurance carrier, whether device(s) should be evaluated by an independent biomedical expert and whether device(s) should be returned to service, repaired, or any other action taken.

     Determine whether a report to comply with the Safe Medical Devices Act is necessary.

- Medical record

  Direct appropriate staff to complete the primary medical record as soon as possible after the event.

  To ensure that future alterations can be identified, make, date, and sequester under lock and key a complete copy of the primary medical record, including any emergency department (ED) or outpatient clinic records.

  Assess any and all secondary medical records (for example, radiology films, fetal monitoring tracings, pathology slides, videotapes, and/or any other pertinent diagnostic electronic monitoring tracings) to determine the need to reproduce these records on different media to prevent fading images, and then sequester them under lock and key.

  Review and assess all primary and secondary medical records and report preliminary findings on potential liability exposure of involved parties to the insurance carrier.

- Other evidence

  Review and sequester under lock and key any and all pertinent third-party contracts (for example, with physicians or outside staffing agencies).

  Sequester expired insurance policies to ensure that the organization can prove who the insurer was at the time of the event and what limits of coverage were in force.

  Maintain a diary review system to periodically review and assess the need for any new or outstanding piece of evidence to ensure that no important part of the claim file is overlooked.

  Copy and sequester under lock and key all pertinent policies, procedures, and protocols.

3. Communicate with appropriate persons.

   - Report the event to the insurance carrier as soon as reasonably possible.
   - Notify the attending physician if he or she is not already involved in or aware of the event.
   - Evaluate the need to notify the vice president for medical affairs (or equivalent position) and physician chairperson(s) for the involved clinical department(s).
   - As necessary, consult the organization policy that describes those patient or resident deaths that need to be reported to the medical examiner or coroner.
   - Evaluate the need for a meeting with the attending physician, the administrator, and the family.
   - As appropriate, notify regulators if an extended care organization is involved.
   - Evaluate the need to notify law enforcement agencies and any agency with whom the organization contracts for clinical personnel.
   - Notify the patient or subscriber satisfaction surveyor so that this individual does not contact the involved patient or subscriber.
   - Evaluate the need to notify the patient or subscriber relations representative to assess whether intervention is necessary.
   - Assess whether immediate notice to senior management is warranted. Issues that should be brought to senior management's attention include, but are not

limited to:

Potential adverse publicity.

Excessive difficulty with personnel.

Any catastrophic event.

- If it is determined that immediate notice of the event to senior management is warranted, assess the need to identify an organization spokesperson, to prepare a response to internal and external inquiries, and to involve the insurance carrier as well as the organization's public relations department.

Investigative Techniques

The investigative process is composed of three steps:

1. Discovery of the facts.
2. Determination of the applicable standard of care.
3. Assessment of the applicable legal principles.

Once these steps have been completed, the risk manager can make a decision to settle or defend the claim. The investigation checklist previously referred to assists in identifying the relevant information. The following techniques facilitate the investigation:

- *Interview the involved staff before interviewing the claimant.* This allows the information provided by the claimant to be put into perspective. The investigator's questions should not be based on the claimant's side of the story; doing so could put the staff being interviewed on the defensive and hinder open response.

- *Do not allow the health care organization's attorney to interview the claimant before the claimant is represented by counsel.* A premature interview may be used against the health care organization at a later date.

- *Always obtain an informal, preliminary expert (for example, peer) review.* This review will assist in identifying the relevant medical issues and the need for additional specialty experts, as well as in determining the applicable standard of care. It also can help in formulating questions to ask the claimant or his or her attorney. Such a review should never be in writing, and the expert providing this initial review does not have to commit to serve later as the identified expert witness for purposes of providing testimony either in deposition or at trial. Most expert reviewers will be physicians; however, if the issue involves nursing care, the expert review should be performed by a qualified nursing expert. Often, quality management staff can perform such reviews. This review should be obtained as soon as possible after notification, as the results will serve as a basis for the claims management strategy.

- *If preliminary information indicates that there is clear liability on the part of the organization, offer to arrange a conference for the claimant and his or her representatives to discuss the situation with physicians and other health care professionals.* This may defuse the claimant's need to "get even" and so avoid the claim. Many times, the claimant is seeking only an acknowledgment that there was an error, as well as an apology. This conference should be arranged before the claimant has retained legal counsel. Although in most instances it is not appropriate for the risk manager to attend this conference, he or she should have a preliminary meeting with the health care professionals and representatives of administration.

- *During the preliminary investigation, do not record interviews with witnesses or request that they write statements.* These activities hinder witnesses from giving the interviewer all the relevant information. Informal interviews are far more likely to produce valuable information that will allow the most appropriate decision to be made in handling the claim.

- *If preliminary information indicates there is clear liability on the part of the organization, make direct contact with the claimant as soon as is practicable.* This may avoid the need for either party to obtain legal counsel and thus eliminate attorneys' fees and reduce the amount of the settlement.

- *Verify all information gathered in the investigation process, especially with regard to the claimant's damages.* It may also be prudent to conduct a *sub rosa* investigation—that is, obtain background information through interviews with neighbors, employers, and coworkers as well as surveillance of the claimant. Such investigations can be time-consuming and should be performed by professional investigators only in those cases warranting the time and expense.

Discovery of Investigative Material

One of the most difficult issues facing health care providers, their insurance carriers, and the defense counsel is how to protect written documents such as incident reports, investigative reports, claim report forms, peer review records, and credentialing files from discovery during the course of civil litigation. These issues will arise more frequently as corporate liability theories expand and injured parties become more aggressive in their pursuit of compensation.

It is important to research statutory provisions and judicial precedent in the relevant jurisdiction in order to develop responses to production requests that comply with applicable statutes and to devise strategies that protect sensitive documents and maintain effective communication. In many jurisdictions, incident reports, investigative reports, and claim report forms will be protected if they are prepared either in anticipation of or during the course of litigation. Thus, it is important to set up a procedure that will maximize such protection. For example, placing "Confidential: Prepared in Anticipation of Litigation" at the top of the incident or investigative report will help ensure protection from discovery. Likewise, forwarding these reports directly to defense counsel will further support the position that such reports should be protected.

Where statutory provisions and judicial precedent provide no protection from discovery, it is critically important that incident reports, investigative reports, and claim report forms contain only objective information. Similarly, peer review records and credentialing file materials should be prepared in such a manner as to maximize availability of protection from discovery and at the same time minimize any adverse impact if such materials become discoverable.

············

CLAIM FILE MANAGEMENT

Well-organized claim files are essential to managing claims effectively. By maintaining all relevant documents in logical order, the risk manager will be able to conduct a thorough diary review on a regular basis and thus keep abreast of the developments in the claim.

Sections of the Claim File

As a claim progresses from initiation to final resolution, documents will be added continually to the claim file. To maintain the information in a logical order, the claim file should be divided into sections.

Correspondence   This section contains the incident report or first notice of the claim, relevant correspondence pertaining to the claim, and follow-up notations by the file handler.

Expenses   This section contains documentation for all loss adjustment costs, such as independent adjusters' fees, fees for expert reviews, billings for independent medical examinations, and legal expenses.

Legal Papers   This section contains copies of the summons and complaint, the answer, interrogatories, transcribed depositions or summaries, and motions.

Expert Reviews and Investigation   This section contains the analyses of medical experts and experts retained for the purpose of assessing damages. The summaries of the investigation also may be contained in this section.

Medical Records   As long as the entire original medical record is easily accessible, only copies of pertinent parts of it need to be kept in the file. In addition, other records, such as computed tomography scans, electroencephalograms, and fetal monitoring strips, should be maintained separately.

Depending on the case, it may be necessary to create additional sections, such as "Damages" or "Medical Literature," if the nature of the injury is severe and permanent or the basis of liability involves a complex and unusual medical issue.

Diary Review

The risk manager should maintain a diary system to review periodically all claim files. By assigning dates for periodic review, he or she can make decisions about handling the case before some new activity mandates action. Each claim file should reflect the next date for review, and there also should be master diaries for all claim files, by date and alphabetically by name. On each review, the following issues should be considered:

- Status of investigation.
- Assessment of liability.
- Documentation of damages.
- Adequacy of reserves.
- Availability of expert witnesses.
- Statute of limitations.
- Status of settlement demands or negotiations, if any.

On diary review, the risk manager should examine each case for recent developments and note them in the file. Each diary review should include an evaluation of the investigation remaining to be completed and recommendations for future handling of the claim. Because most professional and many general liability claims remain open for two to seven years, it is helpful to summarize the information in an organized fashion so that it can be periodically updated. The claim status summary in Exhibit 26.2 provides a format for organizing the facts, the standard of care, the potential liability, and the chronology of legal events.

EXHIBIT 26.2.   Claim Status Summary

MedStar Health, Inc.
Claim Status Summary

Claimant Name _____   Claim No. _____

Address _____

Date of Occurrence _____   Sex _____   Marital Status_____

Dependents _____   Age _____

Employment Status—Current: _____   Income: _____
           At Time of Occurrence _____

Insured Health Care Entity _____

Date Reported to MSRM _____   Reported by _____

MSRM Insured Staff

1. Name _____   Department _____
    Position _____

2. Name _____   Department _____
    Position _____

3. Name _____   Department _____
    Position _____

4. Name _____   Department _____
    Position _____

Non-MSRM Insureds

1. Name _____   Department _____
    Address _____
    Position _____
    Insurance Coverage _____

2. Name _____   Department _____
    Address _____
    Position _____
    Insurance Coverage _____

3. Name _____   Department _____
    Address _____
    Position _____
    Insurance Coverage _____

4. Name _____   Department _____
    Address _____
    Position _____
    Insurance Coverage _____

Synopsis of Case: _____
_____
_____

Claimant's Allegations:_____
_____
_____
_____

Investigation Completed: _____
_____
_____
_____

(Continued)

EXHIBIT 26.2.   **Claim Status Summary** (*Continued*)

Evaluation: _____

_____

_____

_____

Potential Judgment Value: $ _____ % Exposure:_____
% Chance of Losing Case: _____

Reserve History

Reserve	Expense/Indemnity	Date
_____	_____	_____
_____	_____	_____
_____	_____	_____

Excess Carrier Notified: _____ Date: _____

Third-Party Actions: _____

_____

_____

Recommendations for Future Handling: _____

_____

_____

Lawsuit History

Caption:_____

Court: _____ Docket #: _____

Date of Service: _____ Answer Filed: _____

Judge: _____ Trial Date: _____

Jury Trial: _____ Nonjury Trial: _____ Arbitration: _____

Pre-Trial Conference Date: _____

Claimant's Attorney:_____

Address: _____ Phone No.:_____

_____

Defense Attorney: _____

Address: _____ Phone No.:_____

_____ Client: _____

Defense Attorney: _____

Address: _____ Phone No.:_____

_____ Client: _____

Defense Attorney: _____

Address: _____ Phone No.:_____

_____ Client: _____

Defense Attorney: _____

Address: _____ Phone No.:_____

_____ Client: _____

Motions: _____

_____

Interrogatories:
Propounded to Plaintiff, Date: _____ Answers Rec'd, Date: _____
Received from Plaintiff, Date: _____ Answered, Date:_____

Depositions

Deposition _____ Date: _____
Discussion_____

Deposition _____ Date: _____
Discussion_____

Deposition _____ Date: _____
Discussion_____

(*Continued*)

EXHIBIT 26.2.   Claim Status Summary (*Continued*)

Deposition _____ Date: _____
Discussion _____

Deposition _____ Date: _____
Discussion _____

Investigation/Discovery Remaining: _____
_____
_____

Claimant's Expert _____ Specialty _____
Address/Location of Practice _____
Opinion _____

Claimant's Expert _____ Specialty _____
Address/Location of Practice _____
Opinion _____

Claimant's Expert _____ Specialty _____
Address/Location of Practice _____
Opinion _____

Defense Expert (MedStar) _____ Specialty _____
Address/Location of Practice _____
Opinion _____

Defense Expert (MedStar) _____ Specialty _____
Address/Location of Practice _____
Opinion _____

Defense Expert (MedStar) _____ Specialty _____
Address/Location of Practice _____
Opinion _____

Defense Expert (MedStar) _____ Specialty _____
Address/Location of Practice _____
Opinion _____

Defense Expert (MedStar) _____ Specialty _____
Address/Location of Practice _____
Opinion _____

Administrative Actions

Department _____
Action _____
Status _____

Plaintiff's Case Evaluation

Strengths _____
_____
_____

Weaknesses _____
_____
_____

(*Continued*)

EXHIBIT 26.2.   Claim Status Summary (*Continued*)

Defendant's Case Evaluation

Strengths_____

_____

_____

Weaknesses _____

_____

_____

Statutory Caps on Damages: _____

Settlement Negotiations

Medical Specials_____

Lost Wages _____

Demand: _____ Date: _____ Offer: _____ Date: _____

Final Outcome and Discussion: _____

_____

_____

_____

Documentation

To make an informed evaluation of the merits of the claim, the risk manager should include in the claim file:

- Copies of all reports required for establishing and processing claim files, including first-notice-of-claim reports, reserve reports, and claim status reports.
- Summaries of all investigations by claims personnel, independent adjusters, or risk management personnel.
- Summaries of any interviews with involved staff or other parties relating to the subject of the claim.
- Copies of any statements by involved staff that relate to the subject of the claim.
- Copies of all pertinent medical records and other clinical reports. The original medical record should be properly secured at the health care organization. The risk manager, in conjunction with medical records personnel, should review it periodically to see whether attorneys have reviewed it or requested information from it.
- Copies of any expert reports, or summaries of expert evaluations if the expert has not provided a written report.
- If the claim is in suit, copies of all pleadings.
- Reports from defense counsel assigned to the case, including status reports or legal research papers prepared by the attorney, as required by developments in the case.
- Copies of all correspondence with codefendants, their insurers, and excess carriers.
- Copies of all bills, invoices, and records of payments.
- Copies of any other correspondence relating to the claim.

Both the claimant and the health care organization are interested in maintaining confidentiality of the information in the claim file. The file should be made available only to parties with a legitimate need for the information kept in it.

Depending on the nature of the organization's insurance program and the risk manager's role, it is not necessary that the risk manager maintain all the items in the claim file. For example, he or she may prefer to file deposition summaries rather than the complete deposition transcript. However, all involved parties should agree on who is responsible for maintaining what documentation.

The risk manager should keep claim files in a secure location with limited access. All original medical records, x-rays, tracings, equipment, devices, and supplies that may be necessary to the defense of a claim also should be well protected.

Because medical records must be available in the event that patients or subscribers are readmitted, the risk manager must work with the medical records department to have records of patients or subscribers who have filed claims put in a separate file cabinet. When a lawsuit is filed, the medical records department should *sequester* that patient's medical record (that is, keep it separate, with severely limited access) and label it to indicate its special status. The risk manager should periodically review the need to continue to sequester the record. Radiographs should be treated in the same way.

When the risk manager suspects that a claim may be brought, he or she should immediately have copies of pertinent parts of the medical record made and maintained in the claim file. If someone alters the record, the risk manager will have a copy of the unaltered record and will be in a better position to protect the organization or provider.

RESERVING OF CLAIMS

Reserving—that is, setting aside an amount of money that will be paid out in indemnity and loss adjustment costs by the time the case is settled or resolved—is more art than science. Reserving may be funded or unfunded. When reserves are funded, cash or other assets are set aside, before any loss, in an account. If reserves are unfunded, losses are paid out of current operations and then expensed. Reserving can be done by the insurance company, the risk manager, or an outside claims management firm. Because there is no "formula" for establishing a reserve for a case, the risk manager should be involved, especially if the organization is commercially insured, to provide information on the locality where the incident occurred and any additional facts that might affect damages and costs. In addition, the independent adjuster and defense counsel may be able to provide valuable advice to the insurance company (if the organization is commercially insured) or the risk manager (if it is self-insured).

The proper reserving of claims is critical to the financial soundness of the insurer, the risk pool, or the self-insurance fund. Because reserves must accurately reflect the insurance fund's monetary exposure, the health care organization, with active participation of the risk manager, should establish guidelines for appropriately reserving claims.

All claims, whether in suit or not, should be reserved as soon as sufficient information is available to assess the liability exposure. Although some cases may have reserves established within thirty days of notification, others may take years. When possible, all cases should be reserved within ninety to one hundred and eighty days after notification. Where a health care organization is self-insured, either the risk manager or an independent claims management service should establish reserves for both the actual indemnity costs (the amount to be paid in damages) and expenses (the amount to be paid to investigate and settle or defend the claim). Reserves for expenses should be established to cover the cost of investigation and expert review. However, anticipated legal expenses need not be included unless and until legal process has been initiated. Where an organization is commercially insured, the insurance company is responsible for setting reserves.

As the claim develops, new information from experts, defense counsel, or adjusters may necessitate changing the reserve. Part of the diary review mentioned earlier includes reviewing the reserve to make sure it is still accurate, and adjusting it if necessary. Reserves may be increased or decreased; however, it is important to avoid what is referred to as "stepladdering" reserves. *Stepladdering* is the process of steadily increasing reserves at periodic intervals as each new development comes to light. It is important to avoid stepladdering reserves in order to maintain accuracy of actuarial projections. The best way to avoid stepladdering is to complete a thorough investigation as soon as possible so that the initial reserve is valid for the life of the file.

Just as important as the reserve itself is documentation of the process used and the factors considered in establishing or adjusting a reserve.

- *Claimant information:* Age, gender, occupation, annual earnings, dependents, and diagnosis.
- *Information regarding the claimant's injury:* Nature and extent of injury (whether partial, temporary, or permanent), and prospects for rehabilitation.
- *Facts of the occurrence:* As alleged by claimant, as developed by investigator, documentation in the medical record, and statements of witnesses.
- *Parties involved:* Identification, levels of education, and evaluation of credibility.
- *Damages and financial information:* Medical specials (hospital, clinic, or nursing home charges; physician or dentist fees; costs for medication or prosthetics; private-duty nursing care charges), pain and suffering, lost wages, payment status of claimant's counsel, and liens.
- *Expert witnesses:* Reports of expert witnesses, identity and qualifications of experts for claimant and defense, experience of experts with procedure or treatment in question, and experience of experts in litigation. (*Note:* Experts may include physicians, nurses, pharmacists, economists, or others with expertise in a particular area.)
- *Verdict and settlement values:* Outcomes for similar injuries in the particular jurisdiction or geographic area.
- *Information regarding claimant's attorney:* Attorney's experience, both generally and in regard to the type of case in question; plaintiff's attorney's willingness to settle or try the case.
- *Information on codefendants and possible third-party actions:* Includes availability of additional insurance coverage.
- *Intangible factors:* Includes appearance and jury appeal of the claimant, physicians, staff, or other witnesses, and the "sympathy factor."
- *Evaluation of liability issues:* Includes both favorable and unfavorable issues.

The reserve rationale form in Exhibit 26.3 provides a concise method for documenting the reserving process, thereby validating adequacy of the reserve.

············

LITIGATION MANAGEMENT

Appropriate, knowledgeable, and carefully selected defense counsel is essential to successful litigation management. The risk manager's role in working with defense counsel involves selecting or recommending the defense firm, regularly and effectively communicating with

EXHIBIT 26.3. **Reserve Rationale Form**

Reserve Rationale Form
Confidential and Privileged
Attorney Work Product

Case: _____
Date: _____
Preparer: _____

1. **Liability Issues:**
   _____
   _____
   _____
   _____
   _____
   _____
   _____
   _____
   _____

   (Note: + = Favorable Factor
   − = Unfavorable Factor)

2. **Damages:**
   Hospital: _____
   Physicians: _____
   Lost Wages: _____
   Loss of Potential Earning Power:

   _____
   Pain & Suffering: _____
   Rehabilitation: _____
   Future Medicals: _____
   Permanent Injury: _____

3. Worst Case Estimate:
   Probable Adverse Verdict:
   Probability (% of 100)
     of Losing: _____
   Liability (% of 100)
     Our Exposure Only: _____

4. Indemnity Reserve: _____
   Expense Reserve (20%
     Underlying Limits): _____

5. Legal Basis for Allocation
   among Hospital and Defendants:
   _____
   _____
   _____
   _____

6. Hospital:
     Indemnity: _____
   Physicians:
     Indemnity: _____
   Other Defendants:
     Indemnity: _____

7. **Reserve by Coverage:**
   Hospital: _____
   Primary: _____
   Excess: _____

   Physicians: _____
   Primary: _____
   Excess: _____

Case:
Supplemental Analysis Sheet

8. Basis for Allocation of Self-Insured Reserves and Expenses among HUP, CPUP and University:

   _____
   _____
   _____
   _____

9.

	Indemnity	Expense	Total
Hospital:	_____	_____	_____
Physician:	_____	_____	_____
Resident:	_____	_____	_____

the defense attorneys (including providing guidelines for the defense firm to follow), helping to control legal fees, and evaluating the performance of the defense firm.

Selecting the Defense Firm

Underlying successful claims management is the careful selection and effective use of defense counsel. There should be appropriate criteria for assigning defense counsel and procedures for ensuring effective communication between defense counsel and risk manager. Equally important are instructions designed to ensure that defense counsel and risk manager work together to provide the highest-quality legal representation available.

The health care organization may be either self-insured, in which case the risk manager is responsible for selecting defense counsel, or commercially insured, in which case the risk manager merely needs to recommend defense counsel. In either situation, a law firm selected to serve as defense counsel should have:

- Significant experience litigating medical professional liability cases. Factors to consider in evaluating the law firm's level of experience include the number of health care clients represented and the types of legal representation provided; the number of insurance carriers (commercial or captive) or self-insurance trusts represented by the firm, and the nature of the representation provided; the number of medical professional liability actions defended by the firm, including the actual number of trials conducted; and the firm's record in medical professional liability litigation.
- More than one attorney capable of litigating medical professional liability cases, and adequate support staff, including paralegals or trained investigators.
- Representation that has been limited to defense, with no clients preferred over other clients.
- Billing rates that are competitive with other firms of similar experience.
- Reasonable geographical proximity to the insured defendants and court setting.

In assigning or recommending counsel for a case, the risk manager also should take into consideration:

- The attorney's current caseload and ability to handle the litigation effectively and efficiently.
- Prior experience with the subject matter and the allegations raised in the case.
- Prior experience with counsel chosen to represent the plaintiff.

Conflicts of interest in representing clients are common. Often defense counsel may refuse to defend the health care organization *and* individually named defendants who are employees. The principal reason for this position is that if a conflict of interest arises at some point in the litigation, defense counsel may have to withdraw entirely from the representation. Often, employed physicians who are named defendants may be concerned about a potential conflict of interest between the organization's economic interests and their personal reputation. In such cases, it may be appropriate to retain separate counsel to represent the individually named defendants. When a joint defense is not possible and separate counsel is retained, every attempt should be made to select attorneys who are willing to "coordinate" the defense. To ensure that the best possible legal services are provided in all circumstances and that there is no conflict of interest, the risk manager should select at least two law firms to which assignments for representation in litigation may be made.

Communicating with Defense Counsel

It is the risk manager's responsibility to coordinate the defense of lawsuits filed against the health care organization and to communicate effectively with defense counsel. Therefore, it is helpful to develop guidelines to assist defense counsel in maximizing the effectiveness of the litigation process and minimizing misunderstandings. A defense firm's compliance with those guidelines should be part of the risk manager's periodic review and evaluation of defense counsel's effectiveness.

Acknowledgment of Assignment   An acknowledgment letter should be sent immediately upon receipt of a new case. Where the health care organization is commercially insured, this acknowledgment generally is addressed to the insurance company, and a copy is sent to the risk manager.

Designation of Trial Attorney   An individual attorney should be designated to have overall responsibility for a particular case. It is not necessary that the trial attorney conduct all phases of discovery; however, he or she must be familiar with the facts and legal issues, conduct significant depositions, attend hearings on dispositive motions, and be prepared to try the case. This attorney will be the principal negotiator in any settlement discussions handled by defense counsel.

Risk Manager   Defense counsel must maintain a close working relationship with the risk manager and work with him or her in investigation of the facts and development of the defense. The risk manager should assist in arranging interviews; gathering information for answering interrogatories; locating pertinent organization records, policies, and procedures; and so on. Having the risk manager serve as a conduit for communications between defense counsel and the health care organization's staff also minimizes the risk of communication by staff members to unauthorized individuals. All staff involved in the claim should be cautioned to treat the case as confidential and advised not to discuss it with anyone, especially attorneys or adjusters, unless authorized to do so by the risk manager. The risk manager should receive copies of all pertinent correspondence.

Investigation   The risk or claims manager or insurance company (or independent adjusters working on its behalf) will, when appropriate, conduct investigations. Investigative reports are confidential, and defense counsel should make every effort to avoid their production. Any proposed production of such reports must be discussed with the risk manager.

Discovery   The health care organization relies on defense counsel's experience and expertise as to the timing and necessity of depositions, interrogatories, and other discovery; however, all discovery must have prior approval in accordance with the litigation strategy report. (See Exhibit 26.4.)

Medical Reviews   In medical professional liability cases, the risk manager often obtains informal medical reviews in order to identify the applicable medical issues. It is essential that defense counsel discuss potential expert witnesses with the risk manager prior to their retention. Curriculum vitae and fee schedules must be submitted to the risk manager prior to such discussion.

EXHIBIT 26.4.   Litigation Strategy Report

MedStar Health, Inc.
Litigation Strategy Report

SECTION I

File #:   Claims Professional: Insured:

Billing Period: Date Completed: Plaintiff: Defense Counsel:
/ / to / /   /   /

Objective: Estimated
                                              MedStar   Date of
                                         Planned Activities: Completion:

Basis for Objective: _____   / /
                                         _____   / /
                                         _____   / /
                                         _____   / /
                                         _____   / /
                                         _____   / /

SECTION II

Response Activities by Counsel:	Estimated Time:	Activities Initiated by Counsel:	Estimated Time:

Additional Comments Concerning Legal Expenses:

Litigation Strategy Report
page 2

A. Is Service Proper? _____ If Not, State Reason and Recommendation:

B. Is Venue Proper? _____ If Not, State Reason and Recommendation:

(Continued)

EXHIBIT 26.4.   **Litigation Strategy Report** (*Continued*)

C. Is Statute of Limitations an Issue? _____ If So, State Reason and Recommendation:

D. Provide a Brief Synopsis of the Facts:

Litigation Strategy Report
page 3

E. Provide an Analysis of the Legal Issues and Defenses (outlining each party's strengths and weaknesses):

F. What Is the Estimated Judgment Value/Range? _____

     Estimated Settlement Value/Range? _____

     Impact of Statutory Caps on Damages? _____

     Percentage of Insured Exposure? _____

     Rationale: _____

Litigation Strategy Report
page 4

Estimated Trial Date	Probability of a Defense Verdict:	Prejudgment Interest Rate:
___ / ___ / ___	_____ %	_____ %

G. Is Settlement Recommended at This Time? _____

     Rationale:

H. Comment on the Experience and Expertise of:

    • Plaintiff's Counsel:

    • Codefendant's Counsel:

I. Provide Recommendations for Future Handling:

    • Investigation:

    • Discovery:

(*Continued*)

EXHIBIT 26.4.   **Litigation Strategy Report** (*Continued*)

• Expert Reviews:

• Crossclaims, Joinders, etc.:

Trial Attorney: Attorney Preparing Report: Date Report Completed:

                                                            ___ / ___ / ___

Cross-Claims and Joinders   No counterclaims, cross-claims, or third-party actions may be filed unless first discussed with the risk manager. No such actions will be authorized until they have been discussed with the organization's CEO.

Settlements   Defense counsel should not engage in any substantive settlement negotiations with the plaintiff or codefendant before agreeing on a settlement strategy with the risk manager.

Reporting Requirements   The litigation strategy report mandates a collaborative exchange between defense counsel and risk manager by establishing the agreed objective of the litigation process and identifying the specific steps to be taken by both parties to reach that objective. The risk manager will complete Section 1 of the report and forward it to defense counsel for completion of Section 2. Defense counsel will be required to anticipate the major activities to be completed during the service period specified by the risk manager. This report should be completed within thirty days of receipt of a new case. It will be sent out periodically by the risk manager during the course of the litigation.

Deposition Summaries   These reports should include a summary of the testimony, counsel's analysis of the witness's strengths and weaknesses, and counsel's opinion as to how the testimony affects the case. These reports should be submitted within thirty days of the deposition.

Supplemental Reports   Periodic status reports should be provided by defense counsel, when appropriate, and should contain an evaluation as to how the new information affects the case.

Pretrial Litigation Strategy Report   This report (shown in Exhibit 26.5) will be forwarded to defense counsel from the risk manager upon notification of a trial date and will be completed in the same manner as the Litigation Strategy Report. It is a collaborative effort that aims to outline the agreed-upon objective of the trial process as well as those steps needed to reach the objective.

Controlling Legal Fees

To ensure the highest-quality legal representation while maintaining control over legal fees, the health care organization should address billing practices as part of a comprehensive litigation management program. Thus, in addition to the instructions outlined above, guidelines similar to the following should be communicated to all defense counsel.

EXHIBIT 26.5. **Pretrial Litigation Strategy Report**

MedStar Health, Inc.
Pretrial Litigation Strategy Report

SECTION I

File #: Claims Professional: Insured:

Plaintiff: Risk Manager: Defense Counsel:

MedStar's Position Regarding Settlement/Defense of This Case:

SECTION II

Venue:	Plaintiff's Counsel:	Trial: _____	Trial Date:
		Nonjury Trial: ___	
Court:		Arbitration: _____	___ / ___ / ___

A. Is Settlement Recommended? _____ Settlement Value: _____

    Statutory Cap on Damages: _____

    Rationale:

B. What Is the Plaintiff's Demand? _____;

    Special Damages: _____;

    Discuss the Plaintiff's Position Regarding Settlement:

C. What Is the Position of the Codefendants Regarding the Settlement?

Pretrial Litigation Strategy Report
page 2

| Probable Verdict Range: | Probability of a Defense Verdict: | Est. Length of Trial: |
| _____ to _____ | _____ % | _____ days |

D. Discuss the Experience and Expertise of:

    • Plaintiff's Counsel:

    • Codefendant's Counsel:

(Continued)

EXHIBIT 26.5.   Pretrial Litigation Strategy Report (*Continued*)

E. Recommended Course of Action:

Discovery and Pretrial Preparation			
Activity	Time	Activity	Time

Estimated Legal Fees through
  Trial: $ _____

Estimated Expenses through
  Trial: $ _____

Trial Attorney: _____

Date of Report: _____/_____/_____

Proposed Experts   Fees
_____
_____
_____
_____
_____

Hourly Rates   To facilitate an effective bill review process, defense counsel will submit a list of all attorneys working on the organization's cases with their hourly rates. It is the responsibility of defense counsel to update this list when appropriate. All proposed increases in hourly rates must be submitted for approval.

Professional Services

- Only one firm member should be in attendance at hearings, depositions, trials, or conferences. If circumstances demand that two members attend, it must be discussed with and approved by the risk manager.

- If a file is reassigned to another attorney for the benefit of the firm, the health care organization will not pay for the second attorney to become familiar with the case.

- The health care organization will not pay for attorneys or paralegals to perform clerical functions, such as collating, indexing, filing, photocopying, and so on.

- All legal research exceeding three hours must be pre-approved. A report summarizing the final results of this research should be forwarded to the risk manager. Repetitive entries for file review will be carefully examined.

Miscellaneous Expenses

- Whenever possible, invoices for court reporters, copy services, court fees, expert fees, and so on, should be submitted directly to the risk manager for payment.

- Photocopying charges should not exceed fifteen cents per page.
- Fax charges should not exceed one dollar per page.
- Clerical or secretarial overtime charges will be approved only when the case creates an unreasonable drain on the firm's normal spread of clerical duties.
- All costs must be supported by adequate documentation.

Billing Practices   The firm shall process all billing in a timely fashion. All bills should be itemized and should list the attorney or paralegal providing the services, their billable rate, hours worked, and a description of the work performed. General bills submitted without this type of information are not acceptable. Bills may be submitted by the law firm on a monthly basis but must be submitted at least quarterly. Where the health care organization or managed care plan is commercially insured, the law firm may send bills directly to the insurance company; however, risk managers should have the opportunity to review them.

Bill Auditing   All bills submitted by defense counsel will be audited regularly for compliance with these guidelines.

Finally, the health care organization might enter into alternate billing arrangements with its defense firms, such as fees per case and incentive payments based on either the amount of indemnity payment or the stage of litigation at which the claim is resolved. In addition, a discount arrangement whereby the law firm agrees to have its bill discounted by 5 percent if paid within ten days is a simple and effective method for reducing legal expenses.

Evaluating Defense Firm Performance

The risk manager should review the performance of each law firm at least once a year. That review should consider:

- The firm's compliance with the procedural requirements as set forth in the instructions to defense counsel.
- The degree of responsiveness to and cooperation with the health care organization's risk manager.
- The firm's track record in litigation over the previous year.
- The firm's billings over the previous year.
- The firm's ability to understand the underlying medical issues and manage the claim.

See Exhibit 26.6 for a sample defense counsel evaluation form.

∙∙∙∙∙∙∙∙∙∙∙∙

CLAIMS MANAGEMENT WITH REGARD TO INSURANCE COMPANIES AND BROKERS

Working with insurance companies and brokers is an essential part of claims management. To obtain the most effective and efficient service from the insurer(s), it is important for the risk manager to clarify the division of responsibility for reporting claims, investigating, negotiating, and so on.

EXHIBIT 26.6.   Sample Defense Counsel Evaluation Form

MedStar Health, Inc. Claims Department
Defense Counsel Evaluation Form

File #: _____   Date: _____

RE: _____

1. **Responsiveness**

   How accessible was defense counsel throughout the duration of this claim file?

   (1) Inaccessible
   (2) Usually unavailable
   (3) Generally available
   (4) Most accessible, prompt response to all inquiries
   (5) Always accessible, frequently initiated communication

2. **Communication**

   How well did defense counsel keep the file updated regarding significant claim activity throughout the duration of this claim file?

   (1) Infrequently updated, had to request most information
   (2) Erratic information flow
   (3) Moderate information flow
   (4) Prompt information flow
   (5) Superior information flow, updates regardless of activity

3. **Competency**

   How well did defense counsel identify, enunciate, and apply the underlying medical or liability issues most reflective of this claim?

   (1) Poor understanding, seemed to learn as he/she went
   (2) Fair understanding
   (3) Average understanding, subject matter unfamiliar but researched
   (4) Good understanding, file benefitted from attorney's experience
   (5) Excellent understanding, attorney is expert in this field

4. **Management**

   How well did defense counsel govern the progress of this claim?

   (1) Poor control, seemed to *react* to the movement of others
   (2) Fair control
   (3) Average control, not much else he/she could do to speed process
   (4) Good control, aggressive representation
   (5) Excellent control, attorney in command as much as possible

5. **Billing**

   Overall, how well did defense counsel comply with Neumann billing guidelines and how expensive, comparatively, were defense costs?

   (1) Did not follow guidelines, fees excessive
   (2) Occasionally followed guidelines, fees higher than average
   (3) Erratic billing system, fees average
   (4) Usually followed guidelines, fees average or below norm
   (5) Always complied with guidelines, fees always in order and only reflected time spent on file

(Continued)

EXHIBIT 26.6.   **Sample Defense Counsel Evaluation Form**   (*Continued*)

6. **Performance**

What category would best describe the overall performance of defense counsel in the aforementioned claim file?

(1) Poor   (2) Fair   (3) Average

(4) Good   (5) Excellent

TOTAL _____

Comments:

Delineation of Responsibilities

The risk manager may interact with commercial insurance companies in several ways. If the organization is commercially insured and has either no, or a very small, deductible, the insurance company may take a very active role in claims and litigation management. If the organization is commercially insured and has a self-insured retention, the insurance company's role will depend on the amount of the retention. The greater the retention, the less active the insurance company's role. Finally, if the organization is self-insured but has purchased excess commercial coverage, the excess insurance company will most likely assume a passive role.

However, regardless of the level of insurer involvement, the risk manager should clarify the following issues with the commercial carrier:

• Requirements for reporting PCEs, claims, and lawsuits.

• Responsibilities for investigation.

• Responsibilities for negotiation.

• Authority to appoint defense counsel.

• Responsibility for providing periodic status reports.

• Settlement authority.

The risk manager also needs to understand the role of the insurance broker. Insurance brokers can be a valuable resource for the risk manager in the following ways:

• Assisting in evaluating coverage.

• Explaining terms and conditions of coverage.

• Serving as the agent for purposes of reporting PCEs, claims, and lawsuits.

• Maintaining loss runs.

• Acting as an advocate for the insured.

Regardless of the risk-financing arrangement, the risk manager plays a major role in claims and litigation management. It is incumbent upon the risk manager to clarify his or her role with insurance brokers and commercial carriers in order to more effectively execute the position's responsibilities. This clarification should be in writing in order to avoid disputes. Similarly, it should be emphasized that insurance brokers and commercial carriers can provide a service to the health care organization or managed care plan, and the risk manager should take appropriate advantage of that service.

Duty to Defend and Reservation of Rights

Commercial medical professional liability insurance policies (as well as many manuscript insurance policies and trust fund coverage agreements) contain a requirement that the insurer will defend any claim or suit alleging bodily injury or property damage and seeking damages payable under the insurance policy. This provision has become known as the *duty to defend* and is far broader than the duty to pay damages. It extends to any action, even if groundless, false, or fraudulent, in which facts are alleged within the coverage of the policy. Furthermore, the general rule is that the allegations of the complaint constitute the sole test of the insurer's duty to defend.

Where there is a question regarding coverage for a particular claim or suit, the insurer may want to investigate the claim without admitting liability or waiving any of its rights under the policy. One procedural device for achieving this objective is a *reservation of rights* letter. The insurer forwards notice to the insured indicating that it is proceeding with the investigation and defense of the claim, but reserving all rights. Notice is given so that there can be no inference that merely because the insurer is proceeding to investigate the claim, it is waiving any of its rights. Another device used by insurance companies is a "nonwaiver agreement," which is similar to a reservation of rights notice except that it is a bilateral agreement between the parties, rather than a unilateral declaration of nonwaiver by the insurer. Under a nonwaiver agreement, the parties agree that in exchange for the insurer's right to assert policy defenses, the insurer, if found liable, will cover the cost of independent defense counsel so that a conflict of interest can be avoided.

Responsibility for Reporting to Excess Insurers and Reinsurers

Primary responsibility for reporting to all insurers rests with the original insured. All claims that could involve an excess insurer's or reinsurer's coverage should be reported in as timely a manner as reasonably possible. Such claims should be reported according to the reporting requirements of each carrier for the appropriate time periods. Most excess insurers and reinsurers require the reporting of incidents, claims, and lawsuits involving serious injury (as defined by the insurer), coverage disputes, allegations of bad faith, and specified reserves. Periodic reports should be sent to the excess carrier or reinsurer to keep it informed of the case status. Depending on the seriousness of the injury and the amount of the reserve, the excess carrier or reinsurer may participate in managing the claim. It also may serve as a consultant regarding claims management strategy and often can assist in identifying medical and other experts.

Excess insurers and reinsurers may conduct periodic audits of the claim files in order to review and evaluate the insured's claims-handling and management procedures. In fact, the risk manager may wish to conduct a self-assessment to evaluate adherence to the organization's litigation management standards. See Exhibit 26.7 for a sample closed-claim audit form.

....

CLAIMS SETTLEMENT

Settling valid claims as quickly as possible should be the goal of every claims management program. Reaching a settlement requires the risk manager to have knowledge of several negotiation techniques and their appropriateness in various situations. Alternative dispute resolution also is an effective and efficient way to settle professional liability claims.

EXHIBIT 26.7.   Sample Closed-Claim Audit Form

MedStar Health, Inc.
Closed-Claim Audit

Claimant Name: _____   Closed Date: _____

File Number: _____

1.	Investigator Assignment Two Days?	Yes	No	N/A
2.	Investigator Report Received Thirty Days?	Yes	No	N/A
3.	Internal Medical Review Received Thirty Days?	Yes	No	N/A
4.	Internal Medical Review Received Thirty Days?	Yes	No	N/A
5.	Indemnity Reserve Established Ninety Days?	Yes	No	—
6.	Liability Assessment Ninety Days?	Yes	No	—
7.	Plan of Action Established Ninety Days?	Yes	No	—
8.	Settlement Negotiations Handled In-House?	Yes	No	N/A
9.	Indemnity Reserve Adequate?	Yes	No	—
10.	Expense Reserve Adequate?	Yes	No	—
11.	Reduced Expenses Due to MedStar Claim Management?	Yes	No	N/A
Totals				

Score: _____

Reviewer: _____

Review Date: _____

Decision to Settle

Every claims management program should be guided by a philosophy similar to the following:

> It is the goal of the Health Care Organization to handle all claims in a fair and equitable manner. To that end, valid claims shall be settled promptly and for a reasonable amount, and frivolous or nonmeritorious claims shall be defended. It is expected that claims personnel will strive for efficiency and consistency in the handling of claims, and be cognizant of the Health Care Organization's efforts to establish a reputation in the legal community for fairness, honesty, and sound judgment. Likewise, the health care organization wishes to establish a reputation for firmness in resisting nonmeritorious claims.[1]

Even if the health care organization is commercially insured, it should adopt a similar philosophy and share it with its broker and the company providing insurance coverage. This philosophy facilitates valid claims being settled as quickly as possible, when there is a reasonable demand. Such an approach benefits both the injured party and the organization, involved staff, and the insurance program (whether self-insurance or commercial insurance). However, when the claim lacks merit or the demand is unreasonable, the claim should be denied and a vigorous defense prepared.

Effective communication between the insurer (self-insurance program or commercial carrier) and the insured health care organization and others afforded coverage under the program is an essential element in effective claims management. To that end, the insurer must work closely with the organization's administrative staff and risk manager in the investigation, defense, and disposition of claims. Further, there should be clearly defined claims settlement authority guidelines that specify:

- A method for deciding all coverage issues in accord with general insurance principles and specific policies approved by the health care organization (or commercial insurer) in response to specific questions regarding coverage for a particular incident, individual, or situation.

- A listing of individuals or groups of individuals that have varying levels of authority (dollar limits) to settle claims in accord with generally accepted claims management principles and specific policies adopted by the health care organization (or commercial insurer).

- A dispute resolution mechanism for handling internal conflicts over the amount to be paid.

When the health care organization is commercially insured, it is important that no attempt be made to negotiate, settle, or compromise any claim or suit that could result in payment by the insurer under its policy without prior consent of the insurer. Given this approach to claims management, conflicts between the insured health care organization, its employees, and other covered parties, and the insurer regarding the decision to settle should be minimized.

Reporting of Medical Professional Liability Payments

The requirement under the Health Care Quality Improvement Act of 1986[2] to report medical professional liability payments to the National Practitioner Data Bank (NPDB) and the appropriate state licensing board(s) within thirty days of the date that payment was made has caused physicians, dentists, and other licensed health care practitioners great concern. This concern is based in large part on the reality that sometimes claims are settled for economic reasons rather than because of the provision of substandard care. Nevertheless, each person or entity, including a medical professional liability insurer, that makes a payment under an insurance policy, self-insurance program, or otherwise on behalf of a physician, dentist, or other licensed health care practitioner in settlement of, or in satisfaction in whole or in part of, a written claim or judgment against such physician, dentist, or other licensed health care practitioner must report that information to the NPDB. However, because such payments may not reflect on the professional competence or professional conduct of the physician, dentist, or other licensed health care practitioner, the report should clearly state whether there was medical merit to the claim and whether the practitioner in issue met the accepted standard of care in dealing with the patient or subscriber.

The trigger for a report on a particular health care practitioner is that he or she was named in both the written complaint or claim demanding monetary payment for damages and the settlement release or final adjudication. It should be noted, however, that if the complaint or claim is made only against a clinic, group practice, or health care organization (except where a sole practitioner is referred to a professional corporation), no report is necessary. Likewise, if the health care practitioner is dismissed from the lawsuit prior to judgment (except if such dismissal is a condition of settlement), no report is necessary.

To avoid staff problems related to medical professional liability claim payment reports, the risk manager and the claims manager should hold periodic educational programs with medical, dental, and other licensed health care practitioners to minimize misunderstandings regarding the reporting requirements of the NPDB. Health care professionals who are the subject of such a report should be allowed to review it prior to submission to the NPDB.

Negotiation Techniques

As is true of many other skills, experience increases the likelihood of successfully negotiating settlement of a medical professional liability claim. However, the quality of that experience depends in large part on an understanding of the process of negotiation and the various techniques that operate within it.

The filing of a lawsuit initiates an adversarial process referred to as *adjudication*, which involves three parties. The first party justifies its position and attempts to destroy the second party's position. The second party does likewise to the first party. Then a third, uninvolved party, the judge or jury, makes the decision. Negotiation, on the other hand, should be a collaborative effort between two or more involved parties to settle their differences. When settlement negotiations take place after initiation of a lawsuit, negotiations should not be conducted by defense counsel because defense counsel is retained to represent its client in an adversarial process and may not always be in the best position to collaborate in resolving the claim.

Equal in importance to the process of negotiation is an understanding of the substance of the claim. The negotiator must understand the facts, the standard of care, and the applicable legal principles. In brief, the process of negotiation involves:

- *Analyzing the needs of both parties to the negotiation:* In addition to deciding what he or she wants to accomplish and prioritizing those needs, the negotiator should assess the needs of the other party. This will facilitate successful collaboration, which requires that both parties fulfill their needs, rather than each competing to gain the greater advantage over the other.
- *Determining whether expectations are reasonable:* The focus should be on concluding the negotiations satisfactorily to both parties. This result is far more likely when the parties' expectations are reasonable.
- *Setting realistic goals:* Goals are based on needs and expectations; however, they must be tempered by reality. For example, a claims manager's goal may be to settle a claim involving a scar on the face of a five-year-old girl for $1,000 in order to keep average per claim payments under $5,000. Although that goal may meet certain needs, it will be viewed as unrealistic if recent reported settlements or court awards for similar injuries have been in the $20,000 to $30,000 range.
- *Obtaining appropriate authorization for settlement:* The negotiator must have limits to his or her settlement authority in order to enhance flexibility in negotiation. In other words, he or she should not be able to commit the organization above an authorized amount at the negotiation table. When final agreements are subject to ratification, the negotiator can use ratification as a tool to extend the negotiations, seek further concessions, avoid making additional concessions, or finalize the agreement.

When professionals are sued, they believe their competence is at issue. The successful negotiator approaches the task of negotiation objectively, setting aside the ego needs of the people involved. A position based on logic rather than personal issues is far more likely to succeed. In addition, the successful negotiator will have prepared well and enhanced his or her bargaining power by learning all the facts, using documentation to support the position, and being patient.

Negotiators may employ a variety of techniques, including:

- Emphasizing mutual interests.
- Using questions.
- Using delays.
- Creating "straw" issues.
- Using humor and other diversions.
- Presenting "good guys" and "bad guys."
- Walking out in the middle of a negotiation (the "hat trick").
- Using deadlines.
- Using threats.
- Being silent.
- Using alternative positions.
- Using concessions.
- Making the other party appear unreasonable.
- Calling for a caucus or recess.
- Moving to close the arrangement.
- In complex negotiations, carefully documenting what has been agreed to and getting consensus on what has been documented.

Before "structured" settlements were introduced, medical professional liability claims were resolved by cash payments. However, with the introduction of a method whereby payments are paid out, or structured, over a period of years, settlements may be easier to negotiate because the total settlement value can be greatly increased without increasing the cost to the payer. When initially introduced, structured settlements were recommended for cases where the values were in the million-dollar range; however, it is now quite common to structure cases with values of several thousand dollars.

The final step in the settlement process is *executing an appropriate release*. The purpose of the release is to document payment of damages for a particular injury by a named party and to foreclose future claims against that party for injuries arising out of the same occurrence. Thus, all parties having an interest in the subject matter of the claim should be named in the release. The risk manager should consult legal counsel for advice in the drafting and execution of the release because claims involving minors, incompetents, and the deceased may have special requirements. Although there may be small claims in which obtaining a release may not seem necessary, it is always preferable to obtain an appropriate release.

Alternative Dispute Resolution Mechanisms

Medical professional liability litigation is time-consuming and expensive. Alternative dispute resolution (ADR) mechanisms have been suggested as a method to ease the expense and backup in the civil litigation system. Such mechanisms have the advantages of economy, greater speed of resolution, less hostility between the parties, and some degree of privacy. However, a lack of understanding about the various mechanisms and a fear of "losing" certain rights continue to be major roadblocks to more effective use of ADR mechanisms. A drastic change in attitudes on the parts of judges, attorneys, and the public will be required before such mechanisms can be used effectively. The win-lose philosophy must give way to a broader "problem-solving" orientation to disputes.

An article in the *ABA Journal* described dispute resolution as taking many forms: "One way to classify dispute resolution alternatives is by the amount of control the disputants have over the process and the outcome. Viewed in this way, the processes can be lined up from right (much control) to left (very little control). At the extreme right is negotiation. In the middle of the spectrum is mediation; then arbitration. At the extreme left is adjudication."[3]

The major alternative dispute resolution mechanisms are:

- *Negotiation:* Voluntary, usually informal, unstructured process. There is no third-party facilitator, but parties may be represented by legal counsel.
- *Mediation:* Neutral third party is brought in to facilitate mutually acceptable agreement.
- *Arbitration:* Either a private, voluntary process or court related. Neutral third party or panel makes decision. Sometimes there is a written opinion.

The following alternative dispute resolution mechanisms are variations on the themes of negotiation, mediation, and arbitration:

- *Private judging:* The case is referred to a "party-selected," neutral decision maker. There are statutory procedural requirements, and appeal to formal judicial process is available.
- *Neutral fact-finding:* This mechanism can be voluntary or involuntary. A neutral fact finder investigates and submits a report or testifies in court.
- *Ombudsman:* Used generally by organizations. A third party is selected by the organization to investigate complaints. The process is voluntary, private, informal, and nonbinding.
- *Minitrial:* Private, consensual proceeding. Lawyers present their clients' cases, the parties try to resolve the issues, and the advisor or judge renders an opinion.
- *Summary jury trial:* This is the jury equivalent of a minitrial. Jury renders advisory verdict.
- *Moderated settlement:* This procedure is initiated by either counsel or the court. Attorneys present their clients' cases before a panel of impartial third parties (usually attorneys) who evaluate the case and render an advisory, nonbinding opinion for use in settlement negotiations.

Alternative dispute resolution is a mechanism that has not been used often enough. However, it is likely to become an increasingly important mechanism as health care providers design and implement programs to improve their systems for compensating individuals injured in the course of the provision of health care services as part of the effort to deliver high-quality health care in the most cost-effective manner.

....

PROCESS OF A LAWSUIT

A *lawsuit* is the mechanism used by one party (for example, patients or clients) to attempt to establish a legal basis for a claim against another party (for example, a health care professional). In the pursuit of such claims, the U.S. legal system uses the *adversarial process*—that is, a process in which opposing parties produce evidence to support their respective positions. This process demands a neutral forum—the court. For the process to be effective, certain rules have been developed to govern the conduct of the proceeding. Those rules are referred to as *procedural law.* They provide the structure for presenting evidence and the arguments of the parties, and they include rules to determine the court where the lawsuit is to be filed, time limits for filing various legal documents, and limits of the discovery process. Those various rules aid the courts in performing two major functions: resolving disputes between parties in a manner consistent with the applicable law and principles of justice, and accomplishing this within a time frame that makes the relief granted meaningful.[4] *Substantive law,* on the other hand, creates, defines, and regulates the rights and duties that are to be enforced. The trial process can be divided into broad categories: pretrial procedure, trial procedure, and posttrial procedure.

Pretrial Procedure

The patient's, or *plaintiff's,* attorney will evaluate the merits of the patient's claim, and if it has merit, will file a *complaint*, or statement of material facts on which the plaintiff is relying to support the claim. When the complaint is filed, either the court or the attorney issues a *summons,* a notice to the parties named in the complaint that an action has been filed against them and that they are required to answer at a time and place indicated in the summons.

The *defendant* must in turn seek legal counsel. In response to the complaint, the defendant's attorney may choose to file one or more *motions,* asking to have the case dismissed because of lack of jurisdiction, asking for a more definite statement in the complaint, or asking for summary judgment in a case where the facts are not in dispute and the applicable legal principles dictate a decision in favor of the defendant.

The purpose of a motion is not only to obtain the requested relief but also to preserve the record for appeal. Preserving the record is important because the appellate court generally will refuse to consider any legal theories not first presented to the trial court.

The defendant is then required to file an *answer,* in which he or she admits or denies the *allegations* in the complaint and sets forth any additional information regarding the facts of the case. The defendant also may assert various *affirmative defenses* in the answer, such as the plaintiff's contributory negligence, or the *statute of limitations,* indicating that the time limit for the plaintiff to sue has expired.

In some jurisdictions, the plaintiff is then permitted to file a *reply* in response to the defendant's answer. After those documents have been filed with the court the issues of the case are said to be drawn, or *joined.* The basis of the claim is established, and the plaintiff may not later attempt to establish the claim on grounds not presented in those initial pleadings.

The statute of limitations prescribes the time period during which plaintiffs can file a complaint. Generally, if a complaint is not filed within this period, the patient loses the right to proceed with a suit. Once the plaintiff has filed the complaint, other time limits apply to the filing of the remaining pleadings, and because extensions of such time limits are routinely granted, months pass between filing the complaint, the answer, and the reply, adding to the overall length of time required for the processing of a lawsuit from filing to final judgment.

Both parties to the lawsuit use the *discovery process* to gather facts, documents, or other materials that are in the knowledge or possession of the other party and are necessary to that party to develop the case. The mechanisms used to elicit that information include requests for admissions of facts, as well as interrogatories, depositions, and subpoenas or subpoenas *duces tecum,* which means that the witness is required to bring documents with him or her. In addition, defendants in medical professional liability cases have the right to request that the plaintiff undergo an examination by an independent medical expert either designated by the defendant or appointed by the court. That examination may provide vital information substantiating or refuting the plaintiff's claim of injuries.

Interrogatories

Interrogatories are lists of questions to be answered in writing and under oath. Answering interrogatories might well be viewed by risk managers with the same disdain that a billing clerk views the filing of insurance forms. In both cases, however, the tasks are "necessary evils." Just as the cash flow of the health care organization depends in large part on third-party reimbursement, so, too, does the success of the litigation depend on the information provided in the answers to interrogatories.

Interrogatories can be useful or bothersome. Obtaining information by interrogatories may disclose facts that appreciably improve the organization's case. On the other hand, having to answer lengthy and detailed interrogatories can be annoying and expensive. Following are guidelines for responding to interrogatories:

- The risk manager generally should be the one to respond to interrogatories on behalf of the organization. Although some information may not be in his or her immediate possession, letting a member of the senior administrative staff who may have all the information answer interrogatories may subject him or her to a deposition and allow the plaintiff to go on a "fishing" expedition.
- Thus, the risk manager should consult with defense counsel to determine which questions need not be answered for procedural reasons. The risk manager should not be intimidated into answering burdensome questions. It is perfectly appropriate to object to such questions.
- The risk manager should never allow the defense attorney to file answers to interrogatories without reviewing and approving the final answers.

When interrogatories exceed the bounds of reasonableness, the answering party may be excused from compliance by requesting a protective order from the court. Short of a protective order, the answering party has the right to object to answering interrogatories by stating specifically the grounds for the objection. Following are examples of standard objections that can be raised:

- The answers sought are readily known to the inquiring party and the request amounts to an undue burden on the answering party.
- The information sought is in the possession of the party requesting it.
- The information sought is a matter of public record and equally available to both parties.
- The interrogatories are burdensome and time-consuming. (This objection must be supported by detailed reasons.)
- The interrogatories require a legal opinion. Such matters are beyond the scope of "factual" interrogatories.

- The scope of the interrogatories is too broad or vague.
- The interrogatories are inapplicable to the instant case. The plaintiff's attorney may have used "stock" interrogatories without tailoring them to the specific claim.

Although the risk manager may be annoyed by having to answer interrogatories, propounding them on the other party can be a useful tool. Reasons for submitting interrogatories include:

- The aid that they provide in securing preliminary information when first notice of a claim is the lawsuit.
- Their potential for reducing the number of issues so as to avoid extensive and time-consuming depositions.
- The essential facts that can be uncovered during answers to interrogatories, which can result in the obtaining of such additional information as employment records or, if there was subsequent treatment at another facility, health care organization records.
- The disclosing of information contained in the answers to interrogatories, which may show that all the essential parties have not been joined in the lawsuit

Following are reasons for not using interrogatories:

- The complexity of a factual issue may be too involved to provide a clear understanding in a written answer.
- Unlike oral depositions, the plaintiff's attorney will read and approve the language used in answering interrogatories by the plaintiff. Crucial questions of fact might be better asked in an oral deposition.[5]

Depositions

A *deposition* is the testimony of a witness who is examined out of court by a party who has given notice to all other parties so that they can be present to cross-examine the *deponent*. The examination takes place before an official, usually a court reporter, who is empowered to administer an oath. Testimony of a witness being deposed takes the same question-and-answer format as testimony in open court.

Objections to questions may be made but cannot be ruled on at the time because the person before whom the deposition is being taken is not a judge. Such objections will be noted in the stenographic record of the deposition and can then later be ruled on by the court. The taking of testimony by depositions was originally the means of taking testimony of witnesses who would be unable to appear at the trial. However, depositions also may be taken (and today, more commonly are taken) for discovery purposes—that is, as a means for the parties to learn all relevant facts pertaining to their case prior to trial.

The mechanics for taking a deposition are relatively simple. The party desiring to take the deposition is merely required to give written notice to all other parties to the lawsuit of the time and place for taking the deposition and the names of the witnesses to be examined. A subpoena may be used to compel the attendance of a witness, if necessary; such a subpoena also may require the witness to bring specifically designated documents—the medical record and health care organization policies, for example.

Depositions taken on oral examination are more effective than a written examination because an answer to a question may disclose information or suggest a clue to a new line of inquiry, which, in turn, may open up other areas. The only limitation in the scope of questioning during a deposition is that the inquiry be confined to any matter relevant to the subject matter of the suit, including not only what may be evidence at the trial but also what may lead to evidence.

In preparing a witness for a deposition, it is helpful to explain in some detail the process of a deposition, including, for example, who will be present, how the room will be arranged, how those in attendance will be seated, and what the order of questioning will be. That information allows the deponent to become oriented immediately to the surroundings and then to concentrate on the substance of the deposition.

Most depositions are held in the offices of the attorney for the party requesting the deposition. However, in medical professional liability cases involving the depositions of several health care professionals, it is not uncommon to hold depositions on the health care organization's premises, thereby accommodating the schedules of the deponents and avoiding disruption of the delivery of health care services. Because depositions are used for discovery by all parties to a lawsuit, the risk manager may be coordinating them for both the plaintiff and the defendant.

The room chosen should be large enough to accommodate the deponent and his or her attorney, the attorney who requested the deposition, the attorneys for other parties involved in the lawsuit, the court reporter, and the plaintiff(s) or defendant(s), if they choose to attend. The seating for a deposition is dictated by a number of factors. First, the court reporter needs to be in a position to hear clearly the testimony of the deponent. The attorney who has requested the deposition needs to be in a position to be heard by the deponent and to hear the deponent's responses. Usually, the deponent is seated directly across from the attorney who will be asking the questions, and the court reporter is seated off to the side, but facing the deponent. The deponents attorney will be seated immediately beside the deponent. The parties to the lawsuit and any other attorneys will then seat themselves accordingly.

The deposition will commence as soon as all parties are present. At that point, the court reporter will be asked to swear or affirm the witness; from that point on, every word spoken during the course of the deposition is under oath and recorded, unless an attorney for one or more of the parties requests an opportunity to speak "off the record."

The risk manager will help prepare the health care organization's employees for deposition or trial. Following is a list of suggestions for witnesses:

- *The witness should present a good appearance.* The opposing attorney will appraise the witness and evaluate his or her probable impression on the jury. Therefore, it is important that he or she dress neatly and conventionally. A business suit or similar attire is appropriate, as is a uniform if the deposition takes place at the health care organization.
- *The witness should maintain a courteous demeanor.* In answering questions, the witness should be polite and cooperative and avoid showing displeasure at the inconvenience of having to go through the deposition. He or she should rely on the health care organization's attorney for protection against harassment or improper questioning.
- *The witness should speak loudly and enunciate clearly.* This is important so that the court reporter can correctly record what is said. Witnesses who nod their heads or use other body language will be asked to respond audibly. In addition, they should avoid body movements, such as nodding in agreement with the attorney posing questions, as those movements might be misinterpreted by the attorney and lead to a different line of questioning that may either obscure or distort the main issues.

- *The witness should be prepared to give personal and professional information.* This might include information about place of residence, age, and marital status, as well as dates of marriages or divorces. Although such information often seems irrelevant to the issues of a particular lawsuit, it may be relevant to the witness's credibility. Of even greater importance are questions having to do with educational background, including schools attended, dates attended, degrees awarded and additional academic work that may not have led to a degree.

In addition to this general information, attorneys often ask specific questions concerning certain courses taken—mathematics, for instance—and what grade the witness received. This kind of questioning may be intended to show the witness in a bad light.

The witness will be questioned concerning employment background. The witness who reviews this information prior to the deposition will answer questions with confidence and self-assurance.

- *The witness should know the facts.* It is always appropriate for the witness to review the facts of the occurrence, including the medical record and the documentation made by the witness, as well as any notes made at the time of the incident. No purpose is served by an attempt to "play dumb" in a deposition. In fact, professional credibility often is damaged when such tactics are used.

The witness who is asked a question beyond the scope of his or her professional competence should say so in response to the question. Often a plaintiff's attorney will ask a witness who is a nurse to render an opinion on the care provided by a physician. This question is inappropriate and should be objected to by the health care organization's attorney.

- *The witness should prepare diagrams and sketches, if appropriate.* If the particular incident that is the subject of the lawsuit involves placement of persons or objects, and those placements are particularly relevant, it may be helpful to make a sketch or diagram of the scene either before or during the deposition, if requested to do so.

- *The witness should be prepared to answer questions regarding matters of time, amount, and distance.* Often in medical professional liability cases, the time of an event (an order, a transfer to the operating room, a page to the attending physician) is important, as is the amount of certain items (fluids administered intravenously, blood, medication). Thus, the witness might be asked to estimate a time or an amount. If he or she cannot do so reliably, the appropriate response is "I'm only guessing" or even "I don't know."

- *The witness should be prepared to identify exhibits.* The basis of almost every medical professional liability action is the documentation contained in the medical record. Thus, it is quite likely that during a deposition the witness will be handed the medical record of the patient or subscriber involved in the case. If this happens, the witness should take time to review it carefully before either identifying it or saying, "I don't know." In responding to questions concerning the exhibit, the witness should make clear reference to the title of the document and its various parts and make sure that the answers given are related to the documentation provided in the exhibit. Witnesses are not required to interpret notations made by other members of the health care team.

In addition to the medical record, health care organization policies and procedures may be introduced as evidence to prove the standard of care in a particular situation. Again, time should be taken to identify the document, and the effective date of the policy's application should be carefully checked.

- *The witness should understand the questions before answering them.* Often deponents, in an effort not to antagonize the attorney asking questions, will hesitate to ask the attorney to repeat a question. An inaccurate answer in response to a misunderstood question can materially affect the results of the case. In addition, if the clarification does not come until the transcribed deposition is reviewed or even later, as at trial, the witness's motives in changing a response may be questioned.

- *The witness should pause before answering questions.* After being asked a question, the witness should pause for just a few seconds, or longer to reflect on the meaning of the question and to give his or her attorney time to raise any objections. When the organization's attorney objects to a question, the witness should refrain from answering further until the matter has been resolved. The attorney will direct the witness if an answer is required.

- *The witness should give brief answers.* If yes or no will suffice, no further information should be given in response to the question. Lengthy responses give the questioner much more information than asked for; furthermore, it may be information the questioner would not have thought to have extracted. Also, the witness should be coached to answer only the questions asked. Witnesses are not required to guess or speculate as to what the answer might be. "I don't know" or "I don't remember" is a perfectly acceptable response as long as it is truthful.

- *The witness should not qualify favorable facts.* This means that witnesses should avoid expressions such as "I think" or "I guess" in their responses. Each response should convey a sense of authority and definiteness that serves to increase credibility. Vague responses draw into question not only the timing of certain crucial events, but also professional integrity.

- *The witness should tell the truth.* When a witness receives a subpoena notifying him or her to appear for a deposition, he or she typically inquires, "What shall I say?" The response is simple: "Tell the truth." It is unnecessary and often harmful to try to "improve" on the facts of the case. The opposing party invariably recognizes such conduct and can later exploit any inaccuracy to its advantage. Furthermore, if at a subsequent time the judge or jury members believe that a witness has exaggerated on one point, they may well surmise that other points have been exaggerated.

- *The witness should review the transcript.* The witness will be asked to review the deposition transcript and to correct any errors. Often the risk manager will perform a preliminary review and then meet with witnesses to review matters needing clarification. The witness will then sign the transcript, authenticating its accuracy.

Subpoenas, or Subpoenas *Duces Tecum*

A *subpoena,* or *subpoena duces tecum* (meaning, requiring the witness to bring certain documents with him or her) is a process requiring a witness to appear and give testimony or produce documents or property for inspection. All the previous suggestions also apply to testifying at trial. The major difference, of course, is that the witness will be in a courtroom and, in addition to the attorneys and parties, a judge and perhaps a jury will be present, as well as members of the general public, the press, and other interested parties. However, the nature of the questioning is the same. Whoever calls a witness will have the first opportunity to ask questions. Afterward, the opposing party's attorney will have the opportunity to question the witness. By offering to prepare a witness either alone or in conjunction with the defense counsel and sharing with him or her the previous guidelines, the risk manager can assist the witness in presenting a professional and credible image.

The complex nature of a medical professional liability action usually requires the testimony of *expert witnesses*. That requirement, however, adds to the time involved in the discovery process as well as the trial itself.

After each party to the lawsuit has had an opportunity to delineate fully the issues to be addressed and to obtain all necessary information, the judge assigned to the case generally will call a pretrial conference. The purpose of this conference is to attempt to settle the case without resorting to trial. Because all discovery should have been completed by that time, each side should be fully aware of the facts and better able to assess the likelihood of prevailing at trial.

If the attempt at settlement fails, the pretrial conference serves to clarify issues still in dispute. It is also an opportunity for each side to set forth the facts of the case from its point of view, the issues, and the applicable law, and to identify the witnesses who will testify and the exhibits that will be submitted for the court's consideration. At the pretrial conference, the parties also might enter into stipulations agreeing upon particular facts or other matters not in dispute in the proceedings. The parties to the lawsuit generally do not attend such conferences but may attend if they choose.

Trial Procedure

Generally, the case has been set for trial prior to the pretrial conference. By the time the case comes to trial, often a year or more has passed since the filing of the complaint, and at least two or three years have passed since the actual incident occurred.

The plaintiff may, and usually does, ask to have a jury trial. The alternative is a trial by a judge only. In such cases, the court then proceeds to *impanel a jury*. Each prospective juror is questioned by the attorneys representing the plaintiff and the defendant to determine possible bias or partiality. This process, known as *voir dire,* allows each party to attempt to select a jury that will be most favorable, or at least impartial, to the issue at hand. If a juror appears biased, either party may challenge the prospective juror "for cause," and that juror will be dismissed. In addition, all jurisdictions permit a specific number of "peremptory" challenges that allow a prospective juror to be removed without giving any reason.

In a jury trial, the jury's role is to determine the facts of the case from the evidence presented and any conflicting testimony. It is the province of the judge to rule on questions of law, such as scope of pretrial discovery, competency of a witness to testify, or admissibility of evidence. If a plaintiff waives the right to a jury trial, the trial proceeds with the judge deciding questions of fact as well as questions of law.

After the jury has been selected, jurors are sworn in and attorneys for both sides present their *opening statements,* setting forth the basis on which the claim or defense is made and the evidence that the parties intend to present to prove their respective cases. It is important to note that opening statements, however persuasive and well reasoned, are not evidence.

At the conclusion of the opening statements, the plaintiff has the first opportunity to plead the case through the testimony of witnesses and other documentary evidence, such as expert medical reports. Each witness is subject to *direct examination* by the plaintiff's attorney, and then cross-examination by the defendant's attorney, to clarify or challenge statements made during direct testimony.

Rules of evidence govern the questioning of witnesses and the presentation of documentary evidence and exhibits. Attorneys for either the plaintiff or the defendant may *object* to questions asked or exhibits *submitted* for the court's consideration, and the judge will rule on each objection. To be considered admissible, evidence must be relevant and material to the facts at issue in the trial. After the plaintiff has presented all evidence believed necessary to prove the case, both parties have an opportunity to make motions for a *directed verdict*. If the plaintiff makes a motion for a directed verdict, the judge is asked to rule that the evidence or law is so clearly in the plaintiff's favor that it is pointless for the trial to proceed. If the defendant makes a motion for a directed verdict, the judge, assuming all evidence presented by the plaintiff as factually true, is asked to rule that the plaintiff has no case. If the judge grants the motion on behalf of the plaintiff, the judgment is rendered in favor of the plaintiff. If the judge grants the motion on behalf of the defendant, the case is dismissed with *prejudice* and the defendant has prevailed.

If no motion for a directed verdict is made, or if the motion is denied, the defendant presents the evidence to support the case by calling witnesses and presenting exhibits in the same way the plaintiff did. The defendant's witnesses are subject to direct examination by the defendant's attorney and cross-examination by the plaintiff's attorney. After the defendant has concluded, the plaintiff has a right to rebut the evidence presented by the defendant by either recalling witnesses or calling new witnesses. Again, defendant and plaintiff have the opportunity to move for a directed verdict at the close of all the evidence in the case. If no motion is made, or if such a motion is denied, *closing arguments* are presented to the judge or jury. Just as opening statements are summaries of what the respective parties believe the evidence *will show*, closing arguments are summaries of what the respective parties believe the evidence *has shown*. Like opening statements, they are not considered evidence.

The judge then instructs the jury, if there is one, concerning the applicable law. This is referred to as the *charge to the jury*. The judge also may instruct the jury on how to arrive at an amount of damages to be awarded if it finds in favor of the plaintiff. The purpose of those instructions is to provide a framework for the jury to weigh the evidence.

In a jury trial, the jury then retires to consider the evidence and reach a verdict. In a nonjury trial, the judge will retire to review the evidence and reach a decision. Under some circumstances, the judge may decide to take the case away from the jury by *directing a verdict* in favor of one party, by *declaring a mistrial* because of the lack of some requisite, or by *declaring a nonsuit*, terminating the action if the plaintiff failed to present a sufficient case.

The jury (or judge) returns a *verdict*, which may be general or special. A *general verdict* is one in which the jury makes a complete finding and a single conclusion on all issues presented to it. In a *special verdict*, the jury makes only findings of fact. It then becomes the duty of the judge to apply the law to the facts as found by the jury. Most states require unanimous verdicts in civil cases, but a few do not. In cases where the requisite number of votes cannot be obtained after thorough deliberation, a *hung jury* may be declared and a new trial will be ordered.

Posttrial Procedure

Depending on the verdict, either the plaintiff or the defendant may allege errors at the trial that constitute grounds for an appeal to a higher court. The person who files the appeal is the *appellant*, usually the loser in the lower court; the other party is the *appellee*. Again, there are time limits applicable to the filing of the appeal. The appellant will first prepare a written document, referred to as a brief, setting forth the *assignments of error* (made by the trial court) and file it with the appellate court. In addition, the appellant may be required to secure an appeal bond guaranteeing that damages and costs will be paid if the appeal is not successful. The appellee then will respond to the appellant's brief. These briefs will include statements and arguments regarding points of law.

The appellate court will rely on the transcript of the trial court proceedings and the briefs and arguments made by counsel in reaching its decision. Usually, there will be oral arguments as well. The parties rarely attend the appellate hearing. The appellate court will issue a written opinion setting forth the decision, applicable law, and the rationale for the court's decision. The appellate court may affirm or reverse, in whole or in part, the lower court's decision, or it may remand (send the case back to the lower court for a new trial).

An appellate court is a court of review. Its purpose is not to retry the case but, rather, to scrutinize the record of the trial court to determine whether reversible error in law has been committed. Most appellate courts do not review factual issues because determination of such issues is the sole province of the trial judge or jury. In general, a party has a right to a first appeal, but a second appeal to a higher court often requires the consent of the court.

If the final judgment is for the defendant, the case is concluded except for payment of court costs, usually by the plaintiff. If the plaintiff prevails, the defendant must comply with the judgment—in the case of a medical professional liability action, usually the payment of monetary damages. And, depending on the jurisdiction, the defendant may be obligated to pay interest on the judgment calculated from either the date of the original judgment or the final judgment. Failure to do so could result in being cited for *contempt of court* with a *writ of execution,* a written order to put in force the judgment of a court levied against the defendant's property to satisfy the judgment.

············

CONCLUSION

There are few areas of a risk manager's responsibilities where he or she can so positively affect the health care organization's resources as in claims and litigation management. To effectively manage medical professional liability claims, the risk manager must take a proactive approach regardless of the nature of the organization or the risk financing program. The risk manager should be provided with all the tools necessary to either participate actively in or monitor the investigation, documentation, reserving, negotiating, litigating, and settling of medical professional liability claims.

Endnotes

1. MedStar Health, Inc. *Claims Management Policy CM-1.*

2. *Health Care Quality Improvement Act of 1986.* PL 99-660, 100 Stat. 3784 (codified at 42 USC ¤¤ 11101-11152, as amended).

3. "Emerging Options in Dispute Resolution." *ABA Journal, 75,* June 1989, p. 67.

4. Hemelt, M. D., and Mackert, M. E. *Dynamics of Law in Nursing and Health Care.* Reston, Va. Reston Publishing Co., 1978, p. 5.

5. Morrill, A. E. *Trial Diplomacy* (2nd ed.). Chicago: Court Practice Institute, 1972, pp. 188–191.

Suggested Readings

Cohen, E. S. "How to be a Good Witness." *The Coordinator,* *3*(7), Aug. 1984, p. 11.

Cullen, K., and Winnicki, R. "Litigation Management Key to Controlling Claims Costs." *National Underwriter* (Property and Casualty/Risk and Benefits Management Ed.), Apr. 10, 1995, p. 13.

Donaldson, J. H. *Casualty Claim Practice* (3rd ed.). Homewood, Ill.: Richard D. Irwin, 1976.

Greenfield, G. "Harnessing the Cost of Legal Bills." *Risk Management,* *40*(1), Jan. 1993, p. 28.

Hemelt, M. D., and Mackert, M. D. *Dynamics of Law in Nursing and Health Care.* Reston, Va.: Reston Publishing Co., 1978.

Holder, A. R. *Medical Malpractice Law* (2nd ed.). New York: John Wiley & Sons, 1978.

King, J. H. *The Law of Medical Malpractice.* St. Paul, Minn.: West Publishing Co., 1977.

Klimon, E. L. "The Legal Process and Medical Malpractice." *Nursing Economic$,* *3*(1), Jan.–Feb. 1985, pp. 44–48.

Klimon, E. L. "Do You Swear to Tell the Truth." *Nursing Economic$,* *3*(2), Mar.–Apr. 1985, pp. 98–102.

Kraus, G. P. *Health Care Risk Management: Organization and Claims Administration.* Owings Mills, Md.: National Health Publishers, 1986.

Laubach, P. B., and others. *The Process and Technique of Negotiating.* Chicago: Foundation of the American College of Hospital Administrators, 1984.

Lorimer, J. J., and others. *The Legal Environment of Insurance.* vol. 1 (2nd ed.). Malvern, Pa.: American Institute for Property and Liability Underwriters, 1981.

MedStar Health, Inc. *Claims Management Policy and Procedure Manual.* Columbia, Md.: MedStar Health, Inc., 1999.

Miller, C. E. *How Insurance Companies Settle Cases.* Santa Ana, Calif.: James Publishing Group, 1989.

Morrill, A. E. *Trial Diplomacy* (2nd ed.). Chicago: Court Practice Institute, 1972.

Schumaier, S. G. "Controlling Litigation Can Mean Increased Savings." *Risk Management,* Sept. 20, 1987.

Troyer, G. T., and Salman, S. L. *Handbook of Health Care Risk Management.* Rockville, Md.: Aspen, 1986.

Tweedy, D. "A Litigation Management: Systems Take Two Approaches in Identifying Legal Costs." *Business Insurance,* Nov. 18, 1991, p. 43.

U.S. Department of Health and Human Services. *National Practitioner Data Bank Guidebook* (Supplement) (Pub. no. HRSA-94-027). Rockville, Md.: Health Resources and Service Administration, Aug. 1992.

Wade, R. D. *Risk Management HPL: Hospital Professional Liability Primer.* Columbus: Ohio Hospital Insurance Co., 1983.

27

The Risk Manager and Biomedical Technology

Sally T. Trombly

An individual risk manager's official scope of responsibility for "biomedical technology" may vary, depending on the particular health care setting. However, issues relating to biomedical technology can cross health care disciplines, departments, and lines of institutional accountability, exposing potential liabilities. It is also not uncommon for risk management to be charged with responsibility for operationalizing technology decisions made by others—or for dealing with a legacy of risk exposures brought about by prior decisions regarding technology use in health care.

In addition, risk management plays a central role in ensuring compliance with regulations regarding health care technology and, on occasion, dealing with external representatives charged with enforcement of those edicts. Continued flux can be expected as institutional and/or corporate entities continue to expand, contract services, shift the focus of their mission, or alter priorities. This chapter provides practical suggestions for the risk manager who, by choice or default, must cope with the operational issues generated by today's technological advances and those on the way for tomorrow.

....

RISK MANAGEMENT'S ROLE IN ASSESSING THE "FIT" OF TECHNOLOGY

Gone are the days when a clinician could go to a facility administrator, ask that the institution acquire the latest piece of medical equipment, and assume that the request would be fulfilled. Today's cost-conscious administrators are more circumspect about the acquisition of new technology than their predecessors. Whether it be the purchase of a new piece of equipment or the offering of the latest laparoscopic procedure, the technology being proposed is likely to undergo an evaluation process to determine whether it fulfills the needs of the institution and the target population served. Two key factors in the decision-making process are the competitive and fiscal impact of the technology on the institution. To ensure that the technology is a good "fit," decision makers must consider its impact on the institution's corporate vision, philosophy and culture, goals (both long- and short-term), organizational structure, and ability to appropriately provide service to its clientele.

To make a fully informed decision, the institution should consider using a multidisciplinary approach to the assessment, soliciting the views of appropriate nonclinical staff as well as the clinical staff who will use the technology. For example, a representative of the biomedical department, an engineer, the risk manager, and the purchasing officer can bring valuable insights to the discussion. The biomedical representative likely would be aware of training and credentialing associated with successful use of the new technology or procedure, and also would be familiar with the technology's byproducts and the manner in which they should be disposed. The engineer would be familiar with the physical plant's capabilities to accommodate the technology—for example, whether the facility's ventilation and electrical capacity were adequate. The purchasing officer would understand the impact of the technology purchase on the organization's fiscal health. The risk manager would provide valuable insights about what potential risks might result from new adaptations of accepted procedures, how to anticipate potential problems and prevent their occurrence, and whether the facility's insurance would cover losses related to the new technology.

The risk manager also should be involved in the assessment of the fiscal impact of new technology, including its impact on operations. One of the major factors to be evaluated is whether to buy, lease, or enter into a consignment arrangement. These options carry a host of ramifications, including:

- Short- and long-term fiscal or payback implications.
- Potential staff requirements and responsibility to meet personnel training needs (both initial and ongoing).
- Regulatory mandates where responsibility for compliance may hinge on which party actually owns the piece of technology.

Simply because a procedure or piece of technology carries risks is no reason to forego its purchase; likewise, simply because it is new is no reason to obtain it. Prudent weighing of all factors involved requires the risk manager's special skills in knowing how to anticipate potential problems—and how to best avoid or deal with them.

ONGOING TECHNOLOGY MANAGEMENT CONCERNS

Managing the use of technology in health care settings requires a coordinated effort that integrates the expertise of a number of individuals and/or departments. The risk manager should be a central figure in this management effort. The challenge of managing technology can be expected to grow as health care delivery systems change and encompass more diverse sites of care and geographic locales. However, certain basic concerns are likely to remain. For risk management, these include:

- Staff training and education in the use of equipment and procedures.
- Policies and procedures regarding the maintenance, surveillance, and disposal of biomedical equipment.
- Compliance with regulations governing biomedical devices and equipment.

A systematic technology management process ensures that an institution uses its resources to benefit its patient base, meets applicable regulatory edicts, and reduces the likelihood of adverse outcomes and liability exposure. The management process may vary with the type and complexity of both the technology and the facility, but should include appropriate risk management systems and structures to identify and resolve problems generated by the technology in use.

Role of Staff Training in Technology Management

Staff training is crucial to the successful management of the risk exposure inherent in technology use. The institution should be prepared to meet the full spectrum of training needs, from initial training in the use and support of a piece of new equipment, to in-service "refresher" types of training, to individualized remedial training to correct any problems that arise. Training should be made available to not only clinical users but also to engineering personnel and others responsible for equipment maintenance and/or calibration.

In planning training, the institution should not overlook educational materials and services provided by manufacturers, which can broaden its training resources. In addition, it should ensure that the method of training is appropriate to the training objectives. In many cases, the preferred training method is hands-on demonstration and practice with actual equipment. However, interactive computer-assisted instruction (CAI) can be equally effective for learning some types of material. Where necessary, testing and/or certification may be indicated to demonstrate the acquisition of a certain base of knowledge.

Maintenance and Surveillance of Biomedical Equipment

Effective maintenance and surveillance of biomedical equipment can help control potential risk. Issues for risk management to consider include:

- Disposable versus reused products.
- "Modified" products.
- Handling of product recalls.
- Equipment brought in from outside the facility.

For the most part, institutional policies, procedures, and protocols dictate the day-to-day mechanics of handling technology. The answers to less routine management questions depend on an institution's unique circumstances and thus may vary from institution to institution. For example, one institution may prohibit reuse of disposable items or internal modification of products because of the level of potential risk exposure, whereas another may determine that if an opened but unused product can be reprocessed without being a hazard to patient safety, the risks are acceptable. As more health care facilities affiliate and link services, the need to review internal policies for consistency will increase. One of the challenges that integrated delivery systems (IDSs) face is providing a consistent level of care to patients across their network. This need for consistency extends to care involving the use of biomedical technology and medical equipment.

A mechanism to respond to product recalls also should be part of an institution's technology management program. Because the first notice of recall can come from a variety of departments—purchasing, biomedical engineering, safety, risk management, administration—there should be a centralized point of institutional accountability that ensures information is properly disseminated. The next steps of the process depend on the product's location—on-site, off-site, or implanted in a patient of the facility. IDSs may have a corporate protocol that specifies the role to be played by component facilities in this process.

Potential risks also are associated with equipment brought into a facility from outside sources, either formally through consignment or informally by clinicians, sales representatives, or patients who use a particular piece of technology in their home. Because these situations carry risk, it is essential that they be covered by the facility's technology management program.

Some manufacturers of medical devices furnish most of their products to health care facilities and/or individuals under consignment. This method of distribution is common for implantation devices, such as pacemakers and prostheses. In a consignment, ownership and control of the device remains with the original owner (in this case, its manufacturer) until such time that it is taken for use by a particular individual. In most circumstances, the manufacturer retains ownership and control even if it stores the device on location at the institution, because the manufacturer's representative can remove or replace stock without the institution's consent, and because the facility does not actually incur costs for purchase until the time the device is taken from the current consignment for patient use. Generally, consignments involve some type of contractual agreement. The institution should ensure that such an agreement clearly delineates the roles and responsibilities of "both sides" relative to the technology involved.

Today, technology and sophisticated medical devices are found in a variety of locations away from the traditional acute care hospital site. In addition, patients or their families may be taught to use facility-owned equipment as part of their plan of care. The lack of a direct accountability and/or relationship between these users and the risk manager can hamper the effectiveness of institutional technology management programs. Site-specific involvement in the development of the program and ongoing refinement as delivery mechanisms evolve may offer one mechanism for garnering additional support from these groups.

Disposal of Biomedical Equipment

Disposal concerns fall into two general categories: (1) the sale, donation, or abandonment of a facility's equipment to another entity, group, or individual; and (2) acquisition by the facility of a castoff from someone else. Although it may seem altruistic to pass on unneeded or outmoded equipment to others, the institution must evaluate the medicolegal issues and potential risk exposures that could arise should something adverse subsequently be allegedly linked to the piece of equipment.

Although specific cases revolving around this issue have yet to emerge, there are nevertheless potential risk exposure issues to be considered. For example:

- The selling or donating entity could find itself being considered part of the distribution chain, with a potential for product liability exposure.

- Issues such as the existing condition of the equipment, its remaining useful life, and warranty concerns may emerge for parties on both sides of the transaction.

- Donation versus sale may be a factor in how the equipment recycling and/or transfer is viewed, if something adverse subsequently occurs.

- The corporate structure in a health care delivery system may encourage or limit such transfers within its organization.

Presently, there are national and international groups that sponsor and/or facilitate the recycling of medical equipment and independent transfers and donations that occur, such as Recovered Medical Equipment for the Developing World (REMEDY), Resources International, Helen Keller International, and the Albert Schweitzer Foundation of America. Sharing of resources and recycling should not be prohibited; however, assessment of the pros and cons of the particular situation is called for to avoid unwanted or unrecognized liability exposure.

············

DIVERGENT VIEWS ON THE REUSE/REPROCESS ISSUE

There continues to be a lack consensus on the issue of reuse or reprocessing of medical devices. (The term "reuse" involves a device both previously used on a patient and then repackaged and reprocessed for subsequent use on another individual. The term "reprocessing" is used when device packaging has been opened, the device not actually used on a patient, and then is reprocessed.) Not surprisingly, manufacturers of medical devices labeled as "single use" oppose both reuse and reprocessing, while proponents cite waste avoidance and cost savings for the health care system as a beneficial outcome of reuse and/or reprocessing. Neither the Joint Commissions on Accreditation of Healthcare Organizations (JCAHO) nor the Centers for Disease Control and Prevention (CDC) prohibit reuse or reprocessing, leaving health care entities to make their own decisions.

In the past, the Food and Drug Administration (FDA) has taken the position that its existing policies (such as those making hospitals that reprocess single-use devices responsible for their actions, and requiring commercial reprocessors to comply with FDA regulations regarding good manufacturing practices) provide adequate public protection. The FDA has also noted a lack of data linking adverse patient outcomes to reuse of single-use medical devices.[1] Even a review and analysis of published clinical studies by ECRI, a nonprofit health services research agency, concluded that "there is no clear evidence that reuse of single-use medical devices is either safe or unsafe for patients."[2]

With continued growth in the number of entities doing or interested in reprocessing and the complexity of devices being considered for reprocessing, the FDA announced in late 1999 that it would propose a new strategy on reuse of single-use devices. Under consideration is a regulatory approach taking into account the specifics of the device, how complex the reprocessing needs to be, and the potential for infection or other patient harm from use of a reprocessed device. A companion oversight and enforcement process would also be developed by the FDA based on categorization of commonly reprocessed devices as low, moderate, or high risk.[3]

FDA has said that action on the reuse issue is a priority for the agency in 2000. However, until clear guidance becomes available from external sources, health care entities will need to make their decision on reprocessing and reuse based on a thorough cost and benefit analysis of their own particular care setting, patient population, medical device usage and costs, and staff time and resources available for reprocessing and reuse. The potential implications of patient injury resulting in adverse media exposure or litigation should also be considered as part of this analysis.

One way to approach the issue of whether to reuse and/or reprocess is through use of a decision tree model (see Figure 27.1). This detailed model makes it clear that the decision to reuse or reprocess is more complex that it might appear on the surface. The initial decision about whether to proceed with reuse and reprocessing should be

FIGURE 27.1. Decision Tree for Evaluating Single-Use Devices for Reuse

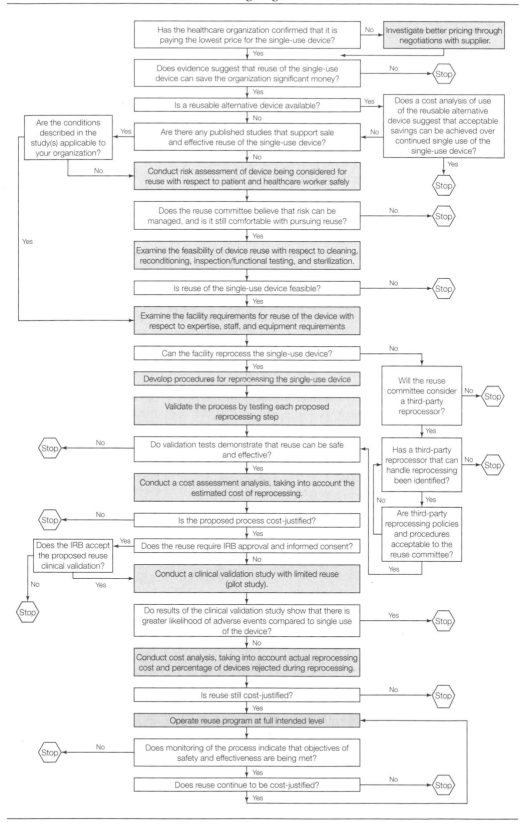

Source: Reprinted with permission from ECRI, copyright 1997. Taken from *Reuse of Single-Use Medical Devices: Making Informed Decisions,* pp.44–45. www.ecri.org

viewed as only the first step in an ongoing process an entity must demonstrate if it is to fulfill the duty to provide safe and appropriate medical care to its patients. An ongoing commitment of committee monitoring time and staff resources should also be anticipated, as the reuse and reprocessing issue will continue to evolve and options could change in the future.

....

WHEN BIOMEDICAL TECHNOLOGY ISSUES BRING AN OUTSIDER CALLING

With their potential for areas of inconsistent external regulatory approaches and overlapping responsibilities, patient- or employee-related problems involving biomedical technology can present the perfect opportunity for an external regulator or accreditation representative to visit an institution. Whether it's the institution's licensing entity, or the delegated reviewer for a state or federal regulator that arrives on the doorstep, having a compliance plan and process in place can help make the experience less traumatic.

With the advent of corporate compliance programs (see Chapter 20 on corporate compliance), risk managers have another opportunity to contribute their expertise, and should keep abreast of regulatory changes in relevant areas. Exhibit 27.1 offers tips to use in dealing with regulatory issues and can be useful in helping broaden the understanding of the regulatory forces increasingly prevalent in today's health care settings. The information in Exhibit 27.2 on shaping the role of risk management to cope with outside

---

EXHIBIT 27.1.   Tips for Coping with Regulatory Issues

1. Try to understand what the goal of the legislation is.
   - One problem is that what comes out at the end of a legislative journey may bear little resemblance to the original goal.
   - Use the "legislative history" (composed of committee reports and other background material) to help provide interpretation.

2. Review the statute and/or regulation with the goal in mind.
   - How does the goal fit in with individual or institutional purposes?
   - Will you choose to interpret the statute and/or regulation broadly or narrowly?
   - What are the costs/benefits of compliance versus challenge? Be aware that courts are generally reluctant to interfere with the legislative and regulatory processes.

3. Note areas where terms are undefined or subject to differing interpretations.
   - These areas may allow you to make reasonable interpretations (either broader or narrower), which may be more favorable in a particular situation. Be sure to substantiate the rationale used in such situations and apply criteria uniformly.

4. Establish appropriate systems to handle the particular regulatory issue in a consistent manner.
   - Identify lines of responsibility and accountability for the issue.
   - Provide education and/or training as necessary.
   - Build feedback loops into the systems.

5. Continue to monitor regulatory issues for subsequent revisions which may necessitate changes in the existing internal systems.
   - Revisions may require revisiting one or more of the "tips."

Source: The Risk Management Foundation of the Harvard Medical Institutions, 101 Main Street, Cambridge, MA 02142. Used with permission.

EXHIBIT 27.2.   Ten Tips for Coping with Inspections

Have a plan in advance!

1. Identify an individual to be responsible for interface with the agency. Designate an alternative backup.
2. Verify the inspector's credentials:
   - Notice of inspection.
   - Identify which inspector is team leader.
   - Review nature and scope of visit.
3. Identify staff and institutional locations involved and notify appropriate management personnel.
4. Gather institutional "inspection team." Team might include:
   - Administrative representative.
   - Risk manager.
   - Legal office representative.
   - Photographer.
   - Technical personnel.
5. Accompany the inspectors.
6. Consider beforehand how you will respond to possible requests by inspectors:
   - Employee interviews.
   - Review and/or copying of documents.
   - Evaluation and/or removal of equipment.
7. Plan your own "paper trail" of the visit:
   - Document inspection.
   - Document individual roles.
   - List items reviewed, copied, released, and so on.
   - If they photograph, you should also.
   - Debrief following visit.
8. At the completion of the visit, find out when you can expect written findings and to whom they will be sent.
9. Submit a written response to the findings if indicated.
10. Keep in mind:
    - You need not offer an agency information beyond the stated scope of the visit.
    - Reports generated by the agency in its inspection are not protected documents.

Source: The Risk Management Foundation of the Harvard Medical Institutions, 101 Main Street, Cambridge, MA 02142. Used with permission.

inspections should be adapted to work within the framework of the corporate compliance plan adopted by the institution.

....

CONCLUSION

Successful management of biomedical technology will continue to be an operational challenge in the health care delivery system. Although fundamental operational processes and structures will remain the backbone of biomedical technology risk management in health care settings, programs must be flexible, farsighted, and open to consideration of innovative options if they are to flourish in this continually changing health care climate.

Endnotes

1. Letter from FDA to Health Industry Manufacturers Association, July 1998.
2. ECRI, *Special Report: Reuse of Single-Use Medical Devices: Making Informed Decisions,* 1997, p. 1.
3. See the FDA Web site at www.fda.gov/cdrh/reuse for latest information.

Suggested Readings

Berry, D. "Medical Technology Risks: Looking Beyond the Obvious." *Journal of Healthcare Risk Management, 13*(4), Fall 1993, pp. 36–42.

ECRI, *Special Report: Reuse of Single-Use Medical Devices: Making Informed Decisions,* 1997.

Food and Drug Administration Web site www.fda.gov

Joint Commission on Accreditation of Healthcare Organizations Web site www.jcaho.org

Lamb-Mechanick, D., and McDonald, C. "How to Successfully Manage an External Agency Inspection." *Journal of Healthcare Risk Management, 14*(1), Winter 1994, pp. 20–28.

Parsons, M. "The Dilemma Over Reprocessing Single-Use Medical Devices." *Journal of Healthcare Risk Management, 18*(4), Fall 1998, pp. 54–61.

Solomon, R. "Medical Devices: A Risk Management Perspective." *Journal of Healthcare Risk Management, 13*(4), Fall 1993, pp. 4–13.

28

Ethics and Patient Care

Sheila Cohen Zimmet

This chapter is intended to provide the reader with an understanding of the ethics and law affecting everyday patient care issues, particularly those that are the most difficult to resolve—decisions to withhold or withdraw medical treatment and experimentation on human subjects. It is hoped that an understanding of the relevant bioethical and legal principles will assist the risk manager in reducing legal exposures by promoting communication among health care providers, patients, and their families as to available treatment options and the benefits and burdens of each. All too often risk management issues arise because patients or their family members or surrogates[1] are uncomfortable about treatment decisions that have been made either with or without their participation; they feel they have been the subject of experimentation without their knowledge; or they simply are not comfortable deciding to forego further treatment because they think it may not be the "right" thing to do.

If the families or surrogates of patients with terminal, incurable illnesses were counseled and understood the benefits and burdens of treatment and understood that it is ethically permissible to withhold futile care, or perhaps preferable when the burdens of treatment outweigh the benefits of that treatment, there would be far less suspicion and even hostility in intensive care units. It is important that patients and their families understand and believe that treatment recommendations are made on the basis of burdens and benefits to the patient, not to the managed care system. It is the rare family dispute or stalemate over treatment options for a terminally ill patient that cannot be resolved by having the health care providers, family members or other surrogates, and religious and ethics consultants together in one room, openly discussing the ethically permissible options, including the option of no further treatment.

Appendix 28.1 on page 656 contains basic ethics and regulatory documents that are useful reference tools for the risk manager. The emphasis is on ethics because that is the source of the law in this area. For example, the legal concept of patient self-determination that is recognized in judicial opinions and codified into law derives from the ethical principle of respect for autonomy that is defined below, as does the law applicable to research on human subjects.

············

ETHICAL PRINCIPLES AND MORAL OBLIGATIONS

The relationships between health care providers and their patients and families are guided by certain basic ethical principles and the morally binding obligations that are derived from those principles. The basic ethical principles that are most relevant to clinical bioethics are described as follows:

1. Beneficence, which creates an obligation to benefit patients and other persons and to further their welfare and interests.

2. A principle of respect for patients' autonomy.*

3. Nonmaleficence, which asserts an obligation to prevent harm or, if risks of harm must be taken, to minimize those risks.

4. Justice, which is relevant to fairness of access to health care and to issues of rationing at the bedside.

The morally binding obligations between patient and clinician, or other health care provider, that derive from these principles are:

• To respect the patient's privacy and maintain a process that protects confidentiality.

• To communicate honestly about all aspects of the patient's diagnosis, treatment, and prognosis.

• To determine whether the patient is capable of sharing in decision making.

• To conduct an ethically valid process of informed consent throughout the relationship.

The concepts of doing good (beneficence), avoiding harm (nonmaleficence), privacy, confidentiality, and justice that are central to these ethical principles and moral obligations were recognized in the Oath of Hippocrates set forth in Appendix 28.5.

············

RESEARCH

In 1990, Executive Editor Dr. Marcia Angell of the *New England Journal of Medicine* reiterated the journal's position that only research conducted in accordance with the rights of human subjects would be published. The results of unethical research would not be published, regardless of scientific merit.

> There are three reasons for our position. First, the policy of publishing only ethical research, if generally applied, would deter unethical work. . . . Furthermore, any other policy would tend to lead to more unethical work. . . . Second, denying publication even when the ethical violations are minor protects the principle of the

---

* Fletcher and others, "Clinical Ethics: History, Content, and Resources," pp. 3–17, 10, in Fletcher, *Introduction to Clinical Ethics*, University Publishing Group, 1995.

primacy of the research subject. If small lapses were permitted we would become inured to them, and this would lead to larger violations. And finally, refusal to publish unethical work serves notice to society at large that even scientists do not consider science the primary measure of a civilization. Knowledge, although important, may be less important to a decent society than the way it is obtained.[3]

The primacy of the human subject of which Dr. Angell wrote is the central concept of the modern system of human subject protection in biomedical research. It has its roots in the basic ethical principles of respect for persons, beneficence, and justice, the hallmarks of the 1979 report of the National Commission for the Protection of Human Subjects in Biomedical and Behavioral Research, known as the Belmont Report, which described the basic ethical principles upon which all biomedical and behavioral research should be based. (See Appendix 28.1 for more on the Belmont Report.) The Belmont Report was not the first to address these important concepts in the context of human research. In developing its report, the National Commission looked to the principles enunciated in the Nuremberg Code, developed during the Nuremberg War Crime Trials as a set of standards to judge the conduct of those physicians and scientists who had conducted biomedical research on imprisoned populations and for whom the results of that research took priority over the human subjects themselves. (See Appendix 28.6 for more on the Nuremberg Code.) The commission also looked to the Declaration of Helsinki, adopted by the World Medical Assembly in 1964 and revised in 1975 as recommendations to guide medical doctors in biomedical research involving human subjects. (See Appendix 28.2 on page 668 for more on the Declaration of Helsinki.)

The three basic ethical concepts of the Belmont Report, and the current regulations governing research on human subjects, are defined in the report as follows:

- *Respect for persons* means a recognition of the personal dignity and autonomy of individuals, and special protection of those persons with diminished autonomy . . . an affirmative obligation to protect vulnerable populations.

- *Beneficence* involves an obligation to maximize benefits and minimize risks of harm (nonmaleficence).

- *Justice* requires a fair distribution of the benefits and burdens of research.

Adherence to these basic ethical concepts ensures that the disadvantaged are not used as research subjects for the benefit of the advantaged and that social progress resulting from human research does not justify overriding the rights of the individual subject.[4]

The Belmont Report (see Appendix 28.1) distinguished between research and practice in discussing which activities require special review. *Practice* includes interventions designed to enhance the well-being of a patient through either diagnosis or treatment and that have a reasonable expectation of success. *Research* was defined as "an activity designed to test a hypothesis, permit conclusions to be drawn, and thereby to develop or contribute to generalizable knowledge (expressed, for example, in theories, principles, and statements of relationships)." A departure from standard practice or the institution of a new treatment was not viewed as research. However, the commission recommended that new procedures should be made part of formal research protocols in order to evaluate safety and efficacy.

Following publication of the Belmont Report, both the Department of Health, Education and Welfare (DHEW; now the Department of Health and Human Services, DHHS) and the Food and Drug Administration (FDA) strengthened their human subject protections, increasing but not altering the role of the Institutional Review Boards (IRBs). The

DHHS human research regulations, including IRB requirements, are codified at Code of Federal Regulations Title 45, Part 46 (including the Federal Policy or "Common Rule" followed by all federal agencies that sponsor research). (See *On the Protection of Human Subjects* in Appendix 28.3 on page 673.) FDA regulations on human research are codified at Code of Federal Regulations Title 21 Parts 50 (informed consent), 56 (Institutional Review Boards), 312 (Investigational New Drug Application), 812 (Investigational Device Exemptions), and 860 (Medical Device Classification Procedures).

Each health care institution that receives federal funding for human research from a department or agency covered by the Federal Policy or "Common Rule," or that is subject to FDA regulation, must have one or more IRBs with authority to review, require modification of, approve, or disapprove the research. The IRB may be established by the institution or, less often, may be an independent IRB under contract to the institution to provide IRB services. A document assuring compliance with human subject protections must be negotiated between the institution and DHHS before DHHS-funded research may be conducted. The document, known as an *assurance,* may be for a single project or, more often, may be a *multiple project assurance.* Applicable regulations are codified at 45 CFR 46.103. DHHS and FDA have the authority to conduct compliance inspections of institutions engaged in research, including the activities of IRBs, and to halt or restrict federally funded research if institutions are found out of compliance with human subject protections. For example, an institution found to be out of compliance may have its multiple project assurance restricted or revoked.

The federal research requirements are founded on respect for the autonomy of the research subject evidenced by stringent informed consent requirements, the protection of vulnerable populations, the absence of coercion, and the reasonable balance of benefits and burdens of the proposed research for the individual subject, not for society at large. An individual's decision not to participate in research may not in any way affect the ability of the individual to receive medical care to which the individual otherwise would be entitled. It is the role of the IRBs to review and monitor the conduct of research and to educate the faculty about the proper conduct of research. A discussion of the role of the IRBs and recent regulatory activity in this area follows.

INSTITUTIONAL REVIEW BOARDS

For Dr. Gary B. Ellis, Ph.D., director of the Office for Protection from Research Risks (OPRR),[5] the relationship between subject and researcher is one based on trust, and that trust must be respected:

> In the final analysis, research investigators, research institutions, and federal regulators are stewards of a trust agreement with the people who are research subjects. For research subjects who are safeguarded by the federal regulations, we have a system in place that (1) minimizes the potential for harm, (2) enables and protects individual, autonomous choice, and (3) promotes the pursuit of new knowledge. By doing so, we protect the rights and welfare of our fellow citizens who make a remarkable contribution to the common good by participating in research studies. We owe them our best effort.[6]

It is the role of the IRBs to safeguard that trust, and to assess research in terms of risks and benefits, the adequacy of informed consent, the adequacy of safeguards to protect the privacy and confidentiality of subjects,[7] and the equitable selection of subjects (is inclusion of vulnerable populations appropriate? are minorities and women of child-bearing potential adequately represented, or is a clear and compelling reason for their exclusion provided?). The IRB must (1) identify risks of the research, (2) determine that the risks will be minimized to the extent possible, (3) identify probable benefits of the research, (4) determine that the risks are reasonable in relation to the benefits to the subject and the knowledge to be gained, (5) ensure that research subjects are provided with an accurate and fair description of the risks, discomforts, and anticipated benefits, (6) ensure that research subjects are offered the opportunity to voluntarily accept or reject participation in the research, or discontinue participation, without coercion or fear of reprisal or deprivation of treatment to which the patient is otherwise entitled,[8] and (7) determine intervals of periodic review and, when necessary, determine the adequacy of mechanisms for monitoring data collection.

In a time of declining clinical revenue there may be increased pressure from principal investigators and administrators to cut corners and speed up the approval process for sponsored research. Such an approach places the welfare of the researcher and the research institution ahead of the welfare of the subject and is inconsistent with the ethical foundation of biomedical research and the regulatory framework derived therefrom. The results of research, whether the return is scientific recognition or financial reward, or both, may never take priority over the research subject. Furthermore, recent compliance activities of OPRR have shown that an approach to research that minimizes protection of the subject can ultimately prove to be very costly, both in revenue and reputation.

OPRR and FDA compliance activities increased significantly in 1999 and are expected to continue at increased intensity, signaling an increase in public interest in the ethical and procedural propriety of biomedical research. Listed below are some of the deficiencies cited as the bases for adverse actions taken against research institutions in 1999:

- Failure to consider safeguards to protect the rights and welfare of vulnerable subjects.

- Failure to document that the IRB reviewed and approved protocol changes in research prior to initiation of the protocol.

- Failure to document required findings at convened meetings of the IRB.

- Failure to conduct annual review of protocols; late annual review of protocols.

- Expedited review of protocols and protocol changes by expedited procedures that exceeded the limitations of expedited review.

- Approval of consent forms that failed to adequately describe reasonably foreseeable risks and discomforts and failed to explain who to contact for answers to questions.

- Unsatisfactory education plan to ensure that all IRB members, IRB staff, and all research investigators are educated about the requirements for the protection of human subjects.

- Allowing individuals with conflicts of interest (such as, the director and assistant director of Office of Grants and Contracts) to serve as voting IRB members.

- Taking action at IRB meetings when there was no quorum present.

- IRB minutes were not sufficiently detailed to show the basis for requiring changes in or disapproving research, and did not include a written summary of the discussion of controverted issues and their resolution.

- Approval of protocols contingent on substantive modifications without requiring additional review.

- Failure of IRB to conduct ongoing monitoring activities.

- Failure of the institution's oversight system to prevent research protocols from being initiated prior to IRB review and approval.

- Failure to document the specific findings required for IRB approval of research involving children (see *Protection of Human Subjects,* p. 684 of Appendix 28.4).

- Required elements of informed consent were omitted from consent forms.

- IRB membership lacked diversity to promote respect for its advice and counsel in safeguarding the rights and welfare of human subjects; membership must include non-scientific member and a member with expertise in the particular subject matter at issue (such as a mental health professional).

At a conference held in Washington, D.C., on October 21, 1999, "IRBs in Crisis: Institutional Responses," cosponsored by the Association of American Medical Colleges and Public Responsibility in Medicine and Research, OPRR Director Dr. Gary Ellis emphasized the responsibilities of IRBs to educate investigators and monitor the conduct of research, as well as the institutional responsibility to provide adequate training to the IRB members themselves. In issuing its required corrective action notification to one institution, OPRR noted that the education plan should include periodic didactic or interactive training for IRB members, periodic in-service training, and institutional certification for investigators. Ultimately the expectation is an increase in institutional support for the IRB infrastructure, including a research compliance officer function that many institutions are implementing for continuous monitoring of research activities.

Each research institution should review its own policies and procedures and its IRB records for compliance with federal regulations to determine whether it is vulnerable to an adverse action on the basis of the above criteria. For example, does the institution have an internal monitoring system to verify that investigators are complying with research protocols, that all subjects have signed consent forms, that IRB policies and procedures satisfy federal requirements, that minutes of IRB meetings are adequate, or that training of IRB members and investigators meet the regulatory compliance emphasis on education that Dr. Ellis appeared to signal? The risk manager should assess whether and how he or she or a research compliance officer or similar official could assist the institution in meeting its obligations in the area of human biomedical research. If compliance is not adequate, the loss to the institution, in terms of funding and reputation, could be enormous. Institutions must be vigilant in their review and monitoring of the activities of the IRB and investigators. If they are not, they can expect that OPRR will be.

· · · · · · · · · · · ·

PATIENT SELF-DETERMINATION ACT

The federal Patient Self-Determination Act of 1990 (PSDA) [P.L. No.101-508, codified at 42 U.S.C. Sections 1395(c)(c) and 1396(a)(a), Section 4206 of the Omnibus Reconciliation Act of 1990] requires institutional health care providers who receive federal funds, such as hospitals, nursing homes, hospices, and home health agencies, to inform patients of their right to make health care decisions.[9] This includes the right to accept or refuse treatment and the right to formulate *advance directives* (commonly referred to as living wills and durable powers of attorney). The law requires hospitals to provide written information to each adult patient at the time of admission concerning the institution's policies for implementing the patient's right to make health care decisions. Advance directives are documents formulated in advance of a period of incapacity in which the individual executing the document sets forth his or her wishes with respect to treatment options and/or delineates who should serve as surrogate decision maker in the event the individual becomes unable to express his or her own wishes.

The PSDA sets forth a mechanism for educating patients about their constitutional right to self-determination that was recognized by the U.S. Supreme Court in its first "right to die" case, *Cruzan v. Director, Missouri Department of Health,* 497 U.S. 261, 110 S.Ct. 2841, 111 L.Ed. 2nd 224, 58 U.S.L.W. 4916 (1990). In *Cruzan,* the court held that the due process clause of the Fourteenth Amendment to the U.S. Constitution gives to each person a constitutionally protected liberty interest in refusing unwanted medical treatment, thereby giving constitutional status to the ethical principle of respect for patients' autonomy. In this context, the right of autonomy and the right of self-determination are synonymous.

If a person is incapacitated, and thereby unable to make and/or express an informed and voluntary choice to accept or refuse treatment, he or she does not lose the right. Rather, the individual's right to make the treatment choices must be exercised by a surrogate. The Durable Power of Attorney for Health Care is the mechanism by which an individual designates who will serve in that surrogate role.[10]

The Patient Self-Determination Act focuses on the right of competent patients to determine and direct the future course of their medical treatment. The act seeks to avoid a situation in which the wishes of a patient are not clearly known and/or there is no legally valid surrogate decision maker available to advise the health care provider what the patient would want under the circumstances. The PSDA does not alter the common law concept of next of kin, nor does it affect substantive state law regarding surrogate decision making. It sets forth a mechanism whereby patients learn about their rights under state law to make treatment decisions and execute advance directives and are offered the opportunity to take advantage of those rights. Under the PSDA, health care institutions must:

1. Provide written information to all adult patients upon admission or initial receipt of care about their rights to make decisions, including the right to accept or refuse treatment, and to execute advance directives, and the written policies of the institution that respect these rights.

2. Comply with state law regarding the rights of patients to make treatment decisions and execute advance directives.

3. Educate the staff and the community about these issues.

4. Document in the patient's medical record whether the individual has executed an advance directive.[11]

5. Not condition the provision of care on the execution of an advance directive.

Even when an individual has executed an advance directive that sets forth the individual's wishes regarding the acceptance or refusal of treatment, including life-sustaining treatment, it is not always clear to the health care provider or the surrogate what the individual intended under particular clinical circumstances. For example, did the individual who specified that life-sustaining treatment be withdrawn in the event of a terminal, incurable disease, or persistent vegetative state, intend that mechanical ventilation and artificial hydration and nutrition be withheld, or just the respirator? If the individual did not address a persistent vegetative state, but addressed only a terminal, incurable disease, did he or she intend the treatment choice to be applied to the former and would state law permit the withdrawal of treatment under these circumstances? State laws differ on the interpretation of when a person is in a terminal, incurable condition so as to invoke the terms of an advance directive. State law may require that an advance directive specify its applicability to a persistent vegetative state in order for the treatment options to apply. Advance directives should specifically address treatment options under these different clinical presentations.

In light of recent court decisions upholding the rights of pregnant women to refuse invasive medical treatment, even if the treatment is deemed lifesaving or otherwise beneficial to the fetus, regardless of gestational age (see *Baby Boy Doe v. Mother Doe,* 260 Ill. App.3d 392, 632 N.E.2d 326 [Ill. App. 1994]; In re A.C., 573 A.2d 1235 [D.C. App. 1990]), advance directives that address the treatment wishes of pregnant patients should be considered, particularly for institutions providing tertiary maternal-fetal medicine or perinatology services. The directive should address the provision of life-sustaining treatments for the mother, including artificial hydration and nutrition, and CPR, both before and subsequent to viability of the fetus, and whether or not the patient authorizes a C-section if it is deemed to be in the best interest of the unborn child. The directive should provide for authorization or refusal of these treatments, and specify that failure to provide the treatments may result in the death of, or harm to, the baby.

∙∙∙∙∙∙∙∙∙∙∙∙

DO NOT RESUSCITATE—WITHHOLDING OR WITHDRAWING TREATMENT

It has been said that the paradox of modern medicine is that treatment intended to save life often ends up prolonging the agony of dying.[12] Whether it is due to the clinician's or family's refusal to accept defeat, or the mistaken belief that the withholding or withdrawing of treatment is ethically abhorrent, or the simple discomfort that accompanies a discussion of the inevitability of death, this issue continues to be one of the most difficult and frequent ethical dilemmas confronting health care providers. It is not a new issue. In his treatise *The Art,* Hippocrates defined the purpose of medicine to include the following:

> . . . to do away with the sufferings of the sick, to lessen the violence of their diseases, and to refuse to treat those who are over-mastered by their diseases realizing in such cases that medicine is powerless. . . . Whenever therefore a man suffers an illness which is too strong for the means at the disposal of medicine he surely must not expect that it can be overcome by medicine.[13]

(See also Appendix 28.5 for the Hippocratic Oath.)

It is clear from the prior discussions of patient autonomy and self-determination that there is a constitutionally protected and ethically sanctioned right to refuse treatment, including life-sustaining treatment. What is important to understand and to put into practice is a process for determining and implementing the treatment decision when the patient cannot make or communicate the choice.

Frameworks for decision making can be found in the 1983 report of the President's Commission for the Study of Ethical Problems in Medicine and Biomedical and Behavioral Research, entitled *A Report on the Ethical, Medical, and Legal Issues in Treatment Decisions: Deciding to Forego Life-Sustaining Treatment* (referred to here as Report),[14] and in the Hastings Center's *Guidelines on the Termination of Life-Sustaining Treatment and the Care of the Dying* (1987).[15]

It is important for health care providers to understand that their patients have the right to make health care decisions based on their own values and experiences, and to have their decisions respected. The first step is determining the appropriate decision maker. The competent adult patient, one who is able to understand the significance of his or her decisions and communicate those decisions effectively, has the right to make the decision. It is the patient's right to balance benefits and burdens, and decide whether to proceed with treatment, based on that patient's own values and personal preferences. As the commission noted, "The moral claim of autonomy supports acting in accord with the patient's preference."[16] It is ethically appropriate to reject treatment when the burdens of treatment outweigh the benefits of treatment, or when treatment is deemed to be futile.

If the patient is unable to make or communicate the decision, it is the role of the appropriate surrogate decision maker to advise the health care provider what the patient would want. This is known as the Substituted Judgment Test. It is not the role of the surrogate to make an independent judgment of what is in the best interest of the patient called (the Best Interest Test), unless a decision could not otherwise be reached, such as where the patient has never had the capacity to form his or her own judgment (such as a newborn). In general, unless the health care provider has reason to believe that the treatment choice of a legally valid surrogate is inconsistent with that which the patient would make or has set forth in an advance directive, the decision of a surrogate should control.

In the event of a disagreement between clinician and surrogate as to the appropriate course of action, internal mechanisms to resolve the matter, including ethics committee consultation, should be attempted. Resorting to a judicial forum to resolve disagreements between health care providers and decision makers regarding the appropriate course of treatment for an incapacitated patient is generally unproductive. "[D]ecision making about life-sustaining care is rarely improved by resort to the courts."[17] It is not the role of the court to substitute its own judgment for the informed substituted judgment of the surrogate, nor will it substitute its own best interest determination for that of the surrogate. Unless the health care provider can establish that the decision of a surrogate to either require or refuse medical treatment, including a *do not resuscitate order* (DNR), constitutes either neglect or abuse, thereby invoking the authority of the state to protect innocent third parties,[18] courts will not override the decisions of legally valid surrogates. For further example, refer to *In re Baby K,* 16 F.3d 590 (4th Cir. 1994), affirming the district court ruling that required the hospital to provide full pulmonary resuscitation for an anencephalic infant when requested by the mother, even though the care was deemed futile and outside the scope of the standard of care. The Court of Appeals held that a refusal by emergency room personnel to provide stabilizing resuscitative measures to the infant, if brought to the emergency department in respiratory distress, would constitute a violation of the requirements of the Emergency Medical Treatment and Active Labor Act (EMTALA), 42 USC sec. 1395dd, that all persons seeking emergency medical treatment receive an appropriate medical screening and stabilizing treatment. The lower court ruling that it could not substitute its judgment for the judgment of the mother, who was the legally valid surrogate, was affirmed. The court also stated, with respect to the moral dilemma facing the health care providers who thought the provision of futile care to Baby K was inappropriate,

> . . . to the extent that [Virginia law] exempts treating physicians in participating hospitals from providing care they consider medically or ethically inappropriate, it is preempted . . . it does not allow the physicians treating Baby K to refuse to provide her with respiratory support.[19]

In a recent decision by the D.C. Court of Appeals, the court recognized that parents have a fundamental constitutional right to the care, custody, and management of their child that is not absolute, but must yield to the best interest and well-being of the child. In the case of *In Re K.I.,* nos. 98-FS-1683 and 98-FS-1767, 1700-1742 (D.C. App. 1999), the parents disagreed as to the appropriateness of resuscitation for their terminally ill child and the medical evidence established that resuscitation would be futile and would result only in pain and discomfort. The lower court concluded that the mother's refusal to consent to the issuance of the DNR order was unreasonably contrary to the child's well being. In affirming the lower court ruling that a DNR order should be entered, the Court of Appeals held

> . . . in cases involving minor respondents who have lacked, and will forever lack, the ability to express a preference regarding their course of medical treatment . . . and where the parents do not speak with the same voice but disagree as to the proper course of action, the best interests of the child standard shall be applied to determine whether to issue a DNR. . . .[20]

··········

CONCLUSION

It is recommended that the risk manager become familiar with the ethical issues discussed in this chapter and promote their dissemination to the health care providers who deal with these difficult issues on a regular basis. An ethics consultation mechanism should be made available at any time it is needed to assist health care providers, patients and their families reach health care decisions that can be implemented with the knowledge that all parties are comfortable with the decision.[21]

Endnotes

1. "Surrogate" refers to the individual who is legally authorized to make health care decisions on behalf of a patient who is unable to make or communicate decisions on his or her own behalf due to incapacity. The surrogate may be the common law next-of-kin or an individual designated by the patient in a Durable Power of Attorney for Health Care to make health care decisions for the patient in the event of temporary or permanent incapacity.

2. The term "autonomy" derives from the Greek *autos,* meaning self, and *nomos,* meaning rule or law—self-rule, or self-law. The concept of autonomy is associated with privacy, free choice, and personal responsibility for one's choices. Beauchamp, T. L., and Walters, L. *Contemporary Issues in Bioethics.* Wadsworth Publishing Company, 1994, p. 22.

3. Angell, M., M.D. "The Nazi Hypothermia Experiments and Unethical Research Today." *New England Journal of Medicine 322,* May 17, 1990, 146–64.

4. Jonsen, A. R. "The Ethics of Research with Human Subjects: A Short History." In A. R. Jonsen, R. M. Veatch, and L. Walters, *Source Book in Bioethics,* Georgetown Georgetown University Press, 1998, pp. 5–9.

5. OPRR is the federal office with human subject research oversight authority. A relocation is pending from National Institutes of Health (NIH) to the Office of Public Health and Science, DHHS. The move is seen as a means of increasing OPRR visibility and access to the Secretary.

6. Ellis, G., Ph.D., "Protecting the Rights and Welfare of Human Research Subjects." *Academic Medicine 74*(9), Sept. 1999, pp. 1008–1009.

7. For particularly sensitive research, such as genetic research where there is a concern that the release of information regarding the results of research could lead to discrimination in the workplace or in the ability of individuals who are found to be carriers of genetic diseases to obtain life or health insurance, there is a mechanism for protection of data. The Secretary of DHHS, or his or her designee, may issue a Certificate of Confidentiality "to protect the privacy of research subjects by withholding their identities from all persons not connected with the research. . . . Persons so authorized to protect the privacy of such individuals may not be compelled in any Federal, State, or local civil, criminal, administrative, legislative, or other proceedings to identify such individuals." 42 USC sec.241(d), Section 301(d) of the Public Health Service Act, Protection of Identity, Research Subjects. For further information, call NIH at (301) 402-7221.

8. For example, is the amount of compensation offered so excessive as to be coercive? Is the subject compensated only at the end of a six-month clinical trial so that the subject cannot withdraw during the trial without loss of all compensation, or is the compensation prorated for the amount of time the subject participated?

9. Subsequent to enactment of the PSDA, which is enforceable only against institutions that participate in Medicare and Medicaid, the Joint Commission on Accreditation of Health Care Organizations (JCAHO) amended its accreditation standards to require all health care organizations that are accredited by the JCAHO to maintain mechanisms for informing patients about their rights to self-determination and honoring those rights. See *JCAHO Comprehensive Accreditation Manual for Hospitals: The Official Handbook,* Patient Rights and Organizational Ethics, RI.1.2.4 (1999).

10. This chapter focuses on the rights of patients and their surrogates to make treatment decisions. It is important for the risk manager to understand that the law presumes consent for medically necessary medical treatment in a medical emergency when consent of the patient cannot be obtained and a surrogate is not available. If the patient's life or future health may be jeopardized if treatment is not instituted immediately, and the treatment has not been refused by the patient, consent will be presumed.

11. While not specified in the law, institutional policies should include a mechanism by which the patient's advance directive is included in the medical record so it is readily available and known to the clinicians before implementation is needed. An advance directive in a safe at the bank or in a drawer at home is not helpful to the health care provider when a decision must be made immediately.

12. Hite, C. A., and others. "Death and Dying." In Fletcher, and others, *Introduction to Clinical Ethics,* University Publishing Group, 1995, pp. 115–138.

13. Hippocrates. *The Art.* In *Hippocrates.* vol. II. Jones W.H.S. (trans.). Loeb Classical Library, Harvard University Press, Cambridge (1967), cited in E. D. Pellegrino, M.D., "Withholding and Withdrawing Treatments: Ethics at the Bedside." *Clinical Neurosurgery 35,* 1989, pp. 164–184.

14. Many of the developments during the decade subsequent to the issuance of this report that shape the law and ethics of patient self-determination as it is understood today, grow out of recommendations of the commission, including, for example, state enactment of legislation providing for advance directives, and the growth of institutional ethics committees to provide consultation to clinicians and patients and their families on issues that have life-or-death consequences for patients.

15. An excellent summary of the decision-making process described in the ethics literature, including reference to the reports by the Hastings Center and the President's Commission, may be found in Dr. Carol Taylor's 1990 article "Ethics in Health Care and Medical Technologies." *Theoretical Medicine 11,* 1990, pp. 111–124.

16. *Report,* at p. 245.

17. *Report,* at p. 247.

18. For example, courts have traditionally ordered medically necessary and appropriate treatment of children over parental objections. See *In the Matter of Adam L.,* 111 Wash. L. Rep. 25 (D.C. Sup. Ct., Jan. 6, 1983). However, in instances where treatment is not likely to preserve life, or is itself highly risky, judges generally will not substitute their judgment for the judgment of patients.

19. *Ibid.*

20. *In the Matter of Adam L.,* p. 1,714. The standard for deciding whether and under what circumstances it is legally permissible to forego life-sustaining treatment for critically ill or handicapped newborns is set forth in the 1984 amendments to the Child Abuse Prevention and Treatment and Adoption Reform Act of 1974. 42 USCA sec. 5102 (3)(A) and (3)(B). Regulations are found at 45 CFR Part 1340. In general, it is not permissible to withhold medically indicated treatment except under certain specified conditions:

    The infant is chronically and irreversibly comatose;

    The provision of such treatment would merely prolong dying;

    Treatment would not be effective in ameliorating or correcting all of the infant's life threatening conditions;

    Treatment would otherwise be futile in terms of the survival of the infant;

    Treatment would be virtually futile in terms of the survival of the infant and the treatment itself would be inhumane.

    To the extent the law prohibits the withholding of artificial hydration and nutrition from these infants, that portion of the law is inconsistent with the Supreme Court holding in *Cruzan* that affords constitutional status to the right to withhold medical treatment, including artificial hydration and nutrition, which was the medical treatment at issue in that case.

21. Whether an ethics consult note should be entered in the patient record, and what its contents should be, are the subject of ongoing debate in the ethics literature. I generally favor a consult note placed in the chart that outlines the ethical dilemma and sets forth the recommendations regarding whether the various treatment options that are available to the practitioner and the patient or surrogate are ethically or morally permissible under the clinical circumstances, but does not dictate treatment decisions. A record of the consult must be maintained, and, in the event of litigation, it is discoverable whether it is in the patient chart or in the records of the consult service. In other words, the content of the note, in terms of objectivity and recognition that the ultimate decision makers are the physician and his or her patient and surrogate, is more important than its location.

Suggested Readings

Federal Policy or "Common Rule,"
www.grants.nih.gov/grants/oprr/humansubjects/45CFR46.htm

Office for Protection from Research Risks, *Protecting Human Research Subjects—Institutional Review Board Guidebook,* 1993,
www.nih.gov/grants/oprr/irb/irb_guidebook.htm

Office for Protection from Research Risks, *OPRR Human Subjects Protections,*
grants.nih.gov/grants/oprr/library_human.htm

Office for Protection from Research Risks, *Human and Animal Protection,*
grants.nih.gov/grants/oprr/oprr.htm

Food and Drug Administration, *Information Sheets, Guidance for Institutional Review Boards and Clinical Investigators*, 1998 Update, www.fda.gov/oha/irb/toc.htm
fda.gov/oc/oha/irb/toc2.html

U.S. Agency for International Development, *How to Interpret the Federal Policy for the Protection of Human Subjects or "Common Rule,"*
www.info.usaid.gov/pop_health/commonrule.htm

U.S. Department of Energy, Office of Science, Office of Biological and Environmental Research, *Protecting Human Subjects,*
www.er.doe.gov/production/ober/humsubj/hsindex/html

President's Commission for the Study of Ethical Problems in Medicine and Biomedical and Behavioral Research, *Deciding to Forego Life-Sustaining Treatment: A Report on the Ethical, Medical, and Legal Issues in Treatment Decisions*, U.S. Government Printing Office, Mar. 1983.

Guidelines on the Termination of Life-Sustaining Treatment and the Care of the Dying, The Hastings Center, Indiana University Press, 1987.

American Medical Association, Current Opinions of the Council on Ethical and Judicial Affairs, www.ama-assn.org/apps/pf_online/pf....HTM&nxt_pol=policy/CEJA

American Medical Association, Principles of Medical Ethics (1980), www.ama-assn.org/ethic/pome.htm

American Nurses Association

    Code for Nurses with Interpretive Statements

    Position Statement on Nursing Care and Do-Not-Resuscitate Decisions

    Position Statement on Nursing and the Patient Self-Determination Act

    Position Statement on Foregoing Artificial Nutrition and Hydration

www.NursingWorld.org

or contact the American Nurses Association in Washington, D.C., at (202) 554-4444.

Appendix 28.1

The Belmont Report (April 18, 1979)

DEPARTMENT OF HEALTH, EDUCATION, AND WELFARE

Office of the Secretary

Protection of Human Subjects

Belmont Report: Ethical Principles and Guidelines for the Protection of Human Subjects of Research, Report of the National Commission for the Protection of Human Subjects of Biomedical and Behavioral Research.

AGENCY: Department of Health, Education, and Welfare.

ACTION: Notice of Report for Public Comment.

SUMMARY: On July 12, 1974, the National Research Act (Pub. L. 93-348) was signed into law, thereby creating the National Commission for the Protection of Human Subjects of Biomedical and Behavioral Research. One of the charges to the Commission was to identify the basic ethical principles that should underlie the conduct of biomedical and behavioral research involving human subjects and to develop guidelines which should be followed to assure that such research is conducted in accordance with those principles. In carrying out the above, the Commission was directed to consider: (i) the boundaries between biomedical and behavioral research and the accepted and routine practice of medicine, (ii) the role of assessment of risk-benefit criteria in the determination of the appropriateness of research involving human subjects, (iii) appropriate guidelines for the selection of human subjects for participation in such research and (iv) the nature and definition of informed consent in various research settings.

The Belmont Report attempts to summarize the basic ethical principles identified by the Commission in the course of its deliberations. It is the outgrowth of an intensive four-day period of discussions that were held in February 1976 at the Smithsonian Institution's Belmont Conference Center supplemented by the monthly deliberations of the Commission that were held over a period of nearly four years. It is a statement of basic ethical principles and guidelines that should assist in resolving the ethical problems that surround the conduct of research with human subjects. By publishing the Report in the Federal Register, and providing reprints upon request, the Secretary intends that it may be made readily available to scientists, members of Institutional Review Boards, and Federal employees. The two-volume

Appendix, containing the lengthy reports of experts and specialists who assisted the Commission in fulfilling this part of its charge, is available as DHEW Publication No. (OS) 78-0013 and No. (OS) 78-0014, for sale by the Superintendent of Documents, U.S. Government Printing Office, Washington, D.C. 20402.

Unlike most other reports of the Commission, the Belmont Report does not make specific recommendations for administrative action by the Secretary of Health, Education, and Welfare. Rather, the Commission recommended that the Belmont Report be adopted in its entirety, as a statement of the Department's policy. The Department requests public comment on this recommendation.

National Commission for the Protection of Human Subjects of Biomedical and Behavioral Research

Members of the Commission

Kenneth John Ryan, M.D., Chairman, Chief of Staff, Boston Hospital for Women.

Joseph V. Brady, Ph.D., Professor of Behavioral Biology, Johns Hopkins University.

Robert E. Cooke, M.D., President, Medical College of Pennsylvania.

Dorothy I. Height, President, National Council of Negro Women, Inc.

Albert R. Jonsen, Ph.D., Associate Professor of Bioethics, University of California at San Francisco.

Patricia King, J.D., Associate Professor of Law, Georgetown University Law Center.

Karen Lebacqz, Ph.D., Associate Professor of Christian Ethics, Pacific School of Religion.

*David W. Louisell, J.D., Professor of Law, University of California at Berkeley.

Donald W. Seldin, M.D., Professor and Chairman, Department of Internal Medicine, University of Texas at Dallas.

Eliot Stellar, Ph.D., Provost of the University and Professor of Physiological Psychology, University of Pennsylvania.

*Robert H. Turtle, LL.B., Attorney, VomBaur, Coburn, Simmons & Turtle, Washington, D.C.

* Deceased.

Table of Contents

BELMONT REPORT

Ethical Principles and Guidelines for Research Involving Human Subjects

Scientific research has produced substantial social benefits. It has also posed some troubling ethical questions. Public attention was drawn to these questions by reported abuses of human subjects in biomedical experiments, especially during the Second World War. During the Nuremberg War Crime Trials, the Nuremberg code was drafted as a set of standards for judging physicians and scientists who had conducted biomedical experiments on concentration camp prisoners. This code became the prototype of many later codes[1] intended to assure that research involving human subjects would be carried out in an ethical manner.

The codes consist of rules, some general, others specific, that guide the investigators or the reviewers of research in their work. Such rules often are inadequate to cover complex situations; at times

[1] Since 1945, various codes for the proper and responsible conduct of human experimentation in medical research have been adopted by different organizations. The best known of these codes are the Nuremberg Code of 1947, the Helsinki Declaration of 1964 (revised in 1975), and the 1971 Guidelines (codified into Federal Regulations in 1974) issued by the U.S. Department of Health, Education, and Welfare Codes for the conduct of social and behavioral research have also been adopted, the best known being that of the American Psychological Association, published in 1973.

they come into conflict, and they are frequently difficult to interpret or apply. Broader ethical principles will provide a basis on which specific rules may be formulated, criticized and interpreted.

Three principles, or general prescriptive judgments, that are relevant to research involving human subjects are identified in this statement. Other principles may also be relevant. These three are comprehensive, however, and are stated at a level of generalization that should assist scientists, subjects, reviewers, and interested citizens to understand the ethical issues inherent in research involving human subjects. These principles cannot always be applied so as to resolve beyond dispute particular ethical problems. The objective is to provide an analytical framework that will guide the resolution of ethical problems arising from research involving human subjects.

This statement consists of a distinction between research and practice, a discussion of the three basic ethical principles, and remarks about the application of these principles.

A. Boundaries Between Practice and Research

It is important to distinguish between biomedical and behavioral research, on the one hand, and the practice of accepted therapy on the other, in order to know what

activities ought to undergo review for the protection of human subjects of research. The distinction between research and practice is blurred partly because both often occur together (as in research designed to evaluate a therapy) and partly because notable departures from standard practice are often called "experimental" when the terms "experimental" and "research" are not carefully defined.

For the most part, the term "practice" refers to interventions that are designed solely to enhance the well-being of an individual patient or client and that have a reasonable expectation of success. The purpose of medical or behavioral practice is to provide diagnosis, preventive treatment or therapy to particular individuals.[2] By contrast, the term "research"

---

[2]Although practice usually involves interventions designed solely to enhance the well-being of a particular individual, interventions are sometimes applied to one individual for the enhancement of the well-being of another (e.g., blood donation, skin grafts, organ transplants) or an intervention may have the dual purpose of enhancing the well-being of a particular individual, and, at the same time, providing some benefit to others (e.g., vaccination, which protects both the person who is vaccinated and society generally). The fact that some forms of practice have elements other than immediate benefit to the individual receiving an intervention, however, should not confuse the general distinction between research and practice. Even when a procedure applied in practice may benefit some other person, it remains an intervention designed to enhance the well-being of a particular individual or groups of individuals; thus, it is practice and need not be reviewed as research.

---

designates an activity designed to test an hypothesis, permit conclusions to be drawn, and thereby to develop or contribute to generalizable knowledge (expressed, for example, in theories, principles, and statements of relationships). Research is usually described in a formal protocol that sets forth an objective and a set of procedures designed to reach that objective.

When a clinician departs in a significant way from standard or accepted practice, the innovation does not, in and of itself, constitute research. The fact that a procedure is "experimental," in the sense of new, untested or different, does not automatically place it in the category of research. Radically new procedures of this description should, however, be made the object of formal research at an early stage in order to determine whether they are safe and effective. Thus, it is the responsibility of medical practice committees, for example, to insist that a major innovation be incorporated into a formal research project.[3]

Research and practice may be carried on together when research is designed to

---

[3]Because the problems related to social experimentation may differ substantially from those of biomedical and behavioral research, the Commission specifically declines to make any policy determination regarding such research at this time. Rather, the Commission believes that the problem ought to be addressed by one of its successor bodies.

evaluate the safety and efficacy of a therapy. This need not cause any confusion regarding whether or not the activity requires review; the general rule is that if there is any element of research in an activity, that activity should undergo review for the protection of human subjects.

B. Basic Ethical Principles

The expression "basic ethical principles" refers to those general judgments that serve as a basic justification for the many particular ethical prescriptions and evaluations of human actions. Three basic principles, among those generally accepted in our cultural tradition, are particularly relevant to the ethics of research involving human subjects: the principles of respect for persons, beneficence and justice.

1. *Respect for Persons*— Respect for persons incorporates at least two ethical convictions: first, that individuals should be treated as autonomous agents, and second, that persons with diminished autonomy are entitled to protection. The principle of respect for persons thus divides into two separate moral requirements: the requirement to acknowledge autonomy and the requirement to protect those with diminished autonomy.

An autonomous person is an individual capable of deliberation about personal goals and of acting under the direction of such deliberation. To respect autonomy is to give weight to autonomous persons' considered opinions and choices while refraining from obstructing their actions unless they are clearly detrimental to others. To show lack of respect for an autonomous agent is to repudiate that person's considered judgments, to deny an individual the freedom to act on those considered judgments, or to withhold information necessary to make a considered judgment, when there are no compelling reasons to do so.

However, not every human being is capable of self-determination. The capacity for self-determination matures during an individual's life, and some individuals lose this capacity wholly or in part because of illness, mental disability, or circumstances that severely restrict liberty. Respect for the immature and the incapacitated may require protecting them as they mature or while they are incapacitated.

Some persons are in need of extensive protection, even to the point of excluding them from activities which may harm them; other persons require little protection beyond making sure they undertake activities freely and with awareness of possible adverse consequences. The extent of protection afforded should depend upon the risk of harm and the likelihood of benefit. The judgement that any individual lacks autonomy should be periodically re-evaluated and will vary in different situations.

In most cases of research involving human subjects, respect for persons demands that subjects enter into the research voluntarily and with adequate information. In some situations, however, application of the principle is not obvious. The involvement of prisoners as subjects of research provides an instructive example. On the one hand, it would seem that the principle of respect for persons requires that prisoners not be deprived of the opportunity to volunteer for research. On the other hand, under prison conditions they may be subtly coerced or unduly influenced to engage in research activities for which they would not otherwise volunteer. Respect for persons would then dictate that prisoners be protected. Whether to allow prisoners to "volunteer" or to "protect" them presents a dilemma. Respecting persons, in most hard cases, is often a matter of balancing competing claims urged by the principle of respect itself.

2. *Beneficence*—Persons are treated in an ethical manner not only by respecting their decisions and protecting them from harm, but also by making efforts to secure their well-being. Such treatment falls under the principle of beneficence. The term "beneficence" is often understood to cover acts of kindness or charity that go beyond strict obligation. In this

document, beneficence is understood in a stronger sense, as an obligation. Two general rules have been formulated as complementary expressions of beneficent actions in this sense: (1) do not harm and (2) maximize possible benefits and minimize possible harms.

The Hippocratic maxim "do no harm" has long been a fundamental principle of medical ethics. Claude Bernard extended it to the realm of research, saying that one should not injure one person regardless of the benefits that might come to others. However, even avoiding harm requires learning what is harmful; and, in the process of obtaining this information, persons may be exposed to risk of harm. Further, the Hippocratic Oath requires physicians to benefit their patients "according to their best judgment." Learning what will in fact benefit may require exposing persons to risk. The problem posed by these imperatives is to decide when it is justifiable to seek certain benefits despite the risks involved, and when the benefits should be foregone because of the risks.

The obligations of beneficence affect both individual investigators and society at large, because they extend both to particular research projects and to the entire enterprise of research. In the case of particular projects, investigators and members of their institutions are obliged to give forethought

to the maximization of benefits and the reduction of risk that might occur from the research investigation. In the case of scientific research in general, members of the larger society are obliged to recognize the longer term benefits and risks that may result from the improvement of knowledge and from the development of novel medical, psychotherapeutic, and social procedures.

The principle of beneficence often occupies a well-defined justifying role in many areas of research involving human subjects. An example is found in research involving children. Effective ways of treating childhood diseases and fostering healthy development are benefits that serve to justify research involving children—even when individual research subjects are not direct beneficiaries. Research also makes it possible to avoid the harm that may result from the application of previously accepted routine practices that on closer investigation turn out to be dangerous. But the role of the principle of beneficence is not always so unambiguous. A difficult ethical problem remains, for example, about research that presents more than minimal risk without immediate prospect of direct benefit to the children involved. Some have argued that such research is inadmissible, while others have pointed out that this limit would rule out much research promising great benefit to

children in the future. Here again, as with all hard cases, the different claims covered by the principle of beneficence may come into conflict and force difficult choices.

3. *Justice*—Who ought to receive the benefits of research and bear its burdens? This is a question of justice, in the sense of "fairness in distribution" or "what is deserved." An injustice occurs when some benefit to which a person is entitled is denied without good reason or when some burden is imposed unduly. Another way of conceiving the principle of justice is that equals ought to be treated equally. However, this statement requires explication. Who is equal and who is unequal? What considerations justify departure from equal distribution? Almost all commentators allow that distinctions based on experience, age, deprivation, competence, merit and position do sometimes constitute criteria justifying differential treatment for certain purposes. It is necessary, then, to explain in what respects people should be treated equally. There are several widely accepted formulations of just ways to distribute burdens and benefits. Each formulation mentions some relevant property on the basis of which burdens and benefits should be distributed. These formulations are (1) to each person an equal share, (2) to each person according to individual need, (3) to each

person according to individual effort, (4) to each person according to societal contribution, and (5) to each person according to merit.

Questions of justice have long been associated with social practices such as punishment, taxation and political representation. Until recently these questions have not generally been associated with scientific research. However, they are foreshadowed even in the earliest reflections on the ethics of research involving human subjects. For example, during the 19th and early 20th centuries the burdens of serving as research subjects fell largely upon poor ward patients, while the benefits of improved medical care flowed primarily to private patients. Subsequently, the exploitation of unwilling prisoners as research subjects in Nazi concentration camps was condemned as a particularly flagrant injustice. In this country, in the 1940's, the Tuskegee syphilis study used disadvantaged, rural black men to study the untreated course of a disease that is by no means confined to that population. These subjects were deprived of demonstrably effective treatment in order not to interrupt the project, long after such treatment became generally available.

Against this historical background, it can be seen how conceptions of justice are relevant to research involving human subjects. For example, the selection of research subjects needs to be scrutinized in order to determine whether some classes (e.g., welfare patients, particular racial and ethnic minorities, or persons confined to institutions) are being systematically selected simply because of their easy availability, their compromised position, or their manipulability, rather than for reasons directly related to the problem being studied. Finally, whenever research supported by public funds leads to the development of therapeutic devices and procedures, justice demands both that these not provide advantages only to those who can afford them and that such research should not unduly involve persons from groups unlikely to be among the beneficiaries of subsequent applications of the research.

C. Applications

Applications of the general principles to the conduct of research leads to consideration of the following requirements: informed consent, risk/benefit assessment, and the selection of subjects of research.

1. *Informed Consent*— Respect for persons requires that subjects, to the degree that they are capable, be given the opportunity to choose what shall or shall not happen to them. This opportunity is provided when adequate standards for informed consent are satisfied.

While the importance of informed consent is unquestioned, controversy prevails over the nature and possibility of an informed consent. Nonetheless, there is widespread agreement that the consent process can be analyzed as containing three elements: information, comprehension, and voluntariness.

Information. Most codes of research establish specific items for disclosure intended to assure that subjects are given sufficient information. These items generally include: the research procedure, their purposes, risks and anticipated benefits, alternative procedures (where therapy is involved), and a statement offering the subject the opportunity to ask questions and to withdraw at any time from the research. Additional items have been proposed, including how subjects are selected, the person responsible for the research, etc.

However, a simple listing of items does not answer the question of what the standard should be for judging how much and what sort of information should be provided. One standard frequently invoked in medical practice, namely the information commonly provided by practitioners in the field or in the locale, is inadequate since research takes place precisely when a common understanding does not exist. Another standard, currently popular in malpractice law, requires the practitioner to reveal the information that reasonable persons would wish to know in order to make a decision regarding their care. This, too, seems insufficient since the research subject, being in essence a volunteer, may wish to know considerably more about risks gratuitously undertaken than do patients who deliver themselves into the hand of a clinician for needed care. It may be that a standard of "the reasonable volunteer" should be proposed: the extent and nature of information should be such that persons, knowing that the procedure is neither necessary for their care nor perhaps fully understood, can decide whether they wish to participate in the furthering of knowledge. Even when some direct benefit to them is anticipated, the subjects should understand clearly the range of risk and the voluntary nature of participation.

A special problem of consent arises where informing subjects of some pertinent aspect of the research is likely to impair the validity of the research. In many cases, it is sufficient to indicate to subjects that they are being invited to participate in research of which some features will not be revealed until the research is concluded. In all cases of research involving incomplete disclosure, such research is justified only if it is clear that (1) incomplete disclosure is truly necessary to accomplish the goals of the research, (2) there are no undisclosed risks to subjects that are more than minimal, and (3) there is an adequate

plan for debriefing subjects, when appropriate, and for dissemination of research results to them. Information about risks should never be withheld for the purpose of eliciting the cooperation of subjects, and truthful answers should always be given to direct questions about the research. Care should be taken to distinguish cases in which disclosure would destroy or invalidate the research from cases in which disclosure would simply inconvenience the investigator.

Comprehension. The manner and context in which information is conveyed is as important as the information itself. For example, presenting information in a disorganized and rapid fashion, allowing too little time for consideration or curtailing opportunities for questioning, all may adversely affect a subject's ability to make an informed choice.

Because the subject's ability to understand is a function of intelligence, rationality, maturity and language, it is necessary to adapt the presentation of the information to the subject's capacities. Investigators are responsible for ascertaining that the subject has comprehended the information. While there is always an obligation to ascertain that the information about risk to subjects is complete and adequately comprehended, when the risks are more serious, that obligation increases. On

occasion, it may be suitable to give some oral or written tests of comprehension.

Special provision may need to be made when comprehension is severely limited—for example, by conditions of immaturity or mental disability. Each class of subjects that one might consider as incompetent (e.g., infants and young children, mentally disabled patients, the terminally ill and the comatose) should be considered on its own terms. Even for these persons, however, respect requires giving them the opportunity to choose to the extent they are able, whether or not to participate in research. The objections of these subjects to involvement should be honored, unless the research entails providing them a therapy unavailable elsewhere. Respect for persons also requires seeking the permission of other parties in order to protect the subjects from harm. Such persons are thus respected both by acknowledging their own wishes and by the use of third parties to protect them from harm.

The third parties chosen should be those who are most likely to understand the incompetent subject's situation and to act in that person's best interest. The person authorized to act on behalf of the subject should be given an opportunity to observe the research as it proceeds in order to be able to withdraw the subject from the research, if such action appears in the subject's best interest.

Voluntariness. An agreement to participate in research constitutes a valid consent only if voluntarily given. This element of informed consent requires conditions free of coercion and undue influence. Coercion occurs when an overt threat of harm is intentionally presented by one person to another in order to obtain compliance. Undue influence, by contrast, occurs through an offer of an excessive, unwarranted, inappropriate or improper reward or other overture in order to obtain compliance. Also, inducements that would ordinarily be acceptable may become undue influences if the subject is especially vulnerable.

Unjustifiable pressures usually occur when persons in positions of authority or commanding influence—especially where possible sanctions are involved—urge a course of action for a subject. A continuum of such influencing factors exists, however, and it is impossible to state precisely where justifiable persuasion ends and undue influence begins. But undue influence would include actions such as manipulating a person's choice through the controlling influence of a close relative and threatening to withdraw health services to which an individual would otherwise be entitled.

2. Assessment of Risks and Benefits.—The assessment of risks and benefits requires a careful arrayal of relevant data, including, in some cases, alternative ways of obtaining the benefits sought in the research. Thus, the assessment presents both an opportunity and a responsibility to gather systematic and comprehensive information about proposed research. For the investigator, it is a means to examine whether the proposed research is properly designed. For a review committee, it is a method for determining whether the risks that will be presented to subjects are justified. For prospective subjects, the assessment will assist the determination whether or not to participate.

The Nature and Scope of Risks and Benefits. The requirement that research be justified on the basis of a favorable risk/benefit assessment bears a close relation to the principle of beneficence, just as the moral requirement that informed consent be obtained is derived primarily from the principle of respect for persons. The term "risk" refers to a possibility that harm may occur. However, when expressions such as "small risk" or "high risk" are used, they usually refer (often ambiguously) both to the chance (probability) of experiencing a harm and the severity (magnitude) of the envisioned harm.

The term "benefit" is used in the research context to refer to something of positive value related to health or welfare. Unlike "risk," "benefit" is not a term that expresses probabilities. Risk is properly contrasted to probability of benefits, and benefits are properly contrasted with harms rather than risks of harm. Accordingly, so-called risk/benefit assessments are concerned with the probabilities and magnitudes of possible harms and anticipated benefits. Many kinds of possible harms and benefits need to be taken into account. There are, for example, risks of psychological harm, physical harm, legal harm, social harm and economic harm and the corresponding benefits. While the most likely types of harms to research subjects are those of psychological or physical pain or injury, other possible kinds should not be overlooked.

Risks and benefits of research may affect the individual subjects, the families of the individual subjects, and society at large (or special groups of subjects in society). Previous codes and Federal regulations have required that risks to subjects be outweighed by the sum of both the anticipated benefit to the subject, if any, and the anticipated benefit to society in the form of knowledge to be gained from the research. In balancing these different elements, the risks and benefits affecting the immediate research subject will normally carry special weight. On the other hand, interests other than those of the subject may on some occasions be sufficient by themselves to justify the risks involved in the research, so long as the subjects' rights have been protected. Beneficence thus requires that we protect against risk of harm to subjects and also that we be concerned about the loss of the substantial benefits that might be gained from research.

The Systematic Assessment of Risks and Benefits. It is commonly said that benefits and risks must be "balanced" and shown to be "in a favorable ratio." The metaphorical character of these terms draws attention to the difficulty of making precise judgments. Only on rare occasions will quantitative techniques be available for the scrutiny of research protocols. However, the idea of systematic, nonarbitrary analysis of risks and benefits should be emulated insofar as possible. This ideal requires those making decisions about the justifiability of research to be thorough in the accumulation and assessment of information about all aspects of the research, and to consider alternatives systematically. This procedure renders the assessment of research more rigorous and precise, while making communication between review board members and investigators less subject to misinterpretation, misinformation and conflicting judgments. Thus, there should first be a determination of the validity of the presuppositions of the research; then the nature, probability and magnitude of risk should be distinguished with as much clarity as possi-

ble. The method of ascertaining risks should be explicit, especially where there is no alternative to the use of such vague categories as small or slight risk. It should also be determined whether an investigator's estimates of the probability of harm or benefits are reasonable, as judged by known facts or other available studies.

Finally, assessment of the justifiability of research should reflect at least the following considerations: (i) Brutal or inhumane treatment of human subjects is never morally justified. (ii) Risks should be reduced to those necessary to achieve the research objective. It should be determined whether it is in fact necessary to use human subjects at all. Risk can perhaps never be entirely eliminated, but it can often be reduced by careful attention to alternative procedures. (iii) When research involves significant risk of serious impairment, review committees should be extraordinarily insistent on the justification of the risk (looking usually to the likelihood of benefit to the subject—or, in some rare cases, to the manifest voluntariness of the participation). (iv) When vulnerable populations are involved in research, the appropriateness of involving them should itself be demonstrated. A number of variables go into such judgments, including the nature and degree of risk, the condition of the particular

population involved, and the nature and level of the anticipated benefits. (v) Relevant risks and benefits must be thoroughly arrayed in documents and procedures used in the informed consent process.

3. Selection of Subjects.—Just as the principle of respect for persons finds expression in the requirement for consent, and the principle of beneficence in risk/benefit assessment, the principle of justice gives rise to moral requirements that there be fair procedures and outcomes in the selection of research subjects.

Justice is relevant to the selection of subjects of research at two levels: the social and the individual. Individual justice in the selection of subjects would require that researchers exhibit fairness: thus, they should not offer potentially beneficial research only to some patients who are in their favor or select only "undesirable" persons for risky research. Social justice requires that distinction be drawn between classes of subjects that ought, and ought not, to participate in any particular kind of research, based on the ability of members of that class to bear burdens and on the appropriateness of placing further burdens on already burdened persons. Thus, it can be considered a matter of social justice that there is an order of preference in the selection of classes of subjects (e.g., adults before children) and that some classes of potential subjects (e.g., the institutionalized mentally infirm or prisoners) may be involved as research subjects if at all, only on certain conditions.

Injustice may appear in the selection of subjects, even if individual subjects are selected fairly by investigators and treated fairly in the course of research. Thus injustice arises from social, racial, sexual and cultural biases institutionalized in society. Thus, even if individual researchers are treating their research subjects fairly, and even if IRBs are taking care to assure that subjects are selected fairly within a particular institution, unjust social patterns may nevertheless appear in the overall distribution of the burdens and benefits of research. Although individual

institutions or investigators may not be able to resolve a problem that is pervasive in their social setting, they can consider distributive justice in selecting research subjects.

Some populations, especially institutionalized ones, are already burdened in many ways by their infirmities and environments. When research is proposed that involves risks and does not include a therapeutic component, other less burdened classes of persons should be called upon first to accept these risks of research, except where the research is directly related to the specific conditions of the class involved. Also, even though public funds for research may often flow in the same directions as public funds for health care, it seems unfair that populations dependent on public health care constitute a pool of preferred research

subjects if more advantaged populations are likely to be the recipients of the benefits.

One special instance of injustice results from the involvement of vulnerable subjects. Certain groups, such as racial minorities, the economically disadvantaged, the very sick, and the institutionalized may continually be sought as research subjects, owing to their ready availability in settings where research is conducted. Given their dependent status and their frequently compromised capacity for free consent, they should be protected against the danger of being involved in research solely for administrative convenience, or because they are easy to manipulate as a result of their illness or socioeconomic condition.

[FR Doc. 90-12065 Filed 4-17-79; 8:45 am]

Appendix 28.2

The Helsinki Declarations of 1964, 1975

....

INTRODUCTION

It is the mission of the doctor to safeguard the health of the people. His knowledge and conscience are dedicated to the fulfillment of this mission.

The Declaration of Geneva of The World Medical Association binds the doctor with the words: "The health of my patient will be my first consideration" and the International Code of Medical Ethics which declares that "Any act or advice which could weaken physical or mental resistance of a human being may be used only in his interest."

Because it is essential that the results of laboratory experiments be applied to human beings to further scientific knowledge and to help suffering humanity, the World Medical Association has prepared the following recommendations as a guide to each doctor in clinical research. It must be stressed that the standards as drafted are only a guide to physicians all over the world. Doctors are not relieved from criminal, civil and ethical responsibilities under the laws of their own countries.

In the field of clinical research a fundamental distinction must be recognized between clinical research in which the aim is essentially therapeutic for a patient, and the clinical research, the essential object of which is purely scientific and without therapeutic value to the person subjected to the research.

I. Basic Principles

1. Clinical research must conform to the moral and scientific principles that justify medical research and should be based on laboratory and animal experiments or other scientifically established facts.

2. Clinical research should be conducted only by scientifically qualified persons and under the supervision of a qualified medical man.

3. Clinical research cannot legitimately be carried out unless the importance of the objective is in proportion to the inherent risk to the subject.

4. Every clinical research project should be preceded by careful assessment of inherent risks in comparison to foreseeable benefits to the subject or to others.

5. Special caution should be exercised by the doctor in performing clinical research in which the personality of the subject is liable to be altered by drugs or experimental procedure.

II. Clinical Research Combined with Professional Care

1. In the treatment of the sick person, the doctor must be free to use a new therapeutic measure, if in his judgment it offers hope of saving life, reestablishing health, or alleviating suffering.

   If at all possible, consistent with patient psychology, the doctor should obtain the patient's freely given consent after the patient has been given a full explanation. In case of legal incapacity, consent should also be procured from the legal guardian; in case of physical incapacity the permission of the legal guardian replaces that of the patient.

2. The doctor can combine clinical research with professional care, the objective being the acquisition of new medical knowledge, only to the extent that clinical research is justified by its therapeutic value for the patient.

III. Non-Therapeutic Clinical Research

1. In the purely scientific application of clinical research carried out on a human being, it is the duty of the doctor to remain the protector of the life and health of that person on whom clinical research is being carried out.

2. The nature, the purpose and the risk of clinical research must be explained to the subject by the doctor.

3a. Clinical research on a human being cannot be undertaken without his free consent after he has been informed; if he is legally incompetent, the consent of the legal guardian should be procured.

3b. The subject of clinical research should be in such a mental, physical and legal state as to be able to exercise fully his power of choice.

3c. Consent should, as a rule, be obtained in writing. However, the responsibility for clinical research always remains with the research worker; it never falls on the subject even after consent is obtained.

4a. The investigator must respect the right of each individual to safeguard his personal integrity, especially if the subject is in a dependent relationship to the investigator.

4b. At any time during the course of clinical research the subject or his guardian should be free to withdraw permission for research to be continued.

   The investigator or the investigating team should discontinue the research if in his or their judgment, it may, if continued, be harmful to the individual.

∙∙∙∙∙∙∙∙∙∙∙∙

2. THE HELSINKI DECLARATION OF 1975

Introduction

It is the mission of the medical doctor to safeguard the health of the people. His *or her* knowledge and conscience are dedicated to the fulfillment of this mission.

The Declaration of Geneva of The World Medical Association binds the doctor with the words "The health of my patient will be my first consideration," and the International Code of Medical Ethics declares that "Any act or advice which could weaken physical or mental resistance of a human being may be used only in his interest."

The purpose of biomedical research involving human subjects must be to improve diagnostic, therapeutic and prophylactic procedures and the understanding of the aetiology and pathogenesis of disease.

In current medical practice most diagnostic, therapeutic, or prophylactic procedures involve hazards. This applies a fortiori to biomedical research.

Medical progress is based on research which ultimately must rest in part on experimentation involving human subjects.

In the field of *biomedical* research a fundamental distinction must be recognized between *medical* research in which the aim is essentially *diagnostic or* therapeutic for a patient, and *medical* research, the essential object of which is purely scientific and without *direct diagnostic or* therapeutic value to the person subjected to the research.

Special caution must be exercised in the conduct of research which may affect the environment, and the welfare of animals used for research must be respected.

Because it is essential that the results of laboratory experiments be applied to human beings to further scientific knowledge and to help suffering humanity, The World Medical Association has prepared the following recommendations as a guide to every doctor in *biomedical* research *involving human subjects. They should be kept under review in the future.* It must be stressed that the standards as drafted are only a guide to physicians all over the world. Doctors are not relieved from criminal, civil and ethical responsibilities under the laws of their own countries.

I. Basic Principles

1. *Biomedical* research *involving human subjects* must conform to *generally accepted* scientific principles and should be based on *adequately* performed laboratory and animal experimentation *and on a thorough knowledge of the scientific literature.*

2. *The design and performance of each experimental procedure involving human subjects should be clearly formulated in an experimental protocol which should be transmitted to a specially appointed independent committee for consideration, comment and guidance.*

3. *Biomedical* research *involving human subjects* should be conducted only by scientifically qualified persons and under the supervision of a *clinically competent* medical *person. The responsibility for the human subject must always rest with a medically qualified person and never rest on the subject of the research, even though the subject has given his or her consent.*

4. *Biomedical* research involving human subjects cannot legitimately be carried out unless the importance of the objective is in proportion to the inherent risk to the subject.

5. Every *biomedical* research project *involving human subjects* should be preceded by careful assessment of *predictable* risks in comparison with foreseeable benefits to the subject or to others. *Concern for the interests of the subject must always prevail over the interests of science and society.*

6. *The right of the research subject to safeguard his or her integrity must always be respected. Every precaution should be taken to respect the privacy of the subject*

and to minimize the impact of the study on the subject's physical and mental integrity and on the personality of the subject.

7. *Doctors should abstain from engaging in research projects involving human subjects unless they are satisfied that the hazards involved are believed to be predictable. Doctors should cease any investigation if the hazards are found to outweigh the potential benefits.*

8. *In publication of the results of his or her research, the doctor is obliged to preserve the accuracy of the results. Reports of experimentation not in accordance with the principles laid down in this Declaration should not be accepted for publication.*

9. *In any research on human beings, each potential subject must be adequately informed of the aims, methods, anticipated benefits and potential hazards of the study and the discomfort it may entail. He or she should be informed that he or she is at liberty to abstain from participation in the study and that he or she is free to withdraw his or her consent to participation at any time. The doctor should then obtain the subject's freely given informed consent, preferably in writing.*

10. *When obtaining informed consent for the research project the doctor should be particularly cautious if the subject is in a dependent relationship to him or her or may consent under duress. In that case the informed consent should be obtained by a doctor who is not engaged in the investigation and who is completely independent of this official relationship.*

11. *In the case of legal incompetence, informed consent should be obtained from the legal guardian in accordance with national legislation. Where physical or mental incapacity makes it impossible to obtain informed consent, or when the subject is a minor, permission from the responsible relative replaces that of the subject in accordance with national legislation.*

12. *The research protocol should always contain a statement of the ethical considerations involved and should indicate that the principles enunciated in the present Declaration are complied with.*

II. Medical Research Combined with Professional Care (Clinical Research)

1. In the treatment of the sick person, the doctor must be free to use a new *diagnostic or* therapeutic measure, if in his *or her* judgment it offers hope of saving life, reestablishing health or alleviating suffering.

2. *The potential benefits, hazards and discomfort of a new method should be weighed against the advantages of the best current diagnostic and therapeutic methods.*

3. *In any medical study, every patient—including those of a control group, if any—should be assured of the best proven diagnostic and therapeutic method.*

4. *The refusal of the patient to participate in a study must never interfere with the doctor-patient relationship.*

5. *If the doctor considers it essential not to obtain informed consent, the specific reasons for this proposal should be stated in the experimental protocol for transmission to the independent committee.* (I, 2).

6. The doctor can combine medical research with professional care, the objective being the acquisition of new medical knowledge, only to the extent that medical research is justified by its *potential diagnostic or* therapeutic value for the patient.

III. Non-Therapeutic Biomedical Research Involving Human Subjects (Non-Clinical Biomedical Research)

1. In the purely scientific application of *medical* research carried out on a human being, it is the duty of the doctor to remain the protector of the life and health of that person on whom *biomedical* research is being carried out.

2. *The subjects should be volunteers—either healthy persons or patients for whom the experimental design is not related to the patient's illness.*

3. The investigator or the investigating team should discontinue the research if in his, *her or their* judgment it may, if continued, be harmful to the individual.

4. *In research on man, the interest of science and society should never take precedence over considerations related to the well-being of the subject.*

Appendix 28.3

On the Protection of Human Subjects: U.S. Department of Health, Education, and Welfare's Institutional Guide

Introduction. In 1971, the Department of Health, Education, and Welfare (DHEW), now known as the Department of Health and Human Services (HHS), issued institutional guidance designed to safeguard the rights and welfare of human subjects of federally funded medical research. This document expanded and formalized guidelines that the National Institutes of Health published in 1966 and revised in 1969. The policies in the DHEW document were also reviewed, and a revised version was published in the Code of Federal Regulations (45 CFR 46) in May 1974. These regulations, the 1974 version of the Guide, were likewise reviewed and revised—this time on the basis of recommendations from the National Commission for the Protection of Human Subjects of Biomedical and Behavioral Research (1974–1978)— and officially promulgated in 1981. The DHEW guidance document remains the bedrock of federal regulations governing the protection of human subjects in research.

Policy

Safeguarding the rights and welfare of human subjects involved in activities supported by grants or contracts from the Department of Health, Education, and Welfare is the responsibility of the institution which receives or is accountable to the DHEW for the funds awarded for the support of the activity. In order to provide for the adequate discharge of this institutional responsibility, it is the policy of the Department that no grant or contract for an activity involving human subjects shall be made unless the application for such support has been reviewed and approved by an appropriate institutional committee.

This review shall determine that the rights and welfare of the subjects involved are adequately protected, that the risks to an individual are outweighed by the potential benefits to him or by the importance of the knowledge to be gained, and that informed consent is to be obtained by methods that are adequate and appropriate.

Reprinted from *The Institutional Guide to DHEW Policy on Protection of Human Subjects.* DHEW Publication No. NIH 72-102, December 1, 1971 (Washington, D.C.: U.S. Government Printing Office, 1971), pp. 2–11.

In addition the committee must establish a basis for continuing review of the activity in keeping with these determinations.

The institution must submit to the DHEW, for its review, approval, and official acceptance, an assurance of its compliance with this policy. The institution must also provide with each proposal involving human subjects a certification that it has been or will be reviewed in accordance with the institution's assurance.

No grant or contract involving human subjects at risk will be made to an individual unless he is affiliated with or sponsored by an institution which can and does assume responsibility for the protection of the subjects involved.

Since the welfare of subjects is a matter of concern to the Department of Health, Education, and Welfare as well as to the institution, no grant or contract involving human subjects shall be made unless the proposal for such support has been reviewed and approved by an appropriate professional committee within the responsible component of the Department. As a result of this review, the committee may recommend to the operating agency, and the operating agency may require, the imposition of specific grant or contract terms providing for the protection of human subjects, including requirements for informed consent.

Applicability

A. General   This policy applies to all grants and contracts which support activities in which subjects may be at risk.

B. Subject   This term describes any individual who may be at risk as a consequence of participation as a subject in research, development, demonstration, or other activities supported by DHEW funds.

This may include patients; outpatients; donors of organs, tissues, and services; informants; and normal volunteers, including students who are placed at risk during training in medical, psychological, sociological, educational, and other types of activities supported by DHEW.

Of particular concern are those subjects in groups with limited civil freedom. These include prisoners, residents or clients of institutions for the mentally ill and mentally retarded, and persons subject to military discipline.

The unborn and the dead should be considered subjects to the extent that they have rights which can be exercised by their next of kin or legally authorized representatives.

C. At Risk   An individual is considered to be "at risk" if he may be exposed to the possibility of harm—physical, psychological, sociological, or other—as a consequence of any activity which goes beyond the application of those established and accepted methods necessary to meet his needs. The determination of when an individual is at risk is a matter of the application of common sense and sound professional judgement to the circumstances of the activity in question. Responsibility for this determination resides at all levels of institutional and departmental review. Definitive determination will be made by the operating agency.

D. Types of Risks and Applicability of the Policy
1. Certain risks are inherent in life itself, at the time and in the places where life runs its course. This policy is not concerned with the ordinary risks of public or private living, or

those risks associated with admission to a school or hospital. It is not concerned with the risks inherent in professional practice as long as these do not exceed the bounds of established and accepted procedures, including innovative practices applied in the interest of the individual patient, student or client.

Risk and the applicability of this policy are most obvious in medical and behavioral science research projects involving procedures that may induce a potentially harmful altered physical state or condition. Surgical and biopsy procedures; the removal of organs or tissues for study, reference, transplantation, or banking; the administration of drugs or radiation; the use of indwelling catheters or electrodes; the requirement of strenuous physical exertion; subjection to deceit, public embarrassment, and humiliation are all examples of procedures which require thorough scrutiny by both the Department of Health, Education, and Welfare and institutional committees. In general those projects which involve risk of physical or psychological injury require prior written consent.

2. There is a wide range of medical, social, and behavioral projects and activities in which no immediate physical risk to the subject is involved; e.g., those utilizing personality inventories, interviews, questionnaires, or the use of observation, photographs, taped records, or stored data. However, some of these procedures may involve varying degrees of discomfort, harassment, invasion of privacy, or may constitute a threat to the subject's dignity through the imposition of demeaning or dehumanizing conditions.

3. There are also medical and biomedical projects concerned solely with organs, tissues, body fluids, and other materials obtained in the course of the routine performance of medical services such as diagnosis, treatment and care, or at autopsy. The use of these materials obviously involves no element of physical risk to the subject. However, their use for many research, training, and service purposes may present psychological, sociological, or legal risks to the subject or his authorized representatives. In these instances, application of the policy requires review to determine that the circumstances under which the materials were procured were appropriate and that adequate and appropriate consent was, or can be, obtained for the use of these materials for project purposes.

4. Similarly, some studies depend upon stored data or information which was often obtained for quite different purposes. Here, the reviews should also determine whether the use of these materials is within the scope of the original consent, or whether consent can be obtained.

E. Established and Accepted Methods
Some methods become established through rigorous standardization procedures prescribed, as in the case of drugs or biologicals, by law or, as in the case of many educational tests, through the aegis of professional societies or nonprofit agencies. Acceptance is a matter of professional response, and determination as to when a method passes from the experimental stage and becomes "established and accepted" is a matter of judgement.

In determining what constitutes an established and accepted method, consideration should be given to both national and local standards of practice. A management procedure may become temporarily established in the routine of a local institution but still fail to win acceptance at the national level. A psychological inventory may be accepted nationally, but still contain questions which are disturbing or offensive to a local population. Surgical procedures which are established and accepted in one part of the country may be considered experimental in another, not due to inherent deficiencies, but because of the lack of proper facilities and trained personnel. Diagnostic procedures which are routine in the United States may pose serious hazards to an undernourished, heavily infected, overseas population.

If doubt exists as to whether the procedures to be employed are established and accepted, the activity should be subject to review and approval by the institutional committee.

F. Necessity to Meet Needs   Even if considered established and accepted, the method may place the subject at risk if it is being employed for purposes other than to meet the needs of the subject. Determination by an attending professional that a particular treatment, test, regimen, or curriculum is appropriate for a particular subject to meet his needs limits the attendant risks to those inherent in the delivery of services, or in training.

On the other hand, arbitrary, random, or other assignment of subjects to differing treatment or study groups in the interests of a DHEW supported activity, rather than in the strict interests of the subject, introduces the possibility of exposing him to additional risk. Even comparisons of two or more established and accepted methods may potentially involve exposure of at least some of the subjects to additional risks. Any alteration of the choice, scope, or timing of an otherwise established and accepted method, primarily in the interests of a DHEW activity, also raises the issue of additional risk.

If doubt exists as to whether the procedures are intended solely to meet the needs of the subject, the activity should be subject to review and approval by the institutional committee.

Institutional Review

A. Initial Review of Projects   1. Review must be carried out by an appropriate institutional committee. The committee may be an existing one, such as a board of trustees, medical staff committee, utilization committee, or research committee, or it may be specially constituted for the purpose of this review. Institutions may utilize subcommittees to represent major administrative or subordinate components in those instances where establishment of a single committee is impracticable or inadvisable. The institution may utilize staff, consultants, or both.

The committee must be composed of sufficient members with varying backgrounds to assure complete and adequate review of projects and activities commonly conducted by the institution. The committee's membership, maturity, experience, and expertise should be such as to justify respect for its advice and counsel. No member of an institutional committee shall be involved in either the initial or continuing review of an activity in which he has a professional responsibility, except to provide information requested by the committee. In addition to possessing the professional competence to review specific activities, the committee should be able to determine acceptability of the proposal in terms of institutional commitments and regulations, applicable law, standards of professional conduct and practice, and community attitudes [note to 21 CFR 130 omitted]. The committee may therefore need to include persons whose primary concerns lie in these areas rather than in the conduct of research, development, and service programs of the types supported by the DHEW.

If an institution is so small that it cannot appoint a suitable committee from its own staff, it should appoint members from outside the institution.

Committee members shall be identified by name, occupation or position, and by other pertinent indications of experience and competence in areas pertinent to the areas of review such as earned degrees, board certifications, licensures, memberships, etc.

Temporary replacement of a committee member by an alternate of comparable experience and competence is permitted in the event a member is momentarily unable to fulfill committee responsibility. The DHEW should be notified of any permanent replacement or additions.

2. The institution should adopt a statement of principles that will assist it in the discharge of its responsibilities for protecting the rights and welfare of subjects. This may be an appropriate existing code or declaration or one formulated by the institution itself [note omitted]. It is to be understood that no such principles supersede DHEW policy or applicable law.

3. Review begins with the identification of those projects or activities which involve subjects who may be at risk. In institutions with large grant and contract programs, administrative staff may be delegated the responsibility of separating those projects which do not involve human subjects in any degree; i.e., animal and nonhuman materials studies. However, determinations as to whether any project or activity involves human subjects at risk is a professional responsibility to be discharged through review by the committee, or by subcommittees.

If review determines that the procedures to be applied are to be limited to those considered by the committee to be established, accepted, and necessary to the needs of the subject, review need go no further; and the application should be certified as approved by the committee. Such projects involve human subjects, but these subjects are not considered to be at risk.

If review determines that the procedures to be applied will place the subject at risk, review should be expanded to include the issues of the protection of the subject's rights and welfare, of the relative weight of risks and benefits, and of the provision of adequate and appropriate consent procedures.

Where required by workload considerations or by geographic separation of operating units, subcommittees or mail review may be utilized to provide preliminary review of applications.

Final review of projects involving subjects at risk should be carried out by a quorum of the committee. . . . Such review should determine, through review of reports by subcommittees, or through its own examination of applications or of protocols, or through interviews with those individuals who will have professional responsibility for the proposal project or activity, or through other acceptable procedures that the requirements of the institutional assurance and of DHEW policy have been met, specifically that:

a. The rights and welfare of the subjects are adequately protected.

Institutional committees should carefully examine applications, protocols, or descriptions of work to arrive at an independent determination of possible risks. The committee must be alert to the possibility that investigators, program directors, or contractors may, quite unintentionally, introduce unnecessary or unacceptable hazards, or fail to provide adequate safeguards. This possibility is particularly true if the project crosses disciplinary lines, involves new and untried procedures, or involves established and accepted procedures which are new to the personnel applying them. Committees must also assure themselves that proper precautions will be taken to deal with emergencies that may develop even in the course of seemingly routine activities.

When appropriate, provision should be made for safeguarding information that could be traced to, or identified with, subjects. The committee may require the project or activity director to take steps to insure the confidentiality and security of data, particularly if it may not always remain under his direct control.

Safeguards include, initially, the careful design of questionnaires, inventories, interview schedules, and other data gathering instruments and procedures to limit the personal information to be acquired to that which is absolutely essential to the project or activity. Additional safeguards include the encoding or enciphering of names, addresses, serial numbers, and of data transferred to tapes, discs, and printouts. Secure, locked spaces and cabinets may be necessary for handling and storing documents and files. Codes and ciphers should always be kept in secure places, distinctly separate from encoded and enciphered data. The shipment, delivery, and transfer of all data, printouts, and files between offices and institutions may require careful controls. Computer to computer transmission of data may be restricted or forbidden.

Provision should also be made for the destruction of all edited, obsolete or depleted data on punched cards, tapes, discs, and other records. The committee may also determine a future date for destruction of all stored primary data pertaining to a project or activity.

Particularly relevant to the decision of the committees are those rights of the subject that are defined by law. The committee should familiarize itself through consultation with legal counsel with these statutes and common law precedents which may bear on its decisions. The provisions of this policy may not be construed in any manner or sense that would abrogate, supersede, or moderate more restrictive applicable law or precedential legal decisions.

Laws may define what constitutes consent and who may give consent, prescribe or proscribe the performance of certain medical and surgical procedures, protect confidential communications, define negligence, define invasion of privacy, require disclosure of records pursuant to legal process, and limit charitable and governmental immunity.

b. The risks to an individual and outweighed by the potential benefits to him or by the importance of the knowledge to be gained.

The committee should carefully weigh the known or foreseeable risks to be encountered by subjects, the probable benefits that may accrue to them, and the probable benefits to humanity that may result from the subject's participation in the project or activity. If it seems probable that participation will confer substantial benefits on the subjects, the committee may be justified in permitting them to accept commensurate or lesser risks. If the potential benefits are insubstantial, or are outweighed by risks, the committee may be justified in permitting the subjects to accept these risks in the interests of humanity. The committee should consider the possibility that subjects, or those authorized to represent subjects, may be motivated to accept risks for unsuitable or inadequate reasons. In such instances the consent procedures adopted should incorporate adequate safeguards.

Compensation to volunteers should never be such as to constitute an undue inducement.

No subject can be expected to understand the issues of risks and benefits as fully as the committee. Its agreement that consent can reasonably be sought for subject participation in a project or activity is of paramount practical importance.

The informed consent of the subject, while often a legal necessity is a goal toward which we must strive, but hardly ever achieve except in the simplest cases.

Henry K. Beecher, M.D.

c. The informed consent of subjects will be obtained by methods that are adequate and appropriate [note to 21 CFR 130 omitted].

Informed consent is the agreement obtained from a subject, or from his authorized representative, to the subject's participation in an activity.

The basic elements of informed consent are:

1. A fair explanation of the procedures to be followed, including an identification of those which are experimental;

2. A description of the attendant discomforts and risks;

3. A description of the benefits to be expected;

4. A disclosure of appropriate alternative procedures that would be advantageous for the subject;

5. An offer to answer any inquiries concerning the procedures;

6. An instruction that the subject is free to withdraw his consent and to discontinue participation in the project or activity at any time.

In addition, the agreement, written or oral, entered into by the subject, should include no exculpatory language through which the subject is made to waive, or to appear to waive, any of his legal rights, or to release the institution or its agents from liability for negligence (the use of exculpatory clauses is contrary to public policy [*Tunkl v. Regents of University of California*]).

Informed consent must be documented. . . .

Consent should be obtained, whenever practicable, from the subjects themselves. When the subject group will include individuals who are not legally or physically capable of giving informed consent, because of age, mental incapacity, or inability to communicate, the review committee should consider the validity of consent by next of kin, legal guardians, or by other qualified third parties representative of the subjects' interests. In such instances, careful consideration should be given by the committee not only to whether these third parties can be presumed to have the necessary depth of interest and concern with the subjects' rights and welfare, but also to whether these third parties will be legally authorized to expose the subjects to the risks involved.

The review committee will determine if the consent required, whether to be secured before the fact, in writing or orally, or after the fact following debriefing, or whether implicit in voluntary participation in an adequately advertised activity, is appropriate in the light of the risks to the subject, and the circumstances of the project.

The review committee will also determine if the information to be given to the subject, or to qualified third parties, in writing or orally, is a fair explanation of the project or activity, of its possible benefits, and of its attendant hazards.

Where an activity involves therapy, diagnosis, or management, and a professional/patient relationship exists, it is necessary "to recognize that each patient's mental and emotional condition is important . . . and that in discussing the element of risk, a certain amount of discretion must be employed consistent with full disclosure of fact necessary to any informed consent" (*Salgo v. Leland Stanford Jr. University Board of Trustees* [154C.A.2nd 560; 317 P.2d 1701]).

Where an activity does not involve therapy, diagnosis, or management, and a professional/subject rather than a professional/patient relationship exists, "the subject is entitled to a full and frank disclosure of all the facts, probabilities, and opinions which a reasonable man might be expected to consider before giving his consent" (*Halushka v. University of Saskatchewan* [1965] 53 D.L.R. [2d]).

When debriefing procedures are considered as a necessary part of the plan, the committee should ascertain that these will be complete and prompt.

B. Continuing Review   This is an essential part of the review process. While procedures for continuing review of ongoing projects and activities should be based in principle on the initial review criteria, they should also be adapted to the size and administrative structure of the institution. Institutions which are small and compact and in which the committee members are in day-to-day contact with professional staff may be able to function effectively with some informality. Institutions which have placed responsibility for review in boards of trustees, utilization committees, and similar groups that meet on frequent schedules may find it possible to have projects reviewed during these meetings.

In larger institutions with more complex administrative structures and specially appointed committees, these committees may adopt a variety of continuing review mechanisms. They may involve systematic review of projects at fixed intervals, or at intervals set by the committee commensurate with the project's risk. Thus, a project involving an untried procedure may initially require reconsideration as each subject completes his involvement. A highly routine project may need no more than annual review. Routine diagnostic service procedures, such as biopsy and autopsy, which contribute to research and demonstration activities generally require no more than annual review. Spot checks may be used to supplement scheduled reviews.

Actual review may involve interviews with the responsible staff, or review of written reports and supporting documents and forms. In any event, such review must be completed at least annually to permit certifications of review on noncompeting continuation applications.

C. Communication of the Committee's Action, Advice, and Counsel
If the committee's overall recommendation is favorable, it may simultaneously prescribe restrictions or conditions under which the activity may be conducted, define substantial changes in the research plans which should be brought to its attention, and determine the nature and frequency of interim review procedures to ensure continued acceptable conduct of the research.

Favorable recommendations by an institutional committee are, of course, always subject to further appropriate review and rejection by institution officials.

Unfavorable recommendations, restrictions, or conditions cannot be removed except by the committee or by the action of another appropriate review group described in the assurance filed with the Department of Health, Education, and Welfare.

Staff with supervisory responsibility for investigators and program directors whose projects or activities have been disapproved or restricted, and institutional administrative and financial officers should be informed of the committee's recommendations. Responsible professional staff should be informed of the reasons for any adverse actions taken by the institutional committee.

The committee should be prepared at all times to provide advice and counsel to staff developing new projects or activities or contemplating revision of ongoing projects or disapproved proposals.

D. Maintenance of an Active and Effective Committee   Institutions should establish policy determining overall committee composition, including provisions for rotation of memberships and appointment of chairmen. Channels of responsibility should be established for implementation of committee recommendations as they may affect the actions of responsible professional staff, grants and contracts officers, business officers, and other responsible staff. Provisions should be made for remedial action in the event of disregard of committee recommendations. . . .

Appendix 28.4

Code of Federal Regulations
Title 45 Public Welfare
Department of Health and Human Services
National Institutes of Health Office for
Protection from Research Risks
Part 46 Protection of Human Subjects
Revised June 18, 1991
Effective August 19, 1991

Subpart A—Federal Policy for the Protection of Human Subjects (Basic DHHS Policy for Protection of Human Research Subjects)

Subpart B—Additional DHHS Protections Pertaining to Research, Development, and Related Activities Involving Fetuses, Pregnant Women, and Human In Vitro Fertilization

Subpart C—Additional DHHS Protections Pertaining to Biomedical and Behavioral Research Involving Prisoners as Subjects

Subpart D—Additional DHHS Protections for Children Involved as Subjects in Research

Authority: 5 U.S.C. 301; Sec. 474(a), 88 Stat. 352 (42 U.S.C. 2891-3(a)).

Note: As revised, Subpart A of the DHHS regulations incorporates the Common Rule (Federal Policy) for the Protection of Human Subjects (56 FR 28003). Subpart D of the HHS regulations has been amended at section 46.401(b) to reference the revised Subpart A.

The Common Rule (Federal Policy) is also codified at

7 CFR Part 1c	Department of Agriculture
10 CFR Part 745	Department of Energy
14 CFR Part 1230	National Aeronautics and Space Administration
15 CFR Part 27	Department of Commerce
16 CFR Part 1028	Consumer Product Safety Commission
22 CFR Part 225	International Development Cooperation Agency, Agency for International Development
24 CFR Part 60	Department of Housing and Urban Development
28 CFR Part 46	Department of Justice
32 CFR Part 219	Department of Defense
34 CFR Part 97	Department of Education
38 CFR Part 16	Department of Veterans Affairs
40 CFR Part 26	Environmental Protection Agency
45 CER Part 690	National Science Foundation
49 CFR Part 11	Department of Transportation

TITLE 45

Code of Federal Regulations
Part 46

PROTECTION OF HUMAN SUBJECTS

***

Revised June 18, 1991
Effective August 19, 1991

***

Subpart A—Federal Policy for the Protection of Human Subjects (Basic DHHS Policy for Protection of Human Research Subjects)

Source: 56 FR 28003, June 18, 1991.

§46.101 To What Does This Policy Apply?

(a) Except as provided in paragraph (b) of this section, this policy applies to all research involving human subjects conducted, supported, or otherwise subject to regulation by any Federal Department or Agency which takes appropriate administrative action to make the policy applicable to such research. This includes research conducted by Federal civilian employees or military personnel, except that each Department or Agency head may adopt such procedural modifications as may be appropriate from an administrative standpoint. It also includes research conducted, supported, or otherwise subject to regulation by the Federal Government outside the United States.

1. Research that is conducted or supported by a Federal Department or Agency, whether or not it is regulated as defined in §46.102(e), must comply with all sections of this policy.

2. Research that is neither conducted nor supported by a Federal Department or Agency but is subject to regulation as defined in §46.102(e) must be reviewed and approved, in compliance with §46.101, §46.102, and §46.107 through §46.117 of this policy, by an Institutional Review Board (IRB) that operates in accordance with the pertinent requirements of this policy.

   (b) Unless otherwise required by Department or Agency heads, research activities in which the only involvement of human subjects will be in one or more of the following categories are exempt from this policy:[1]

1. Research conducted in established or commonly accepted educational settings, involving normal educational practices, such as (i) research on regular and special education instructional strategies, or (ii) research on the effectiveness of or the comparison among instructional techniques, curricula, or classroom management methods.

2. Research involving the use of educational tests (cognitive, diagnostic, aptitude, achievement), survey procedures, interview procedures or observation of public behavior, unless:

   (i) information obtained is recorded in such a manner that human subjects can be identified, directly or through identifiers linked to the subjects; and (ii) any disclosure of the human subjects' responses outside the research could reasonably place the subjects at risk of criminal or civil liability or be damaging to the subjects' financial standing, employability, or reputation.

3. Research involving the use of educational tests (cognitive, diagnostic, aptitude, achievement), survey procedures, interview procedures, or observation of public behavior that is not exempt under paragraph (b)(2) of this section, if: (i) the human subjects are elected or appointed public officials or candidates for public office; or (ii) Federal statute(s) require(s) without exception that the confidentiality of the personally identifiable information will be maintained throughout the research and thereafter.

4. Research involving the collection or study of existing data, documents, records, pathological specimens, or diagnostic specimens, if these sources are publicly available or if the information is recorded by the investigator in such a manner that subjects cannot be identified, directly or through identifiers linked to the subjects.

5. Research and demonstration projects which are conducted by or subject to the approval of Department or Agency heads, and which are designed to study, evaluate, or otherwise examine:

   (i) Public benefit or service programs; (ii) procedures for obtaining benefits or services under those programs; (iii) possible changes in or alternatives to those programs or procedures; or (iv) possible changes in methods or levels of payment for benefits or services under those programs.

6. Taste and food quality evaluation and consumer acceptance studies, (i) if wholesome foods without additives are consumed or (ii) if a food is consumed that contains a

food ingredient at or below the level and for a use found to be safe, or agricultural chemical or environmental contaminant at or below the level found to be safe, by the Food and Drug Administration or approved by the Environmental Protection Agency or the Food Safety and Inspection Service of the U.S. Department of Agriculture.

(c) Department or Agency heads retain final judgment as to whether a particular activity is covered by this policy.

(d) Department or Agency heads may require that specific research activities or classes of research activities conducted, supported, or otherwise subject to regulation by the Department or Agency but not otherwise covered by this policy, comply with some or all of the requirements of this policy.

(e) Compliance with this policy requires compliance with pertinent Federal laws or regulations which provide additional protections for human subjects.

(f) This policy does not affect any State or local laws or regulations which may otherwise be applicable and which provide additional protections for human subjects.

(g) This policy does not affect any foreign laws or regulations which may otherwise be applicable and which provide additional protections to human subjects of research.

(h) When research covered by this policy takes place in foreign countries, procedures normally followed in the foreign countries to protect human subjects may differ from those set forth in this policy. [An example is a foreign institution which complies with guidelines consistent with the World Medical Assembly Declaration (Declaration of Helsinki amended 1989) issued either by sovereign states or by an organization whose function for the protection of human research subjects is internationally recognized.] In these circumstances, if a Department or Agency head determines that the procedures prescribed by the institution afford protections that are at least equivalent to those provided in this policy, the Department or Agency head may approve the substitution of the foreign procedures in lieu of the procedural requirements provided in this policy. Except when otherwise required by statute, Executive Order, or the Department or Agency head, notices of these actions as they occur will be published in the *Federal Register* or will be otherwise published as provided in Department or Agency procedures.

(i) Unless otherwise required by law, Department or Agency heads may waive the applicability of some or all of the provisions of this policy to specific research activities or classes or research activities otherwise covered by this policy. Except when otherwise required by statute or Executive Order, the Department or Agency-head shall forward advance notices of these actions to the Office for Protection from Research Risks, National Institutes of Health, Department of Health and Human Services (DHHS), and shall also publish them in the *Federal Register* or in such other manner as provided in Department or Agency procedures.[1]

---

[1]Institutions with DHHS-approved assurances on file will abide by provisions of Title 45 CFR Part 46 Subparts A–D. Some of the other departments and agencies have incorporated all provisions of Title 45 CFR Part 46 into their policies and procedures as well. However, the exemptions at 45 CFR 46.101(b) do not apply to research involving prisoners, fetuses, pregnant women, or human in vitro fertilization, Subparts B and C. The exemption at 45 CFR 46.101 (b)(2), for research involving survey or interview procedures or observation of public behavior, does not apply to research with children, *Subpart D,* except for research involving observations of public behavior when the investigator(s) do not participate in the activities being observed.

§46.102 Definitions

(a) *Department or Agency* head means the head of any Federal Department or Agency and any other officer or employee of any Department or Agency to whom authority has been delegated.

(b) *Institution* means any public or private entity or Agency (including Federal, State, and other agencies).

(c) *Legally authorized representative* means an individual or judicial or other body authorized under applicable law to consent on behalf of a prospective subject to the subject's participation in the procedure(s) involved in the research.

(d) *Research* means a systematic investigation, including research development, testing and evaluation, designed to develop or contribute to generalizable knowledge. Activities which meet this definition constitute research for purposes of this policy, whether or not they are conducted or supported under a program which is considered research for other purposes. For example, some demonstration and service programs may include research activities.

(e) *Research subject to regulation,* and similar terms are intended to encompass those research activities for which a Federal Department or Agency has specific responsibility for regulating as a research activity, (for example, Investigational New Drug requirements administered by the Food and Drug Administration). It does not include research activities which are incidentally regulated by a Federal Department or Agency solely as part of the Department's or Agency's broader responsibility to regulate certain types of activities whether research or non-research in nature (for example, Wage and Hour requirements administered by the Department of Labor).

(f) *Human subject* means a living individual about whom an investigator (whether professional or student) conducting research obtains

  1. data through intervention or interaction with the individual, or
  2. identifiable private information.

  Intervention includes both physical procedures by which data are gathered (for example, venipuncture) and manipulations of the subject or the subject's environment that are performed for research purposes. *Interaction* includes communication or interpersonal contact between investigator and subject. *Private information* includes information about behavior that occurs in a context in which an individual can reasonably expect that no observation or recording is taking place, and information which has been provided for specific purposes by an individual and which the individual can reasonably expect will not be made public (for example, a medical record). Private information must be individually identifiable (i.e., the identity of the subject is or may readily be ascertained by the investigator or associated with the information) in order for obtaining the information to constitute research involving human subjects.

(g) *IRB* means an Institutional Review Board established in accord with and for the purposes expressed in this policy.

(h) *IRB approval* means the determination of the IRB that the research has been reviewed and may be conducted at an institution within the constraints set forth by the IRB and by other institutional and Federal requirements.

(i) *Minimal risk* means that the probability and magnitude of harm or discomfort anticipated in the research are not greater in and of themselves than those ordinarily encountered in daily life or during the performance of routine physical or psychological examinations or tests.

(j) *Certification* means the official notification by the institution to the supporting Department or Agency, in accordance with the requirements of this policy, that a research project or activity involving human subjects has been reviewed and approved by an IRB in accordance with an approved assurance.

§46.103 Assuring Compliance with This Policy—Research Conducted or Supported by Any Federal Department or Agency

(a) Each institution engaged in research which is covered by this policy and which is conducted or supported by a Federal Department or Agency shall provide written assurance satisfactory to the Department or Agency head that it will comply with the requirements set forth in this policy. In lieu of requiring submission of an assurance, individual Department or Agency heads shall accept the existence of a current assurance, appropriate for the research in question, on file with the Office for Protection from Research Risks, National Institutes Health, DHHS, and approved for Federalwide use by that office. When the existence of a DHHS-approved assurance is accepted in lieu of requiring submission of an assurance, reports (except certification) required by this policy to be made to Department and Agency heads shall also be made to the Office for Protection from Research Risks, National Institutes of Health, DHHS.

(b) Departments and agencies will conduct or support research covered by this policy only if the institution has an assurance approved as provided in this section, and only if the institution has certified to the Department or Agency head that the research has been reviewed and approved by an IRB provided for in the assurance, and will be subject to continuing review by the IRB. Assurances applicable to federally supported or conducted research shall at a minimum include:

1. A statement of principles governing the institution in the discharge of its responsibilities for protecting the rights and welfare of human subjects of research conducted at or sponsored by the institution, regardless of whether the research is subject to Federal regulation. This may include an appropriate existing code, declaration, or statement of ethical principles, or a statement formulated by the institution itself. This requirement does not preempt provisions of this policy applicable to Department- or Agency-supported or regulated research and need not be applicable to any research exempted or waived under *§46.101*(b) or (i).

2. Designation of one or more IRBs established in accordance with the requirements of this policy, and for which provisions are made for meeting space and sufficient staff to support the IRB's review and recordkeeping duties.

3. A list of IRB members identified by name; earned degrees; representative capacity, indications of experience such as board certifications, licenses, etc., sufficient to describe each member's chief anticipated contributions to IRB deliberations; and any employment or other relationship between each member and the institution; for example: full-time employee, part-time employee, member of governing panel or board, stockholder, paid or unpaid consultant. Changes in IRB membership shall be reported to the Department or Agency head, unless in accord with *§46.103*(a) of this policy, the existence of a DHHS-approved assurance is accepted. In this case, change in IRB membership shall

be reported to the Office for Protection from Research Risks, National Institutes of Health, DHHS.

4. Written procedures which the IRB will follow (i) for conducting its initial and continuing review of research and for reporting its findings and actions to the investigator and the institution; (ii) for determining which projects require review more often than annually and which projects need verification from sources other than the investigators that no material changes have occurred since previous IRB review; and (iii) for ensuring prompt reporting to the IRB of proposed changes in a research activity, and for ensuring that such changes in approved research, during the period for which IRB approval has already been given, may not be initiated without IRB review and approval except when necessary to eliminate apparent immediate hazards to the subject.

5. Written procedures for ensuring prompt reporting to the IRB, appropriate institutional officials, and the Department or Agency head of (i) any unanticipated problems involving risks to subjects or others or any serious or continuing noncompliance with this policy or the requirements or determinations of the IRB; and (ii) any suspension or termination of IRB approval.

(c) The assurance shall be executed by an individual authorized to act for the institution and to assume on behalf of the institution the obligations imposed by this policy and shall be filed in such form and manner as the Department or Agency head prescribes.

(d) The Department or Agency head will evaluate all assurances submitted in accordance with this policy through such officers and employees of the Department or Agency and such experts or consultants engaged for this purpose as the Department or Agency head determines to be appropriate. The Department or Agency head's evaluation will take into consideration the adequacy of the proposed IRB in light of the anticipated scope of the institution's research activities and the types of subject populations likely to be involved, the appropriateness of the proposed initial and continuing review procedures in light of the probable risks, and the size and complexity of the institution.

(e) On the basis of this evaluation, the Department or Agency head may approve or disapprove the assurance, or enter into negotiations to develop an approvable one. The Department or Agency head may limit the period during which any particular approved assurance or class of approved assurances shall remain effective or otherwise condition or restrict approval.

(f) Certification is required when the research is supported by a Federal Department or Agency and not otherwise exempted or waived under *§46.101* (b) or (i). An institution with an approved assurance shall certify that each application or proposal for research covered by the assurance and by *§46.103* of this policy has been reviewed and approved by the IRB. Such certification must be submitted with the application or proposal or by such later date as may be prescribed by the Department or Agency to which the application or proposal is submitted. Under no condition shall research covered by *§46.103* of the policy be supported prior to receipt of the certification that the research has been reviewed and approved by the IRB. Institutions without an approved assurance covering the research shall certify within 30 days after receipt of a request for such a certification from the Department or Agency, that the application or proposal has been approved by the IRB. If the certification is not submitted with in these time limits, the application or proposal may be returned to the institution.

(Approved by the Office of Management and Budget under Control Number 9999-0020.)

§§46.104—46.106 [Reserved]
§46.107 IRB Membership

(a) Each IRB shall have at least five members, with varying backgrounds to promote complete and adequate review of research activities commonly conducted by the institution. The IRB shall be sufficiently qualified through the experience and expertise of its members, and the diversity of the members, including consideration of race, gender, and cultural backgrounds and sensitivity to such issues as community attitudes, to promote respect for its advice and counsel in safeguarding the rights and welfare of human subjects. In addition to possessing the professional competence necessary to review specific research activities, the IRB shall be able to ascertain the acceptability of proposed research in terms of institutional commitments and regulations, applicable law, and standards of professional conduct and practice. The IRB shall therefore include persons knowledgeable in these areas. If an IRB regularly reviews research that involves a vulnerable category of subjects, such as children, prisoners, pregnant women, or handicapped or mentally disabled persons, consideration shall be given to the inclusion of one or more individuals who are knowledgeable about and experienced in working with these subjects.

(b) Every nondiscriminatory effort will be made to ensure that no IRB consists entirely of men or entirely of women, including the institution's consideration of qualified persons of both sexes, so long as no selection is made to the IRB on the basis of gender. No IRB may consist entirely of members of one profession.

(c) Each IRB shall include at least one member whose primary concerns are in scientific areas and at least one member whose primary concerns are in nonscientific areas.

(d) Each IRB shall include at least one member who is not otherwise affiliated with the institution and who is not part of the immediate family of a person who is affiliated with the institution.

(e) No IRB may have a member participate in the IRB's initial or continuing review of any project in which the member has a conflicting interest, except to provide information requested by the IRB.

(f) An IRB may, in its discretion, invite individuals with competence in special areas to assist in the review of issues which require expertise beyond or in addition to that available on the IRB. These individuals may not vote with the IRB.

§46.108 IRB Functions and Operations

In order to fulfill the requirements of this policy each IRB shall:

(a) Follow written procedures in the same detail as described in *§46.103*(b)(4) and to the extent required by *§46.103*(b)(5).

(b) Except when an expedited review procedure is used (see *§46.110*), review proposed research at convened meetings at which a majority of the members of the IRB are present, including at least one member whose primary concerns are in nonscientific areas. In order for the research to be approved, it shall receive the approval of a majority of those members present at the meeting.

§46.109 IRB Review of Research

(a) An IRB shall review and have authority to approve, require modifications in (to secure approval), or disapprove all research activities covered by this policy.

(b) An IRB shall require that information given to subjects as part of informed consent is in accordance with *§46.116.* The IRB may require that information, in addition to that specifically mentioned in *§46.116,* be given to the subjects when in the IRB's judgment the information would meaningfully add to the protection of the rights and welfare of subjects.

(c) An IRB shall require documentation of informed consent or may waive documentation in accordance with *§46.117.*

(d) An IRB shall notify investigators and the institution in writing of its decision to approve or disapprove the proposed research activity, or of modifications required to secure IRB approval of the research activity. If the IRB decides to disapprove a research activity, it shall include in its written notification a statement of the reasons for its decision and give the investigator an opportunity to respond in person or in writing.

(e) An IRB shall conduct continuing review of research covered by this policy at intervals appropriate to the degree of risk, but not less than once per year, and shall have authority to observe or have a third party observe the consent process and the research. (Approved by the Office of Management and Budget under Control Number 9999–0020.)

§46.110 Expedited Review Procedures for Certain Kinds of Research Involving No More Than Minimal Risk, and for Minor Changes in Approved Research.

(a) The Secretary, HHS, has established, and published as a Notice in the *Federal Register,* a *list of categories* of research that may be reviewed by the IRB through an expedited review procedure. The list will be amended, as appropriate, after consultation with other departments and agencies, through periodic republication by the Secretary, HHS, in the *Federal Register.* A copy of the list is available from the Office for Protection from Research Risks, National Institutes of Health, DHHS, Bethesda, Maryland 20892.

(b) An IRB may use the expedited review procedure to review either or both of the following:

1. some or all of the research appearing on the list and found by the reviewer(s) to involve no more than minimal risk,

2. minor changes in previously approved research during the period (of one year or less) for which approval is authorized.

Under an expedited review procedure, the review may be carried out by the IRB chairperson or by one or more experienced reviewers designated by the chairperson from among members of the IRB. In reviewing the research, the reviewers may exercise all of the authorities of the IRB except that the reviewers may not disapprove the research. A research activity may be disapproved only after review in accordance with the non-expedited procedure set forth in *§46.108*(b).

(c) Each IRB which uses an expedited review procedure shall adopt a method for keeping all members advised of research proposals which have been approved under the procedure.

(d) The Department or Agency head may restrict, suspend, terminate, or choose not to authorize an institution's or IRB's use of the expedited review procedure.

§46.111 Criteria for IRB Approval of Research

(a) In order to approve research covered by this policy the IRB shall determine that all of the following requirements are satisfied:

1. Risks to subjects are minimized: (i) by using procedures which are consistent with sound research design and which do not unnecessarily expose subjects to risk, and (ii) whenever appropriate, by using procedures already being performed on the subjects for diagnostic or treatment purposes.

2. Risks to subjects are reasonable in relation to anticipated benefits, if any, to subjects, and the importance of the knowledge that may reasonably be expected to result. In evaluating risks and benefits, the IRB should consider only those risks and benefits that may result from the research (as distinguished from risks and benefits of therapies subjects would receive even if not participating in the research). The IRB should not consider possible long-range effects of applying knowledge gained in the research (for example, the possible effects of the research on public policy) as among those research risks that fall within the purview of its responsibility.

3. Selection of subjects is equitable. In making this assessment the IRB should take into account the purposes of the research and the setting in which the research will be conducted and should be particularly cognizant of the special problems of research involving vulnerable populations, such as children, prisoners, pregnant women, mentally disabled persons, or economically or educationally disadvantaged persons.

4. Informed consent will be sought from each prospective subject or the subject's legally authorized representative, in accordance with, and to the extent required by *§46.116*.

5. Informed consent will be appropriately documented, in accordance with, and to the extent required by *§46.117*.

6. When appropriate, the research plan makes adequate provision for monitoring the data collected to ensure the safety of subjects.

7. When appropriate, there are adequate provisions to protect the privacy of subjects and to maintain the confidentiality of data.

(b) When some or all of the subjects are likely to be vulnerable to coercion or undue influence, such as children, prisoners, pregnant women, mentally disabled persons, or economically or educationally disadvantaged persons, additional safeguards have been included in the study to protect the rights and welfare of these subjects.

§46.112 Review by Institution

Research covered by this policy that has been approved by an IRB may be subject to further appropriate review and approval or disapproval by officials of the institution. However, those officials may not approve the research if it has not been approved by an IRB.

§46.113 Suspension or Termination of IRB Approval of Research

An IRB shall have authority to suspend or terminate approval of research that is not being conducted in accordance with the IRB's requirements or that has been associated with unexpected serious harm to subjects. Any suspension or termination or approval shall include a statement of the reasons for the IRB's action and shall be reported promptly to the investigator, appropriate institutional officials, and the Department or Agency head. (Approved by the Office of Management and Budget under Control Number 9999–0020.)

§46.114 Cooperative Research

Cooperative research projects are those projects covered by this policy which involve more than one institution. In the conduct of cooperative research projects, each institution is responsible for safeguarding the rights and welfare of human subjects and for complying with this policy. With the approval of the Department or Agency head, an institution participating in a cooperative project may enter into a joint review arrangement, rely upon the review of another qualified IRB, or make similar arrangements for avoiding duplication of effort.

§46.115 IRB Records

(a) An institution, or when appropriate an IRB, shall prepare and maintain adequate documentation of IRB activities, including the following:

1. Copies of all research proposals reviewed, scientific evaluations, if any, that accompany the proposals, approved sample consent documents, progress reports submitted by investigators, and reports of injuries to subjects.

2. Minutes of IRB meetings which shall be in sufficient detail to show attendance at the meetings; actions taken by the IRB; the vote on these actions including the number of members voting for, against, and abstaining; the basis for requiring changes in or disapproving research; and a written summary of the discussion of controverted issues and their resolution.

3. Records of continuing review activities.

4. Copies of all correspondence between the IRB and the investigators.

5. A list of IRB members in the same detail as described in *§46.103*(b)(3).

6. Written procedures for the IRB in the same detail as described in *§46.103*(b)(4) and *§46.103*(b)(5).

7. Statements of significant new findings provided to subjects, as required by *§46.116*(b)(5).

(b) The records required by this policy shall be retained for at least 3 years, and records relating to research which is conducted shall be retained for at least 3 years after completion of the research. All records shall be accessible for inspection and copying by authorized representatives of the Department or Agency at reasonable times and in a reasonable manner.

(Approved by the Office of Management and Budget under Control Number 9999–0020.)

§46.116 General Requirements for Informed Consent

Except as provided elsewhere in this policy, no investigator may involve a human being as a subject in research covered by this policy unless the investigator has obtained the legally effective informed consent of the subject or the subject's legally authorized representative. An investigator shall seek such consent only under circumstances that provide the prospective subject or the representative sufficient opportunity to consider whether or not to participate and that minimize the possibility of coercion or undue influence. The information that is given to the subject or the representative shall be in language understandable to the subject or the representative. No informed consent, whether oral or written, may include any exculpatory language through which the subject or the representative is made to waive or appear to waive any of the subject's legal rights, or releases or appears to release the investigator, the sponsor, the institution or its agents from liability for negligence.

(a) Basic elements of informed consent. Except as provided in paragraph (c) or (d) of this section, in seeking informed consent the following information shall be provided to each subject:

1. a statement that the study involves research, an explanation of the purposes of the research and the expected duration of the subject's participation, a description of the procedures to be followed, and identification of any procedures which are experimental;
2. a description of any reasonably foreseeable risks or discomforts to the subject;
3. a description of any benefits to the subject or to others which may reasonably be expected from the research;
4. a disclosure of appropriate alternative procedures or courses of treatment, if any, that might be advantageous to the subject;
5. a statement describing the extent, if any, to which confidentiality of records identifying the subject will be maintained;
6. for research involving more than minimal risk, an explanation as to whether any compensation and an explanation as to whether any medical treatments are available if injury occurs and, if so, what they consist of, or where further information may be obtained;
7. an explanation of whom to contact for answers to pertinent questions about the research and research subjects' rights, and whom to contact in the event of a research-related injury to the subject; and
8. a statement that participation is voluntary, refusal to participate will involve no penalty or loss of benefits to which the subject is otherwise entitled, and the subject may discontinue participation at any time without penalty or loss of benefits to which the subject is otherwise entitled.

(b) Additional elements of informed consent. When appropriate, one or more of the following elements of information shall also be provided to each subject:

1. a statement that the particular treatment or procedure may involve risks to the subject (or to the embryo or fetus, if the subject is or may become pregnant) which are currently unforeseeable;
2. anticipated circumstances under which the subject's participation may be terminated by the investigator without regard to the subject's consent;
3. any additional costs to the subject that may result from participation in the research;

4. the consequences of a subject's decision to withdraw from the research and procedures for orderly termination of participation by the subject;
5. a statement that significant new findings developed during the course of the research which may relate to the subject's willingness to continue participation will be provided to the subject; and
6. the approximate number of subjects involved in the study.

(c) An IRB may approve a consent procedure which does not include, or which alters, some or all of the elements of informed consent set forth above, or waive the requirement to obtain informed consent provided the IRB finds and documents that:

1. the research or demonstration project is to be conducted by or subject to the approval of state or local government officials and is designed to study, evaluate, or otherwise examine: (i) public benefit or service programs; (ii) procedures for obtaining benefits or services under those programs; (iii) possible changes in or alternatives to those programs or procedures; or (iv) possible changes in methods or levels of payment for benefits or services under those programs; and
2. the research could not practicably be carried out without the waiver or alteration.

(d) An IRB may approve a consent procedure which does not include, or which alters, some or all of the elements of informed consent set forth in this section, or waive the requirements to obtain informed consent provided the IRB finds and documents that:

1. the research involves no more than minimal risk to the subjects;
2. the waiver or alteration will not adversely affect the rights and welfare of the subjects;
3. the research could not practicably be carried out without the waiver or alteration; and
4. whenever appropriate, the subjects will be provided with additional pertinent information after participation.

(e) The informed consent requirements in this policy are not intended to preempt any applicable Federal, State, or local laws which require additional information to be disclosed in order for informed consent to be legally effective.

(f) Nothing in this policy is intended to limit the authority of a physician to provide emergency medical care, to the extent the physician is permitted to do so under applicable Federal, State, or local law.

(Approved by the Office of Management and Budget under Control Number 9999-0020.)

§46.117 Documentation of Informed Consent

(a) Except as provided in paragraph (c) of this section, informed consent shall be documented by the use of a written consent form approved by the IRB and signed by the subject or the subject's legally authorized representative. A copy shall be given to the person signing the form.

(b) Except as provided in paragraph (c) of this section, the consent form may be either of the following:

1. A written consent document that embodies the elements of informed consent required by *§46.116*. This form may be read to the subject or the subject's legally authorized representative, but in any event, the investigator shall give either the subject or the representative adequate opportunity to read it before it is signed; or

2. A short form written consent document stating that the elements of informed consent required by *§46.116* have been presented orally to the subject or the subject's legally authorized representative. When this method is used, there shall be a witness to the oral presentation. Also, the IRB shall approve a written summary of what is to be said to the subject or the representative. Only the short form itself is to be signed by the subject or the representative. However, the witness shall sign both the short form and a copy of the summary, and the person actually obtaining consent shall sign a copy of the summary. A copy of the summary shall be given to the subject or the representative, in addition to a copy of the short form.

(c) An IRB may waive the requirement for the investigator to obtain a signed consent form for some or all subjects if it finds either:

1. That the only record linking the subject and the research would be the consent document and the principal risk would be potential harm resulting from a breach of confidentiality. Each subject will be asked whether the subject wants documentation linking the subject with the research, and the subject's wishes will govern; or

2. That the research presents no more than minimal risk of harm to subjects and involves no procedures for which written consent is normally required outside of the research context.

In cases in which the documentation requirement is waived, the IRB may require the investigator to provide subjects with a written statement regarding the research. (Approved by the Office of Management and Budget under Control Number 9999-0020.)

§46.118 Applications and Proposals Lacking Definite Plans for Involvement of Human Subjects

Certain types of applications for grants, cooperative agreements, or contracts are submitted to departments or agencies with the knowledge that subjects may be involved within the period of support, but definite plans would not normally be set forth in the application or proposal. These include activities such as institutional type grants when selection of specific projects is the institution's responsibility; research training grants in which the activities involving subjects remain to be selected; and projects in which human subjects' involvement will depend upon completion of instruments, prior animal studies, or purification of compounds. These applications need not be reviewed by an IRB before an award may be made. However, except for research exempted or waived under *§46.101* (b) or (i), no human subjects may be involved in any project supported by these awards until the project has been reviewed and approved by the IRB, as provided in this policy, and certification submitted, by the institution, to the Department or Agency.

§46.119 Research Undertaken Without the Intention of Involving Human Subjects

In the event research is undertaken without the intention of involving human subjects, but it is later proposed to involve human subjects in the research, the research shall first be reviewed and approved by an IRB, as provided in this policy, a certification submitted, by the institution, to the Department or Agency, and final approval given to the proposed change by the Department or Agency.

§46.120 Evaluation and Disposition of Applications and Proposals for Research to Be Conducted or Supported by a Federal Department or Agency

(a) The Department or Agency head will evaluate all applications and proposals involving human subjects submitted to the Department or Agency through such officers and employees of the Department or Agency and such experts and consultants as the Department or Agency head determines to be appropriate. This evaluation will take into consideration the risks to the subjects, the adequacy of protection against these risks, the potential benefits of the research to the subjects and others, and the importance of the knowledge gained or to be gained.

(b) On the basis of this evaluation, the Department or Agency head may approve or disapprove the application or proposal, or enter into negotiations to develop an approvable one.

§46.121 [Reserved]

§46.122 Use of Federal Funds

Federal funds administered by a Department or Agency may not be expended for research involving human subjects unless the requirements of this policy have been satisfied.

§46.123 Early Termination of Research Support: Evaluation of Applications and Proposals

(a) The Department or Agency head may require that Department or Agency support for any project be terminated or suspended in the manner prescribed in applicable program requirements, when the Department or Agency head finds an institution has materially failed to comply with the terms of this policy.

(b) In making decisions about supporting or approving applications or proposals covered by this policy the Department or Agency head may take into account, in addition to all other eligibility requirements and program criteria, factors such as whether the applicant has been subject to a termination or suspension under paragraph (a) of this section and whether the applicant or the person or persons who would direct or has/have directed the scientific and technical aspects of an activity has/have, in the judgment of the Department or Agency head, materially failed to discharge responsibility for the protection of the rights and welfare of human subjects (whether or not the research was subject to Federal regulation).

§46.124 Conditions

With respect to any research project or any class of research projects, the Department or Agency head may impose additional conditions prior to or at the time of approval when in the judgment of the Department or Agency head additional conditions are necessary for the protection of human subjects.

Subpart B—Additional DHHS Protections Pertaining to Research, Development, and Related Activities Involving Fetuses, Pregnant Women, and Human In Vitro Fertilization

Source: 40 FR 33528, Aug. 8, 1975; 43 FR 1758, January 11, 1978; 43 FR 51559, November 3, 1978

§46.201 Applicability

(a) The regulations in this subpart are applicable to all Department of Health and Human - Services grants and contracts supporting research, development, and related activities involving: (1) the fetus, (2) pregnant women, and (3) human *in vitro* fertilization.

(b) Nothing in this subpart shall be construed as indicating that compliance with the procedures set forth herein will in any way render inapplicable pertinent State or local laws bearing upon activities covered by this subpart.

(c) The requirements of this subpart are in addition to those imposed under the other subparts of this part.

§46.202 Purpose

It is the purpose of this subpart to provide additional safeguards in reviewing activities to which this subpart is applicable to assure that they conform to appropriate ethical standards and relate to important societal needs.

§46.203 Definitions

As used in this subpart:

(a) "Secretary" means the Secretary of Health and Human Services and any other officer or employee of the Department of Health and Human Services (DHHS) to whom authority has been delegated.

(b) "Pregnancy" encompasses the period of time from confirmation of implantation (through any of the presumptive signs of pregnancy, such as missed menses, or by a medically acceptable pregnancy test), until expulsion or extraction of the fetus.

(c) "Fetus" means the product of conception from the time of implantation (as evidenced by any of the presumptive signs of pregnancy, such as missed menses, or a medically acceptable pregnancy test), until a determination is made, following expulsion or extraction of the fetus, that it is viable.

(d) "Viable" as it pertains to the fetus means being able, after either spontaneous or induced delivery, to survive (given the benefit of available medical therapy) to the point of independently maintaining heartbeat and respiration. The Secretary may from time to time, taking into account medical advances, publish in the *Federal Register* guidelines to assist in determining whether a fetus is viable for purposes of this subpart. If a fetus is viable after delivery, it is a premature infant.

(e) "Nonviable fetus" means a fetus *ex utero* which, although living, is not viable.

(f) "Dead fetus" means a fetus *ex utero* which exhibits neither heartbeat, spontaneous respiratory activity, spontaneous movement of voluntary muscles, nor pulsation of the umbilical cord (if still attached).

(g) *"In vitro* fertilization" means any fertilization of human ova which occurs outside the body of a female, either through admixture of donor human sperm and ova or by any other means.

§46.204 Ethical Advisory Boards

(a) One or more Ethical Advisory Boards shall be established by the Secretary. Members of these Board(s) shall be so selected that the Board(s) will be competent to deal with medical, legal, social, ethical, and related issues and may include, for example, research scientists, physicians, psychologists, sociologists, educators, lawyers, and ethicists, as well as representatives of the general public. No Board member may be a regular, full-time employee of the Department of Health and Human Services.

(b) At the request of the Secretary, the Ethical Advisory Board shall render advice consistent with the policies and requirements of this part as to ethical issues, involving activities covered by this subpart, raised by individual applications or proposals. In addition, upon request by the Secretary, the Board shall render advice as to classes of applications or proposals and general policies, guidelines, and procedures.

(c) A Board may establish, with the approval of the Secretary, classes of applications or proposals which: (1) must be submitted to the Board, or (2) need not be submitted to the Board. Where the Board so establishes a class of applications or proposals which must be submitted, no application or proposal within the class may be funded by the Department or any component thereof until the application or proposal has been reviewed by the Board and the Board has rendered advice as to its acceptability from an ethical standpoint.

(d) [*Nullified under Public Law 103-43, June 10, 1993*]

§46.205 Additional Duties of the Institutional Review Boards in Connection with Activities Involving Fetuses, Pregnant Women, or Human in Vitro Fertilization

(a) In addition to the responsibilities prescribed for Institutional Review Boards under Subpart A of this part, the applicant's or offeror's Board shall, with respect to activities covered by this subpart, carry out the following additional duties:

1. determine that all aspects of the activity meet the requirements of this subpart;

2. determine that adequate consideration has been given to the manner in which potential subjects will be selected, and adequate provision has been made by the applicant or offeror for monitoring the actual informed consent process (e.g., through such mechanisms, when appropriate, as participation by the Institutional Review Board or subject advocates in: (i) overseeing the actual process by which individual consents required by this subpart are secured either by approving induction of each individual into the activity or verifying, perhaps through sampling, that approved procedures for induction of individuals into the activity are being followed, and (ii) monitoring the progress of the activity and intervening as necessary through such steps as visits to the activity site and continuing evaluation to determine if any unanticipated risks have arisen);

3. carry out such other responsibilities as may be assigned by the Secretary.

(b) No award may be issued until the applicant or offeror has certified to the Secretary that the Institutional Review Board has made the determinations required under paragraph (a) of this section and the Secretary has approved these determinations, as provided in *§46.120* of Subpart A of this part.

(c) Applicants or offerors seeking support for activities covered by this subpart must provide for the designation of an Institutional Review Board, subject to approval by the Secretary, where no such Board has been established under Subpart A of this part.

§46.206 General Limitations

(a) No activity to which this subpart is applicable may be undertaken unless:

1. appropriate studies on animals and nonpregnant individuals have been completed;

2. except where the purpose of the activity is to meet the health needs of the mother or the particular fetus, the risk to the fetus is minimal and, in all cases, is the least possible risk for achieving the objectives of the activity;

3. individuals engaged in the activity will have no part in: (i) any decisions as to the timing, method, and procedures used to terminate the pregnancy, and (ii) determining the viability of the fetus at the termination of the pregnancy; and

4. no procedural changes which may cause greater than minimal risk to the fetus or the pregnant woman will be introduced into the procedure for terminating the pregnancy solely in the interest of the activity.

(b) No inducements, monetary or otherwise, may be offered to terminate pregnancy for purposes of the activity.

Source: 40 FR 33528, Aug. 8, 1975, as amended at 40 FR 51638, Nov .6, 1975.

§46.207 Activities Directed Toward Pregnant Women as Subjects

(a) No pregnant woman may be involved as a subject in an activity covered by this subpart unless: (1) the purpose of the activity is to meet the health needs of the mother and the fetus will be placed at risk only to the minimum extent necessary to meet such needs, or (2) the risk to the fetus is minimal.

(b) An activity permitted under paragraph (a) of this section may be conducted only if the mother and father are legally competent and have given their informed consent after having been fully informed regarding possible impact on the fetus, except that the father's informed consent need not be secured if: (1) the purpose of the activity is to meet the health needs of the mother; (2) his identity or whereabouts cannot reasonably be ascertained; (3) he is not reasonably available; or (4) the pregnancy resulted from rape.

§46.208 Activities Directed Toward Fetuses *In Utero* as Subjects

(a) No fetus *in Utero* may be involved as a subject in any activity covered by this subpart unless: (1) the purpose of the activity is to meet the health needs of the particular fetus and the fetus will be placed at risk only to the minimum extent necessary to meet such needs, or (2) the risk to the fetus imposed by the research is minimal and the purpose of the activity is the development of important biomedical knowledge which cannot be obtained by other means.

(b) An activity permitted under paragraph (a) of this section may be conducted only if the mother and father are legally competent and have given their informed consent, except that the father's consent need not be secured if: (1) his identity or whereabouts cannot reasonably be ascertained; (2) he is not reasonably available; or (3) the pregnancy resulted from rape.

§46.209 Activities Directed Toward Fetuses *Ex Utero,* Including Nonviable Fetuses, as Subjects.

(a) Until it has been ascertained whether or not a fetus *ex utero* is viable, a fetus *ex utero* may not be involved as a subject in an activity covered by this subpart unless:

1. there will be no added risk to the fetus resulting from the activity, and the purpose of the activity is the development of important biomedical knowledge which cannot be obtained by other means, or

2. the purpose of the activity is to enhance the possibility of survival of the particular fetus to the point of viability.

(b) No nonviable fetus may be involved as a subject in an activity covered by this subpart unless:

1. vital functions of the fetus will not be artificially maintained,

2. experimental activities which of themselves would terminate the heartbeat or respiration of the fetus will not be employed, and

3. the purpose of the activity is the development of important biomedical knowledge which cannot be obtained by other means.

(c) In the event the fetus *ex utero* is found to be viable, it may be included as a subject in the activity only to the extent permitted by and in accordance with the requirements of other subparts of this part.

(d) An activity permitted under paragraph (a) or (b) of this section may be conducted only if the mother and father are legally competent and have given their informed consent, except that the father's informed consent need not be secured if: (1) his identity or whereabouts cannot reasonably be ascertained, (2) he is not reasonably available, or (3) the pregnancy resulted from rape.

§46.210 Activities Involving the Dead Fetus, Fetal Material, or the Placenta

Activities involving the dead fetus, mascerated fetal material, or cells, tissue, or organs excised from a dead fetus shall be conducted only in accordance with any applicable State or local laws regarding such activities.

§46.211 Modification or Waiver of Specific Requirements

Upon the request of an applicant or offeror (with the approval of its Institutional Review Board), the Secretary may modify or waive specific requirements of this subpart, with the approval of the Ethical Advisory Board after such opportunity for public comment as the Ethical Advisory Board considers appropriate in the particular instance. In making such decisions, the Secretary will consider whether the risks to the subject are so outweighed by the sum of the benefit to the subject and the importance of the knowledge to be gained as to warrant such modification or waiver and that such benefits cannot be gained except through a modification or waiver. Any such modifications or waivers will be published as notices in the Federal Register.

Subpart C—Additional DHHS Protections Pertaining to Biomedical and Behavioral Research Involving Prisoners as Subjects.

Source: 43 FR 53655, Nov. 16, 1978.

§46.301 Applicability

(a) The regulations in this subpart are applicable to all biomedical and behavioral research conducted or supported by the Department of Health and Human Services involving prisoners as subjects.

(b) Nothing in this subpart shall be construed as indicating that compliance with the procedures set forth herein will authorize research involving prisoners as subjects, to the extent such research is limited or barred by applicable State or local law.

(c) The requirements of this subpart are in addition to those imposed under the other subparts of this part.

§46.302 Purpose

Inasmuch as prisoners may be under constraints because of their incarceration which could affect their ability to make a truly voluntary and uncoerced decision whether or not to participate as subjects in research, it is the purpose of this subpart to provide additional safeguards for the protection of prisoners involved in activities to which this subpart is applicable.

§46.303 Definitions

As used in this subpart:

(a) "Secretary" means the Secretary of Health and Human Services and any other officer or employee of the Department of Health and Human Services to whom authority has been delegated.

(b) "DHHS" means the Department of Health and Human Services.

(c) "Prisoner" means any individual involuntarily confined or detained in a penal institution. The term is intended to encompass individuals sentenced to such an institution under a criminal or civil statute, individuals detained in other facilities by virtue of statutes or commitment procedures which provide alternatives to criminal prosecution or incarceration in a penal institution, and individuals detained pending arraignment, trial, or sentencing.

(d) "Minimal risk" is the probability and magnitude of physical or psychological harm that is normally encountered in the daily lives, or in the routine medical, dental, or psychological examination of healthy persons.

§46.304 Composition of Institutional Review Boards Where Prisoners Are Involved

In addition to satisfying the requirements in *§46.107* of this part, an Institutional Review Board, carrying out responsibilities under this part with respect to research covered by this subpart, shall also meet the following specific requirements:

(a) A majority of the Board (exclusive of prisoner members) shall have no association with the prison(s) involved, apart from their membership on the Board.

(b) At least one member of the Board shall be a prisoner, or a prisoner representative with appropriate background and experience to serve in that capacity, except that where a particular research project is reviewed by more than one Board only one Board need satisfy this requirement.

§46.305 Additional Duties of the Institutional Review Boards Where Prisoners Are Involved

(a) In addition to all other responsibilities prescribed for Institutional Review Boards under this part, the Board shall review research covered by this subpart and approve such research only if it finds that:

1. the research under review represents one of the categories of research permissible under *§46.306*(a)(2);

2. any possible advantages accruing to the prisoner through his or her participation in the research, when compared to the general living conditions, medical care, quality of food, amenities and opportunity for earnings in the prison, are not of such a magnitude that his or her ability to weigh the risks of the research against the value of such advantages in the limited choice environment of the prison is impaired;

3. the risks involved in the research are commensurate with risks that would be accepted by nonprisoner volunteers;

4. procedures for the selection of subjects within the prison are fair to all prisoners and immune from arbitrary intervention by prison authorities or prisoners. Unless the principal investigator provides to the Board justification in writing for following some other procedures, control subjects must be selected randomly from the group of available prisoners who meet the characteristics needed for that particular research project;

5. the information is presented in language which is understandable to the subject population;

6. adequate assurance exists that parole boards will not take into account a prisoner's participation in the research in making decisions regarding parole, and each prisoner is clearly informed in advance that participation in the research will have no effect on his or her parole; and

7. where the Board finds there may be a need for follow-up examination or care of participants after the end of their participation, adequate provision has been made for such examination or care, taking into account the varying lengths of individual prisoners' sentences, and for informing participants of this fact.

(b) The Board shall carry out such other duties as may be assigned by the Secretary.

(c) The institution shall certify to the Secretary, in such form and manner as the Secretary may require, that the duties of the Board under this section have been fulfilled.

§46.306 Permitted Research Involving Prisoners

(a) Biomedical or behavioral research conducted or supported by DHHS may involve prisoners as subjects only if:

(1) the institution responsible for the conduct of the research has certified to the Secretary that the Institutional Review Board has approved the research under *§46.305* of this subpart; and

(2) in the judgment of the Secretary the proposed research involves solely the following:

(A) study of the possible causes, effects, and processes of incarceration, and of criminal behavior, provided that the study presents no more than minimal risk and no more than inconvenience to the subjects;

(B) study of prisons as institutional structures or of prisoners as incarcerated persons, provided that the study presents no more than minimal risk and no more than inconvenience to the subjects;

(C) research on conditions particularly affecting prisoners as a class (for example, vaccine trials and other research on hepatitis which is much more prevalent in prisons than elsewhere; and research on social and psychological problems such as alcoholism, drug addiction, and sexual assaults) provided that the study may proceed only after the Secretary has consulted with appropriate experts including experts in penology, medicine, and ethics, and published notice, in the *Federal Register,* of his intent to approve such research; or

(D) research on practices, both innovative and accepted, which have the intent and reasonable probability of improving the health or well-being of the subject. In cases in which those studies require the assignment of prisoners in a manner consistent with protocols approved by the IRB to control groups which may not benefit from the research, the study may proceed only after the Secretary has consulted with appropriate experts, including experts in penology, medicine, and ethics, and published notice, in the *Federal Register,* of the intent to approve such research.

(b) Except as provided in paragraph (a) of this section, biomedical or behavioral research conducted or supported by DHHS shall not involve prisoners as subjects.

Subpart D Additional DHHS Protections for Children Involved as Subjects in Research

Source: 48 FR 9818, March 8, 1983; 56 FR 28032, June 18, 1991.

§46.401 To What Do These Regulations Apply

(a) This subpart applies to all research involving children as subjects, conducted or supported by the Department of Health and Human Services.

(1) This includes research conducted by Department employees, except that each head of an Operating Division of the Department may adopt such nonsubstantive,

procedural modifications as may be appropriate from an administrative standpoint.

(2) It also includes research conducted or supported by the Department of Health and Human Services outside the United States, but in appropriate circumstances, the Secretary may, under paragraph (i) of *§46.101* of Subpart A, waive the applicability of some or all of the requirements of these regulations for research of this type.

(b) Exemptions at *§46.101*(b)(1) and (b)(3) through (b)(6) are applicable to this subpart. The exemption at *§46.101*(b)(2) regarding educational tests is also applicable to this subpart. However, the exemption at *§46.101*(b)(2) for research involving survey or interview procedures or observations of public behavior does not apply to research covered by this subpart, except for research involving observation of public behavior when the investigator(s) do not participate in the activities being observed.

(c) The exceptions, additions, and provisions for waiver as they appear in paragraphs (c) through (i) of *§46.101* of *Subpart A* are applicable to this subpart.

§46.402 Definitions

The definitions in *§46.102* of Subpart A shall be applicable to this subpart as well. In addition, as used in this subpart:

(a) "Children" are persons who have not attained the legal age for consent to treatments or procedures involved in the research, under the applicable law of the jurisdiction in which the research will be conducted.

(b) "Assent" means a child's affirmative agreement to participate in research. Mere failure to object should not, absent affirmative agreement, be construed as assent.

(c) "Permission" means the agreement of parent(s) or guardian to the participation of their child or ward in research.

(d) "Parent" means a child's biological or adoptive parent.

(e) "Guardian" means an individual who is authorized under applicable State or local law to consent on behalf of a child to general medical care.

§46.403 IRB Duties

In addition to other responsibilities assigned to IRBs under this part, each IRB shall review research covered by this subpart and approve only research which satisfies the conditions of all applicable sections of this subpart.

§46.404 Research Not Involving Greater Than Minimal Risk

DHHS will conduct or fund research in which the IRB finds that no greater than minimal risk to children is presented, only if the IRB finds that adequate provisions are made for soliciting the assent of the children and the permission of their parents or guardians, as set forth in *§46.408*.

§46.405 Research Involving Greater Than Minimal Risk But Presenting the Prospect of Direct Benefit to the Individual Subjects

DHHS will conduct or fund research in which the IRB finds that more than minimal risk to children is presented by an intervention or procedure that holds out the prospect of direct benefit for the individual subject, or by a monitoring procedure that is likely to contribute to the subject's well-being, only if the IRB finds that:

(a) the risk is justified by the anticipated benefit to the subjects;

(b) the relation of the anticipated benefit to the risk is at least as favorable to the subjects as that presented by available alternative approaches; and

(c) adequate provisions are made for soliciting the assent of the children and permission of their parents or guardians, as set forth in *§46.408.*

§46.406 Research Involving Greater Than Minimal Risk and No Prospect of Direct Benefit to Individual Subjects, But Likely to Yield Generalizable Knowledge about the Subject's Disorder or Condition

DHHS will conduct or fund research in which the IRB finds that more than minimal risk to children is presented by an intervention or procedure that does not hold out the prospect of direct benefit for the individual subject, or by a monitoring procedure which is not likely to contribute to the well-being of the subject, only if the IRB finds that:

(a) the risk represents a minor increase over minimal risk;

(b) the intervention or procedure presents experiences to subjects that are reasonably commensurate with those inherent in their actual or expected medical, dental, psychological, social, or educational situations;

(c) the intervention or procedure is likely to yield generalizable knowledge about the subjects' disorder or condition which is of vital importance for the understanding or amelioration of the subjects' disorder or condition; and

(d) adequate provisions are made for soliciting assent of the children and permission of their parents or guardians, as set forth in *§46.408.*

§46.407 Research Not Otherwise Approvable Which Presents an Opportunity to Understand, Prevent, or Alleviate a Serious Problem Affecting the Health or Welfare of Children

DHHS will conduct or fund research that the IRB does not believe meets the requirements of *§46.404. §46.405,* or *§46.406* only if:

(a) the IRB finds that the research presents a reasonable opportunity to further the understanding, prevention, or alleviation of a serious problem affecting the health or welfare of children; and

(b) the Secretary, after consultation with a panel of experts in pertinent disciplines (for example: science, medicine, education, ethics, law) and following opportunity for public review and comment, has determined either:

(1) that the research in fact satisfies the conditions of *§46.404, §46.405,* or *§46.406,* as applicable, or

(2) the following:

(i) the research presents a reasonable opportunity to further the understanding, prevention, or alleviation of a serious problem affecting the health or welfare of children;

(ii) the research will be conducted in accordance with sound ethical principles;

(iii) adequate provisions are made for soliciting the assent of children and the permission of their parents or guardians, as set forth in *§46.408*.

§46.408 Requirements for Permission by Parents or Guardians and for Assent by Children

(a) In addition to the determinations required under other applicable sections of this subpart, the IRB shall determine that adequate provisions are made for soliciting the assent of the children, when in the judgment of the IRB the children are capable of providing assent. In determining whether children are capable of assenting, the IRB shall take into account the ages, maturity, and psychological state of the children involved. This judgment may be made for all children to be involved in research under a particular protocol, or for each child, as the IRB deems appropriate. If the IRB determines that the capability of some or all of the children is so limited that they cannot reasonably be consulted or that the intervention or procedure involved in the research holds out a prospect of direct benefit that is important to the health or well-being of the children and is available only in the context of the research, the assent of the children is not a necessary condition for proceeding with the research. Even where the IRB determines that the subjects are capable of assenting, the IRB may still waive the assent requirement under circumstances in which consent may be waived in accord with *§46.116* of *Subpart A*.

(b) In addition to the determinations required under other applicable sections of this subpart, the IRB shall determine, in accordance with and to the extent that consent is required by *§46.116* of *Subpart A*, that adequate provisions are made for soliciting the permission of each child's parents or guardian. Where parental permission is to be obtained, the IRB may find that the permission of one parent is sufficient for research to be conducted under *§46.404* or *§46.405*. Where research is covered by *§46.406* and *§46.407* and permission is to be obtained from parents, both parents must give their permission unless one parent is deceased, unknown, incompetent, or not reasonably available, or when only one parent has legal responsibility for the care and custody of the child.

(c) In addition to the provisions for waiver contained in *§46.116* of *Subpart A*, if the IRB determines that a research protocol is designed for conditions or for a subject population for which parental or guardian permission is not a reasonable requirement to protect the subject (for example, neglected or abused children), it may waive the consent requirements in Subpart A of this part and paragraph (b) of this section, provided an appropriate mechanism for protecting the children who will participate as subjects in the research is substituted, and provided further that the waiver is not inconsistent with Federal, State, or local law. The choice of an appropriate mechanism would depend upon the nature and purpose of the activities described in the protocol, the risk and anticipated benefit to the research subjects, and their age, maturity, status, and condition.

(d) Permission by parents or guardians shall be documented in accordance with and to the extent required by *§46.117* of *Subpart A*.

(e) When the IRB determines that assent is required, it shall also determine whether and how assent must be documented.

§46.409 Wards

(a) Children who are wards of the State or any other agency, institution, or entity can be included in research approved under *§46.406* or *§46.407* only if such research is:

    1. related to their status as wards; or which the majority of children involved as subjects are not wards.

(b) If the research is approved under paragraph (a) of this section, the IRB shall require appointment of an advocate for each child who is a ward, in addition to any other individual acting on behalf of the child as guardian or in loco parentis. One individual may serve as advocate for more than one child. The advocate shall be an individual who has the background and experience to act in, and agrees to act in, the best interests of the child for the duration of the child's participation in the research and who is not associated in any way (except in the role as advocate or member of the IRB) with the research, the investigator(s) or the guardian organization.

Appendix 28.5

Oath of Hippocrates

Fourth Century B.C.E.

*A*ttributed to Hippocrates, the oath, which exemplifies the Pythagorean school *rather than Greek thought in general, differs from other, more scientific, writ-ings in the Hippocratic corpus. Written later than some of the other treatises in the corpus, the Oath of Hippocrates is one of the earliest and most important state-ments on medical ethics. Not only has the oath provided the foundation for many succeeding medical oaths, such as the Declaration of Geneva, but it is still adminis-tered to the graduating students of many medical schools, either in its original form or in an altered version.*

I swear by Apollo Physician and Asclepius and Hygieia and Panaceia and all the gods and goddesses, making them my witnesses, that I will fulfil according to my ability and judgment this oath and this covenant:

To hold him who has taught me this art as equal to my parents and to live my life in partnership with him, and if he is in need of money to give him a share of mine, and to regard his offspring as equal to my brothers in male lineage and to teach them this art—if they desire to learn it—without fee and covenant; to give a share of precepts and oral instruction and all the other learning to my sons and to the sons of him who has instructed me and to pupils who have signed the covenant and have taken an oath accord-ing to the medical law, but to no one else.

I will apply dietetic measures for the benefit of the sick according to my ability and judgment; I will keep them from harm and injustice.

I will neither give a deadly drug to anybody if asked for it, nor will I make a sugges-tion to this effect. Similarly I will not give to a woman an abortive remedy. In purity and holiness I will guard my life and my art.

I will not use the knife, not even on sufferers from stone, but will withdraw in favor of such men as are engaged in this work.

Whatever houses I may visit, I will come for the benefit of the sick, remaining free of all intentional injustice, of all mischief and in particular of sexual relations with both female and male persons, be they free or slaves.

What I may see or hear in the course of the treatment or even outside of the treat-ment in regard to the life of men, which on no account one must spread abroad, I will keep to myself holding such things shameful to be spoken about.

If I fulfil this oath and do not violate it, may it be granted to me to enjoy life and art, being honored with fame among all men for all time to come; if I transgress it and swear falsely, may the opposite of all this be my lot.

Appendix 28.6

Nuremburg Code 1946

The Nuremberg Military Tribunal's decision in the case of the United States v. Karl Brandt et al. includes what is now called the Nuremberg Code, a ten-point statement delimiting permissible medical experimentation on human subjects. According to this statement, humane experimentation is justified only if its results benefit society and it is carried out in accord with basic principles that "satisfy moral, ethical, and legal concepts." To some extent, the Nuremberg Code has been superseded by the Declaration of Helsinki as a guide for human experimentation.

1. The voluntary consent of the human subject is absolutely essential.

   This means that the person involved should have legal capacity to give consent; should be so situated as to be able to exercise free power of choice, without the intervention of any element of force, fraud, deceit, duress, over-reaching, or other ulterior form of constraint or coercion; and should have sufficient knowledge and comprehension of the elements of the subject matter involved as to enable him to make an understanding and enlightened decision. This latter element requires that before the acceptance of an affirmative decision by the experimental subject there should be made known to him the nature, duration, and purpose of the experiment; the method and means by which it is to be conducted; all inconveniences and hazards reasonably to be expected; and the effects upon his health or person which may possibly come from his participation in the experiment.

   The duty and responsibility for ascertaining the quality of the consent rests upon each individual who initiates, directs or engages in the experiment. It is a personal duty and responsibility which may not be delegated to another with impunity.

2. The experiment should be such as to yield fruitful results for the good of society, unprocurable by other methods or means of study, and not random and unnecessary in nature.

3. The experiment should be so designed and based on the results of animal experimentation and a knowledge of the natural history of the disease or other problem under study that the anticipated results will justify the performance of the experiment.

4. The experiment should be so conducted as to avoid all unnecessary physical and mental suffering and injury.

5. No experiment should be conducted where there is an *a priori* reason to believe that death or disabling injury will occur; except, perhaps, in those experiments where the experimental physicians also serve as subjects.

6. The degree of risk to be taken should never exceed that determined by the humanitarian importance of the problem to be solved by the experiment.

7. Proper preparations should be made and adequate facilities provided to protect the experimental subject against even remote possibilities of injury, disability, or death.

8. The experiment should be conducted only by scientifically qualified persons. The highest degree of skill and care should be required through all stages of the experiment of those who conduct or engage in the experiment.

9. During the course of the experiment the human subject should be at liberty to bring the experiment to an end if he has reached the physical or mental state where continuation of the experiment seems to him to be impossible.

10. During the course of the experiment the scientist in charge must be prepared to terminate the experiment at any stage, if he has probable cause to believe, in the exercise of the good faith, superior skill and careful judgment required of him that a continuation of the experiment is likely to result in injury, disability, or death to the experimental subject.

["Permissible Medical Experiments." *Trials of War Criminals before the Nuremberg Military Tribunals under Control Council Law No. 10: Nuremberg October 1946–April 1949.* Washington: U.S. Government Printing Office (n.d.), vol. 2, pp. 181–182.]

29

Human Resources Issues

Michael P. Warnick

G iven the litigious nature of our society, the high volume of claims for discrimination, harassment, wrongful termination, and other employment-related litigation is not surprising. Health care organizations, like all employers, must be ever mindful of the possibility of legal action from past, present, and prospective employees. For this reason, the role of risk management has expanded beyond the traditional relationship with operations to include a closer relationship with the human resources department. Consider the following facts:

- The Equal Employment Opportunity Commission (EEOC) reported that in 1997 there were more than 80,000 charges filed with the agency.[1]

- A 1992 risk consultant report showed that work-related claims against employers were increasing at a rate of 5,000 per year, and that the average employment practices award was $458,997. A year later, the average award had risen to $536,000.[2]

- The alarming number of violent incidents in the workplace, including homicides, has raised concerns about the extent to which employers should inquire into the backgrounds of employees as a measure to maintain workplace security.

- Congress, through legislation such as the Americans with Disabilities Act (ADA)[3] and the Family Medical Leave Act (FMLA),[4] has created new grounds for suits.

As the number of employment-related claims increases, so does the potential of financial risk to employers. Defense against such claims can be costly, even when the organization is not at fault or the claim is groundless or fraudulent. Moreover, the potential exposure for monetary damages threatens limited financial resources.

This chapter provides a general summary of the laws affecting human resources issues to help health care risk managers better assess the risk of employment-related claims. It also offers suggestions for minimizing exposure from such claims. Although application of the principles described herein cannot guarantee that the health care organization will never be sued by a disgruntled employee (even a groundless suit can be filed and must be defended), adhering to the precautions described will help minimize the risk of litigation and ultimate liability.

Before one analyzes how to control and/or mitigate employment practices exposures, it is first necessary to have a basic understanding of the laws that create the employment exposures.

....

EMPLOYMENT AT-WILL DOCTRINE

Historically, the employer-employee relationship has been "at will"—that is, the employee serves at the exclusive direction and control of the employer. The relationship can be terminated at any time by either party, and the employer does not have to demonstrate just cause in order to discharge the employee.

Most states still adhere to the at-will rule in the absence of a written agreement between employer and employee. However, universal application of the employment at-will rule gradually has eroded as a result of statutes and common law developments in case law that affect the employment relationship.

Employment Statutes Affecting the Employment Relationship

Given the erosion of the employment-at-will rule, it is important that the risk manager be familiar with federal statutes that affect the employment relationship. In addition, risk managers should be familiar with applicable state statutes that prohibit discrimination, such as harassment and wrongful termination, by private employers against individuals within the protected categories defined by those acts. All human resources managers, supervisors, and staff also should be familiar with the requirements of federal and state laws affecting the employment relationship. Exhibit 29.1 lists major federal statutes affecting employment relations and summarizes the key point or points of each.

Title VII of the Civil Rights Act of 1964   Title VII of the Civil Rights Act of 1964 prohibits discrimination on the basis of race, color, religion, sex, or national origin in hiring, discharge, compensation, and any terms, conditions, or privileges of employment.[5] Claims of sexual harassment and pregnancy discrimination also are covered under Title VII's prohibition of discrimination on the basis of sex. Title VII covers health care organizations that have fifteen or more employees for each working day in each of twenty or more calendar weeks in the current or preceding year.

If an employee files suit in federal court under Title VII, he or she may be entitled to reinstatement or front pay; back pay; attorney's fees; an injunction against the prohibited discrimination; compensatory damages for pain and suffering, financial loss, and damages for mental anguish; and punitive damages. The total amount of compensatory and punitive damages available to each plaintiff proving intentional discrimination is subject to caps, based on the size of the work force (see Table 29.1). Note that the caps do not limit the amount of back pay or interest on back pay, front pay, or attorney's fees. In addition, they apply to the damages awarded to each complaining party in a case involving multiple plaintiffs.

EXHIBIT 29.1.   Federal Statutes Regarding Employment

Title VII of the Civil Rights Act of 1964	• Prohibits discrimination on the basis of race, color, religion, sex, or national origin in hiring, discharge, compensation, and any terms, conditions, or privileges of employment.
Americans with Disabilities Act	• Prohibits discrimination against a QIWD when discrimination is based on the individual's disability. • Requires an employer to make "reasonable accommodation" to assure that a QIWD gets or maintains employment.
Age Discrimination in Employment Act of 1967	• Protects employees over the age of forty from discrimination on the basis of age with regard to hiring, discharge, compensation, and other terms, conditions, or privileges of employment.
Sections 1981 and 1983 of the Reconstruction Civil Rights Acts	• Prohibits racial or national origin discrimination in the making and/or enforcement of contracts, which may include any form of employment relationship. • Prohibits all forms of intentional bias in the workplace regarding the hiring, firing, disciplining, promoting, and compensating of employees and in working conditions. • Prohibits the deprivation of constitutionally guaranteed rights by employers under cover of state law.
Family and Medical Leave Act of 1993	• Requires private-sector employers of fifty or more employees to provide up to twelve weeks of unpaid, job-protected leave to eligible employees for qualified family and medical reasons.
Equal Pay Act of 1963	• Prohibits differences in pay between men and women for the performance of "substantially equal jobs," unless the differences are due to a factor other than sex, such as a bona fide merit system, training program, or seniority system.
Fair Labor Standards Act	• Establishes a minimum wage applicable to all employees of covered employers and provides for a mandatory overtime payment for employees working more than forty hours per week.
Employee Polygraph Protection Act	• Prohibits uses of polygraphs by private employers except in certain situations. Private employers can use polygraphs when (1) the employee is suspected of being involved in a workplace incident involving economic loss to the employer (for example, theft); (2) a prospective employee is seeking an armored car, security alarm, or security guard position; or (3) the employee seeks a position with a company authorized to manufacture and/or distribute controlled substances. Government employers and consultants retained by the federal government for national security intelligence can use polygraphs.
Older Workers' Benefit Protection Plan	• 1990 Amendment to the Age Discrimination Act of 1967, which clarified congressional intent regarding age-based distinctions in benefit plans or packages.

TABLE 29.1.   Caps on Damages Available to Plaintiffs Under Title VII

Number of Employees	*Cap*
15 to 100 employees	$50,000
101 to 200 employees	$100,000
201 to 500 employees	$200,000
501 employees or more	$300,000

Americans with Disabilities Act   The ADA prohibits discrimination against a qualified individual with a disability (QIWD) when the discrimination is based on the individual's disability. Like Title VII, the ADA protects only "qualified" individuals who have a disability—that is, "an individual with a disability who, with or without reasonable accommodation, can perform the essential functions of the employment position that such individual holds or desires."[6] The ADA requires an employer to make a "reasonable accommodation" if needed to ensure that a QIWD gets or maintains employment.

The ADA requires reasonable accommodation in three areas: to permit an employee to perform the essential functions of the job; to create fairness in testing an application of procedure; and to permit a disabled individual to enjoy benefits and privileges of employment that are equal to, or substantially equal to, those benefits and privileges afforded similarly situated nondisabled individuals. Reasonable accommodation may include making the existing facilities accessible, restructuring jobs, modifying work schedules, reassigning employees, or making any other workplace modifications that the employer can accomplish without undue hardship. An "undue hardship" consists of any action that requires significant difficulty or expense when considered in light of such factors as the nature and cost of the accommodation needed, the overall financial resources of the facility or employer involved, and the employer's type of operation.

A plaintiff filing suit under the ADA has the right to demand a jury trial. The potential damages on an ADA claim include reinstatement, back pay and benefits, attorney's fees, expert witness fees, and compensatory and punitive damages. The court also may award injunctive relief and order the employer to provide reasonable accommodation. Under the ADA, compensatory and punitive damages are not available if the employer demonstrates good faith efforts, in consultation with the disabled employee, to identify and make reasonable accommodation.

Risk managers should bear in mind that individuals who are participating in drug rehabilitation programs are considered disabled and therefore protected by the ADA, whereas employees who currently are abusing drugs are not protected. Thus, if an employer terminated an employee for being intoxicated on the job, the employer's action would not be considered a violation of the ADA.

Extreme caution must be exercised, however, in employment decisions regarding employed physicians who are suspected of drug impairment. Although such physicians can be summarily suspended if they pose a threat to patient safety, the risk manager must work closely with the credentials officers to ensure that facility bylaws are followed and due process is afforded to the physicians.

Moreover, even though a human resources policy may allow for termination of an employee who refuses to submit to a drug test based on reasonable suspicion of impairment, termination of an employed physician may be construed as constructive termination of medical staff privileges without due process and therefore a violation of the physician's constitutional rights. Risk managers should work closely with legal counsel, credentials officers, and the human resources department in such situations.

Age Discrimination in Employment Act of 1967   The Age Discrimination in Employment Act of 1967 (ADEA) protects employees over the age of forty from discrimination on the basis of age with regard to hiring, discharge, compensation, and other terms, conditions, or privileges of employment.[7] Further, employers are prohibited from retaliating against an employee for asserting his or her rights under the ADEA and from publishing any notice or advertisement that expresses any age preference or limitation. The ADEA applies to any employer that has twenty or more employees.

An employee proving a claim of age discrimination may be entitled to back pay and fringe benefits, including interest; attorney's fees and costs; and reinstatement or front pay. In addition, if the employee can prove that the employer committed a "willful violation" of the ADEA, he or she may recover additional damages in an amount equal to the award for back pay and benefits. These are not considered to be punitive damages. Moreover, lawsuits under the ADEA are not subject to the compensatory and punitive damage caps on Title VII and ADA claims.

In this age of downsizing and rightsizing, some organizations institute policies governing reductions in force or offer early retirement packages. All too often, an employee accepts an early retirement package and then files suit alleging age discrimination. To minimize the risk of lawsuit, it is imperative that risk managers and legal counsel be involved in the development of reduction-in-force or early retirement policies.

Sections 1981 and 1983 of the Reconstruction Civil Rights Acts

Section 1981 of the Civil Rights Act of 1866 prohibits racial or national origin discrimination in the making and/or enforcement of contracts, which may include any form of employment relationship.[8] It prohibits all forms of intentional bias in the workplace regarding the hiring, firing, disciplining, promoting, and compensating of employees and in working conditions. Section 1983 of the Civil Rights Act of 1871 prohibits deprivation of constitutionally guaranteed rights by employers under cover of state law.[9] To bring a section 1983 claim, the plaintiff must demonstrate that deprivation of constitutional rights was the result of "state action." Thus, section 1983 claims usually are directed against government bodies such as municipalities or quasi-government bodies that rely on government funding for their operations. Risk managers should be aware that plaintiff attorneys may file section 1983 claims against a facility that is a Medicare participating provider of health care, alleging that the facility is thus a quasi-government body because it relies on federal Medicare funds. Even if such claims are unsuccessful, they are expensive to defend. Damages in sections 1981 and 1983 cases may include reinstatement, back pay and benefits, punitive damages, attorney's fees, and interest.

Family and Medical Leave Act of 1993

The FMLA requires private-sector employers of fifty or more employees to provide up to twelve weeks of unpaid, job-protected leave to eligible employees for qualified family and medical reasons. An employee is eligible only if:

1. The employer has at least fifty employees within a fifty-mile radius of the employee's work site.

2. The employee has worked for a covered employer for at least one year.

3. The employee has worked for the employer at least 1,250 hours over the previous twelve months.

Employees must give thirty days' advance notice to employers of a request for a medical or family leave when the need for leave is foreseeable, such as for the birth of a child, placement of a child for adoption or in foster care, or planned medical reasons. An employer may require that an employee comply with the employer's usual rules for requesting leave but may not deny medical leave on that basis. In addition, when an employee has a medical emergency, the employer cannot require written notice that complies with the employer's usual medical policy or practice.

An employee who is denied leave under the FMLA may file a federal lawsuit to recover monetary damages and equitable relief, including reinstatement and promotion. An employer who violates the FMLA may be held liable for the monetary damages resulting from a violation of the act. These damages include wages, salary, benefits, or other compensation lost by the employee, as well as attorney's fees, expert witness fees, and other litigation costs. Even if an employee has not suffered any lost wages, he or she can recover monetary damages sustained as a direct result of the violation, including the cost of providing care to a child or parent, up to a sum equal to twelve weeks of wages or salary. In addition, the amount of damages will be doubled unless the employer can prove that it acted in good faith and reasonably believed that it was not violating the FMLA, in which case the court may deny doubling of the damages award.

Risk managers should work closely with legal counsel and the human resources department in the development and application of policies related to family and medical leave. For example, the law states that an employer *may* require an employee to provide a medical certificate. Use of the word *may* is permissive and grants employers latitude in policy development. However, problems arise when the word *may* is actually used within a facility's policy, because it could lead to inconsistent application of the rules by managers. If it is the employer's policy that medical certificates are to be provided by the employee, risk managers could suggest that the policy incorporate the word *shall*, which is construed as obligatory rather than permissive.

The final regulations governing this federal law (60 *Fed. Reg.* 2180) became effective April 6, 1995. They expand the definitions of *serious health condition* to include any period of incapacity because of a chronic condition, even without treatment by a health care provider during the absence and even if the absence is less than three days. This means that employees suffering from asthma and migraine headaches are eligible for leave under the FMLA. The definition of *health care provider* also has been expanded under the final regulations to include midwives and social workers. In addition to the broadening of definitions, the regulations clarify the interaction between the FMLA and workers' compensation laws, an important issue on which to focus.

Finally, in working with legal counsel and human resources personnel, risk managers must check their state's version of the FMLA. Some state laws allow a greater number of weeks for leave than that prescribed by federal law. Although the general rule is that federal law "trumps" state law, state law must be followed when it is more generous than federal law, and failure to do so could result in a lawsuit.

Equal Pay Act of 1963   The Equal Pay Act of 1963 prohibits differences in pay between men and women for the performance of "substantially equal jobs," unless the differences are due to a factor other than sex, such as a bona fide merit system, training program, or seniority system.[10] "Substantially equal jobs" are those that require equal skills, effort, and responsibility and that are performed under similar working conditions. The Equal Pay Act applies to all employers regardless of the number of their employees.

An employee who prevails on a claim under the Equal Pay Act may recover back pay in the amount of the wage differential. If the employer's conduct was willful, the court may double the damage award, unless the employer demonstrates that it acted in a sincere and reasonable belief that its conduct was lawful. The back pay award is generally limited to two years, unless the court determines that the violation was willful, in which case the back pay may be extended to three years. In addition, an award of attorney's fees and costs to the prevailing party is mandatory.

Agency Procedures

The EEOC is the federal agency charged with responsibility for receiving and investigating charges of discrimination arising under Title VII, the ADA, and the ADEA. Before an employee can file suit under those statutes, he or she must file a charge of discrimination with the EEOC or state human rights agency. The EEOC will review the charge and serve a copy upon the employer and any other person named as a respondent in the charge. The EEOC also may file a charge of discrimination on behalf of a person it believes has been the target of discrimination, even though that individual has not filed a charge on his or her own behalf.

A charge of discrimination must be filed with the EEOC within 180 days of the alleged unlawful employment practice. This period may be extended to 300 days, however, in jurisdictions that have a state or local agency charged with enforcing any state or local prohibitions against employment discrimination. Many states have agencies similar to the EEOC and have entered into agreements with the EEOC that allow a charge to be filed with either the EEOC or the comparable state agency.

The EEOC must investigate the allegations contained in the charge, and will invite the employer to file a response to the charge. The EEOC's investigatory powers are very broad. It may request relevant documents from the employer, inspect the employer's premises, interview other employees, and issue subpoenas to enforce compliance with a request for information. The EEOC also may schedule a fact-finding conference to allow for a face-to-face meeting between complainant and employer in order to encourage a settlement of the charge. It is imperative that the employer gather all the pertinent facts and documents prior to the conference. For example, the employee's manager or supervisor, whose presence may be requested at the conference, may have kept a separate file on the employee within the employee's department. Failure to learn of this prior to the conference may place the employer in a disadvantageous position from which it may be difficult to recover. The EEOC does not have the power to force the parties to settle but often encourages them to do so.

The purpose of the EEOC's investigation is to determine whether there is reasonable cause to believe the charge is true. If the EEOC determines that reasonable cause does not exist, it must dismiss the charge and notify the complainant, who then may file a lawsuit in federal court within ninety days of the EEOC's decision. This notice is called a *right-to-sue letter*. The EEOC's findings are not binding upon the court hearing the lawsuit in federal court. A complainant also may request and receive a right-to-sue letter before the EEOC completes its investigation.

If the EEOC determines that there is reasonable cause to support the allegations contained in the charge of discrimination, it must attempt to eliminate the cause of the unlawful practice through conference, conciliation, and persuasion. If conciliation efforts are unsuccessful, the EEOC can file its own suit against the employer, refer the matter to the U.S. attorney general for civil action, or issue a right-to-sue letter to the complainant. As a general rule, the EEOC issues a right-to-sue letter to the complainant and does not file suit, except (1) in a case involving a large number of employees, or (2) in a case in which the EEOC wishes to challenge the way courts have been interpreting the civil rights laws.

Common-Law Exceptions to Employment at Will

In addition to the federal statutes previously described, there are several other common law exceptions to the employment-at-will rule. These include breach of contract actions, public policy protections, and various types of tort claims. The sections that follow describe key points regarding these common-law exceptions.

Breach of Contract Actions   A common exception to the employment-at-will rule arises when an employee can prove that the employment relationship was governed by a written or implied contract. In certain cases in which employer and employee have not entered into a written employment agreement, courts have recognized an implied contract. Often these cases involve employee handbooks, the employee claiming that the handbook sufficiently established the conditions of employment to permit the court to find that a contract can be implied and that the parties should be bound by the handbook's terms and conditions. In addition, employers have been held liable for breaches of verbal promises to applicants or employees. If an employee proves a breach of contract, he or she still has an obligation to mitigate the potential damages by actively seeking comparable employment.

Risk managers should caution supervisors, administrators, and other managers against making statements to employees that could be construed as a promise of employment. In turbulent times, employees are likely to seek reassurance about job security. A comment such as, "As long as you continue to do a good job, you should be with us for a long time," puts the employer at risk for a lawsuit based on implied contract of employment if the employee is later terminated during a period of downsizing.

Public Policy Protections   The courts in many states have determined that employees should not be terminated for exercising their legal rights and have recognized a cause of action for an employee who has been discharged for exercising those rights. These claims often are referred to as *public policy* exceptions to the at-will employment rule. For example, courts have allowed an employee terminated for filing a workers' compensation claim to recover for wrongful discharge. Similarly, many states allow common-law or statutory "whistleblower" claims that allow an employee to recover upon proof that he or she was the subject of an adverse employment action solely because he or she disclosed an unfair or illegal practice by the employer. In addition, courts have recognized a cause of action for wrongful discharge on behalf of an employee who was terminated for refusing to violate a valid law.

Tort Claims   Tort claims constitute another common-law exception to the employment-at-will rule. These claims discover those circumstances, outside the realm of breach of contract, in which a person claims to have been injured as a result of the wrongful conduct of another. Employment-related tort claims may include:

- *Negligence:* In employment-related litigation, negligence theory is commonly applied in cases involving sexual harassment through claims such as negligent hiring, training, retention, or supervision of an employee. Plaintiffs also have used these theories against employers in cases in which they claim they have been injured by violence committed by employees in the workplace.

   Negligent hiring cases arise when a plaintiff maintains that the employer breached its duty to the plaintiff by hiring an employee it knew or should have known had a history of workplace violence or sexual harassment. Under the negligent retention theory, some courts have held an employer liable if it retained an employee that it knew or should have known posed a threat to other employees.

- *Defamation:* Often, this type of claim is brought by a former employee who claims to have been defamed by a former employer's statements to a prospective employer. A defamation claim also may arise when an employee claims to have been fired or demoted on the basis of a false accusation by the employer or another employee. Although the proof requirements vary from state to state, in general, a plaintiff claiming defamation must demonstrate that (1) the defendant made a defamatory statement concerning the plaintiff; (2) the statement was "published," or communicated to others, by the defendant; and (3) the plaintiff was injured by the statement. As a general rule, truth is a defense to a defamation claim.

To avoid liability for defamation, health care organizations should be careful in responding to inquiries from prospective employers of former employees. All responses should be truthful and fully supportable. The organization should avoid inappropriate or unnecessary characterizations of personal habits of former employees. When an employee leaves, the organization should attempt to obtain his or her consent to release information to prospective employers.

Risk managers also may wish to consider suggesting that the facility develop a policy that will allow release of only limited information about a former employee, such as verification of employment, position held, and salary at time of termination. Release of this type of information to prospective employers puts the organization at only minimal risk.

- *Invasion of privacy:* In the employment context, invasion of privacy claims generally rely on the theory of "unreasonable intrusion upon seclusion"; in other words, actions by an employer that unreasonably and intentionally intrude into the private affairs or concerns of an employee. A typical example of an invasion of privacy claim in the employment context might involve the improper disclosure or collection of information in an employee's personnel file. Another area of concern involves surveillance of employees that unreasonably intrudes into their private affairs, including eavesdropping or other monitoring of phone conversations.

- *Fraud or misrepresentation:* Liability for a fraud or misrepresentation claim may arise when an employee alleges that he or she was induced to leave a prior job on the basis of promises by his or her new employer, only to find that they were false. A misrepresentation claim also might arise when an employer makes certain promises that persuade an employee to stay, and the employee later discovers that they were false. Although courts in some states have refused to recognize fraud or misrepresentation claims in the employment context, health care organizations should be aware of this potential source of liability.

- *Intentional infliction of emotional distress:* As a general rule, to prove a cause of action for intentional infliction of emotional distress, a plaintiff must demonstrate that (1) the defendant's conduct was extreme and outrageous; (2) the defendant intentionally and recklessly caused harm; and (3) the plaintiff suffered emotional distress as a result. The proof needed to recover under this theory varies widely among the states. Some do not recognize this cause of action, whereas others will find an employer liable only for truly outrageous conduct. To avoid exposure to this type of claim, health care organization managers and supervisors should refrain from conduct that might embarrass or demean an employee unnecessarily.

- *Interference with business relations:* This category of tort claims is an umbrella for a number of related claims. Often claims of interference with business relations are raised by a former employee who alleges that he or she was denied future employment on the basis of conduct or statements by a former employer. In those cases involving references given to prospective employers, some courts have held that an employer holds a "conditional privilege" when responding to direct inquiries regarding former employees and may not be held liable for truthful responses, so long as the privilege is not abused.

• *Assault and battery charges:* Assault can be established when a person intends to cause a harmful contact with another person and creates a situation in which the plaintiff has a well-founded fear of such contact. A claim for battery arises when the defendant intentionally and offensively touches another. In the employment context, plaintiffs have brought claims for assault and battery in connection with harassment claims and claims involving violence in the workplace.

Claims involving violence include violent acts committed by patients, as well as by employees and visitors. As a result, the organization should develop policies that define procedures to be followed in the event that a patient becomes violent. Routine in-service training should include programs on how employees can recognize potentially violent patients and can protect themselves from acts of violence, and attendance at such programs should be documented.

In addition, all health care facilities should consider developing policies for handling crises. Emergency departments in high-crime areas are especially at risk, but even rural facilities have been known to develop plans to deal with crises such as a hostage situation.

HIRING GUIDELINES

Another area of possible risk exposure is in the hiring of employees. Although the primary focus of the hiring process is, of course, to find the most qualified person for the available position, minimizing the risk of exposure to litigation should be a secondary focus. Like all employers, the health care organization must conduct its interviews within the guidelines established by federal and state antidiscrimination laws. If the position is accurately defined and the hiring process is conducted with these guidelines in mind, the organization will already have put into place one of the most important elements of its defense against any claim of discrimination. The sections that follow provide an overview of the guidelines to follow when conducting the four major steps in the hiring process—defining the job, advertising and recruiting for the position, reviewing applications, and interviewing applicants.

Step 1. Defining the Job

The first step in filling a job vacancy is to create a job description that defines the essential job functions for the position. The job description should articulate the necessary skills for the position and describe the relationship between the available position and facility operations. The position also should be defined in a manner that does not exclude any applicant or group of applicants. This precaution is critical to defending a claim by a disgruntled applicant that he or she was rejected for inappropriate or discriminatory reasons. If litigation ensues, the health care organization will have to demonstrate that its decision was based on legitimate reasons related to its business operations.

Step 2. Advertising and Recruiting

As with the job description, the advertising and recruiting process must be performed in a manner that does not raise any suspicions that the health care organization is attempting to exclude any group protected by state or federal law. Advertisements and job listings should be placed in a wide variety of sources, including newspapers, professional journals, private and public employment agencies, and any other sources that will assist in providing the broadest pool of applicants for the position. In addition, ads and listings should avoid any language that might be construed as indicating a racial or sexual preference. The organization also should avoid references to age, unless a minimum age is required by statute or regulation.

In composing job advertisements, the best practice is to "say what you mean and mean what you say." If a job is advertised as requiring a master's degree and an applicant with lesser credentials is chosen, the employer may face claims by potential applicants with bachelor's degrees that they relied to their detriment on the ad and were therefore foreclosed from the position. Although the potential applicants would have the burden of proving that they would have been selected for the position, the employer still may need to devote treasured time to this issue. Moreover, if the situation occurs with candidates internal to the organization, morale problems could arise that put the organization at risk of poor-quality work.

Step 3. Reviewing the Application

The job application should elicit only that information the organization needs to determine whether the applicant can perform the essential job functions. The application should not request any information that might be construed as violating any laws.

The application should be signed and dated by the applicant. In addition, it should contain a statement of consent by the applicant permitting the organization to contact previous employers about the applicant's employment history and an acknowledgment by the applicant that, if hired, he or she is subject to immediate termination if the organization determines that any of the information provided is false. If the position is not covered by a written employment agreement or collective bargaining agreement, the application also should contain a disclaimer that informs the applicant that, if hired, he or she will be an at-will employee subject to termination at any time.

Step 4. Interviewing the Applicant

Any person involved in interviewing prospective employees must be well versed in the governing the interview process. The interviewer should clearly communicate the essential job functions to the applicant, and interview questions should focus on how the applicant can perform those functions. The interviewer must avoid making inquiries that could suggest that discrimination may affect the process. For example, the health care organization may advise the applicant of its attendance policy but may not ask whether, in the past, the applicant has been able to make appropriate child care arrangements to avoid absenteeism. Similarly, an applicant may be asked whether he or she would be willing to relocate, but not whether his or her spouse would be willing to change employment to accommodate relocation. If the information communicated and elicited during the interview relates to the job requirements and the nature of the position, the risk of potential liability is minimized.

Health care organizations also must be aware of certain areas of specific concern that apply to the interviewing process. These include disability-related inquiries, prohibited questions, privacy concerns, and false or misleading promises.

Disability-Related Inquiries　　The ADA prohibits an employer from asking about the existence, nature, or severity of a disability until after the employer has offered the position to an applicant. At the preoffer stage, the organization may ask about an applicant's ability to perform specific job-related functions but may not ask about the existence, nature, or severity of a disability. Once the job offer has been made, however, the employer may ask about the nature and extent of a disability, so long as the questions pertain to the essential job functions and are asked of all employees in that job category. If a job offer is withdrawn following the interview process, it can be withdrawn only for job-related reasons consistent with business necessity, and the organization should be prepared to demonstrate that the employee cannot perform the essential job functions, even with reasonable accommodation.

In addition, an employer may not require an applicant to submit to a preemployment physical but may require a physical once a job offer has been extended. Any medical information obtained from the physical must be maintained in a file separate and distinct from the employee's general personnel file and must remain confidential.

An employer can also require a prospective employee to submit to a drug test as a condition of employment once an offer of employment has been extended. However, public employers can only require a test when it is "reasonable" under the circumstances, such as when it is necessary to protect public safety. In addition, several states have passed statutes limiting drug testing in private sector workplaces. A risk manager should check his or her particular state law for restrictions on drug screening before implementing a drug screening policy.

Acceptable Versus Prohibited Questions   With these general guidelines in mind, the organization also should be aware that certain questions may not be asked before extending a job offer. The organization may ask:

- Whether the applicant can perform a specific task, such as carrying a heavy object, with or without reasonable accommodation if the position requires the employee to perform the task.

- That an applicant perform a job-related function but must provide a reasonable accommodation to the applicant who requests one or allow the applicant to describe how he or she would perform the job function.

- Whether the applicant can satisfy the organization's attendance requirements and may inquire about his or her prior attendance record.

- Whether an applicant has required certificates or licenses.

- Whatever party may be appropriate, such as a former employer, any questions about the applicant that it could ask the applicant directly.

The organization may not ask:

- About a disability that the applicant voluntarily disclosed before being offered a job.

- During the preoffer stage, if he or she has a disability, even if it would bar the applicant from the particular position at a later stage of the application process.

- During the preoffer stage, if he or she would need reasonable accommodation to perform a particular job, even if the applicant has voluntarily disclosed that a reasonable accommodation will be necessary.

- About current or prior lawful drug use, because these kinds of questions are likely to elicit information about a disability.

Privacy Concerns   The health care organization should be aware of any privacy restrictions under applicable state law. Some states restrict the questions an employer may ask about an applicant's off-duty activities. For example, it may be unlawful to refuse to hire smokers or people who drink alcohol off duty because the law may prohibit an employer from refusing to hire a person for engaging in lawful activities away from work, so long as the activities do not affect the employee's ability to perform his or her duties.

Risk managers should work with legal counsel and human resources personnel to ascertain applicable state laws regarding questions on employment applications specific to arrests and convictions. For example, health care applicants with access to controlled substances may be required to disclose arrest records because the issue is one of "job-relatedness." Further, some laws may allow inquiries regarding convictions so long as the inquiry is accompanied by a statement that a conviction record will not necessarily be a bar to employment. The reality is that many people with criminal records do not respond truthfully to questions on employment applications. Therefore, if state law permits the organization to conduct criminal background checks, the organization should take this precaution and not merely rely on an applicant's word.

Organizations also should be careful when inquiring into an applicant's employment or credit history unless those issues directly relate to the specific job. State law may prohibit any employer from asking an applicant whether he or she has ever filed a workers' compensation claim. Some states, however, have enacted statutes requiring hospitals to run criminal background checks on their employees. The facility should consult the law in its state to determine whether it is required to run criminal checks and which employees are subject to them.

Moreover, to avoid claims based on the common-law tort of invasion of privacy, the organization should not ask questions that might unnecessarily intrude into the applicant's privacy. The general guideline is to ask only about those areas that directly relate to the specific job.

False or Misleading Promises   Finally, the organization should avoid making any statements that might be construed by the applicant as a promise of a specific term or condition of employment. Plaintiffs in employment cases have attempted to use statements made during the interview process as the basis for breach of contract (discussed earlier) and/or misrepresentation of claims. For example, an employee may claim that he or she was induced to leave a prior job because the organization made certain promises the employee claims are untrue.

It also is common for an employer to provide a probationary employment period, which generally is intended to allow an employer to freely terminate an employee's employment if the employee's performance is not satisfactory during that period. It is, however, important not to make any misleading representation that the employee's job status is somehow more protected once the probationary period ends.

The interviewer also should provide accurate information regarding organizational policy on matters such as employee discipline and termination procedures. Additionally, the interviewer should not promise employment for any particular length of time or indicate any restrictions on termination. For instance, the interviewer should not say that the employee will have a job as long as his or her performance is good. Any statement to that effect could serve as a basis for a breach of contract suit.

. . . .

MANAGEMENT OF WORKPLACE RISK

Health care organizations, like all employers, attempt to maintain a productive workplace by minimizing the disruption caused by problem employees and by effectively addressing disciplinary issues as they arise. The following subsections highlight issues that may arise during the course of the employment relationship and suggest measures that organizations can take to minimize the risk of liability. As with all human resources issues, risk management and human resources personnel should consult with an attorney familiar with employment law in general and applicable state laws in particular.

Employment Handbook

The employment handbook generally spells out policies and procedures on matters such as absenteeism, tardiness, vacation, sick days, discipline, performance, reviews, and sexual harassment. Although it may state that it is not an employment contract, some courts have disregarded such disclaimers and treated handbooks as forming the basis of an implied employment contract. Thus, any health care organization that gives its employees a handbook or manual that outlines employment policies and procedures should abide by its terms.

At the beginning of the handbook, a disclaimer in bold print should inform employees that the handbook is not intended to create an employment contract. Some courts continue to recognize a disclaimer of this kind. The handbook also should include a signature page on which the employee acknowledges its receipt and his or her understanding of its contents, including the at-will policy and the fact that the handbook is not a contract. The employer should retain a copy of this acknowledgment. Ideally, the original document should be placed in the employee's personnel file and a copy retained by the employee. This practice will assist the employer if an employee later alleges that it altered objections purportedly noted on the signature page by the employee. Risk managers should work with human resources personnel to develop a method to track the receipt handbook acknowledgments from all employees. The one that "falls through the cracks" may well be the one that is needed to support the employer in a legal action.

As a final precaution, the employer should consult with an experienced labor or employment attorney before issuing a handbook to its employees and should arrange for its periodic review as employment laws change.

Employee Review Process

Since the Joint Commission on Accreditation of Healthcare Organizations (JCAHO) requires documentation of competence assessments of employees, it is important that health care providers establish a standardized and documented employee review process. The employee review process provides a health care organization with the opportunity to document employee deficiencies and to identify areas for improvement. Used properly, it can be an invaluable aid in maintaining and improving employee productivity and recognizing and rewarding positive work performance. At the same time, it can provide valuable documentation for use in defending lawsuits brought by employees.

Although no procedures will prevent a disgruntled employee from filing a lawsuit, an organization can minimize its potential liability by following these guidelines during the review process:

- Establish performance standards that are clearly defined, uniform, job related, and objective, and clearly communicate performance standards to employees to avoid any claim that they did not know how they would be evaluated.

- Assess an employee's competence to perform prescribed tasks, and compare that performance to established performance standards, not with another employee's performance.

- If the employee's performance falls below established performance standards, clearly articulate to the employee areas of improvement and what the employee must do to meet the established standard of performance. The employee's performance should then be revisited at established intervals.

- Enforce performance standards consistently to avoid situations in which an employee who has consistently received above-average evaluations is later discharged for an alleged performance problem. This situation is very difficult to defend if a claim is filed. Inconsistent enforcement also can be used as evidence of unlawful discrimination.

- Apply policies consistently. Disciplining one employee for excessive sick time while ignoring the same conduct from other employees will provide a basis for a discrimination lawsuit against the employer.

- Regularly document performance problems for all employees, not just the employee you intend to discharge. Regular documentation diffuses any argument by a disgruntled employee of being singled out for discipline.

- Instruct supervisors on how to conduct the evaluation and how to complete the review form. In particular, instruct supervisors that reviews should be based on personal observations and not "hearsay" or word-of-mouth reports from other employees. In addition, reviews should focus on the employee's ability to satisfy the objective performance standards and should not include any extraneous personal comments.

- Provide the employee with a copy of any written review and allow him or her the opportunity to address minor problems before they become major headaches.

- Consider instituting a grievance procedure that gives both employee and employer an opportunity to address minor problems before they escalate. If the policy identifies a chain of command to be followed, problems may be resolved at the lowest level.

- Limit disclosure of the substance of an employee's review to those individuals who need to know the information contained in it. Do not use the review procedure to publicly embarrass or ridicule an employee.

Harassment Policy

In today's employment climate, a comprehensive harassment policy addressing sexual and other prohibited harassment is a necessity. The U.S. Supreme Court recently made clear that an employer can avoid liability for some types of harassment by its supervisor if it (1) maintains an accessible avenue for employees to complain of sexual harassment and (2) takes prompt and effective remedial action once a complaint has been made.[11] Thus, health care organizations must develop a harassment policy according to the following principles:

- A comprehensive harassment policy should be prepared and distributed that defines the types of conduct that constitute sexual harassment, identifies the person to whom incidents of harassment should be reported, and outlines the kind of investigation that will be undertaken in response to any charge of harassment.

- The policy should prohibit all forms of harassment, including sexual harassment and harassment on the basis of race, gender, national origin, religion, disability, or age.

- An employee must be able to report an incident of harassment outside the ordinary "chain of command" whenever the incident involves a supervisor.

- Any harassment allegation should be investigated promptly and thoroughly. The extent to which the organization abides by and enforces its own policy is as important as the policy's language.

- The organization must maintain confidentiality regarding its investigation to the extent practical but should not tell employees that absolute confidentiality is possible.

- The organization must adopt appropriate remedial measures and act in a way that minimizes the possibility that the harassing conduct could be repeated. These actions should include possible termination of the harasser.

- The organization should check the laws in its state to see if education regarding sexual harassment must be provided to supervisory personnel within a specified period following their appointment date. Documentation of training and a list of personnel who attended the training should be retained.

- The organization should consider adding a sexual harassment policy to its employee handbook.

Protection Against Violence in the Workplace

Unfortunately, the past several years have seen an increase in workplace violence. As a general rule, employers are not liable for the violent acts of their employees unless the acts are related to job duties or the employer could reasonably foresee that an employee was likely to commit a violent act. Most often, incidents of workplace violence lead to claims that an employer negligently hired, retained, or supervised the employee who committed the violent act or did not take due care to maintain a safe environment. Whether an employer will be held liable depends on whether it had reason to know that an employee had a propensity to violence and, if so, by what means the employer attempted to protect fellow employees from the violent employee. The best protection is to scrutinize an applicant's prior employment history and obtain as accurate a profile as possible before hiring the applicant. The organization also should make sure that it provides proper security for its employees, visitors, and clients and implements policies that prohibit any harassment, intimidation, or threats of violence.

Regulation of Wages and Working Hours

Under the Fair Labor Standards Act (FLSA)[12] and similar state laws, employees must be compensated at or above a set minimum wage for all hours that the employer requires the employee to work, regardless of whether the employee is actually performing work-related duties. For example, an employee must be compensated for waiting time while on duty. The FSLA also requires that an employer pay overtime for work over forty hours in a week on the basis of one and one-half times the employee's regular rates. The FLSA and related state laws contain a number of exempt categories of employees, such as professional and administrative employees, to whom overtime pay does not apply. These laws also establish record-keeping requirements. The U.S. Department of Labor and similar state agencies are authorized to inspect and review an employer's records. These requirements should be carefully reviewed with an attorney familiar with applicable state laws.

Drug and Alcohol Testing

Drug and alcohol testing policies must be implemented with full consideration of the constitutional, statutory, and common-law privacy rights involved. It is essential to be aware of applicable state law as well. For example, some states have a specific statute governing the circumstances under which employees can be tested for drug use, and may penalize employers for violations of the applicable statute. On the other hand, a health care organization may be required to adopt drug-testing procedures if it is a government contractor with affirmative action obligations. One caveat regarding laws applicable to drug testing is use of the phrase *reasonable suspicion* within the law. If an employer tests an employee based on reasonable suspicion that he or she was under the influence of an illegal substance, the employee may file suit against the employer and allege that the suspicion was unreasonable. Risk managers should advise the organization that it is crucial to document the bases of its suspicions.

Personnel Records

Perhaps nothing varies from employer to employer more than policies and practices regarding the information contained in employee personnel records. Some employers document each and every circumstance affecting an employee's status, whereas others maintain little more than a copy of the application and annual review. The guiding principles are to conform to the standards required by regulatory agencies and to be consistent. If the organization requires its supervisors to document each and every absence, performance deficiency, or any other problem affecting employee status, it should do so for all employees and for all circumstances warranting a disciplinary notice. Inconsistency in documenting employee performance and maintaining information in an employee's personnel file may later bolster a plaintiff's claim of discrimination if the file is subject to review by an employee's attorneys during litigation.

Typically, employees have the right to review their personnel files and obtain a copy of them. The organization should ensure that its employee access policies comply with any applicable state statutes or regulations. It also should maintain the appropriate level of confidentiality regarding information contained in the files. Access to employee files should be restricted to supervisors and human resources personnel who rely on the information contained in them.

Employee Polygraph Tests

The Employee Polygraph Protection Act prohibits employers from directly or indirectly requiring, requesting, suggesting, or causing any employee or prospective employee to take or submit to a lie detector test.[13] It also forbids employers from using, accepting, referring to, or inquiring regarding the results of the lie detector test of any employee or prospective employee. An employer cannot discharge, discipline, discriminate against in any manner, deny employment or promotion to, or threaten to take action against any employee or prospective employee who refuses to take a lie detector test or based on the results of any lie detector test. The employee's rights under the act may not be waived by contract or otherwise, except where such waiver is part of a written settlement agreement. An employer may not disclose the results of a lie detector test except to the examinee, a court or similar body pursuant to an order in accord with due process of law, or to a government agency, insofar as the disclosed information is an admission of criminal conduct.

The act also prohibits retaliation. An employer may not take any adverse action in regard to an employee who has filed a complaint, instituted a lawsuit based on the act, testified or plans to testify in a proceeding under the act, or exercised the rights afforded by the act.

The act also contains a limited exemption for ongoing investigations of economic loss or injury to the employer's business and for drug security, drug theft, and drug diversion investigations. There are a number of restrictions on these exemptions, and if lie detector tests are administered pursuant to these exemptions, specific procedures set forth in the act must be followed in conducting the examination.

Any employer who violates the act may be assessed a civil penalty of not more than $10,000. The penalty is assessed by the secretary of the Department of Labor, taking into account the employer's previous record and the gravity of the violation. The Secretary of Labor also may seek injunctive relief to prevent further violations of the act.

An employee or prospective employee may bring a civil action against an employer who violates this act in any state or federal court. He or she may recover such legal or equitable relief as may be appropriate, including but not limited to employment, reinstatement, promotion, lost wages and benefits, and reasonable costs, including attorney's fees.

· · · · · · · · · · · ·

TERMINATION GUIDELINES

Perhaps more than any other aspect of the employment relationship, the end of that relationship has the potential to result in litigation. The potential for litigation extends not just to involuntary terminations, but also to cases in which employees voluntarily give up their jobs. The following procedures can help identify potential problems before they become lawsuits.

Voluntary Termination

Whenever an employee voluntarily gives up his or her job, the health care organization should arrange for an exit interview to verify that the employee's departure is, in fact, voluntary. It may be that an employee may later claim that he or she was constructively discharged from employment. In a constructive discharge case, the employee claims that he or she could no longer tolerate the work environment and was compelled to resign or retire because of harassment or discrimination.

The exit interview allows the organization to verify the reason for resignation. If the resignation is not truly voluntary, the organization can discuss an alternate position or some other arrangement that might circumvent a potential lawsuit. At minimum, the employer should request that the employee submit a resignation letter documenting his or her reasons for resigning. The exit interview also allows the organization to advise the employee of its policies regarding references and of benefits available after termination, such as the Consolidated Omnibus Reconciliation Act (COBRA).

Equally important, the exit interview provides the employer with valuable documentation in the event that an employee later files for unemployment compensation. Depending on state law, an employee who voluntarily leaves gainful employment is ineligible for unemployment compensation. If the organization is self-insured in this respect, money can be saved by challenging the employee's application for funds. If the organization wins the case, the employee will have an opportunity to appeal the decision and may well allege constructive termination. The documentation procured during the exit interview may be helpful to the organization at this time.

Involuntary Termination

Before discharging an employee, the organization should review the facts supporting the discharge and consider any laws that might affect it. A careful review of the decision, based on the following steps, can help prevent the stress and expense of a wrongful discharge suit.

Step 1. Gather All the Facts   If a discharge is the result of a business reorganization or a business decline, make sure that those facts are documented. The guiding principle in employment litigation is that the employer must be able to demonstrate that its decision was based on legitimate reasons related to its business operations. Therefore, the organization should verify all facts supporting the discharge before carrying out the decision. If the discharge is the result of a reduction in force due to a business decline, make sure that the data support the decision to discharge a given employee. Similarly, if the discharge is for performance problems, make sure that they have been properly documented. An objective review of the facts prior to implementing the decision will assist in minimizing the risk of liability.

Step 2. Review the Laws Affecting the Discharge   Once the facts supporting the discharge have been documented, the organization should review the laws that might affect the termination of that employment relationship. Any analysis of an employer's right to terminate must begin with the at-will employment rule. If the at-will rule applies, the employer can terminate the employment relationship at any time. However, before discharging the employee, the employer must determine whether its state courts still apply the employment-at-will rule and whether any of the following exceptions to the at-will rule apply:

- *Written employment agreements:* The employer should determine whether the organization and the employee have entered into a written employment agreement. If the organization has a written agreement with the employee, the grounds and procedure for discharge may be covered by the agreement. Before firing an employee who is subject to a written agreement, the organization should review it and abide by the procedures, if any, it sets forth.

- *Collective bargaining agreements:* If the employee is in a union and/or is subject to a collective bargaining agreement, the employer should be careful to follow its procedures for attempting to discharge the employee. The agreements almost uniformly have "just cause" requirements for discharging an employee and a grievance arbitration mechanism for resolving disputes. However, the employee has no power to enforce the collective bargaining agreement individually unless the union has breached its duty of fair representation to the employee.

- *Implied employment agreements:* If the employee is covered by an employee handbook or manual, the organization should bear in mind the possibility that a court might determine that the handbook formed the basis of an employment contract. Thus, the organization should follow the termination procedures, if any, outlined in the employee handbook to minimize the risk of liability for breach of contract.

- *Potential discrimination claims:* The employer should review the discharge for potential discrimination under federal, state, and local laws. Answering the following questions can help uncover potential problems:

1. After reviewing a list of employees discharged during the previous year, do any patterns emerge, such as a larger number of discharges among any protected groups to which the employee belongs?

2. If an employee is being discharged for a performance problem, have any other employees with a similar problem *not* been discharged? If so, why not?

3. In view of a potential disability discrimination claim, has the organization documented the employee's requests and its own efforts to reasonably accommodate the employee's disability?

4. Does the employer's record contain any statements that indicate a possible bias against the employee on the basis of age, gender, national origin, or any other prohibited discrimination?

By identifying potential problems before carrying out the discharge, the organization can ensure that it is on solid ground. Although there are no guarantees against lawsuits, an informed decision minimizes the risk of potential liability.

Step 3. Discharge the Employee   The discharge should be implemented in a manner that minimizes the risk of liability for the way in which it is carried out. If possible, the employee should be advised in person of the termination in a way that does not unduly embarrass or demean him or her. A "public" termination could give rise to a cause of action for intentional or negligent infliction of emotional distress. The person advising the employee of the termination also should be prepared to discuss any severance pay and benefits available and to advise the employee concerning the return of any company property.

In addition, risk management, in conjunction with the management information systems department, should develop a policy that locks out computer access to employees about to be discharged. Lockout should occur prior to notifying the employee of discharge. Maintenance of a lockout policy prevents potential loss of vital documents or theft of confidential or proprietary information.

Depending on the circumstances, the organization may wish to have a security guard outside the room where the discharge is to take place. If the discharged employee has personal effects on the premises, the guard will be available to accompany the employee as he or she retrieves the items and to escort the employee from the building if security is a concern.

Step 4. Review Release/Separation Agreements   If the employer wants the employee to sign a release of any potential lawsuits or claims, it should ask its attorney to draft or review any release so that the employee's signature will not be obtained on a document that cannot be used against the employee in any litigation that might ensue. For example, any release must be supported by adequate consideration from the employer. In addition, the ADEA and the Older Workers' Benefit Protection Act[14] impose specific requirements for releases from employees over the age of forty.

Risk managers should work with legal counsel and human resources personnel in reviewing state laws regarding these agreements. For example, under some state laws, the employee is automatically eligible for unemployment compensation benefits after signing a release or separation agreement.

....

INSURANCE COVERAGE FOR EMPLOYMENT-RELATED CLAIMS

In the face of growing employment-related litigation and the increased risk of exposure for these claims, risk managers should review current insurance coverage to determine whether it exists for employment-related claims. Typically, employment claims are not covered by existing policies. Although comprehensive general liability policies may afford coverage for defamation claims, such as slander or libel, these policies often specifically exclude claims for wrongful termination, discrimination, and sexual harassment. A directors' and officers' (D&O) policy may offer limited coverage to the individual officers and directors, but will not extend coverage to the health care organization itself unless entity coverage is specifically purchased. Other forms of insurance, such as fiduciary liability coverage, are unlikely to cover these types of claims.

In response to the escalation in employment-related litigation and the threat of exposure to employment-related claims, the insurance industry has seen the recent growth of employment practices liability insurance (EPLI). Typically, the insurer has a duty to defend claims made under the policy. Loss under EPLI generally includes all amounts an insured is obligated to pay, including amounts paid for judgments and settlements, as well as defense costs associated with the claim. In addition, some insurers now are offering endorsements to errors and omissions professional liability policies that extend coverage to employment-related claims. Some D&O insurers are also offering employment practices coverage to the entity by endorsement, even if the entity does not have full coverage under the policy. Risk managers should always read the insurance policy carefully to ascertain what is and is not covered

••••••••••••

CONCLUSION

It is a fact that the number of workplace discrimination and harassment complaints has grown over the past several years. Complaints of age, sex, and racial discrimination, claims of breach of contract, and complaints of harm resulting from workplace violence now are among the potential loss exposures faced by health care organizations in today's litigious climate. As a result, the risk manager's role in relation to human resources issues has increased. Risk managers today must be knowledgeable about federal as well as state statutes that apply to the workplace. They also must be able to ensure that hiring and termination guidelines are followed consistently and objectively, and that employment policies are established, updated regularly, and equitably enforced. Those steps will help protect the organization from potential claims—and, just as important, ensure an atmosphere of fairness in the workplace.

Endnotes

The author would like to acknowledge Daniel Engel, JD, Barbara Calderone, JD, Bonnie Lederman, JD, and Clinton Wesolik, JD, for their previous work which contributed to this chapter.

1. U.S. EEOC, Office of Field Programs, 1997. www.eeoc.gov/stats/index.html

2. Glad, P., and Rupp, R. *Employment-Related Liability Claims and Insurance,* 716 PLI 1 Comm. 121, 195. Commercial Law and Practice Course Handbook Series, Practing Law Institute, 1995, p. 1.

3. Americans with Disabilities Act, 42 USC §12101 et seq.

4. Family Medical Leave Act of 1993, 29 USC §2601 et seq.

5. Title VII of the Civil Rights Act of 1964, 42 USC §2000-e et seq.

6. 42 USC §12111 (8).

7. Age Discrimination in Employment Act of 1967m, 29 USC §621 et seq.

8. Civil Rights Act of 1866, 42 USC §1981.

9. Civil Rights Act of 1871, 42 USC §1983.

10. Equal Pay Act of 1963, 29 USC §206 (d)(1) et seq.

11. *Faragher v. City of Boca Raton,* 524 U.S. 775, 188 S. Ct. 2275, 141 L. Ed. 2d 662 (1998);

    Burlington Industries v. Ellerth, 524 U.S. 742, 118 S. Ct. 2257, 141 L. Ed. 2d 663 (1998).

12. Fair Labor Standards Act of 1938, 29 USC §201 et seq.

13. Employee Polygraph Protection Act of 1988, 29 USC §2001-09.

14. Older Workers' Benefit Protection Act of 1990, 29 USC §621 et seq.

PART V

Risk Financing

The risk financing section has been updated and revised to give the reader a thorough introduction to all aspects of insurance and risk financing. This edition of the handbook presents the genesis and purpose of insurance specifically and risk financing generally. The overview of insurance practices and principles both explains how insurance works as well as discusses the most prevalent insurance coverage found in a health care organization's risk financing program. Finally, the chapter on risk financing techniques is divided into three sections to present a more complete overview of risk financing. In other words, the chapter reviews those tools other than insurance that are available to fund losses. This chapter also includes a discussion on the tax implications of various risk financing methods and actuarial and accounting issues that a risk manager must address when deciding whether his or her organization should retain risk and how to fund for any retained risk.

30

Introduction to Risk Financing

Dominic A. Colaizzo

Chinese merchants were among the earliest known business people to utilize risk financing in the conduct of trade and commerce. Merchants who shipped their goods on the Yangtze River could never be sure that their goods would safely arrive at the trading centers down river. It was not unusual for a merchant boat to sink, losing both the boat and its cargo because some sections of the river were treacherous and difficult to navigate. To avoid total loss, merchants would coordinate their shipping activities and distribute their cargo among several ships. If a boat and its cargo were destroyed during its voyage, then an individual merchant suffered only a partial loss instead of a disastrous total loss. By pooling their interests, these merchants had greater assurance that all would not be lost.

In London in the late 1600s, individuals interested in investing or financially participating in shipping and trade ventures would gather at Lloyd's Coffee House in London. Notices of trade voyages would be posted that identified the type of ship, its cargo, destination, crew, and captain. Individuals would write their names under these notices with the amount of liability they would assume in the event of a loss at sea. Each underwriter pledged his personal assets to cover his percentage of the loss in return for a premium for taking the risk. When the notice or slip was fully subscribed, the contract was complete.

Throughout history, close-knit communities have practiced risk financing in an informal way by pooling their resources. In central Pennsylvania, Amish tradition provided for the entire community to help rebuild a barn or house devastated by fire or storm. In return for each member's pledge and resources to participate in the rebuilding effort, the risk of disaster was transferred and distributed to everyone in the community.

Within the last ten years, health care institutions have faced aggressive audits and investigations of their billing practices under the Medicare program by the Health Care Financing Administration (HCFA) and the Office of the Inspector General (OIG). As billing practices were found to be in noncompliance with the government's interpretation of the reimbursement regulations, many providers were (and still are) faced with the repayment of large amounts to Medicare plus fines and penalties. Providers, for the most part, never anticipated or funded for these business losses, which have had a material negative impact on the financial solvency of their institutions. Traditional insurance for such losses is, for the most part, unavailable. To finance these payments, some providers entered into contracts with insurers that indemnified the provider for the full loss in the year of payment in return for a full repayment of the insurance proceeds, plus the insurer's expenses, over a designated time period. Although this transaction had all the characteristics of a loan, it was structured as an insurance transaction, allowing for a beneficial accounting treatment by the provider and allowing the provider to stabilize their financials.

In the examples above, the Chinese, English, and Amish entrepreneurs, and health care executives all used some form of risk financing to deal with the potential for financial loss associated with adverse events. The basics of risk financing for a trip down the Yangtze River or to address Medicare fraud and abuse are essentially the same, including some or all of the following:

1. The need to anticipate the risks of the group's operations.

2. A plan or means to financially deal with a loss if it occurred.

3. Pooling of resources.

4. Transfer of risk.

5. Spread of risk.

6. Some risk retention.

7. Verbal or written contracts to substantiate financing in the event of a loss.

8. Identifying the simplest, least expensive, and most creative way to finance loss without jeopardizing the financial integrity of their operations.

9. The ultimate goal to protect the assets of their business or personal lives.

Today, risk financing is viewed as a complicated subject involving legal contracts, sophisticated accounting, and myriad government regulations. All sorts of risk financing structures are available, such as: an indemnification clause in a contract; an insurance policy transferring the risk for a given exposure for a given price; the use of a captive insurance company; or a risk securitization plan utilizing corporate bonds triggered by preestablished loss criteria. The types of exposures and losses faced by health care institutions for which a planned approach of risk financing is needed are also numerous and complex. These exposures range from the traditional slip and fall in the parking lot or medical professional liability and employment risks to the business risks of capitation, Medicare fraud and abuse, and interest rate fluctuations.

This chapter will introduce you to the concepts of risk financing within the overall context of the risk management process. It will establish the principles and foundation for structuring and implementing the various risk financing techniques discussed in detail in the chapters that follow. You will gain an appreciation of the importance of risk financing and a framework for a successful program.

RISK FINANCING IN THE CONTEXT OF THE OVERALL RISK MANAGEMENT PROCESS

You have learned by now that the risk management process involves two major areas that are intricately tied to each other—the identification and analysis of exposures and treating the exposures through some form of risk management technique. Figure 30.1 delineates the structure of this process and its key elements.

FIGURE 30.1.   **Risk Management Process Structure**

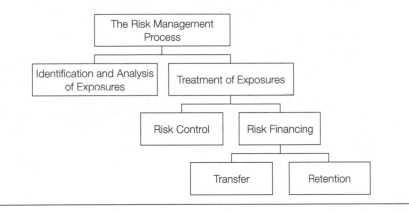

If we are unable to treat these exposures in a manner that significantly eliminates the potential for loss through loss control, we must plan for their treatment through some form of risk financing.

The focus of this chapter is on the risk financing techniques and methods for generating funds to finance loss that the risk control process could not avoid. In some cases, the potential for loss was not identified or anticipated for risk treatment. As the figure depicts, risk can be financed through risk retention or transfer to an outside party.

The decision to utilize the most appropriate method for your organization's risk treatment should be based upon cost efficiency, financial stability and security, and the control over program administration each method affords your organization.

············

RISK RETENTION

Risk retention techniques can vary from the unplanned payment of a loss from operating funds when the loss occurs to a more planned approach such as the use of a captive insurance company. Basically, there are four methods employed by organizations for the financing of loss through retention.

Use of Available Cash

Losses can be paid out of available cash from operations. Neither loss reserves nor funds have been established or designated for these payments. For example, institutions typically pay the $500 deductible for an automobile loss or the $5,000 deductible for a property loss out of available operating cash. These deductible payments are typically treated as unplanned expenditures from operations.

From a risk financing point of view, this technique is acceptable for losses that are small in nature and infrequent in occurrence. For example, this is not an acceptable technique for financing medical professional liability exposures that typically are significant and frequent for most health care organizations. Unplanned or unfunded payments for this exposure could materially affect the financial stability of the organization at any given time.

Loss Reserves

A loss reserve can be established for the potential liability or payment of losses. The reserve is typically based on expected losses and treated as an accounting entry that identifies the potential liability on the organization's financial statements. This liability also can be funded by cash, securities, or other liquid assets that are earmarked for the designated liabilities. This technique recognizes that a liability for loss exists and can go as far as setting aside assets to fund that liability. This is a significant difference from the first technique described above.

An example of the use of this technique is the treatment of the tail liability an organization has when it utilizes a claims-made insurance policy for its professional liability exposures. Accounting standards for health care providers require them to "book" or account for the liability they have for claims that have occurred but have not been reported (IBNR) by the end of their fiscal or accounting year. An accounting entry is made on the financial statements to reflect the liability for this IBNR. This liability may or may not be funded, depending upon the philosophy or resources of the organization.

Use of Borrowed Funds

Borrowed funds can be used to pay for losses when they become payable. For the traditional health care provider, this method is inefficient as it reduces the ability of the organization to borrow funds for more appropriate purchases. Moreover, the cost of unplanned borrowing typically is more expensive when used to fund operating expenses instead of long-term capital improvements. The use of borrowed funds to pay for losses is really a means of borrowing time. Ultimately, the institution must pay for the loss with its own earnings or other resources.

Self-Insurance

Formalized methods of self-insurance can be used when an organization finances its losses through a planned strategy. The most typical forms of self-insurance utilized by health care institutions today are the *self-insurance trust* and *captive insurance company.*

Self-Insurance Trust   A trust is a funding vehicle that, in simplest terms, is a bank account administered by an independent third party (trustee). The funds are designated for the sole and restricted purpose of paying losses. The trustee administers the trust through a formalized agreement and a statement of coverage that outlines the type and limits of loss to be paid. Funding in the trust is typically established at levels determined by an actuarial study and operated in accordance with Medicare requirements. From an accounting perspective, the trust's assets and liabilities are generally declared in a footnote to the parent's financial statements.

Since a trust is not an insurance vehicle, it is strictly limited to the funding purposes for which it was established. A trust typically cannot be utilized for the for-profit subsidiaries of a not-for-profit parent. Also, a trust lacks flexibility to accommodate regulated lines of insurance and cannot accommodate the risks of third parties (those entities or individuals outside the parent's economic family). Such activities would be considered the conduct of insurance and would be subject to state insurance regulations and/or jeopardize the parent's not-for-profit status.

The trust was once was the most common vehicle for self-insurance of the primary professional and general liability exposures of a health care provider. Now, it gradually is being replaced by captive insurance companies because these vehicles can more flexibly accommodate the various exposures and risk financing needs a health care institution faces in today's environment.

Captive Insurance Company A captive is a closely held insurance company whose insurance business is primarily supplied by and controlled by its owners and in which the original insureds are the principal beneficiaries. Simply stated, a captive is a corporation for which the product is the payment of losses and the revenue is premium payments. Because a captive is an insurance vehicle and can be structured in many ways, it has great flexibility to accommodate the numerous and varied risk financing needs of organizations such as third-party businesses, for-profit entities, and other lines of coverage. It is the most formalized method of self-insurance and its separate financial statements (balance sheet and income statement) legitimize and focus the risk management program within a health care organization. This vehicle elevates the risk management function in an organization as its board members typically are drawn from the senior ranks of management and the parent's board. Because of a captive's visibility, there is a greater importance on controlling losses, the primary driver of costs for any program.

A more detailed discussion of these formal methods of self insurance will be presented in later chapters.

············

RISK TRANSFER

By definition, risk transfer techniques transmit an organization's risk to an outside party. The most common method of risk transfer is the purchase of commercial insurance. Risk transfer also can be accomplished through noninsurance techniques, such as the use of an indemnification provision in a noninsurance agreement. Indemnification is the process by which one is restored or reimbursed to the extent of the loss ("made whole again").

Insurance is a contractual relationship that exists when one party (the insurer) for consideration (premium) agrees to reimburse or pay for another party's (insured) fortuitous loss caused by a predefined event (peril). Risk is shifted to others and spread among many parties. In general terms, covering the risks of unrelated parties by a company owned by multiple owners will constitute insurance.

From a practical view, insurance will nearly always involve some form of risk retention on a planned or unplanned basis. The use of a deductible would be an example of a planned retention. Denial of coverage as a result of an adverse policy coverage interpretation by the commercial insurer would certainly be an unplanned retention. The insurance policy, therefore, should never be viewed as a "complete" transfer of risk.

There are many forms and types of insurance that are generally classified in four areas as defined and illustrated in Table 30.1.

Chapter 31 on insurance will provide you with a more detailed discussion of these coverages. It is important to understand the principles and practices of these coverages as you apply them effectively in a risk financing program.

The other method of risk transfer, the use of indemnification provisions in a contact, can be an effective tool to lower the overall cost of risk. A hold-harmless agreement is an agreement between two or more parties defining an obligation or duty resting on one party to make good the liability, loss, or damage that the other party has incurred or may incur. Hold-harmless indemnification provisions can vary significantly. The most common type may read as follows:

Provider agrees to indemnify and hold harmless the managed care organization (MCO) against any negligent act or claim made with respect to items or services provided by Provider under this Agreement to the extent that the negligent act or claim is attributable to any person or activity for which Provider is solely responsible or

TABLE 30.1.   Types of Insurance

Type of Insurance	*Definition*	*Examples*
First Party	Provides coverage for the insured's own property or person. Coverage is intended to indemnify the insured to restore him or her to the same financial position that he or she had prior to the loss.	Fire and Property Business Interruption Boiler and Machinery Builders Risk Flood Earthquake Crime HMO/Capitation Stop Loss
Third-Party or Liability Insurance	Provides coverage to a party other than the insured. Coverage is intended to indemnify the third party for loss or injury caused by the insured. Involves three parties: 1. The insured who caused the harm or damage. 2. The party who is harmed. 3. The insurer.	Professional Liability GL (Premises Liability) Excess/Umbrella Employers Liability Auto Liability D&O E&O Environmental Impairment
Health and Welfare Insurance (Benefits)	Provides coverage for an insured's employees. Coverage is intended to indemnify the employee by restoring his or her health and earnings to the level maintained prior to the loss.	Workers' Compensation Health Benefits Long-Term Disability Short-Term Disability Dental Vision Life
Financial Guarantees (Surety and Bonds)	Provides a guarantee that specific obligations of a contract or performance will be fulfilled. These differ from traditional insurance in that assets are pledged for the full amount of risk transferred.	Surety and Bonds Public Official Bonds Judicial Bonds Contract or Performance Bonds License and Permit Bonds

which arises in connection with the use or maintenance of property, equipment, or facilities under the direction or control of Provider. MCO agrees to indemnify and hold harmless Provider against any negligent act or claim made with respect to items or services provided under this Agreement to the extent that the negligent act or claim is attributable to any person or activity for which MCO is solely responsible or otherwise arises from duties or obligations that are solely the responsibility of MCO under this Agreement.*

This clause states that each of the parties to the agreement will be responsible for indemnifying the other party for loss caused due to their negligence. This method of risk transfer is practical in certain situations such as the execution of construction or supply contracts, but not in others, such as for the professional liability risks of providing care to patients. Patients are unlikely to sign a hold-harmless agreement before agreeing to be admitted to the hospital for care. (Consent-to-treat agreements that patients are asked to sign before surgery or other invasive treatment are not intended to transfer risk but to authorize the particular treatment being proposed.)

As with any risk financing technique, indemnification provisions need to be evaluated for the cost efficiency, financial security, and control they afford in the risk transfer

---

*Bureau of National Affairs. Taken from Health Law and Business Library.

process. Therefore, these agreements need to be supported by the financial resources of the contracting party or some form of insurance or surety. They also need to be written or supported in such a way as to clearly define each party's rights and obligations in the event of a loss. In any event, given the legal uncertainties in enforcing hold-harmless agreements, they should never by relied upon exclusively to accomplish risk transfer.

. . . .

RISK RETENTION VERSUS RISK TRANSFER

The decision whether to transfer rather than retain risk will depend upon many factors, including:

- The size and type of your operation.
- Your financial strength and resources.
- The type of risk to be treated.
- Your risk taking philosophy.
- Your organization's future goals and objectives.
- The overall effectiveness of your risk management and loss control program.

The decision framework and principles discussed here will provide a foundation for choosing between the two.

Risk financing can be viewed as a continuum (see Figure 30.2) between total risk transfer to total retention. The figure provides a framework of the cost efficiency and cost certainty that each technique provides. Total risk transfer through insurance will fix costs with certainty, but cost efficiencies are sacrificed as a result of the insurance carriers' charges for taking on the full risk. The opposite is true for self-insurance of total exposures.

For example, if you purchased insurance for the first dollar of loss for your professional liability exposures, your financing costs for a given period of time would be fixed,

FIGURE 30.2. **Risk Financing Continuum**

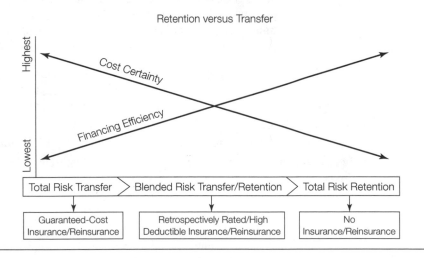

providing you with the highest level of cost certainty. Theoretically, it would also be the most costly approach since your premium would include:

- The insurance company's profit.
- Overhead.
- Estimate of the losses to be paid under the policy.
- Charges for use of their policy form.
- Reinsurance.
- Miscellaneous services.
- A charge for the "risk" they are assuming for this exposure.

Since they are taking the risk for you, they will want to retain control over most or all major decisions involving the coverage. This might be the best risk financing technique for a small organization with limited assets and resources where maximum cost certainty is important for financial well being. It might also be a better technique for financing miscellaneous exposures for which you cannot reasonably predict the frequency or severity of loss. These exposures can usually be insured at a "reasonable" price.

At the other end of the continuum, you could choose to retain all the risk for your professional liability exposures through some method of self-insurance. The cost of financing the risk would be most uncertain and would vary significantly with the frequency and severity of losses. Your cost efficiency would be at a high level since you would not pay an insurer for profit, overhead, and other charges and because you would retain control over all aspects of the risk financing program. This approach may make sense for very large organizations that have the resources to manage their risk management programs in an effective manner and have sufficient assets to accommodate the volatility of loss payments without impairment to the financial strength of the organization.

Typically, risk managers utilize a combination of risk transfer and retention for professional liability exposures, whereby the predicable layer of loss is retained while the unpredictable, catastrophic loss is transferred. This approach strikes a balance between cost efficiency and certainty. By retaining the predictable loss layer, insurance company profit and overhead and other charges are minimized. Transferring the unpredictable, more volatile catastrophic losses to an insurer at a "reasonable" premium prevents significant swings in overall program costs and promotes financial stability over the long term, a key objective of any well run organization. Program control is also balanced in a more effective and appropriate manner between your organization and the insurer.

As you chose between risk transfer and retention, consider the following guidance:

- The risk taking philosophy of your organization affects the goals of the risk financing program. Define the risk you are willing to take versus what you can afford. Senior management needs to be involved in establishing the philosophy.
- Self-insure the predictable layer of loss where possible. To do otherwise would be trading dollars with an insurer with a loss of control over your program.
- Transfer the unpredictable or catastrophic layers of potential loss at limits sufficient to protect the assets of your organization. Excess coverage at sufficient limits is usually available at reasonable prices. Self-insuring this exposure to loss would be risking a lot to save a little.
- If you retain risk, you should have an effective risk management program in place to control or minimize loss. Sound risk information, loss control, claims handling, and

litigation management systems are prerequisites. You also need to involve senior management and all "your" insureds in the process. An effective program will also make your organization an attractive risk for insurance purposes as you purchase coverage for catastrophic exposures. Keep in mind that risk retention through some form of self-insurance is not a cure for poor loss experience.

- Always take a long-term review of your risk transfer versus retention strategy. In a soft marketplace, you may be able to purchase insurance at a cost that is lower than expected losses. What impact does this have on your long-term costs and control over the program? Will the purchase of insurance take focus away from loss control efforts?

- Be prudent and conservative in funding for your self-insurance program. You can always fund less in the future if your loss experience develops better than expected. You always need a buffer to accommodate adverse loss experience in any program.

- When purchasing insurance, know your carrier better than they know themselves. Make sure they have the financial security, stable management, and policy services to be a good partner. Investigate their track record for paying claims and honoring their commitments. Do you have a relationship with your insured to resolve gray areas of coverage?

- Choose your risk financing consultants, brokers, actuaries, legal advisers, defense counsel, and auditors carefully. They need to be your partners and advocates in safeguarding your organization's assets and reputation. They not only have to be qualified through education and experience, but also need the integrity to have your total interest at heart. Make sure they can work together as a team to make your program as effective as possible.

··········

CONCLUSION

The risk financing of losses that occur despite your best risk control efforts may be from the unstructured payment of loss from operating funds, the application of the indemnification provision of a contract, or financed under the structured terms of a formal captive insurance company. The best and most effective method for your organization will depend upon many factors including the type of risk, its predictability for loss, the financial impact on your organization, your risk taking philosophy, the sophistication of your risk management program, and the degree of control you desire over program services.

As a risk management professional, it is your responsibility to guide your organization in making the best choice in meeting the overall mission and objectives of the organization. A sound risk financing program is important in protecting the assets of your organization and ultimately its reputation and ability to serve its customers and patients.

Suggested Readings

"BNA's Health Law & Business Library." Bureau of National Affairs, Inc., October 1999, Washington, D. C. (202) 452-4200. www.bna.com

Gibbons, R., Rejda, G., and Elliott, M. "Insurance Perspectives." American Institute for Charted Property Casualty Underwriters, 1994.

"The Hold Harmless Agreement." Cincinnati: The National Underwriter Co., 1987.

Krauss, G. E. *Essentials of Property and Casualty Insurance* (10th ed.).

31

Insurance Practices and Principles

Kimberly Willis
Judy M. Hart

This chapter presents insurance principles and practices that are applicable to the health care industry. The first section written by Kimberly Willis discusses basic concepts about what insurance is, how it is regulated, and how we purchase insurance in this dynamic marketplace. The second section written by Judy Hart discusses the major types of insurance used by health care institutions.

These topics are important because the most common method of transferring or financing risk is to purchase insurance. Unfortunately, many individuals charged with health care risk management are assigned responsibility for the purchase of insurance but have limited knowledge of its nuances. Many health care risk managers are seeking an insurance product that is a comprehensive and cost-effective method of transferring unwanted risk to an insurer. This dictates a need to understand the nature of insurance, to how to read an insurance policy, to understand traditional health care coverages, and to be able to determine when changes are necessary. Insurance alone cannot prevent risk, but it can provide security against loss.

DEFINITION OF INSURANCE

Barry Smith defines insurance as "a system by which a risk is transferred by a person, business, or organization to an insurance company, which reimburses the insured for covered losses and provides for sharing of costs or losses among all insureds. Risk, transfer, and sharing are vital elements of insurance."[1] It is risk, or the possibility of loss, that creates the need for insurance. An organization can retain risk or transfer its risk to another organization. Risk is commonly transferred to an insurance company. By accepting and sharing in the risk of many organizations, the insurance company is able to statistically calculate the likelihood that losses will or will not occur. It can also calculate their likely severity. This calculation results in a premium that is then charged back to the organization wishing to transfer their risk. If the method of premium calculation is sound, the insurer should be able to pay the claims that are incurred and still return a profit.

An insurance policy is a legal contract that creates obligations for both the insured (organization wishing to transfer risk) and the insurer (insurance company accepting the risk). Under this contract, the insurer promises to pay certain amounts if defined events take place. For example, the insuring agreement of a professional liability policy obligates the insurer to pay on behalf of the insured sums, which the insured shall become legally obligated to pay as damages for the rendering or failure to render professional health care services. This obligation is modified by various other clauses, coverage terms, exclusions, and definitions within the insurance contract. An insured's obligations vary but most frequently they are required to pay a premium, report claims or likely losses in a speedy manner, and minimize the likelihood for loss. Insured losses must usually be fortuitous events—sudden and accidental. Intentional acts that result in loss are generally not covered by the insurance contract.

While insurance contracts vary, they usually contain four standard elements: the declarations page, insuring agreement, conditions of the policy, and exclusions.

The *declarations page* identifies the named insured and describes the property or activity to be insured. Components of the page include the policy number, coverage inception and expiration date, insured address, policy limit, applicable deductible, and premium. The declarations page may also identify the various forms to be attached to the policy.

The *insuring agreement* provides the language wherein the insurer states its obligations under the terms of the contract. In general, the insuring agreement is often broadly stated but later narrowed based on additional wording elsewhere in the policy. The insuring agreement contains conditional promises to pay. For example, if the policy states the insurer will pay sums related to the rendering or failure to render "professional services," the meaning of professional services is defined elsewhere in the policy. If the claim does not fall within this definition, it will not be covered. When interpreting the policy, the insured should remember the insuring agreement is subject to the declarations, conditions, exclusions, and definitions contained elsewhere in the policy.

The *conditions of the policy* spell out many of the obligations of the insured and the insurer. Examples of important conditions include:

- The insured's obligation to provide prompt notice of loss.
- The insured's obligation to cooperate with the insurer in investigation and settlement of loss.
- The insured's obligation to pay premium in a timely manner.
- The conditions under which the policy may be canceled or nonrenewed.
- The insurer's right to inspect the premises.
- The coverage territory of the policy.
- The applicability of limits, deductibles, and defense expenses.

Failure of an insured to adhere to the policy's conditions could result in the insurer's refusal to honor a claim.

Exclusions refer to policy provisions that eliminate or minimize coverage the insurer does not intend to provide. Exclusions are usually identified in a specific section of the policy; however, additional exclusions may be dispersed throughout the wording and terms of the contract. In some cases, exclusions are added by endorsement(s) attached to the main policy form. While exclusions appear punitive, they may not be. In some cases, an exclusion is added to eliminate the potential for duplicate coverage or coverage not needed by a typical insured. In either case, by adding the exclusion the insured could receive a premium credit or lower premium. Under other circumstances, an insurer may add an exclusion for their own benefit. Such is the case when the carrier is trying to limit risk they consider undesirable, a morale hazard, or outside their reinsurance arrangements. Typical exclusions include intentional acts, war, pollution or nuclear energy, and criminal acts.

Many liability policies exclude or minimize coverage provided for sexual misconduct, antitrust, punitive damages, and discrimination.

Insureds should work closely with the broker, agent, consultant, and/or carrier to make certain their insurance policy(s) provide comprehensive, cost-effective, and financially secure transfer of risk.

. . . .

HOW INSURANCE IS REGULATED

Insurance is a highly regulated industry. The majority of the regulation is mandated at the state level. The rules and regulations vary by state. Nearly all states give their insurance departments the power to regulate rates, to license insurers and insurance company representatives, to approve policy forms, and to respond to consumer complaints.

Insurance brokers and agents must be licensed in their state(s) of operation. This usually involves a state examination and continuing education requirements.

Most insurance carriers must apply and financially qualify in every state in which they wish to solicit or conduct business. Once a carrier is approved by the state, it is considered admitted. As an admitted insurer, the carrier must obey all state laws regulating the operation of an insurance company. In addition, they must file their current policy forms, any changes in forms, and any premium rate increases or decreases with the state for approval by the insurance department. Most states have established insolvency funds. These guaranty funds are designed to protect insureds if their admitted insurer becomes insolvent. These funds generally cover only the failure of insurers that are licensed to do business in the state and are typically financed by assessments against those insurers.

For various reasons, some carriers operate as nonadmitted or surplus lines carriers in a state. These companies are exempt from rigorous state regulations. Neither their premium rates nor the contents of their policies are subject to regulation and review. Since these carriers are exempt from various state regulations, they are not allowed to participate in the guaranty fund.

. . . .

INSURANCE COMPANY FINANCIAL SECURITY

The financially stability of an insurance carrier should be a key consideration in an insured's decision to transfer risk. If an admitted carrier fails, their insureds may have access to the state guaranty fund. Unfortunately, the protection offered by these funds is limited. Not all state funds cover all policies or claims. For example, some guaranty funds exclude medical malpractice policies. Others limit the time in which a claim can be reported to the fund. The duration may be shorter than the time provided under the original insurance policy. In some cases, the limits of liability provided by the fund are lower than the limits the defunct insurance carrier provided. For example, the fund may only pay thirty-three cents on each dollar of the policy limit. In this scenario, the insured is still responsible for the remainder of any claim.

It is critical that insureds carefully evaluate the financial position of their insurance carriers. Due to this, a rating system has been developed to categorize the financial condition of carriers. The most frequently cited rating resource for insurance companies is A. M. Best. Best has a two-tiered rating system consisting of quantitative analysis as well as qualitative review.

Financial Strength and Size

Under quantitative analysis, each carrier's financial performance is examined and more than 100 financial tests are performed. These tests primarily focus on profitability, leverage and capitalization, and liquidity. Based on the ratios, Best assigns a value from "A++" to "F."

Best's qualitative review includes an evaluation of (1) the company's spread of risk exposures; (2) appropriateness of reinsurance; (3) quality and diversification of assets; (4) adequacy of loss reserves; (5) adequacy of surplus; (6) capital structure; (7) management experience; (8) market presence; and (9) policyholders' confidence. Based on these factors, Best assigns a class ranking of 1 to 15. An insured can obtain an insurer's Best rating by asking his or her insurance carrier, agent, or broker for a copy of the current report. In addition, the Best manuals are usually available at large public or university libraries. A second source for financial information is Standard & Poor's as well as Moody's.

....
HOW INSURANCE IS PURCHASED

Most health care risk managers gain access to the commercial insurance market through the use of an insurance broker or independent agent.

Traditionally, brokers are independent insurance professionals who represent the insurance buyer to the insurance company. In this role, they participate in the evaluation of risk potential, gathering of exposure and loss information, presentation of the data to the insurance community, negotiation of coverage terms and premium pricing, and evaluation of quotations. Brokers may also provide assistance in loss mitigation, as well as alternative means of financing risk. Historically, agents have legally and contractually represented the interest of the insurance carrier, not the insured. An agent may represent one or many insurance carriers. In practice, the line between a broker and agent has blurred. Both act as facilitators to the evaluation and purchase of insurance.

Brokers and agents are commonly compensated on a commission basis. The amount of commission varies by line of coverage and carrier. Brokers are frequently willing to accept compensation on a flat fee basis. This removes any bias the broker might have regarding their commission level with a particular carrier. Some brokers are willing to work on a fee plus incentive basis. Regardless of the method of compensation, your broker or agent should be willing to openly discuss compensation.

············

DRAFTING COVERAGE SPECIFICATIONS

Risk managers often have the responsibility of securing cost-efficient, comprehensive policies from a financially secure insurer. This is not an easy task. The process of securing coverage often needs to begin at least six months prior to policy inception. The first step is an evaluation of exposures and the insurance products available to cover the exposures. Once the exposure(s) to be transferred and potential carriers have been identified, an application for coverage is prepared. This application is often called an underwriting submission. The submission serves as a tool to present your organization's business strategies, risk exposures, and insurance desires to the insurance marketplace.

Some carriers will allow the insured to develop their own application for coverage. Others require that the submission be prepared based on a standard format developed by the carrier. The submission is then submitted to the carrier's underwriting department. A quotation is developed. The insured, broker or agent, and insurer then negotiate through coverage terms, services, and pricing considerations. Upon agreement the coverage is bound.

Components of the underwriting submission frequently include:

- A description of operations and organizational chart.
- Listing of named insureds and additional insureds.
- Location listing.
- Current exposure information.
- Currently valued historical loss experience (three to ten years of loss experience).
- Large claim summary.
- Signed application (as requested by the carrier).
- Current annual report or other financial statements.
- Description of risk management department procedures including loss prevention and claims management.
- Description of desired coverage—limits, deductible, coverage extensions, pricing guidelines, policy period, and key coverage terms or services.

Key criteria to consider when selecting a carrier include:

- Does the purchase of this policy support the short-term and/or long-term objectives of the health care organization and risk management department?
- Is the insurance carrier financially secure? What is their financial rating according to A. M. Best or other rating organization?
- Is the carrier knowledgeable in health care operations?
- Is the carrier flexible?
- Is the pricing competitive?
- How will future pricing be impacted by the organization's favorable or unfavorable loss experience?
- How will future pricing be impacted by losses within or outside of the health care industry?
- Is the carrier capable of meeting claims administration, loss prevention, risk management information system (RMIS), and education needs?

- How long has this carrier been offering this type of coverage? What is their past history in the marketplace?
- What is the carrier's claims handling philosophy? Will they allow input from your organization?
- Who do they use for legal counsel?

Insurance policies vary in terms and conditions, but key coverage considerations should include:

- Is the quotation based on complete and accurate exposure and loss information? If the information is not complete, could the pricing change based on the outstanding data?
- What is the limit of the policy? How does it apply?
- Is there a deductible or retention and how does it apply?
- Does the policy include a coinsurance provision?
- What are the policy period, effective date, and expiration of coverage?
- What is the premium? Is there a minimum premium? Is the premium flat, assessable, or auditable?
- Is coverage claims-made or occurrence?
- If coverage is claims-made, what is the retroactive date?
- What is the intent of coverage? Has the carrier released sample forms and endorsements?
- What are the key exclusions? Are these common? Can they be amended?
- Who is covered by the policy? Organizations as well as individuals?
- What is the coverage territory?
- What is the procedure for reporting claims?
- What is the definition of a claim?
- Does the application become warranty to the policy?
- How are defense costs handled? Are they within or outside of the limit and/or retention?
- Are there provisions for adding or deleting exposures during the policy period?
- Under what circumstances can the insured and insurer cancel or nonrenew the policy?

Once coverage has been bound, the broker or carrier will issue a binder of insurance coverage. The binder serves as evidence the coverage was purchased. Once the actual policy is issued, the binder is no longer needed. It may also be helpful to have your broker or agent prepare an insurance summary. This tool highlights key components of your insurance policy. The summary will often include a schedule of the types of policies purchased, policy numbers, policy period, limits of coverage, deductibles, premiums, and a summary of the coverage intent, as well as major exclusions.

PREPARING FOR THE HARD MARKET

The insurance industry is cyclical. It is characterized by periods of low premium, flexible terms, and generous capacity later to be fraught with escalating premiums, strict underwriting procedures, and limited availability of coverage. Since the late 1980s, the industry has generally been in a soft cycle. Carriers have been willing to offer flexible and competitively priced programs. This will not always be the case. While no one can predict a turn to a hard market or the best position to take in a hard market, certain considerations should be evaluated. These include:

- What is the overall business strategy of the carrier?
- Have they historically been committed to the health care industry?
- Are they committed to the organization?
- How has the carrier reacted to other pricing cycles?
- Is it time to lock in a multiyear program based on today's pricing?
- What is the financial status of the carrier?
- What is the carrier's loss ratio for similar accounts? Is the exposure profitable for them?
- Does it make sense to put all the organization's exposures with one carrier and hope the economies of scale prove beneficial, or is it more appropriate to disperse the exposures throughout the marketplace and create numerous relationships?

The potential for a hard market also dictates that a health care organization reevaluate their current risk financing program. Analysis should include:

- Review of limits purchased: Are they enough? Should they be reduced or restructured?
- Review of retentions: Should the retentions be restructured?
- Should our organization continue to transfer this risk? Could it be better accommodated by an alternative risk financing vehicle or retention of the risk?
- Review of the organization's risk and claims management program: Is it in order?

The hard market is eminent. Because of this certainty, health care risk managers should constantly be reviewing their risk financing techniques for short-term as well as long-term benefits.

CLAIMS-MADE VERSUS OCCURRENCE POLICIES

Certain health care-related policies are often written on a claims-made basis. Examples include directors' and officers' (D&O) liability, and managed care errors and omissions (E&O). Other policies are offered on an occurrence basis. Automobile, property, and workers' compensation are usually written on occurrence forms. Still other coverages, such as professional liability, are commonly written on either claims-made or occurrence.

An occurrence policy covers an insured for incidents that occur while the policy is in effect, regardless of when the incident is reported to the insurer. Unlike claims-made, there is no need for an insured to obtain an additional policy endorsement or extension when they wish to move to a new insurer. The date the claim or incident is filed has no impact on the applicable policy period. The date the claim occurred determines the applicable policy period.

A claims-made policy covers an insured for incidents that both occur and are reported to the insurer while the policy is in force. This method of tracking claims can be burdensome because claims or incidents may occur during one policy period but are not reported until after the policy period has ended. If this happens, no coverage will apply towards the claim. This potential gap in coverage can be minimized through the maintenance of an original retroactive date (nose) and/or the purchase of an extended reporting period (tail).

For coverage under a claims-made policy to apply, the incident or claim must have occurred after the retroactive date of the policy. The retroactive date is usually the first date the insured purchased claims-made coverage. It is usually recommended that this date be maintained as the policy years progress.

For example, assume a physician purchased her first claims-made policy on 7/1/96, from XYZ Insurance. The policy will cover those claims that are incurred and reported from 7/1/96 through 7/1/97. Since this is the first claims-made policy the physician has purchased, it will have a 7/1/96 retroactive date. Now assume three years pass. The physician has maintained claims-made coverage with XYZ for the entire three-year period. In addition, she has maintained her original retroactive date of 7/1/96. Unbeknownst to the physician, an incident that ultimately results in a claim occurred on 8/1/96 but was not reported to the physician until the current policy period (7/1/98–7/1/99). Even though the claim occurred on 8/1/96, it will be paid under the current claims-made policy rather than the original 7/1/1996–1997 policy. This is due to the fact that the physician has maintained her retroactive date of 7/1/96 on the current policy. The current policy covers those claims incurred and reported for the 7/1/96 through 7/1/99 period; however, the current policy would not cover claims reported to a previous policy. If the physician had not maintained her 7/1/96 retroactive date, the claim would not have been covered by either policy. In contrast, if the physician had purchased occurrence coverage, the claim would be paid under the 7/1/1996–1997 occurrence policy regardless of when the claim was reported.

Nose

Under a claims-made form, the nose is the period of time between an insured's retroactive date and the current policy period. In the example above, the nose is the period 7/1/96 to 7/1/98. The policy will respond to claims that have been incurred during the period 7/1/96 through 7/1/98 but are not reported until the 7/1/1998–1999 policy year. In addition, the 1998–1999 policy will also provide protection for those claims incurred and reported during the 7/1/1998–1999 policy year.

Tail

A tail is also known as an extended reporting period (ERP). An ERP may need to be purchased if an insured changes carriers or various other scenarios. The ERP essentially converts a claims-made policy to an occurrence policy by extending coverage to all claims that arise from care rendered during the policy period (and nose period, if applicable), regardless of when the claim is reported.

It is preferable to purchase an unlimited extended reporting period. Some carriers may limit the ERP and only allow claims to be reported within twelve months, thirty-six months, and so on.

The carrier will usually charge an additional premium for the ERP. The premium is often in the range of 100 percent—200 percent of the annual premium for the current policy period. During a soft-market cycle, carriers may be more willing to offer this extension at a more reasonable price. An ERP can be purchased from the expiring carrier, the new carrier, or a third carrier who was previously not involved in the risk. Generally, the new carrier is the most cost-effective option because they see the potential for a new long-term relationship.

An additional item to consider when purchasing claims-made coverage is the definition of a claim. Most claims-made policies define a claim as a suit or an incident likely to result in a suit. This allows the insured to report incidents that may become a suit under the current policy period and minimizes the likelihood of a gap in coverage. Some policies, however, define a claim as only a suit. Care must be taken when moving from one claims-made insurance carrier to another. Even if the new carrier agrees to maintain the insured's original retroactive date, it is possible for a gap in coverage to result if each carrier defines a claim in different terms.

HOW MUCH SHOULD WE PURCHASE?

Health care risk managers are often concerned as to whether they are purchasing the appropriate amount of insurance coverage. This question is not easily answered. Guidelines are provided by reviewing the limits historically purchased by the organization, the loss history of the organization, analysis of the regulatory and legal climate, evaluation of exposures created by the organization's business strategies, and benchmarking these factors against other similar organizations. Included in this analysis is a review of what limits are being purchased as well as risk retained through a deductible or self-insured retention.

LIMITS OF LIABILITY

The policy limits of liability state the maximum obligation of the insurer. Limits are frequently quoted on a per occurrence and annual aggregate basis. For example, coverage might be bound providing $1 million per occurrence with a $3 million annual aggregate. These limits are commonly represented $1,000,000/$3,000,000. Under this scenario, the most the carrier will pay is $1 million for a single occurrence during the policy year. In addition, the most the carrier will pay for all claims in the policy year is $3 million regardless of the number of claims filed.

Defense costs can play a critical role in determining the actual policy limits. It is preferable to have defense costs outside of the policy limits. Under these circumstances, the carrier will pay up to $1 million plus all defense costs. The less desirable method is to have defense costs within the limit. In these cases, the most the insurer will pay is $1 million regardless of amount of defense and supplementary payments due.

In addition to per occurrence and aggregate limits, some policies contain sublimits. A sublimit caps the most the policy will pay for a particular peril. This limit is usually within the limits provided by the policy. The sublimit is not in addition to the policy limits.

Deductibles or self-insured retentions (SIRs) state the amounts the insured has agreed to retain. Deductibles or SIRs may apply to each claim, each occurrence, or in aggregate to all losses for the policy period. Both serve to reduce premiums. Under a deductible, claims handling usually remains within the authority and responsibility of the insurance carrier. The actual limit provided by the policy is usually the per occurrence limit less the deductible. To explain, if the policy contains a $1 million limit and a $100,000 deductible, the most the policy will actually pay is $900,000. In contrast, if the policy includes an SIR, the policy will pay the full limit described excess of the insured's SIR. The SIR obligates the insured to pay the first $100,000 then the carrier will pay up to $1 million. SIRs usually allow the insured influence or control over the claims administration process.

············

SPECIFIC TYPES OF INSURANCE FOR THE HEALTH CARE INDUSTRY

Several broad categories of insurance are offered by the insurance industry. These types of coverage are categorized by the kinds of loss they insure against. The most common types of coverage relating to losses inherent to the health care industry are first-party coverage, third-party or liability coverage, health and welfare insurance, and financial guarantees provided by carriers in various forms of bonds such as surety bonds. Other types of coverage include named peril, all risk, time element, and so on.

First-Party Insurance

First-party insurance provides financial reimbursement as the result of damage or destruction to the insured's own property. This type of insurance is also called "direct damage" coverage.

One of the significant exposures to loss faced by a health care organization is direct damage to owned or leased buildings, business personal property, attached equipment, building service equipment, and the loss of income should all or a portion of the facility be unusable as the result of a loss. Such losses can result from fire and lightning, windstorm, hail, explosion, smoke, water, sprinkler leakage, riot, vandalism or malicious mischief, falling aircraft or other vehicles, sudden freeze, weight of ice and snow, earthquake, and other perils.

The common risk treatment for property losses is the purchase of commercial insurance. Property insurance for health care organizations has traditionally been readily available in the insurance market due to the positive nature of health care industry property risks. Most health care property is classified as highly protected risk (HPR), meaning that the risk is adequately protected and that management has a preventative attitude toward loss avoidance and life safety. Health care property risks are considered well below the national average.

The property insurance marketplace for these HPR risks has been stable and very competitive for the past several years. However, recent catastrophic losses have caused a restriction in the market thus causing increased premiums and limited availability of high-limit catastrophic coverage for losses attributable to wind, flood, and earthquake. Most HPR property carriers provide loss control engineering services to their policyholders. These value-added services can assist the risk manager in maintaining the status of the current facilities, as well as provide input on new construction. Generally these carriers provide inspections and recommendations on an ongoing basis. The benefits of complying with the insurers' recommendations should be measured against the cost of compliance.

The majority of property policies available to the health care industry are comprehensive in form. A single policy can incorporate coverage such as:

- Physical damage to real and business personal property.
- Time element coverage.
- Boiler and machinery.
- Transit coverage.
- Automatic builders' risk protection.
- Fine arts coverage.

- Valuable papers coverage.
- Electronic data processing coverage.

Property policies specify the exact property and business personal property to be covered, the dollar amount of coverage afforded, and the types of loss covered under the policy. Property insurance may protect any covered person or organization that has an "insurable interest" in the property.

Property coverage can be written on an actual cash value (ACV) basis or replacement cost basis. Protection afforded on an ACV basis will provide replacement less depreciation. Under a replacement cost basis, claim payments will be based on the cost to repair or replace the property without any deduction for depreciation. Because this preferred option requires that you carry enough coverage to replace damaged or destroyed property, it is very important to determine the correct property limit. Most replacement cost policies contain a "coinsurance" provision. This provision requires the insured to carry insurance equal to a specified percentage of the replacement cost of the value of the property covered. If the amount of coverage is inadequate, a coinsurance penalty is assessed at the time of loss. This may result in reimbursement for loss that is less than the replacement cost or cost to repair.

....

NAMED PERIL VERSUS ALL RISK COVERAGE

Insurance to protect against direct damage losses can be purchased on a named peril or all risk basis. Under a named-peril policy, only losses that fall under the specific perils named in the policy are covered. The burden of proof to prove a loss is on the insured. The preferred form of coverage is the all risk form. Its broad, blanket insuring agreement covers all loss unless eliminated by specific exclusion. In the all risk form, the burden of proof is on the insurance carrier to prove a loss is not covered.

Even with the new comprehensive all risk forms, there are a number of perils that are difficult to insure, or are noninsurable. These include earthquake, flood, nuclear reaction, volcanic eruption, war perils, intentional losses, wear and tear perils, and business perils such as marketing and political losses.

Where significant exposure exists for perils such as earthquake, wind, and flood, carriers will provide sublimits of coverage, or exclude coverage period. In such instances, excess, or wrap-around, coverage can be provided by purchasing a difference in conditions (DIC) policy. In these policies, the definition of earthquake includes landslide, quake, and other similar movements. The definition of flood includes surface water, rides, tidal waves, mud slides, mud flow, backing up of sewer or drains, or underground water flowing or seeping through foundations, walls, doors, windows, or other openings.

....

TIME ELEMENT COVERAGE

In addition to direct damage losses, a health care organization faces the peril of losing revenues as a result of an insured loss. Coverage for this kind of loss is provided by consequential loss or time element insurance.

Major wind damage, a fire, or flood could result in either a partial or total shutdown of a hospital's operation. During the shutdown, revenues generated by those operations are lost and there would probably be additional expenses in attempting to continue as nearly as possible the normal conduct of business. A time element coverage, business interruption insurance, pays for the loss of earnings as well as continuing expenses resulting from a covered loss. These expenses can include ordinary payroll if included in the limit determination. It will also reimburse the insured for extra expenses incurred to keep a facility in operation while repairs are being made or to mitigate further damage. These "extraordinary" expenses are those considered above and beyond the insured's ordinary expenses of operation for the time the interruption of ordinary operations to the time of the assumption of ordinary operations. Examples include the expense of transferring patients to another facility, or the loss of income as the result of closing the emergency room while repairs are being made.

This coverage can provide a contribution clause that operates much like a coinsurance clause. To ensure the limit of coverage applicable to the risk meets the policy's requirements, limits should be reviewed annually with the carrier or broker. The deductible for this form of insurance is typically stated as a specified number of hours or days following the actual loss.

BOILER AND MACHINERY

Boiler and machinery insurance provides protection for the explosion of boilers and other pressure vessels, as well as the accidental damage to equipment. It covers owned property as well as resulting damage to other property, including property in your care, custody, and control for which you are liable. Accidents to boilers and machinery are, in most instances, directly related to the energy inherent in their operations such as heat, pressure, electrical energy, centrifugal force, and reciprocating motion.

Standard property policies cover losses to boilers and machinery, as well as to other property, when caused by perils insured against in the policy. However, these forms do not cover damage to boilers and machinery or anything else when the loss is caused by uninsured or excluded perils. These might include explosions or other sudden breakdowns in the boilers and machinery. Where such losses are excluded, a separate boiler and machinery policy is necessary. Many of the newer comprehensive property policies have limited boiler and machinery exclusions eliminating the need to carry separate coverage.

BUILDER'S RISK

Property risk associated with new construction is typically covered under a builder's risk policy. Buildings under construction face unique hazards. Building materials on the premises are subject to theft or destruction. Because fire protection systems, such as sprinkler systems, may not be fully installed and operational, the risk characteristics for a fire loss are modified.

A builder's risk policy may be issued to cover the interest of the building owner, the interest of the contractor, or the owner and the contractor jointly as their interest may appear. A separate builder's risk policy may be provided by the contractor, or purchased by the health care organization. Under the new comprehensive property policy forms, automatic builder's risk coverage is generally extended to construction on any existing premises. Coverage can be added to cover exposure at an off-site location, subject to carrier notification and acceptance.

ELECTRONIC DATA PROCESSING AND MEDIA COVERAGE

Electronic data processing (EDP) equipment is subject to loss from all the perils to which other equipment is exposed, such as fire, windstorm, and so on, and is sensitive to perils that have little effect on other property. These include dust, temperature, and humidity changes that can affect the equipment enough to result in an actual loss. Recorded media data is vulnerable to the same losses including magnetic storms. They can also be lost, stolen, erased, or tampered with.

In addition to direct loss, the temporary loss of data processing facilities could result in a serious interruption to the organization. The extra expense coverage in an EDP policy could reimburse for equipment rental or use of time-sharing facilities, additional payroll, temporary office equipment, or temporary help.

Separate EDP policies, or an EDP extension on a standard property policy, provide protection for the added risks associated with these exposures. Standard property policies pay for the loss of media but not the loss of information. EDP coverage will pay for replacement of information displayed on cards, disks, drums, or tapes.

COMMERCIAL CRIME INSURANCE AND EMPLOYEE DISHONESTY

Crime insurance covers two broad categories of risk—crimes committed by outsiders, and crimes committed by employees. While there is some overlap of coverage between crime and property policies, most policies exclude or severely restrict coverage for money and securities. Most property policies do not cover employee dishonesty and certain kinds of robbery.

Separate crime insurance can cover money and securities against burglary, robbery, theft, destruction, disappearance, and employee dishonesty. Crime insurance also covers property other than money and securities against loss due to specified crime perils such as burglary, robbery, theft, computer fraud, extortion, and employee dishonesty. Crime coverage also extends to loss as the result of property damaged, but not stolen by burglars or robbers.

Probably the most significant financial risk for health care providers is employee dishonesty. This can include embezzlement, the theft of drugs or other hospital supplies, and the alteration of financial records for personal gain. Along with the rapid growth in technology has come a new opportunity for criminal loss. Computer fraud is at an all-time high and is rapidly increasing. Computer crime includes electronic theft of money and securities, embezzlement, fraud, or erased or modified information.

THIRD-PARTY INSURANCE

Third-party insurance provides coverage to a party other than the insured to make that person whole for loss or injury caused by the negligence of the insured. It involves three parties—one who is harmed, the insurer, and the insured that caused harm or damage. Unlike first-party coverage, the named insured is never a direct recipient of the payment for loss responded to by a liability policy. The most common third-party coverage applicable to health care organizations are:

- Medical professional liability.
- General liability (premises liability, personal injury, and contractual liability).

- Umbrella excess liability.
- Employment practices liability.
- Automobile liability.
- Directors' and officers' (D&O) liability.
- Miscellaneous errors and omissions (E&O) coverage, including managed care E&O.
- Environmental impairment liability.
- Fiduciary liability.
- Heliport and nonowned aircraft liability.

············

MEDICAL PROFESSIONAL LIABILITY

Medical professional liability insurance provides coverage for claims arising from the providing or the failure to provide professional services. Professional services are typically described as "any act or omission in the furnishing of professional health care services, including the furnishing of food, medications or appliances, the postmortem handling of bodies, or arising out of the service by any persons as members of a formal accreditation board. Medical professional liability policies are written on a bodily injury or personal injury basis. They generally exclude damage to property.

The named insured should be broadened to cover all corporate entities, the insureds' interest in joint ventures, the board of directors or board of trustees, members of committees, employees, students, volunteer workers, and members of religious organizations. In the event interns, residents, fellows, or employed or contracted physicians and surgeons are to be covered for their personal interest, basic policy wording requires an amendment. The basic policy form should also be reviewed to make certain physicians are covered for administrative responsibilities without a requirement to specifically extend the coverage to include that exposure. Coverage extended to employees including physicians and surgeons typically extends to negligent acts occurring within the scope of their duties on behalf of the named insured. Even though there are a number of insureds covered under the policy, the limit of liability applicable to each medical incident applies on a per event or per occurrence basis. The aggregate limit on the policy is the sum of all losses in any particular year. Defense costs may or may not be included in the policy limits, depending on the carrier's form.

Health care entity employees, particularly nurses, frequently ask the risk manager whether they should carry their own insurance. In responding to that question, the risk manager should inform employees who and what the entity's policy covers. The risk manager should also review the other insurance provision of the organization's medical professional liability policy to see how the coverage would respond in the event an employee carries individual coverage. In some instances, the policy would be excess over and above the employee's personal insurance. In other instances, the policy would contribute to the claim proportionately with the employee's carrier based on the limits carried on each policy. The entity's policy usually will cover employees for negligent acts and omissions within the scope of their employment. Coverage would not extend to a second job or moonlighting activities. If those activities are present, a separate policy should be purchased. Additionally, the risk manager should remind entity employees that although the entity's policy protects them from costs of defense and indemnity, they will have no decision-making authority over how their defense is conducted—something they may have with their own policy.

Most hospital bylaws require all voluntary attending physicians to carry their own medical professional liability coverage at stated minimum limits. If the physician and health care entity are found to be negligent, the entity may be held financially liable for the inadequacy of the physician's limits under the theory of joint and several liability. Where physicians have challenged the entity's ability to impose minimum insurance requirements as a condition of staff membership, the courts have said the entity may do so as long as the requirement is not applied arbitrarily or capriciously.

Medical professional liability insurance is considered a "specialty coverage." In view of that, most carriers have developed customized policy forms, many of which do not resemble the other in terms and conditions. It is critical the risk manager performs a thorough evaluation and comparison of coverage terms and conditions in selecting a professional liability carrier. A broker, agent, or insurance company representative can be very helpful in this process. In addition to the product itself, most carriers provide a portfolio of risk management services that are available to assist risk meet his or her risk management objectives. These services should be evaluated based on their perceived effectiveness and need on the part of the risk manager.

Two forms of medical professional liability coverage are available in the industry—claims-made and occurrence. In purchasing this coverage, it is critical the risk manager be knowledgeable of the differences in the forms insuring that all claims—those reported and those that have occurred but are not yet reported are covered by a single or by continuous policies. Please refer to the section called Claims-Made versus Occurrence Policies on page 751 of this chapter.

Changes in the health care environment associated with the delivery of health care services in an integrated setting have presented additional exposures the risk manager must address. Basic medical professional liability policies need to be reviewed to make certain they are broad enough to extend to new exposures. Some of these are:

- Miscellaneous errors and omissions coverage, such as data processing E&O, employed attorney's E&O, and hospital or physician management E&O.
- Contractual liability as it relates to professional liability assumed on behalf of others if liability would not have been present in the absence of the agreement.
- Utilization management and review—particularly as it relates to gatekeepers liability.
- Marketing, advertising, and Internet exposures.
- Confidentiality issues.
- Credentialing of physicians and allied health care providers for others.
- Antitrust or restraint of trade issues.
- Third-party claim administration and claims management for others.
- Enterprise liability—vicarious liability for all aspects of delivery in an integrated network.
- Coverage for day care centers, special health care events, and volunteer activities.
- Architects or design or build legal liability.
- Telemedicine and the associated licensing issues.
- Medicare billing errors and Medicare fraud and abuse issues.

············

COMMERCIAL GENERAL LIABILITY

Medical professional liability covers injury to patients on or about the premises for the purpose of receiving medical treatment. A health care provider is subject to third-party claims from members of the public other than patients for injury as the result of negligence in connection with the nonmedical aspects of their premises. This would include nonmedical related contractual obligations, injury to visitors, product liability, independent contractors liability, personal injury allegations such as libel, slander, false arrest, defamation of character, and sexual abuse to nonpatients.

Commercial general liability protects the named insured against financial loss resulting from liability to third parties arising out of the premises owned or occupied, acts of independent contractors hired, products sold that leave the premises, and liability assumed under contract, subject to the exclusions in the policy. Coverage applies to bodily injury, property damage, and personal injury allegations.

General liability coverage is usually provided by the same insurer providing the medical professional liability coverage to the health care entity. Those two types of protection frequently are combined in a single policy avoiding a "gray" area as to what is a professional versus what is a general liability claim. Where coverage is purchased separately, the general liability carrier will include an amendment excluding injury to patients. This limitation will typically read "coverage is excluded for bodily injury to any person who is in your building, or on your premises for the purpose of receiving any type of medical evaluation, care, or treatment." In some instances the coverage can be modified with the following additional language: ". . . except for injuries caused by windstorm or fire, including any injury from smoke, fumes or panic, earthquake, lightening, or explosion." This extension of coverage provides the risk manager additional protection in the event of a catastrophic loss injuring patients as well as visitors.

Additional commercial general liability exposures can exist for organizations providing child care centers. These exposures may include such things as corporal punishment, molestation, or failure to maintain sanitary conditions resulting in the spread of disease. In addition, many health care entities are affiliated with academic universities that require special protection for claims that may arise out of an educational setting. Examples of those claims are failure to educate, wrongful suspension from a program, or inadequate supervision. Commercial general liability policies should be reviewed to make certain coverage is included for these exposures, or a separate policy must be purchased.

The risk manager is challenged to keep informed about the health care entity's activities so that he or she can ensure the policy is broad enough to cover new ventures and operations. Common areas of concern are increased advertising including e-marketing, environmental impairment or hazardous waste disposal exposure, asbestos removal, and the general liability exposures applicable to patient-owned premises in home health operations.

············

MANAGED CARE E&O COVERAGE

The emergence of managed care has significantly increased the need to purchase managed care E&O coverage. Managed care entities such as preferred provider organizations, management service organizations, physician and hospital organizations, health maintenance organizations, independent practice associations, foundations and legal entities like 501a have presented new exposures areas for health care risk managers to address. As stated earlier, a medical professional liability policy responds to bodily injury allegations. Many of the allegations against these organizations are for "wrongful acts" in the design and administration of managed care plans. These allegations may or may not allege bodily injury.

Some of these allegations can result from:

- Improper design or administration of cost control systems.
- Physician incentive agreements.
- Breach of patient confidentiality.
- Employment Retirement Income Security Act of 1974 (ERISA) violations.
- Antitrust.
- Economic credentialing.
- Denial of benefits/services.
- Failure to refer—delay in referral.
- Discrimination.
- Violation of state insurance regulations.
- Invasion of privacy.
- Insolvency or bankruptcy.

The insurance industry has responded to this risk with separate managed care E&O policy forms. Some forms will include coverage for the administrative risk associated with managed care and extend to provide direct medical professional liability coverage for employed providers. Other forms are intended to cover the administrative risk associated with managed care and provide vicarious liability coverage for the organization facilitating the delivery of health care services. The typical insuring agreement of these policies covers damages because of personal injury in the performance of professional services including but not limited to, utilization review, peer review, claims processing, enrollment, and marketing of services.

Managed care E&O policy forms contain a number of exclusions or coverage limitations applicable to the risk associated with managed care contracting and managed care health care delivery. It is important the risk manager review these restrictions to have a clear understanding of what portion of the risk is insurable and what portion cannot be covered by insurance.

....

EXCESS UMBRELLA LIABILITY

Catastrophic losses can have a major impact on the bottom line of a health care entity, threatening their own financial survival. Excess umbrella liability coverage can be purchased to provide additional coverage after the first layer—the primary layer—of liability coverage has been exhausted. The primary layer is typically considered $1 million per medical incident and $30 million annual aggregate. The excess policy picks up over and above the primary limits afforded per medical incident or claim and if so written will drop down to effect coverage in the event of aggregate exhaustion of the underlying coverage. Umbrella excess liability coverage is a comprehensive form of excess liability coverage, providing coverage excess of a number of third-party exposures such as medical professional liability, commercial general liability, automobile liability, employer's liability, and nonowned aircraft and heliport liability.

In order to maintain concurrency (avoiding gaps in coverage), primary and excess should maintain the same effective date. If the coverage is claims made, policies should also maintain the same retroactive date. In addition it is important the primary and umbrella excess medical professional and commercial general liability coverage be written on concurrent coverage forms. If the primary is claims-made, the excess coverage should be written on a claims-made form to avoid gaps and overlaps in coverage. If the primary is written or self-insurance funded on an occurrence basis, the excess should be maintained on an occurrence basis. If primary coverage is afforded on an occurrence basis and the excess coverage written on a claims-made basis, it is necessary for the risk manager to maintain two sets of loss data, one on an occurrence basis as required by the primary carrier and one on a claims made basis to meet the requirements of the claims made excess carrier.

As with primary medical professional liability policies, all umbrella excess liability carriers have customized policy forms. Most of these forms are "stand-alone" in nature, and do not necessarily follow form of the primary policies or self-insured trust document they sit over. It is important the risk manager do a through evaluation of policy forms to make certain continuity of coverage does indeed exist.

While we have seen the frequency of losses decrease in the past few years, loss severity has continued to increase. In view of this, it is important the risk manager continually review the limits of liability insurance purchased, making certain they adequately protect the assets of the organization.

············

AUTOMOBILE LIABILITY

Health care entities are exposed to liability as the result of owned or leased automobiles as well as nonowned and hired automobiles. In addition, automobile exposure can exist from the operation of parking garages including valet parking. A commercial automobile policy protects against loss arising out of the ownership, maintenance, or use of automobiles and their equipment. It extends to vehicles you own, hire, or borrow, and those you do not own but may be responsible for, such as the personal car of an employee used in your home health operation. Coverage provided for vehicles you do not own is excess over any coverage the owner may have.

Uninsured motorists coverage and personal injury protection is also included subject to limits required by each state. This covers bodily injury only in most states and will not pay for repairs to your vehicles caused by an uninsured driver. The policy should provide automatic coverage for newly acquired or leased vehicles, including those used for emergency or patient transport. Automobile physical damage—comprehensive and collision coverage—should be considered for owned and long-term leased vehicles.

Insurers determine rates for automobile coverage based on loss experience, territory of operation, garaging location of the vehicle, and type and use of the vehicle. Loss prevention activities, such as safe driver programs, and minimum insurance requirements for individuals using their personal vehicles on behalf of the organization are taken into consideration in the final pricing determination.

The risk associated with employees using their personal vehicles associated with home health organizations has materialized into a major exposure for many health care risk managers. In some instances automobile carriers are adding premium surcharges to accounts with this exposure. It is important the health care organization maintain insurance requirements for all individuals using their personal vehicles in business at an adequate level of liability coverage. Certificates of insurance should be required and maintained on a current basis for all drivers. In addition, motor vehicle registrations should be obtained on all drivers on an annual basis.

GARAGE LIABILITY EXPOSURE

Some health care organizations provide valet parking for emergency room patients and visiting family members. Two significant exposures have been created by this service. A third-party liability exposure develops when hospital employees operate the vehicles. The hospital can also be held responsible for damage to patient vehicles while parked in hospital-owned or -operated parking garages. While difficult to quantify, this ultimate exposure can be determined by the maximum value of all vehicles parked in the garage. Protection for this risk can be found in both the automobile and commercial general liability policy. The risk manager should review coverage afforded in their commercial general liability and automobile policy before purchasing a separate garage liability policy.

Most general liability policies respond to garage operations as the result of damages such as a parking garage entrance arm malfunction causing damage to a third-party vehicle. It also responds to injury due to the "existence" exposure of the premises, such as a visitor slip and fall in the parking garage. An automobile policy can protect the insured for the ownership, maintenance, and use of *any* vehicle. A garagekeeper's legal liability policy provides coverage for physical damage (comprehensive and collision) for automobiles in the care, custody, and control of the insured. The basic coverage in this form applies to damages for which you are legally liable. The policy can be endorsed to provide "goodwill" coverage providing reimbursement for damages where there is a question of legal negligence. This can be used as a public relations tool for the risk manager. The coverage can be modified to respond on either a primary or excess basis. If written on a primary basis, coverage for damage to the third-party vehicle is provided automatically regardless of any other insurance. Coverage on an excess basis only applies excess of the owner's automobile coverage.

The risk manager can take several steps to reduce the probability of loss. Garage security and key protection should minimize vandalism and theft. A driver recruiting program, including motor vehicle record verification for all employees driving third-party autos, may reduce exposures. Contracting the garage operations to a third party will shift the majority of the exposure to the garage management company.

D&O LIABILITY

Decisions made by directors, trustees, and key executives have a significant impact on the financial health and daily operations of a health care entity. It is essential they have the freedom to make wise, responsible, and sometimes difficult decisions without risk to their personal assets.

The board delegates authority to conduct affairs on a day-to-day basis to the administrative and medical staff officers. However, the board is ultimately responsible for the establishment and maintenance of appropriate standards relating to all activities associated with the delivery of health care services. This governance responsibility cannot be delegated. The purpose of D&O insurance is to protect directors, trustees, and key executives in the event of personal liability litigation, or to insure the health care entity itself from its obligation to provide indemnity from such litigation.

Staff-related issues are becoming a more significant exposure for directors and officers, who are increasingly being held accountable for medical staff selection and decisions regarding staff privileges. In making these decisions they may be accused of lack of due process or interference with a person's right to practice their profession. What were once routine denials of staff privileges, can now give rise to antitrust allegations with charges of restraint of trade by denying an individual the right to practice his or her profession, or favoring one group of competing interests over another.

Statutory immunity laws have been enacted in a number of states granting immunity from personal liability to directors of not-for-profit health care facilities. However, this relief does not guarantee immunity from being sued. Also, state laws provide no protection from legal actions under federal statutes involving, for example, antitrust, discrimination, and environmental protection.

Changes in the health care industry have opened new areas of risk for health care executives. Those organizations developing integrated delivery networks are engaged in joint ventures with physicians, private enterprises, and/or other health care providers. These alliances hold a strong potential for antitrust allegations from excluded providers or suppliers who claim a cooperative arrangement restricts their ability to compete in the community. Heightened competition for patients, managed care contracts, and other revenue sources present a restraint of trade exposure.

The continued trend for mergers, acquisitions, and divestiture activities among hospitals and physicians is another area of concern. Companies involved in these ventures experience a significantly heightened frequency and severity of D&O claims.

Another relatively new source of exposure is third-party contractual relationships. As health care organizations increasingly take advantage of outpatient care opportunities, it is often difficult to maintain the same quality standards across their owned and managed facilities as well as their off-site delivery facilities such as surgi-centers and home health operations.

The directors' and officers' liability policy, typically written on a claims-made form, pays on behalf of the organization all losses for which the organization grants indemnification to the insured persons and which the insured persons have become legally obligated to pay on account of any claim for a *wrongful act*. A wrongful act means any error, misstatement, misleading statement, act, omission, neglect, or breach of duty.

D&O insurance policies typically have three distinct insuring agreements. The first agreement pays on behalf of the individual insureds claims for wrongful acts, which are nonindemnifiable events under the organization's bylaw indemnification agreement. The second reimburses the entity for wrongful acts on the part of the individual insureds, which are indemnifiable under the corporate bylaws. These insuring agreements are considered "Individual" coverage (Part A), "Corporate Reimbursement" (Part B), and "Entity Coverage" (Part C). If extended to provide entity coverage, protection is afforded the entity in the event it is held legally responsible for wrongful acts covered in the individual coverage sections of the policy.

. . . .

EMPLOYMENT PRACTICES LIABILITY

Employment practices liability (EPL) coverage can be included in the D&O policy by endorsement, or purchased as a separate policy. The risk manager should evaluate this risk and determine if a combined D&O approach is appropriate, or if separate coverage should be purchased.

The EPL policy is designed to reimburse an organization for alleged negligence in selection and hiring as well as employment issues associated with all current health care personnel. Recent legislative changes and increased public awareness have expanded liability risk for employment related claims, making it easier to file claims and secure greater compensation. Some of these exposures are discrimination, sexual harassment, wrongful termination, violation of the American with Disabilities Act, and hostile work environment.

FIDUCIARY LIABILITY

The need for insurance protection for individuals who exercise management or administrative responsibilities for employee benefit plans was redefined by the Employment Retirement Income Security Act of 1974 (ERISA).

ERISA defined the principle responsibilities of individuals who are fiduciaries of employee benefit plans while making the fiduciaries personally responsible for their actions. Employers with more than twenty-five employees are subject to ERISA with limited exceptions. Two of these exceptions are plans providing government sponsored benefits, (including Medicare) and some plans sponsored by religious affiliated organizations.

Every plan subject to ERISA must have a written plan document that defines the benefits provided, the eligible participants, the vesting rights, and the claim process, and it must identify by name the individuals responsible for the management of the plan. An annual update to plan participants is required.

Fiduciaries are defined by ERISA as individuals named as fiduciaries in the plan documents, and any other persons or organizations responsible for administering benefits or claims or collecting or handling funds relating to the plan. Fiduciary liability insurance covers the alleged breach of fiduciary responsibility under common law or ERISA for directors and administrators of the plans.

EMPLOYEE BENEFIT LEGAL INSURANCE

In addition to management responsibilities, individuals with duties relating to the administration of employee benefit plans can create situations in which they or their employees may become liable for misadministration of an employee benefit program.

Administrative risk arising from workers' compensation, social security, unemployment compensation, or statutorily required nonoccupational disability benefit programs exist even though they do not fall under the ERISA regulations.

Insurance protection against this administrative risk is called employee benefit liability. This coverage is usually endorsed on to a commercial general liability policy.

ENVIRONMENTAL IMPAIRMENT LIABILITY

There is an increased awareness and concern among insureds over the extent of potential liabilities related to the transfer of properties that might be contaminated.

Exposures include the particularly serious cases of gradual pollution that can occur in the course of normal operations of a hospital entity as well as liability for sudden and accidental exposure. Impairment is considered to be in place when substances (shock, noise, pressure, radiation, gases, vapors, heat, or other phenomena such as light) propagate or spread through soil, air, or water. Examples in the hospital environment include underground storage tanks, hazardous waste incinerators, or radioactive, hazardous, medical, pathological, and infectious wastes.

Since 1973, most commercial general liability policies have excluded contamination and pollution except when sudden and accidental. This exclusion created a gap in basic liability coverage that very few insurers have filled, even under specialty coverage or in the excess and surplus lines marketplace. Certain specialty underwriters, however, have developed environmental impairment liability coverage, which insures liability for environmental impairment, including clean-up costs. "Sudden and accidental" contamination or pollution is excluded unless the insured cannot obtain the coverage under the commercial general liability policy.

AVIATION COVERAGE—NONOWNED AIRCRAFT AND HELIPORT COVERAGE

Many health care facilities have landing sites available for helicopter landings. If such a site is delegated as a helipad for use by life-flight operators or other emergency helicopter landings, a separate heliport liability policy should be carried. The exposures associated with this risk depends on the hospital's role in the operation and use of the heliport premises along with any contractual obligations they assume as the result of its operation.

Heliport liability policies cover bodily injury and physical damage arising out of the use, ownership, or operation of a helipad, including slips and falls that occur during the loading and unloading of patients, bodily injury to bystanders, and damage to the property of others. Operation and use of the helipad is excluded from a commercial general liability policy.

Nonowned aircraft liability policies cover bodily injury and property damage caused by an "accident" involving a nonowned helicopter or an accident involving a nonowned aircraft for which the organization is responsible.

The frequency of air travel by employees or health care executives should be evaluated to determine the need for this type of coverage. Claims have been made against corporate entities arising out of their sponsorship of meetings wherein employees were victims in commercial air disasters as well as chartered aircraft crashes. Risk managers should also evaluate the adequacy of insurance provided by charter companies and helicopter services.

HEALTH AND WELFARE INSURANCE-EMPLOYEE BENEFIT INSURANCE

While most employee benefit insurance plans are coordinated by the human resources department, it is important the risk manager be familiar with the types of plans provided by their employer. Some risk managers may have responsibility for coordinating such programs, or be involved in the decision-making process for carrier selection. These coverage can include long- and short-term disability, life, health, accident, dental, and vision insurance.

············

WORKERS' COMPENSATION

All states create a statutory obligation on the part of employers to provide compensation to employees for injuries arising out of, and in the course of their employment. All employers are subject to the applicable workers' compensation of the states in which they operate, and under the appropriate circumstances to federal statutes. Failure to comply with these laws can result in fines and penalties, one of which is statutory removal of the employer's defense to suit by employees alleging injury as a result of thcir work. Workers' compensation insurance is a pure form of no-fault insurance. Adherence to the workers' compensation statute is governed by each state's division of workers' compensation.

Employers who fall under the workers' compensation statutes are required to purchase insurance, qualify as a self-insured, or reject the act, which is permissible in a limited number of states. Workers' compensation insurance provides statutory benefit coverage with virtually unlimited medical benefits to work accident victims. It also replaces a portion of lost wages defined as indemnity payments. Employers' liability, part of the standard workers' compensation policy, protects employers from suits brought by injured employees to recover monetary damages separate and distinct from claims for statutory benefits. Employers' liability claims can arise from:

- Employees who reject the act (which is possible in some states).
- Injuries not covered by the act (questionable claims relating to scope of employment).
- Suits by a spouse for loss of consortium or companionship.
- Suits by a third party that has been held liable for the injury and seeks reimbursement from the employer.

The premium for workers' compensation insurance is determined with the application of rates established on a state-by-state basis to employee remuneration. The rates are based on classifications determined by the risk associated with the responsibilities of the employee. Individual claim history is used to modify the ultimate premium based on experience rating models for each classification of employee. Risk managers should work closely with the human resources and employee health departments in identifying, measuring, and addressing workers' compensation risks.

············

FINANCIAL GUARANTEES

Surety bonds are frequently required to comply with laws associated with a number of health care exposures. In a surety contract, one party (the surety) agrees to be bound, along with the principal, to a third party in the same agreement. The surety and the principal on the bond become the promisor to a third-party promisee. The third-party would be able to collect the obligation from the surety, if the principle cannot meet the financial responsibility. In the event the surety is called upon to meet the obligations under the bond, they attempt to collect the obligation (seek reimbursement) from the principal. This is the major difference in financial guarantee insurance versus other insurance contracts.

Health care organizations are required to post surety bonds to comply with laws in a number of areas. They include but are not limited to:

- Patients' valuables.
- Durable medical equipment.

- Home health bonds.
- Liquor bonds.
- Residents' funds bonds.
- Performance and payment bonds for construction projects.
- License bonds.
- Various court bonds such as appeal bonds.
- Notary bonds.
- Pharmacy.

PROVIDER STOP-LOSS COVERAGE

Provider stop-loss coverage may be needed by those organizations that have agreed in advance to bear financial risk for the provision of health care services under full or partial capitated managed care contracts. Provider stop-loss coverage reimburses a health care provider, subject to daily limitations and coinsurance requirements, for losses in excess of a stipulated amount per member per year.

There are two avenues for the risk manager to consider in purchasing such coverage. Some managed care organizations are willing to include a certain amount of stop-loss protection in the provider's capitated agreement. The coverage can also be purchased from the commercial insurance industry. This line of coverage represents a rapidly growing new product to the industry.

Risk managers should evaluate both options to make certain what avenue selected has maximum protection to the financial performance of their organization. (See Chapter 22 on providers and managed care.)

CONCLUSION

Insurance is only one of the many tools available to the health care risk manager to manage the financial aspects of risk. The risk manager's primary insurance responsibility is to identify his or her organization's risk exposures and determine whether the transfer of risk to an insurance company is the appropriate method for treatment of that risk. Utilizing insurance products for risk treatment requires the risk manager to develop a level of insurance knowledge, as well as a good working relationship with agents or brokers and the insurance industry. The risk manager's role should also include the preparation of statistical risk data, including rating data, and up-to-date historical loss data for use by the carriers in determining the appropriate premium. He or she should also be familiar with the resources, such as brokers, agents, and consultants, available to assist in the placement of coverage, the analysis of carriers, and the proposals submitted by those carriers.

Endnote

1. Smith, B. D. *How Insurance Works: An Introduction to Property and Liability Insurance.* Malvern, Pa. Insurance Institute of America, 1984, p. 4.

Suggested Readings

Best's Insurance Reports. Oldwick, N.J.: A. M. Best (published annually).

Head, G. L., Elliot, M. W. and Blinn, J. D. *Essentials of Risk Financing,* vol. I (3rd ed.). Malvern, Pa.: Insurance Institute of America, 1996.

MacDonald, M. G., Meyer, K. C., and Essig, B. *Health Care Law: A Practical Guide.* New York: Mathew Bender, 1987.

Malecki, D. S., Horn, R. C., Wiening, E. A., and Donaldson, J. H. *Commercial Liability Risk Management and Insurance,* vol. II (2nd ed.). Malvern, Pa.: American Institute for Property and Liability Underwriters, 1986.

Rodda, W. H., Trieschmann, J. S., Wiening, E. A., and Hedges, B. A. *Commercial Property Risk Management and Insurance*, vol. I (3rd ed.). Malvern, Pa.: American Institute for Property and Liability Underwriters, 1988.

Smith, B. D., Trieschmann, J. S., and Wiening, E. A. *Property and Liability Insurance Principles* (2nd ed.). Malvern, Pa.: Insurance Institute of America, 1994.

Troyer, G., and Salman, S. *Handbook of Health Care Risk Management.* Rockville, Md. Aspen, 1986.

32

Risk Financing Techniques

Brad R. Norrick
Thomas M. Jones
Thomas M. Hermes

This chapter presents an introduction to risk financing. It is written in three sections beginning with an overview of risk financing including a description of the various mechanisms used to fund retained risk; a discussion of related tax issues; and finally a discussion of pertinent actuarial and accounting issues related to risk financing. The objective of this chapter is to provide the risk manager with insight into the various key issues that must be resolved when designing a risk financing program.

OVERVIEW OF RISK FINANCING TECHNIQUES

As health care organizations have grown, claims of all types have grown, and insurance premiums have become a larger expense for health care organizations, causing the financing of risk to become more sophisticated. Where, in the past, a community hospital might have purchased medical professional liability insurance for a few thousand dollars, the cost today could be in the millions. As premium dollars have increased, several alternatives to traditional insurance purchasing have been developed. These alternatives may enhance cash flow, receive preferred accounting and tax treatment, or may allow an organization to take more control over the way claims are handled. This chapter will provide an overview of the more traditional approaches to financing risk and give the reader a flavor for the wide variety of the more interesting options available.

GUARANTEED COST

Guaranteed cost programs are also known as "fixed cost" programs. The elements that encompass the pricing of the insurance product are discussed here. Some of these elements include: prospective rating, loss exposure, pure premium, experience rating, expense loss, and risk charge.

Insurance Pricing

The premium one pays for insurance is based on a number of factors—in the case of life insurance, one's age, health, gender, and amount of coverage requested all impact the premium. For those coverages of greatest interest to the health care risk manager, premiums are dependent upon similar calculations of "exposure to loss." Exposures are a proxy for the probability that claims will occur. The individual at the insurance company who analyzes exposures and arrives at a premium is the underwriter. Underwriting consists of counting exposures and applying rates to achieve a premium indication. This indication can then be adjusted based on other factors that will be discussed later.

Automobile liability coverage is based on number, type, and use of vehicles. As the size of a fleet increases, the probability that an accident will occur also increases. Workers' compensation premium is calculated from payrolls. As a firm's payroll increases, insurers assume that more employees are working more hours, resulting in greater potential for an accident. Medical professional liability pricing is based on occupied beds, numbers of deliveries, and other similar measurements of the risk of loss or exposure.

In an effort to be as accurate as possible, insurers weight or "rate" the various exposures. In the automobile fleet example, a tractor trailer receives a higher weighting or rate than a private passenger vehicle. A Ferrari is rated higher than a Hugo—the insurer sees a greater chance for theft or damage with a very expensive, high-performance car. A car in New York City is viewed as having a higher loss potential than one driven in Lima, Ohio, so it receives a higher rate. A Ferrari in New York driven by a sixteen-year-old male is an underwriter's worst nightmare.

In the case of medical professional liability, geography is as important as the types of services or procedures provided. For example, an OB/GYN in rural Indiana may pay only 10 percent of the premium that they would pay if they were in Detroit, Michigan. This differential has more to do with insurers' past experience with the high jury verdicts awarded in the courts of Wayne County than any difference in the quality of medicine practiced in the two settings. However, an OB/GYN in any jurisdiction will be rated higher than a pathologist because insurers see a large difference in their potential for claims.

Commercial insurance coverage pricing is also affected by whether coverage "attaches" at the first dollar or if the organization retains some of the risk of loss. The term "guaranteed cost" is insurance industry jargon for coverage that provides protection from the first dollar. However, most coverages, from homeowner's to group medical, have a retained amount or deductible that the policyholder pays in event of loss.

The size of the deductible on the physical damage protection provided by a personal automobile policy affects the premium. A deductible discourages a policyholder from reporting small claims and provides the insurer with a contribution on larger losses. Therefore, an insurer might give a policyholder a 10-percent credit for a $250 deductible. If the deductible were increased to $2000 the credit might be 25 percent.

Prospective Rating   Unlike most industries, an insurance company does not know the cost of its product until well after it is sold. Insurers must price their policies prospectively, making the assumption that the past is a reasonably accurate predictor of the future. In offering insurance, an underwriter looks at a blend of industry-wide information and the characteristics of the particular risk. For example, in pricing property coverage for a hospital, an insurer will look at general actuarial information that forecasts the probability of fires, windstorms, earthquakes, and other hazards potentially affecting the hospital facilities. The insurer will also especially look at the construction, fire protection, and past loss experience of the hospital they are underwriting.

Loss Exposure   An insurer tries to evaluate the risk that they will pay claims under the policies they provide. They try to answer the question, "What is our exposure to loss?" In property insurance the insurer tries to evaluate the insured property's exposure to loss by particular perils. Perils include fire, windstorm, earthquake, flood, and so on. Therefore, if an office building could be replaced for $1 million, the underwriter has a one-million-dollar exposure. If the office building is on the coast, the underwriter especially evaluates the risk presented by the perils of windstorm and flood. In liability coverages the primary peril is the possibility of a lawsuit or claim for damages. The exposures that could create a claim are the actions of employees, the products produced, services rendered, or other business operations that could lead to injuries or damages.

In the case of a hospital, exposures include the number of employed medical staff, the number of occupied beds, and other measurable data. Depending on the particular underwriter, different approaches to measuring or evaluating loss potential are used. Some underwriters simply count the various exposures presented to arrive at a premium. Others will thoroughly analyze loss information for inclusion in their pricing. Others will try to evaluate the overall commitment to quality and safety that an organization displays. Still others will attempt to size up an organization by meeting with its senior management. In all cases the insurers are trying to select the organizations that will allow them to collect enough premiums to pay all claims presented.

Pure Premium   The insurance industry is unique in that it is allowed to share pricing information among competitors. Data from across the country is collected and compiled to help insurers establish rates. They begin with loss information—claims for each type of coverage by industry segment. For example, over the past ten years the industry may have data that suggest that an average neurosurgeon will experience two claims every three years and that they will cost on average $18,000. Therefore, an underwriter might anticipate that a typical neurosurgeon will cost $36,000 over a three-year period or $12,000 per year. This number represents only the claims costs and is known in the industry as the "pure premium." This average then may be adjusted by region, or it may take in other factors.

An underwriter has several sources for a "pure premium" for the risk(s) he is evaluating. The pure premium is the best estimate of the prospective cost of investigating, defending, and settling claims covered by the policy. This figure may be generated by an insurance industry rating bureau, a governmental agency, or by a carrier's internal actuarial department. Regardless of the source, the pure premium represents an average rate for like exposures. For example, a state bureau of workers' compensation insurance may publish a pure premium rate of three dollars per one hundred dollars of payroll for sheet metal workers within that state. The rate for an automobile driven for pleasure might only be $1,000 for a $1 million limit of liability coverage. The underwriter can use this average rate as the basis for developing a final premium.

Experience Rating   An insurer will take into consideration an organization's own loss experience if they feel the data are accurate and credible. To achieve the goal of accuracy, an underwriter will request five or even ten years of past experience, recently valued—meaning that the status and evaluation of all claims has been conducted within the past thirty to ninety days. To be considered credible, the volume of losses has to be sufficient to reasonably predict the future. For example, the credibility of property loss information showing a claim once a decade is much lower than the credibility of 2,000 workers' compensation claims spread relatively evenly over the past eight years.

Underwriters will use accurate, credible data to adjust the pure premium to better reflect the characteristics of the specific risk. In the case of workers' compensation, a mandatory calculation of an "experience modifier" is done. The exact method for performing this calculation is proscribed by a regulatory body of each state. The modifier adjusts the average rate to one modified by the risk's own past loss experience. For example, the calculation may determine that the risk presented by the sheet metal shop mentioned previously is significantly better than average, and use a .66 experience modifier to adjust their pure premium rate to two dollars from the three dollars average rate. There is a cliché in the insurance industry: "Over the long haul, you pay your own losses," either directly, within a deductible-type arrangement, or indirectly through experience rating. Therefore, a health care risk manager can impact the cost of insurance by (1) preventing and/or mitigating losses to the greatest extent possible, and (2) tracking loss information carefully to be certain that the data given to underwriters truly reflect the organization's experience.

Expense Load   In addition to collecting enough premium to adjudicate claims, insurers also need to cover their costs and generate a profit. Depending on the type of coverage, the expense loading may be 25–50 percent of the final cost. For example, many insurers use a 65/35 ratio for workers' compensation. They hope that no more than sixty-five cents of each premium dollar they collect will be needed to investigate, defend, and pay claims, leaving the other thirty-five cents for overhead (things like heat, light, employees, computers, taxes, and agent commissions), and a profit margin.

Risk Charge   It is possible to break an insurer's charges down into even smaller component pieces. For example, overhead may contain a specific number of premium dollars set aside for loss control services. It may be possible to break out the cost associated with installment payments and remove this cost by prepaying premiums in a lump sum. Another cost that can be isolated is the "risk charge" or insurance charge for the truly catastrophic potential for loss. By collecting a small risk charge from every insured policy, the insurer hopes to have enough money set aside for the catastrophic claim that some insured will suffer somewhere, sometime. Spreading the funding of this loss potential over a large population of policies is really the fundamental building block of insurance.

When these elements are combined—pure premium (losses + loss adjustment costs) + expense load + risk charge · experience credits or debits—the result is a guaranteed cost or first-dollar insurance premium (see Exhibit 32.1).

Aviation insurance and some small premium programs are written on a guaranteed cost basis. However, most major programs of interest to health care risk managers include a "loss-responsive" component. The following sections provide an overview of some of these alternatives.

· · · · · · · · · · · ·
RETROSPECTIVE RATING

This approach to pricing insurance coverage attempts to adjust premiums based on actual loss experience during the policy term. Retro rating begins with a calculation of guaranteed cost premium. The insurer and insured then negotiate the parameters of the retro plan.

EXHIBIT 32.1.   Premium Dollar Pie Chart

Typically a retro includes a minimum premium, a maximum premium, an "each claim" stop-loss, and a subject premium. For example, a workers' compensation program might begin with $1 million in guaranteed cost premium. Negotiations might result in a minimum premium of 50 percent, a maximum of 125 percent, a stop-loss of $100,000, and subject premium of $900,000.

This means that regardless of actual experience, the most the insured will pay is $1,250,000 (the max) and the least is $500,000 (the min), and no one loss will be counted as more than $100,000 against the calculation. The $100,000 "nonsubject" premium (total premium of $1 million minus subject premium of $900,000) covers insurer overhead and the insurance charge for "capping" losses at $100,000.

The calculation of retro premium takes place six months after policy expiration and then every twelve months thereafter or some other predetermined time frame, until both parties agree to close the program. The calculation might look like this:

(Losses + nonsubject premium) · taxes = retro premium (subject to min and max)

Let us try three scenarios, each with 5 percent (1.05) as the tax loading. Assuming $700,000 in losses, the calculation is as follows:

$$(700,000 + 100,000) \cdot 1.05 = \$840,000 \text{ (or \$160,000 less than guaranteed cost coverage)}$$

Assuming $50,000 in losses:

$$(50,000 + 100,000) \cdot 1.05 = \$500,000 \text{ (program minimum)}$$

Assuming $2,100,000 in losses:

$$(2,100,000 + 100,000) \cdot 1.05 = \$1,250,000 \text{ (program maximum)}$$

Intuitively, the concept of a retro is very attractive. Premium ultimately paid comes reasonably close to actual costs, within a "risk corridor" (the min and max) that makes budgeting possible. Many organizations used retro plans for their workers' compensation coverage until deductible and self-insurance plans became more popular. Unfortunately, retros require significant administration and do not readily lend themselves to "long-tail" insurance coverages like medical professional liability or to "short-tail" coverages like property. Therefore, their applicability to health care risk management is somewhat limited.

Large Deductibles

A more straightforward approach to retaining risk is to utilize a deductible. Virtually every type of insurance may be written with a deductible. As the deductible increases, the credit against guaranteed cost coverage should also increase. Recognize, however, retaining a deductible "costs" something. Although increasing a $100 deductible to a $250 deductible on your automobile physical damage coverage may appear to save money, if you have dozens of $200 and $250 fender benders each year the higher deductible may ultimately "cost" more. As health care organizations retain larger deductibles, accounting and tax issues, as well as issues of "risk appetite," and budget-ability become more complex. Large deductibles of $1 million or more demand that an organization create a formal approach for meeting these obligations, especially as they aggregate over time. Choosing the most appropriate and cost-effective deductible or retention and the method for funding the claims that will fall within it is an art and science that will be discussed in detail later.

Normally when a deductible program is proposed, the insurer intends to continue to provide all traditional services, such as loss control and claims administration. They will typically provide a system for the insurer to first pay and then be reimbursed for deductible losses. The insurer may require an escrow deposit to cover the lag time between their payment of a claim and reimbursement. They may also require collateral guaranteeing that deductible claims will be paid. See "meeting collateral requirements" below for a further discussion. In some cases, the responsibility for handling claims and other services within a deductible program can be "unbundled" to an organization other than the insurer. Under a guaranteed cost or first-dollar approach, the insurer typically provides bundled services—policy issuance, claims adjusting, loss control, auditing, and other related items. Some insureds prefer to unbundle these services—buying only "risk transfer" from an insurance company and ancillary services from multiple vendors or handling them in-house. By unbundling, some organizations believe they gain greater control over the cost and quality of the transfer and the services, so a side benefit of retaining risk is the enhanced control an organization may gain over service providers.

Some deductible programs include an "annual aggregate stop-loss," a feature that requires the insurer to step in to pay claims when all claims within the deductible reach a predetermined value. There are several other variations on this theme, including disappearing deductibles, maintenance deductibles, and deductibles that diminish as additional claims are paid.

SELF-INSURANCE

Self-insurance is hard to distinguish from large deductible programs in many respects. Both allow the insured a premium credit for accepting the responsibility for paying claims up to a certain level; both assume that some risk transfer or insurance excess of the retention will continue to be purchased; both approaches may have collateral and escrow requirements; both can feature stop-loss protection; and so on. There are a few subtle differences, however.

In many cases state regulations must be met for an organization to become a "qualified" self-insurer. Often the insured is given the responsibility for determining how claims will be administered within a self-insured program. The insured may handle claims themselves or purchase services from a claims administration firm. It is also important to note that a $100,000 deductible on a $1 million limit program results in

$900,000 of insurance, while a $1 million excess insurance policy over a self-insured retention of $100,000 actually provides $1 million in protection. Exhibit 32.2 displays a deductible program and a self-insured program with excess coverage.

············
MEETING LOCAL REGULATIONS

Certain highly regulated types of insurance, like workers' compensation and automobile liability, may only be self-insured with the permission of the states' insurance regulators. States typically require that an organization wishing to self-insure its workers' compensation meet size and financial responsibility thresholds. They may also require the submittal of a comprehensive employee safety plan, the credentials of the proposed claims administrator, and so on.

Self-insuring medical professional liability coverage is complicated by the requirements imposed by Medicare or Medicaid reimbursement. If an organization wants reimbursement for the expense of setting aside funds to pay self-insurance obligations, they must follow federal guidelines that require a formal program with very specific rules about how funds are invested, how they can be disbursed, and so on. Many health care organizations set up self-insurance trusts to meet these regulations. With the various changes in reimbursement over the past several years, some organizations have decided that meeting these guidelines is no longer a priority.

Meeting Collateral Requirements

If the deductible or self-insured retention is large and a significant volume of claims is expected, the insurer will ask the organization to secure its ability to pay these claims with collateral. One underwriter calculates collateral requirements by estimating expected losses for the policy period and subtracting the amount expected to be paid by the end of the period. Therefore, if expected losses are $1 million and 20 percent of incurred losses are typically paid in the first year, the collateral amount would be set at $800,000.

EXHIBIT 32.2.   Umbrella Coverage

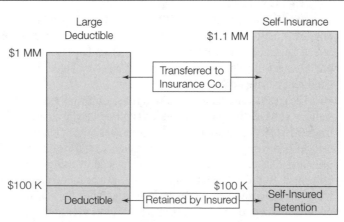

In either case, "umbrella" or excess coverage can be purchased
to provide additional protection.

In the second year of the program, this figure might be reduced by an additional 15 percent for claims expected to be paid in the second year (to $680,000), but the second year would have a new collateral requirement of $800,000 ($1 million–20 percent), resulting in total collateral of $1,480,000. Collateral might be expected to continue to increase for five or six years and then level out, all other things being equal.

Collateral may be cash, securities, promissory notes, or most often, letters of credit. Insurers tend to be inflexible about collateral because regulators require them to account for any liabilities unsupported by collateral. Since the amount of collateral required tends to grow as multiple policy years' deductibles or retentions accumulate, some organizations replace letters of credit with surety bonds to free up their lines of credit.

∙∙∙∙∙∙∙∙∙∙∙∙

CAPTIVE INSURANCE COMPANIES

A captive is a limited purpose insurance company, set up in a jurisdiction that is favorable to such companies, to provide insurance to entities that are also the company's owners. "Limited purpose" means that the captive has been incorporated, capitalized, and organized with the intent of providing coverage to a single entity (and possibly its affiliates) or a single group. Unlike a traditional insurance company, the captive does not intend to provide multiple lines of insurance to unrelated entities.

Jurisdictions of choice for captives recognize the limited nature of captives' missions and do not hold them to the same standards as insurance companies serving the general public. For example, Vermont's captive insurance company laws allow for minimal capitalization, and streamlined annual reports, audits, and business plans.

The concept of a hospital, a system, or a group of health care providers setting up an insurance subsidiary is well established. Health care captives have been operating successfully since the 1970s. Usually a captive is created to replace the deductible or self-insurance that an organization would retain. The captive becomes an investment vehicle for funds set aside to pay future expected losses.

In the past, the driving force for health care captive implementation was the non-availability of affordable commercial professional liability coverage for either a health system or for its independent medical staff. Since a captive is not subject to strict insurance company regulations, it can often provide these coverages more efficiently than commercial carriers. In the 1970s and 1980s when the country went through a "malpractice crisis," captives provided the only mechanism available to deal with liability losses. Several of these programs born in crisis have thrived by providing aggressive risk management initiatives and using the synergies available through joint claims defense to continue to drive down costs.

The classic sales pitch for considering a captive stresses the flexibility, the control, the stability, and the strategic positioning a captive can help an owner achieve. Flexibility results from the ability to insure multiple entities, customers, suppliers, and affiliates in a single vehicle. Control comes from unbundled services and the discretion to invest funds until they are needed to pay claims. Stability is enhanced by using the captive as a market "shock absorber." By this we mean that the captive can be funded conservatively in times when the market is expensive and aggressively in times when the market is "soft," allowing the parent organization to smooth its risk transfer costs over time. A captive can provide a strategic risk transfer platform that makes acquisitions easier, solves potential insurance problems, and builds funding for enhanced services. The captive's ability to access all potential insurers and reinsurers without constraint also gives an organization the assurance that it has the lowest possible cost for excess insurance or reinsurance over its retention.

No other loss-responsive approach offers all these potential benefits. However, there is a price. Even the most frugal captives cost their parent organizations $50,000 to 100,000 per year in overhead and management fees. The key to captive feasibility for an organization is, "Do we need all of the captive's benefits?" A careful assessment of an organization's needs, future plans, current competitive position, and so on is needed to determine if a captive should be considered.

Single Parent

A single parent captive is incorporated and owned by one organization. Single ownership allows the captive maximum flexibility in meeting its owner's needs. It can, however, offer coverage to other entities in certain circumstances. For example, it might extend liability coverage to a 50–50 percent joint venture. Exhibit 32.3 displays captive insurance company mechanics.

Group Captives

The benefits of captives are their flexibility, stability, control, and strategic positioning advantages. The down side is their cost. A potential "best of both worlds" is a group captive. A group captive can share the costs among several participants. An ancillary benefit of a group approach can be the benchmarking and information sharing that occurs as organizations come together to share risk. Dozens of group captives have been created and are operating effectively. However, this "best of both worlds" looks a little better on paper than in reality.

A group captive does not offer the same level of benefits as a single-owner captive, because the group must reach consensus on issues of flexibility and strategic positioning. For example, an organization may desire to include coverage for employment-related liabilities within its program, but the other group members may not be comfortable sharing this risk. Each participant may find itself compromising its own desires for the good of the group.

EXHIBIT 32.3.   **Direct Issue Captive**

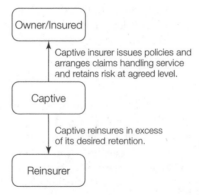

To ensure fairness, most group captives decide they need extensive planning for, and documentation of, their risk sharing agreements, their governance, and so on. At the end of the day, many groups discover the costs of negotiating these arrangements, and having legal counsel document them costs more than they expected. The goal of saving money through a group approach may not pan out. The group may also be uncomfortable sharing financial data and loss information from member to member. On the other hand, if risk sharing, potential tax deductibility, or other goals are envisioned, a group captive approach may be an ideal solution.

Fronts

In many cases, a captive insurance company can issue a policy to its parent organization without any problem. However, certain types of insurance are highly regulated by the fifty states. Workers' compensation and automobile liability coverages are often required by law. Insurers offering these policies must be licensed and admitted to provide insurance by each state. Some states (such as Pennsylvania and Florida) require that medical professional liability coverage be purchased only from licensed carriers. If an organization that owns a captive wants to extend coverage to affiliated entities, like independent medical staff, it must not solicit on behalf of an unlicensed insurer. Therefore, if a captive wants to provide regulated coverages or conduct any marketing in the Unites States, it must do it in conjunction with a licensed carrier.

To meet these regulatory requirements, the approach usually taken is for an admitted carrier to act as a "front" for the captive's reinsurance of the all or some portion of the risk. The "fronting" carrier charges a fee for the use of its insurance policy and any additional services that are negotiated. For example, the front might provide certificate issuance or claims administration services as well as a policy. Costs could be expressed as a percent of premium flowing to the captive or a flat fee. Pure fronting fees may be as high as 10 percent of premium, but most programs pay a flat amount in the $25,000 to $100,000 range.

Several carriers are willing to consider fronting arrangements. Along with their fee, they will request evidence that the captive is well funded and managed, and want appropriate collateral to protect themselves against the potential insolvency of the captive. Like collateral for a deductible or self-insurance program, collateral could take the form of a letter of credit (LOC), securities, bonds, or cash.

Some state insurance regulators are uncomfortable with the concept of fronting. They worry that certificates and policies issued by insurance companies that do not really bear any risk could mislead third parties. They also dislike their own lack of control over the captives providing the reinsurance behind the fronts. There have been several attempts to outlaw, or at least control the use of fronts and/or offshore reinsurance. Exhibit 32.4 displays a fronted captive program.

Domicile Selection

The Cayman Islands became the most popular domicile for health care captives throughout the 1970s and 1980s. Within the past few years more captive owners are considering Bermuda, Vermont, Hawaii, and other locales. The cost of incorporating and maintaining a captive is substantial, regardless of domicile. The capitalization requirements range from a low of $120,000 in Bermuda and Cayman to $250,000 in Vermont. Initial set-up

EXHIBIT 32.4.   Fronted Reinsurance Captive

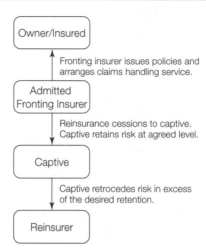

costs of $25,000 to $50,000 are consistent from domicile to domicile. In all jurisdictions, annual operating costs are between $50,000 and $100,000. Therefore, a domicile is rarely chosen exclusively on the basis of cost or capitalization requirement.

All domiciles have the various professional service providers necessary to support captive insurance companies. These include legal, accounting, bookkeeping, investment management, and banking services. The difference in cost, operational fees, and availability of professional consultants from any of the domiciles to the next has become negligible, so the selection often comes down to accessibility, frequency of flights, time zone changes from the domicile to the owner's location, or personal preferences between skiing or scuba diving.

In certain cases one domicile offers flexibility in an area that matches with the organization's business plan. For example, an organization might choose Dublin, Ireland, as a domicile because they have European operations. Another entity might choose Bermuda because they purchase their excess liability coverage from one or more of the major insurers located there. If a multistate system wanted to aggressively pursue enrollment of its independent medical staff in a captive program, it might want to choose Vermont as the captive domicile. This is because a captive in Vermont might qualify as a risk retention group (RRG) and offer the system marketing advantages in multiple states. The next section will provide additional information about RRGs.

A captive insurance company can help an organization solve business problems. A quality consultant will help a health care organization assess its unique risks and business issues to determine whether a captive can help and choose the domicile with the greatest benefits to the organization.

Captives—The Next Generation

Savvy risk managers, working in conjunction with insurance brokers and consultants, continually tweak existing approaches or create new ones to meet their evolving needs. What was cutting edge yesterday is passé today. A continuing trend is the development and utilization of captive-like vehicles to achieve specific objectives.

....

RISK RETENTION GROUPS (RRG)S

In 1986, Congress enacted amendments to the Product Liability Risk Retention Act of 1981 that expanded the act to apply to all liability risks. Those amendments created the concept of RRGs. An RRG is an insurance company that provides liability coverage to its members and owners. Members must be "similar or related entities" with respect to the liabilities to which they are exposed. This language has been interpreted to allow a wide variety of health care providers to be members of the same RRG (such as physicians and hospitals).

An RRG must be licensed as an insurance company in at least one of the fifty states. Offshore domiciles, like Bermuda, do not qualify. The states that have chosen to attract captive insurance companies are logical choices for licensing RRGs because their capitalization requirements and regulatory climates are attractive to start-up insurance companies. In fact, many domestically domiciled group captives could automatically qualify as RRGs. Unlike a captive, which must be licensed or fronted by a licensed insurance company in every state in which it desires to conduct business, the Risk Retention Act provides that an RRG need be licensed in *one* state only to conduct business in *any* state. This difference significantly lessens the regulatory requirements an RRG must meet to solicit members in multiple states.

The mechanics of an RRG are identical to a direct policy-issuing captive. The difference is in the group ownership of the insurance company.

Due to these differences between offshore captives and onshore RRGs, some health care organizations have created both. A single-parent captive might be set up offshore and owned by the health care system for tax and regulatory reasons, while the RRG is set up onshore with system and physician ownership, so that multistate physician groups or other entities which the organization wants to attract, can be legally solicited. The RRG issues the policies to its owner and members and purchases reinsurance from the offshore captive, receiving benefits from both.

After some initial skepticism due to a few RRG liquidations and an uncertain state regulatory environment, it is now clear that an RRG can provide health care organizations with another option for retaining and financing risk.

Reciprocals

Within the past several years creation of "onshore" reciprocal insurance companies as alternatives to "offshore" captives has become popular. Most commercial insurance companies are "stock" companies and look like other publicly traded firms. Most health care organization-owned insurance companies, whether onshore or offshore, use this model. Some insurers are "mutual" companies where the policyholders are the company owners. Reciprocals are a third type of insurance vehicle that, like a mutual insurer, allows ownership by policyholders. Several states (such as Vermont and Michigan) offer a reciprocal option within their insurance statutes.

In at least two cases, reciprocals are owned jointly by a health care system and its independent medical staff. These companies were created to allow physicians to come together with a health care system and share in the profitability of their medical professional insurance programs without causing adverse tax consequences. Like captives or RRGs, reciprocals can offer owners certain tax and/or regulatory benefits that will be covered in the tax section of this chapter.

Purchasing Groups

Group programs can be especially attractive to smaller entities because larger retentions can be entertained than by single organizations. The fact that risk is "pooled" or spread among multiple organizations can bring some comfort to an entity that, in contrast to a stand-alone program, one bad year of one's own loss experience will not bankrupt the program. And this same spreading of loss is attractive to for-profit entities because it helps meet the IRS's requirement for up-front tax deductibility of prefunding amounts. On the other hand, sharing claims with others can be an exercise in faith. The prospective group participant should do its homework very carefully.

Purchasing groups are a sort of a hybrid of conventional insurance and RRGs, and were also created by the Risk Retention Act. Purchasing groups allow members to purchase insurance from traditional insurance companies on a group basis, without state regulation. Purchasing groups must be composed of "similar or related" entities and one of their purposes must be to group purchase liability insurance. Existing groups, such as trade associations, may, by board resolution, become purchasing groups. Per the act, a purchasing group is not subject to state insurance regulators' examination, but the insurance company providing coverage to the group is subject to all typical state controls.

Purchasing groups provide an opportunity for individual organizations to pool their buying power to achieve more competitive pricing than they could individually. Purchasing groups also sidestep the difficult issues of capitalization, organization, risk sharing, and governance that group captives and RRGs face. As a result, purchasing groups can form with little lead time.

Unfortunately, purchasing groups are subject to all the vagaries of working with the conventional insurance market, albeit with enhanced purchasing power. Also, by teaming with others, a purchasing group member may find that it is forced to accept a standard menu of coverage that has not been tailored to its individual needs. However, for the organization with little or no appetite for risk retention and no specialized needs, the purchasing group format offers an opportunity to find coverage at a more reasonable price than it could as a single entity.

············

SOFT MARKET INNOVATIONS

As discussed in other sections of this chapter and in other chapters of this book, significant competition exists in the general insurance marketplace. Since 1988 we have had a "soft" or buyers' market for professional liability insurance. As the cost of coverage has declined over these years, several organizations ask the question, "Why should we retain risk when we can buy 'cheap' insurance?" In fact, some organizations have retreated from self-insurance and captive programs and returned to traditional, guaranteed-cost coverage during this soft market. When the health care risk manager has the opportunity to transfer risk for premiums at, or below, expected losses, they may justifiably shun loss-responsive plans and sophisticated funding approaches. However, there are potential benefits to the more sophisticated alternatives beyond up-front premium cost.

The ultimate cost or value of an alternative is a combination of:

- The breadth of the protection provided.
- The net present value (after taxes, if applicable) of the up-front cost.

- The cashflow and accounting implications of the program.
- The value of services and administration provided.
- The ease of administration and efficiency of the program.
- The specifically tailored nuances that make the program unique to the insured's needs.

The next section will attempt to give a sense of some additional nuances that are possible.

············

INTEGRATED RISK FINANCING AND INTEGRATED HEALTH CARE

As various health care providers come together in "vertically integrated systems" or "horizontal conglomerates," health care risk managers will be asked to deal with a wide spectrum of risk. From the claims-made tail on a physician practice acquisition, to the insolvency of a recently purchased entity's liability insurer, the risk manager will have the opportunity to help solve their organization's problems—from employed physicians' benefits plans to the nightmare of funding for pension programs. The successful risk manager will apply liability solutions to capitation issues, and keep up to date on captive taxation issues. The risk manager will be challenged with risks from pollution claims, wrongful termination claims, and the financial risks of underpricing (or overexpensing) capitation plans. Can any risk-funding plan meet these potentially conflicting needs, and do it cost effectively?

Several attempts have been made to offer integrated systems integrated insurance programs. Rather than purchasing each type or "line" of insurance on a stand-alone basis with different renewal dates, different limits, and different deductibles, these multirisk approaches combine several coverages together into integrated plans. An integrated program created in excess of self-insured retentions or a captive might include professional liability, general liability, automobile liability, employers' liability, employee benefits liability, environmental liability, directors' and officers' (D&O) liability, miscellaneous errors and omissions (E&O), employment practices liability, managed care liability, heliport liability, and property, marine, and crime insurance. Or it might even go beyond "traditionally insured" risks to pick up products-recall coverage, foreign currency exchange, residual values, and interest rate or commodity price fluctuations.

Three basic concepts stand behind these approaches:

Efficiency—Risk managers want to spend more time on risk prevention and mitigation and less time on annual insurance renewals for multiple programs or coverages.

The "Portfolio Effect"—By pulling a group or portfolio of risks together, they tend to offset or "hedge" each other, making the whole less volatile than the sum of the parts.

Combined Purchasing Power—Just as a purchasing group can use its size to negotiate improved coverage and pricing, an organization can enhance its "market clout" by placing its insurance as a package.

To date only the largest corporate insurance buyers have implemented integrated risk financing programs; however, if the past predicts the future, these concepts will become available to all buyers of insurance in no time. Exhibit 32.5 displays a traditional program and an integrated program.

EXHIBIT 32.5. **Integrated and Nonintegrated Programs**

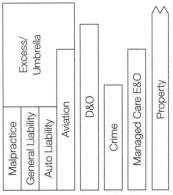

Traditional "Nonintegrated" Program   Integrated Program

············
MULTIYEAR SINGLE LIMIT

The use of multiyear policies has been popular in recent years. Insurers recognize the benefit of "locking up" a client for two, three, or even five years, so they offer a reduced premium. If the organization is willing to prepay the entire multiyear premium, carriers will offer a further discount.

Some health care organizations have decided to purchase multiyear single limit (MYSL) coverage for those coverages they purchase every year, but make claims against it very infrequently (such as D&O or excess coverages purchased well above expected loss levels). They feel coverages with these characteristics can be bought for multiple years with a single-aggregate policy limit. That is, instead of purchasing "fresh" limits at each annual anniversary, a single-aggregate limit is put in place for the entire multiyear policy term.

Often insurers will offer a three-year single-limit program for about the cost of two consecutive annual limit plans. Since one limit has to cover a longer period, some organizations have used the single limit savings to significantly increase the multiyear limit. Exhibit 32.6 displays the concept using a MYSL approach for excess coverage.

By combining integrated risk financing with MYSL programs, an organization can further concentrate its buying power. Insurers recognize the "three dimensional" benefits of the portfolio effect of multiple risks over longer periods of time. Recognize that multiple-year commitments provide stability, which can be positive or negative to both parties. If the insurance market continues to "soften," locking in a multiyear arrangement could prevent an organization from receiving the benefits of the competitive market at future program anniversaries. If the market "hardens," the insurer misses the opportunity to increase premiums at future anniversaries.

············
THE USE OF REINSURANCE

Insurance companies understand the benefits of spreading and sharing risks. They typically share the risks they assume with other insurance companies or reinsurers. They may purchase reinsurance on a "treaty" or a "facultative" basis. Treaty reinsurance might

EXHIBIT 32.6.   Traditional Program Structure and MYSL Structure

Traditional Structure				MYSL Structure		
Excess	Excess	Excess		Excess		
Primary	Primary	Primary		Primary	Primary	Primary
1997	1998	1999		1997	1998	1999

automatically provide protection against all claims above $250,000 in exchange for the reinsurer accepting 30 percent of all premiums collected. Or the reinsurer may automatically accept 20 percent of every premium dollar and losses from the first dollar. Treaty reinsurance protects an insurer across its book of business. Facultative reinsurance is arranged on a risk-by-risk basis. A primary commercial insurance company might write a $5 million policy for a hospital, but only keep $500,000 of the risk, passing $4,500,000 along to one or more reinsurers.

Some health care organizations have decided to sidestep primary commercial insurers and go directly to reinsurers. Accessing the reinsurance market directly can offer an organization certain advantages. Reinsurers typically do not have extensive branch office systems to support, nor do they provide the level of claims and loss control service consumers expect from the firms like St. Paul, CNA, or Zurich. Therefore, reinsurers can offer large limits of coverage (known in the industry as "capacity") at wholesale costs. A few of the best-known reinsurers have been quietly providing the lion's share of liability capacity to health care providers for decades.

In some cases commercial primary insurers are taking so little risk that they look like "fronts" rather than insurance companies. By purchasing reinsurance directly, health care entities cut out this middleman, and save the retail mark up. Savings could be in the same 10-percent range charged by some fronting carriers. Some health care risk managers have decided that building a direct relationship with these reinsurers can save them money *and* provide greater stability as primary insurers come and go.

Some organizations use their captive insurance companies to "front" the insurance policies they need and then reinsure or pass off all or most of the risk to one or more large capacity reinsurers. This approach is the mirror image of using a commercial front and reinsuring with a captive. Using a captive to front in this way only works for unregulated lines of coverage. Several health care organizations created captive insurance companies expressly for the purpose of insuring medical professional liability insurance with reinsurers—bearing no risk in the captive, using it only as an access point to reinsurers' capacity.

This section was included to give readers a flavor for the broad spectrum of risk financing alternatives available. However, this information was obsolete even before this book was printed. Every day new strategies are created and old ones are modified and improved. The health care risk managers who wants to add value to their organization will be well served by constantly searching for the new and unique, reading the journals, asking the questions, and devouring all sources of information to continue to gain risk financing expertise.

TAX ASPECTS OF RISK FINANCING

The threshold tax issue for health care providers forming or participating in a risk financing mechanism is always the same: Is it really "insurance" for federal and state tax purposes? Although economists and insurance academics long ago reached a general consensus on the meaning of the term "insurance," the tax law definition to this day continues to evolve.

Why Presence or Absence of "Insurance" Matters

A key distinction emanates from whether the founder or participant in a risk financing program is itself a taxable entity or a tax-exempt organization. Because the tax law precedent on this subject developed primarily in the world of taxable multinational corporations, we will start the discussion with taxable health care entities, such as for-profit hospitals, the majority of physicians' professional service corporations, and most "continuum of care" assisted living on nursing homes.

Benefits of "Insurance" to Taxpayers   The most obvious advantage of "insurance" being present is the ability to deduct the payment to the insurer. A long established tax law principle is that setting money aside in a pure self-funding reserve earmarked for future contingent losses is not tax deductible since in effect the taxpayer is merely moving the funds "from its left to its right pocket." To achieve tax deductibility, the payment must be an insurance premium that constitutes an "ordinary and necessary" business expense. In contrast, payments into a reserve fund are generally not deductible until the fund actually pays out money for a loss or for loss adjustment expenses. Although this difference is only one of timing, an organization able to accelerate deductions and defer tax in effect benefits from an interest-free loan by the government.

A corollary benefit from "insurance" inures to the risk funding vehicle itself. As stated, a regular taxpayer cannot deduct internal loss reserves. The Internal Revenue Code, however, affords insurance companies a special statutory advantage. They alone are eligible to take a current tax deduction for a "reasonable and fair" estimate of future contingent losses and loss adjustments expenses. So if a funding vehicle is subject to tax and if it can be classified as an insurance company, its tax burden will be substantially reduced, especially in the case of "long-tailed" exposures such as medical malpractice insurance where years pass between the prefunding (premium) and the payout (claim satisfaction). As will be described below, this loss reserve deduction is beneficial to both onshore and offshore captives.

One other benefit redounds to an offshore captive that constitutes an insurance company. Should it decide for tax minimization or compliance reasons that it prefers to be treated as a domestic taxpayer, it can make an essentially irrevocable election to this effect. But only true insurance or reinsurance companies are permitted to so elect.

Disadvantages of "Insurance" to Taxpayers   A significant disadvantage of falling within the definition of "insurance" to programs involving offshore insurers should be mentioned. Premiums paid to an offshore carrier (whether or not a "captive") are subject to a federal excise tax (unless a tax treaty applies) of 4 percent of the premium for "direct" (unfronted) insurance and 1 percent of premium for reinsurance. No tax treaty relief exists for any of the common offshore captive domiciles (such as Bermuda, the Cayman Islands, or Barbados). Further, many states have a special type of premium tax, often called a "self-procurement" tax, applicable to insurance premiums paid to both onshore and offshore captives. In many (but not all) cases, this tax is not applicable if no "insurance" exists such that the payment, at least arguably, is not really a "premium."

Another disadvantage will be described in more detail further on. An amendment to the Internal Revenue Code effective in 1996 automatically classifies "insurance" income of offshore captives owned by tax-exempt organizations as unrelated business taxable income (UBTI) in the hands of those organizations. By definition, UBTI is income derived from an activity unrelated to the organization's tax-exempt purpose and thus is subject to income tax at normal corporate rates. As a result, tax-exempt health providers now are treated in the same manner as their taxable counterparts—their offshore group captive's underwriting and investment income is currently subject to federal income tax.

Two General Tax Rules of Thumb   In contrast to taxable entities, tax-exempt organizations generally prefer that their risk retention and funding programs not constitute "insurance." Premium and loss reserve deductions are irrelevant to them. If the program involves an offshore captive, they want to avoid federal excise tax (only applicable to insurance) and hopefully also state self-procurement tax. As mentioned, "insurance income" of an offshore group captive owned by a U.S. tax-exempt organization is treated as UBTI in the hands of that owner. But if the offshore captive generates no insurance income, this unfavorable provision is inapplicable.

Consistent with the foregoing, it generally is the case that taxable entities struggle to create insurance, and tax-exempt organizations strive to avoid it. Surprising to nontax practitioners, however, is the fact that a trust, captive, or any other risk-bearing entity insuring more than one unrelated tax-exempt organization is considered engaged in a true "insurance" business under the Internal Revenue Code's strict rules, and therefore is *per se* a taxable entity. The unfavorable decisions in three litigated cases have been applied to tax-exempt hospitals and other charities, which logically but erroneously believed their risk pools would inherit the participants' tax-exempt status.

Another major complication for health care providers and managed care organizations is the relatively recent advent of integrated delivery systems (IDSs) composed of both taxable and tax-exempt members in varying ownership configurations. The result usually is the need for a case-by-case analysis of alternative risk financing structures, consistent with the organizational goals and regulatory constraints, to determine whether it is preferable to fall within or escape from a characterization for tax purposes as an "insurance" program. But the two general rules usually remain valid: tax-exempt organizations are better off without "insurance," and taxpaying entities are better off with it. With this lengthy introduction, we now turn to how insurance is defined for tax purposes.

The Tax Definition of Insurance

Surprisingly, neither the Internal Revenue Code nor other official pronouncements actually define the term "insurance." To find insurance, both the Internal Revenue Service and the numerous courts of law have required the presence of both risk shifting and risk distribution. In 1977, the seminal IRS revenue ruling was released in which the single "economic family" doctrine was enunciated, denying premium and loss-reserve deductibility to a single-parent captive covering only the captive's parent and its subsidiaries.[1] A year later, the IRS conceded that if a sufficient number of unrelated parties pool their loss exposures (thirty one in that case), then sufficient risk distribution exists to create "insurance."[2] A gray area exists between one and thirty one, but an unofficial rule of thumb has emerged that more than ten unrelated participants truly pooling risks almost surely will suffice for insurance and perhaps as few as three or four is enough.

Risk shifting connotes the transfer of risk to a separate party. Risk distribution mandates that enough independent risks of unrelated parties are being pooled to invoke the "actuarial law of large numbers." Application of these concepts is illustrated by the two theories, which have caused the courts to conclude "insurance" is present: the "unrelated risk" approach and the "brother-sister risk" theory. Rather than try to recite the complex facts of the pertinent cases, the discussion here will set forth a distillation of the basic principles derived from them.

Unrelated Risk   Although the IRS in a still-outstanding revenue ruling disagrees,[3] the courts have determined that if a risk-funding vehicle (such as a captive) covers a sufficiently large percentage of unrelated risk, then the entire risk pool should be treated as an insurance company. This judicial rule came from a trilogy of cases decided contemporaneously against the IRS in 1992. At one extreme, the IRS alleged that Allstate was not an "insurance company" relative to its then parent, Sears, notwithstanding that well over 99 percent of Allstate's insureds were completely unrelated parties.[4] In a companion case also decided for the taxpayer, Harper Group, only 29 percent of the retained premiums were attributable to unrelated parties. Nevertheless, that taxpayer also prevailed.[5] Thus, with a considerable degree of trepidation, 30 percent of retained premium has become the unofficial rule of thumb for finding enough risk transfer and risk distribution to support a finding of "insurance." It should be noted, however, that the IRS supported an unsuccessful 1998 legislative proposal in Congress that would have raised the minimum unrelated risk threshold to 50 percent of retained premium.

Brother-Sister Theory   While the battle over unrelated risk was underway, an ingenious lawyer for Humana Corporation in 1986 presented to the court a then novel theory that a captive's coverage of brother-sister corporations, although under common ownership by the parent, could result in a finding of insurance. The argument was built on a long-standing tax principle that separate corporations should be treated separately in spite of their common ownership, and stated that risk indeed had been distributed among the numerous sister subsidiaries of the captive even though they belonged to the same economic family. Although the Tax Court rejected this approach, the Sixth Circuit Court of Appeals accepted it,[6] and other circuit courts subsequently have cited this case with approval.[7] More recently, the Federal Circuit in Washington, D.C., also concurred, giving this theory national viability.[8] So siblings of even a single-parent captive, if there are enough of them, apparently can deduct premiums paid to the captive (although the parent itself cannot) and further the captive should be able to deduct its loss reserves.

Tax as a Factor in Captive Domicile and Form Selection

The basic dichotomy in captive domicile selection is onshore versus offshore. Nontax factors often rightly predominate in making the "proper" choice. The conventional wisdom is that offshore insurance regulation, for example in Bermuda and the Cayman Islands, generally is more flexible and reporting requirements less stringent than onshore. Captive friendly states, however, such as Vermont and Hawaii, also have made great strides in accommodating the ever-changing uses and objectives of captives and their owners.

From a tax perspective, a few fundamental tax principles will assist in analyzing domiciles for the optimal tax outcome. First, corporations formed under the law of any U.S. state generally are subject to federal income tax on worldwide income. Recall that a domestic captive writing "insurance" can take a tax deduction for loss reserves, but a captive functioning as a noninsurance funding vehicle cannot. An exception to the world wide taxation rule is that in theory, and sometimes in practice, a domestic captive wholly owned by a single tax-exempt organization and writing only controlled risks can itself obtain a tax exemption if properly structured. In this respect, such a limited purpose captive could be thought of as an incorporated, hospital-medical-malpractice trust fund.

In contrast, an offshore corporation is itself taxable in the United States only if it does business here. A narrow exception is that if it is an "insurance company," it can voluntarily elect to be taxed as a domestic corporation. But most offshore captives diligently avoid engaging a U.S. business both to avoid federal income tax and to stay out of insurance regulatory trouble (as "alien" insurers without a certificate of authority from any state, they are prohibited from conducting an insurance business onshore).

An offshore captive, if controlled by U.S. persons or if writing in significant part risk of it owners, will be subject to a complex imputed federal income tax regime under Subpart F of the Internal Revenue Code. Basically, to prevent deferral of tax by operating offshore, the captive's underwriting and investment income will be deemed distributed annually as a hypothetical dividend to its U.S. shareholders *pro rata* to their percentage share ownership. For taxable owners, this regime is extremely difficult to avoid, regardless whether the captive is carrying on an "insurance" business. Tax-exempt captive owners have an easier task. As stated, if they can avoid characterization as "insurance," then the previously referenced 1996 tax law amendment is inapplicable and their deemed dividend under Subpart F is excludible from UBTI just as an ordinary cash dividend would be. Alternatively, offshore group hospital programs under a special rule can escape UBTI by returning any profits to participants via a policyholder rather than a shareholder dividend.

Other Tax and Legal Issues

Two other important tax issues relevant to health care risk funding should be mentioned. The first is the federal income tax concept of private inurement, which dictates that a tax-exempt organization cannot deploy its tax-exempt assets in a manner that unduly benefits taxable parties. The penalty to the exempt organization can be as harsh as loss of its tax exemption. The antidote is for the tax-exempt organization to treat private parties, regardless of their relationship or status with respect to the organization, on a verifiable arm's length basis (meaning, as if they were unrelated parties). The application of this principle to risk funding is that no subsidies or other concessions materially deviating from the actuarial determination of the appropriate premium range should be allowed to occur.

A second issue is to avoid violation of the Medicare "fraud and abuse" rules. In essence, it is a civil and sometimes a criminal offense to offer or provide something of value to a physician in exchange for Medicare-covered patient referrals or admissions. In the context of professional liability insurance, again the key is to have verifiable actuarial support for the premium rates charged. As applied to hospital and physician insurance programs, if carefully and properly conceived and documented, it may be permissible to offer an insurance premium discount to physicians who participate in preventative and loss reduction programs. It may even be permissible to offer a premium discount to those physicians who direct more of their practice to the sponsoring institution of the insurance plan. The latter discount, however, must be bolstered by credible, contemporaneous, and reasonably documented evidence that by subjecting more of the professionals' admissions and procedures to an enhanced loss quality program, improved loss results will justify the reduction in premiums.

Application to the Health Care Industry

The complexity of the analysis of whether one or more particular candidates for a risk funding program should create an "insurance" program for tax purposes and, if so, using which structure is apparent. A trust is appropriate for the vast majority of tax-exempt providers that wish to cover only institutional risks. Under legal and tax principles, risks of employees, whether physicians, nurses, or other paraprofessionals, are considered part and parcel of the employer's risk. Once the desire to cover nonemployees emerges, such as voluntary medical staff, managed care organizations, including independent physician associations (IPAs) or physician-hospital organizations (PHOs), the unavoidable consequence is a need to consider and choose from a wide variety of structural alternatives, each with its own pros and cons. Given the trend toward system integration, joint ventures and "strategic alliances," and the failure of tort reform to alleviate liability exposures, the need to consider a vehicle for risk funding becomes ever more compelling. The 1990s "soft" insurance market lulled some into the comforting belief that adequate medical malpractice always would be available at reasonable prices. But history dispels that notion, and when another professional liability insurance "crisis" erupts, many of today's purchasers of guaranteed cost commercial coverage will scramble to put together a self-funding program, often with a captive, equally dependable in a "hard" insurance market.

....

ACTUARIAL AND ACCOUNTING APPLICATIONS FOR RISK FINANCING

Guaranteed cost insurance is the preferred risk-financing technique when coverage costs are unpredictable or relatively small. However, as health care systems continue to merge and grow, their costs become more predictable and risk-financing techniques employed by these systems tend to be more sophisticated and complex.

This section will focus on the actuarial and accounting application concepts underlying the advanced risk-financing techniques previously described.

Expected Losses

Most of the advanced risk-financing techniques, such as large deductibles, self-insurance, or captive insurance, involve self-retention of significant risk. It is important, therefore, to have a good understanding of a program's underlying expected losses at all levels in evaluating the optimal combination of commercial and self-insured risk-financing techniques for that particular program. Loss projection techniques will often vary by line of business, limits of coverage, size of risk under consideration, coverage form, and the availability and credibility of risk-specific historical loss and exposure data.

The estimation of program expected losses is a somewhat complex process involving estimation and evaluation of a number of parameters.

Trends (Frequency, Severity)   Trends reflect the changes in average loss costs from year to year due to inflation (severity) and the propensity to sue (frequency). Severity trends are generally calculated by measuring the change in average loss costs each year where average loss costs are the total loss costs divided by the number of claims.

For example, if the average claim size in 1995 is $100 and in 1996 is $105, the implied severity trend is 5 percent. Frequency is defined as the number of claims divided by the number of exposure units. Frequency trends measure the change in frequency each year. For example, if the number of claims in 1995 is 100 and in 1996 is 105, and the exposures remain constant for both years, the implied frequency trend is 5 percent.

Loss Development Patterns (Paid, Reported Incurred)   Loss development patterns reflect changes in historic incurred (or paid) losses for a given policy year, accident year, or report year (for the purpose of this discussion, we will refer to *policy year*) at various evaluation points (twelve months from inception, twenty-four months, thirty-six months, and so on). These patterns are used to estimate the ultimate value of current years losses that have not fully matured. In order to analyze historical loss development patterns, loss data are organized in a format known as a "loss development triangle," where the rows represent policy years and columns represent evaluation points (you can see the "triangle" format in the simple example described here).

In a "long-tail" line of coverage such as medical malpractice, a long period of time may pass before the ultimate value of a claim is known, and the loss development triangle provides a convenient format for observing the aggregate changes in loss patterns as the years mature. It is generally assumed that the historical pattern will be repeated in the future. For example, if all losses are paid by twenty four months and history indicates that 50 percent of the losses are paid as of twelve months, then we would expect the current year twelve-month paid losses to double by the twenty-four–month valuation.

In some situations, there is a change in the environment (such as tort reform) that causes a shift in loss development. In such a case, explicit adjustments need to be made to the historical pattern for use in projecting ultimate losses.

Exposure Units   Exposure unit changes measure the changes in expected loss from year to year due to changes in the size of the entity or the mix of business. While the appropriate "exposure bases" for measuring relative changes in risk varies by coverage, exposure bases generally have three ideal characteristics: readily available, objective, and varies directly with risk. For example, professional liability exposure bases include occupied beds by type, outpatient visits, deliveries, and doctors by specialty. Generally multiple exposure bases for a single coverage such as professional liability will be converted to a single index by using relative weights or relativities.

For example, one primary care physician may be equivalent to three occupied acute care beds. Combining 100 primary care physicians with 100 acute care occupied beds would produce 400 exposure units where a unit is defined as an acute care occupied bed-equivalent. When projecting current loss costs based on historical losses it is important to adjust the historical losses for the relative change in underlying exposures.

Limit Adjustment Factors   Limit adjustment factors are derived from size of loss distributions and are used to adjust "basic limits" losses to various specific or per claim retention limits. Typically, most evaluations of expected program losses, where large limits are retained, are split between two levels: basic limits losses and retained limits losses. The basic limit loss cutoff is intended to capture the predictable losses, while the limit adjustment factors are used to provide for the "fortuitous" or unpredictable losses at higher retentions. Basic limits definitions vary by coverage and tend to increase over time. For example, the professional liability basic limit loss cutoff in the 1970s was $25,000 whereas in the 1990s it ranges from $200,000 to $500,000.

Data Credibility   Data credibility pertains to both the quality and predictability of the data. Before relying on underlying data to project expected losses, reviewing the data for consistency and reasonableness is important. Substantial swings in exposure units by year, declining claim counts or declining paid losses in subsequent valuations are usually red flags for data problems. Even if the data are deemed reliable it may not be a good predictor for some of the parameters underlying expected losses. For example, most trend indications are done on a state or regional basis. Very few health care organizations are both sufficiently large and located in the same geographic region (state) such that their data produce credible trend indications. Likewise, limit adjustment factors are generally derived on a regional basis. Generally the weight given to individual risk experience compared with broader industry experience will be directly proportional to the size of the individual risk and the quality of the data.

Confidence Levels   Confidence levels reflect the potential variation of actual losses from the expected loss projections. Generally loss projections are done on an expected value basis or an approximate 55-percent confidence level basis. The confidence level reflects the theoretical probability that the expected losses will not be exceeded by the actual losses. At expected value, we expect fifty-five times out of 100 that our actual losses will be lower than expected and forty-five times out of 100 actual losses will be above expected. Usually self-insured programs are funded at higher than a 55-percent confidence level (70 percent to 90 percent) to protect against adverse fluctuations in loss experience. Confidence levels are usually derived by simulating the expected losses of a hypothetical risk of similar size using loss parameters derived from the entity being evaluated.

Pure Premiums   Pure premiums are defined as the expected loss costs per exposure unit. Evaluating expected losses for current or future policy periods usually involves developing an expected pure premium for the policy period under review and extending that pure premium by the anticipated number of exposure units. Techniques to develop pure premium estimates vary based on the coverage provided and availability of historical data but are usually derived using the parameters discussed here. Typically, basic limits historical losses are developed to an ultimate basis and divided by the applicable exposure units to produce historical basic limits pure premiums. The historical basic limits pure premiums are then adjusted to current level with trend factors and adjusted to the retained limits under consideration using limit adjustment factors.

Retention Levels (Specific, Aggregate)   Retention levels for a self-insured program reflect the point at which self-retained losses are "stopped." Self-insured retention levels are usually determined on a specific (per claim, per occurrence) basis, an aggregate basis, or a combination of both. A program with a $1 million/$3 million self-insured limit retains up to the first $1 million for each individual claim in a given policy year with a further restriction that all retained losses for that policy year not exceed $3 million in aggregate. Selecting appropriate self-insured retention levels requires an evaluation of the following considerations:

- Willingness of commercial market to attach at various retention levels.
- Comparison of self-insured funding costs with corresponding commercial market costs at various retentions.
- Willingness and ability of the health care institution to accept the risk of adverse or worst case outcomes.

As a practical matter, most self-insured retentions are driven by commercial market decisions on their appropriate attachment point. During a soft market, commercial underwriters are looking for premium volume and will set their best price at lower attachment points. During a hard market, underwriters are looking for profits and will generally seek to raise attachment points while maintaining premium volume. While price plays an important part in determining appropriate retention levels, risk of adverse outcome should be considered particularly for low-frequency or high-severity coverages such as D&O coverage. Generally with low-frequency or high-severity coverages, the premium cost saved does not warrant the risk taken.

Usually, retention levels are selected to coordinate with commercial excess or reinsurance coverage. Care should be taken to avoid gaps in coverage by using consistent policy periods, terms, forms and coverage documents, and confirming treatment of allocated loss adjustment expense (in or out of limits). Further, excess or reinsurance agreements often have coinsurance clauses or surviving retention requirements after aggregate exhaustion. Each of these may extend the actual self-insured losses beyond the stated retention.

Coverage Form—Claims Made, Occurrence, or Prior Acts   Program losses will vary considerably based on the coverage form under consideration. Claims made coverage losses are based on claims *reported* during the coverage period regardless of when the incident actually occurred, subject to the retroactive inception date. Occurrence coverage losses are based on incidents that *occur* during the coverage period regardless of when the claim is reported. Prior acts (or tail) coverage losses are based on incidents that occurred before the prior acts coverage period and are subsequently reported during the prior acts coverage period. Prior acts coverage is used in conjunction with claims made coverage to essentially provide occurrence coverage by covering any unreported or IBNR claims.

Estimating program losses as of a certain valuation date for a selected coverage period usually involves evaluation of three components: known losses, development on known losses (IBNE), and unknown losses (IBNR).

Known losses for a selected coverage period at any valuation date reflects the sum, at that valuation date, of all paid losses plus all outstanding case basis (adjusters) reserves for all known coverage period claims (both open or closed).

Typically as claims are reported, claims adjusters establish a case reserve amount reflecting their current estimate of the ultimate claim value. These reserves may change over time as the adjuster learns more about the claim. When a claim is settled, the case basis reserve is ultimately replaced with actual paid amounts. Often, the final paid amount will vary from the adjusters' reserve amount—sometimes higher, sometimes lower. The difference between the adjusters' case basis reserves and the final paid amounts is often referred to as development on known losses, or incurred but not enough (IBNE).

The final component, unknown losses or incurred but not reported (IBNR), refers to the ultimate value of claims that have occurred as of a valuation date, but have not yet been identified through the claims reporting system.

Typically, loss estimates for claims-made coverage will focus on known losses and development on known losses since by definition, claims-made coverage encompasses only reported or known claims. There are some exceptions, however, such as extended reporting periods.

Loss estimates for occurrence coverage include evaluation of known losses, development on known losses, and unknown losses.

Occasionally individuals will ignore these parameters and estimate expected losses using simplistic approaches (such as selecting the three-year average paid or reported losses). These simple approaches may understate the actual value significantly, especially for long tail lines such a professional liability or workers' compensation or for programs or coverages with limited historical data. Usually evaluations of expected losses giving full consideration to the above parameters are conducted by individuals with an actuarial background.

....

ACTUARIAL PROJECTIONS

An actuary is an individual who analyzes current financial implications of future contingent events. To achieve professional designations in the various actuarial societies (casualty, life, and so on), actuaries are required to pass a series of exams that test their knowledge on all aspects of insurance and risk. These exams include traditional actuarial topics (probability and statistics, mortality, for example), insurance law, underwriting, policy forms, coverage, insurance accounting, asset and liability management, risk management, claims management, strategic planning, and general management.

Typically, health care organizations that retain significant risk will engage an actuary to assist in evaluating the self-retained losses for a variety of reasons.

Medicare/Medicaid Reimbursement   Health care organizations that self-insure coverages through captive programs or self-insurance trusts are required to obtain annual actuarial reviews of their funding levels to obtain reimbursement of their funding costs to the extent applicable.

Regulatory Requirements   Laws governing insurance and self-insurance vary considerably by coverage and domicile. Most captive domiciles require an annual actuarial certification of loss reserves, particularly for long-tail lines such as professional liability. Regulators typically review actuarial reports when approving retained limits and collateral and security for workers' compensation and other self-insured programs.

Bond Covenants   Bond covenants and loan agreements will often require specific limits of insurance coverage to be in place throughout the life of the agreement. Where a portion or all the required insurance coverage is provided through some form of self-insurance, actuarial evaluations of the self-insurance program are often requested.

Audit Support   Typically auditors will request, and rely on, independent actuarial reviews of self-insurance programs to support financial statement accrual of self-insurance liabilities.

Excess Insurers and Reinsurers   Excess insurers and reinsurers of captive programs usually request copies of the independent actuarial reviews before committing to coverage, attachment level, and pricing for a program. The health care organization will also rely on actuarial projections to determine appropriate retention levels.

Fiduciary Responsibility   Generally when health care organizations or their captives retain significant risk, board members will require annual actuarial reviews to support the reasonableness of their decisions.

Actuarial Reports

Actuarial guidelines regarding communications suggest that actuarial reports should identify the underlying data, assumptions, and methods with sufficient clarity that another actuary practicing in the same field could make an objective assessment of reasonableness and validity of the report. Typically, an actuarial report will contain the following sections:

- *Purpose or Scope*—Briefly outlines the scope of the report.
- *Distribution and Use*—Outlines and limits who is authorized to review and/or rely on the report as well as the uses for which the report is intended.
- *Reliances and Limitations*—Provides general discussion of where the actuary has relied on others for information or data supporting the analysis as well as a description of underlying limitations of the analysis.
- *Summary and Conclusions*—Provides discussion of the report findings generally including references to key supporting exhibits.
- *Methodology*—Description of the methodology underlying the analysis usually with references to supporting exhibits.
- *Major Assumptions*—Detailed assumptions underlying the selection of parameters affecting the analysis.
- *Exhibits and Graphs*—Usually provides a summary of findings as well as sufficient detail to support the analysis.

When reviewing an actuarial report, the reader should first confirm that the purpose or scope is appropriate as well as the intended distribution and usage. While portions of the text may be viewed as "boilerplate language," it is intended to provide the reader with sufficient insight to understand the findings and conclusions of the report. Generally the reader should also focus on the assumptions, which outline most of the parameters underlying the analysis. Wherever possible, the reader should confirm that the assumptions are both reasonable and appropriate. Finally, the reader should focus on the summary or conclusions section to determine the findings of the report.

Actuarial reports tend to be technical in nature and are often confusing to the novice reader. Quite often executive summary extracts are prepared from the full report, which exclude most of the reliances, limitations, and methodology discussion as well as most of the supporting exhibits. These usually focus on the key issues and concerns without all the technical support.

Accounting Issues

Historically accounting for insurance or self-insurance liability was a relatively straightforward process usually involving expensing the premiums paid for commercial coverage or the actual funds set aside for self-insurance. However, as the self-insured liability of individual health care organizations grew through a variety of advanced risk financing techniques, it became apparent that this method of expensing often produces inaccurate, inconsistent results.

For example, prior to 1987, the financial statement accrual for a health care system funding its occurrence basis self-insurance program at a 90-percent confidence level would be significantly higher than the financial statement accrual for an identical system with an unfunded self-insured liability expensing on a pay-as-you-go basis. A set of accounting guidelines (SOP 87-1) was initially established in 1987 to provide guidance on generally accepted accounting principals (GAAP) underlying the determination of appropriate financial statement accrual liability independent of the various self-insured funding approaches. These guidelines level the playing field by requiring a consistent approach to accruing uninsured asserted and unasserted liabilities for all health care organizations. The current guidelines are described in the American Institute of Certified Public Accountants (AICPA) publication, *Audits of Providers of Healthcare Services*.

The guidelines address appropriate financial statement accruals under a number of risk financing scenarios including uninsured programs, trust funds, captives, and commercial insurance (claims-made and tail coverage, retrospectively rated policies).

Generally, the guidelines state that the ultimate cost of liability should be accrued when incidents resulting in claims occur if it is probable that the liability has been incurred and the amount of the liability can reasonably be determined. Generally, the "most likely" or expected value estimate of liability is the amount accrued. However, if within a range of estimates liability no amount is more likely than any other, the minimum liability estimate is accrued. If the range of liability cannot be reasonably estimated, no liability is accrued; however, a contingency may be disclosed in the notes to the financial statements.

Often actuarial reports used to determine appropriate funding for self-insured liabilities can also be used to support appropriate financial statement accruals. However, several adjustments are usually required to convert "actuarially sound" funding indications to appropriate GAAP accruals. Typical adjustments include the following:

Claims Made Versus Occurrence   While many self-insured programs are funded on a claims-made basis, accrual guidelines require that all losses that have occurred, both known and unknown, should be accrued if the liability can be reasonably determined. For claims-made programs, this requires a separate determination of IBNR claim accrual amounts.

Confidence Levels   Typically self-insured programs are funded at higher (70 percent to 90 percent) confidence levels whereas loss accruals are generally fixed at expected value (55 percent).

Retained Limits   Self-insured programs are usually funded for the full self-insured retained limits, whereas loss accruals usually reflect only actual known losses and unknown losses limited to a "predictable loss" layer (or "working" layer). If, for example, a self-insured program retains and funds a per-claim limit of $5 million, but the historical losses for the self-insured program have never exceeded $1 million, the accrual "limit" for unreported losses may be established at $1 million per claim with a financial statement disclosure for the contingent liability in excess of $1 million per claim.

Data Reliance   While actuarial funding reports often rely on broader-based industry data to supplement individual risk experiences and parameter selections, accrual guidelines emphasizes more reliance on individual risk experience. This can result in different weights given to industry experience for funding and accrual projections.

Discounting   While the accounting guidelines have not taken a position on discounting, they do require disclosure. Occasionally a self-insured program will take different positions on discounting for funding and accrual purposes.

Endnotes

1. *Rev. Rul. 77-316*, 1977-2 C.B. 53.
2. *Rev. Rul. 78-338*, 1978-2 C.B. 107.

3. *Rev. Rul. 88-72,* 1988-2 C.B. 31.

4. *Sears, Roebuck and Co. v. Commissioner,* 972 F.2d 858 (7th Cir. 1992).

5. *Harper Group v. Commissioner,* 979 F.2d 1341 (9th Cir. 1992).

6. *Humana, Inc. v. Commissioner,* 881 F.2d 247 (6th Cir. 1989).

7. See, e.g., *Gulf Oil Corporation v. Commissioner,* 914 F2d 396 (3d Cir. 1990).

8. *Kidde Industries, Inc. v. U.S.,* 40 Fed. Cl. 42 (1997).

PART VI

Monitoring and Evaluating

C hapters in this section describe the various ways in which risk managers are involved in the monitoring and evaluation of systems' and providers' performance, including the performance of the risk management (RM) program itself. The section begins with a general discussion of performance improvement (PI) and its relationship to the risk management function. Next, a special and useful PI tool, benchmarking, is described, including the use of cost of risk as criteria for evaluating an RM program's financial performance. A more thorough discussion of tools to use specifically in RM program evaluation is presented.

The three remaining chapters discuss more specific tools and functions that can and should be used for PI efforts in all health care delivery settings. These tools emphasize the importance of using feedback from others to help in the monitoring and evaluating of system and RM program performance: accreditation, licensure, and surveying bodies; customer and client satisfaction measures; and the request for proposals process for the selection of insurance brokers, a generic process that can be used to create new avenues of support for an internal RM program.

33

Risk Management's Role in Performance Improvement

Peggy Berry Martin
Robert J. Marder

As developed and practiced in health care organizations today, any "quality related" or "performance improvement" efforts share a fundamental goal with the risk management function: to improve overall organizational performance by monitoring, evaluating, and addressing problems in essential patient care and the performance of health care systems on which providers depend to deliver quality care. For the health care risk manager, achieving this goal means preventing and eliminating losses that can occur when those processes and outcomes are malfunctional, absent, or otherwise inadequate. Malfunctioning processes can present liability exposures to the organization and its practitioners. As suggested by the examples in Table 33.1, a breach in a standard of care resulting in patient injury or death is frequently associated with a malfunctioning process or system.

When identified as chronic, process failures such as lack of adherence to standard treatment protocols, risk management staff are presented with opportunities to lead or participate in efforts to eliminate the root causes of these problems. In this way, risk management can reduce both the likelihood of process failures recurring and their demonstrated loss-generating potential.

This chapter touches on the evolution of quality efforts in health care, then discusses how and why risk management has an important role in any efforts to improve organizational performance.

ORGANIZATIONAL EFFORTS TO IMPROVE QUALITY

The quality of care rendered to patients and the performance of staff and systems in health care facilities have been formally reviewed and studied with the goal to improving them for at least one hundred years. In 1914, Dr. Ernest Codman, a surgeon at Massachusetts

TABLE 33.1.   Loss as a Function of Process Failure

Source of Loss	*Potential Process Failure*
Child's death due to delay in treatment of epiglottis—$1.31 million settlement.	Failure to adhere to standard treatment protocols.
Wrong type of blood administered to thirty-eight-year-old man resulting in death—$1.35 million verdict.	Improperly performed cross-matching procedure.
Cause of child's brain damage concealed from parents by physicians—$6 million verdict.	Questionable credentialing and privileging processes.

General Hospital, recommended that patients be examined one year after surgery to determine whether the operation had alleviated symptoms. His efforts led to the creation of the American College of Surgeons Hospital Standardization Program in 1918. This program included preestablished standards, hospital evaluation surveys, and the granting of accreditation for recognized compliance with the standards. The basics of this program were used by the Joint Commission on Accreditation of Healthcare Organizations (JCAHO) several decades later when their accreditation program was established.[1]

Through the decades, different terms have been used; processes, techniques, and tools have become more sophisticated. In the 1970s and 1980s, the (then) JCAH defined quality assurance as "a formal, systematic program by which care rendered to patients is measured against established criteria."[2] The 1980s and 1990s brought variations on the organizational quality efforts developed from concepts introduced by Deming,[3] Juran,[4] and others. With those concepts brought the terms *total quality management* (TQM), which is the organization-wide environment in which quality efforts could thrive, and *continuous quality improvement* (CQI), the systematic, team-based approach to process and performance improvement, into the health care environment from other industries.

At present, despite the proliferation of TQM principles in health care organizations, the actual use of TQM as a brand name is not as apparent and may now be referred to collectively as quality improvement (QI) initiatives or performance improvement or process improvement (PI) efforts. The question then for the risk manager is not whether their organization is a TQM organization; but rather how TQM principles are operationalized into PI approaches in the organization, how they relate to the risk management function, and how risk managers can be part of the process.

For many organizations, even a partial shift to a TQM environment represents a significant philosophical change. In the "traditional" environment, the organization reacted to individual events and often to individual providers mistake. In the TQM environment, the organization focuses on systems and their improvement. Although the TQM environment's essential characteristics have been enumerated and described in a variety of ways, it is easy to find agreement on a number of essential features, including:

- Establishment of a fear-free atmosphere in which staff are unafraid to question the status quo, openly and frankly discuss problems and opportunities for improvement, and freely share information vital to understanding and improving important clinical, management, and governance processes.

- Staff-wide understanding of and access to a formal, in-place, team-based process improvement mechanism.

- Staff-wide recognition of internal and external customer-supplier relationships, and the value of customer satisfaction as a driving force behind improving performance.

- Visible top-down leadership of and support for ongoing efforts to measure and improve organizational performance.

- Staff accountability for and empowerment to take actions essential to achieving optimum performance.

- Focus on looking at performance issues proactively rather than reactively.

- Focus on discovering common causes of problems inherent to a process, rather than blaming individuals for aberrant performance.

- Focus on a systematic, organized method of problem solving that uses data and statistical quality control tools as integral components of the problem identification, analysis, and resolution processes.

Most health care organizations now identify some QI or PI methods that they can adapt for their own use, based on models from the quality literature and standards enumerated by accrediting bodies. Such methods include: Focus-Plan, Do, Check, Act (Focus-PDCA) the process improvement model created by Walter Shewhart and W. Edwards Deming; Focus, Analyze, Develop, and Execute (FADE), a process improvement model created by Organizational Dynamics, Inc., of Burlington, Mass.; as well as the Xerox method. Although these methods differ in some respects, they share four essential steps:

1. Identify a goal.

2. Analyze systems and processes.

3. Plan appropriate action or actions and implementation methods.

4. Monitor performance to sustain improvement.

So, while the adoption of an improvement process is a required component in many regulatory and accrediting agencies, few mandate a specific approach. The 1998 *JCAHO Accreditation Manual* states: "While there are many approaches to improving organization performance, all have essential processes in common: process design; performance measurement; performance assessment; and performance improvement."[5]

The mandate of accrediting bodies alone make the connection between any type of quality initiatives and the risk management function an obvious one. More important, the organization-wide nature of the risk management (RM) function combined with the motivation of that program to reduce potential liability by proactively assessing the quality of care rendered and monitoring efforts of improvement make the connection between quality and risk management a near necessity for the survival of the health care facility.

JCAHO's chapter entitled "Improving Organizational Performance" contains specific standards for quality efforts as well as RM: "[d]ata on important processes and outcomes are also collected from PI.3.3.2 risk management activities." The scoring guidelines for RM Standard PI.3.3.2 include the question, "Do operational links to patient care and safety activities include the exchange of relevant information?"[6]

In addition, the similarities between steps in the QI process and in the risk management process make RM professionals logical choices to lead quality initiative efforts. One common view of the risk management process espoused by George Head of the Insurance Institute of America is:

1. Identify and analyze the exposures to loss.

2. Examine the feasibility of alternative techniques, such as risk control to stop losses, risk financing to pay for losses, and so on.

3. Select the best technique.

4. Implement the apparent best technique.

5. Monitor and improve the risk management program.[7]

There can be little argument that the steps in the risk management process overlap and complement the essential steps in a QI or PI function. But how can the overlap be translated into some practical activities that the risk manager can perform or encourage so as to be seen as an integral part of the quality initiatives in his or her organization?

The ten guidelines that follow summarize the activities that each of the components of the PI function requires using an example of a problem identified from traditional risk management data.

Identify a Goal

1. Describe in objectively verifiable terms the known or suspected problem that represents an opportunity to reduce potential liability exposure and improve an aspect of the organization's performance. (See Table 33.2 for a list of potential liability situations that may be appropriate for PI projects.)

   Example: Four claims within three years with allegation of failure to diagnose an MI. No evidence of written discharge instructions for these patients found in their record.

2. Clearly state what undesired situation or event(s) the project will seek to reduce and/or eliminate.

   Example: Lack of time and condition specific discharge instructions make defending claims with allegations of failure to diagnose difficult.

3. State how much the problem is expected to be reduced within a specified time frame in response to (corrective) intervention.

   Example: Eighty percent of patients that present to the emergency room have time- and condition-specific discharge instructions.

Analyze Systems and Processes

4. Specify the baseline data needed to demonstrate how frequently and/or severely the undesired situation or event is being seen within a specified time frame and the causes (that is, malfunctioning processes or functions or parts thereof) that are contributing to it.

TABLE 33.2.   Problems Appropriate for Risk Management CQI Projects

- Excessive delays in responding to fetal distress.
- Excessive number of missed ED diagnoses of cerebral or spinal injuries, MI, appendicitis, ectopic pregnancy, or meningitis.
- Slow response time to trauma patients requiring surgery for orthopedic, abdominal, or head injuries.
- High unplanned-return rate to the OR within forty-eight hours of initial surgery.
- Intubation mishaps (failure to maintain airway).
- High psychiatric patient suicide rate.
- Frequent failure to monitor or observe adverse effects of psychiatric (or other) medications.
- Informed consent often improperly obtained.
- High rate of CNS complications during or within two days of procedures involving anesthesia administration.
- High rate of adverse occurrences or claims involving HIV/AIDS patients.
- Inadequate credentialing procedures.
- High rate of IRB-related occurrences or claims.
- High rate of claims for which the risk-identification or reporting system failed to provide warning.

---

5. State the measures (that is, indicators) that have been or will be used to collect the baseline data and to monitor performance for signs of improvement subsequent to taking action.

   Example: Use of emergency department (ED) generic screening elements.

6. Collect the specified data, and use statistical process control data-display techniques (CQI tools) to prepare them for team review and analysis.
   - To display frequency or volume of occurrences, use run charts, control charts, pie charts, or histograms.
   - To display causes, use cause-and-effect (fishbone) diagrams, flowcharts, or Pareto charts.

Plan Appropriate Action or Actions and Implementation Methods

7. Propose (corrective) intervention based on the team's analysis of findings concerning the problem's frequency or severity and causes. QI tools that may be used include:
   - Flowchart (to design or propose the desired elements of a process or function).
     Example: Discharge process.
   - Cause-and-effect diagram (to delineate factors and situations vital to achieving the desired state).
     Example: How many patients leave without being seen by a physician?
   - Force-field analysis (to delineate pros and cons of contemplated actions).
   - Multivoting and/or selection chart (to prioritize the team's proposed actions when several options appear viable).

8. Pilot test the selected action(s) for a specified period, and monitor performance to determine whether it has had a desired effect, a negative effect, or no effect.

Monitor Performance to Sustain Improvements

9. Solidify the solutions (that is, make them permanent) if data reveal performance has improved. Continue to monitor performance until it is within acceptable levels and the problem's causes have been either eliminated permanently or otherwise brought under control. Thereafter, monitor performance as needed to make sure the desired improvement is being sustained.

10. If the actions taken are not followed by evidence of improved performance, revisit the team's analysis of the problem (in case any causes have been overlooked):
    - Reassess the performance indicator(s). Are the data being generated truly reflective of actual performance?
    - Identify on implement alternative intervention.
    - Continue monitoring performance for signs of improvement.

. . . .

RISK MANAGEMENT FUNCTIONS AND PERFORMANCE IMPROVEMENT

Health care risk managers are most concerned with the role that systems problems and individual provider performance play in the quality of care rendered to patients and also in the frequency and severity of claims. While it is not always easy to prove, liability is likely to be decreased by addressing those performance issues proactively.

Quality initiatives, especially those that use information from generic screening activities, incident reports, or potential claims, can be designed to address the very issues that lead to malpractice claims. Therefore, the risk manager can not only support the quality initiatives but actually supply the data that help define the problem to be addressed. The added benefit to having the risk manager supply data to the initiative is that providers may believe that reporting incidents or reporting near-misses are important activities as a starting point to address quality concerns. More providers may be encouraged to report if they are shown that the risk management data are used for improvement.

A variety of accrediting and regulatory bodies require some evidence of a process improvement or performance improvement or quality improvement function. By participating actively in the function the risk manager can be seen as a leader in helping facilities or practices comply, thereby not only getting issues addressed through the process that may reduce liability but may also avoid the liability of noncompliance with regulatory bodies and the risk of financial loss and damage to reputation that such noncompliance could cause.

The current rate of change in the delivery of health care creates additional stress, distraction, turmoil, inefficiency, and discontent among providers, administrators, and patients, an atmosphere that breeds increased liability. Downsizing, mergers, the performance of more complicated procedures in less controlled environments, and increasing demands by regulators add to the likelihood that care will be fragmented, patients will be displeased, and that mistakes will be made. Risk managers have a vested interest in helping all parties cope effectively with change. Through performance improvement initiatives, risk managers can help sort out causes and solutions and can play an active part in improvement projects that seek to objectively assess how changes are affecting care. The risk manager can assist personnel to adjust data collection tools to reflect new realities, to look at different types of problems created by new organizational structures, and to identify new areas of training that may help to alleviate some anxiety and reduce potential liability at the same time.

Risk management departments and functions are certainly effected by changes in the health care delivery system. Risk managers can use the PI process to look closely and periodically at their own operation. Publicly using such a process, including involving other health care providers to assess some part of the risk management function, can spread the word that the process is valued for its own sake, that the risk manager is interested in improving his or her own department performance, and that results of the initiatives will be shared with other providers to help them improve their own systems. For example, if the goal of the risk management function is to have a 0-percent surprise rate (that is, knowing about all potential claims before they become real claims or suits), looking at risk management data collection systems on a periodic basis would be useful. Such a process may lead to greater efficiencies in what is reported and to whom, and may indicate opportunities for capturing information that could be fed back into other quality initiatives.

Likewise if the risk managers' duties have increased as a result of mergers or other organizational changes, looking at some of the routine processes again may be necessary to ensure efficiency with the larger operation. For example, change in organizational structure may prompt a review of claims and litigation management to ensure such things as appropriate economies, relevant communication efforts with defendants during the litigation process, and appropriate monitoring of defense attorneys.

While PI projects for the risk management function and for the wider organization are valuable and are nearly a necessity, misapplication of the process could lead to some other kinds of risk. The risk manager is an appropriate person to monitor the PI function as a whole and make recommendations when necessary, while guarding against being thought an obstructionist to the process. Some examples of misapplication may include:

- *Organizational arrogance,* which is most often manifested by the implementation of a process change because someone (most commonly a powerful person within the organization) thought it was a great idea without planning for benchmarking to see how others do it or to learn others experiences with it. Obviously the goal of proceeding carefully with proposed solutions is not to stifle true creativity or innovation but to view new ideas in the light of prior knowledge and experience.

- *Silo mentality* is best defined as redesigning a process without considering its impact on other related processes or personnel. Hallmarks of this problem are design teams that exclude key players or the selection of performance measures that focus only on process efficiency without measures of clinical quality or customer satisfaction.

- The *"damn the torpedoes, full speed ahead" mentality* is the rush to implement solutions even after successfully benchmarking without some form of pilot testing to work out the kinks before full-scale implementation is attempted. While the desire to pilot test is sometimes seen as a delaying tactic, implementation can actually be quicker and easier after the potential risks of implementation on a wider scale are known.

- *Excessive reaction to anecdotal occurrences* happens most often when reliable data are not available or not used well. This can be particularly dangerous for a risk manager who is tempted to advocate for change on the basis of one disastrous occurrence without assessing whether the circumstances are what is called in the quality literature a "special variation"—a rare occurrence that needs to be analyzed and treated differently than an occurrence that has happened several times before and is likely to happen again, therefore amenable to PI efforts.[8] This does not mean that root-cause analysis of a critical systems failure that resulted in a sentinel event should not be used as the basis for further study within the PI program. However, when routine processes are changed without having data to understand the source of the process variation, new risks can be introduced through tampering with the system without first going through careful data analysis. One of the most common examples of "tampering with the system" is introducing a new policy or procedure to try to prevent an adverse event without thinking through the effect of that change on the rest of the system.

ENGAGING PHYSICIANS IN THE PI PROCESS

Since physicians are an important part of the functioning of any health care system and since the quality of their performance often equates with the quality of patient care, risk managers can help to bring the physicians into the whole PI process by using examples from potential or actual claims as fodder for PI efforts.

Physicians can become disillusioned quickly with processes that seem to be initiated without supporting data or that seem irrelevant to improving the quality of the care they can render to their patients. Risk managers can help get physicians involved and keep their interest by using the PI process to address potential liability issues. For example:

- Proactively improving systems that physicians rely on can help them to deliver better patient care and can help them better defend that care should claims arise anyway.

While physicians are thought of as part of the hospital health care team, they are actually more of a customer of the hospital's systems and may have only limited input into how those systems are designed. A good example is the patient care documentation system. While documentation is the physicians' responsibility, by viewing the physician as a customer the risk manager can work with medical records and other systems to make it easier to document key information.

- Systematically obtaining and distributing outcomes data that can be used to modify physician practice can get and keep the physicians' attention. Physicians tend to be very responsive to data if presented in the right context. By organizing claims or incident reporting data into clinically relevant information, risk managers can interest the physician in PI efforts. Risk managers can also demonstrate to them ways that such data can help them improve the quality of patient care as well as attempt to prevent potential liability situations. Working with key physician opinion leaders to analyze and distribute data is usually the best approach.

- Closely related to distributing outcomes data, physicians can be encouraged to be involved in PI efforts if information on best practices is shared with them in a non-judgmental way. Physicians are likely to be most interested in PI teams organized to address either specific diseases or specific clinical pathways. With the increased accessibility of information on best practices (whether through formal benchmarking programs, literature searches, or personal experiences), risk managers can get this information into the hands of the appropriate PI team.

- Risk managers can be seen as professionals who can successfully bridge the gap between clinical and administrative concerns. This is especially valuable for organizations and physicians alike in this era of reengineering, downsizing, cost-cutting, merging, and acquiring. In this particularly confusing time, physicians need reassurance that the results of such changes in the systems are being tracked to determine how patient care is being affected. Risk managers are in a good position to help providers look for the problems that can occur with change—training issues, communication lapses, policy and procedure confusion, low morale—and help assess how or if those problems are negatively impacting patient care. Even more important to the physicians and the organization, the risk manager can help to design solutions to the problems identified.[9]

············

CONCLUSION

Risk management issues can become even more visible (or visible for the first time) when portrayed in the context of PI projects, especially if the topics chosen include the possibility of measurable positive outcomes. In this way, PI can help demonstrate the value of risk management to the organization.

In turn, increased visibility for risk management issues can mean greater visibility for the risk manager, whose credibility tends to be increased when he or she is seen as a part of the management team. Specific skills the risk manager already possess can be readily employed, such as expertise in data collection and analysis, and conflict resolution, and as an advocate for controversial issues. These positive attributes can be demonstrated even more forcefully when the PI project is aimed directly at enhancing the operations of the risk management function itself.

Opportunities for decreasing losses and enhancing performance through improvement of these and other processes make risk managers important stakeholders in the success of their organizations' quality initiatives. And to the extent that they choose to join, lead, or otherwise actively participate in such efforts, they can become welcome members of the vanguard of staff involved in ensuring that those initiatives succeed. Conversely, if they choose not to participate, they may be seen as irrelevant, or expendable to the organization.

Endnotes

1. Meisenheimer, C. G. *Quality Assurance.* Rockville, Md.: Aspen Systems Corp., 1985, pp. 4–5.

2. *Ibid.,* pp. 5–6.

3. Walton, M. *The Deming Management Method.* New York: The Putnam Publishing Co., 1986.

4. Juran, J. *Juran on Leadership for Quality: an Executive Handbook.* New York: The Free Press, 1989.

5. Weber, D. R. "Incorporating Quality Improvement Strategies and Benchmarking into Risk Management." In Youngberg, B. (ed.), *The Risk Manager's Desk Reference.* Rockville, Md.: Aspen Systems Corp., 1994, pp. 119–123.

6. *1988 Hospital Accreditation Standards.* Chicago: Joint Commission on Accreditation of Healthcare Organizations, 1997, p. 129.

7. *Ibid.,* p. 321.

8. Head, G. L., and Horn, S. *Essentials of Risk Management,* vol. 1 (2nd ed.). Malvern, Pa.: Insurance Institute of America, 1991. pp. 5, 11.

9. Tan, M. W. "TQM in Health Care: A Time of Transition." *FORUM, 12*(5), Sept.–Oct. 1991, p. 1.

10. Knox, G. E., Kelley, M., and Simpson, K. R. "Downsizing, Reengineering, and Patient Safety: Numbers, Newness, and Resultant Risk." *Journal of Healthcare Risk Management, 19*(3), Fall 1999, p. 19.

Suggested Reading

Berwick, D. M. "The Clinical Process and the Quality Process." *Quality Management in Health Care, 1*(1), Fall 1992, pp. 1–8.

Berwick, D. M. "Commentary: Peer Review and Quality Management: Are They Compatible?" *Quality Review Bulletin, 16*(7), July 1990, pp. 246–251.

Berwick, D. M. "Continuous Improvement as an Ideal in Health Care." *New England Journal of Medicine, 320*(1), Jan. 5, 1989, pp. 53–56.

Challan, B. "A Risk Manager's Evolving Experience with CQI." *Journal of Healthcare Risk Management, 13*(3), Summer 1993, pp. 25–30.

Collins, K., Quinlan, A., Farrell, M., and Snyder, L. M. "Influencing Physician Behavior with CQI: A Case Study." *Quality Management in Health Care, 2*(3), Spring 1994, pp. 27–35.

Deragon, J. T. *Fourth Generation Risk Management.* Chicago: Chicago Quality Insurance Congress, 1994.

Friedmann, P., and Selbovitz, L. G. "Continuous Quality Improvement and Physician Training." *Quality Management in Health Care, 1*(1), Fall 1992, pp. 13–19.

Gates, P. E. "Clinical Quality Improvement: Getting Physicians Involved." *Quality Review Bulletin, 19*(2), Feb. 1993, pp. 56–61.

Goldsmith, J. "A Radical Prescription for Hospitals." *Harvard Business Review, 67*(3), May–June 1989, pp. 104–111.

Hopkins, J. L. "What TQM Is and Isn't." *QRC Advisor, 7*(8), June 1991, pp. 1, 4–6.

Joseph, E., and Meyers, D. *Healthcare Risk Management/Total Quality Management: Making the Connection.* Chicago: Care Communications, 1993.

Moen, R. D., and Nolan, T. W. "Process Improvement: A Step-by-Step Approach to Analyzing and Improving a Process." *Quality Progress*, Sept. 1987, pp. 62–68.

Plsek, P. E. "Notes on Selecting Quality Improvement Projects." National Demonstration Project, Boston, 1989.

Plsek, P. E. "Organization and Infrastructure for QI Methods and Tools of Quality Management." National Demonstration Project, 1988.

34

Benchmarking

Kathleen M. Roman

Every day the health care risk manager grapples with change. On an ongoing basis, the risk manager identifies potential changes, analyzes the benefits and/or risks associated with change, and implements change in a manner designed to produce the intended effects. As a change agent, the health care risk manager uses a variety of tools to address risk and to improve quality. Benchmarking is one of these tools.

BENCHMARKING AS A QUALITY IMPROVEMENT TOOL

This chapter demystifies the benchmarking process by providing an overview of its role, as an independent measure, and as part of the quality improvement function. A general discussion of benchmarking as it can be used by the risk manager offers examples of several benchmarking models and their applicability in a variety of health care environments. A walkthrough of the benchmarking process includes pragmatic advice and strategies risk managers can use to increase their chances for successful results. And finally, a financial benchmarking known as the "cost of risk" will also be discussed.

Benchmarking is a comparative process used by organizations to collect and measure internal or external data that may ultimately be used for the purpose of developing, implementing, and sustaining quality improvements. It can be used to: target opportunities for improvement; research successful methods for implementing proposed improvements; and to measure their impact on the environment.[1] Thus, benchmarking *most often* includes three components: (1) planning; (2) data collection and comparative analysis; and (3) for some projects, introduction and monitoring of improvement processes.[2] Some benchmarking projects may terminate with the identification of partners' best practices. Some, however, may fold into and become part of the quality improvement function and continue to provide comparative data throughout the monitoring and improvement phases of the project.

Benchmarking can be implemented in two ways. *Internally,* a department or organization may use benchmarking to measure and compare its own processes or outcomes over time. When using *external* benchmarking, the learning organization seeks the expertise of another organization, referred to as the benchmark partner. Using a formal protocol, the two (or sometimes more) organizations delineate the process to be studied. The benchmark partners then reveal their solution to the learning partner. All participants share information throughout the study, including final results.

Given the uncertainty and change (some might call it chaos) inherent in this turn-of-the-century health care environment, benchmarking could produce beneficial results. They can provide tangible evidence of the importance of systems-wide strategic goals. They can foster development of realistic objectives. They can help tear down old boundaries and forge new interorganizational alliances. They can empower employees to join in the drive for excellence.[3] Finally, benchmarking enhances the visibility and influence of the risk manager. It helps the risk manager coalesce clinical information, insurance issues, liability data, and administrative goals. The benchmark project can translate these diverse technical jargons into the "bottom line" language of today's health care boardroom.

....
ORIGINS OF BENCHMARKING

Benchmarking arose out of the work of W. Edwards Deming, an American generally credited as the pioneer of total quality management (TQM). Deming taught that if organizations want to improve, they must adhere to these basic principles:

1. Quality improvement (QI) cannot occur without the full support of senior management.
2. People do not malfunction; processes do.
3. The reduction of process variation reduces the potential for error and inefficiency.
4. All processes and outcomes must be measurable.
5. Problem solving must include multidisciplinary approaches that empower all employees to participate in the quality process.[4]

Deming believed that errors occur because too many process variables clog the workplace. Identify and reduce variables through implementation of consistent processes, and workers will succeed, Deming predicted. Measure outcomes, he reasoned, and employees will discover further ways to reduce variation and to improve efficiency. Deming proposed that the workplace must evolve beyond production mandates, price-driven purchasing choices, and the use of blame as a quality assurance mechanism. In their place, he proffered a team approach in which every member of the organization contributes to its transformation. Benchmarking proves useful in a quality improvement environment because it lends itself to monitoring outcomes and the ongoing measurement of incremental improvements. Thus, the components of benchmarking (planning, data analysis and comparison, and measurement) dovetail perfectly with Deming's theories of quality improvement.[5]

Benchmarking: Slow Transition into the Health Care Setting

To date, few hospitals or health care systems have implemented benchmarking initiatives. Of those that have engaged in benchmarking, most became involved because their TQM/CQI/QI departments spearheaded the projects. Another reason that benchmarking has not made a smooth transition into health care is the insistence by traditionalists that quality-enhancing initiatives work only when implemented in a rigid, industrial-style approach. This mindset may have arisen because of the conventional view that medicine is an art requiring an endless series of processes so intricate and demanding that it is impossible to reduce process variation; thus, benchmarking proves futile. In fact, reduction of variance has been thwarted more often by flawed data collection and analysis than by the differences between mechanized or human process implementation. This obstacle will be addressed elsewhere in the chapter.

Under the old order, risk managers tiptoed around issues related to clinical outcomes, sticking close to cost of risk assessment, such as claims handling, insurance needs assessment, and liability prevention. If TQM staff initiated projects associated with liability issues, or the costs of addressing them, they did so without risk management input. In many instances, neither service has understood or recognized benefits the other provides to the organization. In worst-case scenarios, each has zealously guarded its "turf."

The traditional separation of risk management from quality initiatives is evident in a classic example of sporadic safety improvements that resulted not from studies of quality improvement but, rather, from the costs associated with liability issues. In *Health Care Quality Management for the 21st Century,* Couch discusses the development of electrically controlled hospital beds following a long string of attempts to address related liability issues.[6] As losses mounted because of the number of patients who had fallen out of bed, a new industry evolved—the manufacture of bed rails. Initially, hospitals purchased only one rail for each bed—and patients fell out of bed between the bed and the wall.

Consequently, hospitals began to install rails on both sides of beds. However, the severity of injuries actually increased because patients climbed over the bed rails, falling an even greater distance. New technology led to the development of hi-lo beds, which nurses were required to crank up and down. Although this lessened patient risk, the number of nurses applying for workers' compensation soared as a result of back injuries. A subsequent innovation, the electrically-controlled bed, was eventually fine-tuned with the introduction of half rails.

Restraints, staff training on patient assistance, and other advances related to fall prevention soon followed. These safety improvements occurred because the costs associated with these injuries led to analyses of *processes* (in accordance with Deming's theories) and not, as Couch emphasizes, because of efforts to identify medical staff or hospital personnel misconduct.

··········

BENCHMARKING, TOTAL QUALITY MANAGEMENT, AND RISK MANAGEMENT

The American Society for Healthcare Risk Management (ASHRM) advocates the cooperation of risk management and TQM in team efforts to broaden the perspective on and approaches to change. At ASHRM's 1992 annual meeting, then president-elect Jane C. McConnell told attendees: "In the past, risk managers have been viewed in some quarters as people who are concerned (only) with preventing financial losses. We need to demonstrate how they also play an important role in improving the quality of patient care."[7] Yet in most health care institutions, risk managers and quality experts have not yet taken this evolutionary step in TQM implementation. By doing so, each will find its role strengthened by the other. Together they are likely to achieve greater visibility and influence throughout the organization. Benchmarking provides a format for this crucial growth step.

For yet another reason, it makes sense for risk management and TQM to join forces. They can foster needed change within organizations already fearful of too much change. Budgetary considerations serve as a good starting point. When a risk manager's recommendation is accompanied by data predicting substantial savings, the project's approval chances increase. However, when a recommendation (based either on liability prevention or quality improvement) bears a *higher* price tag, it becomes more difficult to convince the powers-that-be of the potential long-term benefits of the plan. But an alliance between risk management and quality, each supportive of the proposed change from their unique perspective, presents a much clearer picture of the proposed plan. The quality picture can focus on the advantages related to long-term improvements in care, patient satisfaction, and reduction in staff workload. At the same time, the risk management perspective will highlight cost of risk analyses such as expenses related to litigation and claims resolution, insurance fees, and administrative costs associated with risk management— including prevention initiatives. The likelihood of success is greater when the two services unite in their analyses and recommendations.

....

EXTERNAL OVERSIGHT OF HEALTH CARE QUALITY

Progressive health care organizations recognize that external forces will continue to play a larger role in patient satisfaction and cost containment. Managed care, employers, and legislative bodies will penalize entities that ignore quality-risk management initiatives. Suggestions from policymakers outside the health care community stress the importance of patient satisfaction, the elimination of waste, inefficiency, and inappropriate or fraudulent billing practices.[8] This systems-improvement approach is supported in part by the *Accreditation Manual for Hospitals,* published by the Joint Commission on Accreditation of Healthcare Organizations (JCAHO).[9] JCAHO acknowledged this trend when it published *The Measurement Mandate: On the Road to Performance Improvement in Health Care* (1993).

Health care risk managers are also keeping an eye on the ever-growing number of American organizations seeking quality compliance standing with the International Organization for Standardization (ISO). This worldwide federation of national standards committees works cooperatively to establish identical processes that apply from supplier to purchasing organization to customer, regardless of the industry, regardless of the country. A small but growing number of health care entities in the United States are abandoning JCAHO for ISO compliance status. The new ISO9000:2000 Standards for Quality Management and Quality Assurance are expected to draw further interest and participation from the health care community.[10] (See Chapter 37 for more information on ISO.)

While the United States is always at the forefront of advances in medical technology, it may not be keeping up with other countries' quality measurement initiatives. In England, for example, benchmarking took a public turn when the Secretary of State for Health mandated compulsory risk-adjusted audits in every hospital and for every specialty. Support for publicizing hospital outcomes information is gaining momentum in the United States as well.[11] It seems reasonable to expect that such studies, made available to the public, would have significant market impact. The prudent health care risk manager might interpret this increased level of external oversight and expectation as "the writing on the wall."

As support builds for quality initiatives, health care professionals are increasingly turning to the manufacturing and industrial texts on quality. Increased government attention to drug errors has spurred some hospitals to search for ways to shift from *departmental* problem solving to *function-oriented* problem solving. For example, a problem identified as the late arrival of medication from the pharmacy to a particular floor might spearhead an internal benchmark study to compare ways in which medications are ordered by, and delivered to, other departments. According to Deming's theories, this type of project identifies process (rather than personnel) failure. It should help lay the groundwork for development of measurable steps to improve medication ordering and delivery. In turn, these steps can support a consistent system-wide manner of implementation (thus fulfilling Deming's mandate to eliminate variability).

One tool risk managers may consider as a means of "working into" benchmarking is the *Risk Management Self-Assessment Manual.*[12] Using a format that analyzes activities, process measures, and outcomes that should culminate in action plans, the manual is a useful tool for internal measurement and will help the novice benchmarker transition into external benchmarking projects. Although the approach focuses on health care risk management, the design is also ideal for risk management-quality "benchmarking joint ventures." (Further information about this manual can be found in Chapter 35.)

···········
BENCHMARKING BASICS FOR RISK MANAGERS

Health care risk managers are familiar with processes involving comparison of present and past performance. Risk managers who have studied for Associate in Risk Management (ARM) designation are familiar with the risk management matrix developed by the Insurance Institute of America (Exhibit 34.1). This matrix encompasses Deming's requisite components of the benchmarking process—planning, collecting and analyzing data, and monitoring improvement.

Incorporating these same components, benchmarking also may be used to compare the performance of the individual, group, department, task force, hospital, or organization against acknowledged industry leaders. Usually, external benchmarking involves

EXHIBIT 34.1.   Risk Management Matrix

Decision Axis \ Managerial Axis	Plan	Organize	Lead	Control
Identify and analyze loss exposures				
Examine alternative risk management techniques				
Select risk management technique (s)				
Implement technique (s)				
Monitor results				

Source: Insurance Institute of America, Malvern, Pa. Reprinted with permission.

comparison(s) of similar process(es) between similar organizations. By identifying how the elite address specific challenges, a learning organization may discover how to incorporate these best practices into its own protocols, thereby avoiding the necessity to reinvent the wheel.

Internal benchmarking, which can be accomplished by comparing results of a specified process over a period of time, might be an ideal way for the novice to begin. Internal benchmarking increases the comfort level for further projects by helping the inexperienced benchmark team acquire skill through basic experiments without the more stringent requirements of time and resources required for external benchmarking.

Selection of an Internal Benchmarking Project

The value of an internal benchmarking project is exemplified in the litigation evaluation form developed by the University of Pittsburgh Medical Center (Exhibit 34.2). This form addresses a classic risk management issue—adequate preparation of a witness or defendant for deposition and/or trial. What potential benefits could result from the consistent completion of this form? Over time, the risk manager should be able to effect a number of positive changes in litigation preparation, drawing upon responses provided in earlier evaluations.

Building adequate time into the project is important. This kind of benchmark probably should be implemented over several years, rather than months. Blips in the system (such as a class action suit) can be factored; additionally, categories of improvements will be evident if responses to each question are recorded over the long haul.

Internal staff issues to be addressed in this example include:

- What kinds of training should risk analysts receive to adequately prepare deponents?

- Are these training protocols in writing?

- Are they administered on a timely basis and recorded?

- If respondents give negative responses regarding risk analyst support, what kinds of training redesign should occur?

- If negative responses correspond to interaction with attorneys, what kinds of protocols should be developed to assist attorneys to do a better job?

- Are expectations for attorney-related services in writing, appropriately disseminated, and updated in a timely fashion?

- Of the questions that relate specifically to the deponent's behavior, what processes might be developed to assist the improvement process in these areas?

- If a physician responds that, as a result of the litigation procedure, he or she has learned the importance of complete documentation, should the offer of a risk management class that addresses this issue be automatically forthcoming?

- Should a follow-up inquiry at an appropriate interval ask the physician if he or she has been able to implement and sustain the hoped-for record-keeping changes?

- Will random spot-checks be made of the physician's documentation?

Processes altered as a result of responses to the questionnaire should, over time, provide a quantifiable record of improvements as well as spotlight new challenges. Because this program will record the development and continuous improvement of the litigation preparation process, it poses a legitimate internal benchmarking opportunity. Over time,

EXHIBIT 34.2.   Litigation Evaluation

Caption: _____ Date of incident: _____

The purpose of this questionnaire is to evaluate the service provided by the attorneys and risk management staff, in an effort to correct or improve the quality and service provided to the hospital staff.

How were you made aware that there was a legal suit filed by this patient?
_____ Letter from risk management
_____ Phone call from risk management
_____ Notified by supervisor phone call from _____
_____ Other _____

_____ Yes _____ No _____ N/A When you talked with the risk analyst, were you treated courteously?
_____ Yes _____ No _____ N/A Was the nature of the suit explained to you?
_____ Yes _____ No _____ N/A Did you remember this patient or occurrence?
_____ Yes _____ No _____ N/A Was the litigation process explained to you?
_____ Yes _____ No _____ N/A Were you reminded not to discuss the case with anyone?
_____ Yes _____ No _____ N/A Were you provided with a phone number or business card in case you had questions?
_____ Yes _____ No _____ N/A Were you asked to appear at a deposition?
_____ Yes _____ No _____ N/A Was a deposition explained to you?
_____ Yes _____ No _____ N/A Did you meet with the attorney prior to the deposition?
_____ Yes _____ No _____ N/A Was the purpose of the predeposition meeting explained to you?
_____ Yes _____ No _____ N/A Were you prepared appropriately for the deposition?
_____ Yes _____ No _____ N/A Were you nervous prior to the deposition?
_____ Yes _____ No _____ N/A Did a risk analyst accompany you to the deposition?
_____ Yes _____ No _____ N/A Did the risk analyst help to make you feel at ease?
_____ Yes _____ No _____ N/A Did the attorney help to make you feel at ease?
_____ Yes _____ No _____ N/A If the case did go to trial, were you informed of the outcome?
_____ Yes _____ No _____ N/A Did you learn anything through the litigation process (in general, or regarding your role in the care of the patient) that ill affect how you practice?
_____ Yes _____ No _____ N/A Do you have any suggestions for risk management with regard to helping the witness to understand the process better? If yes, please write comments on back.

Do you think the staff should have more education with regard to the:

_____ Yes _____ No _____ N/A Litigation process?
_____ Yes _____ No _____ N/A Documentation?
_____ Yes _____ No _____ N/A Other: _____

Other comments: _____

Name (optional) (please print) _____

Source: University of Pittsburgh Medical Center. Reprinted, with permission, from *Hospital Risk Management*, Dec. 1994.

the department can also identify areas in which the hoped-for results have been less-than-satisfactory. At this point, the risk manager might decide to engage in exterior benchmarking—looking at methods used by other health care organizations to handle litigation preparation. Once the risk manager is assured of administrative support, he or she will first want to develop an internal team to cooperatively define the problem, share the research tasks, and identify potential benchmarking partners whose reputations reflect outstanding claims-handling ability.

When undertaking a long-term benchmarking study, the team should conduct an initial assessment to identify processes or technology that may be altered before the study is completed. The team will want to determine if such changes could alter or degrade the data being collected. Example: Will a software upgrade, implemented halfway through the study, alter the way in which data are obtained or analyzed, and will the alterations skew the results?[13]

The Internal Benchmarking Team—and Member Roles

The risk manager who has developed the most extensive networking skills will have an advantage when initiating a benchmarking project.[14] Numerous individuals throughout the organization may offer valuable leads on potential partners (Exhibit 34.3). Depending on the nature of the project, various professional societies should be able to identify contacts. Local and/or state chapters of ASHRM or quality improvement associations will lend assistance. Literature searches, including database access, also will prove valuable. By forming a committee to analyze the internal process that needs improvement, the risk manager will broaden the group's perspective and increase the number of details available about the process.

The team approach works best when its members are encouraged to identify potential obstacles as well as possible improvement strategies. Dividing various aspects of the project among team members can lead to positive results for the current project but it can also gather information that will enhance future projects. The many variations in health care systems will continue to cause problems unless they are addressed—and physicians are not the parties solely responsible for these variations. Health care is becoming increasingly competitive, and hospitals and other health care facilities that are comfortably ensconced in their various communities today may not even exist in a few years. Increasingly, benchmarking is being used (not always accurately) to identify top performers by "proving" the value of services, the consistent quality of care, and financial strength.

The internal team also is an important component of external benchmarking. The risk manager needs to "sell" the idea in order to build a group of advocates who will support and participate from beginning to end. The models that follow provide suggestions the novice benchmark team can use to establish the "who" as well as the "what" of their project.

SunHealth Alliance Model

A care-specific benchmark format was designed by the SunHealth Alliance of Charlotte, N.C. Called Benchmarking Process (Figure 34.1),[15] this outline breaks the phases into eleven separate processes, enabling the team to divide tasks and set priorities. For example, the tenth step (Implement new practices), could be broken into smaller components, including needed materials, staffing, budget, interaction with other functions, storage, and processes themselves. Depending on their areas of expertise and interest, various members of the benchmarking team might participate in as few as one—or as many as all—of these stages. Implementation timing, including finding the bugs, can be built into the overall process.

Kaiser Permanente Model

Breaking the potential team into groups and identifying the specific roles they might play in the project provided a map for an initial benchmarking experience for the Southern California Kaiser Permanente Medical Group. The novice Kaiser team utilized Deming's processes as they tackled a project aimed at improving appointment access

EXHIBIT 34.3.   Criteria for Selecting Potential Anesthesia Benchmarking Partners

	Yes	No
I. Does your anesthesia department have written protocols that address the following:		
A. Staffing requirements per number of procedures.	☐	☐
B. Supervision, delegation, and discipline of those who provide anesthesia or anesthesia-related services.	☐	☐
C. Assessment of anesthesia risk and its relationship to the procedure(s) to be performed.	☐	☐
D. Time-frames within which certain anesthesia-related services should be provided.	☐	☐
E. Means of indentifying deviation from protocols, causes for the deviation, and processes for addressing these issues.	☐	☐
F. Stipulation of procedures to be followed by anesthesia staff while a patient is in the recovery room.	☐	☐
G. Guidelines for patient education, informed consent procedures and documentation thereof.	☐	☐
H. Stipulation of procedures to be followed by anesthesia staff during shift changes.	☐	☐
I. Stipulation of procedures to be followed by anesthesia staff when patient is released from the recovery room:		
1. On an out-patient basis	☐	☐
2. And sent to a room	☐	☐
J. Procedures for dealing with the unexpected, such as patient emergency, patient violence, equipment malfunction, and so on.	☐	☐
K. A medical staff committee oversees anesthesia-related services, continuing education, peer review, and quality assurance.	☐	☐
II. Does your department document that the above-named protocols are consistently and accurately implemented?		
A. Staffing requirements per number of procedures.	☐	☐
B. Supervision, delegation, and discipline of those who provide anesthesia or anesthesia-related services.	☐	☐
C. Documentation of your assessment of anesthesia risk and its relationship to the procedure(s) to be performed.	☐	☐
D. Means of identifying deviation from protocols, causes for the deviation, and processes for addressing these issues of procedures to be followed by anesthesia staff during shift changes.	☐	☐
E. Stipulation of procedures to be followed by anesthesia staff while a patient is in the recovery room.	☐	☐
F. Guidelines for patient education, informed consent procedures, and documentation thereof.	☐	☐
G. Stipulation of procedures to be followed by anesthesia staff during shift changes.	☐	☐
H. Stipulation of procedures to be followed by anesthesia staff when patient is released from the recovery room:		
1. On an out-patient basis.	☐	☐
2. And sent to a room.	☐	☐
I. Procedures for dealing with the unexpected, such as patient emergency, patient violence, equipment malfunction, and so on.	☐	☐
J. Medical staff meeting notes, recommendations, guidelines, and policies and procedures, including peer review, continuing education, and quality assurance activities.	☐	☐

(Continued)

EXHIBIT 34.3.   **Criteria for Selecting Potential Anesthesia Benchmarking** (*Continued*)

III. Does your department use the documentation it collects to implement a regularly
scheduled review and/or revision of the following:

		Review/ revision occurs
A.	Staffing requirements per number of procedures.	_____
B.	Supervision, delegation, and discipline of those who provide anesthesia or anesthesia-related services.	_____
C.	Data collected regarding assessment of anesthesia risk and its relationship to the procedure(s) to be performed.	_____
D.	Time frames within which certain anesthesia-related services should be provided. _____	
E.	Means of indentifying deviation from protocols, causes for the deviation and processes for addressing these issues.	_____
F.	Stipulation of procedures to be followed by anesthesia staff while a patient is in the recovery room.	_____
G.	Guidelines for patient education, informed consent procedures, and documentation thereof.	_____
H.	Stipulation of procedures to be followed by anesthesia staff during shift changes.	_____
I.	Stipulation of procedures to be followed by anesthesia staff when patient is released from the recovery room:	
	1. On an outpatient basis	_____
	2. And sent to a room	_____
J.	Procedures for dealing with the unexpected, such as patient emergency, patient violence, equipment malfunction, and so on.	_____
K.	Medical staff guidelines, policies, and/or other requirements regarding anesthesia-related services, continuing education, peer review, and quality assurance activities.	_____

(Figure 34.2). A. Vicki Lewis, assistant director of service assessment for the medical group, said, "We were all new to this and learning from each other. For us, the [extra] detail we developed in our model was very useful, especially when we talked with others about our results."[16] Even though the Kaiser team was inexperienced, the data it was able to develop were valuable to its external partners as well.

A special feature of the Kaiser Permanente model is its graphic depiction of potential participants, each of whom offered useful suggestions. For example, Lewis emphasized the importance of the champion or advocate role. "Risk management fits into the model in a number of places, depending on what they want to know," she said. "There are times when risk management needs to be the advocate in order to sell the idea to those people who will actually end up implementing the changes. Our job was to provide information and to gain acceptance for the study." But on another occasion, she said, the champion was an operations staffer who was able to run initial pilot studies. "Our advocate ran interference for the project all along," Lewis said. "When naysayers said, 'That will never work,' our advocate was able to say, 'I tried it; it did work—and here are the results.' This helps overcome objections and really helped build consensus."[17]

Although the Kaiser Permanente model may appear complicated, Lewis and her group found its detail was its major strength. "We believe that other people can benefit from our model because we broke it down into little pieces; it's easier to see what we want to know about ourselves and our processes, and it's easier to identify who needs to be involved and what we need to do next."[18] Lewis and her group acknowledged that most

FIGURE 34.1. **Benchmarking Process**

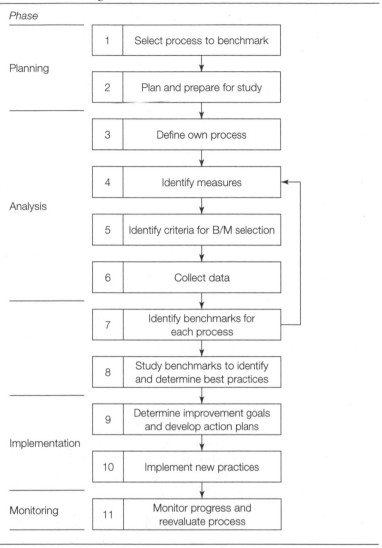

Source: Joint Commission on Accreditation of Healthcare Organizations. *Journal on Quality Improvement 20*(5), May 1994. Reprinted with permission.

benchmarking literature emphasizes the importance of identifying partners who are best in class; however, that is not always possible. In fact, complications can be anticipated, but also addressed, in the search for benchmark partners.

Selection of External Benchmarking Partners

How can the best potential benchmarking partners be identified? Literature searches and networking, both within and outside the organization, usually produce some good leads. Many health care organizations, particularly those embarking on their first external benchmarking projects, include a consultant advisor who is experienced in the target area. However, identifying ideal partners may not always work out; some will not be

FIGURE 34.2.   Kaiser Permanente Benchmarking Model

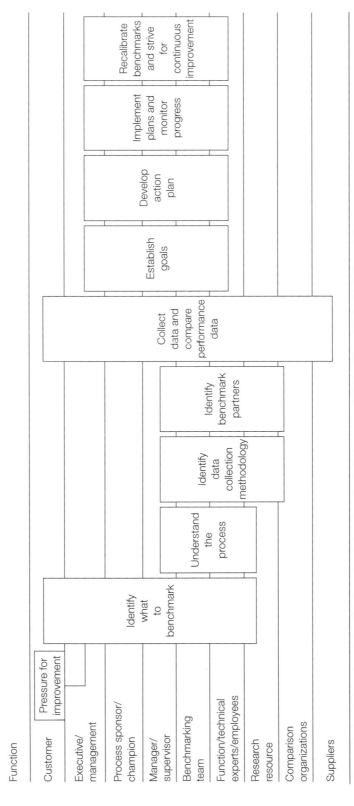

Source: Joint Commission on Accreditation of Healthcare Organizations. *Journal on Quality Improvement 20(5),* May 1994, p. 287. Reprinted with permission.

interested in participating and some may not be able to. Others, having been identified, may function in an environment so foreign that their methods are incompatible with the project. The risk manager who has experience with internal benchmarking may find it easier to identify compatible organizations—and weed out the incompatible. Data collection and analysis processes of the potential benchmarking partner(s) should also be examined to determine their "fit" with the risk manager's organization. Many organizations gather data, but not all of them do so accurately; others interpret data incorrectly; and still others gather data but never seem to do anything productive with it.[19] It is one thing to discover that apples are being compared with oranges; it is an entirely different challenge to discover that apples are being compared with alligators.

An advantage to benchmarking with very similar organizations over time is the potential for role reversal in future studies. While Hospital A may be the learning organization in a study of staph infections, in a later study on parking structure security, Hospital B might become the learning organization and Hospital A become the benchmark partner.[20]

Some quality experts claim that benchmarking studies should remain within the same industry—for example, manufacturing companies should benchmark only with other manufacturers. But another school of thought contends that a project may actually benefit from dealing with diverse experts. For example, one hospital that wanted to provide door-to-door transportation for elderly volunteers undertook a benchmarking study and was unable to identify other hospitals that had successfully dealt with similar problems. The risk manager suggested benchmarking with a community transit authority that offered a senior shopping-day program for residents of a local retirement home. After working with the transit authority, the hospital team identified a number of ways to improve its new program.

When searching for a benchmarking partner that has technical knowledge, the team might benefit from building relationships with organizations that have similar philosophies about problem solving, regardless of the industry. These compatibilities may also help the learning organization discover if outcome improvements were associated with process changes or if they had also been affected by organizational characteristics or policies.[21] The failure of health care mergers is often associated with cultures that can't blend. Regardless of the similarity of their processes, it may be impossible for a rigid, highly vertical organization to partner with an open, reengineered model.

When working with external benchmark partners it is advisable to conduct basic and internal research first. This will avoid wasting partners' time. Have questions ready; if several people will be contacting various partners, ensure consistency of approach by using the same format. If partner organizations will be asked to complete a form or questionnaire, streamline it.

They'll willingly complete a questionnaire that consists of a series of check-off boxes rather than have to draft a lengthy report. Further data can be obtained through subsequent meetings or phone calls, if necessary.

If site visits to partner facilities are planned, use initial verbal and written contacts to weed out those organizations that are least compatible. Administrators will be more likely to sign off on travel requests when they know that screening has reduced the number of potential sites to those few most likely to produce relevant results. Although it is not necessary for the entire benchmark team to participate in all site visits, it is advisable to ensure that different perspectives are represented. For example, one hospital found that site visits were more productive when a risk manager and a representative of the quality team traveled to the partner facility. Another benchmark team reported that it benefited when a site visit team included one clinical and one administrative representative—in their case, a financial analyst. Wherever the site visit may occur and regardless of the composition of the visitation team, each team should obtain responses to a predetermined set of questions. However, teams should also be free to gather additional pertinent information, particularly in areas of members' specific expertise.

Another important factor in establishing partnerships is the matter of *protocol,* or the process of rewarding participants for their cooperation and input. What is the incentive for participation in the project if the benchmarking partner accrues no results or benefits? This critical distinction marks the difference between benchmarking and tutoring.[22] Results of a benchmark project should be made freely available to *all* participants. The report, or results, or whatever formal outcome is generated should be provided to each benchmark partner, along with the courtesy of a formal thank-you. Conversely, one party should never share results of the study with nonparticipating organizations without permission of the other partner(s).

It is possible that, during the course of a benchmarking project, one organization may discover competitive advantage information about a partner. The ethics of benchmarking is an important issue that has been addressed by the American Productivity and Quality Center. Its Benchmarking Code of Conduct provides guidelines for addressing the ethical and legal issues involved (see Exhibit 34.4). No benchmarking project should ever be used as a means of gaining an advantage over a competitor generous enough to share its time, data, and expertise.

IMPLEMENTING THE BASIC STEPS IN BENCHMARKING

What do experienced benchmark teams say about benchmarking? The following tips can guide risk managers new to the process through the three major steps of identifying and planning a benchmarking project, collecting and analyzing data, and monitoring improvement.

Step 1. Building Consensus

From a multitude of potential projects, a critical challenge may prove easy to identify— for example, the neonatal intensive care unit (NICU) that has an ongoing problem with staph infections. Without such a choice, a few general considerations may prove useful. Risk managers are adept at gaining support for proposals based on analysis of the risks and benefits. What may be gained by undertaking this project? What might be lost if the proposal is dismissed?

Health care risk managers become experts at the art of consensus building. Negotiation techniques stress the importance of using a win-win approach. This process emphasizes

EXHIBIT 34.4.   Benchmarking Code of Conduct

• Keep it legal.	• Be prepared from the start.
• Be willing to give what you get.	• Understand expectations.
• Respect confidentiality.	• Act in accordance with expectations.
• Keep Information internal.	• Be honest.
• Do not refer without permission.	

Reprinted, with permission, from "The Benchmarking Code of Conduct"; published by the American Productivity & Quality Center (APQC). For more information about the APQC International Benchmarking Clearinghouse, call 800-776-9676 or 713-681-4020.

potential benefits for the decision makers without ignoring possible risks. Successful risk managers will adopt the problem-solving language of the decision maker to clarify the mission and to obtain support.

In the following example, the risk manager wants to conduct a benchmarking study that will identify ways to improve security in the hospital's nursery. She has asked the four administrators who must sign off on the project to attend a meeting: the hospital CEO, the vice president of legal affairs, the vice president of nursing, and the CFO. The risk manager elects to divide the presentation into four components.

The first part of the presentation focuses on liabilities attached to lax nursery security with examples of recent problems and unsuccessful attempts to design a satisfactory solution. Claims related to nursery security may also be included. While the risk manager shares this information with everyone at the meeting, the increased eye contact, compatible body language, and principle points of this part of the presentation are geared toward the vice president of legal affairs whose interests in the project will center on liability issues.

During the second phase of the presentation, the risk manager emphasizes the concerns of clinical staff, discussing research and literature related to security methodologies that don't hinder nurses' ability to care for their patients. The obvious "target" for this portion of the presentation will be the vice president of nursing.

Next, the risk manager turns to the third decision maker, the CFO, and the focus switches to money. The risk manager outlines past expenses for dealing with security, such as, insurance, equipment, staff training, and so on. Projected costs for a new system are discussed and the attendant possible reductions in insurance premiums, claims handling, redundant security procedures, and so on, will be outlined for all the group members—but especially for the CFO.

Finally, the risk manager transitions to the hospital's reputation, to its focus as a place where the weak and ill will be protected and kept safe. The CEO, whose reputation is vested in the reputation of the hospital, is the principal audience for this summation. The hospital's standing in the community is a critical factor for the CEO. The safety of newborns and their families' peace of mind are critical marketing concerns the CEO will include in his or her considerations, along with the board's view of the hospital's role as a community asset.

The overall presentation was delivered to all four decision makers, but the risk manager was careful to gear its different elements to each of the four hospital officers—with the obvious intention of speaking to that person's specialized skills and responsibilities. By "speaking the language" of the listener, the risk manager has addressed the group members' individual concerns while, at the same time, providing a clear picture of the overall plan. This approach doesn't guarantee project approval—but it can help.

Most health care organizations are looking for value-added service; money is always an issue. Possible areas for risk management benchmarking might include: number of potential claims; administrative fee adjustments; claims handling; premium increases; and defense costs.[23] A rationale for risk management benchmarking might be its ability to prove that potential claims were averted through use of a tracking system that would identify: types of complaints; administrative costs associated with handling them; and their actual outcomes (for example, whether a suit occurred and, if so, with what result). Such data, compiled over time, also might be useful in a comparative analysis with similar allegations, left unaddressed, that ended up in court, with the attendant costs, including legal expenses, awards, and/or settlements.

Step 2. Collect and Analyze Data

If a health care facility is experiencing many process problems, it probably should conduct a number of internal measurement studies, concentrating on incremental gains. Experienced benchmarkers advise analyzing each function, breaking it down into all its components, and measuring each step. Studying the incremental results of internal projects also will increase a risk manager's skill in assessing partners' strengths and various organizations' compatibility. It is not necessary to do "world-class" benchmarking in order to benefit; in fact, participating in best-of-the-best benchmarking early on may be a mistake because the team may not yet know what to look for—and it may inadvertently test the good will of its partners.[24]

Analysis of subjective data requires caution. It is easier to verify the reliability of objective results because data fall into delineated categories. Subjective data may invite a variety of interpretations, particularly if terms have not been clearly defined, or if the method of obtaining, recording, and analyzing material is open to individual interpretation. In some instances, however, subjective data may be all that are available. In these cases, the team should be scrupulous about developing and consistently implementing one approach.

Variability of data and concerns regarding the applicability of one organization's data within the measurement processes of another organization were addressed earlier in this chapter. Comparisons of outcomes may prove useless without comparisons of the processes that led to the outcomes. Therefore, data analysis will be only as useful as the definitions of the variables. For example, it is not sufficient to simply gather information, either internally or externally, on the number of incidents that occur. If patients are falling, it is not enough to count the falls. Benchmark analysis will be inadequate if locations of the falls are not identified. In addition, the risk manager should ask: Did the falls occur pre- or post-op? Was the patient who fell being treated for a terminal illness? Was he or she involved in long-term care? Was the patient recalcitrant? Was he or she mentally competent? What medications was the patient receiving? Could they have played a role in the incident? What were the patient's activity orders? Were they being followed? Did the patient's vision, access to eyeglasses or blood sugar level, contribute to the injury? Was anyone else present when the patient fell? If so, was that person a guest or an employee of the facility?[25] As this example shows, the basic question asked by the original study proposal ultimately may be broken down into numerous subquestions.

In another example analyzing needle sticks, it would be worthwhile to segregate incidents that occur in the midst of an emergency or complicated procedure from incidents in which carelessness or failure to follow established protocols contributed to the injury.

Partners from other industries may prove helpful in projects involving failure to follow established guidelines. Contrary to some assumptions, industrial quality improvement techniques have proven useful in health care benchmarking—with one caveat. In an industrial environment, many processes are automated, whereas the majority of medical processes involve multiple human interactions—thereby increasing the potential for variation. While there are only a few ways to manufacture a widget, health care providers may follow a dozen clinically accepted routes to accomplish a successful treatment.[26] Techniques for reducing variation will prove instructive but they usually must convert into an environment in which a human, rather than a machine, performs the actual processes.

A further example of the variability of process outcomes resulting from human interaction is highlighted in a proposed benchmark study whose goal is to improve employee return-to-work policies. The project team has identified a number of factors that might improve outcomes.

- Is there a light-duty or return-to-work program?
- Are there formal, written job descriptions for normal- and light-duty functions?
- Does management support the program?
- Are there written return-to-work guidelines?
- Are supervisors trained to administer the program?
- Have employees been educated about the program?
- Do industrial health or rehab clinics know about the program and the range of light-duty job functions?
- Are claims administrators fully informed about the program?
- How soon after the initial claim report does the claim administrator and industrial health or human resources personnel discuss return-to-work potential?
- Are claim files audited for compliance with the program?
- Are injured employees called at home to check recovery progress? If so, who places the calls, and is a consistent format followed?
- Is the light-duty program coordinated with any physical or vocational rehabilitation programs? If so, how?
- Does the program comply with the Americans with Disabilities Act?
- Is there a system to track disability claims and the return-to-work program? If so, does it capture enough data to determine program effectiveness in returning employees to work?
- Does the system track program cost-effectiveness?[27]

While benchmarking projects may vary in their approaches to similar issues, participants analyzing responses to studies like the return-to-work questionnaire, will soon identify: (1) areas in which no policies and procedures exist, (2) programs whose processes are highly sophisticated or streamlined, and (3) programs or processes very similar to or very different from their own. Depending on the project, some potential partners may be eliminated at this point, while others will become even more significant to the project.

Step 3. Implement and Monitor Process Improvements

At this stage, benchmarking projects sometimes bog down. Several factors may contribute to this. First, team members have invested considerable time and effort in the planning, collection, and analysis phases. They are simply running out of enthusiasm. If they become less conscientious during the implementation phase, the value of the entire project may be threatened.

Second, this is the time when hidden agendas sometimes rear their ugly heads. During the research and analysis phases, it is possible for diverse interests to align. But at the point where it becomes obvious that some faction may lose authority, turf, or money—even if all have agreed that the plan is in the best interest of the organization—objections, stalling tactics, or political machinations may occur.

The best way to deal with these possibilities is to preempt them early in team development. Each team member should be encouraged to air his or her concerns, fears, and reservations. In addition to clearing the air, these conversations may actually strengthen the overall project. By legitimizing these issues, a more effective and cooperative team may result.

One benchmarking veteran participated in a project that took more than three years to reach the implementation stage. Because the leaders anticipated the need for long-term commitment, and because most participants expected that the outcome would alter group autonomy, turf issues were identified early on and individuals were encouraged to share their reservations or concerns. Those concerns were then included as priority items during research phases and site visits. As a result, these individuals had more opportunities to see how benchmark partners addressed similar challenges. Overall, the concerns were satisfactorily addressed and the group experienced greater consensus and esprit de corps. The early team development effort paid off in the ultimate success of the project.[28]

A further bonus resulting from team-focused benchmarking is the opportunity to ask for participant feedback during the early stages of implementation. While a new procedure may be working wonderfully for one part of the team, complications may occur for others. The vigilance of team members will identify the "bugs" before they turn into monsters. Mini-tests of segments of the plan may also prove successful before the whole system is linked together. Analysis of data, especially if the team has the luxury of conducting a pilot test (or tests), provides graphic evidence to support the group's working hypothesis. It is less stressful to fix a slow leak than to steer through a blowout. The results of initial "tests" should identify areas that require additional fine-tuning. Using these tests to monitor the final implementation will also provide a record of improvement that can be used to verify the success to administrators, to thank the team and its advocates for their efforts, and to encourage their continued support for future projects.

Throughout the benchmarking process, but especially when projects may extend over several years, participation of various team members may increase or decrease, depending on current project phase. All team members need to be updated on the current status of the project and, even those whose responsibilities are ended or yet-to-come. For very large projects, team meetings at set times and locations prove helpful. Brief update memos also fill the need to keep participants (as well as administration and the overall employee population) in the loop.

············
SYSTEMS BARRIERS TO BENCHMARKING

The "dragons" that threaten the success of benchmarking within a health care organization are the same ones that risk managers skirmish with almost daily. Often called *systems barriers,* they are referred to by one expert as system-by-system barriers to quality improvement.[29] These include technical, structural, psychosocial, managerial, and cultural barriers.

Technical or Technology Barriers

Although the technology of medicine is sophisticated, the ability to monitor and assess processes is still relatively unsophisticated. Much of medicine continues to be practiced on "gut" or intuition level. As a result, it currently is unrealistic to expect that all decisions can be codified or standardized. Additionally, many health care professionals, including a number of administrators, believe that sufficient quality practices are already in place.[30] Risk managers must address this challenge by educating and by consensus building from within.

Strategies include: individual and team networking with other departments and services; volunteering to provide value-added programs (such as training); conducting pilot studies and sharing the results; recruiting participants in small internal benchmarking projects and "marketing" the outcomes within the organization; and developing a reputation as a resource center for cooperative projects.

Further benchmarking challenges may be identified by studying the information technology resources of the organization. Many health care organizations are struggling with their information technology systems. Incompatible software and/or hardware prevent the collection and analysis of pertinent data. Problems also arise when updates are inconsistent and equipment becomes obsolete or irreparable—and the data it contains may be lost or contaminated. Mergers of entities with incompatible platforms have led to communications Towers of Babel. The problem is exacerbated when various "kingdoms" within the entity fail to share information that could be useful to others; don't take into account useful information reported by others; or duplicate projects whose data could be generated once to multiple users.

Advances in information technology occur almost daily. Risk managers need to be aware of changes in the marketplace. They need to include IT departments in risk management education. Corporate decision making should factor possible risks that may threaten implementation or effectiveness, based on the capabilities of the present system. Failure to pay close attention to the organization's information technology evolution will increase liabilities for corruption or loss of patient information; violation of confidentiality requirements; loss of access to data during emergent situations; failure to comply with legislative mandates; billing errors; and inability to obtain, analyze, and store data critical to the ongoing functions of the hospital itself.

Structural Barriers

Structural barriers comprise a formidable challenge that risk managers must address if their benchmarking proposals are to be taken seriously. Status quo administrations may cling to the opinion that quality concerns should be centralized and should function through one individual or group. This belief is contrary to Deming's philosophy that specifies that every member of the organization is a potential participant in quality initiatives and thus a possible benchmark resource. Aside from administrative concerns about losing control (authority) over the definition of quality, resistance also may occur if clinicians assume that the elimination of variance threatens them with enforced conformity, the dreaded "cookbook medicine."

As hospitals agglomerate into systems, individuals within these new organizations are unable to stay abreast of resources, services, and the myriad functions fulfilled by multiple groups within the overall entity. Internal benchmarking will be complicated when the risk manager no longer knows where and by whom certain processes are performed. The likelihood of this occurrence increases in direct proportion to the number of entities in the holding corporation, the number and dispersal of multiple cites, the duplication of processes, and the sometimes hostile reaction to the new environment by those who have been "assimilated." Because the majority of health care organizations have provided insufficient quality training within their ranks, quality initiatives, including benchmarking, may become more difficult to initiate. Finally, the much-touted economies of scale may be overshadowed by the inefficiencies of communication, resulting in a whole new level of learning and teaching the risk manager must address before benchmarking can be considered.[31]

Psychosocial Barriers

Human nature generally seeks to avoid conflict. But in the uncertain times that have befallen U.S. health care, anxiety about being "judged" as a result of benchmarking (or other quality initiatives) leads to hesitance. Additionally, expectations that quality-related projects will lead to upheaval and turf wars are challenges that risk managers must plan to address with their most diplomatic approaches. If quality improvement allows participation of the previously disenfranchised, will those farther up the "organizational food chain" forfeit their professional prerogatives?[32] These internalized concerns are not always easy to identify; the risk manager may be torn between the demands emanating from the boardroom and the frustrations of the folk in the trenches.

An initial benchmarking project in such an environment might begin with a survey asking representatives of numerous services and departments to share their suggestions for improving quality. Repeating this survey over a number of years might record improvements or, quite the opposite, point out the unaddressed issues that continue to cause concern—and that undoubtedly contribute to the organization's liability exposures. In either case, it could help establish an agenda, leverage administration support, and build consensus among the troops. Additional benefits include: cooperative planning and implementation of educational projects with other services and more comprehensive updates or reports to administration. These outreach activities enhance morale and highlight the risk management function as the place where the action is. These team members comprise the advocates and organization opinion leaders for future projects. By "bragging" on the accomplishments of the team, when the team has been composed of a multidisciplinary group of volunteers, the risk manager offers proof that change can be controlled and that it really can be beneficial.

Managerial Barriers

A supportive administration is critical to the success of the risk management function. In fact, research has shown that the risk management function is likely to be ineffective without the necessary support.[33] Instead of being a catalyst for positive change, instead of building transorganizational consensus, instead of documenting the success and achievements of the organization, the risk manager will probably be busy shopping for additional liability limits.

Which is worse, lack of planning or lack of leadership? Or are they one and the same thing? Without the foresight to recognize the development needs of both system and personnel, a health care organization undoubtedly will lack resources for quality improvement as well.[34] In such an environment, the risk manager often seems to be speaking a foreign language. Unfortunately, it is not always possible to effect change under such circumstances—unless the board revolts or a merger occurs.

Cultural Barriers

The end of the twentieth century has witnessed an unprecedented amalgamation of health care organizations. Hospitals buy out or merge with their competitors. Health care systems expand into neighboring cities and states. Doctors sell their practices and become part of a corporate monolith. Defining the scope and nature of a benchmarking project may be complicated by the size of multilayer and multisite systems in which former competitors may view benchmarking as a report card or as a battle for budget, staff, or authority.

Within the health care environment, traditionalists, including some clinicians, refuse to believe that quality initiatives are necessary. These individuals, regardless of where they may be within the organization, will not support change. They assert that the organization's privacy is paramount and that outside sources should have no access to information about internal processes. Additionally, although they may be forced at some level to acknowledge that there are instances in which the care provided is inferior, this admission will be gained only after a lengthy battle—and will not be forgiven.[35] Fear is the greatest enemy of change—especially if past change has failed to provide positive results.

. . . .

FINANCIAL BENCHMARKING: COST OF RISK

Two critical health care issues for the twenty-first century are cost and quality. These issues proffer both the biggest challenges and the greatest opportunities for risk managers. If the risk manager is to be effective, he or she will need to draw upon a variety of analytical tools. One of these tools is called *cost of risk* (COR). It includes a variety of measurements that provide a complete picture of the organization's investment in addressing risk.

Cost of Risk

Cost of risk analyses were formalized in the early 1960s and have been generally accepted as consisting of four components:

1. Net insurance premiums: workers' compensation, property and liability exposures, and related taxes.

2. Retained or uninsured losses, deductibles, or self-insured retentions.

3. Administrative costs: risk management and insurance department services, broker fees and other related services (such as education).

4. Risk control and loss prevention expenses: safety, fire protection, and so on.[36]

Cost of risk is most often expressed as a cost per unit of revenue. By adding up the costs for the four components and dividing them by the organization's annual revenue (expressed in thousands of dollars), the risk manager can determine the organization's COR.

Cost of Risk as a Benchmarking Tool

Implementing a consistent plan to track these costs, the risk manager will identify numerous opportunities for benchmarking. Internal benchmarking will provide dollars and cents pictures of exposures or losses that require preventive action. Internal benchmarking can also provide graphic proof of improvements and savings. Perhaps the most effective benefit to consistent measures over time will be the risk manager's ability to look at five years' worth of data and identify legitimate trends—with the highs of shock losses leveled off and the lows of market shifts accounted for. The risk manager's credibility will be enhanced in an organization that has come to rely on the variety of data that can be compiled through COR analyses.

Internal Comparisons with National COR Data

Annually, a national COR survey has been conducted by the Risk and Insurance Management Society (RIMS) in conjunction with the actuarial firm Tillinghast Towers Perrin. These reports offer the risk manager an opportunity to benchmark against national averages. Survey results are based on data provided for the previous year. Until 1999 the surveys had reflected downward COR expenditures per $1,000 of revenue. However, the 1999 RIMS Benchmark Survey, conducted in conjunction with Ernst & Young, reported a $5.71 COR per $1,000 of revenue in 1998, an 8.8-percent increase from the previous year.

Through most of the 1990s, the RIMS Benchmark Survey reported continuous reductions in CORs. For example, the 1997 COR was $5.25, a 10-percent reduction over the previous year's COR of $6.49. This reduction, in turn, comprised an 11-percent decrease from the $7.30 COR for 1995.

Analysts, speculating on the increases noted in the 1999 survey suggest that a few respondents may have suffered very large losses. Or, the increase may have occurred because of a shift in the demographics of the respondent corporations. If participants in earlier surveys had been very large corporations, whose COR could be expected to be lower, the upward shift could be expected if several of these companies did not provide their 1998 data.

The RIMS studies provide the risk manager the opportunity to conduct mini-benchmarking projects that take into account national data–without having to seek external partners. In fact, many COR benchmarking projects will rely on internal benchmarking. This is true for several reasons.

Challenges to COR Benchmarking:

Proprietary Data   First, while another health care organization may be willing to share information about its project to reduce the number of slips-and-falls, it may be loathe to reveal how much it is paying for professional liability insurance or broker fees. A thin border divides shareable information from proprietary information—and that border most often consists of a row of dollar signs.

Inconsistent Data   A second challenge to external COR benchmarking is the variability of data collection processes from one organization to another. The best cost-related studies gather and plot data over extended periods of time. While consistency may have been built into the original project design, inadvertent alterations may affect outcomes. For example, a midwestern hospital had been conducting an ongoing benchmarking project with a hospital in their network. The project, designed to reduce neonatal incidents, had implemented numerous improvements over several years. Out of the blue, a monthly program designed to calculate progress at both hospitals reported significant deterioration in quality measures. Near panic ensued before the team was finally able to discover the cause of the problem—a regularly-scheduled software update had been implemented without any concern that it might affect the project. But the new software computed data differently and could not measure against the old reports; thus all the new data had been corrupted.

Incomplete Data   In a third instance, a risk manager missed a critical factor when determining the results of an educational project. A program was implemented to provide fall-reduction education for all employees. Follow-up indicated that falls had been reduced by more than 60 percent. Some time later, however, the risk manager discovered that another factor might have contributed to the reduction in the number of falls. At the same time that the education project was being implemented, the housekeeping staff coincidentally began using a new nonslip floor wax. The COR had not included a factor that undoubtedly helped reduce the number of falls.

The floor wax confusion occurred because two well-intentioned services failed to communicate. But more often than not, "missing" data results from conscious efforts of a group to control its own territory. In some hospitals, for example, workers' compensation data are gathered by, and protected, by the human resources department, which is loath to share data with other departments.

Unreliable Data   Relying solely on money as an indicator of improvement may not provide an accurate picture of the organization's risk-related efforts. For example, a risk manager might report that a reduction in the amount of money spent on medication-related claims constitutes an achieved quality goal. However, if that same risk manager were to compare the internal data with jury verdict review (JVR) data and with claims data reported by the Physicians Insurance Association of America (PIAA), the results might reveal that the hospital is still on the dangerous side of the bell curve. "Money basically tells you about money," cautions risk management expert John Groskopf. "Use it as one of the factors under consideration but don't assume that it can be used to answer all other questions."[37] In general, Groskopf recommends that risk managers stick to smaller projects that provide one answer at a time rather than attempt to use a series of complicated processes to determine one figure (such as a dollar-based COR) to assign one quality and cost designation to the entire organization.

From his years of experience consulting with a variety of health care organizations, Groskopf believes that few risk managers have the actuarial skill to engage in an all-encompassing cost of risk assessment. Further, even when the answer is accurate, it does not necessarily provide the organization with a clear picture.[38] For example, a saved-dollar figure probably will not identify the savings source. It also may be difficult to determine whether the savings really resulted from a reduction in claims or from an unidentified factor—such as the nonslip floor wax.

Administrative Biases or Misunderstandings   The vision established by each organization's leadership will, to some degree, effect the kind of information the risk manager is asked to provide; it will also influence the administration's response. Many risk managers report that they have inadequate staff to gather and analyze all the data that a complete COR process would entail. In fact, administrators may rigidly delineate the reports they want to see. If nothing else, risk managers are a pragmatic lot and they will generate the reports most likely to effect support for needed action(s).

An additional concern voiced by many risk managers is the fear that administrators will assume that a lower COR is synonymous with a satisfactory assessment of quality. Obviously, this is not always the case. Senior management's need to hear "good news" should not preclude the risk manager's ability to sound an appropriate alarm.

Recommendations

The following points are efforts to enhance the effectiveness of benchmarking COR.

Translate the Information for the Listener   As with other benchmarking processes, the risk manager can gain support by implementing the technical language of the listener. This approach can be especially beneficial in COR presentations when the risk manager uses graphic displays, providing the audience with a visual breakdown of multicomponent information that might otherwise be difficult for segments of the intended audience to grasp.

Build Consensus   Working with other departments the risk manager can build a data-gathering network resulting in a balanced picture of all four COR components. While administrators may not place equal value on each measurement, the risk manager can take the organization's pulse and base his or her recommendations on a broader spectrum of data. In addition, the risk manager will be in a better position to initiate internal and, ultimately, external benchmarking practices.

While risk managers may not conduct all COR analyses on a regular basis or with the same degree of detail, nonetheless, certain measurements should be conducted at set intervals. This information should be shared with, and analyzed by, multiple departments or services. Plans to act on the results should be seen as the starting point for quality initiatives, some of which may provide distinct opportunities for benchmarking. Cost of risk programs are most valuable when they are conducted over time. So if resources, staff, and time are limited, it is all the more important to prioritize. Design efforts should concentrate on critical needs (most frequently-occurring or highest lost claims); vision and mission statements (the organization's service goals for the next several years); and results of quality improvement and customer satisfaction data.

Confidentiality   Should an external benchmark partner be willing to share confidential financial information, the risk manager and other team members must be especially proactive about protecting this information. A threat to the confidentiality of the material may arise from within the walls of the organization. Education, appropriate policies and procedures, and oversight of protected information are critical.

Resources   The RIMS Benchmark Survey provides a basic measurement opportunity. However, other entities also assess COR and may offer additional information and suggestions for risk managers. One such entity is the University HealthSystem Consortium with conducts its own COR survey through its membership. Teaching hospitals or other members of the UHC can access data available through its published COR reports.

Seen in a broad perspective, COR provides the framework for all measurement within the risk management function. It gathers and analyzes the data necessary to define and fine-tune quality initiatives. It determines whether monies spent on training, education, technology, and equipment did or did not add value to services provided by the organization. It measures improvement in ways that can be visualized. Without COR assessments as a continuous quality and/or benchmarking process, the organization will be forced to make decisions based on hunches. Just as health care itself requires the intelligent use of hunches backed by technology and clinical skill, so too will risk management in the new century learn and benefit from implementing COR as a diagnostic tool.

. . . .

CONCLUSION

Benchmarking as part of an ongoing, pervasive TQM policy is still in its infancy in the health care environment. Change occurs slowly in deeply conservative systems, and medicine remains a bastion of conservatism. Even when enthusiasm levels are high, risk managers should avoid overshooting the mark. First lay the groundwork, by assessing the market, by networking, and by building consensus. In hidebound organizations, risk managers will want to "sell" risk management as an ally and resource. The risk manager must heighten administrator and board awareness of the progress that other entities are making. The TQM staff may prove the risk manager's closest allies in advocating change. Together they should choose small initial benchmark projects that will build one success on another. The multitude of analytical processes involved with building a risk management program dictate a minimal comfort level with the mathematical and computer technologies essential for measuring—and accurately reporting—progress. Facility in statistical analysis will be an increasingly necessary risk management tool. Risk managers should remember to mind the money, spending less time on processing claims and more time on identifying and measuring the processes for preventing them. Most of all, they should share their benchmarking experiences with one another. Risk msanagement is an eclectic profession. It has attracted nurses, lawyers, safety experts, health care administrators, educators, and a host of other talented and dedicated people. Although some view this "patchwork" background as a weakness, it may prove to be the profession's greatest strength.

Endnotes

1. Roskopf, J. F. "Benchmarking Risk Management Standards." *The John Liner Review: The Quarterly Review of Advanced Risk Management Strategies, 9*(1), pp. 60–102.

2. Barnes, R. V., and Lawton, L. "Clinical Benchmarking Improves Clinical Paths: Experience with Coronary Artery." *Journal on Quality Improvement, 20*(5), May 1994, pp. 267–276.

3 Roskopf, J. F. "Benchmarking Risk Management Standards." *The John Liner Review: The Quarterly Review of Advanced Risk Management Strategies, 9*(1), p. 57.

4. DePorter, J., and Youngberg, B. J. "Understanding Total Quality Management in Health Care." *Critical Issues Shaping Medical Practice.* Chicago: The University Hospital Consortium, 1994, pp. 10.1–10.13.

5. Melum, M. M., and Sinioris, M. K. *Total Quality Management: The Health Care Pioneers.* Chicago: American Hospital Publishing, 1992, pp. 325–334.

6. Couch, J. B.(ed.). *Health Care Quality Management for the 21st Century.* Tampa: American College of Physician Executives, 1991, p. 310.

7. Hudson, T. "ASHRM Takes Steps to Educate Members." *Hospitals, 66*(20), Oct. 20, 1992, p. 32.

8. Hudson, T. "Hospitals Find Ways to Integrate Risk Management Functions." *Hospitals, 66*(20), Oct. 20, 1992, pp. 32, 34–36.

9. Joint Commission on Accreditation of Healthcare Organizations. *Accreditation Manual for Hospitals.* vol. 1. Oakbrook Terrace, Ill.: JCAHO, 1996.

10. ISO Central Secretariat. *ISO 9001: 2000 Quality Management Systems.* Geneva: International Organization for Standardization, 1999, pp. 1–27.

11. Richardson, D., Tarnow-Mordi, W. O., and Lee, S. K. "Risk Adjustment for Quality Improvement: Measurement." *Pediatrics, 103*(1), Jan. 1999, p. 263.

12. American Hospital Association. *Risk Management Self-Assessment Manual.* Chicago: AHA, 1991, pp. 1–16.

13. Richardson, D., Tarnow-Mordi, W. O., and Lee, S. K. "Risk Adjustment for Quality Improvement: Measurement." *Pediatrics, 103*(1), Jan. 1999, p. 263.

14. Roskopf, J. F. "Benchmarking Risk Management Standards." *The John Liner Review: The Quarterly Review of Advanced Risk Management Strategies, 9*(1), p. 57.

15. Berkey, T. "Benchmarking in Health Care: Turning Challenges into Success." *Journal on Quality Improvement, 20*(5), May 1994, pp. 277–284.

16. Interview with A. V. Lewis, Jan. 4, 1996.

17. *Ibid.*

18. *Ibid.*

19. Interview with J. F. Roskopf, Jan. 23, 1996.

20. Richman, V. V. "Setting Goals for Reductions in Canadian Cesarean Delivery Rates: Benchmarking Medical Practice Patterns." *American Journal of Obstetrics and Gynecology, 181*(3), Sept. 1999, p. 212.

21. Richardson, D., Tarnow-Mordi, W. O., and Lee, S. K. "Risk Adjustment for Quality Improvement: Measurement." *Pediatrics, 103*(1), Jan. 1999, p. 263.

22. Roskopf, J. F. "Risk Management Excellence." ASHRM Conference, Miami, Fla., Oct. 31, 1995.

23. "Can You Prove Your Worth? Benchmarking Can Effectively Show the Results of Risk Management." *Hospital Risk Management*, Dec. 1994, pp. 161–65.

24. Benson, T. E. "Quality is Not What You Think It Is." *Industry Week*, Oct. 5, 1992, p. 22.

25. Interview with J. F. Roskopf, Jan. 23, 1996.

26. Gardner, E. "Putting Guidelines into Practice: Benchmarking Efforts Are Leading to a Growing Number of Guidelines, But Despite Cost and Quality Benefits, They Often Still Require a Hard Sell." *Modern Healthcare*, Sept. 7, 1992, p. 24.

27. Roskopf, J. F. "Benchmarking Risk Management Standards." *The John Liner Review: The Quarterly Review of Advanced Risk Management Strategies, 9*(1), pp. 61–62.

28. Interview with M. J. Brewer, Division Director of Quality/Clinical Risk Management, Parkview Memorial Hospital, Ft. Wayne, Ind., Dec. 15, 1995.

29. Ziegenfuss, J. T., Jr. *The Organizational Path to Health Care Quality.* Ann Arbor, Mich.: Health Administration Press, 1993, p. 195.

30. *Ibid.*

31. *Ibid.*

32. Delbecq, A. L. "The Hidden Competitive Weapon Supporting Innovation in Health Care." *Physician Executive, 21*(5), May 1995, p. 18.

33. Ruroede, K. "Predictive Model for Healthcare Risk Management Personal Investment Initiatives within a Managed Care Environment." Ph.D. Dissertation, The Chicago Medical School, 1998.

34. Ziegenfuss, J. T., Jr. *The Organizational Path to Health Care Quality.* Ann Arbor, Mich.: Health Administration Press, 1993, p. 195.

35. *Ibid.*

36. Gara, K. G. "Tools Can Help Reduce Risk Management Costs." *Atlanta Business Chronicle*, Aug. 8, 1997. p. 2.

37. Garaskopf, J. Interview on Oct. 22, 1999.

38. Youngberg, B. "Measuring Performance." *The Risk Manager's Desk Reference* (2nd ed.). Gaithersburg, Md.: Aspen Publishers. 1998, pp. 236–238.

35

Risk Management Program Evaluation

Christopher Cassirer

Since the medical professional liability insurance crises of the 1970s and 1980s, risk management programs have been regarded by many as one of the most promising responses to the problem of medical malpractice. In general, risk management programs are defined as the systems designed to prevent and control patient injury, enhance quality, promote safety, and minimize the losses associated with medical malpractice claims.

NEED FOR RISK MANAGEMENT PROGRAM EVALUATION

The objectives of these programs are to: (1) design and implement activities to reduce the risk of injury associated with medical management of the patient, (2) reduce and control the number and size of payments for medical malpractice claims and losses, (3) identify the most economical approaches to financing risk whether it is through purchased insurance and/or a variety of self-insurance alternatives, and (4) enhance quality and improve patient safety.[1]

During the past thirty years, support for hospital risk management programs has come from both federal and state legislatures, insurance companies, policy makers, managers, and members of the patient care community. For example, in response to the medical malpractice insurance crisis of the 1970s, the Health Care Financing Administration (HCFA) introduced changes to the Medicare reimbursement policy which enabled hospitals to consider alternative methods of financing risk.[2] A condition of eligibility for reimbursement was that hospitals had to provide evidence that a risk management program was in place to control losses.

In response to the crises of the 1970s and 1980s, many state legislatures passed mandates requiring hospitals to implement risk management programs as a condition of eligibility for licensure. Although mandates and regulations varied among the states, there was a clear commitment to promote risk management as one of the more promising responses to the medical malpractice problem.[3]

Health care provider associations and groups also demonstrated support for risk management. The Department of Health and Human Services Task Force on Medical Liability and Malpractice and the American Hospital Association's Medical Malpractice Task Force issued statements advocating the strengthening and continued expansion of risk management programs in hospitals. Further, the Joint Commission on the Accreditation of Healthcare Organizations (JCAHO) introduced language requiring hospitals to implement various risk management program activities, such as linking risk management with quality assurance activities in hospitals as a condition of continued accreditation.[4]

Despite the wealth of support that has been generated for risk management, there is an absence of data or reliable information to suggest that risk management programs are effective. In part this is due to the relative recency of risk management programs in the health care industry. Second, there is little to no agreement among the professional community about what is an effective risk management program. Third, there are real difficulties associated with demonstrating the impact of risk management program activities on incidents and rates of adverse events and patient injuries and the frequency and severity of medical malpractice claims. Fourth, measuring what is prevented continues to be the most elusive goal in proving the value of risk management. Medical chart reviews, occurrence screens, and incident reports made verbally or in writing can be important sources of information about medical injury. Losses associated with malpractice claims tend to be the focus of our evaluation activities. Risk managers, however, can begin to enhance their skills and assume a leadership role by learning more about the basic tools currently available to design, implement, and evaluate risk management program effectiveness.

To help enable practicing risk managers with a better set of tools, this chapter will: (1) present an empirically based conceptual framework to define risk management program goals and objectives, (2) present information about the American Society for Healthcare Risk Management's (ASHRM) past efforts to develop a comprehensive risk management program evaluation model that incorporates a systems perspective, a continuous quality improvement approach to program design, and evaluation, (3) review recent research regarding hospitals' efforts to implement the ASHRM model, (4) discuss other studies and ongoing research efforts to evaluate risk management program effectiveness, and (5) discuss future trends that will continue to affect efforts by professional risk managers to develop tools and strategies, and recommend partnership strategies and roles for the profession in building an evaluation model to demonstrate the effectiveness of risk management programs in practice.

··········

SETTING RISK MANAGEMENT PROGRAM OBJECTIVES

While risk management programs have a defined role in many types of health care provider organizations, much of the history and current effort to evaluate programs is based on our knowledge of hospital risk management practices. Since the 1970s, studies have continued to show that approximately 80 percent of malpractice claims are the result of hospital-based adverse events and injuries to patients. Thus, efforts to develop research-driven models, tools, and strategies to manage risk have been largely hospital-based. Similarly, evaluation research and recommendations regarding the effective design and development of risk management programs for health care organizations have been largely hospital-focused.

The generally accepted frame guiding current efforts to conceptualize the goals and objectives of risk management programs is based on the accumulating evidence drawn from twenty years of research on rates of adverse events involving hospitalized patients and the accumulating literature on medical malpractice closed claims studies. The most important studies to date were conducted in the 1970s and 1980s. The results of these investigations have impacted national policy formulation and state-enacted legislative activities. Operationally, these studies have shaped the currently accepted framework for defining the problem of medical malpractice and the goals and objectives of hospital and health care risk management programs.

● ● ● ● ● ● ● ● ● ● ● ●
NATIONAL ASSOCIATION OF INSURANCE COMMISSIONERS

In response to the medical malpractice insurance crisis of the 1970s, the National Association of Insurance Commissioners (NAIC) began a comprehensive study based on the malpractice claims files of all U.S. insurers that had written premiums of $1 million or more in any year since 1970.[5,6] The complete database included information on 71,788 claims closed by 128 insurers between 1975 and 1978.

Analysis of filed claims indicated that 78 percent of all incidents resulting in paid claims occurred in hospitals and accounted for approximately 87 percent of all payments to claimants. The majority of these claims were filed based on incidents and adverse events occurring in operating rooms and emergency departments. Approximately one-third of all paid claims alleged improperly performed procedures.

A similar analysis was conducted by the U.S. General Accounting Office (GAO) following the medical malpractice insurance crisis of the 1980s. In 1987, the GAO published a study of 1,706 closed malpractice claims. Data were obtained from twenty-five professional liability insurance companies. This group was selected to represent a population of 73,000 closed claims involving more than 100,000 providers and 102 insurance companies as of 1984. The findings were similar to those of the NAIC researchers. Approximately 80 percent of closed malpractice claims were determined to be the result of medical care related to injuries involving hospitalized patients.

● ● ● ● ● ● ● ● ● ● ● ●
CALIFORNIA HOSPITAL ASSOCIATION STUDY

The emerging evidence that most injuries occurred to hospitalized patients led to two major studies of patient injury rates in hospitals in the 1970s and the 1980s. These studies measured rates of adverse events and adverse events due to probable negligence occurring among hospitalized patients.

The first comprehensive investigation to estimate rates of adverse events and injuries due to negligence was conducted by the California Medical Association and the California Hospital Association in the 1970s. The purpose of the study was to determine the cost and feasibility of a no-fault compensation system for medical malpractice. The analysis involved reviews of 20,864 medical records drawn from a sample of twenty-three acute care hospitals in California. Medical records represented patient differences in age, gender, race, and payment source. Hospitals included in the sample represented differences in size, location, region, ownership, and teaching status. Reviewed medical records were assumed to represent all California hospital discharges during 1974.

Examination of the medical records involved the application of twenty screening criteria. Trained medical chart reviewers applied the criteria and identified hospitalized patient charts where there was evidence of an adverse event. Screened charts were then subjected to a second review by teams of physicians and physician-attorneys to determine if a potentially compensable malpractice event (PCE) had occurred. PCEs were defined for the study as adverse events in which patients suffered temporary or permanent disability due to errors in health care management. Physician-attorneys then reviewed all charts with evidence of a PCE to determine if a jury would be likely to decide in favor of the injured patient in a legal review of the malpractice claim.

The researchers estimated that 970 or 4.65 percent of medical charts provided evidence of patient injuries likely due to errors in health care management of the patient, either prior to or during hospitalization. From those initial 970 records it was determined that 17 percent would have been likely to result in a legal determination of negligence. Based on this research, it was later estimated that one out of every 126 patients hospitalized in California in 1974 suffered a potentially compensable injury.[7]

············

HARVARD MEDICAL PRACTICE STUDY

The medical malpractice crisis of the mid-1980s prompted a second major study to measure hospitalized patient injury rates. Similar to the study conducted in California, a team of researchers at the Harvard University developed a population-based measure of the incidence of hospitalized patient injuries and produced an estimate of the percentage of medical care-related injuries due to probable negligence.

To estimate the incidence of patient injuries, the Harvard research team selected a random sample of fifty-one acute care hospitals in New York in 1984. Hospitals were stratified by size, geographic location, teaching status, and ownership. Second, a random sample of approximately 31,000 medical records was selected from among the fifty-one hospitals.

Medical records were reviewed by trained medical record analysts (MRAs) and nurses to screen for adverse events. Adverse events were defined in the Harvard study as evidence of substandard care, inappropriately performed medical procedures, or errors in health care management. The MRAs relied on eighteen screens to identify adverse events. In total, 1,133 adverse events were detected. Teams of physician-attorneys then reviewed the adverse events to decide if there was any indication of probable negligence. Of the 1,133 records initially selected, 280 were determined to be the result of probable negligence in health care management of the patient.[8,9]

Based on their analysis, the Harvard research team estimated that 3.7 percent of patients discharged from the fifty-one hospitals in New York in 1984 suffered an adverse event. Of these adverse events, approximately 1 percent was determined to be due to probable negligence. Initial findings indicated that adverse events ranged in hospitals from .2 percent to 7.9 percent with a mean of 3.2 percent. Rates of adverse events due to negligence ranged from 1 percent to 60 percent with a mean of 24.9 percent. Further analysis indicated that rates were not normally distributed among the hospitals. Characteristics of hospitals examined for their possible association with rates of adverse events (AEs) and negligent adverse events (NAEs) included hospital ownership, location, size, proportion of minority discharges, and the teaching status of the hospitals.

The results of a multivariate regression analysis indicated that university teaching hospitals had a higher rate of adverse events than affiliated and nonteaching hospitals. Hospitals in upstate, nonmetropolitan statistical areas had significantly fewer adverse events than hospitals closer to the major cities. Large hospitals had fewer adverse events than medium-size hospitals. The only hospital characteristic, however, significantly associated with negligent adverse events among the hospitals was the proportion of minority discharges.

In the most recent studies conducted by another Harvard Medical Practice Study team, approximately 15,000 medical charts were examined from hospitals in Colorado and Utah in 1995. Methods of chart review to identify AEs and NAEs were similar to those utilized in the studies examining rates of medical injury in New York hospitals. Patient injury rates ranged from 3 to 4 percent.[10] Similar to the findings of the New York medical practice study, the rate of NAEs was determined to be less than 1 percent.

Based on this data, the Institute of Medicine (IOM) estimates that as many as 44,000 to 98,000 patients experience a preventable medical injury in the process of receiving medical care in hospitals in the United States per year.[11]

············
RELATIONSHIPS BETWEEN PATIENT INJURIES AND MALPRACTICE CLAIMS

Data on rates of patient injuries, however, provide only partial insight into the full scope of the medical malpractice problem. Studies have shown that not all injuries result in the filing of medical malpractice claims or legal determinations in favor of patients, even when there has been evidence of probable negligence.

The first studies to examine relationships between patient injuries and malpractice claims were conducted in the early 1980s. Danzon, for example, examined the early findings of the California researchers with the goal of determining the number of patients who were injured in the process of receiving medical treatment that later filed a malpractice claim.[12] A second goal of the study was to estimate the number of patients who recovered damages when an adverse event was determined to be the result of probable negligence.

The results of these analyses indicated that less than one in ten patients suffered an adverse event due to negligence in California hospitals in 1974 went on to file a medical malpractice claim. Of those claims that were filed, slightly less than 40 percent resulted in payments to claimants.[13,14]

The second major set of studies focusing on relationships between patient injuries and malpractice claims was conducted by the research team at Harvard. They evaluated in detail the 280 medical charts that suggested patients were injured due to probable negligence. Based on their research, it was determined that only forty-seven, or one out of every 7.6 negligent adverse events resulted in filing claims for injuries due to probable negligence, only one out of sixteen received compensation.

Similar to the findings of Danzon, the Harvard research team concluded that of all those patients discharged from New York hospitals in 1984 who suffered an adverse event due to probable negligence, few went on to file malpractice claims or recover damages for their injuries. Although several medical malpractice insurance crises had occurred in the past, the data suggest that the problem of medical malpractice may have been much worse than indicated during the crises of the 1970s and 1980s.

....

CONCEPTUALIZING RELATIONSHIPS, PATIENT INJURIES, AND MALPRACTICE CLAIMS

Relationships between the incidence of patient injuries, the rate of provider error, and malpractice claims are represented by Figure 35.1.[15–17] Area A represents all medical injuries among hospitalized patients. Results of the California study, for example, indicate that 4.65 percent of all patients discharged from hospitals in California in 1974 were injured as a result of medical mismanagement of the patient. Similarly, the results of the Harvard Medical Practice Study indicate that 3.7 percent of patients discharged from hospitals in New York in 1984 suffered an adverse event.

Area B represents the extent of legal misconduct in medicine. Although the scope of this dimension is unknown, the incidence of negligence in medical care that results in patient injury can be identified. The Harvard studies, for example, indicate that approximately 1 percent of patients hospitalized in New York in 1984 suffered an adverse event due to negligence. This percentage represents all of those patient injuries that should result in the filing of medical malpractice claim.

Area D represents the estimates of negligent adverse events that have emerged as medical malpractice claims. It suggests that the actual number of claims that emerge is significantly less than the number expected if current systems for addressing injury and claims were operating effectively. It also overlaps Area B to indicate that some claims are filed when there is no evidence of negligence. Moreover, it suggests that claims are filed

FIGURE 35.1.   Relationships Among Patient Injuries, Provider Errors, and Malpractice Claims

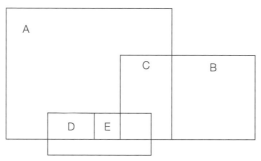

A = Incidence of patient injuries = Unknown
B = Incidence of errors during medicine = Estimates of 3–4 percent (Harvard Studies)
C = Patient injuries due to errors in medical care = Less than 1 percent (Harvard Studies)
D = Filed malpractice claims (1 out of 8—Danzon; Harvard Studies)
E = Filed claims resulting in claimant compensation (1 out of 10—Danzon; Harvard)

Adapted from: National Association of Insurance Commissioners. *NAIC Malpractice Claims: Medical Malpractice Closed Claims, 1975–1978.* Milwaukee, WIS. National Association of Insurance Commissioners, 1980; Orlikoff, J. E., Vanagunas, A. M. *Malpractice Prevention and Liability Control for Hospitals* (2nd ed.). Chicago, Ill.: American Hospital Association, 1988; Morlock, L. L., Cassirer, C., Malitz, F. E. "Hospital Risk Management and Professional Liability Claims Experience in Maryland." *Final Report: Agency for Health Care Policy & Research,* Grant Number 1 RO1 HS06735, 1997; Cassirer, C. *Hospital Risk Management Programs in Maryland (1995).* Baltimore: Johns Hopkins University, 1997.

due to legal misconduct by health care providers when no evidence of medical care related injury appeared in the medical record.

Finally, Area E represents the number of claims that result in compensation to claimants who are injured due to negligence in the process of receiving medical treatment. Consistent with the findings from the major studies of medical injury and malpractice, it suggests that fewer patients are compensated than expected. As noted, in the Harvard studies, only one out of every sixteen patients who suffered an injury due to negligence received compensation under the current liability system.

This adapted framework (Figure 35.1) initially proposed by the National Association of Insurance Commissioners (NAIC) in the late 1970s continues to provide the most comprehensive paradigm for characterizing the multidimensional nature of the medical malpractice problem in hospitals and highlights the major goals and objectives that hospital risk management programs attempt to address. Referring to Figure 35.1, in theory, hospital risk management programs have the potential to: (1) reduce the frequency of preventable adverse events (Area A), (2) reduce the number of patient injuries due to provider errors (Area B), (3) decrease the number of malpractice claims (Area C), (4) manage the number of claims that do emerge to control losses (Area D), and (5) finance risk through the most economical methods to ensure an adequate source of funds is available to pay for malpractice claims and expenses (Areas D and E).

....

ASHRM MODEL FOR RM EVALUATION

Prior to the 1980s, hospitals and other health care provider organizations had little guidance or access to resources to help them respond to state mandates and other requirements to develop risk management programs. To facilitate hospitals' efforts, the American Hospital Association (AHA) chartered a subsidiary organization, named the American Society for Healthcare Risk Management (ASHRM). For the past twenty years, ASHRM has assumed a leadership role in helping to define the professional practice of health care risk management.

Following the medical malpractice insurance crisis of the 1980s, ASHRM organized a task force of experts to define a model and approach to developing and implementing a hospital risk management program assessment tool. By 1991, the ASHRM task force had produced a *Hospital Risk Management Self-Assessment Manual* for risk managers. Included in the manual is a tool called the ASHRM Assessment Abstract. The abstract includes a listing and description of the types of program elements and related activities that ASHRM believes every hospital should have in place as part of developing an effective program. These recommendations were designed to apply to all hospitals in every state, regardless of whether or not states had a mandate.

The approach defined by ASHRM represents "better practices" in the profession as defined by a leading society of risk management professionals. These better practices reflect the accumulated wisdom of the experts serving on the task force and the experience of practicing risk managers. The history and support for the ideas synthesized in the abstract can be found in the trade and professional literature, numerous published articles and books on the subject of health care risk management, as well as the limited scientific research on the effectiveness of these approaches.[18–25] The objectives of risk management programs that are the focus of the ASHRM model have been described. The recommendations of ASHRM are designed to represent the basics, a starting point for risk management program development.

··········

THE ASHRM MODEL PHILOSOPHY

The ASHRM Model for risk management is based on risk management theory, a systems approach and a continuous quality improvement philosophy of program improvement.[26–30] Each activity recommended by ASHRM should have a structure in place to support it, an associated set of processes to accomplish the activity, and a set of defined outcome measures for evaluating performance. Consistent with the theory of CQI, emphasis is placed on the development of process measures. Accumulated data and information about performance is to be used to guide ongoing improvement to accomplish risk management program goals.

··········

THE ASHRM MODEL ASSESSMENT PROGRAM

According to ASHRM, an effective hospital risk management program comprises five basic program elements, each of which is delineated into specific dimensions of activity. The five elements and related dimensions of activity recommended by ASHRM are as follows:

Organizational Structure

ASHRM recommends that a hospital risk management program should have an organizational structure to support the risk management function. Dimensions of the organizational structure that should be in place include activities to promote governing board commitment, establishing the role and responsibilities for a designated hospital risk manager, and activities to promote medical staff involvement in the hospital risk management program.

Governing Board Support   Activities of the governing board assessed with the ASHRM Assessment Abstract focused on whether the governing board supports the risk management program, whether a written policy statement or plan describing the risk management program has been developed, and if formal approval of the plan has been secured from the governing board. Another activity assessed is whether the governing board receives reports from risk management at least twice per year.

Process measures for assessing governing board support focus on the content of the written risk management plan. For example, whether goals and objectives have been defined for risk management, whether the position of the risk manager in the organizational structure is identified in the plan, as well as other plan characteristics.

Other measures of process assessed whether there are established communication channels between risk management and other organizational components and if there is a description of the institutional policy of risk financing. Process measures also focused on the written risk management reports to the governing body. The processes assessed were whether the report to the governing body included information on insurance issues, risk financing issues, and adverse events, as well as the hospital's claims experience, among other measures.

Outcome measures focused on whether there is documentation of the governing board approval of the risk management program and whether the governing board updates the risk management plan at least annually. Another outcome measure assessed is whether the governing body takes appropriate action on data from risk management and if those actions are documented in the governing body meeting minutes.

Designated Risk Manager   One activity was assessed on this dimension of hospital risk management programs. It focused on whether there is a designated person(s) responsible for the hospital risk management program.

Process measures focused on the contents of the written job description for the risk manager. Assessments pertained to the role of the risk manager in loss identification, quality assurance, safety management, claims handling, risk financing, security, and patient relations, among other roles. No outcome measures were assessed on this dimension of hospital risk management programs.

Medical Staff Involvement   The ASHRM Assessment Abstract assessed whether medical staff involvement in the hospital risk management program was structured. Process measures further delineated the attributes of this structured involvement and included items such as whether the medical staff had developed criteria in at least three clinical areas to identify adverse patient events.

Other process measures assessed were whether there was a process for the medical staff to review variations from these established criteria, whether the medical staff identified risk management problems in the delivery of patient care, whether the medical staff recommended corrective action to resolve problems, whether the medical staff ensured that problems were resolved, whether the medical staff participated in risk management policy development, and whether the medical staff participated in the design of educational programs directed toward loss prevention.

Three outcome measures assessed on this dimension focused on whether the medical staff had identified at least three risk management problems annually, whether the medical staff had resolved at least three problems, and whether the number of claims involving the medical staff had decreased over time.

Incident Identification and Analysis

The second element that ASHRM recommends should be in place is an incident identification and analysis system. This element comprises two dimensions of activity including activities designed to identify incidents of adverse events and activities directed toward the analysis of incidents.

Risk Identification Systems   Assessments of the risk identification system focused on whether the hospital had developed systematic methods for reporting patient, visitor, and employee-related adverse events. Assessments also focused on whether there was a system to identify adverse events in high risk clinical areas and whether there was a system developed to report adverse events to local and state entities.

Process measures for patient, visitor, employee and clinical high risk incident identification systems focused on whether reports produced by these systems identified the number of incidents that occurred each month as compared to an activity base. Process measures for the system for reporting adverse events to state and local entities were concerned with whether the system identified an individual with reporting responsibility, whether there was a process in place for determining which events were reportable, and if a format had been established for reporting adverse events.

Outcome measures for incident reporting systems pertaining to patient, visitor, employee, and high risk clinical areas focused on whether the reporting method in each of the four areas increased the percentage of claims identified at the time of occurrence. The outcome measure for the system of reporting adverse events focused on whether local and state requirements were followed.

Risk Analysis   One activity was assessed on this dimension of hospital risk management programs. The item focused on whether a process had been developed to analyze and trend risk identification data. Assessments of process measures related to this activity focused on whether the analysis of identified risk was stratified by location, type of occurrence, patient characteristics, and other characteristics. The outcome measurement focused on whether loss prevention activities had been initiated as a result of the identified problems.

Loss Prevention

The third basic element recommended by ASHRM is loss prevention, which comprises several dimensions of activity: education programs to prevent incidents from occurring, updating informed consent policies, monitoring hospital compliance with regulatory and accreditation requirements, analyzing claims data, and engaging in activities around patient and family relations.

Educational Programs   Risk management educational activities assessed included whether risk management information was presented to new employees, residents, and medical staff during orientation programs and whether continuing medical education (CME) programs were conducted on risk management at least annually.

Process measures assessed focused on whether comparison data had been developed to examine the number of employees, residents, and medical staff exposed to risk management out of the total number of these individuals who were hired annually. A process measure was also defined as whether the risk manager compares the number of physicians in attendance at CME programs out of the total number of medical staff.

The one outcome measure assessed was whether heightened awareness had been observed regarding the institutional risk management program, risk manager functions, and related policies and procedures.

Informed Consent   One activity and one process measure were assessed pertaining to informed consent. There were no outcome measures assessed. The activity assessed focused on whether the hospital provided a current, updated policy and procedure for obtaining and documenting informed consent. The process measure assessed was defined as whether the informed consent policy and procedure had been updated within the last two years.

Compliance with Regulations   One activity pertaining to compliance with regulations was assessed. The item focused on whether the hospital monitored local, state, federal, and JCAHO requirements for risk management. Process measures assessed focused on whether the number and type of standards were monitored and if the hospital tracked the amount of time spent in reviewing requirements, educating staff, providing consultation, preparing for survey visits, and developing and implementing plans to improve compliance with risk management program requirements. Outcome measures assessed focused on whether monitoring activities and processes resulted in the absence or reduction of the frequency and severity of regulatory citations, the frequency and severity of JCAHO contingencies, and the frequency and severity of claims related to noncompliance with risk management regulations.

Claims Data Analysis Activities   The ASHRM Assessment Abstract assessed whether hospitals had implemented a mechanism for analyzing claims and or incident data and whether loss prevention issues had been identified. Process measures focused on whether this information was reviewed periodically by specific categories including, allegation, service, specialty, and location. The one outcome measure assessed focused on whether claims reviews resulted in a lower frequency and severity of claims in areas targeted by loss prevention efforts.

Patient and Family Relations   Activities pertaining to patient and family relations focused on whether institutional mechanisms had been developed to assist and respond to patients and families following an adverse event, the filing of a complaint, or notification of lost or stolen property. The process measure assessed focused on whether the hospital risk management program tracked the number and type of patient and family interactions. The outcome measure assessed was whether claims had been averted due to positive patient and family interventions.

- - - - - - - - - - - -
RISK FINANCING POLICIES AND PROCEDURES

The fourth basic element that ASHRM recommends should be in place is a risk financing policy and process for analyzing decisions about risk funding. Activities pertaining to the risk financing dimension were defined as whether the hospital had implemented a mechanism for calculating the overall cost of risk, monitoring the cost of risk, comparing the cost of risk with other institutions, and conveying findings to senior management and the governing body.

Process measures focused on whether this data was compiled annually and included information on risk financing costs, loss prevention costs, risk management program administration costs, and information on underfunded losses. Another process measure assessed focused on whether the cost of risk was tracked as a percentage of overall operating budget.

Assessments of outcome measures focused on whether the cost of risk was similar to or lower than comparable institutions and whether the cost of risk was controlled or reduced overtime.

Claims Management Policies and Procedures

The fifth basic element of a hospital risk management assessment program is developing a claims management program. Claims management activities assessed with the ASHRM Assessment Abstract focused on whether the hospital had developed a written claims management policy and claims management process. Process measures assessed included whether the policy was developed with senior management input, whether the policy was reviewed at least annually, and whether the policy reflects a comprehensive review of the process for conducting claims investigation, case analysis, settlement processes, litigation management processes, and claims file maintenance.

Outcome measures assessed focus on whether the policy and policy review process result in a lower frequency of claims involving wrongful claims management practices, a lower frequency of claims involving "bad faith," and favorable audit reports from external sources such as excess insurance carriers.

Each program assessment element ASHRM Assessment Abstract is identified. The number of recommended activities, processes, and outcome measures appears in summary form in Table 35.1.

TABLE 35.1. Hospital Risk Management Elements Measured on ASHRM Assessment Abstract

	Structures/ Activities	*Process Measures*	*Outcome Measures*	*Total*
Organizational Structure				
Governing Board	3	16	3	22
Hospital Risk Manager	1	18	0	19
Medical Staff Involvement	1	10	3	14
TOTAL	5	44	6	55
Risk Identification and Analysis				
Risk Identification	5	7	5	17
Risk Analysis	1	4	1	6
TOTAL	6	11	6	23
Loss Prevention				
Education	4	4	1	9
Informed Consent	1	1	0	2
Compliance	1	6	3	10
Claims Data Analysis	2	4	1	7
Patient and Family Programs	3	1	1	5
TOTAL	11	16	6	33
Risk Financing	4	6	2	12
Claims Management	1	7	3	11
TOTAL ITEMS ASSESSED	27	84	23	134

COMMITMENT TO THE ASHRM ASSESSMENT MODEL AMONG HOSPITALS IN THREE STATES

Despite the wealth of support that has been generated for hospital risk management programs there is a dearth of empirical evidence describing their effectiveness. One dimension of assessing risk management program effectiveness is to determine organizational commitment to developing a risk management program in the first place.

Although the ASHRM Assessment Model and tool have been available since the mid-1980s, it does not appear to have been widely utilized in practice. Several recent studies undertaken by researchers from the Harvard and Johns Hopkins University have utilized the ASHRM Assessment Abstract to evaluate the effectiveness of hospital risk management programs. The results of the following investigations examined the extent to which hospitals have developed effective risk management programs based on the model and approach defined by ASHRM.[31] Two key questions addressed in this research are: To what extent do hospitals have risk management programs in place that incorporate the basic elements and dimensions of an effective program as defined by ASHRM? And, what are the barriers to adoption of the ASHRM model?

DEVELOPING AN EFFECTIVE ASHRM RISK MANAGEMENT ASSESSMENT PROGRAM

In 1995, researchers from Johns Hopkins University and Harvard University conducted a study to describe the level of hospital risk management program activity in three states: Colorado, Utah, and Maryland. In this study, a modification of the ASHRM self-assessment tool was administered to risk managers in seventy-seven acute care hospitals along with a second survey designed to collect information about perceived "better practices," including barriers and facilitators to enhancing program performance. In total, thirteen hospitals in Utah, fifteen hospitals in Colorado, and forty-nine hospitals in Maryland completed a slightly modified version of the ASHRM Assessment Abstract and the second survey. The hospital risk management programs studied in Colorado and Utah are the same hospitals studied in the recent findings on patient injury rates presented in the Institute of Medicine report on medical error.[32]

Participation in the 1995 study of hospital risk management programs was motivated by involving state chapters of ASHRM: the Utah Healthcare Associated Risk Managers (USHRM), the Colorado Healthcare Associated Risk Managers (CHARM), and the Maryland Society for Healthcare Risk Management (MSHRM). Each state chapter of ASHRM supported the project by presenting their members with information about the study including its design, specific aims, and benefits to the members. Each chapter published an announcement of the study in their respective newsletters and/or sent a letter of endorsement signed by the president of the local state chapter.

Informed consent to participate was a two-stage process. First, a letter describing the study was sent to the hospital CEOs in each state. Follow-up phone calls were made to each hospital to verify that the letter had been received and to determine if there were any questions or concerns about participating in the study. Then, each hospital risk manager received a telephone call to describe the project and request that the ASHRM Assessment abstract be completed. Hospital risk managers had the opportunity to review the abstract and to discuss the project internally with other hospital administrators prior to giving their consent to participate.

Responding to the abstract required risk managers to indicate whether specific program activities were "in-place" or "needed development." To estimate the level of hospital risk management program activity, total raw scores were computed for each hospital by counting the number of program activities "in place" and dividing that number by 134 (the total number of activities, processes, and outcome measures included in the abstract). Sub-scores were also computed to estimate the level of activity on individual program elements and dimensions of activity within each program element. Variation in mean abstract activity scores are reported in the tables.

Total ASHRM Activity Scores

The results of the study of hospital risk management activity based on responses to the ASHRM Assessment Abstract suggest that, on average, hospitals in these three states have approximately 65 percent of the recommended risk management programs and activities in place (Table 35.2).

Structure, Process, Outcome

Across the states, on average, hospitals had the greatest commitment to developing structures and activities to support the risk management function. The results indicate that, on average, hospitals in the three states had 71 percent of the structures and activities in place. There was, however, somewhat lesser commitment to developing the processes associated with those activities. Hospitals in the three states had 64 percent of the processes in place associated with structures and activities identified in the abstract. The least amount of activity was in hospitals' efforts to implement outcome measures to assess risk management program performance. On average, hospitals in the three states had 60 percent of the outcome measures in place recommended in the abstract.

TABLE 35.2.   **Mean and Range of Hospital Risk Management Program Activity Scores (%)**

Based on Risk Managers' Responses to the ASHRM Assessment Abstract (1995): Structure, Process, Outcome, and Total Scores*

	Utah		*Colorado*		*Maryland*		*TOTAL*	
	Mean	*Range*	*Mean*	*Range*	*Mean*	*Range*	*Mean*	*Range*
Structure/ Activities	69	(21–97)	62	(44–82)	74	(37–96)	71	(22–96)
Processes	61	(14–91)	54	(15–83)	66	(29–94)	64	(14–94)
Outcomes	70	(9–100)	68	(39–91)	56	(9–100)	60	(9–100)
TOTAL	64	(15–90)	58	(26–93)	66	(28–94)	65	(15–94)

*Activity scores (%) are defined as the total number of items "in-place" divided by the total number possible per dimension, multiplied by 100.

ASHRM Program Elements

Across the states, 73 percent of the hospitals had the recommended organizational structures in place; 77 percent had implemented suggested risk identification and analysis systems; 65 percent had appropriate claims management functions in operation; 62 percent had implemented suggested loss prevention strategies; but only 30 percent had adopted recommended risk financing mechanisms (Table 35.3).

Barriers to Developing an Effective ASHRM Risk Management Assessment Program

In addition to administering the ASHRM Assessment Abstract, a second survey was completed by the seventy-seven hospitals. Hospital risk managers responded to both open- and closed-ended questions and participated in key-informant interviews in which they discussed barriers to developing a program consistent with ASHRM's recommendations.

Key issues that emerged regarding barriers to utilization and implementation of the ASHRM Abstract focused on the following:

● *Awareness:* Although the ASHRM Assessment Abstract had been in publication since 1991, many risk managers were not aware that this instrument and guidance was available through the professional association. Others had copies of the Self-Assessment Manual which included the abstract but had not put it into use.

● *Turnover:* Risk managers reported that turnover in responsibility for the risk management function or set of activities within their organizations limited the opportunity to implement and follow through on many of the activities recommended by ASHRM.

● *Competing priorities:* Risk managers reported that increasing market pressure to control costs has resulted in budget and/or staff reductions to support risk management activities. Designated risk managers found themselves with an increasing array of responsibilities and insufficient time to focus on more than claims management and conducting providing the basic in-services programs.

● *Alternative models in place:* Some risk managers reported that while they had many of the dimensions and activities recommended by ASHRM, their programs were based on a different philosophy or organizational arrangement that affected how risk

TABLE 35.3.   Major Program Elements and Dimensions

Mean and Range of Hospital Risk Management Program Activity Scores (Percent)

Based on Risk Managers' Responses to the ASHRM Assessment Abstract (1995): Major Program Elements and Related Dimensions*

	Utah		Colorado		Maryland		TOTAL	
	Mean	Range	Mean	Range	Mean	Range	Mean	Range
Organizational Structure	72	(15–98)	64	(16–96)	75	(23–100)	73	(15–100)
Governing Board Support	66	(0–96)	68	(39–96)	80	(23–100)	76	(0–100)
Hospital Risk Manager	77	(5–100)	63	(5–100)	79	(16–100)	76	(5–100)
Medical Staff Involvement	74	(0–100)	57	(0–100)	62	(0–100)	63	(0–100)
Risk Identification	75	(39–100)	82	(48–100)	77	(26–100)	77	(26–100)
Risk Identification System	73	(41–100)	82	(65–100)	74	(35–100)	75	(35–100)
Risk Analysis System	83	(0–100)	80	(0–100)	84	(0–100)	83	(30–100)
Loss Prevention	54	(9–90)	57	(21–85)	65	(15–94)	62	(9–94)
Education	46	(0–67)	41	(0–100)	40	(11–100)	45	(0–100)
Informed Consent	82	(0–100)	94	(50–100)	88	(0–100)	88	(0–100)
Compliance	38	(0–100)	59	(10–100)	53	(0–100)	51	(0–100)
Patient/Family Relations	84	(20–100)	60	(20–100)	89	(40–100)	84	(20–100)
Claims Data Analysis	62	(0–100)	62	(0–100)	82	(0–100)	76	(0–100)
Risk Financing	31	(0–92)	19	(0–100)	33	(0–100)	30	(0–100)
Claims Management	70	(0–100)	30	(0–100)	47	(0–100)	65	(0–100)

*Activity scores (percent) are defined as the total number of items "in-place" divided by the total number possible per dimension, multiplied by 100.

management activities were implemented. For example, among those hospitals participating in integrated delivery systems, many reported that the corporate entity had centralized the risk management function. Specific activities may have been available through the corporate office, but implemented specifically within their institutions. Other programs reported they did not have formal and separate risk management programs. Instead, risk management activities were part of a patient advocate or patient ombudsman function. Still another program reported that increased competition, consolidation, and integration in the local market had led to a corporate decision to fold the risk management function into the human resources department. Issues of physician credentialing, review, and response to incidents of patient injury that are tied to risk management program activities were considered by this institution to be "employee" performance issues and best housed within the human resources function.

In general, there did not appear to be any consensus among the risk managers in the three states regarding "one best way" to design or implement a risk management program within their institutions. Instead, there were perceptions about "better practices" and a suggestion that there may be a range of alternative models that have the potential to improve quality, safety, and reduce risk. Other models include insurer-based initiatives and medical specialty-focused risk management interventions, among others.

Risk managers did, however, identify opportunities to enhance the ASHRM model. One suggestions was to review the relevance of the criteria defined by ASHRM. It has been ten years since the abstract was published. Another recommendation was that while the ASHRM model is conceptually sound, the model reflects errors of commission rather than errors of omission. Much of the marketplace is highly penetrated by managed care organizations and payment arrangements, which create incentives to omit certain approaches to diagnosis and related treatments. The consequences of these actions may not be apparent for many years to come, creating concerns about how to best manage this emerging exposure. The model designed by AHSRM is based on the assumption that injuries are the result of committed acts. Thus, in the ASHRM model, an important focus of an effective risk management program, is to design systems that utilize incident reporting to identify and manage potentially compensable events.

Regardless of the approach or area of activity in medicine that is the focus of a hospital- or organization-based risk management intervention, there remains an ongoing substantive and empirical challenge to defining appropriate measures of risk management program outcomes. The successful evaluation of risk management program effectiveness to promote evidence-based management is dependent upon defining and measuring outcomes. There are few if any who have been successful in reaching consensus on what is an acceptable set of measures for assessing organizational risk and defining measures that can be utilized to inform decision making, prevent injury, and improve the management of claims. Identification of incidents of patient injury continues to be a challenge. Providers remain reluctant to report adverse events. Data and systems to review and share information are under development. However, developing acceptable measures of adverse event rates, relevant measurements of claims frequency, and severity that can be compared within and across organizations remains an important challenge. Fundamentally, risk management programs are designed to prevent patient injury from occurring in the first place. Measuring the impact of injuries prevented remains a largely undeveloped area of research and program evaluation.

············
RISK MANAGEMENT PROGRAM OUTCOME MEASURES?

Consistent with the objectives of hospital risk management programs, there are a limited set of agreed upon, scientifically valid outcome measures that are both timely and meaningful in practice. As noted, the ASHRM Assessment Abstract provides a starting point for hospitals seeking to develop an effective program. However, these measures are largely subjective, relying on self-assessment using a crude scale. Other measures that are of interest but difficult to develop and compute include analysis of adverse events, measurements of claims risk and claims management practices, as well as measures of safety and quality.

Adverse Events

A primary objective of hospital risk management programs is to prevent and control patient injuries. Historically, the methods utilized to detect incidents of injury include incident reports and occurrence screens. Incident reports are limited in that providers are traditionally unwilling to report information. Occurrence screens have been broad and poorly specified, often providing more data than information. The studies conducted in California and by the Harvard researchers in which criteria were utilized to screen medical charts formed the basis of much of the early work on occurrence screens. Medical chart review to collect data on injuries continues to warrant substantial criticism.

Currently, the shift to managed care and related strategies to shape and direct provider decision making is creating a climate in which more treatments and services are omitted. Increasingly, incident identification requires an understanding of the clinical decision making process and tracking and analysis of services omitted, as well as acts committed to detect adverse events. Standardized measures of clinical decision making processes are not sufficiently developed to promote interhospital or interorganizational comparisons.

Claims Risk Assessment

Efforts to assess hospital and organizational risk of experiencing a medical malpractice claim are poor and challenging. A key issue for liability insurers is to estimate the likelihood that a provider will be exposed to a malpractice claim. Lack of consensus exists among the professional community about when an adverse event becomes a claim and what the organizational and clinical indicators are that suggest differences in risk among institutions. Traditionally, types of services offered has provided a starting point. Hospitals providing obstetrical, surgery, and emergency services are at greater risk than hospitals that do not offer these services. The Harvard studies have provided some recent evidence to suggest that certain organizational characteristics are associated with greater risk of exposure to claims and lawsuits. Understanding organizational risk and the development of measures to assess risk remains an important area of development. This information is critical to ensure that comparisons among organizations regarding the impact of risk management programs are relevant.

Claims Management

Another important objective of hospital risk management programs is to prevent and control losses associated with medical malpractice claims. Malpractice claims management is itself a complex phenomenon with an intricate array of processes and players. Decisions about how to address a claim once it is filed are critical for ensuring that funds are managed efficiently and effectively. Traditional measures have focused on the frequency and severity of malpractice claims—that is, the number of claims and the amount spent on claims. Opportunities exist in defining more specific and standardized measures of claims management practices particularly ones that incorporate a time dimension. For example, early intervention to address an adverse event before it becomes a claim is critical. Once a claim is made, managing financial losses and reducing time to resolution of a claim can lower expenses.

Safety and Quality

Since the 1980s, there has been an important and ongoing discussion and belief among policy makers and managers that risk management should overlap with quality management initiatives within organizations. Currently, the discussion of both risk and quality has evolved into a discussion of patient safety.[33] The recent report from the Institute of Medicine (IOM) on error in medicine provides a detailed discussion of the emerging literature on patient injury rates, and risk and quality approaches to improving patient safety. In its current form, the discussion of safety should be treated as a core value within organizations. For the first time in history, health care providers are attempting to define and measure how this value is transmitted and managed within organizations. Efforts to produce assessments of safety and safe cultures are currently underway. For example, models of how complex systems fail, adapted from other industries, are helping to frame our approach to addressing medical injury and improving patient safety.[34] Outcome measures of safety and quality should be developed and assessed for their relevance and use in managing risk.

Evaluation Studies of Risk Management Program Effectiveness

Despite the difficulties in measuring outcomes of risk management programs, to date there have been a handful of research studies that have attempted to relate health care risk management activities in hospitals to improvements in malpractice claims experience. As noted, these investigations only provide limited insight into the true impact of risk management programs, given the complex relationship that exists between injuries and claims.

MARYLAND HOSPITAL STUDY

One of the most influential studies of hospital risk management program effectiveness was conducted by Morlock and Malitz.[35] In this study, researchers examined relationships between hospital risk management activity among forty acute care hospitals in Maryland and their medical malpractice claims experience. Using data from a 1980 survey of hospital risk management activity, the researchers described risk management program components including policies for handling medical incidents and characteristics of educational programs offered on quality, safety, and risk. The medical malpractice claims experience of hospitals was assessed based on closed claims data for incidents occurring between 1980 and 1982. All claims utilized in the analysis were closed by 1987.

Malpractice claims were aggregated for each hospital. Indicators were constructed to measure the total number of filed malpractice claims per hospital bed, the number of filed claims per 100 hospital beds, the number of filed claims settled privately per 100 hospital beds, total dollars awarded by the court system per bed, and total dollars in private settlements per bed. These claims were examined for both claims arising from all hospital incidents and for those claims in which hospitals were named as defendants. Claims were adjusted for hospital bed size and the volume of services provided by developing an index measure. Although crude, this measure was assumed to adjust for differences in hospital exposure to risk.

The analysis indicated that after adjusting for differences in risk, the malpractice claims experience of hospitals with the following risk management activities in place was significantly better:

1. A policy of notifying clinical chiefs of adverse medical incidents.
2. A policy of specifying who had responsibility for informing patients and families of errors.
3. Governing board receipt of risk management reports on a regular basis.
4. Governing board oversight of risk management or quality assurance activities.
5. Education efforts concerning the responsibilities of physicians and nurses in quality assurance and risk management.

The results of this academic research investigation of Maryland hospitals remain the only empirical support for hospital risk management programs.[36,37]

CLINICAL INDICATOR RESEARCH

The most recent evidence of risk management effectiveness has come from the professional liability insurance provider community. It reflects ongoing work in the area of risk management services research including design, development, implementation, and creation of clinical indicators of program performance. MMI Companies, Inc., recently published a report examining the impact of its risk management approach on the malpractice claims experience of its clients.

A key element of the MMI approach to risk management is the development of clinical indicator programs in high risk medical specialties. According to a recent report from MMI in which twelve years of data are summarized and analyzed, there is strong evidence to suggest that their clinical risk modification programs are helping to lower the cost of malpractice claims. For example, in one of several analyses over time, MMI indicates that hospitals in full compliance with their clinical guidelines in emergency services, perinatal, and perioperative services have a significantly lower average cost per malpractice claim than hospitals with less than full compliance. Further analysis of this data suggested that full adherence to MMI guidelines in all three areas combined reduced the average cost per claim by almost $70,000. Moreover, hospitals in this category had average claims costs of $2,834 in comparison to average claims costs of $72,767 among hospitals with no compliance.

···········

FUTURE OF RISK MANAGEMENT EFFECTIVENESS STUDIES—EVALUATION IN A CHANGING ENVIRONMENT

Evaluating the effectiveness of health care risk management programs continues to present a number of challenges. The marketplace continues to change. Integration and managing care remain quixotic goals. In the profession of health care risk management, there no consensus among the profession regarding the design and development of risk management programs. As noted, recent studies indicate there is wide variation in commitment in the level of risk management activity among hospitals. In addition, defining outcome measures that can be tied to specific risk management activities in a meaningful way is difficult and a relatively new area of research and risk management program administration. Further, much of our knowledge about what works in risk management continues to come from expert opinion, descriptive research, and a very small number of scientifically based studies of the effectiveness of risk management programs.

Although "better practices" in the profession are evident, it is clear that insufficient attention has been directed toward the continued development of new tools that help demonstrate value-added risk management. The ASHRM Assessment Abstract, for example, has been available for nearly a decade. Its use by professionals seems limited. Evaluation of the tool has only recently been initiated, an activity that should be led by the profession.

As market pressure continues to increase and risk managers are called to demonstrate the value-added of their programs, an important issue for the profession is to consider taking on the challenge of defining the next steps in risk management program evaluation. Similar to the past, perhaps a first step toward this goal is to utilize the professional association of ASHRM and its state-affiliated chapters to create an interdisciplinary group of professionals including physicians, nurses, risk managers, and health service researchers, among others, to begin to address these issues.

As this group comes together, they should start by recognizing and defining the areas of overlap with quality and patient safety inherent in risk management. Although well appreciated conceptually, risk management is not independent of activities to improve quality of patient care or to enhance efforts to improve patient safety. In fact, from a historical perspective, safety and risk have been linked as organizational program activities since the early 1970s.[38] As part of its effort to define the next direction for risk management program development and measures of effectiveness, attention needs to be directed toward developing operational definitions of differences and core sets of activities that are independent of safety and quality and unique to managing risk. Then, risk managers can begin to lead the design and development of an evaluation strategy that can integrate and manage across these core functions in the related areas of quality, safety, and risk.

As noted, the history of risk management is currently tied in large part to success stories based on faith and anecdote rather than quantitative assessments of program performance. The future of risk management program success, however, will require that the profession develop a strategy that begins with evidenced-based management practices. Again, risk managers themselves must respond to the call for action to share the learning about defining the models, tools, and approaches to measuring the impact of their activities.

To continue the dialogue and enhance professional practice in evaluating risk management program effectiveness, risk management professionals must also continue to utilize and work in partnership with ASHRM and other professional risk organizations to create and experiment with new models and tools to help demonstrate value-added risk management. As the nation continues to struggle with issues surrounding patient injury, patient safety, and improving quality, the call goes out to the profession to reactivate its historical role as a leader role in patient injury prevention.

....
CONCLUSION

The purpose of this chapter has been to highlight some of the key issues that pertain to the evaluation of health care risk management programs. Hospitals played a major role in this discussion. Despite many efforts to create change in factors that contribute to incidents of patient injury in hospitals, these institutions continue to be a place where many of the most severe and disabling medical injuries occur.

To help risk managers begin to reframe and rethink approaches to developing hospital risk management program assessment tools in the future, this chapter also presented some of the history of medical injury in hospitals and a conceptual framework for defining the objectives of hospital risk management program interventions. To date, this framework remains one of the most comprehensive approaches to describing the multidimensional character of the problem of medical injury. Although the focus here has been to identify the role and objectives of hospital risk management programs, it also provides a powerful framework for areas of opportunity to think through strategies for relating to quality improvement and emerging patient safety initiatives.

In addition, this chapter presented information and reviewed recent research on current efforts to adopt a hospital risk management program assessment model based on the recommendations of ASHRM. A key finding from the research, noted previously, is that there is wide variation in institutional commitment to development hospital risk assessment programs. Further research is needed to identify and understand the factors that may help explain this observed variation.

Finally, this chapter discussed the future of health care risk management and issued a call to the profession to continue to pursue a partnership strategy and to reactivate its role as a leader in the patient injury prevention and patient safety movement.

Endnotes

1. Morlock, L. L., and others. "Medical Liability and Clinical Risk Management." *Managing Quality of Care in a Cost Focused Environment.* Tampa, Fla.: American College of Physician Executives, 1999.

2. HCFA Manual, 1978.

3. U.S. General Accounting Office. *Health Care Initiatives in Hospital Risk Management.* Washington, D.C.: GAO/HRD-89-79, 1989.

4. Morlock, L. L., and others. "Medical Liability and Clinical Risk Management." *Managing Quality of Care in a Cost Focused Environment.* Tampa, Fla.: American College of Physician Executives, 1999.

5. Nat'l Assoc. of Ins. Comm., 1980.

6. Morlock, L. L., and others. "Medical Liability and Clinical Risk Management." *Managing Quality of Care in a Cost Focused Environment.* Tampa, Fla.: American College of Physician Executives, 1999.

7. Danzon, P. M. *Medical Malpractice: Theory, Evidence, and Public Policy.* Cambridge, Mass.: Harvard University Press, 1985.

8. Brennan, T. A., and others. "Incidence of Adverse Events and Negligence in Hospitalized Patients. Results of the Harvard Medical Practice Study-I." *New England Journal of Medicine, 324*(6), Feb. 7, 1991, pp. 370–376.

9. Weiler, P. C. "Toward No-Fault Compensation/Organizational Liability." *Medical Malpractice On Trial.* Cambridge, Mass.: Harvard University Press, 1990.

10. Thomas, E. J., Studdert, D. M., Newhouse, J. P., and others. "Costs of Medical Injuries in Utah and Colorado." *Inquiry, 36,* 1999, pp. 255–264.

11. Kohn, L. T., Corrigan, J. M., Donaldson, M. S. "To Err is Human: Building a Safer Health System." Institute of Medicine, Washington, D.C.: National Academy Press, 1999.

12. Danzon, P. M. *Medical Malpractice: Theory, Evidence, and Public Policy.* Cambridge, Mass.: Harvard University Press, 1985.

13. *Ibid.*

14. Morlock, L. L., and others. "Medical Liability and Clinical Risk Management." *Managing Quality of Care in a Cost Focused Environment.* Tampa, Fla.: American College of Physician Executives, 1999.

15. Mills, D. H (ed.). *California Medical Association and California Hospital Association's Report on Medical Insurance Feasibility Study.* Sacramento, Calif.: Sutter Publications, 1980.

16. Orlikoff, J. E., and Vanagunas, A. M. *Malpractice Prevention and Liability Control for Hospitals* (2nd ed.). Chicago: American Hospital Association, 1988.

17. Morlock, L. L., and others. "Medical Liability and Clinical Risk Management." *Managing Quality of Care in a Cost Focused Environment.* Tampa, Fla.: American College of Physician Executives, 1999.

18. Wade, R. D. *Risk Management HPL: Hospital Professional Liability Primer* (1st ed.). Columbus: Ohio Hospital Insurance Company, 1983.

19. Monagle, J. F. *Risk Management: A Guide for Health Care Professionals.* Rockville, Md.: Aspen Publications, 1985.

20. Troyer, G. T., Salman, S. L. (eds.). *Handbook of Healthcare Risk Management.* Rockville, Md.: Aspen Systems Corp., 1986.

21. Orlikoff and Vanagunas, 1977.

22. Orlikoff, J. E., and Vanagunas, A. M. *Malpractice Prevention and Liability Control for Hospitals* (2nd ed.). Chicago: American Hospital Association, 1988.

23. Harpster, L. M., and Veach, M. S. (eds.). *Risk Management Handbook for Health Care Facilities.* American Society for Health Care Risk Management: American Hospital Association, 1989.

24. Morlock and Malitz, 1991.

25. Morlock, L. L., and others. "Medical Liability and Clinical Risk Management." *Managing Quality of Care in a Cost Focused Environment.* Tampa, Fla.: American College of Physician Executives, 1999.

26. American Society for Healthcare Risk Management (ASHRM). *Hospital Risk Management Self-Assessment Manual.* Chicago: American Hospital Association, 1991.

27. Monagle, J. F. *Risk Management: A Guide for Health Care Professionals.* Rockville, Md.: Aspen Publications, 1985.

28. Orlikoff, J. E., and Vanagunas, A. M. *Malpractice Prevention and Liability Control for Hospitals* (2nd ed.). Chicago: American Hospital Association, 1988.

29. Wade, R. D. *Risk Management HPL: Hospital Professional Liability Primer* (1st ed.). Columbus: Ohio Hospital Insurance Company, 1983.

30. Ziegenfuss, J. T., and Perlman, H. "Decreasing Medical Malpractice." *Health Care Management Review, 14*(4), 1989, pp. 67–75.

31. Morlock, L. L., Cassirer, C., and Malitz, F. E., "Hospital Risk Management and Professional Liability Claims Experience in Maryland." *Final Report: Agency for Health Care Policy & Research,* Grant Number 1 RO1 HS06735, 1997.

32. Kohn, L. T., Corrigan, J. M., Donaldson, M. S. "To Err is Human: Building a Safer Health System." Institute of Medicine, Washington, D.C.: National Academy Press, 1999.

34. *Ibid.*

35. Cook, R. I. *A Brief Look at the New Look in Error, Safety and Failure of Complex Systems.* Cognitive Technologies Laboratory. Chicago: University of Chicago, 1999.

36. Morlock and Malitz, 1991.

37. U.S. General Accounting Office. *Health Care Initiatives in Hospital Risk Management.* Washington, D.C.: GAO/HRD-89-79, 1989.

38. U.S. General Accounting Office. *Testimony-Medical Malpractice: Experience With Efforts To Address Problems.* Washington, D.C.: GAO/T-HRD-93-24, 1993.

39. Wade, R. D. *Risk Management HPL: Hospital Professional Liability Primer* (1st ed.). Columbus: Ohio Hospital Insurance Company, 1983.

Suggested Readings

American Hospital Association. *Medical Malpractice Task Force Report on Tort Reform and Compendium of Professional Liability Early Warning Systems for Health Care Providers.* Chicago: American Hospital Association, 1986.

American Society for Healthcare Risk Management (ASHRM). *Hospital Risk Management Self-Assessment Manual.* Chicago: American Hospital Association, 1991.

Brennan, T. A., and others. "Incidence of Adverse Events and Negligence in Hospitalized Patients. Results of the Harvard Medical Practice Study-I." *New England Journal of Medicine, 324*(6), Feb. 7, 1991, pp. 370–376.

Cassirer, C. *Hospital Risk Management Programs in Maryland (1995).* Baltimore: Johns Hopkins University, 1997.

Cook, R. I. *A Brief Look at the New Look in Error, Safety and Failure of Complex Systems.* Cognitive Technologies Laboratory. Chicago: University of Chicago, 1999.

Danzon, P. M. *Medical Malpractice: Theory, Evidence, and Public Policy.* Cambridge, Mass.: Harvard University Press, 1985.

Harpster, L. M., and Veach, M. S. (eds.). *Risk Management Handbook for Health Care Facilities.* American Society for Health Care Risk Management: American Hospital Association, 1989.

Institute of Medicine. Joint Commission on Accreditation of Healthcare Organizations (JCAHO). *Accreditation Manual for Hospitals.* Chicago, Ill., 1989.

Kohn, L. T., Corrigan, J. M., Donaldson, M. S. "To Err is Human: Building a Safer Health System." Institute of Medicine, Washington, D.C.: National Academy Press, 1999.

Mills, D. H (ed.). *California Medical Association and California Hospital Association's Report on Medical Insurance Feasibility Study.* Sacramento, Calif.: Sutter Publications, 1980.

Monagle, J. F. *Risk Management: A Guide for Health Care Professionals.* Rockville, Md.: Aspen Publications, 1985.

Morlock, L. L., and Malitz, F. E. "Do Hospital Risk Management Programs Make A Difference?: Relationships Between Risk Management Program Activities and Hospital Malpractice Claims Experience." *Law and Contemporary Problems, 54*(2), Nov. 1991, pp. 1–22.

Morlock, L. L., and others. "Medical Liability and Clinical Risk Management." *Managing Quality of Care in a Cost Focused Environment.* Tampa, Fla.: American College of Physician Executives, 1999.

Morlock, L. L., Cassirer, C., and Malitz, F. E., "Hospital Risk Management and Professional Liability Claims Experience in Maryland." *Final Report: Agency for Health Care Policy & Research,* Grant Number 1 RO1 HS06735, 1997.

National Association of Insurance Commissioners. *Malpractice Claims: Medical Malpractice Closed Claims, 1975–1980.* Milwaukee, Wis.: National Association of Insurance Commissioners, 1978.

Orlikoff, J. E., and Vanagunas, A. M. *Malpractice Prevention and Liability Control for Hospitals* (2nd ed.). Chicago: American Hospital Association, 1988.

Smith, D. G., and Wheeler, J. R. C. "Strategies and Structures for Hospital Risk Management Programs." *Health Care Management Review, 17*(3), Summer 1992, pp. 9–17.

Thomas, E. J., Studdert, D. M., Newhouse, J. P., and others. "Costs of Medical Injuries in Utah and Colorado." *Inquiry 36,* 1999, pp. 255–264.

Troyer, G. T., Salman, S. L. (eds.). *Handbook of Healthcare Risk Management.* Rockville, Md.: Aspen Systems Corp., 1986.

U.S. General Accounting Office. *Medical Malpractice: Characteristics of Claims Closed in 1984.* Washington, D.C.: GAO/HRD-87-55, 1987.

U.S. General Accounting Office. *Insurance: Profitability of the Medical Malpractice and General Liability Lines.* Washington, D.C.: GAO/GGD-87-67, 1987a.

U.S. General Accounting Office. *Health Care Initiatives in Hospital Risk Management.* Washington, D.C.: GAO/HRD-89-79, 1989.

U.S. General Accounting Office. *Testimony-Medical Malpractice: Experience With Efforts To Address Problems.* Washington, D.C.: GAO/T-HRD-93-24, 1993.

Wade, R. D. *Risk Management HPL: Hospital Professional Liability Primer* (1st ed.). Columbus: Ohio Hospital Insurance Company, 1983.

Weiler, P. C. "Toward No-Fault Compensation/Organizational Liability." *Medical Malpractice On Trial.* Cambridge, Mass.: Harvard University Press, 1990.

Ziegenfuss, J. T., and Perlman, H. "Decreasing Medical Malpractice." *Health Care Management Review, 14*(4), 1989, pp. 67–75.

36

Client and Customer Satisfaction

Frances Kurdwanowski
Maria D. Lain

Health care organizations must make customer satisfaction a guiding principle in today's competitive environment. It makes good business sense to strive for excellent service and positive provider-patient relationships. Maintaining good relationships requires an effort to understand and meet the expectations of those who depend on the health care delivery system. In turn, systems need providers to deliver that care. Health care providers not only exercise their skills, but must do so by creating a positive environment for the patient.

When assuming a patient-centered approach to risk management—that is, that all endeavors of a health care system are ultimately intended to benefit the patient—it makes sense to concentrate on the patient side of the customer satisfaction equation. Patients realize that rapid change is occurring in the health care field. They are not sure how or why, but they do know that price and cost containment are at the root of health care reform and that patients and their expectations seem to have lost their preeminent place in the minds of health care providers.

IMPORTANCE OF CUSTOMER SATISFACTION

Recent research indicates that the critical factor in consumer satisfaction with health care providers is quality of service. Customers' perceptions of their interactions with their health care provider are every bit as important to them as the provider's clinical reputation.[1] What people expect and care about is consistent, timely service from caring, competent professionals. From a purely risk-management perspective, dissatisfied customers represent an exposure to financial loss. In today's competitive environment, customers are more likely to sever their relationship with the health care provider with whom they are dissatisfied and seek out one who meets their expectations of service. Loss of customers is compounded by word of mouth. The provider loses not only the dissatisfied customer, but potentially everyone to whom customers voice their dissatisfaction, such as family members and friends.[2]

···········

MEASUREMENT OF CUSTOMER SATISFACTION

The simplest and best way to find out what the customer expects from his or her health care provider is to ask and then listen. This can be done in various ways. For example:

- Surveying customers after a health care encounter to determine if their expectations were met.

- Conducting administrative rounds within the facility to determine if customers' expectations are being met.

- Employing focus groups of noncustomers to describe what they expect from a health care organization; inquiries might focus on certain demographic groups or groups that have certain purchasing characteristics that the health care organization wishes to capture or penetrate.

- Conducting exit polls or telemarketing surveys within the organization's service area.

Surveys may be quantitative or qualitative. Quantitative surveys use close-ended questions that measure patient satisfaction by counting or by use of scales. They are best suited to determining the degree of satisfaction with various attributes and to assessing change as health care services are modified. Qualitative surveys use open-ended questions that allow patients to express their thoughts and concerns in their own words. Qualitative answers are adequate for obtaining patients' attitudes; however, a quantifiable rating scale attaching numbers to performance, such as a, rating from one to ten, yields a more refined response. The most commonly used scales are five-point scales, asking for ratings from excellent to poor or extremely satisfied to not satisfied.

Measurement and listening systems that will allow the organization to provide valid and reliable feedback can be very helpful to the risk manager with risk identification. These can include:

- *One-on-one interaction with the customer.* This can be done face to face or by telephone.

- *Data collection via surveys, mail, phone, or e-commerce.* All are effective when the response rate is at least 50 percent. Random sampling can be used to secure economies of scale. Reputable market research companies are able to provide assistance to ensure that the survey instrument is valid and reliable.

- *Internal customer surveys.* Within an organization there are departments that serve each other. An internal survey can determine how effectively needs are being met and exceeded.

- *Focus groups.* They may also be used to dig deeper into an area that requires performance improvement, and also to better understand customers' expectations and the organization's performance against them.

- *Positive commendation and complaint resolution systems.* These provide a balanced perspective on current "hot spots" and areas of excellence within an organization. The objective of focusing on both the positive and the negative is to place in perspective the strength of positive feedback health care organizations receive by comparison to the negatives and then, among the negatives, how many result in significant risk to the hospital. Using this mechanism, an evaluation of an issue will become a learning experience and not a blaming experience. Multidisciplinary performance improvement teams may focus on positively impacting the work environment and each of the customers served. Some of these teams may do the following:

Communicate the vision and measurement importance for the organization's success.

Communicate results using a balance score card approach that reports frequently and honestly on performance against satisfaction, and promotes the opportunity for employee learning and growth, operations' effectiveness, and better financial performance.

Communicate best practices so that others in the organization may learn.

- *Rewards and recognition.* Create opportunities to celebrate with each of the jobs well done.

- *"Just do it" groups.* This *can* work at getting rid of the irritants and barriers that impact how service is delivered.

- *Coordinated teams.* Organize teams to: (1) evaluate products and services and provide those that best meet the needs of the customers, (2) positively impact the staff through performance evaluations that measure service quality, competency, and accountability for overall organizational performance, and (3) seek ways to involve the community at large to improve communication, share knowledge, and provide the ability for continuous feedback.

The value of creating a positive work environment may be seen when:

- Everyone understands each other's needs and there is no guesswork about the mission or goals of the organization.

- Positive standards are endorsed by positive behaviors.

- Systems and processes are in alignment with customer needs.

- Everyone is accountable for doing the right thing.

Professionals from the academic environment and marketing industry can help the organization decide what sampling technique best fits the organization's needs. They are also best suited to help with the development of survey instruments. The most important consideration in developing a strategy for understanding customer expectations is knowing what questions to ask. Exactly what the organization wants to find out and what questions will elicit that information must be carefully considered. Questioning must be done in such a way that the potential for bias is minimized and the objectivity of the inquiry is maximized. Typically, the development of questions is best left to professionals who specialize in this type of inquiry.

SURVEY ADMINISTRATION

Surveys may be conducted in person, by telephone, or through direct mail. The strengths and weaknesses of each method should be weighed before selecting one.

In-person and telephone surveys afford certain advantages to both the patient and the organization. With these methods of gathering feedback, the patient has the opportunity to ask questions about the survey and the interviewer has the opportunity to clarify questions and to probe for more information. In addition, because the interaction between patient and interviewer is more personal than that afforded by a written survey, in-person and telephone surveys may project a more "caring" image for the organization. On the other hand, interaction between patient and interviewer can be a double-edged sword. The interviewer must be well trained and pleasant to talk to, or the calls can do more harm than good. Moreover, if calls are lengthy or come at an inconvenient time, the respondent may become impatient. Studies show that as calls approach the fifteen-minute mark, respondents become uncomfortable.[3]

Some organizations prefer to use direct mail questionnaires because they are less intrusive. That is, patients can complete them at their convenience. However, response rates are usually less than 30 percent. Response rates may be raised if multiple mailings occur and the organization makes follow-up phone calls requesting that patients respond to the questionnaire. In addition, patients are more likely to respond if the questionnaire is well-designed, short, easy to complete, and simple to return. Organizations should include a stamped, self-addressed envelope or use a business reply envelope so that only those questionnaires that are returned will be charged to the health care organization's postal account.

Written questionnaires can also be distributed to patients during their stay at the health care facility or during the discharge process. An advantage of this distribution method is that it can raise response rates. A drawback is that patients who are asked to complete a questionnaire in an office or hospital setting may fear that their anonymity may not be preserved. This fear can compel patients to rate services more favorably than they otherwise might. Patients may also feel pressured to complete the questionnaire quickly. Less candid responses may result in high satisfaction rate, but they undermine the effort's validity.

Drafting the Survey Questions

Precise survey questions produce reliable responses; ambiguous questions yield confusing answers. For example, in response to the ambiguous question, "How would you like to hear more about our services?," some patients will answer "yes" or "no," while others will say, "In the mail."[4] Also to be avoided are double-barreled questions—that is, single questions that ask about two different aspects of service. The double-barreled question, "Was the receptionist friendly and knowledgeable?" is unsuitable because a patient may wish to answer "yes" to one part of the question and "no" to the other.

Interpreting Responses

Once data are collected, they must be interpreted. Interpretation is usually performed by the professionals hired to draft the survey and interview respondents. As an alternative, organizations may wish to use one of the software packages specifically formulated to assist health care organizations in tracking and trending customers' reactions to the services they provide. Some of these packages are quite sophisticated.

FACCT Performance Measurement

There are many good reasons for organizations to evaluate how well they are meeting customers' expectations. One of the most compelling reasons is that the financial well being of the organization depends on its retaining and enhancing market share. But in these days of managed care, there is another compelling reason: purchasers are evaluating organizational performance.

Consider the growing number of coalitions formed by purchasers and health care consumer groups concerned about quality and cost. One of these coalitions, the

Foundation for Accountability (FACCT,) was founded for the purposes of evaluating, endorsing, and promoting a common set of patient-oriented measures of health care quality focused on the outcome of care.[5] The overriding goal of this initiative is to provide health care consumers with reliable indicators of the extent to which health care systems provide and manage care for entire populations, and detail outcomes data for specific conditions. Although the group's initial concern was increasing costs, its focus has broadened to include quality. FACCT defines value as a combination of costs and quality.

FACCT has developed a guidebook for performance measurement that provides an accountability framework. This framework has been designed to facilitate the collection and reporting of uniform health care information through analysis of data on consumers' health status, satisfaction, and risk factors, as well as measures for specific conditions. The framework consists of twelve global assessments that measure how well a system provides services to its enrolled population through the measurement of demographic characteristics, health status, health behaviors, and enrollee satisfaction. The framework also examines more isolated incidents or subsets of care by measuring how effectively the system provides care for enrollees when they are ill as assessed through comprehensive data-specific illnesses. The measures address five questions for each specific condition:

- How does the condition affect patients' physical and emotional abilities to live normal lives?

- How effectively do health care services delivered affect the progression of certain diseases?

- How satisfied are affected patients with the care, services, and information they have received?

- How effectively and appropriately is the health care system delivering important preventive, diagnostic, and/or treatment services?

- Are affected patients receiving care in a way that enhances functioning in their work and personal lives?[6]

These measures have been designed to transcend all health care delivery forms, but they are intended to be flexible enough to encompass all forms of care yet specific enough to take into account differing structures.

The heath care field's two main accrediting agencies, the Joint Commission on Accreditation of Healthcare Organizations (JCAHO) and the National Committee for Quality Assurance (NCQA), have incorporated FACCT measures in their respective performance measurement initiatives. The Indicator Management System (IMS), part of the JCAHO's initiative, and the Health Plan Employer Data and Information Set (HEDIS), part of the NCQA's initiatives, place importance on performance information based on the outcomes of care. From the consumer's point of view, the end result is an evaluation system that establishes uniformity, reduces the burden on health care systems, and generates comparable information on what works and who is doing the best job. This information permits customers to make meaningful comparisons about providers and plans.

INTERNALIZING A CUSTOMER-CENTERED PHILOSOPHY

Assuming that an organization has selected a valid survey technique, sampled a statistically valid and representative number of customers, and properly interpreted the collected data, the organization will have a fairly clear idea of the service expectations of the targeted customer group. How then should the organization communicate this information to the people responsible for meeting customer expectations? If follow-through does not occur, the organization will, at best, achieve only short-term gains in customer satisfaction. At worst, the organization stands to lose credibility not only with its customers, but also with its staff.

Formalizing the Philosophy

Health care organizations' efforts to improve and maintain customer satisfaction must begin with the very highest levels of authority—the board and senior management. The governing body must emphasize its commitment to customer satisfaction in the organiza-tion's mission statement, and in its statement of vision and values. This commitment must be clearly and unequivocally communicated by the chief executive officer to every level of management and through them to each and every employee, agent, contractor, physician, staff member, supplier, vendor, and consultant.

Providing the Information

The organization's marketing materials, by-laws, medical staff rules, regulations, brochures, and so on should reflect its commitment to customer satisfaction. These mate-rials can serve as a constant reminder to both the staff and the public of the importance of the customer in the institution's philosophical foundation. By committing to writing its belief in customer satisfaction, the organization provides patients and staff with a bench-mark by which to measure the service received and the care provided.

Operationalizing the Philosophy

Once the organization's customer satisfaction philosophy is formalized, it must be oper-ationalized. This is the point at which all staff, clinical as well as nonclinical, learn the skills necessary to identify and satisfy customer expectations. Essentially, the object of this step is to teach staff how to identify and respond to customer needs. Provisions should be made for instructing all employees and physicians:

- A behavioral focus emphasizing customer service and the availability of a system to assist in the resolution of conflict is an important aspect.

- Every interaction with a patient is an opportunity to represent the organization in a positive fashion.

- Patients, as customers, are not at their best. They are sick, frightened, and alone in a foreign environment. Health care providers must take customers as they find them and do their best to relieve their anxiety and exceed their expectations. The overwhelming message at this stage is that it is health care providers' privilege and responsibility to help the customers, not the other way around.

- Training and orientation must define the limits of each person's authority to address patient expectations. If problems are to be resolved early, everyone must be empow-ered to assist in the resolution process.

Most patients talk more willingly with family and friends than with hospital staff and health care providers. A recent Technical Assistance Research Program's (TARP) study indicates that only 1–5 percent of patients direct complaints to top management or designated patient advocates; 45 percent voice concerns to staff working directly with them; and 50 percent never make complaints to anyone.[7] Why is this so? Because patients:

- Think that their complaints are insignificant.
- Do not know where to direct their complaints.
- Do not think that complaints will do any good.
- Fear retribution.

The idea that customers fear communicating with their providers should be anathema to the health care field. Regardless of the setting in which health care providers consider this dilemma—hospital, physician's office, managed care organization (MCO), and so on—providers must determine why patients fear communicating with them. The availability of a multidimensional grievance process can help by providing several avenues for the recognition and resolution of patient complaints.

Grievance System

A grievance system should involve all staff, including risk management and patient relations (in the physician's office, this might be the office manager, or in the MCO, the customer relations staff), in the effort to help resolve customer satisfaction issues. The system should facilitate daily informal communication within and between departments, and it should enable the organization to track and trend issues on a periodic basis (computerized systems are of great benefit in this area).

Most important, the system should enable the organization to identify and handle grievances when they are still minor. Most litigation results from an accumulation of grievances that are never addressed; therefore, every aspect of the system should strive to improve communication between the customer and the provider and provide alternative avenues for resolution of problems. The idea throughout the process is to avoid the "mushrooming" of complaints.

Providing a Listening Ear

Most customer concerns stem from the quality of the communication between the provider and the patient. Typically, the patient feels that the physician or other provider is not listening. The key is to provide the patient with opportunities to gain a sense of control. Forums such as "care conferences," which allow the patient and/or the patient's family to address the assembled care team, go a long way toward achieving this goal. Sound preadmission teaching and the use of clinical pathways also help the patient feel that he or she is a part of the process.

The risk manager need not be the central focus of the grievance resolution process. Instead, risk management staff may serve in a facilitator role in the response to individual patient concerns, referring them to the most appropriate resource for resolution.

The organization's general grievance policy should reflect its stated philosophy regarding customer satisfaction, as well as the training and orientation provided to those who are expected to implement it. The policy should:

- List resources available for response.
- Acknowledge that every situation is different.
- Be flexible to allow for the appropriate response of individuals and resources.

Important guidelines to follow when developing the organization's general grievance policy are to:

- Treat the patient as a valued customer.
- Find out what the customer wants.
- Empathize with the customer.
- Remember that there is always more than one side to a story.
- Avoid becoming defensive.

Last, but certainly not least, the grievance system should strive to discover unexpressed complaints. Despite cutbacks and changes in health care, patients' expectations are much higher today. They understand the fallibility of the system much better than they used to and they fear being lost in it. The health care organization that is able to meet patients' expectations and allay their concerns is more likely to avoid claims stemming from an accumulation of grievances.

············

CONCLUSION

The risk manager should use survey methods for determining patient satisfaction as a risk identification tool. Someone else usually does trending and tracking of patient complaints; the risk manager should receive regular reports about those outcomes. Continual problem areas should be addressed through education and/or corrective measures.

Proficiency and tact in dealing with people are essential in maintaining good relationships with groups within the health care organization, as well as with those outside it—the valued customers.

Endnotes

1. Krowinski, W., and Steiber, S. *Measuring and Managing Patient Satisfaction.* Chicago: American Hospital Publishing, 1996, pp. 43–44.
2. *Ibid.,* p. 11.
3. Anwar, R. "Get the Most From Your Patient Satisfaction Survey." *The Physician's Advisor,* June 1996, pp. 6–7.
4. *Ibid.,* p. 10.
5. Wilson, E. "The Last Word on Patient Satisfaction: Getting the FACCTS Straight." *Health Systems Review,* Nov./ Dec. 1995, p. xx.
6. *Ibid.,* p. 15.
7. Krowinski, W., and Steiber, S. *Measuring and Managing Patient Satisfaction.* Chicago: American Hospital Publishing, 1996, pp. 43–44.

Suggested Readings

"A Week in the Life of Hospital." *Time Magazine, 15*, Oct. 12, 1998, p. 152.

Aiken, and others. "Downsizing the Hospital Nursing Workforce." *Health Affairs, 15*, Fall 1996, pp. 13–15.

Buckingham, M., and Coffman, C. *First, Break All The Rules: What the World's Greatest Managers Do Differently.* The Gallup Organization: Simon & Schuster, 1999.

Carroll, R. (ed.). *Risk Management Handbook for Healthcare Organizations* (2nd ed.). Chicago: American Society for Healthcare Risk Management and American Hospital Publishing Co., 1977, pp. 66–73.

Lickerman, D. "Reducing Managed Care Risk Through Better Communication." *Journal of Healthcare Risk Management,* Fall 1994, pp. 24–29.

National Committee for Quality Assurance (NCQA) www.ncqa.org

Para, P. "Patient Relations for Modern Times." *Journal of Healthcare Risk Management,* Fall 1997, pp. 23–29.

"Risk Management Pearls for Physicians: Managing Risk in a Managed Care Environment." *ASHRM/AHA,* 1995, pp. 4–5, 9.

Rozovsky, L. "Risk Management and the Media." *Journal of Healthcare Risk Management,* Summer 1995, pp. 24–29.

"Service Excellence: Service Quality Strategies of America's Leading Health Systems." Washington, D.C.: The Advisory Board Company, 1998.

Shindul-Rothschild, J., and others. "Where Have All the Nurses Gone? Final Results of Our Patient Care Survey." *American Journal of Nursing,* March 1996, pp. 5–6.

St. Paul Fire and Marine Insurance Co. "The Digest: A Medical Liability and Risk Management Newsletter: Physician Behaviors that Lead to Malpractice Claiming," Spring 1997.

The National Coalition on Health Care. "How Americans Perceive the Health Care System," January 1997.

37

Accreditation, Licensure, Certification, and Surveying Bodies

Kathleen Stillwell

The health care industry has undergone tremendous transition during recent years. One of the most significant changes has been the shift of substantial portions of the population into integrated managed care delivery systems. With these changes there has been an increased emphasis on measuring the quality of care provided by the health care systems. Additionally, there has been increased public and private attention on the organizations assigned or related to health care organizational oversight.

Accrediting organizations, licensure, certification, and surveying bodies have continued their efforts to establish requirements and regulatory standards that are subject to review by federal, state, and private organizations. While it may not be the risk manager's job to manage or monitor compliance with published standards, it is incumbent upon the risk manager to be familiar with the organizations responsible for oversight. Failure to meet standards may adversely impact the health care organization's ability to operate, provide services, meet contract requirements, or to receive funding from sources that require compliance with specific standards.

The purpose of this chapter is to provide an overview of the topic to acquaint the risk manager with resources and information appropriate to meet the challenge of identifying and understanding the variety of organizations responsible for health care organizational licensure, accreditation, certification, and survey.

This chapter reviews the major bodies that oversee both mandatory and voluntary activities associated with licensure, accreditation, certification, and survey. It examines the rationales for participating in these activities and the role that the risk management program may play in the process. In some cases, states and local jurisdictions maintain the right to regulate health care through licensure of institutions as well as individual practitioners. In all states, there are prescriptive regulations and rules that describe the compliance elements that must be in place before a health care enterprise can do business. Health care organizations are subject to specific mandatory review and may also participate in voluntary accreditation and inspection programs that apply to either the organization as a whole or specialized areas within the health care industry.

RISK MANAGEMENT RESPONSIBILITIES

Risk management program requirements shall continue to expand. It is important to note that nearly every single accreditation, certification, and regulatory requirement requires some form of risk management activity. At the same time it should be recognized that health care organizations must demonstrate an intent and willingness to comply with published standards and regulations if they intend to succeed in stay in the industry.

Patient safety, protection, and compliance with standards and regulations require management of outcomes data. The best qualified health care organizations are focusing how to deliver safe, effective, and efficient care without compromising essential elements of control. One way to improve is to identify the inefficient areas of the system and devote attention to the process of continuous improvement. This means health care organizations working together to identify opportunities to improve and then designing program infrastructures that support the design. Health care organizations that do not attend to this priority shall suffer the consequences of increased risks, diminished financial return, and of course, a lack of public confidence.

The health care risk manager is in a unique position to make a difference when he or she is knowledgeable and resourceful about the issues that must be addressed by the health care organization. The risk manager who understands how to effectively integrate risk management techniques for achieving compliance with standards and regulatory requirements will be viewed as a true value-added component to the health care delivery system.

WHY PARTICIPATE IN VOLUNTARY ACCREDITATION ACTIVITIES?

Given the staggering amount of mandated regulation in health care, it is reasonable to ask why organizations participate in additional programs, most of which are "voluntary." There are significant reasons to participate voluntarily. Perhaps the best reason is that it is the right thing to do to demonstrate an organization's commitment to following established standards and regulations. The principle of providing the best possible service and looking for ways to constantly improve that service is a core part of the medical ethic for individual caregivers as well as provider organizations. Moreover, the public demands it. Public accountability is fulfilled through a number of different activities. Licensure, accreditation, and certification make up just one category but are important in ensuring that an organization meets or exceeds contemporary expectations of quality, safety, and performance improvement.

Participation also makes good business sense. Although participation in many of the basic programs is necessary just to be in business, other programs enhance the organization in important ways. Through ongoing benchmarking and performance improvement programs, service quality and cost-effectiveness are addressed. Participation in voluntary programs can also present marketing and recruiting advantages. From a risk management perspective, failure to meet licensure, accreditation, certification, and survey requirements may directly impact on the health care organization's loss exposure.

LICENSURE, ACCREDITATION, AND CERTIFICATION ACTIVITIES

Licensure, accreditation, and certification activities can be divided between mandatory and voluntary functions, although some, such as deemed status relationships, play a dual role. Mandatory functions include organizational licensure; individual health care professional licensure; specific licensure for activities such as handling radioactive materials or preparing and shipping blood or blood components; approval to participate in federal funding programs through either government inspection or deemed status; and compliance with broadly applicable regulatory programs such as workplace safety, equal rights, and the Americans with Disabilities Act.

Accreditation and certification programs make up the "voluntary" activities and generally are self-sponsored by the industry or by specialty organizations. Virtually all these entities are nongovernmental.

THE RISK MANAGEMENT ROLE

The health care risk manager should make it a priority to be aware of the multitude of organizations performing licensure, accreditation, certification, and survey of health care organizations. The risk management program description may include participation in the processes associated with the oversight activities. Loss of funding due to any violation of regulatory or accreditation standards and/or public disclosure of a failure to meet established standards may result in an adverse effect on the health care organization's business operations and/or pending or future litigation.

It is critical for the risk manager to understand the impact of compliance with regulatory, licensure, certification, and accrediting bodies.

MANDATORY SURVEYING BODIES

Mandatory surveying bodies are required for health care organizations to operate and obtain a license. This is a requirement in every state in the United States.

Department of Health and Human Services

The Department of Health and Human Services (DHHS) is the United States government's principal agency for protecting the health of all Americans and providing essential human services, especially for the population of those least able to help themselves.

The DHHS includes more than 300 programs covering a wide spectrum of activities. The DHHS works closely with all state and local governments, and many of the DHHS funded services are provided at the local level by state or county agencies. The Public Health Service Operating Divisions of the DHHS includes such organizations as:

- National Institutes of Health.
- Centers for Disease Control and Prevention.
- Indian Health Services.
- Substance Abuse and Mental Health Services Administration.
- Food and Drug Administration.
- Agency for Toxic Substances and Disease Registry.

- Health Resources and Services Administration.
- Agency for Health Care Policy and Research.

The Human Services Operating Divisions include such organizations as:

- Health Care Financing Administration.
- Administration for Children and Families.
- Administration on Aging.

Health Care Financing Administration

In the public sector, the most visible certification organization is the Health Care Financing Administration (HCFA), which oversees payment for most of the health care covered by the federal government. This federal agency administers the Medicare, Medicaid, and Child Health Insurance programs. HCFA provides health insurance for more than 74 million Americans. In addition to providing health insurance, HCFA performs a number of quality-focused activities, including regulation of laboratory testing, surveys and certification of health care facilities (including nursing homes, home health agencies, intermediate care facilities for the mentally retarded, and hospitals), development of coverage policies, and quality of care improvement.

HCFA oversees payments that can make up more than 50 percent of a health care organization's revenue. With the onset of federal Medicare and Medicaid law in the mid-1960s, federal statutes and regulations defined the requirements for health care organizations to participate in these programs. These requirements, known as Conditions for Participation, define the organization structure and function requirements, with particular attention paid to service quality and appropriateness.

Many of the HCFA requirements focus on documentation required in the clinical record to justify care and the payment for care. HCFA oversees these requirements by either inspecting organizations directly, contracting with state health departments to inspect them, or relying on private accrediting organizations such as the Joint Commission for Healthcare Organizations (JCAHO) or the American Osteopathic Association (AOA).

To ensure public and expert involvement in its programs, HCFA maintains standing committees. Meetings of the committees are open to the public and utilized as a mechanism at provide advice or to make recommendations on a variety of issues related to HCFA's responsibilities. Additionally, HCFA sponsors special projects and initiatives in response to national issues challenging the health care industry. The following standing committees have been established:

- Practicing Physicians Advisory Council.
- Citizens Advisory Panel on Medicare Education.
- Negotiated Rulemaking Committee on the Medicare Ambulance Fee Schedule.
- Negotiated Rulemaking Committee on Coverage and Administrative Policies for Clinical Diagnostic Laboratory Tests.
- Medicare Coverage Advisory Committee.
- Competitive Pricing Advisory Committee.
- Health Care Financing Administration Management Advisory Committee.
- Negotiated Rulemaking Committee on Solvency Standards for Provider Sponsored Organizations.

When HCFA grants deemed status to private organizations, it reserves the right to assess their performance. It does this through an ongoing effort known as a validation survey, in which HCFA conducts the inspection of a health care entity that has been privately accredited and compares its results with those of the deemed accrediting organization. HCFA also monitors individual patient care through a series of contracted relationships with professional review organizations (PROs), and through its own compliance programs, monitored by its inspector general.

Health care organizations can be excluded from participation in Medicare if they fail to comply with any element of these activities. For more information, visit www.hcfa.gov, the Web site of the Health Care Financing Administration. For a list of regional offices of the HCFA, see Exhibit 37.1.

State Health Department

The other highly visible public entity is the state health department, which is the agency generally charged with overseeing health care organizations' right to do business. Not surprisingly, the approach taken by states varies tremendously and often is reflective of the "culture" of the state with respect to regulation. These activities include review activities that are regularly scheduled, independent inspections or surveys, to deemed status

EXHIBIT 37.1.   Regional Offices of the Health Care Financing Administration

Region I	*Region VI*
CT, ME, MA, NH, RI, VT	AR, LA, NM, OK, TX
Room 1211	Room 1935
JFK Federal Building	1200 Main Tower Building
Boston, MA 02203	Dallas, TX 75202
617-565-1322	214-767-6301
Region II	*Region VII*
NJ, NY, PR, VI	IA, KS, MO, NE
Room 3821	New Federal Office Building
26 Federal Plaza	601 East 12th Street, Room 242
New York, NY 10278	Kansas City, MO 64106
212-264-1121	816-426-2408
Region III	*Region VIII*
DE, DC, MD, PA, VA, WV	CO, MT, ND, SD, UT, WY
3535 Market Street	Federal Building
P.O. Box 7760	1961 Stout Street, Room 1185
Philadelphia, PA 19101	Denver, CO 80294
215-596-6571	303-844-4721
Region IV	*Region IX*
AL, FL, GA, KY, MS, NC, SC, TN	AZ, CA, HI, NV, US Pacific Islands
Suite 601	75 Hawthorne Street
101 Marietta Tower	4th Floor
Atlanta, GA 30323	San Francisco, CA 94105
404-841-2361	415-744-3679
Region V	*Region X*
IL, IN, MI, OH, WI	AK, ID, OR, WA
105 West Adams Street	2201 Sixth Avenue
15th Floor	Mail Stop RX-42
Chicago, IL 60603-6201	Seattle, WA 98121
312-353-9804	206-553-0511

relationships with private accrediting bodies, to simply reacting to tragic or highly publicized events.

In some states the inspection is directed towards high-priority areas such as credentials review and privileging programs; others take a collaborative approach that might include the JCAHO and the state medical association as a part of the review process.

············

VOLUNTARY SURVEYING BODIES

Voluntary surveying bodies are invited to participate in survey processes at the request of the health care organization. These organizations charge a fee for their services.

Joint Commission on Accreditation of Healthcare Organizations

In 1951, the American College of Physicians, the American Hospital Association, the American Medical Association, and the Canadian Medical Association joined with the American College of Surgeons to create the Joint Commission on Accreditation for Healthcare Organizations (JCAHO). This independent, not-for-profit organization was established for the primary purpose of providing voluntary accreditation.

JCAHO is dedicated to improving the quality of care in organized health care settings. The organization provides evaluation, accreditation, and consultation, and establishes standards for long-term care facilities, ambulatory health care organizations, home care agencies, hospices, hospitals, health care delivery networks, and organizations offering major mental health services. JCAHO offers accreditation to health care organizations throughout the United States.

On-site accreditation surveys are intended to assess the extent of the health care organization's compliance with applicable standards and to provide information and guidance to assist the organization with continuing performance improvement. The surveys are conducted every three years, or more frequently if a follow-up survey or revisit for compliance with recommendations is required.

As new technologies and demands impact health care organizations, JCAHO may respond with the development of a standard corresponding to identified needs. Consumer demands for accountability have influenced revisions of standards as well as the evolution of new standards. JCAHO is a major supplier of education and consultation to the health care industry and conducts more than 400 educational programs for accredited organizations and those seeking accreditation. The standards for each JCAHO accreditation program are published in a separate standards manual. JCAHO also publishes reference manuals, guides to quality improvement, accreditation survey scoring guidelines, and periodicals.

The JCAHO's official monthly journal is the *Joint Commission Journal on Quality Improvement*. The journal is available from the JCAHO Customer Service office.[1]

American Osteopathic Association

The American Osteopathic Association (AOA) has been accrediting health care facilities in the United States for more than fifty years. Since 1965, the AOA has had deemed status authority from HCFA to survey hospitals under the Medicare Conditions of Participation. The AOA is one of the only two voluntary accreditation programs in the United States authorized by HCFA to survey hospitals under Medicare. The AOA conducts an on-site survey to verify compliance with published AOA standards. The AOA has also developed published accreditation requirements for the following areas:

- Ambulatory care and surgery.
- Mental health.
- Substance abuse.
- Physical rehabilitation medicine facilities.[2]

National Committee for Quality Assurance

The National Committee for Quality Assurance (NCQA) is a private, not-for-profit organization that assesses and reports on the quality of managed care plans. NCQA's mission is to provide information to purchasers and consumers of managed health care to distinguish the health plan's quality. NCQA has led national efforts to promote accountability for managed care health plans. The managed care organization (MCO) accreditation program is voluntary. Currently nearly half of the health maintenance organizations (HMOs) in the United States participate in the NCQA accreditation process. In order for an organization to become accredited by NCQA it must go through a survey and meet standards that are designed to evaluate the health plan's administrative and clinical systems. As part of the accreditation process, the health plan must also submit specific data as part of the accreditation process. During an accreditation survey health plans must provide data on specific areas that include the following areas:

- Access and service to plan.
- Qualified providers in plan.
- Staying healthy: preventative health measures.
- Getting better: effective treatments, drugs, devices.
- Living with illness: management of chronic illness.

Hedis

NCQA has been viewed as a leader in health plan performance measurement since 1991. The Health Plan Employer Data and Information Set (HEDIS) was developed by NCQA as a set of specific standard measures for comparing health plans. The HEDIS data set includes more than fifty performance measures. A consumer survey and survey to evaluate parents' experiences with their children's care is included in the survey process. HEDIS evaluates the results a health plan actually achieves in approximately fifty key areas of care and service such as immunization rates, cholesterol management, and member satisfaction. The results of HEDIS data are published and made available to prospective buyers and to the public.[3]

ISO 9000

The International Organization for Standardization (ISO) comprises ninety-one member countries with each country entitled to one vote. The United States's representative to the ISO is the American National Standards Institute (ANSI). The intent of the ISO is to create a universal approach to evaluating, managing, and directing quality based on global standards. ISO quality management standards were first published in 1987 as a quality management system. ISO publishes a set of standards that outline procedures to establish performance standards, designate responsibilities, organize processes, and demand management accountability. The standards were revised in 1994; the ISO 9000:2000 standards are planned for publication in early 2001. Based on the draft standards that have been circulated, there will be a reduction in the number of standards. However, the proposed standards are expected to cover the same essential areas and will include any requirements specific to the health care industry. The focus of the new standards will be to encourage continuous performance improvement and documentation of process and procedures. ISO standards are intended to apply to a wide range of industries. The standards are not industry specific.

The ISO standards were designed to provide a vehicle for quality management standards applicable to a variety of industries. The intent is to assist organizations to achieve quality outcomes and results based on a consistent, reliable, and cost-efficient model. The ISO standards are used throughout the world by service industries, manufacturing, environmental industries, space and aviation industries, and their suppliers.

In recent years, the health care industry has recognized ISO standards as both an alternative and adjunct to existing quality management systems. Perhaps the greatest influence of ISO for the health care industry has been the growing movement for ISO-certified industry organizations to require ISO certification from suppliers, including health care providers. Health care providers and payers, viewed as major tier-one suppliers to organizations around the world, are appropriately responding to this requirement.

The ISO standards support business process improvement for all industries. The health care industry worldwide has increasingly embraced the ISO standards as an alternative to existing quality management systems.

....
WHY ADOPT ISO 9000 IN HEALTH CARE?

Health care organizations choose to adopt ISO 9000 standards for a variety of reasons. An organization's reasons for doing so may include:

- To comply with customers who require ISO 9000.
- To compete in global and domestic markets.
- To improve the quality system.
- To minimize repetitive auditing by accrediting organizations.
- To improve subcontractors' and vendors' performance.

The benefits of ISO certification for health care organizations include but are not limited to the following:

- Enhanced understanding of quality practices throughout the organization.
- A mechanism to improve documentation of process and procedure.
- A tool to strengthen and improve supplier and customer confidence.
- Cost savings and improved profitability.

- Improved organizational awareness of quality.
- Strengthened and continuous performance improvement.

Complying with ISO 9000 standards does not indicate that every product or service meets the customers' requirements, only that the quality system in use is capable of meeting them. Consistently measuring customer satisfaction and striving to continually improve processes is the key to a successful quality management system.

What Is the ISO 9000 Series?

The core of the ISO 9000 Quality Systems Standard is a series of five international standards that provide guidance in the development and implementation of an effective quality management system. Not specific to any particular product or service, these standards are applicable to both manufacturing and service industries. The ISO 9001 standard, directed at service industries, is the most common standard applied to health care organizations.

ISO 9001   This standard is a model for use by organizations (both manufacturing and service) to certify their quality system from initial design and development of a desired product or service through production, installation, and servicing.

ISO 9002   This standard is identical to ISO 9001 except it omits the requirement of documenting the design and development process.

ISO 9003   This standard is for use by organizations that need only to show, through inspection and testing, that they are delivering the desired product or service.

ISO 9004   This standard is a basic set of guidelines that organizations can use to help them develop and implement their quality management system.

············

WHAT DO THE ISO STANDARDS INCLUDE?

The ISO 9001, applicable to health care, consists of twenty sections called clauses (standards). The clauses identify elements of performance required for ISO certification; however, the clauses do not stipulate how an organization must reach compliance thresholds. The clauses include:

4.1 Management responsibility

4.2 Quality system

4.3 Contract review

4.4 Design control

4.5 Document and data control

4.6 Purchasing

4.7 Control of customer-supplied product

4.8 Product identification and traceability

4.9 Process control

4.10 Inspection and testing

4.11 Control of inspection, measuring, and test equipment

4.12 Inspection and test status

4.13 Control of nonconforming product

4.14 Corrective and preventive action

4.15 Handling, storage, packaging, preservation, and delivery

4.16 Control of quality records

4.17 Internal quality audits

4.18 Training

4.19 Servicing

4.20 Statistical techniques

....

DRAFT STANDARDS FOR ISO 9000:2000 PUBLISHED

In the draft of ISO 9000:2000 standards it is anticipated these twenty clauses will be blended to reflect eight primary standards. A quality management system refers to the activities carried out within an organization to satisfy the quality-related expectations of customers. To ensure that a quality management system is in place, customers or regulatory agencies may insist that your organization demonstrate that your quality management system conforms to ISO 9000 quality system models.

There are three audit levels for ISO. The "first-party" audit is performed by individuals internal to the organizations. "Second-party" audits are performed by the customer or an independent auditor. "Third-party" audits are performed by a registrar coming into the organization to audit, or verify, that a system in place. When a third-party registrar finds an organization fulfills the requirements of the ISO 9000 standards, the organization becomes "registered" and receives a certificate indicating registration is complete.

ISO 9000 registration requires annual audits to monitor continuing compliance. Overall, it has been well demonstrated that if a health care provider is ISO qualified and/or registered, any other survey process is simpler and less costly regarding both preparation and compliance demonstration. While ISO registration is not intended to replace JCAHO or NCQA accreditation, it does make the compliance demonstration process appreciably less difficult, time consuming, and costly.

Many health care organizations have turned to ISO registration as an efficient mechanism to demonstrate the presence and functioning capacity of a quality management system that is working throughout the organization.

....

STEPS TO ISO REGISTRATION

The following is a generic process that health care organizations may follow to achieve ISO quality system registration.[4]

Phase I—Organization for Registration

- Obtain management commitment.
- Establish steering committee.

- Begin internal quality auditing.
- Select a registrar.

Phase II—Preparing for Registration

- Document existing processes with procedures and work instruction.
- Identify areas needing improvement.
- Adopt improved procedures and work instructions.
- Prepare the quality manual.
- Apply to your registrar for an assessment.
- Consider a preassessment.
- Conduct a "dress rehearsal" audit.
- Submit revised manual to the registrar.
- Modify and finalize quality practices; train personnel.

Phase III—Experiencing the ISO Registration Audit

- Arrange for your registrar to conduct the assessment and identify findings (discrepancies).
- Respond to findings.
- Submit to the registrar for review the corrective actions you will take.
- The registration certificate is awarded.

Phase IV—Continuing ISO Registration Through Surveillance Audits

- Maintain quality practice to ensure continuing compliance.
- Notify your registrar of major changes in practice.
- Arrange for registrar to conduct semi-annual surveillance audits.
- Continue to improve.

············

COLLEGE OF AMERICAN PATHOLOGISTS

The College of American Pathologists (CAP) is a medical society serving more than 15,000 physician members and the laboratory community throughout the world.[5] Established in 1922, CAP is the world's largest association composed exclusively of pathologists and is widely considered the leader in providing laboratory quality improvement programs.

In 1951, CAP published the first laboratory standards. In 1964, CAP performed the first laboratory accreditation, and by 1979, CAP was designated as the official laboratory accreditation program.

The mission of the college, the principal organization of board-certified pathologists, is to represent the interests of patients, the public, and pathologists by fostering excellence in the practice of pathology and in laboratory medicine worldwide.

············

CLINICAL LABORATORY IMPROVEMENT AMENDMENT

The Clinical Laboratory Improvement Amendments (CLIA) of 1988 is a federal regulation passed by the U.S. Congress. CLIA does not apply to the use of laboratory test results or to the medical decision-making process. It focuses specifically on standards for laboratory test performance. The CLIA standards were designed to improve quality in laboratory testing and include specifications for quality control, quality assurance, patient test management, personnel, and proficiency testing.

The CLIA regulations establish minimum standards for laboratory practice and quality. These regulations concern all laboratory testing used for the assessment of human health or the diagnosis, prevention, or treatment of disease. CLIA applies to every laboratory and testing site in the United States, even if only a few basic tests are performed as part of physical examinations.

Some simple tests are waived from specific CLIA requirements. If a laboratory performs only these tests, the laboratory can obtain a certificate of waiver (CLIA HCFA Waiver Registration) to show that the laboratory is exempt from specific CLIA requirements. The following laboratory procedures are included among the eight tests exempt from specific CLIA standards:

- Dipstick or tablet urinalysis (nonautomated).
- Fecal occult blood.
- Ovulation test using visual color comparison.
- Urine pregnancy test using visual color comparison.
- Erythrocyte sedimentation rate.
- Hemoglobin by copper sulfate method.
- Spun microhematocrit.
- Blood glucose using certain devices cleared by the Food and Drug Administration (FDA) specifically for home use.
- Hemoglobin by single anaylte instruments self-contained specimen or reagents interaction with direct measurement and readout.

A laboratory with a certificate of waiver will not be inspected routinely. The laboratory may be inspected as part of complaint investigations and on a random basis to determine whether only the waived tests are being performed. CLIA registration certificates are valid for a maximum of two years or until such time as an inspection can be conducted to determine program compliance, whichever is shorter.

Certificates are issued to laboratories complying with the CLIA standards. Certificates of accreditation are issued to those complying with department-approved, private, non-profit accreditation programs. In addition, in states with federally approved licensure programs, a laboratory may obtain a state license in lieu of a certificate or certificate of accreditation. If a laboratory is located in a state with an approved program and the laboratory obtains a state license, it is only necessary to comply with the state rules, not the federal CLIA regulations.

In choosing which type of certification to seek, you may consider factors such as cost, convenience, professional affiliations, and other considerations beyond the scope of this discussion. The major costs to all laboratories involve fees for certification and compliance and enrollment in proficiency testing (PT) programs. These costs will vary, depending on the amount of testing conducted in the laboratory and on the types of PT programs in which the laboratory enrolls.

A copy of the Federal Register containing the CLIA standards for laboratories can be ordered by contacting:

National Technical Information Services
5285 Port Royal Road
Springfield, VA 22161
800-553-6847

Be sure to specify the date of the issue that you are requesting (for example, February 28, 1992) and your choice of paper or microfiche format. Enclose a check or money order payable to the Superintendent of Documents. Credit card orders can also be placed by calling or faxing the order desk. In addition, you may view and photocopy the Federal Register document at most libraries designated as U.S. Government Depository Libraries and at many other public and academic libraries throughout the country.

....

COMMISSION ON ACCREDITATION OF REHABILITATION FACILITIES

The Commission on Accreditation of Rehabilitation Facilities (CARF) is a private, not-for-profit organization that accredits programs and services in adult day services, behavioral health, employment and community services, and medical rehabilitation. CARF develops and maintains practical and relevant standards of quality for such programs.

The Rehabilitation Accreditation Commission was formed in 1966 by two national organizations—the Association of Rehabilitation Centers and the National Association of Sheltered Workshops and Homebound Programs. In September 1966, the two organizations agreed to pool their interests in assuring quality in rehabilitation facilities, there by forming CARF.

The purpose of CARF is to promote the quality, value, and optimal outcomes of services through a consultative accreditation process that centers on enhancing the lives of the persons served. Facilities accredited by CARF demonstrate that they have substantially met nationally recognized standards for quality of services, including customer service. The standards are developed by the field, which consists of the persons served, rehabilitation professionals, and purchasers of services. The CARF standards are applied through a peer review process to determine how well an organization is serving its consumers.

Every year the CARF standards are reviewed and new ones are developed to keep pace with changing conditions and current consumer needs. CARF's accreditation, research, and educational activities are conducted in accordance with CARF's core values and standards. In addition, CARF is committed to:

- The continuous improvement of both organizational management and service delivery.
- Diversity and cultural competence in all CARF activities and associations.
- Recognizing organizations that achieve accreditation through a consultative peer-review process and demonstrating their commitment to the continuous improvement of their programs and services with a focus on the needs and outcomes of the persons served.
- Conducting accreditation research emphasizing outcomes measurement and management, and providing information on common program strengths as well as areas needing improvement.

- Providing consultation, education, training, and publications that support organizations in achieving and maintaining accreditation of their programs and services.

In 1997, CARF and JCAHO initiated a combined accreditation survey process to freestanding rehabilitation hospitals. The CARF standards (rewritten in 1988 to be unidemensional) represent the Standard Conformance Rating System. A Standards Manual and Survey Preparation Guide are available from CARF.[6]

....
AMERICAN ACCREDITATION HEALTHCARE COMMISSION

The American Accreditation Healthcare Commission (URAC) is a nonprofit organization founded in 1990 to establish standards for the managed care industry. URAC membership includes representation from a variety of constituencies affected by managed care: employers, consumers, regulators, health care providers, and the workers' compensation and managed care industries. Member organizations of URAC participate in the development of standards, and are eligible to sit on the board of directors.

URAC offers nine different accreditation programs for managed health care organizations including:

- Case Management Organization Standards.
- Credential Verification Organization (CVO) Standards.
- Health Call Center Standards.
- Health Network Standards.
- Health Plan Standards.
- Health Utilization Management Standards.
- Network Practitioner Credentialing Standards.
- Workers' Compensation Network Standards.
- Workers' Compensation Utilization Management Standards.

Several new accreditation programs also are under development. Once a managed care organization decides to seek accreditation from URAC, they first obtain application materials from URAC and submit documentation of compliance with each standard. This documentation is then reviewed by a member of URAC accreditation staff, who works with the applicant to resolve any issues that have been identified. URAC staff follow up with a site visit to the applicant in order to ensure operations are consistent with the documentation that was submitted. Finally, the application is reviewed by the Accreditation Committee and the Executive Committee, which are composed of representatives of URAC's member organizations.

Since 1991, URAC has issued more than 1,200 accreditation certificates to over 300 organizations doing business in all fifty states. In addition, regulators in over half of the states recognize URAC's accreditation standards in the regulatory process. In addition to its commitment to evaluating and accrediting managed health care organizations, URAC participates in a number of research projects related to performance improvement in the health care system.

URAC has also published a number of books and reports to assist with better understanding the many complex regulations, requirements, codes and laws related to the health care delivery system, such as *The Survey of State Health Utilization Review Laws and Regulations* (1999), *The PPO Guide* (1999), *Case Management State Laws: A 50-State Survey of Health & Insurance Statutory Codes* (1999), and *Models of Care: Case Studies in Healthcare Delivery Innovation* (1999).

In support of its mission to educate the public about quality and best practice in health care, URAC offers a variety of educational seminars throughout the country. To find out more information, contact their office or visit their Web site.[7]

············

ACCREDITATION ASSOCIATION FOR AMBULATORY HEALTH CARE

The Accreditation Association for Ambulatory Health Care (AAAHC), incorporated in 1979, is a nonprofit corporation that serves as an advocate for the provision and documentation of high quality health services in ambulatory health care organizations. AAAHC accreditation is a voluntary process involving several steps.

Once an organization has decided to pursue AAAHC accreditation it conducts a self-assessment using published AAAHC guidelines and standards. The next step is to participate in an on-site survey conducted by trained AAAHC surveyors. Following the on-site survey the accreditation team makes recommendations that is then reviewed by the AAAHC Board of Directors. The board of directors makes the final accreditation. AAAHC accreditation may be awarded for six months, one year, or three years, depending on the level of compliance with the published standards.

The AAAHC is dedicated to educating providers for both quality improvement and the accreditation standards and procedures. Educational sessions are held throughout the year. To date, more than 900 organizations nationwide have been accredited by the AAAHC. The AAAHC standards include the following areas for review:

- Patient rights.
- Governance.
- Administration.
- Quality of care.
- Quality management and improvement.
- Clinical records.
- Professional improvement.
- Facilities and environment.

Accreditation offers both quantitative as well as intangible benefits to an ambulatory surgery center, rather than public recognition alone. The letter of accreditation can actually enhance a health care center's success by providing a process by which the organization examines its internal processes and controls. The added value of accreditation is in its ability to strengthen public confidence as the organization has voluntarily submitted to an external review and evaluation.

The AAAHC has worked collaboratively with health care accrediting organizations and has been approved by the American Medical Association's physician credentialing program to provide Environment of Care surveys.[8]

············

FOOD AND DRUG ADMINISTRATION

The Food and Drug Administration (FDA) is one of the oldest U.S. consumer protection agencies. The FDA serves as a primary defense for the protection and safety of U.S. food, drugs, and medical devices. The agency is responsible for the manufacture, import, transport, storage, and sale of about $1 trillion worth of products each year. The FDA is a public health agency, charged with protecting U.S. consumers by enforcing the Federal Food, Drug, and Cosmetic Act and several related public health laws. The FDA is an agency within the Public Health Service, which in turn is a part of the Department of Health and Human Services.[9]

The FDA annually regulates more than $1 trillion worth of products used by U.S. consumers. It is the responsibility of the FDA to manage the manufacturing, labeling, and distribution of the following: food; cosmetics; medicines; medical devices; blood supply; radiation-emitting products; animal feed; and animal drugs.

The FDA sends investigators and inspectors to visit more than 15,000 facilities a year. For any company found in violation of any of the laws that the FDA enforces, the FDA can ask the company to voluntarily correct the problem or to recall a faulty product from the market. Recall is usually the fastest and most effective manner to protect the public from an unsafe product. This is also a very costly and time-consuming process. The FDA does not issue recalls unless it believes public safety is threatened.

If a company will not or cannot correct a condition of public safety, the FDA has jurisdiction to impose legal sanctions. The agency can go to court to force a company to stop selling a product and can issue a demand that any product already produced and distributed be seized and destroyed. The FDA has authority to hold imported products if warranted. The agency can impose criminal penalties, including prison sentences, against manufacturers and distributors in violation of the laws enforced by the FDA.

In addition to its oversight authorities, the FDA provides scientific research and testing of products. The National Center for Toxicological Research, which investigates the biological effects of widely used chemicals, is operated by the FDA. Assessing and weighing risks against benefits is a primary focus of the FDA's public health protection duties. The FDA scrutiny of drugs and devices does not end once a product is on the market. The agency continues to collect and analyze reports on drugs, devices, and consumers.

....

U.S. EQUAL EMPLOYMENT OPPORTUNITY COMMISSION

The U.S. Equal Employment Opportunity Commission (EEOC) was established by Title VII of the Civil Rights Act of 1964 and began operating on July 2, 1965. The mission of the EEOC is to promote equal opportunity in employment through administrative and judicial enforcement of the federal civil rights laws and through education and technical assistance. The EEOC enforces the principal federal statutes prohibiting employment discrimination, including:

- *Title VII of the Civil Rights Act of 1964,* as amended, which prohibits employment discrimination on the basis of race, color, religion, sex, or national origin.

- *The Age Discrimination in Employment Act (ADEA) of 1967,* as amended, which prohibits employment discrimination against individuals forty years of age and older.

- *The Equal Pay Act (EPA) of 1963,* which prohibits discrimination on the basis of gender in compensation for substantially similar work under similar conditions.

- *The Title I of the Americans with Disabilities Act (ADA) of 1990,* which prohibits employment discrimination on the basis of disability in both the public and private sector, excluding the federal government.

- *The Civil Rights Act of 1991,* which includes provisions for monetary damages in cases of intentional discrimination and clarifies provisions regarding disparate impact actions.

- *Section 501 of the Rehabilitation Act of 1973,* as amended, which prohibits employment discrimination against federal employees with disabilities.

The EEOC maintains offices throughout the United States.[10] Individuals who believe they have been subject to discrimination in relation to their employment may file an administrative charge. Additionally, individual EEOC commissioners may initiate charges that the discrimination laws have been violated. Once a claim is filed, the EEOC initiates an investigation to determine if there is "reasonable cause" to believe that discrimination has occurred.

Through the investigation the EEOC determines if there is "reasonable cause" to support the discrimination charges. The EEOC must then seek to conciliate the charge to reach a voluntary resolution between the charging party and the respondent. In the event that conciliation is not successful, the EEOC may bring suit in federal court. Whenever the EEOC concludes its processing of a case, or earlier upon the request of a charging party, it issues a "notice of right to sue," which enables the charging party to bring an individual action in court.

The EEOC also issues regulatory and other forms of guidance interpreting the laws it enforces. The EEOC is responsible for the federal sector employment discrimination program, provides funding and support to state and local fair employment practices agencies (FEPAs), and conducts broad-based outreach and technical assistance programs.

In February 1996, the EEOC approved its National Enforcement Plan (NEP). This plan sets forth a framework for the EEOC's enforcement strategy as follows:

- Prevention of discrimination through education and outreach.

- Voluntary resolution of disputes when possible.

- Strong and fair enforcement when resolution fails.

. . . .

CONCLUSION: THE FUTURE FOR ACCREDITATION, LICENSURE, CERTIFICATION, AND SURVEYING BODIES

In the future, oversight and regulation of the health care industry will continue to expand. U.S. consumer groups and a variety of special interest groups have clearly indicated their concerns for health care industry performance and accountability. Based on this trend for expanding government oversight in the health care industry, it is safe to anticipate the industry shall continue to be subject to increased demands for health care provider and payer accountability. This will include compliance with published standards and regulations.

It is also reasonable to expect that government, regulatory, and accrediting bodies will expand requirements for the health care industry. Compliance program components will be critical to the future of the health care delivery system. The primary areas of concern for risk management relate to patient safety, patient rights, product safety, provider qualifications, and fiscal responsibility (of both payers and providers).

The movement towards increased managed care contacting and selection of providers will necessitate strong programs of compliance and formal quality management of processes to identify, mediate, and reduce risk through the implementation of loss prevention programs.

Fraud and abuse has become a focus of interest for the government, with both criminal and civil monetary penalties being assessed for violations. The threat of criminal charges, resulting in prison sentences, will result in the growing fear and concern that health care programs are appropriately established and carried out under the direction and oversight of governing boards.

Accreditation and certification of health care programs are expected to develop in the areas of networks, independent contractors, and employer purchasing groups. Enhanced participation of consumer groups and public interest groups will also drive this process of ensuring that the industry is responsive to recognized areas of risk and loss.

New areas of risk for consideration shall include but not be limited to health e-commerce, confidentiality of data, unauthorized access and disclosure of patient data, provider qualifications, and customer satisfaction. As the population ages, the health care industry will increasingly focus on resources directed at wellness rather than acute and episodic health care. This shift shall result in both providers and payers being faced with decreasing financial resources to ensure compliance with administrative and clinical program requirements.

It has become an imperative that health care organizations identify efficient and effective methods for achieving compliance and satisfying the multitude of oversight requirements. In the future there must be a continued focus on the evaluation of existing risk management programs with the development of policies, procedures, and programs to safeguard data and compliance initiatives. Performance measures and tracking of risk-related data requires sophisticated information systems. The health care organizations of the future must address the information requirements and respond accordingly.

Managing risk is an organizational responsibility. The shift to managing enterprise risk should prompt the health care risk manager to focus on serving the organization as a reliable resource for a variety of compliance issues. Organizations working together, as a team, will obtain the best results.

Endnotes

1. Joint Commission on Accreditation of Healthcare Organizations
   One Renaissance Boulevard
   Oakbrook Terrace, IL 60181-4294
   630-792-5000
   www.jcaho.org

2. American Osteopathic Association
   142 E. Ontario Street
   Chicago, IL 60611
   800-621-1773
   www.am-osteo-assn.org

3. National Committee for Quality Assurance
   2000 L Street NW, Suite 500
   Washington, D.C. 20036
   202-955-3500
   www.ncqa.org

4. American Society for Quality
   www.asq.org

5. College of American Pathologists
   325 Waukegan Road
   Northfield, IL 60093
   800-323-4040
   www.cap.org

6. CARF
   4891 E. Grant Road
   Tucson, AZ 85712
   Phone: 520-325-1044
   www.carf.org

7. American Accreditation Healthcare Commission (URAC)
   1275 K Street NW #1100
   Washington, D.C. 20005
   202-216-9010
   www.urac.org

8. Accreditation Association for Ambulatory Health Care (AAAHC)
   3201 Old Glenview Road
   Wilmette, IL 60091
   847-853-6060
   www.aaahc.org

9. Food and Drug Administration
   Rockville, MD 20857
   www.fda.gov

10. U.S. Equal Employment Opportunity Commission
    1801 L Street, N.W.
    Washington, D.C. 20507
    202-663-4900
    www.eeoc.gov

Suggested Readings

www.marshall.usc.edu/library/Industries/health.html

Grass, S. *Of Foxes and Hen Houses.* Quorum Books, 1984.

Pare, M. (ed.). "Certification and Accreditation Programs Directory: A Descriptive Guide to National Voluntary Certification and Accreditation Programs for Professionals," Research, September 1998.

38

Request for Proposals

Roberta Carroll

A s health care continues to change, so does the relationship between health care entities and their independent service providers. Many risk and insurance management professionals are reevaluating these relationships and taking the opportunity to create new avenues of support for their internal risk management programs. Increased pressure for cost efficiencies and cost-effectiveness has further enhanced this opportunity.

This chapter will outline for the risk manager the process and necessary steps for requesting proposals from professionals outside their organization. This process known as *request for proposals* (RFPs) can be utilized for special projects, insurance broking and consulting, outsourcing, and a wide variety of other projects described later in this chapter. It is meant to be a guide for the risk manager who has never participated in an RFP as well as for the more "seasoned" risk manager.

The drafting of an RFP (generally written by the risk manager or insurance buyer) and evaluating responses from interested parties is only one part of a cycle of services rendered by others at the risk manager's request. This "broker service cycle," as described by Judith Morgan, a retired principal with Tillinghast-Towers Perrin in a 1996 educational session, is a six-step process that includes as its fourth step "the selection of a new broker or a refinement of the existing broker relationship."[1] The service cycle shares many characteristics with the risk management decision-making process and the quality cycle of the continuous quality improvement (CQI) process described in Chapter 33 (see Table 38.1). It is within that broad scope that this chapter is drafted.

TABLE 38.1.   Comparison of Quality Cycle with Risk Management Process and Broker Service Cycle

Quality Cycle	*RM Decision-Making Process*	*Broker Service Cycle*
Plan	Identify and analyze	Determine service needs
Do	Evaluate alternate techniques	Evaluate current broker
Check	Choose technique	Weigh benefits of change or introduction of competition
Act	Implement technique(s)	Select broker or refine relationship
	Monitor results	Manage relationship measure performance

··············

TYPES OF SERVICES REQUESTED

Although this chapter was written to examine and document the process for the selection of insurance brokers, the information can be applied to a wide variety of other relationships with which a health care risk manager may engage. Health care entities may require assistance on a project basis. The process and tools identified within this chapter can be adapted easily for other projects as well. The RFP process can be utilized to evaluate outside providers for the following services or projects:

- Third-party administrators (TPA's) for claims administration.
- Actuaries for funding levels or risk retention levels.
- Accountants for self-insured programs.
- Legal defense firms.
- Loss control specialists (both clinical and nonclinical).
- Independent adjusters with an expertise in a variety of coverage specialties.
- Captive feasibility studies.
- Risk management information systems.
- Insurance brokerage.
- Strategic planning consultation.
- Risk management program auditing.
- Legal bill review and auditing.
- Medical group benefits brokerage.
- Medical group managed care contract analysis.
- Drafting grievance procedures for an HMO.
- Integrated delivery system (IDS) evaluation of claims adjudication systems.
- A hospital or health care system that wants to review the marketplace for insurance consultants.
- Evaluating the relative merits of an internal risk management program versus outsourcing the risk management program or portions thereof.

TYPES OF PROPOSALS

In selecting brokers, two types of proposals are requested most frequently: a *market proposal* and a *conceptual proposal*. In the market proposal, specific lines of coverage are assigned to a specific broker who is assigned to a market or markets. The broker candidates must then access only the markets assigned to them for price and coverage. In the conceptual proposal, broker candidates are asked only for recommendations for changes to enhance the current insurance program; brokers are not allowed to access specific markets.

Market Proposal

A market proposal is one in which the client wishes to assign the marketplace by line of coverage. Brokers are generally asked to list by priority the markets with which they would best like to work. Each broker chosen to bid on the account is then given an identified number of markets that it may access on the client's behalf in attempting to get the best coverage, terms, conditions, and price. Once a market has been identified, it is assigned to only one broker. A market proposal is best used on smaller, easier-to-place coverage lines, where there is no lack of capacity in the marketplace or the proposal process can be used by individual lines of coverage.

Having all insurance policy renewals on the same date makes the process easier. If the renewal dates are staggered and the risk manager is assigning all lines of coverage to brokers by markets at the same time, the proposals will not reflect the true cost of the program because the market will hold its quotes open for a limited period of time. By the time the new broker goes to place coverage at the time of renewal, the bid or quote or indication it originally received may have to be renegotiated. Renegotiations could increase or decrease not only the cost of coverage, but also the dollars that the placing broker receives as compensation.

In the market method, compensation is usually paid on a commission basis. In many instances, the dollars paid to a broker by way of commissions are reasonable from the buyers and brokers standpoint. However, in some scenarios, the dollars generated by a fixed commission may not pay for the services rendered by the broker on the account. In other cases, the premiums paid to the carrier will generate dollars significant enough in commission to the broker to be viewed by the buyer as not being worth the value given. Commission dollars can also be considered over compensation by the buyer if they consider themselves to be instrumental in assisting the broker place the business. Activities that a savvy risk manager can and many times do assist with are: gathering required underwriting information; drafting coverage specifications; packaging submission materials; analyzing coverage, terms, limits, and price; and even visiting markets with the broker.

In using the market method, the risk manager must evaluate whether each individual insurance carrier assigned needs to be contacted by the risk management department and notified as to what broker it has been assigned. If the incumbent carrier is assigned to a broker other than the one currently handling that line of risk, it will not respond to a new broker without the client's permission. Even then, the process could be delayed while the incumbent broker is given an opportunity for the client to change the assignment and for the incumbent broker to maintain the market. It would be wise to allow the incumbent broker to use all current insurance carriers with whom it has placed business on the risk manager's behalf.

The *advantages* of the market method are:

- The broker with the ability to get the best cost is identified.
- The selection process is made simpler and more straightforward.
- The cost of insurance coverage is the "key" determinant to winning.

The *disadvantages* of the market approach are:

- Pricing all lines of coverage by market assignments is difficult for a program that has multiple renewal dates.
- Identifying the total cost of compensation can be difficult.
- There is strong potential that multiple brokers will be on the account.
- There is no reward for innovation or creativity, particularly with alternate risk financing options.

Another method of market proposal is to prepare a "mini-market" RFP for a single line of coverage as it comes up for renewal. The RFP then is given to a limited number of brokers, with a list of identifiable markets assigned to each. Again, only one broker is given access to a given market. For a large, complex account, the fragmented nature of this method generally renders it impractical. The mini-market approach is more time-consuming as each line of coverage is marketed by multiple brokers and markets.

Conceptual Proposal

With the conceptual proposal, respondents are asked to offer suggestions on improvements and changes to the current program without actually going to the insurance marketplace for costs or coverage. This type of proposal is particularly beneficial if the insurance program has multiple renewal dates, has difficult lines of coverage to place, has limited markets available to underwrite the risks, or is large or complex. In a conceptual proposal, it is assumed that all participating brokers will have the technical expertise to place the coverage lines, enjoy solid market contacts, and have the wherewithal to service the account. In evaluating conceptual proposals received, emphasis should be on the areas of creativity, innovation, and personality fit, as opposed to cost and specific market contacts.

Many proposals in the health care arena, particularly for larger accounts, are conceptual. This type of proposal does not require market notification because the markets will not be approached. In fact, the written RFP should state that the broker candidate does not have permission to access the marketplace on the risk manager's behalf, that this is only a conceptual proposal and not one in which the insurance products and/or coverage will be priced. Penalties for failing to adhere to this rule need to be clearly spelled out and may include the broker being eliminated from the process. Having the marketplace hear about proposed changes before the risk manager has a chance to evaluate the recommendations and take action is to be avoided at all costs. It is important to remember that the risk manager controls this process.

Advantages of the conceptual proposal include:

- The conceptual approach is less complicated than the market approach.
- This approach is less subject to chance (in a market bid process, the broker may find the insurer with the best price purely by chance, which reveals nothing about the quality of that broker's services).

- The conceptual approach does not give the chosen broker full-market access and thus is less disruptive to the market.
- It allows and encourages determinants other than cost for the selection process.
- Creativity and innovation are encouraged and rewarded.
- The risk manager can implement the program over time and spread marketing of the program over the year without having to do all the work up front, unless renewal dates are all the same.
- Team collaboration is encouraged.
- Brokers have the opportunity to showcase their individual firms' expertise, and the risk manager can see different brokers' capacity for innovation.

Among the *disadvantages* of the conceptual approach are:

- It is very subjective.
- After being selected, the broker may fail to be as aggressive as they suggested in the RFP process.
- Pricing compensation can be difficult, as the structure of the final program is yet to be determined. Until a program is structured and a determination made as to what services are needed, pricing at best can be offered as a "best guess."

Interviews

Another avenue or additional way to evaluate and select service providers or consultants is through an interview process. This process eliminates the need for drafting a formal RFP, a process that if done correctly takes time and resources to prepare. Risk managers, while they may find it a challenging and educational process, are generally pressed for time and therefore do not relish preparing a formal RFP. In many instances, particularly with well-seasoned risk managers, the brokerage and consulting community is well known. Relationships with a variety of professionals have been forged over time. With the recent consolidation of insurance brokerage and consulting companies, the need to blanket the community to see *who is out there* and *who is doing what* has diminished. Many risk managers already know the community. For those new to the profession brokerage interviews, the least formal RFP process may be the most appropriate learning model.

In the interview method of evaluating and choosing a broker or consultant, the process is greatly compressed and the emphasis becomes much more relationship driven. For the national companies responding, it is generally a given that they all have the capabilities to handle almost any size account regardless of the complexities. During the interview process it is still vital that the buyer focus in on those services, skills, and technical capabilities that will be necessary to manage the account regardless of their national or community standing. Many smaller regional brokers are quite capable of handling health care accounts.

It is incumbent upon the risk manager in an interview selection process to draft questions that all respondents will need to address. This process tends not to be as reliant upon what resources and services are available, as are the composition and compatibility of the team.

It is rare that an account will be "won" utilizing just one of the methods described here. In most instances, it will be some combination of methods. Usually an interview will be conducted even if it is to just meet the broker chosen through a written RFP.

· · · · · · · · · · · ·

INITIAL STEPS IN THE RFP PROCESS

As important as the actual RFP document is the groundwork that should come beforehand. The initial steps in the process are assessing the goals of the RFP process, setting a time line, choosing a broker selection committee, and deciding on evaluation criteria.

Setting the Goals

The key to a successful RFP process is an accurate assessment of where the risk management program is and an understanding of what the risk manager hopes to accomplish through this process. A helpful first step is for the risk manager to answer certain questions. The answers will assist in writing the RFP, evaluating the responses received, and choosing a broker that best fits the needs of the organization. The questions include:

- What does your current broker do? What would you like it to do that it is not doing now? Can you set priorities for your needs and concerns?

- Why are you asking for proposals at this time? Are you unhappy with current services? Can you reduce your concerns to writing? Have you tried to resolve them with your current broker? Do you prepare a RFP routinely every three to six years regardless of the experience? Have you recently merged or acquired another entity, and are you trying to combine programs? Have the key service players on your account team changed? You need to be very clear about why you are initiating this process at this time. Preparing an RFP is very time-consuming and should not be taken lightly. The time required translates into a cost that can be significant for all parties.

- What risk and insurance management programs do you currently have in place? Are they in writing? Does your broker place and service all lines of insurance? Do you go directly to the market on some lines of coverage? Are you in any group purchasing programs, risk retention groups, or other alternate risk-financing programs? Can you clearly articulate what the broker's role will be with these other insurance professionals on your behalf, if any?

- In your health care organization, who has responsibility for engaging or changing a broker, or expanding its current role? If you do not have this responsibility, you need the approval of senior management (or whoever has authority) to delegate the process to you, your staff, or a selection committee to make the process meaningful and to avoid wasting anyone's time. If the authority and responsibility are not delegated prior to starting the RFP process, you and your organization could be embarrassed in the insurance community as the process continues. At the very least, you may not obtain the desired result.

- Have you thought through the politics of the situation? From a credibility standpoint, it is vital that, to the extent possible, you maintain and encourage a "level playing field," avoiding bias in your approach. If competing brokers believe you have been fair and ethical in your dealings with them, they will respect you and your team, regardless of the outcome.

- From what companies are you requesting a proposal? Is your account large enough (premium dollars) or complicated enough requiring special expertise that a national/international broker would be helpful? How is it determined, and who determines, which brokers are asked to bid or submit proposals? In many cases this is a political decision made outside risk management. While the individual brokers may not need to know the thought process behind who receives the RFP, the buyer should. Do you only want to go to the largest five brokers by revenue volume? Do you want to access only brokers that have health care expertise? Do you want to only access brokers with a local or regional presence? Who is the contact at each firm? Do you have the person's name, address, phone and fax numbers, and e-mail address?

● Are you required to have a formal bidding process because of some types of contracts or because of your organization's structure? Are you a government or public entity? (Although this chapter does not specifically address the more formal or mandatory bidding process, the information should be helpful from a general standpoint.)

● What specific areas of the insurance program are important to your operation, have the most potential for volatility, and/or are at the highest risk? These probably are areas where you want the broker candidate to concentrate most of its efforts, which needs to be identified in the RFP through questions. Is the RFP going to have any limitations on what you want the broker to do? These also need to be spelled out clearly.

● Do you have access to all the information you need to proceed? It may seem easy to answer yes to that question; however, until you start gathering all the information you need to forward to the company preparing the proposal, you may be unaware that not all the information needed is at your fingertips. You may need to request information from sources outside the risk and insurance management department, such as annual reports from the marketing and public relations department. The more information you can share with the broker candidates, the more informative and relevant their response will be.

● What type of RFP will you be drafting: market, conceptual, or for consulting services only (in which case your request and the response will be dramatically streamlined)? The answer to this question will determine the type and kind of information you need to give to and receive from the respondents. Again, depending on the answer, this process can be extremely complex and time-consuming, especially for a health care system with multiple entities and subsidiaries and a fully integrated network of services looking for a new broker. A single-project RFP, or one in which the compensation is relatively small, may not require a complicated, lengthy process. It is important that the process be as simple as possible to meet your needs. If the potential respondents believe it is too cumbersome, complicated, and time-consuming for the perceived benefits, they may not respond. When this occurs, you lose the opportunity to evaluate a wide range of experts.

● Is there an ideal time for this process? Do you have the time and staff support to manage the project now? Remember that the process requires time on the part of both parties. Is it reasonable to make a change at this time if that is what the final outcome determines? Are you in the midst of a merger or acquisition? If so, you may want to wait until that process is completed to see how it may affect the decision to go forward. At a minimum, you may be adding another potential respondent. Remember that you need to finish what you start!

The answers to these questions will lay the foundation for the RFP that needs to be drafted. The more specifically the risk manager can identify needs and objectives, the more likely it is that the responses received will adequately address key issues.

Establishing a Time Line

As mentioned previously, the RFP process requires time on the part of all parties. Depending on the project size and complexity, it can take six to nine months to complete, from drafting the RFP language to beginning a contractual relationship.

To encourage innovative and creative responses that are individualized for the risk manager's organization, it is important to allow adequate time for brokers to review the information forwarded to them, clarify any open questions, assemble a response team, and draft and finalize their response. Failing to allow sufficient time encourages a "cookie-cutter" or "off-the-shelf" approach, which is not appropriate in most cases. Following is a guide for identifying key dates in the RFP process:

- *Date the RFP is distributed to the potential respondents.* If the person to whom the RFP is addressed is no longer at the company or is unable to respond, the RFP should be forwarded to someone who can respond appropriately on the company's behalf if the company indeed chooses to respond.

- *Date the risk manager will be available in person or by telephone for questions regarding the information contained in the RFP.* Regardless of the method of communication, it is always helpful to limit the time frame in which questions will be answered.

- *Date the written response is due.* It is important to be specific—for example, on or before 5:00 p.m. PST, October 1. To simply say on October 1 may imply that proposals will be accepted after 5:00 p.m. It also is important to state how many copies are required and to whom responses should be addressed, along with the correct delivery addresses for each recipient.

- *Time frame in which responses will be evaluated.* This period of time should be used not only to review the written response, but also to ask any open questions that are relevant and require an answer before a decision to go forward can be made. This time frame also will allow for clarification of information that appears to be misunderstood. If it becomes necessary to clarify misunderstood information, it is important that the same information be relayed to all participants. The risk manager who is working with a selection committee may want to involve members at this point to assist in reviewing all the respondents and choosing the finalist.

- *Date respondents will be notified of results.* At this point, it usually is appropriate to invite the finalist(s) to make oral presentations to selection committee. If the risk manager is unable to respond when promised, it is important that respondents be notified of the delay and offered an appropriate explanation. A new date then should be identified and communicated to them. Adherence to this date is critical. It is always helpful to share with respondents how the results will be communicated—by fax, by phone, or in writing. (For sample notification letters to respondents, see Exhibits 38.1 and 38.2.)

- *Date or period of time set aside for oral presentations.* If time permits, it usually is best to schedule all oral presentations to take place on the same day. To finalists in the RFP process, this is a period of excitement as well as great anxiety. Therefore, providing finalists with thorough information on how the presentations will be managed and the logistics can help alleviate some of this anxiety. (See Exhibits 38.3 and 38.4.)

- *Date by which a final decision will be made.* Again, it is important to share with respondents how the decision will be communicated and when.

- *Date the engagement is to commence and length of the assignment (one year or multiple years).* If a change will be made in brokerage representation, a transition period must be planned. The length of time for this transition period varies depending on the contract's complexity. Markets need to be contacted regarding this change through a "broker of record" letter (see Exhibit 38.5).

The time line also can list the actual date the risk management department began the process, such as drafting and finalizing the RFP and gathering all the information needed to send with the proposals. This date is not generally given to the bidding broker but may be presented for future RFP use.

EXHIBIT 38.1.   **Sample Congratulatory Letter Finalist**

Dear_____,

Congratulations! Our broker selection committee has reviewed all the written proposals received in response to our RFP for brokerage services, and your firm has been chosen as a finalist.

We were delighted by the quality of all the proposals received; it was apparent our RFP was thoroughly read, seriously evaluated and researched, allowing for thought-provoking responses.

The other companies that have been asked to make presentations are (other company name) and (other company name). Dates for the oral presentations have not been decided. We will contact you with possible dates as soon as we can coordinate the selection committee members' schedules.

Once again, congratulations. We look forward to meeting with you and your account team.

Sincerely,

_____

EXHIBIT 38.2.   **Sample Rejection Letter**

Dear_____ ,

Our broker selection committee has reviewed the proposals received in response to our RFP.

We were very pleased by the quality of all the proposals. It was obvious that you took our request seriously, and we sincerely thank you. Your account team is to be commended. After a thorough review of the written proposals by the selection committee, our decision, albeit a difficult one, does not include (proposing company) as a finalist to the oral presentations.

All respondents did an exemplary job in showcasing their firm's capabilities and we appreciate the time you took in drafting your response. The relationship between our companies has been enhanced by your efforts, and we are desirous of keeping in touch periodically. While our decision is final, I would be pleased to entertain any questions you may have regarding our decision or the process.

We thank you again for your participation.

Cordially,

_____

EXHIBIT 38.3.   Sample Presentation and Clarification Letter

Dear_____ ,

We look forward to your visit to our corporate offices and in expanding upon your written proposal. You will be given one hour for your presentation. You may use any format you believe is appropriate; however, we ask that you leave time for questions. Please let us know if you have any special audiovisual needs; we will do our best to accommodate them. We anticipate meeting the account team that will be responsible for the day-to-day servicing of our account. In addition, if you plan to use any consultants or subcontractors for any portion of your engagement, we request that you include them in your presentation.

We anticipate that the broker selection committee will comprise six to eight people (depending on scheduling). The following are those who have been invited to participate in this process:

name	title	entity/facility
name	title	entity/facility
(etc.)		

Two dates are offered for the final presentations: Friday, May 19, and Tuesday, May 23. Please let us know as soon as possible by fax if your team is unavailable for either those dates. If we do not hear from you by Friday, April 28, we will assume that either date is acceptable. The actual date and time for your presentation will then be scheduled.

Our corporate offices are located at (give full address including floor number and ZIP code. It is also helpful to add directions from the major highways and airport in your area). Visitor parking is available and we will provide your team with validation. A full-service cafeteria, which is open for breakfast at 7:00 a.m. and lunch at 11:30 a.m., is located on the ground floor.

As most of you are aware, we hope to have all brokerage placed on a fixed-fee basis, even on those lines that are routinely placed on a commission basis. We anticipate that if a market will not quote net, commission dollars received would offset the fixed fee. The only line where we are considering allowing commission dollars is in the placement of bonds (surety, appeal, patient trust fund, notary, and so on).

Although we at (your company) are extremely cost conscious and want to evaluate services rendered in relationship to dollars paid, it is equally important to us that compensation paid our brokerage and consultant partner is fair and equitable while commensurate with services provided.

During your oral presentation, we expect you to address what services are covered in your fixed fee. Are there any lines of coverage on which you anticipate receiving commission? Please let us know how you anticipate receiving compensation for hospital and medical group provider excess/stop-loss, professional, and general liability for our medical groups, and all lines of coverage currently being placed through and by (current provider). Are there dollars in your fixed fee for these coverages? How do you propose being compensated for new business placed during the year?

We thank you for your interest and look forward to seeing you at the oral presentations.

Cordially,

Use this letter to add information inadvertently left out previously or to clarify information that may have been misunderstood. Some risk managers tell the finalist by what criteria they will be judged. This is very helpful to the participants and should be included if that is your preference.

EXHIBIT 38.4.   Sample Presentation Confirmation Letter

RE: Broker Selection Process/Oral Presentations

Dear_____ ,

We look forward to your presentation on Tuesday, May 23, from 1:00 p.m. to 2:00 p.m. PST. The presentation will take place in our boardroom on the twenty-first floor. For your information, the enclosed business cards* represent the selection committee members who are available to participate from our organization.

Please let us know as soon as possible who will be attending the presentation from your company. It is requested that attendance be limited only to those that will have an active role in the presentation.

We thank you for your interest and look forward to seeing you on May 23 at 1:00 p.m. PST.

Cordially yours,

_____

*There are notebook-sheet-size business card holders that work well for this purpose.

EXHIBIT 38.5.   Broker of Record Letter

To whom it may concern:

This will confirm that we have appointed (name of broker) as our exclusive insurance broker with respect to our insurance program, effective (date). The appointment of (broker) rescinds all previous appointments, and the authority contained herein shall remain in full force until canceled in writing.

(Broker) is hereby authorized to negotiate directly with any interested company with respect to changes in existing insurance policies and in closing, changing, increasing, or canceling insurance carried under temporary binders or cover notes. We understand, however, that (broker) has no responsibility for any deficiencies in the insurance program to which this letter applies until it has had a reasonable opportunity to coordinate a review and to provide us with its recommendations.

This letter constitutes your authority to furnish (broker) representatives with all information they may request as it pertains to our insurance contracts, rates, rating schedules, surveys, reserves, and retentions. It also allows you to release all other financial data they may wish to obtain for their study of our present and future requirements in connection with the insurance program to which this letter applies. We request that you not communicate such information to anyone else. Attached is a list of policies (your company) has in place with (company of addressee).

Very truly yours,

_____

Establishing a Broker Selection Committee

A broker selection committee can lend invaluable support and assistance to the risk management department as they go through the brokerage review process. It is particularly helpful to seek the ideas of people who may not be involved in the organization's day-to-day risk activities.

The RFP process can be used as a tool in educating those who are directly affected by high premiums or those areas that are considered high risk. It also provides an opportunity to obtain a wide variety of opinions on issues that are key to the organization, encourages a new perspective on insurance from those outside the department, and enhances collective support and buy-in among constituents.

Composition of the selection committee requires careful deliberation. Those invited to participate must commit to being active members of the team, supporting the time frames and amount of work necessary to accomplish objectives. Thus, clear objectives for this process must be communicated to the committee participants. As in any committee, an identifiable team leader or process facilitator is essential. In most cases, that role is delegated to the risk manager, although it could be delegated to another individual.

Determine Evaluation Criteria

It is helpful to determine the evaluation criteria in advance. In the long run, taking the extra time to draft an evaluation tool for the RFP process can help streamline the amount of time spent. The broker selection committee can play a vital role in this process by helping the risk management staff to develop meaningful and relevant criteria. Established criteria also assist in maintaining a level playing field for all parties and provide a useful guide in reviewing the written materials and oral presentations.

The evaluation criteria need not be complicated, lengthy, or detailed, but merely relevant to the organization's requirements. If the selection committee will assist in developing evaluation criteria, the entire group should agree on the definitions of terms used in the proposals.

The following areas can be used to compare the respondents with each other and in relationship to the insurance program objectives. Not all these areas are pertinent throughout the whole process; some may lend themselves to either the oral presentation or written materials, or may be general comments on how candidates comported themselves throughout the process (see Exhibit 38.6).

- Health care expertise.
- Reputation.
- Listening skills.
- Innovation and creativity.
- Reference checks.
- Location of service team.
- Ease of access to the service team (voice mail, e-mail, 800 numbers).
- Computer expertise and support.
- Personality fit among the players within their own team and with the risk manager's team.

EXHIBIT 38.6.   RFP Presentation Evaluation Form

Overall Score _____
Average Score _____

Category (1 is lowest, 5 is highest)	*1*	*2*	*3*	*4*	*5*
Availability or accessibility of team					
Expertise in health care					
Expertise in managed care					
Commitment to your account					
Communication skills					
Information systems savvy					
Innovation					
Domestic and international market					
Reputation					
Office location					
Pricing					
Creativity					

- Cultural and organizational fit.
- Adherence to the RFP process.
- Compensation.
- Communication skills and style.
- Commitment to the risk manager's account.
- Enthusiasm and energy level.
- Presentation style.
- Ability to follow direction.
- Consulting services available.

....
WHAT TO INCLUDE IN THE RFP

It is critical that in requesting proposals, risk managers provide brokers with general information on the health care organization itself as well as specific information about the project or services to be provided. If it is a brokerage, RFP information on the organization's risk financing program needs to be forwarded to all participants.

Executive Summary

An executive summary or an overview of the organization with accompanying annual reports, organizational charts, a brief description of all operating divisions, financial statements, organizational vision and mission statements, market share evaluation, and similar material will assist brokers in drafting a response that will meet the risk manager's needs while highlighting their own expertise and competence. It can be difficult for brokers to sense the culture and tone of an organization for which they are preparing a proposal while highlighting their own company. Usually, any information they can be provided is appreciated.

Insurance Information

In addition to general information on their organization, risk managers need to provide brokers with information on the organization's insurance program (or whatever project the brokers are being asked to respond to). Obviously, the information forwarded will depend on the type of proposal. Following are general items that can be forwarded: schedules of insurance, declaration pages to policies, insurance policies, loss runs, coverage specifications, named insureds, organizational structure and biographical sketches of staff, and open issues or a "wish list" of coverages.

....

WHAT TO LOOK FOR IN RESPONSES TO THE RFP

In response to an RFP, a broker should demonstrate technical competence and skill in accessing markets. Also, several important items of information to include are references, suggested composition of the team that will service the account, and types of services the broker offers. Other information the risk manager may wish to have can include proof of the broker's own insurance coverage and evidence of the broker's social responsibility toward the community.

Technical Competence

It is critical that an insurance broker has a competency that the department either does not have within its organization or does not have time to use to the fullest extent. As risk management roles change over time, many of these distinctions become blurred—a broker today, a risk manager tomorrow, and vice versa. Even if the expertise exists within the risk manager's organizational structure to perform many of the same duties requested in an RFP, it may still make sense to outsource some functions related to risk and insurance management. These functions need to be evaluated as to the cost benefit of in-house versus outsourcing. In many cases, it is very difficult to maintain critical market contacts while keeping abreast of new product development and the cyclical nature of the insurance marketplace.

Market Access and Marketing Philosophy

Skill in marketing the account to company underwriters is an important aspect of the brokerage role and not one to be minimized. It is helpful if the risk manager understands his or her broker's relationship with the marketplace. Asking the following questions will help:

- Does the broker have an exclusive relationship with a particular market? Brokers who are unfamiliar with markets other than the one with which they have an exclusive relationship may not provide as broad a technical expertise as the risk manager may wish to have, and their ability to place business with other markets may be hampered.

- In terms of premium dollars, how much business does the broker place with a particular carrier?

- Is the broker a managing general agent (MGA) for a company or a specific program? Does it have the underwriting pen for a particular company? Is it an agent representing a company? In its response, the broker should identify any conflicts it may have with a market(s) and what they may be.

- Does the broker's marketing philosophy fit with the corporate culture and how the organization does business? Does the broker have access to the key players in all the markets in which the organization currently does, or would like to do, business? What is the broker's philosophy in bringing the risk manager to visit the markets on renewal? In many cases, it can be helpful if the risk manager is part of this process. It also is a great learning experience. Education is a two-way street, particularly in health care. The risk manager has an obligation to assist in educating the broker on the delivery of health care, just as the broker has an obligation to educate the risk manager on insurance and marketplace issues. Education should be viewed as a commitment by both parties to enhance the level of expertise. Brokers always try to place business with insurance carriers that are, and will continue to be, financially viable into the future. Risk managers should question brokers as to how they evaluate a market for its financial security. Does the broker have an independent committee that evaluates the financial viability of specific markets?

- What are the broker's criteria for placing business with a given market? Is it the expectation that clients will do business only with carriers rated A6 or better by A. M. Best, the rating agency? Does the broker use waivers in placing difficult-to-place business if the rating is below A6 or some other predetermined set of guidelines? If so, under what circumstances? By buying insurance, risk managers are transferring financial liability for a loss to another party; it is incumbent upon the risk manager and the placing broker to use due diligence in selecting and placing business with a viable market.

Account Team

The composition of the team suggested to manage the risk manager's account is a critical component of a successful partnership. An organizational chart showing the names of team members with accompanying biographical sketches is helpful for reviewing each team member's technical competency and depth of experience. Another useful element is if the broker identifies each team member's assigned responsibilities and accountabilities. The amount of time contemplated for each team member to work on the risk manager's account can provide insight into how the broker may have priced its services and identify who the risk manager's primary contact will be on a daily basis. The risk manager should not be afraid to ask for or suggest changes to the account team; the broker should be willing to accommodate the request if at all possible.

A key question to ask is whether the proposed account team is computer literate. What types of computer programs is the account team familiar with? Which ones does it routinely use? Are they compatible with the organization's programs? Does the team have any software programs that it is proposing to support the organization's account? If so, does that require any additional expense on organization's part? (Such costs may not be identified in the broker's response to the RFP.)

It also is helpful to know where the account team members are located. With e-mail, fax capabilities, voice mail, and the Internet, this is perhaps less of an issue than in the past. Nevertheless, it is important if the risk manager needs or wants to be able to meet with the broker in person. Related questions include whether team members are near a major airport, and how often that airport is served. Can the team members rent a car nearby, or is taxi service available? Backup support for the team also should be identified before it is needed. What happens if a key team player is suddenly unavailable? Can the team continue to handle the day-to-day operations related to the account in a timely and appropriate manner?

Account Services

During the RFP process, it is important that the risk manager be able to evaluate the services required or desired to manage his or her account on an ongoing basis. Some of the tools that will assist in that evaluation are:

- A well-drafted RFP that clearly articulates service needs and objectives.
- A proposal that is responsive to service needs and objectives and is articulated in writing.
- A service agreement that spells out the relationship and responsibilities of both parties.
- A transition plan that will outline for both the service team and the client those steps that will be taken to ensure a smooth and seamless transition from one broker to another, if a change is indeed to be made. The transition plan should include an effective date for the change over, a timeline for at least the first ninety (90) days of the account and a listing of responsible parties by task.
- Periodic meetings on open issues. These are best scheduled with written agendas covering all open items identifying responsible parties. For large accounts, these meetings can be every two weeks or monthly. On a limited project basis, instead of a personal meeting, status reports could be presented in writing; on a smaller brokerage account, it may be a combination of both written communication and personal meetings.
- Stewardship reporting to the client. Usually conducted on a yearly basis, this gives the broker an opportunity to recap the year's accomplishments on the client's behalf and also memorializes objectives and goals for the next year on which the broker and client have mutually agreed.
- Quality control is the responsibility of both parties, individually and together. The responding brokers should be asked what type of quality control monitoring process they have in-house to evaluate services rendered. Is this process written? Can clients obtain a copy of the broker's internal procedures for quality control? (In many cases, clients may receive a copy of this internal report; risk managers should ask for one.) What monitors are to be set up for clients to evaluate the services the broker is rendering on their behalf? It is not unusual today for part of the broker's compensation to be at risk and based on quality control monitors. Quality control monitoring of the account should be ongoing from the perspective of both parties. Obviously, risk managers would not wait until the contract expired to identify key areas that need to be changed; rather, they would expect those changes to be made as they are identified and as soon as practical.

Consulting Services

Brokers today, particularly the large national brokerage firms, offer a wide variety of consulting services that compliment and support their brokerage business. Among those services are

- Claims analysis.
- Reporting and adjusting.

- Full TPA services.
- Claims auditing.
- Reserve analysis.
- Actuarial analysis.
- Funding analysis.
- Claims information systems.
- A full gamut of loss control services, both clinical and nonclinical, such as engineering studies and surveys; licensing and accreditation preparedness surveys; educational seminars; workshops and conferences; and disaster preparedness.
- Capitation risk management.
- Assistance in reengineering efforts and outsourcing activities.
- Review and analysis of alternate risk-financing methods.
- Captive management.

The list is limited only by the lack of an identified need on the part of the client. If a broker does not offer a service that a client believes is necessary to manage the account, in most cases the broker will develop the in-house expertise or subcontract that service to a third party. A question to include in the written RFP is, "Do you plan to engage the services of any third parties or subcontractors to assist in the servicing or management of this account?" If so, please identify the role you envision them performing on our behalf, who will manage the process, and how they will be compensated. As health care entities evaluate ways to cut costs and improve efficiencies, many are looking to the broker with whom they have an established relationship for assistance. Many of these consulting projects can be short term, requiring technical expertise the health care organization may not have internally.

References

A broker's reputation in the marketplace is as important as the volume of written premiums it places or the size of its account portfolio. Obviously, the more business it places with a given market or carrier, the more important the broker is to the carrier and the more weight the broker carries in negotiating on the risk manager's behalf. Reputation is meaningful because insurance brokerage is still very much a relationship business. In many cases, a broker's reputation precedes it in the marketplace and permeates the industry and its specialty niche. The risk manager's role as the client is to determine whether the broker's reputation is as good as he or she has been led to believe. (A broker with a bad or poor reputation probably would not be invited to respond to an RFP.) This can be accomplished by requesting current references and contacting knowledgeable individuals at those organizations to obtain their opinions. Ask such questions as: Does the broker have a reputation in the industry as being proactive? Are they responsive to identified needs? Are they customer friendly? Are they timely? (Several other areas to ask the broker's current clients about were mentioned earlier in the chapter section titled "Deciding on Evaluation Criteria.") This feedback should be used as part of the evaluation process.

It is always of interest to ask respondents to identify new business obtained over the past two calendar or fiscal years, as well as about accounts lost over the same period of time. Asking for the primary reason(s) they won or lost an account also could provide helpful information. In addition, it can be useful for risk managers to ask for references on accounts that are similar to their health care organization in size, complexity, culture, and structure. Reference checks are easier if the broker has identified a reference contact person by name, with the address as well as phone and fax numbers and e-mail addresses.

It then is incumbent upon the risk manager to telephone the references before any of the parties make oral presentations. However, it should be kept in mind that although references can provide valuable insight, they have been provided by the responding broker, and it is highly unlikely that the broker would provide names of clients who would not give good references. Risk managers should be sure to identify issues that are of particular importance to their organization and then draft specific questions to address them.

Many buyers will ask the broker during the RFP process or during the interview process to list three accounts that they have lost in the past two years and the reasons why.

Service Contracts

Service contracts or agreements should be drafted and approved by both parties. They spell out account expectations for service, the responsibilities and accountabilities of the account service team, the contract period, and the compensation basis, as well as any bonus arrangements, and offer the risk manager a method of evaluation. The terms under which the service contract can be terminated also are identified in this written document. Cancellation should always benefit the client, as the client is the one who will be responsible for engaging a new broker and the transition from one broker to another takes time. This necessitates that cancellation or nonrenewal of the brokerage contract be handled in an orderly, smooth manner.

Compensation

Health care entities can compensate their brokers in several ways: fixed fee, commission time and expense, retainer fees, bonuses, and compensation dollars at risk.

Fixed Fee   In the past, the primary method of payment was commission dollars calculated as a percentage of premium. However, the increasing belief is that the compensation a broker receives should be for services rendered and should not be contingent on premium dollars paid. Premiums, particularly in professional liability, workers' compensation, employment practices liability, and environmental impairment liability, have had wide fluctuations over the past few years. As a result, over the past five to ten years, more and more health care accounts have begun requesting brokerage on a fixed-fee basis. Compensation based on fixed fees not only allows clients to identify the compensation paid, but also encourages them to evaluate the services received in light of what it is costing them. It also allows clients to budget the cost and allows them to allocate the cost among operating entities or units.

Compensation paid to a broker should be fair and equitable and for identifiable services rendered (or contemplated to be rendered). Obviously, brokers want to receive a profit from doing business; however, it should be reasonable and not outrageous. A fixed fee allows the parties to reach a consensus on fairness, reasonableness, and equitability.

Multiple-year service contracts may enhance the client's ability to negotiate more favorable fixed-fee rates over a single-year fee. Most brokers who know they will have a client's account for a minimum of three years will average their fee and spread it over the term of the contract. Another way to offer compensation on a fixed-fee basis is to set a minimum and maximum fixed fee for the year and pay out the average quarterly. At the end of the contract period, both parties mutually determine the final compensation for the year. This scenario allows clients to expand or contract the volume of service during the year and still pay an equitable fee. This is equitable where the program changes are fairly nominal; however, in situations in which clients are merging and acquiring new organizations or where the servicing of their account otherwise dramatically increases, this may not be adequate compensation. Fixed-fee arrangements can be individualized to meet both the client's and broker's needs and can be as varied as their programs.

The following questions should be addressed in the RFP or at the oral presentation:

- How will new business be handled over the course of the contract? Will the broker be allowed to receive commission dollars on the original placement the first year, then renegotiate the next year's fixed fee?
- On a fixed-fee basis, will there be any exception(s) for the placement of business under different payment methods, such as commission dollar on bond placements?
- If a market pays commission dollars to the broker, has it been clearly articulated how those dollars are to be handled? Will they be used to offset fixed fees? Will they be kept throughout the year by the broker and reconciled at the end of the contract period, or could they be used to offset next year's fixed fee?

Commission   There are still many accounts that receive compensation on a commission basis. An accurate accounting of commission dollars paid should be made at least yearly. The client then needs to determine whether the compensation paid is equitable and fair. In some situations, it may be considered low; in others, high. Commission dollars are calculated as a percentage of the premium dollars and are paid by the insurance carriers.

The biggest concern with brokerage compensation on a commission basis is that there is no direct relationship to the volume or level of service performed or required. Commission dollars are very effective in several situations such as small accounts, single-line insurance placements, and the placement of bond.

Time and Expense Accounts, and Retainer Fees   Time and expense accounts as well as retainer accounts require tracking the activities of the account team and pricing them on a preapproved hourly rate. It is important that client and broker have a mutual understanding as to how expenses are to be managed, as well as which ones are authorized and which ones are not. Fixed-fee accounts should have a trigger point, determined by the client, at which time the client is to be notified of the dollars spent on the project and a projection for future costs until project closure. These forms of payment can be particularly effective in special-project or consulting accounts. For large accounts, tracking time and expense can be particularly cumbersome for account teams On a new large account that was obtained on a fixed fee, it would not be inappropriate to have time and expenses tracked for the first year to verify the fixed fee's adequacy.

It is important that the risk manager and broker agree or certainly understand the definition of terms and the basic ways in which fees are developed. As an example, some brokers consider a full-time equivalent (FTE) to be 1,950 hours a year. They may then take off for vacation, holiday, and an average use of sick time leaving a lower number of hours available. Many health care entities still use 2,080 hours as the basis for a full-time equivalent (FTE).

Bonus Arrangements and Compensation Dollars at Risk   With compensation dollars at risk, the client holds back a percentage of the fixed dollars until the end of the contact period, at which time an evaluation of the year's activities is made. Built-in incentives and placement of part of the compensation at risk are quite the norm today. However, these approaches require identifying in advance what criteria will be used to pay bonus arrangements or evaluating when and how the compensation that is at risk will be paid. Nevertheless, bonus arrangements and compensation dollars at risk can be very effective in rewarding the account team for exceptional services rendered. Conversely, they can be used to penalize an account team for not maintaining an adequate level of service or not reaching identifiable targets.

There can be as many different compensation arrangements as there are client and broker arrangements; the only requirements are that they be fair, easily understood by all team members, attainable through controllable activities as opposed to changes in the marketplace, memorialized in writing, and based on identifiable criteria. Bonus arrangements as well as compensation dollars at risk can be based on a percentage of a fixed fee.

Other Issues Related to Compensation   Other issues regarding compensation that need to be reviewed and agreed upon are:

- Frequency of billing and invoicing.
- The date clients will be billed. A billing date of the thirty-first of the month (as compared to the first) could put an invoice due into a different quarter or fiscal year, where the dollars may not have been budgeted.
- To whom to address the invoice(s). What signature authorizations will be necessary? What is the client's turnaround time for the processing of payment? How long does the client have before payment(s) is due? When is it due to the company? Who gets the benefit of the time value of premium dollars? (If the premium dollars are large, this can be a significant issue.)
- If the client allocates premium and brokerage compensation among different operating units, it is helpful to determine how the allocations will be made and build spreadsheets to accomplish this task in an expeditious and consistent manner before the invoice is due.

Miscellaneous

Two other issues that are appropriate to ask during the RFP process are related to the responding brokers' insurance coverages and their social responsibility to the public and community at large.

The respondents should show proof of coverage for insurance they have in place while handling the client's account. It is appropriate to request certificates of insurance on errors and omissions (E&O)insurance coverage, automobile liability, and workers' compensation, to name the more common exposures.

If how an organization responds to social responsibility issues is a significant issue for the risk manager, the executive management team, or to fit the culture of the health care organization, the RFP may ask questions related to the respondents volunteerism, corporate giving and matching programs, employee and community assistance programs, and other like activities that benefit society through financial aid or human resources support.

············

ORAL PRESENTATIONS

Any information that can be provided to those brokers participating in oral presentations is appreciated. At this point, all respondents have all expended considerable time in responding to the written RFP and are eager to get the account and "close the deal." General information, such as availability of parking, location of dining facilities, client capabilities for handling audiovisual requests, number and names of people who will attend the presentation, as well as their role in the organization, can go a long way toward making the process go smoothly. Other general information that could be helpful to share with the brokers is whether a room is available where they can rehearse and whether participants can be separated while waiting or scheduled so that they do not have to wait together in the same area. The presentations should be scheduled so that the selection team can take a break between sessions. This is so that the selection committee does not forget the specific details and can complete its evaluations immediately following the presentations. Name tags or place tags for the committee and the account team, if known ahead of time, are helpful. Taking care of some of the mundane housekeeping arrangements in advance will be greatly appreciated. It is important to remember that in most cases, brokers are guests at the client's facility and should be treated as such. If time permits, brokers also usually appreciate a tour of the facility. (See Exhibits 38.3 and 38.4.)

Any specific questions the selection team has should be written down so as not to be forgotten. If appropriate, they may be forwarded to all the participants in advance so that responses can be prepared before the presentation.

Specific questions that perhaps should be saved for the presentation are: How does the broker plan to make a smooth transition from the existing broker (if a change is to be made)? What does the broker see as the account's top priorities? What does the broker believe will be the most difficult tasks to accomplish?

In terms of whether brokers should be told whom they are competing against, opinions vary. It probably is easier, and really does no harm, to inform them as to who received the RFP, who responded, who the finalists are, and who was awarded the account. Like any field, the brokerage industry has its own internal grapevine; brokers appreciate receiving this information officially from the client rather than secondhand from another source. Also, this enables the client to control what information is given out and in what manner. For sample letters to participants of the case presentations, see Exhibits 38.7 and 38.8.

············

MONITORING RESULTS AND EVALUATING SERVICES

Once the RFP process is complete and a new service provider has been selected, it is equally important to periodically evaluate those services. The criteria established audit tools uses and formal reports are all monitoring elements to be considered.

Establish Criteria

In order to monitor or evaluate the services performed by outside service providers, it is first necessary to review what services the outside provider was engaged to perform. It is hoped that these performance standards are documented and memorialized in a service agreement, stewardship report, response to a request, or some other similar document. Other documents that outline the agreement between the two parties with respect

EXHIBIT 38.7.   Sample Congratulation Letter to Winner

Dear_____,

While I realize you that have already been give the good news by phone just this morning as to the outcome of the oral presentations, I wanted to officially notify you in writing of the committee decision. We are pleased to tell you that the committee's decision was favorable to your firm. This change is effective October 1, and is for a (mention the time frame, one year, two years, for example).

In order to plan for the transition, it is requested that you call me the first part of next week so that we can schedule our first planning session.

Congratulations! The efforts of your team are to be commended. Please pass on my comments and the committee's decision to the team, as you all did an excellent job. We look forward to working with you and anticipate a close working relationship.

Cordially yours,

_____

EXHIBIT 38.8.   Sample Rejection Letter

Dear_____,

The broker selection committee convened the day following your oral presentation. The committee reviewed their evaluation forms and discussed all the finalists in detail. After an in-depth evaluation and group discussion, the decision has been made to award our broker business to (name of company.) We feel (new broker company) will best meet our strategic objectives and will add value to our risk management program through a partnering arrangement.

I would be remiss in not telling you that this decision was by no means an easy one. The caliber of all the participants was outstanding, and your firm is to be commended for an excellent job in responding to the RFP.

I want to take this opportunity to thank you and your firm for the services you have rendered over the past (# of years) years. We anticipate a smooth transition to (name of new broker) and would appreciate your usual cooperation. I will call you next week to set up a planning session convenient to you and your team.*

While the decision of the selection committee is final and the new broker has been appointed, I would be pleased to discuss our decision or the selection process in more detail, should you desire.

Cordially yours,

_____,

*This paragraph can be eliminated if the addressee is not the incumbent broker.

to services to be performed could be appropriate. These could include signed and dated file notes, confirmed faxes, meeting notes, and other written correspondence. Having the performance standard agreed to ahead of time diminishes the possibility of disagreements later and makes the evaluation process a meaningful one. It also lets the service provider know up-front what the expectations are, allows them to determine if they can meet them in a timely fashion and solicits their agreement as to whether or not they can accomplish them. In many situations the evaluation criteria is developed in conjunction with the performance standards in a service agreement. In this manner the service team not only knows what the expectations for service are but by what criteria they will be judged. It is not unusual for the evaluation criteria to be tied into compensation dollars. These dollars can be at risk due to not meeting objectives or for additional bonus monies depending on the outcome of the evaluation. Regardless of the size of the account or the complexities of the service to be provided, or if the account compensation is on a fixed fee or commission, it is important that the client give feedback to the outside service provider on how they are performing. As with any type of performance review, it is also helpful to give periodic status reports. If it is judged that they are doing well, timely feedback will encourage the continuation of positive performance. If improvement is warranted, it will allow the service provider to modify the service to meet the client's expectation or amend with the client the service agreement and accompanying evaluation criteria (see Exhibit 38.9).

Auditing Tools   Performance standards are one of the platforms of any audit tool. If one of the performance standards, as an example, is to provide certificates of insurance (COIs) within one working day of the request, this then becomes an evaluation criteria element. In developing the criteria for this one element, issues to be taken into account are: how many COIs are contemplated to be issued yearly, how many are actually requested and completed, the complexity of the request, completeness of necessary information received from the client, and so on. Needless to say, if the account generates 250 COIs yearly, the performance criteria may be based on a percentage of the time that they are completed with in the appropriate time frame—for examples 95 percent of the time. If it were anticipated that the account would only generate approximately fifty COIs a year and in reality the client requested 250, the evaluation of this performance criteria would need to be tempered by the change or increase in the services required. The account team may not be set up to handle the additional work

Evaluation criteria can be complex or simple. It can be as simple as having only three categories for each performance standard: (1) criteria met, (2) criteria not met, and (3) criteria exceed. It is best to keep it as simple as possible. Just remember that the service provider needs to show task completion and the client needs to evaluate the performance. Both require some sort of audit and paper trail.

Develop a Timeline   Timelines are another area where performance standards can be set. As an example, one performance standard may be that coverage specifications are drafted ninety days before renewal. This standard requires the cooperation of both the broker and the client. The broker may develop the first draft of specifications and then gain approval from the client as to the thoroughness of the specifications, adding where necessary. Timelines can be generic for some functions. With insurance renewals, a standard timeline may be that renewal submissions be to the marketplace ninety days before the renewal date. This can be standard for all lines of coverage.

EXHIBIT 38.9.   **Sample Insurance Brokers Evaluation Criteria**

Period: _____ Broker: _____

Rating System   (5) Outstanding   (4) Commendable   (3) Acceptable   (2) Fair   (1) Poor

	2000	2001
I. Creativity		
A. Presents new and/or alternative methods for loss avoidance or reduction.	_____	_____
B. Develops plans for nontraditional methods of loss financing.	_____	_____
C. Devises equitable allocation or rating methodologies.	_____	_____
D. Creates solutions and alternatives to legislative and regulatory initiatives.	_____	_____
II. Service		
A. Prompt response to requests for coverage or changes.	_____	_____
B. Easily accessible for consultation.	_____	_____
C. Reference source for insurance information.	_____	_____
D. Timely and effective interoffice coordination.	_____	_____
III. Technical Expertise and Support		
A. Legislative and regulatory updates.	_____	_____
B. Current analysis and communication of new policy forms and endorsements.	_____	_____
C. Continuing education of staff.	_____	_____
D. Thorough understanding of makeup and goals.	_____	_____
IV. Technical Expertise and Support		
A. Appropriate fee for services rendered.	_____	_____
B. Services performed as agreed upon.	_____	_____
C. Fees for additional services negotiated in advance.	_____	_____
V. Communication		
A. Meet with local management at least annually.	_____	_____
B. Accurate and timely reports.	_____	_____
C. Current update on insurance industry.	_____	_____
D. Prompt response or acknowledgement to inquiries.	_____	_____
E. Timely notification of personnel changes.	_____	_____
VI. Quality of Service		
A. Secures coverage as reqeusted.	_____	_____
B. Visits to sites		
1. Account representatives	_____	_____
2. Professional liability loss control	_____	_____
3. Claims representative	_____	_____
C. Accurate billings and allocations.	_____	_____
D. Accurate reports of coverage.	_____	_____
E. Prompt delivery of policies.	_____	_____
F. Policies reviewed for:		
1. Intended coverage	_____	_____
2. Proper rates and values	_____	_____
G. Annual stewardship report.	_____	_____

(Continued)

EXHIBIT 38.9.   Sample Insurance Brokers Evaluation Criteria (*Continued*)

Period: _____ Broker: _____

Rating System   (5) Outstanding   (4) Commendable   (3) Acceptable   (2) Fair   (1) Poor

	2000	2001
VII. Staffing		
A. Appointment of account managers with approval of management.	_____	_____
B. Account team has adequate health care experience.	_____	_____
C. Continuity of team.	_____	_____
D. Appropriate level of team members for nature of work performed.	_____	_____
E. Effective interface between account team	_____	_____
VIII. Reporting		
A. Annual stewardship report.	_____	_____
B. Timely reports on market conditions.	_____	_____
C. Special project reports as indicated.	_____	_____
D. Summaries of coverage.	_____	_____
IX. Confidentiality		
A. Maintains confidentiality of information unless prior approval for release is granted by the president.	_____	_____
X. Carrier Performance		
A. Management		
1. Financial strength	_____	_____
2. Underwriting philosophy	_____	_____
3. Accessibility to insured	_____	_____
B. Timely reports on market conditions.		
1. Timeliness of policies and endorsements	_____	_____
2. Accuracy of issuances	_____	_____
3. Flexibility of mid-term exposure changes	_____	_____
C. Claims handling		
1. Timely acknowledgement of claims notice	_____	_____
2. Prompt assignment of adjuster or counsel	_____	_____
3. Adequate or fair reserves	_____	_____
4. Timely settlement or disposition	_____	_____

Timelines can lend valuable assistance in planning the servicing needs of an account and a factor in determining the staffing requirements. If all the renewals center around a central date of July 1 or January 1, it may not be prudent to give the marketing staff time off the month before renewal.

Stewardship   Stewardship reports are prepared by the broker and given to the clients as an evaluative tool or report card on their performance. They also are used as a tool to plan for the near-term future. Please keep in mind that a stewardship report is not a marketing brochure for the broker. They are, however, a meaningful and productive way to offer the client account results in a complete and concise manner. If the results have been particularly good, both the risk management department and the broker win. The stewardship report is an excellent tool for the risk manager to circulate among senior management as an FYI. It is crucial, therefore that the risk manager signs off on a draft report before publication.

Stewardship reports can be written for any time frame indicated or agreed upon. The most frequent time frame seems to be yearly. For programs that are multiyear placements or integrated programs, the publication of a stewardship report can vary depending on the needs of the client. The stewardship report written right after a major multiyear renewal may be a large-scale undertaking and would outline the marketing activities and results. During the nonrenewal years of a multiyear program, the stewardship report can be condensed and may be used only as an evaluation tool for performance standards previously set. Personnel changes on the account team also need to be addressed in the stewardship report. Stewardship reports generally give the following information:

1. Executive overview.
2. Program highlights and accomplishments.
3. Schedule of insurance and coverage detail by line of coverage.
4. Account service team.
5. Goals and objective for the next year.
6. Markets and security.
7. Compensation.

·············

CONCLUSION

Risk managers should bear in mind that the broker who did not obtain their business today may be the broker of choice for their organization tomorrow. People move, organizations change, and the increase in mergers, acquisitions, and divestitures requires that we maintain contacts and good relationships beyond only those performing work for us. Thus, every attempt should be made to play the game fairly, giving everyone an equal opportunity. How the risk manager played the game may be remembered longer than his or her organization's final decision.

As the pressures continue to increase for health care risk management activities to be cost efficient and effective, the efforts of risk managers must reflect shareholder value to the organization. Risk managers can add value by better understand the RFP process, how to customize it for their organization, and how to position themselves with their outside service providers to the best advantage of all.

Endnotes

1. Morgan, J. "Implementing a TQM Broker-Client Relationship." *Presentation to the Harvard Risk Management Series,* Module 3, May 22, 1996.

Suggested Readings

Charron, M. P. "Insurance Broker Services in the 1990s." *Forecast,* Betterley Risk Consultants, Apr. 1990, pp. 3–4.

Cox, C. H. "Risk Primer: Planning for the Bidding Process." *Risk and Insurance Magazine,* July 1995.

Feldman, M. R. "Broker Evaluation and Selection." *Perspectives in Healthcare Risk Management* (monograph), ASHRM, Winter 1986, pp. 1–3.

Griffin, G. "Developing Broker-Services Agreements." *The Risk Management Letter 16*(9), pp. 5–8.

Lefenfeld, M. S. "Fee-Based Compensation Replaces Shrinking Income." *Best's Review (Property/Casualty),* Mar. 1996, pp. 68–69.

Perez, J. R. "Comparing Fees and Commissions." *Risk Management,* June 1995, pp. 39, 42.

Quinley, K. M. "The ABCs of RFPs." *Commercial Claims,* Spring 1996, pp. A18–21.

Rakich, R. "Competitive Selection of Group Health and Dental Programs: Part I—Broker Competition." *The Risk Management Letter, 15*(6), 1994, a publication of Warren, McVeigh & Griffin, Inc., pp. 1–4.

Sinclair, R. L. "A Broker Selection Process" (monograph #6). *Risk Financing Compendium,* Chicago: American Society for Health Care Risk Management, pp. 1–4.

Tenaglia, S. "Broker Selection and Service Requirements." Presented at ASHRM Annual Conference, Phoenix, Arizona, Oct. 12, 1988.

West, K. Z. "How Do You Select and Work with an Insurance Broker? RIMS New Manual May Have Some Answers." *Risk Management,* Feb. 1996, pp. 30–32.

Wiebe, M. A. "Re-Engineering the Broker/Risk Manager Relationship." *The John Liner Review, 9*(4), Winter 1996, pp. 15–20.

"Salad Days: A Corporate Finance Survey Finds That Risk Management is Pleased with Their Brokers and International Carriers." *FW's Corporate Finance,* Summer 1995, pp. 38–38.

Index